2011
Novel & Short Story Writer's Market®

includes a 1-year online subscription to
Novel & Short Story Writer's Market on **WritersMarket.com**

WritersMarket.com
Where & How to Sell What You Write

THE ULTIMATE MARKET RESEARCH TOOL FOR WRITERS

To register your *2011 Novel & Short Story Writer's Market* book and **start your 1-year online genre only subscription**, scratch off the block below to reveal your activation code, then go to www.WritersMarket.com. Click on "Sign Up Now" and enter your contact information and activation code. It's that easy!

UPDATED MARKET LISTINGS FOR YOUR INTEREST AREA
EASY-TO-USE SEARCHABLE DATABASE
RECORD KEEPING TOOLS
INDUSTRY NEWS
PROFESSIONAL TIPS AND ADVICE

Your purchase of *Novel & Short Story Writer's Market* gives you access to updated listings related to this genre of writing (valid through 1/31/12). For just $9.99, you can upgrade your subscription and get access to listings from all of our best-selling Market books. Visit **www.WritersMarket.com** for more information.

WritersMarket.com

Where & How to Sell What You Write

ACTIVATE YOUR WRITERSMARKET.COM SUBSCRIPTION TO GET INSTANT ACCESS TO:

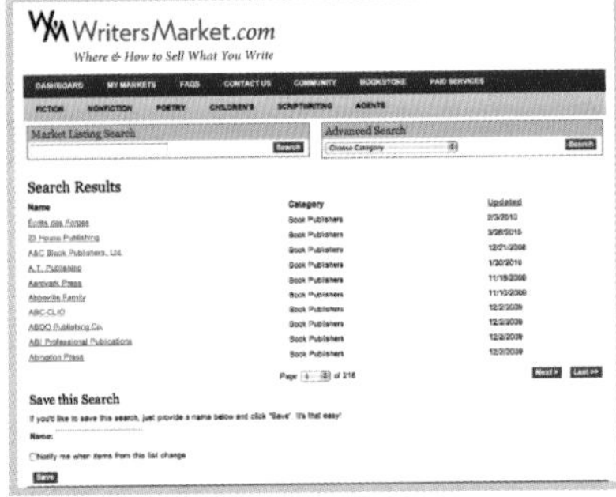

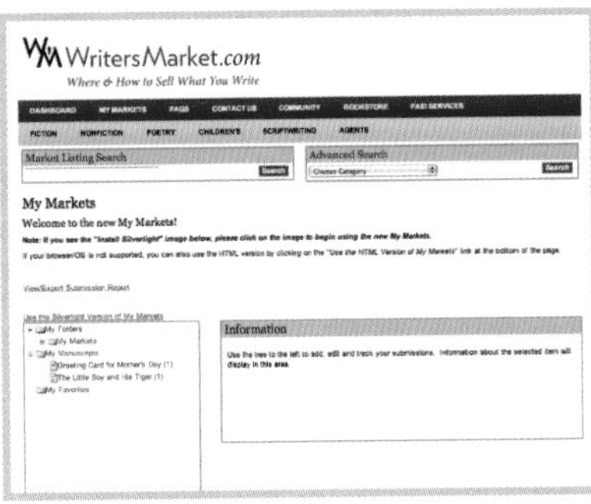

11NMI0M

- **UPDATED LISTINGS IN YOUR WRITING GENRE** — Find additional listings that didn't make it into the book, updated contact information and more. WritersMarket.com provides the most comprehensive database of verified markets available anywhere.
- **EASY-TO-USE SEARCHABLE DATABASE** — Looking for a specific magazine or book publisher? Just type in its name. Or widen your prospects with the Advanced Search. You can also search for listings that have been recently updated!
- **PERSONALIZED TOOLS** — Store your best-bet markets, and use our popular record-keeping tools to track your submissions. Plus, get new and updated market listings, query reminders, and more – every time you log in!
- **PROFESSIONAL TIPS & ADVICE** — From pay rate charts to sample query letters, and from how-to articles to Q&A's with literary agents, we have the resources freelance writers need.
- **INDUSTRY UPDATES** — Debbie Ridpath Ohi's Market Watch column keeps you up-to-date on the latest publishing industry news, so you'll always be in-the-know.

YOU'LL GET ALL OF THIS WITH YOUR INCLUDED SUBSCRIPTION TO

WritersMarket.com

To put the full power of WritersMarket.com to work for you, upgrade your subscription and get access to listings from all of our best-selling Market books. Find out more at **www.WritersMarket.com**

2011 Novel & Short Story Writer's Market®

30TH ANNUAL EDITION

ALICE POPE, EDITOR

WRITER'S DIGEST
BOOKS
WritersDigest.com
Cincinnati, Ohio

Complaint Procedure

If you feel you have not been treated fairly by a listing in *Novel & Short Story Writer's Market*, we advise you take the following steps:

- First try to contact the listing. Sometimes one phone call or a letter can quickly clear up the matter.
- Document all your correspondence with the listing. When you write us with a complaint, provide the details of your submission, the date of your first contact with the listing and the nature of your subsequent correspondence.
- We will enter your letter into our files and attempt to contact the listing. The number and severity of complaints will be considered in our decision whether or not to delete the listing from the next edition.

Novel & Short Story Writer's Market website: www.novelandshortstory.com
Writer's Market website: www.writersmarket.com
Writer's Digest website: www.writersdigest.com
Writer's Digest Bookstore: www.writersdigestshop.com

Distributed in Canada by Fraser Direct
100 Armstrong Avenue
Georgetown, ON, Canada L7G 5S4
Tel: (905) 877-4411

Distributed in the U.K. and Europe by David & Charles
Brunel House, Newton Abbot, Devon, TQ12 4PU, England
Tel: (+44) 1626 323200, Fax: (+44) 1626 323319
E-mail: mail@davidandcharles.co.uk

Distributed in Australia by Capricorn Link
Loder House, 126 George Street
Windsor, NSW 2756 Australia
Tel: (02) 4577-3555

ISSN: 0897-9812
ISBN-13: 978-1-58297-951-9
ISBN-10: 1-58297-951-0

Cover design by Claudean Wheeler
Production coordinated by Greg Nock

Attention Booksellers: This is an annual directory of F + W Media, Inc. Return deadline for this edition is December 31, 2011.

Contents

INTERVIEWS

MARKETS

RESOURCES

INDEXES

You've Got a Story

So Now What?

To make the most of *Novel & Short Story Writer's Market*, you need to know how to use it. And with more than 600 pages of fiction publishing markets and resources, a writer could easily get lost amid the information. This quick-start guide will help you wind your way through the pages of *Novel & Short Story Writer's Market*, as well as the fiction publishing process, and emerge with your dream accomplished—to see your fiction in print.

1. Read, read, read. Read numerous magazines, fiction collections and novels to determine if your fiction compares favorably with work currently being published. If your fiction is at least the same caliber as that you're reading, then move on to step two. If not, postpone submitting your work and spend your time polishing your fiction. Writing and reading the work of others are the best ways to improve craft.

For help with craft and critique of your work:

You'll find advice and inspiration from best-selling authors and top fiction editors in the Articles section, beginning on page 4, and in the Interviews section, beginning on page 58. You'll find Contest listings beginning on page 471. You'll find Conference & Workshop listings beginning on page 496.

2. Analyze your fiction. Determine the type of fiction you write to best target markets most suitable for your work. Do you write literary, genre, mainstream or one of many other categories of fiction? For definitions and explanations of genres and subgenres, see the Glossary beginning on page 542 and the Genre Glossary beginning on page 550. There are magazines and presses seeking specialized work in each of these areas as well as numerous others.

For editors and publishers with specialized interests, see the Category Index beginning on page 591.

3. Learn about the market. Read *Writer's Digest* magazine (F+W Media, Inc.); Publishers Weekly, the trade magazine of the publishing industry; and Independent Publisher, which contains information about small- to medium-sized independent presses. And don't forget the Internet. The number of sites for writers seems to grow daily, and among them you'll find www.writersmarket.com and www.writersdigest.com.

4. Find markets for your work. There are a variety of ways to locate markets for fiction. The periodicals sections of bookstores and libraries are great places to discover new journals and magazines that might be open to your type of short stories. Read writing-related magazines and newsletters for information about new markets and publications seeking fiction submissions. Also, frequently browse bookstore shelves to see what novels and short story collections are being published and by whom. Check acknowledgment pages for names of editors and agents, too. Online journals often have links to the Web sites of other journals that may publish fiction. And last but certainly not least, read the listings found here in Novel & Short Story Writer's Market.

Also, don't forget to utilize the Category Indexes at the back of this book to help you target your market for your fiction.

5. Send for guidelines. In the listings in this book, we try to include as much submission information as we can get from editors and publishers. Over the course of the year, however, editors' expectations and needs may change. Therefore, it is best to request submission guidelines by sending a self-addressed stamped envelope (SASE). You can also check each magazine's and press' website, which usually contains a page with guideline information. And for an even more comprehensive and continually updated online markets list, you can obtain a subscription to www.writersmarket.com.

6. Begin your publishing efforts with journals and contests open to beginners. If this is your first attempt at publishing your work, your best bet is to begin with local publications or those you know are open to beginning writers. Then, after you have built a publication history, you can try the more prestigious and nationally distributed magazines. For markets most open to beginners, look for the ☐ symbol preceding listing titles. Also, look for the ◩ symbol that identifies markets open to exceptional work from beginners as well as work from experienced, previously published writers.

7. Submit your fiction in a professional manner. Take the time to show editors that you care about your work and are serious about publishing. By following a publication's or book publisher's submission guidelines and practicing standard submission etiquette, you can increase your chances that an editor will want to take the time to read your work and consider it for publication. Remember, first impressions last, and a carelessly assembled submission packet can jeopardize your chances before your story or novel manuscript has had a chance to speak for itself. For help with preparing submissions read "The Business of Fiction Writing," beginning on page 49.

8. Keep track of your submissions. Know when and where you have sent fiction and how long you need to wait before expecting a reply. If an editor does not respond by the

EASY-TO-USE REFERENCE ICONS

E-MAIL ADDRESSES AND WEB SITES

$◩◪THE SOUTHERN REVIEW

Old President's House, Louisiana State University, Baton Rouge LA 70803. (225)578-5108. Fax: (225)578-5098. E-mail: southernreview@lsu.edu. Web site: www.lsu.edu/thesouthernreview. **Contact:** Jeanne Leiby, editor. Magazine: 6¼ × 10; 240 pages; 50 lb. Glatfelter paper; 65 lb. #1 grade cover stock. Quarterly. Estab. 1935. Circ. 3,000.

SPECIFIC CONTACT NAMES

• Several stories published in *The Southern Review* were Pushcart Prize selections.

Needs Literary. "We desire fiction that crystalizes immediately the author's voice and vision." Receives approximately 300 unsolicited mss/month. Accepts 6-7 mss/issue. Reading period: September-May. Publishes ms 6 months after acceptance. Agented fiction 1%. **Publishes 10-12 new writers/year.** Recently published work by Jill McCorkle, James Lee Burke, Robin Black, James Fowler. Also publishes literary essays, literary criticism, poetry.

DETAILED SUBMISSION GUIDELINES

How to Contact Send complete ms with cover letter and SASE. No queries. "Prefer brief letters giving information on author concerning where he/she has been published before, biographical info and what he/she is doing now." Responds in 2 months to mss. Sample copy for $8. Writer's guidelines online. Reviews fiction, poetry.

TIPS ON APPROACHING EACH SPECIFIC PUBLISHER

Payment/Terms Pays $30/page. Pays on publication for first North American serial rights. Sends galleys to author via e-mail. Sponsors awards/contests.

Advice "Careful attention to craftsmanship and technique combined with a compelling sense of the importance of story will always make us pay attention."

time indicated in his market listing or guidelines, wait a few more months and then follow up with a letter (and SASE) asking when the editor anticipates making a decision. If you still do not receive a reply from the editor within a month or two, send a letter withdrawing your work from consideration and move on to the next market on your list.

9. Learn from rejection. Rejection is the hardest part of the publication process. Unfortunately, rejection happens to every writer, and every writer needs to learn to deal with the negativity involved. On the other hand, rejection can be valuable when used as a teaching tool rather than a reason to doubt yourself and your work. If an editor offers suggestions with his or her rejection slip, take those comments into consideration. You don't have to automatically agree with an editor's opinion of your work. It may be that the editor has a different perspective on the piece than you do. Or, you may find that the editor's suggestions give you new insight into your work and help you improve your craft.

10. Don't give up. The best advice for you as you try to get published is be persistent, and always believe in yourself and your work. By continually reading other writers' work, constantly working on the craft of fiction writing, and relentlessly submitting your work, you will eventually find that magazine or book publisher that's the perfect match for your fiction. *Novel & Short Story Writer's Market* will be here to help you every step of the way.

GUIDE TO LISTING FEATURES

On page 2 you will find an example of the market listings contained in *Novel & Short Story Writer's Market* with call-outs identifying the various format features of the listings. (For an explanation of the symbols used, see the sidebar on this page.)

2011 NOVEL & SHORT STORY WRITER'S MARKET KEY TO SYMBOLS

N market new to this edition

A publisher accepts agented submissions only

market is closed to submissions

actively seeking new writers

seeks both new and established writers

prefers working with established writers, mostly referrals

only handles specific types of work

award-winning market

Canadian market

market located outside of U.S. and Canada

imprint, subsidiary or division of larger book publishing house (in book publishers section)

C publisher of graphic novels or comics

$ market pays (in magazine sections)

● comment from the editor of *Novel & Short Story Writer's Market*

ms, mss manuscript(s)

SASE self-addressed, stamped envelope

SAE self-addressed envelope

IRC International Reply Coupon, for use in countries other than your own

(For definitions of words and expressions relating specifically to writing and publishing, see the Glossary in the back of this book.)

ARTICLES

Giving Writer's Block the Finger

& Nine Other Writing Pitfalls You Need to Deal With

by I.J. Schecter

There are a number of writing demons just lying in wait to trip up aspiring wordsmiths. You're probably familiar with a number of them (the demons, not the wordsmiths). I'm here to tell you that none of these alleged obstacles are legitimate, and that you're well within your rights to punch each one of them in the nose on your way to literary fame and fortune.

Of course, to be able to overcome an obstacle, you have to be able to recognize it. Here are the top ten excuses I've heard writers offer for not being able to stick with the program, the reasons each of them are totally unfounded, and the steps you need to take to get past them. And by past them, I mean right *through* the suckers.

EXCUSE #1

I can't tell which of my ideas is the bestselling one.

Why it isn't legit: All writers are constantly bombarded by story ideas. That's practically what *makes* you a writer. If you didn't have ideas, you'd have nothing to write. So having *too many* ideas is not a good excuse.

What you need to do: Stop worrying about which idea is the *perfect* one and just pick *any* one. Test it. See if it has legs. You'll know quickly enough. Or maybe you won't. Maybe you won't discover until page 150 that it's dead on the vine. But that's okay. As you write more, not only will your writing get better and better, so will your ability to pick out the great ideas from the average ones.

Tip: If you're having trouble judging the quality of a certain manuscript, put it aside for at least a week and then come back to it. When you look at it with fresh eyes, you'll know.

EXCUSE #2

Writing chapter two seems wickedly intimidating.

Why it isn't legit: Writing chapter one is like running the first ten minutes of a marathon—you're on adrenaline. After that, it becomes a true test to see whether you have what it takes.

I.J. SCHECTER (www.ijschecter.com) is an award-winning author, interviewer and essayist based in Toronto. His bestselling collection, *Slices: Observations From the Wrong Side of the Fairway* (John Wiley & Sons) is available in bookstores and online.

What you need to do: Stop fretting about whether you know the characters well enough or can envision exactly where the plot is going over the next 250 pages. Just write. Write whatever comes. Force yourself to meet a certain number of pages or words per day. Do it. Don't not do it.

Tip: Don't write in chapters. Write the entire manuscript as a complete story first, beginning to end. Don't break it up or assign chapters until you're done. Thinking too much about chapter breaks, scene transitions and so on can serve as an inadvertent hindrance to the actual writing—which should be paramount.

EXCUSE #3

I don't know what made me think I could write a whole novel.

Why it isn't legit: After the energetic burst of chapter one, chapter two seems daunting as heck. After the concerted effort to get chapter two down, the rest of the book seems downright impossible. But writer's block, in all its supposed forms, is just plain bogus. If you've written 50 pages, how could it make sense that you can't write another 50—and another 50 after that? You know the only way to shut up that voice that tells you you can't write? Write.

What you need to do: Remember the true reason you're writing a novel in the first place: the irrepressible need that's going to make you write whether you like it or not. Take it a chunk at a time; don't let yourself get intimidated by the whole looming beast. A thousand words here, a few pages there—you'll get there. Because, actually, you have no choice.

Tip: Plot the story backwards. I'm serious. Start with the ending and then work in reverse. When you're finished, you'll have a full outline.

EXCUSE #4

This all made sense a hundred pages ago. Now I don't know what the hell I'm talking about.

Why it isn't legit: Every writer in history has had to deal with the psychological roller coaster that is writing, whether it's a 2,000-word short story or sprawling epic. One minute your writing is spellbinding, the next it's a dog's breakfast. On page 50, everything seems cohesive and fluid; on page 100, it seems threadbare and disjointed. It goes with the territory.

What you need to do: Remind yourself that every writer writes to a certain level of ability every time he or she sits down to compose. Yes, to your eyes the writing might seem wonderful one moment and miserable the next, but that's just your perception playing tricks on you. How you evaluate your writing on a given day likely has more to do with how fat or thin you feel, whether your new relationship is going well or poorly, and how many copies of your most loved/hated author's new book just sold in its first week of release. Just get the story down. Later, when you go back to it fresh, you'll have a more objective view. Slightly more objective, anyway.

Tip: Before you get too deep into the manuscript, chart some basic elements to keep you in control: each character's age, general personality, reason for being in the story, and specific motivations; an overall description of the setting, including anything special or unusual about it; and any important date or event references, so that you can always go back and check that you aren't contradicting something you've written earlier.

EXCUSE #5

I don't know how to end it.

Why it isn't legit: If you started it, you can finish it.

What you need to do: Also, take a good hard look at whether your story can end before you've currently ended it. It's said that most stories actually begin on page two, which I firmly believe. I also believe most stories end before the last page. Go have a look and see if I'm right.

Tip: Take half a dozen books you've read before and re-read their final 20 pages. Then, if you don't already know where your own story is going to end, sketch out three possible endings. The right denouement will probably make itself obvious.

EXCUSE #6

I can't bring myself to change these words. They're like my babies. Plus, how do I know I won't end up cutting out the best parts?

Why it isn't legit: Revision aversion is strictly about ego, and the sooner you put that ego aside, the sooner you'll improve your manuscripts by leaps and bounds. Beginning writers often ask me the number-one hardest thing for a writer to learn, and I always tell them the same thing: learning to enjoy tearing apart your own work.

What you need to do: When you plunge in and start to edit your manuscript, don't think of it as detraction; think of it as enhancement—because it is. Any first draft is just a prototype. It's the *final* version of the product that counts. So embrace the editing process. It can be exhilarating, liberating, empowering and, ultimately—when you sit down to read the improved manuscript—tremendously gratifying. Also, learning to write and learning to revise are two different, but equally important, skills. There isn't a successful writer on the planet who's only a good writer or only a good reviser. Every great writer has worked hard to be both.

Tip: Avoid the edit-as-you-go syndrome. I'm not talking about deleting the word you've just written and replacing it with a better one; I'm talking about scrapping and rewriting entire paragraphs or sections as a substitute for getting words down on the page. There is nothing more important as a writer than conditioning yourself to produce drafts first, then edit them.

EXCUSE #7

I freak out when I think about sending my work anywhere. I don't know if I can stand the rejection.

Why it isn't legit: You have two choices in this business. Grow a thick hide and start sending your work out, or write material for the rest of your life and never share it with anyone. The thing is, that latter choice is incompatible with the reasons you write in the first place: to express your feelings and opinions, to share them with others, hopefully through publication, and to have lots and lots of people pay money to read them. You don't want to deal with the rejection? Then let me ask you this. What's worse in your mind: having to hear "no" lots of times on the way to publishing success, or never having tried?

What you need to do: If you love them, set them free. Get your work to a level you believe is spit-polish fantabulous, listen to the voice in your head when it tells you it's time to submit, take the time to study your *Writer's Market*, proofread a zillion times, make sure your query is short and great (and that you've spelled the editor's name right), inhale deeply, and then let yourself click Send or drop the envelope into the mail. It isn't an easy moment, but you'll survive it. And, like revising your own work, the more often you force yourself to do it, the less of a big deal it will become. Tip: When your work does get rejected—and it will—it's okay to let yourself get angry, frustrated or mildly homicidal. But it's only okay if you put a time limit on this reaction. I impose on myself a ten-minute limit. When I get a reply I didn't want to hear, I allow my emotions to boil to the surface in whatever form, but I give them only ten minutes to fester. Then I turn them into productive energy.

EXCUSE #8

It's hard to make a living writing.

Why it isn't legit: It's *definitely* hard to make enough money from writing to do it full-time. But who says you have to do it full-time to call yourself a writer? If we measured writing success only by the ability to do it professionally, there would be very few writers. More writers than you think have their fingers in other pies.

What you need to do: Put aside any hard-and-fast definitions of "success" you may be clinging to, like "I will write a bestselling novel" or "I will make X amount of dollars from my writing." Those kinds of concrete feats are largely beyond your control. Instead, take control of the things you *can* influence, like how much you write, when you write, and what ideas you submit when. Build your credentials and your profile over time. Yes, there are the Stephenie Meyer and John Grisham stories that happen every once in a while. And I wish that kind of success for you. But look at your writing career as a long-term thing. Think of all those actors who say "It took me 20 years to become an overnight success." They became overnight successes because they had the right attitude in the first place.

Tip: Whatever your day job is, when you're at work, be about work. When you're writing, be about writing. Try not to spend all your time at work talking about "what you really want to do," because you then preclude yourself from the upward progression you deserve. You might not even think about, or be aware of, how good you actually are at your job, but other people probably recognize it, so, while you're waiting for that big writing strike, allow yourself the possibility of reaping the rewards of your other talents and efforts, too.

Articles

EXCUSE #9

It seems impossible to keep track of everything.

Why it isn't legit: Creative people constantly use the excuse that their creativity is at odds with the instinct for good organization. I don't buy it, and neither should you. Let's look at this simply. As I've often been heard to say, when you're well organized, you can spend more time writing and less time trying to find the stapler. And don't you want to spend your time writing?

What you need to do: Create a simple system of organization. First, buy some folders, hanging files, vertical organizers—whatever works best for your working area—and label them according to logical categories. For example, I use categories like Contracts, Submissions and Correspondence, and then I have sub-folders for each. Next, organize yourself electronically. Create e-mail folders that precisely match the physical folders you've created (or at least align them as closely as possible), and start filing individual e-mails. Do the same for all your manuscripts and other documents. Don't let them sit among a vast pool of stuff, making them difficult to find, reference and keep track of. If it's warranted, make multiple sub-folders. Go as many layers down as you need to until everything is where it belongs and easy to find. It will make your life immensely easier and your writing time infinitely more fruitful.

Tip: The busier you get, the more you'll benefit from following the one-spot-for-one-thing rule. The rule is simple: Designate one spot for each important item you use, and always put it away in that same spot. Oh, sure, it seems easy, but it isn't. Try it. I guarantee you'll adore it once you get good at it. Memory sticks, pens, rulers, stamps, envelopes, CDs, keys, wallets, manuscripts—the list of things we all have to keep track of day to day is almost endless. But follow this rule and you'll want to kiss yourself for the ease with which you can locate things. Now if I could just convince my wife to follow it.

EXCUSE #10

I want my writing to be read and adored by millions, but I don't want to have to be an "Author."

Why it isn't legit: You know how you get all annoyed when you hear movie stars whining about how they don't get any privacy? What do you say to the TV when you watch them say these things? Right: "So why did you become an actor in the first place, jerk?"

What you need to do: Understand that writers today need to put themselves out there in order to sell. You need to be a social marketer. You need to be a strategic (read: shameless) self-promoter. You need to force yourself to talk proudly and commercially about your writing at social gatherings. You need to embrace the aspirational spotlight. One of my goals is to change the perception that authors don't make good talk-show guests. Make it one of your goals, too.

Tip: Attend readings by visiting writers—at libraries, community centers, bookstores, auditoriums, wherever. Watching other authors in action will help you learn how some use the public eye to their advantage and some don't. Study the ones who do, and emulate them.

ARTICLES

Which Arc Are We On?

How to Keep Your Stories Straight

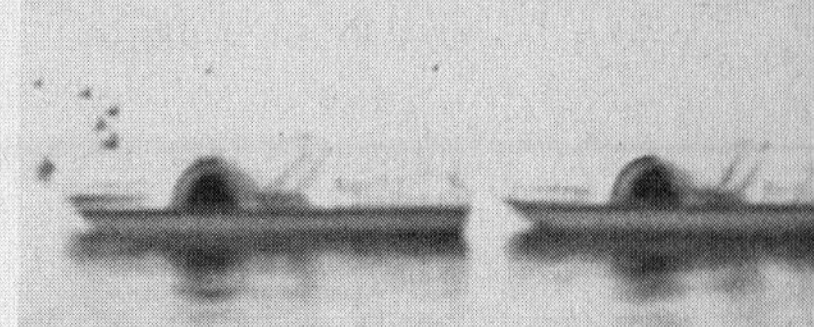

by Janice Hussein

Novel writers face a number of complexities when writing the dramatic arcs of their stories. The dramatic arcs involve the major elements of the novel: plot, structure, character, conflict. And like the composer of music, who drafts the right notes, phrases, and movements for an orchestra, the writer creates the words, scenes and arcs to be played in harmony in the reader's mind. There are many arcs in play, at any time in a novel; they are all intertwined, and they must all work together in harmony.

So, in the middle of writing your novel, you might find yourself thinking something like: Which (damn) arc am I on? Story arc? Character arc? Romantic? Subplot? And how many are in play at any particular point in this novel? Especially when they are all entwined. So how can we better understand these dramatic arcs? What are their roles, their interrelationships? What determines when each arc begins and ends within the larger structure, and how does that affect suspense? What's involved with creating a piece of fiction with great dramatic arcs that keep the reader interested from beginning to end? Obviously, to some extent, the answer depends on the story, on how the story is told, but it also depends on the structure and those arcs.

What is an arc? The word "arc" implies both a unity and a progression, both a noun and a verb. As a verb, the word means "to follow an arc-shaped course"—*Merriam-Webster's Collegiate Dictionary,* 11th Ed. As a noun, arc is defined several ways: "the apparent path...; something arched or curved; a curved path; a sustained... discharge... across a gap ...; a continuous progression or line of development in a story's dramatic arc." For our purposes, that "progression or line of development" implies a beginning and end, and then in-between, growth and/or progression, suggesting that change has occurred, that we aren't in the same place at the end of the novel. Thus, dramatic arcs provide cohesiveness, a unity that defines what a novel is—plot, character and so on. But within that unity lies action, movement; these dramatic arcs also house the engine of fiction—the conflict, complications, turning points, character growth.

What exactly are the Story, Character, Romantic, and Subplot arcs? The Story arc is the essential or main plot, the "line of development "of the story, the external conflict which poses the Central question that becomes the focus of the hero, through which all the conflict is played—until the goal is reached at the end, and that Central question

JANICE HUSSEIN is a professional editor and freelance writer. Learn more at www.documentdriven.com.

is answered. By contrast, the Character arcs are the process of change that a character undergoes over the course of a story, so that by story end, the characters have grown by struggling against the conflict and are thus prepared and able to meet and overcome the "forces of antagonism." Similar to the Story arc, the Romantic arc is a "line of development "in the novel by which the hero and heroine meet, face obstacles to their relationship, and finally come together. This arc can be the main story arc, as in romance novels, or it can be a subplot arc, as in *Fatal Burn*, by Lisa Jackson. And finally, the Subplot arcs are the secondary plots, story lines that are less important in both scope and length. But in the novel, all these arcs are interrelated, woven together.

STORY ARC

Let's start with Story arc, as it is probably the dramatic arc that everyone knows the best. This is the external conflict, involving the protagonist's main goal, the obstacles that must be overcome, and the consequences that must be faced from decisions the protagonists must make to reach that goal.

The Story arc shows a progression of conflict. A novel begins by establishing the protagonist's Ordinary world, and then moves the action ahead with the Inciting Incident, the escalating conflict—1st turning point, the midpoint or 2nd turning point, and the last or 3rd turning point—the black moment, and then concludes with the climax, resolution, and perhaps an epilogue. So basically, the setup, complications and turning points, and then the resolution of the conflict.

Conflict unifies and drives the story. Without conflict, and without a unifying plot, there is no novel. A novel must have a plot. If it doesn't have a plot, then it's not a novel—it's an essay. For the conflict in a novel to work correctly, there must be momentum. There must be conflict in each scene; the scenes must build on other scenes—what happens must occur or be based upon what has already occurred, must build on what has occurred in previous scenes. The story arc must build to the climatic moment.

The story arc is set up in Act One, by introducing all the story elements—characters, plot, setting, tone, Inciting Incident. The setup orients the reader and focuses the story line. The story arc should ideally begin in the first chapter, with the inciting incident, which begins the main plotline or at least leads the reader to the main plotline—the major conflict may not be revealed until chapter two or three. Regardless, the inciting incident must happen within the first 3 chapters. However, it should not occur too far into the story, as this will make the beginning too long without a distinct purpose, and will lose the readers' interest. Otherwise there is no set formula for when it should happen—it depends on the story. The inciting incident occurs through chance or the antagonist's actions or through the protagonist's decision or actions.

But the setup of the story arc is not completed when the Inciting Incident happens, unless the Central question has been raised. The Central question is, will the protagonist reach or attain their central goal. For example, in *Dream Man* by Linda Howard, the inciting incident is the first murder, in chapter one, with the heroine aware of the incident, but the Central question isn't raised until she decides whether or not to become involved, which happens in chapter three.

How this arc affects suspense

The story arc and the suspense are powered by the turning points, obstacles, barriers, reversals and complications, which the protagonist faces over the course of the novel. These turning points, obstacles, barriers, reversals and complications are usually caused by four things: the antagonist's actions and goals; the protagonist's actions and reactions; interaction with the subplot and characters; and chance. The suspense, as a function of that external conflict or story arc, should be strong enough, palpable enough to carry the reader through to the end of the book. If the story arc ends too soon, the novel, action, and characters would then have no direction, no purpose. There is nothing more to keep the reader interested in the novel—the conflict ends, the suspense ends, and you've lost the reader.

The story arc of the novel should have at least 2 turning points or reversals—the three-act structure, the minimum structure for the novel—but more are often used. The turning points focus the story and help create momentum. Each turning point performs these 4 major functions: raises the Central question again; creates time for the character's decision or enlightenment; raises the stakes; and pushes the story into the next act. The second turning point performs an additional function by creating greater momentum.

For the Story arc in the novel with a three-act structure, there are five major scenes that must be shown, not told: the Inciting Incident; the climax of Act I (Turning point 1); the black moment; the climax of Act II (Turning point 2); and the novel's climax in Act III (the climatic moment). These scenes should not be summarized. The turning point at the end of Act One should not happen more than one-fifth to one-fourth into the book; otherwise the beginning is too long. The last turning point should occur about three-quarters of the way through the book, leaving room for complications, for building suspense and rising action. In the three-act structure, the second turning point should not occur so late in the novel that the middle continues too long without a major complication or reversal.

One way to shore up the sagging middle—besides barriers, complications and reversals—is to add subplots or another turning point. So an example of adding a turning point or act would be to add a midpoint; then the novel would have a four-act structure. There can be up to 5 or more turning points, but too many acts can make the events of the novel too repetitious, and the novel may become too unwieldy for the writer... and the reader. There has to be a balance; but that balance has to serve the story, not limit it.

The Story arc shows a progression of conflict in relation to the protagonist, and the dynamic between those two. It provides the obstacles that force the growth of the character (character arc), so that when all the forces of antagonism converge, and the final face-off occurs, the character will achieve the goal. The external conflict (story arc) and internal conflict (character arc) are intertwined throughout the plot. They are interdependent, each playing off the other.

CHARACTER ARC

Each major character should have their own story line—a plot or subplot with a goal, motivation, obstacles and some kind of antagonist. But this plot or subplot is different from the Character arc, which is internal conflict.

Any major characters—protagonists or antagonists—in the main plot or subplots can have a character arc. It's better if at least one of the protagonists have a character arc. This gives depth to the character and to the story.

Internal conflict is the emotional facet of conflict. It puts the character's inner mind on stage, showing the interplay between emotion and reason, between the character arc and the story arc. The more the reader knows and identifies with the protagonist, the more they will bond with the character and the story emotionally. It allows the readers to more fully empathize and identify with the characters, and to identify with their struggles on a more personal level. Thus, it makes the characters more sympathetic and believable. It draws the readers into the story more completely, since readers respond to emotion and to the intimacy of the character arc. It dimensionalizes the story arc and the characters. And readers remember compelling, multidimensional characters.

Character growth propels the novel forward, because changing circumstances (obstacles, reversals, and so on) will force change in the character, and will force that changing character to face obstacles by attempting new strategies to achieve the goal—they will think differently based on those changing circumstances and what has or hasn't worked for them. Character arcs begin with the introduction of major or subplot characters, usually in the first few chapters, and they end with the resolution, or with the end of the story arc or the subplot. It shows the character's transformation. Character arcs more fully reveal the true nature of each character, through actions and decisions that change the characters as they go through obstacles, so that by the novel's end, the reader finally sees who the characters really are and sees how they've been forced to change in response to events.

How this arc affects suspense

Character drives plot and plot drives character. The character should be someone who we as readers can empathize with, identify with, and root for, and this pairing of character and plot—and what could happen—keeps us turning the pages. The character arc functions to drive the action and the suspense, because changing, growing characters must change their strategies to meet the escalating efforts of the antagonists, until at the climax, the protagonists finally succeed.

Further, without a character arc, the character may seem unsympathetic, unredeemable and static, less interesting. And readers won't feel as involved in the story, and might lose interest. A novel that doesn't have a character arc may seem to lack sufficient character development. Characters should be compelling; thus, showing—not telling—character development in the form of a character arc is an excellent means of making this happen.

ROMANTIC ARC

The romantic arc can be either the story arc or the subplot arc. In a romance, the romantic arc would follow the "rules" of a story arc. In other fiction, such as mainstream, thrillers, and so on, the romantic arc begins when the hero or heroine meets the love interest, usually during or after the inciting incident. In such cases, the romantic arc would end—following the guidelines for subplots—usually before the main story arc.

The romantic arc, like the story arc, becomes intertwined with the character arc. One or both protagonists must change and grow to achieve the romantic goal.

How this arc affects suspense

Problems may occur with the romantic arc. In a romance, ideally, the hero and heroine should meet in the first chapter, but at least by the third chapter. If they meet too late in the novel's beginning, then the story arc—in this case, the romantic arc—would begin too late. The suspense would flounder. The suspense is also affected by the obstacles to the hero and heroine getting together, both through the romantic arc and the character arc. But if the romantic arc ends too soon, then the novel loses suspense, loses tension. And then one of the elements that kept the reader solidly involved in the story would be gone.

SUBPLOT ARC(S)

Subplot arcs are comprised of the secondary plots, involving the secondary characters, who aren't as well developed as the main characters; generally these arcs begin after the main plot and end before the main plot. The subplots usually help to carry the theme of the novel or complement the theme of the novel, yet offer some contrast to the main plot and characters. Subplots provide a sense of real characters in a real world within the novel, a sense of community.

The subplots may be presented in a one-act, two-act or three-act structure. Ideally, the subplots have setup, complications, turning points and resolution just like the main plot. A subplot may begin before the Inciting Incident, but usually they begin during or after that Incident, and they end before or during the novel's climax. In a novel other than a romance, one of the subplots may be the romance involving the protagonist. Examples of this occur in *The Bourne Identity*, between Jason & Marie, and in the movie *Witness*, between John and Rachel.

The novel *Bet Me*, by New York Times bestselling author Jennifer Crusie, offers an excellent illustration of how the subplot arcs intersect with the romantic arc. The romantic arc begins in chapter one, scene two, in a reversal where Min, the heroine, makes a decision about whether or not to date the hero, Cal. Then two of the subplots begin and end in this order:

Subplot 1 begins: Chapter 1, Scene 2. Liza and Tony.

Subplot 2 begins: Chapter 1, Scene 2. Roger and Bonnie.

Subplot 1 ends: Chapter 12, Scene 5. Liza and Tony.

Subplot 2 ends: Chapter 15, Scene 4. Roger and Bonnie.

The main romantic arc ends in chapter 16, and chapter 17 serves as an Epilogue.

The movie *Witness* provides another example of subplot turning points within the framework of a main plot and its turning points. The first turning point occurs when Rachel nurses John after he is shot, at the beginning of Act II. The second turning point occurs when they kiss. The turning points of the subplot occur right after the turning points of the main plot. The turning points of the main plot arc are the shooting in the garage, with the second turning point occurring when John's whereabouts are discovered.

How this arc affects suspense

Subplots should intersect the Central plot in some way, either to resonate or accentuate the suspense. If the subplot runs parallel to the Central plot, then it is not serving the story. All elements must work together into a cohesive whole; otherwise the readers will wonder where the story is going and become confused and disinterested.

Secondary characters in subplots help with the character and plot development in the main plot and characters. An example of this kind of plot development through secondary characters appears in *Bet Me*: the heroine, Min, would never have approached the hero and overheard "the bet" if she hadn't been pushed to do so by her best friends—the characters in the subplots.

The use of subplots must be balanced against the exigencies of the story arc, of the suspense. The more subplots there are, the stronger the main plot should be. Three subplots are a good number for a novel, but more than five subplots would be too complicated for most books. A subplot should be given fewer scenes and less page space than the Central plot, so that the subplot doesn't take over the story. One way to do this is to summarize parts of the subplot rather than to tell them. The beginnings and endings of subplots can be staggered to create interest, depth, and suspense in the middle of the novel, and keep the readers turning the pages.

SUMMARY: THE ARCS

Combining all these Arcs into a tightly woven novel can be somewhat daunting. It requires juggling a number of elements at the same time and making decisions, based on your characters and the conflict in your novel, about how to multi-layer to produce that seamless cohesion of arcs—story, character, romantic and subplot—that is a great novel. Observe how other authors incorporate these elements into their novels. How do they make them come together? How are the elements interrelated? What works and what doesn't work? Only by understanding how the parts work together do we understand what makes a great novel.

ARTICLES

Exploring the World of Flash Fiction

by Kelcey Parker

Grab your notebook, pack your binoculars, squirt some bug spray, and don your hat; we're headed out in search of that ubiquitous but elusive form: flash fiction. We might begin our quest with a few questions about flash fiction's identifying features. How big is it? (250-1000 words) What are the different breeds? (short short, smoke-long, quick fiction, microfiction) What is its natural habitat? (print magazines, online journals, hand-held electronics) How has the species evolved over time? (from surprise endings to stylized truths) And what do we do if we think we've found one of these creatures? (take good notes!) Lucky for us, we've got the perfect resource to tuck into our sacks: *The Rose Metal Press Field Guide to Writing Flash Fiction*. The *Field Guide* helps readers capture "this rather wild-running flash adolescent and settle it down a bit to get a better understanding of its past, present, and future" before releasing it back into the wild.

Published in 2009, the *Field Guide* is the first source to provide a wide-ranging history of flash fiction that points to its roots in chants and myth, in Boccaccio and Shakespeare, and in Asian picture-stories—"miniatures in India, and ukiyo-e (or 'pictures of the floating world') in Japan." In her introduction to the *Field Guide*, editor Tara L. Masih moves her investigation from flash fiction's roots to its early practitioners in the West (Washington Irving, Edgar Allan Poe, Kate Chopin, O.Henry), to Asia's contribution, and then to the effects of the twentieth century's technological innovations on very short stories. In the 25 essays that follow the introduction, readers are introduced to definitions, musings, encouragement, writing prompts, and even sample stories from some of the biggest names in flash fiction.

In the following interview, you'll meet the publishers, editor, and three contributors of *The Rose Metal Press Field Guide to Flash Fiction*. Kathleen Rooney and Abigail Beckel are co-founders of Rose Metal Press; Tara L. Masih is the book's editor and author of the historical introduction; Pamela Painter is a writer and teacher who Masih credits with being one of the first to offer courses focused exclusively on flash fiction; and Kim Chinquee and Deb Olin Unferth are both exciting, up-and-coming writers of flash fiction who also contributed to the *Field Guide*. Here, each of them shares a little about their own pursuit of flash fiction.

KELCEY PARKER (www.kelceyparker.com) is the author of *For Sale By Owner* (Kore Press, 2011), a collection of short stories.

How did you come to write and publish flash fiction? What draws you to the form?

Pamela Painter: I was serving on an arts panel with James Thomas and afterwards we crossed paths in the Chicago airport. Along with writer/editor Robert Shapard, James had published a story of mine in the superb collection *Sudden Fiction*—a story that was shorter than most I wrote, but I hadn't been thinking of length at the time. James said they were working on a new anthology titled *Flash Fiction* and suggested I send him a story. I hadn't written anything that short—ever. But I gave it a try, and my story "I Get Smart" started me down the path of writing very short stories. [I guess I "got smart." Thanks, James.] Intriguing how these collections, and the magazine *Quick Fiction*, have "renamed" the short short story. In fact, last summer I titled my course at the Provincetown Fine Arts Work Center "Quick, Sudden, Flash: Writing the Short Short Story."

Abby Beckel & Kathleen Rooney: Curiously, although both of us write creatively, neither of us writes flash fiction. And while it might be the opposite of what you'd expect, our not writing it is a big part of why we publish so much of it. Even though we are not practitioners of the form, we get to act as collectors, building up our holdings and exhibiting them to the broadest possible audiences. Like curators of an awesome flash fiction museum. One particular aspect that draws us to the form is the narrative and creative punch the brevity of flash offers at the time that you read it, while also setting the story bouncing around in your mind for days, even years to come.

Tara L. Masih: I was writing in the very short form for years before it became popular. I learned to write what were called "vignettes," or "fragments" (the term still used in France), from my high school teacher Kathy Collins. Her style of stringing together these shorts to make a complete story worked for me. I'm drawn to it because it is comfortable territory, and I love the distillation of words and ideas the form demands.

Kim Chinquee: I wrote my first piece of flash fiction in Mary Robison's fiction writing workshop at the University of Southern Mississippi's Center for Writers. She challenged us to write a story in less than five pages. After that story ("The Top Shelf") was accepted for publication in NOON, I started reading more shorter works, becoming more fascinated with the form: how the short length invites the reader to focus more closely on each word, each detail, the essence of the work.

Deb Olin Unferth: I like the way each successful example of the form is a perfect single unit of experience, almost like a raindrop. It expresses one thing—whether the story spans an entire year's time or only a moment, or contains five characters or two—the piece is unified by one thought or idea.

Describe a time when you've revised a longer story into a flash fiction—or vice versa, when you've expanded a flash story into something longer? How do you make decisions about story length?

Painter: I've never condensed a longer story into a flash fiction. My very short stories begin short and end that way. Somehow, for me, the final length of a story is contained in the story's beginning. I never know how a story is going to develop or end when I begin, but I do know after writing a paragraph or a page whether a story will be one or two pages or seventeen or twenty-five pages. The arc and length of a new story announce themselves almost immediately, and mysteriously—no, of course—it has a lot to do with language.

Masih: Before I begin a story, I know it's going to be standard or flash. It takes a different mindset, for me, to put myself into flash mode. Immediately I'm thinking condensation, and my editing self is on high alert. I drastically slash and burn as I write sentences. I also pay more attention to my opening line. I know in a longer story I have space to meander and wander till I get the opening right, but in flash, the story has to explode out of the starting gate, as it helps guide me and the reader quickly to the conclusion, which also has to be strong. As Nathan Leslie writes in the *Field Guide*, "This is a slop-free zone."

Chinquee: Usually, for me, it's revising a flash story into something longer. I write flash almost every day, as part of my routine. On the other hand, I have taken some elements of longer stories, and created flashes from them. It usually depends upon whatever project I'm working on at the time, how much time I have, how much energy I'm able to invest in a particular piece or project.

Unferth: The first time I wanted to write a novel, I spent six months writing a hundred and fifty pages and then I stopped and starting revising. I cut a little here and a little there, and a little more and a little more, until I'd whittled it down to a page and a half, and then I published it. A friend said I should call it "My Novel." I find I have to decide in advance how long I want a piece to be or else all my work would be that way. I once read that Giacometti's *Standing Woman* and *Walking Man* pieces wouldn't exist if his brother Diego didn't run in and grab them before Giacometti whittled them down to nothing. He'd start with a large bronze slab and a chisel. Left on his own—and this had actually happened—he'd carve away at it to the point where all that was left was a tiny speck on a huge base, and then he'd take one last poke and the figure would collapse into dust. Those sculptures have an enormous power to them.

Tara's introduction to the Field Guide tracks the history of manuals and anthologies devoted to flash fiction. In the U.S., she identifies a flourish of activity in the first half of the twentieth century with the rise of magazines and printing technologies. After a few decades in which readers were lost to television, Masih says, the decade of the 1980s "was to become the decade of the rebirth of the literary short short story." Most recently, she cites flash fiction's particular fit with online and hand-held technologies. What do you think makes flash fiction an especially relevant form today?

Painter: It can fit on an iPhone. I almost feel like adding "alas." Though I want new technologies to celebrate and publish very short stories, I don't want them to decree what art should be or do. They should serve as an inspiration not as a prescription.

Beckel & Rooney: We hesitate to make any particular claims for the form's relevance or worthiness right-now-today as opposed to its relevance or worthiness in the past or the future. One of the best things about Tara's intro is that it shows that the form is a (perhaps surprisingly) enduring one. Flash fiction, under various names, has been around for a very long time. We're happy that it's so popular now, and hope it will continue to be so in the future. You could say that "relevance" is defined more by writers than by readers, as in: is this form the most effective way to tell my stories? Judging by the growing number of practitioners and the exceptional talent we saw during the creation of *The Field Guide* and see during our short short story chapbook contest each year, writers are finding flash fiction quite relevant and fruitful.

Masih: I've obviously given my theories already. I'll let the others weigh in on theirs. But I will say I don't think there is only one answer. And what does make me happy is that it is becoming a relevant and an accepted genre. There is still a lot of grumbling about this, but more and more teachers are offering it as a separate section or course. Pam Painter gets credit for being one of the first in this country to do so and to champion it at Emerson College. Her students have spread out like flash disciples, helping to create a revitalized audience.

As editors and teachers, what makes a piece of flash fiction rise to the top of the slush pile or stand out in a stack of student stories?

Painter: I want to be drawn in by the language of the first sentence, the set-up. And finally, I admire "fall away endings." I've co-authored a textbook on writing fiction, *What If? Writing Exercises for Fiction Writers,* that discusses beginnings, characterization, plot—the usual suspects. But in my short short class there are only a few questions we ask of a short short: Is the language doing its job? Does the story work? And does the last sentence memorably close the story down?

Masih: Each flash story has to be judged on its own merit. I find there are many styles that work well. What is consistent is the amount of story that a writer manages to cram, artfully, into a small space; or, vice versa, a small idea or feeling that is captured and elongated and holds your attention in a way that you just can't stop reading for a page or two.

Chinquee: Work that says something in a new way, that uses fresh language, images, and makes sensory details come alive. Work that sings, and hums, and dances!

Unferth: I like urgency and sound. I like to feel as though the writer went through a lot to get this down on the page, that this object exists not only to entertain, that there is something philosophical, emotional, and aesthetic at stake—and also that the piece is engaging with the history of humor as well (that is different from, but necessitates, being funny). And a short piece should sound like a song or a series of heartbeats: rhythmic, pulsing. Any sentence that doesn't use vowels or consonants as echoes, that doesn't use stressed syllables to its advantage is going to fall flat.

What is a successful tip you've given to students or writers about composing or publishing flash fiction?

Painter: Listen. Look. Very short stories are everywhere for the taking. And every syllable, not just every word, must count. Sometimes my class knows that a student's last sentence needs three more syllables—that the sound is not quite right.

Masih: Focus on one small truth.

Chinquee: Write from the heart, in the heart of the event/conflict/dissonance. Publish only your best work; don't publish just to be published.

What surprised you, or what did you learn about flash fiction as you participated in the making of the Field Guide?

Painter: Tara's introduction to the Field Guide is, in itself, an education in the evolution of the short short story; it should be read by everyone curious about or devoted to that form.

Beckel & Rooney: It's not quite accurate to call it "surprise" exactly since it keeps happening and since we should be used to it by now, but whenever Rose Metal Press embarks on a flash-related project, we are overwhelmed and inspired by how many people are so totally into and supportive of flash as a form. The community of people who love to read and write it is tight-knit and enthusiastic, and we're psyched to get to be a part of that movement.

Masih: I mention in the intro that I had no idea what I was in for when I took on the history of what I strongly believe is its own genre. I had no idea how far back the history went, and how many respected authors were experimenting with it at the end of the 1800s. I also didn't realize O. Henry was the driving force early on, or that writers could make a living off of placing their short shorts in magazines.

(Besides Rose Metal Press, of course...) What are some of your favorite journals and publishers of flash fiction? What are they doing well?

Painter: Quite a few writers and editors—Robert Shapard, James Thomas, Dinty Moore, Tom Hazuka, Randall Brown, Mark Budman—are publishing short short story collections and also assembling rich, wide-ranging anthologies. I greatly admire the journal *Quick Fiction*. One of the founding editors, Jennifer Pieroni, was in my short short class at Emerson. Instead of going on to an MFA program she started *Quick Fiction*, which soon became one of the places to publish very short stories. The late Jerome Stern's superb *Micro Fiction* collected some of the best entries to his World's Best Short Short Story contest.

Masih: What the best journals are doing is weeding through a lot of bad flash to find those "comet sightings" that Robert Shapard and James Thomas, in their introduction to *New Sudden Fiction*, rightly claim are so rare.

Chinquee: *NOON, Quick Fiction, Willow Springs, wigleaf, Conjunctions, elimae, Denver Quarterly*. These journals are consistent and surprising.

Unferth: My favorites are *NOON* and *McSweeney's*. I read them cover to cover, most issues. There is very little patience in those two journals for sheer storytelling. The editors demand a commitment to the modern. You can hear in the background their editorial voice. I believe in the editorial voice: the journal as artistic editorial expression.

MORE ABOUT YOUR GUIDES

Pamela Painter is the author of two story collections, *Getting to Know the Weather*, and *The Long and Short of It, and* co-author of *What If? Writing Exercises for Fiction Writers*. Her flash fiction has appeared in *Sudden Fiction, Flash Fiction, Flash Fiction Forward*, and *MicroFiction*. Painter teaches at Emerson College in Boston. Her first collection of flash fiction, *Wouldn't You Like to Know*, was published in 2010 by Carnegie Mellon University Press.

Kathleen Rooney is the editor and co-founder of Rose Metal Press. Her latest book is the essay collection *For You, For You I Am Trilling These Songs* (Counterpoint, 2010).

Abby Beckel is the publisher and co-founder of Rose Metal Press. She has worked professionally in publishing for more than nine years and is a published poet.

Tara L. Masih is editor of the *Rose Metal Press Field Guide to Writing Flash Fiction* (2009), and her debut story collection, *Where the Dog Star Never Glows*, was published in 2010. She received an MA in Writing and Publishing from Emerson College, and has published fiction, poetry, and essays in numerous anthologies and literary magazines. She now works as a freelance book editor in Andover, Massachusetts. www.taramasih.com

Kim Chinquee is the author of *Oh Baby* (Ravenna Press) and *Pretty* (White Pine Press). She is the recipient of a Pushcart Prize, and lives in Buffalo, New York.

Deb Olin Unferth is the author of the flash fiction collection *Minor Robberies* and the novel *Vacation*, both from McSweeney's. Her next book, *Revolution*, is forthcoming in 2011 from Henry Holt. She is an assistant professor at Wesleyan University in Connecticut.

ARTICLES

Conferences, Workshops & Retreats

Should You Go?

by Jack Smith

If you're serious about your craft, you spend a lot of time working at it—alone. Writing, as any writer knows, is a very solitary activity. If you're a member of a writing group or guild, or have writer friends who provide feedback and encouragement, you're already connected to other writers. But still, if you don't attend conferences, you may be missing out on the chance to make important professional contacts. Plus more: valuable information about craft and marketing from presentations and panels; creative writing workshops and professional criticism of your work; an opportunity to meet with agents and publishers. There's the cost, of course, and possibly the time away from work. But if you can swing those two, a good conference may be well worth the investment.

For one thing, there's the spark of inspiration.

"I've often left conferences feeling energized and renewed, committed to completing a writing project," says Anjali Banerjee, a commercial success in both young adult and literary women's fiction. For literary fiction writer Phyllis Westover, "Perhaps one of the biggest benefits of writers conferences is just the stoking of one's own furnace by virtue of being in an energetic writing environment totally protected from all the distractions of business as usual and the many obligations of life."

To make your conference experience this positive, choose well. Banerjee emphasizes that different conferences have different focuses—some on craft, some on marketing and promotion, and some on a combination of craft and marketing. Which one is right for you? Start with the current issue of *Novel & Short Story Writer's Market*, which has about fifty pages of Conferences & Workshops. Visit the conference website and, if need be, email or call for more information. Check with colleagues for advice on good ones to attend. If you are working in a specific genre (e.g., romance, mystery, Christian, science fiction and fantasy), it may be best to choose a conference devoted to that area.

What you want out of a conference can probably be boiled down to two basic benefits: personal and professional.

CONNECTING WITH OTHER WRITERS

Tom LaMarr, author of *Hallelujah City*, sees conferences as a way out of the typical writer's alienated existence: "Like many writers, I produced my first novel in a vacuum.

JACK SMITH's satirical novel *Hog to Hog* (Texas Review Press) won the George Garrett Fiction Prize. His stories and essays have appeared in many publications, including North American Review, The Southern Review, Georgia Review and Ploughshares. Besides his writing, he co-edits The Green Hills Literary Lantern.

A conference would have been helpful, if only to offset that feeling of isolation." Joe Benevento, co-editor of *The Green Hills Literary Lantern*, notes the sense of camaraderie one sometimes feels in the presence of fellow writers. "Even a few people who I rejected for *GHLL* ended up saying things like, 'Yours was the nicest rejection letter I ever received,' or things of that sort."

Besides the chance to socialize with other writers, there's of course the professional benefit, as Nathan Leslie, author of six volumes of fiction, points out: "One can establish connections through writing conferences that can help advance one's writing career." But with which writers? "Conferences are a great way to meet fellow writers who are a step or two beyond you in your career," says Steven Wingate, author of the prize-winning *Wifeshopping*. "You can learn as much from them about getting where you want to be as you can from people who have already reached the top of the totem pole because they've recently gone through what you're going through."

You should be aware of the hierarchy, especially at large conferences, as far as writers several career notches above you. Wingate cautions against "expecting that you'll hobnob with the big authors," which "isn't realistic because they are inundated with requests from people and want to protect their time just as any other writer does." Benevento has noted the hierarchical nature of such large conferences as the annual AWP. DeWitt Henry, founder of *Ploughshares*, and workshop leader at several conferences, applauds The Squaw Valley Writer's Conference for eliminating this very problem: "The tenor of the entire conference is engaging and egalitarian, rather than hierarchical. Financial aid is available on a merit basis. When a staff member discovers exciting work, word quickly spreads throughout the conference."

PRESENTATIONS, PANELS, BOOKS FAIRS

Depending on the conference, presentations and panels can cover a wide variety of topics, from craft to marketing to promotion in several genres. Nathan Leslie identifies these program elements as "the bread and butter of most conferences." Conference offerings should be available on the conference website. "What an opportunity to learn from those farther along the writing path!" exclaims Mary-Lane Kamberg, author of nonfiction as well as poetry and fiction. "Don't be afraid to ask questions. Writers conferences are also good places to learn what's hot and what's not." Kamberg says of The Maui Writers Conference and Retreat: "Every presenter had multiple bestseller titles and was happy to share the nuts and bolts."

Phyllis Westover appreciates one informative aspect of the Iowa Summer Writing Festival—the "Elevenses": "Between 11 and noon each day, a different member of the teaching staff speaks on a different topic or aspect of writing. Not only is that informative, but it gives you a good taste of presenters/instructors with whom you might want to take a workshop with another year."

Panels are another highlight of conferences, and agents often sit on panels. The tips they offer can sometimes be surprising. Midge Raymond, author of the prize-winning *Forgetting English*, recalls one example: "One thing I remember well was an agent in a panel saying that a first-time author does NOT want a big, six- or seven-figure advance ("you're screwing yourself" were her exact words) because the chances of earning it back in sales were slim, and it would forever be a struggle to sell your next book. This is a surprise to most writers (everyone thinks they want a big advance), but it's such an important thing to consider and I was glad to hear it mentioned."

Janna Cawrse Esarey, author of the memoir *The Motion of the Ocean*, mentions another surprising agent comment: "I remember one agent who announced at an Agent/Editor Panel that the reason they were all here was to meet us, the writers. Don't be shy, she said, about pitching at lunch, in the hall, in the bathroom. She was kidding about the bathroom. But you could almost see the rest of the panel cringe as she spoke. Her point was a good one, though," says Esarey. "Writers who politely approach agents and editors are helping them do their job—regardless of how intently agents and editors may examine their shoes as they walk down the hall."

Of course, you might pick up such tips or comments in a creative writing craft book or magazine article. But when a conference has an agent presence, and agents serve on panels, they're right there to drop nuggets of wisdom—and if you have questions, you can direct these questions right at them.

One advantage of large-scale conferences is book fairs. Simmons Buntin, Editor/Publisher, *Terrain.org: A Journal of the Built & Natural Environments*, emphasizes the importance of book fairs at large conferences like AWP: "Visiting tables/booths and talking with editorial staff (and sometimes contributors) is the best way to learn about the publication short of actually purchasing it (or, in our case, visiting it online)." But one shouldn't get the idea that this is a forum "for submitting work," says Buntin. Instead, book fairs provide a good opportunity "for identifying publications you're interested in submitting your work to (whether individual literary journals or book publishers), talking with the editors to get a sense of what they're interested in for upcoming issues, and rubbing elbows with other inquiring writers."

WORKSHOPS

Many conferences—as well as workshops and retreats—offer writing workshops. Check to be sure that the one you're interested in does. AWP, for instance, doesn't. If you're planning on participating in a writing workshop, be sure to find out the set-up before you go. Robert Garner McBrearty, a recent winner of the Sherwood Anderson Foundation Fiction Award for his short story collection *Episode* (Pocol Press), has had fellowships at MacDowell Colony and the Fine Arts Work Center, in Provincetown, MA., as well as taught at several conferences. According to McBrearty, one should find out what is meant by the term "Workshop" prior to attending a planned-on conference. This may mean directed creative writing exercises—not a critique of your work. Don't disallow craft workshops, though. Midge Raymond has taught revision workshops at Get Lit! in Spokane as well as at the Southern California Writers' Conference in San Diego. "I was happily surprised to find that the revision workshops were very well attended (often when teaching I find that this is a least favorite aspect of writing). But perhaps," says Raymond, "because conferences focus on getting your work sold, attendees see the value in it."

But let's say a craft workshop doesn't meet your present needs. You want professional feedback on a particular story or novel-in-progress. If so, be sure you know the exact workshop set-up. Workshops that provide critiques of writers' work may be "run like grad school workshops, where one's work is critiqued by a teacher and fellow students," says McBrearty. If this is the case, you should find out in advance the answers to three basic questions: "How many people will be in the workshop; how many stories will one be able to present to the workshop; and how long and thoroughly will one's story be discussed?"

"Chances are," McBrearty points out, "in many conference workshops, you may only have an opportunity to have one of your stories, or a novel chapter discussed." But this presents another question: "Will the stories be read ahead of time, or will they be read out loud in class?" If the latter, "don't expect the level of critique to be very high. Much of the value of this type of workshop will depend upon the adeptness of the teacher and one's fellow students and also on one's own ability to take and give criticism."

Make sure, says McBrearty, to find out about the workshop leader. "What are his or her credentials? If possible, read some of his or her work. If you're writing a detective novel, and the teacher writes absurdist short stories, it may not be a good fit."

Finally, McBrearty advises writers not to "trust everything that is said, either positively or negatively, about one's work."

Three basic points to keep in mind, then: Know the workshop set-up, and decide if it's right for you. Check out the workshop leader's credentials. Go to the workshop hoping to get solid feedback—not "the answer."

Writers have certainly had rewarding experiences from workshop activities. Cliff Garstang, author of *In an Uncharted Country*, states: "The most useful workshops I've attended are those with workshop faculty who are genuinely interested in teaching and helping writers improve their craft. My experiences at Sewanee Writers' Conference and Bread Loaf Writers' Conference have been uniformly positive. Not only are the attendees generally serious about their craft, but the workshops are dedicated." Garstang also attended the Tinker Mountain Writers' Workshop twice. "It's a well-organized smaller conference that attracts good faculty, but the student writers aren't all experienced. The advantage is that the size allows for plenty of interaction with the faculty and sometimes closer attention than you might get at a bigger conference." Under the Volcano, in Tepoztlán, Mexico, was also a good experience, says Garstang. "It's small, with excellent faculty, so you get a lot of face time with them."

Steven Wingate appreciates this face-to-face quality in Sozopol Fiction Seminars, held in Sozopol, Bulgaria. It's "very new and intimate, and it's developing its personality as it moves forward. The founder, Elizabeth Kostova, even workshops her own fiction alongside those of the seminar participants."

Dana Wood, Chicago literary author, recently attended Writing Away Retreats. It met her definition of a successful workshop: "A successful workshop does not mean that you will walk away signed with an agent or a bona fide contract from an editor. What comes from a successful workshop is that you learned something, something that will help you be a better writer, something imparted to you by the carefully-selected literary professionals in attendance."

MEETING AGENTS & EDITORS

As with workshops, don't go in blind. If the conference blurb or website doesn't mention agents and editors, don't assume they'll be there. If agents and editors will be present, or "participate," what does this mean? If the conference blurb isn't more specific than this, then, says Robert Garner McBrearty, you have to wonder about the various scenarios possible: "Does it mean that writers need to be lucky or aggressive enough to meet one at a cocktail party, or does it mean the agents and editors will be giving talks, or does it mean that there will be some system set up where one can meet the agents/editors and have one's work reviewed? Ideally, one will have a chance to set up an appointment, which may mean paying an extra fee." Check all this out in advance, McBrearty urges.

McBrearty himself had a good experience at the Aspen Summer Words Writing Retreat and Literary Festival. "There was an organized system for signing up to meet agents and editors and to have one's work reviewed. There was an added fee to meet agents or editors, though it seemed quite reasonable. After reading my opening chapter, the agent that I met asked me to send the rest of my novel to her."

Cliff Garstang has found that Sewanee and Bread Loaf are great conferences to meet with agents and editors. "Faculty members have been known to recommend their workshop participants to visiting agents, which is an invaluable foot in the door. And it frequently happens that agents and editors will approach writers whose readings they've heard and liked."

Dana Wood praises Writing Away Retreats: "They differ from other conferences because the publishing professionals are very accessible. Like other retreats, you get consult time with the agents and editors and you get to make your pitch. But at Writing Away Retreats, the professionals are embedded with you all weekend. You eat meals with them, drink wine with them, play Scrabble with them, banter around a bonfire with them. This is unprecedented access compared to other conferences."

Sorche Elizabeth Fairbank, of Fairbank Literary Representation, advises authors to choose wisely amongst the range of agent and editor interactions available across the board: "It may come down to quality vs. quantity: the week-long retreat and limited attendance weekend workshops mean much more one-on-one time with fewer agents, whereas mega conferences and one-day pitch sessions tend to get you a short time with a greater variety of agents."

If you do have the opportunity to pitch your work, regardless of session type, you should consider this sound advice from Mary-Lane Kamberg: "Be sure you're pitching to someone who represents what you have written." And once that matter is settled, says Kamberg, consider what you're getting into in case the agent takes an interest in your work. Two key questions to ask yourself: Is this someone you'd like to work with? Is this "someone you would trust with your money?"

Definitely do not head off to a conference with plans to sign with an agent, cautions Steven Wingate. "Remember that the path to your agent can go through many steps, and remember that your goal in meeting an agent is not an instant 'yes' but an invitation to send a manuscript—that's all you need to do on a first meeting."

Janna Cawrse Esarey puts it this way: "They don't have to love it. They don't have to gush about it. You simply want the right to put these three words on your correspondence: Requested Materials Enclosed. That will keep you out of the slush pile."

MEETING WITH SMALL PRESS PUBLISHERS

"Writing conferences can be a useful source for finding out about publishers," states Nathan Leslie. "I personally haven't found a publisher per se through this route, but I've discovered publishers who I've later submitted my work to." As to bringing your work "to pass around," Leslie discourages this practice since many editors seem to "frown on this." What he finds most helpful about the small press publisher presence "is the fact that the editors are right there to assist with questions, to clarify what they publish and so on."

Says Barry Kitterman, author of *The Baker's Boy*, "I have connected with editors of magazines and with the publisher of my novel [SMU Press]. I think AWP is a good opportunity to try to talk to the people who are representing small presses. I also see representatives from the self-publishing enterprises there, so I'm sure a writer could arrange for someone to publish a book that way, if that's the sort of thing someone wants to do."

Joe Benevento has also appreciated the small press presence at conferences. "I met the publisher of my second novel, Lynn Price of Behler Publications, just when she was starting out with that press, and so was able to have her agree to look at *The Odd Squad*." Behler eventually published this novel, and it was a finalist, says Benevento, for the 2006 John Gardner Fiction Book Award.

SOME FINAL THOUGHTS

No two conferences are the same, so you need to be sure the conference you choose satisfies whatever goals or objectives you have. Doug Crandell, author of several works of fiction at commercial presses, cautions writers to be careful in selecting workshops: "Anybody can put up a shingle, but the staff should be people who've published recently, or agents who are actively selling books. There are some scams out there, some that may not technically be scams but are hosted by people who are not actively engaged in writing, publishing, and helping others get published." A second, different kind of caution, from Anjali Banerjee: "Ultimately, writing is a solitary pursuit. I believe that in some ways, conferences can be a distraction from facing the true work of actually completing a manuscript, revising, and sending out your work." The lesson here? Do take advantage of every opportunity to attend a good conference, but be prepared to get back to your cloister, to start cranking again, facing that computer screen alone. Inspired, of course, by all you gained at a valuable conference.

'Creating Good Old-Fashioned Buzz'

Alyson B. Stanfield's Action Plan for Self-Promotion

by Kelcey Parker

"I don't want to bother people." "I don't know where to begin." "I'm an introvert." "There aren't enough hours in the day to do it all." "I'd rather be in the studio." These are the excuses Alyson B. Stanfield hears from artists who would rather, as she says, "dive headfirst off a cliff than do anything related to self-promotion." But Stanfield knows that "if you want recognition and compensation for your work, you need to stick your neck out start telling people" about it.

Stanfield is an artist's consultant—an "art biz coach"—who has created a unique business of teaching artists how to promote and sell their work by "creating good old-fashioned buzz." Through her national workshops, newsletters, book, blog, and website, Stanfield provides artists with "no-excuse" action plans to achieve their goals. While Stanfield earned degrees in art history and has served as a museum curator, she has also worked in the U.S. Senate, and she maintains that the principles and tools she shares with artists are the same she witnessed in politics and that she now uses to run her own very successful business.

I asked Stanfield how these same principles might be applied to writers. The following Action Plan is adapted, in consultation with Stanfield and in her voice, from her book, *I'd Rather Be in the Studio: The Artist's No-Excuse Guide to Self-Promotion*, and from her website, www.artbizcoach.com, and blog, www.artbizblog.com.

ACTION 1: ACCEPT THE PRINCIPLES OF NO-EXCUSE SELF-PROMOTION

The first step in self-promotion is to accept and "own" six principles. These principles have become the foundation for my classes, writings, and workshops.

- You are in charge of your career. You have control over the submissions, sales, and descriptions of your work.
- Connections are critical to your success.
- Life isn't fair, the writing world isn't fair, and no one owes you anything. Building a successful career and reputation is hard work.
- If you ignore the latest technology, you'll quickly fall behind.

KELCEY PARKER (www.kelceyparker.com) is the author of *For Sale By Owner* (Kore Press, 2011), a collection of short stories.

- Your story or novel is not your only form of communication. The right cover letter, biographical statement, and web presence can help you sell your fiction.
- No one can promote your work better than you. No one believes in it more than you do. You must set your own goals.

ACTION 2: DEFINE SUCCESS FOR YOURSELF

What is your definition of success? Do you know what you want to achieve? If you don't, how will you know when you get it? And how will you know what you're supposed to be doing to get it? Everyone defines success differently. To some, success is finishing their novel. To others, it might be making $100,000 a year from the sale of their writing or being nominated for a Pulitzer Prize. What does your vision of success look like? Define it. Be specific enough that you can visualize your dream and make it come true.

Use the following list to think about success in the various areas of your life and career, and revise your list as your goals change. Define your success in terms of:

Quantity of writing (number of stories or books you write each year or number of hours you spend writing each week)

- Quality of writing (improvement, mastery)
- Publication venues Submission schedule
- Teaching venues and opportunities
- Travel Home, office, and environment
- Physical and spiritual health
- Leadership roles
- Published work
- Visits to your website or blog
- Sales of your book
- Grants received
- Solicitations from editors
- Other?

ACTION 3: DEVOTE YOURSELF TO YOUR WRITING TIME

You can't write a few stories and sit back in the easy chair. You have to work, work, work. While I don't believe that a writer needs an MFA to succeed, I do know that universities give writers a leg up on creating the habit of writing regularly and meeting deadlines. Follow these two guidelines for your writing time:

Make it regular. Whether it's the same time every day, the same number of hours each week, or on the same days of the week. Schedule your writing time when you are most creative and productive.

Keep it sacred. Don't let anyone or anything interfere with your writing time. Writers can be particularly vulnerable to email; keep your email program closed while you write. It's also important to be able to turn down requests and invitations that would take you away from your writing time.

ACTION 4: DIFFERENTIATE YOURSELF

Most writers would rather be writing about their characters than about themselves. But writing about your work and about yourself is nonnegotiable. You need to communicate with interested readers, editors, and reviewers. Before an agent or a small press editor reads your fiction, she will read your query letter. Your query letter includes a description of your manuscript (the "pitch") and a brief biography.

Pitch. Think of your pitch as the description that will be found on the back cover of your book. A well-written pitch empowers you. It helps you define your writing before others do it for you. Above all, your pitch should compel agents and editors to read your work.

Bio. Your short biography should include a list of recent or prominent publications, degrees (if applicable), and a mention of where you live. But when writing for public consumption, you may want to spice up your bio to make it memorable. Your bio shouldn't read like everyone else's bio. What is quirky about you? What can you say about yourself that will set you apart from other writers? Or how can you give just the facts using colorful language and storytelling techniques? Apply your storytelling skills to your own bio!

Differentiating yourself includes creating an effective website and blog, and writing press releases, grants, and newsletters. Take time to craft a description of your work and a memorable bio, and be sure to keep it updated, as this material will be used in a variety of other contexts as you build your career.

ACTION 5: SUBMIT YOUR WORK

Even as a number of writers opt for self-publishing, it remains important to have your work published and supported by other people. This not only legitimizes your work, it expands your network of resources. When literary journals publish emerging writers, they often nominate the works for awards like the Pushcart Prize or for inclusion in anthologies like Best American Short Stories. Having your work available to the larger public may also lead to a solicitation from the editor of another journal or even from a literary agent looking to represent a book manuscript. If and when you get a book published, you can contact the editor of a journal that published your work and ask her to make an announcement online or include a review in a future issue. To obtain any of these benefits, however, you must submit your work.

Be smart about your submissions. As you write about yourself and your writing (see above), you will become more aware of your unique vision, and of your style and subject matter. Not all publishers will share your vision, so be sure to target your submissions to journals and presses with similar sensibilities. Study their websites, read their publications, follow their guidelines, and remember to keep good records.

ACTION 6: AMPLIFY YOUR ONLINE PRESENCE

If potential editors or publishers want to find out more about you, they should be able to find you online. While you can't control everything about your online presence, you are in control of how you want to represent yourself, which explains why securing a website is one of the first steps writers take toward self-promotion. The next steps include starting a blog and applying the strategies below to leave a virtual footprint.

Website

As you develop your website, the most important question to consider is: What would you like your website to do for you? Is it a place you send people so they can see samples of your work—an online portfolio? Will you use it for aggressive e-marketing to generate website traffic and, ultimately, enthusiasm for your work? Or will you use it to sell books directly to customers? Maybe it's a combination of all of the above. Another important consideration is: How much do you have to spend? If you're on a budget, consider contacting the art department of a local university to hire a graduate student designer. Remember, though, that a web designer is like the photographer at a wedding, and it might be worth paying more for the best.

After you know what you want your site to do for you and how much you can or should spend, you can select the pages and layout you'll need. The navigation menu, which is composed of your major links, should look the same and appear in the same place on every page of your site. Try to keep the number of major links to as few as possible so that your site isn't cluttered and you aren't confusing visitors. There are five categories that must be on the navigation menu of your web site.

- **Home.** Your name should be prominent and links to pages inside your site should be easy to navigate. Ask yourself: What can I put on this page that has a wow factor and will draw people in? You have to capture web surfers' attention immediately.
- **Writing.** Depending on where you are in your career, this page might include a list of publications, links to stories published online, links to journals that have published your work, excerpts of stories, summaries of novels-in-progress, or a list of published books with information and links for how to purchase. Some writers include reviews of their work on this page; other writers have a separate navigation link to reviews.
- **About.** The "about" page is home to your memorable biography (see above) and your author photograph. The most intriguing photographs of writers are those taken in a setting specific to their style or subject matter. Urban writers are often featured with their city in the background; rural writers may have trees and sky behind them. Travel writers are often photographed in a particular location.
- **Contact.** You want to make it easy for people to find you. Post your email address, making the link "hot," which means it will launch a self-addressed e-mail message for your visitors' convenience. Include a phone number and a conventional mailing address.
- **Blog.** Your blog might be hosted on your website or just linked, but it should be prominent.

Start a blog

Blogs help you build an audience by connecting with readers on a very personal level. Whereas websites are mostly static, blogs are ever changing and more personal. They give you a platform for a more intimate dialogue with your readers. One of the most frequent excuses I hear from people who haven't started a blog is that they don't necessarily want to share their personal lives with the world. Guess what? You don't have to! The majority of blog readers don't care what you had for breakfast or what you're watching on TV. People want to read about subjects that interest them. You'll build a following if you write about something that your likely readers can relate to or something they want to know about. To make your blog successful:

- Give it a purpose.
- Visit other blogs. See what you like and don't like.
- Start a file folder for blogging ideas. Gather content over months and years.
- Include attractive images for visual appeal.
- Use your contact list (see below) to get the first subscribers to your blog updates.
- Let people in on secrets as you're discovering them yourself. People love secrets and obscure facts!

Leave your virtual footprint all over the Internet

Sending emails that say you have updated your website or blog and fine and good, but they don't do the trick over the long haul. What you need are loyal, raving fans. If you want to amplify your online presence—to attract people to your website and blog—you have some work to do. Here are some activities you can do during your office hours:

- Post as often as possible to your blog.
- Read and comment on other blogs.
- Link to other blogs in your posts.
- Use keywords and phrases throughout your website and blog so you can be found through search engines.
- Create meaningful text links: make hot links to keywords rather than to URLs.
- Make your blog visible on your website.
- Ask people to leave comments on your blog.
- Make use of social media: develop a profile on LinkedIn, create a fan page or just connect with people you know on Facebook.

ACTION 7: CREATE YOUR CONTACT LIST

Your contact list is your most important asset. No one knows the same people you do. The people you know–regardless of whether or not they are part of the literati–will help you succeed. And no one can succeed on his or her own. In the simplest terms, a contact list contains names and contact information of people you know or might like to know. For the writer, a contact list usually begins with friends and family, and then expands to fellow writers and potential readers. Use your contact list to stay in touch with all of these people–to keep them informed of your goings-on. In a nutshell, your contact list–something unique to you and your career–is the primary tool you use to share your writing with the world. Sharing in a sincere way is much easier and much more effective than trying to sell.

These days, the writer's contact list contains both bricks-and-mortar addresses along with email addresses and phone numbers. You need all three types of information in order to keep your name in front of people and to conduct critical follow-up. Your contact list should:

- Be easy to access at a moment's notice. A computerized database gives you this advantage.
- Contain between 200 and 250 names at the bare minimum. That's how many people you probably already know and everyone you know should be on your list.
- Be updated regularly.
- Be used. Your contact list is worthless if it's not used! You don't need to contact your list every time you publish a story, but you can certainly let them know if you are giving a reading or if your book is being released. If you don't continue putting your name in front of people, you are likely to be forgotten.

ACTION 8: ESTABLISH A MARKETING ROUTINE

A marketing routine will help you create opportunities and expand your contact list. A solid commitment to regular marketing actions seems particularly important for the writer who would much rather dive head first off a cliff than do anything related to self-promotion. Your marketing routine might include variations of the following activities: Set a schedule with regular office hours Review goals Post blog entry Comment on five other blogs Read literary journals and magazines for two hours at the library Send email messages to five contacts just to stay in touch Attend a reading at a local bookstore or university Have coffee or lunch with one writer or business contact Take a computer or technology class Update website

ACTION 9: CONNECT WITH OTHER WRITERS

Being around other writers builds your confidence and sustains you emotionally. In addition, you will hear about opportunities you never knew existed if you hadn't been part of a group. You'll hear about them before they are ever published! If you join an organization, you will also be eligible to apply for grants and awards sponsored by the organization; be introduced to new products and materials; and receive business advice in many areas (software, accounting, taxes, copyright, and more). Most importantly, you'll make contacts that lead to the next step on your career path.

If you aren't familiar with organizations in your area, contact local libraries, universities, or bookstores. Or, create your own group of writers who meet regularly for the purpose of trading work and supporting each other. You might also consider "joining" a community on a part-time basis in a distant locale. You can escape once or twice a year to be around like-minded writers and artists in communities, sometimes called "colonies." Some people think of spending time at writers' colonies as vacations, but they are working vacations. You attend to be inspired and to learn from your peers. Learn about these opportunities in writers' magazines, discussion groups, and online lists. The more you're connected with other writers, the more opportunities you'll discover—and the more people will know you.

ARTICLES

What Not to Tweet

Managing Your Online Persona

by Brian Farrey

Scene: 9th of June, 1870—Gads Hill Place, Kent, England.
Charles Dickens sits in a high backed chair, watching the fire in the hearth dwindle. Reaching across the desk, his hand moves past the inkwell and quill and settles instead on his laptop keyboard, poised to tweet.

> TheRealBoz: OMG! Not sure how to finish MYSTERY OF EDWIN DROOD. Stuck for an ending. ROFL! Not really. Should be EZ to see. Everyone knows the killer is

And for want of more than 140 characters, the conclusion of Dickens' unfinished novel would forever be shrouded in mystery.

Absurd? Of course. But Dickens *was* an inveterate self-promoter. He travelled across Britain, America, and Europe to read his work, perform his plays, and be as ubiquitous as possible. Given his penchant for shameless self-promotion, I fully believe old Boz would be Web 2.0 savvy and doing YouTube videos, had the technology existed in Victorian London. Alas, Dickens didn't have to worry about tweeting or updating his blog or being unfriended on Facebook by Louisa May Alcott.

But you do.

THE INTERNET AS FRIEND

The proliferation of the Internet over the past decade opened up countless opportunities for writers. It meant greater and immediate access to the works of other writers, offering a source of inspiration and hope for those in need. Researching agents and editors became easier as these elusive creatures put themselves out in cyberspace, many providing sage wisdom on how to work the system. And perhaps the most important thing the Internet has done for writers is it provided a more direct means of communicating with potential readers.

Within the last few years, the meteoric rise of social networking alone has granted writers the ability to promote forthcoming books, announce personal appearances, and

---

BRIAN FARREY is the acquiring editor for Flux, the young adult imprint of Llewellyn Worldwide. Prior to his work as an editor, he spent several years as a book publicist and uses that experience helping his first time authors to start thinking about their public personas. He has a Twitter account he uses for work (@EyeOnFlux) and is dreading the need for a Facebook account to help publicize his debut YA novel, coming from Simon Pulse in 2011.

relate to their readers on a slightly more personal level. Blog tours are trumping the far more expensive cross-country book tours. Live chats are becoming an acceptable substitute for hard-to-land radio and TV interviews. Skype allows even the most remote libraries and schools to stream in authors from around the world for book discussions and questions. While it's not (yet) enforced by law that writers should maintain an online presence, the ones who do often find themselves with a distinct advantage in the world of public relations.

By design or by accident, writers now play a larger role in managing their public persona. The days where all writers had to do was write are becoming obsolete in a world where publishers rely more and more on authors to be proactive in the promotion of their work. It's become increasingly important not only to create and maintain a web presence but also interact in the online community. Participating in discussion forums, commenting on blogs, hosting blog tours—these all contribute to positioning yourself not only as a writer but a trusted member of a unique society.

But with this new autonomy comes a price. Entering the online arena presents not only opportunity but challenges for writers. It's always been hard for most writers knowing that their every published word comes under scrutiny from a battery of critical readers. As writers begin making their cyber-presence known, most find themselves cited, studied, and vilified in ways they never imagined.

THE INTERNET AS FOE

Remember the salad days of the Internet? When it was just *fun?* Before it became recognized as a legitimate medium, people gave themselves distinctive usernames to reflect their interests or personalities. People could interact under assumed identities, often taking on behaviors that they might not manage if anyone knew who they were. In fact, many people continue to go by the identities they assumed ten or more years ago. (I can't help but wonder if HottGuy69@prodigy.com has any regrets today about his hastily chosen sobriquet.)

It's becoming harder and even less desirable to proceed with complete anonymity, especially for writers. In an effort to reach potential readers, more and more writers are turning to social networking to zero in on people who might be interested in their work. So it's now important to drop the likes of HottGuy69 in favor of yourname@gmail.com. The Internet has evolved and we must evolve with it, understanding the tool for both the good and harm it can do.

The early days of online interaction left us with two enduring legacies. First, those people who still choose to participate with confrontational, ill-argued anonymity purely for the sake of riling cyberfeathers (we call them, quite appropriately, trolls). Second, and most damaging, despite its worldwide prominence, some people still labor under the illusion of intimacy and privacy in regards to what they post online.

A common mistake is to see your little corner of the Internet—be it website, blog, Facebook or Twitter account—as an island. No one can safely assume that the little blog they started just to update family on their latest escapades isn't being read by thousands of people. Many writers stockpile "friends" on Facebook in a strategic effort to reach as many people as possible, not stopping to think how it compromises the candor they may use on their posts. It only takes one off-the-cuff, angry tweet to start the downward spiral where you're either scrambling to do damage control or—worst case scenario—charging deeper into a flame war with no clear exit strategy. The best course, naturally, means taking steps to avoid either situation. And that means making conscious, carefully measured choices about what to post online.

TAKING CHARGE

Managing one's public persona can be tricky. Thousands of public relations professionals around the world devote their careers to media coaching, offering tips on how to present oneself in an interview, handle aggressive interviewers, and convey your message concisely. And while I can't cram everything you'd ever need to know about media coaching into the confines of this article, I can share a few tips on navigating what can become (but doesn't have to be) a publicity minefield.

It all starts with remembering this: *You are a writer. You are also a brand.* There should be little difference between what General Mills or Proctor & Gamble do to defend the image of their brands and what you do when you present yourself in cyberspace. And while I understand the allure of using Twitter to vent frustration (*believe me* I understand) or the desire to rail against anyone who decides your work isn't their cup of tea, taking the high road supersedes any short term gratification garnered from the low road. Because, in the end, what's more important is protecting your brand and the best way to do that is not come across as a raving loon.

To wit:

1) Avoid TMI (aka stuff that's waaaay too personal)

Your blog/Facebook/Twitter account is not and *should not* be your personal journal. These aren't the places to bemoan that Author X seemingly got a better book deal than you (when your book is *obviously* just as good, if not better, thank you very much). They shouldn't be a sounding board for relationship difficulties or a cheap substitute for therapy. To be clear: I don't advocate being someone you're not. Relating to potential readers often means revealing a bit of who you are, offering samples of your personality that shred the "mysterious author aura" and put a face to a work. Be yourself but exercise discretion.

2) Eschew the illusion of privacy and intimacy.

The most curious phenomenon to emerge from the advent of social networking is the concept of the "friend." Naturally, for a writer, there can be a direct correlation between the number of friends and the number of potential readers. And if that's the route you choose—amassing friends regardless of how well you're actually acquainted with them—then don't make the mistake of assuming that anything you say will be just between you and them. I actually applaud this method of accepting any friend who is interested in you and your writing. Having a wide network can be beneficial. The danger comes in taking "friend" too literally. I know a writer who locked certain blog posts when he/she wanted to vent, making the posts only available to their "friends." Problem was they had 2,000 friends. And some of those friends were friends of the people the writer would go off on in the locked posts. And that material *always* got back to the person they were complaining about. And suddenly the bestselling author they were hoping to get a blurb from for their debut book wasn't as interested once they found out the things the writer was saying in their "locked" posts. Save yourself a lot of time and frustration by just assuming that everyone will read every word you post online, no matter how secure you think it is.

3) Avoid attacks

Recent years have seen a series of episodes that some might describe as "authors behaving badly." Like the fairly recent brouhaha with Alice Hoffman who, following a lukewarm review in the Boston Globe, took to Twitter where she impugned the reviewer's credentials (of which Ms. Hoffman wasn't fully aware) and provided the reviewer's contact information in an attempt to marshal her supporters into protesting

What to Tweet

Enough of the "don'ts" already. So you've got your very own cyber bully pulpit—what now? Here are some suggestions on how to use social networking to your advantage:

Semi-regular blog posts: Some writers manage to blog every day. Some, once a month. If you decide blogging is right for you (it's not for everyone), give yourself a goal: one post a day/week/month. Blogs are like newspapers/magazines/TV shows in that they thrive on regular new content. Share your thoughts on the state of the publishing industry, gush about the last five books you just read, write a thoughtful analysis of the online controversy du jour. Just keep the content coming.

Use Twitter to direct people to new blog posts (yours or others), interesting articles, or information on upcoming appearances.

(no doubt giving her publicist an aneurysm in the process). Or romance author Candace Sams who engaged in an all-out flame war on Amazon over a bad review, the results of which were ridiculed throughout cyberspace. Any artist—regardless of medium—possesses an instinct to defend their work but the execution of that defense is critical. You stand a greater chance of coming through unscathed by not taking such a defense to a public forum.

4) Avoid feuds

I have a writer friend who would disagree with me on this. He loves a good literary feud. Writers showing their true colors, wielding their words as finely honed broadswords. History is rife with literary scandals and feuds. Henry Wadsworth Longfellow v. Edgar Allan Poe. Mario Vargas Llosa v. Gabriel Garcia Marquez. Truman Capote v. Gore Vidal. It used to be that these feuds were carried out in newspapers and magazines, with authors writing op ed pieces by which they'd vivisect a rival's latest work. Today, the Internet endows its children with a sense of invincibility and a bravery most would not possess when facing down the object of their derision in person. While they may be tempting to use as publicity, I recommend staying away from taking another author on. *Especially* if you're an emerging writer.

5) Avoid an excess of negativity

No one likes to be around a sad sack. Nothing will send readers running faster than a writer who consistently complains or criticizes, often without merit or the proper facts to back up their grievances. This is not to say that you should avoid mentioning difficult topics. Some of the best conversations occurring online are thoughtful, articulate discussions of controversial subject matters. In fact, the online community was directly responsible for prompting a major publisher to re-design two of their books when an uproar ensued over the portrayal of the protagonist on the cover. But there's a clear difference between raising important issues and just wallowing in self-pity. Don't be that writer.

6) Avoid cries for attention

I'll admit: there is some personal bias in this one. I get frustrated by writers who do things simply for attention. But there is also a practical reason to avoid this behavior.

By "cries for attention," I'm talking about those tweets that simply say: "Oh my god." Or "Holy crap." And nothing else. Then the attention-seeking writer sits back and feels loved as all the @writersname tweets show up, begging for more details. Aside from coming off as needy, the risk of doing these types of announcements is that you become the writer who tweeted wolf. When you're constantly introducing a bit of forced drama, people are going to get bored with it soon and you'll be hemorrhaging followers in no time.

7) Don't tweet/blog in anger

Think twice, tweet once. I'm as guilty as anyone when it comes to firing off a blog post in the heat of the moment. It's remarkably cathartic. Thankfully, I've learned to hit save rather than send, giving myself time to consider what I'm saying. Nine times out of ten, I delete the post before putting it out there. That remaining one time out of ten, I do some heavy editing. As I've mentioned, the Internet offers a sense of invulnerability because you're not necessarily seeing the people to whom you're talking. Just like in real life—you remember that, don't you?—things said on the impulse of anger carry consequences.

There are many writers who've used the Internet in creative and innovative ways to open a dialogue with readers and engender a sense of camaraderie that's more about a shared experience than it is selling books. John Green—through a combination of blogging, tweeting, and most notably vlogging—has not only unified a community of like-minded individuals but he's managed to raise money for good causes in the process (and all without emitting an endless stream of infomercials for his work). Hasn't hurt his image (or book sales) any.

TWO FINAL THOUGHTS

First, everything I've discussed here applies to published and unpublished writers alike. Whether you're awaiting publication of your fourth book or are still on tenterhooks for the e-mail from an editor proclaiming your brilliance, it's never too soon/late to start crafting your image. In fact, by investing the time to participate in forums and commenting on blogs, you become a familiar face and someone people are more likely to support than an upstart who just shows up online one day with a new book to plug. Be a member of the community first, a promoter second.

Finally, no, I'm not forgetting that, for a lot of people, social networking is still *fun*. In fact, bleeding it of that fun factor to produce a completely sterile, button-down web presence can be just as damaging as the TMI. But temper the fun with reason and you won't be blushing with shame as your inbox ignites over last night's rage-fueled Facebook post. To quote old Boz: "Regrets are the natural property of grey hairs." Not bad. Would've made a great tweet.

Organizing Your Book Launch

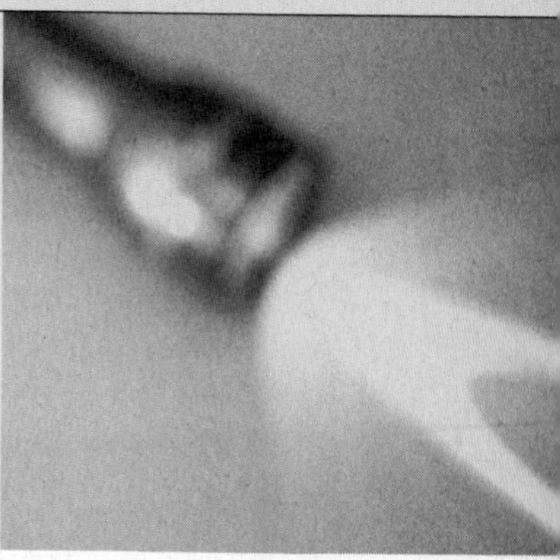

The Critical Checklist

by I.J. Schecter

As you may have heard, writing a book is the easy part. Okay, it isn't exactly easy. Let me start over. As you may have heard, writing a book is only the first step in a longer process, which includes finding an agent and/or publisher, working with that agent/or publisher to turn your initial manuscript into the best, most marketable final product possible, and, finally—swallow hard—getting out there and marketing the book.

I've been promoting my own books for a good while now, and I can't say it's gotten any easier. While I do admit to enjoying the recognition and status authorship confers, I still feel icky sending an e-mail blast to everyone I know whenever I have a new release to announce. And while I do get a rush from talking about my work, I take no pleasure in having to trigger my 30-second spiel in the hopes of moving copies whenever my wife and I are at a dinner party and someone asks "How's the writing?" I do that sort of thing because I'd be foolish not to, and because I trust that the people I'm speaking to understand the reason for it.

But there is one part of the marketing process I love: the launch. I don't mean the fictional launch, that date upon which the book is made available by your publisher, Amazon and the scads of other discount booksellers you discover when you Google yourself. I mean the actual physical event, the one where you get to enjoy the spotlight and really feel like an author for a few hours. Not that you don't feel like a real author when you're sitting at your laptop. But this you get to dress up for.

Besides being fun, your book launch provides a golden opportunity for both you and your book. It takes effort to assemble an effective launch, but the effort is more than worthwhile. Here are a baker's dozen important things to keep in mind.

Start noodling it earlier than you think you have to.

As with all aspects of book marketing, start wrapping your head around the launch as far in advance as possible. This is especially true for certain types of books and certain types of venues. For my golf book, *Slices: Observations from the Wrong Side of the Fairway*, I wanted to hold the launch at a nearby golf and country club. The book came out in May, high season for corporate golf events and other typical club functions. I got my butt in gear in October—and still almost missed the boat.

I.J. SCHECTER (www.ijschecter.com) is an award-winning author, interviewer and essayist based in Toronto. His bestselling collection, *Slices: Observations From the Wrong Side of the Fairway* (John Wiley & Sons) is available in bookstores and online.

Set a budget.

You can't know how many copies of your book you're going to sell at the launch, but you can at least run a few projections and decide how much risk you'd like to assume. Say it's $500 to book the room for the event and $1,000 for the refreshments you're going to provide. Your book retails for $24.99, but you're going to sell it at the launch for a "Special Launch Price of $20." That means you're going to have to sell 75 copies at the launch to break even ($20 x 75 = $1,500). The good news about a launch is that pretty much everyone who attends is going to buy a copy (not counting couples), and many people will buy more than one. It's vital that you make it as easy as possible for people to pay, if for no other reason than to make the line move as fast as possible. That's why $20 works nicely.

It's unlikely your publisher will finance the entire book launch if it's over a certain amount, but they may be able to throw you a bit of cash to help defray the overall costs. Then again, you won't know if you don't ask. So ask.

Choose a venue.

It's more important for the launch venue to be relevant and distinct than for it to be splashy. I held my first-ever book launch at a place called The Academy of Spherical Arts, an old warehouse converted to a bar that contained a collection of vintage billiards tables. People still mention it to me, not because of the book or my reading, but because the place was cool.

Assemble an exhaustive invitation list.

My favorite element about each of my book launches has been the same: my delight at the surprise attendees—those people who were on the invitation list but who I never thought would show. My lesson has been this: You never know who's interested in coming to a book launch. Yes, we writers spend plenty of private time moaning about the challenges of publishing, but the fact is that once you're a published author, a certain sheen attaches itself to you which is intriguing to the outside world. Dozens of people have told me quite frankly that they came to one of my events just because "they wanted to see what a book launch was like." And the truth is that most people have never attended one. So, unless someone has sent you a message in blood saying they want off your distribution list, include them.

Create and send the invitation.

Send the invitation electronically, unless you're inviting royalty or dignitaries who expect something engraved and printed. (Actually, just e-blast them, too.) Certain things can make your e-invitation more compelling. First, ask your publisher if their graphics team would mind creating the invitation for you. If they have graphics people, the answer will probably be yes. Ask them to include your favorite blurb for the book somewhere prominent. And, of course, the book cover. Write some brief copy—yourself; don't let the graphics people do it—that lets your invitees know when and where the event will take place. Add a note about pre-ordering a signed copy, to (a) create a sense of ordering urgency and (b) allow yourself to pre-inscribe some books ahead of time, giving people the enjoyment of having their "reserved" copy handed to them at the launch instead of having a "generic" copy pulled from the pile. Send the invitation two months in advance and track responses (or have your publisher track responses) for the next few weeks. Send it again a month in advance, then again one week in advance. If you can, try to remove from each subsequent wave those who have already responded.

Make nice with your contact.
Whoever you're dealing with at the venue—the food and beverage manager, head librarian, whatever—treat them extra kindness, patience and professionalism from the moment you first make contact until the last second of the launch. On the day of the event, there may be snafus, and you're going to want someone in your corner willing to find a back-up mike in a hurry.

Get someone from the publisher to come out and represent.
Part of being an author is building up prestige around yourself. (Sorry.) A terrific way to do this is by having someone from the publishing house attend the launch to say a few words about you and the book before you take the mike. Even if your editor can't attend, the publisher would probably be only too happy to send someone in his or her place. And even if that person is more junior, the crowd isn't going to notice. What they're going to notice is that the publisher thinks enough of you as an author and the book you've written to send someone to talk about both. Ideally, the publisher will send two people—one to introduce you, one to handle book sales. Remember to ask if they can process credit or debit cards, even though most people will pay in cash.

As uncomfortable as it may seem, you need to consider yourself the guest of honor.
That means delegating as much responsibility as possible to others so you can spend your time talking to people instead of checking on the cheese-and-cracker platters. Your parents, your siblings, your friends—all of them will be only too happy to take on tasks to help you make the event a success. Let them.

Align with a charity.
Think about what kind of charitable organization is a germane match for your book, then call up that charity, tell them you'd like to donate a dollar for every book sold at your launch to the organization, and invite someone to attend and say a few words on its behalf. This not only looks great to the crowd, but it connects you to more people, associates your writing with benevolent giving, creates the opportunity for yet another person to talk about how you're not only super-talented but also kind, and, sometimes, creates a more fun atmosphere. For the Slices launch, I aligned with Right to Play, who sent to the event not only a senior representative from the organization but also tons of their fun, bright-red paraphernalia, including key chains and soccer balls—at no cost to me.

Tell the media.
You aren't likely to get Matt Lauer to drop in, but that doesn't mean you shouldn't try to let all of your local media outlets know about the launch—especially the charity angle. They're always looking for items to fill air time or column inches. Think of any friends, family or associates you have who are in media—at newspapers, TV stations, in radio, social marketing gurus, and so on. Have your publisher send them a press release about the launch and then follow up with a personal phone call a day or two later. Even a 15-second spot on your local station is great publicity.

Think about inscriptions.
The first thing most people will do after you hand them their copy is open it to see what you've written. You're an alleged writer, so they're going to be expecting something clever, or cute, or both. To avoid panicking every time someone new steps up and hands you a copy to sign, take some time prior to the launch to come up with half a dozen different inscription "templates" that you can use as defaults on the day of the

launch. Make them different lengths, so you can choose accordingly depending on how many people are buying and how long the line is. For instance, for *Slices*, I used default templates ranging from "Happy swinging!" to "May your drives fly straight, your approaches stick and your putts find the heart of the cup." Try to avoid merely signing your name; it's a letdown. Also, try to avoid using the same inscription for people you know are friends with each other—because they are going to compare.

Rock the mike.

Whether you like it or not, you're the star attraction—which means at some point you've got to get up to that podium. (Oh, remember to ask them to supply a podium.) A good length of time for a book launch is two and a half to three hours, and a good time to do your reading is about an hour in so that people have had a chance to drink and nosh, mingle, and get their copy purchased and signed. Thank everyone for coming out to support not only you but books and publishing in general, thank the publisher and your editor and production team, and then read an excerpt from the book, absolutely no longer than ten minutes. Ideally, pick something funny, if your book contains funny. Rehearse—out loud—before the event in order to be aware of any tongue-trips and to perfect your tone and pacing. Speak slower than you think you need to. We all go too fast once we get up there. And don't be surprised if you get emotional during the reading, with the whole crowd listening just to the words you've written and had published. Wait, it's only me?

Expect the comedown.

Like the publication of your book itself, the launch entails both a serious amount of effort and a pretty significant mix of anxiety and anticipation. Once it's done, even if it's a huge success, you're likely going to experience a sense of anticlimax ranging anywhere from mild to profound. To help minimize this feeling, view your book launch like you view every other part of the book process—as just one component of a much broader effort. Just as this book is only one book in what will hopefully be a multi-title career, the launch is only one feature of what will be a multi-pronged marketing campaign. So enjoy it, make the most of it, take a deep breath when it's done—and then get back to promoting that book! By the way, remember to include me on the invitation list.

ARTICLES

Advice from Agents

Literary Agents Answer Some of Fiction FAQs

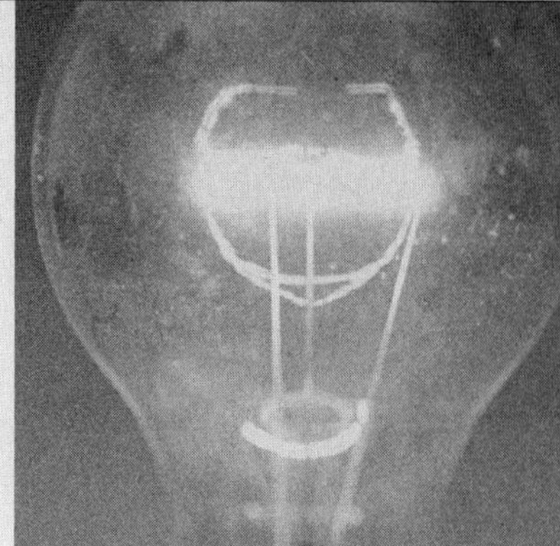

by Chuck Sambuchino

Whether during their travels to conference or on their personal blogs, literary agents get a lot of questions from writers, some over and over. Below is a roundup of such questions answered by some of the top agents in the business.

ON QUERIES & PITCHING

If I submit a novel to a publisher who agrees to publish it, would it be in bad taste to write to an agent who had rejected me earlier and ask for representation again? I don't know anything about publishing contracts and would like someone to help walk me through it should the time come.

It's fine to approach an agent at any point in the process. We've taken on new clients in cases where we're the first person to see the work and also in cases where there's already an offer on the table. In fact, sometimes, the editor who has made the offer will recommend the author contact us. As your question implies, agents do more than just secure an offer. They also negotiate contracts, act as the author's advocate and champion, and help the author navigate the path after publication. It's an agent's job to deal with issues and (sometimes) the problems that can arise after a publishing contract is secured. That way, the author can have a productive and creative relationship with her editor. A good agent will also think not just about fostering the success of a single book but also the big picture of a client's career.

—**Laura Rennert**, *senior agent, Andrea Brown Literary Agency*

What are the most common problems you see in a query letter from an unknown author?

First, mistakes in grammar, spelling, word usage or sentence structure. Anything like that is going to put me right off. Second, not saying what the book is about right away. I am only able to spend a minute at most reading your query letter—tell me exactly what I should know immediately, because I may not read all the way to the end. Third, being boring or unoriginal—writers don't seem to realize how many query letters we read in

---

CHUCK SAMBUCHINO (guidetoliteraryagents.com/blog) is the editor of *Guide to Literary Agents* and the author of *Formatting & Submitting Your Manuscript*, 3rd Ed. Follow him on Twitter @chucksambuchino.

a day or a week. We've seen everything and are looking, more than anything, for our attention to be caught, to be taken by surprise. Be surprising!

—**Ellen Pepus**, *co-founder, Signature Literary*

Let's say you're looking through the slush pile at query letters. What are common elements you see in a query letter that don't truly need to be there?
If your query letter is more than one page long, there are things in there that are superfluous. The most common unnecessary addition is a description of the writer's family/personal life if the book is not a memoir. Some personal background is good, but I would much prefer to know about the amazing novel you wrote. The personal information can come later. The other most common misstep is listing weak qualifications for writing the book. What I mean by that is when someone says, "I have a daughter, so I am qualified to write this very general book about how to raise daughters." In today's very crowded book market, you must have a strong platform to write nonfiction.

—**Abigail Koons**, *literary agent, The Park Literary Group*

I've heard that you shouldn't (can't?) have two different agents represent your work, but what if your varying genres demand it? I write chick lit and thrillers, but my agent handles only the latter. What should I do?
Most agents handle a smattering of fiction and nonfiction, and so in most cases, there won't be a problem with an agent handling whatever work, categorically, his or her client turns to. However, if one's agent, obviously wanting to serve each and every book optimally, says honestly that he or she truly wouldn't do the job for whatever reason—they don't, let's say, understand the genre in question, or they really don't know the editors who publish it to make the proper targeted submissions—then the client should certainly feel free to seek appropriate representation for the book in the "new" genre. What's more, if the situation is succinctly explained to the new agent(s) being approached, they will certainly be understanding (in my view, anyway), and evaluate the submission on merit. And if the writer plans to continue in the new genre, so that the submission in question is not a one-shot, the new agent is even more likely to be open to acting as the writer's "second" agent—even if he or she won't be doing the usual, representing all of that writer's work.

—**John Ware**, *founder, John A. Ware Literary Agency*

Do you see many query letters that come in too long?
Length is an issue. Even though I accept online queries, I still want the query to come in somewhere close to one page. I think that writers often think that because it's online, I have no way of knowing that it's more than a page. Believe me, I do. Queries that are concise and compelling are the most intriguing.

—**Regina Brooks**, *founder, Serendipity Literary Agency*

ON FICTION & GENRES

With literary fiction, what do you look for? What gets you to keep reading?
With literary fiction, I often look for a track record of previous publications. If you've been published in Tin House or McSweeney's or GlimmerTrain, I want to know. It tells me that the writer is, in fact, committed to their craft and building an audience out there in the journals. But if you have a good story and are a brilliant writer, I wouldn't mind if you lived in a cave in the Ozarks. For the record, I have yet to sign anyone who lives in a cave in the Ozarks.

—**Michelle Brower**, *literary agent, Folio Literary*

If you were speaking to someone who was sitting down to write a romance book but had never done so before, what would you tell them about the basics of the genre?

The word count should range from 50,000 to about 100,000. There is a formula to writing good romance. The hero must be a man the reader would like to date, and the heroine should be the type of girl who is bigger than life, who the reader would like to be like. They should meet, overcome obstacles and in the end get together. There are dozens of different kind of romances. The author could join the Romance Writers of America for support and get into critique groups. All my published authors have critique groups.

—**Mary Sue Seymour**, *founder, The Seymour Agency*

How does a writer know if her writing falls into the category of women's fiction, as opposed to perhaps literary fiction?

I think I have a fairly good definition of women's fiction. These are not simply stories with female characters but stories that tell us the female journey. Women's fiction is a way for women to learn and grow, and to relate to others what it is to be a woman. When I think of literary fiction, the emphasis is placed more on the telling of a good story instead of making the female journey the centerpiece.

—**Scott Eagan**, *founder, Greyhaus Literary*

Can you help define the category "Christian Living" and give a few examples?

The Christian Living category of books represents a huge umbrella that covers a multitude of topics. Christian Living works can include books on issues of importance to women, men and teenagers; Christian Living books can be about parenting, marriage, family life, divorce, breast cancer, healing, health, faith journeys, spiritual challenges, leadership and devotionals. [One] series that I've contracted is for three books with a theme of taking faith to the next level. These were written by a pastor of a large church, and the audience will be members of churches across the country who are interested in working through a study program that deals with parenting and other similar topics.

—**Janet Benrey**, *founder,Benrey Literary*

ON OTHER AGENT MATTERS

Do agents usually hold out for a good deal on a book, or do they take the first acceptable offer that comes along?

Well, an offer in your pocket is always better than none. Certainly, if an agent feels she can demand more for a book, she should hold out; however, usually the editor who makes the first offer is the most enthusiastic and thoroughly understands the book, and may turn out to be the best editor and in-house advocate for that book. The most money is not necessarily the best deal for an author. That enthusiasm, commitment and support from all divisions within a publishing house often means more than those dollars in your bank account. An agent's experience regarding what editors are looking to buy, what publishers are currently paying and what the marketplace is like should lead that agent to advise her client regarding whether or not an offer on the table is the best (whatever its true meaning) that can be expected. We do see editors on a regular basis. Again, working from experience, an agent helps her client make the best possible decision. We all want our authors to accomplish their goals.

—**Laura Langlie**, *founder, Laura Langlie, Literary Agent*

Do you need a conservative agent to represent a conservative-minded book?

A liberal agent to represent a liberal book? Do agents cross over?

I suspect many agents prefer to work only with political authors whose views are at least in the same quadrant as their own. Some, though, including myself, are open to and enjoy the chance to work with clients whose views challenge us, and are no less effective at selling those books to the right editor and publisher. I have represented a number of liberal, conservative and libertarian authors writing on a range of interesting topics, and sold their books to a mix of publishers. As always, the best way for an author to see if an agent might be right for them, regardless of their political views, is to read the good directories/guides to agents and then visit any prospective agent's website to get a more thorough understanding of their work with other clients.

—**Ted Weinstein**, *founder, Ted Weinstein Literary*

What advice would you give writers who have had work rejected by agents?

It still surprises me how many writers are angry or defensive when agents reject their work. It's a wasted opportunity. We invest countless hours reading book proposals and giving each proposal careful thought. We have firsthand knowledge of what's selling (or easy to sell) and what's not. Rather than firing off a counter-response (which has probably never convinced an agent in the history of agenting), authors should use the opportunity to find out why they were rejected and improve their future chances of success. It is not rude to ask for more detailed feedback following a rejection, as long as the request is polite. We may be able to give advice or point out character, dialogue, pacing, pitch or structural issues that you might have missed. It could also lead to a referral or a request to resubmit.

—**Brandi Bowles**, *literary agent, Howard Morhaim Literary*

I've read some articles that say "Agents agent," meaning that their job is to sell your work, rather than do other tasks such as assisting to edit a manuscript. But other articles say agents are now responsible for lots of editing throughout the process. Which is correct?

I can only speak for what we do at our agency, but it's been a long time since any good agent I know has just sold books. Agenting is a full-service business and, in this day and age, when editors sometimes seem to be playing musical chairs and projects are orphaned almost as soon as they're bought, providing editorial feedback for our clients is increasingly important. Here at Dystel & Goderich, we edit an author's work before it goes out on submission in order to optimize its chances in the marketplace. Occasionally, we also offer editorial support once the book is sold and the acquiring editor is unable or unwilling to edit. We like to think that our role is to "cause" books to be published, and for that to happen, we need to be involved at every step of the way.

—**Miriam Goderich**, *founding agent, Dystel & Goderich Literary Management*

Is it wise to follow trends?

It's always tempting to write something that seems trendy. Much of this business is about the selling aspect, so writers often think that if they write what publishers seem to be publishing, or what seems to be appearing on bestseller lists, then they have a greater chance of getting a contract—but I honestly don't think it's the wisest way to go. Sure, a writer needs to be aware of what's out there, both so you're not reinventing the wheel (i.e., writing a book that's essentially already been published), as well as so you know how to position your book—but you really need to write what you write best. This means if you've never written for the YA market and have little sense of that audience, then starting now probably doesn't make sense, nor for that matter does reinventing yourself as a political writer if you don't already have a column or blog that's well known in that arena. You're not likely to "fool" publishers simply by trying to do what's hot.

Beyond this, though, there's the issue of timing. This is a business where things move slowly, so whatever it is you'd be selling today most likely won't come out for a year to two-and-a-half years. Who knows where the market will be at that point? Being conscious of the market is key—but above all, your book needs to be the best it can be. Who knows—maybe if it's terrific, you'll start the next trend.

—**Felicia Eth**, *founder, Felicia Eth Literary Representation*

I'm talking with an agent who politely refused to share a list of who he represents and what he's recently sold. Is this normal?

I understand agencies that don't list clients in directories and public access places. That's a personal choice. Hartline (my agency) lists authors and books sold right on their website. To get down to the point of considering representation, however, not knowing anything about who they have represented and what success they've had would, to me, be like agreeing to surgery without knowing for sure that my doctor has a medical degree. If someone applies for a job, they have to provide a résumé and show their experience and qualifications. An agent is not going to take on a client without knowing the critical details about them, and I believe the client is entitled to the same consideration. Before you sign with an agent, know who they are, who they represent and what titles they've sold.

—**Terry W. Burns**, *literary agent, Hartline Literary Agency*

Let's say an acquaintance calls you and says, "An agent wants to represent me, but she's new to the scene and has no sales. Is that OK?" How would you answer that?

An agent with little or no sales who has been an assistant at a leading agency will have just as much clout getting to an editor perhaps as an established agent, at least initially. One of the things I always advise writers to do is to ask an interested agent—that is, one who's made an offer of representation—"Why do you want to be my agent?" They will then hear a very clear thumbnail sketch of how that agent will sound agenting.

—**Katharine Sands**, *literary agent, Sarah Jane Freymann Literary Agency*

ARTICLES

Genre Fiction Resources

For Romance, Mystery, Speculative Fiction & Horror

Below is a list of invaluable resources for fiction writers organized by genre. To order any of the Writer's Digest Books titles visit the Writer's Digest Shop www.writersdigestshop.com or call (800)448-0915 or. Writer's Digest titles are also available at Amazon.com or www.barnesandnoble.com.

FOR ROMANCE WRITERS

Magazines

Romance Writers Report, Romance Writers of America, 16000 Stuebner Airline Rd., Suite 140, Spring TX 77379. (832)717-5200. Fax: (832)717-5201. E-mail: info@rwanational.org.

Romantic Times Bookclub Magazine, 55 Bergen St., Brooklyn NY 11201. (718)237-1097. Web site: www.romantictimes.com.

Books

On Writing Romance: How to Craft a Novel That Sells, by Leigh Michaels.

Writing Romances: A Handbook by the Romance Writers of America, edited by Rita Clay Estrada and Rita Gallagher.

You Can Write a Romance, by Rita Clay Estrada and Rita Gallagher (Writer's Digest Books)

Writing the Christian Romance, by Gail Gaymer Martin

Organizations & Online

Canadian Romance Authors' Network. Web site: www.canadianromanceauthors.com.

Romance Writers of America, Inc. (RWA), 16000 Stuebner Airline Rd., Suite 140, Spring TX 77379. (832)717-5200. Fax: (832)717-5201. E-mail: info@rwanational.org. Web site: www.rwanational.org.

Romance Writers of America regional chapters. Contact National Office (address above) for information on the chapter nearest you.

The Romance Club. Web site: http://theromanceclub.com.

Romance Central. Web site: www.romance-central.com. Offers workshops and forum where romance writers share ideas and exchange advice about romance writing.

Writer's Market Web site: www.writersmarket.com.

Writer's Digest Web site: www.writersdigest.com.

FOR MYSTERY WRITERS

Magazines

Mystery Readers Journal, Mystery Readers International, P.O. Box 8116, Berkeley CA 94707. Web site: www.mysteryreaders.org.
Mystery News, Black Raven Press, PMB 152, 105 E. Townline Rd., Vernon Hills IL 60061-1424. Web site: www.blackravenpress.com.
Mystery Scene, 331 W. 57th St., Suite 148, New York NY 10019. Web site: www.mysteryscenemag.com.

Books

Howdunit series (Writer's Digest Books):

Modus Operandi: A Writer's Guide to How Criminals Work, by Mauro V. Corvasce and Joseph R. Paglino
Missing Persons: A Writer's Guide to Finding the Lost, the Abducted and the Escaped, by Fay Faron
Book of Poisons, by Serita Stevens and Anne Bannon
Scene of the Crime: A Writer's Guide to Crime Scene Investigation, by Anne Wingate, Ph.D.
Book of Police Procedure and Investigation, by Lee Lofland

Other Writer's Digest Books for mystery writers:

The Criminal Mind, A Writer's Guide to Forensic Psychology, by Katherine Ramsland
Writing Mysteries: A Handbook by the Mystery Writers of America, edited by Sue Grafton
Writing and Selling Your Mystery Novel: How to Knock 'em Dead With Style, by Hallie Ephron
You Can Write a Mystery, by Gillian Roberts

Organizations & Online

Crime Writers of Canada. Web site: www.crimewriterscanada.com.
Crime Writers' Association. Web site: www.thecwa.co.uk.
Mystery Writers of America, 17 E. 47th St., 6th Floor, New York NY 10017. Web site: www.mysterywriters.org
The Private Eye Writers of America, 4342 Forest DeVille Dr., Apt. H, St. Louis MO 63129. Web site: http://hometown.aol.com/rrandisi/myhomepage/writing.html
Sisters in Crime, P.O. Box 442124, Lawrence KS 66044-8933. Web site: www.sistersincrime.org
Writer's Market Web site: www.writersmarket.com.
Writer's Digest Web site: www.writersdigest.com.

FOR SCIENCNE FICITION, FANTASY & HORROR WRITERS

Magazines

Locus, P.O. Box 13305, Oakland CA 94661. E-mail: locus@locusmag.com. Web site: www.locusmag.com.
The Horror Writer, P.O. Box 1188, Long Beach NY 11561. Web site: www.bloodmoonrisingmagazine.com/horrorwritermag.html.
SPECFICME! (bimonthly PDF newsletter). Web site: www.specficworld.com.

Books (by Writer's Digest Books):

How to Write Science Fiction & Fantasy, by Orson Scott Card

The Writer's Complete Fantasy Reference, from the editors of Writer's Digest Books
On Writing Horror, edited by Mort Castle

Organizations & Online

Fantasy-Writers.org. Web site: www.fantasy-writers.org.
Horror Writers Association, P.O. Box 50577, Palo Alto CA 94303. Web site: www.horror.org.
Science Fiction & Fantasy Writers of America, Inc., P.O. Box 877, Chestertown MD 21620. E-mail: execdir@sfwa.org. Website: www.sfwa.org/.
SF Canada, 303-2333 Scarth St., Regina SK S4P 2J8. Web site: www.sfcanada.ca.
SpecFicWorld. Web site: www.specficworld.com. Covers all 3 speculative genres (science fiction, fantasy and horror).
Books and Writing Online. Web site: www.interzone.com/Books/books.html.
Writer's Market Web site: www.writersmarket.com.
Writer's Digest Web site: www.writersdigest.com.

The Business of Fiction Writing

It's true there are no substitutes for talent and hard work. A writer's first concern must always be attention to craft. No matter how well presented, a poorly written story or novel has little chance of being published. On the other hand, a well-written piece may be equally hard to sell in today's competitive publishing market. Talent alone is just not enough.

To be successful, writers need to study the field and pay careful attention to finding the right market. While the hours spent perfecting your writing are usually hours spent alone, you're not alone when it comes to developing your marketing plan. *Novel & Short Story Writer's Market* provides you with detailed listings containing the essential information you'll need to locate and contact the markets most suitable for your work.

Once you've determined where to send your work, you must turn your attention to presentation. We can help here, too. We've included the basics of manuscript preparation, along with information on submission procedures and how to approach markets. We also include tips on promoting your work. No matter where you're from or what level of experience you have, you'll find useful information here on everything from presentation to mailing to selling rights to promoting your work—the "business"' of fiction.

APPROACHING MAGAZINE MARKETS

While it is essential for nonfiction markets, a query letter by itself is usually not needed by most magazine fiction editors. If you are approaching a magazine to find out if fiction is accepted, a query is fine, but editors looking for short fiction want to see *how* you write. A cover letter can be useful as a letter of introduction, but it must be accompanied by the actual piece. The key here is brevity. A successful cover letter is no more than one page (20 lb. bond paper). It should be single spaced with a double space between paragraphs, proofread carefully and neatly typed in a standard typeface (not script or italic). The writer's name, address and phone number appear at the top, and the letter is addressed, ideally, to a specific editor. (If the editor's name is unavailable, address to "Fiction Editor.")

The body of a successful cover letter contains the name and word count of the story, a brief list of previous publications if you have any, and the reason you are submitting to this particular publication. Mention that you have enclosed a self-addressed, stamped envelope or postcard for reply. Also let the editor know if you are sending a disposable manuscript that doesn't need to be returned. (More and more editors prefer disposable manuscripts that save them time and save you postage.) Finally, don't forget to thank the editor for considering your story. See the sample short story cover letter on page 51.

Note that more and more publications are open to receiving electronic submissions, both as e-mail attachments and through online submission forms. See individual listings for specific information on electronic submission requirements and always visit magazines' Web sites for up-to-date guidelines.

APPROACHING BOOK PUBLISHERS

Some book publishers do ask for queries first, but most want a query plus sample chapters or an outline or, occasionally, the complete manuscript. Again, make your letter brief. Include the essentials about yourself—name, address, phone number, e-mail and publishing experience. Include a three or four sentence "pitch" and only the personal information related to your story. Show that you have researched the market with a few sentences about why you chose this publisher. See the sample book query on page 52.

BOOK PROPOSALS

A book proposal is a package sent to a publisher that includes a cover letter and one or more of the following: sample chapters, outline, synopsis, author bio, publications list. When asked to send sample chapters, send up to three *consecutive* chapters.

An outline covers the highlights of your book chapter by chapter. Be sure to include details on main characters, the plot and subplots. Outlines can run up to 30 pages, depending on the length of your novel. The object is to tell what happens in a concise, but clear, manner.

A synopsis is a shorter summary of your novel, written in a way that expresses the emotion of the story in addition to just explaining the essential points. Evan Marshall, literary agent and author of *The Marshall Plan for Getting Your Novel Published* (Writer's Digest Books), suggests you aim for a page of synopsis for every 25 pages of manuscript. Marshall also advises you write the synopsis as one unified narrative, without section, subheads or chapters to break up the text. The terms synopsis and outline are sometimes used interchangeably, so be sure to find out exactly what each publisher wants.

A FEW WORDS ABOUT AGENTS

Agents are not usually needed for short fiction and most do not handle it unless they already have a working relationship with you. For novels, you may want to consider working with an agent, especially if you intend to market your book to publishers who do not look at unsolicited submissions. For more on approaching agents and to read listings of agents willing to work with beginning and established writers, see our Literary Agents section beginning on page 106 and refer to this year's edition of *Guide to Literary Agents*, edited by Chuck Sambuchino.

MANUSCRIPT MECHANICS

A professionally presented manuscript will not guarantee publication. But a sloppy, hard-to-read manuscript will not be read—publishers simply do not have the time. Here's a list of suggested submission techniques for polished manuscript presentation:

- **Use white, 8½×11 bond paper,** preferably 16 or 20 lb. weight. The paper should be heavy enough so it will not show pages underneath it and strong enough to take handling by several people.
- **Type your manuscript** on a computer and print it out using a laser or ink jet printer (or, if you must, use a typewriter with a new ribbon).
- **Proofread carefully.** An occasional white-out is okay, but don't send a marked-up

Short Story Cover Letter

Lauren Mosko
4700 East Galbraith Rd.
Cincinnati, OH 45236
Phone (513) 531-2690
Fax (513) 531-2687
lauren.mosko@fwpubs.com

March 2, 2010

Toni Graham
Cimarron Review
Oklahoma State University
205 Morrill Hall
Stillwater, OK 74078-0135

Dear Toni Graham:

I am submitting my short story, "Things From Which You can Never Recover" (6,475 words), for your consideration in *Cimarron Review*.

I am currently an editor for Writer's Digest Books and my essays, interviews and reviews have been published in several books in the Writer's Market series, as well as *The Writer's Digest Handbook of Magazine Article Writing* (2nd ed.), *I.D. Magazine*, and the alt weeklies *Louisville Eccentric Observer* and (Cincinnati's now-defunct) *Everybody's News*.

Enclosed you will also find an SASE for you response; you may recycle the manuscript. This is a simultaneous submission.

Your listing in *Novel & Short Story Writer's Market* says you are seeking work with "unusual perspective, language, imagery and character," and I think my story fits this description. I hope you enjoy it. Thank you in advance for your time and consideration.

Sincerely,

Lauren Mosko

Encl: Short story, "Things from Which You Can Never Recover"
SASE

This sample cover letter is professional, brief an succinct. It doesn't waste a second of the editor's time and allows the writer's work to speak for itself. The power is in the precise details: the name of the editor, the title of the story, the word count, the writer's publishing history, and attention to the journal's submission guidelines (noting that a SASE is enclosed, and that this is a simultaneous submission).

Articles

Query to Publisher: Novel

Teresa McClain
273 Chesterfield Lane
Sacramento, CA 99999
(7144)555-6262
teresawriter@email.com

November 20, 1996

1 line

Addressed to specific editor

Steven T. Murray, Editor-in-Chief
Fjord Press
P.O. Box 16349
Seattle, WA 98116

1 line

Dear Mr. Murrary:

1 line

Please consider reviewing a novel that I have completed concerning the emotional struggles a thirteen-year-old African-American boy endures when his mother declares that he must leave his native Harlem and move down south (Florida) to live with a father he has never known. Entitled *Plenty Good Room*, the manuscript is written entirely from the viewpoint of the thirteen-year-old (a la *Catcher in the Rye*) and is a first-person account replete with emotion and stingingly blunt dialogue. This book is not a children's book. The language is contemporary and often raw and unrelenting. The book is, however, a timely exposé on a young black male growing up in a single-parent home where the parent is too young, too inexperienced, and too poor to adequately parent and where the father is not at all involved.

Sounds good

She got me here!

Got me again!

Now I'm hooked—got to read this

Single-spaced text

1 line

The manuscript is divided into three stages of the young man's life: His life in New York and the events that subsequently lead to his mother's insistence that his father shoulder the remaining responsibility of rearing him; the not so clear-cut path he takes to become a part of his father's life; and his life with his father and the ultimate unraveling of a dream he thought had come true.

Good that she gives a clear idea of the overall structure of the novel

I have enclosed the first twenty pages of my thirteen-chapter manuscript. Please notify me if you are interested in reviewing my complete text for possible publishing considerations. I have enclosed an SASE for your prompt response.

Details enclosures in the body of the letter—perfectly fine

Sincerely,

Signature

Teresa McClain

Comments provided by Steven Murray of Fjord Press.

manuscript with many typos. Keep a dictionary, thesaurus and stylebook handy and use the spellcheck function on your computer.

• **Always double space and leave a 1-inch margin** on all sides of the page.

• **For a short story manuscript,** your first page should include your name, address, phone number and e-mail address (single-spaced) in the upper left corner. In the upper right, indicate an approximate word count. Center the name of your story about one-third of the way down, skip a line and center your byline (byline is optional). Skip four lines and begin your story. On subsequent pages, put last name and page number in the upper right hand corner.

• **For book manuscripts,** use a separate title page. Put your name, address, phone number and e-mail address in the lower right corner and word count in the upper right. If you have representation, list your agent's name and address in the lower right. (This bumps your name and contact information to the upper left corner.) Center your title and byline about halfway down the page. Start your first chapter on the next page. Center the chapter number and title (if there is one) one-third of the way down the page. Include your last name and the novel's title in all caps in the upper left and put the page number in the upper right of this page and each page to follow. Start each chapter with a new page.

• **Include a word count.** If you work on a computer, chances are your word processing program can give you a word count. (If you are using a typewriter, there are a number of ways to count the number of words in your piece. One way is to count the words in five lines and divide that number by five to find an average. Then count the number of lines and multiply to find the total words. For long pieces, you may want to count the words in the first three pages, divide by three and multiply by the number of pages you have.)

• **Always keep a copy.** Manuscripts do get lost. To avoid expensive mailing costs, send only what is required. If you are including artwork or photos but you are not positive they will be used, send photocopies. Artwork is hard to replace.

• **Suggest art where applicable.** Most publishers do not expect you to provide artwork and some insist on selecting their own illustrators, but if you have suggestions, please let them know. Magazine publishers work in a very visual field and are usually open to ideas.

• **Enclose a self-addressed, stamped envelope (SASE)** if you want a reply or if you want your manuscript returned. For most letters, a business-size (#10) envelope will do. Avoid using any envelope too small for an 8½ × 11 sheet of paper. For manuscripts, be sure to include enough postage and an envelope large enough to contain it. If you are requesting a sample copy of a magazine or a book publisher's catalog, send an envelope big enough to fit.

• **Consider sending a disposable manuscript** that saves editors time and saves you money.

• **When sending electronic submissions** via e-mail or online submission form, check the publisher's website or contact them first for specific information and follow the directions carefully.

• **Keep accurate records.** This can be done in a number of ways, but be sure to keep track of where your stories are and how long they have been "out." Write down submission dates. If you do not hear about your submission for a long time—about one to two months longer than the reporting time stated in the listing—you may want to contact the publisher. When you do, you will need an accurate record for reference.

MAILING TIPS

When mailing short correspondence or short manuscripts:

- Fold manuscripts under five pages into thirds and send in a business-size (#10) envelope.
- Mail manuscripts five pages or more unfolded in a 9 × 12 or 10 × 13 envelope.
- Mark envelopes in all caps, FIRST CLASS MAIL or SPECIAL FOURTH CLASS MANUSCRIPT RATE.
- For return envelope, fold it in half, address it to yourself and add a stamp or, if going to a foreign country, International Reply Coupons (available at the main branch of your local post office).
- Don't send by certified mail. This is a sign of an amateur and publishers do not appreciate receiving unsolicited manuscripts this way.
- For the most current postage rates, visit the United States Postal Service online at www.usps.com.

When mailing book-length manuscripts:

First Class Mail over 11 ounces (about 65 8½ × 11 20 lb.-weight pages) automatically becomes **PRIORITY MAIL**.

Metered Mail may be dropped in any post office box, but meter strips on SASEs should not be dated.

The Postal Service provides, free of charge, tape, boxes and envelopes to hold up to two pounds for those using PRIORITY and EXPRESS MAIL. Requirements for mailing FOURTH CLASS and PARCEL POST have not changed.

Main branches of local banks will cash foreign checks, but keep in mind payment quoted in our listings by publishers in other countries is usually payment in their currency. Also note reporting time is longer in most overseas markets. To save time and money, you may want to include a return postcard (and IRC) with your submission and forgo asking for a manuscript to be returned. If you live in Canada, see "Canadian Writers Take Note" on page 539.

Important note about IRCs: Foreign editors sometimes find IRCs have been stamped incorrectly by the U.S. post office when purchased. This voids the IRCs and makes it impossible for foreign editors to exchange the coupons for return postage for your manuscript. When buying IRCs, make sure yours have been stamped correctly before you leave the counter. (Each IRC should be stamped on the bottom *left* side of the coupon, not the right.) More information about International Reply Coupons, including an image of a correctly stamped IRC, is available on the USPS website (www.usps.com).

RIGHTS

The Copyright Law states that writers are selling one-time rights (in almost all cases) unless they and the publisher have agreed otherwise. A list of various rights follows. Be sure you know exactly what rights you are selling before you agree to the sale.

Copyright is the legal right to exclusive publication, sale or distribution of a literary work. As the writer or creator of a written work, you need simply to include your name, date and the copyright symbol © on your piece in order to copyright it. Be aware, however, that most editors today consider placing the copyright symbol on your work the sign of an amateur and many are even offended by it.

To get specific answers to questions about copyright (but not legal advice), you can call the Copyright Public Information Office at (202)707-3000 weekdays between 8:30 a.m. and 5 p.m. EST. Publications listed in *Novel & Short Story Writer's Market* are

About Our Policies

We occasionally receive letters asking why a certain magazine, publisher or contest is not in the book. Sometimes when we contact listings, the editors do not want to be listed because they:

- do not use very much fiction.
- are overwhelmed with submissions.
- are having financial difficulty or have been recently sold.
- use only solicited material.
- accept work from a select group of writers only.
- do not have the staff or time for the many unsolicited submissions a listing may bring.

Some of the listings do not appear because we have chosen not to list them. We investigate complaints of unprofessional conduct in editors' dealings with writers and misrepresentation of information provided to us by editors and publishers. If we find these reports to be true, after a thorough investigation, we will delete the listing from future editions.

There is no charge to the companies that list in this book. Listings appearing in *Novel & Short Story Writer's Market* are compiled from detailed questionnaires, phone interviews and information provided by editors, publishers, and awards and conference directors. The publishing industry is volatile and changes of address, editor, policies and needs happen frequently. To keep up with the changes between editions of the book, we suggest you check the market information on the *Writer's Market* website at www.writersmarket.com, or on the *Writer's Digest* website at www.writersdigest.com. Many magazine and book publishers offer updated information for writers on their Web sites. Check individual listings for those website addresses.

Organization newsletters and small magazines devoted to helping writers also list market information. Several offer online writers' bulletin boards, message centers and chat lines with up-to-the-minute changes and happenings in the writing community.

We rely on our readers, as well, for new markets and information about market conditions. E-mail us if you have any new information or if you have suggestions on how to improve our listings to better suit your writing needs.

copyrighted *unless* otherwise stated. In the case of magazines that are not copyrighted, be sure to keep a copy of your manuscript with your notice printed on it. For more information on copyrighting your work see *The Copyright Handbook: How to Protect & Use Written Works*, 8th edition, by Stephen Fishman (Nolo Press, 2005).

Some people are under the mistaken impression that copyright is something they have to send away for, and that their writing is not properly protected until they have "received"' their copyright from the government. The fact is, you don't have to register your work with the Copyright Office in order for your work to be copyrighted; any piece of writing is copyrighted the moment it is put to paper.

Although it is generally unnecessary, registration is a matter of filling out an application form (for writers, that's Form TX) and sending the completed form, a nonreturnable copy of the work in question and a check for $45 to the Library of Congress, Copyright Office, Register of Copyrights, 101 Independence Ave. SE, Washington DC 20559-6000. If the thought of paying $45 each to register every piece you write does not appeal to you, you can cut costs by registering a group of your works with one form, under one title for one $45 fee.

Most magazines are registered with the Copyright Office as single collective entities themselves; that is, the individual works that make up the magazine are *not* copyrighted individually in the names of the authors. You'll need to register your article yourself if you wish to have the additional protection of copyright registration.

For more information, visit the United States Copyright Office online at www.copyright.gov.

First Serial Rights—This means the writer offers a newspaper or magazine the right to publish the article, story or poem for the first time in a particular periodical. All other rights to the material remain with the writer. The qualifier ``North American'' is often added to this phrase to specify a geographical limit to the license.

When material is excerpted from a book scheduled to be published and it appears in a magazine or newspaper prior to book publication, this is also called first serial rights.

One-time Rights—A periodical that licenses one-time rights to a work (also known as simultaneous rights) buys the *nonexclusive* right to publish the work once. That is, there is nothing to stop the author from selling the work to other publications at the same time. Simultaneous sales would typically be to periodicals without overlapping audiences.

Second Serial (Reprint) Rights—This gives a newspaper or magazine the opportunity to print an article, poem or story after it has already appeared in another newspaper or magazine. Second serial rights are nonexclusive; that is, they can be licensed to more than one market.

All Rights—This is just what it sounds like. All rights means a publisher may use the manuscript anywhere and in any form, including movie and book club sales, without further payment to the writer (although such a transfer, or *assignment*, of rights will terminate after 35 years). If you think you'll want to use the material later, you must avoid submitting to such markets or refuse payment and withdraw your material. Ask the editor whether he is willing to buy first rights instead of all rights before you agree to an assignment or sale. Some editors will reassign rights to a writer after a given period, such as one year. It's worth an inquiry in writing.

Subsidiary Rights—These are the rights, other than book publication rights, that should be covered in a book contract. These may include various serial rights; movie, television, audiotape and other electronic rights; translation rights, etc. The book contract should specify who controls these rights (author or publisher) and what percentage of sales from the licensing of these sub rights goes to the author.

Dramatic, Television and Motion Picture Rights—This means the writer is selling his material for use on the stage, in television or in the movies. Often a one-year option to buy such rights is offered (generally for 10% of the total price). The interested party then tries to sell the idea to other people—actors, directors, studios or television networks, etc. Some properties are optioned over and over again, but most fail to become dramatic productions. In such cases, the writer can sell his rights again and again—as long as there is interest in the material. Though dramatic, TV and motion picture rights are more important to the fiction writer than the nonfiction writer, producers today are

Important Listing Information

- Listings are not advertisements. Although the information here is as accurate as possible, the listings are not endorsed or guaranteed by the editors of *Novel & Short Story Writer's Market*.
- *Novel & Short Story Writer's Market* reserves the right to exclude any listing that does not meet its requirements.

increasingly interested in nonfiction material; many biographies, topical books and true stories are being dramatized.

Electronic Rights—These rights cover usage in a broad range of electronic media, from online magazines and databases to CD-ROM magazine anthologies and interactive games. The editor should specify in writing if—and which—electronic rights are being requested. The presumption is that unspecified rights are kept by the writer.

Compensation for electronic rights is a major source of conflict between writers and publishers, as many book publishers seek control of them and many magazines routinely include electronic rights in the purchase of print rights, often with no additional payment. Alternative ways of handling this issue include an additional 15 percent added to the amount to purchase first rights and a royalty system based on the number of times an article is accessed from an electronic database.

MARKETING AND PROMOTION

Everyone agrees writing is hard work whether you are published or not. Yet, once you achieve publication the work changes. Now, not only do you continue writing and revising your next project, you must also concern yourself with getting your book into the hands of readers. It becomes time to switch hats from artist to salesperson.

While even best-selling authors whose publishers have committed big bucks to marketing are asked to help promote their books, new authors may have to take it upon themselves to plan and initiate some of their own promotion, sometimes dipping into their own pockets. While this does not mean that every author is expected to go on tour, sometimes at their own expense, it does mean authors should be prepared to offer suggestions for promoting their books.

Depending on the time, money and personal preferences of the author and publisher, a promotional campaign could mean anything from mailing out press releases to setting up book signings to hitting the talk-show circuit. Most writers can contribute to their own promotion by providing contact names—reviewers, hometown newspapers, civic groups, organizations—that might have a special interest in the book or the writer.

Above all, when it comes to promotion, be creative. What is your book about? Try to capitalize on it. Focus on your potential audiences and how you can help them to connect with your book.

Daniel Lazar

Submissions Tips From a Literary Agent

by Leigh Hamrick

There seems to be no step in a writer's career that is as baffling, as puzzling or as insurmountable as the query letter. It's a seemingly impenetrable wall that stands between our work, which we personally love and have spent the past weeks, months, or even years creating, and the right person taking the time to read it and uncover its potential.

Rejection after rejection has us pulling out our hair. How do they do it? We ask ourselves when we see another book hit the stands. What are they saying that I'm not? Am I being too professional? Not professional enough? Should I relax my guard and let my personality shine through? Should I stop being chatty and get to the point? Should I give up and write another book? Go for vanity publishing?

Surrender and get a job with retirement before it's too late?

Every one of us has experienced this frustration. Fortunately, powerhouse literary agent Daniel Lazar made himself available to shed some light on this subject.

Having worked in publishing for eight years, Lazar started at the illustrious Writers House in New York as an intern and quickly made his way up to senior agent. In that time he's become familiar with the common mistakes writers make when creating, and submitting, query letters.

In this interview he gives us, the ones furiously typing away at our computers, a chance to look at the query process from the other side of the desk. He helps us identify the reasons why our letters were a miss rather than a hit and what we can do to narrow the beam on our target agent or publisher.

Additionally we get to hear from Lazar's star client, Jennifer McMahon. She began as humbly as the rest of us and has since become a New York Times bestseller. Dreams can, and do, come true.

Know who you're sending your work to

It's often been said that familiarizing yourself with an agent or publisher is one of the most important steps to take in your quest for publication. In spite of that fact, a clear lack of knowledge is the biggest reason hopefuls get sent on their way.

"My taste is pretty broad," Lazar begins by way of introduction, "and my list fluctuates as a result, depending on what comes in during any given time. Sometimes it's half non-fiction, half fiction. As we're talking right now my list happens to be mostly fiction,

LEIGH HAMRICK is a freelance writer.

Reprinted with permission.

Juliet, by Anne Fortier, is an example of novel that appeals to agent Daniel Lazar.

Reprinted with permission.

The Little Giant of Aberdeen County, by Tiffany Baker, is another example.

split evenly between adult and children's books, with the remaining amount being nonfiction.

"For fiction, I'm drawn to literary fiction, women's fiction and historical fiction. I'd point to my books Juliet by Anne Fortier, or *The Little Giant of Aberdeen County* by Tiffany Baker, or New York Times bestseller *Island of Lost Girls* by Jennifer McMahon as some great examples.

"In children's books my taste runs the gamut, from literary to commercial. Terrific examples would be Newbery Honor winner and New York Times bestseller *Savvy* by Ingrid Law, and New York Times bestseller *The Dork Diaries* by Rachell Renee Russell, as well as newer books like the hilarious and hearty *The Popularity Papers* by Amy Ignatow and the mind-blowing *Meanwhile* by Jason Shiga."

Doing the research necessary to know this about an agent is important. Being familiar with the books they have recently helped find publication gives you a sense of what that agent is looking for and what they're successful at selling. Scattershot queries—named so because they are like spraying bullets at a target in a desperate attempt to hit something—are only a waste of your own time, not to mention the agent's. You're much less likely to land an agent when you've made it obvious you didn't make even a rudimentary attempt to learn about their tastes and interests.

Not every agent takes offense at this type of querying. "In a typical day, my office probably receives between fifty and seventy-five queries—that's combining e-mail and hardcopy. 80% of these are just writers casting their net wide, and frankly, I don't have a problem with that. Hey, I don't like to narrow down the kind of books I take on, so I'm casting my net wide, too." However, "10% of the letters are clearly and pointedly written by a writer who has researched my list, read some of my books (or even just ten

Jennifer McMahon: A Success Story

Jennifer McMahon, who burst out onto the literary scene with her book Promise Not to Tell, is one of Lazar's clients, and she was thrilled to participate in this interview. "I remember reading features like this in Writer's Market when I was agent shopping (both times!)," she says, "and getting a lot of information and inspiration from them. How fun to be part of one!"

Lazar says, "Jennifer McMahon is a great success story. Her first book took us about two years and probably fifty submissions (not to mention a few rewrites) to finally get it sold for a modest sum to Harper Collins as a paperback original. It was just a hard book to categorize and that befuddled so many editors. But that book literally took off on day one."

How many queries had you sent out before you landed your agent? Did you face many rejections?

"I sent my queries out in batches of ten. After sending out my first batch I got a couple of requests for a synopsis and sample chapters, and I was lucky enough to have an agent offer to represent me right away. She was very enthusiastic about the book but, sadly, she didn't have any luck selling it. I wrote a second book, and she couldn't sell that one either. Book three was a disaster and I was too ashamed to show it to her. I then wrote book four, determined that this would be The One—it eventually became *Promise Not to Tell*.

"It just didn't work for my agent and as she hadn't been able to sell my earlier books she decided it was time we parted company. I was devastated! That was the biggest rejection of my writing life, to be essentially fired by my own agent! I thought about giving up.

"But then I thought about all I'd put into this. I dusted myself off, wrote a brand new query letter for the most recent book and sent out a fresh batch of ten."

Is this when you met Daniel Lazar?

"Yes. One of my queries went to Simon Lipskar at Writers House. Dan Lazar was his assistant at the time. They asked to see the beginning of the book, then the whole book. With Dan's help, I revised the manuscript before it went on to Simon. Dan had brilliant suggestions for ways to make the book better. Simon ended up passing, but Dan was taking on his own clients and offered to represent me. I was absolutely thrilled!

"I should point out that in my batch of ten queries for Promise Not to Tell, Dan was the only one who asked to see more. The other responses varied from a hand-written apologetic rejection letter to my query letter being returned to me with 'REJECTED' stamped on it. One agency I simply never heard from. I count myself lucky that I only had to suffer through as much rejection as I did before connecting with Dan."

Did you revise your query letter many times before you were successful?

"I think I worked almost as hard on my query letter as I did on the book! Obvious, it's a shorter document, but I was trying to pack as much into a couple of brief paragraphs as I could. I showed draft after draft to friends, got their responses, then worked on it some more. I wanted it to do everything a good query letter is supposed to: hook the reader right away, give a sense of my writing style and capture the essence of the story. And of course, no typos!"

Reprinted with permission.

Island of Lost Girls is McMahon's second novel, following up the success of *Promise Not to Tell*.

What do you feel made your query catch Lazar's eye?

"I don't know exactly—of course I'd like to think it was the concise, intriguing description of a great story! But then again nine other agents saw the very same letter and passed. There is certainly an element of luck in all this. My query fell into the right hands at the right time, and something in it sparked Dan's interest."

Did you experience anxiety and doubt wabout your work?

"Tons! Especially after my first agent ended our relationship after reading Promise Not to Tell. But I still believed that it was a good story. I'd written a book that I would want to read and I believed other people would feel the same way, if I could just get it out there. Honestly, I still experience plenty of anxiety and doubt even after having four books published with a fifth on the way, foreign rights deals, the New York Times bestseller list and the rest of it!

"Ultimately you have to find a way to let that go long enough to get down to the work of writing well, and then to the even harder (for me) task of marketing that writing."

The act of crafting a query letter that will strike a chord with the right agent is also an act of salesmanship. We as writers have to learn how to shift from being authors—a profession that is so personal it's almost secretive—to being our own publicists. With confidence, the right amount of modesty and a clear presentation of our individual voice we need to convey: "Yes, I am a writer. And I'm a good one. This is why you should take a chance on my work."

pages of some of my books) and targeted me for a specific, personal reason that makes sense. And I have to say these letters really stand out."

The other 10%? "Just out to lunch." More on that later.

The question we agonize over: are our queries even being read?

"We do read every letter, yes," Lazar answers. "Personally I read all my e-mail queries and my assistant filters the hardcopy ones. He rejects the no's and hands me the yes's. Sometimes I'll take it from there, sometimes I'll ask him to read it first. That's just me. Other agents here at Writers House handle their submissions differently.

"Do we read every word of every letter? Honestly, not always. It's like dating—if you've ever been on a series of blind dates, you know you can usually tell in the first minute or two if this person is a real prospect or if you'll just need to grin and bear it for the forty-five minutes of coffee. After you've read thousands of letters over the years, you start to get an instinctive grasp of where even a one-page letter is going.

"So we do open every e-mail query and letter and give them a fair shot, but sometimes you can tell after a paragraph that it's already a no. And sometimes we can tell after a paragraph that it's a big, resounding YES!"

Lazar genuinely does keep his eyes open for that promising manuscript, no matter how buried it may be on his desk. "I've been very lucky with my slush pile. Most of my clients came to me via good old fashioned query letters. I know other agents sometimes gripe about unsolicited queries and the flood of writers, but I take the influx of letters very, very seriously. Probably to the point of distraction for my poor (and very brilliant) assistant! He and I spent about three months going over his yes and no piles when he first started, until I felt I could completely trust him.

"By the way," he points out, "I'm very type A about responding to my queries. If you don't get a response, it's either because your e-mail got caught in our spam, or ours got caught in yours. Often people e-mail me but their e-mail programs don't allow 'unapproved' messages, and since they didn't add my e-mail address, or that of my assistant, our messages get bounced out. Honestly, the best advice I can give you is to not use these kinds of programs for your queries. Use a regular hotmail, yahoo or google account, because the agent could pass along your e-mail and you might hear from another agent in the office, or their assistant." That is one e-mail you do not want to miss.

So just what are those published authors doing that we aren't?

How does a query letter catch the eye of someone like Daniel Lazar? "The best queries don't try too hard to pin down every aspect of the plot. I'm talking more about fiction and memoirs here." As opposed to nonfiction, where a detailed synopsis and outline is crucial. "I know this drives authors crazy, trying to sum up their book in just a few sentences. I'd advise you not to do that. Instead, try to inject atmosphere into the letter. The point of the query letter is to give the agent or editor a taste of your idea and an even richer sense of your voice as a writer. Trying to get evocative details and specifics into the letter are much more helpful, because if in just a few lines you can paint a real picture, then even if the plot is a bit hazy in the letter I'll be curious to check out the full manuscript and see what it delivers."

What if we've never been published before? "Not having a publishing history is not a liability if your letter and your manuscript deliver—in fact, being a 'debut' is pretty exciting."

Can we hear about those "out to lunch" letters now?

"In terms of car wrecks, aside from the obvious 'To Whom it May Concern' letters, some of the more outrageous mistakes include:

Having a query letter sent on behalf of the author by a lawyer or assistant. E-mailing the agent to ask "do you accept e-mail queries?" E-mailing every agent at the same agency—with the same query letter. Authors who don't add me to their approved e-mail list. I've had my requests for a manuscript blocked as spam. These writers have no idea now that I was even interested. Authors who call ahead to pitch the book. It may or may not be intrusive; but, more importantly, the letter is so vital because it's a written form of introduction and that's how you're trying to present yourself at this early stage: as a writer. I can't tell if your book is amazing just by the sound of a voice."

INTERVIEWS

Ralph Nader

Turning to Fiction

Photo Mike Simons/Corbis

by Jack Smith

When most people think of Ralph Nader, they probably think of his four runs for President on the independent ticket. Beyond his presidential campaigns, he's well-known, of course, as a consumer advocate, influencing such consumer protection areas as auto safety and insurance reform. An attorney with a law degree from Harvard, Nader has been a college professor, served in government (consultant to the U.S. Department of Labor, 1964-1965), and been a political activist for nearly a half century, forming many non-profit, public-interest groups, most notably Public Citizen, and influencing a significant amount of federal legislation, including the Freedom of Information Act and the Clean Air Act. His work has led to the formation of such governmental agencies as the Occupational Safety and Health Administration (OSHA) and the Environmental Protection Agency.

Ralph Nader has authored and co-authored many nonfiction books including the classic work, *Unsafe at Any Speed*, published in 1965. Recently Nader turned to fiction writing, debuting with *Only the Super-Rich Can Save Us!* Though it's commonly referred to as a novel, Nader himself calls it a practical utopia. Set in the period following Katrina, the book is based on the premise that it would take the super-rich to save the poor and needy—the title referring to a cry of gratitude from a fictitious Katrina victim who is delivered, not by government assistance, but by Nader's fictionalized Warren Buffett, a megabillionaire who arrives in a convoy loaded down with critically needed supplies. Afterwards, in reflecting over the national shame, Buffett gathers a team of billionaires to meet at Maui to change the American economic and political system—that is, to mount an attack strong enough to reverse the present corporatist state, a state in which lobbyists for big business influence legislators to vote for the interests of the rich over those of the ordinary citizen.

For his tale, Nader uses seventeen real-life billionaires, among them Ted Turner, Bill Cosby, and Yoko Ono, each of them having decided to give back to society and change America's present trend, in which more and more citizens are being reduced to serfdom. With Warren Buffett as general coordinator, they soon develop numerous projects, including Recruitment (of hundreds of lecturers); the Congress Project (a multibillion dollar buyout to replace the money of lobbyists with small contributions

JACK SMITH's satirical novel *Hog to Hog* (Texas Review Press) won the George Garrett Fiction Prize. His stories and essays have appeared in many publications, including *North American Review*, *The Southern Review*, *Georgia Review* and *Ploughshares*. Besides his writing, he co-edits *The Green Hills Literary Lantern*.

from millions of ordinary voters); and CUBS (citizen utility boards addressing a broad range of consumer and public concerns). The billionaires decide to call themselves the Meliorists, with their various goals summed up in a legislation package called the Agenda for the Common Good. This Agenda includes what they consider to be basics for each citizen of a democratic society: a living wage, health insurance, tax reform, sustainable energy, more equitable distribution of wealth, electoral reform, and the seeding of deeper forms of democracy. The Meliorists have fifteen billion dollars behind them to make all this happen.

The book's conflict comes when big business strikes back, or at least tries to, but, since this is utopian fiction, they are fated to lose, for all their grand counterattack schemes. They lose within one year, in 2006. The mobilization against them is much too strong—too much support from below, from the massive grassroots movement countrywide. Fitting with Nader's own politics, *Only the Super-Rich* is populist and progressive: "Top down, bottom up. The Meliorists knew they wouldn't get anywhere unless they mobilized the community. They had to draw and energize the political and civic activities of millions of people back home." The book doesn't close with a victorious, rest-on-your laurels smugness, however. Implementation still remains, and final success—meaning total eradication of social injustice and innumerable societal ills—will only come, as Nader's closing chapter reveals, with considerable work and eternal vigilance against further oligarchic offensives.

While *Only the Super-Rich* runs 733 pages and presents detailed strategies needed to effect democratic change, as Nader conceives this, it's also a book with striking conflict and colorful scenes and characters: Ted Turner organizes Billionaires Against Bullshit; Warren Beatty challenges Arnold Schwarzenegger for the California gubernatorial race; Lancelot Lobo, the firebrand hired by eleven powerful CEOs to fight for big business and squelch the Agenda, shows up at the CEO organizational meeting with his pit bull. Speaking of Lobo, Nader states: "I put in a lot of my distaste for corporate lawyers in one man." Lobo's counterattack strategies include spreading fear of corporate flight and vast unemployment. Much of the book's main drama centers on Lobo and his CEOs, but Nader also gets a lot of dramatic mileage and suspense out of the Meliorists' implementation of their Agenda, with July 4 a climactic date, and Labor Day festivities demonstrating grassroots populism in action. Nader spices his book with plenty of humor, including many humorous plays on names, perhaps the most memorable being Bush Bimbaugh and Pawn Vanity, the two kings of talk radio. A provocative mix of humor and seriousness occurs when the Meliorists push to change the Pledge of Allegiance to "liberty and justice for some"—deeds must match words, they argue.

Nader would like to see *Only the Super-Rich* become a movie. "Warren Beatty thought it could be a good movie. He said it would be stripped down, obviously." And this raises a question about the book itself—when it's translated. "My publisher was at the Frankfurt Book Fair, and they're all fascinated by the book; of course they asked for the abridged because they won't translate a book that size. So it's going to be abridged." With so much specific detail needed to spell out the political play-by-play transformation narrated in this practical utopia, abridgment could, of course, lead to loss of important material. Yet Nader is confident: "They say there are skilled abridgers who can avoid most of that. So we'll see."

Once *Only the Super-Rich* comes out in paperback, Ralph Nader hopes it will be adopted by small book clubs. Even though it's not the standard "novel," as he points out, it's nonetheless fiction, which is what book clubs go for, and he sees it as meeting people's present needs. "It's really a very fertile ground for discussion. Anyone can relate to what's discussed in this book because of the dialogue among citizens, the grassroots effort, and the issues that people often think about—their livelihood, their country."

Recently, long-time nonfiction author and former Presidential candidate Ralph Nader turned to writing fiction.

What drew you into writing fiction after such a long career of nonfiction writing?

Well, I think it gives the writer more imaginative flexibility in having the reader envision real possibilities for our country. Had I done it in nonfiction, it would have been more like a policy book, which wouldn't have had the drama and the narrative and certainly wouldn't have been able to detail the step-by-step approach without an extraordinary amount of tedium.

But you don't call it a novel.

A novel would be very restrictive. Because it would be restricted by the character whose personality you have to develop, and that's why it's called a practical utopia. A work of practical utopian fiction. Just the way *1984* and *Brave New World* were dystopias. As a high school student, I was inspired when my teacher suggested that I read Edward Bellamy's *Looking Backward*, which came out in the late 1880s and sold a million copies. It was a sensation at the time. There's one survey that said it was the second most influential book after Karl Marx's *Das Kapital* in the U.S. because it invigorated the imagination of the blossoming populist, progressive movement of that era.

I'd like to see more authors use practical utopian fiction. I came across a book called *The End of Utopia* by Russell Jacoby; it came out in 1999. He's a professor of history at UCLA. He took his academic colleagues and others to task for not writing practical utopian fiction and not being imaginative about scenarios for the future and just wallowing in pseudo social science research—you know, trivial surveys and regression analysis, case studies, existing situations. I talked to him several times after the book came out, and he was quite delighted that his book helped as a way to make my point.

A practical utopian work. So that's different, you're saying, from a utopian novel like Looking Backward?

The difference between utopian fiction of this kind—*Only the Super-Rich Can Save Us!*—is that it doesn't describe an existing utopia. By contrast, Thomas More's Utopia was described as way in the South Seas somewhere. Someone had left England and then come back and told about this happy society. Mine isn't really utopian in that sense because it shows step by step how to get to a higher level of humanity.

What's a one-sentence definition of a practical utopia?
A practical utopia basically is envisioning a much improved, humane, efficient, self-correcting, sustainable society for us and posterity that is within our means, within our values, within our constitution. And within a relatively short time period. So it's not like the 22nd century.

***Only the Super-Rich* seems pretty satirical at times.**
Some of it is satirical, obviously with Lobo. And some of the behavior of the senior members of Congress, but a lot of it is just straight humor—with the collision of interests, the collision of power, how they behaved when the entrenched CEOs and their political allies saw this tidal wave of popular organized power with muscle and money behind it coming toward them, how they began to dialogue differently among one another, and you know, one or two would start straying from the party line, challenging the other.

Would you say, then, that the satire in this work is the soft kind, the playful kind?
Very soft, very intermittent. There's more humor than satire.

Speaking of humor, how did you come up with the names for the opposition—e.g. Lobo?
And Theresa Tieknots? Actually I got a letter from a linguist. He's an expert in names that sound like their activities. Kind of a nice letter. Which ones are phonetic, which ones are metaphorical. I thought that with the size of the book—and there are some serious discussions there—that it enlivened it, and it produced a chuckle every few pages, and it just made it easier to read.

You use seventeen actual billionaires as characters in your book. Did you take fictional liberties with them?
I started with their activities in life. I know over half of them. I've read biographies of them. I read other books, like Soros's book, biographies of Buffett, an autobiography of Bernie Rapoport, a book on the law by Joe Jamail, *The Power of the Peddler* by Jeno Paulucci, and on and on. So I had it set. I didn't want to disembody them and create new characters with their names. And I really extended them to a much higher, more intense level of impact—that's what I did.

So they are pretty much as they are in real life.
Yes, and in fact Bernie Rapoport was delighted that his father was smeared as a communist. How he reacted was almost exactly how he *would* have reacted.

Did you do all your research before you wrote, or did you find that you were doing some research as you wrote?
Very little as I wrote—mostly just checking. Checking numbers, checking dates, checking facts.

Who is your intended audience for this work?
Well, the intended audience . . . first of all, the woman who typed this book owns a small diner in New England, and she types on the side to make some extra money, and I asked her at the end when I gave her the book, "Jean, why did you like this book so much?" and she said, "Because I got a good feeling of very powerful, rich people caring about the problems of people like us, and giving us a role to participate in, turning our

country around." So that was almost the perfect answer to your question. Obviously, I do want the super-rich to read this, many of them, and there are lots of them around the country, and you don't have to be super-rich from a national point of view like the Meliorists are; you can be regionally or locally super-rich. But also I want the general audience to read it, and I want the business person to read it on their commutes from Pelham, New York, to Wall Street, and from Long Island to Wall Street. So I want it to be a general reader book, a business reader book, and a super-rich reader book. And I wouldn't mind if some of the media read it.

Is part of your mission is to get people more politically active?
Yes. I want to show them that while corporate power and their political cohorts in Washington forming the corporate state are very powerful, a lot of their power is the reflection of the extent of powerlessness by the people whom they don't represent and often exclude, rip off and marginalize, and underpay and overcharge, so as people develop a sense of civic self-confidence, and political self-confidence in this book, the gigantic opposition wouldn't seem so gigantic. So I do want to lift the people's morale. A lot of people in this country are demoralized, discouraged—due to recession, unemployment, war, deficits, and so on—and I want to lift their morale and raise their imagination, but above all, I want to raise their expectation levels, as to what they believe this country can become very quickly, with long overdue changes and improvements, more than a few which have been in Western Europe and Canada for decades.

Can we call this political fiction?
One of my colleagues calls it political science fiction to contrast it with science fiction utopias. Most utopias now are considered in the science fiction mode. And so it's like political science fiction because it *could* be nonfiction, and that's why Tom Peters [author of *In Search of Excellence*] put on the cover the comment that he'd like to see this become nonfiction. It's a very realistic book. I don't want the reader to read a page without saying, "This could happen." And once you accept the predicate of fifteen billion dollars of input and muscle of the super-rich and their Rolodexes and their contacts and their bottom-up strategy, with community and political organizations like the Clean Elections Party and so on—once you accept that, it could happen. And so there's a political science fiction story or play or book inside a lot of people around the country, people who've been trying to change things in their neighborhood or trying to change city hall or trying to change some dominant corporation's behavior in a city or town—whether it's a copper mine or a paper mill, or oil refinery—they all have that in them. I've done twenty-three city tours so far, and I get nods in the audience. I said, "You know, when you're defeated after struggling for months or years, don't you say to yourself 'If only we had more media, if only we had more organizers, if only we had more money,' and, well," I said, "if your answers to those are 'yes,' if you do say that to yourself, you've got the kernel of this kind of a short story, play, or book." It's a whole new genre of fiction. I've never been overwhelmed by contemporary novels.

Would you say that *Only the Super-Rich* is a work of social protest much in the vein of *The Grapes of Wrath*?
Basically it's social action, political action. It goes beyond social protest. The Meliorists, as you can see from their dialogue earlier in the year at Maui, already understood what had to be protested, but they went to the next step, which is to change it. That's the contribution of the book. You know, we live in a golden age of protest documentaries—*Sicko*, *Fahrenheit 9/11*, *Iraq for Sale*, *Why We Fight*, on and on and on—we live in the

golden age of muckraking books. Contrary to popular impression, they're pouring out by the week on almost every industry, every abuse: Enron, Goldman Sachs, Wall Street, every political shenanigan. They're pouring out, and almost nothing is happening. Especially since the conditions covered in these books and documentaries are festering, getting worse, and in the case of Wall Street, and health insurance, producing a lot of disasters—but then nothing's happening. And so I say to the people who are writing them, "You've got to go to the next step." I can't even get these people to read my book. Even my friends say, "Oh, it's too long—and I'm too busy." I say, "You're too busy spinning your wheels; you're on a treadmill. This is a real strategy for change." They say, "Oh, it's just fiction; it'll never happen." I say, "Let me give you some advice. What you're doing day after day, spinning your wheels with these books and testimony and not changing the electoral system, and voting for the least worse of the two parties, you're the ones who are living in a dystopia, a real dystopia—on the ground. So between a real dystopia on the ground and my practical utopia in this book, I think the probabilities are greater that some super-rich people will step up to the plate as envisioned in this book than your getting somewhere with your dystopia."

There is a position out there which says that fiction should not be agenda-driven. And yet some notable fiction certainly has been. You mentioned *1984*, for instance.

Yes. And how about Ayn Rand's books? Look how much they've sold, although they are subsidized and promoted by the Ayn Rand Institute.

Would you have any suggestions for people who want to write political science fiction?

Write it from your own experience. If you've been struggling to correct some injustice or to advance some practice—health, safety, fair dealing, worker . . . whatever . . ., the environment—write it from your own experience because that's the easiest way to do it; otherwise, you have to become more novelistic in your craft if you don't write it from your experience.

Did you ever outline at any stage, or did you just write?

I used just a little bit of an outline sketch, in pieces—like I'd say, this is what has to occur in March, April, May; they have to throw the gauntlet down on July Fourth weekend to the corporate executives, and so on. It wasn't in any detail at all. I couldn't do the detail—I don't think that way. It's just basically a time sketch of what happens in one year.

How did you work on characterization? Did you plan that out, or did it just happen as you wrote?

Well, someone told me that Lobo was the only character who would have risen to the status of a character in a novel. That he was the most interesting character. But I didn't want readers to start focusing on character—I wanted them to focus on the strategy of pending collision of power and the power struggle and how they anticipated, how they forecast, how they responded, how they decoyed Bush Bimbaugh and Pawn Vanity, and distracted them.

You use a lot of dialogue with the eleven CEOs and Lobo. Did the dialogue just come to you as you were writing, or did you have to think about it?

Because I'm in the business of persuading people who aren't persuaded, I have to project myself and empathize with their mental framework and their practiced syllogisms, slogans and all, so it wasn't hard to go back and forth.

What was your process like in writing this 733-page book? Did you set goals and deadlines?

Well, I had to write it intermittently because I have so many other commitments and activities, so I wrote about twenty to twenty-five manuscript pages at a time. And it was easy basically because for forty years I've been putting in my mental reservoir "What if, what if, what if?" You know, when you tend to lose, you say: what if there were more media, more organizers, more money, more wherewithal, more people of influence making calls to people who have to return them. Making calls to members of Congress. And so if you took all the time I spent on this book and put it together, it's about nine full months.

And mind you, it's a little larger print. It would have come in at about a hundred pages less if I hadn't insisted on larger print. I want older people to read it too.

Do you have plans for any more works of fiction at this time?

Obviously, you know, when you do something of this scope, you envision a lot of smaller but very important, similar movements. So yes, I have a number of ideas.

Now that you've completed your first work of fiction, which do you like to write better—fiction or nonfiction?

Well, I could tell you after I've written several more. I'm just comparing many nonfiction books I've done with one work of fiction. So it might not be a fair comparison. But it's really delightful to type from your own imagination and knowledge base and not have to worry about footnotes.

INTERVIEWS

Merline Lovelace

Military Discipline Applied to Romance Writing

by Deborah Bouziden

When Merline Lovelace retired from the United States Air Force in 1991, it seemed only natural for her to become a writer. She had been an avid reader all her life and often wove stories in her head.

"I thought about writing while I was still on active duty, but didn't have time," Lovelace said, "but I was determined to do something new and totally different as a second career, so the week after I hung up my uniform for the last time I started pounding out my first book."

After that initial book was finished, Lovelace kept pounding. That consistency rewarded her with 81 books published as of January 2010 in 28 different languages.

She has faced the ups and downs of publishing as a soldier would face a battle on the front. Lovelace says she hasn't come up against any challenges other than the usual ones writers face—getting an agent, sending manuscripts and proposals out and learning not to take rejection personally.

"I overcame the first two by sheer persistence and the last was a matter of understanding agents and editors had a better feel for the market than I did.

"Now I find the hardest part about my writing is maintaining my interest in a book right up to the end. I always have so many ideas percolating that I get halfway through one book and start itching to dive in to the next."

But discipline always wins and Lovelace finishes those books, one after another. Peers, friends, and family know she is one of the most disciplined writers out there today. She claims to use a "carrot and stick" approach to her writing, but over eighty books in less than twenty years requires fortitude and discipline most writers only wish for.

"I'm a morning person so I'm generally at my desk about 6:30 or 7:00 a.m. I write until I run out of steam-usually around noon or 1:00 p.m.-then I go exercise. Afternoons I get back to work if I'm behind schedule. On the calendar hanging above my desk I mark the day I need to finish each chapter to finish a book on time. If I get the chapter done ahead of schedule, I kick back and relax. If not, I keep my butt in the chair until I'm on track again."

Lovelace has written for a number of series through her career like Harlequin's Lone Star Country Club and Holiday Honeymoon by invitation. The Code Name: Danger and

DEBORAH BOUZIDEN is a full time freelance writer, speaker, teacher, certified Journal Technique Instructor, and creative coach.

Samantha Spade mysteries were initiated by Lovelace herself. She has been on the USA Today Bestselling Author's List, has won a Romance Writers' of America RITA award, been named Oklahoma's Writer of the Year and Oklahoma's Female Veteran of the Year. As Lovelace's book list grows so does her integrity, generosity, and the respect she receives from her peers. She takes it all in stride.

"My writing career has been an amazing journey that's brought me fantastic friends and experiences," Lovelace said. "I've learned from every rejection and rejoiced in every book with my name on the cover."

Now You See Her, by Merline Lovelace, is a mystery novel featuring Samantha Spade.

No writer ever forgets her first sale. Please share the story of yours. What book was it? How did you meet your editor? Where were you when you received "the call"? The date? Did you have to do rewrites?

My first sale was a 25,000 word novella that was part of Harlequin's Short Reads program. I heard about the program at a writer's conference in Albuquerque way back in late September 1991, just a week after I retired from the Air Force. The deadline for submissions was the 15th of October, so I sat down, pounded out a story, and zinged it off—blithely unaware that manuscripts languish in the slush pile for months on end. By the time I got *the call* in July 1992, I'd finished two additional full length contemporary romances and one long historical. All eventually sold.

As to rewrites on my first sale, my editor commented that my point of view (POV) transitions were kind of rough in places and asked me to smooth them out. I'd never taken a writing course and was so new to the business that I didn't have a clue what the heck she was referring to. (In the Air Force, POV stands for Privately Owned Vehicle!). I thought about asking her but didn't want to appear too ignorant, so I did some quick research and figured it out for myself.

What is the favorite thing about what you do? What is your least favorite? Why?

I love the research! I could lose myself forever in distant eras, cultures, or places. I also get tons of plot ideas while researching. My least favorite is always having a deadline hanging over me. I try to space out my projects enough to give me time to travel and play but always end up taking on more than I intended to. One of these days I'm going to slow down.

You have traveled quite extensively, first in your Air Force career and now as a private citizen. Most of your books are set in exotic locations. When you are preparing to travel, do you already have a plot/book in mind or do the locations tell you about the story that takes place? When you travel, do you take notes, pictures, etc.?

Travel is both a passion and a main source for story ideas. I usually don't have a plot in mind when I plan an itinerary but something always catches my attention and sparks an idea. For example, as soon as I stepped onto Hadrian's Wall in northern England that I *had* to write a book about Roman Britain. Same thing happened when I stood on the windswept parade ground at Fort Laramie, WY. I swear I could almost hear the bugles. Then I noticed a building labeled "laundresses" on a map of the fort, asked the Park Ranger about it, and—boom!—The plot for *The Horse Soldiers* leaped into my head.

In *All the Wrong Moves* there are a lot of acronyms. In your other books, there are a lot of details whether you are describing a location or writing about government agencies. Is this information in your head or do you maintain a reference source? How do you research your books and how do you keep all the research organized?

I used to write based on my personal experience in government circles. But I've been out of that world so long now that I do extensive research for all my books, contemporary or historical. The internet has made that research so much easier—whole books like Teddy Roosevelt's account of the Spanish American War or Eddie Rickenbacker's WWI memoirs are now in the public domain and available on the 'Net'. Also, you can pull up uniform requirements, training guides, organization charts, regulations and all kinds of other info on government agencies like the FBI, Border Patrol, Air Force, etc.

When I find an article or info that might pertain to my story, I print it out and put it in a 4"or 5" D-ring binder with tabs for various subtopics. The darn binders get so full and heavy they make the bookshelves in my office closet sag! But I keep them because they're reusable. For example, some years ago I wrote several books set in the 11th and 12 century. Just last week I dug my medieval binder out again for a historical I'm doing for Blaze.

How did the Samantha Spade Series come about?

The idea of a series featuring a young, smart-mouthed AF lieutenant had been simmering for quite a while. Then I read an article about some of the far-out, ultra-weird technologies being developed by the Defense Advanced Research Projects Agency. The two concepts just clicked together in my mind.

Since I'm a total non-techie, Samantha had to be one, too. And that made it all the more fun plopping her down among braniac civilians with very distinct personalities. All in all, I've had a ball with this series.

In the Samantha Spade series, you write the stories in first person. In your other books, you write in third. Why? Which one do you prefer? Was it/is it difficult for you to switch from one to the other?

After eighty plus books using third person point of view, it was great fun and so refreshing to write in the first. It took some getting used to though, as I couldn't jump into another character's head and tell readers what he or she was thinking. Now I switch back and forth between books and very much enjoy the variety.

With all your successes, have you ever been rejected? If so, what advice do you have for other writers on handling rejection?

You're not a real writer until you've had a book rejected 18 times, as happened to my first historical before it finally sold! I might have gotten discouraged if I'd submitted and been rejected eighteen separate times. But I'd shot gunned the proposal all at once. So for every rejection that came in, I could hope for the others that were still out there.

That's the real trick to handling rejection. Having so many ideas and proposals in the works that if one falls flat, you can float another and another and another....

Quite honestly, though, if I hadn't hit within a few years I probably would have given up the idea of a second career as a writer. I love the creative process, but I'm not driven to write and wouldn't do it if I wasn't paid well for my efforts.

How did you meet your agent? What tips can you give other writers looking for an agent? How important to you feel an agent is to a writer's career?

I didn't actually meet my first agent until several years after we'd started working together. Before I signed with her, I constructed a list of 20 potential agents and shotgunned queries to all of them. Two of those twenty were interested. I went with the one that fit my personality. My suggestion to other writers looking for an agent is to do the same. Just keep sending those queries until you find an agent you click with.

As to whether you need an agent, I would say yes when you first start out. Publishing is a tough business and it helps to have someone guide you through those early pitfalls. An agent is also a good idea if you're targeting a mainstream publisher as there are so many variables in those contracts to negotiate. Not so much if you're targeting category/series lines in Harlequin or Silhouette since their contracts are pretty much boilerplate.

The characters in your stories are strong willed and determined. How do you come up with your characters? You write so many books, how do you keep their characteristics separated?

Some writers envision a character first. I tend to come up with a plot, and then build my characters around it. For example, I'll ask myself why he or she would do that. What's in their background that would make them react that way? What's their motivation for acting the way they do?

How do I keep their characteristics separated? I construct a chart with their physical attributes, personal history, personality quirks, and motivation/conflict, then pin it to the bulletin board right above my computer. Without that chart I'd be lost—especially when I have to do edits or galleys on one book while I'm in the middle of writing another.

You have so many books out and more in the works. Why do you think you are so successful?

I view writing as both a craft *and* a business. I keep spreadsheets on everything—one with the number of copies of each book printed and sold by country; another showing the dates I submit manuscripts, proposals and contracts that calculates expected payment dates; a 3-year production timeline built around ms, proposal and pub dates so I can plan promo and trips; an income/expense spreadsheet that I keep up regularly and can simply transfer to a Schedule C & E come tax time; and many more!

I think these spreadsheets satisfy the disciplined military type in me. I like to see exactly where I'm going and what I need to do to get there. I also believe a writer has to be professional. I've only missed one deadline in 80 plus books. It killed me to be late, even though it was only two weeks and I knew my editor wouldn't get around to reading the manuscript for months.

Day Leclaire

Writing Life: 'Good Days Are Fairy Dust and Magic'

by Leigh Hamrick

If you read romance then you know Day Leclaire. With more than 50 published books, ten RITA nominations and a host of writing awards to her credit, her name is virtually synonymous with the genre. She is one of Harlequin's most popular authors and her loyal fan base continues to grow. Leclaire generously allowed me to pin her down long enough for an in-depth interview about her writing history, what's she's learned about publishing and how she manages to keep up her terrific pace. Her insights and experiences are real, funny and unflinching. With great candor Leclaire opens up about her own journey as a writer and gives those of us still struggling to realize our dreams of becoming published sound and realistic advice. Look for her upcoming releases, *Dante's Temporary Fiancée* (September 2010) and *Dante's Marriage Pact* (December 2010).

A tough career choice: writer or princess?

"There is no career or profession, no activity or hobby, no ability or talent I'd rather have than that of a writer," says Day Leclaire from her home in the Outer Banks, a thin chain of islands off the coast of North Carolina, where she lives with her husband and their dogs. "Even on those days when I'm pulling out my hair, swearing at my computer, dropkicking my laptop or watching an old Rambo flick while picturing my editor on the receiving end of all those blows and bullets, I'd still rather fight to get the words out than anything else. Anything.

"And on the good days? It's transcendent. Good days are fairy dust and magic. They more than make up for the bad days." She doesn't mind taking that fairy dust with a serving of realism, though. "If you're reading this," she says, "you either want to write, in which case you have my sympathies, or you are—God help you—already in the business. "If you want to be a writer, this is not a blueprint. There is no such thing. This is just one person's journey, mostly boring, except for the parts where I'm lying to make it more interesting."

Writing wasn't always what Leclaire had in mind for herself. In fact, she had much bigger plans. "I wanted to be a princess." Unfortunately for her "Leia had dibs on that. So, instead, I was born just one of the herd, no blue blood in me, though I do have a spit or two of Irish, which I treasure.

LEIGH HAMRICK is a freelance writer.

Day Leclaire FAQs

Here are some answers to questions every reader and potential writer asks the author.

Which of your own books are your favorites?
"I love all my Fairytale Wedding books. I love all my Dante books. I love all my Salvatore books. I loved my first two books, *Jinxed* and *Where There's A Will*. But I'd have to say my all-time favorite is *Her Secret Santa*. I can't even tell you why. It's a really sweet story that I enjoyed writing and that just came together well for me."

Which of your books is your least favorite?
"My least favorite book (I actually had to go look up the title because I dislike the book so much) is *Shotgun Bridegroom*. I dislike it because I set it where I currently live, which doesn't work for me because it's too 'real.' In other words, I could see the warts. Additionally, the ending was awkward. I've never been able to figure out how I could have written it differently."

Did you consider getting an agent?
"Because I write for Harlequin, I haven't needed an agent. I negotiate my own contract since I know what I want and have no problem asking for it or hanging tough. If I submit a manuscript elsewhere, though, I will absolutely look for an agent."

How much was the advance on your first book?
"My first advance was $4,000. After that first book, my advances per contract, which range from three to five books each, usually increased by about $500."

Did you earn royalties on your first book?
"I've received royalties on every book I've written. As it turns out, I have made more off Jinxed than any other book (fast approaching six figures) mainly because Harlequin did a special promotion with it. It's rare, but it does happen, even in category."

What advances are you commanding now?
"Right now I receive an advance of about $10,000 per book, but since the advances are deducted from your royalties it doesn't matter what you receive unless you need the money up front. This is vastly different from single title where high advances equal publisher support, mind you. I'd demand far higher advances if I were writing single title."

What advice can you give aspiring writers?
"What brings in the steady, dependable money is writing really good books that appeal to readers and to do that repeatedly over time. It's important to have regular releases; in other words, two or more books a year (in category), every year. Just keep the quality as high as possible. "I make a very comfortable living off my books by writing three a year. It's put a roof over my head, food on the table, has enabled me to be a stay-at-home mom while still having a very nice career and it keeps my dogs in kibble. "Plus I don't have to work nine-to-five. What more could you want?"

"I discovered at a fairly young age that I wanted to write. I don't think at that point I fully grasped the concept of what an actual job entailed; and even when I did come to terms with that rather horrifying nine to five concept, I quickly realized that working wasn't something I ever really wanted to do.

"So you can understand why the idea of becoming a writer appealed. That wasn't work! That was scribbling in a book while sitting at a café table on the Champs-Élysées sipping wine. Little did I know that as a writer I would work more hours and more days than any nine-to-fiver on the planet. Maybe I should have held out for that princess position."

What inspired Leclaire at such a young age to write? "For me, the path to becoming a writer actually started with discovering books and that wondrous feeling of being transported to another place and time and world through its pages. "A teacher in my second grade had a reading session every day. I remember she read *Old Yeller* and I had to bury my head in my arms to hide the tears when Travis had to shoot his dog. I pretended I was laughing so I wouldn't get beaten up."

Then she read *A Wrinkle in Time* and I was utterly captivated. Thanks to that book I became a serious reader. The instant the teacher finished it I went to the library and checked it out. After that I checked out half a dozen books a week. "The next step in the process was going from reader to writer. That happened in the fourth grade. We had a teacher who incorporated creative writing as a part of her English program. My class was given an assignment to complete a Halloween story that she had provided a few starter paragraphs to.

"I'd love to say that I went wild and wrote this amazing piece of fiction. In truth, one of my classmates did. I was literally blown away when the teacher read it to us. It was at that point that I made the connection between books and the people who write them. More importantly I discovered that if this boy could write this wonderful story, so could I! It gave me chills to realize I could choose any subject I wanted. I could even make things up (in other words, lie). It was the most wonderful, liberating, amazing feeling in the world. I still react that way when I sit down to begin writing a new book. I can make up anything I want and earn a living doing it (in other words, lie *big* time). How cool is that?"

The road to publication

"At the time I decided I wanted to be a writer, professionally, I was in my mid-twenties and living in Seattle with my husband. We owned a couple of produce markets. "Now, my husband is Mr. Retail. He's outgoing and loves being around people and running his own place. Me? I'm the exact opposite. I'm Ms. Hermit." Not good when your business is as customer oriented as retail is. "You have to deal with customers *all the time*. That means being nice to them *all the time*." She admits: "I don't do 'nice'. Okay, I can, but it's a struggle to behave for six days a week, twelve hours a day. As in, pelt a rude customer with tomatoes type of serious struggle.

"Right about then I discovered I was pregnant and told my husband I was tired of being nice. Since he was tired of cleaning up the tomatoes he asked me what I wanted to do instead.

"Without a second's hesitation out came: I want to write. I hadn't even realized the idea had been sitting in the back of my head, bubbling away until I opened my mouth and out it came. The next day my husband took me downtown and bought me a computer. He really is a wonderful man!"

Rejection? For Day Leclaire?

Sometimes even the best have to pay their dues. "My first manuscript was a partial," she recalls. "It was a romance, of course, and a terrible story of revenge. I called it *Vengence[sic] is Mine*. In those days there wasn't a spell checker and so every single page had that title on it, misspelled. Cracks me up every time I see the word. "I sent it off to Harlequin's Toronto office. About three months later I received a personalized rejection letter. It basically said: though your writing is competent, your characters are stereotypical and your plot is melodramatic and it pretty much sucks. Now go away."

Obviously she didn't. In fact, the rejection didn't slow her down a bit. "I was over the moon! All I saw was that my writing was competent. I could fix the rest. I guess when you're passionate about something you find the silver lining in all those clouds. That's not to say I wasn't seriously disappointed, though. I was."

Day Leclaire has more than 50 published books and a host of writing awards to her credit.

After their son Matthew was born, Leclaire spent some time enjoying her new role as a mother, but returned to writing when he was about two years old. "Again, it was a romance. Again, it was fairly dramatic." The plot was centralized around the wheelchair-bound hero, who, contrary to romance books at the time, doesn't recover the use of his legs. "The problem was, I was writing a romance, not a story about men dealing with paralysis and so, even though I received a long letter requesting revisions, it was ultimately rejected. "But now I knew I was close. Very close. I could practically smell that first sale."

A book of laughter borne of tragedy

"Then my younger sister, Nancy, was diagnosed with a brain tumor and died the following year. I spent that summer sequestered in my condo with the drapes drawn. It was a hideous time. I mean really bad. My husband, at his wit's end, finally informed me that I could either write or go get a job and, by the way, the local McDonald's was hiring. I took the hint.

"Oddly enough, I had just picked up a Harlequin that I was very excited to read." The heroine worked at a toy factory. "What a great idea! I was so envious. Why, think of all the fun. What if she got to test all the toys? What if she was a total klutz or a jinx? The hero, who would have to be the owner, wouldn't be happy. And here this other woman had written a story that—even before I read it—I could see clearly in my head." A surprise was in store, though. "The story was nothing like I'd imagined, which meant...I could write it!

"This is where my writing took a turn. Instead of melodrama it was a slapstick, screwball comedy. It was fun. It was funny. It was different. "Writing that book, and the humor in it, literally saved me. I don't think I realized just how depressed I was by the loss of my sister until I found the ability to laugh again. I gave the book the title *Jinxed* and dedicated it to Nancy.

"It took me three months to write the book." Three or four months later "I received a letter asking for revisions. I was beyond disappointed at this point. I put *Jinxed* aside." A mistake, as she later realized. "When an editor asks for revisions," she says emphatically, "*make the revisions and send them in!* For an editor to take the time to detail a number of revisions, it means they are extremely interested.

"When I finally got around to doing the revisions, I sent it back. I received a phone call not long after telling me that *Jinxed* had been accepted. I thought she was calling to tell me that she wanted more revisions, so when she said, 'We'd like to publish your novel,' I didn't say a word, mainly because I was waiting for the other shoe to drop. You know, like 'but first you have to climb Mt Everest and then swim with Jaws in chummed water.' I think I said, 'Okaaaay.' Then she went silent, too. Finally she said, 'This is the part of the phone call when you're supposed to scream for joy.' Poor thing. I'd totally deflated the big moment that all editors love—calling the author with a first sale. I think I made up for it once I understood she was really serious, though. I mean, who wouldn't be thrilled? Harlequin was buying my book!

Now it's time to act like a writer

With the sale of *Jinxed* Leclaire settled into becoming a writer in every sense of the word, and it didn't bear much similarity to enjoying a glass of wine in a Parisian café. "Since I was now earning my income writing, I needed to behave professionally, which meant I had to get my butt in the chair and write on a regular basis. That often interferes with what friends and family expect from you.

"The problems for most writers are the deadlines and the self-discipline required to succeed. We tend to overestimate how much we can accomplish in X amount of time. Dangle a contract in front of me and I instantly start to salivate. That can be a problem when you say, 'Sure I can fit that extra book in!' when you're barely meeting your deadlines as it is.

"If you're not passionate about your story," she cautions, "or you're trying to write just for the money, it doesn't work well and your writing shows it. "But when you find your voice...when the stories that spring naturally from your imagination are the stories that readers clamor for, that editors can't put down, writing is the best life there is. It becomes more than a career. It's your way of contributing to the world, and sharing a part of yourself, and doing what you're driven to do. It's an act that completes you and satisfies you, fills you up and drains you dry, excites you and wrings every emotion from you.

"That's what you try—to the best of your ability—to share with readers."

INTERVIEWS

James Rollins

Blending History with Cutting Edge Science

by Janice Gable Bashman

James Rollins looks for two things when he's starting a novel: "a bit of history that ends in a question mark and some cutting-edge science that makes [him] think 'What if...?'" He takes that information, combines it with exotic locales, and creates thrillers that continually hit the New York Times bestseller list.

Rollins is the author of the Sigma Force thrillers (*The Doomsday Key*, *Sandstorm*, *Map of Bones*, *Black Order*, *The Judas Strain*, and *The Last Oracle*), the novelization of the film *Indiana Jones and the Kingdom of The Crystal Skull*, *Jake Ransom and the Skull King's Shadow* (the first of a young adult series), and six other thrillers. He also writes fantasy under the name James Clemens.

In your thrillers you love "merging the ancient and the modern, then stirring that pot and seeing what develops." Why does this process make a great thriller?
The primary goal of any thriller should be to entertain, but for a novel to have an impact, it must also have some resonance that lasts beyond that final page. Pulp entertainment will sell books, but I believe to build a readership that there must be a lasting impression. For each thriller writer, this will be different and should be a reflection of his or her passion. I love history, archaeology, mythology, so these are the elements that I fold into my stories. It allows me to imbue a modern pulp tale with the weight of history, to raise intriguing questions that make readers look at the past in a new light. When you have readers scratching their heads wondering what's true and what's not, you've engaged them at a new level. I end each book with an author's note, where I lay out what's real and what's fiction. So if a concept intrigues a reader, I offer them a steppingstone to continue their own investigation. It is such interactivity that can be a key to keeping that novel alive in readers' minds, to keep them talking about it long after they've finished it. If you can do that, your audience will continue to grow.

It seems like it should be easy to take a piece of history, blend in cutting-edge science, add an exotic location, develop a "what if" question, and take the

---

JANICE GABLE BASHMAN is co-author (with Jonathan Maberry) of *Wanted Undead or Alive: Vampire Hunters and Other Kick-Ass Enemies of Evil* (Citadel Press 2010). She is a contributing editor of the *Big Thrill*, the newsletter of the International Thriller Writers, and she also writes for other leading publications. Visit Janice at www.janicegablebashman.com or contact her at janicebashman@yahoo.com.

result and create a plot. But it's not. How do you combine these divergent elements to craft an exciting story?

Unfortunately that means outlining. Most thrillers lean toward a more plot-oriented structure. For a story to unfold with surprises, cliffhangers, red herrings, and suspenseful turns, some roadmap should be in place before you write your first word. That doesn't mean every twist and turn must be established beforehand. In my case, I know where the story starts and where it ends, along with several key steppingstones in between. I don't necessarily know how A connects to B connects to C. I prefer to explore that as I write. That's one of the joys of the craft for me.

As to specifics of combining multiple elements (science, history, setting), it's an act of layering. None of my stories are built the same way. For my novel *Amazonia*, I started with the setting: the Brazilian rainforest. Then I went in search of the region's mythology, read about the ongoing pharmaceutical research going on in the forest, and began putting the story together. For my novel *The Judas Strain*, it started with a historical mystery: whatever happened to Marco Polo's lost fleet? From there, I researched where to set the story and figured out a scientific explanation to answer that historical question. For my novel *Black Order*, it started with a controversial bit of science: the debate between evolution and creationism. Then I set about finding a historical context to have this debate unfold and a modern place to tell it. So it's all about layering and outlining.

What do you find most difficult about this process, and how do you resolve the difficulty?

The most difficult process is finding that right balance of these thematic elements and to fuse them into a seamless whole. It is all too easy (and lazy) to let the historical or scientific details overwhelm your story. It is an easy trap to fall into. Booklovers enjoy reading thrillers for the *thrill* of the story. They're not looking for a historical lecture or a scientific discourse. Always keep that in mind.

I find a great way of avoiding this trap is by focusing on the characters, to deeply establish that point of view for each scene. It is *characters in conflict* that move your story forward. If you've populated your novel with a set of real, flawed, and three-dimensional characters, two things will happen. First, when you're writing in these characters' viewpoints—when you're living in their shoes and thinking in their heads—you'll have a greater sense when your story is getting too bogged down and heavy-handed. If your character is real, you'll sense when the situation is false.

Second, by creating well-rounded and sympathetic characters, when you put them in jeopardy, the readers will be invested in the outcome. And story is all about conflict. Keep those characters in jeopardy and you're less likely to let the story slip into a lecture.

How do you make it seem plausible to the reader that the history and cutting-edge science you have combined are possible?

It's actually a simple two-step process.

The first step is to *ground the story* in reality as you open the book. Begin the novel with real people in a modern setting plagued by a plausible threat. Next, over the course of the novel, weave in the historical and scientific elements—again these should be factual and well supported. Only then should you allow your story to drift into the land of speculation and conjecture, to take those factual details and extrapolate an exciting adventure. But to get there, you must start firmly grounded in reality.

The second step is to seed the story with *telling details*, those wonderful tidbits that make the story feel real. There is magic in such details. For example, if I'm setting a story in Katmandu and my character needs a caffeine fix, I will look up the exact address of a Starbucks in that city and send my character there. Now if your reader has been to Katmandu and realizes "Hey, there really is a Starbucks on that corner," then that reader will believe almost anything you write after that—even that there are telepathic marsupials living under Antarctica. So do your research and seed those details throughout your novel. It will make the story all the more plausible.

When combining history with science, what other things are important to know and why?

A few additional items to keep in mind:

Just because a bit of history or science appeals to you, don't forget your audience. Certainly you should look for a subject that you can write about passionately. If something bores you, it will show in your writing. But search for some aspect of that subject that will strike a chord with a large audience, something that has some broad appeal.

Controversy never hurts. If there's an element of history or science that lends itself to a controversial subject matter, all the better. It's a way to make the science or history instantly relatable and pertinent.

Science and history are all good, but who cares? It's what writer Steve Berry calls the "so what?" of a story. Whatever science or history is raised in a book should have some applicability to modern times and should matter.

Finally, keep in mind that the cogs and wheels of science can make for an exciting story, but the true impact lies in how these cogs and wheels challenge your characters at an emotional level. The edge of the scientific exploration is fraught with questions of spirituality and morality (cloning, stem cells, etc), and these questions should be equally explored in a novel for it to have true emotional resonance.

You conduct an extraordinary amount of research (90 days) before sitting down to write. How do you incorporate this information into your work without overburdening the reader with too much historical or scientific fact?

That is another common trap for writers: I've done all this research, now I'm going to make you read it. I talked a little bit about how to avoid this by focusing on your characters, but there are times when you do need to pass on information to educate your reader about some aspect of the story. How do you do this without stopping the story dead in its tracks? This can be tricky, but there are two tools that can help smooth this over. First and foremost, keep explanations as simple as possible. Rather than info-dumping for several pages, split such information into smaller bits and spread them out. Second—and this is very important—*present such information in conflict*. Have a heated argument between characters where this information is debated. Have a detail revealed that solves an immediate physical threat. Never stop the story just to have a group of characters amicably discuss a subject. Make it a fight, infuse it with conflict. In such situations, readers may not even realize you're secretly filling their heads with necessary information. So spread those details out and introduce them in conflict.

What advice can you give to other writers about combining history and cutting-edge science?

Begin building a library of resources and ideas. I subscribe to dozens of magazines: *Scientific American, National Geographic, Smithsonian, New Science, Archaeology,* and scores of others. I scour the science sections of newspapers and watch hour after hour of the History Channel. I search for tidbits that might make for a good story, basically looking for an intriguing location, or a piece of history that ends in a question mark, or a bit of science that makes me go "what if?" When I come across an article I cut it out or jot a note, then it gets tossed into a cardboard file box. I don't have any filing system in that box. It's all jumbled and random and chaotic (and probably somewhere at the bottom there are mice nesting in there). I like that chaos because by pure chance odd pieces of science and history end up together, bits that I would never have thought to connect in my wildest fantasies. It's a great tool for building a wealth of ideas for hundreds of books. Plus it's just plain fun.

What about craft? What else is important for writers to know?

One last bit of craft to learn is discipline. No story gets written without hours in front of the keyboard. I'm a slow writer. It takes me an hour to write one double-spaced page of a manuscript. Yet, I still write two novels a year. Does that mean writing like a crazed banshee, sacrificing quality for quantity? No, it just means setting up a schedule that works for you. Early in my career, while working full-time as a veterinarian, I made a personal commitment to write THREE pages a day (for five out of seven days of the week). Mind you, that's double-spaced pages and I took weekends off. On that schedule, you can produce 800 manuscript pages, plenty for two novels. But to accomplish that means making a commitment to yourself—and sticking to it. I prefer committing to a number of pages versus a number of hours. *Hours* can be frittered away; *pages* must be finished. Even writing only ONE page a day, you'll have a novel done by year's end. So there's no reason not to start today.

INTERVIEWS

Eric Van Lustbader

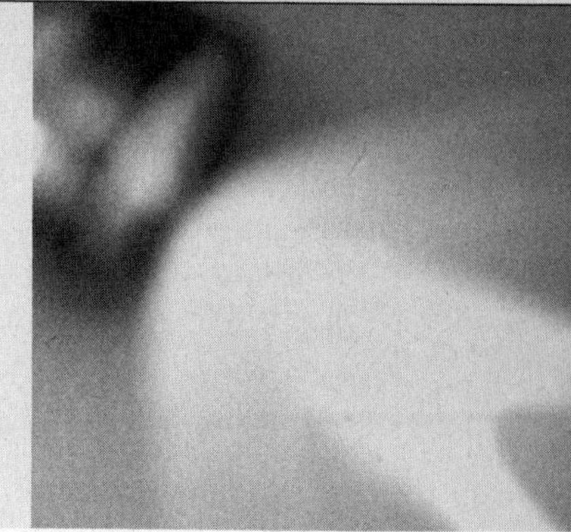

Great Characters Make for Great Thrillers

by Janice Gable Bashman

New York Times best-selling author Eric Van Lustbader knows how to build a character. He uses his well-tested techniques (identification with characters, the inciting incident, action, making it personal, caring, and building a flow) to create three dimensional characters that keep his readers glued to the pages and wanting to read more.

Lustbader is the author of more than 20 thrillers, including six novels in the Nicholas Linnear *Ninja* series, and two novels, *First Daughter* and *Last Snow*, in a new series starring Jack McClure and Alli Carson. He is also the author of the last five books in the Jason Bourne series, which include *The Bourne Legacy*, *The Bourne Betrayal*, *The Bourne Sanction*, *The Bourne Deception*, and *The Bourne Objective*. His novels have been translated into more than 20 languages.

You stress that it is extremely important to build a solid character in the first 100 pages of a novel. To achieve that goal, the reader must identify with the character. How do you accomplish this in your writing?

The primary thing to keep in mind is that readers project themselves into the novels they read. People are flawed—they see themselves as flawed. When the character you create is also flawed, your readers tend to identify more closely with the character, drawing them into the story more easily and, eventually, more deeply.

Beyond this, the flaw serves another vital function. In the beginning of your story, your main character is incomplete (whether or not she or he knows it): this can mean many things, such as, the character has lost a loved one, has been abused in youth, is an orphan, etc. His or her story arc is to be complete (or at least be on the right road) by story's end. This gives your story its emotional drive and resonance over and above the plot line.

What happens when the reader experiences a flawed character whose story arc is not complete (or on the right road) by the story's end?

Frustration. The only way to make this work is if you're writing a series and the character will be extended into the next book. Frankly, writing a series is a whole

---

JANICE GABLE BASHMAN is co-author (with Jonathan Maberry) of *Wanted Undead or Alive: Vampire Hunters and Other Kick-Ass Enemies of Evil* (Citadel Press 2010). She is a contributing editor of the *Big Thrill*, the newsletter of the International Thriller Writers, and she also writes for other leading publications. Visit Janice at www.janicegablebashman.com or contact her at janicebashman@yahoo.com.

different animal, which I learned the hard way when I wrote *The Ninja*. I had no thought that this might become a series, so with each book it became more and more difficult to find new things in Nicholas' life. I mean, you can't all of a sudden bring on a brother or a sister in book four, without straining the reader's sense of credibility in the world you have created.

That's why, when I was asked to take over the Bourne series from my friend, the late Bob Ludlum, I took a macro approach. This is, I reimagined Bourne's new world over the course of several novels, projecting into the future where I wanted him to go and who he might meet, battle against, fall in love with, etc. For instance, I knew there would be a tremendous number of readers coming to my books because of the success of the films. I also had to think of the long-time Ludlum fans. So I took two of Bob's recurring Bourne characters and killed them off in the first twenty pages, the inciting incident, that set the first book rolling. This way, older readers felt on familiar ground before Bourne's world was turned upside down. They felt for him. At the same time, current events immediately pulled the new readers into Bourne's reimagined world. Similarly, with Bourne's wife and children. Something had to be done with them, otherwise they'd be in constant peril and the books would be in danger of becoming repetitious. Keep in mind that Bob never meant for Bourne to be a recurring character. I decided that Marie be accidentally killed between Legacy and Betrayal. The children were sent off to her parents' farm in rural Canada. Now Bourne was free to meet a wider range of characters and interact with them in a more natural way.

You've stated that the inciting incident "turns the protagonist's world upside down." What is an inciting incident and how does it build character?

The classic example I like to give is in the beginning of Alfred Hitchcock's masterpiece, *North By Northwest*. Roger Thornhill (Cary Grant) is sitting in a hotel lobby in New York City, waiting to have lunch with his mother (right off the bat we see that he's not your typical movie hero). It happens that just at the moment he sees her and raises his arm in greeting, a page comes around calling another man's name. Thus, to the agents following this (as it turns out) mythical man, Thornhill is mistaken for that man, is kidnapped by foreign agents, and off we go. The twist is that during the course of the film this mild-mannered advertising exec *becomes* the mythical.

Through the inciting incident, Thornhill's world is turned upside down—he's thrust into the unfamiliar and frightening world of espionage. "Unfamiliar" and "frightening" are the two more important words in defining and creating the inciting incident. The situation you create for your character is one in which she or he must reveal traits—cleverness, resourcefulness, guts, and relentlessness that are not at first apparent. In other words, the character learns about himself or herself along with the reader.

Action isn't just about physical change—it's also about conflict between characters. How does conflict through action transform characters and make thmake them more real?Conflict is the way to haem more real?

Conflict is the way to have characters learn about themselves. They're thrust into new situations against their will. This creates a conflict within themselves that must be resolved. The immediacy of the situation ensures that it can't be put off, so they are forced to act outside their comfort zone, to do things they assumed (or were afraid) they couldn't do. Change is what novels are all about. A plot twist is nothing more than a change that your characters must confront. In confronting the unknown and the frightening, your characters change. In this way, they grow, deepen, and become whole people.

Why is it important to make emotion personal to the reader, and in what way does this transform character?

It is essential to understand that emotion doesn't exist (at least in a novel) in any other form than the personal. How to bring home the horror of war to a reader? Is it through a description of a battlefield, a massacre, or mass killings? Possibly, but wouldn't it be better to bring it home through, say, the choice a prisoner has to make between saving her own life and that of her child's, or the terror of a child as he or she sees the family being killed? This is the way to make big issues both compelling and understandable to your reader.

Let's say, for instance, your novel is set in the present, during the recession. Do you describe all the people out of work? Or is that the backdrop to your protagonist losing his or her job for reasons he or she doesn't understand, and doesn't want to understand? The mystery here, the way you've hooked your reader, is why the character is in denial. There must be a reason and, if you've done your job correctly, your reader wants to find out.

You also stress "building a flow." Explain what this means and how it affects both the reader and the characters.

It's useful to think of your novel as if it were a roller-coaster ride. That is, alternating sections of tension and release (up and down, in visual terms). Tension doesn't always mean physical action. In fact, unlike in the movies, constant action in a novel merely fatigues the reader. Rather, tension between characters is what is meant here. Face-offs over differences in philosophy, in one character trying to bend the other to his or her will: a boss to a subordinate, one lover to another. Psychological tension, in other words.

You've stated "heroes have flaws, though never fatal ones, otherwise they'd be dull as dishwater." Can you expand on that statement?

Fatal flaws make readers wish they had never invested their time (and money) in a character. They feel cheated, and rightly so. Readers are looking for their heroes to find redemption, because that's what we're all looking for. Redemption for mistakes we've made, errors in judgement, errors in trust, the disappointments accumulated in life. Whatever mistakes your character has made in the past have to be at least partially rectified in the course of his or her arc.

Your characters are "people [you'd] like to know." Do you think that's why your characters are so strong?

Absolutely. Unless you are a dyed-in-the-wool nihilist, chances are your favorite novels are the ones that feature characters you'd like to meet. Why? Not only do they embody the attributes you yourself would like to have, but even more importantly, the characters feel real to you. That's the highest compliment you can pay a fiction author: that his characters seem like real people. I have a fetish about this, both in my writing and my reading. I can't abide characters I can't conceive of as being real people. In my opinion, the two worst offenses a writer can commit is creating a female character that doesn't seem authentic (a man in a skirt, in other words) and creating an antagonist (or a villain, if you like) that is one-dimensional. I insist that my antagonists be flawed just as I insist that my protagonists be flawed. Why not? They're both human beings. If you don't see it that way, you've made a crucial error. Pure evil, like pure good, is without depth, and, therefore, just plain boring.

Each author has his own process for creating characters. What's yours?
That's like asking a musician what his process is for creating a melody. The process as a mysterious as it is complex. A lot depends on what the book is about. For instance, my new series features Jack McClure, advisor to the president, and the president's daughter Alli Carson. The books are about the relationship between these two people. Alli was the best friend of Jack's daughter, Emma, who dies at the beginning of *First Daughter*, the first book in the series. Both *First Daughter* and *Last Snow*, the second novel in the series, as well as the third I'm working on now, are, at heart, about the exploitation of young women. Therefore, I need to imagine characters who fit into that world, i.e., the exploited and the exploiters. The important factor here is to ensure that the characters aren't black-and-white, to ensure that they are three-dimensional, capable of good and evil, that they don't always make the right or the wrong choices. That they live and breath just like you or I do.

Do you find your characters' voices or do they find you?
In the beginning I usually have a rough idea of a character's voice, but I write organically. Though I do sketch out an outline, it's just that, a sketch. I figure out what the book is about, the skeleton of the plot, like towns on a map, but by what route I get to each town is up in the air. During the course of the writing, characters often surprise me. I've had characters meant to be bit players who turn in virtuoso cameos, or even, every once in a while, shoulder their way into a lead role. There comes a point in the book usually around the 100 page mark, when my characters become full-voiced. I know who they are. A certain thrill occurs when these events take place, because I know my world is alive and breathing on its own. It's off author life support.

What advice can you give to other writers about building solid characters?
Don't go to extremes. Don't build your characters on clichés. Do take the time to speak to each of your characters (either out loud or in your mind) until you know how each of them will react to situations. Don't have a character act against his/her personality just because it will help move the plot along. (See virtually any episode of *Heroes*, just about the worst offender on this score of any TV show currently on the air.) That's simply lazy writing.

The primary thing to keep in mind is that readers project themselves into the novels they read. People are flawed—they see themselves as flawed. When the character you create is also flawed, your readers tend to identify more closely with the character, drawing them into the story more easily and, eventually, more deeply.

Beyond this, the flaw serves another vital function. In the beginning of your story, your main character is incomplete (whether or not she or he knows it): this can mean many things, such as, the character has lost a loved one, has been abused in youth, is an orphan, etc. His or her story arc is to be complete (or at least be on the right road) by story's end. This gives your story its emotional drive and resonance over and above the plot line.

What happens when the reader experiences a flawed character whose story arc is not complete (or on the right road) by the story's end?
Frustration. The only way to make this work is if you're writing a series and the character will be extended into the next book. Frankly, writing a series is a whole different animal, which I learned the hard way when I wrote *The Ninja*. I had no thought that this might become a series, so with each book it became more and more difficult to find new things in Nicholas' life. I mean, you can't all of a sudden bring on

a brother or a sister in book four, without straining the reader's sense of credibility in the world you have created.

That's why, when I was asked to take over the Bourne series from my friend, the late Bob Ludlum, I took a macro approach. This is, I reimagined Bourne's new world over the course of several novels, projecting into the future where I wanted him to go and who he might meet, battle against, fall in love with, etc. For instance, I knew there would be a tremendous number of readers coming to my books because of the success of the films. I also had to think of the long-time Ludlum fans. So I took two of Bob's recurring Bourne characters and killed them off in the first twenty pages, the inciting incident, that set the first book rolling. This way, older readers felt on familiar ground before Bourne's world was turned upside down. They felt for him. At the same time, current events immediately pulled the new readers into Bourne's reimagined world. Similarly, with Bourne's wife and children. Something had to be done with them, otherwise they'd be in constant peril and the books would be in danger of becoming repetitious. Keep in mind that Bob never meant for Bourne to be a recurring character. I decided that Marie be accidentally killed between Legacy and Betrayal. The children were sent off to her parents' farm in rural Canada. Now Bourne was free to meet a wider range of characters and interact with them in a more natural way.

You've stated that the inciting incident "turns the protagonist's world upside down." What is an inciting incident and how does it build character?

The classic example I like to give is in the beginning of Alfred Hitchcock's masterpiece, *North By Northwest*. Roger Thornhill (Cary Grant) is sitting in a hotel lobby in New York City, waiting to have lunch with his mother (right off the bat we see that he's not your typical movie hero). It happens that just at the moment he sees her and raises his arm in greeting, a page comes around calling another man's name. Thus, to the agents following this (as it turns out) mythical man, Thornhill is mistaken for that man, is kidnapped by foreign agents, and off we go. The twist is that during the course of the film this mild-mannered advertising exec *becomes* the mythical.

Through the inciting incident, Thornhill's world is turned upside down—he's thrust into the unfamiliar and frightening world of espionage. "Unfamiliar" and "frightening" are the two more important words in defining and creating the inciting incident. The situation you create for your character is one in which she or he must reveal traits—cleverness, resourcefulness, guts, and relentlessness that are not at first apparent. In other words, the character learns about himself or herself along with the reader.

Action isn't just about physical change—it's also about conflict between characters. How does conflict through action transform characters and make them more real?

Conflict is the way to have characters learn about themselves. They're thrust into new situations against their will. This creates a conflict within themselves that must be resolved. The immediacy of the situation ensures that it can't be put off, so they are forced to act outside their comfort zone, to do things they assumed (or were afraid) they couldn't do. Change is what novels are all about. A plot twist is nothing more than a change that your characters must confront. In confronting the unknown and the frightening, your characters change. In this way, they grow, deepen, and become whole people.

Why is it important to make emotion personal to the reader, and in what way does this transform character?

It is essential to understand that emotion doesn't exist (at least in a novel) in any other form than the personal. How to bring home the horror of war to a reader? Is it through a description of a battlefield, a massacre, or mass killings? Possibly, but wouldn't it be better to bring it home through, say, the choice a prisoner has to make between saving her own life and that of her child's, or the terror of a child as he or she sees the family being killed? This is the way to make big issues both compelling and understandable to your reader.

Let's say, for instance, your novel is set in the present, during the recession. Do you describe all the people out of work? Or is that the backdrop to your protagonist losing his or her job for reasons he or she doesn't understand, and doesn't want to understand? The mystery here, the way you've hooked your reader, is why the character is in denial. There must be a reason and, if you've done your job correctly, your reader wants to find out.

You also stress "building a flow." Explain what this means and how it affects both the reader and the characters.

It's useful to think of your novel as if it were a roller-coaster ride. That is, alternating sections of tension and release (up and down, in visual terms). Tension doesn't always mean physical action. In fact, unlike in the movies, constant action in a novel merely fatigues the reader. Rather, tension between characters is what is meant here. Face-offs over differences in philosophy, in one character trying to bend the other to his or her will: a boss to a subordinate, one lover to another. Psychological tension, in other words.

You've stated "heroes have flaws, though never fatal ones, otherwise they'd be dull as dishwater." Can you expand on that statement?

Fatal flaws make readers wish they had never invested their time (and money) in a character. They feel cheated, and rightly so. Readers are looking for their heroes to find redemption, because that's what we're all looking for. Redemption for mistakes we've made, errors in judgement, errors in trust, the disappointments accumulated in life. Whatever mistakes your character has made in the past have to be at least partially rectified in the course of his or her arc.

Your characters are "people [you'd] like to know." Do you think that's why your characters are so strong?

Absolutely. Unless you are a dyed-in-the-wool nihilist, chances are your favorite novels are the ones that feature characters you'd like to meet. Why? Not only do they embody the attributes you yourself would like to have, but even more importantly, the characters feel real to you. That's the highest compliment you can pay a fiction author: that his characters seem like real people. I have a fetish about this, both in my writing and my reading. I can't abide characters I can't conceive of as being real people. In my opinion, the two worst offenses a writer can commit is creating a female character that doesn't seem authentic (a man in a skirt, in other words) and creating an antagonist (or a villain, if you like) that is one-dimensional. I insist that my antagonists be flawed just as I insist that my protagonists be flawed. Why not? They're both human beings. If you don't see it that way, you've made a crucial error. Pure evil, like pure good, is without depth, and, therefore, just plain boring.

Each author has his own process for creating characters. What's yours?

That's like asking a musician what his process is for creating a melody. The process as a mysterious as it is complex. A lot depends on what the book is about. For instance, my new series features Jack McClure, advisor to the president, and the president's daughter

Alli Carson. The books are about the relationship between these two people. Alli was the best friend of Jack's daughter, Emma, who dies at the beginning of *First Daughter*, the first book in the series. Both *First Daughter* and *Last Snow*, the second novel in the series, as well as the third I'm working on now, are, at heart, about the exploitation of young women. Therefore, I need to imagine characters who fit into that world, i.e., the exploited and the exploiters. The important factor here is to ensure that the characters aren't black-and-white, to ensure that they are three-dimensional, capable of good and evil, that they don't always make the right or the wrong choices. That they live and breath just like you or I do.

Do you find your characters' voices or do they find you?

In the beginning I usually have a rough idea of a character's voice, but I write organically. Though I do sketch out an outline, it's just that, a sketch. I figure out what the book is about, the skeleton of the plot, like towns on a map, but by what route I get to each town is up in the air. During the course of the writing, characters often surprise me. I've had characters meant to be bit players who turn in virtuoso cameos, or even, every once in a while, shoulder their way into a lead role. There comes a point in the book usually around the 100 page mark, when my characters become full-voiced. I know who they are. A certain thrill occurs when these events take place, because I know my world is alive and breathing on its own. It's off author life support.

What advice can you give to other writers about building solid characters?

Don't go to extremes. Don't build your characters on clichés. Do take the time to speak to each of your characters (either out loud or in your mind) until you know how each of them will react to situations. Don't have a character act against his/her personality just because it will help move the plot along. (See virtually any episode of *Heroes*, just about the worst offender on this score of any TV show currently on the air.) That's simply lazy writing.

And while I'm on the subject, never create characters in the service of your plot. Your characters must move the plot along, not the other way around. Otherwise, all you're left with is cardboard cutouts. Lastly, believe in your characters. If you don't, neither will your readers.

Kij Johnson

Creating Heroes, Creating Worlds

by Janice Gable Bashman

Monkeys, dogs, aliens, and other beings are every bit as compelling as humans in Kij Johnson's fiction, and her characters resonate with readers long after they finish reading her work. An image, a bit of dialogue, or a title incite Johnson's stories, but it is her deep understanding of character that makes her work continually receive the recognition it deserves.

Winner of the World Fantasy Award, the Theodore Sturgeon Memorial Award, and the International Association for the Fantastic in the Arts Crawford Award, and nominated for the Hugo, Nebula, and World Fantasy Awards, Kij Johnson is the author of dozens of short stories and novelettes, as well as the novels *The Fox Woman* and *Fudoki*. Her short fiction has appeared in *Amazing Stories, Analog, Asimov's, Duelist Magazine, Fantasy & Science Fiction, Realms of Fantasy*, and *The Twilight Zone Magazine*; online at www.clarkesworld.com, www.tor.com, www.scifi.com, and her own website, www.kijjohnson.com; and in numerous anthologies, including *The Coyote Road*, and numerous "Best Of" collections.

Kij has taught a science fiction and fantasy novel writing workshop at the University of Kansas since 2005. She worked as managing editor at Tor Books, as a collections and special editions editor for Dark Horse Comics, and as an editor and managing editor for Wizards of the Coast. Kij is currently vice chair on the board of the Clarion West Writers' Workshop.

Why do you think your characters stay with your readers for so long?

I always write about myself. I'm ticking back through the stories I've written in recent years, and they're always about something I'm thinking about, and the characters are the sorts of people who would be thinking about those things. They're nearly always women (though Kaya no Yoshifuji, one of the three voices in *The Fox Woman* [Tor, 1999], was not). They usually think way too much.

I have been thinking lately that a good challenge for me is to create a convincing male character. Who is not also a dog or a monkey or a sentient bush or some freakish thing that might cover up any weak spots.

JANICE GABLE BASHMAN is co-author (with Jonathan Maberry) of *Wanted Undead or Alive: Vampire Hunters and Other Kick-Ass Enemies of Evil* (Citadel Press 2010). She is a contributing editor of the *Big Thrill*, the newsletter of the International Thriller Writers, and she also writes for other leading publications. Visit Janice at www.janicegablebashman.com or contact her at janicebashman@yahoo.com.

Which of your characters are your favorites and why?

Favorites is hard. I am fascinated by whomever I am writing at the moment or I guess I wouldn't be writing about her. There are characters I like returning to in my mind. I deeply respect the princess Harueme from the novel *Fudoki* (Tor, 2003), who is someone I wish were real so that I could meet her. I love Aimee from "26 Monkeys, Also The Abyss" (*Asimov's*, July 2008), because she has a bunch of monkeys and an adorable boyfriend, and what's not to like about that? I love the Linna of "At the Mouth of the River of Bees" (scifi.com), because Linna and I have this in common, that we have watched a dog we love dying, and wished there were something we could do; except that Linna succeeds where I have failed.

The Linnas are interesting to me. I have written two stories with a main character named Linna, hardly a common name: "At the Mouth of the River of Bees" and "The Evolution of Trickster Stories Among the Dogs of North Park After the Change" (*Coyote Road*, Firebird, 2007) and I am pretty sure there will be another Linna story. The two Linnas are not the same person, though they have many resemblances and they are both deeply aware of and engaged in the human/dog connection.

So why name them the same thing? And if they are named the same thing, why not make them the same person? Some of it is that the Linnas have symbolic roles. Linnas relate to their world in a single very concrete, specific way, but Linna in "River of Bees" eases death; Linna in "Trickster Stories" is a witness. They are essentially the same person, even if it manifests differently: isolated women who have turned to dogs.

You stated you "usually start a story with an image in [your] mind, or an exchange of dialogue." Sometimes, your story begins with a title. At what point do your characters reveal themselves, and how do you perceive them initially?

The spur to the story may be the image or the dialogue or the title; if I did not have that spur, I would not write a story about a travelling monkey show ("26 Monkeys") or a semi-mythological Japanese empress ("The Empress Jingu Fishes" [*Conqueror Fantastic*, Roc]), or horse and dog cultures ("The Horse Raiders" [Analog]). But these three stories are just examples of a story I return to all the time, about women who lose everything and then put the pieces back together, or don't. If I didn't have those spurs, I would have found others and written different stories, but the women would have been the same women, even if in different situations. Like the Linnas.

In preparation for writing *The Fox Woman*, you wrote extensively from each character's point of view. You previously stated, "[you] would sit down to say—okay, who is Shikujo? If I'm the woman, Shikujo, what am I feeling? Okay, I'm mad, but I can't admit it. I'm hurt, but I can't admit it. I want desperately to be good. I want to be a good wife because that's how I identify myself. If I'm not a good wife, then I don't know what I am." Why was this exercise so important to creating character, and how did the results effect your writing process?

I wrote those characters endlessly because that was the first book I had written, and I didn't know how else to get inside them. It worked out, because that's what those three do anyway—write extensively about themselves, Yoshifuji, especially. Harueme from *Fudoki* is similar in that she is examining her life closely as she lets it go, and I could have written tens of thousand more words of her.

Characters in my short fiction don't seem to require this sort of chewing over, because they're usually direct responses to specific questions coming up in my own life.

Some of your main characters are not human, such as the fox in *The Fox Woman*, the monkeys in "26 Monkeys," and the alien in "Spar." What factors must you consider when creating these characters to make them realistic to the reader?

I've said before that I am fascinated by the where the line is drawn between human and Other. Writing about dogs is about this—they're as close to us as you can get, really, and yet we don't understand what's really going on for them, and never will.

Kitsune in *The Fox Woman* is very human, very much a teenaged girl. Kagaya-hime from Fudoki, on the other hand, is very *in*human—a cat in human form who loses none of her solitary, amoral, feline character—but I think Kagaya-hime works in the story only because she is balanced by her amanuensis, the very human Harueme.

I think the heart of writing the Other is to understand that it *is* Other. We're not going to understand it. The most we will ever get is a flicker of insight. But we will never see ourselves clearly unless we try to get outside ourselves. For me, writing about the Other is a very formal exercise encouraging me to do this.

Many of your characters remain nameless, identified by their role in the story, i.e. the manager or the wife. You obviously created three dimensional characters yet you chose to keep the character nameless. Why did you choose to create nameless characters?

I'm terrible at names. Here's another answer: they are people, but their importance in the story is rooted in their role. Also, I guess I'm intrigued by how far you can strip out the conventional markers for character and still have that person feel real and specific.

You stated, "stories should not be cheap; they should cost the writer something, and the reader something else." Explain.

Whatever else it is, this statement is an admonition to myself. I can be a glib writer. I was lucky enough to be raised reading the sorts of books that gave me a vast vocabulary and a deep intuitive understanding of language, and I can sometimes drop a thousand words on the page that are lovely and emotionally resonant. In the past I have written stories that were creations of craft rather than internally driven works. (No, I'm not going to tell you which ones.)

It used to be that I was cool with writing stuff like that, but lately it's been bugging me. It seems dishonest when I do this because I feel as though I am tricking people into caring for something that I don't care as much about.

The reader pays a price when she reads a story, when she puts herself into the power of the writer. Fiction is an author manipulating a reader: an author makes the reader see or feel or think something she might not otherwise have seen or felt or thought. It seems as though the least I can do is get down there in the weeds with the reader, and experience things I maybe wasn't ready to, either.

"Spar" is a good example of this, I think. A reviewer called it "aggressively unpleasant," and I think that person was exactly right. I don't like relentlessly grim stories. I don't like tentacle porn. It's not a story I would enjoy reading if I stumbled on it online or in a magazine, though I think I would have had a hard time putting it down, and a harder time forgetting it. It plays against a lot of my strengths—the prose is brutish, there's no dialogue except in flashback, there's no descriptions, the character is not a thinker. It was not a cheap story to write, and it's not a cheap story to read.

Why is it so important for characters to change throughout the story, and do you know how this will occur prior to writing or is it a process that occurs while you are writing?

Change is what makes a story. The situation almost always changes, and the characters usually change, though they don't have to—James Bond, for an easy example. I think we like reading stories where characters change because we like to see that people *can* change, and that changing can improve their world. It gives us courage.

I have written characters who have not changed much, but writing is a tool for self-exploration for me. I continue to change for better or worse, and I would have a hard time understanding why a character would not, and staying engaged with someone who was uninterested in change.

What advice can you give to other writers about creating realistic characters?

The better I know myself, the more likely is it that I will be able to write someone who is *not* myself. The more you know about yourself, the better your characters will become. If you know enough about yourself, you can see the holes in your understanding of human nature. When you see these gaps you can start to extrapolate - or interpolate—and take educated guesses at the things you don't know.

This is also why I love thinking about Other intelligences, dogs and monkeys and the like. If I compare how I think with how a dog (who is definitely not me) thinks, I may learn something that will help me when I compare how I think with how another human (who is no more me than the dog is) thinks.

Characters are real. They are the heroes of their own stories. However tidily we try to sew things up, their lives are not tidy. Something comes after "happily ever after."

They are not you, not even the ones who are exactly like you. And they are all you, even the ones who are utterly different.

INTERVIEWS

Delia Sherman

Creating Fantasy in a Real-life Urban Setting

Photo Beth Gwinn

by Janice Gable Bashman

For Delia Sherman, grounding a setting in the real world, knowing what makes a setting right for a story, and using details to make the setting believable are the keys to successfully creating fantasy in a real-life urban setting. Time and time again, Sherman draws her readers into incredible worlds filled with wonder and excitement, the new and old, the real and the fantastic.

Sherman is the author of *Through a Brazen Mirror*, which led to a nomination for the Campbell Award for Best New Science Fiction Writer, and *The Porcelain Dove*, winner of the Mythopoeic Award and a New York Times Notable Book. She also wrote The Fall of the Kings with Ellen Kushner. The novels in her New York Between Series, *Changeling* and *The Magic Mirror of the Mermaid Queen*, are aimed at younger readers. The Freedom Maze, a middle-grade time-travel fantasy set in Louisiana, will be published by Big Mouth Press in 2010.

In addition to her novels, Sherman has published numerous short stories and poems in magazines, such as the *Magazine of Fantasy & Science Fiction*, and in anthologies, including *Firebirds*, *Trolls Eye View*, *Poe*, and *Salon Fantastique*. Her stories have been reprinted in fourteen volumes of *The Year's Best Fantasy & Horror*. Sherman also edits books and anthologies, teaches science fiction and fantasy writing at the Clarion and Odyssey workshops, and has served as a judge for the Crawford Award for Best First Fantasy Novel, The James Tiptree, Jr. Award, and the World Fantasy Award.

You've set many fantasy stories in real-life modern cities. Do you find the story first or the setting?

Settings are very important to me. If I get interested in a setting, I can usually find characters and build a story for it. But if all I have is an idea and no interesting place to set it, I can't write the story.

For me, where something happens is at least as important as the event itself, and I especially enjoy pairings that are unusual or even counterintuitive. My historical novel The Porcelain Dove is a literary fairy tale/romance in the French Age of Enlightenment. And my New York Between series is set in an alternate New York populated by the folklore brought to America by immigrants from all over the world—with the addition

---

JANICE GABLE BASHMAN is co-author (with Jonathan Maberry) of *Wanted Undead or Alive: Vampire Hunters and Other Kick-Ass Enemies of Evil* (Citadel Press 2010). She is a contributing editor of the *Big Thrill*, the newsletter of the International Thriller Writers, and she also writes for other leading publications. Visit Janice at www.janicegablebashman.com or contact her at janicebashman@yahoo.com.

of some home-grown New York folklore culled from 20th century literature, current popular culture, and my own experience of growing up in Manhattan in the 60's.

When creating a fantasy that occurs in a real-life setting, what things are important to know and why?

You have to know what it is about the setting that makes it the right one for your story. A story about a mermaid set in Tucson, AZ would be very different from one set in San Francisco, which would be different again from one set in Chicago. All of them would be possible to write. But the Tucson story would probably be about how a mermaid got there in the first place and why and how difficult it would be to keep her alive. The San Francisco story wouldn't have to deal with these issues, and so the plot would be likely to focus less on survival and more on another kind of adventure. The Chicago one might be about displacement or adaptation or the loneliness of being the only mermaid in the Great Lakes, but you wouldn't have to work quite so hard to make it believable as with the Tucson story.

You also need to know your real-life setting very well. Visiting the city you're writing about is, of course, the ideal preparation. Maps, pictures, travel books, even other novels set in the same city are extremely useful, even if you live there. But they can't tell you what midtown New York smells like in winter (butter and sugar, from caramel-coated peanut vendors) or what the wind feels like blowing up from Riverside Drive (a tiger trying to rip your face off).

How do you make it seem plausible to the reader that the fantasy occurring within the real-life setting is possible?

The key to truly successful urban fantasy, I think, is to make both the city and the fantasy as real as possible. Every detail that grounds your setting in the real world will make the fantastic parts of your story much more believable.

At the very least, you have to get the street names right and know enough about the neighborhoods your characters visit to know if they'd be able to buy a hot dog from a street vendor or from a storefront if they get hungry. In order to build a solid sense of atmosphere, it's always good to appeal to all the senses: smell and touch (which includes temperature) and taste as well as the more obvious sight and hearing. Think of how a city is different at different times of day—what it looks like, who is out on the streets, how they're dressed, how they act. Culture is part of a setting, too: what people wear, how they greet each other, what is considered acceptable or unacceptable behavior in a given situation. If you set a scene in a museum, realize that a guard will probably notice if one of his exhibits is missing—although he may not notice if a statue has changed its pose.

It sounds like a contradiction in terms to say that your fantastic elements have to be realistic, too, but they do. Formal magic is wound around with rules and rituals and warnings. In fairy tales, events tend to follow certain patterns, and magic, even the most powerful, works according to an internal logic that can be baffled by trickery as well as overcome by superior force. All-powerful magic that always does exactly what you want it to does not make for an interesting story. In Changeling, I modeled my elves and fairies on the elves of traditional folk lore, who are easily distracted, touchy, greedy, tricky, and obsessive as well as being beautiful, charming, artistic, and able to grant wishes.

Your Changeling series of urban-fantasy novels takes place in an alternate, fairy New York. How does creating fantasy in a real-life urban setting differ from creating fantasy in an alternate (or fictional) setting?

I can't stretch the laws of probability as much when I'm working with a completely real-world setting. Characters—even the magical ones—have to travel on real buses and subways and spend real time and money doing it. Holly Black's Modern Fairy Tale trilogy is a wonderful example of how to do this. Her fairies live in a New York that is absolutely real, struggling not only with the internecine intrigue that drives the plot, but also with having to maintain the glamors that let them pass as human and take potions to keep themselves from dying from ironsickness.

Not that there aren't laws in fairyland. In Changeling, Neef never pays for anything with money, but she has to barter or bargain for everything she needs according to the rules and conventions of fairy tale. And while the New York neighborhoods my characters live in aren't exactly like the neighborhoods of real-life New York, they are based on old novels, legends, and history. The presiding spirit of the neighborhood is The Producer of Broadway, for instance, who looks and talks like a character from Damon Runyon, who wrote the stories that inspired the Broadway musical (and later, movie) Guys and Dolls.

Do you find it easier to create fantasy in a real-life setting or an alternate (or fictional) setting?

I like working with real settings for my fantasies because I find it easier to look things up than to make them up. If I need to find out whether flooding a fresh water lake with river water will poison the lake (which is a big plot point in The Magic Mirror of the Mermaid Queen), I don't have to learn about rivers and estuaries and draw maps to make sure what I want to happen could happen. All I have to do is look up the salt content of the Hudson River as it passes Manhattan Island, and I'm all set. The same goes for every major physical detail of New York Between, from where my characters live to how they get from place to place.

Of course, when I'm working in an alternate real-world setting, I get to be more playful. For instance, in New York Between, the Fairy Folk get around by taking a magical transportation system called the Betweenways. I imagine it as being a little like a moving sidewalk, a little like a Star Trek transporter, and a little like a subway. It's noisy, confusing, crowded, and only takes you where you want to go if you really, really want to go there and are absolutely focused. Which is pretty much how the New York Subway feels to someone who isn't familiar with it. It is also inspired by the descriptions in many, many fairy tales, of mortals being whirled through space by demons, djinn, witches, wizards, and goblins, to be deposited, disoriented and reeling, at their destinations.

You've stated that "the trick in successful speculative fiction (both fantasy and science fiction) is to make the invented world seem as real as the world in which we shop for our groceries." How do you accomplish this?

You have to pay attention to details. The real world has variety: cities and towns and empty wastes, mountains and rivers, different kinds of people living in different cultures, speaking different languages. Two of the greatest fantasists of all time, J.R.R. Tolkein and Ursula K. LeGuin, display the variety of their invented worlds by sending their characters on long journeys that pass through many different lands. You can also bring characters from different places together in one central location, as Terry Pratchett often brings characters to Ankh-morpork in his Discworld books. I talked earlier about using sensory details. Real places have temperature, characteristic smells (some good, some not so much), recognizable sounds of animals or machines or wind through the leaves. Invented ones should too.

It's also important to pay attention to how real people behave. In the real world, people eat and sleep and get tired. When they sprain an ankle or get a skinned knee, they won't be able to run fast for several days. And getting hurt or even getting hungry is certainly a part of even the most magical adventures. Many beginning writers forget to let their characters rest or eat or sleep because they think writing about mundane things like getting a hot dog or taking a nap is boring and will bore the reader. Nothing could be farther from the truth.

Take food. It can be a danger (eating fairy food traps you in fairyland forever). It can be a challenge (what do you offer a hungry dragon to keep it from eating you?). It can be a friendship offering (feeding a hungry demon). It can be a bonding experience (adventurers pooling whatever is in their pockets and planning together while they eat it). These scenes not only make your characters more real, they can also advance the plot or complicate it.

What elements affect the authenticity of the worlds you create?
Internal coherence is central to making any fantasy believable. If you have established that only one character has the power to see vampires for what they really are, you had better have a very good and cogent reason for another character to be able to see them, too. And "It was convenient for the plot that she see vampires" is not a good or cogent reason.

In my New York Between stories, I was very careful to make the behavior and habits of the immigrant supernatural creatures consistent with their behavior and habits in folk tales.

What advice can you give to other writers about creating fantasy in a real-life urban setting?
Well, you've got to know your urban setting—how it looks, sounds, smells, feels. You have to be familiar enough with the sociology of the city you've chosen to know where a pale guy wandering the streets at night is going to go unnoticed (if you want him unnoticed) or stick out (if you want him to stick out).

All the realism I've been talking about will help your reader believe in the fantastic parts of your story. But it's also important that the fantasy itself be believable, by which I mean it needs to have some consistent rules and abide by them. This does not mean you have to invent a coherent magic system or look up what people believed about vampires in medieval Europe (unless you want to). It means that you have imagine what effect a dragon appearing in the middle of a real city would actually have. Would it burn down buildings? Would the fire department come? How long would it take the army and the navy to get involved? How about if the dragon was in human form? Would it still want to eat virgins? Or would it be happy just to amass a huge fortune? You get to decide, but you have to abide by the limitations of your decision.

What about character interaction with setting? How does that affect the story?
The most important element of any novel of any genre is, of course, the characters. Without characters a reader can care about, be irritated by, fall in love with, hate, want to spend time with, maybe even be, a novel is just an intellectual exercise. The best urban fantasists—John Crowley, Emma Bull, Holly Black—use setting the same way they use their characters. Their characters not only live in their settings. They interact with them, they are formed by them, they hate them or love them. If you create your setting with the same care and attention you give your characters, your whole fantastic story will be far more believable than it would be if you just threw in a couple of street names and a landmark or two and called it a day.

INTERVIEWS

Premiere Voices

by Travis Adkins

By the time you read this, many of the freshman writers featured in this year's issue of Premiere Voices will have already become sophomores. Jamie Ford, author of the *New York Times*-bestseller *Hotel at the Corner of Bitter and Sweet*, will be looking to duplicate the success of his debut. Barb Johnson, whose first short-story collection *More of This World or Maybe Another* was published to wide acclaim, could have graduated to the status of "novelist and short-story writer." Dennis Tafoya, author of *Dope Thief*, has already completed his second novel, so perhaps he'll have a whole shelf at your local bookstore. And James Klise, who switched genres from literary fiction to young adult to write his first book *Love Drugged*, may be on to a new genre altogether.

But in accomplishing that hoped-for second book, they'll each draw upon the same lessons that made them successful the first time around: take it one day at a time, focus on writing each story as it comes, and the rest will take care of itself.

Barb Johnson
More of This World or Maybe Another (Harper Perennial)

Barb Johnson has a piece of advice that might seem contrary to the mission of *Novel & Short Story Writer's Market*: don't take the process of submitting your work too seriously.

"Writing what makes me happy is all that matters," declares Johnson, author of the short story collection *More of This World or Maybe Another*. "Participating, showing up, those things are crucial. Submitting, editing, revising—all very important. But enjoying the act of writing is the most essential of all. I submit a lot of work. I get rejected a lot. I'm much happier when I'm engaged in the process of writing and submitting and disengaged from the outcome—rejection or publication."

Her attitude and approach must work. Johnson has enjoyed almost a lifetime's worth of recognition and success in the five years since she decided to abandon her

---

TRAVIS ADKINS is a freelance writer in Brooklyn, New York and a frequent contriutor to *Novel & Short Story Writer's Market*.

previous career of carpentry—which she'd been practicing for more than 20 years—and enter the MFA program at the University of New Orleans. Since she made that momentous decision, nothing has distracted Johnson from her goal of becoming a writer—not the daunting task of starting a new career, not the hurdles of breaking into publication, not even losing her livelihood to Hurricane Katrina.

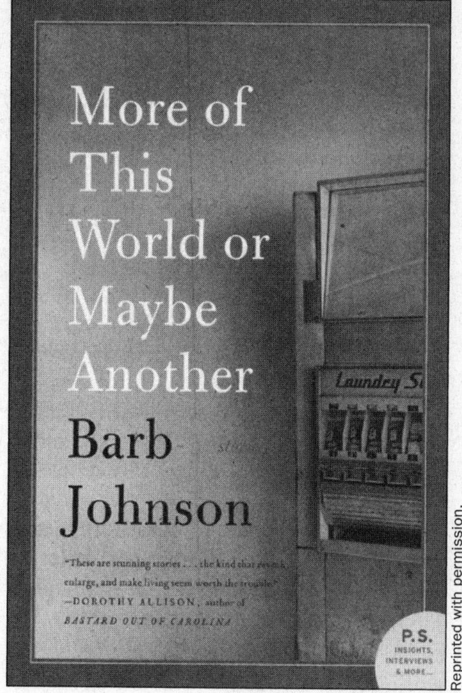

Reprinted with permission.

It was during the aftermath of Katrina, in fact, that Johnson wrote her breakthrough story "Killer Heart," which won *Glimmer Train's* Short Story Award for New Writers. "I had sneaked back into New Orleans after Katrina, and I was living on my balcony," says Johnson. "The story is set years before the hurricane, and that helped me get away from the immediate scenery. Writing it restored me. It kept me from losing my mind and caving in to the intense sorrow of that time. It became clear to me that I didn't just want to, but in fact *needed* to, make writing the focus of my life."

Though getting published and winning an award was a vindication, it was the process of writing an earlier story, "St. Luis of Palmyra," that convinced Johnson that she had become a full-fledged writer. "Like many, it took awhile for me to be able to assess what I had written," she says. "Was it a good story? A bad story? I couldn't tell. Then I wrote 'St. Luis of Palmyra.' I loved the character and I loved his adventures. And I learned how a character can engage me and make me want to write more about him. All this happened, not in the first draft, but many drafts into it. It was the first time that I was able to demystify writing. I realized that stories weren't magic, that they were neither good nor bad at conception. They required shaping. And it was conceivable to me that I could get better at shaping. This gave me great hope for the whole endeavor, and it still does."

The characters that Johnson writes about in the nine stories that comprise *More of This World or Maybe Another* are of a type that is becoming increasingly rare in contemporary fiction. They're economically lower-class, but aren't one-dimensional caricatures defined by their social standing; they lead lives full of difficult circumstances and suffering, but are neither victims or saints. They're the people that Johnson knows best, the ones that she's lived with all her life. Realizing that they could be the subjects of stories was a moment of revelation for her.

"For a long time I thought of fiction as being about fancy places and well-educated, slightly bored people," says Johnson. "I thought I was going to write about those people, but writing about people and places you don't really know will put you on the express train to clichéd writing. I didn't appreciate the land and the circumstances of my early years. Rice fields. Oil and gas wells. Refineries. Swamps. Life in the lower class. My appreciation got kick-started when I drove across the bridge that's in my hometown. I hadn't seen it in almost thirty years. It's a beautiful bridge that, today, would never be built because of its steep grade. At the top, I looked down at the petrochemical plants that line the shore of the river. It was a surreal landscape. The obvious danger of it made my heart beat really fast. Growing up, everyone's father worked there. We were surrounded by explosive materials and never thought a thing of it. I used that landscape in the story, "More of This World or Maybe Another," and, even though none of the things in the story actually happened to me, it felt like the truest thing I'd ever written. I'd been resisting that landscape, those feelings. I thought of them as embarrassing and ersatz artifacts. But everyone's place, all our experiences—even the most benign, maybe especially the most benign—are important. They shape how we see the world, and rather than limit, they expand the fictional worlds we are able to create."

With a $50,000 Gift of Freedom award from A Room Of Her Own Foundation, a grant from the Astraea Foundation, and the distinction of having *More of This World or Maybe Another* named a Barnes & Noble Discover pick, Johnson has come a long way from her days as a carpenter. She's not taking any of it for granted.

"Writers get to choose how they view the world of writing," Johnson says. "It is far more productive to believe that what we write has its own meaning, its own value. And it makes for a much happier existence if we bring a super-sized bucket of faith to the writing table. It is as demanding as any spiritual practice. Writers understand being broke. We know all about exhaustion and sacrifice. Early on, we realize that there will never be enough time to write. So it is tempting to believe that writing is about suffering. But nothing is about suffering unless we believe it is. Writing is about lucky us. We distill our experiences, process our emotions and make sense of our worlds by writing it all down. It's how we're made. So lucky us."

Dennis Tafoya
Dope Thief (Minotaur Books)

As many writers have learned, the time that elapses between inspiration and creation can often stretch over years, as the original idea changes and matures until it's finally ready to be told. That was the case for Dennis Tafoya, whose first novel had its origins in an experience from his youth that has stayed with him for years.

"When I was a kid I was an EMT in an emergency room," says Tafoya. "Biker gangs used to rent farm houses and set up speed labs in the countryside not far from where I lived. One night, one of the labs burned, and we got calls all night from people asking how to take care of burns. A few days later a badly-burned body showed up in the woods. That stuck in my head, and ever since I've wondered how somebody ends up in a burning meth lab in the middle of the night. I wonder, too, if you've come to that place is there any way back? Is it possible to create characters who get involved in that kind of life and who can still claim our sympathy?"

Pondering those questions led Tafoya to write *Dope Thief*, which tells the story of a thief named Ray and partner-in-crime and best friend, Manny. Ray and Manny's specialty is posing as DEA enforcers and ripping off small-time drug dealers for their money and drugs and then disappearing before anyone finds them out. Their scam works until they accidentally hit up the wrong person—a major dealer with a violent streak and connections to New England biker gangs. As they try to stay one step ahead of their pursuer, Ray begins to question the life he's leading and how he can escape it—provided he doesn't get killed first.

Reprinted with permission.

Beyond the true-life event that sparked the story, Tafoya also found himself drawn to the subject matter by his abiding interest in the crime and noir genres. "I've always been fascinated by crime," he says. "When I was a kid, my grandfather gave me a copy of *Beyond Belief,* by Emlyn Williams, a very stylized telling of the story of Ian Brady and Myra Hindley, the Moors Murderers. I've always read a ton of true crime ever since. I love guys like Elmore Leonard and Charles Willeford and Lawrence Block, too. I think of their books as not just great entertainment, but lessons on writing; on economy, and how to let characters drive the story."

Although the idea for *Dope Thief* had been gestating for a long time, when he began writing it Tafoya still found that a lot of the pieces didn't quite fit during the first draft. "I didn't do a very detailed outline for Dope Thief, and found a lot of the story elements and characters as I wrote the first draft," he says. "I ended up creating some of the pivotal characters on the fly, and had to make several passes to deal with that. It changed the way I write, so that now I do create more detailed outlines and try to work out more in advance. That said, I still enjoy finding important elements in the writing. I think all writers like at least a little spontaneity in the process."

Tafoya learned another way to get around those tough spots when inspiration is running a little slow: move on to something else. "Getting stuck is common, but there are a few simple tricks that usually work for me," he says. "I can work on other scenes or other stories. Sometimes I'll read poetry or some favorite writers, and sometimes I'll just let myself write what I know is placeholder material that I'll have to go back and replace when I feel like I've got a more interesting idea for the scene."

The important thing, he says, is to follow the advice he once read Anne Lamott give: "finish your sh...ty first draft."

"I say that as someone who started a dozen novels over many years before I had the motivation to actually complete a manuscript through to 'The End," Tafoya says. "There are going to be obstacles—my friend Greg Frost always refers to the 100-page wall, for instance. But you have to keep going. Write through it, or around it, but keep going. You'll have many chances to improve or edit later. Just get it done."

Tafoya, who also cites such "writer's writers" as Annie Proulx and Cormac McCarthy as influences, originally planned for *Dope Thief* to be more of a literary novel about criminals than a crime novel, per se. But in revising it, he downplayed the literary novel aspects in favor of a structure that hewed closer to the conventions of the crime novel genre, and found that doing so improved the novel on both fronts.

"I wanted to deliver more of the experience that readers who picked up the book in the crime section of the bookstore would expect," he says. "I think it's actually a much better book for having made the changes."

Tafoya counts himself lucky to have as his agent Alex Glass at Trident Media Agency—"a tremendous advocate, and a real asset in the writing process"—and to have as his editor Kelley Ragland at St. Martin's Minotaur. "More than anything, Kelley allowed me the freedom to do the things I think I do best, and not worry unnecessarily about commercial considerations," he says. "We were so in sync on "Dope Thief" it's hard to remember what she recommended and what I changed on my own."

One word describes Tafoya's feeling when he learned that *Dope Thief* had been bought: "amazing."

"I was in my car when Alex called me," he recounts. I remember it every time I pass the place where I got the news. I had to pull over to call everyone I knew. I've always written, but I never thought seriously about having a book in print until the opportunity kind of dropped into my lap."

He has one more piece of advice for other first time authors: "Just believe it can happen for you, keep going, and don't give up."

Jamie Ford
Hotel at the Corner of Bitter and Sweet
(Ballantine Books)

First-time authors dream about having the kind of success enjoyed by Jamie Ford, whose debut novel *Hotel at the Corner of Bitter and Sweet* hit the *New York Times* bestseller list en route to having 100,000 copies in print. Ford's success is all the more improbable when one considers that his novel, a romantic drama set in the milieu of World War II-era Chinese-American and Japanese-American cultures, is the kind of work that often gets pigeonholed by its ethnicity. For Ford, who is Chinese-American, one of the most incredible parts of the experience has been discovering just how much universal appeal a love story can hold.

"I guess I'd assumed that these experiences of family conflict and assimilation were somehow proprietary," Ford says. "I was humbled and delighted to be so wrong."

Hotel at the Corner of Bitter and Sweet takes place during a tragic episode in American history. The novel's protagonist is Henry Lee, a Chinese-American who as a youth falls in love with Keiko Okabe, a Japanese-American girl who along with her family is rounded up and sent to an internment camp during World War II. More than 40 years later, Lee happens upon a parasol that once belonged to Keiko. His love reawakened by the discovery, he sets out to learn what happened to Keiko and along the way revisits the painful choices he's made to fit in to his adopted country.

Ford chalks up the wide appeal of *Hotel at the Corner of Bitter and Sweet* to the common human urge to connect to characters and plots with a heart. "So often plotlines, especially in film, are some variation of this: You hurt me. I get even. The end," he says. "When I see those kinds of stories, I don't feel better in the end, I actually feel kind of sad. I think that characters that are quietly noble always resonate more. Think of *It's a Wonderful Life.* We all want a George Bailey moment, where our sacrifices are rewarded with kindness. Redemption is always a more satisfying outcome than revenge."

Readers may find some truths about the human condition in *Hotel at the Corner of Bitter and Sweet*, but for Ford, writing the book also revealed a thing or two about himself, both as a person and as a writer. "I set out to write a noble romantic tragedy, with a bit of a redemptive ending," he says. What I hadn't planned was this father-son conflict—that just sort of elbowed its way onto the stage. Obviously I have some latent father-son issues. That was a cathartic surprise, for sure."

"I also learned that I love research, which is rather odd. You never in a million years grow up thinking you'll say, 'Hey, I love research!' That's akin to saying, "Hey, I love doing my taxes!" But there you go. My research is almost archeological. I sift the sand for hours and occasionally find a bone. Then it's party time."

In shaping the book's structure, Ford was helped immensely by his stint at the "Literary Boot Camp" workshop run by Orson Scott Card, the bestselling author of such sci-fi classics as *Ender's Game*. It may seem unlikely that a sci-fi author would have much advice on writing romantic drama, but Ford says that, again, the universal nature of storytelling trumped differences between genre.

"What I love about Card's work, starting with *Ender's Game*, is that despite whatever fantastical world is depicted, he still manages to sink deep emotional hooks with his characters," he says. "Basically, his stories are still complicated human (or at least humanoid) dramas. It was during his workshop that he mentioned the concept of a noble romantic tragedy, and talked about it as if it were this unicorn—this mythical creature. I guess I heard that as a challenge and set out to find one. Beyond that, he really champions storytelling over performance writing—something that was refreshing to hear in an MFA-lauded field of prose-driven work. I think the emphasis on performance writing over actual storytelling is why critically acclaimed books often draw blank stares from readers, and why YA books like Suzanne Collins' *Hunger Games*, are filling that void with adults."

After "writing like a madman for three months, with a week or two in the mix to travel out to Seattle for more research," Ford was ready to begin shopping the novel around to agents. He landed with Kristin Nelson of Nelson Literary Agency—a fortuitous choice, he says. "I had offers from NYC-based agents, but really clicked with Kristin. She's relentlessly nice, though don't be fooled—she's a TOUGH negotiator."

While Ford's success may seem hard to emulate, he has some simple words of encouragement for first-time authors. "Anyone can do this if you work hard enough and are honest with yourself. You don't necessarily need an MFA. Hemingway never went to college—he was too busy telling stories. You need a pulse and a pen. If you can write, then write."

James Klise

Love Drugged (Flux)

James Klise has traveled a long and winding road throughout his writing career. After getting his MFA in 1993, Klise set out on his journey to becoming an author by submitting his short stories to small-but-respected literary publications, a well-trod path that has been followed by many writers. Klise enjoyed solid success along the way, getting published in such notable magazines as *StoryQuarterly*, *New Orleans Review*, *Ascent*, *Sou'wester*, and *Southern Humanities Review*. But it was a change of direction to another genre—young adult fiction—that led to his first novel.

That change in his course was preceded by a change in careers. "About seven years ago, I became a high school librarian," Klise says. "Just like that, my imagination was overwhelmed with all that high school drama, that crazy energy. The novel came easily, because high school was an old familiar world that I was revisiting with fresh eyes and a little wisdom. I had never written about teens before, and likely wouldn't now, if they weren't so often literally in my line of vision."

The rich supply of high school drama resulted in *Love Drugged*, the story of 15-year old Jamie Bates. A high school freshman, Jamie is just discovering that he's gay, but he isn't ready to come out. When another gay classmate learns his secret, Jamie panics and tried to avoid being outed by dating another classmate, Celia Gamez—only the beginning of a series of spontaneous bad decisions and risky behaviors.

"*Love Drugged* started with an idea I couldn't shake, an image of frightening confinement: a teenage boy held against his will in an enormous house with a library," says Klise. "At first I thought this image might be a metaphor for being a closeted gay teenager—discomfort, isolation, unlimited information combined with limited opportunities. Then I jumped to the very logical conclusion that the boy I imagined was, in fact, a closeted gay teenager. It did not take long for the boy to become my narrator."

With a plot that hinges on Jamie's discovery of a mysterious new drug that promises to "cure" homosexuality—a drug invented by Celia's physician father—and a widening net of deception, revelations and consequences, *Love Drugged* combines the young adult novel with the structure of thrillers, one of Klise's favorite genres.

"Strong voice and compelling plot are both essential elements of a good YA novel, says Klise." "I knew something about voice, thanks to years of writing short stories, but I had never written a novel before. I needed to learn about plot. I wanted to keep readers on the edge of their seats. While I was working on the first draft, I read thrillers for inspiration—writers like Patricia Highsmith, Donna Tartt, Scott Smith, Gillian Flynn. My goal, always, was to get readers to turn the page. At the same time, the narrator's voice sets the tone; *Love Drugged* is a comic novel. Maybe any novel, whatever the genre, can benefit from having the heart of a thriller."

During the first draft of *Love Drugged*, Klise learned some valuable lessons about the craft of novel writing. "I wrote the first draft without an outline, so there were quite a few unnecessary detours before I got to the end," he says. "Long stretches of byways, roadside stops without attractions. A writing teacher gave me a valuable piece of advice. If you ever feel lost or stuck during the first draft—and you will—just skip ahead to the next part of the story that you are *dying* to write. Proceed directly to the next essential scene. She reminded me that unlike short stories, novels are rarely written start to finish, in chronological order."

Klise had some beginners luck as he shopped the novel around. Foregoing an agent, he sent *Love Drugged* out to publishing houses, where it got picked up off the slush pile. His career came in handy, too.

"When it came to selling the book, my day job offered an important advantage," he says. "I manage a library for teenagers, run a teen book group, and enjoy reading YA fiction with them. Because of this exposure, I have a pretty good sense of the various publishers and even the tastes of specific editors. In retrospect, the book might have sold faster if I had sent it to a bunch of publishers rather than one at a time. I wasn't smart about the business of book selling, which is why I intend to use an agent in the future. But I'm happy with the way it all turned out because *Love Drugged* ended up with exactly the right editor."

Klise's editor is Brian Farrey at Flux, the young adult imprint of Llewellyn Worldwide. Flux is a relatively new imprint—it launched in 2006—but one that has enjoyed a lot of success. "*Love Drugged* benefited enormously from Brian's suggestions, both structurally and within individual scenes," says Klise. "He helped streamline the opening and he encouraged me to move a major plot element from the middle to closer to the front. Working with Brian felt like having a very smart, very funny, very blunt friend come to my aid."

Having finally reached his destination of becoming an author, Klise has some pointers for fellow journeymen writers.

"Cultivate patience," he says. "Superhuman, unreasonable, shrug-at-the-passing-of-another-year patience. I look back on my early years as the time I needed to grow up, read a lot, write all sorts of things, and discover the kind of writer I was meant to be. It was like turning a radio dial slowly back and forth, searching for a frequency that came in loud and clear. Also, I stayed open to all the new material that my life presented. And those years of writing and polishing stories gave me the skills I needed to reshape and revise *Love Drugged* to the point that I could sell it. Success, however a writer defines it, may take a while, so the trick is to have fun with the process. Year after year, I keep putting new stories out there, knocking on doors. This is going to sound like one of those cheesy *Parade* magazine cover quotes, but oh, what the heck: I enjoy being a dreamer. I like the fact that I go to bed each night thinking about what good news might arrive the next day. It's one of the best things about being a writer."

MARKETS

Literary Agents

Many publishers are willing to look at unsolicited submissions but most feel having an agent is in the writer's best interest. In this section, we include agents who specialize in or represent fiction.

The commercial fiction field is intensely competitive. Many publishers have small staffs and little time. For that reason, many book publishers rely on agents for new talent. Some publishers are even relying on agents as ``first readers'' who must wade through the deluge of submissions from writers to find the very best. For writers, a good agent can be a foot in the door—someone willing to do the necessary work to put your manuscript in the right editor's hands.

It would seem today that finding a good agent is as hard as finding a good publisher. Yet those writers who have agents say they are invaluable. Not only can a good agent help you make your work more marketable, an agent also acts as your business manager and adviser, protecting your interests during and after contract negotiations.

Still, finding an agent can be very difficult for a new writer. If you are already published in magazines, you have a better chance than someone with no publishing credits. (Some agents read periodicals searching for new writers.) Although many agents do read queries and manuscripts from unpublished authors without introduction, referrals from their writer clients can be a big help. If you don't know any published authors with agents, attending a conference is a good way to meet agents. Some agents even set aside time at conferences to meet new writers.

Almost all the agents listed here have said they are open to working with new, previously unpublished writers as well as published writers. They do not charge a fee to cover the time and effort involved in reviewing a manuscript or a synopsis and chapters, but their time is still extremely valuable. Only send an agent your work when you feel it is as complete and polished as possible.

USING THE LISTINGS

It is especially important that you read individual listings carefully before contacting these busy agents. The first information after the company name includes the address and phone, fax, e-mail address (when available) and website. **Member Agents** gives the names of individual agents working at that company. (Specific types of fiction an agent handles are indicated in parentheses after that agent's name). The **Represents** section lists the types of fiction the agency works with. Reading the **Recent Sales** gives you the names of writers an agent is currently working with and, very importantly, publishers the agent has placed manuscripts with. **Writers' Conferences** identifies conferences an agent attends (and where you might possibly meet that agent). **Tips** presents advice directly from the agent to authors.

Also, look closely at the openness to submissions icons that precede most listings. They will indicate how willing an agency is to take on new writers.

ACACIA HOUSE PUBLISHING SERVICES, LTD.

62 Chestnut Ave., Brantford ON N3T 4C2 Canada. (519)752-0978. **Contact:** (Ms.) Frances Hanna or Bill Hanna. Represents 100 clients. Currently handles: nonfiction books 30%, novels 70%.

- Ms. Hanna has been in the publishing business for 30+ years, first in London as a fiction editor with Barrie & Jenkins and Pan Books, and as a senior editor with a packager of mainly illustrated books. She was condensed books editor for 6 years for *Reader's Digest* in Montreal and senior editor and foreign rights manager for William Collins & Sons (now HarperCollins) in Toronto. Mr. Hanna has more than 40 years of experience in the publishing business.

Member Agents Frances Hanna; Bill Hanna, vice president (self-help, modern history, military history).

Represents Nonfiction books, novels. **Considers these nonfiction areas:** animals, biography, language, memoirs, military, music, nature, film, travel. **Considers these fiction areas:** adventure, detective, literary, mainstream, mystery, thriller.

- This agency specializes in contemporary fiction—literary or commercial. Actively seeking outstanding first novels with literary merit. Does not want to receive horror, occult or science fiction.

How to Contact Query with outline, SASE. *No unsolicited mss.* No phone queries. Responds in 6 weeks to queries.

Terms Agent receives 15% commission on English language sales; 20% commission on dramatic sales; 25% commission on foreign sales. Charges clients for photocopying, postage, courier.

Recent Sales This agency prefers not to share information on specific sales.

Tips "We prefer that writers be previously published, with at least a few short stories or articles to their credit. Strongest consideration will be given to those with three or more published books. However, we would take on an unpublished writer of outstanding talent."

THE AHEARN AGENCY, INC.

2021 Pine St., New Orleans LA 70118. E-mail: pahearn@aol.com. Website: www.ahearnagency.com. **Contact:** Pamela G. Ahearn. Other memberships include MWA, RWA, ITW. Represents 35 clients. 20% of clients are new/unpublished writers. Currently handles: novels 100%.

- Prior to opening her agency, Ms. Ahearn was an agent for 8 years and an editor with Bantam Books.

Represents Considers these nonfiction areas: animals, child guidance, cultural interests, current affairs, ethnic, film, gay, health, history, investigative, lesbian, medicine, parenting, personal improvement, popular culture, self-help, theater, true crime, women's issues. **Considers these fiction areas:** action, adventure, contemporary issues, crime, detective, ethnic, family saga, feminist, glitz, historical, humor, literary, mainstream, mystery, police, psychic, regional, romance, supernatural, suspense, thriller.

- "This agency specializes in historical romance and is also very interested in mysteries and suspense fiction. Does not want to receive category romance, science fiction or fantasy."

How to Contact Query with SASE. Accepts simultaneous submissions. Responds in 8 weeks to queries. Responds in 10 weeks to mss. Obtains most new clients through recommendations from others, solicitations, conferences.

Terms Agent receives 15% commission on domestic sales. Agent receives 20% commission on foreign sales. Offers written contract, binding for 1 year; renewable by mutual consent.

Recent Sales *Red Chrysanthemum*, by Laura Rowland; *Only a Duke Will Do*, by Sabrina Jeffries; *The Alexandria Link*, by Steve Berry.

Writers Conferences Moonlight & Magnolias; RWA National Conference; Thriller Fest; Florida Romance Writers; Bouchercon; Malice Domestic.

Tips "Be professional! Always send in exactly what an agent/editor asks for—no more, no less. Keep query letters brief and to the point, giving your writing credentials and a very brief summary of your book. If one agent rejects you, keep trying—there are a lot of us out there!"

AITKEN ALEXANDER ASSOCIATES

18-21 Cavaye Place, London England SW10 9PT UK. (44)(207)373-8672. Fax: (44)(207)373-6002. E-mail: reception@aitkenalexander.co.uk. Website: www.aitkenalexander.co.uk. **Contact:** Submissions Department. Estab. 1976. Represents 300+ clients. 10% of clients are new/unpublished writers.

Member Agents Gillon Aitken, agent; Clare Alexander, agent; Andrew Kidd, agent; Lesley Thorne, film/television.

Represents Nonfiction books, novels. **Considers these nonfiction areas:** current affairs, government, history, law, memoirs, popular culture, politics. **Considers these fiction areas:** historical, literary.

- "We specialize in literary fiction and nonfiction."

How to Contact Query with SASE. Submit synopsis, first 30 pages. Responds in 6-8 weeks to queries. Obtains most new clients through recommendations from others, solicitations.

Terms Agent receives 15% commission on domestic sales. Agent receives 20% commission on foreign sales. Offers written contract; 28-day notice must be given to terminate contract. Charges for photocopying and postage.

Recent Sales Sold 50 titles in the last year. *My Life With George*, by Judith Summers (Voice); *The Separate Heart*, by Simon Robinson (Bloomsbury); *The Fall of the House of Wittgenstein*, by Alexander Waugh (Bloomsbury); *Shakespeare's Life*, by Germane Greer (Picador); *Occupational Hazards*, by Rory Stewart.

Tips "Before submitting to us, we advise you to look at our existing client list to establish whether your work will be of interest. Equally, you should consider whether the material you have written is ready to submit to a literary agency. If you feel your work qualifies, then send us a letter introducing yourself. Keep it relevant to your writing (e.g., tell us about any previously published work, be it a short story or journalism; you may be studying or have completed a post-graduate qualification in creative writing; when it comes to nonfiction, we would want to know what qualifies you to write about the subject)."

ALIVE COMMUNICATIONS, INC.

7680 Goddard St., Suite 200, Colorado Springs CO 80920. (719)260-7080. Fax: (719)260-8223. E-mail: submissions@alivecom.com. Website: www.alivecom.com. **Contact:** Rick Christian. Member of AAR. Other memberships include Authors Guild. Represents 100+ clients. 5% of clients are new/unpublished writers. Currently handles: nonfiction books 50%, novels 40%, juvenile books 10%.

Member Agents Rick Christian, president (blockbusters, bestsellers); Lee Hough (popular/commercial nonfiction and fiction, thoughtful spirituality, children's); Andrea Christian (thoughtful/inspirational nonfiction, women's fiction/nonfiction, popular/commercial nonfiction & fiction); Joel Kneedler popular/commercial nonfiction and fiction, thoughtful spirituality, children's).

Represents Nonfiction books, novels, short story collections, novellas. **Considers these nonfiction areas:** autobiography, biography, business, child guidance, economics, how-to, inspirational, parenting, personal improvement, religious, self-help, women's issues, women's studies. **Considers these fiction areas:** adventure, contemporary issues, crime, family saga, historical, humor, inspirational, literary, mainstream, mystery, police, religious, satire, suspense, thriller.

- This agency specializes in fiction, Christian living, how-to and commercial nonfiction. Actively seeking inspirational, literary and mainstream fiction, and work from authors with established track records and platforms. Does not want to receive poetry, scripts or dark themes.

How to Contact Query via e-mail. "Be advised that this agency works primarily with well-established, bestselling, and career authors. Always looking for a breakout, blockbuster author with genuine talent." New clients come through recommendations from others.
Terms Agent receives 15% commission on domestic sales. Offers written contract; 2-month notice must be given to terminate contract.
Recent Sales Sold 300+ titles in the last year. *A spiritual memoir* by Eugene Peterson (Viking); *A biography of Rwandan president Paul Kagame*, by Stephen Kinzer (St. Martin's Press); *Ever After*, by Karen Kingsbury (Zondervan); *A Hole in our Gospel*, by Rich Stears (Nelson); *My Life Outside the Ring*, by Hulk Hogan (St. Martins Press), Tim Pawlenty (Tyndale).
Tips Rewrite and polish until the words on the page shine. Endorsements and great connections may help, provided you can write with power and passion. Network with publishing professionals by making contacts, joining critique groups, and attending writers' conferences in order to make personal connections and to get feedback. Alive Communications, Inc., has established itself as a premiere literary agency. We serve an elite group of authors who are critically acclaimed and commercially successful in both Christian and general markets.

AMBASSADOR LITERARY AGENCY

P.O. Box 50358, Nashville TN 37205. (615)370-4700. E-mail: Wes@AmbassadorAgency.com. Website: www.AmbassadorAgency.com. **Contact:** Wes Yoder. Represents 25-30 clients. 10% of clients are new/unpublished writers. Currently handles: nonfiction books 95%, novels 5%.

- Prior to becoming an agent, Mr. Yoder founded a music artist agency in 1973; he established a speakers bureau division of the company in 1984.

Represents Nonfiction books, novels. **Considers these nonfiction areas:** biography, current affairs, ethnic, government, history, how-to, memoirs, popular culture, religion, self-help, women's.

"This agency specializes in religious market publishing dealing primarily with A-level publishers." Actively seeking popular nonfiction themes, including the following: practical living; Christian spirituality; literary fiction. Does not want to receive short stories, children's books, screenplays or poetry."

How to Contact Query with SASE. Submit proposal package, outline, synopsis, 6 sample chapters, author bio. Accepts simultaneous submissions. Responds in 2-4 weeks to queries. Obtains most new clients through recommendations from others.
Terms Agent receives 15% commission on domestic sales. Agent receives 20% commission on foreign sales. Offers written contract.
Recent Sales Sold 20 titles in the last year. *The Death and Life of Gabriel Phillips*, by Stephen Baldwin (Hachette); *Amazing Grace: William Wilberforce and the Heroic Campaign to End Slavery*, by Eric Mataxas (Harper San Francisco); *Life@The Next Level*, by Courtney McBath (Simon and Schuster); *Women, Take Charge of Your Money*, by Carolyn Castleberry (Random House/ Multnomah).

MARCIA AMSTERDAM AGENCY

41 W. 82nd St., Suite 9A, New York NY 10024-5613. (212)873-4945. **Contact:** Marcia Amsterdam. Signatory of WGA. Currently handles: nonfiction books 15%, novels 70%, movie scripts 5%, TV scripts 10%.

- Prior to opening her agency, Ms. Amsterdam was an editor.

Represents Novels, movie scripts, feature film, sitcom. **Considers these fiction areas:** adventure, detective, horror, mainstream, mystery, romance (contemporary, historical), science, thriller, young adult. **Considers these script areas:** comedy, romantic comedy.
How to Contact Query with SASE. Responds in 1 month to queries.
Terms Agent receives 15% commission on domestic sales. Agent receives 20% commission on foreign sales. Agent receives 10% commission on film sales. Offers written contract, binding for 1 year. Charges clients for extra office expenses, foreign postage, copying, legal fees (when agreed upon).
Recent Sales *Hidden Child*, by Isaac Millman (FSG); *Lucky Leonardo*, by Jonathan Canter (Sourcebooks).

Tips "We are always looking for interesting literary voices."

BETSY AMSTER LITERARY ENTERPRISES

P.O. Box 27788, Los Angeles CA 90027-0788. **Contact:** Betsy Amster. Estab. 1992. Member of AAR. Represents more than 65 clients. 35% of clients are new/unpublished writers. Currently handles: nonfiction books 65%, novels 35%.

- Prior to opening her agency, Ms. Amster was an editor at Pantheon and Vintage for 10 years, and served as editorial director for the Globe Pequot Press for 2 years.

Represents Nonfiction books, novels. **Considers these nonfiction areas:** art & design, biography, business, child guidance, cooking/nutrition, current affairs, ethnic, gardening, health/medicine, history, memoirs, money, parenting, popular culture, psychology, science/technology, self-help, sociology, travelogues, social issues, women's issues. **Considers these fiction areas:** ethnic, literary, women's, high quality.

> "Actively seeking strong narrative nonfiction, particularly by journalists; outstanding literary fiction (the next Richard Ford or Jhumpa Lahiri); witty, intelligent commerical women's fiction (the next Elinor Lipman or Jennifer Weiner); mysteries that open new worlds to us; and high-profile self-help and psychology, preferably research based." Does not want to receive poetry, children's books, romances, Western, science fiction, action/adventure, screenplays, fantasy, techno thrillers, spy capers, apocalyptic scenarios, or political or religious arguments.

How to Contact For adult titles: b.amster.assistant@gmail.com. See submission requirements online at website. The requirements have changed and only e-mail submissions are accepted. Accepts simultaneous submissions. Responds in 1 month to queries. Responds in 2 months to mss. Obtains most new clients through recommendations from others, solicitations, conferences.

Terms Agent receives 15% commission on domestic sales. Agent receives 20% commission on foreign sales. Offers written contract, binding for 1 year; 3-month notice must be given to terminate contract. Charges for photocopying, postage, long distance phone calls, messengers, galleys/books used in submissions to foreign and film agents and to magazines for first serial rights.

Writers Conferences USC Masters in Professional Writing; San Diego State University Writers' Conference; UCLA Extension Writers' Program; Los Angeles Times Festival of Books; The Loft Literary Center.

EDWARD ARMSTRONG LITERARY AGENCY

Fiction, PO Box 3343, Fayville MA 01745. (401)569-7099. **Contact:** Edward Armstrong. Currently handles: other 100% fiction.

- Prior to becoming an agent, Mr. Armstrong was a business professional specializing in quality and regulatory compliance. **This agency has not been taking submissions since 2007.** Please continue to check back.

Represents Novels, short story collections, novellas. **Considers these fiction areas:** mainstream, romance, science, thriller, suspense.

> **This agency is not taking submissions at this time (5/3/07).** Please continue to check back. Does not want to receive nonfiction or textbooks.

How to Contact Obtains most new clients through solicitations.

Terms Agent receives 5% commission on domestic sales. Agent receives 5% commission on foreign sales. This agency charges for photocopying and postage.

ARTISTS AND ARTISANS INC.

244 Madison Ave., Suite 334, New York NY 10016. Website: www.artistsandartisans.com. **Contact:** Adam Chromy and Jamie Brenner. Represents 70 clients. 80% of clients are new/unpublished writers. Currently handles: nonfiction books 50%, fiction 50%.

Member Agents Adam Chromy (fiction and narrative nonfiction); Jamie Brenner (thrillers, commercial and literary fiction, memoir, narrative nonfiction, Young Adult); Gwendolyn Heasley (Young Adult).

Represents Nonfiction books, novels. **Considers these nonfiction areas:** biography, business, child, current affairs, ethnic, health, how-to, humor, language, memoirs, money, music, popular culture, religion, science, self-help, sports, film, true crime, women's, fashion/style. **Considers these fiction areas:** confession, family, humor, literary, mainstream.

- "My education and experience in the business world ensure that my clients' enterprise as authors gets as much attention and care as their writing." Working journalists for nonfiction books. No scripts.

How to Contact Query by email only. Accepts simultaneous submissions. Responds to queries only if interested. Obtains most new clients through recommendations from others, solicitations, conferences.

Terms Agent receives 15% commission on domestic sales. Agent receives 25% commission on foreign sales. Offers written contract; 1-month notice must be given to terminate contract. "We only charge for extraordinary expenses (e.g., client requests check via FedEx instead of regular mail)."

Recent Sales *New World Monkeys*, (Shaye Areheart); *World Made by Hand* (Grove Atlantic); *House of Cards*, by David Ellis Dickerson (Penguin).

Writers Conferences ASJA Writers Conference, Pacific Northwest Writers Conference, Newbury Port Writers Conference.

Tips "Please make sure you are ready before approaching us or any other agent. If you write fiction, make sure it is the best work you can do and get objective criticism from a writing group. If you write nonfiction, make sure the proposal exhibits your best work and a comprehensive understanding of the market."

AVENUE A LITERARY

419 Lafayette St., Second Floor, New York NY 10003. Fax: (212)228-6149. E-mail: submissions@avenuealiterary.com. Website: www.avenuealiterary.com. **Contact:** Jennifer Cayea. Represents 20 clients. 75% of clients are new/unpublished writers. Currently handles: nonfiction books 40%, novels 45%, story collections 5%, juvenile books 10%.

- Prior to opening her agency, Ms. Cayea was an agent and director of foreign rights for Nicholas Ellison, Inc., a division of Sanford J. Greenburger Associates. She was also an editor in the audio and large print divisions of Random House.

Represents Nonfiction books, novels, short story collections, juvenile. **Considers these nonfiction areas:** cooking, cultural interests, current affairs, dance, ethnic, film, foods, health, history, medicine, memoirs, music, nutrition, personal improvement, popular culture, self-help, sports, theater. **Considers these fiction areas:** contemporary issues, family saga, feminist, historical, literary, mainstream, thriller, young adult, women's/chick lit.

- "Our authors are dynamic and diverse. We seek strong new voices in fiction and nonfiction, and are fiercely dedicated to our authors." We are actively seeking new authors of fiction and nonfiction.

How to Contact Query via e-mail only. Submit synopsis, publishing history, author bio, full contact info. Paste info in e-mail body. No attachments. Accepts simultaneous submissions. Responds in 8 weeks to queries. Obtains most new clients through recommendations from others, solicitations, conferences.

Terms Agent receives 15% commission on domestic sales. Agent receives 15% commission on foreign sales. Offers written contract; 30-day notice must be given to terminate contract.

Recent Sales *Gunmetal Black*, by Daniel Serrano.

Tips "Build a résumé by publishing short stories if you are a fiction writer."

THE AXELROD AGENCY

55 Main St., P.O. Box 357, Chatham NY 12037. (518)392-2100. E-mail: steve@axelrodagency.com. **Contact:** Steven Axelrod. Member of AAR. Represents 15-20 clients. 1% of clients are new/unpublished writers. Currently handles: novels 95%.

- Prior to becoming an agent, Mr. Axelrod was a book club editor.

Represents Novels. **Considers these fiction areas:** mystery, romance, women's.

How to Contact Query with SASE. Accepts simultaneous submissions. Responds in 3 weeks to queries. Responds in 6 weeks to mss. Obtains most new clients through recommendations from others.

Terms Agent receives 15% commission on domestic sales. Agent receives 20% commission on foreign sales. No written contract.

Writers Conferences RWA National Conference.

BAKER'S MARK LITERARY AGENCY

P.O. Box 8382, Portland OR 97207. (503)432-8170. E-mail: info@bakersmark.com. Website: www.Bakersmark.com. **Contact:** Bernadette Baker-Baughman or Gretchen Stelter. Currently handles: nonfiction books 35%, novels 25%, 40% graphic novels.

Represents Nonfiction books, novels, scholarly books, graphic novels. **Considers these nonfiction areas:** anthropology, archeology, autobiography, biography, business, cultural interests, economics, ethnic, gay, government, how-to, humor, investigative, law, lesbian, popular culture, politics, satire, true crime, women's issues, women's studies, comics/graphic novels. **Considers these fiction areas:** cartoon, comic books, contemporary issues, crime, detective, erotica, ethnic, experimental, fantasy, feminist, gay, glitz, historical, horror, humor, lesbian, literary, mainstream, mystery, police, psychic, regional, satire, supernatural, suspense, thriller, women's, chick literature.

- "Baker's Mark specializes in graphic novels and popular nonfiction with an extremely selective taste in commercial fiction." Actively seeking graphic novels, nonfiction, fiction (YA/Teen and magical realism in particular). Does not want to receive Westerns, poetry, sci-fi, novella, high fantasy, or children's picture books.

How to Contact Query with 1 page with no attachments and no chapters in the email. Send SASE if mailing by post. "If interested, we will request representative materials from you." Accepts simultaneous submissions. Responds in 4-6 weeks. Obtains most new clients through recommendations from others, solicitations.

Terms Agent receives 15% commission on domestic sales. Agent receives 20% commission on foreign sales. Offers written contract, binding for 18 months; 30-day notice must be given to terminate contract.

Recent Sales *Never After*, by Dan Elconin (Simon Pulse); *Boilerplate: History's Mechanical Marvel*, by Paul Guinan and Anina Bennet (Abrams Image); *War Is Boring*, by David Axe with illustration by Matt Bors (New American Library); *The Choyster Generation*, by Amalia mcGibbon, Claire Williams, and Lara Vogel (Seal Press).

Writers Conferences New York Comic Convention, BookExpo of America, San Diego Comic Con, Stumptown Comics Fest, Emerald City Comic Con.

Tips "Baker's Mark is also looking to help pioneer new media models for books, and is especially interested in books that experiment with social media, open source software (and other digital technologies) as we help establish new business paradigms for the ebook revolution."

BARER LITERARY, LLC

270 Lafayette St., Suite 1504, New York NY 10012. Website: www.barerliterary.com. **Contact:** Julie Barer. Estab. 2004. Member of AAR.

- Before becoming an agent, Julie worked at Shakespeare & Co. Booksellers in New York City. She is a graduate of Vassar College.

Member Agents Julie Barer.

Represents Nonfiction books, novels, short story collections, Julie Barer is especially interested in working with emerging writers and developing long-term relationships with new clients. **Considers these nonfiction areas:** biography, ethnic, history, memoirs, popular culture, women's. **Considers these fiction areas:** contemporary issues, ethnic, historical, literary, mainstream.

- This agency no longer accepts young adult submissions. No Health/Fitness, Business/Investing/Finance, Sports, Mind/Body/Spirit, Reference, Thrillers/Suspense, Military, Romance, Children's Books/Picture Books, Screenplays

How to Contact Query with SASE; no attachments if query by email. We do not respond to queries via phone or fax.

Terms Agent receives 15% commission on domestic sales. Agent receives 20% commission on foreign sales. Offers written contract. Charges for photocopying and books ordered.
Recent Sales *The Unnamed*, by Joshua Ferris (Reagan Arthur Books); *Tunneling to the Center of the Earth*, by Kevin Wilson (Ecco Press); *A Disobedient Girl*, by Ru Freeman (Atria Books); *A Friend of the Family*, by Lauren Grodstein (Algonquin); *City of Veils*, by Zoe Ferraris (Little, Brown).

LORETTA BARRETT BOOKS, INC.

fiction and non-fiction, 220 E. 23rd St., 11th Floor, New York NY 10010. (212)242-3420. E-mail: query@lorettabarrettbooks.com. Website: www.lorettabarrettbooks.com. **Contact:** Loretta A. Barrett, Nick Mullendore. Estab. 1990. Member of AAR. Currently handles: nonfiction books 50%, novels 50%.

- Prior to opening her agency, Ms. Barrett was vice president and executive editor at Doubleday and editor-in-chief of Anchor Books.

Member Agents Loretta A. Barrett; Nick Mullendore.
Represents Nonfiction books, novels. **Considers these nonfiction areas:** biography, child guidance, current affairs, ethnic, government, health/nutrition, history, memoirs, money, multicultural, nature, popular culture, psychology, religion, science, self-help, sociology, spirituality, sports, women's, young adult, creative nonfiction. **Considers these fiction areas:** contemporary, psychic, adventure, detective, ethnic, family, fantasy, historical, literary, mainstream, mystery, thriller, young adult.

O→ "The clients we represent include both fiction and non-fiction authors for the general adult trade market. The works they produce encompass a wide range of contemporary topics and themes including commercial thrillers, mysteries, romantic suspense, popular science, memoirs, narrative fiction and current affairs." No children's, juvenile, cookbooks, gardening, science fiction, fantasy novels, historical romance.

How to Contact See guidelines online. Use email or if by post, query with SASE. Accepts simultaneous submissions. Responds in 3-6 weeks to queries.
Terms Agent receives 15% commission on domestic sales. Agent receives 20% commission on foreign sales. Offers written contract. Charges clients for shipping and photocopying.

BARRON'S LITERARY MANAGEMENT

4615 Rockland Drive, Arlington TX 76016. E-mail: barronsliterary@sbcglobal.net. **Contact:** Adele Brooks, president.
Represents Nonfiction books, novels. **Considers these nonfiction areas:** business/investing/finance, health/exercise/nutrition, history, cook books, psychology, science, true crime. **Considers these fiction areas:** historical, horror, all mysteries, detective/pi/police, romance: suspense, paranormal, historical, chick lit and lady lit, science fiction, thriller, crime thriller, medical thriller.

O→ Barron's Literary Management is a small Dallas/Fort Worth-based agency with good publishing contacts tightly written, fast moving fiction, as well as authors with a significant platform or subject area expertise for nonfiction book concepts.

How to Contact Contact by e-mail initially. Send bio and a brief synopsis of your story or a nonfiction proposal. Obtains most new clients through e-mail submissions.
Tips "Have your book tightly edited, polished and ready to be seen before contacting agents. I respond quickly and if interested may request an electronic or hard copy mailing."

FAYE BENDER LITERARY AGENCY

fiction and non-fiction equally., 337 W. 76th St., #E1, New York NY 10023. E-mail: info@fbliterary.com. Website: www.fbliterary.com. **Contact:** Faye Bender. Estab. 2004. Member of AAR.
Represents Nonfiction books, novels, juvenile. **Considers these nonfiction areas:** biography, memoirs, popular culture, women's issues, women's studies, young adult, narrative; health; popular science. **Considers these fiction areas:** commercial, literary, women's, young adult (middle-grade).

O⁻ "I choose books based on the narrative voice and strength of writing. I work with previously published and first-time authors." Faye does not represent picture books, genre fiction for adults (western, romance, horror, science fiction, fantasy), business books, spirituality or screenplays.

How to Contact Query with SASE and 10 sample pages via mail or e-mail. Guidelines online.

Tips "Please keep your letters to the point, include all relevant information, and have a bit of patience."

BENREY LITERARY

P.O. Box 12721, New Bern NC 28561. (252)638-5787. Fax: (886)297-9483. E-mail: query@benreyliterary.com. Website: www.benreyliterary.com. **Contact:** Janet Benrey. Represents 20 clients. 5% of clients are new/unpublished writers. Currently handles: nonfiction books 20%, novels 80%.

- Prior to her current position, Ms. Benrey was with the Hartline Literary Agency.

Represents Novels, nonfiction books with a narrow focus. **Considers these nonfiction areas:** religious, true crime. **Considers these fiction areas:** literary, mystery, religious, romance, thriller, women's.

O⁻ This agency's specialties include inspirational romance, women's fiction, mystery, true crime, thriller (secular and Christian), as well as Christian living, church resources, inspirational.

How to Contact Query via e-mail only. Submit proposal package, synopsis, 3 sample chapters, author bio. More submission details available online. Accepts simultaneous submissions. Responds only if there is interest Obtains most new clients through recommendations from others, conferences.

Terms Agent receives 15% commission on domestic sales. Agent receives 20% commission on foreign sales. Offers written contract; 30-day notice must be given to terminate contract. "Understand the market as best you can. Don't create a new genre."

Tips Understand the market as best you can. Attend conferences and network. Don't create a new genre.

MEREDITH BERNSTEIN LITERARY AGENCY

2095 Broadway, Suite 505, New York NY 10023. (212)799-1007. Fax: (212)799-1145. Member of AAR. Represents 85 clients. 20% of clients are new/unpublished writers. Currently handles: nonfiction books 50%, other 50% fiction.

- Prior to opening her agency, Ms. Bernstein served at another agency for 5 years.

Represents Nonfiction books, novels. **Considers these fiction areas:** literary, mystery, romance, thriller, young adult.

O⁻ "This agency does not specialize. It is very eclectic."

How to Contact Query with SASE. Accepts simultaneous submissions. Obtains most new clients through recommendations from others, conferences, developing/packaging ideas.

Terms Agent receives 15% commission on domestic sales. Agent receives 20% commission on foreign sales. Charges clients $75 disbursement fee/year.

Recent Sales More of the best-selling New York Times, USA Today, and Wall Street Journal; *House of Nighy* series, by P.C. Cast and Kristin Cast; *The No Cry Separation Anxiety Solution*, by Elizabeth Pantrey, and *Following the Waters,* by David Carroll (a McArthur Genius Award Winner) and nominee for National Book Award in 2009.

Writers Conferences Southwest Writers' Conference; Rocky Mountain Fiction Writers' Colorado Gold; Pacific Northwest Writers' Conference; Willamette Writers' Conference; Surrey International Writers' Conference; San Diego State University Writers' Conference.

BLEECKER STREET ASSOCIATES, INC.

532 LaGuardia Place, #617, New York NY 10012. (212)677-4492. Fax: (212)388-0001. E-mail: bleeckerst@hotmail.com. **Contact:** Agnes Birnbaum. Member of AAR. Other memberships include RWA, MWA. Represents 60 clients. 20% of clients are new/unpublished writers. Currently handles: nonfiction books 75%, novels 25%.

- Prior to becoming an agent, Ms. Birnbaum was a senior editor at Simon & Schuster, Dutton/ Signet, and other publishing houses.

Represents Nonfiction books, novels. **Considers these nonfiction areas:** newage, animals, biography, business, child, computers, cooking, current affairs, ethnic, government, health, history, how-to, memoirs, military, money, nature, popular culture, psychology, religion, science, self-help, sociology, sports, true crime, women's. **Considers these fiction areas:** ethnic, historical, literary, mystery, romance, thriller, women's.

O→ "We're very hands-on and accessible. We try to be truly creative in our submission approaches. We've had especially good luck with first-time authors." Does not want to receive science fiction, westerns, poetry, children's books, academic/scholarly/professional books, plays, scripts, or short stories.

How to Contact Query with SASE. No email, phone, or fax queries. Accepts simultaneous submissions. Responds in 2 weeks to queries. Responds in 1 month to mss. "Obtains most new clients through recommendations from others, solicitations, conferences, plus, I will approach someone with a letter if his/her work impresses me."

Terms Agent receives 15% commission on domestic sales. Agent receives 25% commission on foreign sales. Offers written contract; 1-month notice must be given to terminate contract. Charges for postage, long distance, fax, messengers, photocopies (not to exceed $200).

Recent Sales Sold 14 titles in the last year. *Following Sarah*, by Daniel Brown (Morrow); *Biology of the Brain*, by Paul Swingle (Rutgers University Press); *Santa Miracles*, by Brad and Sherry Steiger (Adams); *Surviving the College Search*, by Jennifer Delahunt (St. Martin's).

Tips "Keep query letters short and to the point; include only information pertaining to the book or background as a writer. Try to avoid superlatives in description. Work needs to stand on its own, so how much editing it may have received has no place in a query letter."

BLISS LITERARY AGENCY INTERNATIONAL, INC.

1601 N. Sepulveda Blvd, #389, Manhattan Beach CA 90266. E-mail: info@blissliterary.com. Website: www.blissliterary.com. **Contact:** Jenoyne Adams.

Member Agents Prior to her current position, Ms. Adams was with Levine Greenberg Literary Agency.

Represents Nonfiction books, novels, juvenile, Willy Blackmore. **Considers these nonfiction areas:** parenting, narrative nonfiction, women's. **Considers these fiction areas:** literary, multicultural, commercial.

O→ "Middle grade, YA fiction and nonfiction, young reader? Bring it on. We are interested in developing and working on projects that run the gamut—fantasy, urban/edgy, serious, bling-blingy? SURE. We love it all." "I haven't found it yet, but with a deep appreciation for anime and martial arts flicks, we are looking for the perfect graphic novel."

How to Contact Query via e-mail or snail mail. Send query, synopsis, one chapter, contact info. No attachments. One Word document via e-mail is preferred. No pdf files. Responds in 6-8 weeks to queries, sometimes longer.

Tips "Non-query related matters can be addressed by e-mailing info@blissliterary.com."

BOOKENDS, LLC

136 Long Hill Rd., Gillette NJ 07933. Website: www.bookends-inc.com; bookendslitagency.blogspot.com. **Contact:** Jessica Faust, Kim Lionetti. Member of AAR. RWA, MWA Represents 50+ clients. 10% of clients are new/unpublished writers. Currently handles: nonfiction books 50%, novels 50%.

Member Agents Jessica Faust (fiction: romance, erotica, women's fiction, mysteries and suspense; nonfiction: business, finance, career, parenting, psychology, women's issues, self-help, health, sex); Kim Lionetti (women's fiction, mystery, true crime, pop science, pop culture, and all areas of romance).

Represents Nonfiction books, novels. **Considers these nonfiction areas:** business, child, ethnic, gay, health, how-to, money, psychology, religion, self-help, sex, true crime, women's. **Considers these fiction areas:** detective, cozies, mainstream, mystery, romance, thriller, women's.

- "BookEnds is currently accepting queries from published and unpublished writers in the areas of romance (and all its sub-genres), erotica, mystery, suspense, women's fiction, and literary fiction. We also do a great deal of nonfiction in the areas of self-help, business, finance, health, pop science, psychology, relationships, parenting, pop culture, true crime, and general nonfiction." BookEnds does not want to receive children's books, screenplays, science fiction, poetry, or technical/military thrillers.

How to Contact Review website for guidelines, as they change.

BOOKS & SUCH LITERARY AGENCY

52 Mission Circle, Suite 122, PMB 170, Santa Rosa CA 95409. E-mail: representation@booksandsuch.biz. Website: www.booksandsuch.biz. **Contact:** Janet Kobobel Grant, Wendy Lawton, Etta Wilson, Rachel Zurakowski. Member of AAR. Member of CBA (associate), American Christian Fiction Writers. Represents 150 clients. 5% of clients are new/unpublished writers. Currently handles: nonfiction books 50%, novels 50%.

- Prior to becoming an agent, Ms. Grant was an editor for Zondervan and managing editor for *Focus on the Family*; Ms. Lawton was an author, sculptor and designer of porcelain dolls. Ms. Wilson emphasizes middle grade children's books. Ms. Zurakowski concentrates on material for 20-something or 30-something readers.

Represents Nonfiction books, novels, juvenile books. **Considers these nonfiction areas:** child, humor, religion, self-help, women's. **Considers these fiction areas:** contemporary, family, historical, mainstream, religious, romance, African American adult.

- This agency specializes in general and inspirational fiction, romance, and in the Christian booksellers market. Actively seeking well-crafted material that presents Judeo-Christian values, if only subtly.

How to Contact Query via e-mail only, no attachments. Accepts simultaneous submissions. Responds in 1 month to queries. "*If you don't hear from us asking to see more of your writing within 30 days after you have sent your email, please know that we have read and considered your submission but determined that it would not be a good fit for us.*" Obtains most new clients through recommendations from others, conferences.

Terms Agent receives 15% commission on domestic sales. Agent receives 20% commission on foreign sales. Offers written contract; 2-month notice must be given to terminate contract. No additional charges.

Recent Sales Sold 125 titles in the last year. *One Simple Act*, by Debbie Macomber (Howard Books); *Victim of Grace*, by Robin Jones Gunn (Zondervan); *Paradise Valley*, by Dale Cramer (Bethany House). Other clients include: Lauraine Snelling, Lori Copeland, Rene Gutteridge, Dale Cramer, BJ Hoff, Diann Mills.

Writers Conferences Mount Hermon Christian Writers' Conference; Society of Childrens' Writers and Illustrators Conference; Writing for the Soul; American Christian Fiction Writers' Conference; San Francisco Writers' Conference.

Tips "The heart of our agency's motivation is to develop relationships with the authors we serve, to do what we can to shine the light of success on them, and to help be a caretaker of their gifts and time."

THE BARBARA BOVA LITERARY AGENCY

3951 Gulf Shore Blvd. No. PH 1-B, Naples FL 34103. (239)649-7263. Fax: (239)649-7263. E-mail: michaelburke@barbarabovaliteraryagency.com. Website: www.barbarabovaliteraryagency.com. **Contact:** Ken Bova, Michael Burke. Represents 30 clients. Currently handles: nonfiction books 20%, fiction 80%.

Represents Nonfiction books, novels. **Considers these nonfiction areas:** biography, history, science, self-help, true crime, women's, social sciences. **Considers these fiction areas:** adventure, crime, detective, mystery, police, science fiction, suspense, thriller, women's, young adult, teen lit.

- This agency specializes in fiction and nonfiction, hard and soft science.

How to Contact Query through website. Obtains most new clients through recommendations from others.
Terms Agent receives 15% commission on domestic sales. Agent receives 20% commission on foreign sales. Charges clients for overseas postage, overseas calls, photocopying, shipping.
Recent Sales Sold 24 titles in the last year. *The Green Trap* and *The Aftermath*, by Ben Bova; *Empire and A War of Gifts*, by Orson Scott Card; *Radioman*, by Carol E. Hipperson.
Tips "We also handle foreign, movie, television, and audio rights."

BRADFORD LITERARY AGENCY

5694 Mission Center Road, #347, San Diego CA 92108. (619)521-1201. E-mail: laura@bradfordlit.com. Website: www.bradfordlit.com. **Contact:** Laura Bradford. Represents 35 clients. 20% of clients are new/unpublished writers. Currently handles: nonfiction books 10%, novels 90%.

- Ms. Bradford started with her first literary agency straight out of college and has 14 years of experience as a bookseller in parallel.

Represents Nonfiction books, novels, novellas, within a single author's collection, anthology. **Considers these nonfiction areas:** business, child care, current affairs, health, history, how-to, memoirs, money, popular culture, psychology, self-help, women's interest. **Considers these fiction areas:** adventure, detective, erotica, ethnic, historical, humor, mainstream, mystery, romance, thriller, psychic/supernatural.

Actively seeking romance (including category), romantica, women's fiction, mystery, thrillers and young adult. Does not want to receive poetry, short stories, children's books (juvenile) or screenplays.

How to Contact Query with SASE. Submit cover letter, first 30 pages of completed ms., synopsis and SASE. Send no attachments via e-mail; only send a query letter. Accepts simultaneous submissions. Responds in 10 weeks to queries. Responds in 10 weeks to mss. Obtains most new clients through solicitations.
Terms Agent receives 15% commission on domestic sales. Agent receives 20% commission on foreign sales. Offers written contract, non-binding for 2 years; 45-day notice must be given to terminate contract. Charges for photocopies, postage, extra copies of books for submissions.
Recent Sales Sold 53 titles in the last year. *Tempting Eden*, by Margaret Rowe (Berkley Heat); *Princess Poltergeist*, by Stacey Kade (Hyperion Children's); *Ruthless Heart*, by Emma Lang (Kensington Brava); *Deadly Fear*, by Cynthia Eden(Grand Central); *Precious and Fragile Things*, by meganart 9 HMira Hart (Mira Books); *Cruel Enchantment*, by Anya Bast (Berkley Sensation); *Razorland*, by Elisabeth Naughton (Dorchestser); *His Darkest Craving*, by Juliana Stone (Avon).
Writers Conferences RWA National Conference; Romantic Times Booklovers Convention.

CURTIS BROWN, LTD.

10 Astor Place, New York NY 10003-6935. (212)473-5400. Website: www.curtisbrown.com. Alternate address: Peter Ginsberg, president at CBSF, 1750 Montgomery St., San Francisco CA 94111. (415)954-8566. Member of AAR. Signatory of WGA.
Member Agents Ginger Clark; Katherine Fausset; Holly Frederick; Emilie Jacobson, senior vice president; Elizabeth Hardin; Ginger Knowlton, vice president; Timothy Knowlton, CEO; Laura Blake Peterson; Maureen Walters, senior vice president; Mitchell Waters. San Francisco Office: Nathan Bransford, Peter Ginsberg (President).
Represents Nonfiction books, novels, short story collections, juvenile. **Considers these nonfiction areas:** agriculture horticulture, americana, crafts, interior, juvenile, New Age, young, animals, anthropology, art, biography, business, child, computers, cooking, current affairs, education, ethnic, gardening, gay, government, health, history, how-to, humor, language, memoirs, military, money, multicultural, music, nature, philosophy, photography, popular culture, psychology, recreation, regional, religion, science, self-help, sex, sociology, software, spirituality, sports, film, translation, travel, true crime, women's, creative nonfiction. **Considers these fiction areas:** contemporary, glitz, newage, psychic, adventure, comic, confession, detective, erotica, ethnic, experimental, family, fantasy, feminist, gay, gothic, hi lo, historical, horror, humor, juvenile, literary, mainstream,

military, multicultural, multimedia, mystery, occult, picture books, plays, poetry, regional, religious, romance, science, short, spiritual, sports, thriller, translation, western, young, women's.
How to Contact Prefers to read materials exclusively. *No unsolicited mss.* Responds in 3 weeks to queries. Responds in 5 weeks to mss. Obtains most new clients through recommendations from others, solicitations, conferences.
Terms Offers written contract. Charges for some postage (overseas, etc.)
Recent Sales This agency prefers not to share information on specific sales.

BROWNE & MILLER LITERARY ASSOCIATES

410 S. Michigan Ave., Suite 460, Chicago IL 60605-1465. (312)922-3063. E-mail: mail@browneandmiller.com. Website: www.brownandmiller.com. **Contact:** Danielle Egan-Miller. Estab. 1971. Member of AAR. Other memberships include RWA, MWA, Author's Guild. Represents 150 clients. 2% of clients are new/unpublished writers. Currently handles: nonfiction books 25%, novels 75%.
Represents Nonfiction books, most genres of commercial adult fiction and non-fiction, as well as select young adult projects. **Considers these nonfiction areas:** agriculture, animals, anthropology, archeology, autobiography, biography, business, child guidance, cooking, crafts, cultural interests, current affairs, economics, environment, ethnic, finance, foods, health, hobbies, horticulture, how-to, humor, inspirational, investigative, medicine, memoirs, money, nature, nutrition, parenting, personal improvement, popular culture, psychology, religious, satire, science, self-help, sociology, sports, technology, true crime, women's issues, women's studies. **Considers these fiction areas:** contemporary issues, crime, detective, erotica, ethnic, family saga, glitz, historical, inspirational, literary, mainstream, mystery, police, religious, romance, sports, suspense, thriller, paranormal.

"We are partial to talented newcomers and experienced authors who are seeking hands-on career management, highly personal representation, and who are interested in being full partners in their books' successes. We are editorially focused and work closely with our authors through the whole publishing process, from proposal to after publication." "We are most interested in commercial women's fiction, especially elegantly crafted, sweeping historicals, edgy, fresh teen/chick/mom/lady lit, and CBA women's fiction by established authors. We are also very keen on literary historical mysteries and literary YA novels. Topical, timely non-fiction projects in a variety of subject areas are also of interest, especially prescriptive how-to, self-help, sports, humor, and pop culture." Does not represent poetry, short stories, plays, original screenplays, articles, children's picture books, software, horror or sci-fi novels.

How to Contact Query with SASE. *No unsolicited mss.* Prefers to read material exclusively. Put submission in the subject line. Send no attachments. Responds in 6 weeks to queries. Obtains most new clients through referrals, queries by professional/marketable authors.
Terms Agent receives 15% commission on domestic sales. Agent receives 20% commission on foreign sales. Offers written contract, binding for 2 years. Charges clients for photocopying, overseas postage.
Writers Conferences BookExpo America; Frankfurt Book Fair; RWA National Conference; ICRS; London Book Fair; Bouchercon, regional writers conferences.
Tips "If interested in agency representation, be well informed."

PEMA BROWNE, LTD.

11 Tena Place, Valley Cottage NY 10989. E-mail: ppbltd@optonline.net. Website: www.pemabrowneltd.com. **Contact:** Pema Browne. Signatory of WGA. Other memberships include SCBWI, RWA. Represents 30 clients. Currently handles: nonfiction books 25%, novels 50% novels/romance, juvenile books 25%.

- Prior to opening her agency, Ms. Browne was an artist and art buyer.

Represents Nonfiction books, novels, juvenile, reference books. **Considers these nonfiction areas:** business, child guidance, cooking, cultural interests, economics, ethnic, finance, foods, gay, health, how-to, inspirational, juvenile nonfiction, lesbian, medicine, metaphysics, money, New Age, nutrition, parenting, personal improvement, popular culture, psychology, religious, self-help, spirituality, women's issues, women's studies, reference. **Considers these fiction areas:** contemporary, glitz, adventure, feminist, gay, historical, juvenile, literary, mainstream, commercial, mystery, picture books, religious, romance, contemporary, gothic, historical, regency, young.

O→ "We are not accepting any new projects or authors until further notice."

How to Contact Query with SASE. No attachments for e-mail.

Terms Agent receives 20% commission on domestic sales. Agent receives 20% commission on foreign sales.

Recent Sales *The Champion*, by Heather Grothaus (Kensington/Zebra); *The Highlander's Bride*, by Michele Peach (Kensington/Zebra); *The Daring Harriet Quimby*, by Suzanne Whitaker (Holiday House); *One Night to Be Sinful*, by Samantha Garver (Kensington); *Taming the Beast*, by Heather Grothaus (Kensington/Zebra); *Kisses Don't Lie*, by Alexis Darin (Kensington/Zebra).

Tips "We do not review manuscripts that have been sent out to publishers. If writing romance, be sure to receive guidelines from various romance publishers. In nonfiction, one must have credentials to lend credence to a proposal. Make sure of margins, double-space, and use clean, dark type."

BROWN LITERARY AGENCY

410 Seventh St. NW, Naples FL 34120. Website: www.brownliteraryagency.com. **Contact:** Roberta Brown. Member of AAR. Other memberships include RWA, Author's Guild. Represents 45 clients. 5% of clients are new/unpublished writers.

Represents Novels. **Considers these fiction areas:** erotica, romance, women's, single title and category.

O→ "This agency is selectively reading material at this time."

How to Contact Query via e-mail only. Send synopsis and two chapters in Word attachment. Response time varies.

Terms Agent receives 15% commission on domestic sales. Agent receives 20% commission on foreign sales. Offers written contract; 30-day notice must be given to terminate contract.

Writers Conferences RWA National Conference.

Tips "Polish your manuscript. Be professional."

ANDREA BROWN LITERARY AGENCY, INC.

1076 Eagle Drive, Salinas CA 93905. E-mail: andrea@andreabrownlit.com; caryn@andreabrownlit.com. Website: www.andreabrownlit.com. **Contact:** Andrea Brown, president. 10% of clients are new/unpublished writers.

- Prior to opening her agency, Ms. Brown served as an editorial assistant at Random House and Dell Publishing and as an editor with Knopf.

Member Agents Andrea Brown; Laura Rennert (laura@andreabrownlit.com); Kelly Sonnack; Caryn Wiseman; Jennifer Rofé; Jennifer Laughran, associate agent; Jamie Weiss Chilton, associate agent, and Jennifer Mattson, associate agent, and Mary Kole.

Represents Juvenile Nonfiction books, novels. **Considers these nonfiction areas:** juvenile nonfiction, memoirs, young adult, narrative. **Considers these fiction areas:** juvenile, literary, picture books, women's, young adult, middle-grade, all juvenile genres.

O→ This agency specializes in children's books, though each agent has differing tastes.

How to Contact For picture books, submit complete ms, SASE. For fiction, submit short synopsis, SASE, first 3 chapters. For nonfiction, submit proposal, 1-2 sample chapters. For illustrations, submit 4-5 color samples (no originals). "We only accept queries via e-mail. No attachments, with the exception of jpeg illustrations from illustrators." Visit the agents' bios on our website and choose only one agent to whom you will submit your e-query. Send a short email query letter to that agent with QUERY in the subject field. Accepts simultaneous submissions. If we are interested in your work, we will certainly follow up by email or by phone. However, if you haven't heard from us within 6 to 8 weeks, please assume that we are passing on your project. Obtains most new clients through referrals from editors, clients and agents. Check website for guidelines and information.

Terms Agent receives 15% commission on domestic sales. Agent receives 20% commission on foreign sales. Offers written contract.

Recent Sales *Chloe*, by Catherine Ryan Hyde (Knopf); Sasha Cohen Autobiography (HarperCollins); *The Five Ancestors*, by Jeff Stone (Random House); *Thirteen Reasons Why*, by Jay Asher (Penguin); *Identical*, by Ellen Hopkins (S&S)

Writers Conferences SCBWI; Asilomar; Maui Writers' Conference; Southwest Writers' Conference; San Diego State University Writers' Conference; Big Sur Children's Writing Workshop; William Saroyan Writers' Conference; Columbus Writers' Conference; Willamette Writers' Conference; La Jolla Writers' Conference; San Francisco Writers' Conference; Hilton Head Writers' Conference: Pacific Northwest Conference; Pikes Peak Conference.

TRACY BROWN LITERARY AGENCY

P.O. Box 88, Scarsdale NY 10583. (914)400-4147. Fax: (914)931-1746. E-mail: tracy@brownlit.com. **Contact:** Tracy Brown. Represents 35 clients. Currently handles: nonfiction books 90%, novels 10%.

- Prior to becoming an agent, Mr. Brown was a book editor for 25 years.

Represents Nonfiction books, novels, anthologies. **Considers these nonfiction areas:** animals, autobiography, biography, business, cooking, current affairs, dance, economics, environment, finance, foods, government, health, history, how-to, humor, inspirational, law, medicine, memoirs, military, money, music, nature, nutrition, personal improvement, popular culture, politics, psychology, religious, satire, science, self-help, sociology, sports, technology, war, women's issues, women's studies. **Considers these fiction areas:** contemporary issues, feminist, literary, mainstream, women's.

O→ Specializes in thorough involvement with clients' books at every stage of the process from writing to proposals to publication. Actively seeking serious nonfiction and fiction. Does not want to receive YA, sci-fi or romance.

How to Contact Submit outline/proposal, synopsis, author bio. Accepts simultaneous submissions. Responds in 2 weeks to queries. Obtains most new clients through referrals.

Terms Agent receives 15% commission on domestic sales. Agent receives 20% commission on foreign sales. Offers written contract.

Recent Sales *Super in the City: A Novel*, by Daphne Uviller (Bantam); *The Purity Myth*, by Jessica Valenti (Seal Press); *Jane Addams: Spirit In Action*, by Louise W. Knight (Norton).

SHEREE BYKOFSKY ASSOCIATES, INC.

PO Box 706, Brigantine NJ 08203. E-mail: submitbee@aol.com. Website: www.shereebee.com. **Contact:** Sheree Bykofsky. Member of AAR. Other memberships include ASJA, WNBA. Currently handles: nonfiction books 80%, novels 20%.

- Prior to opening her agency, Ms. Bykofsky served as executive editor of The Stonesong Press and managing editor of Chiron Press. She is also the author or co-author of more than 20 books, including *The Complete Idiot's Guide to Getting Published*. Ms. Bykofsky teaches publishing at NYU and SEAK, Inc.

Member Agents Janet Rosen, associate.

Represents Nonfiction books, novels. **Considers these nonfiction areas:** Americana, animals, architecture, art, autobiography, biography, business, child guidance, cooking, crafts, creative nonfiction, cultural interests, current affairs, dance, design, economics, education, environment, ethnic, film, finance, foods, gardening, gay, government, health, history, hobbies, humor, language, law, lesbian, memoirs, metaphysics, military, money, multicultural, music, nature, New Age, nutrition, parenting, philosophy, photography, popular culture, politics, psychology, recreation, regional, religious, science, sex, sociology, spirituality, sports, translation, travel, true crime, war, anthropology; creative nonfiction. **Considers these fiction areas:** contemporary issues, literary, mainstream, mystery, suspense.

O→ This agency specializes in popular reference nonfiction, commercial fiction with a literary quality, and mysteries. "I have wide-ranging interests, but it really depends on quality of writing, originality, and how a particular project appeals to me (or not). I take on fiction when I completely love it - it doesn't matter what area or genre." Does not want to receive poetry, material for children, screenplays, westerns, horror, science fiction, or fantasy.

How to Contact E-mail short queries to submitbee@aol.com. Please, no attachments, snail mail, or phone calls. Accepts simultaneous submissions. Responds in 3 weeks to queries with SASE. Responds in 1 month to requested mss. Obtains most new clients through recommendations from others.

Terms Agent receives 15% commission on domestic sales. Agent receives 20% commission on foreign sales. Offers written contract, binding for 1 year. Charges for postage, photocopying, fax.

Recent Sales *Red Sheep: The Search for my Inner Latina*, by Michele Carlo (Citadel/Kensington); *Bang the Keys: Four Steps to a Lifelong Writing Practice*, by Jill Dearman (Alpha, Penguin); *Signed, Your Student: Celebrities on the Teachers Who Made Them Who They Are Today*, by Holly Holbert (Kaplan); *The Five Ways We Grieve*, by Susan Berger (Trumpeter/Shambhala).

Writers Conferences ASJA Writers Conference; Asilomar; Florida Suncoast Writers' Conference; Whidbey Island Writers' Conference; Florida First Coast Writers' Festibal; Agents and Editors Conference; Columbus Writers' Conference; Southwest Writers' Conference; Willamette Writers' Conferece; Dorothy Canfield Fisher Conference; Maui Writers' Conference; Pacific Northwest Writers' Conference; IWWG.

Tips "Read the agent listing carefully and comply with guidelines."

N ◙ KIMBERLEY CAMERON & ASSOCIATES

1550 Tiburon Blvd., #704, Tiburon CA 94920. Fax: (415)789-9177. E-mail: info@kimberleycameron.com. Website: www.kimberleycameron.com. **Contact:** Kimberley Cameron. Member of AAR. 30% of clients are new/unpublished writers. Currently handles: nonfiction books 50%; fiction 50%.

- Kimberley Cameron & Associates (formerly The Reece Halsey Agency) has had an illustrious client list of established writers, including the estate of Aldous Huxley, and has represented Upton Sinclair, William Faulkner, and Henry Miller.

Member Agents Kimberley Cameron, April Eberhardt, Amy Burkhardt.

Represents Nonfiction, fiction. **Considers these nonfiction areas:** biography, current affairs, foods, humor, language, memoirs, popular culture, science, true crime, women's issues, women's studies, lifestyle. **Considers these fiction areas:** adventure, contemporary issues, ethnic, family saga, historical, horror, mainstream, mystery, interlinked short story collections, thriller, women's, and sophisticated/crossover young adult.

O→ "We are looking for a unique and heartfelt voice that conveys a universal truth."

How to Contact Query via email. See our website for submission guidelines. Obtains new clients through recommendations from others, solicitations.

Terms Agent receives 15% on domestic sales; 10% on film sales. Offers written contract, binding for 1 year.

Writers Conferences Pacific Northwest Writers Association Conference, Aspen Summer Words, Willamette Writers Conference, San Diego State University Writers Conference, San Francisco Writers Conference, Killer Nashville, Left Coast Crime, Bouchercon, Book Passage Mystery and Travel Writers Conferences, Antioch Writers Workshop, Florida Writers Association Conference, and others.

Tips "Please consult our submission guidelines and send a polite, well-written query to our email address."

◙ MARIA CARVAINIS AGENCY, INC.

1270 Avenue of the Americas, Suite 2320, New York NY 10019. (212)245-6365. Fax: (212)245-7196. E-mail: mca@mariacarvainisagency.com. **Contact:** Maria Carvainis, Chelsea Gilmore. Member of AAR. Signatory of WGA. Other memberships include Authors Guild, Women's Media Group, ABA, MWA, RWA. Represents 75 clients. 10% of clients are new/unpublished writers. Currently handles: nonfiction books 35%, novels 65%.

- Prior to opening her agency, Ms. Carvainis spent more than 10 years in the publishing industry as a senior editor with Macmillan Publishing, Basic Books, Avon Books, and Crown Publishers. Ms. Carvainis has served as a member of the AAR Board of Directors and AAR Treasurer, as well as serving as chair of the AAR Contracts Committee. She presently serves on the AAR Royalty Committee. Ms. Gilmore started her publishing career at Oxford University Press, in the Higher Education Group. She then worked at Avalon Books as associate editor. She is most interested in women's fiction, literary fiction, young adult, pop culture, and mystery/suspense.

Member Agents Maria Carvainis, president/literary agent; Chelsea Gilmore, literary agent.

Represents Nonfiction books, novels. **Considers these nonfiction areas:** autobiography, biography, business, economics, history, memoirs, science, technology, women's issues, women's studies. **Considers these fiction areas:** contemporary issues, historical, literary, mainstream, mystery, suspense, thriller, women's, young adult, middle grade.

⊶ Does not want to receive science fiction or children's picture books.

How to Contact Query with SASE. Responds in up to 3 months to mss and to queries. Obtains most new clients through recommendations from others, conferences, query letters.

Terms Agent receives 15% commission on domestic sales. Agent receives 20% commission on foreign sales. Offers written contract. Charges clients for foreign postage and bulk copying.

Recent Sales *A Secret Affair*, by Mary Balogh (Delacorte); *Tough Customer*, by Sandra Brown (Simon & Schuster); *A Lady Never Tells*, by Candace Camp (Pocket Books); *The King James Conspiracy*, by Phillip Depoy (St. Martin's Press).

Writers Conferences BookExpo America; Frankfurt Book Fair; London Book Fair; Mystery Writers of America; Thrillerfest; Romance Writers of America.

◪ CASTIGLIA LITERARY AGENCY

1155 Camino Del Mar, Suite 510, Del Mar CA 92014. (858)755-8761. Fax: (858)755-7063. Website: home.earthlink.net/~mwgconference/id22.html. Member of AAR. Other memberships include PEN. Represents 50 clients. Currently handles: nonfiction books 55%, novels 45%.

Member Agents Julie Castiglia; Winifred Golden; Sally Van Haitsma; Deborah Ritchken.

Represents Nonfiction books, novels. **Considers these nonfiction areas:** animals, anthropology, archeology, autobiography, biography, business, child guidance, cooking, cultural interests, current affairs, economics, environment, ethnic, finance, foods, health, history, inspirational, language, literature, medicine, money, nature, nutrition, psychology, religious, science, technology, women's issues, women's studies. **Considers these fiction areas:** contemporary issues, ethnic, literary, mainstream, mystery, suspense, women's.

⊶ Does not want to receive horror, screenplays, poetry or academic nonfiction.

How to Contact Query with SASE. Obtains most new clients through recommendations from others, solicitations, conferences.

Terms Agent receives 15% commission on domestic sales. Agent receives 25% commission on foreign sales. Offers written contract; 6-week notice must be given to terminate contract.

Recent Sales *Germs Gone Wild*, by Kenneth King (Pegasus); *The Insider*, by Reece Hirsch (Berkley/Penguin); *The Leisure Seeker*, by Michael Zadoorian (Morrow/HarperCollins); *Beautiful: The Life of Hedy Lamarr*, by Stephen Shearer (St. Martin's Press); *American Libre*, by Raul Ramos y Sanchez (Grand Central); *The Two Krishnas*, by Ghalib Shiraz Dhalla (Alyson Books).

Writers Conferences Santa Barbara Writers' Conference; Southern California Writers' Conference; Surrey International Writers' Conference; San Diego State University Writers' Conference; Willamette Writers' Conference.

Tips "Be professional with submissions. Attend workshops and conferences before you approach an agent."

◪ JANE CHELIUS LITERARY AGENCY

548 Second St., Brooklyn NY 11215. (718)499-0236. Fax: (718)832-7335. E-mail: queries@janechelius.com; jane@janechelius.com. Website: www.janechelius.com. Member of AAR.

Represents Nonfiction books, novels. **Considers these nonfiction areas:** biography, humor, medicine, parenting, popular culture, satire, women's issues, women's studies, natural history; narrative. **Considers these fiction areas:** literary, mystery, suspense, women's, men's adventure.

- Does not want to receive fantasy, science fiction, children's books, stage plays, screenplays, or poetry.

How to Contact Please see website for submission procedures. We do not consider email queries with attachments. No unsolicited sample chapters or mss. Responds in 3-4-weeks usually.

ELYSE CHENEY LITERARY ASSOCIATES, LLC

270 Lafayette St., Suite 1504, New York NY 10012. Website: www.cheneyliterary.com. **Contact:** Elyse Cheney, Nicole Steen.

- Prior to her current position, Ms. Cheney was an agent with Sanford J. Greenburger Associates.

Represents Nonfiction, novels. **Considers these nonfiction areas:** autobiography, biography, business, cultural interests, current affairs, finance, history, memoirs, multicultural, politics, science, sports, women's issues, women's studies, narrative; journalism. **Considers these fiction areas:** commercial, family saga, historical, literary, romance, short story collections, suspense, thriller, women's.

How to Contact Query this agency with a referral. Include SASE or IRC. No fax queries. Snail mail or e-mail (submissions@cheneyliterary.com) only.

Recent Sales *Moonwalking with Einstein: A Journey into Memory and the Mind*, by Joshua Foer; *The Coldest Winter Ever*, by Sister Souljah (Atria); *A Heartbreaking Work of Staggering Genius*, by Dave Eggers (Simon and Schuster).

THE CHOATE AGENCY, LLC

1320 Bolton Road, Pelham NY 10803. E-mail: mickey@thechoateagency.com. Website: www.thechoateagency.com. **Contact:** Mickey Choate. Estab. 2004. Member of AAR.

Represents Nonfiction books, novels. **Considers these nonfiction areas:** history, memoirs, by journalists, military or political figures, biography; cookery/food; journalism; military science; narrative; politics; general science; natural science, wine/spirits. **Considers these fiction areas:** historical, mystery, thriller, select literary fiction, strong commercial fiction.

- The agency does not handle genre fiction, chic-lit, cozies, romance, self-help, confessional memoirs, spirituality, pop psychology, religion, how-to, New Age titles, children's books, poetry, self-published works or screenplays.

How to Contact Query with brief synopsis and bio. This agency prefers e-queries, but accepts snail mail queries with SASE.

WM CLARK ASSOCIATES

186 Fifth Avenue, Second Floor, New York NY 10010. (212)675-2784. Fax: (347)-649-9262. E-mail: general@wmclark.com. Website: www.wmclark.com. Estab. 1997. Member of AAR. 50% of clients are new/unpublished writers. Currently handles: nonfiction books 50%, novels 50%.

- Prior to opening WCA, Mr. Clark was an agent at the William Morris Agency.

Represents Nonfiction books, novels. **Considers these nonfiction areas:** architecture, art, autobiography, biography, cultural interests, current affairs, dance, design, ethnic, film, history, inspirational, memoirs, music, politics, popular culture, religious, science, sociology, technology, theater, translation, travel memoir, (Eastern Philosophy only). **Considers these fiction areas:** contemporary issues, ethnic, historical, literary, mainstream, Southern fiction.

- William Clark represents a wide range of titles across all formats to the publishing, motion picture, television, and new media fields on behalf of authors of first fiction and award-winning, best-selling narrative nonfiction,, international authors in translation, chefs, musicians, and artists. Offering individual focus and a global presence, the agency undertakes to discover, develop, and market today's most interesting content and the talent that create it, and forge sophisticated and innovative plans for self-promotion, reliable revenue streams, and an enduring creative career. Referral partners are available to provide services including editorial consultation, media training, lecture booking, marketing support, and public relations. Agency does not respond to screenplays or screenplay pitches. It is advised that before querying you become familiar with the kinds of books we handle by browsing our Book List, which is available on our website.

How to Contact Accepts queries via online form only at www.wmclark.com/queryguidelines.html. Email queries will be deleted. Responds in 1-2 months to queries.

Terms Agent receives 15% commission on domestic sales. Agent receives 20% commission on foreign sales. Offers written contract.

Tips "WCA works on a reciprocal basis with Ed Victor Ltd. (UK) in representing select properties to the US market and vice versa. Translation rights are sold directly in the German, Italian, Spanish, Portuguese, Latin American, French, Dutch, and Scandinavian territories in association with Andrew Nurnberg Associates Ltd. (UK); through offices in China, Bulgaria, Czech Republic, Latvia, Poland, Hungary, and Russia; and through corresponding agents in Japan, Greece, Israel, Turkey, Korea, Taiwan, and Thailand."

THE DOE COOVER AGENCY

P.O. Box 668, Winchester MA 01890. (781)721-6000. Fax: (781)721-6727. E-mail: info@doecooveragency.com. Website: http://doecooveragency.com. Represents more than 100 clients. Currently handles: nonfiction books 80%, novels 20%.

Member Agents Doe Coover (general nonfiction, including business, cooking/food writing, health and science); Colleen Mohyde (literary and commercial fiction, general nonfiction), Member AAR; Amanda Lewis (YA & children's books); Associate: Frances Kennedy.

Represents **Considers these nonfiction areas:** autobiography, biography, business, cooking, economics, foods, gardening, health, history, nutrition, science, technology, social issues, narrative nonfiction. **Considers these fiction areas:** commercial, literary.

- This agency specializes in general nonfiction, particularly biography, business, cooking and food writing, health, history, popular science, social issues, gardening, and humor. The agency does not accept romance, fantasy, science fiction, poetry or screenplays.

How to Contact Query with SASE. E-mail queries are acceptable—please check website for submission guidelines. No unsolicited manuscripts, please. Accepts simultaneous submissions. Responds in 4-6 weeks to queries. Obtains most new clients through recommendations from others, solicitations.

Terms Agent receives 15% commission on domestic sales. Agent receives 10% of original advance commission on foreign sales. No reading fees.

Recent Sales Sold 25-30 titles in the last year. *As Always, Julia, Letters of Julia Child and Avis De Voto-Food, Friendship and the Making of a Masterpiece*, selected and edited by Joan Reardon (Houghton Mifflin Harcourt), *Confessions of a Tarot Card Reader*, by Jane Stern (The Globe Pequot Press) *The Farm*, by Ian Knauer (Houghton Mifflin Harcourt), *Bottling the Gods: Why Global Development has gone Unnecessarily Wrong for So Long*, by Edward Carr (Palgrave/St. Martin's), *The Sewing Book*, by Tanya Whelan (Potter Craft), *The Gourmet Cookie Book: The Single Best Cookie Recipe from 1941-2009*, by Gourmet Magazine (Houghton Mifflin Harcourt), *Shades of Grey*, by Clea Simon (Severn House UK), *Cloud County Revival: How Wind Energy is Breathing New Life into America's Heartland*, by Philip Warburg (Beacon Press). Movie/TV MOW script(s) optioned/sold: *Keeper of the House*, by Rebecca Godwin, *Mr. White's Confession* by Robert Clark. Other clients include: WGBH, New England Aquarium, Blue Balliett, David Allen, Jacques Pepin, Deborah Madison, Rick Bayless, Suzanne Berne, Adria Bernardi, Paula Poundstone

CRICHTON & ASSOCIATES

6940 Carroll Ave., Takoma Park MD 20912. (301)495-9663. Fax: (202)318-0050. E-mail: query@crichton-associates.com. Website: www.crichton-associates.com. **Contact:** Sha-Shana Crichton. 90% of clients are new/unpublished writers. Currently handles: nonfiction books 50% fiction 50%.

- Prior to becoming an agent, Ms. Crichton did commercial litigation for a major law firm.

Represents Nonfiction books, novels. **Considers these nonfiction areas:** child guidance, cultural interests, ethnic, gay, government, investigative, law, lesbian, parenting, politics, true crime, women's issues, women's studies, African-American studies. **Considers these fiction areas:** ethnic, feminist, inspirational, literary, mainstream, mystery, religious, romance, suspense, chick lit.

O→ Actively seeking women's fiction, romance, and chick lit. Looking also for multicultural fiction and nonfiction. Does not want to receive poetry.

How to Contact For fiction, include short synopsis and first 3 chapters with query. Send no e-attachments. For nonfiction, send a book proposal. Responds in 3-5 weeks to queries.

Terms Agent receives 15% commission on domestic sales. Agent receives 20% commission on foreign sales. Offers written contract, binding for 45 days. Only charges fees for postage and photocopying.

Recent Sales *The African American Entrepreneu*, by W. Sherman Rogers (Praeger); *The Diversity Code*, by Michelle Johnson (Amacom); *Secret & Lies*, by Rhonda McKnight (Urban Books); *Love on the Rocks*, by Pamela Yaye (Harlequin). Other clients include Kimberley White, Beverley Long, Jessica Trap, Altonya Washington, Cheris Hodges, Pamela Yaye.

Writers Conferences Silicon Valley RWA; BookExpo America.

D4EO LITERARY AGENCY

7 Indian Valley Road, Weston CT 06883. (203)544-7180. Fax: (203)544-7160. E-mail: d4eo@optonline.net. **Contact:** Bob Diforio. Represents more than 100 clients. 50% of clients are new/unpublished writers. Currently handles: nonfiction books 70%, novels 25%, juvenile books 5%.

- Prior to opening his agency, Mr. Diforio was a publisher.

Represents Nonfiction books, novels. **Considers these nonfiction areas:** juvenile, art, biography, business, child, current affairs, gay, health, history, how-to, humor, memoirs, military, money, psychology, religion, science, self-help, sports, true crime, women's. **Considers these fiction areas:** adventure, detective, erotica, historical, horror, humor, juvenile, literary, mainstream, mystery, picture books, romance, science, sports, thriller, western, young.

How to Contact Query with SASE. Accepts and prefers e-mail queries. Prefers to read material exclusively. Responds in 1 week to queries. Obtains most new clients through recommendations from others.

Terms Agent receives 15% commission on domestic sales. Agent receives 25% commission on foreign sales. Offers written contract, binding for 2 years; 60-day notice must be given to terminate contract. Charges for photocopying and submission postage.

DANIEL LITERARY GROUP

1701 Kingsbury Drive, Suite 100, Nashville TN 37215. (615)730-8207. E-mail: submissions@danielliterarygroup.com. Website: www.danielliterarygroup.com. **Contact:** Greg Daniel. Represents 45 clients. 30% of clients are new/unpublished writers. Currently handles: nonfiction books 85%, novels 15%.

- Prior to becoming an agent, Mr. Daniel spent 10 years in publishing - six at the executive level at Thomas Nelson Publishers.

Represents Nonfiction books, novels. **Considers these nonfiction areas:** autobiography, biography, business, child guidance, current affairs, economics, environment, film, health, history, how-to, humor, inspirational, medicine, memoirs, nature, parenting, personal improvement, popular culture, religious, satire, self-help, sports, theater, women's issues, women's studies. **Considers these fiction areas:** action, adventure, contemporary issues, crime, detective, family saga, historical, humor, inspirational, literary, mainstream, mystery, police, religious, satire, suspense, thriller.

O→ The agency currently accepts all fiction topics, except for children's, romance and sci-fi. "We take pride in our ability to come alongside our authors and help strategize about where they want their writing to take them in both the near and long term. Forging close relationships with our authors, we help them with such critical factors as editorial refinement, branding, audience, and marketing." Nonfiction. The agency is open to submissions in almost every popular category of nonfiction, especially if authors are recognized experts in their fields. No screenplays, poetry or short stories.

How to Contact Query via e-mail only. Submit publishing history, author bio, brief synopsis of work, key selling points. E-queries only. Send no attachments. For fiction, send first 5 pages pasted in e-mail. Responds in 2-3 weeks to queries.

DAVIS WAGER LITERARY AGENCY

419 N. Larchmont Blvd., #317, Los Angeles CA 90004. E-mail: submissions@daviswager.com. Website: www.daviswager.com. **Contact:** Timothy Wager. Estab. 2004. Represents 12 clients.

- Prior to his current position, Mr. Wager was with the Sandra Dijkstra Literary Agency, where he worked as a reader and associate agent.

Represents Nonfiction books, novels. **Considers these fiction areas:** literary.

- Actively seeking: literary fiction and general-interest nonfiction. "I do not handle screenplays, children's books, romance, or science fiction. Memoirs and most genre fiction (other than crime or noir) are a serious long shot, too."

How to Contact Query with SASE. Submit author bio, synopsis for fiction, book proposal or outline for nonfiction. Query via e-mail. No author queries by phone.

THE JENNIFER DECHIARA LITERARY AGENCY

31 East 32nd St., Suite 300, New York NY 10016. (212)481-8484. E-mail: jenndec@aol.com. Website: www.jdlit.com. **Contact:** Jennifer DeChiara, Stephen Fraser. Represents 100 clients. 50% of clients are new/unpublished writers. Currently handles: nonfiction books 25%, novels 25%, juvenile books 50%.

- Prior to becoming an agent, Ms. DeChiara was a writing consultant, freelance editor at Simon & Schuster and Random House, and a ballerina and an actress.

Member Agents Jennifer DeChiara, Stephen Fraser, Dorothy Spencer (adult fiction and nonfiction).

Represents Nonfiction books, novels, juvenile. **Considers these nonfiction areas:** autobiography, biography, child guidance, cooking, crafts, criticism, cultural interests, current affairs, dance, decorating, education, environment, ethnic, film, finance, foods, gay, government, health, history, hobbies, how-to, humor, interior design, investigative, juvenile nonfiction, language, law, lesbian, literature, medicine, memoirs, military, money, music, nature, nutrition, parenting, personal improvement, photography, popular culture, politics, psychology, satire, science, self-help, sociology, sports, technology, theater, true crime, war, women's issues, women's studies, celebrity biography. **Considers these fiction areas:** confession, crime, detective, ethnic, family saga, fantasy, feminist, gay, historical, horror, humor, juvenile, lesbian, literary, mainstream, mystery, picture books, police, regional, satire, sports, suspense, thriller, young adult, chick lit; psychic/supernatural; glitz.

- "We represent both children's and adult books in a wide range of ages and genres. We are a full-service agency and fulfill the potential of every book in every possible medium—stage, film, television, etc. We help writers every step of the way, from creating book ideas to editing and promotion. We are passionate about helping writers further their careers, but are just as eager to discover new talent, regardless of age or lack of prior publishing experience. This agency is committed to managing a writer's entire career. For us, it's not just about selling books, but about making dreams come true. We are especially attracted to the downtrodden, the discouraged, and the downright disgusted." Actively seeking literary fiction, chick lit, young adult fiction, self-help, pop culture, and celebrity biographies. Does not want westerns, poetry, or short stories.

How to Contact Query with SASE. Accepts simultaneous submissions. Responds in 3-6 months to queries. Responds in 3-6 months to mss. Obtains most new clients through recommendations from others, conferences, query letters.

Terms Agent receives 15% commission on domestic sales. Agent receives 20% commission on foreign sales. Offers written contract.

Recent Sales Sold over 100 titles in the past year. *The Chosen One*, by Carol Lynch Williams (St. Martin's Press); *The 30-Day Heartbreak Cure*, by Catherine Hickland (Simon & Schuster); *Naptime for Barney*, by Danny Sit (Sterling Publishing); *The Screwed-Up Life of Charlie the Second*, by

Drew Ferguson (Kensington); *Heart of a Shepherd*, by Rosanne Parry (Random House); *Carolina Harmony*, by Marilyn Taylor McDowell (Random House); *Project Sweet Life*, by Brent Hartinger (HarperCollins). Movie/TV MOW scripts optioned/sold: *The Elf on the Shelf*, by Carol Aebersold and Chanda Bell (Waddell & Scorsese); *Heart of a Shepherd*, by Rosanne Parry (Tashtego Films); *Geography Club*, by Brent Hartinger (The Levy Leder Company). Other clients include Sylvia Browne, Matthew Kirby, Sonia Levitin, Susan Anderson, Michael Apostolina.

JOELLE DELBOURGO ASSOCIATES, INC.

101 Park St., 3rd Floor, Montclair NJ 07042. (973)783-6800. Fax: (973)783-6802. E-mail: info@delbourgo.com. Website: www.delbourgo.com. **Contact:** Joelle Delbourgo, Molly Lyons, Jacquie Flynn. Represents more than 100 clients. Currently handles: nonfiction books 75%, novels 25%.

- Prior to becoming an agent, Ms. Delbourgo was an editor and senior publishing executive at HarperCollins and Random House.

Member Agents Joelle Delbourgo (narrative nonfiction, serious "expert-driven" nonfiction, self-help, psychology, business, history, science, medicine, quality fiction); Molly Lyons (memoir, narrative nonfiction, biography, current events, cultural issues, pop culture, health, psychology, smart, fresh practical nonfiction, fiction, young adult and middle grade); Jacquie Flynn (thought-provoking and practical business, parenting, education, personal development, current events, science and other select nonfiction and fiction titles).

Represents Nonfiction books, novels. **Considers these nonfiction areas:** autobiography, biography, business, child guidance, cooking, cultural interests, current affairs, decorating, diet/nutrition, economics, education, environment, ethnic, foods, gay/lesbian, government, health, history, how-to, inspirational, interior design, investigative, law, medicine, metaphysics, money, New Age, popular culture, politics, psychology, religious, science, sociology, technology, true crime, women's issues, women's studies, New Age/metaphysics, interior design/decorating. **Considers these fiction areas:** historical, literary, mainstream, mystery, suspense.

- "We are former publishers and editors, with deep knowledge and an insider perspective. We have a reputation for individualized attention to clients, strategic management of authors' careers, and creating strong partnerships with publishers for our clients." Actively seeking history, narrative nonfiction, science/medicine, memoir, literary fiction, psychology, parenting, biographies, current affairs, politics, young adult fiction and nonfiction. Does not want to receive genre fiction, science fiction, fantasy, or screenplays.

How to Contact Query by mail with SASE. Accepts simultaneous submissions. Responds in 3 weeks to queries. Responds in 2 months to mss.

Terms Agent receives 15% commission on domestic sales. Agent receives 20% commission on foreign sales. Offers written contract. Charges clients for postage and photocopying.

Recent Sales *Tabloid Medicine*, by Robert Goldberg, Ph.D. (Kaplan); *The Lost Gospel*, by Simcha Jacobovichi (represented by the Elaine Markson Agency) and Barrie Wilson (Overlook Press); *Risk and the Smart Investor*, by David Martin (McGraw-Hill); *Dragon Bone Hill*, by Lindsay Tam Holland (Simon and Schuster Books for Young Readers).

Tips "Do your homework. Do not cold call. Read and follow submission guidelines before contacting us. Do not call to find out if we received your material. No e-mail queries. Treat agents with respect, as you would any other professional, such as a doctor, lawyer or financial advisor."

DHS LITERARY, INC.

10711 Preston Road, Suite 100, Dallas TX 75230. (214)363-4422. Fax: (214)363-4423. Website: www.dhsliterary.com. **Contact:** David Hale Smith, president. Represents 35 clients. 15% of clients are new/unpublished writers. Currently handles: nonfiction books 60%, novels 40%.

- Prior to opening his agency, Mr. Smith was an agent at Dupree/Miller & Associates.

Represents Nonfiction books, novels. **Considers these nonfiction areas:** autobiography, biography, business, child guidance, cooking, cultural interests, current affairs, diet/nutrition, economics, ethnic, foods, investigative, parenting, popular culture, sports, true crime. **Considers these fiction areas:** crime, detective, ethnic, frontier, literary, mainstream, mystery, police, suspense, thriller, westerns.

○ This agency is not actively seeking clients and usually takes clients on by referral only.

How to Contact We accept new material by referral only. Only responds if interested. *No unsolicited mss.*

Terms Agent receives 15% commission on domestic sales. Agent receives 25% commission on foreign sales. Offers written contract; 10-day notice must be given to terminate contract. This agency charges for postage and photocopying.

Recent Sales Safer, by Sean Doolittle; Person of Interest, by Theresa Schwegel; Monday Morning Choices, by David Cottrell

Tips "Remember to be courteous and professional, and to treat marketing your work and approaching an agent as you would any formal business matter. If you have a referral, always query first via e-mail. Sorry, but we cannot respond to queries sent via mail, even with a SASE. Visit our website for more information."

THE JONATHAN DOLGER AGENCY

49 E. 96th St., Suite 9B, New York NY 10128. Fax: (212)369-7118. Member of AAR.

Represents Nonfiction books, novels. **Considers these nonfiction areas:** biography, history, women's, cultural/social. **Considers these fiction areas:** women's, commercial.

How to Contact Query with SASE. No e-mail queries.

Terms Agent receives 15% commission on domestic sales. Agent receives 25% commission on foreign sales.

Tips "Writers must have been previously published if submitting fiction. We prefer to work with published/established authors, and work with a small number of new/previously unpublished writers."

JIM DONOVAN LITERARY

4515 Prentice St., Suite 109, Dallas TX 75206-5028. E-mail: jdlqueries@sbcglobal.net. **Contact:** Melissa Shultz, agent. Represents 30 clients. 10% of clients are new/unpublished writers. Currently handles: nonfiction books 75%, novels 25%.

Member Agents Jim Donovan (history—particularly American, military and Western; biography; sports; popular reference; popular culture; fiction—literary, thrillers and mystery); Melissa Shultz (parenting, women's issues, memoir.

Represents Nonfiction books, novels. **Considers these nonfiction areas:** autobiography, biography, business, child guidance, current affairs, economics, environment, health, history, how-to, investigative, law, medicine, memoirs, military, money, music, parenting, popular culture, politics, sports, true crime, war, women's issues, women's studies. **Considers these fiction areas:** action, adventure, crime, detective, literary, mainstream, mystery, police, suspense, thriller.

○ This agency specializes in commercial fiction and nonfiction. "Does not want to receive poetry, children's, short stories, inspirational or anything else not listed above."

How to Contact "For nonfiction, I need a well-thought query letter telling me about the book: What it does, how it does it, why it's needed now, why it's better or different than what's out there on the subject, and why the author is the perfect writer for it. For fiction, the novel has to be finished, of course; a short (2 to 5 page) synopsis—not a teaser, but a summary of all the action, from first page to last—and the first 30-50 pages is enough. This material should be polished to as close to perfection as possible." Accepts simultaneous submissions. Responds in 3 weeks to queries. Responds in 1 month to mss. Obtains most new clients through recommendations from others.

Terms Agent receives 15% commission on domestic sales. Agent receives 20% commission on foreign sales. Offers written contract, binding for 1 year; 30-day notice must be given to terminate contract. This agency charges for things such as overnight delivery and manuscript copying. Charges are discussed beforehand.

Recent Sales Sold 27 titles in the last year. *The Last Gunfight*, by Jeff Guinn (Simon and Schuster); *Resurrection*, by Jim Dent (St. Martin's Press); *The Battling Bastards of Bataan*, by Bill Sloan (Simon and Schuster); *Perfect*, by Lew Paper (NAL); *Honor in the Dust*, by Gregg Jones (NAL);

First in War, by David Clary (Simon and Schuster);*Desperadoes,* by Mark Gardner (HarperCollins); *Apocalypse of the Dead,* by Joe McKinney (Kensington).
Tips "Get published in short form—magazine reviews, journals, etec.—first. This will increase your credibility considerably, and make it much easier to sell a full-length book."

DOYEN LITERARY SERVICES, INC.

1931 660th St., Newell IA 50568-7613. (712)272-3300. Website: www.barbaradoyen.com. **Contact:** (Ms.) B.J. Doyen, president. Represents over 100 clients. 20% of clients are new/unpublished writers. Currently handles: nonfiction books 100%.

- Prior to opening her agency, Ms. Doyen worked as a published author, teacher, guest speaker, and wrote and appeared in her own weekly TV show airing in 7 states. She is also the co-author of *The Everything Guide to Writing a Book Proposal* (Adams 2005) and *The Everything Guide to Getting Published* (Adams 2006).

Represents Nonfiction for adults, no children's. **Considers these nonfiction areas:** agriculture, Americana, animals, anthropology, archeology, architecture, art, autobiography, biography, business, child guidance, computers, cooking, crafts, cultural interests, current affairs, diet/nutrition, design, economics, education, environment, ethnic, film, foods, gardening, government, health, history, hobbies, horticulture, language, law, medicine, memoirs, metaphysics, military, money, multicultural, music, parenting, photography, popular culture, politics, psychology, recreation, regional, science, self-help, sex, sociology, software, technology, theater, true crime, women's issues, women's studies, creative nonfiction, computers, electronics.

- This agency specializes in nonfiction. Actively seeking business, health, science, how-to, self-help—all kinds of adult nonfiction suitable for the major trade publishers. Does not want to receive pornography, children's books, fiction, or poetry.

How to Contact Prefer email query through our website, using the contact button. Please read the wesite before submitting a query. Include your background information in a bio. Send no unsolicited attachments. Accepts simultaneous submissions. Responds immediately to queries. Responds in 3 weeks to mss.
Terms Agent receives 15% commission on domestic sales. Agent receives 20% commission on foreign sales. Offers written contract, binding for 2 years.
Recent Sales *Stem Cells For Dummies*, by Lawrence S.B. Goldstein and Meg Schneider; *The Complete Idiot's Guide to Country Living*, by Kimberly Willis; *The Complete Illustrated Pregnancy Companion,* by Robin Elise Weiss; *The Complete Idiot's Guide to Playing the Fiddle*, by Ellery Klein; *Healthy Aging for Dummies*, by Brent Agin, M.D. and Sharon Perkins, R.N.
Tips "Our authors receive personalized attention. We market aggressively, undeterred by rejection. We get the best possible publishing contracts. We are very interested in nonfiction book ideas at this time and will consider most topics. Many writers come to us from referrals, but we also get quite a few who initially approach us with query letters. Do not call us regarding queries. It is best if you do not collect editorial rejections prior to seeking an agent, but if you do, be upfront and honest about it. Do not submit your manuscript to more than 1 agent at a time—querying first can save you (and us) much time. We're open to established or beginning writers—just send us a terrific letter!"

DUNHAM LITERARY, INC.

156 Fifth Ave., Suite 625, New York NY 10010-7002. (212)929-0994. Website: www.dunhamlit.com. **Contact:** Jennie Dunham. Member of AAR. Represents 50 clients. 15% of clients are new/unpublished writers. Currently handles: nonfiction books 25%, novels 25%, juvenile books 50%.

- Prior to opening her agency, Ms. Dunham worked as a literary agent for Russell & Volkening. The Rhoda Weyr Agency is now a division of Dunham Literary, Inc.

Represents Nonfiction books, novels, short story collections, juvenile. **Considers these nonfiction areas:** anthropology, archeology, autobiography, biography, cultural interests, environment, ethnic, government, health, history, language, law, literature, medicine, popular culture, politics, psychology, science, technology, women's issues, women's studies. **Considers these fiction areas:** ethnic, juvenile, literary, mainstream, picture books, young adult.

How to Contact Query with SASE. Responds in 1 week to queries. Responds in 2 months to mss. Obtains most new clients through recommendations from others, solicitations.
Terms Agent receives 15% commission on domestic sales. Agent receives 20% commission on foreign sales.
Recent Sales America the Beautiful, by Robert Sabuda; Dahlia, by Barbara McClintock; Living Dead Girl, by Tod Goldberg; In My Mother's House, by Margaret McMulla; Black Hawk Down, by Mark Bowden; Look Back All the Green Valley, by Fred Chappell; Under a Wing, by Reeve Lindbergh; I Am Madame X, by Gioia Diliberto.

DUPREE/MILLER AND ASSOCIATES INC. LITERARY

100 Highland Park Village, Suite 350, Dallas TX 75205. (214)559-BOOK. Fax: (214)559-PAGE. Website: www.dupreemiller.com. **Contact:** Submissions Department. Other memberships include ABA. Represents 200 clients. 20% of clients are new/unpublished writers. Currently handles: nonfiction books 90%, novels 10%.
Member Agents Jan Miller, president/CEO; Shannon Miser-Marven, senior executive VP; Annabelle Baxter; Nena Madonia; Cheri Gillis.
Represents Nonfiction books, novels, scholarly, syndicated, religious, inspirational/spirituality. **Considers these nonfiction areas:** animals, anthropology, archeology, architecture, art, autobiography, biography, business, child guidance, cooking, crafts, current affairs, dance, diet/nutrition, design, economics, education, environment, ethnic, film, foods, gardening, government, health, history, how-to, humor, language, literature, medicine, memoirs, money, multicultural, music, parenting, philosophy, photography, popular culture, psychology, recreation, regional, satire, science, self-help, sex, sociology, sports, technology, theater, translation, true crime, women's issues, women's studies. **Considers these fiction areas:** action, adventure, crime, detective, ethnic, experimental, family saga, feminist, glitz, historical, humor, inspirational, literary, mainstream, mystery, picture books, police, psychic, religious, satire, sports, supernatural, suspense, thriller.

O→ This agency specializes in commercial fiction and nonfiction.

How to Contact Submit 1-page query, outline, SASE. Obtains most new clients through recommendations from others, conferences, lectures.
Terms Agent receives 15% commission on domestic sales. Offers written contract.
Writers Conferences Aspen Summer Words Literary Festival.
Tips "If interested in agency representation, it is vital to have the material in the proper working format. As agents' policies differ, it is important to follow their guidelines. Work on establishing a strong proposal that provides sample chapters, an overall synopsis (fairly detailed), and some biographical information on yourself. Do not send your proposal in pieces; it should be complete upon submission. Your work should be in its best condition."

DWYER & O'GRADY, INC.

Agents for Writers & Illustrators of Children's Books, P.O. Box 790, Cedar Key FL 32625-0790. (352)543-9307. Fax: (603)375-5373. Website: www.dwyerogrady.com. **Contact:** Elizabeth O'Grady. Estab. 1990. Other memberships include SCBWI. Represents 30 clients. Currently handles: juvenile books 100%.

- Prior to opening their agency, Mr. Dwyer and Ms. O'Grady were booksellers and publishers.

Member Agents Elizabeth O'Grady; Jeff Dwyer.
Represents Juvenile. **Considers these nonfiction areas:** juvenile. **Considers these fiction areas:** juvenile, picture books, young.

O→ "We are not accepting new clients at this time. This agency represents only writers and illustrators of children's books." No juvenile books.

How to Contact *No unsolicited mss.* Obtains most new clients through recommendations from others, Direct approach by agent to writer whose work they've read.
Terms Agent receives 15% commission on domestic sales. Agent receives 20% commission on foreign sales. Offers written contract; 1-month notice must be given to terminate contract. This agency charges clients for photocopying of longer mss or mutually agreed upon marketing expenses.

Writers Conferences BookExpo America; American Library Association Annual Conference; SCBWI.

Tips "This agency previously had an address in New Hampshire. Mail all materials to the new Florida address."

EAMES LITERARY SERVICES

4117 Hillsboro Road, Suite 251, Nashville TN 37215. Fax: (615)463.9361. E-mail: info@eamesliterary.com; John@eamesliterary.com; Ahna@eamesliterary.com. Website: www.eamesliterary.com. **Contact:** John Eames.

Member Agents John Eames, Jonathan Rogers.

Represents Nonfiction books, novels. **Considers these nonfiction areas:** inspirational, memoirs, religious, young adult. **Considers these fiction areas:** inspirational, religious, young adult.

This agency specializes in the Christian marketplace. Actively seeking "adult and young adult fiction that sparks the imagination, illuminates some angle of truth about the human condition, causes the reader to view the world with fresh eyes, and supports a Christian perspective on life in all its complexities. Stories might be redemptive, or tragic. Characters might be noble, or flawed. Situations might be humorous, or dark. And many manuscripts might contain some combination of all of the above. We also seek adult and young adult nonfiction that is anecdotal as well as instructional, utilizes a 'show, don't tell' philosophy of writing, and offers a unique and biblically sound perspective on a given topic. If the submission is a nonfiction narrative (e.g., memoir), the work should follow most of the same recommendations for a work of fiction, as listed above. We look for proposals that are very well written and (especially for nonfiction) are from authors with an expansive platform and processing some literary notoriety."

How to Contact Query through email along with a book proposal; author bio (including publishing history); plot synopsis or chapter summary; and 2-3 chapters of sample content (attached as a Microsoft Word document). Responds in 3-5 weeks.

EAST/WEST LITERARY AGENCY, LLC

1158 26th St., Suite 462, Santa Monica CA 90403. (310)573-9303. Fax: (310)453-9008. E-mail: query@eastwestliteraryagency.com. Estab. 2000. Represents 100 clients. 70% of clients are new/unpublished writers. Currently handles: nonfiction books 25%, juvenile books 75%.

Member Agents Deborah Warren, founder; Mary Grey James, partner literary agent (special interest: southern writers and their stories, literary fiction); Rubin Pfeffer, partner content agent and digital media strategist.

How to Contact By referral only. Submit proposal and first 3 sample chapters, table of contents (2 pages or fewer), synopsis (1 page). For picture books, submit entire ms. Requested submissions should be sent by mail as a Word document in Courier, 12-pt., double-spaced with 1.20 inch margin on left, ragged right text, 25 lines per page, continuously paginated, with all your contact info on the first page. Only responds if interested, no need for SASE. Responds in 60 days. Obtains new clients through recommendations from others.

Terms Agent receives 15% commission on domestic sales. Agent receives 25% commission on foreign sales. Offers written contract; 30-day notice must be given to terminate contract. Charges for out-of-pocket expenses, such as postage and copying.

ANNE EDELSTEIN LITERARY AGENCY

20 W. 22nd St., Suite 1603, New York NY 10010. (212)414-4923. Fax: (212)414-2930. E-mail: info@aeliterary.com. Website: www.aeliterary.com. Member of AAR.

Member Agents Anne Edelstein; Krista Ingebretson.

Represents Nonfiction books, Fiction. **Considers these nonfiction areas:** history, inspirational, memoirs, psychology, religious, Buddhist thought. **Considers these fiction areas:** literary.

This agency specializes in fiction and narrative nonfiction.

How to Contact Query with SASE; submit 25 sample pages.

Recent Sales *Confessions of a Buddhist Atheist*, by Stephen Batchelor (Spiegel & Grau); *April & Oliver*, by Tess Callahan (Doubleday).

ANN ELMO AGENCY, INC.

305 Seventh Avenue, # 1101, New York NY 10001. (212)661-2880. Fax: (212)661-2883. E-mail: aalitagent@sbcgobal.net. **Contact:** Lettie Lee. Member of AAR. Other memberships include Authors Guild.

Member Agents Lettie Lee; Mari Cronin (plays); A.L. Abecassis (nonfiction).

Represents Nonfiction books, novels. **Considers these nonfiction areas:** biography, current affairs, health, history, how-to, popular culture, science. **Considers these fiction areas:** ethnic, family, mainstream, romance, contemporary, gothic, historical, regency, thriller, women's.

How to Contact Only accepts mailed queries with SASE. Do not send full ms unless requested. Responds in 3 months to queries. Obtains most new clients through recommendations from others.

Terms Agent receives 15% commission on domestic sales. Agent receives 20% commission on foreign sales. Offers written contract.

Tips "Query first, and **only** when asked send a double-spaced, readable manuscript. Include a SASE, of course."

THE ELAINE P. ENGLISH LITERARY AGENCY

4710 41st St. NW, Suite D, Washington DC 20016. (202)362-5190. Fax: (202)362-5192. E-mail: elaine@elaineenglish.com; naomi@elaineenglish.com. Website: www.elaineenglish.com. **Contact:** Elaine English; Naomi Hackenberg. Member of AAR. Represents 20 clients. 25% of clients are new/unpublished writers. Currently handles: novels 100%.

- Ms. English has been working in publishing for more than 20 years. She is also an attorney specializing in media and publishing law.

Member Agents Elaine English (novels); Naomi Hackenberg (Young Adult fiction).

Represents Novels. **Considers these fiction areas:** historical, multicultural, mystery, suspense, thriller, women's, romance (single title, historical, contemporary, romantic, suspense, chick lit, erotic), general women's fiction. The agency is slowly but steadily acquiring in all mentioned areas.

O→ Actively seeking women's fiction, including single-title romances, and young adult fiction. Does not want to receive any science fiction, time travel, or picture books.

How to Contact Generally prefers e-queries sent to queries@elaineenglish.com or YA sent to naomi@elaineenglish.com. If requested, submit synopsis, first 3 chapters, SASE. Please check website for further details. Responds in 4-8 weeks to queries; 3 months to requested submissions Obtains most new clients through recommendations from others, conferences, submissions.

Terms Agent receives 15% commission on domestic sales. Agent receives 20% commission on foreign sales. Offers written contract; 30-day notice must be given to terminate contract. Charges only for shipping expenses; generally taken from proceeds.

Recent Sales Have been to Sourcebooks, Tor, Harlequin.

Writers Conferences RWA National Conference; Novelists, Inc.; Malice Domestic; Washington Romance Writers Retreat, among others.

FELICIA ETH LITERARY REPRESENTATION

555 Bryant St., Suite 350, Palo Alto CA 94301-1700. (650)375-1276. Fax: (650)401-8892. E-mail: feliciaeth@aol.com. **Contact:** Felicia Eth. Member of AAR. Represents 25-35 clients. Currently handles: nonfiction books 85%, novels 15% adult.

Represents Nonfiction books, novels. **Considers these nonfiction areas:** animals, anthropology, autobiography, biography, business, child guidance, cultural interests, current affairs, economics, ethnic, gay/lesbian, government, health, history, investigative, law, medicine, parenting, popular culture, politics, psychology, science, sociology, technology, true crime, women's issues, women's studies. **Considers these fiction areas:** literary, mainstream.

⊶ This agency specializes in high-quality fiction (preferably mainstream/contemporary) and provocative, intelligent, and thoughtful nonfiction on a wide array of commercial subjects.

How to Contact Query with SASE. Accepts simultaneous submissions. Responds in 3 weeks to queries. Responds in 4-6 weeks to mss.

Terms Agent receives 15% commission on domestic sales. Agent receives 20% commission on foreign sales. Agent receives 20% commission on film sales. Charges clients for photocopying and express mail service.

Recent Sales Sold 70-10 titles in the last year. *Bumper Sticker Philosophy*, by Jack Bowen (Random House); *Boys Adrift*, by Leonard Sax (Basic Books); *A War Reporter*, by Barbara Quick (HarperCollins); Pantry, by Anna Badkhen (Free Press/S&S).

Writers Conferences "Wide Array - from Squaw Valley to Mills College."

Tips "For nonfiction, established expertise is certainly a plus—as is magazine publication—though not a prerequisite. I am highly dedicated to those projects I represent, but highly selective in what I choose."

FAIRBANK LITERARY REPRESENTATION

199 Mount Auburn St., Suite 1, Cambridge MA 02138-4809. (617)576-0030. Fax: (617)576-0030. E-mail: queries@fairbankliterary.com. Website: www.fairbankliterary.com. **Contact:** Sorche Fairbank. Member of AAR. Represents 45 clients. 20% of clients are new/unpublished writers. Currently handles: nonfiction books 60%, novels 22%, story collections 3%, other 15% illustrated.

Member Agents Sorche Fairbank (narrative nonfiction, commercial and literary fiction, memoir, food and wine); Matthew Frederick (scout for sports nonfiction, architecture, design).

Represents Nonfiction books, novels, short story collections. **Considers these nonfiction areas:** agriculture, architecture, art, autobiography, biography, cooking, crafts, cultural interests, current affairs, decorating, diet/nutrition, design, environment, ethnic, foods, gay/lesbian, government, hobbies, horticulture, how-to, interior design, investigative, law, memoirs, photography, popular culture, politics, science, sociology, sports, technology, true crime, women's issues, women's studies. **Considers these fiction areas:** action, adventure, feminist, gay, lesbian, literary, mainstream, mystery, sports, suspense, thriller, women's, Southern voices.

⊶ "I have a small agency in Harvard Square, where I tend to gravitate toward literary fiction and narrative nonfiction, with a strong interest in women's issues and women's voices, international voices, class and race issues, and projects that simply teach me something new about the greater world and society around us. We have a good reputation for working closely and developmentally with our authors and love what we do." Actively seeking literary fiction, international and culturally diverse voices, narrative nonfiction, topical subjects (politics, current affairs), history, sports, architecture/design and pop culture. Does not want to receive romance, poetry, science fiction, young adult or children's works.

How to Contact Query with SASE. Submit author bio. Accepts simultaneous submissions. Responds in 6 weeks to queries. Responds in 10 weeks to mss. Obtains most new clients through recommendations from others, solicitations, conferences, ideas generated in-house.

Terms Agent receives 15% commission on domestic sales. Agent receives 20% commission on foreign sales. Offers written contract, binding for 12 months; 45-day notice must be given to terminate contract.

Writers Conferences San Francisco Writers' Conference, Muse and the Marketplace/Grub Street Conference, Washington Independent Writers' Conference, Murder in the Grove, Surrey International Writers' Conference.

Tips "Be professional from the very first contact. There shouldn't be a single typo or grammatical flub in your query. Have a reason for contacting me about your project other than I was the next name listed on some website. Please do not use form query software! Believe me, we can get a dozen or so a day that look identical—we know when you are using a form. Show me that you know your audience—and your competition. Have the writing and/or proposal at the very, very best it can be before starting the querying process. Don't assume that if someone likes it enough they'll 'fix' it. The biggest mistake new writers make is starting the querying process before they—and the work—are ready. Take your time and do it right."

FARRIS LITERARY AGENCY, INC.

P.O. Box 570069, Dallas TX 75357. (972)203-8804. E-mail: farris1@airmail.net. Website: www.farrisliterary.com. **Contact:** Mike Farris, Susan Morgan Farris. Represents 30 clients. 60% of clients are new/unpublished writers. Currently handles: nonfiction books 40, novels 60.

- Both Mr. Farris and Ms. Farris are attorneys.

Represents Nonfiction books, novels. **Considers these nonfiction areas:** autobiography, biography, business, child guidance, cooking, current affairs, dance, economics, government, health, history, how-to, humor, inspirational, memoirs, military, music, parenting, popular culture, religious, satire, self-help, sports, war, women's issues, women's studies. **Considers these fiction areas:** action, adventure, crime, detective, frontier, historical, humor, inspirational, mainstream, mystery, police, religious, romance, satire, sports, suspense, thriller, westerns.

- "We specialize in both fiction and nonfiction books. We are particularly interested in discovering unpublished authors. We adhere to AAR guidelines." Does not want to receive science fiction, fantasy, gay and lesbian, erotica, young adult or children's.

How to Contact Query with SASE or by e-mail. Accepts simultaneous submissions. Responds in 2-3 weeks to queries. Responds in 4-8 weeks to mss. Obtains most new clients through recommendations from others, solicitations, conferences.

Terms Agent receives 15% commission on domestic sales. Agent receives 20% commission on foreign sales. Offers written contract; 30-day notice must be given to terminate contract. Charges clients for postage and photocopying.

Recent Sales *The Yard Dog* and The Insane Train, by Sheldon Russell (St. Martin's Press); *Eurostorm*, by Payne Harrison (Variance Publishing); *Relative Chaos*, by Kay Finch (Avalon Books); *Call Me Lucky: A Texan in Hollywood*, by Robert Hinkle and Mike Farris (University of Oklahoma Press); *Sketch Me If You Can* (the first book in a three book deal for the A Portrait of Crime mystery series), by Sharon Pape (Berkley Books); film rights options for *Balaam Gimble's Gumption*, by Mike Nichols (John M. Hardy Publishing).

Writers Conferences The Screenwriting Conference in Santa Fe; La Jolla Writers Conference; east Texas Christian Writers Conference.

DIANA FINCH LITERARY AGENCY

116 W. 23rd St., Suite 500, New York NY 10011. (646)375-2081. E-mail: diana.finch@verizon.net. Website: dianafinchliteraryagency.blogspot.com/. **Contact:** Diana Finch. Member of AAR. Represents 40 clients. 20% of clients are new/unpublished writers. Currently handles: nonfiction books 65%, novels 25%, juvenile books 5%, multimedia 5%.

- Prior to opening her agency, Ms. Finch worked at Ellen Levine Literary Agency for 18 years.

Represents Nonfiction books, novels, scholarly. **Considers these nonfiction areas:** autobiography, biography, business, child guidance, computers, cultural interests, current affairs, dance, economics, environment, ethnic, film, government, health, history, how-to, humor, investigative, juvenile nonfiction, law, medicine, memoirs, military, money, music, parenting, photography, popular culture, politics, psychology, satire, science, self-help, sports, technology, theater, translation, true crime, war, women's issues, women's studies, computers, electronic. **Considers these fiction areas:** action, adventure, crime, detective, ethnic, historical, literary, mainstream, police, thriller, young adult.

- Actively seeking narrative nonfiction, popular science, and health topics. "Does not want romance, mysteries, or children's picture books."

How to Contact Query with SASE or via e-mail (no attachments). Accepts simultaneous submissions. Obtains most new clients through recommendations from others.

Terms Agent receives 15% commission on domestic sales. Agent receives 20% commission on foreign sales. Offers written contract. "I charge for photocopying, overseas postage, galleys, and books purchased, and try to recap these costs from earnings received for a client, rather than charging outright."

Recent Sales *Genetic Rounds* by Robert Marion, M.D. (Kaplan); *Honeymoon In Tehran* by Azadeh Moaveni (Random House); *Darwin Slept Here* by Eric Simons (Overlook); *The Tyranny of Oil* by Antonia Juhasz (HarperCollins); *Stalin's Children* by Owen Matthews (Bloomsbury); *Radiant Days* by Michael Fitzgerald (Shoemaker & Hoard); *The Queen's Soprano* by Carol Dines (Harcourt Young Adult); *What To Say to a Porcupine* by Richard Gallagher (Amacom).
Tips "Do as much research as you can on agents before you query. Have someone critique your query letter before you send it. It should be only 1 page and describe your book clearly—and why you are writing it—but also demonstrate creativity and a sense of your writing style."

FINEPRINT LITERARY MANAGEMENT

240 West 35th St., Suite 500, New York NY 10001. (212)279-1282. E-mail: stephany@fineprintlit.com. Website: www.fineprintlit.com. Member of AAR.
Member Agents Peter Rubie, CEO (nonfiction interests include narrative nonfiction, popular science, spirituality, history, biography, pop culture, business, technology, parenting, health, self-help, music, and food; fiction interests include literate thrillers, crime fiction, science fiction and fantasy, military fiction and literary fiction); Stephany Evans, president (nonfiction interests include health and wellness - especially women's health, spirituality, lifestyle, home renovating/decorating, entertaining, food and wine, popular reference, and narrative nonfiction; fiction interests include stories with a strong and interesting female protagonist, both literary and upmarket commercial — including chick lit, romance, mystery, and light suspense); June Clark (nonfiction: entertainment, self-help, parenting, reference/how-to books, teen books, food and wine, style/beauty, and prescriptive business titles); Diane Freed (nonfiction: health/fitness, women's issues, memoir, baby boomer trends, parenting, popular culture, self-help, humor, young adult, and topics of New England regional interest); Meredith Hays (both fiction and nonfiction: commercial and literary; she is interested in sophisticated women's fiction such as urban chick lit, pop culture, lifestyle, animals, and absorbing nonfiction accounts); Janet Reid (mysteries and offbeat literary fiction); Colleen Lindsay; Marissa Walsh; Ward Calhoun; Laura Wood.
Represents Nonfiction books, novels. **Considers these nonfiction areas:** business, child guidance, cooking, dance, diet/nutrition, economics, foods, government, health, history, humor, law, medicine, memoirs, music, parenting, politics, psychology, science, spirituality, true crime, women's issues, women's studies, narrative nonfiction, young adult, popular science. **Considers these fiction areas:** crime, detective, fantasy, literary, military, mystery, police, romance, science fiction, suspense, war, women's, young adult.
How to Contact Query with SASE. Submit synopsis and first two chapters for fiction; proposal for nonfiction. Do not send attachments or manuscripts without a request. Obtains most new clients through recommendations from others, solicitations.
Terms Agent receives 15% commission on domestic sales. Agent receives 20% commission on foreign sales.

FOUNDRY LITERARY + MEDIA

33 West 17th St., PH, New York NY 10011. (212)929-5064. Fax: (212)929-5471. Website: www.foundrymedia.com.
Member Agents Peter H. McGuigan (smart, offbeat nonfiction, particularly works of narrative nonfiction on pop culture, niche history, biography, music and science; fiction interests include commercial and literary, across all genres, especially first-time writers); Yfat Reiss Gendell (favors nonfiction books focusing on all manners of prescriptive: how-to, science, health and well-being, memoirs, adventure, travel stories and lighter titles appropriate for the gift trade genre. Yfat also looks for commercial fiction highlighting the full range of women's experiences - young and old - and also seeks science fiction, thrillers and historical fiction); Stéphanie Abou (in fiction and nonfiction alike, Stéphanie is always on the lookout for authors who are accomplished storytellers with their own distinctive voice, who develop memorable characters, and who are able to create psychological conflict with their narrative. She is an across-the-board fiction lover, attracted to

both literary and smart upmarket commercial fiction. In nonfiction she leans towards projects that tackle big topics with an unusual approach. Pop culture, health, science, parenting, women's and multicultural issues are of special interest); Chris Park (memoirs, narrative nonfiction, Christian nonfiction and character-driven fiction); David Patterson (outstanding narratives and/or idea-driven works of nonfiction); Hannah Brown Gordon (fiction, YA, memoir, narrative nonfiction, history, current events, science, psychology and pop-culture); Lisa Grubka; Mollie Glick (literary fiction, narrative non-fiction, YA, and a bit of practical non-fiction); Stephen Barbara (all categories of books for young readers in addition to servicing writers for the adult market); Brandi Bowles (idea and platform-driven nonfiction in all categories, including music and pop-culture, humor, business, sociology, philosophy, health, and relationships. Quirky, funny, or contrarian proposals are always welcome in her inbox, as are big-idea books that change the way we think about the world. Brandi also represents fiction in the categories of literary fiction, women's fiction, urban fantasy, and YA).

Represents Considers these nonfiction areas: biography, child, health, memoirs, multicultural, music, popular culture, science. **Considers these fiction areas:** literary, religious.

How to Contact Query with SASE. Should be addressed to one agent only. Submit synopsis, 3 sample chapters, author bio, For nonfiction, submit query, proposal, sample chapter, TOC, bio. Put submisssions on your snail mail submission.

FOX LITERARY

168 Second Ave., PMB 180, New York NY 10003. E-mail: submissions@foxliterary.com. Website: www.foxliterary.com.

Represents Considers these nonfiction areas: memoirs, biography, pop culture, narrative nonfiction, history, science, spirituality, self-help, celebrity, dating/relationships, women's issues, psychology, film & entertainment, cultural/social issues, journalism. **Considers these fiction areas:** erotica, fantasy, literary, romance, science, young adult, science fiction, thrillers, historical fiction, literary fiction, graphic novels, commercial fiction, women's fiction, gay & lesbian, erotica, historical romance.

- Does not want to receive screenplays, poetry, category Westerns, horror, Christian/inspirational, or children's picture books.

How to Contact E-mail query and first five pages in body of e-mail. E-mail queries preferred. For snail mail queries, must include an e-mail address for response. Do not send SASE.

LYNN C. FRANKLIN ASSOCIATES, LTD.

1350 Broadway, Suite 2015, New York NY 10018. (212)868-6311. Fax: (212)868-6312. **Contact:** Lynn Franklin, President; Claudia Nys, Foreign Rights; Michelle Andelman, Agent/Children's. Other memberships include PEN America. Represents 30-35 clients. 50% of clients are new/unpublished writers. Currently handles: nonfiction books 90%, novels 10%.

Represents Nonfiction books, novels. **Considers these nonfiction areas:** newage, biography, current affairs, health, history, memoirs, psychology, religion, self-help, spirituality. **Considers these fiction areas:** literary, mainstream, commercial; juvenile, middle-grade, and young adult.

- "This agency specializes in general nonfiction with a special interest in self-help, biography/memoir, alternative health, and spirituality."

How to Contact Query via e-mail to agency@franklinandsiegal.com. No unsolicited mss. No attachments. For nonfiction, query letter with short outline and synopsis. For fiction, query letter with short synopsis and a maximum of 10 sample pages (in the body of the e-mail). Please indicate "query adult" or "query children's) in the subject line. Accepts simultaneous submissions. Responds in 2 weeks to queries. Responds in 6 weeks to mss. Obtains most new clients through recommendations from others, solicitations.

Terms Agent receives 15% commission on domestic sales. Agent receives 20% commission on foreign sales. Offers written contract.

Recent Sales Adult: *Made for Goodness*, by Archbishop Desmond Tutu and Reverend Mpho Tutu (HarperOne); *Children of God Storybook Bible*, by Archbishop Desmond Tutu (Zondervan for originating publisher Lux Verbi); *Playing Our Game: Why China's Economic Rise Doesn't Threaten* *the West*, by Edward Steinfeld (Oxford University Press); *The 100 Year Diet*, by Susan Yager (Rodale); Children's/YA: HILDREN'S/YA: *I Like Mandarin*, by Kirsten Hubbard (Delacorte/Random House; *A Scary Scene in a Scary Movie*, by Matt Blackstone (Farrar, Straus & Giroux).

SARAH JANE FREYMANN LITERARY AGENCY

59 W. 71st St., Suite 9B, New York NY 10023. (212)362-9277. E-mail: sarah@sarahjanefreymann.com; Submissions@SarahJaneFreymann.com. Website: www.sarahjanefreymann.com. **Contact:** Sarah Jane Freymann, Steve Schwartz. Represents 100 clients. 20% of clients are new/unpublished writers. Currently handles: nonfiction books 75%, novels 23%, juvenile books 2%.

Member Agents Sarah Jane Freymann; (nonfiction books, novels, illustrated books); Jessica Sinsheimer, Jessica@sarahjanefreymann.com (young adult fiction).

Represents Considers these nonfiction areas: animals, anthropology, architecture, art, autobiography, biography, business, child guidance, cooking, current affairs, decorating, diet/nutrition, design, economics, ethnic, foods, health, history, interior design, medicine, memoirs, parenting, psychology, self-help, women's issues, women's studies, lifestyle. **Considers these fiction areas:** ethnic, literary, mainstream.

How to Contact Query with SASE. Responds in 2 weeks to queries. Responds in 6 weeks to mss. Obtains most new clients through recommendations from others.

Terms Agent receives 15% commission on domestic sales. Agent receives 20% commission on foreign sales. Offers written contract. Charges clients for long distance, overseas postage, photocopying. 100% of business is derived from commissions on ms sales.

Recent Sales *How to Make Love to a Plastic Cup: And Other Things I Learned While Trying to Knock Up My Wife*, by Greg Wolfe (Harper Collins); *I Want to Be Left Behind: Rapture Here on Earth*, by Brenda Peterson (a Merloyd Lawrence Book); *That Bird Has My Name: The Autobiography of an Innocent Man on Death Row*, by Jarvis Jay Masters with an Introduction by Pema Chodrun (HarperOne); *Perfect One-Dish Meals*, by Pam Anderson (Houghton Mifflin); *Birdology*, by Sy Montgomery (Simon & Schuster); *Emptying the Nest: Launching Your Reluctant Young Adult*, by Dr. Brad Sachs (Macmillan); *Tossed & Found*, by Linda and John Meyers (Steward, Tabori & Chang); *32 Candlesl*, by Ernessa Carter; *God and Dog*, by Wendy Francisco.

Tips "I love fresh, new, passionate works by authors who love what they are doing and have both natural talent and carefully honed skill."

FREDRICA S. FRIEDMAN AND CO., INC.

136 E. 57th St., 14th Floor, New York NY 10022. (212)829-9600. Fax: (212)829-9669. E-mail: info@fredricafriedman.com; submissions@fredricafriedman.com. Website: www.fredricafriedman.com/. **Contact:** Ms. Chandler Smith. Represents 75+ clients. 50% of clients are new/unpublished writers. Currently handles: nonfiction books 95%, novels 5%.

Represents Nonfiction books, novels, anthologies. **Considers these nonfiction areas:** art, biography, business, child, cooking, current affairs, education, ethnic, gay, government, health, history, how-to, humor, language, memoirs, money, music, photography, popular culture, psychology, self-help, sociology, film, true crime, women's, interior design/decorating. **Considers these fiction areas:** literary.

- "We represent a select group of outstanding nonfiction and fiction writers. We are particularly interested in helping writers expand their readership and develop their careers." Does not want poetry, plays, screenplays, children's books, sci-fi/fantasy, or horror.

How to Contact Submit e-query, synopsis; be concise, and include any pertinent author information, including relevant writing history. If you are a fiction writer, we also request a one-page sample from your manuscript to provide its voice. We ask that you keep all material in the body of the email. Accepts simultaneous submissions. Responds in 4-6 weeks to queries. Responds in 4-6 weeks to mss. Obtains most new clients through recommendations from others.

Terms Agent receives 15% commission on domestic sales. Agent receives 25% commission on foreign sales. Offers written contract. Charges for photocopying and messenger/shipping fees for proposals.

Recent Sales *A World of Lies: The Crime and Consequences of Bernie Madoff*, by Diana B. Henriques (Times Books/Holt); *Polemic and Memoir: The Nixon Years*, by Patrick J. Buchanan (St. Martin's Press); *Angry Fat Girls: Five Women, Five Hundred Pounds, and a Year of Losing It..Again*, by Frances Kuffel (Berkley/Penguin); *Life With My Sister Madonna*, by Christopher Ciccone with Wendy Leigh (Simon & Schuster Spotlight); *The World Is Curved: Hidden Dangers to the Global Economy*, by David Smick (Portfolio/Penguin); *Going to See the Elephant*, by Rodes Fishburne (Delacorte/Random House); *Seducing the Boys Club: Uncensored Tactics from a Woman at the Top*, by Nina DiSesa (Ballantine/Random House); *The Girl from Foreign: A Search for Shipwrecked Ancestors, Forgotten Histories, and a Sense of Home*, by Sadia Shepard (The Penguin Press).
Tips "Spell the agent's name correctly on your query letter."

FULL CIRCLE LITERARY, LLC

7676 Hazard Center Dr., Suite 500, San Diego CA 92108. E-mail: submissions@fullcircleliterary.com. Website: www.fullcircleliterary.com. **Contact:** Lilly Ghahremani, Stefanie Von Borstel. Represents 55 clients. 60% of clients are new/unpublished writers. Currently handles: nonfiction books 70%, novels 10%, juvenile books 20%.

- Before forming Full Circle, Ms. Von Borstel worked in both marketing and editorial capacities at Penguin and Harcourt; Ms. Ghahremani received her law degree from UCLA, and has experience in representing authors on legal affairs.

Member Agents Lilly Ghahremani (young adult, pop culture, crafts, "green" living, narrative nonfiction, business, relationships, Middle Eastern interest, multicultural); Stefanie Von Borstel (Latino interest, crafts, parenting, wedding/relationships, how-to, self-help, middle grade/teen fiction/YA, green living, multicultural/bilingual picture books); Adriana Dominguez (fiction areas of interest: children's books - picture books, middle grade novels, and (literary) young adult novels; on the adult side, she is looking for literary, women's, and historical fiction.Nonfiction areas of interest: multicultural, pop culture, how-to, and titles geared toward women of all ages).
Represents Nonfiction books, juvenile. **Considers these nonfiction areas:** animals, autobiography, biography, business, child guidance, crafts, cultural interests, current affairs, dance, diet/nutrition, ethnic, foods, health, hobbies, how-to, humor, juvenile nonfiction, medicine, parenting, popular culture, satire, self-help, women's issues, women's studies. **Considers these fiction areas:** ethnic, literary, young adult.

- "Our full-service boutique agency, representing a range of nonfiction and children's books (limited fiction), provides a one-stop resource for authors. Our extensive experience in the realms of law and marketing provide Full Circle clients with a unique edge." "Actively seeking nonfiction by authors with a unique and strong platform, projects that offer new and diverse viewpoints, and literature with a global or multicultural perspective. We are particularly interested in books with a Latino or Middle Eastern angle and books related to pop culture." Does not want to receive "screenplays, poetry, commercial fiction or genre fiction (horror, thriller, mystery, Western, sci-fi, fantasy, romance, historical fiction)."

How to Contact Agency accepts e-queries. See website for fiction guidelines, as they are in flux. For nonfiction, send full proposal Accepts simultaneous submissions. Responds in 1-2 weeks to queries. Responds in 4-6 weeks to mss. Obtains most new clients through recommendations from others, solicitations, conferences.
Terms Agent receives 15% commission on domestic sales. Agent receives 20% commission on foreign sales. Offers written contract; up to 30-day notice must be given to terminate contract. Charges for copying and postage.
Tips "Put your best foot forward. Contact us when you simply can't make your project any better on your own, and please be sure your work fits with what the agent you're approaching represents. Little things count, so copyedit your work. Join a writing group and attend conferences to get objective and constructive feedback before submitting. Be active about building your platform as an author before, during, and after publication. Remember this is a business and your agent is a business partner."

DON GASTWIRTH & ASSOCIATES

265 College St., New Haven CT 06510. (203)562-7600. Fax: (203)562-4300. E-mail: Donlit@snet.net. **Contact:** Don Gastwirth. Signatory of WGA. Represents 26 clients. 10% of clients are new/unpublished writers. Currently handles: nonfiction books 30%, scholarly books 60%, other 10% other.

- Prior to becoming an agent, Mr. Gastwirth was an entertainment lawyer and law professor.

Represents Nonfiction books, scholarly. **Considers these nonfiction areas:** business, current affairs, history, military, money, music, nature, popular culture, psychology, translation, true crime. **Considers these fiction areas:** mystery, thriller.

O- This is a selective agency and is rarely open to new clients that do not come through a referral.

How to Contact Query with SASE.

Terms Agent receives 15% commission on domestic sales. Agent receives 10% commission on foreign sales.

GELFMAN SCHNEIDER LITERARY AGENTS, INC.

250 W. 57th St., Suite 2122, New York NY 10107. (212)245-1993. Fax: (212)245-8678. E-mail: mail@gelfmanschneider.com. **Contact:** Jane Gelfman, Deborah Schneider. Member of AAR. Represents 300+ clients. 10% of clients are new/unpublished writers.

Represents Fiction and nonfiction books. **Considers these fiction areas:** literary, mainstream, mystery, women's.

O- Does not want to receive romance, science fiction, westerns, or children's books.

How to Contact Query with SASE. Send queries via snail mail only. Responds in 1 month to queries. Responds in 2 months to mss.

Terms Agent receives 15% commission on domestic sales. Agent receives 20% commission on foreign sales. Agent receives 15% commission on film sales. Offers written contract. Charges clients for photocopying and messengers/couriers.

BARRY GOLDBLATT LITERARY, LLC

320 Seventh Ave., #266, Brooklyn NY 11215. Fax: (718)360-5453. Website: www.bgliterary.com/contactme.html. **Contact:** Barry Goldblatt. Member of AAR. SCBWI

Member Agents Barry Goldblatt, Joe Monti, Beth Fleisher (kids work and graphic novels; she is particularly interested in finding new voices in middle grade and young adult fantasy, science fiction, mystery, historicals and action adventure).

Represents Juvenile books. **Considers these fiction areas:** picture books, young adult, middle grade, all genres.

O- This agency specializes in children's books of all kinds.

How to Contact E-mail queries query@bgliterary.com, and include the first five pages and a synopsis of the novel pasted into the text of the e-mail. No attachments or links.

Recent Sales *The Infernal Devices* trilogy, by Cassandra Clare (McElderry Books); *Kat by Moonlight* trilogy, by Stephanie Burgis (Atheneum Books), *Giving Up a Ghost*, by Samantha Schutz (Scholastic).

THE SUSAN GOLOMB LITERARY AGENCY

875 Avenue of the Americas, Suite 2302, New York NY 10001. Fax: (212)239-9503. E-mail: susan@sgolombagency.com. **Contact:** Susan Golomb. Represents 100 clients. 20% of clients are new/unpublished writers. Currently handles: nonfiction books 50%, novels 40%, story collections 10%.

Member Agents Susan Golomb (accepts queries); Sabine Hrechdakian (accepts queries); Kim Goldstein (no unsolicited queries).

Represents Nonfiction books, novels, short story collections, novellas. **Considers these nonfiction areas:** animals, anthropology, archeology, autobiography, biography, business, current affairs, economics, environment, government, health, history, law, memoirs, military, money, popular culture, politics, psychology, science, sociology, technology, war, women's issues, women's studies.

Considers these fiction areas: ethnic, historical, humor, literary, mainstream, satire, thriller, women's, young adult, chick lit.

- "We specialize in literary and upmarket fiction and nonfiction that is original, vibrant and of excellent quality and craft. Nonfiction should be edifying, paradigm-shifting, fresh and entertaining." Actively seeking writers with strong voices. Does not want to receive genre fiction.

How to Contact Query with SASE. Submit outline/proposal, synopsis, 1 sample chapters, author bio, SASE. Query via mail or e-mail. Responds in 2 week to queries. Responds in 8 weeks to mss. Obtains most new clients through recommendations from others, solicitations.

Terms Agent receives 15% commission on domestic sales. Agent receives 20% commission on foreign sales. Offers written contract.

Recent Sales Sold 20 titles in the last year. *Sunnyside*, by Glen David Gold (Knopf); *How to Buy a Love of Reading*, by Tanya Egan Gibson (Dutton); *Telex From Cuba*, by Rachel Kushner (Scribner); *The Imperfectionists,* by Tom Rachman (Dial).

IRENE GOODMAN LITERARY AGENCY

27 W. 24th Street, Suite 700B, New York NY 10010. E-mail: queries@irenegoodman.com. Website: www.irenegoodman.com. **Contact:** Irene Goodman, Miriam Kriss. Member of AAR.

Member Agents Irene Goodman; Miriam Kriss; Barbara Poelle; Jon Sternfeld.

Represents Nonfiction books, novels. **Considers these nonfiction areas:** narrative nonfiction dealing with social, cultural and historical issues; an occasional memoir and current affairs book, parenting, social issues, francophilia, anglophilia, Judaica, lifestyles, cooking, memoir. **Considers these fiction areas:** historical, intelligent literary, modern urban fantasies, mystery, romance, thriller, women's.

- "Specializes in the finest in commercial fiction and nonfiction. We have a strong background in women's voices, including mysteries, romance, women's fiction, thrillers, suspense. Historical fiction is one of Irene's particular passions and Miriam is fanatical about modern urban fantasies. In nonfiction, Irene is looking for topics on narrative history, social issues and trends, education, Judaica, Francophilia, Anglophilia, other cultures, animals, food, crafts, and memoir." Barbara is looking for commercial thrillers with strong female protagonists; Miriam is looking for urban fantasy and edgy sci-fi/young adult.

How to Contact Query. Submit synopsis, first 10 pages. E-mail queries only! See the website submission page. No e-mail attachments. Responds in 2 months to queries.

Recent Sales *The Ark*, by Boyd Morrison; *Isolation*, by C.J. Lyons; *The Sleepwalkers*, by Paul Grossman; *Dead Man's Moon*, by Devon Monk; *Becoming Marie Antoinette*, by Juliet Grey; *What's Up Down There*, by Lissa Rankin; *Beg for Mercy*, by Toni Andrews; *The Devil Inside*, by Jenna Black.

Tips "We are receiving an unprecedented amount of email queries. If you find that the mailbox is full, please try again in two weeks. Email queries to our personal addresses will not be answered. Emails to our personal in-boes will be deleted."

SANFORD J. GREENBURGER ASSOCIATES, INC.

55 Fifth Ave., New York NY 10003. (212)206-5600. Fax: (212)463-8718. E-mail: queryHL@sjga.com. Website: www.greenburger.com. Member of AAR. Represents 500 clients.

Member Agents Heide Lange; Faith Hamlin; Dan Mandel; Matthew Bialer; Courtney Miller-Callihan, Michael Harriot, Brenda Bowen (authors and illustrators of children's books for all ages as well as graphic novelists); Lisa Gallagher.

Represents Nonfiction books and novels. **Considers these nonfiction areas:** Americana, animals, anthropology, archeology, architecture, art, biography, business, computers, cooking, crafts, current affairs, decorating, diet/nutrition, design, education, environment, ethnic, film, foods, gardening, gay/lesbian, government, health, history, horticulture, how-to, humor, interior design, investigative, juvenile nonfiction, language, law, literature, medicine, memoirs, metaphysics, military, money, multicultural, music, New Age, philosophy, photography, popular culture, psychology, recreation, regional, science, sex, sociology, software, sports, theater, translation, travel, true crime, women's issues, women's studies, young adult, software. **Considers these fiction areas:** action, adventure, crime, detective, ethnic, family saga, feminist, gay, glitz, historical, humor, lesbian, literary, mainstream, mystery, police, psychic, regional, satire, sports, supernatural, suspense, thriller.

O→ No romances or Westerns.

How to Contact Submit query, first 3 chapters, synopsis, brief bio, SASE. Accepts simultaneous submissions. Responds in 2 months to queries and mss. Responds to mss. Obtains most new clients through recommendations from others.

Terms Agent receives 15% commission on domestic sales. Agent receives 20% commission on foreign sales. Charges for photocopying and books for foreign and subsidiary rights submissions.

THE GREENHOUSE LITERARY AGENCY

11308 Lapham Drive, Oakton VA 22124. E-mail: submissions@greenhouseliterary.com. Website: www.greenhouseliterary.com. **Contact:** Sarah Davies. Other memberships include SCBWI. Represents 20 clients. 100% of clients are new/unpublished writers. Currently handles: juvenile books 100%.

- Prior to becoming an agent, Ms. Davies was the publishing director of Macmillan Children's Books in London.

Represents Juvenile. **Considers these fiction areas:** juvenile, young adult.

O→ "We exclusively represents authors writing fiction for children and teens. The agency has offices in both the USA and UK, and Sarah Davies (who is British) personally represents authors to both markets. The agency's commission structure reflects this – taking 15% for sales to both US and UK, thus treating both as 'domestic' market." All genres of children's and YA fiction - ages 5+. Does not want to receive nonfiction, poetry, picture books (text or illustration) or work aimed at adults.

How to Contact E-queries only as per guidelines given on website. Query should contain one-paragraph synopsis, one-paragraph bio, up to 5 sample pages pasted into e-mail. Replies to all submissions mostly within 2 weeks, but leave 6 weeks before chasing for response. Responds in 6-8 weeks to requested full manuscripts. Responds in 6 week to queries. Obtains most new clients through recommendations from others, solicitations, conferences.

Terms Agent receives 15% commission on domestic sales. Agent receives 25% commission on foreign sales. Offers written contract. This agency charges very occasionally for copies for submission to film agents or foreign publishers.

Writers Conferences Bologna Children's Book Fair, SCBWI conferences, BookExpo America.

Tips "Before submitting material, authors should read the Greenhouse's 'Top 10 Tips for Authors of Children's Fiction,' which can be found on our website."

KATHRYN GREEN LITERARY AGENCY, LLC

250 West 57th St., Suite 2302, New York NY 10107. (212)245-2445. Fax: (212)245-2040. E-mail: query@kgreenagency.com. **Contact:** Kathy Green. Other memberships include Women's Media Group. Represents approximately 20 clients. 50% of clients are new/unpublished writers. Currently handles: nonfiction books 50%, novels 25%, juvenile books 25%.

- Prior to becoming an agent, Ms. Green was a book and magazine editor.

Represents Nonfiction books, novels, short story collections, juvenile, middle grade and young adult only). **Considers these nonfiction areas:** autobiography, biography, business, child guidance, cooking, current affairs, diet/nutrition, economics, education, foods, history, how-to, humor, interior design, investigative, juvenile nonfiction, memoirs, parenting, popular culture, psychology, satire, self-help, sports, true crime, women's issues, women's studies, juvenile. **Considers these fiction areas:** crime, detective, family saga, historical, humor, juvenile, literary, mainstream, mystery, police, romance, satire, suspense, thriller, women's, young adult, women's.

O→ Keeping the client list small means that writers receive my full attention throughout the process of getting their project published. Does not want to receive science fiction or fantasy.

How to Contact Query to query@kgreenagency.com. Send no samples unless requested. Accepts simultaneous submissions. Responds in 1-2 months to mss. Obtains most new clients through recommendations from others, solicitations, conferences.

Terms Agent receives 15% commission on domestic sales. Agent receives 20% commission on foreign sales. No written contract.
Recent Sales *The Touch Series,* by Laurie Stolarz; *How Do You Light a Fart*, by Bobby Mercer; *Creepiosity*, by David Bickel; *Hidden Facets: Diamonds For the Dead,* by Alan Orloff; *Don't Stalk the Admissions Officer*, by Risa Lewak; *Designed Fat Girl*, by Jennifer Joyner.
Tips "This agency offers a written agreement."

GREGORY & CO. AUTHORS' AGENTS

3 Barb Mews, Hammersmith, London W6 7PA England. (44)(207)610-4676. Fax: (44)(207)610-4686. E-mail: info@gregoryandcompany.co.uk. Website: www.gregoryandcompany.co.uk. **Contact:** Jane Gregory. Other memberships include AAA. Represents 60 clients. Currently handles: nonfiction books 10%, novels 90%.
Member Agents Stephanie Glencross.
Represents Nonfiction books, novels. **Considers these nonfiction areas:** autobiography, biography, history. **Considers these fiction areas:** crime, detective, historical, literary, mainstream, police, thriller, contemporary women's fiction.

- As a British agency, we do not generally take on American authors. Actively seeking well-written, accessible modern novels. Does not want to receive horror, science fiction, fantasy, mind/body/spirit, children's books, screenplays, plays, short stories or poetry.

How to Contact Query with SASE. Submit outline, first 10 pages by email or post, publishing history, author bio. Send submissions to Mary Jones, submissions editor: maryjones@gregoryandcompany.co.uk Accepts simultaneous submissions. Returns materials only with SASE. Obtains most new clients through recommendations from others, conferences.
Terms Agent receives 15% commission on domestic sales. Agent receives 20% commission on foreign sales. Offers written contract; 1-month notice must be given to terminate contract. Charges clients for photocopying of whole typescripts and copies of book for submissions.
Recent Sales *Ritual*, by Mo Hader (Bantam UK/Grove Atlantic); *A Darker Domain*, by Val McDermid (HarperCollins UK); *The Chameleon's Shadow*, by Minette Walters (Macmillan UK/ Knopf Inc); *Stratton's War*, by Laura Wilson (Orion UK/St. Martin's).
Writers Conferences CWA Conference; Bouchercon.

JILL GROSJEAN LITERARY AGENCY

1390 Millstone Road, Sag Harbor NY 11963-2214. (631)725-7419. Fax: (631)725-8632. E-mail: jill6981@aol.com. **Contact:** Jill Grosjean. Represents 40 clients. 100% of clients are new/ unpublished writers. Currently handles: novels 100%.

- Prior to becoming an agent, Ms. Grosjean was manager of an independent bookstore. She has also worked in publishing and advertising.

Represents Novels. **Considers these fiction areas:** historical, literary, mainstream, mystery, regional, romance, suspense.

- This agency offers some editorial assistance (i.e., line-by-line edits). Actively seeking literary novels and mysteries.

How to Contact E-mail queries only, no attachments. No cold calls, please. Accepts simultaneous submissions. Responds in 1 week to queries. Responds in 1 month to mss. Obtains most new clients through recommendations from others, solicitations.
Terms Agent receives 15% commission on domestic sales. Agent receives 20% commission on foreign sales. No written contract. Charges clients for photocopying and mailing expenses.
Recent Sales *Single Thread* and *Thread of Truth, A Thread So Thin, Snow Angels*, by Marie Bostwick (Kensington); *Greasing the Pinata* and *Jump*, by Tim Maleeny (Poison Pen Press); *Stealing the Dragon and Beating the Babushka, Midnight Ink, Emma and the Vampires*, by Wayne Josephson; *Shame and No Idea*, by Greg Garrett, David C. Cook; *The Reluctant Journey* of David Conners; *The Summer the Wind Whispered My Name*, by Don Locke; *Cyber Crime Fighters*, by Felicia Donovan and Kristyn Bernier.
Writers Conferences Book Passage's Mystery Writers' Conference; Agents and Editors Conference; Texas Writers' and Agents' Conference.

LAURA GROSS LITERARY AGENCY

75 Clinton Pl., Newton MA 02459. (617)964-2977. Fax: (617)964-3023. E-mail: query@lauragrossliteraryagency.com; lgross@lauragrossliteraryagency.com. **Contact:** Laura Gross. Represents 30 clients. Currently handles: nonfiction books 40%, novels 50%, scholarly books 10%.

- Prior to becoming an agent, Ms. Gross was an editor.

Represents Nonfiction books, novels. **Considers these nonfiction areas:** autobiography, biography, child guidance, cultural interests, current affairs, ethnic, government, health, history, law, medicine, memoirs, parenting, popular culture, politics, psychology, sports, women's issues, women's studies. **Considers these fiction areas:** historical, literary, mainstream, mystery, suspense, thriller.

How to Contact Query with SASE or by email. Submit author bio. Responds in several days to queries. Obtains most new clients through recommendations from others.

Terms Agent receives 15% commission on domestic sales. Agent receives 20% commission on foreign sales. Offers written contract.

HALSTON FREEMAN LITERARY AGENCY, INC.

140 Broadway, 46th Floor, New York NY 10005. E-mail: queryhalstonfreemanliterary@hotmail.com. **Contact:** Molly Freeman, Betty Halston. Currently handles: nonfiction books 65%, novels 35%.

- Prior to becoming an agent, Ms. Halston was a marketing and promotion director for a local cable affiliate; Ms. Freeman was a television film editor and ad agency copywriter.

Member Agents Molly Freeman, Betty Halston.

Represents Nonfiction books, novels. **Considers these nonfiction areas:** autobiography, biography, business, child guidance, cultural interests, current affairs, economics, ethnic, gay/lesbian, government, health, history, horticulture, how-to, humor, investigative, law, medicine, memoirs, metaphysics, New Age, parenting, politics, psychology, satire, self-help, true crime, women's issues, women's studies. **Considers these fiction areas:** action, adventure, crime, detective, ethnic, feminist, frontier, historical, horror, humor, literary, mainstream, mystery, police, romance, satire, science fiction, suspense, thriller, westerns, women's.

- "We are a hands-on agency specializing in quality nonfiction and fiction. As a new agency, it is imperative that we develop relationships with good writers who are smart, hardworking and understand what's required of them to promote their books." Does not want to receive children's books, textbooks or poetry. Send no e-mail attachments.

How to Contact Query with SASE. For nonfiction, include sample chapters, synopsis, platform, bio and competitive titles. For fiction, include synopsis, bio and three sample chapters. No e-mail attachments. Accepts simultaneous submissions. Responds in 2-6 weeks to queries. Responds in 1-2 months to mss. Obtains most new clients through recommendations from others, solicitations, conferences.

Terms Agent receives 15% commission on domestic sales. Agent receives 20% commission on foreign sales. This agency charges clients for copying and postage directly related to the project.

HALYARD LITERARY AGENCY

Chicago IL E-mail: submissions@halyardagency.com. Website: www.halyardagency.com. **Contact:** Alaina Grayson.

Member Agents Alaina Grayson.

Represents Nonfiction books, novels. **Considers these nonfiction areas:** autobiography, biography, history, science, technology. **Considers these fiction areas:** fantasy, historical, juvenile, science fiction, young adult, general, paranormal.

- Based out of Chicago, Halyard Literary Agency is a new agency on the lookout for authors who have the same passion for innovation that we do. Halyard is small, but provides assistance through every stage of book production. We're dedicated to building relationships with our authors, not just for one book or one year, but throughout their publishing life.

How to Contact *Closed to all submissions*. Query with SASE. E-mail queries only to submissions@halyardagency.com. Send requested materials as e-mail attachments only if requested from query.

THE MITCHELL J. HAMILBURG AGENCY

149 S. Barrington Ave., #732, Los Angeles CA 90049. (310)471-4024. Fax: (310)471-9588. **Contact:** Michael Hamilburg. Estab. 1937. Signatory of WGA. Represents 70 clients. Currently handles: nonfiction books 70%, novels 30%.

Represents Nonfiction books, novels. **Considers these nonfiction areas:** anthropology, biography, business, child, cooking, current affairs, education, government, health, history, memoirs, military, money, psychology, recreation, regional, self-help, sex, sociology, spirituality, sports, travel, women's, creative nonfiction; romance; architecture; inspirational; true crime. **Considers these fiction areas:** glitz, New Age, adventure, experimental, feminist, humor, military, mystery, occult, regional, religious, romance, sports, thriller, crime; mainstream; psychic.

How to Contact Query with outline, 2 sample chapters, SASE. Responds in 1 month to mss. Obtains most new clients through recommendations from others, conferences, personal search.

Terms Agent receives 10-15% commission on domestic sales.

☑ HARTLINE LITERARY AGENCY

123 Queenston Dr., Pittsburgh PA 15235-5429. (412)829-2483. Fax: (412)829-2432. E-mail: joyce@hartlineliterary.com. Website: www.hartlineliterary.com. **Contact:** Joyce A. Hart. Represents 40 clients. 20% of clients are new/unpublished writers. Currently handles: nonfiction books 40%, novels 60%.

Member Agents Joyce A. Hart, principal agent; Terry Burns; Tamela Hancock Murray; Diana Flegal.

Represents Nonfiction books, novels. **Considers these nonfiction areas:** business, child guidance, cooking, diet/nutrition, economics, foods, inspirational, money, parenting, religious, self-help, women's issues, women's studies. **Considers these fiction areas:** action, adventure, contemporary issues, family saga, historical, inspirational, literary, mystery, regional, religious, suspense, thriller, amateur sleuth, cozy, contemporary, gothic, historical, and regency romances.

- This agency specializes in the Christian bookseller market. Actively seeking adult fiction, self-help, nutritional books, devotional, and business. Does not want to receive erotica, gay/lesbian, fantasy, horror, etc.

How to Contact Submit summary/outline, author bio, 3 sample chapters. Accepts simultaneous submissions. Responds in 2 months to queries. Responds in 3 months to mss. Obtains most new clients through recommendations from others.

Terms Agent receives 15% commission on domestic sales. Offers written contract.

Recent Sales Aurora, An American Experience in Quilt, Community and Craft, and A Flickering Light, by Jane Kirkpatrick (Waterbrook Multnomah); Oprah Doesn't Know My Name, by Jane Kirkpatric (Zondervan); Paper Roses, Scattered Petals, and Summer Rains, by Amanda Cabot (Revell Books); Blood Ransom, by Lisa Harris (Zondervan); I Don't Want a Divorce, by David Clark (Revell Books); Love Finds You in Hope, Kansas, by Pamela Griffin (Summerside Press); Journey to the Well, by Diana Wallis Taylor (Revell Books); Paper Bag Christmas, The Nine Lessons, by Kevin Milne (Center Street); When Your Aging Parent Needs Care, by Arrington & Atchley (Harvest House); Katie at Sixteen, by Kim Vogel Sawyer (Zondervan); A Promise of Spring, by Kim Vogel Sawyer (Bethany House); The Big 5-OH!, by Sandra Bricker (Abingdon Press); A Silent Terror & A Silent Stalker, by Lynette Eason (Steeple Hill); Extreme Devotion series, by Kathi Macias (New Hope Publishers); On the Wings of the Storm, by Tamira Barley (Whitaker House); Tribute, by Graham Garrison (Kregel Publications); The Birth to Five Book, by Brenda Nixon (Revell Books); Fat to Skinny Fast and Easy, by Doug Varrieur (Sterling Publishers).

☑ JOHN HAWKINS & ASSOCIATES, INC.

71 W. 23rd St., Suite 1600, New York NY 10010. (212)807-7040. Fax: (212)807-9555. E-mail: jha@jhalit.com. Website: www.jhalit.com. **Contact:** Moses Cardona (moses@jhalit.com). Member of AAR. Represents over 100 clients. 5-10% of clients are new/unpublished writers. Currently handles: nonfiction books 40%, novels 40%, juvenile books 20%.

Member Agents Moses Cardona; Anne Hawkins (ahawkins@jhalit.com); Warren Frazier (frazier@jhalit.com); William Reiss (reiss@jhalit.com).

Represents Nonfiction books, novels, young adult. **Considers these nonfiction areas:** agriculture, Americana, anthropology, archeology, architecture, art, autobiography, biography, business, cultural interests, current affairs, design, economics, education, ethnic, film, gardening, gay/lesbian, government, health, history, horticulture, how-to, investigative, language, law, medicine, memoirs, money, multicultural, music, philosophy, popular culture, politics, psychology, recreation, science, self-help, sex, sociology, software, theater, travel, true crime, young adult, music, creative nonfiction. **Considers these fiction areas:** action, adventure, crime, detective, ethnic, experimental, family saga, feminist, frontier, gay, glitz, hi-lo, historical, inspirational, lesbian, literary, mainstream, military, multicultural, multimedia, mystery, police, psychic, religious, short story collections, sports, supernatural, suspense, thriller, translation, war, westerns, women's, young adult.

How to Contact Submit query, proposal package, outline, SASE. Accepts simultaneous submissions. Responds in 1 month to queries. Obtains most new clients through recommendations from others.

Terms Agent receives 15% commission on domestic sales. Agent receives 20% commission on foreign sales. Charges clients for photocopying.

Recent Sales *Celebration of Shoes*, by Eileen Spinelli; *Chaos*, by Martin Gross; *The Informationist*, by Taylor Stevens; *The Line*, by Olga Grushin

HIDDEN VALUE GROUP

1240 E. Ontario Ave., Ste. 102-148, Corona CA 92881. (951)549-8891. Fax: (951)549-8891. E-mail: bookquery@hiddenvaluegroup.com. Website: www.hiddenvaluegroup.com. **Contact:** Nancy Jernigan. Represents 55 clients. 10% of clients are new/unpublished writers.

Member Agents Jeff Jernigan, jjernigan@hiddenvaluegroup.com (men's nonfiction, fiction, Bible studies/curriculum, marriage and family); Nancy Jernigan, njernigan@hiddenvaluegroup.com (nonfiction, women's issues, inspiration, marriage and family, fiction).

Represents Nonfiction books and adult fiction. **Considers these nonfiction areas:** autobiography, biography, business, child guidance, economics, history, how-to, inspirational, juvenile nonfiction, language, literature, memoirs, money, parenting, psychology, religious, self-help, women's issues, women's studies. **Considers these fiction areas:** action, adventure, crime, detective, fantasy, frontier, inspirational, literary, police, religious, thriller, westerns, women's.

- "The Hidden Value Group specializes in helping authors throughout their publishing career. We believe that every author has a special message to be heard and we specialize in getting that message out." Actively seeking established fiction authors, and authors who are focusing on women's issues. Does not want to receive poetry or short stories.

How to Contact Query with SASE. Submit synopsis, 2 sample chapters, author bio, and marketing and speaking summary. Accepts queries to bookquery@hiddenvaluegroup.com. No fax queries. Accepts simultaneous submissions. Responds in 1 month to queries. Responds in 1 month to mss. Obtains most new clients through recommendations from others, solicitations.

Terms Agent receives 15% commission on domestic sales. Agent receives 15% commission on foreign sales. Offers written contract.

Writers Conferences Glorieta Christian Writers' Conference; CLASS Publishing Conference.

HOPKINS LITERARY ASSOCIATES

2117 Buffalo Rd., Suite 327, Rochester NY 14624-1507. (585)352-6268. **Contact:** Pam Hopkins. Member of AAR. Other memberships include RWA. Represents 30 clients. 5% of clients are new/unpublished writers. Currently handles: novels 100%.

Represents Novels. **Considers these fiction areas:** mostly women's genre romance, historical, contemporary, category, women's.

- This agency specializes in women's fiction, particularly historical, contemporary, and category romance, as well as mainstream work.

How to Contact Regular mail with synopsis, 3 sample chapters, SASE. Accepts simultaneous submissions. Responds in 2 weeks to queries. Responds in 1 month to mss. Obtains most new clients through recommendations from others, solicitations, conferences.

Terms Agent receives 15% commission on domestic sales. Agent receives 20% commission on foreign sales. No written contract.
Recent Sales Sold 50 titles in the last year. *The Wilting Bloom Series*, by Madeline Hunter (Berkley); *The Dead Travel Fast*, by Deanna Raybourn; *Baggage Claim*, by Tanya Michna (NAL).
Writers Conferences RWA National Conference.

ANDREA HURST LITERARY MANAGEMENT

P.O. Box 19010, Sacramento CA 95819. E-mail: andrea@andreahurst.com. Website: www.andreahurst.com. **Contact:** Andrea Hurst, Judy Mikalonis, Amberly Finarelli, Gordon Warnock. Represents 100+ clients. 50% of clients are new/unpublished writers. Currently handles: nonfiction books 50%, novels 50%.

- Prior to becoming an agent, Ms. Hurst was an acquisitions editor as well as a freelance editor and published writer; Ms. Mikalonis was in marketing and branding consulting; Amberly Finarelli was a freelance editor, and Gordon Warnock was a freelance editor and marketing consultant.

Member Agents Andrea Hurst, andrea@andreahurst.com (adult fiction, women's fiction, nonfiction—including personal growth, health and wellness, science, business, parenting, relationships, women's issues, animals, spirituality, women's issues, metaphysical, psychological, cookbooks and self-help); Judy Mikalonis, judy@andreahurst.com (YA fiction, Christian fiction, Christian nonfiction); Amberly Finarelli, amberly@andreahurst.com (Nonfiction: humor/gift books, crafts, how-to, Relationships/advice, Self-help, psychology, Travel writing, Narrative nonfiction. Fiction: Commercial women's fiction, Comic and cozy mysteries, Literary fiction with a focus on the arts, culture, and/or history, Contemporary young adult); Represents nonfiction books. Considers these nonfiction areas: crafts, interior, juvenile, newage, animals, art, biography, business, child, cooking, education, health, humor, memoirs, military, money, music, business, child. Represents nonfiction books, true crime, women's, giftbooks, nature, photography, popular culture, psychology, religion, science, self-help, sociology, true crime, women's, giftbooks. Gordon Warnock, gordon@andreahurst.com, PO Box 29380, Sacramento CA 95829. Gordon represents nonfiction: Memoir, political and current affairs, health, humor and cookbooks. Fiction: Commercial narrative with a literary edge. Writers Conferences: San Francisco Writers Conference, Willamette, American Independent Writers Conference, Wyoming Writers Conference, East of Eden, Algonkian Write and Pitch.
Represents Nonfiction books, novels, juvenile. **Considers these fiction areas:** inspirational, juvenile, literary, mainstream, psychic, religious, romance, supernatural, thriller, women's, young adult.

- "We work directly with our signed authors to help them polish their work and their platform for optimum marketability. Our staff is always available to answer phone calls and e-mails from our authors and we stay with a project until we have exhausted all publishing avenues." Actively seeking "well written nonfiction by authors with a strong platform; superbly crafted fiction with depth that touches the mind and heart and all of our listed subjects." Does not want to receive sci-fi, horror, Western, poetry or screenplays.

How to Contact Email query with SASE. Submit outline/proposal, synopsis, 2 sample chapters, author bio. Query a specific agent after reviewing website. Use (agentfirstname)@andreahurst.com Accepts simultaneous submissions. Obtains most new clients through recommendations from others, solicitations, conferences.
Terms Agent receives 15% commission on domestic sales. Agent receives 20% commission on foreign sales. Offers written contract, binding for 6 to 12 months; 30-day notice must be given to terminate contract. This agency charges for postage. No reading fees. Visit our new blog. www.andreahurst.com
Recent Sales *A Year of Miracles*, by Dr. Bernie Siegel, NWL; *Selling Your Crafts on Etsy* (St. Martins); *The Underground Detective Agency*, (Kensington); *Alaskan Seafood Cookbook*, (Globe Pequot); *Faith, Hope and Healing*, by Dr. Bernie Siegel (Rodale); *Code Name: Polar Ice*, by Jean-

Michel Cousteau and James Fraioli (Gibbs Smith); *How to Host a Killer Party*, by Penny Warner (Berkley/Penguin).

Writers Conferences San Francisco Writers' Conference; Willamette Writers' Conference; PNWA; Whidbey Island Writers Conference.

Tips "Do your homework and submit a professional package. Get to know the agent you are submitting to by researching their website or meeting them at a conference. Perfect your craft: Write well and edit ruthlessly over and over again before submitting to an agent. Be realistic: Understand that publishing is a business and be prepared to prove why your book is marketable and how you will market it on your own. Be Persistent!"

INTERNATIONAL TRANSACTIONS, INC.

P.O. Box 97, Gila NM 88038-0097. (845)373-9696. Fax: (845)373-7868. E-mail: info@intltrans.com. Website: www.intltrans.com. **Contact:** Peter Riva. Represents 40+ clients. 10% of clients are new/unpublished writers. Currently handles: nonfiction books 60%, novels 25%, story collections 5%, juvenile books 5%, scholarly books 5%.

Member Agents Peter Riva (nonfiction, fiction, illustrated; television and movie rights placement); Sandra Riva (fiction, juvenile, biographies); JoAnn Collins (fiction, women's fiction, medical fiction).

Represents Nonfiction books, novels, short story collections, juvenile, scholarly, illustrated books, anthologies. **Considers these nonfiction areas:** anthropology, archeology, architecture, art, autobiography, biography, computers, cooking, cultural interests, current affairs, diet/nutrition, design, ethnic, foods, gay/lesbian, government, health, history, humor, investigative, language, law, literature, medicine, memoirs, military, music, photography, politics, satire, science, sports, translation, true crime, war, women's issues, women's studies. **Considers these fiction areas:** action, adventure, crime, detective, erotica, experimental, family saga, feminist, gay, historical, humor, lesbian, literary, mainstream, mystery, police, satire, spiritual, sports, suspense, thriller, women's, young adult, chick lit.

- "We specialize in large and small projects, helping qualified authors perfect material for publication." Actively seeking intelligent, well-written innovative material that breaks new ground. Does not want to receive material influenced by TV (too much dialogue); a rehash of previous successful novels' themes or poorly prepared material.

How to Contact First, e-query with an outline or synopsis. E-queries only!. Responds in 3 weeks to queries. Responds in 5 weeks to mss. Obtains most new clients through recommendations from others, solicitations.

Terms Agent receives 15% (25% on illustrated books) commission on domestic sales. Agent receives 20% commission on foreign sales. Offers written contract; 120-day notice must be given to terminate contract.

Tips "'Book'—a published work of literature. That last word is the key. Not a string of words, not a book of (TV or film) 'scenes,' and never a stream of consciousness unfathomable by anyone outside of the writer's coterie. A writer should only begin to get 'interested in getting an agent' if the work is polished, literate and ready to be presented to a publishing house. Anything less is either asking for a quick rejection or is a thinly disguised plea for creative assistance—which is often given but never fiscally sound for the agents involved. Writers, even published authors, have difficulty in being objective about their own work. Friends and family are of no assistance in that process either. Writers should attempt to get their work read by the most unlikely and stern critic as part of the editing process, months before any agent is approached. In another matter: the economics of our job have changed as well. As the publishing world goes through the transition to e-books (much as the music industry went through the change to downloadable music) - a transition we expect to see at 95% within 10 years - everyone is nervou and wants "assured bestsellers" from which to eke out a living until they know what the new e-world will bring. This makes the sales rate and, especially, the advance royalty rates, plummet. Hence, our ability to take risks and take on new clients' work is increasingly perilous financially for us and all agents."

JABBERWOCKY LITERARY AGENCY

P.O. Box 4558, Sunnyside NY 11104-0558. (718)392-5985. Website: www.awfulagent.com. **Contact:** Joshua Bilmes. Other memberships include SFWA. Represents 40 clients. 15% of clients are new/unpublished writers. Currently handles: nonfiction books 15%, novels 75%, scholarly books 5%, other 5% other.

Member Agents Joshua Bilmes; Eddie Schneider.

Represents Novels. **Considers these nonfiction areas:** autobiography, biography, business, cooking, current affairs, diet/nutrition, economics, film, foods, gay/lesbian, government, health, history, humor, language, law, literature, medicine, money, popular culture, politics, satire, science, sociology, sports, theater, war, women's issues, women's studies, young adult. **Considers these fiction areas:** action, adventure, contemporary issues, crime, detective, ethnic, family saga, fantasy, gay, glitz, historical, horror, humor, lesbian, literary, mainstream, police, psychic, regional, satire, science fiction, sports, supernatural, thriller.

- This agency represents quite a lot of genre fiction and is actively seeking to increase the amount of nonfiction projects. It does not handle children's or picture books. Book-length material only—no poetry, articles, or short fiction.

How to Contact Query with SASE. Please check our website as there may be times during the year when we are not accepting queries. Query letter only; no manuscript material unless requested. Accepts simultaneous submissions. Responds in 3 weeks to queries. Obtains most new clients through solicitations, recommendation by current clients.

Terms Agent receives 15% commission on domestic sales. Agent receives 20% commission on foreign sales. Offers written contract, binding for 1 year. Charges clients for book purchases, photocopying, international book/ms mailing.

Recent Sales Sold 30 US and 100 foreign titles in the last year. *Dead in the Family*, by Charlaine Harris; *The Way of Kings*, by Brandon Sanderson; *The Desert Spear*, by Peter V. Brett; Oath of Fealty, by Elizabeth Moon. Other clients include Tanya Huff, Simon Green, Jack Campbell, Kat Richardson and Jon Sprunk.

Writers Conferences World SF Convention, September 2009; World Fantasy, October 2009; Boucheron, September 2009; full schedule of appearances can be found on our website.

Tips "In approaching with a query, the most important things to us are your credits and your biographical background to the extent it's relevant to your work. I (and most agents) will ignore the adjectives you may choose to describe your own work."

JCA LITERARY AGENCY

27 West 20th St., New York NY 10011. (212)727-0190. E-mail: tonyouthwaite@yahoo.com. Website: www.jcalit.com. **Contact:** Tony Outhwaithe. Tony's mailing address: Midpoint Trade Books, 27 West 20th Street, New York, NY 10011; Member of AAR. Represents 100 clients.

Member Agents Tony Outhwaite, Tom Cushman.

Represents Nonfiction books, novels. **Considers these nonfiction areas:** autobiography, biography, current affairs, film, government, history, investigative, language, law, literature, memoirs, popular culture, politics, sociology, sports, theater, translation, true crime. **Considers these fiction areas:** action, adventure, contemporary issues, crime, detective, family saga, historical, literary, mainstream, mystery, police, sports, suspense, thriller.

- Does not want to receive screenplays, poetry, children's books, science fiction/fantasy, textbooks, or genre romance.

How to Contact Query with SASE. No unsolicited mss. Materials not returned without proper envelope/postage.

Terms Agent receives 15% commission on domestic sales. Agent receives 20% commission on foreign sales. No written contract.

J DE S ASSOCIATES, INC.

9 Shagbark Road, Wilson Point, South Norwalk CT 06854. (203)838-7571. **Contact:** Jacques de Spoelberch. Represents 50 clients. Currently handles: nonfiction books 50%, novels 50%.

- Prior to opening his agency, Mr. de Spoelberch was an editor with Houghton Mifflin.

Represents Nonfiction books, novels. **Considers these nonfiction areas:** biography, business, cultural interests, current affairs, economics, ethnic, government, health, history, law, medicine, metaphysics, military, New Age, personal improvement, politics, self-help, sociology, sports, translation. **Considers these fiction areas:** crime, detective, frontier, historical, juvenile, literary, mainstream, mystery, New Age, police, suspense, westerns, young adult.
How to Contact Query with SASE. Responds in 2 months to queries. Obtains most new clients through Recommendations from authors and other clients.
Terms Agent receives 15% commission on domestic sales. Agent receives 20% commission on foreign sales. Charges clients for foreign postage and photocopying.

JET LITERARY ASSOCIATES

2570 Camino San Patricio, Santa Fe NM 87505. (505)474-9139. E-mail: etp@jetliterary.com. Website: www.jetliterary.com. **Contact:** Liz Trupin-Pulli. Represents 75 clients. 35% of clients are new/unpublished writers.
Member Agents Liz Trupin-Pulli (adult and YA fiction/nonfiction; romance, mysteries, parenting); Jim Trupin (adult fiction/nonfiction, military history, pop culture); Jessica Trupin, associate agent based in Seattle (adult fiction and nonfiction, children's and young adult, memoir, pop culture.
Represents Nonfiction books, novels, short story collections. **Considers these nonfiction areas:** autobiography, biography, business, child guidance, cultural interests, current affairs, economics, ethnic, gay/lesbian, government, humor, investigative, law, memoirs, military, parenting, popular culture, politics, satire, sports, true crime, war, women's issues, women's studies. **Considers these fiction areas:** action, adventure, crime, detective, erotica, ethnic, gay, glitz, historical, humor, lesbian, literary, mainstream, mystery, police, romance, suspense, thriller, women's, young adult.

- "JET was founded in New York in 1975, so we bring a wealth of knowledge and contacts, as well as quite a bit of expertise to our representation of writers." Actively seeking women's fiction, mysteries and narrative nonfiction. Does not want to receive sci-fi, fantasy, horror, poetry, children's or religious.

How to Contact An e-query is preferred; if sending by snail mail, include an SASE. Responds in 1 week to queries. Responds in 8 weeks to mss. Obtains most new clients through recommendations from others, solicitations, conferences.
Terms Agent receives 15% commission on domestic sales. Agent receives 10% commission on foreign sales. Offers written contract, binding for 3 years. This agency charges for reimbursement of mailing and any photocopying.
Recent Sales Sold 22 books in 2009 including several ghostwriting contracts. Mom-In-chief, by Jamie Woolf (Wiley, 2009); Dangerous Games, by Charlotte Mede (Kensington, 2009); So You Think You Can Spell!, by David Grambs and Ellen Levine (Perigee, 2009); Cut, Drop & Die, by Joanna Campbell Slan (Midnight Ink, 2009).
Writers Conferences Women Writing the West; Southwest Writers Conference; Florida Writers Association Conference.
Tips Do not write 'cute' queries—stick to a straightforward message that includes the title and what your book is about, why you are suited to write this particular book, and what you have written in the past (if anything), along with a bit of a bio.

CAREN JOHNSON LITERARY AGENCY

132 East 43rd St., No. 216, New York NY 10017. Fax: (718)228-8785. E-mail: caren@johnsonlitagency.com. Website: www.johnsonlitagency.com. **Contact:** Caren Johnson Estesen, Elana Roth. Represents 20 clients. 50% of clients are new/unpublished writers. Currently handles: nonfiction books 35%, juvenile books 35%, romance/women's fiction 30%.

- Prior to her current position, Ms. Johnson was with Firebrand Literary and the Peter Rubie Agency.

Member Agents Caren Johnson Estesen, Elana Roth.
Represents Nonfiction books, novels. **Considers these nonfiction areas:** history, popular culture, science, technology. **Considers these fiction areas:** detective, erotica, ethnic, romance, young adult, middle grade, women's fiction.

- Does not want to receive poetry, plays or screenplays/scripts. Elana Roth will consider picture books but is very selective of what she takes on.

How to Contact Query via e-mail only, "directing your query to the appropriate person; responds in 12 weeks to all materials sent. Include 4-5 sample pages withing the body of your email when pitching us. Accepts simultaneous submissions. Responds in 4-6 weeks to queries. Responds in 6-8 weeks to mss. Obtains most new clients through recommendations from others.
Terms Agent receives 15% commission on domestic sales. Agent receives 20% commission on foreign sales. Offers written contract; 30-day notice must be given to terminate contract. This agency charges for postage and photocopying, though the author is consulted before any charges are incurred.
Recent Sales Please check out website for a complete client list.
Writers Conferences RWA National; BookExpo America; SCBWI.

VIRGINIA KIDD AGENCY, INC.

538 E. Harford St., P.O. Box 278, Milford PA 18337. (570)296-6205. Fax: (570)296-7266. Website: www.vk-agency.com. Other memberships include SFWA, SFRA. Represents 80 clients.
Member Agents Christine Cohen.
Represents Novels. **Considers these fiction areas:** fantasy, historical, mainstream, mystery, science fiction, suspense, women's, speculative.

- This agency specializes in science fiction and fantasy.

How to Contact *This agency is not accepting unpublished authors at this time.* Query with SASE. Submit synopsis (1-3 pages), cover letter, first chapter, SASE. Snail mail queries only. Responds in 6 weeks to queries.
Terms Agent receives 15% commission on domestic sales. Agent receives 20-25% commission on foreign sales. Agent receives 20% commission on film sales. Offers written contract; 2-month notice must be given to terminate contract. Charges clients occasionally for extraordinary expenses.
Recent Sales *Sagramanda*, by Alan Dean Foster (Pyr); *Incredible Good Fortune*, by Ursula K. Le Guin (Shambhala); *The Wizard and Soldier of Sidon*, by Gene Wolfe (Tor); *Voices and Powers*, by Ursula K. Le Guin (Harcourt); *Galileo's Children*, by Gardner Dozois (Pyr); *The Light Years Beneath My Feet* and *Running From the Deity*, by Alan Dean Foster (Del Ray); *Chasing Fire*, by Michelle Welch. Other clients include Eleanor Arnason, Ted Chiang, Jack Skillingstead, Daryl Gregory, Patricia Briggs, and the estates for James Tiptree, Jr., Murray Leinster, E.E. "Doc" Smith, R. A. Lafferty.
Tips "If you have a completed novel that is of extraordinary quality, please send us a query."

HARVEY KLINGER, INC.

300 W. 55th St., Suite 11V, New York NY 10019. (212)581-7068. E-mail: queries@harveyklinger.com. Website: www.harveyklinger.com. **Contact:** Harvey Klinger. Member of AAR. Represents 100 clients. 25% of clients are new/unpublished writers. Currently handles: nonfiction books 50%, novels 50%.
Member Agents David Dunton (popular culture, music-related books, literary fiction, young adult, fiction, and memoirs); Sara Crowe (children's and young adult authors, adult fiction and nonfiction, foreign rights sales); Andrea Somberg (literary fiction, commercial fiction, romance, sci-fi/fantasy, mysteries/thrillers, young adult, middle grade, quality narrative nonfiction, popular culture, how-to, self-help, humor, interior design, cookbooks, health/fitness).
Represents Nonfiction books, novels. **Considers these nonfiction areas:** autobiography, biography, cooking, diet/nutrition, foods, health, investigative, medicine, psychology, science, self-help, spirituality, sports, technology, true crime, women's issues, women's studies. **Considers these fiction areas:** action, adventure, crime, detective, family saga, glitz, literary, mainstream, mystery, police, suspense, thriller.

- This agency specializes in big, mainstream, contemporary fiction and nonfiction.

How to Contact Query with SASE. No phone or fax queries. Don't send unsolicited manuscripts or e-mail attachments. Responds in 2 months to queries and mss Obtains most new clients through recommendations from others.

Terms Agent receives 15% commission on domestic sales. Agent receives 25% commission on foreign sales. Offers written contract. Charges for photocopying mss and overseas postage for mss.

Recent Sales *Woman of a Thousand Secrets*, by Barbara Wood; *I am Not a Serial Killer*, by Dan Wells; untitled memoir, by Bob Mould; *Children of the Mist*; by Paula Quinn; *Tutored*, by Allison Whittenberg; *Will You Take Me As I Am*, by Michelle Mercer. Other clients include: George Taber, Terry Kay, Scott Mebus, Jacqueline Kolosov, Jonathan Maberry, Tara Altebrando, Alex McAuley, Eva Nagorski, Greg Kot, Justine Musk, Alex McAuley, Nick Tasler, Ashley Kahn, Barbara De Angelis.

ELAINE KOSTER LITERARY AGENCY, LLC

55 Central Park W., Suite 6, New York NY 10023. (212)362-9488. Fax: (212)712-0164. **Contact:** Elaine Koster, Stephanie Lehmann, Ellen Twaddell. Estab. 1998. Member of AAR. Other memberships include MWA, Author's Guild, Women's Media Group. Represents 40 clients. 10% of clients are new/unpublished writers. Currently handles: nonfiction books 10%, novels 90%.

- Prior to opening her agency, Ms. Koster was president and publisher of Dutton-NAL, part of the Penguin Group.

Represents Nonfiction books, novels. **Considers these nonfiction areas:** autobiography, biography, business, child guidance, cooking, current affairs, diet/nutrition, economics, environment, ethnic, foods, health, history, how-to, medicine, money, parenting, popular culture, psychology, self-help, spirituality, women's issues, women's studies. **Considers these fiction areas:** contemporary issues, crime, detective, ethnic, family saga, feminist, historical, literary, mainstream, mystery, police, regional, suspense, thriller, young adult, chick lit.

O→ This agency specializes in quality fiction and nonfiction. Does not want to receive juvenile, screenplays, or science fiction.

How to Contact Fiction: a query letter (hard copy only) which includes publishing credentials, 3 sample chapters, outline and a SASE. Non-fiction: query letter (hard copy only) with proposal and SASE. Prefers to read materials exclusively. Responds in 3 weeks to queries. Responds in 1 month to mss. Obtains most new clients through recommendations from others.

Terms Agent receives 15% commission on domestic sales. Bills back specific expenses incurred doing business for a client.

Recent Sales The Lost and Forgotten Languages of Shanhai, by Ruiyan Xu (St. Martin's Press);

Tips "We prefer exclusive submissions. Don't e-mail or fax submissions. Please include biographical information and publishing history."

KRAAS LITERARY AGENCY

E-mail: irenekraas@sbcglobal.net. Website: www.kraasliteraryagency.com. **Contact:** Irene Kraas. Represents 35 clients. 75% of clients are new/unpublished writers. Currently handles: novels 100%.

Member Agents Irene Kraas, principal.

Represents Novels. **Considers these fiction areas:** literary, thriller, young adult.

O→ This agency is interested in working with published writers, but that does not mean self-published writers. "Actively seeking psychological thrillers, medical thrillers, some literary fiction and young adult. With each of these areas, I want something new. No Da Vinci Code or Harry Potter ripoffs. I am especially not interested in storylines that include the Mafia or government. Not interested in personal stories of growth, stories about generation hangups and stories about drugs, incest, etc." Does not want to receive short stories, plays or poetry. This agency no longer represents adult fantasy or science fiction.

How to Contact Query and e-mail the first 10 pages of a completed ms. Requires exclusive read on mss. Accepts simultaneous submissions.

Terms Offers written contract.

Tips "I am interested in material - in any genre - that is truly, truly unique."

EDITE KROLL LITERARY AGENCY, INC.

20 Cross St., Saco ME 04072. (207)283-8797. Fax: (207)283-8799. E-mail: ekroll@maine.rr.com. **Contact:** Edite Kroll. Represents 45 clients. 20% of clients are new/unpublished writers. Currently handles: nonfiction books 40%, novels 5%, juvenile books 40%, scholarly books 5%, other.

- Prior to opening her agency, Ms. Kroll served as a book editor and translator.

Represents Nonfiction books, novels, very selective, juvenile, scholarly. **Considers these nonfiction areas:** juvenile, selectively, biography, current affairs, ethnic, gay, government, health, no diet books, humor, memoirs, selectively, popular culture, psychology, religion, selectively, self-help, selectively, women's, issue-oriented nonfiction. **Considers these fiction areas:** juvenile, literary, picture books, young adult, middle grade, adult.

"We represent writers and writer-artists of both adult and children's books. We have a special focus on international feminist writers, women writers and artists who write their own books (including children's and humor books)." Actively seeking artists who write their own books and international feminists who write in English. Does not want to receive genre (mysteries, thrillers, diet, cookery, etc.), photography books, coffee table books, romance or commercial fiction.

How to Contact Query with SASE. Submit outline/proposal, synopsis, 1-2 sample chapters, author bio, entire ms if sending picture book.No phone queries. Responds in 2-4 weeks to queries. Responds in 4-8 weeks to mss. Obtains most new clients through recommendations from others.

Terms Agent receives 15% commission on domestic sales. Agent receives 20% commission on foreign sales. Offers written contract; 30-day notice must be given to terminate contract. Charges clients for photocopying and legal fees with prior approval from writer.

Recent Sales Sold 12 domestic/30 foreign titles in the last year. This agency prefers not to share information on specific sales. Clients include Shel Silverstein estate, Suzy Becker, Geoffrey Hayes, Henrik Drescher, Charlotte Kasl, Gloria Skurzynski, Fatema Mernissa.

Tips "Please do your research so you won't send me books/proposals I specifically excluded."

☐ KT LITERARY, LLC

9249 S. Broadway, #200-543, Highlands Ranch CO 80129. (720)344-4728. Fax: (720)344-4728. E-mail: queries@ktliterary.com. Website: www.ktliterary.com. **Contact:** Kate Schafer Testerman. Member of AAR. Other memberships include SCBWI. Represents 20 clients. 60% of clients are new/unpublished writers. Currently handles: nonfiction books 5%, novels 5%, juvenile books 90%.

- Prior to her current position, Ms. Schafer was an agent with Janklow & Nesbit.

Represents Nonfiction books, novels, juvenile books. **Considers these nonfiction areas:** popular culture. **Considers these fiction areas:** action, adventure, fantasy, historical, juvenile, romance, science fiction, women's, young adult.

"I'm bringing my years of experience in the New York publishing scene, as well as my lifelong love of reading, to a vibrant area for writers, proving that great work can be found, and sold, from anywhere." "Actively seeking brilliant, funny, original middle grade and young adult fiction, both literary and commercial; witty women's fiction (chick lit); and pop-culture, narrative nonfiction. Quirky is good." Does not want picture books, serious nonfiction, and adult literary fiction.

How to Contact E-mail queries only. Responds in 2 weeks to queries. Responds in 2 months to mss. Obtains most new clients through recommendations from others, solicitations, conferences.

Terms Agent receives 15% commission on domestic sales. Agent receives 20% commission on foreign sales. Offers written contract; 30-day notice must be given to terminate contract.

Writers Conferences Various SCBWI conferences, BookExpo.

Tips "If we like your query, we'll ask for (more). Continuing advice is offered regularly on my blog 'Ask Daphne', which can be accessed from my website."

☐ KT PUBLIC RELATIONS & LITERARY SERVICES

1905 Cricklewood Cove, Fogelsville PA 18051. (610)395-6298. Fax: (610)395-6299. Website: www.ktpublicrelations.com; Blog: http://newliteraryagents.blogspot.com. **Contact:** Jon Tienstra.

Represents 12 clients. 75% of clients are new/unpublished writers. Currently handles: nonfiction books 50%, novels 50%.

- Prior to becoming an agent, Kae Tienstra was publicity director for Rodale, Inc. for 13 years and then founded her own publicity agency; Mr. Tienstra joined the firm in 1995 with varied corporate experience and a master's degree in library science.

Member Agents Kae Tienstra (health, parenting, psychology, how-to, women's fiction, general fiction); Jon Tienstra (nature/environment, history, cooking/foods/nutrition, war/military, automotive, health/medicine, gardening, general fiction, science fiction/contemporary fantasy, popular fiction).

Represents Nonfiction books, novels. **Considers these nonfiction areas:** animals, child guidance, cooking, decorating, diet/nutrition, environment, foods, health, history, hobbies, horticulture, how-to, interior design, medicine, military, parenting, popular culture, psychology, science, self-help, technology, interior design/decorating. **Considers these fiction areas:** action, adventure, crime, detective, family saga, historical, literary, mainstream, mystery, police, romance, science fiction, suspense, thriller, contemporary fantasy (no swords or dragons).

O→ "We have worked with a variety of authors and publishers over the years and have learned what individual publishers are looking for in terms of new acquisitions. We are both mad about books and authors and we look forward to finding publishing success for all our clients. Specializes in parenting, history, cooking/foods/nutrition, war, health/medicine, psychology, how-to, gardening, science fiction, contemporary fantasy, women's fiction, and popular fiction." Does not want to see unprofessional material.

How to Contact Query with SASE. Prefers snail mail queries. Will accept e-mail queries. Responds in 3 months to chapters; 6-9 months for mss. Accepts simultaneous submissions. Responds in 4 weeks to queries.

Terms Agent receives 15% commission on domestic sales. Agent receives 20% commission on foreign sales. Offers written contract. Charges clients for long-distance phone calls, fax, postage, photocopying (only when incurred). No advance payment for these out-of-pocket expenses.

THE LA LITERARY AGENCY

P.O. Box 46370, Los Angeles CA 90046. (323)654-5288. E-mail: laliteraryag@mac.com. **Contact:** Ann Cashman, Eric Lasher.

- Prior to becoming an agent, Mr. Lasher worked in publishing in New York and Los Angeles.

Represents Nonfiction books, novels. **Considers these nonfiction areas:** animals, anthropology, archeology, architecture, art, autobiography, biography, business, child guidance, cooking, cultural interests, current affairs, diet/nutrition, design, economics, environment, ethnic, foods, government, health, history, how-to, investigative, law, medicine, parenting, popular culture, politics, psychology, science, self-help, sociology, sports, technology, true crime, women's issues, women's studies, narrative nonfiction. **Considers these fiction areas:** action, adventure, crime, detective, family saga, feminist, historical, literary, mainstream, police, sports, thriller.

How to Contact Query with outline, 1 sample chapter. No fax or e-mail queries.

Recent Sales *Full Bloom: The Art and Life of Georgia O'Keeffe*, by Hunter Druhojowska-Philp (Norton); *And the Walls Came Tumbling Down*, by H. Caldwell (Scribner); *Italian Slow & Savory*, by Joyce Goldstein (Chronicle); *A Field Guide to Chocolate Chip Cookies*, by Dede Wilson (Harvard Common Press); *Teen Knitting Club* (Artisan); *The Framingham Heart Study*, by Dr. Daniel Levy (Knopf).

PETER LAMPACK AGENCY, INC.

551 Fifth Ave., Suite 1613, New York NY 10176-0187. (212)687-9106. Fax: (212)687-9109. E-mail: alampack@verizon.net. **Contact:** Andrew Lampack. Represents 50 clients. 10% of clients are new/unpublished writers. Currently handles: nonfiction books 20%, novels 80%.

Member Agents Peter Lampack (president); Rema Delanyan (foreign rights); Andrew Lampack (new writers).

Represents Nonfiction books, novels. **Considers these fiction areas:** adventure, crime, detective, family saga, literary, mainstream, mystery, police, suspense, thriller, contemporary relationships.

- "This agency specializes in commercial fiction and nonfiction by recognized experts." Actively seeking literary and commercial fiction, thrillers, mysteries, suspense, and psychological thrillers. Does not want to receive horror, romance, science fiction, westerns, historical literary fiction or academic material.

How to Contact Query via e-mail. *No unsolicited mss.* Responds within 2 months to queries. Obtains most new clients through referrals made by clients.

Terms Agent receives 15% commission on domestic sales. Agent receives 20% commission on foreign sales.

Recent Sales *Spartan Gold*, by Clive Cussler with Grant Blackwood; *The Wrecker*, by Clive Cussler with Justin Scott; *Medusa*, by Clive Cussler and Paul Kemprecos; *Silent Sea*, by Clive Cussler with Jack Dubrul; *Summertime*, by J.M. Coetzee; *Dreaming in French*, by Megan McAndrew; *Time Pirate*, by Ted Bell.

Writers Conferences BookExpo America; Mystery Writers of America.

Tips "Submit only your best work for consideration. Have a very specific agenda of goals you wish your prospective agent to accomplish for you. Provide the agent with a comprehensive statement of your credentials - educational and professional accomplishments."

LAURA LANGLIE, LITERARY AGENT

239 Carroll St., Garden Apartment, Brooklyn NY 11231. (718)855-8102. Fax: (718)855-4450. E-mail: laura@lauralanglie.com. **Contact:** Laura Langlie. Represents 25 clients. 50% of clients are new/unpublished writers. Currently handles: nonfiction books 15%, novels 58%, story collections 2%, juvenile books 25%.

- Prior to opening her agency, Ms. Langlie worked in publishing for 7 years and as an agent at Kidde, Hoyt & Picard for 6 years.

Represents Nonfiction books, novels, short story collections, novellas, juvenile. **Considers these nonfiction areas:** autobiography, biography, cultural interests, current affairs, environment, film, history, language, law, literature, memoirs, popular culture, politics, psychology, satire, theater, women's issues, women's studies, history of medicine and science, animals (not how-to). **Considers these fiction areas:** crime, detective, ethnic, feminist, historical, humor, juvenile, literary, mainstream, mystery, police, suspense, thriller, young adult, mainstream.

- "I'm very involved with and committed to my clients. I also employ a publicist to work with all my clients to make the most of each book's publication. Most of my clients come to me via recommendations from other agents, clients and editors. I've met very few at conferences. I've often sought out writers for projects, and I still find new clients via the traditional query letter." Does not want to receive how-to, children's picture books, science fiction, poetry, men's adventure or erotica.

How to Contact Query with SASE. Accepts queries via fax. Accepts simultaneous submissions. Responds in 1 week to queries. Responds in 1 month to mss. Obtains most new clients through recommendations, submissions.

Terms Agent receives 15% commission on domestic sales. Agent receives 20% commission on foreign and dramatic sales. No written contract.

Recent Sales Sold 15 titles in the last year. *Alice I Have Been*, by Melanie Benjamin (Delacorte Press); *Here Lies Linc*, by Delia Ray (Alfred A. Knopf Books for Young Readers); *Livvie Owen Lived Here*, by Sarah Dooley (Feiwel & Friends/Macmillan); *Miss Dimple Disappears*, by Mignon F. Ballard (St. Martin's Press); *Insatiable*, by Meg Cabot (William Morrow); *Gemma*, by Meg Tilly (St. Martin's Press); *Girl's Best Friend*, by Leslie Margolis (Bloomsbury); *The Elite Gymnasts*, by Dominique Moceanu and Alicia Thompson (Disney/Hyperion); *Safe From the Sea*, by Peter Geye (Unbridled Books).

Tips "Be complete, forthright and clear in your communications. Do your research as to what a particular agent represents."

LANGTONS INTERNATIONAL AGENCY

124 West 60th St., #42M, New York NY 10023. (646)344-1801. E-mail: langtonsinternational@gmail.com. Website: www.langtonsinternational.com. **Contact:** Linda Langton, President.

- Prior to becoming an agent, Ms. Langton was a co-founding director and publisher of the international publishing company, The Ink Group.

Represents Nonfiction books and literary fiction. **Considers these nonfiction areas:** biography, health, history, how-to, politics, self-help, true crime. **Considers these fiction areas:** literary, political thrillers, young adult and middle grade books.

- "Langtons International Agency is a multi-media literary and licensing agency specializing in nonfiction, thrillers and children's middle grade and young adult books as well as the the visual world of photography."

How to Contact Query with SASE. Submit outline/proposal, synopsis, publishing history, author bio. Only published authors should query this agency Accepts simultaneous submissions.

Recent Sales *Talking With Jean-Paul Sartre: Conversations and Debates*, by Professor John Gerassi (Yale University Press); *The Obama Presidency and the Politics of Change*, by Professor Stanley Renshon (Routledge Press); *I Would See a Girl Walking*, by Diana Montane and Kathy Kelly (Berkley Books); *Begin 1913-1992*, by Avi Shilon (Yale University Press); *This Borrowed Earth*, by Robert Emmet Hernan (Palgrave McMillan); *The Perfect Square*, by Nancy Heinzen (Temple Uni Press); *The Honey Trail*, by Grace Pundyk (St. Martins Press); *Dogs of Central Park*, by Fran Reisner (Rizzoli/Universe Publishing).

MICHAEL LARSEN/ELIZABETH POMADA, LITERARY AGENTS

1029 Jones St., San Francisco CA 94109-5023. (415)673-0939. E-mail: larsenpoma@aol.com. Website: www.larsen-pomada.com. **Contact:** Mike Larsen, Elizabeth Pomada. Member of AAR. Other memberships include Authors Guild, ASJA, PEN, WNBA, California Writers Club, National Speakers Association. Represents 100 clients. 40-45% of clients are new/unpublished writers. Currently handles: nonfiction books 70%, novels 30%.

- Prior to opening their agency, Mr. Larsen and Ms. Pomada were promotion executives for major publishing houses. Mr. Larsen worked for Morrow, Bantam and Pyramid (now part of Berkley); Ms. Pomada worked at Holt, David McKay and The Dial Press. Mr. Larsen is the author of the 4th edition of *How to Write a Book Proposal* and *How to Get a Literary Agent* as well as the coauthor of *Guerilla Marketing for Writers: 100 Weapons for Selling Your Work*, which was republished in September 2009.

Member Agents Michael Larsen (nonfiction); Elizabeth Pomada (fiction & narrative nonfiction).

Represents Considers these nonfiction areas: anthropology, archeology, architecture, art, autobiography, biography, business, current affairs, diet/nutrition, design, economics, environment, ethnic, film, foods, gay/lesbian, health, history, how-to, humor, inspirational, investigative, law, medicine, memoirs, metaphysics, money, music, New Age, popular culture, politics, psychology, religious, satire, science, self-help, sociology, sports, travel, women's issues, women's studies, futurism. **Considers these fiction areas:** action, adventure, contemporary issues, crime, detective, ethnic, experimental, family saga, feminist, gay, glitz, historical, humor, inspirational, lesbian, literary, mainstream, mystery, police, religious, romance, satire, suspense, chick lit.

- We have diverse tastes. We look for fresh voices and new ideas. We handle literary, commercial and genre fiction, and the full range of nonfiction books. Actively seeking commercial, genre and literary fiction. Does not want to receive children's books, plays, short stories, screenplays, pornography, poetry or stories of abuse.

How to Contact Query with SASE. Responds in 8 weeks to pages or submissions.

Terms Agent receives 15% commission on domestic sales. Agent receives 20% (30% for Asia) commission on foreign sales. May charge for printing, postage for multiple submissions, foreign mail, foreign phone calls, galleys, books, legal fees.

Recent Sales Sold at least 15 titles in the last year. *Secrets of the Tudor Court*, by D. Bogden (Kensington); *Zen & the Art of Horse Training*, by Allan Hamilton, M.D. (Storey Pub.); *The Solemn Lantern Maker*, by Merlinda Bobis (Delta); *Bite Marks*, the fifth book in an urban fantasy series by J.D. Rardin (Orbit/Grand Central); *The Iron King*, by Julie Karawa (Harlequin Teen).

Writers Conferences This agency organizes the annual San Francisco Writers' Conference (www.sfwriters.org).

Tips "We love helping writers get the rewards and recognition they deserve. If you can write books that meet the needs of the marketplace and you can promote your books, now is the best time ever to be a writer. We must find new writers to make a living, so we are very eager to hear from new writers whose work will interest large houses, and nonfiction writers who can promote their books. For a list of recent sales, helpful info, and three ways to make yourself irresistible to any publisher, please visit our website."

THE STEVE LAUBE AGENCY

5025 N. Central Ave., #635, Phoenix AZ 85012. (602)336-8910. E-mail: krichards@stevelaube.com. Website: www.stevelaube.com. **Contact:** Steve Laube. Other memberships include CBA. Represents 60+ clients. 5% of clients are new/unpublished writers. Currently handles: nonfiction books 48%, novels 48%, novella 2%, scholarly books 2%.

- Prior to becoming an agent, Mr. Laube worked 11 years as a Christian bookseller and 11 years as editorial director of nonfiction with Bethany House Publishers.

Represents Nonfiction books, novels. **Considers these nonfiction areas:** religious. **Considers these fiction areas:** religious.

- Primarily serves the Christian market (CBA). Actively seeking Christian fiction and religious nonfiction. Does not want to receive children's picture books, poetry or cookbooks.

How to Contact Submit proposal package, outline, 3 sample chapters, SASE. No email submissions. Consult website for guidelines. Accepts simultaneous submissions. Responds in 6-8 weeks to queries. Obtains most new clients through recommendations from others, solicitations, conferences.

Terms Agent receives 15% commission on domestic sales. Agent receives 20% commission on foreign sales. Offers written contract; 30-day notice must be given to terminate contract.

Recent Sales Sold 80 titles in the last year. Other clients include Deborah Raney, Bright Media, Allison Bottke, H. Norman Wright, Ellie Kay, Jack Cavanaugh, Karen Ball, Tracey Bateman, Susan May Warren, Lisa Bergren, John Rosemond, David Gregory, Cindy Woodsmall, Karol Ladd, Judith Pella, Michael Phillips, Margaret Daley, William Lane Craig, Vicki Hinze, Tosca Lee, Ginny Aiken.

Writers Conferences Mount Hermon Christian Writers' Conference; American Christian Fiction Writers' Conference.

ROBERT LECKER AGENCY

4055 Melrose Ave., Montreal QC H4A 2S5 Canada. (514)830-4818. Fax: (514)483-1644. E-mail: leckerlink@aol.com. Website: www.leckeragency.com. **Contact:** Robert Lecker. Represents 20 clients. 20% of clients are new/unpublished writers. Currently handles: nonfiction books 80%, novels 10%, scholarly books 10%.

- Prior to becoming an agent, Mr. Lecker was the co-founder and publisher of ECW Press and professor of English literature at McGill University. He has 30 years of experience in book and magazine publishing.

Member Agents Robert Lecker (popular culture, music); Mary Williams (travel, food, popular science).

Represents Nonfiction books, novels, scholarly, syndicated material. **Considers these nonfiction areas:** autobiography, biography, cooking, cultural interests, dance, diet/nutrition, ethnic, film, foods, how-to, language, literature, music, popular culture, science, technology, theater. **Considers these fiction areas:** action, adventure, crime, detective, erotica, literary, mainstream, mystery, police, suspense, thriller.

- RLA specializes in books about popular culture, popular science, music, entertainment, food and travel. The agency responds to articulate, innovative proposals within 2 weeks. Actively seeking original book mss only after receipt of outlines and proposals.

How to Contact Query first. Only responds to queries of interest. Discards the rest. Accepts simultaneous submissions. Responds in 2 weeks to queries. Responds in 1 month to mss. Obtains most new clients through recommendations from others, conferences, interest in website.

Terms Agent receives 15% commission on domestic sales. Agent receives 15-20% commission on foreign sales. Offers written contract, binding for 1 year; 6-month notice must be given to terminate contract.

LESCHER & LESCHER, LTD.

346 E. 84th St., New York NY 10028. (212)396-1999. Fax: (212)396-1991. **Contact:** Robert Larson; Carolyn Larson. Member of AAR. Represents 150 clients. Currently handles: nonfiction books 80%, novels 20%.

Represents Nonfiction books, novels. **Considers these nonfiction areas:** biography, cooking, current affairs, history, law, memoirs, popular culture, cookbooks/wines, narrative nonfiction. **Considers these fiction areas:** commercial, literary, mystery, suspense.

Does not want to receive screenplays, science fiction or romance.

How to Contact Query with SASE. Obtains most new clients through recommendations from others.

Terms Agent receives 15% commission on domestic sales. Agent receives 10% commission on foreign sales.

LEVINE GREENBERG LITERARY AGENCY, INC.

307 Seventh Ave., Suite 2407, New York NY 10001. (212)337-0934. Fax: (212)337-0948. Website: www.levinegreenberg.com. Member of AAR. Represents 250 clients. 33% of clients are new/unpublished writers. Currently handles: nonfiction books 70%, novels 30%.

- Prior to opening his agency, Mr. Levine served as vice president of the Bank Street College of Education.

Member Agents James Levine, Daniel Greenberg, Stephanie Kip Rostan, Lindsay Edgecombe, Danielle Svetcov, Elizabeth Fisher, Victoria Skurnick.

Represents Nonfiction books, novels. **Considers these nonfiction areas:** New Age, animals, art, biography, business, child, computers, cooking, gardening, gay, health, money, nature, religion, science, self-help, sociology, spirituality, sports, women's. **Considers these fiction areas:** literary, mainstream, mystery, thriller, psychological, women's.

This agency specializes in business, psychology, parenting, health/medicine, narrative nonfiction, spirituality, religion, women's issues, and commercial fiction.

How to Contact See website for full submission procedure at "How to Submit. Or use our email address if you prefer. Do not submit directly to agents." Obtains most new clients through recommendations from others.

Terms Agent receives 15% commission on domestic sales. Agent receives 20% commission on foreign sales. Offers written contract. Charges clients for out-of-pocket expenses—telephone, fax, postage, photocopying—directly connected to the project.

Writers Conferences ASJA Writers' Conference.

Tips "We focus on editorial development, business representation, and publicity and marketing strategy."

PAUL S. LEVINE LITERARY AGENCY

1054 Superba Ave., Venice CA 90291-3940. (310)450-6711. Fax: (310)450-0181. E-mail: paul@paulslevinelit.com. Website: www.paulslevinelit.com. **Contact:** Paul S. Levine. Other memberships include the State Bar of California. Represents over 100 clients. 75% of clients are new/unpublished writers. Currently handles: nonfiction books 60%, novels 10%, movie scripts 10%, TV scripts 5%, juvenile books 5%.

Member Agents Paul S. Levine (children's and young adult fiction and nonfiction, adult fiction and nonfiction except sci-fi, fantasy, and horror); Loren R. Grossman (archaeology, art/photography/architecture, gardening, education, health, medicine, science).

Represents Nonfiction books, novels, episodic drama, movie, TV, movie scripts, feature film, TV movie of the week, sitcom, animation, documentary, miniseries, syndicated material, reality show. **Considers these nonfiction areas:** architecture, art, autobiography, biography, business, child guidance, computers, cooking, crafts, cultural interests, current affairs, diet/nutrition, design, economics, education, ethnic, film, foods, gay/lesbian, government, health, history, hobbies, how-to, humor, investigative, language, law, medicine, memoirs, military, money, music, New Age, parenting, photography, popular culture, politics, psychology, science, self-help, sociology, sports, theater, true crime, women's issues, women's studies, creative nonfiction, animation. **Considers**

these fiction areas: action, adventure, comic books, confession, crime, detective, erotica, ethnic, experimental, family saga, feminist, frontier, gay, glitz, historical, humor, inspirational, lesbian, literary, mainstream, mystery, police, regional, religious, romance, satire, sports, suspense, thriller, westerns. **Considers these script areas:** action, biography, cartoon, comedy, contemporary, detective, erotica, ethnic, experimental, family, feminist, gay, glitz, historical, horror, juvenile, mainstream, multimedia, mystery, religious, romantic comedy, romantic drama, sports, teen, thriller, western.

O- Does not want to receive science fiction, fantasy, or horror.

How to Contact Query with SASE. Accepts simultaneous submissions. Responds in 1 day to queries. Responds in 6-8 weeks to mss. Obtains most new clients through conferences, referrals, listings on various websites and in directories.

Terms Agent receives 15% commission on domestic sales. Offers written contract. Charges for postage and actual, out-of-pocket costs only.

Recent Sales Sold 10 books in the last year and 5 script projects. *Apocalypse Never*, by Tad Daley (Rutgers University Press); movie rights to *Vampire High*, by Douglas Rees (1492 Productions); *Silver*, by Steven Savile (Variance Publishing); *Romancing the Runway*, by Linda Hudson-Smith (Harlequin). Other clients include David Seidman, Patricia Santos, Carol Jones.

Writers Conferences Willamette Writers Conference; San Francisco Writers Conference; Santa Barbara Writers Conference and many others.

Tips "Write good, sellable books."

LINDSTROM LITERARY MANAGEMENT, LLC

871 N. Greenbrier St., Arlington VA 22205. Fax: (703)527-7624. E-mail: submissions@lindstromliterary.com. Website: www.lindstromliterary.com. **Contact:** Kristin Lindstrom. Other memberships include Author's Guild. Represents 9 clients. 30% of clients are new/unpublished writers. Currently handles: nonfiction books 30%, novels 70%.

- Prior to her current position, Ms. Lindstrom started her career as an editor of a monthly magazine in the energy industry, and was employed as a public relations manager for a national software company before becoming an independent marketing and publicity consultant.

Represents Nonfiction books, novels. **Considers these nonfiction areas:** animals, autobiography, biography, business, current affairs, economics, history, investigative, memoirs, popular culture, science, technology, true crime. **Considers these fiction areas:** action, adventure, crime, detective, erotica, inspirational, mainstream, mystery, police, religious, suspense, thriller, women's.

O- "In 2006, I decided to add my more specific promotion/publicity skills to the mix in order to support the marketing efforts of my published clients." Actively seeking commercial fiction and narrative nonfiction. Does not want to receive juvenile or children's books, or books of poetry.

How to Contact Query via e-mail only. Submit author bio, synopsis and first four chapters if submitting fiction. For nonfiction, send the first 4 chapters, synopsis, proposal, outline and mission statement. *You will only hear from us again if we decide to ask for a complete manuscript or further information.* Accepts simultaneous submissions. Responds in 6 weeks to queries. Responds in 8 weeks to requested mss Obtains most new clients through referrals and solicitations.

Terms Agent receives 15% commission on domestic sales. Agent receives 20% commission on performance rights and foreign sales. Offers written contract. This agency charges for postage, UPS, copies and other basic office expenses.

Recent Sales A memoir by Agathe von Trapp (It Books/Harper). Two book deal for Alice Wisler (Bethany House); a thriller by J.C. Hutchins (St. Martin's Press).

Tips "Do your homework on accepted practices; make sure you know what kind of book the agent handles."

LINN PRENTIS LITERARY

155 East 116th St., #2F, New York NY 10029. Fax: (212)875-5565. E-mail: ahayden@linnprentis.com; linn@linnprentis.com. Website: www.linnprentis.com. **Contact:** Amy Hayden, acquisitions director; Linn Prentis, agent; Jordana Frankel assistant. Represents 18-20 clients. 25% of clients are

new/unpublished writers. Currently handles: nonfiction books 5%, novels 65%, story collections 7%, novella 10%, juvenile books 10%, scholarly books 3%.

- Prior to becoming an agent, Ms. Prentis was a nonfiction writer and editor, primarily in magazines. She also worked in book promotion in New York. Ms. Prentis then worked for and later ran the Virginia Kidd Agency. She is known particularly for her assistance with manuscript development."

Represents Nonfiction books, novels, short story collections, novellas, from authors whose novels I already represent, juvenile, for older juveniles, scholarly, anthology. **Considers these nonfiction areas:** juvenile, animals, art, biography, current affairs, education, ethnic, government, how-to, humor, language, memoirs, music, photography, popular culture, sociology, women's. **Considers these fiction areas:** adventure, ethnic, fantasy, feminist, gay, glitz, historical, horror, humor, juvenile, lesbian, literary, mainstream, mystery, thriller.

O→ "Because of the Virginia Kidd connection and the clients I brought with me at the start, I have a special interest in sci-fi and fantasy, but, really, fiction is what interests me. As for my nonfiction projects, they are books I just couldn't resist." Actively seeking hard science fiction, family saga, mystery, memoir, mainstream, literary, women's. Does not want to "receive books for little kids."

How to Contact Query with SASE. Submit synopsis. No phone or fax queries. No snail mail. E-mail queries to ahayden@linnprentis.com. Include first ten pages and synopsis as either attachment or as text in the e-mail. Accepts simultaneous submissions. Obtains most new clients through recommendations from others, solicitations.

Terms Agent receives 15% commission on domestic sales. Agent receives 20% commission on foreign sales. Offers written contract; 60-day notice must be given to terminate contract.

Recent Sales Sold 15 titles in the last year. *The Sons of Heaven*, *The Empress of Mars*, and *The House of the Stag*, by Kage Baker (Tor); the last has also been sold to Dabel Brothers to be published as a comic book/graphic novel; *Indigo Springs* and a sequel, by A.M. Dellamonica (Tor); Wayne Arthurson's debut mystery plus a second series book; *Bone Crossed* and *Cry Wolf* for New York Times #1 bestselling author Patricia Briggs (Ace/Penguin). "The latter is the start of a new series."

Tips "Consider query letters and synopses as writing assignments. Spell names correctly."

◪ LIPPINCOTT MASSIE MCQUILKIN

27 West 20th Street, Suite 305, New York NY 10011. Fax: (212)352-2059. E-mail: info@lmqlit.com. Website: www.lmqlit.com. **Contact:** Rob McQuilkin. Represents 90 clients. 30% of clients are new/unpublished writers. Currently handles: nonfiction books 40%, novels 40%, story collections 10%, scholarly books 5%, poetry 5%.

Member Agents Maria Massie (fiction, memoir, cultural criticism); Will Lippincott (politics, current affairs, history); Rob McQuilkin (fiction, history, psychology, sociology, graphic material); Jason Anthony (pop culture, memoir, true crime, and general psychology).

Represents Nonfiction books, novels, short story collections, scholarly, graphic novels. **Considers these nonfiction areas:** animals, anthropology, archeology, architecture, art, autobiography, biography, business, child guidance, cultural interests, current affairs, design, economics, ethnic, film, gay/lesbian, government, health, history, inspirational, language, law, literature, medicine, memoirs, military, money, music, parenting, popular culture, politics, psychology, religious, science, self-help, sociology, technology, true crime, women's issues, women's studies. **Considers these fiction areas:** action, adventure, cartoon, comic books, confession, family saga, feminist, gay, historical, humor, lesbian, literary, mainstream, regional, satire.

O→ "LMQ focuses on bringing new voices in literary and commercial fiction to the market, as well as popularizing the ideas and arguments of scholars in the fields of history, psychology, sociology, political science, and current affairs. Actively seeking fiction writers who already have credits in magazines and quarterlies, as well as nonfiction writers who already have a media platform or some kind of a university affiliation." Does not want to receive romance, genre fiction or children's material.

How to Contact "We accepts electronic queries only. Only send additional materials if requested." Accepts simultaneous submissions. Responds in 1 week to queries. Responds in 1 month to mss. Obtains most new clients through recommendations from others, solicitations, conferences.
Terms Agent receives 15% commission on domestic sales. Agent receives 20% commission on foreign sales. Offers written contract; 30-day notice must be given to terminate contract. Only charges for reasonable business expenses upon successful sale.
Recent Sales Clients include: Peter Ho Davies, Kim Addonizio, Don Lee, Natasha Trethewey, Anatol Lieven, Sir Michael Marmot, Anne Carson, Liza Ward, David Sirota, Anne Marie Slaughter, Marina Belozerskaya, Kate Walbert.

LITERARY AGENCY FOR SOUTHERN AUTHORS

2123 Paris Metz Road, Chattanooga TN 37421. E-mail: southernlitagent@aol.com. **Contact:** Lantz Powell. Represents 20 clients. 60% of clients are new/unpublished writers. Currently handles: nonfiction books 50%, novels 50%.

- Prior to becoming an agent, Mr. Powell was in sales and contract negotiation.

Represents Nonfiction books, novels, juvenile, for ages 14 and up. **Considers these nonfiction areas:** architecture, art, biography, business, crafts, cultural interests, current affairs, economics, education, ethnic, government, history, hobbies, how-to, humor, inspirational, language, law, metaphysics, military, New Age, photography, popular culture, politics, religious, satire, true crime, young adult. **Considers these fiction areas:** cartoon, comic books, humor, literary, mainstream, regional, religious, satire, young adult.

"We focus on authors that live in the Southern U.S. We have the ability to translate and explain complexities of publishing for the Southern author." "Actively seeking quality projects by authors with a vision of where they want to be in 10 years and a plan of how to get there." Does not want to receive unfinished, unedited projects that do not follow the standard presentation conventions of the trade. No romance.

How to Contact Query via e-mail first and include a synopsis. Accepts simultaneous submissions. Responds in 2-3 days to queries. Responds in 1 week to mss. Obtains most new clients through recommendations from others.
Terms Agent receives 15% commission on domestic sales. Agent receives 25% commission on foreign sales. Offers written contract. "We charge when a publisher wants a hard copy overnight or the like. The client always knows this beforehand."
Recent Sales Sold 10+ titles in the last year. List of other clients and books sold will be available to authors pre-signing, but is not for public knowledge.
Writers Conferences Conference for Southern Literature; Tennessee Book Fair.
Tips "If you are an unpublished author, join a writers group, even if it is on the Internet. You need good honest feedback. Don't send a manuscript that has not been read by at least five people. Don't send a manuscript cold to any agent without first asking if they want it. Try to meet the agent face to face before signing. Make sure the fit is right."

THE LITERARY GROUP INTERNATIONAL

14 Penn Plaza, Suite 925, New York NY 10122. (646)442-5896. E-mail: js@theliterarygroup.com. Website: www.theliterarygroup.com. **Contact:** Frank Weimann. 65% of clients are new/unpublished writers. Currently handles: nonfiction books 50%, other 50% fiction.
Member Agents Frank Weimann.
Represents Nonfiction books, novels, graphic novels. **Considers these nonfiction areas:** animals, anthropology, biography, business, child guidance, crafts, creative nonfiction, current affairs, education, ethnic, film, government, health, history, humor, juvenile nonfiction, language, memoirs, military, multicultural, music, nature, popular culture, politics, psychology, religious, science, self-help, sociology, sports, travel, true crime, women's issues, women's studies. **Considers these fiction areas:** adventure, contemporary issues, detective, ethnic, experimental, family saga, fantasy, feminist, historical, horror, humor, literary, multicultural, mystery, psychic, romance, sports, thriller, young adult, regional, graphic novels.

This agency specializes in nonfiction (memoir, military, history, biography, sports, how-to).

How to Contact Query with SASE. Prefers to read materials exclusively. Only responds if interested. Obtains most new clients through referrals, writers' conferences, query letters.
Terms Agent receives 15% commission on domestic sales. Agent receives 20% commission on foreign sales. Offers written contract; 30-day notice must be given to terminate contract.
Recent Sales *One From the Hart*, by Stefanie Powers with Richard Buskin (Pocket Books); *Sacred Trust, Deadly Betrayal*, by Keith Anderson (Berkley); *Gotti Confidential*, by Victoria Gotti (Pocket Books); Anna Sui's illustrated memoir (Chronicle Books); *Mania*, by Craig Larsen (Kensington); *Everything Explained Through Flowcharts*, by Doogie Horner (HarperCollins); *Bitch*, by Lisa Taddeo (TOR); film rights for *Falling Out of Fashion*, by Karen Yampolsky to Hilary Swank and Molly Smith for 2S Films.
Writers Conferences San Diego State University Writers' Conference; Maui Writers' Conference; Agents and Editors Conference; NAHJ Convention in Puerto Rico, among others.

JULIA LORD LITERARY MANAGEMENT

38 W. Ninth St., #4, New York NY 10011. (212)995-2333. Fax: (212)995-2332. E-mail: query@juliallordliterary.com. Website: julialordliterary.com. Member of AAR.
Member Agents Julia Lord, owner.
Represents Nonfiction, fiction. **Considers these nonfiction areas:** autobiography, biography, environment, history, humor, science, sports, travel, African-American; lifestyle; narrative nonfiction; reference. **Considers these fiction areas:** action, adventure, historical, literary, mainstream.
How to Contact Query letter or Recommendation. All hard copy query letters will be answered. Query emails will only be answered if we are interested. email: query@julialordliterary.com. Obtains most new clients through recommendations from others, solicitations.

LOWENSTEIN ASSOCIATES INC.

121 W. 27th St., Suite 601, New York NY 10001. (212)206-1630. Fax: (212)727-0280. Website: www.lowensteinassociates.com. **Contact:** Barbara Lowenstein. Member of AAR. Represents 150 clients. 20% of clients are new/unpublished writers. Currently handles: nonfiction books 60%, novels 40%.
Member Agents Barbara Lowenstein, president (nonfiction interests include narrative nonfiction, health, money, finance, travel, multicultural, popular culture and memoir; fiction interests include literary fiction and women's fiction); Kathleen Ortiz, Associate Agent and Foreign Rights Manager at Lowenstein Associates. She is seeking children's books (chapter, middle grade, and young adult) and young adult non-fiction.
Represents Nonfiction books, novels. **Considers these nonfiction areas:** animals, anthropology, archeology, autobiography, biography, business, child guidance, current affairs, education, ethnic, film, government, health, history, how-to, language, literature, medicine, memoirs, money, multicultural, parenting, popular culture, psychology, science, sociology, travel, music; narrative nonfiction; science; film. **Considers these fiction areas:** crime, detective, erotica, ethnic, fantasy, feminist, historical, literary, mainstream, mystery, police, romance, suspense, thriller, young adult.

> "This agency specializes in health, business, creative nonfiction, literary fiction and commercial fiction—especially suspense, crime and women's issues. We are a full-service agency, handling domestic and foreign rights, film rights and audio rights to all of our books." Barbara Lowenstein is currently looking for writers who have a platform and are leading experts in their field, including business, women's issues, psychology, health, science and social issues, and is particularly interested in strong new voices in fiction and narrative nonfiction.

How to Contact Query with SASE or via electronic form on each agent's page. Submit to only one agent. Prefers to read materials exclusively. For fiction, send outline and first chapter. *No unsolicited mss.* Responds in 4 weeks to queries. Obtains most new clients through recommendations from others, solicitations, conferences.

Terms Agent receives 15% commission on domestic sales. Agent receives 20% commission on foreign sales. Offers written contract. Charges for large photocopy batches, messenger service, international postage.
Writers Conferences Malice Domestic
Tips Know the genre you are working in and read! Also, please see our website for details on which agent to query for your project.

LYONS LITERARY, LLC

27 West 20th St., Suite 10003, New York NY 10011. (212)255-5472. Fax: (212)851-8405. E-mail: info@lyonsliterary.com. Website: www.lyonsliterary.com. **Contact:** Jonathan Lyons. Member of AAR. Other memberships include The Author's Guild, American Bar Association, New York State Bar Associaton, New York State Intellectual Property Law Section. Represents 37 clients. 15% of clients are new/unpublished writers. Currently handles: nonfiction books 60%, novels 40%.
Represents Nonfiction books, novels. **Considers these nonfiction areas:** animals, autobiography, biography, cooking, crafts, cultural interests, current affairs, diet/nutrition, ethnic, foods, gay/lesbian, government, health, history, hobbies, how-to, humor, law, medicine, memoirs, military, money, multicultural, popular culture, politics, psychology, science, sociology, sports, technology, translation, travel, true crime, women's issues, women's studies. **Considers these fiction areas:** contemporary issues, crime, detective, fantasy, feminist, gay, historical, humor, lesbian, literary, mainstream, mystery, police, psychic, regional, satire, science fiction, sports, supernatural, suspense, thriller, women's, chick lit.

- "With my legal expertise and experience selling domestic and foreign language book rights, paperback reprint rights, audio rights, film/TV rights and permissions, I am able to provide substantive and personal guidance to my clients in all areas relating to their projects. In addition, with the advent of new publishing technology, Lyons Literary, LLC is situated to address the changing nature of the industry while concurrently handling authors' more traditional needs."

How to Contact Only accepts queries through online submission form. Accepts simultaneous submissions. Responds in 8 weeks to queries. Responds in 12 weeks to mss. Obtains most new clients through recommendations from others.
Terms Agent receives 15% commission on domestic sales. Agent receives 20% commission on foreign sales. Offers written contract.
Writers Conferences Agents and Editors Conference.
Tips "Please submit electronic queries through our website submission form."

DONALD MAASS LITERARY AGENCY

121 W. 27th St., Suite 801, New York NY 10001. (212)727-8383. E-mail: info@maassagency.com. Website: www.maassagency.com. Member of AAR. Other memberships include SFWA, MWA, RWA. Represents more than 100 clients. 5% of clients are new/unpublished writers. Currently handles: novels 100%.

- Prior to opening his agency, Mr. Maass served as an editor at Dell Publishing (New York) and as a reader at Gollancz (London). He also served as the president of AAR.

Member Agents Donald Maass (mainstream, literary, mystery/suspense, science fiction, romance); Jennifer Jackson (commercial fiction, romance, science fiction, fantasy, mystery/suspense); Cameron McClure (literary, mystery/suspense, urban, fantasy, narrative nonfiction and projects with multicultural, international, and environmental themes, gay/lesbian); Ms. J.L. Stermer (fiction, memoir, narrative nonfiction, pop-culture [cooking, fashion, style, music, art], smart humor, upscale erotica/erotic memoir and multi-cultural fiction/nonfiction); Amy Boggs (fantasy and science fiction, especially urban fantasy, paranormal romance, steampunk, YA/children's, and alternate history. historical fiction, multi-cultural fiction, Westerns).
Represents Novels. **Considers these nonfiction areas:** narrative nonfiction (and see J.L's bio for subject interest). **Considers these fiction areas:** crime, detective, fantasy, historical, horror, literary, mainstream, mystery, police, psychic, science fiction, supernatural, suspense, thriller, women's, romance (historical, paranormal, and time travel).

- This agency specializes in commercial fiction, especially science fiction, fantasy, mystery and suspense. Actively seeking to expand in literary fiction and women's fiction. Does not want to receive nonfiction, picture books, prescriptive nonfiction, or poetry.

How to Contact Query with SASE. Returns material only with SASE. Accepts simultaneous submissions. Responds in 2 weeks to queries. Responds in 3 months to mss.

Terms Agent receives 15% commission on domestic sales. Agent receives 20% commission on foreign sales.

Recent Sales *Codex Alera 5: Princep's Fury*, by Jim Butcher (Ace); *Fonseca 6: Bright Futures*, by Stuart Kaimsky (Forge): *Fathom*, by Cherie Priest (Tor); *Gospel Grrls 3: Be Strong and Curvaceous*, by Shelly Adina (Faith Words); *Ariane 1: Peacekeeper*, by Laura Reeve (Roc); *Execution Dock*, by Anne Perry (Random House).

Writers Conferences Donald Maass: World Science Fiction Convention; Frankfurt Book Fair; Pacific Northwest Writers Conference; Bouchercon. Jennifer Jackson: World Science Fiction Convention; RWA National Conference.

Tips We are fiction specialists, also noted for our innovative approach to career planning. Few new clients are accepted, but interested authors should query with a SASE. Works with subagents in all principle foreign countries and Hollywood. No prescriptive nonfiction, picture books or poetry will be considered.

MACGREGOR LITERARY

2373 N.W. 185th Ave., Suite 165, Hillsboro OR 97214. (503)277-8308. E-mail: submissions@macgregorliterary.com. Website: www.macgregorliterary.com. **Contact:** Chip MacGregor. Signatory of WGA. Represents 40 clients. 10% of clients are new/unpublished writers. Currently handles: nonfiction books 40%, novels 60%.

- Prior to his current position, Mr. MacGregor was the senior agent with Alive Communications. Most recently, he was associate publisher for Time-Warner Book Group's Faith Division, and helped put together their Center Street imprint.

Member Agents Chip MacGregor, Sarah Bishop.

Represents Nonfiction books, novels. **Considers these nonfiction areas:** business, current affairs, economics, history, how-to, humor, inspirational, parenting, popular culture, satire, self-help, sports, marriage. **Considers these fiction areas:** crime, detective, historical, inspirational, mainstream, mystery, police, religious, romance, suspense, thriller, women's, chick lit.

- "My specialty has been in career planning with authors—finding commercial ideas, then helping authors bring them to market, and in the midst of that assisting the authors as they get firmly established in their writing careers. I'm probably best known for my work with Christian books over the years, but I've done a fair amount of general market projects as well." Actively seeking authors with a Christian worldview and a growing platform. Does not want to receive fantasy, sci-fi, children's books, poetry or screenplays.

How to Contact Query with SASE. Accepts simultaneous submissions. Responds in 3 weeks to queries. Obtains most new clients through recommendations from others. Not looking to add unpublished authors except through referrals from current clients.

Terms Agent receives 15% commission on domestic sales. Agent receives 15% commission on foreign sales. Offers written contract; 30-day notice must be given to terminate contract. Charges for exceptional fees after receiving authors' permission.

Writers Conferences Blue Ridge Christian Writers' Conference; Write to Publish.

Tips "Seriously consider attending a good writers' conference. It will give you the chance to be face-to-face with people in the industry. Also, if you're a novelist, consider joining one of the national writers' organizations. The American Christian Fiction Writers (ACFW) is a wonderful group for new as well as established writers. And if you're a Christian writer of any kind, check into The Writers View, an online writing group. All of these have proven helpful to writers."

CAROL MANN AGENCY

55 Fifth Ave., New York NY 10003. (212)206-5635. Fax: (212)675-4809. Website: www.carolmannagency.com/. **Contact:** Eliza Dreier. Member of AAR. Represents roughly 200 clients.

15% of clients are new/unpublished writers. Currently handles: nonfiction books 90%, novels 10%.

Member Agents Carol Mann (health/medical, religion, spirituality, self-help, parenting, narrative nonfiction); Laura Yorke; Gareth Esersky; Myrsini Stephanides (Nonfiction areas of interest: pop culture and music, humor, narrative nonfiction and memoir, cookbooks; fiction areas of interest: offbeat literary fiction, graphic works, and edgy YA fiction).

Represents Nonfiction books, novels. **Considers these nonfiction areas:** anthropology, archeology, architecture, art, autobiography, biography, business, child guidance, cultural interests, current affairs, design, ethnic, government, health, history, law, medicine, money, music, parenting, popular culture, politics, psychology, self-help, sociology, sports, women's issues, women's studies. **Considers these fiction areas:** commercial, literary.

- This agency specializes in current affairs, self-help, popular culture, psychology, parenting, and history. Does not want to receive genre fiction (romance, mystery, etc.).

How to Contact Keep initial query/contact to no more than two pages. Responds in 4 weeks to queries.

Terms Agent receives 15% commission on domestic sales. Agent receives 20% commission on foreign sales. Offers written contract.

MANUS & ASSOCIATES LITERARY AGENCY, INC.

425 Sherman Ave., Suite 200, Palo Alto CA 94306. (650)470-5151. Fax: (650)470-5159. E-mail: manuslit@manuslit.com. Website: www.manuslit.com. **Contact:** Jillian Manus, Jandy Nelson, Penny Nelson. Member of AAR. Represents 75 clients. 30% of clients are new/unpublished writers. Currently handles: nonfiction books 70%, novels 30%.

- Prior to becoming an agent, Ms. Manus was associate publisher of two national magazines and director of development at Warner Bros. and Universal Studios; she has been a literary agent for 20 years.

Member Agents Jandy Nelson, jandy@manuslit.com (self-help, health, memoirs, narrative nonfiction, women's fiction, literary fiction, multicultural fiction, thrillers). She is currently on sabbatical and not taking on new clients; Jillian Manus, jillian@manuslit.com (political, memoirs, self-help, history, sports, women's issues, Latin fiction and nonfiction, thrillers); Penny Nelson, penny@manuslit.com (memoirs, self-help, sports, nonfiction); Dena Fischer (literary fiction, mainstream/commercial fiction, chick lit, women's fiction, historical fiction, ethnic/cultural fiction, narrative nonfiction, parenting, relationships, pop culture, health, sociology, psychology); Janet Wilkens Manus (narrative fact-based crime books, religion, pop psychology, inspiration, memoirs, cookbooks); Stephanie Lee (not currently taking on new clients).

Represents Nonfiction books, novels. **Considers these nonfiction areas:** autobiography, biography, business, child guidance, cultural interests, current affairs, economics, environment, ethnic, health, how-to, medicine, memoirs, money, parenting, popular culture, psychology, science, self-help, technology, women's issues, women's studies, Gen X and Gen Y issues; creative nonfiction. **Considers these fiction areas:** literary, mainstream, multicultural, mystery, suspense, thriller, women's, quirky/edgy fiction.

- "Our agency is unique in the way that we not only sell the material, but we edit, develop concepts, and participate in the marketing effort. We specialize in large, conceptual fiction and nonfiction, and always value a project that can be sold in the TV/feature film market." Actively seeking high-concept thrillers, commercial literary fiction, women's fiction, celebrity biographies, memoirs, multicultural fiction, popular health, women's empowerment and mysteries. No horror, romance, science fiction, fantasy, Western, young adult, children's, poetry, cookbooks or magazine articles.

How to Contact Query with SASE. If requested, submit outline, 2-3 sample chapters. All queries should be sent to the California office. Accepts simultaneous submissions. Responds in 3 months to queries. Responds in 3 months to mss. Obtains most new clients through recommendations from others, solicitations, conferences.

Terms Agent receives 15% commission on domestic sales. Agent receives 20-25% commission on foreign sales. Offers written contract, binding for 2 years; 60-day notice must be given to terminate contract. Charges for photocopying and postage/UPS.

Recent Sales *Nothing Down for the 2000s* and *Multiple streams of Income for the 2000s*, by Robert Allen; *Missed Fortune 101*, by Doug Andrew; *Cracking the Millionaire Code*, by Mark Victor Hansen and Robert Allen; *Stress Free for Good*, by Dr. Fred Luskin and Dr. Ken Pelletier; *The Mercy of Thin Air*, by Ronlyn Domangue; *The Fine Art of Small Talk*, by Debra Fine; *Bone Men of Bonares*, by Terry Tamoff.

Writers Conferences Maui Writers' Conference; San Diego State University Writers' Conference; Willamette Writers' Conference; BookExpo America; MEGA Book Marketing University.

Tips "Research agents using a variety of sources."

THE EVAN MARSHALL AGENCY

Six Tristam Place, Pine Brook NJ 07058-9445. (973)882-1122. Fax: (973)882-3099. E-mail: evanmarshall@optonline.net. **Contact:** Evan Marshall. Member of AAR. Other memberships include MWA, Sisters in Crime. Currently handles: novels 100%.

Represents Novels. **Considers these fiction areas:** action, adventure, erotica, ethnic, frontier, historical, horror, humor, inspirational, literary, mainstream, mystery, religious, satire, science fiction, suspense, westerns, romance (contemporary, gothic, historical, regency).

How to Contact Query first with SASE; do not enclose material. No e-mail queries. Responds in 1 week to queries. Responds in 3 months to mss. Obtains most new clients through recommendations from others.

Terms Agent receives 15% commission on domestic sales. Agent receives 20% commission on foreign sales. Offers written contract.

Recent Sales *Blood Vines*, by Erica Spindler (St. Martin's Press); *Breakneck*, by Erica Spindler (St. Martin's Press); *Such a Pretty Face*, by Cathy Lamb (Kensington); *If He's Sinful*, by Hannah Howell (Zebra).

THE MARTELL AGENCY

1350 Avenue of the Americas, Suite 1205, New York NY 10019. Fax: (212)317-2676. E-mail: afmartell@aol.com. **Contact:** Alice Martell.

Represents Nonfiction books, novels. **Considers these nonfiction areas:** business, economics, health, history, medicine, memoirs, multicultural, psychology, self-help, women's issues, women's studies. **Considers these fiction areas:** commercial, mystery, suspense, thriller.

How to Contact Query with SASE. Submit sample chapters. Submit via snail mail. No e-mail or fax queries.

Recent Sales *Peddling Peril: The Secret Nuclear Arms Trade,* by David Albright and Joel Wit (Five Press); *America's Women: Four Hundred Years of Dolls, Drudges, Helpmates, and Heroines*, by Gail Collins (William Morrow). Other clients include Serena Bass, Thomas E. Ricks, Janice Erlbaum, David Cay Johnston, Mark Derr, Barbara Rolls, Ph.D.

MAX AND CO., A LITERARY AGENCY AND SOCIAL CLUB

3929 Coliseum St., New Orleans LA 70115. (201)704-2483. E-mail: mmurphy@maxlit.com. Website: www.maxliterary.org. **Contact:** Michael Murphy.

- Max & Co. was established in the Fall of 2007 by Michael Murphy. Prior to the literary agency, Michael began in book publishing in 1981 at Random House. He left in '95 as a Vice President and later ran William Morrow as their Publisher. Co-agent Jack Perry joined publishing in 1994 and has been a Vice President in Sales & Marketing for Random House, Source Books, and Scholastic

Member Agents Michael Murphy, Nettie Hartsock (literary & commercial fiction. business books & popular nonfiction, and the occasional Southern fiction book), Jack Perry (nonfiction books with a foundation in history, sports, business, politics, narrative nonfiction, math, & science).

Represents Considers these nonfiction areas: business, history, humor, memoirs, politics, science, sports, narrative nonfiction. **Considers these fiction areas:** commercial, literary.

- Seeking work in literary or eclectic fiction. In nonfiction, seeks narrative or creative nonfiction. Does not represent romance, science fiction, fantasy, tea-cozy or who-dunnit mysteries. Does not represent self-help or prescriptive (how-to) nonfiction. Represents no children's or YA work.

How to Contact Agency desires on-line submissions and will not accept nor respond to mailed submissions. There are four agents—two in New York, one in Austin, Texas and Michael Murphy in New Orleans.

MARGRET MCBRIDE LITERARY AGENCY

7744 Fay Ave., Suite 201, La Jolla CA 92037. (858)454-1550. Fax: (858)454-2156. E-mail: staff@mcbridelit.com. Website: www.mcbrideliterary.com. **Contact:** Michael Daley, submissions manager. Member of AAR. Other memberships include Authors Guild. Represents 55 clients.

- Prior to opening her agency, Ms. McBride worked at Random House, Ballantine Books, and Warner Books.

Represents Nonfiction books, novels. **Considers these nonfiction areas:** autobiography, biography, business, cooking, cultural interests, current affairs, dance, diet/nutrition, economics, ethnic, foods, government, health, history, how-to, law, medicine, money, music, popular culture, politics, psychology, science, self-help, sociology, technology, women's issues, women's studies, style. **Considers these fiction areas:** action, adventure, crime, detective, ethnic, frontier, historical, humor, literary, mainstream, mystery, police, satire, suspense, thriller, westerns.

- This agency specializes in mainstream fiction and nonfiction. Does not want to receive screenplays, romance, poetry, or children's/young adult.

How to Contact Query with synopsis, bio, SASE. No e-mail or fax queries. Accepts simultaneous submissions. Responds in 4-6 weeks to queries. Responds in 6-8 weeks to mss.

Terms Agent receives 15% commission on domestic sales. Agent receives 25% commission on foreign sales. Charges for overnight delivery and photocopying.

THE MCCARTHY AGENCY, LLC

7 Allen St., Rumson NJ 07660. Phone/Fax: (732)741-3065. E-mail: mccarthylit@aol.com. **Contact:** Shawna McCarthy. Member of AAR. Currently handles: nonfiction books 25%, novels 75%.

Member Agents Shawna McCarthy.

Represents Nonfiction books, novels. **Considers these nonfiction areas:** biography, history, philosophy, science. **Considers these fiction areas:** fantasy, juvenile, mystery, romance, science, women's.

How to Contact Query via e-mail only. Accepts simultaneous submissions.

THE MCGILL AGENCY, INC.

10000 N. Central Expressway, Suite 400, Dallas TX 75231. (214)390-5970. E-mail: info.mcgillagency@gmail.com. **Contact:** Jack Bollinger. Estab. 2009. Represents 10 clients. 50% of clients are new/unpublished writers.

Member Agents Jack Bollinger (eclectic tastes in nonfiction and fiction); Amy Cohn (nonfiction interests include women's issues, gay/lesbian, ethnic/cultural, memoirs, true crime; fiction interests include mystery, suspense and thriller).

Represents Considers these nonfiction areas: biography, business, child guidance, current affairs, education, ethnic, gay, health, history, how-to, memoirs, military, psychology, self-help, true crime, women's issues. **Considers these fiction areas:** historical, mainstream, mystery, romance, thriller.

How to Contact Query via e-mail. Responds in two weeks to queries and 6 weeks to manuscript. Obtains new clients through conferences

Terms 15%

MENDEL MEDIA GROUP, LLC

115 West 30th St., Suite 800, New York NY 10001. (646)239-9896. Fax: (212)685-4717. E-mail: scott@mendelmedia.com. Website: www.mendelmedia.com. Member of AAR. Represents 40-60 clients.

- Prior to becoming an agent, Mr. Mendel was an academic. "I taught American literature, Yiddish, Jewish studies, and literary theory at the University of Chicago and the University of Illinois at Chicago while working on my PhD in English. I also worked as a freelance technical writer and as the managing editor of a healthcare magazine. In 1998, I began working for the late Jane Jordan Browne, a long-time agent in the book publishing world."

Represents Nonfiction books, novels, scholarly, with potential for broad/popular appeal. **Considers these nonfiction areas:** Americana, animals, anthropology, architecture, art, biography, business, child guidance, cooking, current affairs, dance, diet/nutrition, education, environment, ethnic, foods, gardening, gay/lesbian, government, health, history, how-to, humor, investigative, language, medicine, memoirs, military, money, multicultural, music, parenting, philosophy, popular culture, psychology, recreation, regional, religious, science, self-help, sex, sociology, software, spirituality, sports, true crime, war, women's issues, women's studies, Jewish topics; creative nonfiction. **Considers these fiction areas:** action, adventure, contemporary issues, crime, detective, erotica, ethnic, feminist, gay, glitz, historical, humor, inspirational, juvenile, lesbian, literary, mainstream, mystery, picture books, police, religious, romance, satire, sports, thriller, young adult, Jewish fiction.

- "I am interested in major works of history, current affairs, biography, business, politics, economics, science, major memoirs, narrative nonfiction, and other sorts of general nonfiction." Actively seeking new, major or definitive work on a subject of broad interest, or a controversial, but authoritative, new book on a subject that affects many people's lives." I also represent more light-hearted nonfiction projects, such as gift or novelty books, when they suit the market particularly well." Does not want "queries about projects written years ago that were unsuccessfully shopped to a long list of trade publishers by either the author or another agent. I am specifically not interested in reading short, category romances (regency, time travel, paranormal, etc.), horror novels, supernatural stories, poetry, original plays, or film scripts."

How to Contact Query with SASE. Do not e-mail or fax queries. For nonfiction, include a complete, fully-edited book proposal with sample chapters. For fiction, include a complete synopsis and no more than 20 pages of sample text. Responds in 2 weeks to queries. Responds in 4-6 weeks to mss. Obtains most new clients through recommendations from others.

Terms Agent receives 15% commission on domestic sales. Agent receives 20% commission on foreign sales.

Writers Conferences BookExpo America; Frankfurt Book Fair; London Book Fair; RWA National Conference; Modern Language Association Convention; Jerusalem Book Fair.

Tips "While I am not interested in being flattered by a prospective client, it does matter to me that she knows why she is writing to me in the first place. Is one of my clients a colleague of hers? Has she read a book by one of my clients that led her to believe I might be interested in her work? Authors of descriptive nonfiction should have real credentials and expertise in their subject areas, either as academics, journalists, or policy experts, and authors of prescriptive nonfiction should have legitimate expertise and considerable experience communicating their ideas in seminars and workshops, in a successful business, through the media, etc."

HENRY MORRISON, INC.

105 S. Bedford Road, Suite 306A, Mt. Kisco NY 10549. (914)666-3500. Fax: (914)241-7846. **Contact:** Henry Morrison. Signatory of WGA. Represents 54 clients. 5% of clients are new/unpublished writers. Currently handles: nonfiction books 5%, novels 95%.

Represents Nonfiction books, novels. **Considers these nonfiction areas:** anthropology, archeology, autobiography, biography, government, history, law, politics. **Considers these fiction areas:** action, adventure, crime, detective, family saga, historical, police.

How to Contact Query with SASE. Responds in 2 weeks to queries. Responds in 3 months to mss. Obtains most new clients through recommendations from others.
Terms Agent receives 15% commission on domestic sales. Agent receives 25% commission on foreign sales. Charges clients for ms copies, bound galleys, finished books for submissions to publishers, movie producers and foreign publishers.

MORTIMER LITERARY AGENCY

52645 Paui Road, Aguanga CA 92536. E-mail: kmortimer@mortimerliterary.com. Website: www.mortimerliterary.com. **Contact:** Kelly Gottuso Mortimer. Romance Writers of America. Represents 16 clients. 80% of clients are new/unpublished writers. Currently handles: nonfiction books 40%, novels 40%, young adult books 20%.

- Prior to becoming an agent, Ms. Mortimer was a freelance writer and the CFO of Microvector, Inc. She has a degree in contract law, finance and is a winner of The American Christian Fiction Writers Literary Agent of the Year Award in 2008 and the OCC-RAW Volunteer of the Year award. Was top 5: Publishers marketplace top 100 Dealmakers- Romance category, 2008.

Represents Nonfiction books, novels, young adult. **Considers these nonfiction areas:** Please refer to submissions page on website, as the list changes. **Considers these fiction areas:** Please refer to submissions page on website, as the list changes.

- "I keep a short client list to give my writers personal attention. I edit my clients' manuscripts as necessary. I send manuscripts out to pre-selected editors in a timely fashion, and send my clients monthly reports. I only sign writers not yet published, or not published in the last 3 years. Those are the writers who need my help the most."

How to Contact See website for submission guidelines. Accepts simultaneous submissions. Responds in 3 months to mss. Obtains most new clients through query letters.
Terms Agent receives 15% commission on domestic sales. Agent receives 20% commission on foreign sales. Offers written contract. "I charge for postage - only the amount I pay and it comes out of the author's advance. The writer provides me with copies of their manuscripts if needed."
Writers Conferences RWA, several conference. See schedule on website.
Tips "Follow submission guidelines on the website, submit your best work and don't query unless your manuscript is finished. Don't send material or mss that I haven't requested."

DEE MURA LITERARY

269 West Shore Drive, Massapequa NY 11758-8225. (516)795-1616. Fax: (516)795-8797. E-mail: query@deemuraliterary.com. **Contact:** Dee Mura. Signatory of WGA. 50% of clients are new/unpublished writers.

- Prior to opening her agency, Ms. Mura was a public relations executive with a roster of film and entertainment clients and worked in editorial for major weekly news magazines.

Member Agents Dee Mura, Karen Roberts, Bobbie Sokol, David Brozain.
Represents Considers these nonfiction areas: animals, anthropology, biography, business, child guidance, computers, current affairs, education, ethnic, finance, gay, government, health, history, how-to, humor, juvenile nonfiction, law, lesbian, medicine, memoirs, military, money, nature, personal improvement, politics, science, self-help, sociology, sports, technology, travel, true crime, women's issues, women's studies. **Considers these fiction areas:** action, adventure, contemporary issues, crime, detective, ethnic, experimental, family saga, fantasy, feminist, gay, glitz, historical, humor, juvenile, lesbian, literary, mainstream, military, mystery, psychic, regional, romance, science fiction, sports, thriller, westerns, young adult, political. **Considers these script areas:** action, cartoon, comedy, contemporary, detective, (and espionage), family, fantasy, feminist, gay/lesbian, glitz, historical, horror, juvenile, mainstream, mystery, psychic, romantic comedy, romantic drama, science, sports, teen, thriller, western.

- "Some of us have special interests and some of us encourage you to share your passion and work with us." Does not want to receive "ideas for sitcoms, novels, films, etc., or queries without SASEs."

How to Contact Query with SASE. Accepts e-mail queries (no attachments). If via e-mail, please include the type of query and your genre in the subject line. If via regular mail, you may include the first few chapters, outline, or proposal. No fax queries. Accepts simultaneous submissions. Only responds if interested; responds as soon as possible. Obtains most new clients through recommendations from others, queries.

Terms Agent receives 15% commission on domestic sales. Agent receives 20% commission on foreign sales. Offers written contract. Charges clients for photocopying, mailing expenses, overseas/long distance phone calls/faxes.

Recent Sales Sold more than 40 titles and 35 scripts in the last year.

Tips "Please include a paragraph on your background, even if you have no literary background, and a brief synopsis of the project."

MUSE LITERARY MANAGEMENT

189 Waverly Place, #4, New York NY 10014. (212)925-3721. E-mail: museliterarymgmt@aol.com. Website: www.museliterary.com/. **Contact:** Deborah Carter. Associations: NAWE, International Thriller Writers, Historical Novel Society, Associations of Booksellers for Children, The Authors Guild, Children's Literature Network, and American Folklore Society. Represents 5 clients. 80% of clients are new/unpublished writers.

- Prior to starting her agency, Ms. Carter trained with an AAR literary agent and worked in the music business and as a talent scout for record companies in artist management. She has a BA in English and music from Washington Square University College at NYU.

Represents Novels, short story collections, poetry books. **Considers these nonfiction areas:** , narrative nonfiction (no prescriptive nonfiction), children's. **Considers these fiction areas:** adventure, detective, juvenile, mystery, picture books, suspense, thriller, young adult, espionage; middle-grade novels; literary short story collections, literary fiction with popular appeal.

- Specializes in manuscript development, the sale and administration of print, performance, and foreign rights to literary works, and post-publication publicity and appearances. Actively seeking "writers with formal training who bring compelling voices and a unique outlook to their manuscripts. Those who submit should be receptive to editorial feedback and willing to revise during the submission provess in order to remain competitive. " Does not want "manuscripts that have been worked over by book doctors (collaborative projects ok, but writers must have chops); category romance, chick lit, sci-fi, fantasy, horror, stories about cats and dogs, vampires or serial killers, fiction or nonfiction with religious or spiritual subject matter."

How to Contact Query with SASE. Query via e-mail (no attachments). Discards unwanted queries. Responds in 2 weeks to queries. Responds in 2-3 weeks to mss. Obtains most new clients through recommendations from others, conferences.

Terms Agent receives 15% commission on domestic sales. Agent receives 20% commission on foreign sales. One-year contract offered when writer and agent agree that the manuscript is ready for submission; manuscripts in development are not bound by contract. Sometimes charges for postage and photocopying. All expenses are preapproved by the client.

JEAN V. NAGGAR LITERARY AGENCY, INC.

216 E. 75th St., Suite 1E, New York NY 10021. (212)794-1082. E-mail: jvnla@jvnla.com. Website: www.jvnla.com. **Contact:** Jean Naggar. Member of AAR. Other memberships include PEN, Women's Media Group, Women's Forum. Represents 80 clients. 20% of clients are new/unpublished writers. Currently handles: nonfiction books 35%, novels 45%, juvenile books 15%, scholarly books 5%.

- Ms. Naggar has served as president of AAR.

Member Agents Jean Naggar (mainstream fiction, nonfiction); Jennifer Weltz, director (subsidiary rights, children's books); Alice Tasman, senior agent (commercial and literary fiction, thrillers, narrative nonfiction); Jessica Regel, agent (young adult fiction and nonfiction); Elizabeth Evans.

Represents Nonfiction books, novels. **Considers these nonfiction areas:** biography, child guidance, current affairs, government, health, history, juvenile nonfiction, law, medicine, memoirs, New Age, parenting, politics, psychology, self-help, sociology, travel, women's issues, women's studies. **Considers these fiction areas:** action, adventure, crime, detective, ethnic, family saga, feminist, historical, literary, mainstream, mystery, police, psychic, supernatural, suspense, thriller.

- This agency specializes in mainstream fiction and nonfiction and literary fiction with commercial potential.

How to Contact Query via e-mail. Prefers to read materials exclusively. No fax queries. Responds in 1 day to queries. Responds in 2 months to mss. Obtains most new clients through recommendations from others.

Terms Agent receives 15% commission on domestic sales. Agent receives 20% commission on foreign sales. Offers written contract. Charges for overseas mailing, messenger services, book purchases, long-distance telephone, photocopying—all deductible from royalties received.

Recent Sales Night Navigation, by Ginnah Howard; After Hours At the Almost Home, by Tara Yelen; An Entirely Synthetic Fish: A Biography of Rainbow Trout, by Anders Halverson; The Patron Saint of Butterflies, by Cecilia Galante, Wondrous Strange, by Lesley Livingston, 6 Sick Hipsters, by Rayo Casablanca, The Last Bridge, by Teri Coyne; Gypsy Goodbye, by Nancy Springer, Commuters, by Emily Tedrowe; The Language of Secrets, by Dianne Dixon, Smiling to Freedom, by Martin Benoit Stiles; The Tale of Halcyon Crane, by Wendy Webb, Fugitive, by Phillip Margolin; BlackBerry Girl, by Aidan Donnelley Rowley; Wild girls, by Pat Murphy.

Writers Conferences Willamette Writers Conference; Pacific Northwest Writers Conference; Bread Loaf Writers Conference; Marymount Manhattan Writers Conference; SEAK Medical & Legal Fiction Writing Conference.

Tips "Use a professional presentation. Because of the avalanche of unsolicited queries that flood the agency every week, we have had to modify our policy. We will now only guarantee to read and respond to queries from writers who come recommended by someone we know. Our areas are general fiction and nonfiction—no children's books by unpublished writers, no multimedia, no screenplays, no formula fiction, and no mysteries by unpublished writers. We recommend patience and fortitude: the courage to be true to your own vision, the fortitude to finish a novel and polish it again and again before sending it out, and the patience to accept rejection gracefully and wait for the stars to align themselves appropriately for success."

NAPPALAND LITERARY AGENCY

A Division of Nappaland Communications, Inc., P.O. Box 1674, Loveland CO 80539-1674. Fax: (970)635-9869. Website: www.NappalandLiterary.com. **Contact:** Mike Nappa, chief agent. Represents 8 clients. 0% of clients are new/unpublished writers. Currently handles: nonfiction books 45%, novels 50%, scholarly books 5%.

- Prior to becoming an agent, Mr. Nappa served as an acquisition editor for three major Christian publishing houses.

Represents Nonfiction books, novels. **Considers these nonfiction areas:** child guidance, current affairs, inspirational, parenting, popular culture, religious, women's issues, women's studies. **Considers these fiction areas:** adventure, crime, detective, literary, police, religious, thriller.

- This agency will not consider any new authors unless they come with a recommendation from a current Nappaland client. All queries without such a recommendation are immediately rejected. "Interested in thoughtful, vivid, nonfiction works on religious and cultural themes. Also, fast-paced, well-crafted fiction (suspense, literary, women's) that reads like a work of art. Established authors only; broad promotional platform preferred." Does not want to receive children's books, movie or television scripts, textbooks, short stories, stage plays or poetry.

How to Contact Query with SASE. Submit author bio. Include the name of the person referring you to us. Do *not* send entire proposal unless requested. Send query and bio only. Not currently accepting new clients. To reach either Mike Nappa or Alec Smart at Nappaland Literary Agency, please visit www.NappalandLiterary.com. Accepts simultaneous submissions. Responds in 1 month to queries. Responds in 3 months to mss.

Terms Agent receives 15% commission on domestic sales. Agent receives 20% commission on foreign sales. Offers written contract; 30-day notice must be given to terminate contract.

Recent Sales *Family Matters*, by Dr. Timothy Paul Jones (Wesleyan Publishing House); *Drift*, by Sharon Carter Rogers (Howard Books/Simon & Schuster); *Interactive Illustrations*, by Mike Nappa (Standard Publishing).

Writers Conferences Colorado Christian Writers' Conference in Estes Park.

NELSON LITERARY AGENCY

1732 Wazee St., Suite 207, Denver CO 80202. (303)292-2805. E-mail: query@nelsonagency.com. Website: www.nelsonagency.com. **Contact:** Kristin Nelson, president and senior literary agent; Sara Megibow, associate literary agent. Member of AAR. RWA, SCBWI, SFWA

- Prior to opening her own agency, Ms. Nelson worked as a literary scout and subrights agent for agent Jody Rein.

Represents Novels, select nonfiction. **Considers these nonfiction areas:** memoirs. **Considers these fiction areas:** commercial, literary, mainstream, women's, chick lit (includes mysteries), romance (includes fantasy with romantic elements, science fiction, fantasy, young adult).

- NLA specializes in representing commercial fiction and high caliber literary fiction. Actively seeking Latina writers who tackle contemporary issues in a modern voice (think *Dirty Girls Social Club*). Does not want short story collections, mysteries (except chick lit), thrillers, Christian, horror, or children's picture books.

How to Contact Query by e-mail only.

Recent Sales New York Times Bestselling author of *I'd Tell You I Love You, But Then I'd Have to Kill You*, Ally Carter's fourth novel in the Gallagher Girls series; *Hester* (historical fiction), by Paula Reed, *Proof by Seduction* (debut romance), by Courtney Milan, *Soulless* (fantasy debut), by Gail Carriger, *The Shifter* (debut children's fantasy), by Janice Hardy, *Real Life & Liars* (debut women's fiction), by Kristina Riggle, *Hotel on the Corner of Bitter and Sweet* (debut literary fiction), by Jamie Ford.

NORTHERN LIGHTS LITERARY SERVICES, LLC

2721 Tulip Tree Rd., Suite A, Nashville IN 47448-9128. (888)558-4354. Fax: (208)265-1948. E-mail: queries@northernlightsls.com. Website: www.northernlightsls.com. **Contact:** Sammie Justesen. Represents 25 clients. 35% of clients are new/unpublished writers. Currently handles: nonfiction books 90%, novels 10%.

Member Agents Sammie Justesen (fiction and nonfiction); Vorris Dee Justesen (business and current affairs).

Represents Nonfiction books, novels. **Considers these nonfiction areas:** animals, autobiography, biography, business, child guidance, cooking, crafts, current affairs, diet/nutrition, economics, environment, ethnic, foods, health, inspirational, investigative, memoirs, metaphysics, New Age, parenting, popular culture, psychology, religious, self-help, sports, true crime, women's issues, women's studies. **Considers these fiction areas:** action, adventure, crime, detective, ethnic, family saga, feminist, glitz, historical, inspirational, mainstream, mystery, police, psychic, regional, religious, romance, supernatural, suspense, thriller, women's.

- "Our goal is to provide personalized service to clients and create a bond that will endure throughout the writer's career. We seriously consider each query we receive and will accept hardworking new authors who are willing to develop their talents and skills. We enjoy working with healthcare professionals and writers who clearly understand their market and have a platform." Actively seeking general nonfiction—especially if the writer has a platform. Does not want to receive fantasy, horror, erotica, children's books, screenplays, poetry or short stories.

How to Contact Query with SASE. Submit outline/proposal, synopsis, 3 sample chapters, author bio. E-queries preferred. No phone queries. All queries considered, but the agency only replies if interested. If you've completed and polished a novel, send a query letter, a one-or-two page synopsis of the plot, and the first chapter. Also include your biography as it relates to your writing experience. Do not send an entire mss unless requested. If you'd like to submit a nonfiction book, send a query letter, along with the book proposal. Include a bio showing the background that will enable you to write the book. Accepts simultaneous submissions. Responds in 2 months to queries. Responds in 2 months to mss. Obtains most new clients through solicitations, conferences.

Terms Agent receives 15% commission on domestic sales. Agent receives 20% commission on foreign sales. Offers written contract; 30-day notice must be given to terminate contract.

Recent Sales *Intuitive Parenting*, by Debra Snyder, Ph.D. (Beyond Words); *The Confidence Trap*, by Russ Harris (Penguin); *The Never Cold Call Again Toolkit*, by Frank Rumbauskas, Jr. (Wiley); *Thank You for Firing Me*, by Candace Reed and Kitty Martini (Sterling); *The Wal-Mart Cure: Ten Lifesaving Supplements for Under $10* (Sourcebooks).
Tips "If you're fortunate enough to find an agent who answers your query and asks for a printed manuscript, always include a letter and cover page containing your name, physical address, e-mail address and phone number. Be professional!"

KATHI J. PATON LITERARY AGENCY

P.O. Box 2236 Radio City Station, New York NY 10101. (212)265-6586. E-mail: kjplitbiz@optonline.net. **Contact:** Kathi Paton. Currently handles: nonfiction books 85%, novels 15%.
Represents Nonfiction books, novels, short story collections, book-based film rights. **Considers these nonfiction areas:** business, child guidance, economics, environment, humor, investigative, money, parenting, psychology, religious, satire, personal investing. **Considers these fiction areas:** literary, mainstream, multicultural, short stories.

This agency specializes in adult nonfiction.

How to Contact Accepts e-mail queries only. Accepts simultaneous submissions. Accepts new clients through recommendations from current clients.
Terms Agent receives 15% commission on domestic sales. Agent receives 20% commission on foreign sales. Offers written contract. Charges clients for photocopying.
Writers Conferences Attends major regional panels, seminars and conferences.

ALISON J. PICARD, LITERARY AGENT

P.O. Box 2000, Cotuit MA 02635. Phone/Fax: (508)477-7192. E-mail: ajpicard@aol.com. **Contact:** Alison Picard. Represents 48 clients. 30% of clients are new/unpublished writers. Currently handles: nonfiction books 40%, novels 40%, juvenile books 20%.

- Prior to becoming an agent, Ms. Picard was an assistant at a literary agency in New York.

Represents Nonfiction books, novels, juvenile. **Considers these nonfiction areas:** animals, autobiography, biography, business, child guidance, cooking, cultural interests, current affairs, diet/nutrition, economics, education, environment, ethnic, foods, gay/lesbian, government, health, history, how-to, humor, inspirational, juvenile nonfiction, law, medicine, memoirs, metaphysics, military, money, multicultural, New Age, parenting, popular culture, politics, psychology, religious, science, self-help, technology, travel, true crime, war, women's issues, women's studies, young adult. **Considers these fiction areas:** action, adventure, contemporary issues, crime, detective, erotica, ethnic, family saga, feminist, gay, glitz, historical, horror, humor, juvenile, lesbian, literary, mainstream, multicultural, mystery, New Age, picture books, police, psychic, romance, sports, supernatural, thriller, young adult.

"Many of my clients have come to me from big agencies, where they felt overlooked or ignored. I communicate freely with my clients and offer a lot of career advice, suggestions for revising manuscripts, etc. If I believe in a project, I will submit it to a dozen or more publishers, unlike some agents who give up after four or five rejections." No science fiction/fantasy, Western, poetry, plays or articles.

How to Contact Query with SASE. Accepts simultaneous submissions. Responds in 2 weeks to queries. Responds in 4 months to mss. Obtains most new clients through recommendations from others, solicitations.
Terms Agent receives 15% commission on domestic sales. Agent receives 20% commission on foreign sales. Offers written contract, binding for 1 year; 1-week notice must be given to terminate contract.
Recent Sales *Zitface*, by Emily Ormand (Marshall Cavendish); *Totally Together*, by Stephanie O'Dea (Running Press); *The Ultimate Slow Cooker Cookbook*, by Stephanie O'Dea (Hyperion); *Two Untitled Cookbooks*, by Erin Chase (St. Martin's Press); *A Journal of the Flood Year*, by David Ely (Portobello Books — United Kingdom, L'Ancora — Italy); *A Mighty Wall*, by John Foley (Llewellyn/Flux); *Jelly's Gold*, by David Housewright (St. Martin's Press).

Tips "Please don't send material without sending a query first via mail or e-mail. I don't accept phone or fax queries. Always enclose an SASE with a query."

PROSPECT AGENCY, LLC

285 Fifth Ave., PMB 445, Brooklyn NY 11215. (718)788-3217. E-mail: esk@prospectagency.com. Website: www.prospectagency.com. **Contact:** Emily Sylvan Kim. Represents 15 clients. 50% of clients are new/unpublished writers. Currently handles: novels 66%, juvenile books 33%.

- Prior to starting her agency, Ms. Kim briefly attended law school and worked for another literary agency.

Member Agents Emily Sylvan Kim; Becca Stumpf (adult and YA literary, mainstream fiction; nonfiction interests include narrative nonfiction, journalistic perspectives, fashion, film studies, travel, art, and informed analysis of cultural phenomena. She has a special interest in aging in America and environmental issues); Rachel Orr (fiction and nonfiction, particularly picture books, beginning readers, chapter books, middle-grade, YA novels); Teresa Kietlinski (artists who both write and illustrate).

Represents Nonfiction books, novels, juvenile. **Considers these nonfiction areas:** art, biography, history, juvenile nonfiction, law, memoirs, popular culture, politics, science, travel, prescriptive guides. **Considers these fiction areas:** action, adventure, detective, erotica, ethnic, frontier, juvenile, literary, mainstream, mystery, picture books, romance, suspense, thriller, westerns, young adult.

"We are currently looking for the next generation of writers to shape the literary landscape. Our clients receive professional and knowledgeable representation. We are committed to offering skilled editorial advice and advocating our clients in the marketplace." Actively seeking romance, literary fiction, and young adult submissions. Does not want to receive poetry, short stories, textbooks, or most nonfiction.

How to Contact Upload outline and 3 sample chapters to the website. Accepts simultaneous submissions. Responds in 3 weeks to queries. Responds in 1 month to mss. Obtains most new clients through recommendations from others, conferences, unsolicited mss.

Terms Agent receives 15% commission on domestic sales. Agent receives 20% commission on foreign sales. Offers written contract.

Recent Sales *BADD*, by Tim Tharp (Knopf); *Six*, by Elizabeth Batten-Carew (St. Martin's); *Rocky Road*, by Rose Kent (Knopf); *Mating Game*, by Janice Maynard (NAL); *Golden Delicious*, by Aaron Hawkins (Houghton Mifflin Harcourt); *Damaged*, by Pamela Callow (Mira); *Seduced by Shadows*, by Jessica Slade (NAL), *Identity of Ultraviolet*, by Jake Bell (Scholastic); *Quackenstein*, by Sudipta Bardhan-Quallen (Abrams); *Betraying Season*, by Marissa Doyle (Holt); *Sex on the Beach*, by Susan Lyons (Berkley), more.

Writers Conferences "Please see our website for a complete list of attended conferences."

P.S. LITERARY AGENCY

520 Kerr St., #20033, Oakville ON L6K 3C7 Canada. E-mail: query@psliterary.com. Website: www.psliterary.com. **Contact:** Curtis Russell. Represents 10 clients. 25% of clients are new/unpublished writers. Currently handles: nonfiction books 50%, novels 50%.

Represents Nonfiction books, novels, juvenile. **Considers these nonfiction areas:** biography, business, child, cooking, current affairs, government, health, how-to, humor, memoirs, military, money, nature, popular culture, science, self-help, sports, true crime, women's. **Considers these fiction areas:** adventure, detective, erotica, ethnic, family, historical, horror, humor, juvenile, literary, mainstream, mystery, picture books, romance, sports, thriller, young, women's.

"What makes our agency distinct: We take on a small number of clients per year in order to provide focused, hands-on representation. We pride ourselves in providing industry leading client service." Does not want to receive poetry or screenplays.

How to Contact Query via mail or e-mail. Prefers e-mail. Submit synopsis, author bio. Accepts simultaneous submissions. Responds in 6 weeks to queries. Responds in 6 weeks to mss. Obtains most new clients through solicitations.

Terms Agent receives 15% commission on domestic sales. Agent receives 25% commission on foreign sales. Offers written contract; 30-day notice must be given to terminate contract. "This agency charges for postage/messenger services only if a project is sold."
Tips "Please review our website for the most up-to-date submission guidelines."

QUICKSILVER BOOKS: LITERARY AGENTS

508 Central Park Ave., #5101, Scarsdale NY 10583. Phone/Fax: (914)722-4664. E-mail: quickbooks@optonline.net. Website: www.quicksilverbooks.com. **Contact:** Bob Silverstein. Represents 50 clients. 50% of clients are new/unpublished writers. Currently handles: nonfiction books 75%, novels 25%.

- Prior to opening his agency, Mr. Silverstein served as senior editor at Bantam Books and managing editor at Dell Books/Delacorte Press.

Represents Nonfiction books, novels. **Considers these nonfiction areas:** anthropology, archeology, autobiography, biography, business, child guidance, cooking, cultural interests, current affairs, diet/nutrition, economics, environment, ethnic, foods, health, history, how-to, inspirational, language, medicine, memoirs, New Age, parenting, popular culture, psychology, religious, science, self-help, sociology, sports, true crime, women's issues, women's studies. **Considers these fiction areas:** action, adventure, glitz, mystery, suspense, thriller.

O→ This agency specializes in literary and commercial mainstream fiction and nonfiction, especially psychology, New Age, holistic healing, consciousness, ecology, environment, spirituality, reference, self-help, cookbooks and narrative nonfiction. Does not want to receive science fiction, pornography, poetry or single-spaced mss.

How to Contact Query with SASE. Authors are expected to supply SASE for return of ms and for query letter responses. Accepts simultaneous submissions. Responds in 2 weeks to queries. Responds in 1 month to mss. Obtains most new clients through recommendations, listings in sourcebooks, solicitations, workshop participation.
Terms Agent receives 15% commission on domestic sales. Agent receives 20% commission on foreign sales. Offers written contract.
Recent Sales *Simply Mexican*, by Lourdes Castro (Ten Speed Press); *Indian Vegan Cooking*, by Madhu Gadia (Perigee/Penguin); *Selling Luxury*, by Robin Lent & Genevieve Tour (Wiley); *Get the Job You Want, Even When No One's Hiring*, by Ford R. Myers (Wiley); *Matrix Meditations*, by Victor & Kooch Daniels (Inner Traditions Bear & Co.); *Macrobiotics for Dummies* (Wiley); *The Power of Receiving* (Tarcher); *Eat, Drink, Think in Spanish* (Ten Speed Press); *Nice Girls Don't Win at Life* (Broadway).
Writers Conferences National Writers Union.
Tips "Write what you know. Write from the heart. Publishers print, authors sell."

RAINES & RAINES

103 Kenyon Road, Medusa NY 12120. (518)239-8311. Fax: (518)239-6029. **Contact:** Theron Raines (member of AAR); Joan Raines; Keith Korman. Member of AAR. Represents 100 clients.
Represents Nonfiction books, novels. **Considers these nonfiction areas:** Action/Adventure, Autobiography/Biography, Finance/Investing, History, Military/War, NarrativePsychology, All subjects. **Considers these fiction areas:** action, adventure, crime, detective, fantasy, frontier, historical, mystery, picture books, police, science fiction, suspense, thriller, westerns, whimsical.
How to Contact Query with SASE. Responds in 2 weeks to queries.
Terms Agent receives 15% commission on domestic sales. Agent receives 20% commission on foreign sales. Charges for photocopying.

THE REDWOOD AGENCY

4300 SW 34th Avenue, Portland OR 97239. (503)219-9019. E-mail: info@redwoodagency.com. Website: www.redwoodagency.com. **Contact:** Catherine Fowler, founder. Adheres to AAR canon of ethics. Currently handles: nonfiction books 100%.

- Prior to becoming an agent, Ms. Fowler was an editor, subsidiary rights director and associate publisher for Doubleday, Simon & Schuster and Random House for her 20 years in NY Publishing. Content exec for web startups Excite and WebMD.

Represents Nonfiction books, novels. **Considers these nonfiction areas:** business, cooking, diet/nutrition, environment, gardening, health, humor, medicine, memoirs, parenting, popular culture, psychology, satire, self-help, women's issues, women's studies, narrative, parenting, aging, reference, lifestyle, cultural technology. **Considers these fiction areas:** literary, mainstream, suspense, women's, quirky.

"Along with our love of books and publishing, we have the desire and commitment to work with fun, interesting and creative people, to do so with respect and professionalism, but also with a sense of humor." Actively seeking high-quality, nonfiction works created for the general consumer market, as well as projects with the potential to become book series. Does not want to receive fiction. Do not send packages that require signature for delivery.

How to Contact Query via e-mail only. While we redesign website, submit "quick query" to: query@redwoodagency.com. See all guidelines online. Obtains most new clients through recommendations from others, solicitations.

Terms Offers written contract. Charges for copying and delivery charges, if any, as specified in author/agency agreement.

HELEN REES LITERARY AGENCY

14 Beacon St., Suite 710, Boston MA 02108. (617)227-9014. Fax: (617)227-8762. E-mail: reesagency@reesagency.com. **Contact:** Joan Mazmanian, Ann Collette, Helen Rees, Lorin Rees. Estab. 1983. Member of AAR. Other memberships include PEN. Represents more than 100 clients. 50% of clients are new/unpublished writers. Currently handles: nonfiction books 60%, novels 40%.

Member Agents Ann Collette (literary, mystery, thrillers, suspense, vampire, and women's fiction; in non-fiction, she prefers true crime, narrative non-fiction, military & war, work to do with race & class, and work set in or about Southeast Asia. Ann can be reached at: Agent10702@aol.com). Lorin Rees (literary fiction, memoirs, business books, self-help, science, history, psychology and narrative non-fiction. lorin@reesagency.com).

Represents Nonfiction books, novels. **Considers these nonfiction areas:** autobiography, biography, business, current affairs, economics, government, health, history, law, medicine, money, politics, women's issues, women's studies. **Considers these fiction areas:** historical, literary, mainstream, mystery, suspense, thriller.

How to Contact Query with SASE, outline, 2 sample chapters. No unsolicited e-mail submissions. No multiple submissions. Responds in 3-4 weeks to queries. Obtains most new clients through recommendations from others, conferences, submissions.

Terms Agent receives 15% commission on domestic sales. Agent receives 20% commission on foreign sales.

Recent Sales Sold more than 35 titles in the last year. *Get your Shipt Together*, by Capt. D. Michael Abrashoff; *Overpromise and Overdeliver*, by Rick Berrara; *Opacity*, by Joel Kurtzman; *America the Broke*, by Gerald Swanson; *Murder at the B-School*, by Jeffrey Cruikshank; *Bone Factory*, by Steven Sidor; *Father Said*, by Hal Sirowitz; *Winning*, by Jack Welch; *The Case for Israel*, by Alan Dershowitz; *As the Future Catches You*, by Juan Enriquez; *Blood Makes the Grass Grow Green*, by Johnny Rico; *DVD Movie Guide*, by Mick Martin and Marsha Porter; *Words that Work*, by Frank Luntz; *Stirring It Up*, by Gary Hirshberg; *Hot Spots*, by Martin Fletcher; *Andy Grove: The Life and Times of an American*, by Richard Tedlow; *Girls Most Likely To*, by Poonam Sharma.

JODY REIN BOOKS, INC.

7741 S. Ash Ct., Centennial CO 80122. (303)694-4430. Fax: (303)694-0687. Website: www.jodyreinbooks.com. **Contact:** Winnefred Dollar. Member of AAR. Other memberships include Authors' Guild. Currently handles: nonfiction books 70%, novels 30%.

- Prior to opening her agency, Ms. Rein worked for 13 years as an acquisitions editor for Contemporary Books and as executive editor for Bantam/Doubleday/Dell and Morrow/Avon.

Represents Nonfiction books, novels. **Considers these nonfiction areas:** business, child guidance, cultural interests, current affairs, dance, economics, environment, ethnic, film, government, history, humor, law, music, parenting, popular culture, politics, psychology, satire, science, sociology, technology, theater, women's issues, women's studies. **Considers these fiction areas:** literary, mainstream.

O→ *This agency is no longer actively seeking new clients.*

Terms Agent receives 15% commission on domestic sales. Agent receives 25% commission on foreign sales. Agent receives 20% commission on film sales. Offers written contract. Charges clients for express mail, overseas expenses, photocopying mss.

Recent Sales *How to Remodel a Man*, by Bruce Cameron (St. Martin's Press); *8 Simple Rules for Dating My Teenage Daughter*, by Bruce Cameron (ABC/Disney); *Unbound*, by Dean King (Little, Brown); *Halfway to Heaven*, by Mark Obmascik (The Free Press); *The Rhino with Glue-On Shoes*, by Dr. Lucy Spelman (Random House); *When She Flew*, by Jennie Shortridge (NAL).

Tips "Do your homework before submitting. Make sure you have a marketable topic and the credentials to write about it. We want well-written books on fresh and original nonfiction topics that have broad appeal, as well as novels written by authors who have spent years developing their craft. Authors must be well established in their fields and have strong media experience."

JODIE RHODES LITERARY AGENCY

8840 Villa La Jolla Drive, Suite 315, La Jolla CA 92037-1957. Website: jodierhodesliterary.com. **Contact:** Jodie Rhodes, president. Member of AAR. Represents 74 clients. 60% of clients are new/unpublished writers. Currently handles: nonfiction books 45%, novels 35%, juvenile books 20%.

- Prior to opening her agency, Ms. Rhodes was a university-level creative writing teacher, workshop director, published novelist, and vice president/media director at the N.W. Ayer Advertising Agency.

Member Agents Jodie Rhodes; Clark McCutcheon (fiction); Bob McCarter (nonfiction).

Represents Nonfiction books, novels. **Considers these nonfiction areas:** autobiography, biography, child guidance, cultural interests, ethnic, government, health, history, law, medicine, memoirs, military, parenting, politics, science, technology, war, women's issues, women's studies. **Considers these fiction areas:** ethnic, family saga, historical, literary, mainstream, mystery, suspense, thriller, women's, young adult.

O→ "Actively seeking witty, sophisticated women's books about career ambitions and relationships; edgy/trendy YA and teen books; narrative nonfiction on groundbreaking scientific discoveries, politics, economics, military and important current affairs by prominent scientists and academic professors." Does not want to receive erotica, horror, fantasy, romance, science fiction, religious/inspirational, or children's books (does accept young adult/teen).

How to Contact Query with brief synopsis, first 30-50 pages, SASE. Do not call. Do not send complete ms unless requested. This agency does not return unrequested material weighing a pound or more that requires special postage. Include e-mail address with query. Accepts simultaneous submissions. Responds in 3 weeks to queries. Obtains most new clients through recommendations from others, agent sourcebooks.

Terms Agent receives 15% commission on domestic sales. Agent receives 20% commission on foreign sales. Offers written contract; 1-month notice must be given to terminate contract. Charges clients for fax, photocopying, phone calls, postage. Charges are itemized and approved by writers upfront.

Recent Sales Sold 42 titles in the last year. *The Ring*, by Kavita Daswani (HarperCollins); *Train to Trieste*, by Domnica Radulescu (Knopf); *A Year With Cats and Dogs*, by Margaret Hawkins (Permanent Press); *Silence and Silhouettes*, by Ryan Smithson (HarperCollins); *Internal Affairs*, by Constance Dial (Permanent Press); *How Math Rules the World*, by James Stein (HarperCollins); Diagnosis of Love, by Maggie Martin (Bantam); Lies, Damn Lies, and Science, by Sherry Seethaler (Prentice Hall); Freaked, by Jeanne Dutton (HarperCollins); The Five Second Rule, by Anne Maczulak (Perseus Books); The Intelligence Wars, by Stephen O'Hern (Prometheus); Seducing the Spirits, by Louise Young (The Permanent Press), and more.

Tips "Think your book out before you write it. Do your research, know your subject matter intimately, and write vivid specifics, not bland generalities. Care deeply about your book. Don't imitate other writers. Find your own voice. We never take on a book we don't believe in, and we go the extra mile for our writers. We welcome talented, new writers."

ANN RITTENBERG LITERARY AGENCY, INC.

30 Bond St., New York NY 10012. (212)684-6936. Fax: (212)684-6929. Website: www.rittlit.com. **Contact:** Ann Rittenberg, President and Penn Whaling, Associate. Member of AAR. Currently handles: fiction 75%, nonfiction 25%.

Represents Considers these nonfiction areas: memoirs, women's issues, women's studies. **Considers these fiction areas:** literary, thriller, upmarket fiction.

- This agent specializes in literary fiction and literary nonfiction. Does not want to receive screenplays, straight genre fiction, poetry, self-help.

How to Contact Query with SASE. Submit outline, 3 sample chapters, SASE. Query via postal mail *only*. Accepts simultaneous submissions. Responds in 6 weeks to queries. Responds in 2 months to mss. Obtains most new clients through referrals from established writers and editors.

Terms Agent receives 15% commission on domestic sales. Agent receives 20% commission on foreign sales. Offers written contract. This agency charges clients for photocopying only.

Recent Sales *The Given Day*, by Dennis Lehane; *My Cat Hates You*, by Jim Edgar; *Never Wave Goodbye*, by Doug Magee; *House and Home*, by Kathleen McCleary; *Nowhere to Run*, by CJ Box; and *Daughter of Kura*, by Debra Austin.

RLR ASSOCIATES, LTD.

Literary Department, 7 W. 51st St., New York NY 10019. (212)541-8641. Fax: (212)262-7084. E-mail: sgould@rlrassociates.net. Website: www.rlrliterary.net. **Contact:** Scott Gould. Member of AAR. Represents 50 clients. 25% of clients are new/unpublished writers. Currently handles: nonfiction books 70%, novels 25%, story collections 5%.

Represents Nonfiction books, novels, short story collections, scholarly. **Considers these nonfiction areas:** animals, anthropology, archeology, art, autobiography, biography, business, child guidance, cooking, cultural interests, current affairs, decorating, diet/nutrition, economics, education, environment, ethnic, foods, gay/lesbian, government, health, history, humor, inspirational, interior design, language, law, memoirs, money, multicultural, music, parenting, photography, popular culture, politics, psychology, religious, science, self-help, sociology, sports, technology, translation, travel, true crime, women's issues, women's studies. **Considers these fiction areas:** action, adventure, cartoon, comic books, crime, detective, ethnic, experimental, family saga, feminist, gay, historical, horror, humor, lesbian, literary, mainstream, multicultural, mystery, police, satire, sports, suspense.

- "We provide a lot of editorial assistance to our clients and have connections." Actively seeking fiction, current affairs, history, art, popular culture, health and business. Does not want to receive screenplays.

How to Contact Query by either e-mail or mail. Accepts simultaneous submissions. Responds in 4-8 weeks to queries. Obtains most new clients through recommendations from others.

Terms Agent receives 15% commission on domestic sales. Agent receives 20% commission on foreign sales. Offers written contract.

Recent Sales Clients include Shelby Foote, The Grief Recovery Institute, Don Wade, Don Zimmer, The Knot.com, David Plowden, PGA of America, Danny Peary, George Kalinsky, Peter Hyman, Daniel Parker, Lee Miller, Elise Miller, Nina Planck, Karyn Bosnak, Christopher Pike, Gerald Carbone, Jason Lethcoe, Andy Crouch.

Tips "Please check out our website for more details on our agency."

B.J. ROBBINS LITERARY AGENCY

5130 Bellaire Ave., North Hollywood CA 91607-2908. E-mail: Robbinsliterary@gmail.com. **Contact:** (Ms.) B.J. Robbins. Member of AAR. Represents 40 clients. 50% of clients are new/unpublished writers. Currently handles: nonfiction books 50%, novels 50%.

Represents Nonfiction books, novels. **Considers these nonfiction areas:** autobiography, biography, cultural interests, current affairs, dance, ethnic, film, health, humor, investigative, medicine, memoirs, music, popular culture, psychology, self-help, sociology, sports, theater, travel, true crime, women's issues, women's studies. **Considers these fiction areas:** crime, detective, ethnic, literary, mainstream, mystery, police, sports, suspense, thriller.
How to Contact Query with SASE. Submit outline/proposal, 3 sample chapters, SASE. Accepts e-mail queries (no attachments). Accepts simultaneous submissions. Responds in 2-6 weeks to queries. Responds in 6-8 weeks to mss. Obtains most new clients through conferences, referrals.
Terms Agent receives 15% commission on domestic sales. Agent receives 20% commission on foreign sales. Offers written contract; 3-month notice must be given to terminate contract. This agency charges clients for postage and photocopying (only after sale of ms).
Recent Sales Sold 15 titles in the last year. *Getting Stoned With Savages*, by J. Maarten Troost (Broadway); *Hot Water*, by Kathryn Jordan (Berkley); *Between the Bridge and the River*, by Craig Ferguson (Chronicle); *I'm Proud of You*, by Tim Madigan (Gotham); *Man of the House*, by Chris Erskine (Rodale); *Bird of Another heaven*, by James D. Houston (Knopf); *Tomorrow They Will Kiss*, by Eduardo Santiago (Little, Brown); *A Terrible Glory*, by James Donovan (Little, Brown); *The Writing on My Forehead*, by Nafisa Haji (Morrow); *Seen the Glory*, by John Hough Jr. (Simon & Schuster); *Lost on Planet China*, by J. Maarten Troost (Broadway).
Writers Conferences Squaw Valley Writers Workshop; San Diego State University Writers' Conference.

THE ROSENBERG GROUP

23 Lincoln Ave., Marblehead MA 01945. (781)990-1341. Fax: (781)990-1344. Website: www.rosenberggroup.com. **Contact:** Barbara Collins Rosenberg. Estab. 1998. Member of AAR. Other memberships include recognized agent of the RWA. Represents 25 clients. 15% of clients are new/unpublished writers. Currently handles: nonfiction books 30%, novels 30%, scholarly books 10%, other 30% college textbooks.

- Prior to becoming an agent, Ms. Rosenberg was a senior editor for Harcourt.

Represents Nonfiction books, novels, textbooks, college textbooks only. **Considers these nonfiction areas:** current affairs, foods, popular culture, psychology, sports, women's issues, women's studies, women's health, wine/beverages. **Considers these fiction areas:** romance, women's.

Ms. Rosenberg is well-versed in the romance market (both category and single title). She is a frequent speaker at romance conferences. Actively seeking romance category or single title in contemporary romantic suspense, and the historical subgenres. Does not want to receive inspirational, time travel, futuristic or paranormal.

How to Contact Query with SASE. No e-mail or fax queries; will not respond. See guidelines online at website. Responds in 2 weeks to queries. Responds in 4-6 weeks to mss. Obtains most new clients through recommendations from others, solicitations, conferences.
Terms Agent receives 15% commission on domestic sales. Agent receives 15% commission on foreign sales. Offers written contract; 1-month notice must be given to terminate contract. Charges maximum of $350/year for postage and photocopying.
Recent Sales Sold 24 titles in the last year.
Writers Conferences RWA National Conference; BookExpo America.

JANE ROTROSEN AGENCY LLC

318 E. 51st St., New York NY 10022. (212)593-4330. Fax: (212)935-6985. E-mail: lcohen@janerotrosen.com. Website: www.janerotrosen.com. Estab. 1974. Member of AAR. Other memberships include Authors Guild. Represents over 100 clients. Currently handles: nonfiction books 30%, novels 70%.
Member Agents Jane R. Berkey; Andrea Cirillo; Annelise Robey; Margaret Ruley; Christina Hogrebe; Suzanna Best; Peggy Gordijn, director of rights.
Represents Nonfiction books, novels. **Considers these nonfiction areas:** autobiography, biography, business, child guidance, cooking, current affairs, diet/nutrition, economics, environment, foods, health, how-to, humor, investigative, medicine, money, parenting, popular culture, psychology,

satire, self-help, sports, true crime, women's issues, women's studies. **Considers these fiction areas:** crime, family saga, historical, mystery, police, romance, suspense, thriller, women's.

How to Contact Query with SASE to the attention of Submissions. Responds in 2 weeks to writers who have been referred by a client or colleague. Responds in 2 months to mss. Obtains most new clients through recommendations from others.

Terms Agent receives 15% commission on domestic sales. Agent receives 20% commission on foreign sales. Offers written contract, binding for 3 years; 2-month notice must be given to terminate contract. Charges clients for photocopying, express mail, overseas postage, book purchase.

MARLY RUSOFF & ASSOCIATES, INC.

P.O. Box 524, Bronxville NY 10708. (914)961-7939. E-mail: mra_queries3@rusoffagency.com. Website: www.rusoffagency.com. **Contact:** Marly Rusoff.

- Prior to her current position, Ms. Rusoff held positions at Houghton Mifflin, Doubleday and William Morrow.

Member Agents Marly Rusoff.

Represents Nonfiction books, novels. **Considers these nonfiction areas:** architecture, art, autobiography, biography, business, design, economics, health, history, medicine, memoirs, popular culture, psychology. **Considers these fiction areas:** commercial, historical, literary.

"While we take delight in discovering new talent, we are particularly interested in helping established writers expand readership and develop their careers."

How to Contact Query with SASE. Submit synopsis, publishing history, author bio, contact information. For e-queries, include no attachments or pdf files. "We cannot read DOCXs." This agency only responds if interested. Responds to queries. Obtains most new clients through recommendations from others.

Recent Sales *The Thieves of Manhattan*, by Adam Langer (fiction, Spiegel & Grau); *The Kabul Beauty School*, by Deborah Rodriguez & Kristen Ohlson (memoir, Random House); *The Death of Santini*, by Pat Conroy (memoir, Nan Talese/Doubleday); *31 Bond Street*, by Ellen Horan (historical fiction, Harper); *My Name is Mary Sutter*, by Robin Oliveira (historical fiction, Viking); *Sweet Blasphemy*, by Elif Shafak (fiction). Other clients include: Thrity Umrigar, Elif Shafak, Arthur Phillips, Ron Rash, and Roland Merullo.

RUSSELL & VOLKENING

50 W. 29th St., #7E, New York NY 10001. (212)684-6050. Fax: (212)889-3026. Website: www.randvinc.com. **Contact:** Jesseca Salky (adult, general fiction & nonfiction, memoirs: jesseca@randvinc.com) Carrie Hannigan (children's & YA), Josh Getzler (mysteries, thrillers, literary and commercial fiction, young adult and middle grade (particularly adventures and mysteries for boys). Email queries only with cover letter & first 5 pages: josh@randvinc.com), Joy Azmitia (Chick-lit, multicultural fiction, romance, humor, and non-fiction in the areas of travel, pop-culture, and philosophy; joy@randvinc.com.). Member of AAR. Represents 140 clients. 20% of clients are new/unpublished writers. Currently handles: nonfiction books 45%, novels 50%, story collections 3%, novella 2%.

Represents Nonfiction books, novels, short story collections. **Considers these nonfiction areas:** anthropology, architecture, art, autobiography, biography, business, cooking, cultural interests, current affairs, design, education, environment, ethnic, film, gay/lesbian, government, health, history, language, law, military, money, music, photography, popular culture, politics, psychology, science, sociology, sports, technology, true crime, war, women's issues, women's studies, creative nonfiction. **Considers these fiction areas:** action, adventure, crime, detective, ethnic, literary, mainstream, mystery, picture books, police, sports, suspense, thriller.

This agency specializes in literary fiction and narrative nonfiction. novels

How to Contact Query only with SASE to appropriate person. Responds in 4 weeks to queries.

Terms Agent receives 15% commission on domestic sales. Agent receives 20% commission on foreign sales. Charges clients for standard office expenses relating to the submission of materials.

Tips If the query is cogent, well written, well presented, and is the type of book we'd represent, we'll ask to see the manuscript. From there, it depends purely on the quality of the work.

VICTORIA SANDERS & ASSOCIATES

241 Avenue of the Americas, Suite 11 H, New York NY 10014. (212)633-8811. Fax: (212)633-0525. E-mail: queriesvsa@hotmail.com. Website: www.victoriasanders.com. **Contact:** Victoria Sanders, Diane Dickensheid. Estab. 1992. Member of AAR. Signatory of WGA. Represents 135 clients. 25% of clients are new/unpublished writers. Currently handles: nonfiction books 30%, novels 70%.

Member Agents Tanya McKinnon, Victoria Sanders, Chris Kepner (open to all types of books as long as the writing is exceptional. include the first three chapters in the body of the email. At the moment, he is especially on the lookout for quality nonfiction.).

Represents Nonfiction books, novels. **Considers these nonfiction areas:** autobiography, biography, cultural interests, current affairs, dance, ethnic, film, gay/lesbian, government, history, humor, language, law, literature, music, popular culture, politics, psychology, satire, theater, translation, women's issues, women's studies. **Considers these fiction areas:** action, adventure, contemporary issues, ethnic, family saga, feminist, gay, lesbian, literary, thriller.

How to Contact Query by e-mail only.

Terms Agent receives 15% commission on domestic sales. Agent receives 20% commission on foreign sales. Offers written contract. Charges for photocopying, messenger, express mail. If in excess of $100, client approval is required.

Recent Sales Sold 20+ titles in the last year.

Tips "Limit query to letter (no calls) and give it your best shot. A good query is going to get a good response."

SCHIAVONE LITERARY AGENCY, INC.

236 Trails End, West Palm Beach FL 33413-2135. (561)966-9294. Fax: (561)966-9294. E-mail: profschia@aol.com. Website: www.publishersmarketplace.com/members/profschia; Blog Site: www.schiavoneliteraryagencyinc.blogspot.com. **Contact:** Dr. James Schiavone. CEO, corporate offices in Florida; Jennifer DuVall, president, New York office. New York office: 3671 Hudson Manor Terrace, No. 11H, Bronx, NY, 10463-1139, phone: (718)548-5332; fax: (718)548-5332; e-mail: jendu77@aol.com Other memberships include National Education Association. Represents 60+ clients. 2% of clients are new/unpublished writers. Currently handles: nonfiction books 50%, novels 49%, textbooks 1%.

- Prior to opening his agency, Dr. Schiavone was a full professor of developmental skills at the City University of New York and author of 5 trade books and 3 textbooks. Jennifer DuVall has many years of combined experience in office management and agenting.

Represents Nonfiction books, novels, juvenile, scholarly, textbooks. **Considers these nonfiction areas:** animals, anthropology, archeology, autobiography, biography, child guidance, cultural interests, current affairs, education, environment, ethnic, gay/lesbian, government, health, history, how-to, humor, investigative, juvenile nonfiction, language, law, literature, medicine, military, parenting, popular culture, politics, psychology, satire, science, sociology, spirituality, true crime. **Considers these fiction areas:** ethnic, family saga, historical, horror, humor, juvenile, literary, mainstream, science fiction, young adult.

- This agency specializes in celebrity biography and autobiography and memoirs. Does not want to receive poetry.

How to Contact Query with SASE. Do not send unsolicited materials or parcels requiring a signature. Send no e-attachments. Accepts simultaneous submissions. Responds in 2 weeks to queries. Responds in 6 weeks to mss. Obtains most new clients through recommendations from others, solicitations, conferences.

Terms Agent receives 15% commission on domestic sales. Agent receives 20% commission on foreign sales. Offers written contract. Charges clients for postage only.

Writers Conferences Key West Literary Seminar; South Florida Writers' Conference; Tallahassee Writers' Conference, Million Dollar Writers' Conference; Alaska Writers Conference.

Tips "We prefer to work with established authors published by major houses in New York. We will consider marketable proposals from new/previously unpublished writers."

SUSAN SCHULMAN LITERARY AGENCY

454 West 44th St., New York NY 10036. (212)713-1633. Fax: (212)581-8830. E-mail: queries@schulmanagency.com. **Contact:** Susan Schulman. Estab. 1980. Member of AAR. Signatory of WGA. Other memberships include Dramatists Guild. 10% of clients are new/unpublished writers. Currently handles: nonfiction books 50%, novels 25%, juvenile books 15%, stage plays 10%.

Member Agents Linda Kiss, director of foreign rights; Katherine Stones, theater; Emily Uhry, submissions editor.

Represents **Considers these nonfiction areas:** anthropology, archeology, autobiography, biography, business, child guidance, cooking, cultural interests, current affairs, dance, diet/nutrition, economics, education, environment, ethnic, foods, gay/lesbian, government, health, history, how-to, inspirational, investigative, language, law, literature, medicine, memoirs, money, music, parenting, popular culture, politics, psychology, religious, self-help, sociology, sports, true crime, women's issues, women's studies. **Considers these fiction areas:** action, adventure, crime, detective, feminist, historical, humor, inspirational, juvenile, literary, mainstream, mystery, picture books, police, religious, suspense, women's, young adult.

- "We specialize in books for, by and about women and women's issues including nonfiction self-help books, fiction and theater projects. We also handle the film, television and allied rights for several agencies as well as foreign rights for several publishing houses." Actively seeking new nonfiction. Considers plays. Does not want to receive poetry, television scripts or concepts for television.

How to Contact Query with SASE. Submit outline, synopsis, author bio, 3 sample chapters, SASE. Accepts simultaneous submissions. Responds in 6 weeks to queries. Responds in 6 weeks to mss. Obtains most new clients through recommendations from others, solicitations, conferences.

Terms Agent receives 15% commission on domestic sales. Agent receives 20% commission on foreign sales. Offers written contract; 30-day notice must be given to terminate contract.

Recent Sales Sold 50 titles in the last year; hundred of subsidiary rights deals.

Writers Conferences Geneva Writers' Conference (Switzerland); Columbus Writers' Conference; Skidmore Conference of the Independent Women's Writers Group.

Tips "Keep writing!"

SCRIBBLERS HOUSE, LLC LITERARY AGENCY

P.O. Box 1007, Cooper Station, New York NY 10276-1007. (212)714-7744. E-mail: query@scribblershouse.net. Website: www.scribblershouse.net. **Contact:** Stedman Mays, Garrett Gambino. 25% of clients are new/unpublished writers.

Member Agents Stedman Mays, Garrett Gambino.

Represents Nonfiction books, novels, occasionally. **Considers these nonfiction areas:** biography, business, diet/nutrition, economics, health, history, how-to, language, literature, medicine, memoirs, money, parenting, popular culture, politics, psychology, self-help, sex, spirituality, the brain; personal finance; writing books; relationships; gender issues;. **Considers these fiction areas:** crime, historical, literary, suspense, thriller, women's.

How to Contact Query via e-mail. Put "nonfiction query" or "fiction query" in the subject line followed by the title of your project (send to our submissions email on our website). Do not send attachments or downloadable materials of any kind with query. We will request more materials if we are interested. Usually respond in 2 weeks to 2 months to email queries if we are interested (if we are not interested, we will not respond due to the overwhelming amount of queries we receive). We are only accepting email queries at the present time. Accepts simultaneous submissions.

Terms Agent receives 15% commission on domestic sales. Charges clients for postage, shipping and copying.

Tips "If you must send by snail mail, we will return material or respond to a U.S. Postal Service-accepted SASE. (No international coupons or outdated mail strips, please.) Presentation means a lot. A well-written query letter with a brief author bio and your credentials is important. For query letter models, go to the bookstore or online and look at the cover copy and flap copy on other books in your general area of interest. Emulate what's best. Have an idea of other notable books that will be perceived as being in the same vein as yours. Know what's fresh about your project and articulate it in as few words as possible. Consult our website for the most up-to-date information on submitting."

☐ SCRIBE AGENCY, LLC

5508 Joylynne Dr., Madison WI 53716. E-mail: queries@scribeagency.com. Website: www.scribeagency.com. **Contact:** Kristopher O'Higgins. Represents 11 clients. 18% of clients are new/unpublished writers. Currently handles: novels 98%, story collections 2%.

- "We have 17 years of experience in publishing and have worked on both agency and editorial sides in the past, with marketing expertise to boot. We love books as much or more than anyone you know. Check our website to see what we're about and to make sure you jive with the Scribe vibe."

Member Agents Kristopher O'Higgins; Jesse Vogel.

Represents Nonfiction books, novels, short story collections, novellas, anthologies. **Considers these nonfiction areas:** cooking, diet/nutrition, ethnic, foods, gay/lesbian, humor, memoirs, popular culture, satire, women's issues, women's studies. **Considers these fiction areas:** detective, erotica, experimental, fantasy, feminist, gay, horror, humor, lesbian, literary, mainstream, mystery, psychic, science fiction, thriller.

O→ Actively seeking excellent writers with ideas and stories to tell.

How to Contact E-queries only: submissions@scribeagency.com. See the website for submission info, as it may change. Responds in 3-4 weeks to queries. Responds in 5 months to mss.

Terms Agent receives 15% commission on domestic sales. Agent receives 20% commission on foreign sales. Offers written contract. Charges for postage and photocopying.

Recent Sales Sold 3 titles in the last year.

Writers Conferences BookExpo America; The Writer's Institute; Spring Writer's Festival; WisCon; Wisconsin Book Festival; World Fantasy Convention.

SECRET AGENT MAN

P.O. Box 1078, Lake Forest CA 92609-1078. (949)698-6987. E-mail: scott@secretagentman.net. Website: www.secretagentman.net. **Contact:** Scott Mortenson.

Represents Novels. **Considers these fiction areas:** detective, mystery, religious, thriller.

O→ Actively seeking selective mystery, thriller, suspense and detective fiction. Does not want to receive scripts or screenplays.

How to Contact Query with SASE. Query via e-mail or snail mail; include sample chapter(s), synopsis and/or outline. Prefers to read the real thing rather than a description of it. Obtains most new clients through recommendations from others, solicitations.

LYNN SELIGMAN, LITERARY AGENT

400 Highland Ave., Upper Montclair NJ 07043. (973)783-3631. **Contact:** Lynn Seligman. Other memberships include Women's Media Group. Represents 32 clients. 15% of clients are new/unpublished writers. Currently handles: nonfiction books 60%, novels 40%.

- Prior to opening her agency, Ms. Seligman worked in the subsidiary rights department of Doubleday and Simon & Schuster, and served as an agent with Julian Bach Literary Agency (which became IMG Literary Agency). Foreign rights are represented by Books Crossing Borders, Inc.

Represents Nonfiction books, novels. **Considers these nonfiction areas:** interior, anthropology, art, biography, business, child, cooking, current affairs, education, ethnic, government, health, history, how-to, humor, language, money, music, nature, photography, popular culture, psychology, science, self-help, sociology, film, true crime, women's. **Considers these fiction areas:** detective, ethnic, fantasy, feminist, historical, horror, humor, literary, mainstream, mystery, romance, contemporary, gothic, historical, regency, science fiction.

O→ "This agency specializes in general nonfiction and fiction. I also do illustrated and photography books and have represented several photographers for books."

How to Contact Query with SASE. Prefers to read materials exclusively. Accepts simultaneous submissions. Responds in 2 weeks to queries. Responds in 2 months to mss. Obtains most new clients through referrals from other writers and editors.

Terms Agent receives 15% commission on domestic sales. Agent receives 25% commission on foreign sales. Charges clients for photocopying, unusual postage, express mail, telephone expenses (checks with author first).

Recent Sales Sold 15 titles in the last year. Lords of Vice series, by Barbara Pierce; Untitled series, by Deborah Leblanc.

THE SEYMOUR AGENCY

475 Miner St., Canton NY 13617. (315)386-1831. E-mail: marysue@twcny.rr.com. Website: www.theseymouragency.com. **Contact:** Mary Sue Seymour. Member of AAR. Signatory of WGA. Other memberships include RWA, Authors Guild. Represents 50 clients. 5% of clients are new/unpublished writers. Currently handles: nonfiction books 50%, other 50% fiction.

- Ms. Seymour is a retired New York State certified teacher.

Represents Nonfiction books, novels. **Considers these nonfiction areas:** business, health, how-to, self-help, Christian books; cookbooks; any well-written nonfiction that includes a proposal in standard format and 1 sample chapter. **Considers these fiction areas:** religious, Christian books, romance, any type.

How to Contact Query with SASE, synopsis, first 50 pages for romance. Accepts e-mail queries. Accepts simultaneous submissions. Responds in 1 month to queries. Responds in 3 months to mss.

Terms Agent receives 12-15% commission on domestic sales.

Recent Sales Dinah Bucholz's *The Harry Potter Cookbook* to Adams Media.com; Vannetta Chapman's *A Simple Amish Christmas* to Abingdon Press; Shelley Shepard Gray's current book deal to Harper Collins; Shelley Galloway's Multibook Deal to Zondervan; Beth Wiseman's Christmas Two Novellas and Multibook Deal to Thomas Nelson; Mary Ellis's Multibook Deal to Harvest House, Barbara Cameron's Novellas to Thomas Nelson and Multibook Deal to Abingdon Press.

WENDY SHERMAN ASSOCIATES, INC.

27 W. 24th St., New York NY 10010. (212)279-9027. Website: www.wsherman.com. **Contact:** Wendy Sherman. Member of AAR. Represents 50 clients. 30% of clients are new/unpublished writers. Currently handles: nonfiction books 50%, novels 50%.

- Prior to opening the agency, Ms. Sherman served as vice president, executive director, associate publisher, subsidiary rights director, and sales and marketing director for major publishers.

Member Agents Wendy Sherman (board member of AAR).

Represents Nonfiction, fiction. **Considers these nonfiction areas:** memoirs, psychology, narrative; practical. **Considers these fiction areas:** literary, suspense, women's.

- "We specialize in developing new writers, as well as working with more established writers. My experience as a publisher has proven to be a great asset to my clients."

How to Contact Query via e-mail to submissions@wsherman.com Accepts simultaneous submissions. Responds in 1 month to queries. Obtains most new clients through recommendations from others.

Terms Agent receives 15% commission on domestic sales. Agent receives 20% commission on foreign and film sales. Offers written contract.

Recent Sales *Daughters of the Witching Hill*, by Mary Sharratt; *The Measure of Brightness*, by Todd Johnson; *Supergirls Speak Out*, by Liz Funk; *Love in 90 Days*, by Diana Kirschner; *A Long Time Ago and Essentially*, by Brigid Pasulka; *Changing Shoes*, by Tina Sloan.

Tips "The bottom line is: Do your homework. Be as well prepared as possible. Read the books that will help you present yourself and your work with polish. You want your submission to stand out."

JEFFREY SIMMONS LITERARY AGENCY

15 Penn House, Mallory St., London NW8 8SX England. (44)(207)224-8917. E-mail: jasimmons@unicombox.co.uk. **Contact:** Jeffrey Simmons. Represents 43 clients. 40% of clients are new/unpublished writers. Currently handles: nonfiction books 65%, novels 35%.

- Prior to becoming an agent, Mr. Simmons was a publisher. He is also an author.

Represents Nonfiction books, novels. **Considers these nonfiction areas:** autobiography, biography, current affairs, film, government, history, language, memoirs, music, popular culture, sociology, sports, translation, true crime. **Considers these fiction areas:** action, adventure, confession, crime, detective, family saga, literary, mainstream, mystery, police, suspense, thriller.

"This agency seeks to handle good books and promising young writers. My long experience in publishing and as an author and ghostwriter means I can offer an excellent service all around, especially in terms of editorial experience where appropriate." Actively seeking quality fiction, biography, autobiography, showbiz, personality books, law, crime, politics, and world affairs. Does not want to receive science fiction, horror, fantasy, juvenile, academic books, or specialist subjects (e.g., cooking, gardening, religious).

How to Contact Submit sample chapter, outline/proposal, SASE (IRCs if necessary).Prefers to read materials exclusively. Responds in 1 week to queries. Responds in 1 month to mss. Obtains most new clients through recommendations from others, solicitations.

Terms Agent receives 10-15% commission on domestic sales. Agent receives 15% commission on foreign sales. Offers written contract, binding for lifetime of book in question or until it becomes out of print.

Tips "When contacting us with an outline/proposal, include a brief biographical note (listing any previous publications, with publishers and dates). Preferably tell us if the book has already been offered elsewhere."

BEVERLEY SLOPEN LITERARY AGENCY

131 Bloor St. W., Suite 711, Toronto ON M5S 1S3 Canada. (416)964-9598. Fax: (416)921-7726. E-mail: beverly@slopenagency.ca. Website: www.slopenagency.ca. **Contact:** Beverley Slopen. Represents 70 clients. 20% of clients are new/unpublished writers. Currently handles: nonfiction books 60%, novels 40%.

- Prior to opening her agency, Ms. Slopen worked in publishing and as a journalist.

Represents Nonfiction books, novels, scholarly, textbooks, college. **Considers these nonfiction areas:** anthropology, archeology, autobiography, biography, business, current affairs, economics, investigative, psychology, sociology, true crime, women's issues, women's studies. **Considers these fiction areas:** literary, mystery, suspense.

"This agency has a strong bent toward Canadian writers." Actively seeking serious nonfiction that is accessible and appealing to the general reader. Does not want to receive fantasy, science fiction, or children's books.

How to Contact Query with SAE and IRCs. Returns materials only with SASE (Canadian postage only). Accepts simultaneous submissions. Responds in 2 months to queries.

Terms Agent receives 15% commission on domestic sales. Agent receives 10% commission on foreign sales. Offers written contract, binding for 2 years; 3-month notice must be given to terminate contract.

Recent Sales *Solarl Dance*, by Modris Eksteins (Knopf Canada); *God's Brain*, by Lionel Tiger & Michael McGuire (Prometheus Books); *What They Wanted*, by Donna Morrissey (Penguin Canada, Premium/DTV Germany); *The Age of Persuasion*, by Terry O'Reilly & Mike Tennant (Knopf Canada, Counterpoint US); *Prisoner of Tehran*, by Marina Nemat (Penguin Canada, Free Press US, John Murray UK); *Race to the Polar Sea*, by Ken McGoogan (HarperCollins Canada, Counterpoint US); *Transgression*, by James Nichol (HarperCollins US, McArthur Canada, Goldmann Germany); *Vermeer's Hat*, by Timothy Brook (HarperCollins Canada, Bloomsbury US); *Distantly Related to Freud*, by Ann Charney (Cormorant).

Tips "Please, no unsolicited manuscripts."

VALERIE SMITH, LITERARY AGENT

1746 Route 44-55, Modena NY 12548. **Contact:** Valerie Smith. Represents 17 clients. Currently handles: nonfiction books 2%, novels 75%, story collections 1%, juvenile books 20%, scholarly books 1%, textbooks 1%.

Represents Nonfiction books, novels, juvenile, textbooks. **Considers these nonfiction areas:** agriculture horticulture, cooking, how-to, self-help. **Considers these fiction areas:** fantasy, historical, juvenile, literary, mainstream, mystery, science, young, women's/chick lit.

- "This is a small, personalized agency with a strong long-term commitment to clients interested in building careers. I have strong ties to science fiction, fantasy and young adult projects. I look for serious, productive writers whose work I can be passionate about." Does not want to receive unsolicited mss.

How to Contact Query with synopsis, bio, 3 sample chapters, SASE. Contact by snail mail only. Obtains most new clients through recommendations from others.

Terms Agent receives 15% commission on domestic sales. Agent receives 20% commission on foreign sales. Offers written contract; 6-week notice must be given to terminate contract.

SPECTRUM LITERARY AGENCY

320 Central Park W., Suite 1-D, New York NY 10025. Fax: (212)362-4562. Website: www.spectrumliteraryagency.com. **Contact:** Eleanor Wood, president. Estab. 1976. SFWA Represents 90 clients. Currently handles: nonfiction books 10%, novels 90%.

Member Agents Eleanor Wood, Justin Bell.

Represents Nonfiction books, novels. **Considers these fiction areas:** fantasy, historical, mainstream, mystery, romance, science fiction, suspense.

How to Contact Query with SASE. Submit author bio, publishing credits. No unsolicited mss will be read. Snail mail queries **only**. Eleanor and Lucienne have different addresses - see the website for full info. Responds in 1-3 months to queries. Obtains most new clients through recommendations from authors.

Terms Agent receives 15% commission on domestic sales. Deducts for photocopying and book orders.

Tips "Spectrum's policy is to read only book-length manuscripts that we have specifically asked to see. Unsolicited manuscripts are not accepted. The letter should describe your book briefly and include publishing credits and background information or qualifications relating to your work, if any."

SPENCERHILL ASSOCIATES

P.O. Box 374, Chatham NY 12037. (518)392-9293. Fax: (518)392-9554. E-mail: submissions@spencerhillassociates.com. Website: www.spencerhillassociates.com. **Contact:** Karen Solem or Jennifer Schober (and please refer to our website for the latest information). Member of AAR. Represents 96 clients. 10% of clients are new/unpublished writers.

- Prior to becoming an agent, Ms. Solem was editor-in-chief at HarperCollins and an associate publisher.

Member Agents Karen Solem; Jennifer Schober.

Represents Novels. **Considers these fiction areas:** crime, detective, historical, inspirational, literary, mainstream, police, religious, romance, thriller, young adult.

- "We handle mostly commercial women's fiction, historical novels, romance (historical, contemporary, paranormal, urban fantasy), thrillers, and mysteries. We also represent Christian fiction only—no nonfiction." No nonfiction, poetry, science fiction, children's picture books, or scripts.

How to Contact Query submissions@spencerhillassociates.com with synopsis and first three chapters attached as a .doc or .rtf file. Please note we no longer accept queries via the mail. Responds in 6-8 weeks to queries if we are interested in pursuing.

Terms Agent receives 15% commission on domestic sales. Agent receives 20% commission on foreign sales. Offers written contract; 3-month notice must be given to terminate contract.

THE SPIELER AGENCY

154 W. 57th St., Suite 135, New York NY 10019. E-mail: eric@spieleragency.com. **Contact:** Katya Balter. Represents 160 clients. 2% of clients are new/unpublished writers.

- Prior to opening his agency, Mr. Spieler was a magazine editor.

Member Agents Joe Spieler.

Represents Nonfiction books, novels, children's books. **Considers these nonfiction areas:** autobiography, biography, business, child guidance, current affairs, economics, environment, film, gay/lesbian, government, history, law, memoirs, money, music, parenting, politics, sociology, spirituality, theater, travel, women's issues, women's studies. **Considers these fiction areas:** detective, feminist, gay, lesbian, literary, mystery, children's books, Middle Grade and Young Adult novels.

How to Contact Accepts electronic submissions (spieleragency@spieleragency.com), or send query letter and sample chapters. Prefers to read materials exclusively. Returns materials only with SASE; otherwise materials are discarded when rejected. Accepts simultaneous submissions. Responds in 2 weeks to queries. Responds in 2 months to mss. Obtains most new clients through recommendations, listing in *Guide to Literary Agents.*

Terms Agent receives 15% commission on domestic sales. Charges clients for messenger bills, photocopying, postage.

Writers Conferences London Book Fair.

Tips "Check http://www.publishersmarketplace.com/members/spielerlit/."

NANCY STAUFFER ASSOCIATES

P.O. Box 1203, 1540 Boston Post Road, Darien CT 06820. (203)202-2500. Fax: (203)655-3704. E-mail: StaufferAssoc@optonline.net. Website: publishersmarketplace.com/members/nstauffer. **Contact:** Nancy Stauffer Cahoon. Other memberships include Authors Guild. 5% of clients are new/unpublished writers. Currently handles: nonfiction books 15%, novels 85%.

Represents Considers these nonfiction areas: cultural interests, current affairs, ethnic, creative nonfiction (narrative). **Considers these fiction areas:** contemporary, literary, regional.

How to Contact Obtains most new clients through referrals from existing clients.

Terms Agent receives 15% commission on domestic sales. Agent receives 20% commission on foreign sales. Agent receives 15% commission on film sales.

Recent Sales *The Magic and Tragic Year of My Broken Thumb*, by Sherman Alexie; *Bone Fire*, by Mark Spragg; *Claiming Ground*, by Laura Bell, *The Best Camera is the One That's With You*, by Chase Jarvis.

STEELE-PERKINS LITERARY AGENCY

26 Island Ln., Canandaigua NY 14424. (585)396-9290. Fax: (585)396-3579. E-mail: pattiesp@aol.com. **Contact:** Pattie Steele-Perkins. Member of AAR. Other memberships include RWA. Currently handles: novels 100%.

Represents Novels. **Considers these fiction areas:** romance, women's, All genres: category romance, romantic suspense, historical, contemporary, multi-cultural, and inspirational.

How to Contact Submit synopsis and one chapter via e-mail (no attachments) or snail mail. Snail mail submissions require SASE. Accepts simultaneous submissions. Responds in 6 weeks to queries. Obtains most new clients through recommendations from others, queries/solicitations.

Terms Agent receives 15% commission on domestic sales. Offers written contract, binding for 1 year; 1-month notice must be given to terminate contract.

Recent Sales Sold 130 titles last year. This agency prefers not to share specific sales information.

Writers Conferences RWA National Conference; BookExpo America; CBA Convention; Romance Slam Jam.

Tips "Be patient. E-mail rather than call. Make sure what you are sending is the best it can be."

STERNIG & BYRNE LITERARY AGENCY

2370 S. 107th St., Apt. #4, Milwaukee WI 53227-2036. (414)328-8034. Fax: (414)328-8034. E-mail: jackbyrne@hotmail.com. Website: www.sff.net/people/jackbyrne. **Contact:** Jack Byrne. Other memberships include SFWA, MWA. Represents 30 clients. 10% of clients are new/unpublished writers. Currently handles: nonfiction books 5%, novels 90%, juvenile books 5%.

Represents Nonfiction books, novels, juvenile. **Considers these fiction areas:** fantasy, horror, mystery, science fiction, suspense.

- "Our client list is comfortably full and our current needs are therefore quite limited." Actively seeking science fiction/fantasy and mystery by established writers. Does not want to receive romance, poetry, textbooks, or highly specialized nonfiction.

How to Contact Query with SASE. Prefers e-mail queries (no attachments); hard copy queries also acceptable. Responds in 3 weeks to queries. Responds in 3 months to mss.

Terms Agent receives 15% commission on domestic sales. Agent receives 20% commission on foreign sales. Offers written contract; 2-month notice must be given to terminate contract.

Tips "Don't send first drafts, have a professional presentation (including cover letter), and know your field. Read what's been done - good and bad."

STRACHAN LITERARY AGENCY

P.O. Box 2091, Annapolis MD 21404. E-mail: query@strachanlit.com. Website: www.strachanlit.com. **Contact:** Laura Strachan.

- Prior to becoming an agent, Ms. Strachan was (and still is) an attorney.

Represents Nonfiction books, novels. **Considers these nonfiction areas:** narrative. **Considers these fiction areas:** literary and up-market commercial.

- "This agency specializes in literary fiction and narrative nonfiction."

How to Contact Email queries only with brief synopsis and bio.; no attachments or samples unless requested.

Recent Sales *The Interventionist* (Hazelden); The Golden Bristled Boar (UVA Press); *Poser* (Walker).

THE STROTHMAN AGENCY, LLC

Specializes in narrative nonfiction and literary fiction, young adult and middle grade fiction and nonfiction., Six Beacon St., Suite 810, Boston MA 02108. (617)742-2011. Fax: (617)742-2014. E-mail: info@strothmanagency.com. Website: www.strothmanagency.com. **Contact:** Wendy Strothman, Lauren MacLeod. Member of AAR. Other memberships include Authors' Guild. Represents 50 clients. Currently handles: nonfiction books 70%, novels 10%, scholarly books 20%.

- Prior to becoming an agent, Ms. Strothman was head of Beacon Press (1983-1995) and executive vice president of Houghton Mifflin's Trade & Reference Division (1996-2002).

Member Agents Wendy Strothman; Lauren MacLeod.

Represents Nonfiction books, novels, scholarly, young adult and middle grade. **Considers these nonfiction areas:** current affairs, environment, government, history, language, law, literature, politics. **Considers these fiction areas:** literary, young adult, middle grade.

- "Because we are highly selective in the clients we represent, we increase the value publishers place on our properties. We specialize in narrative nonfiction, memoir, history, science and nature, arts and culture, literary travel, current affairs, and some business. We have a highly selective practice in literary fiction, young adult and middle grade fiction, and nonfiction. We are now opening our doors to more commercial fiction but ONLY from authors who have a platform. If you have a platform, please mention it in your query letter." "The Strothman Agency seeks out scholars, journalists, and other acknowledged and emerging experts in their fields. We are now actively looking for authors of well written young-adult fiction and nonfiction. Browse the Latest News to get an idea of the types of books that we represent. For more about what we're looking for, read Pitching an Agent: The Strothman Agency on the publishing website www.strothmanagency.com." Does not want to receive commercial fiction, romance, science fiction or self-help.

How to Contact Open to email (strothmanagency@gmail.com) and postal submissions. See submission guidelines. Accepts simultaneous submissions. Responds in 4 weeks to queries. Responds in 6 weeks to mss. Obtains most new clients through recommendations from others.

Terms Agent receives 15% commission on domestic sales. Agent receives 20% commission on foreign sales. Offers written contract; 30-day notice must be given to terminate contract.

EMMA SWEENEY AGENCY, LLC

245 East 80th St., Suite 7E, New York NY 10075. E-mail: queries@emmasweeneyagency.com. Website: www.emmasweeneyagency.com. **Contact:** Eva Talmadge. Member of AAR. Other memberships include Women's Media Group. Represents 80 clients. 5% of clients are new/unpublished writers. Currently handles: nonfiction books 50%, novels 50%.

- Prior to becoming an agent, Ms. Sweeney was director of subsidiary rights at Grove Press. Since 1990, she has been a literary agent.

Member Agents Emma Sweeney, president; Eva Talmadge, rights manager and agent (Represents literary fiction, young adult novels, and narrative nonfiction. Considers these nonfiction areas: popular science, pop culture and music history, biography, memoirs, cooking, and anything relating to animals. Considers these fiction areas: literary (of the highest writing quality possible), young adult. eva@emmasweeneyagency.com); Justine Wenger, junior agent/assistant (justine@emmasweeneyagency.com).

Represents Nonfiction books, novels.

"We specialize in quality fiction and non-fiction. Our primary areas of interest include literary and women's fiction, mysteries and thrillers; science, history, biography, memoir, religious studies and the natural sciences." Does not want to receive romance and westerns or screenplays.

How to Contact Send query letter and first ten pages in body of e-mail (no attachments) to queries@emmasweeneyagency.com. No snail mail queries.

Terms Agent receives 15% commission on domestic sales. Agent receives 10% commission on foreign sales.

Writers Conferences Nebraska Writers' Conference; Words and Music Festival in New Orleans.

TALCOTT NOTCH LITERARY

276 Forest Road, Milford CT 06460. (203)877-1146. Fax: (203)876-9517. E-mail: editorial@talcottnotch.net. Website: www.talcottnotch.net. **Contact:** Gina Panettieri, president. Represents 35 clients. 25% of clients are new/unpublished writers. Currently handles: nonfiction books 25%, novels 55%, story collections 5%, juvenile books 10%, scholarly books 5%.

- Prior to becoming an agent, Ms. Panettieri was a freelance writer and editor.

Member Agents Gina Panettieri (nonfiction, mystery); Rachel Dowen (children's fiction, mystery); Ann Rought (romance, women's fiction, paranormal).

Represents Nonfiction books, novels, juvenile, scholarly, textbooks. **Considers these nonfiction areas:** animals, anthropology, art, biography, business, computers, cooking, current affairs, decorating, education, environment, ethnic, gay/lesbian, government, health, history, interior design, investigative, juvenile nonfiction, memoirs, metaphysics, military, money, music, New Age, popular culture, psychology, science, sociology, sports, technology, true crime, women's issues, women's studies. **Considers these fiction areas:** action, adventure, crime, detective, fantasy, juvenile, mystery, police, romance, suspense, thriller, young adult.

How to Contact Query via e-mail (preferred) with first ten pages of the ms within the body of the e-mail, not as an attachment, or with SASE. Accepts simultaneous submissions. Responds in 1 week to queries. Responds in 4-6 weeks to mss.

Terms Agent receives 15% commission on domestic sales. Agent receives 20% commission on foreign sales. Offers written contract, binding for 1 year.

Recent Sales Sold 36 titles in the last year. *Delivered from Evil*, by Ron Franscell (Fairwinds); *Outlaw Texas: The Crime Buff's Guide to Texas*, by Ron Franscell (Globe Pequot); *God Goes to Work*, by Tom Zender (John Wiley & Sons); *CPR For Your Plants*, by Sandra Dark and Dean Hill (University Press of Florida); *Now Is The Time To Do What You Love: How To Make The Career Move That Will Change Your Life*, by Nancy Whitney-Reiter (Adams Media Corp); *Green Collar Jobs*, by Scott Deitche (Praeger/Greenwood), and more. Other clients include Tracy Tamborra,

William Brennan, Melissa Ellis, Nancy Hawks-Miller, Koos Verkaik, Kim Bookout, Karen Williams, Kevin Wolf, Jay (Dr. J) Stratoudakis, and more.

Tips "Present your book or project effectively in your query. Don't include links to a Web page rather than a traditional query, and take the time to prepare a thorough but brief synopsis of the material. Make the effort to prepare a thoughtful analysis of comparison titles. How is your work different, yet would appeal to those same readers?"

ANN TOBIAS: A LITERARY AGENCY FOR CHILDREN'S BOOKS

520 E. 84th St., Apt. 4L, New York NY 10028. E-mail: AnnTobias84@hotmail.com. **Contact:** Ann Tobias. Represents 25 clients. 10% of clients are new/unpublished writers. Currently handles: juvenile books 100%.

- Prior to opening her agency, Ms. Tobias worked as a children's book editor at Harper, William Morrow and Scholastic.

Represents Juvenile and young adult. **Considers these nonfiction areas:** juvenile nonfiction, young adult. **Considers these fiction areas:** picture books, poetry, poetry in translation, young adult, illustrated mss; mid-level novels.

O→ This agency specializes in books for children.

How to Contact For all age groups and genres: Send a one-page letter of inquiry accompanied by a one-page writing sample, double-spaced. No attachments will be opened. Other Responds in 2 months to mss. Obtains most new clients through recommendations from editors.

Terms Agent receives 15% commission on domestic sales. Agent receives 20% commission on foreign sales. This agency charges clients for photocopying, overnight mail, foreign postage, foreign telephone.

Tips "Read at least 200 children's books in the age group and genre in which you hope to be published. Follow this by reading another 100 children's books in other age groups and genres so you will have a feel for the field as a whole."

TRANSATLANTIC LITERARY AGENCY

72 Glengowan Road, Toronto Ontario M4N 1G4 Canada. E-mail: info@tla1.com. Website: www.tla1.com. **Contact:** Lynn Bennett. Represents 250 clients. 10% of clients are new/unpublished writers. Currently handles: nonfiction books 30%, novels 15%, juvenile books 50%, textbooks 5%.

Member Agents Lynn Bennett, Lynn@tla1.com, (juvenile and young adult fiction); Shaun Bradley, Shaun@tla1.com (literary fiction and narrative nonfiction); Marie Campbell, Marie@tla1.com (literary juvenile and young adult fiction); Andrea Cascardi, Andrea@tla1.com (literary juvenile and young adult fiction); Samantha Haywood, Sam@tla1.com (literary fiction, narrative nonfiction and graphic novels); Don Sedgwick, Don@tla1.com (literary fiction and narrative nonfiction).

Represents Nonfiction books, novels, juvenile. **Considers these nonfiction areas:** autobiography, biography, business, current affairs, economics, environment. **Considers these fiction areas:** juvenile, literary, mainstream, mystery, suspense, young adult.

O→ "In both children's and adult literature, we market directly into the United States, the United Kingdom and Canada." Actively seeking literary children's and adult fiction, nonfiction. Does not want to receive picture books, poetry, screenplays or stage plays.

How to Contact Submit E-query with synopsis, 2 sample chapters, bio. Always refer to the website as guidelines will change. Responds in 2 weeks to queries. Obtains most new clients through recommendations from others.

Terms Agent receives 15% commission on domestic sales. Agent receives 20% commission on foreign sales. Offers written contract; 45-day notice must be given to terminate contract. This agency charges for photocopying and postage when it exceeds $100.

Recent Sales Sold 250 titles in the last year.

TRIADA U.S. LITERARY AGENCY, INC.

P.O. Box 561, Sewickley PA 15143. (412)401-3376. E-mail: uwe@triadaus.com. Website: www.triadaus.com. **Contact:** Dr. Uwe Stender. Member of AAR. Represents 65 clients. 20% of clients are new/unpublished writers.

Represents Fiction, nonfiction. **Considers these nonfiction areas:** biography, business, cooking, diet/nutrition, economics, education, foods, health, how-to, memoirs, popular culture, science, sports, advice, relationships, lifestyle. **Considers these fiction areas:** action, adventure, crime, detective, ethnic, historical, horror, juvenile, literary, mainstream, mystery, occult, police, romance, women's, young adult.

- "We are looking for great writing and story platforms. Our response time is fairly unique. We recognize that neither we nor the authors have time to waste, so we guarantee a 5-day response time. We usually respond within 24 hours. " Actively looking for both fiction and nonfiction in all areas.

How to Contact E-mail queries preferred; otherwise query with SASE. Accepts simultaneous submissions. Responds in 1-5 weeks to queries. Responds in 2-6 weeks to mss. Obtains most new clients through recommendations from others, conferences.

Terms Agent receives 15% commission on domestic sales. Agent receives 20% commission on foreign sales. Offers written contract; 30-day notice must be given to terminate contract.

Recent Sales *Whatever Happened To Pudding Pops*, by Gael Fashingbauer Cooper and Brian Bellmont (Penguin/Perigee); *86'd*, by Dan Fante (Harper Perennial); *Hating Olivia*, by Mark SaFranko (Harper Perennial); *Everything I'm Not Made Me Everything I Am*, by Jeff Johnson (Smiley Books).

Tips "I comment on all requested manuscripts that I reject."

UPSTART CROW LITERARY

P.O. Box 25404, Brooklyn NY 11202. E-mail: michael (at) upstartcrowliterary (dot) com. Website: www.upstartcrowliterary.com. **Contact:** Michael Stearns. Estab. 2009.

Member Agents Michael Stearns; Chris Richman (special interest in books for boys, books with unforgettable characters, and fantasy that doesn't take itself too seriously); Danielle Chiotti (books ranging from contemporary women's fiction to narrative nonfiction, from romance to relationship stories, humorous tales and young adult fiction); Ted Malawer (accepting queries only through conference submissions and client referrals).

Represents Considers these fiction areas: women's, young adult, middle grade.

How to Contact This agency likes submissions sent through its online form, rather than e-mails to agents.

VANGUARD LITERARY AGENCY

81 E. Jefryn Blvd., Suite E, Deer Park NY 11729. (718)710-3662. Fax: (917)591-7088. E-mail: sandylu@vanguardliterary.com; sandy@lperkinsagency.com. Website: www.vanguardliterary.com. **Contact:** Sandy Lu. Represents 15 clients. 60% of clients are new/unpublished writers. Currently handles: nonfiction books 20%, novels 80%.

- Prior to becoming an agent, Ms. Lu held managerial positions in commercial theater. "Ms. Lu is also an associate agent at the L. Perkins Agency. Please only send queries to one of her e-mail addresses."

Represents Nonfiction books, novels, short story collections, novellas. **Considers these nonfiction areas:** anthropology, archeology, autobiography, biography, cooking, cultural interests, diet/nutrition, ethnic, foods, gay/lesbian, history, investigative, memoirs, music, popular culture, psychology, science, sociology, technology, translation, true crime, women's issues, women's studies. **Considers these fiction areas:** action, adventure, confession, crime, detective, ethnic, historical, horror, humor, literary, mainstream, mystery, police, regional, short story collections, suspense, thriller, women's, urban fantasy.

- "Very few agents in the business still edit their clients' manuscripts, especially when it comes to fiction. Vanguard Literary Agency is different. I care about the quality of my clients' works and will not send anything out to publishers without personally going through each page first to ensure that when the manuscript is sent out, it is in the best possible shape." Actively seeking literary and commercial fiction with a unique voice. Does not want to receive movie or TV scripts, stage plays or poetry; unwanted fiction genres include science fiction/fantasy, Western, YA, children's; unwanted nonfiction genres include self-help, how-to, parenting, sports, dating/relationship, military/war, religion/spirituality, New Age, gift books.

How to Contact Only accepts e-mail queries. No fax queries. Accepts simultaneous submissions. Responds in 2 weeks to queries. Responds in 6-8 weeks to mss. Obtains most new clients through recommendations from others, solicitations, conferences.

Terms Agent receives 15% commission on domestic sales. Agent receives 20% commission on foreign sales. Offers written contract, binding for 1 year; 30-day notice must be given to terminate contract. This agency charges for photocopying and postage, and discusses larger costs (in excess of $100) with authors prior to charging.

Tips "Do your research. Do not query an agent for a genre he or she does not represent. Personalize your query letter. Start with an interesting hook. Learn how to write a succinct yet interesting synopsis or proposal."

CHRISTINA WARD LITERARY AGENCY

PO Box 7144, Lowell MA 01852. (978)656-8389. E-mail: christinawardlit@mac.com.

Represents Books and proposals, and novels. **Considers these nonfiction areas:** biography, health, history, medicine, memoirs, nature, alternative and "green" lifestyle, psychology, science, literary nonfiction, including narrative nonfiction. **Considers these fiction areas:** literary, mystery, suspense, thriller.

JOHN A. WARE LITERARY AGENCY

392 Central Park W., New York NY 10025-5801. (212)866-4733. Fax: (212)866-4734. **Contact:** John Ware. Represents 60 clients. 40% of clients are new/unpublished writers. Currently handles: nonfiction books 75%, novels 25%.

- Prior to opening his agency, Mr. Ware served as a literary agent with James Brown Associates/ Curtis Brown, Ltd., and as an editor for Doubleday.

Represents Nonfiction books, novels. **Considers these nonfiction areas:** Americana, anthropology, biography, current affairs, history, investigative journalism sports, language, music, nature, popular culture, psychology (academic credentials required), true crime, women's issues, social commentary, folklore. **Considers these fiction areas:** detective, mystery, thriller, accessible literary noncategory fiction.

Does not want personal memoirs.

How to Contact Query with SASE. Send a letter only. Responds in 2 weeks to queries.

Terms Agent receives 15% commission on domestic sales, 20% commission on foreign sales, film. Charges clients for courier and messenger service and photocopying.

Recent Sales *Where Men Win Glory: The Odyssey of Pat Tillman*, by Jon Krakauer (Doubleday); *Abundance of Valor* (military history), by Will Irwin (Ballantine); *Velva Jean Learns to Drive* (novel), by Jennifer Niven (Plume); *The Art of the Game* (basketball), by Chris Ballard (Sports Illustrated/Simon & Schuster); *The Aquanet Diaries: Big Hair, Big Dreams, Small Town* (high school memoir), by Jennifer Niven (Gallery); *Spent: A Memoir of Shopaholism*, by Avis Cardella (Little, Brown); *To Kill a Page: A Memoir of Becoming Literate*, by Travis Hugh Culley (Random House); *The Pledge (of Allegiance)*, by Jeffrey Jones and Peter Mayer (Thomas Dunne/St. Martin's Press); Conversions (religious), by Craig Harline (Yale).

Tips "Writers must have appropriate credentials for authorship of proposal (nonfiction); no publishing track record required. I am open to good writing and interesting ideas by new or veteran writers."

CHERRY WEINER LITERARY AGENCY

28 Kipling Way, Manalapan NJ 07726-3711. (732)446-2096. Fax: (732)792-0506. E-mail: cherry8486@ aol.com. **Contact:** Cherry Weiner. Represents 40 clients. 10% of clients are new/unpublished writers. Currently handles: nonfiction books 10-20%, novels 80-90%.

Represents Nonfiction books, novels. **Considers these nonfiction areas:** self-help. **Considers these fiction areas:** action, adventure, contemporary issues, crime, detective, family saga, fantasy, frontier, historical, mainstream, mystery, police, psychic, romance, science fiction, supernatural, thriller, westerns.

- *This agency is currently not accepting new clients except by referral or by personal contact at writers' conferences.* Specializes in fantasy, science fiction, Western's, mysteries (both contemporary and historical), historical novels, Native-American works, mainstream and all genre romances.

How to Contact Query with SASE. Prefers to read materials exclusively. Responds in 1 week to queries. Responds in 2 months to mss.

Terms Agent receives 15% commission on domestic sales. Agent receives 15% commission on foreign sales. Offers written contract. Charges clients for extra copies of mss, first-class postage for author's copies of books, express mail for important documents/mss.

Recent Sales Sold 60 titles in the last year. This agency prefers not to share information on specific sales.

Tips "Meet agents and publishers at conferences. Establish a relationship, then get in touch with them and remind them of the meeting and conference."

THE WEINGEL-FIDEL AGENCY

310 E. 46th St., 21E, New York NY 10017. (212)599-2959. **Contact:** Loretta Weingel-Fidel. Currently handles: nonfiction books 75%, novels 25%.

- Prior to opening her agency, Ms. Weingel-Fidel was a psychoeducational diagnostician.

Represents Nonfiction books, novels. **Considers these nonfiction areas:** art, autobiography, biography, dance, memoirs, music, psychology, science, sociology, technology, women's issues, women's studies, investigative journalism. **Considers these fiction areas:** literary, mainstream.

- This agency specializes in commercial and literary fiction and nonfiction. Actively seeking investigative journalism. Does not want to receive genre fiction, self-help, science fiction, or fantasy.

How to Contact Accepts writers by referral only. *No unsolicited mss.*

Terms Agent receives 15% commission on domestic sales. Agent receives 20% commission on foreign sales. Offers written contract, binding for 1 year with automatic renewal. Bills sent back to clients are all reasonable expenses, such as UPS, express mail, photocopying, etc.

Tips "A very small, selective list enables me to work very closely with my clients to develop and nurture talent. I only take on projects and writers about which I am extremely enthusiastic."

LARRY WEISSMAN LITERARY, LLC

526 8th St., #2R, Brooklyn NY **Contact:** Larry Weissman. Represents 35 clients. Currently handles: nonfiction books 80%, novels 10%, story collections 10%.

Represents Nonfiction books, novels, short story collections. **Considers these fiction areas:** literary.

- "Very interested in established journalists with bold voices. Interested in anything to do with food. Fiction has to feel "vital" and short stories are accepted, but only if you can sell us on an idea for a novel as well." Nonfiction, including food & lifestyle, politics, pop culture, narrative, cultural/social issues, journalism. No genre fiction, poetry or children's.

How to Contact Send e-queries only. If you don't hear back, your project was not right for our list.

Terms Agent receives 15% commission on domestic sales. Agent receives 20% commission on foreign sales.

WHIMSY LITERARY AGENCY, LLC

New York/Los Angeles E-mail: whimsynyc@aol.com. **Contact:** Jackie Meyer. Other memberships include Center for Independent Publishing Advisory Board. Represents 30 clients. 20% of clients are new/unpublished writers. Currently handles: nonfiction books 100%.

- Prior to becoming an agent, Ms. Meyer was with Warner Books for 19 years; Ms. Vezeris and Ms. Legette have 30 years experience at various book publishers.

Member Agents Jackie Meyer; Olga Vezeris (fiction and nonfiction); Nansci LeGette, senior associate in LA.

Represents Nonfiction books. **Considers these nonfiction areas:** agriculture, art, biography, business, child guidance, cooking, education, health, history, horticulture, how-to, humor, interior design, memoirs, money, New Age, popular culture, psychology, religious, self-help, true crime, women's issues, women's studies. **Considers these fiction areas:** mainstream, religious, thriller, women's.

- "Whimsy looks for projects that are concept and platform driven. We seek books that educate, inspire and entertain." Actively seeking experts in their field with good platforms.

How to Contact Send a query letter via e-mail. Send a synopsis, bio, platform and proposal. No snail mail submissions. Responds "quickly, but only if interested" to queries. Obtains most new clients through recommendations from others, solicitations.

Terms Agent receives 15% commission on domestic sales. Agent receives 20% commission on foreign sales. Offers written contract. Charges for posting and photocopying.

WOLFSON LITERARY AGENCY

P.O. Box 266, New York NY 10276. E-mail: query@wolfsonliterary.com. Website: www.wolfsonliterary.com/. **Contact:** Michelle Wolfson. Other memberships include Adheres to AAR canon of ethics. Currently handles: nonfiction books 70%, novels 30%.

- Prior to forming her own agency, Michelle spent two years with Artists & Artisans, Inc. and two years with Ralph Vicinanza, Ltd.

Represents Nonfiction books, novels. **Considers these nonfiction areas:** business, child guidance, economics, health, how-to, humor, medicine, memoirs, parenting, popular culture, satire, self-help, women's issues, women's studies. **Considers these fiction areas:** action, adventure, crime, detective, family saga, mainstream, mystery, police, romance, suspense, thriller, women's, young adult.

- Actively seeking commercial fiction, mainstream, mysteries, thrillers, suspense, women's fiction, romance, YA, practical nonfiction (particularly of interest to women), advice, medical, pop culture, humor, business.

How to Contact E-queries only! Accepts simultaneous submissions. Responds only if interested. Positive response is generally given within 2-4 weeks. Responds in 3 months to mss. Obtains most new clients through recommendations from others, solicitations.

Terms Agent receives 15% commission on domestic sales. Agent receives 25% commission on foreign sales. Offers written contract; 30-day notice must be given to terminate contract.

Writers Conferences SDSU Writers' Conference; New Jersey Romance Writers of America Writers' Conference; American Independent Writers Conference in Washington DC.

Tips "Be persistent."

YATES & YATES

1100 Town & Country Road, Suite 1300, Orange CA 92868. Website: www.yates2.com. Represents 60 clients.

Represents Nonfiction books, novels. **Considers these nonfiction areas:** animals, autobiography, biography, business, current affairs, dance, economics, gay/lesbian, government, health, history, how-to, investigative, language, law, literature, medicine, memoirs, money, music, politics, psychology, science, self-help, sports, technology, true crime, women's issues, women's studies. **Considers these fiction areas:** contemporary issues, crime, detective, ethnic, feminist, gay, historical, lesbian, literary, mainstream, mystery, police, regional, religious, suspense, thriller.

Recent Sales *No More Mondays*, by Dan Miller (Doubleday Currency).

SUSAN ZECKENDORF ASSOC., INC.

171 W. 57th St., New York NY 10019. (212)245-2928. **Contact:** Susan Zeckendorf. Estab. 1979. Member of AAR. Represents 15 clients. 25% of clients are new/unpublished writers. Currently handles: nonfiction books 50%, novels 50%.

• Prior to opening her agency, Ms. Zeckendorf was a counseling psychologist.

Represents Nonfiction books, novels. **Considers these nonfiction areas:** biography, child guidance, health, history, medicine, music, parenting, psychology, sociology, technology, women's issues, women's studies. **Considers these fiction areas:** crime, detective, ethnic, historical, literary, mainstream, mystery, police, suspense, thriller.

O→ Actively seeking mysteries, literary fiction, mainstream fiction, thrillers, social history, classical music, and biography. Does not want to receive science fiction, romance, or children's books.

How to Contact Query with SASE. No e-mail or fax. Accepts simultaneous submissions. Responds in 10 days to queries. Responds in 3 weeks to mss.

Terms Agent receives 15% commission on domestic sales. Agent receives 20% commission on foreign sales. Charges for photocopying and messenger services.

Writers Conferences Frontiers in Writing Conference; Oklahoma Festival of Books.

Tips "We are a small agency giving lots of individual attention. We respond quickly to submissions."

HELEN ZIMMERMANN LITERARY AGENCY

3 Emmy Lane, New Paltz NY 12561. (845)256-0977. Fax: (845)256-0979. E-mail: helen@zimmagency.com. Website: www.zimmermannliterary.com. **Contact:** Helen Zimmermann. Estab. 2003. Represents 25 clients. 50% of clients are new/unpublished writers. Currently handles: nonfiction books 80%, other 20% fiction.

• Prior to opening her agency, Ms. Zimmermann was the director of advertising and promotion at Random House and the events coordinator at an independent bookstore.

Represents Nonfiction books, novels. **Considers these nonfiction areas:** animals, child guidance, diet/nutrition, how-to, humor, memoirs, popular culture, sports. **Considers these fiction areas:** family saga, historical, literary, mystery, suspense.

O→ "As an agent who has experience at both a publishing house and a bookstore, I have a keen insight for viable projects. This experience also helps me ensure every client gets published well, through the whole process." Actively seeking memoirs, pop culture, women's issues and accessible literary fiction. Does not want to receive horror, science fiction, poetry or romance.

How to Contact Accepts e-mail queries only. E-mail should include a short description of project and bio, whether it be fiction or nonfiction. Accepts simultaneous submissions. Responds in 2 weeks to queries. Responds in 1 month to mss. Obtains most new clients through recommendations from others, solicitations.

Terms Agent receives 15% commission on domestic sales. Offers written contract; 30-day notice must be given to terminate contract. Charges for photocopying and postage (reimbursed if project is sold).

Recent Sales *She Bets Her Life: Women and Gambling*, by Mary Sojourner (Seal Press); *Seeds: One Man's Quest to Preserve the Trees of America's Mot Famous People*, by Rick Horan (HarperCollins); *Saddled*, by Susan Richards (Houghton Mifflin Harcourt); *Final Target*, by Steven Gore (HarperPerennial); *Liberated Body, Captive Mind: A WWII POW Memoir*, by Normal Bussel (Pegasus Books).

Writers Conferences BEA/Writer's Digest Books Writers' Conference, Portland, ME Writers Conference, Berkshire Writers and Readers Conference

Literary Magazines

This section contains markets for your literary short fiction. Although definitions of what constitutes "literary" writing vary, editors of literary journals agree they want to publish the best fiction they can acquire. Qualities they look for in fiction include fully developed characters, strong and unique narrative voice, flawless mechanics, and careful attention to detail in content and manuscript preparation. Most of the authors writing such fiction are well read and well educated, and many are students and graduates of university creative writing programs.

Please also review our Online Markets section, page 336, for electronic literary magazines. At a time when paper and publishing costs rise while funding to small and university presses continues to be cut or eliminated, electronic literary magazines are helping generate a publishing renaissance for experimental as well as more traditional literary fiction. These electronic outlets for literary fiction also benefit writers by eliminating copying and postage costs and providing the opportunity for much quicker responses to submissions. Also notice that some magazines with Web sites give specific information about what they offer online, including updated writer's guidelines and sample fiction from their publications.

STEPPING STONES TO RECOGNITION

Some well-established literary journals pay several hundred or even several thousand dollars for a short story. Most, though, can only pay with contributor's copies or a subscription to their publication. However, being published in literary journals offers the important benefits of experience, exposure and prestige. Agents and major book publishers regularly read literary magazines in search of new writers. Work from these journals is also selected for inclusion in annual prize anthologies. (See next page for a list of anthologies.)

You'll find most of the well-known prestigious literary journals listed here. Many, including *The Southern Review* and *Ploughshares*, are associated with universities, while others like *The Paris Review* are independently published.

SELECTING THE RIGHT LITERARY JOURNAL

Once you have browsed through this section and have a list of journals you might like to submit to, read those listings again carefully. Remember this is information editors provide to help you submit work that fits their needs. You've Got a Story, starting on page 1, will guide you through the process of finding markets for your fiction.

Note that you will find some magazines that do not read submissions all year long.

Whether limited reading periods are tied to a university schedule or meant to accommodate the capabilities of a very small staff, those periods are noted within listings (when the editors notify us). The staffs of university journals are usually made up of student editors and a managing editor who is also a faculty member. These staffs often change every year. Whenever possible, we indicate this in listings and give the name of the current editor and the length of that editor's term. Also be aware that the schedule of a university journal usually coincides with that university's academic year, meaning that the editors of most university publications are difficult or impossible to reach during the summer.

FURTHERING YOUR SEARCH

It cannot be stressed enough that reading the listings for literary journals is only the first part of developing your marketing plan. The second part, equally important, is to obtain fiction guidelines and to read with great care the actual journal you'd like to submit to. Reading copies of these journals helps you determine the fine points of each magazine's publishing style and sensibility. There is no substitute for this type of hands-on research.

Unlike commercial periodicals available at most newsstands and bookstores, it requires a little more effort to obtain some of the magazines listed here. The super-chain bookstores are doing a better job these days of stocking literaries, and you can find some in independent and college bookstores, especially those published in your area. The Internet is an invaluable resource for submission guidelines, as more and more journals establish an online presence. You may, however, need to send for a sample copy. We include sample copy prices in the listings whenever possible. In addition to reading your sample copies, pay close attention to the **Advice** section of each listing. There you'll often find a very specific description of the style of fiction the editors at that publication prefer.

Another way to find out more about literary magazines is to check out the various prize anthologies and take note of journals whose fiction is being selected for publication in them. Studying prize anthologies not only lets you know which magazines are publishing award-winning work, but it also provides a valuable overview of what is considered to be the best fiction published today. Those anthologies include:

- *Best American Short Stories*, published by Houghton Mifflin.
- *New Stories from the South: The Year's Best*, published by Algonquin Books of Chapel Hill.
- *The O. Henry Prize Stories*, published by Doubleday/Anchor.
- *Pushcart Prize: Best of the Small Presses*, published by Pushcart Press.

At the beginnings of listings, we include symbols to help you narrow your search. Keys to those symbols can be found on the inside covers of this book.

ACM (ANOTHER CHICAGO MAGAZINE)

Left Field Press, 3709 N. Kenmore, Chicago IL 60613. E-mail: anotherchicagomagazine@yahoo.com. Website: www.anotherchicagomag.org. **Contact:** Jacob S. Knabb, Managing/Fiction editor. Magazine: 5½ × 8½; 200-220 pages; "art folio each issue." Biannual. Estab. 1977. Circ. 2,000.

Needs Ethnic/multicultural, experimental, feminist, gay, lesbian, literary, translations, contemporary, prose poem. No religious, strictly genre or editorial. Receives 300 unsolicited mss/month. Reads mss from February 1-August 31. Publishes ms 6-12 months after acceptance. **Publishes 10 new writers/year.** Recently published work by Stuart Dybek and Steve Almond.

How to Contact Responds in 3 months to queries; 6 months to mss. Accepts simultaneous, multiple submissions. Sample copy for $8 ppd. Writer's guidelines online.

Payment/Terms Pays small honorarium when possible, contributor's copies and 1 year subscription.

Acquires first North American serial rights.
Tips "Support literary publishing by subscribing to at least one literary journal—if not ours, another. Get used to rejection slips, and don't get discouraged. Keep introductory letters short. Make sure manuscript has name and address on every page, and that it is clean, neat and proofread. We are looking for stories with freshness and originality in subject angle and style, and work that encounters the world and is not stuck in its own navel."

$ AFRICAN AMERICAN REVIEW

Humanities 317, 3800 Lindell Boulevard, St. Louis MO 63108-3414. (314)977-3688. E-mail: keenanam@slu.edu. Website: aar.slu.edu. **Contact:** Aileen Keenan. Magazine: 7X10; 200 pages; 55 lb., acid-free paper; 100 lb. skid stock cover; illustrations; photos. "Essays on African-American literature, theater, film, art and culture generally; interviews; poetry and fiction; book reviews." Quarterly. Circ. 2,000.

- *African American Review* is the official publication of the Division of Black American Literature and Culture of the Modern Language Association. The magazine received American Literary Magazine Awards in 1994 and 1995.

Needs Ethnic/multicultural, experimental, feminist, literary, mainstream. "No children's/juvenile/young adult/teen." Receives 35 unsolicited mss/month. Accepts 10 mss/year. Publishes ms 1 year after acceptance. Agented fiction 0%. Recently published work by Solon Timothy Woodward, Eugenia Collier, Jeffery Renard Allen, Patrick Lohier, Raki Jones, Olympia Vernon. Length: 2,500-5,000 words; average length: 3,000 words. Also publishes literary essays, literary criticism, poetry. Sometimes comments on rejected mss.
How to Contact Submit complete ms via online submission manager. Responds in 1 week to queries; 3 months to mss. Sample copy for $12. Writer's guidelines online. Reviews fiction.
Payment/Terms Pays $25-75, 1 contributor's copy and 5 offprints. Pays on publication for first North American serial rights. Sends galleys to author.

$ ALASKA QUARTERLY REVIEW

University of Alaska-Anchorage, 3211 Providence Dr, Anchorage AK 99508. (907)786-6916. E-mail: ayaqr@uaa.alaska.edu. Website: www.uaa.alaska.edu/aqr/. Magazine: 6 × 9; 232-300 pages; 60 lb. Glatfelter paper; 12 pt. C15 black ink or 4-color; varnish cover stock; photos on cover and photo essays. AQR "publishes fiction, poetry, literary nonfiction and short plays in traditional and experimental styles." Semiannual. Circ. 2,700.

- Two stories selected for inclusion in the 2004 edition of *The O'Henry Prize Stories*.

Needs Experimental, literary, translations, contemporary, prose poem. "If the works in *Alaska Quarterly Review* have certain characteristics, they are these: freshness, honesty and a compelling subject. What makes a piece stand out from the multitude of other submissions? The voice of the piece must be strong—idiosyncratic enough to create a unique persona. We look for the demonstration of craft, making the situation palpable and putting it in a form where it becomes emotionally and intellectually complex. One could look through our pages over time and see that many of the pieces published in the *Alaska Quarterly Review* concern everyday life. We're not asking our writers to go outside themselves and their experiences to the absolute exotic to catch our interest. We look for the experiential and revelatory qualities of the work. We will, without hesitation, champion a piece that may be less polished or stylistically sophisticated, if it engages me, surprises me, and resonates for me. The joy in reading such a work is in discovering something true. Moreover, in keeping with our mission to publish new writers, we are looking for voices our readers do not know, voices that may not always be reflected in the dominant culture and that, in all instances, have something important to convey." Receives 200 unsolicited mss/month. Accepts 7-18 mss/issue; 15-30 mss/year. Does not read mss May 10-August 25. Publishes ms 6 months after acceptance. **Publishes 6 new writers/year.** Recently published work by Howard Norman, Douglas Light, Courtney Angela Brkic, Alison Baker, Lindsay Fitz-Gerald, John Fulton, Ann Stapleton, Edith Pearlman. Publishes short shorts.
How to Contact Responds in 4 months to queries; 4 months to mss. Simultaneous submissions "undesirable, but will accept if indicated." Sample copy for $6. Writer's guidelines online.

Payment/Terms Pays $50-200 subject to funding; pays in contributor's copies and subscriptions when funding is limited. Honorariums on publication when funding permits. Acquires first North American serial rights. Upon request, rights will be transferred back to author after publication.
Tips "Professionalism, patience and persistence are essential. One needs to do one's homework and know the market. The competition is very intense, and funding for the front-line journals is generally inadequate, so staffing is low. It takes time to get a response, and rejections are a fact of life. It is important not to take the rejections personally, and also to know that editors make decisions for better or worse, and they make mistakes too. Fortunately there are many gatekeepers. *Alaska Quarterly Review* has published many pieces that had been turned down by other journals—including pieces that then went on to win national awards. We also know of instances in which pieces *Alaska Quarterly Review* rejected later appeared in other magazines. We haven't regretted that we didn't take those pieces. Rather, we're happy that the authors have made a good match. Disappointment should *never* stop anyone. Will counts as much as talent, and new writers need to have confidence in themselves and stick to it."

ALIMENTUM

P.O. Box 210028, Nashville TN 37221, Nashville TN 37221. Website: www.alimentumjournal.com. **Contact:** Submissions editor. Literary magazine/journal: 6 × 7½, 128 pages, matte cover. Contains illustrations. "All of our stories, poems and essays have food or drink as a theme." Semiannual.
Needs Literary. Special interests: food related. Receives 100 mss/month. Accepts 20-24 mss/issue. Manuscript published one to two years after acceptance. **Publishes average of 2 new writers/year.** Published Mark Kurlansky, Oliver Sacks, Dick Allen, Ann Hood, Carly Sachs. Length: 3,000 words (max). Average length: 1,000-2,000 words. Publishes short shorts. Also publishes literary essays, poetry, spot illustrations. Rarely comments on/critiques rejected mss.
How to Contact Send complete ms with cover letter. Snail mail only. No previously published work. 5-poem limit per submission. Simultaneous submissions okay." Responds to queries and mss in 1-3 months. Send either SASE (or IRC) for return of ms or disposable copy of ms and #10 SASE for reply only. Sample copy available for $10. Guidelines available on website. Check for submission reading periods as they vary from year to year.
Payment/Terms Writers receive 1 contributor's copy. Additional contributor's copies $8. Pays on publication. Acquires first North American serial rights. Publication is copyrighted.
Tips "Write a good story, no clicheés, attention to style, strong voice, memorable characters and scenes."

THE ALLEGHENY REVIEW

Box 32 Allegheny College, Meadville PA 16335. E-mail: review@allegheny.edu. Website: http://review.allegheny.edu. **Contact:** Senior editor. Magazine: 6 × 9; 100 pages; illustrations; photos. "The Allegheny Review is one of America's only nationwide literary magazines exclusively for undergraduate works of poetry, fiction and nonfiction. Our intended audience is persons interested in quality literature." Annual. Estab. 1983.
Needs Adventure, ethnic/multicultural, experimental, family saga, fantasy, feminist, gay, historical, horror, humor/satire, lesbian, literary, mainstream, military/war, mystery/suspense, New Age, psychic/supernatural/occult, religious/inspirational (general), romance, science fiction, western. No "fiction not written by undergraduates—we accept nothing but fiction by currently enrolled undergraduate students. We consider anything catering to an intellectual audience." Receives 50 unsolicited mss/month. Accepts 3 mss/issue. Publishes ms 2 months after deadline. **Publishes roughly 90% new writers/year.** Recently published work by Dianne Page, Monica Stahl and DJ Kinney. Publishes short shorts (up to 20 pages). Also publishes literary nonfiction and poetry.
How to Contact Send complete mss with a cover letter. Accepts submissions on disk. Responds in 2 weeks to queries; 4 months to mss. Send disposable copy of ms and #10 SASE for reply only. Sample copy for $4. Writer's guidelines for SASE, by e-mail or on website.
Payment/Terms Pays 1 contributor's copy; additional copies $3. Sponsors awards/contests; reading fee of $5.

Tips "We look for quality work that has been thoroughly revised. Unique voice, interesting topic and playfulness with the English language. Revise, revise, revise! And be careful how you send it—the cover letter says a lot. We definitely look for diversity in the pieces we publish."

ALLIGATOR JUNIPER

Prescott College, 220 Grove Ave., Prescott AZ 86301. (928) 350-2012. Fax: (928) 776-5137. E-mail: aj@prescott.edu. Website: www.prescott.edu/highlights/alligator_juniper/index.html. **Contact:** Jeff Fearnside, managing editor. Literary magazine/journal: 7.5 × 10.5; 182 pages; photographs. "Alligator Juniper was founded with the intention of furthering the environmental and experimental mission of Prescott College, its sponsoring institution, by featuring environmentally-aware and socially-conscious writing and art. Since its premiere issue in 1995, AJ has provided regional, national, and international artists, both established and emerging, a forum in which to publish writing with timely, emotional themes. AJ is proud to showcase a perennially diverse range of artisits." Annual. Estab. 1995. Circ. 1500. Member CLMP.

- AJhas received the AWP Director's Award for Content (2001 & 2004), annual funding from the Arizona Commission on the Arts, and a Gregory Kolovakos Seed Grant from the Council of Literary Magazines and Presses (1997).

Needs Experimental, literary. Does not want genre fiction or children's literature. "Includes an open submissions section on a special theme in each issue. The theme for the 2010 special section is "International Writing," complete information available on website." Accepts 5-6 mss/year. Does not read November-April. Mss published 4 months after acceptance.

How to Contact Primarily accepts submissions via annual *Alligator Juniper* National Writing Contest. See separate listing under Contests and Awards.

THE AMERICAN DRIVEL REVIEW

3561 SE Cora Drive, Portland OR 97202. (503) 236-6377. E-mail: info@americandrivelreview.com. Website: www.americandrivelreview.com. **Contact:** Tara Blaine and David Wester, editors. Magazine: 6 × 9; 90-100 pages; black and white illustrations and photos. The American Drivel Review is a journal of literary humor dedicated to formulating a Unified Field Theory of Wit. Estab. 2004. Circ. 200.

Needs "We are delighted to consider any categories, styles, forms or genres—real or imagined. We are interested in quality humorous writing in every conceivable form." Receives 75-100 unsolicited mss/month. Accepts 20-30 mss/issue; 60-80 mss/year. Publishes ms 2 months after acceptance. **Publishes 10-15 new writers/year.** Recently published work by Willie Smith, Laird Hunt, Matthew Summers-Sparks, Jack Collom, Richard Froude, Guy R. Beining, and Larry Fagin. Publishes short shorts. Also publishes literary essays, literary criticism, poetry.

How to Contact Send complete ms. Accepts submissions by e-mail, disk. Send SASE for return of ms. Responds in 2-3 months to queries. Accepts multiple submissions. No simultaneous submissions. Sample copy for $6.50. Writer's guidelines for #10 SASE, online or by e-mail.

Payment/Terms Pays 2 contributor's copies. Pays on publication for one-time rights.

Tips "We look primarily for sublime, funny, brilliant writing and a unique or experimental voice."

AMERICAN LITERARY REVIEW

University of North Texas, P.O. Box 311307, Denton TX 76203-1307. E-mail: americanliteraryreview@gmail.com. Website: www.engl.unt.edu/alr/. Magazine: 6 × 9; 128 pages; 70 lb. Mohawk paper; 67 lb. Wausau Vellum cover. "Publishes quality, contemporary poems and stories." Semiannual. Circ. 1,200.

Needs Literary, mainstream. "No genre works." Receives 150-200 unsolicited mss/month. Accepts 5-6 mss/issue; 12-16 mss/year. Reading period: October 1-May 1. Publishes ms within 2 years after acceptance. Recently published work by Dana Johnson, Bill Roorbach, Cynthia Shearer, Mark Jacobs and Sylvia Wantanabe. Also publishes literary essays, poetry. Critiques or comments on rejected mss.

How to Contact Send complete ms with cover letter. Responds in 2-4 months to mss. Accepts simultaneous submissions. Sample copy for $8. Writer's guidelines for #10 SASE.

Payment/Terms Pays in contributor's copies. Acquires one-time rights.

Tips "We would like to see more short shorts and stylistically innovative and risk-taking fiction. We like to see stories that illuminate the various layers of characters and their situations with great artistry. Give us distinctive character-driven stories that explore the complexities of human existence." Looks for "the small moments that contain more than at first possible, that surprise us with more truth than we thought we had a right to expect."

$ AMERICAN SHORT FICTION

E-mail: editors@americanshortfiction.org. Literary magazine/journal. 6X9.5, 140 pages. Contains illustrations. Includes photographs. "American Short Fiction (ASF) strives to discover and publish new fiction in which transformations of language, narrative, and character occur swiftly, deftly, and unexpectedly. We are drawn to evocative language, unique subject matter, and an overall sense of immediacy. We target readers who love literary fiction, are drawn to independent publishing, and enjoy short fiction. ASF is one of the few journals that focuses solely on fiction." Quarterly. Circ. 2,500. Member CLMP.

- ASF has had a selection included in *Best Nonrequired Reading*, 2007 and *New Stories from the Southwest*, 2008. Awards from the previous incarnation of ASF (when published by The University of Texas, 1991-1998) include selections in *Best American Short Stories*, *The O. Henry Prize Stories*, the *Graywolf Annual*, the *Pushcart Prize* anthology, and two time finalist for the National Magazine Award.

Needs Experimental, literary, translations. Does not want young adult fiction or genre fiction. "However, we are open to publishing mystery or speculative fiction if we feel it has literary value." Receives 300-400 mss/month. Accepts 5-6 mss/issue; 20-25 mss/year. Manuscript published 3 months after acceptance. Agented fiction 20%. **Publishes 2-3 new writers/year.**Published Joice Carol Oates, Maud Casey, Chris Bachelder, Vendela Vida, Benjamin Percy, Jack Pendarvis, Paul Yoon, and Dagoberto Gilb. Length: 2,000 words (min)-15,000 words (max). Average length: 6,000 words. Publishes short shorts. Average length of short shorts: 500 words. Also publishes literary essays, literary criticism. Sometimes comments on/critiques rejected mss.

How to Contact Submit complete ms electronically on website. Include estimated word count, brief bio. Responds to queries in 2 weeks. Responds to mss in 4-5 months. Guidelines available for SASE, via e-mail, on website. Regular submissions are open. "**To help defray the administrative costs of this new system, we ask that our submitters pay a submission fee of $2 per story.** Submitters should visit our publisher's online store to pay the submission fee. When the transaction is complete, submitters will be directed to our Submission Manager, where they can upload their stories. Our **Submission Manager requires that uploaded files be less than 500 KB**. Send complete ms."

Payment/Terms Writers receive $250-500, 2 contributor's copies, free subscription to the magazine. Additional copies $5. Pays on publication. Acquires first North American serial rights, electronic rights. Sends galleys to author. Publication is copyrighted. Sponsors Short Story Contest. See separate listing or website.

Tips "We publish fiction that speaks to us emotionally, uses evocative and precise language, and takes risks in subject matter and/or form. Try to read an issue or two of *American Short Fiction* to get a sense of what we like. Also, to be concise is a great virtue."

AMOSKEAG, THE JOURNAL OF SOUTHERN NEW HAMPSHIRE UNIVERSITY

2500 N. River Road, Manchester NH 03106. E-mail: m.brien@snhu.edu. Website: www.amoskeagjournal.com. **Contact:** Michael J. Brien, editor. Magazine has revolving editor and occasional themes (see website). Editorial term: 3 yrs. Literary magazine/journal. 6 × 9, 105-140 pages. Contains photographs. "We select fiction, creative nonfiction and poetry that appeals to general readers, writers, and academics alike. We accept work from writers nationwide, but also try to include New England writers. We tend not to accept much experimental work, but the language of poetry or prose must nevertheless be dense, careful and surprising." Annual.

Needs Ethnic/multicultural (general), experimental, feminist, gay, humor/satire, literary. Does not want genre fiction. Receives 200 mss/month. Accepts 10 prose mss and 15-20 poems/issue. Does not read December-August. Reading period is Sept-Dec. Ms published in late April. Published Ann Hood, Maxine Kumin, Paul Hostovsky, Mary Elizabeth Parker, Jessica Bacal, Merle Drown, Pat Parnell, Octavio Quintanilla, Darryl Halbrooks, Simon Perchik and Baron Wormser. Fiction and Creative Nonfiction. Publishes short shorts. Also publishes poetry. Sometimes comments on/critiques rejected mss.

How to Contact Send complete ms with cover letter. Include brief bio, list of publications. Responds to queries in 1 month. Responds to mss in 4-5 months. Send either SASE (or IRC) for return of ms or disposable copy of ms and #10 SASE or email address for reply only. Considers simultaneous submissions, multiple submissions. Sample copy available for $6. Guidelines on website.

Payment/Terms Writers aren't paid, but receive 2 contributor's copies. Additional copies $6. Acquires one-time rights. Publication is copyrighted.

Tips "We're looking for quality and pizzazz. Stories need good pacing, believable characters and dialogue, as well as unusual subjects to stand out. Most stories we get are 'domestic fiction;' middle-class family dramas. Read the news, live an exciting life. Write about remarkable people."

$ THE ANTIGONISH REVIEW

St. Francis Xavier University, P.O. Box 5000, Antigonish NS B2G 2W5 Canada. (902)867-3962. Fax: (902)867-5563. Website: www.antigonishreview.com. **Contact:** Bonnie McIsaac, office manager. Literary magazine for educated and creative readers. Quarterly. Estab. 1970. Circ. 1,000.

Needs Literary, translations, contemporary, prose poem. No erotica. Receives 50 unsolicited mss/month. Accepts 6 mss/issue. Publishes ms 4 months after acceptance. **Publishes some new writers/year.** Recently published work by Calvin Wharton, Stephen Morison jr., Rebecca Rosenblum. Sometimes comments on rejected mss.

How to Contact Send complete ms. Accepts submissions by fax. Accepts electronic (disk compatible with WordPerfect/IBM and Windows) submissions. Prefers hard copy. Responds in 1 month to queries; 6 months to mss. No simultaneous submissions. Sample copy for $7 or online. Writer's guidelines for #10 SASE or online.

Payment/Terms Pays $100 per accepted story. Pays on publication. Rights retained by author.

Tips "Learn the fundamentals and do not deluge an editor."

$ ANTIOCH REVIEW

P.O. Box 148, Yellow Springs OH 45387-0148 United States. E-mail: mkeyes@antioch.edu. Website: www.antiochreview.org. **Contact:** Muriel Keyes. Magazine: 6 × 9; 200 pages; 50 lb. book offset paper; coated cover stock; illustrations "seldom." "Literary and cultural review of contemporary issues, and literature for general readership." Quarterly. Circ. 3,000.

Needs Literary, experimental, contemporary, translations. No science fiction, fantasy or confessions. Receives 275 unsolicited mss/month. Accepts 5-6 mss/issue; 20-24 mss/year. No mss accepted June 1-September 1. Publishes ms 10 months after acceptance. Agented fiction 1-2%. **Publishes 1-2 new writers/year.** Recently published work by Edith Pearlman, Peter LaSalle, Rosellen Brown, Nathan Oates, Stephen O'Connor, and Susan Miller.

How to Contact Send complete ms with SASE, preferably mailed flat. Responds in 4-6 months to mss. Sample copy for $7. Writer's guidelines online.

Payment/Terms Pays $15/printed page. Pays on publication.

Tips "Our best advice always is to read the *Antioch Review* to see what type of material we publish. Quality fiction requires an engagement of the reader's intellectual interest supported by mature emotional relevance, written in a style that is rich and rewarding without being freaky. The great number of stories submitted to us indicates that fiction still has great appeal. We assume that if so many are writing fiction, many must be reading it."

APALACHEE REVIEW

Apalachee Press, P.O. Box 10469, Tallahassee FL 32302. (850)644-9114. Website: http://apalacheereview.org/index.html. **Contact:** Michael Trammell, editor; Mary Jane Ryals, fiction editor. Literary magazine/journal: trade paperback size, 100-140 pages. Includes photographs. "At Apalachee Review, we are interested in outstanding literary fiction, but we especially like poetry, fiction, and nonfiction that addresses intercultural issues in a domestic or international setting/ context." Annual. Circ. 500. Member CLMP.

Needs Ethnic/multicultural, edgy, experimental, fantasy/sci-fi (with a literary bent), feminist, historical, humor/satire, literary, mainstream, mystery/suspense, New Age with a literary bent, translations. Does not want cliché-filled genre-oriented fiction. Receives 60-100 mss/month. Accepts 5-10 mss/issue. Manuscript published 1 yr after acceptance. Agented fiction 0.5%. **Publishes 1-2 new writers/year.** Recently published Lu Vickers, Joe Clark, Joe Taylor, Jane Arrowsmith Edwards, Vivian Lawry, Linda Frysh, Charles Harper Webb, Reno Raymond Gwaltney. Length: 600 words (min)-5,500 words (max). Average length: 3,500 words. Publishes short shorts. Average length of short shorts: 250 words. Also publishes literary essays, book reviews, poetry. Send review copies to Michael Trammell, editor. Sometimes comments on/critiques rejected mss.

How to Contact Send complete ms with cover letter. Include brief bio, list of publications. Responds to queries in 4-6 weeks. Responds to mss in 3-14 months. Send either SASE (international authors should see website for "international" guidelines, no IRCs, please) for return of ms or disposable copy of ms and #10 SASE for reply only. Considers simultaneous submissions. Sample copy available for $8 (current issue), $5 (back issue). Guidelines available for SASE, or check the website.

Payment/Terms Writers receive 2 contributors copies. Additional copies $5/each. Pays on publication. Acquires one-time rights, electronic rights. Publication is copyrighted.

APPALACHIAN HERITAGE

(859)985-3699. E-mail: george_brosi@berea.edu; appalachianheritage@berea.edu. Magazine: 6 × 9; 104 pages; 60 lb. stock; 10 pt. Warrenflo cover; drawings; b&w photos. "Appalachian Heritage is a Southern Appalachian literary magazine. We try to keep a balance of fiction, poetry, essays, scholarly works, etc., for a general audience and/or those interested in the Appalachian mountains." Quarterly.

Needs Historical, literary, regional. "We do not want to see fiction that has no ties to Southern Appalachia." Receives 60-80 unsolicited mss/month. Accepts 2-3 mss/issue; 12-15 mss/year. Publishes ms 3-6 months after acceptance. **Publishes 8 new writers/year.** Recently published work by Wendell Berry, Sharyn Mcrumb, Jayne Anne Phillips, Silas House, Ron Rash, and Jim Wayne Miller. Publishes short shorts. Occasionally comments on rejected mss.

How to Contact Send complete ms. Send SASE for reply, return of ms or send a disposable copy of ms. Responds in 1 month to queries; 6 weeks to mss. Sample copy for $8. Writer's guidelines free.

Payment/Terms Pays 3 contributor's copies; $8 charge for extras. Acquires first North American serial rights.

Tips "Get acquainted with *Appalachian Heritage*, as you should with any publication before submitting your work."

APPARATUS MAGAZINE

Burning Poetry Productions, 2013 W. Farragut, Unit #2, Chicago IL 60625. (773)571-2297. E-mail: Editor@apparatusmagazine.com; submissions @apparatusmagazine.com. Website: apparatusmagazine.com. **Contact:** Adam W. Hart, publisher/editor.

Needs Adventure.

How to Contact Send complete ms with a cover letter including estimated word count, brief bio, list of publications to submissions@apparatusmagazine.com. Accepts submissions by e-mail. Label subject line with "fiction submission." Responds in 2-3 months. Accepts multiple submissions; no simultaneous or previously published submissions. Sample copy on website.

Payment/Terms Acquires first rights, first North American serial rights, electronic rights, including the right to archive work online, option for possible inclusion in print anthology with writer's permission. Publication is copyrighted.

Tips Offers annual apparatus award of $100 for the best fiction piece published in *apparatus magazine* during the publication year. Fiction must have been accepted and published in the journal during this time frame (June to June). Award will be decided upon by a panel. Fiction must be 500 words or less. Don't be afraid to take chances, but make sure the story is not too abstract that the reader cannot enjoy it. Avoid work that is comprised only of dialogue, as such pieces, if not done well, can be quite flat. Mss. that stand out are those that present unique takes on themes— something I have not previously run across. Above all, the voice of the piece must be true—work that is forced will read that way on the page, so listen to what the characters are trying to tell you."

ARGESTES LITERARY REVIEW

Collen Tree Press, 2941 170th St., South Amana IA 52334. (319) 899-0994. E-mail: ctp_argestes@yahoo.com. Website: www.collentreepress.com. **Contact:** Robert Bruce Kelsey, Fiction Editor. Literary magazine/journal. 100-150 pages. Contains illustrations. Includes photographs. "Argestes is a literary review of poetry and short story. We are a print-only journal. We are open to most forms of poetry and short story. We publish work of both established and new writers. We are an independent journal with no university affiliations." Semiannual. Circ. 200.

Needs Ethnic/multicultural (general), experimental, fantasy, feminist, gay, lesbian, literary, science fiction (soft/sociological), translations. Does not want gratuitous violence. Receives 30-60 mss/month. Accepts 3-6 mss/issue; 6-12 mss/year. Ms published 3-6 months after acceptance. **Publishes 3-6 new writers/year.** Published Joseph Hart, J. Cochran, Martin Galvin, Robert Parham, Tim Hurley and Joanne Lowery. Length: 2500 words (max). Average length: 1,700 words. Publishes short shorts. Average length of short shorts: 1,000 words. Also publishes literary essays, literary criticism, book reviews, poetry. Send review copies to Robert Bruce Kelsey-short story collections only. Sometimes comments on/critiques rejected mss.

How to Contact Send complete ms with cover letter. Include estimated word count, brief bio. Responds to queries in 4-8 weeks. Responds to mss in 4-8 weeks. Send disposable copy of ms and #10 SASE for reply only. Considers simultaneous submissions, multiple submissions. Sample copy available for $7. Guidelines available for SASE. Reads all year round.

Payment/Terms Writers receive 2 contributor's copies. Additional copies $7. Pays on publication. Acquires first North American serial rights. Publication is copyrighted.

Tips "We look for a unique voice; an ear for language, dialogue; an obviously unique perception or emotional engagement with the subject matter. Read broadly and deeply, but craft your own stories in your own voice."

ARKANSAS REVIEW

A Journal of Delta Studies, Department of English and Philosophy, P.O. Box 189, State University AR 72467-1890. (501)972-3043. Fax: (501)972-3045. E-mail: jcollins@astate.edu. Website: www.clt.astate.edu/arkreview. **Contact:** General editor. Magazine: 8¼ × 11; 64-100 pages; coated, matte paper; matte, 4-color cover stock; illustrations; photos. Publishes articles, fiction, poetry, essays, interviews, reviews, visual art evocative of or responsive to the Mississippi River Delta. Triannual. Circ. 700.

Needs Literary (essays and criticism), regional (short stories). "No genre fiction. Must have a Delta focus." Receives 30-50 unsolicited mss/month. Accepts 2-3 mss/issue; 5-7 mss/year. Publishes ms 6-12 months after acceptance. Agented fiction 1%. **Publishes 3-4 new writers/year.** Recently published work by Susan Henderson, George Singleton, Scott Ely and Pia Erhart. Also publishes literary essays, poetry. Sometimes comments on rejected mss.

How to Contact Accepts submissions by e-mail, fax. Send SASE for reply, return of ms or send a disposable copy of ms. Responds in 1 week to queries; 4 months to mss. Sample copy for $7.50. Writer's guidelines for #10 SASE.

Payment/Terms Pays 3 contributor's copies; additional copies for $5. Acquires first North American serial rights.

Tips "We see a lot of stories set in New Orleans but prefer fiction that takes place in other parts of the Delta. We'd love more innovative and experimental fiction too but primarily seek stories that involve and engage the reader and evoke or respond to the Delta natural and/or cultural experience."

THE ARMCHAIR AESTHETE

Pickle Gas Press, 19 Abbotswood Crescent, Penfield NY 14526. (585)248-8617. E-mail: bypaul@frontiernet.net; thearmchairaesthete@yahoo.com. **Contact:** Paul Agosto, editor. Magazine: 5½ × 8½; 145-175 pages; 20 lb. paper; 110 lb. card stock color cover and plastic spiral bound. "The Armchair Aesthete seeks quality writing that enlightens and entertains a thoughtful audience (ages 9-90) with a 'good read."' 2 issues per year.

Needs Adventure, fantasy (science fantasy, sword and sorcery), historical (general), horror, humor/satire (satire), mainstream (contemporary), mystery/suspense (amateur sleuth, cozy, police procedural, private eye/hard-boiled, romantic suspense), science fiction (soft/sociological), western (frontier, traditional). "No racist, pornographic, overt gore; no religious or material intended for or written by children. Receives 60 unsolicited mss/month. Accepts 16-24 mss/issue; 60-80 mss/year. Publishes ms 1-12 months after acceptance. Agented fiction 5%. **Publishes 15-25 new writers/year.** Recently published work by Chris Brown, Laverne and Carol Frith, Lydia Williams, Andrew Bynom, Douglas Empringham, Frank Andreotti, Alan Reynolds, and Douglas Empringham. Average length: 4,500 words. Publishes short shorts. Also publishes poetry. Sometimes comments on rejected mss.

How to Contact Accepts submissions by e-mail. Send SASE for reply, return of ms or send a disposable copy of ms. Responds in 2-3 weeks to queries; 3-9 months to mss. Accepts simultaneous, multiple submissions and reprints. Sample copy for $8 (paid to P. Agosto, Ed.) and 5 first-class stamps. Writer's guidelines for #10 SASE. No longer reviews fiction or poetry chapbooks.

Payment/Terms Pays 1 contributor's copy; additional copies for $8 (pay to P. Agosto, editor). Pays on publication for one-time rights.

Tips "Clever, compelling storytelling has a good chance here. We look for a clever plot, thought-out characters, something that surprises or catches us off guard. Write on innovative subjects and situations. Submissions should be professionally presented and technically sound."

$ ARTFUL DODGE

College of Wooster, Department of English, Wooster OH 44691. E-mail: artfuldodge@wooster.edu (inquiries only). Website: www.wooster.edu/artfuldodge/home.htm. **Contact:** Daniel Bourne, editor. Magazine: 180 pages; illustrations; photos. "There is no theme in this magazine, except literary power. We also have an ongoing interest in translations from Central/Eastern Europe and elsewhere." Annual. Circ. 1,000.

Needs Experimental, literary, translations, prose poem. "We judge by literary quality, not by genre. We are especially interested in fine English translations of significant prose writers. Translations should be submitted with original texts." Receives 50 unsolicited mss/month. Accepts 5 mss/year. **Publishes 1 new writer/year.** Recently published work by Nin Andres, Vénus Khoury-Ghata, KEva Marie Ginsburg, Philip Metres, and Daniel Tobin. Average length: 2,500 words. Also publishes literary essays, literary criticism, poetry. Occasionally comments on rejected mss.

How to Contact Send complete ms with SASE. Do not send more than 30 pages at a time. Responds in 1 year to mss. Accepts simultaneous submissions if contacted immediately after being accepted elsewhere. Sample copy/1 year subscription for $7; two year subscriptions are $14. Writer's guidelines for #10 SASE.

Payment/Terms Pays 2 contributor's copies and honorarium of $5/page, "thanks to funding from the Ohio Arts Council." Acquires first North American serial rights.

Tips "If we take time to offer criticism, do not subsequently flood us with other stories no better than the first. If starting out, get as many *good* readers as possible. Above all, read contemporary fiction and the magazine you are trying to publish in."

THE BALTIMORE REVIEW

P.O. Box 36418, Towson MD 21286. Website: www.baltimorereview.org. **Contact:** Susan Muaddi Darraj, managing editor. Magazine: 6 × 9; 150 pages; 60 lb. paper; 10 pt. CS1 gloss film cover. Showcase for the best short stories, creative nonfiction and poetry by writers in the Baltimore area and beyond. Semiannual.

Needs Ethnic/multicultural, literary, mainstream. "No science fiction, westerns, children's, romance, etc." Accepts 20 mss/issue; approx. 40 mss/year. Publishes ms 1-9 months after acceptance. **Publishes "at least a few" new writers/year.** Average length: 3,000 words. Publishes short shorts. Also publishes poetry.

How to Contact Accepts submissions via online system only. Please visit website. Responds in 4-6 months to mss. Accepts simultaneous submissions. Sample copy: $10, which included postage/handling.

Payment/Terms Pays 2 contributor's copies. Acquires first North American serial rights.

Tips "We look for compelling stories and a masterful use of the English language. We want to feel that we have never heard this story, or this voice, before. Read the kinds of publications you want your work to appear in. Make your reader believe and care."

BARBARIC YAWP

Bone World Publishing, 3700 County Rt. 24, Russell NY 13684-3198. (315)347-2609. **Contact:** Nancy Berbrich, fiction editor. Magazine: digest-size; 60 pages; 24 lb. paper; matte cover stock. "We publish what we like. Fiction should include some bounce and surprise. Our publication is intended for the intelligent, open-minded reader." Quarterly. Estab. 1997. Circ. 120.

Needs Adventure, experimental, fantasy (science, sword and sorcery), historical, horror, literary, mainstream, psychic/supernatural/occult, regional, religious/inspirational, science fiction (hard, soft/sociological). "We don't want any pornography, gratuitous violence or whining." Wants more suspense and philosophical work. Receives 30-40 unsolicited mss/month. Accepts 10-12 mss/issue; 40-48 mss/year. Publishes ms up to 6 months after acceptance. **Publishes 4-6 new writers/year.** Recently published work by Francine Witte, Jeff Grimshaw, Thaddeus Rutkowski and Holly Interlandi. Length: 1,500 words; average length: 600 words. Publishes short shorts. Also publishes literary essays, literary criticism, poetry. Often comments on rejected mss.

How to Contact Send SASE for reply, return of ms or send a disposable copy of ms. Responds in 2 weeks to queries; 4 months to mss. Accepts simultaneous, multiple submissions and reprints. Sample copy for $4. Writer's guidelines for #10 SASE.

Payment/Terms Pays 1 contributor's copy; additional copies $3. Acquires one-time rights.

Tips "Don't give up. Read much, write much, submit much. Observe closely the world around you. Don't borrow ideas from TV or films. Revision is often necessary—grit your teeth and do it. Never fear rejection."

BATHTUB GIN

Pathwise Press, 2311 Broadway St, New Orleans, LA 70125. (812) 327-2855. E-mail: pathwisepress@hotmail.com. Website: www. pathwisepress.com. **Contact:** Fiction Editor. Magazine: 8½ × 5½; 60 pages; recycled 20-lb. paper; 80-lb. card cover; illustrations; photos. "Bathtub Gin is looking for work that has some kick to it. We are very eclectic and publish a wide range of styles. Audience is anyone interested in new writing and art that is not being presented in larger magazines." Semiannual. Estab. 1997. Circ. 250.

Needs Condensed novels, experimental, humor/satire, literary. "No horror, science fiction, historical unless they go beyond the usual formula." "We want more experimental fiction." Receives 20 unsolicited mss/month. Accepts 2-3 mss/issue. Reads mss for two issues June 1st-September 15th. "We publish in mid-October and mid-April." **Publishes 10 new writers/year.** Recently published work by J.T. Whitehead and G.D. McFetridge. Publishes short shorts. Also publishes literary essays, literary criticism, poetry. Often comments on rejected mss.

How to Contact Accepts submissions by e-mail. Send cover letter with a 3-5 line bio. Send SASE for reply, return of ms or send a disposable copy of ms. Responds in 1-2 months to queries. Accepts simultaneous, multiple submissions and reprints. Sample copy for $5. Writer's guidelines for #10 SASE. Reviews fiction.

Payment/Terms Pays 2 contributor's copies; discount on additional copies. Rights revert to author upon publication.

Tips "Please be advised that magazine is currently on hiatus and not accepting work until at least 2009."

☐ BELLEVUE LITERARY REVIEW

A Journal of Humanity and Human Experience, 550 First Avenue, OBV-A612, New York NY 10016. (212)263-3973. E-mail: info@blreview.org; stacy.bodziak@nyumc.org. Website: blreview.org. Magazine: 6 × 9; 160 pages. "The BLR is a literary journal that examines human existence through the prism of health and healing, illness and disease. We encourage creative interpretations of these themes." Semiannual. Member CLMP.

Needs Literary. No genre fiction. Receives 100 unsolicited mss/month. Accepts 12 mss/issue; 24 mss/year. Publishes ms 3-6 months after acceptance. Agented fiction 1%. **Publishes 3-6 new writers/year.** Recently published work by Amy Hempel, Sheila Kohler, Martha Cooley. Length: 5,000 words; average length: 2,500 words. Publishes short shorts. Also publishes literary essays, poetry. Sometimes comments on rejected mss.

How to Contact Submit online at www.blreview.org (preferred). Also accepts mss via regular mail. Send complete ms. Send SASE (or IRC) for return of ms or disposable copy of the ms and #10 SASE for reply only. Responds in 3-6 months to mss. Accepts simultaneous submissions. Sample copy for $7. Writer's guidelines for SASE, e-mail or on website.

Payment/Terms Pays 2 contributor's copies, 1-year subscription and 1 year gift subscription; additional copies $6. Pays on publication for first North American serial rights. Sends galleys to author.

◪ BELLINGHAM REVIEW

Mail Stop 9053, Western Washington University, Bellingham WA 98225. Website: www.wwu.edu/~bhreview. Magazine: 6 × 8¼; 150 pages; 60 lb. white paper; four-color cover." *Bellingham Review* seeks literature of palpable quality; stories, essays and poems that nudge the limits of form or execute traditional forms exquisitely. Annual. Circ. 1,600.

- The editors are actively seeking submissions of creative nonfiction, as well as stories that push the boundaries of the form. The Tobias Wolff Award in Fiction Contest runs December 1-March 15; see website for guidelines or send SASE.

Needs Experimental, humor/satire, literary, regional (Northwest). Does not want anything nonliterary. Accepts 3-4 mss/issue. Does not read ms February 2-September 14. Publishes ms 6 months after acceptance. Agented fiction 10%. **Publishes 10 new writers/year.** Recently published work by Patricia Vigderman, Joshua Rolnick, and A.G. Harmon. Publishes short shorts. Also publishes poetry.

How to Contact Send complete ms. Responds in 1-6 months to mss. Accepts simultaneous submissions. Sample copy for $12. Two year subscription is $20. Writer's guidelines online.

Payment/Terms Pays on publication when funding allows. Acquires first North American serial rights.

Tips "We look for work that is ambitious, vital and challenging both to the spirit and the intellect."

◪ ◘ BELLOWING ARK

A Literary Tabloid, P.O. Box 55564, Shoreline WA 98155. E-mail: bellowingark@bellowingark.org. **Contact:** Robert R. Ward, editor. Tabloid: 11½ × 17½; 32 pages; electro-brite paper and cover stock; illustrations; photos. "We publish material we feel addresses the human situation in an affirmative way. We do not publish academic fiction." Bimonthly. Circ. 650.

- Work from *Bellowing Ark* appeared in the *Pushcart Prize* anthology.

Needs Literary, mainstream, serialized novels. "No science fiction or fantasy." Receives 30-70 unsolicited mss/month. Accepts 2-5 mss/issue; 700-1,000 mss/year. Publishes ms 6 months after acceptance. **Publishes 6-10 new writers/year**. Recently published work by Tom Cook, Tanyo Ravicz, Jan Johnson, Jane Lawless, and E.R. Romaine. Also publishes literary essays, literary criticism, poetry. Sometimes comments on rejected mss.

How to Contact Send complete ms and SASE. Responds in 6 weeks to mss. No simultaneous submissions. Sample copy for $4, 9½ × 12½ SAE and $1.43 postage.

Payment/Terms Pays in contributor's copies. Acquires one-time rights.

Tips "*Bellowing Ark* began as (and remains) an alternative to the despair and negativity of the workshop/ academic literary scene; we believe that life has meaning and is worth living—the work we publish reflects that belief. Learn how to tell a story before submitting. Avoid 'trick' endings; they have all been done before and better. *Bellowing Ark* is interested in publishing writers who will develop with the magazine, as in an extended community. We find good writers and stick with them. This is why the magazine has grown from 12 to 32 pages."

BELOIT FICTION JOURNAL

Box 11, 700 College St., Beloit College WI 53511. (608)363-2079. E-mail: bfj@beloit.edu. Website: www.beloit.edu/english/fictionjournal/. **Contact:** Chris Fink, editor-in-chief. Literary magazine: 6 × 9; 250 pages; 60 lb. paper; 10 pt. C1S cover stock; illustrations; photos on cover; ad-free. "We are interested in publishing the best contemporary fiction and are open to all themes except those involving pornographic, religiously dogmatic or politically propagandistic representations. Our magazine is for general readership, though most of our readers will probably have a specific interest in literary magazines." Annual.

- Work first appearing in *Beloit Fiction Journal* has been reprinted in award-winning collections, including the Flannery O'Connor and the Milkweed Fiction Prize collections, and has won the Iowa Short Fiction award.

Needs Literary, mainstream, contemporary. Wants more experimental and short shorts. Would like to see more "stories with a focus on both language and plot, unusual metaphors and vivid characters. No pornography, religious dogma, science fiction, horror, political propaganda or genre fiction." Receives 200 unsolicited mss/month. Accepts 20 mss/year. Publishes ms 9 months after acceptance. **Publishes 3 new writers/year.** Recently published work by Dennis Lehane, Silas House and David Harris Ebenbach. Length: 250-10,000 words; average length: 5,000 words. Sometimes comments on rejected mss.

How to Contact "Our reading period is from August 1st to December 1st only. " No fax, e-mail or disk submissions. Responds in 2 weeks to queries; 2 months to mss. Accepts simultaneous submissions if identified as such. Please send one story at a time. Always include SASE. Sample copy for $ 10 (new issue), $8 (back issue, double issue), $ 6 (back issue, single issue). Writer's guidelines for #10 SASE or on website.

Payment/Terms Buys first North American serial rights only. Payment in copies.

Tips "Many of our contributors are writers whose work we had previously rejected. Don't let one rejection slip turn you away from our—or any—magazine."

BERKELEY FICTION REVIEW

10B Eshleman Hall, University of California, Berkeley CA 94720. (510)642-2892. E-mail: bfictionreview@yahoo.com. Website: OCF.Berkeley.EDU/~bfr/. **Contact:** Caitlin McGuire, editor. Magazine: 5½ × 8½; 180 pages; perfect-bound; glossy cover; some b&w art; photographs. "The mission of Berkeley Fiction Review is to provide a forum for new and emerging writers as well as writers already established. We publish a wide variety of contemporary short fiction for a literary audience." Annual. Circ. 1,000.

Needs Experimental, literary, mainstream. "Quality, inventive short fiction. No poetry or formula fiction." Receives 100 unsolicited mss/month. Accepts 10-15 mss/issue. **Publishes 10-15 new writers/year.** Publishes short shorts. Occacionally comments on rejected mss.

How to Contact Responds in 2-4 months to mss. Accepts simultaneous, multiple submissions. Sample copy for $10. Writer's guidelines for SASE. Accepts e-mail submissions in.pdf or word attachments.

Payment/Terms Pays one contributor's copy. Acquires first rights. Sponsors awards/contests.

Tips "Our criteria is fiction that resonates. Voices that are strong and move a reader. Clear, powerful prose (either voice or rendering of subject) with a point. Unique ways of telling stories-these capture the editors. Work hard, don't give up. Ask an honest person to point out your writing weaknesses, and then work on them. We look forward to reading fresh new voices."

$ BIBLIOPHILOS

The Bibliophile Publishing Co., Inc., 200 Security Building, Fairmont WV 26554. (304)366-8107. **Contact:**Gerald J. Bobango, editor. Literary magazine: 5½ × 8; 68-72 pages; white glossy paper; illustrations; photos. "We see ourself as a forum for new and unpublished writers, historians, philosophers, literary critics and reviewers, and those who love animals. Audience is academic-oriented, college graduate, who believes in traditional Aristotelian-Thomistic thought and education and has a fair streak of the Luddite in him/her. Our ideal reader owns no television, has never sent or received e-mail, and avoids shopping malls at any cost. He loves books." Quarterly. Estab. 1981. Circ. 400.

Needs Adventure, ethnic/multicultural, family saga, historical (general, US, Eastern Europe), horror (psychological, supernatural), humor/satire, literary, mainstream, military/war, mystery/suspense (police procedural, private eye/hard -boiled, courtroom), novel excerpts, regional (New England, Middle Atlantic), romance (gothic, historical, regency period), slice-of-life vignettes, suspense, thriller/espionage, translations, western (frontier saga, traditional), utopian, Orwellian. "No 'I found Jesus and it turned my life around'; no 'I remember Mama, who was a saint and I miss her terribly'; no gay or lesbian topics; no drug culture material; nothing harping on political correctness; nothing to do with healthy living, HMOs, medical programs, or the welfare state, unless it is against statism in these areas." *No unsolicited submissions.* .Accepts 5-6 mss/issue; 25-30 mss/year. Publishes ms 12-18 months after acceptance. **Publishes 2-6 new writers/year.** Recently published work by Mardelle Fortier, Clevenger Kehmeier, Gwen Williams, Manuel Sanchez-Lopez, Janet Tyson, Andrea C. Poe, Norman Nathan. Also publishes literary essays, literary criticism, poetry. Often comments on rejected mss.

How to Contact Query with clips of published work. Include bio, SASE and $5.25 for sample issue. Responds in 2 weeks to queries; 1 month to mss. Sample copy for $5.25. Writer's guidelines for 9½ × 4 SAE and 2 first-class stamps.

Payment/Terms Pays $15-40. Pays on publication for first North American serial rights.

Tips "Write for specifications, send for a sample issue, then *read* the thing, study the formatting, and follow the instructions, which say query first before sending anything. We shall not respond to unsolicited material. We don't want touchy-feely maudlin stuff where hugging kids solves all of life's problems, and we want no references anywhere in the story to e-mail, the Internet, or computers, unless it's to berate them."

BIG MUDDY: A JOURNAL OF THE MISSISSIPPI RIVER VALLEY

Southeast Missouri State University Press, MS2650 English Dept., Southeast MO State University, Cape Girardeau MO 63701. E-mail: sswartwout@semo.edu. Website: www6.semo.edu/universitypress/bigmuddy. **Contact:** Susan Swartwout, publisher/editor. Magazine: 8½ × 5½ perfect-bound; 150 pages; acid-free paper; color cover stock; layflat lamination; illustrations; photos. "Big Muddy explores multidisciplinary, multicultural issues, people, and events mainly concerning, but not limited to, the 10-state area that borders the Mississippi River. We publish fiction, poetry, historical essays, creative nonfiction, environmental essays, biography, regional events, photography, art, etc." Semiannual. Estab. 2001. Circ. 500.

Needs Adventure, ethnic/multicultural, experimental, family saga, feminist, historical, humor/satire, literary, mainstream, military/war, fiction, non fiction, poetry, mystery/suspense, regional (Mississippi River Valley; Midwest), translations. "No romance, fantasy or children's." Receives 50 unsolicited mss/month. Accepts 20-25 mss/issue. Publishes ms 6-12 months after acceptance.

How to Contact Send SASE for return of ms or send a disposable copy of ms and #10 SASE for reply only. Responds in 12 weeks to mss. Accepts multiple submissions. Sample copy for $6. Writer's guidelines for SASE, e-mail, fax or on website. Reviews fiction, poetry, nonfiction.

Payment/Terms Pays 2 contributor's copies; additional copies $5. Acquires first North American serial rights.

Tips "We look for clear language, avoidance of clichés except in necessary dialogue, a fresh vision of the theme or issue. Find some excellent and honest readers to comment on your work-in-progress and final draft. Consider their viewpoints carefully. Revise if needed."

THE BITTER OLEANDER

4983 Tall Oaks Dr., Fayettville NY 13066-9776. (315) 637-3047. Fax: (315) 637-5056. E-mail: info@bitteroleander.com. Website: www.bitteroleander.com. **Contact:** Paul B. Roth. Zine specializing in poetry and short fiction: 6 × 9; 128 pages; 55 lb. paper; 12 pt. CIS cover stock; photos. "We're interested in the surreal; deep image particularization of natural experiences." Bi-annual. Estab. 1974. Circ. 1,200.

Needs Experimental, translations. "No pornography; no confessional; no romance." Receives 200 unsolicited mss/month. Accepts 4-5 mss/issue; 8-10 mss/year. Does not read in July. Publishes ms 4-6 months after acceptance. Recently published work by Mark Joseph Kiewlak, Judith Taylor Gold, Edwin García Lopez, Eros Alegra Clarke, Norberto Luis Romero (Spain), and Samanta Schweblin (Argentina). Max length: 2,500 words. Publishes short shorts. Also publishes literary essays, poetry. Always comments on rejected mss.

How to Contact Send SASE for reply, return of ms. Responds in 1 week to queries; 1 month to mss. Accepts multiple submissions. Sample copy for $10. Writer's guidelines for #10 SASE.

Payment/Terms Pays 1 contributor's copy; additional copies $10. Acquires first rights.

Tips "If within the first 100 words my mind drifts, the rest rarely makes it. Be yourself and listen to no one but yourself."

$ BLACK WARRIOR REVIEW

P.O. Box 862936, Tuscaloosa AL 35486-0027. (205)348-4518. E-mail: bwr@ua.edu. Website: www.bwr.ua.edu. **Contact:** Stephen Gropp-Hess, fiction editor. Magazine: 6 × 9; 160 pages; color artwork. "We publish contemporary fiction, poetry, reviews, essays and art for a literary audience. We publish the freshest work we can find." Semiannual. Circ. 2,000.

- Work that appeared in the *Black Warrior Review* has been included in the *Pushcart Prize* anthology, *Harper's Magazine, Best American Short Stories, Best American Poetry* and *New Stories from the South.*

Needs Literary, contemporary, short and short-short fiction. Wants "work that is conscious of form and well crafted. We are open to good experimental writing and short-short fiction. No genre fiction, please." Receives 300 unsolicited mss/month. Accepts 5 mss/issue; 10 mss/year. Unsolicited novel excerpts are not considered unless the novel is already contracted for publication. Publishes ms 6 months after acceptance. **Publishes 5 new writers/year.** Recently published work by Lily Hoang, Brian Evenson, Peter Markus, Aimee Bender, Lance Olson, Laird Hunt, Pamela Ryder, Michael C. Boyko, James Grinwis. Length: 7,500 words; average length: 2,000-5,000 words. Occasionally comments on rejected mss.

How to Contact Send complete ms with SASE (1 story per submission). Responds in 4 months to mss. Accepts simultaneous submissions if noted. Sample copy for $10. Writer's guidelines online.

Payment/Terms Pays up to $100, copies, and a 1-year subscription. Pays on publication for first rights.

Tips "We look for attention to language, freshness, honesty, a convincing and sharp voice. Send us a clean, well-printed, proofread manuscript. Become familiar with the magazine prior to submission."

BLUELINE

125 Morey Hall, Dept. of English and Communication, Postdam NY 13676. (315)267-2043. E-mail: blueline@potsdam.edu. Website: http://www2.potsdam.edu/blueline/blue.html. **Contact:** fiction editor. Magazine: 6 × 9; 200 pages; 70 lb. white stock paper; 65 lb. smooth cover stock; illustrations; photos. "Blueline is interested in quality writing about the Adirondacks or other places similar in geography and spirit. We publish fiction, poetry, personal essays, book reviews and oral history for those interested in Adirondacks, nature in general, and well-crafted writing." Annual.

Needs Adventure, humor/satire, literary, regional, contemporary, prose poem, reminiscences, oral history, nature/outdoors. No urban stories or erotica. Receives 8-10 unsolicited mss/month. Accepts 6-8 mss/issue. Does not read January-August. Publishes ms 3-6 months after acceptance. **Publishes 2 new writers/year.** Recently published work by Joan Connor, Laura Rodley and Ann Mohin. Length: 500-3,000 words; average length: 2,500 words. Also publishes literary essays, poetry. Occasionally comments on rejected mss.

How to Contact Accepts simultaneous submissions. Sample copy for $6.

Payment/Terms Pays 1 contributor's copy; charges $7 each for 3 or more copies. Acquires first rights.

Tips "We look for concise, clear, concrete prose that tells a story and touches upon a universal theme or situation. We prefer realism to romanticism but will consider nostalgia if well done. Pay attention to grammar and syntax. Avoid murky language, sentimentality, cuteness or folkiness. We would like to see more good fiction related to the Adirondacks and more literary fiction and prose poems. If manuscript has potential, we work with author to improve and reconsider for publication. Our readers prefer fiction to poetry (in general) or reviews. Write from your own experience, be specific and factual (within the bounds of your story) and if you write about universal features such as love, death, change, etc., write about them in a fresh way. Triteness and mediocrity are the hallmarks of the majority of stories seen today."

☐ ◙ BLUE MESA REVIEW

MSC03 2170, 1 University of New Mexico, Alburquerque NM 87131-0001. Fax: (505)277-5573. E-mail: bmrinfo@unm.edu; bmrfictn@unm.edu; bmreditr@unm.edu. Website: www.unm.edu/~bluemesa. **Contact:** Suzanne Richardson. Magazine: 6 × 9; 200 pages; 55 lb. paper; 10 pt CS1 photos. Blue Mesa Review publishes the best/most current creative writing on the market. Annual. Circ. 1,000.

Needs Literary fiction, including but not limited to ethnic/multicultural, experimental, feminist, gay, historical, humor/satire, lesbian, literary, mainstream, regional, western themes. "Seeking strong voices and lively, compelling narrative with a fine eye for craft." Accepts mss August 1-April 30. Publishes approximately 25 mss/year. Also publishes literary essays, poetry, author interviews, and book reviews.

How to Contact Send SASE for reply. Sample copy for $10 for current issue; back issue $5. Writer's guidelines online.

Payment/Terms Pays 2 contributor's copies. Acquires first North American serial rights.

◪ BOGG

A Journal of Contemporary Writing Bogg Publications, 422 N. Cleveland St., Arlington VA 22201-1424. E-mail: boggmag@aol.com. Contact: John Elsberg, US editor. Magazine: 6 × 9; 72 pages; 70 lb. white paper; 70 lb. cover stock; line illustrations. "Poetry (to include prose poems, haiku/tanka and experimental forms), experimental short fiction, reviews." Published 2 times a year. Estab. 1968. Circ. 800.

Needs Very short experimental fiction and prose poems. Receives 25 unsolicited prose mss/month. Accepts 4-6 mss/issue. Publishes ms 3-18 months after acceptance. **Publishes 40-80 new writers/year.** Recently published work by Linda Bosson, Brian Johnson, Katrina Holden Bronson, Karen Rosenberg, Carla Mayfield, and Elizabeth Bernays. Also occasionally publishes interviews and essays on small press history. Rarely comments on rejected mss.

How to Contact Responds in 1 week to queries; 2 weeks to mss. Sample copy for $4 or $6 (current issue). Reviews fiction. Does not consider e-mail or simultaneous submissions.

Payment/Terms Pays 2 contributor's copies; reduced charge for extras. Acquires one-time rights.

Tips "We look for voice and originality. Read magazine first. Bogg is mainly a poetry journal, and we look for prose poems and short experimental or wry fiction that works well with the poetry."

▦ ☐ BOOK WORLD MAGAZINE

2 Caversham Street, London En SW3 4AH United Kingdom. 0207 351 4995. E-mail: leonard.holdsworth@btopenworld.com. **Contact:** James Hughes. Magazine: 64 pages; illustrations; photos. "Subscription magazine for serious book lovers, book collectors, librarians and academics." Monthly. Circ. 6,000.

Needs Also publishes literary essays, literary criticism.

How to Contact Query. Send IRC (International Reply Coupon) for return of ms. Responds in 3 months to queries; 3 months to mss. Accepts simultaneous submissions. Sample copy for $7.50. Writer's guidelines for IRC.
Payment/Terms Pays on publication for one-time rights.
Tips "Always write to us before sending any mss."

$ BOULEVARD

6614 Clayton Rd., Box 325, Richmond Heights MO 63117. E-mail: richardburgin@att.net; richardburgin@netzero.net; kellyleavitt@boulevardmagazine.org. Website: www.boulevardmagazine.org. **Contact:** Richard Burgin, founding editor; Kelly Leavitt, managing editor. Magazine: 5½ × 8½; 150-250 pages; excellent paper; high-quality cover stock; illustrations; photos. "Boulevard is a diverse literary magazine presenting original creative work by well-known authors, as well as by writers of exciting promise." Triannual. Circ. 11,000.
Needs Confessions, experimental, literary, mainstream, novel excerpts. "We do not want erotica, science fiction, romance, western or children's stories." Receives over 600 unsolicited mss/month. Accepts about 10 mss/issue. Does not accept manuscripts between May 1 and October 1. Publishes ms 9 months after acceptance. **Publishes 10 new writers/year.** Recently published work by Joyce Carol Oates, Floyd Skloot, Alice Hoffman, Stephen Dixon and Frederick Busch. Length: 9,000 words maximum; average length: 5,000 words. Publishes short shorts. Also publishes literary essays, literary criticism, poetry. Sometimes comments on rejected mss.
How to Contact Send complete ms. Accepts submissions on disk. SASE for reply. Responds in 2 weeks to queries; 3-4 months to mss. Accepts multiple submissions. No simultaneous submissions. Sample copy for $9. Writer's guidelines online.
Payment/Terms Pays $50-500. Pays on publication for first North American serial rights.
Tips "We pick the stories that move us the most emotionally, stimulate us the most intellectually, are the best written and thought out. Don't write to get published—write to express your experience and vision of the world."

THE BRIAR CLIFF REVIEW

3303 Rebecca St., Sioux City IA 51104-0100. (712)279-5477. E-mail: curranst@briarcliff.edu. Website: www.briarcliff.edu/bcreview. **Contact:** Phil Hey or Tricia Currans-Sheehan, fiction editors. Magazine: 8½ × 11; 120 pages; 70 lb. 100# Altima Satin Text; illustrations; photos. "The Briar Cliff Review is an eclectic literary and cultural magazine focusing on (but not limited to) Siouxland writers and subjects. We are happy to proclaim ourselves a regional publication. It doesn't diminish us; it enhances us." Annual. Circ. 1,000.
Needs Ethnic/multicultural, feminist, historical, humor/satire, literary, mainstream, regional. "No romance, horror or alien stories." Accepts 5 mss/year. Reads mss only between August 1 and November 1. Publishes ms 3-4 months after acceptance. **Publishes 10-14 new writers/year.** Recently published work by Siobhan Fallon, Shelley Scaletta, Jenna Blum, Brian Bedard, Rebecca Tuch, Scott H. Andrews, and Josip Novakovich. Length: 2,500-5,000 words; average length: 3,000 words. Also publishes literary essays, literary criticism, poetry. Sometimes comments on rejected mss.
How to Contact Send SASE for return of ms. Does not accept electronic submissions (unless from overseas). Responds in 4-5 months to mss. Accepts simultaneous submissions. Sample copy for $15 and 9 × 12 SAE. Writer's guidelines for #10 SASE. Reviews fiction.
Payment/Terms Pays 2 contributor's copies; additional copies available for $12. Acquires first rights.
Tips "So many stories are just telling. We want some action. It has to move. We prefer stories in which there is no gimmick, no mechanical turn of events, no moral except the one we would draw privately."

BRILLANT CORNERS

Lycoming College, Williamsport PA 17701. (570) 321-4279. Fax: (570) 321-4090. E-mail: feinstein@lycoming.edu. **Contact**: Sascha Feinstein, editor. Journal: 6 × 9; 90 pages; 70 lb. Cougar opaque, vellum, natural paper; photographs. "We publish jazz-related literature—fiction, poetry and nonfiction." Semiannual. Estab. 1996. Circ. 1,200.

Needs Condensed novels, ethnic/multicultural, experimental, literary, mainstream, romance (contemporary). Receives 10-15 unsolicited mss/month. Accepts 1-2 mss/issue; 2-3 mss/year. Does not read mss May 15-September 1. Publishes ms 4-12 months after acceptance. Publishes short shorts. Also publishes literary essays, literary criticism, poetry. Rarely comments on rejected mss.

How to Contact SASE for return of ms or send a disposable copy of ms. Accepts unpublished work only. Responds in 2 weeks to queries; 1-2 months to mss. Sample copy for $7. Reviews fiction.

Payment/Terms Acquires first North American serial rights. Sends galleys to author when possible.

Tips "We look for clear, moving prose that demostrates a love of both writing and jazz. We primarily publish established writers, but we read all submissions carefully and welcome work by outstanding young writers."

☐ THE BROADKILL REVIEW, A JOURNAL OF LITERATURE

John Milton and Company Quality Used Books, 104 Federal Street, Milton DE 19968. (302) 684-0174. E-mail: the_broadkill_review@earthlink.net. **Contact:** Jamie Brown, Publisher/Editor. PDF Literary magazine/journal. Contains illustrations, photographs. "Quality is the most important factor. This isn't to suggest that we are snobs, for I'm not talking about subject matter, but about the bell-like resonance of the work (evoked within the reader) and clarity. We want the reader left with the feeling that it matters to the reader personally that they read the story. Writing is the first interactive medium, after all, and although 100% communication cannot ever be achieved, owing to all sorts of internal and unconscious filters and the differences between two peoples' perceptions of the same thing, the stories we like are those that understand that and which encourage a kind of divestiture of the self and an investment in the story with whatever they, the reader, can bring to it of an emotional commitment. We are fans of John Gardner's On Becoming a Novelist, and firmly believe in establishing 'the waking dream' as the responsibility of the author." Bimonthly. Estab. 2007. Circ. 12,000. Member CLMP, Delaware Press Assn.

Needs Literary. Does not want anything gratuitous. Receives 8-20 mss/month. Accepts 1-4 mss/issue; 16-20 mss/year. Manuscript published 1-3 months after acceptance. **Publishes 30 new writers/year**. Published Thom Wade Myers, Chad Clifton, Tina Hession, Joshua D. Isard, Maryanne Khan, Richard Myers Peabody, H. A. Maxson, Bob Yearick, Gaylene Carbis, Louise D'Arcy, and Andee Jones. Length: 6,000 words (max). Average length: 3,300 words. Publishes short shorts. Also publishes literary essays, literary criticism, book reviews, poetry. Send two review copies to Editor, The Broadkill Review, 104 Federal Street, Milton, DE 19968. Sometimes comments on/critiques rejected mss, if requested by the author.

How to Contact Send complete ms with cover letter—preferably by e-mail. Include estimated word count, brief bio, list of publications. Responds to queries in 1 week. Responds to mss in 4-26 weeks. Send either SASE (or IRC) for return of ms or disposable copy of ms and #10 SASE for reply only. Considers simultaneous submissions, multiple submissions. Sample copy delivered electronically free upon request. Guidelines available via e-mail.

Payment/Terms Writers receive contributor's copy. Pays on publication. Acquires first rights. Publication is copyrighted.

Tips "Finish the work. Getting to the end of your first draft may be emotionally satisfying and physically enervating, but that is the point where the WORK of writing begins. Don't stint on the effort it may take you to revise your work. We are interested in publishing in our pages that which rises above the ordinary. We are not, on the other hand, interested in stories about your three-headed cat, zombies, flesh-eating bacteria, BEMs from outer-space, or psychopathic axe murderers. In short, your stories and poems should not rely on the unusual circumstance in place of actually having work which is finely crafted, insightful of the human condition, or which manages to make the reader continue to think about it after they have finished reading it. We are open to almost everything that does what Literature should do, which is to exact a price greater than the effort required to read it. The selection process is entirely subjective. We are not representative of the whole world. We publish what moves US. "

BROKEN SOUL'S INTERNATIONAL LITERARY ARTS JOURNAL

158 Spencer Ave., Suite 100, Pittsburgh PA 15227. (412) 668-0691. E-mail: brokensoulsinternational@comcast.net. Website: http://brokensoulsinternationalliteraryartsjournal.webs.com. **Contact:** John Thompson, editor/publisher. An online literary arts journal. "Broken Soul's International Literary Arts Journal" is dedicated to the emotional intellectual with a creative perception of life." Quarterly. Will begin publishing in the spring of 2010.

Needs Literary mainstream, historical, adventure, erotica, humor/satire, inspirational, senior citizen/retirement, sports. Average length: 2,500 words. Also publishes literary essays, literary criticism, photography, poetry, nonfiction, and haiku/senryu.

How to Contact How to Contact: If submitting by snail mail, enclose SASE for return of mss. Responds within 6 months to mss. Accepts simultaneous submissions and previously published work (let us know when & where). Send SASE for writer's guidelines or go to our website for guidelines. Does not pay at this time. Will offer a print on demand service quarterly. Copyright reverts to author upon publication. Retains First North American Serial rights.

Tips "Read a lot of what you write - study the market. Don't fear rejection, but use it as learning tool to strengthen your work before resubmitting."

BUFFALO CARP

Quad City Arts, 1715 2nd Avenue, Rock Island IL 61201. (309)793-1213. Fax: 309-793-1265. E-mail: buffalocarp@gmail.com. Website: www.quadcityarts.com. Literary magazine/journal: 6x9, 100 pages, 60 lb. paper, glossy, four-color with original artwork cover. "Buffalo Carp is a hybrid, an amalgam, unique, surprising and yet somehow inevitable. The works range from the factual to the fanciful, from fascinating to frightening, and everything in between." Annual. Circ. 350.

Needs High quality fiction of any style, genre, etc. "We are more concerned with the quality of the work than the classification of the work." Receives 15 mss/month. Accepts 8-10 mss/issue. Does not read May-August. Manuscript published 6-12 months after acceptance. Agented fiction 5%. Publishes 1-2 new writers/year. Length: 3,000 words (max). Average length: 1,500-3,000 words. Publishes short shorts. Also publishes poetry. Rarely comments on/critiques rejected mss. Flash Fiction Contest opens for submissions September 1 of each year; contest guidelines available on website.

How to Contact Send complete ms with cover letter. Accepts submissions by e-mail. Include estimated word count, brief bio. Responds to queries in 2 weeks. Responds to mss in 6-12 weeks. Send disposable copy of ms and #10 SASE for reply only. Considers simultaneous submissions, multiple submissions. Sample copy available for $7. Guidelines available on website.

Payment/Terms Writers receive 2 contributors copies. Pays on publication. Publication is copyrighted.

Tips "Send us your best, most interesting work. Worry less about how you would classify the work and more about it being high-quality and stand-out. We are looking to go in new directions with upcoming issues, so send us what you think best represents you and not who your influences are. *Buffalo Carp* is not interested in blending in, and has no interest in homogenized work. Blow us away!"

BUTTON

New England's Tiniest Magazine of Poetry, Fiction and Gracious Living, Box 77, Westminster MA 01473. Website: www.moonsigns.net. **Contact:** W.M. Davies, fiction editor. Magazine: 4 × 5; 34 pages; bond paper; color cardstock cover; illustrations; photos. "Button is New England's tiniest magazine of poetry, fiction and gracious living, published once a year. As 'gracious living' is on the cover, we like wit, brevity, cleverly conceived essay/recipe, poetry that isn't sentimental or song lyrics. I started Button so that a century from now, when people read it in landfills or, preferably, libraries, they'll say, 'Gee, what a great time to have lived. I wish I lived back then."' Annual. Estab. 1993. Circ. 1,500.

Needs Literary. "No genre fiction, science fiction, techno-thriller." Wants more of "anything Herman Melville, Henry James or Betty MacDonald would like to read." Receives 20-40 unsolicited mss/month. Accepts 1-2 mss/issue; 3-5 mss/year. Publishes ms 3-9 months after acceptance. Recently published work by Ralph Lombreglia, John Hanson Mitchell, They Might Be Giants and Lawrence Millman. Also publishes literary essays, poetry. Sometimes comments on rejected mss. "Only reads between April 1 and September 30. We will send samples but will discard mss not sent during those periods."

How to Contact Send complete ms with bio, list of publications and explain how you found magazine. Include SASE. Responds in 1 month to queries; 2 months to mss. Sample copy for $2.50 and 1 first class stamp. Writer's guidelines for #10 SASE. Reviews fiction.

Payment/Terms Honorarium, subscription and copies. Pays on publication for first North American serial rights.

Tips "What makes a manuscript stand out? Flannery O'Connor once said, 'Don't get subtle till the fourth page,' and I agree. We look for interesting, sympathetic, believable characters and careful setting. I'm really tired of stories that start strong then devolve into dialogue uninterrupted by further exposition. Also, no stories from a mad person's POV unless it's really tricky and skillful. Advice to prospective writers: Continue to read at least 10 times as much as you write. Read the best, and read intelligent criticism if you can find it. *No beginners please*. Please don't submit more than once a year; it's more important that you work on your craft rather than machine-gunning publications with samples, and don't submit more than 3 poems in a batch (this advice goes for other places, you'll find)."

CAIRN: THE SAINT ANDREWS REVIEW

1700 Dogwood Mile, Laurinburg NC 28352. (910)277-5310. Fax: (910)277-5020. E-mail: pressemail@sapc.edu. Website: www.sapc.edu/sapress.html. Magazine: 50-60 lb. paper. "*Cairn* is a nonprofit, national/international literary magazine which publishes established as well as emerging writers." Member CLMP and AWP.

Needs Literary, short stories and short-short fiction. "We're looking for original, imaginative short fiction with style and insight." **Publishes 10-15 new writers/year.**

How to Contact Send a recyclable copy of ms. by postal mail. Include SASE for reply only. Submissions are accepted September 1-February 1. Accepts simultaneous submissions with notice. Responds in 3-4 months.

Payment/Terms Pays 1 contributor copy.

CALLALOO

Dept. of English, TAMU 4212, Texas A&M University, College Station TX 77843-4227. (979) 458-3108. Fax: (979) 458-3275. E-mail: callaloo@tamu.edu. Website: http://callaloo.tamu.edu. **Contact:** Charles H. Rowell, editor. Magazine: 7X10; 250 pages. "Devoted to publishing fiction, poetry, drama of the African diaspora, including North, Central and South America, the Caribbean, Europe and Africa. Visually beautiful and well-edited, the journal publishes 3-5 short stories in all forms and styles in each issue." Quarterly. Estab. 1976. Circ. 2,000.

- One of the leading voices in African-American literature, Callaloo has recieved NEA literature grants. Several pieces every year are chosen for collections of the year's best stories, such as Beacon's Best John Wideman's "Weight" from Callaloo won the 2000 O. Henry Award.

Needs Ethnic/multicultural (black culture), feminist, historical, humor/satire, literary, regional, science fiction, serialized novels, translations, contemporary, prose poem. "No romance, confessional. Would like to see more experimental fiction, science fiction and well-crafted literary fiction particularly dealing with the black middle class, immigrant communities and/or the black South." Accepts 3-5 mss/issue; 10-20 mss/year. **Publishes 5-10 new writers/year.** Recently published work by Charles Johnson, Edwidge Danticat, Thomas Glave, Nallo Hopkinson, John Edgar Wideman, Jamaica Kincaid, Percival Everett and Patricia Powell. Also publishes poetry.

How to Contact Generally accepts unpublished work, rarely accepts reprints. Responds in 2 weeks to queries; 6 months to mss. Accepts multiple submissions. Sample copy for $12. Writer's guidelines online.

Payment/Terms Pays in contributor's copies. Aquires some rights. Sends galleys to author.

Tips "We look for freshness of both writing and plot, strength of characterization, plausibilty of plot. Read what's being written and published, especially in journals such as *Callaloo*."

CALYX

A Journal of Art & Literature by Women, P.O. Box B, Corvallis OR 97339. (541)753-9384. Fax: (541)753-0515. E-mail: editor@calyxpress.com. Website: www.calyxpress.org. **Contact:** The Editor. Magazine: 6 × 8; 128 pages per single issue; 60 lb. coated matte stock paper; 10 pt. chrome coat cover; original art. Publishes prose, poetry, art, essays, interviews and critical and review articles. "Calyx exists to publish fine literature and art by women and is committed to publishing the work of all women, including women of color, older women, working class women and other voices that need to be heard. We are committed to discovering and nurturing beginning writers." Biannual.

Needs Receives approximately 1,000 unsolicited prose and poetry mss when open. Accepts 4-8 prose mss/issue; 9-15 mss/year. Reads mss October 1-December 31; submit only during this period. Mss received when not reading will be returned. Publishes ms 4-12 months after acceptance. **Publishes 10-20 new writers/year.** Recently published work by M. Evelina Galang, Chitrita Banerji, Diana Ma, Catherine Brady. Also publishes literary essays, literary criticism, poetry.

How to Contact Responds in 4-12 months to mss. Accepts simultaneous submissions. Sample copy for $ 10 plus $4 postage. Include SASE.

Payment/Terms "Combination of free issues and 1 volume subscription."

Tips Most mss are rejected because "The writers are not familiar with *Calyx*. Writers should read *Calyx* and be familar with the publication. We look for good writing, imagination and important/interesting subject matter."

$ THE CAPILANO REVIEW

2055 Purcell Way, North Vancouver BC V7J 3H5 Canada. E-mail: tcr@capilanou.ca. Website: www.thecapilanoreview.ca. Magazine: 7 × 9; 90-120 pages; book paper; glossy cover; perfect-bound; visual art. "Triannual visual and literary arts magazine that publishes experimental art and writing."

Needs "No traditional, conventional fiction. Want to see innovative, genre-blurring work." Receives 100 unsolicited mss/month. Accepts 1 mss/issue; 3 mss/year. Publishes ms 4-6 months after acceptance. **Publishes some new writers/year.** Recently published work by Michael Turner, Lewis Buzbee, George Bowering. Also publishes literary essays, poetry.

How to Contact Include 2- to 3-sentence bio and brief list of publications. Send Canadian SASE or IRCs for reply. Responds in 1 month to queries; 4 months to mss. No simultaneous submissions. Sample copy for $14.70. Writer's guidelines online.

Payment/Terms Pays $50-200. Pays on publication for first North American serial rights.

Tips "Read the magazine before submitting."

CAROLINA QUARTERLY

Greenlaw Hall CB #3520, University of North Carolina, Chapel Hill NC 27599-3520. (919)962-0244. Fax: (919)962-3520. E-mail: cquarter@unc.edu. Website: www.unc.edu/depts/cqonline. **Contact:** Elena Oxman, editor-in-chief. Literary journal: 80-100 pages; illustrations. Publishes fiction for a "general literary audience." Triannual. Estab. 1948. Circ. 900-1,000.

- Work published in *Carolina Quarterly* has been selected for in inclusion in *Best American Short Stories*, in *New Stories for the South: The Year's Best*.

Needs Literary. "We would like to see more short/micro-fiction and more stories by minority/ethnic writers." Receives 150-200 unsolicited mss/month. Accepts 4-5 mss/issue; 14-16 mss/year. Does not read mss May-August. Publishes ms 4 months after acceptance. **Publishes 5-6 new writers/year.** Recently published work by Pam Durban, Elizabeth Spencer, Brad Vice, Wendy Brenner, and Nanci Kincaid. Publishes short shorts. Also publishes literary essays, poetry. Occasionally comments on rejected mss.

How to Contact Responds in 3 months to queries; 6 months to mss. Does not accept e-mail submissions. No simultaneous submissions. Sample copy for $6. Writer's guidelines for SASE.

Payment/Terms Pays in contributor's copies. Acquires first rights.

CC&D, CHILDREN, CHURCHES & DADDIES MAGAZINE: THE UNRELIGIOUS,

NONFAMILY-ORIENTED LITERARY AND ART MAGAZINE

Scars Publications and Design, 829 Brian Court, Gurnee IL 60031-3155. (847)281-9070. E-mail: ccandd96@scars.tv. Website: scars.tv. **Contact:** Janet Kuypers. Literary magazine/journal: 5.5x8.5 perfect-bound, 84-page book. Contains illustrations & photographs as well as short stories, essays, and poetry. Monthly.

Needs "Our biases are works that relate to issues such as politics, sexism, society, and the like, but are definitely not limited to such. We publish good work that makes you think, that makes you feel like you've lived through a scene instead of merely reading it. If it relates to how the world fits into a person's life (political story, a day in the life, coping with issues people face), it will probably win us over faster. We have received comments from readers and other editors saying that they thought some of our stories really happened. They didn't, but it was nice to know they were so concrete, so believable people thought they were nonfiction. Do that to our readers." Interested in many topics including adventure, ethnic/multicultural, experimental, feminist, gay, historical, lesbian, literary, mystery/suspense, new age, psychic/supernatural/occult, science fiction. Does not want religious or rhyming or family-oriented material. Manuscript published 1 yr after acceptance. Published Mel Waldman, Kenneth DiMaggio, Pat Dixon, Robert William Meyers, Troy Davis, G.A. Scheinoha, Ken Dean. Average length: 1,000 words. "Contact us if you are interested in submitting very long stories, or parts of a novel (if you are accepted, it would appear in parts in multiple issues)." Publishes short shorts, essays and stories. Also publishes poetry. Always comments on/critiques rejected mss if asked.

How to Contact Send complete ms with cover letter or query with clips of published work. Prefers submissions by e-mail. "If you have email and send us a snail-mail submission, we will accept writing only if you email it to us." Responds to queries in 2 weeks; mss in 2 weeks. "Responds much faster to e-mail submissions and queries." Send either SASE (or IRC) for return of ms or disposable copy of ms and #10 SASE for reply only, but if you have e-mail PLEASE send us an electronic submission instead. (If we accept your writing, we'll only ask for you to e-mail it to us anyway.) Considers simultaneous submissions, previously published submissions, multiple submissions. Sample copy available of issues before 2010 for $6. Guidelines available for SASE, via e-mail, on website. Reviews fiction, essays, journals, editorials, short fiction.

◪ CENTER

A Journal of the Literary Arts, 107 Tate Hall, Columbia MO 65211. E-mail: cla@missouri.edu. Website: center.missouri.edu. **Contact:** Managing editor. Magazine: 6 × 9; 150-250 pages; perfect bound, with 4-color card cover. "Center publishes poetry, fiction, creative nonfiction, and occasionally, translations. We publish work from a broad range of aesthetic categories and privilege work that is deliberately crafted, engaging, and accessible." Annual. Circ. 500.

Needs Ethnic/multicultural, experimental, humor/satire, literary. Receives 40-60 unsolicited mss/month. Accepts 2-4 mss/year. Reads mss from July 1-December 1 only. Publishes ms 6 months after acceptance. **Publishes 35% new writers/year.** Recently published work by Kim Chinquee, William Eisner, and April Ayers Lawson. Publishes short shorts. Also publishes literary essays, poetry. Sometimes comments on rejected mss.

How to Contact Send SASE (or IRC) for return of ms or send a disposable copy of ms and #10 SASE for reply only. Responds in 1 month to queries; 3-4 months to mss. Accepts simultaneous, multiple submissions. Sample copy for $3.50, current copy $7. Writer's guidelines online.

Payment/Terms Pays 2 contributor's copies; additional copies $3.50. Pays on publication for one-time rights.

N ◪ CHAFFIN JOURNAL

English Department, Eastern Kentucky University, C, Richmond KY 40475-3102. (859)622-3080. E-mail: robert.witt@eku.edu. Website: www.english.edu/chaffin_journal. **Contact:** Robert Witt, editor. Magazine: 8 × 5½; 120-130 pages; 70 lb. paper; 80 lb. cover. "We publish fiction on any subject; our only consideration is the quality." Annual. Circ. 150.

Needs Ethnic/multicultural, historical, humor/satire, literary, mainstream, regional (Appalachia). "No erotica, fantasy." Receives 20 unsolicited mss/month. Accepts 6-8 mss/year. Does not read mss

October 1 through May 31. Publishes ms 6 months after acceptance. **Publishes 2-3 new writers/year.** Recently published work by Meridith Sue Willis, Marie Manilla, Raymond Abbott, Marjorie Bixler, Chris Helvey. Length: 10,000 words per submission period; average length: 5,000 words.
How to Contact Send SASE for return of ms. Responds in 1 week to queries; 3 months to mss. Accepts simultaneous, multiple submissions. Sample copy for $6.
Payment/Terms Pays 1 contributor's copy; additional copies $6. Pays on publication for one-time rights.
Tips "All manuscripts submitted are considered."

$ CHAPMAN

4 Broughton Place, Edinburgh Scotland EH1 3RX United Kingdom. E-mail: chapman-pub@blueyonder.co.uk. Website: www.chapman-pub.co.uk. **Contact:** Joy Hendry, editor. "Chapman, Scotland's quality literary magazine, is a dynamic force in Scotland—publishing poetry; fiction; criticism; reviews; articles on theatre, politics, language and the arts. Our philosophy is to publish new work, from known and unknown writers, mainly Scottish, but also worldwide." Published three times a year. Circ. 2,000.
Needs Experimental, historical, humor/satire, literary, Scottish/international. "No horror, science fiction." Accepts 10-14 mss/issue. Publishes ms 6 months after acceptance. **Publishes 50 new writers/year.**
How to Contact No simultaneous submissions. Writer's guidelines by e-mail or send SASE/IRC.
Payment/Terms Pays by negotiation. Pays on publication for first rights.
Tips "Keep your stories for six months and edit carefully. We seek challenging work which attempts to explore difficult/new territory in content and form, but lighter work, if original enough, is welcome."

CHICAGO QUARTERLY REVIEW

517 Sherman Ave., Evanston IL 60202-2815. Website: chicagoquarterlyreview.com. **Contact:** Syed Afzal Haider and Elizabeth McKenzie, editors. Magazine: 6 × 9; 125 pages; illustrations; photos. Annual. Estab. 1994. Circ. 300.
Needs Literary. Receives 60-80 unsolicited mss/month. Accepts 8-10 mss/issue; 16-20 mss/year. Publishes ms 6 months-1 year after acceptance. Agented fiction 5%. **Publishes 8-10 new writers/year.** Length: 5,000 words; average length: 2,500 words. Publishes short shorts. Also publishes literary essays, poetry. Sometimes comments on rejected mss.
How to Contact Send a disposable copy of ms and #10 SASE for reply only. Responds in 2 months to queries; 6 months to mss. Accepts simultaneous submissions. Up to 5 poems in a single submission; does not accept multiple short story submissions. Sample copy for $9.
Payment/Terms Pays 2 contributor's copies; additional copies $9. Pays on publication for one-time rights.
Tips "The writer's voice ought to be clear and unique and should explain something of what it means to be human. We want well-written stories that reflect an appreciation for the rhythm and music of language, work that shows passion and commitment to the art of writing."

CHICAGO REVIEW

5801 S. Kenwood Ave., Chicago IL 60637. E-mail: chicago-review@uchicago.edu. Website: humanities.uchicago.edu/orgs/review. **Contact:** P. Genesius Durica. Magazine for a highly literate general audience: 6 × 9; 128 pages; offset white 60 lb. paper; illustrations; photos. Quarterly. Circ. 3,500.
Needs Experimental, literary, contemporary. Receives 200 unsolicited mss/month. Accepts 2 mss/issue; 8 mss/year. Recently published work by Harry Mathews, Tom House, Viet Dinh and Doris Doörrie. Also publishes literary essays, literary criticism, poetry. Does not generall publish pieces over 5,000 words.
How to Contact Submit ms with SASE. Does not accept e-mail or fax submissions. Responds in 3-6 months to mss. No simultaneous submissions. Sample copy for $10. Guidelines via website or SASE.

Payment/Terms Pays 3 contributor's copies and subscription.
Tips "We look for innovative fiction that avoids cliché."

$ CHROMA, AN INTERNATIONAL QUEER LITERARY JOURNAL

P.O. Box 44655, London, England N16 0WQ. +44-20-7193-7642. E-mail: editor@chromajournal.co.uk. Website: www.chromajournal.co.uk. **Contact:** Shaun Levin, editor. Literary magazine/journal. 52 pages. Contains illustrations. Includes photographs. "Chroma is the only international queer literary and arts journal based in Europe. We publish poetry, short prose and artwork by lesbian, gay, bisexual and transgendered writers and artists. We are always looking for new work and encourage work in translation. Each issue is themed, so please check the website for details. Past themes have included: Foreigners, Beauty, Islands, and Tormented." Semiannual. Estab. 2004. Circ. 1,000.
Needs Comics/graphic novels, erotica, ethnic/multicultural, experimental, feminist, gay, lesbian, literary. Receives 100 mss/month. Accepts 12 mss/issue; 24 mss/year. Ms published 3 months after acceptance. **Publishes 20 new writers/year.** Length: 2,000 words (min)-5,000 words (max). Average length: 3,000 words. Publishes short shorts. Average length of short shorts: 1,000 words. Also publishes book reviews, poetry. Send review copies to Eric Anderson, books editor. Sometimes comments on/critiques rejected mss.
How to Contact Send complete ms with cover letter. Include brief bio. Responds to queries in 1 month via email. Considers simultaneous submissions, multiple submissions. Guidelines available on website.
Payment/Terms Writers receive up to $150. Additional copies $7. Pays on publication. Acquires first rights. Publication is copyrighted. "The *Chroma* International Queer Writing Competition runs every two years. The first was in 2006. Check guidelines on our website."
Tips "We look for a good story well told. We look for writers doing interesting things with language, writers who are not afraid to take risks in the stories they tell and the way they tell them. Read back issues. If you like what we do, send us your work."

$ CHRYSALIS READER

1745 Gravel Hill Road, Dillwyn VA 23936. (434)983-3021. Fax: (434)983-1074. E-mail: chrysalis@hovac.com. Website: www.swedenborg.com. Book series: 7½ × 10; 192 pages; coated cover stock; illustrations; photos. "*The Chrysalis Reader* audience includes people from numerous faiths and backgrounds. Many of them work in psychology, education, religion, the arts, sciences, or one of the helping professions. The style of writing may be humorous, serious, or some combination of these approaches. Essays, poetry, and fiction that are not evangelical in tone but that are unique in addressing the Chrysalis Reader theme are more likely to be accepted. Our readers are interested in expanding, enriching, or challenging their intellects, hearts, and philosophies, and many also just want to enjoy a good read. For these reasons the editors attempt to publish a mix of writings. Articles and poetry must be related to the theme; however, you may have your own approach to the theme not written in our description." Circ. 3,000.

- "This journal explores contemporary questions of spirituality from a Swedenborgian multifaith perspective. This journal explores contemporary questions of spirituality from the perspective of Swedenborg theology."

Needs Adventure, experimental, historical, literary, mainstream, mystery/suspense, science fiction, fiction (leading to insight), contemporary, spiritual, sports. No religious works. Upcoming theme: "Lenses" (Fall 2009). Receives 50 unsolicited mss/month. Accepts 20-40 mss/year. Publishes ms 9 months after acceptance. **Publishes 10 new writers/year.** Recently published work by Robert Bly, William Kloefkorn, Raymond Moody, Virgil Suárez, Carol Lem, Alan Magee, John Hitchcock. Also publishes literary essays, literary criticism, poetry. Sometimes comments on rejected mss.
How to Contact Query with SASE. Accepts submissions by e-mail and USPS. Responds in 1 month to queries; 4-6 months to mss. No previously published work. Sample copy for $10 and 8½ × 11 SAE. Writer's guidelines and themes for issues for SASE or on website.
Payment/Terms Pays $25-100. Pays at page-proof stage. Acquires first rights, makes work-for-hire assignments. Sends galleys to author.

Tips Looking for "1: Quality; 2. appeal for our audience; 3. relevance to/illumination of an issue's theme."

CIMARRON REVIEW

205 Morrill Hall, OSU, Stillwater OK 74078-0135. (405)744-9476. E-mail: cimarronreview@yahoo.com. Website: cimarronreview.okstate.edu. **Contact:** Toni Graham, fiction editor. Magazine: 6 × 9; 110 pages. "Poetry and fiction on contemporary themes; personal essays on contemporary issues that cope with life in the 21st century. We are eager to receive manuscripts from both established and less experienced writers who intrigue us with their unusual perspective, language, imagery and character." Quarterly. Estab. 1967. Circ. 600.

Needs Literary-quality short stories and novel excerpts. No juvenile or genre fiction. Accepts 3-5 mss/issue; 12-15 mss/year. Publishes ms 2-6 months after acceptance. **Publishes 2-4 new writers/year.** Recently published work by Molly Giles, Gary Fincke, David Galef, Nona Caspers, Robin Beeman, Edward J. Delaney. Also publishes literary essays, literary criticism, poetry.

How to Contact Send complete ms with SASE. Responds in 2-6 months to mss. Accepts simultaneous submissions. Sample copy for $7. Reviews fiction.

Payment/Terms Pays 2 contributor's copies. Acquires first North American serial rights.

Tips "In order to get a feel for the kind of work we publish, please read an issue or two before submitting."

$ THE CINCINNATI REVIEW

P.O. Box 210069, Cincinnati OH 45221-0069. (513)556-3954. E-mail: editors@cincinnatireview.com. Website: www.cincinnatireview.com. **Contact:** Brocke Clarke or Nicola Mason. Magazine: 6 × 9; 180-200 pages; 60 lb. white offset paper. "A journal devoted to publishing the best new literary fiction and poetry as well as book reviews, essays and interviews." Semiannual.

Needs Literary. Does not want genre fiction. Accepts 10-15 mss/year. Reads submissions September 1-May 31. Manuscripts arriving during June, July and August will be returned unread.

How to Contact Send complete ms with SASE. Does not consider e-mail submissions. Responds in 2 weeks to queries; 6 weeks to mss. Accepts simultaneous submissions with notice. Sample copy for $9, subscription $15. Writer's guidelines online or send SASE.

Payment/Terms Pays $25/page. Pays on publication for first North American serial, electronic rights. All rights revert to author upon publication.

THE CLAREMONT REVIEW

The Contemporary Magazine of Young Adult Writers, 4980 Wesley Rd., Victoria BC V8Y 1Y9 Canada. (250)658-5221. Fax: (250)658-5387. E-mail: editor@theClaremontReview.ca. Website: www.theClaremontReview.ca. **Contact:** Lucy Bashford, managing editor; Susan Stenson; Janice McCachen, Terence Young, editors. Magazine: 6 × 9; 110-120 pages; book paper; soft gloss cover; b&w illustrations. "We are dedicated to publishing emerging young writers aged 13-19 from anywhere in the English-speaking world, but primarily Canada and the U.S." Biannual. Circ. 500.

Needs Young adult/teen ("their writing, not writing for them "). No science fiction, fantasy. Receives 20-30 unsolicited mss/month. Accepts 10-12 mss/issue; 20-24 mss/year. Publishes ms 3 months after acceptance. **Publishes 100 new writers/year.** Recently published work by Selina Boan, Blaise Lucey, Gillian Harper, Julianne Yip. Length: 5,000 words; average length: 1,500-3,000 words. Publishes short shorts. Also publishes poetry. Always comments on rejected mss.

How to Contact Responds in 3 months to mss. Accepts multiple submissions. Sample copy for $10.

Payment/Terms Pays 1 contributor's copy. Additional copies for $8. Acquires first North American serial, one-time rights. Sponsors awards/contests.

Tips Looking for "good concrete narratives with credible dialogue and solid use of original detail. It must be unique, honest and have a glimpse of some truth. Send an error-free final draft with a short cover letter and bio. Read us first to see what we publish."

☐ COAL CITY REVIEW

Coal City Press, University of Kansas, Lawrence KS 66045. E-mail: coalcity@sunflower.com. Website: www.coalcityreview.com. **Contact:** Mary Wharff, fiction editor. Literary magazine/ journal: 812 X 512, 124-150 pages, heavy cover. Includes b&w photographs. Annual. Circ. 200.

Needs Experimental, literary, contemporary. Does not want erotica, horror, romance, mystery. Receives 20-30 mss/month. Accepts 8-12 mss/issue. Reads year round. Manuscript published up to 1 year after acceptance. Agented fiction 0%. **Publishes new writers every year.** Published Catherine Bell, Tasha Haas, Bill Church, Aimee Parkison, Thomas Zurwellen, John Talbird. Length: 50 words (min)—4,000 words (max). Average length: 2,000 words. Also publishes literary criticism, poetry. Sometimes comments on/critiques rejected manuscripts.

How to Contact Submit via e-mail to coalcity@sunflower.com. Attach Word file. Include estimated word count, brief bio, list of publications. Responds to mss in 4 months. Send disposable copy of ms and #10 SASE for reply only. Considers simultaneous submissions. Guidelines available via e-mail.

Payment/Terms Writers receive 2 contributor's copies. Additional copies $5. Pays on publication. Acquires one-time rights. Publication is copyrighted.

Tips "We are looking for artful stories—with great language and great heart. Please do not send work that has not been thoughtfully and carefully revised or edited."

◪ $ COLORADO REVIEW

Department of English, 9105 Campus Delivery, Colorado State University, Fort Collins CO 80523-9105. (970)491-5449. E-mail: creview@colostate.edu. Website: coloradoreview.colostate.edu. **Contact:** Stephanie G'Schwind, editor. Literary journal: 200 pages; 60 lb. book weight paper. Circ. 1,100.

Needs Ethnic/multicultural, experimental, literary, mainstream, contemporary. "No genre fiction." Receives 1,000 unsolicited mss/month. Accepts 4-5 mss/issue. Does not read mss May-August. Publishes ms within 1 year after acceptance. Recently published work by Paul Mandelbaum, Ann Hood, Kent Haruf, Charles Baxter, and Bret Lott. Also publishes poetry and creative nonfiction.

How to Contact Send complete ms. Responds in 2 months to mss. Sample copy for $10. Writer's guidelines online. Reviews fiction, poetry, and nonfiction.

Payment/Terms Pays $5/page plus two contributor's copies. Pays on publication for first North American serial rights. Rights revert to author upon publication. Sends galleys to author.

Tips "We are interested in manuscripts that show craft, imagination and a convincing voice. If a story has reached a level of technical competence, we are receptive to the fiction working on its own terms. The oldest advice is still the best: persistence. Approach every aspect of the writing process with pride, conscientiousness—from word choice to manuscript appearance. Be familiar with the *Colorado Review*; read a couple of issues before submitting your manuscript."

CONCHO RIVER REVIEW

ASU Station #10894, San Angelo TX 76909-0894. Website: www.angelo.edu/dept/english/concho_river_review.html. **Contact:** Mary Ellen Hartje, editor. Magazine: 6½ × 9; 100-125 pages; 60 lb. Ardor offset paper; Classic Laid Color cover stock; b&w drawings. "We publish any fiction of high quality—no thematic specialties." Semiannual. Circ. 300.

Needs Ethnic/multicultural, historical, humor/satire, literary, regional, western. Also publishes poetry, nonfiction, book reviews. "No erotica; no science fiction." Receives 10-15 unsolicited mss/ month. Accepts 3-6 mss/issue; 8-10 mss/year. Publishes ms 4-6 months after acceptance. **Publishes 4 new writers/year.** Recently published work by Gordon Alexander, Riley Froh, Gretchen Geralds, Kimberly Willis Holt. Length: 1,500-5,000 words; average length: 3,500 words.

How to Contact Send electric copy upon acceptance. Responds in 3 weeks to queries. Accepts simultaneous submissions (if noted). Sample copy for $4. Writer's guidelines for #10 SASE. Reviews fiction.

Payment/Terms Pays in contributor's copies; $5 charge for extras. Acquires first rights.

Tips "We prefer a clear sense of conflict, strong characterization and effective dialogue."

CONFRONTATION

Long Island University, Brookville NY 11548. (516)299-2720. Fax: (516)299-2735. **Contact:** Jonna Semeiks. Magazine: 6 × 9; 250-350 pages; 70 lb. paper; 80 lb. cover; illustrations; photos. "We are eclectic in our taste. Excellence of style is our dominant concern." Semiannual. Estab. 1968. Circ. 2,000.

- *Confrontation*has garnered a long list of awards and honors, including the Editor's Award for Distinguished Achievement from CCLP and NEA grants. Work from the magazine has appeared in numerous anthologies including the *Pushcart Prize, Best Short Stories*and *The O. Henry Prize Stories*.

Needs Experimental, literary, mainstream, novel excerpts (if they are self-contained stories), regional, slice-of-life vignettes, contemporary, prose poem s. "No 'proselytizing' literature or genre fiction." Receives 250-300 unsolicited mss/month. Accepts 30 mss/issue; 60 mss/year. Does not read June-September. Publishes ms 6 months to 1 year after acceptance. Agented fiction approximately 10-15%. **Publishes 20-30 new writers/year.** Recently published work by Susan Vreeland, Lanford Wilson, Tom Stacey, Elizabeth Swados and Sallie Bingham. Publishes short shorts. Also publishes literary essays, poetry.

How to Contact Send complete ms to Confrontation, English Dept., C.W. Post campus of Long Island University, 720 Northern Blvd., Brookville NY 11548. Accepts e-mail for international submissions only (martin.tucker@liu.edu). "Cover letters acceptable, not necessary. We accept simultaneous submissions but do not prefer them." Responds in 3 weeks to queries; 6-8 weeks to mss. Sample copy for $3. Writer's guidelines not available. Reviews fiction, poetry, nonfiction.

Payment/Terms Pays $25-250. Pays on publication for first North American serial, first, one-time rights.

Tips "We look for literary merit. Keep trying."

CONNECTICUT REVIEW

39 Woodland St., Hartford CT 06105. E-mail: ctreview@ct.edu; ctreview@easternct.edu. Website: www.ct.edu/ctreview/. Magazine: 6x9; 208 pages; white/heavy paper; glossy/heavy cover; color and b&w illustrations and photos; artwork. Connecticut Review presents a wide range of cultural interests that cross disciplinary lines. "We're looking for the best in literary writing in a variety of genres. Some issues contain sections devoted to announced themes. The editors invite the submission of academic articles of general interest, creative essays, translations, short stories, short-shorts, plays, poems and interviews." Annual. Circ. 2,500. Member CLMP.

- Work published in *Connecticut Review* has won the Pushcart Prize and inclusion in Best American Poetry, Best American Short Stories (2000). CR has also received the Phoenix Award for Significant Editorial Achievement and National Public Radio's Award for Literary Excellence (2001).

Needs Literary. "Content must be under 4,000 words and suitable for circulation to libraries and high schools." Receives 250 unsolicited mss/month. Accepts 40 mss/issue; 80 mss/year. Does not accept mss to read May 15-September 1. Publishes ms 1-2 years after acceptance. **Publishes 15-20 new writers/year.** Has published work by John Searles, Michael Schiavone, Norman German, Tom Williams, Paul Ruffin, Dick Allen.

How to Contact Send two disposable copies of ms and #10 SASE for reply only. Responds in 6 months to queries. Considers simultaneous submissions. Sample copy for $12. Writer's guidelines for SASE, but forms for submissions and guidelines available on website.

Payment/Terms Pays 2 contributor's copies; additional copies $10. Pays on publication for first rights. Rights revert to author on publication. Sends galleys to author.

CONTROLLED BURN

Kirtland Community College, 10775 N. St. Helen Rd. Roscommon MI 48653. (989) 275-5000, ext. 386. E-mail: cburn@kirtland.edu. **Contact:** Carol Finke. Literary magazine/journal: 150 pages. "Our job is to take the best writing we get without regard to style, subject matter or form." Annual. Estab. 1995. Circ. 600.

Needs Literary fiction, whether serious or humorous. Does not want badly written work. Receives

100 mss/month. Accepts 3-5 mss/issue; 3-5 mss/year. Reads mss from May 1 through December 1. Manuscript published 4-6 months after acceptance. **Publishes 4-5 new writers/year.** Published Jim Daniels, Dennis Hinrichsen, David Dodd Lee, Brenda Flanagan. Length: 100-8,000. Average length: 5,000. Publishes short shorts. Average length of short shorts: 500. Also publishes poetry.
How to Contact Send complete ms with cover letter. Include brief bio, list of publications. Responds to queries in 4-6 weeks. Responds to mss in 4-6 weeks. Send disposable copy of ms and #10 SASE for reply only. Also accepts email submissions. Considers multiple submissions if identified as such. Sample copy available for $3. Guidelines available for SASE.
Payment/Terms Writers receive 2 contributors copies. Pays on publication. Acquires one-time rights.
Tips "Read our magazine to get a feel for what we publish. Then send us your best work."

COTTONWOOD

Box J, 400 Kansas Union, University of Kansas, Lawrence KS 66045-2115. (785)864-2516. Fax: (785)864-4298. E-mail: tlorenz@ku.edu. **Contact:** Tom Lorenz, fiction editor. Magazine: 6 × 9; 100 pages; illustrations; photos. "Cottonwood publishes high quality prose, poetry and artwork and is aimed at an audience that appreciates the same. We have a national scope and reputation while maintaining a strong regional flavor." Semiannual. Circ. 500.
Needs "We publish literary prose and poetry." Receives 25-50 unsolicited mss/month. Accepts 5-6 mss/issue; 10-12 mss/year. Publishes ms 6-18 months after acceptance. Agented fiction 10%. **Publishes 1-3 new writers/year.** Recently published work by Connie May Fowler, Oakley Hall, Cris Mazza. Length: 1,000-8,000 words; average length: 2,000-5,000 words. Publishes short shorts. Also publishes literary essays, literary criticism, poetry.
How to Contact SASE for return of ms. Responds in 6 months to mss. Accepts simultaneous submissions. Sample copy for $8.50, 9 × 12 SAE and $1.90. Reviews fiction.
Payment/Terms Acquires one-time rights.
Tips "We're looking for depth and/or originality of subject matter, engaging voice and style, emotional honesty, command of the material and the structure. *Cottonwood* publishes high quality literary fiction, but we are very open to the work of talented new writers. Write something honest and that you care about and write it as well as you can. Don't hesitate to keep trying us. We sometimes take a piece from a writer we've rejected a number of times. We generally don't like clever, gimmicky writing. The style should be engaging but not claim all the the attention itself."

$ CRAB ORCHARD REVIEW

A Journal of Creative Works, Southern Illinois University Carbondale, Faner Hall 2380, Mail Code 4503 Eng. Dept., Carbondale IL 62901-4503. (618)453-6833. Fax: (618)453-8224. E-mail: jtribble@siu.edu. Website: www.craborchardreview.siuc.edu. **Contact:** Jon Tribble, managing editor. Magazine: 5½ × 8½; 275 pages; 55 lb. recycled paper, card cover; photo on cover. "We are a general interest literary journal published twice/year. We strive to be a journal that writers admire and readers enjoy. We publish fiction, poetry, creative nonfiction, fiction translations, interviews and reviews." Circ. 2,500.

- *Crab Orchard Review* has won Illinois Arts Council Literary Awards and a 2009 Program Grant from the Illinois Arts Council.

Needs Ethnic/multicultural, literary, excerpted novel. No science fiction, romance, western, horror, gothic or children's. Wants more novel excerpts that also stand alone as pieces. List of upcoming themes available on website. Receives 900 unsolicited mss/month. Accepts 15-20 mss/issue; 20-40 mss/year. Reads February-April and August-October. Publishes ms 9-12 months after acceptance. Agented fiction 1%. **Publishes 4 new writers/year.** Recently published work by Francisco Aragón, Kerry Neville Bakken, Timothy Crandle, Amina Gautier, Jodee Stanley, Alia Yunis. Length: 1,000-6,500 words; average length: 2,500 words. Also publishes literary essays, poetry. Rarely comments on rejected mss.
How to Contact Send SASE for reply, return of ms. Responds in 3 weeks to queries; 9 months to mss. Accepts simultaneous submissions. Sample copy for $12. Writer's guidelines for #10 SASE.
Payment/Terms Pays $100 minimum; $25/page maximum, 2 contributor's copies and a year

subscription. Acquires first North American serial rights.
Tips "We look for well-written, provocative, fully realized fiction that seeks to engage both the reader's senses and intellect. Don't submit too often to the same market, and don't send manuscripts that you haven't read over carefully. Writers can't rely on spell checkers to catch all errors. Always include a SASE. Read and support the journals you admire so they can continue to survive."

$ CRAZYHORSE

College of Charleston, Dept. of English, 66 George St., Charleston SC 29424. E-mail: crazyhorse@cofc.edu. Website: crazyhorse.cofc.edu. **Contact:** Anthony Varallo, fiction editor. Semiannual literary magazine: 8¾ × 8¼; 150 pages; illustrations; photos. Submit up to two manuscripts per year between August 1 and May 31. The journal's mission is to publish the entire spectrum of today's fiction, essays, and poetry—from the mainstream to the avant-garde, from the established to the undiscovered writer. The editors are especially interested in original writing that engages in the work of honest communication. Crazyhorse publishes writing of fine quality regardless of style, predilection, subject. Raymond Carver called *Crazyhorse* "an indispensable literary magazine of the first order."

Needs Receives 200 unsolicited mss/month. Accepts 8-10 mss/issue; 16-20 mss/year. Publishes ms 6-12 months after acceptance. Recently published work by Luke Blanchard, Karen Brown, E. V. Slate, Melanie Rae Thon, Lia Purpura, Carolyn Walker. Length: 25 pages; average length: 15 pages. Publishes short shorts. Pays $20-35 per page of layout, depending on annual budget and grants received.

How to Contact No longer accepts submissions by mail. Responds in 1 week to queries; 3 months to mss. Accepts simultaneous submissions. Sample copy for $5; year subscription for $16. Writer's guidelines for SASE or by e-mail. Acquires first North American serial rights. Sends galleys to author. Click online to use our Submission Manager.

Tips "Write to explore subjects you care about. Clarity of language; subject is one in which something is at stake."

◪ THE CREAM CITY REVIEW

University of Wisconsin-Milwaukee, Box 413, Milwaukee WI 53201. (414)229-4708. E-mail: info@creamcityreview.org. Website: www.creamcityreview.org. **Contact:** Monica Rausch and Ann Stewart, fiction editors. Magazine: 5½ × 8½; 150-300 pages; 70 lb. offset/perfect bound paper; 80 lb. cover stock; illustrations; photos. "General literary publication—an eclectic and electric selection of the best fiction we can find." Semiannual. Estab. 1975. Circ. 2,000.

Needs Ethnic/multicultural, experimental, literary, regional, translations, flash fiction, literary humor, magical realism, prose poem. "Would like to see more quality fiction. No horror, formulaic, racist, sexist, pornographic, homophobic, science fiction, romance." Receives 300 unsolicited mss/month. Accepts 6-10 mss/issue. Does not read fiction, nonfiction or poetry April-September. **Publishes 10 new writers/year.** Recently published work by Ben Percy, Yannick Murphy, Michael Martone, Stuart Dybek, Laurence Goldstein, Harold Jaffe, Bradford Morrow, Gordon Weaver, Gordon Henry, Louis Owens, Arthur Boozhoo, George Makana Clark, Kyoko Mori. Publishes short shorts. Also publishes literary essays, book reviews, literary criticism, poetry, memoir, comics.

How to Contact Responds in 6 months to mss. Accepts simultaneous, multiple submissions. Sample copy for $7 (back issue), $12 (current issue). Reviews fiction.

Payment/Terms Pays 1-year subscription. Acquires first rights. Rights revert to author after publication. Sponsors awards/contests.

Tips "The best stories are those in which the reader doesn't know what is going to happen or what the writer is trying to do. Avoid formulas. Surprise us with language and stunning characters."

N ◪ CUTTHROAT, A JOURNAL OF THE ARTS

P.O. Box 2414, Durango CO 81302. (970) 903-7914. E-mail: cutthroatmag@gmail.com. Website: www.cutthroatmag.com. **Contact:** William Luvaas, fiction editor. Literary magazine/journal and "one separate online edition of poetry, translations, short fiction, and book reviews yearly. 6 × 9, 180+ pages, fine cream paper, slick cover. Includes photographs. "We publish only high quality fiction and poetry. We are looking for the cutting edge, the endangered word, fiction with wit, heart, soul and meaning." Annual. Estab. 2005. Member CCLMP.

Needs Ethnic/multicultural, experimental, feminist, humor/satire, literary, mainstream. Does not want romance, horror, historical, fantasy, religious, teen, juvenile. List of upcoming themes available on website. Receives 100+ mss/month. Accepts 6 mss/issue; 10-12 mss/year. Does not read from October 1st-March 1st and from June 1st-July 15th. **Publishes 5-8 new writers/year.** Published Michael Schiavone, Rusty Harris, Timothy Rien, Summer Wood, Peter Christopher, Jamey Genna, Doug Frelke, Sally Bellerose, Marc Levy. Length: 500 words (min)-5,000 words (max). Publishes short shorts. Also publishes book reviews. Send review copies to Pamela Uschuk. Sometimes comments on/critiques rejected mss.

How to Contact Send complete ms with cover letter. Accepts submissions by e-mail for online edition and from authors living overseas only. Include estimated word count, brief bio. Responds to queries in 1-2 weeks. Responds to mss in 6-8 months. Send either SASE (or IRC) for return of ms or disposable copy of ms and #10 SASE for reply only. Considers simultaneous submissions, multiple submissions. Sample copy available for $10. Guidelines available for SASE, on website.

Payment/Terms Writers receive contributor's copies. Additional copies $10. Pays on publication. Acquires first North American serial rights. Sends galleys to author. Publication is copyrighted. "Sponsors the Rick DeMarinis Short Fiction Prize ($1250 first prize). See separate listing and website for more information."

Tips "Read our magazine and see what types of stories we've published. The piece must have heart and soul, excellence in craft. "

DESCANT

Ft. Worth's Journal of Fiction and Poetry, TCU Box 297270, Ft. Worth TX 76129. (817)257-6537. Fax: (817)257-6239. E-mail: descant@tcu.edu. Website: www.descant.tcu.edu. **Contact:** David Kuhne, editor. Magazine: 6 × 9; 120-150 pages; acid free paper; paper cover. "descant seeks high quality poems and stories in both traditional and innovative form." Annual. Circ. 500-750. Member CLMP.

- Offers four cash awards: The $500 Frank O'Connor Award for the best story in an issue; the $250 Gary Wilson Award for an outstanding story in an issue; the $500 Betsy Colquitt Award for the best poem in an issue; the $250 Baskerville Publishers Award for outstanding poem in an issue. Several stories first published by *descant* have appeared in *Best American Short Stories*.

Needs Literary. "No horror, romance, fantasy, erotica." Receives 20-30 unsolicited mss/month. Accepts 25-35 mss/year. Publishes ms 1 year after acceptance. **Publishes 50% new writers/year.** Recently published work by William Harrison, Annette Sanford, Miller Williams, Patricia Chao, Vonesca Stroud, and Walt McDonald. Length: 1,000-5,000 words; average length: 2,500 words. Publishes short shorts. Also publishes poetry.

How to Contact Send complete ms with cover letter. Include estimated word count and brief bio. Responds in 6-8 weeks to mss. Accepts simultaneous submissions. Sample copy for $10. SASE, e-mail or fax.

Payment/Terms 2 Contributor's copies, additional copies $6. Pays on publication for one-time rights. Sponsors awards/contests.

Tips "We look for character and quality of prose. Send your best short work."

DISLOCATE

English Department, University of Minnesota, 222 Lind Hall, 207 Church St. SE, Minneapolis MN 55455. E-mail: dislocate.magazine@gmail.com. Website: http://dislocate.org. **Contact:** Shantha Susman. Magazine has revolving editor. Editorial term: 2006-2007. Literary magazine/journal: 512 x 812, 128 pages. Annual. Estab. 2005. Circ. 2,000.

Needs Literary fiction. Receives 25-50 mss/month. Accepts 2-3 mss/year. Publishes short shorts. Also publishes literary essays, poetry.

How to Contact Send complete ms with cover letter. Send SASE for reply or return of ms. Considers simultaneous submissions, multiple submissions. Guidelines available on website.

Payment/Terms Pays on publication.
Tips "Looking for excellent writing that rearranges the world."

$ DOWNSTATE STORY

1825 Maple Ridge, Peoria IL 61614. E-mail: ehopkins7@prodigy.net. Website: www.wiu.edu/users/mfgeh/dss. **Contact:** Elaine Hopkins. Magazine: includes illustrations. "Short fiction—some connection with Illinois or the Midwest." Annually in the Fall. Circ. 250.

- Fiction received the Best of Illinois Stories Award.

Needs Adventure, ethnic/multicultural, experimental, historical, horror, humor/satire, literary, mainstream, mystery/suspense, psychic/supernatural/occult, regional, romance, science fiction, suspense, western. No porn. Accepts 10 mss/issue. Publishes ms 1 year after acceptance. Publishes short shorts. Also publishes literary essays.
How to Contact Send complete ms with a cover letter and SASE for return of ms. Responds "ASAP" to mss. Deadline June 30th for each issue. Accepts simultaneous submissions. Sample copy for $8. Writer's guidelines online.
Payment/Terms Pays $50. Pays on acceptance for first rights.

ECLIPSE

A Literary Journal, Glendale College, 1500 N. Verdugo Rd., Glendale CA 91208. (818)240-1000. Fax: (818)549-9436. E-mail: eclipse@glendale.edu. Magazine: 8½ × 5½; 150-200 pages; 60 lb. paper. "Eclipse is committed to publishing outstanding fiction and poetry. We look for compelling characters and stories executed in ways that provoke our readers and allow them to understand the world in new ways." Annual. Circ. 1,800. CLMP.
Needs Ethnic/multicultural, experimental, literary. "Does not want horror, religious, science fiction or thriller mss." Receives 50-100 unsolicited mss/month. Accepts 10 mss/year. Publishes ms 6-12 months after acceptance. **Publishes 8 new writers/year.** Recently published work by Amy Sage Webb, Ira Sukrungruang, Richard Schmitt, George Rabasa. Length: 6,000 words; average length: 4,000 words. Publishes short shorts. Also publishes poetry. Sometimes comments on rejected mss.
How to Contact Send complete ms. Responds in 2 weeks to queries; 4-6 weeks to mss. Accepts simultaneous submissions. Sample copy for $8. Writer's guidelines for #10 SASE or by e-mail.
Payment/Terms Pays 2 contributor's copies; additional copies $ 7. Pays on publication for first North American serial rights.
Tips "We look for well crafted fiction, experimental or traditional, with a clear unity of elements. A good story is important, but the writing must transcend the simple act of conveying the story."

$ ELLIPSIS MAGAZINE

Westminster College of Salt Lake City, 1840 S. 1300 E., Salt Lake City UT 84105. (801)832-2321. Website: www.westminstercollege.edu/ellipsis. **Contact:** Stephanie Peterson (revolving editor; changes every year). Magazine: 6 × 9; 110-120 pages; 60 lb. paper; 15 pt. cover stock; illustrations; photos. Ellipsis Magazine needs good literary poetry, fiction, essays, plays and visual art. Annual. Estab. 1967. Circ. 2,000.
Needs Receives 110 unsolicited mss/month. Accepts 4 mss/issue. Does not read mss November 1-July 31. Publishes ms 3 months after acceptance. **Publishes 2 new writers/year.** Length: 6,000 words; average length: 4,000 words. Also publishes poetry. Rarely comments on rejected mss.
How to Contact Send complete ms. Send SASE (or IRC) for return of ms or send disposable copy of the ms and #10 SASE for reply only. Responds in 6 months to mss. Accepts simultaneous submissions. Sample copy for $7.50. Writer's guidelines online.
Payment/Terms Pays $50 per story and one contributor's copy; additional copies $3.50. Pays on publication for first North American serial rights. Not copyrighted.
Tips "Have friends or mentors read your story first and make suggestions to improve it."

EMRYS JOURNAL

P.O. Box 8813, Greenville SC 29604. E-mail: jenglertcopeland@gmail.com. Website: www.emrys.org. The Emrys Foundation, P.O. Box 8813, Greenville SC 29604. E-mail: lydia.dishman@gmail.

com. Website: www.emrys.org. Contact: L.B. Dishman. Catalog: 9 × 9¾; 120 pages; 80 lb. paper. "We publish short fiction, poetry and creative nonfiction. We are particularly interested in hearing from women and other minorities." Annual. Estab. 1984. Circ. 400.

Needs Literary, contemporary. No religious, sexually explicit or science fiction mss. Accepts approx 18 mss/issue. Reading period: August 1-November 1, no ms will be read outside the reading period. Publishes mss in April. **Publishes several new writers/year.** Recently published work by Jessica Goodfellow and Ron Rash. Length: 5,000 words; average length: 3,500 words. Publishes short shorts.

How to Contact Send complete ms with SASE. Responds after end of reading period. Does not accept simultaneous submissions. Accepts multiple submissions. Sample copy for $15 and 7 × 10 SAE with 4 first-class stamps. Writer's guidelines for #10 SASE.

Payment/Terms Pays in contributor's copies. Acquires first rights.

Tips Looks for previously unpublished literary fiction.

$ EPOCH

251 Goldwin Smith Hall, Cornell University, Ithaca NY 14853. (607)255-3385. Fax: (607)255-6661. Website: www.arts.cornell.edu/english/publications/epoch. **Contact:** Joseph Martin, senior editor. Magazine: 6 × 9; 128 pages; good quality paper; good cover stock. "Well-written literary fiction, poetry, personal essays. Newcomers always welcome. Open to mainstream and avant-garde writing." Circ. 1,000.

- Work originally appearing in this quality literary journal has appeared in numerous anthologies including *Best American Short Stories, Best American Poetry, Pushcart Prize, The O. Henry Prize Stories, Best of the West* and *New Stories from the South.*

Needs Ethnic/multicultural, experimental, literary, mainstream, novel excerpts, literary short stories. "No genre fiction. Would like to see more Southern fiction (Southern US)." Receives 500 unsolicited mss/month. Accepts 15-20 mss/issue. Does not read in summer (April 15-September 15). Publishes ms an average of 6 months after acceptance. **Publishes 3-4 new writers/year.** Recently published work by Antonya Nelson, Doris Betts, Heidi Jon Schmidt. Also publishes poetry. Sometimes comments on rejected mss.

How to Contact Send complete ms. Responds in 2 weeks to queries; 6 weeks to mss. No simultaneous submissions. Sample copy for $5. Writer's guidelines for #10 SASE.

Payment/Terms Pays $5 and up/printed page. Pays on publication for first North American serial rights.

Tips "Read the journals you're sending work to."

EUREKA LITERARY MAGAZINE

300 E. College Ave., Eureka College, Eureka IL 61530-1500. (309)467-6591. E-mail: elm@eureka.edu. **Contact:** Zeke Jarvis, editor. Magazine: 6 × 9; 120 pages; 70 lb. white offset paper; 80 lb. gloss cover; photographs (occasionally). "We seek to be open to the best stories that are submitted to us. Our audience is a combination of professors/writers, students of writing and literature, and general readers." Semiannual. Estab. 1992. Circ. 500.

Needs Ethnic/multicultural, experimental, fantasy (science), feminist, historical, humor/satire, literary, mainstream, mystery/suspense (private eye/hard-boiled, romantic), science fiction (soft/sociological), translations. Would like to see more "good literary fiction stories, good magical realism, historical fiction. We try to achieve a balance between the traditional and the experimental. We look for the well-crafted story, but essentially any type of story that has depth and substance to it is welcome." Receives 100 unsolicited mss/month. Accepts 10-12 mss/issue; 20-30 mss/year. Does not accept mss in summer (May-August). **Publishes 5-6 new writers/year.** Recently published work by Jane Guill, Sarah Strickley, Ray Bradbury, Patrick Madden, Virgil Suarez, Cynthia Gallaher, Wendell Mayo, Tom Noyes, and Brian Doyle. Length: 4,000-6,000 words; average length: 5,000 words. Also publishes short shorts, flash fiction and poetry.

How to Contact Accepts submissions by e-mail. Send SASE for reply, return of ms or send disposable copy of ms. Responds in 2 weeks to electronic queries; 4 months to mss. Accepts simultaneous submissions. Sample copy for $7.50.

Tips "Do something that hasn't been done a thousand times already. Give us unusual but believable characters in unusual but believable conflicts—clear resolution isn't always necessary, but it's nice. We don't hold to hard and fast rules about length, but most stories could do with some cutting. Make sure your title is relevant and eye-catching. Please do not send personal gifts or hate mail. We're a college-operated magazine, so we do not actually exist in summer. If we don't take a submission, that doesn't automatically mean we don't like it—we try to encourage authors who show promise to revise and resubmit. Order a copy if you can."

EVANSVILLE REVIEW

University of Evansville English Dept., 1800 Lincoln Ave., Evansville IN 47722. (812)488-1402. E-mail: evansvillereview@evansville.edu. Website: evansvillereview.evansville.edu. **Contact:** Fiction Editor. Magazine: 6 × 9; 180 pages; 70 lb. white paper; glossy full-color cover; perfect bound. Annual. Circ. 1,000.

Needs Does not want erotica, fantasy, experimental or children's fiction. "We're open to all creativity. No discrimination. All fiction, screenplays, nonfiction, poetry, interviews and anything in between." Receives 70 unsolicited mss/month. Does not read mss December-August. Agented fiction 2%. **Publishes 20 new writers/year.** Recently published work by John Updike, Arthur Miller, X.J. Kennedy, Jim Barnes, Rita Dove. Also publishes literary essays, poetry.

How to Contact Send SASE for reply, or send a disposable copy of ms. Responds in 1 month to queries; 3 months to mss. Accepts simultaneous, multiple submissions and reprints. Sample copy for $5. Writer's guidelines free.

Payment/Terms Pays 2 contributor's copies. Pays on publication for one-time rights. Not copyrighted.

Tips "Because editorial staff rolls over every 1-2 years, the journal always has a new flavor."

EVENING STREET REVIEW

Evening Street Press, Inc., 7652 Sawmill Rd. #352, Dublin OH 43016-9296. E-mail: editor@eveningstreetpress.com. Website: www.eveningstreetpress.com. **Contact:** Gordon Grigsby, editor.

Needs "Intended for a general audience, Evening Street Press, published semiannually, is centered on Elizabeth Cady Stanton's 1848 revision of the Declaration of Independence: "that all men—and women—are created equal," with equal rights to "life, liberty, and the pursuit of happiness." It focuses on the realities of experience, personal and historical, from the most gritty to the most dreamlike, including awareness of the personal and social forces that block or develop the possibilities of this new culture." Circulation: 300.

How to Contact Send complete ms. by mail or e-mail. Wants confession, ethnic, experimental, mainstream, and novel excerpts. Does not want "male chauvinism."

Payment/Terms Pays contributor copies. Rights revert to author upon publication.

FAULTLINE

Dept. of English and Comparative Literature, University of California Irvine, Irvine CA 92697-2650. (949) 824-1573. E-mail: faultline@uci.edu. Website: www.humanities.uci.edu/faultline. **Contact:** Editors change in September each year. Literary magazine: 6 × 9; 200 pages; illustrations; photos. "We publish the very best of what we recieve. Our interest is quality and literary merit." Annual. Estab. 1992.

Needs Translations, literary fiction, nonfiction up to 20 pages. Receives 150 unsolicited mss/month. Accepts 6-9 mss/year. Does not read mss April-September. Publishes ms 9 months after acceptance. Agented fiction 10-20%. **Publishes 30-40% new writers/year.** Recently published work by Maile Meloy, Aimee Bender, David Benioff, Steve Almond, Helen Maria Viramontes, Thomas Keneally. Publishes short shorts. Also publishes literary essays, poetry.

How to Contact Send SASE for reply, return of ms or send a disposable copy of ms. Responds in 2 weeks to queries; 4 months to mss. Accepts simultaneous submissions. Sample copy for $5. Writer's guidelines for business-size envelope.

Payment/Terms Pays 2 contributor's copies. Pays on publication for one-time rights.

Tips "Our commitment is to publish the best work possible from well-known and emerging authors with vivid and varied voices."

FEMINIST STUDIES

0103 Taliaferro, University of Maryland, College Park MD 20742-7726. (301) 405-7415. Fax: (301) 405-8395. E-mail: creative@feministstudies.org. Website: www.feministstudies.org. **Contact:** Minnie Bruce Pratt, creative writing editor. Magazine: journal-sized; about 200 pages; photographs. "We are interested in work that addresses questions of interest to the feminist studies audience, particularly work that pushes past the boundaries of what has been done before. We look for creative work that is intellectually challenging and aesthetically adventurous, that is complicated in dialogue with feminist ideas and concepts, and that shifts our readers into new perspectives on women/gender." Triannual. Estab. 1974. Circ. 7,500.

Needs Ethnic/multicultural, feminist, LGBT, contemporary. Receives 20 unsolicited mss/month. Accepts 2-3 mss/issue. "We review fiction and poetry twice a year. Deadline dates are May 1 and December 1. Authors will recieve notice of the board's decision by July 15 and February 15, respectively." Recently published work by Grace M. Cho, Dawn McDuffie, Susanne Davis, Liz Robbins, Maria Mazziotti Gillan, Cathleen Calbert, and Mary Ann Wehler. Sometimes comments on rejected mss.

How to Contact No simultaneous submissions. Sample copy for $15. Writer's guidelines at website.

Payment/Terms Pays 2 contributor's copies and 10 tearsheets.

$ FICTION

Dept. of English, The City College of New York, 138th St. & Convent Ave., New York NY 10031. (212)650-6319. E-mail: fictionmagazine@yahoo.com. Website: www.fictioninc.com. **Contact:** Mark J. Mirsky, editor. Magazine: 6 × 9; 150-250 pages; illustrations; occasionally photos. "As the name implies, we publish only fiction; we are looking for the best new writing available, leaning toward the unconventional. Fiction has traditionally attempted to make accessible the unaccessible, to bring the experimental to a broader audience." Semiannual. Estab. 1972.

- Stories first published in *Fiction* have been selected for inclusion in the *Pushcart Prize, Best of the Small Presses* anthologies and more recently *Best American Short Stories.*

Needs Experimental, humor/satire (satire), literary, translations, contemporary. No romance, science fiction, etc. Receives 250 unsolicited mss/month. Accepts 12-20 mss/issue; 24-40 mss/year. Reads mss September 15-April 15. Publishes ms 1 year after acceptance. Agented fiction 10-20%. Recently published work by Joyce Carol Oates, John Barth, Robert Musil, Romulus Linney. Publishes short shorts. Sometimes comments on rejected mss.

How to Contact To submit, please send a complete manuscript with cover letter and SASE. No e-mail submissions. Responds in 3 months to mss. Accepts simultaneous submissions. Sample copy for $5. Writer's guidelines online.

Payment/Terms Pays $75 plus subscription. Acquires first rights.

Tips "The guiding principle of *Fiction* has always been to go to terra incognita in the writing of the imagination and to ask that modern fiction set itself serious questions, if often in absurd and comical voices, interrogating the nature of the real and the fantastic. It represents no particular school of fiction, except the innovative. Its pages have often been a harbor for writers at odds with each other. As a result of its willingness to publish the difficult, experimental, unusual, while not excluding the well known, *Fiction* has a unique reputation in the U.S. and abroad as a journal of future directions."

$ THE FIDDLEHEAD

University of New Brunswick, Campus House, 11 Garland Court, Box 4400, Fredericton NB E3B 5A3 Canada. (506)453-3501. Fax: (506) 453-5069. E-mail: fiddlehd@unb.ca; scl@unb.ca. Website: www.thefiddlehead.ca. **Contact:** Kathryn Taglia, Managing Editor. Magazine: 6 × 9; 128-180 pages; ink illustrations; photos. "No criteria for publication except quality. For a general audience, including many poets and writers." Quarterly.

Needs Literary. Receives 100-150 unsolicited mss/month. Accepts 4-5 mss/issue; 20-40 mss/year. Publishes ms within 1 year after acceptance. Agented fiction: small percentage. **Publishes high percentage of new writers/year.** Recently published work by Julie Curwin, Steven Heighton, Rebecca Rosenblum and Nicholasl Ruddock. Average length: 3,000 words. Publishes short shorts. Occasionally comments on rejected mss.
How to Contact Send SASE and *Canadian* stamps or IRCs for return of mss. Responds in 6 months to mss. No email submissions. Simultaneous submissions only if stated on cover letter; must contact immediately if accepted elsewhere. Sample copy for $15 (US).
Payment/Terms Pays up to $40 (Canadian)/published page and 2 contributor's copies. Pays on publication for first or one-time serial rights.
Tips "The best way to get a sense of what our editors are looking for is to read a recent issue."

FIRST CLASS

Four-Sep Publications, P.O. Box 86, Friendship IN 47021. E-mail: christopherm@four-sep.com. Website: www.four-sep.com. **Contact:** Christopher M, editor. Magazine: 4¼ × 11; 48-60+ pages; 24 lb./60 lb. offset paper; craft cover; illustrations; photos. "First Class features short fiction and poetics from the cream of the small press and killer unknowns—mingling before your very hungry eyes. I publish plays, too." Biannual. Circ. 200-400.
Needs Erotica, literary, science fiction (soft/socialogical), satire, drama. "No religious or traditional poetry, or 'boomer angst'—therapy-driven self loathing." Receives 50-70 unsolicited mss/month. Accepts 12-17 mss/issue; 20-30 mss/year. Publishes ms 1 month after acceptance. **Publishes 10-15 new writers/year.** Recently published work by Alan Catlin, Gary Every, John Bennet, B.Z. Niditch. Length: 5,000-8,000; average length: 2,000-3,000 words. Publishes short shorts. Also publishes poetry. Sometimes comments on rejected mss.
How to Contact Send SASE or send a disposable copy of ms and #10 SASE for reply only. Responds in 4-8 week to queries. Accepts simultaneous submissions and reprints. Sample copy for $6. Writer's guidelines for #10 SASE. Reviews fiction.
Payment/Terms Pays 1 contributor's copy; additional copies $5. Acquires one-time rights.
Tips "Don't bore me with puppy dogs and the morose/sappy feeling you have about death. Belt out a good, short, thought-provoking, graphic, uncommon piece."

$ FIVE POINTS

A Journal of Literature and Art, P.O. Box 3999, Georgia State University, Atlanta GA 30302-3999. Website: www.webdelsol.com/Five_Points. Magazine: 6 × 9; 200 pages; cotton paper; glossy cover; photos. Five Points is "committed to publishing work that compels the imagination through the use of fresh and convincing language." Triannual. Circ. 2,000.

- Fiction first appearing in *Five Points* has been anthologized in *Best American Fiction*, Pushcart anthologies, and *New Stories from The South*.

Needs List of upcoming themes available for SASE. Receives 250 unsolicited mss/month. Accepts 4 mss/issue; 15-20 mss/year. Does not read mss April 30-September 1. Publishes ms 6 months after acceptance. **Publishes 1 new writer/year.** Recently published work by Frederick Busch, Ursula Hegi, Melanie Rae Thon. Average length: 7,500 words. Publishes short shorts. Also publishes literary essays, poetry. Sometimes comments on rejected mss.
How to Contact Use online submission manager. Sample copy for $7.
Payment/Terms Pays $15/page minimum ($250 maximum), free subscription to magazine and 2 contributor's copies; additional copies $4. Acquires first North American serial rights. Sends galleys to author. Sponsors awards/contests.
Tips "We place no limitations on style or content. Our only criteria is excellence. If your writing has an original voice, substance and significance, send it to us. We will publish distinctive, intelligent writing that has something to say and says it in a way that captures and maintains our attention."

FLINT HILLS REVIEW

Dept. of English, Box 4019, Emporia State University, Emporia KS 66801-5087. Website: www.emporia.edu/fhr/. Magazine: 9 × 6; 115 pages; 60 lb. paper; glossy cover; illustrations; photos. "FHR seeks work informed by a strong sense of place or region, especially Kansas and the Great Plains region. We seek to provide a publishing venue for writers of the Great Plains and Kansas while also publishing authors whose work evidences a strong sense of place, writing of literary quality, and accomplished use of language and depth of character development." Annual. Circ. 300. CLMP.

Needs Ethnic/multicultural, gay, historical, regional (Plains), translations. "No religious, inspirational, children's." Want to see more "writing of literary quality with a strong sense of place." List of upcoming themes online. Receives 5-15 unsolicited mss/month. Accepts 2-5 mss/issue; 2-5 mss/year. Does not read mss April-December. Publishes ms 4 months after acceptance. **Publishes 4 new writers/year.** Recently published work by Kim Stafford, Elizabeth Dodd, Bart Edelman, and Jennifer Henderson. Length: 1 page-5,000; average length: 3,000 words. Publishes short shorts. Also publishes literary essays, literary criticism, poetry.

How to Contact Send a disposable copy of ms and #10 SASE for reply only. Responds in 5 weeks to queries; 6 months to mss. Accepts simultaneous, multiple submissions. Sample copy for $5.50. Writer's guidelines for SASE, by e-mail, fax or on website. Reviews fiction.

Payment/Terms Pays 2 contributor's copies; additional copies $5.50. Acquires one-time rights.

Tips "Strong imagery and voice, writing that is informed by place or region, writing of literary quality with depth of character development. Hone the language down to the most literary depiction that is possible in the shortest space that still provides depth of development without excess length."

FLYWAY

Iowa State University, 206 Ross Hall, Ames IA 50011. (515)294-8273. Fax: (515)294-6814. E-mail: flyway@iastate.edu. Website: www.flyway.org. **Contact:** Stephen Pett, editor. Literary magazine: 6 × 9; 120 pages; quality paper; cover stock; some illustrations; photos. "We publish quality fiction with a particular interest in place as a component of 'story,' or with an 'enviromental' sensibility. Our stories are accompanied by brief commentaries by their authors, the sort of thing a writer might say introducing a piece at a reading." Biannual. Estab. 1995. Circ. 500.

Needs Literary. Receives 50 unsolicited mss/month. Accepts 2-5 mss/issue; 10-12 mss/year. Reads mss September 1-May. Publishes ms 5 months after acceptance. **Publishes 7-10 new writers/year.** Recently published work by Naomi Shihab Nye, Gina Ochsner, Ted Kooser, Michael Martone. Length: 5,000; average length: 3,500 words. Publishes short shorts. Often comments on rejected mss.

How to Contact Send SASE. Sample copy for $8. Writer's guidelines for SASE.

Payment/Terms Pays 2 contributor's copies; additional copies $6. Acquires one-time rights.

Tips "Quality, originality, voice, drama, tension. Make it as strong as you can."

FOLIATE OAK LITERARY MAGAZINE

Foliate Oak Online, University of Arkansas-Monticello, MCB 113, Monticello AR 71656. (870)460-1247. E-mail: foliateoak@uamont.edu. Website: www.foliateoak.uamont.edu. **Contact:** Diane Payne, faculty advisor. Magazine: 6 × 9; 80 pages. Monthly. Estab. 1980. Circ. 500.

Needs Adventure, comics/graphic novels, ethnic/multicultural, experimental, family saga, feminist, gay, historical, humor/satire, lesbian, literary, mainstream, science fiction (soft/sociological). No religious, sexist or homophobic work. Receives 80 unsolicited mss/month. Accepts 20 mss/issue; 160 mss/year. Does not read mss May-August. Publishes ms 1 month after acceptance. **Publishes 130 new writers/year.** Recently published work by David Barringer, Thom Didato, Joe Taylor, Molly Giles, Patricia Shevlin, Tony Hoagland. Length: 50-2,500 words; average length: 1,500 words. Publishes short shorts. Also publishes literary essays, literary criticism, poetry. Rarely comments on rejected mss.

How to Contact Send complete ms as an e-mail attachment (Word or RTF). Postal submissions will not be read. Please include author's name and title of story/poem/essay in e-mail header. In the e-mail, please send contact information and a short bio. Responds in 4 weeks. Only accepts submissions August through April. Accepts simultaneous submissions and multiple submissions. Please contact ASAP if work is accepted elsewhere. Sample copy for SASE and 6 × 8 envelope. Writer's guidelines online. Reviews fiction.

Payment/Terms Pays contributor's copy. Acquires electronic rights. Sends galleys to author. Not copyrighted.

Tips "We're open to honest, experimental, offbeat, realistic and surprising writing, if it has been edited. Limit poems to five per submission, and one short story or creative nonfiction (less than 2,500 words. You may send up to three flash fictions. PLease put your flash fiction in one attachment. Please don't send more writing until you hear from us regarding your first submission. We are also looking for artwork sent as.jpg or.gif files."

FOLIO

A Literary Journal at American University, Department of Literature, American University, Washington DC 20016. E-mail: folio.editors@gmail.com. Website: www.foliojournal.org. **Contact:** Greta Schuler. Magazine: about 70 pages; illustrations; photos. "Folio is a journal of poetry, fiction and creative nonfiction; illustrations; photos. "Folio is a nationally recognized literary journal sponsored by the College of Arts and Sciences at American University in Washington, D. C. Since 1984, we have published original creative work by both new and established authors. Past issues have included work by Michael Reid Busk, Billy Collins, William Stafford, and Bruce Weigl, and interviews with Michael Cunningham, Charles Baxter, Amy Bloom, Ann Beattie, and Walter Kirn. We look for well-crafted poetry and prose that is bold and memorable." Does not read submissions May-July. Publishes 2-3 new writers/year. Length: 5,000 words; average length: 2,500 words. Publishes short shorts. How to submit. Send a SASE for reply only. Responds in 3-4 months to submission. Accepts simultaneous submissions. Sample copy for $6. "Visit our website and read the journal for more information." We look for work that ignites and endures, is artful and natural, daring and elegant." Semiannual.

Needs Literary. Does not want anything that is sexually offensive. Receives 50-60 unsolicited mss/month.

How to Contact Send complete ms. Send a SASE (or IRC) for reply only.

Payment/Terms Pays 2 contributor's copies. Pays on publication for first North American serial rights.

FREEFALL MAGAZINE

The Alexandra Writers' Centre Society, 922 Ninth Ave. SE, Calgary AB T2G 0S4 Canada. E-mail: michelinem@shaw.ca; freefallmagazine@yahoo.com. Website: www.freefallmagazine.ca. **Contact:** Micheline Maylor, editor-in-chief; Lynn Fraser, managing editor. Magazine: 8½ × 5¾; 100 pages; bond paper; bond stock; b&w illustrations; photos. "FreeFall features the best of new, emerging writers and gives them the chance to get into print along with established writers. Now in its 18th year, FreeFall seeks to attract readers looking for well-crafted stories, poetry, non-fiction, reviews, and artwork." Semiannual. Member: Alberta Magazine Publishers Association (AMPA). Canadian Magazines. Accepts 3-5 mss/issue; 6-10 mss/year. Reads July and January. Publishes ms 4-6 months after acceptance. **Publishes 40% new writers/year.** Length: 500-3,000 words. Send SASE (or IRC) for return of ms, or send a disposable copy of ms with e-mail address or #10 SASE for reply only. Responds in 3 months to mss. Sample copy for $10 (US). Writer's guidelines for SASE, e-mail or on website. Pays 1 contributor's copy; additional copies $10 (US). Acquires first North American serial, one-time rights.

Tips "We look for thoughtful word usage, craftsmanship, strong voice and unique expression coupled with clarity and narrative structure. Professional, clean presentation of work is essential. Carefully read *FreeFall* guidelines before submitting. Do not fold manuscript, and submit 9 × 11 envelope. Include SASE/IRC for reply and/or return of manuscript. You may contact us by e-mail after initial hardcopy submission. For accepted pieces a request is made for disk or e-mail copy. Strong Web presence attracts submissions from writers all over the world."

FRONT & CENTRE

573 Gainsborough Ave., Ottawa ON K2A 2Y6 Canada. (613)729-8973. E-mail: firth@istar.ca. Website: ardentdreams.com/bbp. **Contact:** Matthew Firth, editor. Magazine: half letter-size; 40-50 pages; illustrations; photos. "We look for new fiction from Canadian and international writers—bold, aggressive work that does not compromise quality." Three issues per year. Circ. 500.

Needs Literary ("contemporary realism/gritty urban"). "No science fiction, horror, mainstream, romance or religious." Receives 20 unsolicited mss/month. Accepts 6-7 mss/issue; 10-20 mss/year. Publishes ms 6 months after acceptance. Agented fiction 10%. **Publishes 8-9 new writers/year.** Recently published work by Len Gasparini, Katharine Coldiron, Salvatore Difalco, Gerald Locklin, Amanda Earl, Tom Johns. Length: 50-4,000 words; average length: 2,500 words. Publishes short shorts. Always comments on rejected mss.

How to Contact Send SASE (from Canada) (or IRCs from USA) for return of ms or send a disposable copy of ms with #10 SASE for reply only. Responds in 2 weeks to queries; 4 months to mss. Accepts multiple submissions. Sample copy for $5. Writer's guidelines for SASE or by e-mail. Reviews fiction.

Payment/Terms Acquires first rights. Not copyrighted.

Tips "We look for attention to detail, unique voice, not overtly derivative, bold writing, not pretentious. We should like to see more realism. Read the magazine first—simple as that!"

$ FUGUE

E-mail: fugue@uidaho.edu. Magazine: 6 × 9; 175 pages; 70 lb. stock paper. By allowing the voices of established writers to lend their authority to new and emerging writers, Fugue strives to provide its readers with the most compelling stories, poems, essays, interviews and literary criticism possible. Semiannual.

- Work published in *Fugue* has won the Pushcart Prize and has been cited in *Best American Essays*.

Needs Ethnic/multicultural, experimental, humor/satire, literary. Receives 80 unsolicited mss/month. Accepts 6-8 mss/issue; 12-15 mss/year. Does not read mss May 1-August 31. Publishes ms 6 months after acceptance. **Publishes 4-6 new writers/year.** Recently published work by Kent Nelson, Marilyn Krysl, Cary Holladay, Padgett Powell, Dean Young, W.S. Merwin, Matthew Vollmer. Publishes short shorts. Also publishes literary essays, literary criticism, poetry. Sometimes comments on rejected mss.

How to Contact Send complete ms. Send SASE (or IRC) for return of the ms or disposable copy of the ms and #10 SASE for reply only. Responds in 3-4 months to mss. Accepts simultaneous submissions. Sample copy for $8. Writer's guidelines for SASE or on website.

Payment/Terms Pays $10 minimum and 1 contributor copy as well as a one-year subscription to the magazine; additional copies $5. Pays on publication for first North American serial, electronic rights.

Tips "The best way, of course, to determine what we're looking for is to read the journal. As the name *Fugue* indicates, our goal is to present a wide range of literary perspectives. We like stories that satisfy us both intellectually and emotionally, with fresh language and characters so captivating that they stick with us and invite a second reading. We are also seeking creative literary criticism which illuminates a piece of literature or a specific writer by examining that writer's personal experience."

GARGOYLE

3819 N. 13th St., Arlington VA 22201. (703)525-9296. E-mail: gargoyle@gargoylemagazine.com. Website: www.gargoylemagazine.com. Literary magazine: 5½ × 8½; 200 pages; illustrations; photos. "Gargoyle Magazine has always been a scallywag magazine, a maverick magazine, a bit too academic for the underground and way too underground for the academics. We are a writer's magazine in that we are read by other writers and have never worried about reaching the masses." Annual. Circ. 2,000.

Needs Erotica, ethnic/multicultural, experimental, gay, lesbian, literary, mainstream, translations. "No romance, horror, science fiction." Wants "edgy realism or experimental works. We run both."

Wants to see more Canadian, British, Australian and Third World fiction. Receives 50-200 unsolicited mss/month. Accepts 10-15 mss/issue. Accepts submissions during June, July, and Aug. Publishes ms 6-12 months after acceptance. Agented fiction 5%. **Publishes 2-3 new writers/year.** Recently published work by Nin Andrews, Toby Barlow, Nicole Blackman, Myronn Hardy, Nik Houser, Elise Levine, Dora Malech, Mark Maxwell, Holly Prado, Kit Reed, Eleanor Ross Taylor. Length: 30 pages maximum; average length: 5-10 pages. Publishes short shorts. Also publishes literary essays, literary criticism, poetry. Sometimes comments on rejected mss.

How to Contact "We prefer electronic submissions. Please use submission engine online." For snail mail, send SASE for reply, return of ms or send a disposable copy of ms. Responds in 2 weeks to queries; 3 months to mss. Accepts simultaneous submissions. Sample copy for $12.95.

Payment/Terms Pays 1 contributor's copy; additional copies for 12 price. Acquires first North American serial, and first British rights. Sends galleys to author.

Tips "We have to fall in love with a particular fiction."

☐ GEORGETOWN REVIEW

Box 227, 400 East College St., Georgetown KY 40324. (502)863-8308. Fax: (502)868-8888. E-mail: gtownreview@georgetowncollege.edu. Website: http://georgetownreview.georgetowncollege.edu. **Contact:** Steven Carter, editor. Literary magazine/journal: 6 × 9, 192 pages, 20 lb. paper, four-color 60 lb. glossy cover. "We publish the best fiction we receive, regardless of theme or genre." Annual. Estab. 1993. Circ. 1,000. Member CLMP.

Needs Ethnic/multicultural (general), experimental, literary. Does not want adventure, children's, fantasy, romance. Receives 100-125 mss/month. Accepts 8-10 mss/issue; 15-20 mss/year. Does not read March 16-August 31. Manuscript published 1 month-2 years after acceptance. Agented fiction 0%. **Publishes 3-4 new writers/year.**Published Andrew Plattner, Sallie Bingham, Alison Stine. Average length: 4,000 words. Publishes short shorts. Average length of short shorts: 500-1,500 words. Also publishes literary essays, poetry. Sometimes comments on/critiques rejected manuscripts.

How to Contact Send complete ms with cover letter. Include brief bio, list of publications. Responds to queries in 1 month. Responds to mss in 1-3 months. Send either SASE (or IRC) for return of ms or disposable copy of ms and #10 SASE for reply only. Considers simultaneous submissions. Sample copy available for $7. Guidelines available on website.

Payment/Terms Writers receive 2 contributor's copies, free subscription to the magazine. Additional copies $5. Pays on publication. Acquires first North American serial rights. Publication is copyrighted. "Sponsors annual contest with $1,000 prize. Check website for guidelines."

Tips "We look for fiction that is well written and that has a story line that keeps our interest. Don't send a first draft, and even if we don't take your first, second, or third submission, keep trying."

◪ $ ☐ THE GEORGIA REVIEW

The University of Georgia, Athens GA. (706)542-3481. Fax: (706)542-0047. Journal: 7 × 10; 180-200 pages (average); 50 lb. woven old-style paper; 80 lb. cover stock; illustrations; photos. "Our readers are educated, inquisitive people who read a lot of work in the areas we feature, so they expect only the best in our pages. All work submitted should show evidence that the writer is at least as well educated and well read as our readers. Essays should be authoritative but accessible to a range of readers." Quarterly. Estab. 1947. Circ. 3,000.

- Stories first published in *The Georgia Review* have been anthologized in *Best American Short Stories, Best American Mystery Stories, New Stories from The South* and the *Pushcart Prize. The Georgia Review* won the National Magazine Award in essays in 2007.

Needs "Ordinarily we do not publish novel excerpts or works translated into English, and we strongly discourage authors from submitting these." Receives 300 unsolicited mss/month. Accepts 3-4 mss/issue; 12-15 mss/year. Does not read unsolicited mss May 5-August 15. Publishes ms 6 months after acceptance. **Publishes some new writers/year.** Recently published work by Lee K. Abbot, Kevin Brockmeier, Ann Pancake, Janisse Ray, George Singleton. Also publishes literary essays, reviews, poetry. Occasionally comments on rejected mss.

How to Contact Send complete ms. Responds in 2 weeks to queries; 2-4 months to mss. No simultaneous submissions or electronic submissions. Sample copy for $10. Writer's guidelines online.
Payment/Terms Pays $50/published page. Pays on publication for first North American serial rights. Sends galleys to author.

GERTRUDE

PO Box 83948, Portland OR 97283. **Contact:** Eric Delehoy, editor. Magazine: 5 × 8½; 64-72 pages; perfect bound; 60 lb. paper; glossy card cover; illustrations; photos. Gertrude is a "annual publication featuring the voices and visions of the gay, lesbian, bisexual, transgender and supportive community." Estab. 1999. Circ. 400.
Needs Ethnic/multicultural, feminist, gay, humor/satire, lesbian, literary, mainstream. "No romance, pornography or mystery." Wants more multicultural fiction. "We'd like to publish more humor and positive portrayals of gays—steer away from victim roles, pity." Receives 15-20 unsolicited mss/month. Accepts 4-8 mss/issue; 4-8 mss/year. Publishes ms 1-2 months after acceptance. **Publishes 4-5 new writers/year.** Recently published work by Carol Guess, Demrie Alonzo, Henry Alley and Scott Pomfret. Length: 200-3,000 words; average length: 1,800 words. Publishes short shorts. Also publishes poetry.
How to Contact Send SASE for reply to query and a disposable copy of ms. Responds in 6-9 months to mss. Accepts multiple submissions Simultaneous submissions okay. Sample copy for $5, 6 × 9 SAE and 4 1st class stamps. Writer's guidelines for #10 SASE.
Payment/Terms Pays 1-2 contributor's copies; additional copies $4. Pays on publication. Author retains rights upon publication. Not copyrighted.
Tips "We look for strong characterization, imagery and new, unique ways of writing about universal experiences. Follow the construction of your work until the ending. Many stories start out with zest, then flipper and die. Show us, don't tell us."

$ THE GETTYSBURG REVIEW

Gettysburg College, Gettysburg PA 17325. (717)337-6770. Fax: (717)337-6775. Website: www.gettysburgreview.com. Magazine: 614 × 10; 170 pages; acid free paper; full color illustrations. "Our concern is quality. Manuscripts submitted here should be extremely well written." Reading period September-May. Quarterly. Estab. 1988. Circ. 4,000.

- Work appearing in *The Gettysburg Review* has also been included in *Prize Stories: The O. Henry Awards, Pushcart Prize* anthology, *Best American Fiction, New Stories from The South, Harper's,* and elsewhere. It is also the recipient of a Lila Wallace-Reader's Digest grant and NEA grants.

Needs Experimental, historical, humor/satire, literary, mainstream, novel excerpts, regional, serialized novels, contemporary. "We require that fiction be intelligent and esthetically written." Receives 350 unsolicited mss/month. Accepts 15-20 mss/issue; 60-80 mss/year. Publishes ms within 1 year after acceptance. **Publishes 1-5 new writers/year.** Recently published work by Nicholas Montemarano, Victoria Lancelotta, Leslie Pietrzyk, Kyle Minor, Kerry Neville-Bakken, Margot Singer. Length: 2,000-7,000 words; average length: 3,000 words. Publishes short shorts. Also publishes literary essays, literary criticism, poetry. Sometimes comments on rejected mss.
How to Contact Send complete ms with SASE. Responds in 1 month to queries; 3-6 months to mss. Accepts simultaneous submissions. Sample copy for $10. Writer's guidelines online.
Payment/Terms Pays $30/page. Pays on publication for first North American serial rights.
Tips "Reporting time can take more than three months. It is helpful to look at a sample copy of *The Gettysburg Review* to see what kinds of fiction we publish before submitting."

GINOSKO

P.O. Box 246, Fairfax CA 94978. E-mail: ginoskoeditor@aol.com. Website: www.ginoskliteraryjournal.com. "Ghin-oce-koe: to perceive, understand, come to know; knowledge that has an inception, an attainment; the recognition of truth by personal experience." Published semiannually. Selects material from ezine for Kindle anthology. Circ. 4,500. Member: CLMP.

- *Listed in Best of the Web 2008.

Needs Short fiction, poetry, creative non-fiction interviews, and excerpts. Receives 80-100 unsolicited mss/month. **Publishes 4 new writers/year.** Also publishes artwork and photography.
How to Contact Send complete ms. Accepts submissions by mail and e-mail. Accepts simultaneous, excerpts, and reprints submissions.
Payment/Terms Copyright reverts to author.
Tips "Check downloadable issues on website for style and tone: use latest version of Adobe Reader."

$ GLIMMER TRAIN STORIES

1211 NW Glisan St. #207, Portland OR 97209. (503)221-0836. Fax: (503)221-0837. E-mail: eds@glimmertrain.com. Website: www.glimmertrain.com. **Contact:** Susan Burmeister-Brown and Linda B. Swanson-Davies. Magazine: 225 pages; recycled; acid-free paper; 12 photographs. "We are interested in literary short stories published by new and established writers." Quarterly. Estab. 1991. Circ. 16,000.

- The magazine also sponsors a short story contest for new writers, a very short fiction (under 3,000 words) contest and a family-themed contest.

Needs Literary. Receives 4,000 unsolicited mss/month. Accepts 10 mss/issue; 40 mss/year. Publishes ms up to 18 months after acceptance. Agented fiction 5%. **Publishes 20 new writers/year.** Recently published work by Charles Baxter, Thisbe Nissen, Herman Carrillo, Andre Dubus III, William Trevor, Patricia Henley, Alberto Rios, Ann Beattie. Sometimes comments on rejected mss.
How to Contact Submit work online at www.glimmertrain.org. Different submission categories are open each month of the year. Accepted work published in *Glimmer Train Stories*. Responds in 2 months to mss. Accepts simultaneous submissions. Sample copy for $12 on website. Writer's guidelines online.
Payment/Terms Pays $700 for standard submissions, up to $2,000 for contest winning stories. Pays on acceptance for first rights.
Tips "We are very open to the work of new writers. Of the 100 Distinguished Short Stories listed in the current edition of Best American Short Stories, 10 first appeared in *Glimmer Train Stories*, more than in any other publication, including the *New Yorker*. Three of those 10 were the author's first publication."

GLOBAL CITY REVIEW

City College of New York, 138th St. and Convent Ave., New York NY 10031. E-mail: globalcityreview@ccny.cuny.edu. Website: www.webdelsol.com/globalcityreview. **Contact:** Linsey Abrams. Magazine: 140 pages; stock paper; cardstock cover. "The perspective of GCR is feminist—women are an important focus, as are writers who write from a gay and lesbian or minority position, culturally decentralized voices because of age or culture, international perspectives, the silenced, the poor, etc. The point is an opening of literary space." Semiannual. Estab. 1993. Circ. 500. CLMP.
Needs Ethnic/multicultural (general), experimental, feminist, gay, lesbian, literary, translations. "No genre fiction." Receives 25-30 unsolicited mss/month. Accepts 4-6 mss/issue; 8-12 mss/year. Publishes short shorts. Also publishes literary essays, literary criticism, poetry.
How to Contact Send a disposable copy of ms and #10 SASE for reply only. Responds in 2-6 months to mss. Accepts simultaneous submissions. Sample copy for $8.50. Writer's guidelines for SASE or on website. Reviews fiction.
Payment/Terms Pays 2 contributor's copies; additional copies $8.50. Acquires one-time rights.

$ GRAIN LITERARY MAGAZINE

Saskatchewan Writers Guild, P.O. Box 67, Saskatoon SK S7K 3K1 Canada. (306)244-2828. Fax: (306)244-0255. E-mail: grainmag@sasktel.net (inquiries only). Website: www.grainmagazine.ca. **Contact:** Mike Thompson, business administrator (inquiries only). Literary magazine: 6 × 9; 128 pages; Chinook offset printing; chrome-coated stock; some photos. "Grain is an internationally acclaimed literary journal that publishes engaging, surprising, eclectic, and challenging writing and images by Canadian and international writers and artists." Quarterly. Circ. 1,500.

Needs Experimental, literary, mainstream, contemporary, prose poem, poetry. "No romance, confession, science fiction, vignettes, mystery." Receives 80 unsolicited mss/month. Accepts 8-12 mss/issue; 32-48 mss/year. Publishes ms 11 months after acceptance. Recently published work by Yann Martel, Tom Wayman, Lorna Crozier. Also publishes poetry. Occasionally comments on rejected mss.
How to Contact Send complete ms with SASE (or IRC) and brief letter. Accepts queries by e-mail, mail, fax, phone. Responds in 1 month to queries; 4 months to mss. No simultaneous submissions. Sample copy for $13 or online. Writer's guidelines for #10 SASE or online.
Payment/Terms Pays $50-225. Pays on publication for first Canadian serial rights.
Tips "Submit a story to us that will deepen the imaginative experience of our readers. *Grain* has established itself as a first-class magazine of serious fiction. We receive submissions from around the world. Do not use U.S. postage stamps on your return envelope. Without sufficient Canadian postage or an International Reply Coupon, we *will not* read or reply to your submission. We look for attention to detail, credibility, lucid use of language and metaphor and a confident, convincing voice. Make sure you have researched your piece, that the literal and metaphorical support one another."

GRANTA

The Magazine of New Writing, 12 Addison Ave, London WA W11 4QR Australia. +44 (0)2076 051 360. E-mail: editorial@granta.com. Website: www.granta.com. **Contact:** John Freeman, Editor. Magazine: paperback, 278 pages approx; photos. "Granta magazine publishes fiction, reportage, biography and autobiography, history, travel and documentary photography. It does not publish 'writing about writing.' The realistic narrative—the story—is its primary form." Quarterly. Estab. 1979. Circ. 80,000.
Needs Literary, novel excerpts. No genre fiction. Themes decided as deadline approaches. Receives 100 unsolicited mss/month. Accepts 0-1 mss/issue; 1-2 mss/year. **Publishes 2-3 new writers/ year.**
How to Contact Send SAE and IRCs for reply, return of ms or send a disposable copy of ms. Responds in 3 months to mss. Accepts simultaneous submissions. Sample copy for $14.95. Writer's guidelines online.
Payment/Terms Payment varies. Pays on publication. Buys world English language rights, first serial rights (minimum). "We hold more rights in pieces we commission." Sends galleys to author.
Tips "We are looking for the best in realistic stories; originality of voice; without jargon, connivance or self-conscious 'performance'—writing that endures."

GRASSLIMB

P.O. Box 420816, San Diego CA 92142. E-mail: editor@grasslimb.com. Website: www.grasslimb.com. **Contact:** Valerie Polichar, editor. Magazine: 14 × 20; 8 pages; 60 lb. white paper; illustrations. "Grasslimb publishes literary prose, poetry and art. Fiction is best when it is short and avant-garde or otherwise experimental." Semiannual. Circ. 200.
Needs Ethnic/multicultural, experimental, literary, mystery/suspense (crime), regional, thriller/ espionage, translations. Does not want romance or religious writings. Accepts 2-4 mss/issue; 4-8 mss/year. Publishes ms 3-6 months after acceptance. **Publishes 4 new writers/year.** Recently published work by Kuzhali Manickavel, Parker Dorris. Length: 500-2,000 words; average length: 1,500 words. Publishes short shorts. Also publishes poetry. Rarely comments on rejected mss.
How to Contact Send complete ms. Send SASE for return of ms or disposable copy of ms and #10 SASE for reply only. Responds in 3-4 months to mss. Accepts simultaneous and reprints, multiple submissions. Sample copy for $2.50. Writer's guidelines for SASE, e-mail or on website. Reviews fiction.
Payment/Terms Writers receive $10 minimum; $70 maximum, and 2 contributor's copies; additional copies $3. Pays on acceptance for first print publication serial rights.
Tips "We publish brief fiction work that can be read in a single sitting over a cup of coffee. Work is generally 'literary' in nature, rather than mainstream. Experimental work welcome. Remember

to have your work proofread and to send short work. We cannot read over 2,500 and prefer under 2,000 words. Include word count."

GREEN MOUNTAINS REVIEW

Johnson State College, Johnson VT 05656. (802)635-1350. E-mail: gmr@jsc.vsc.edu. Website: http://greenmountainsreview.jsc.vsc.edu/submissions. **Contact:** Leslie Daniels, fiction editor. JMagazine: digest-sized; 160-200 pages. Semiannual. Estab. 1975.

- *Green Mountains Review* has received a Pushcart Prize and Editor's Choice Award.

Needs Adventure, experimental, humor/satire, literary, mainstream, serialized novels, translations. Receives 100 unsolicited mss/month. Accepts 6 mss/issue; 12 mss/year. "Manuscripts received between March 1 and September 1 will not be read and will be returned." Publishes ms 6-12 months after acceptance. **Publishes 0-4 new writers/year.** Recently published work by Tracy Daugherty, Terese Svoboda, Walter Wetherell, T.M. McNally, J. Robert Lennon, Louis B. Jones, and Tom Whalen. Publishes short shorts. Also publishes literary criticism, poetry. Sometimes comments on rejected mss.

How to Contact Send complete ms and SASE. Responds in 1 month to queries; 6 months to mss. Accepts simultaneous submissions if advised. Sample copy for $7.

Payment/Terms Pays contributor's copies, 1-year subscription and small honorarium, depending on grants. Acquires first North American serial rights. Rights revert to author upon request.

Tips The editors read manuscripts September 1 through March 1. During that period, we make every attempt to respond within three months. If received outside the reading period, manuscripts will be returned unread.

THE GREENSBORO REVIEW

3302 Hall for Humanities, UNC Greensboro, P, Greensboro NC 27402-6170. (336)334-5459. E-mail: jlclark@uncg.edu. Website: www.greensbororeview.org. **Contact:** Jim Clark, editor. Magazine: 6 × 9; approximately 128 pages; 60 lb. paper; 80 lb. cover. Literary magazine featuring fiction and poetry for readers interested in contemporary literature. Semiannual. Circ. 1000.

- Stories for *The Greensboro Review* have been included in *Best American Short Stories, The O. Henry Awards Prize Stories, New Stories from The South,* and *Pushcart Prize.*

Needs Accepts 6-8 mss/issue; 12-16 mss/year. Unsolicited manuscripts must arrive by September 15 to be considered for the spring issue and by February 15 to be considered for the fall issue. Manuscripts arriving after those dates may be held for the next consideration. **Publishes 10% new writers/year.** Recently published work by Renee Ashley, Michael Cadnum, Carl Dennis, Jack Gilbert, Chard diNiord, Curtis Smith, and Kevin Wilson.

How to Contact Responds in 4 months to mss. Accepts simultaneous submissions. No e-mail submissions. Sample copy for $8.

Payment/Terms Pays in contributor's copies. Acquires first North American serial rights.

Tips "We want to see the best being written regardless of theme, subject or style."

THE GRIFFIN

P.O. Box 901, 1325 Sumneytown Pike, Gwynedd Valley PA 19437-0901. (215)641-5518. Fax: (215)641-5552. E-mail: allego.d@gmc.edu. **Contact:** Donna Allegro, editor. Literary magazine: 8½ × 5½; 112 pages. "The Griffin is an annual literary journal sponsored by Gwynedd-Mercy College. Its mission is to enrich society by nurturing and promoting creative writing that demonstrates a unique and intelligent voice. We seek writing which accurately reflects the human condition with all its intellectual, emotional and ethical challenges." Needs Short stories, essays and poetry. Open to genre work. "No slasher, graphic violence or sex." Accepts mss depending on the quality of work submitted. Receives 20-30 unsolicited mss/month. Publishes ms 6-9 months after acceptance. Publishes 10-15 new writers/year. Length: 2,500 words; average length: 2,000 words. Publishes short shorts. Also publishes literary essays, poetry. Send complete ms. All submissions must be on disk and include a hard copy. Send disposable copy of ms, disk and #10 SASE for reply only. Responds in 2-3 months to queries; 6 months to mss. Accepts simultaneous submissions "if notified." Sample copy for $10. Change to $10. The Griffin will be published on line.

GUD MAGAZINE

Greatest Uncommon Denominator Publishing, P.O. Box 1025, Acton CA 93510-1025. E-mail: editor@gudmagazine.com. Website: www.gudmagazine.com. **Contact:** Julia Bernd, Sal Coraccio, editors. Literary magazine/journal. "*GUD Magazine* transcends and encompasses the audiences of both genre and literary fiction. We're selling content, not media. If people want to buy just one story, they'll get it. If they want a PDF magazine, they'll get the whole issue. If they want a beautifully bound paper mag, they'll pay a little extra, but they'll get it. *GUD* features fiction (from flash to 15,000 word stories), art, poetry, essays, comics, reports and short drama. See website for more."

Needs Adventure, erotica, ethnic/multicultural, experimental, fantasy, horror, humor/satire, literary, science fiction, alternate history, mystery, why. Accepts 40 mss/year. Manuscript published 6 months after acceptance. Length: 15,000 words (max).

How to Contact Submit via online form only. Responds to mss in up to 6 months. Considers simultaneous submissions, previously published submissions, and multiple submissions (art and poetry only). Guidelines available on website.

Tips "Be warned: We read a lot. We've seen it all before. We are not easy to impress. Is your work original? Does it have something to say? Read it again. If you genuinely believe it to be so, send it. But first read the guidelines."

GUERNICA

A Magazine of Art and Politics, Attn: Michael Archer, 165 Bennett Ave., 4C, New York NY 10040. E-mail: editors@guernicamag.com. Website: www.guernicamag.com. **Contact:** Meakin Armstrong, Fiction Editor.

Needs Literary, preferably with an international approach. No genre fiction.

How to Contact Submit complete ms with cover letter Attn: Meakin Armstrong to fiction@guernicamag.com. In subject line (please follow this format exactly): "fiction submission."

$ GULF COAST

A Journal of Literature & Fine Arts, Dept. of English, University of Houston, Houston TX 77204-3013. (713)743-3223. E-mail: editors@gulfcoastmag.org. Website: www.gulfcoast.uh.edu. **Contact:** Fiction Editor. Magazine: 7 × 9; approx. 300 pages; stock paper, gloss cover; illustrations; photos. "Innovative fiction for the literary-minded." Estab. 1987.

- Work published in Gulf Coast has been selected for inclusion in the *Pushcart Prize* anthology, *The O'Henry Prize Stories* anthology and *Best American Short Stories*.

Needs Ethnic/multicultural, experimental, literary, regional, translations, contemporary. "No children's, genre, religious/inspirational." Wants more "cutting-edge, experimental" fiction. Receives 300 unsolicited mss/month. Accepts 4-8 mss/issue; 12-16 mss/year. Publishes ms 6 months-1 year after acceptance. Agented fiction 5%. **Publishes 2-8 new writers/year.** Recently published work by Justin Cronin, Cary Holladay, Holiday Reinhorn, Michael Martone, Joe Meno, Karen An-hwei Lee. Publishes short shorts. Sometimes comments on rejected mss.

How to Contact Gulf Coast reads general submissions, submitted by post or through the online submissions manager, from August 15 through March 15. Submissions e-mailed directly to the editors, or postmarked between March 15 and August 15, will not be read or responded to. Please visit our contest page for contest submission guidelines. Responds in 4-6 months to mss. Accepts simultaneous submissions. Back issue for $7, 7 × 10 SASE with 4 first-class stamps. Writer's guidelines for #10 SASE or on website.

Payment/Terms Acquires one-time rights. Please do not send multiple submissions; we will read only one submission per author at a given time, except in the case of our annual contests. **Payment for accepted work** varies depending on availability of funds, but is a minimum of $30 per poem, $20 per page of prose up to $150, $50 per review, and $100 per interview.

Tips "Rotating editorship, so please be patient with replies. As always, please send one story at a time."

GULF STREAM MAGAZINE

Florida International University, English Dept., Biscayne Bay Campus, 3000 N.E. 151st St., N. Miami FL 33181-3000. (305)919-5599. E-mail: gulfstreamfiu@yahoo.com. **Contact:** Corey Ginsberg, editor. Magazine: 5½ × 8½; 124 pages; recycled paper; 80 lb. glossy cover; cover illustrations. "We publish good quality —fiction, nonfiction and poetry for a predominately literary market." Semiannual. Estab. 1989. Circ. 300.

Needs Literary, mainstream, contemporary. Does not want romance, historical, juvenile or religious work. Receives 250 unsolicited mss/month. Accepts 5 mss/issue; 10 mss/year. Does not read mss during the summer. Publishes ms 3-6 months after acceptance. **Publishes 2-5 new writers/year.** Recently published work by Leonard Nash, Jesse Millner, Lyn Millner, Peter Meinke, Susan Neville. Length: 7,500 words; average length: 5,000 words. Publishes short shorts. Also publishes poetry.

How to Contact Responds in 6 months to mss. Accepts simultaneous submissions "if noted." Sample copy for $5. Writer's guidelines for #10 SASE.

Payment/Terms Pays in gift subscriptions and contributor's copies. Acquires first North American serial rights.

Tips "Looks for fresh, original writing—well plotted stories with unforgettable characters, fresh poetry and experimental writing. Usually longer stories do not get accepted. There are exceptions, however."

N HAPA NUI: READER-DRIVEN CONTENT

967 Garden Street, East Palo Alto CA 94303. E-mail: editors@hapanui.com. Website: www.hapanui.com. **Contact:** Julianne Bonnet, editor. Print and online literary magazine/journal. Size: 4.25 X 5.5, 200 pages. Contains illustrations. Includes photographs. "In Hawaiian, 'hapa nui' means majority or large part. The concept of the reader-driven lit mag is at the heart of what we see as a new movement in literature. One part on-line venue and one part print journal, Hapa Nui is a placce where readers determine through a democratic voting process what they like and, ultimately, which work makes it into print. Submit your work or just come back and vote to participate in this new literary revolution." Annual. Estab. 2008. Circ. 250. Member CLMP.

Needs Ethnic/multicultural (general), experimental, family saga, feminist, gay, historical (general), humor/satire, lesbian, literary, mainstream, mystery. Does not want space fantasy, sword and sorcery, religious, overly spiritual or children's/juvenile. Receives 100 mss/month. Accepts up to 52 mss/year. Ms published 1-12 months after acceptance. **Publishes 37% new writers/year.** Published Joyce Nower, Changming Yuan and Rob Carney. Length: 2,500 words (max). Average length: 1,500 words. Publishes short shorts. Average length of short shorts: 250 words. Also publishes literary essays, poetry. Sometimes comments on/critiques rejected mss.

How to Contact Send complete ms with cover letter by e-mail. Include estimated word count, brief bio. Responds to mss in 12 weeks. Considers previously published submissions, multiple submissions. Sample copy available for $5. Guidelines available on website.

Payment/Terms Writers receive 2 contributer's copies. Additional copies $5. Pays on publication. Acquires first North American serial rights, anthology rights. Sends galleys to author. Publication is copyrighted.

Tips "The first paragraph really needs to pull the reader in. The ending has to support a conclusion to everything leading up to that point. We tend to look for work that really speaks to the human struggle-no matter what the circumstances or surroundings. Read the publication or visit the website often to get a idea for editorial preferences."

HARPUR PALATE

A Literary Journal at Binghamton University, English Department, P.O. Box 6000, Binghampton University, Binghamton NY 13902-6000. E-mail: harpur.palate@gmail.com. Website: harpurpalate.binghamton.edu. Magazine: 6 × 9; 180-200 pages; coated or uncoated paper; 100 lb. coated cover; 4-color art portfolio insert. "We have no restrictions on subject matter or form. Quite simply, send us your highest-quality prose or poetry." Semiannual. Circ. 800.

Needs Adventure, ethnic/multicultural, experimental, historical, humor/satire, mainstream, mystery/suspense, novel excerpts, literary, fabulism, magical realism, metafiction, slipstream.

Receives 400 unsolicited mss/month. Accepts 5-10 mss/issue; 12-20 mss/year. Publishes ms 1-2 months after acceptance. **Publishes 5 new writers/year.** Recently published work by Darryl Crawford and Tim Hedges, Jesse Goolsby, Ivan Faute, and Keith Meatto. Length: 250-8,000 words; average length: 2,000-4,000 words. Publishes short shorts. Also publishes poetry. Sometimes comments on rejected mss.

How to Contact Send complete ms with a cover letter. Fiction and flash fiction should be 250-8,000 words. Include e-mail address on cover. Include estimated word count, brief bio, list of publications. Send a disposable copy of ms and #10 SASE for reply only. Submission periods are: July 15-November 15 for the winter issue, and December 15-April 15 for summer. Responds in 1-3 week to queries; 4- 8 months to mss. Accepts simultaneous submissions if stated in the cover letter. Sample copy for $10. Writer's guidelines online.

Payment/Terms Pays 2 copies. Pays on publication for first North American serial, electronic rights. Sponsors awards/contests.

Tips "*Harpur Palate* accepts submissions between July 15 and November 15 for the winter issue, between December 15 and April 15 for the summer issue. *Harpur Palate* sponsors a fiction contest for the summer issue and a poetry contest for the winter issue. We do not accept submissions via e-mail. Almost every literary magazine already says this, but it bears repeating: Look at a recent copy of our publication to get an idea of the kind of writing published."

HARVARD REVIEW

Lamont Library, Cambridge MA 02138. (617)495-9775. E-mail: harvrev@fas.harvard.edu. Website: hcl.harvard.edu/harvardreview. **Contact:** The Editors. Magazine: 6 × 9; 256-272 pages; b&w illustrations; photographs. Semiannual. Circ. 2,000.

Needs Literary. Receives 200 unsolicited mss/month. Accepts 4 mss/issue; 8 mss/year. Publishes ms 3-6 months after acceptance. **Publishes 3-4 new writers/year.** Recently published work by Joyce Carol Oates, Alice Hoffman, William Lychack, Jim Crace, and Karen Bender. Length: 1,000-7,000 words; average length: 3,000-5,000 words. Publishes short shorts. Also publishes literary essays, literary criticism, poetry, and plays. Sometimes comments on rejected mss.

How to Contact Send SASE for return of ms or disposable copy of ms and SASE for reply only. Responds within 6 months to queries. Accepts simultaneous submissions. Writer's guidelines online.

Payment/Terms Pays 2 contributor's copies; additional copies $7. Pays on publication for first North American serial rights. Sends galleys to author.

HAWAI'I PACIFIC REVIEW

1060 Bishop St., Honolulu HI 96813. (808)544-1108. Fax: (808)544-0862. E-mail: pwilson@hpu.edu. Website: www.hpu.edu. **Contact:** Patrice M. Wilson, editor. Magazine: 6 × 9; 100 pages; glossy coated cover. "*Hawai'i Pacific Review* is looking for poetry, short fiction and personal essays that speak with a powerful and unique voice. We encourage experimental narrative techniques and poetic styles, and we welcome works in translation." Annual.

Needs Ethnic/multicultural (general), experimental, fantasy, feminist, historical (general), humor/satire, literary, mainstream, regional (Pacific), translations. "Open to all types as long as they're well done. Our audience is adults, so nothing for children/teens." Receives 30-50 unsolicited mss/month. Accepts 5-10 mss/year. Reads mss September- December each year. Publishes ms 10 months after acceptance. **Publishes 2-4 new writers/year.** Recently published work by Wendell Mayo, Elizabeth Crowell, Janet Flora, Mary Ann Cain, and Jean Giovanetti. Publishes short shorts. Also publishes literary essays, poetry. Sometimes comments on rejected mss.

How to Contact Send SASE for return of ms or send a disposable copy of ms and SASE for reply only. Responds in 2 weeks to queries; 15 weeks to mss. Accepts simultaneous submissions but must be cited in the cover letter. Sample copy for $5.

Payment/Terms Pays 2 contributor's copies; additional copies $5. Pays on publication for first North American serial rights.

Tips "We look for the unusual or original plot; prose with the texture and nuance of poetry. Character development or portrayal must be unusual/original; humanity shown in an original insightful way (or characters); sense of humor where applicable. Be sure it's a draft that has gone through substantial changes, with supervision from a more experienced writer, if you're a beginner. Write about intense emotion and feeling, not just about someone's divorce or shaky relationship. No soap-opera-like fiction."

$ HAYDEN'S FERRY REVIEW

Box 875002, Arizona State University, Tempe AZ 85287-1502. E-mail: hfr@asu.edu. Website: www.haydensferryreview.org. **Contact:** Beth Staples, managing editor. Editors change every 1-2 years. Magazine: 6¾ × 9¾; 150 pages; fine paper; illustrations; photos. "Hayden's Ferry Review publishes best quality fiction, poetry, translations, and creative nonfiction from new, emerging and established writers." Semiannual. Circ. 1,300.

- Work from *Hayden's Ferry Review* has been selected for inclusion in *Pushcart Prize* anthologies, Best of the West, and *Best Creative Nonfiction*.

Needs Ethnic/multicultural, experimental, humor/satire, literary, regional, slice-of-life vignettes, contemporary, prose poem. Possible special issue. Receives 250 unsolicited mss/month. Accepts 5 mss/issue; 10 mss/year. Publishes ms 6 months after acceptance. Recently published work by Joseph Heller, Ron Carlson, Norman Dubie, John Updike, Richard Ford, Yusef Komunyakaa, Joel-Peter Witkin, Ai, David St. John, Gloria Naylor, Tess Gallagher, Ken Kesey, Naomi Shihab Nye, Allen Ginsberg, T.C. Boyle, Raymond Carver, Rita Dove, Chuck Rosenthal, Rick Bass, Charles Baxter, Pam Houston, Mary Ruefle, and Denise Duhamel. Publishes short shorts.

How to Contact Accepts submissions online. Responds in 2-3 days to queries; 2-4 months to mss. Accepts simultaneous submissions. Sample copy for $7.50. Writer's guidelines online.

Payment/Terms Pays $50-100, 2 copies, and 1-year subscription. Pays on publication for first North American serial rights. Sends galleys to author.

HEAVEN BONE

Heaven Bone Press, 62 Woodcock Mtn. Dr. Washingtonvile, NY 10992. (845)496-4109. E-mail: heavenbone@hvc.rr.com. **Contact:** Steven Hirsch and Kirpal Gordon, editors. Magazine: 8½ × 11; 96-116 pages; 60 lb. recycled offset paper; full color cover; computer clip art, graphics, line art, cartoons, halftones and photos scanned in.tif format. "Expansive, fine surrealist and experimental literary, earth and nature, spiritual path. We use current reviews, essays on spiritual and esoteric topics, creative stories. Also: reviews of current poetry releases and expansive literature." Readers are "scholars, surrealists, poets, artists, musicians, students." Annual. Estab. 1987. Circ. 2,500.

Needs Experimental, fantasy, regional, esoteric/scholarly, spiritual. "No violent, thoughtless, exploitive or religious fiction." Receives 45-110 unsolicited mss/month. Accepts 5-15 mss/issue; 12-30 mss/year. Publishes ms 2 weeks-10 months after acceptance. **Publishes 3-4 new writers/ year.** Recently published work by Keith Abbot and Stephen-Paul Martin. Length: 1,200-5,000 words; average length: 3,500 words. Publishes short shorts. Also publishes literary essays, literary criticism, poetry. Sometimes comments on rejected mss.

How to Contact Send SASE for reply or return of ms. Responds in 3 weeks to queries; 10 months to mss. Accepts reprints submissions. Sample copy for $10. Writer's guidelines for SASE. Reviews fiction.

Payment/Terms Pays in contributor's copies; charges for extras. Acquires first North American serial rights. Sends galleys to author.

Tips "Read a sample issue first. Our fiction needs are temperamental, so please query first before submitting. We prefer shorter fiction. Do not send first drafts to test them on us. Please refine and polish your work before sending. Always include SASE. We are looking for the unique, unusual and excellent."

$ HOBART, ANOTHER LITERARY JOURNAL

PO Box 1658, Ann Arbor MI 48106. (206) 399-0410. E-mail: aaron@hobartpulp.com. Website: http://www.hobartpulp.com. **Contact:** Aaron Burch, Editor. Literary magazine/journal. 6 × 9, 200 pages. Contains illustrations. Includes photographs. "We publish non-stuffy, unpretentious, high quality fiction that never takes itself too serious and always entertains." Semiannual. Estab. 2002. Circ. 1000. Member CLMP.

- Inclusion in *Best American Nonrequired Reading* and *Best American Fantasy*, as well as multiple notable mentions in *Best American Nonrequired Reading* and *Best American Essays*.

Needs Literary. Receives 200 mss/month. Accepts 20 mss/issue; 40 mss/year. Ms published 2-8 months after acceptance. **Publishes 2-5 new writers/year.** Published Benjamin Percy, Tod Goldberg, Chris Bachelder, Sheila Heti, Stephany Aulenback, Catherine Zeidler and Ryan Call. Length: 1000 words (min)-7000 words (max). Average length: 3000 words. Publishes short shorts. Also publishes literary essays. Sometimes comments on/critiques rejected mss.
How to Contact Send complete ms with cover letter. Accepts submissions by e-mail. Responds to queries in 2 weeks. Responds to mss in 1-4 months. Send disposable copy of ms and #10 SASE for reply only. Considers simultaneous submissions. Sample copy available for $2. Guidelines available for SASE, via e-mail, on website.
Payment/Terms Writers receive $50-150, 2 contributor's copies, free subscription to the magazine. Additional copies $5. Pays on publication. Acquires first rights. Publication is copyrighted.
Tips "We'd love to receive fewer run-of-the-mill relationship stories and more stories concerning truck drivers, lumberjacks, carnival workers, and gunslingers. In other words: surprise us. Show us a side of life rarely depicted in literary fiction."

HOME PLANET NEWS

P.O. Box 455, High Falls NY 12440. (845)687-4084. Website: http://www.homeplanetnews.org. **Contact:** Donald Lev, editor. Tabloid: 11½ × 16; 24 pages; newsprint; illustrations; photos. "Home Planet News publishes mainly poetry along with some fiction, as well as reviews (books, theater and art) and articles of literary interest. We see HPN as a quality literary journal in an eminently readable format and with content that is urban, urbane and politically aware." Triannual. Circ. 1,000.

- *HPN* has received a small grant from the Puffin Foundation for its focus on AIDS issues.

Needs Ethnic/multicultural, experimental, feminist, gay, historical, lesbian, literary, mainstream, science fiction (soft/sociological). No "children's or genre stories (except rarely some science fiction)." Publishes special fiction issue or anthology. Receives 12 unsolicited mss/month. Accepts 1 mss/issue; 3 mss/year. Publishes ms 1 year after acceptance. Recently published work by Hugh Fox, Walter Jackman, Jim Story. Length: 500-2,500 words; average length: 2,000 words. Publishes short shorts. Also publishes literary criticism.
How to Contact Send complete ms. Send SASE for reply, return of ms or send a disposable copy of the ms. Responds in 6 months to mss. Sample copy for $4. Writer's guidelines for SASE.
Payment/Terms Pays 3 contributor's copies; additional copies $1. Acquires one-time rights.
Tips "We use very little fiction, and a story we accept just has to grab us. We need short pieces of some complexity, stories about complex people facing situations which resist simple resolutions."

HYCO REVIEW ARTS AND LITERARY JOURNAL

Piedmont Community College, P.O. Box 1197, Roxboro NC 27573. (336)599-1181. E-mail: reflect@piedmont.cc.nc.us. Website: www.piedmontcc.edu. **Contact:** Dawn Langley, editor. Online magazine. 100-150 pages.
Needs Literary. "Accepts mss from Person and Caswell county, NC authors only (residents or natives). If time and space permit, we'll consider submissions from other North Carolina authors." Publishes mss 6-10 months after acceptance. **Publishes 3-5 new writers/year.** Recently published work by Maureen Sherbondy, Dainiel Green, Betty Moffett, Lian Gouw, Sejal Badani Ravani, Donna Conrad. Max Length: 4,000 words; average length: 2,500 words. Publishes short shorts. Also publishes poetry and essays, photographs, videos, digital animation, and artwork.
How to Contact Send SASE for return of ms or #10 SASE for reply only. Sample copy for $5. Writer's guidelines for SASE or by e-mail.
Payment/Terms Publication is online. Acquires first North American serial rights. Sponsors awards/contests.

Tips "We look for good writing with a flair, which captivates an educated lay audience. Don't take rejection letters personally. We turn away many submissions simply because we don't have room for everything we like or because the author is not from our region. For that reason, we're more likely to accept shorter well-written stories than longer stories of the same quality. Also, stories containing profanity that doesn't contribute to the plot, structure or intended tone are rejected immediately."

$ THE IDAHO REVIEW

Boise State University, English Dept., 1910 University Dr., Boise ID 83725. (208)426-1002. Fax: (208)426-4373. E-mail: mwieland@boisestate.edu. **Contact:** Mitch Wieland, editor. Magazine: 6 × 9; 180-200 pages; acid-free accent opaque paper; coated cover stock; photos. "A literary journal for anyone who enjoys good fiction." Annual. Estab. 1998. Circ. 1,000. Member CLMP.

- Recent stories reprinted in *The Best American Short Stories, The O. Henry Prize Stories, The Pushcart Prize,* and *New Stories from The South.*

Needs Experimental, literary. "No genre fiction of any type." Receives 150 unsolicited mss/month. Accepts 5-7 mss/issue; 5-7 mss/year. "We do not read from May 1-August 31." Publishes ms 1 year after acceptance. Agented fiction 5%. **Publishes 1 new writer/year.** Recently published work by Rick Bass, Melanie Rae Thon, Ron Carlson, Joy Williams, Madison Smartt Bell, Carolyn Cooke. Length: open; average length: 7,000 words. Publishes short shorts. Also publishes literary essays, poetry. Sometimes comments on rejected mss.

How to Contact Send SASE for return of ms or send a disposable copy of ms and #10 SASE for reply only. Responds in 3-5 months to mss. Accepts simultaneous, multiple submissions. Sample copy for $8.95. Writer's guidelines for SASE. Reviews fiction.

Payment/Terms Pays $100 when funds are available plus 2 contributor's copies; additional copies $5. Pays on publication for first North American serial rights. Sends galleys to author.

Tips "We look for strongly crafted work that tells a story that needs to be told. We demand vision and intlligence and mystery in the fiction we publish."

ILLUMINATIONS

Dept. of English, College of Charleston, 66 George St., Charleston SC 29424-0001. (843)953-1920. Fax: (843)953-1924. E-mail: lewiss@cofc.edu. Website: www.cofc.edu/illuminations. **Contact:** Simon Lewis, editor. Magazine: 5 × 8; 80 pages; illustrations. "Illuminations is one of the most challengingly eclectic little literary magazines around, having featured writers from the United States, Britain and Romania, as well as Southern Africa." Annual. Estab. 1982. Circ. 500.

Needs Literary. Receives 5 unsolicited mss/month. Accepts 1 mss/year. **Publishes 1 new writer/year.** Recently published work by John Michael Cummings. Also publishes poetry. Sometimes comments on rejected mss.

How to Contact Send SASE for reply, return of ms or send a disposable copy of ms. Responds in 2 weeks to queries; 2 months to mss. No simultaneous submissions. Sample copy for $10 and 6 × 9 envelope. Writer's guidelines free.

Payment/Terms Pays 2 contributor's copies of current issue; 1 of subsequent issue. Acquires one-time rights.

$ IMAGE

Art, Faith, Mystery, 3307 Third Ave. W, Seattle WA 98119. (206)281-2988. E-mail: gwolfe@imagejournal.org. Website: www.imagejournal.org. **Contact:** Gregory Wolfe. Magazine: 7 × 10; 136 pages; glossy cover stock; illustrations; photos. "Image is a showcase for the encounter between religious faith and world-class contemporary art. Each issue features fiction, poetry, essays, memoirs, reviews, an in-depth interview and articles about visual artists, film, music, etc. and glossy 4-color plates of contemporary visual art." Quarterly. Circ. 4,500. Member CLMP.

Needs Literary, essays. Receives 100 unsolicited mss/month. Accepts 2 mss/issue; 8 mss/year. Publishes ms 1 year after acceptance. Agented fiction 5%. Recently published work by Annie Dillard, David James Duncan, Robert Olen Butler, Bret Lott, Melanie Rae Thon. Length: 4,000-6,000 words; average length: 5,000 words.

How to Contact Send SASE for reply, return of ms or send disposable copy of ms. Responds in 1 month to queries; 3 months to mss. Sample copy for $16. Reviews fiction.
Payment/Terms Pays $10/page and 4 contributor's copies; additional copies for $6. Pays on acceptance. Sends galleys to author.
Tips "Fiction must grapple with religious faith, though the settings and subjects need not be overtly religious."

$ INDIANA REVIEW

Ballantine Hall 465, 1020 E. Kirkwood, Bloomington IN 47405-7103. (812)855-3439. E-mail: inreview@indiana.edu. Website: www.indianareview.org. **Contact:** Fiction Editor. Magazine: 6 × 9; 160 pages; 50 lb. paper; Glatfelter cover stock. "*Indiana Review*, a nonprofit organization run by IU graduate students, is a journal of previously unpublished poetry and fiction. Literary interviews and essays also considered. We publish innovative fiction and poetry. We're interested in energy, originality and careful attention to craft. While we publish many well-known writers, we also welcome new and emerging poets and fiction writers." Semiannual. Estab. 1976. Circ. 2,000.

- Work published in *Indiana Review* received a Pushcart Prize (2001) and was included in *Best New American Voices* (2001). *IR* also received an Indiana Arts Council Grant and a NEA grant.

Needs Ethnic/multicultural, experimental, literary, mainstream, novel excerpts, regional, translations. No genre fiction. Receives 300 unsolicited mss/month. Accepts 7-9 mss/issue. Reads year round, but refer to web site for closed submission periods. Publishes ms an average of 3-6 months after acceptance. **Publishes 6-8 new writers/year.** Recently published work by Kim Addonizio, Stuart Dybek, Marilyn Chin, Ray Gonzalez, Michael Martone, Melanie Rae Thon. Also publishes literary essays, poetry.
How to Contact Send complete ms. Accepts online submissions. Cover letters should be *brief* and demonstrate specific familiarity with the content of a recent issue of *Indiana Review*. Include SASE. Responds in 4 months to mss. Accepts simultaneous submissions if notified *immediately* of other publication. Sample copy for $9. Writer's guidelines online.
Payment/Terms Pays $5/page, plus 2 contributor's copies. Pays on publication for first North American serial rights. Sponsors awards/contests.
Tips "Because our editors change each year, so do our literary preferences. It's important that potential contributors are familiar with our most recent issue of *Indiana Review* via library, sample copy or subscription. Beyond that, we look for prose that is well crafted and socially relevant. Dig deep. Don't accept your first choice descriptions when you are revising. Cliché and easy images sink 90% of the stories we reject. Understand the magazines you send to—investigate!"

INKWELL MAGAZINE

Manhattanville College, 2900 Purchase St., Box 1379, Purchase NY 10577. (914)323-7239. Fax: (914)323-3122. E-mail: inkwell@mville.edu. Website: www.inkwelljournal.org. **Contact:** Fiction Editor. Literary Journal: 5½ × 7½; 120-170 pages; 60 lb. paper; 10 pt C1S, 4/c cover; illustrations; photos. "Inkwell Magazine is committed to presenting top quality poetry, prose and artwork in a high quality publication. Inkwell is dedicated to discovering new talent and to encouraging and bringing talents of working writers and artists to a wider audience. We encourage diverse voices and have an open submission policy for both art and literature." Annual. Circ. 1,000. Member CLMP.
Needs Experimental, humor/satire, literary. "No erotica, children's literature, romance, religious." Receives 120 unsolicited mss/month. Accepts 45 mss/issue. Does not read mss December-July. Publishes ms 2 months after acceptance. **Publishes 3-5 new writers/year.** Recently published work by Alice Quinn, Margaret Gibson, Benjamin Cheever, Paul Muldoon, Pablo Medina, Carol Muske-Dukes. Length: 5,000 words; average length: 3,000 words. Publishes short shorts. Also publishes poetry.
How to Contact Send a disposable copy of ms and #10 SASE for reply only. Responds in 1 month to queries; 4-6 months to mss. Sample copy for $6. Writer's guidelines for SASE.
Payment/Terms Pays $10/page and 2 contributor's copies; additional copies $8. Acquires first

North American serial, first rights. Sponsors awards/contests.
Tips "We look for well-crafted original stories with a strong voice."

$ THE IOWA REVIEW

308 EPB, University of Iowa, Iowa City IA 52242. Website: www.uiowa.edu/~iareview/. **Contact:** Russell Scott Valentino, editor. Magazine: 5½ × 8½; 200 pages; first-grade offset paper; Carolina CS1 10-pt. cover stock. "Stories, essays, poems for a general readership interested in contemporary literature." Triannual magazine. Circ. 2,500.
Needs "We are open to a range of styles and voices and always hope to be surprised by work we then feel we need." Receives 600 unsolicited mss/month. Accepts 4-6 mss/issue; 12-18 mss/year. Does not read mss January-August. Publishes ms an average of 12-18 months after acceptance. Agented fiction less than 2%. **Publishes some new writers/year.** Recently published work by Benjamin Chambers, Pierre Hauser, Stellar Kim. Also publishes literary essays, literary criticism, poetry.
How to Contact Send complete ms with cover letter. "Don't bother with queries." SASE for return of ms. Responds in 3 months to queries; 3 months to mss. "We discourage simultaneous submissions." Sample copy for $9 and online; subscription $25. Writer's guidelines online. Reviews fiction.
Payment/Terms Pays $.08 per word with a $100 minimum, plus 2 contributor's copies; additional copies 30% off cover price. Pays on publication for first North American serial, nonexclusive anthology, classroom, online serial rights.
Tips "We have no set guidelines as to content or length; we look for what we consider to be the best writing available to us and are pleased when writers we believe we have discovered catch on with a wider range of readers. It is never a bad idea to look through an issue or two of the magazine prior to a submission."

JABBERWOCK REVIEW

Drawer E, Dept. of English, Mississippi State MS 39762. E-mail: jabberwockreview@english.msstate.edu. Website: www.msstate.edu/org/jabberwock. **Contact:** Michael Kardos, editor. Literary magazine/journal: 6x9; 120 pages; 60 lb paper; 80 lb cover. "J Journal publishes literary fiction, creative nonfiction and poetry on the subjects of crime, criminal justice, law and law enforcement. While the themes are specific, they need not dominate the work. We're interested in questions of justice from all perspectives." Semiannual. Circ. 500.
Needs Ethnic/multicultural, experimental, feminist, gay, literary, mainstream, regional, translations. "No science fiction, romance." Receives 150 unsolicited mss/month. Accepts 7-8 mss/issue; 15 mss/year. "We do not read March 15 to September 1." Publishes ms 4-6 months after acceptance. **Publishes 1-5 new writers/year.** Recently published work by Robert Morgan, Charles Harper Webb, Ted Kooser, Alison Baker, Alyce Miller, Lorraine Lopez, J.D. Chapman. Length: 250-5,000 words; average length: 4,000 words. Publishes short shorts. Also publishes literary essays, poetry. Sometimes comments on rejected mss.
How to Contact Send SASE (or IRC) for return of ms. Does not accept e-mail submissions. Responds in 5 months to mss. Accepts simultaneous submissions "with notification of such." Sample copy for $6. Writer's guidelines for SASE.
Payment/Terms Pays 2 contributor's copies. Sponsors awards/contests.
Tips "It might take a few months to get a response from us, but your manuscript will be read with care. Our editors enjoy reading submissions (really!) and will remember writers who are persistent and commited to getting a story 'right' through revision."

J JOURNAL: NEW WRITING ON JUSTICE

445 West 59th Street, New York NY 10019. (212) 327-8697. Fax: (212) 237-8564. E-mail: jjournal@jjay.cuny.edu. Website: www.jjournal.org. **Contact:** Adam Berlin and Jeffrey Heiman, editors. New Writing on Justice Dept. of English, John Jay College of Criminal Justice, 619 West 54th Street, 7th Floor, New York NY 10019. E-mail: journal@jjay.cuny.edu. **Contact:** Adam Berlin and Jeffrey Heiman, editors. Literary magazine/journal: 6x9; 120 pages; 60 lb paper; 80 lb cover. "J Journal publishes literary fiction, creative nonfiction and poetry on the subjects of crime, criminal justice,

law and law enforcement. While the themes are specific, they need not dominate the work. We're interested in questions of justice from all perspectives." Semiannual. Estab. 2008.

Needs Experimental, gay, historical (general), literary, military/war, regional. Receives 100 mss/month. Accepts 5 mss/issue; 10 mss/year. Ms. published 6 months after acceptance. Length: 750-6,000 words (max). Average length: 4,000 words. Also publishes poetry. Sometimes comments on/critiques rejected mss.

How to Contact Send complete ms with cover letter. Include estimated word count, brief bio, list of publications. Responds to queries in 4 weeks; mss in 12 weeks. Send recyclable copy of ms and #10 SASE for reply only. Considers simultaneous submissions. Sample copy available for $10.

Payment/Terms Writers receive 2 contributor's copies. Additional copies $10. Pays on publication. Acquires first rights. Publication is copyrighted.

Tips "We're looking for literary fiction/memoir with a connection, direct or tangential, to the theme of justice."

$ THE JOURNAL

The Ohio State University, 164 W. 17th Ave., Columbus OH 43210. (614)292-4076. Fax: (614)292-7816. E-mail: thejournal@osu.edu. **Contact:** Kathy Fagan (poetry); Michelle Herman (fiction). Magazine: 6 × 9; 150 pages. "We're open to all forms; we tend to favor work that gives evidence of a mature and sophisticated sense of the language." Semiannual. Estab. 1972. Circ. 1,500.

Needs Novel excerpts, literary short stories. No romance, science fiction or religious/devotional. Receives 100 unsolicited mss/month. Accepts 2 mss/issue. Publishes ms 1 year after acceptance. Agented fiction 10%. **Publishes some new writers/year.** Recently published work by Michael Martone, Gregory Spatz and Stephen Graham Jones. Sometimes comments on rejected mss.

How to Contact Send complete ms with cover letter and SASE. Responds in 2 weeks to queries; 2 months to mss. Accepts simultaneous submissions. No electronic submissions. Sample copy for $7 or online. Writer's guidelines online.

Payment/Terms Pays $20. Pays on publication for first North American serial rights. Sends galleys to author.

Tips "Manuscripts are rejected because of lack of understanding of the short story form, shallow plots, undeveloped characters. Cure: Read as much well-written fiction as possible. Our readers prefer 'psychological' fiction rather than stories with intricate plots. Take care to present a clean, well-typed submission."

$ THE KENYON REVIEW

102 W. Wiggin St., Finn House, Gambier OH 43022. (740)427-5208. Fax: (740)427-5417. E-mail: kenyonreview@kenyon.edu. Website: www.kenyonreview.org. **Contact:** Marlene Landefeld. An international journal of literature, culture and the arts dedicated to an inclusive representation of the best in new writing (fiction, poetry, essays, interviews, criticism) from established and emerging writers. Circ. 6,000.

- Work published in the *Kenyon Review* has been selected for inclusion in *The O. Henry Prize Stories, Pushcart Prize* anthologies, *Best American Short Stories,* and *Best American Poetry*.

Needs Excerpts from novels, condensed novels, ethnic/multicultural, experimental, feminist, gay, historical, humor/satire, lesbian, literary, mainstream, translations, contemporary. Receives 900 unsolicited mss/month. Unsolicited mss read only from September 15-January 15. Publishes ms 1 year after acceptance. Recently published work by Alice Hoffman, Beth Ann Fennelly, Romulus Linney, John Koethe, Albert Goldbarth, Erin McGraw.

How to Contact Only accepting mss via online submissions program. Please visit website for instructions. Do not submit via e-mail or snail mail. No simultaneous submissions. Sample copy $12 single issue, includes postage and handling. Please call or e-mail to order. Writer's guidelines online.

Payment/Terms Pays $15-40/page. Pays on publication for first rights.

Tips "We look for strong voice, unusual perspective, and power in the writing."

KEREM

Creative Explorations in Judaism, Jewish Study Center Press, 3035 Porter St. NW, Washington DC 20008. (202)364-3006. E-mail: langner@erols.com; kerem@simpatico.ca. Website: www.kerem.org. **Contact:** Gilah Langner, co-editor. Magazine: 6 × 9; 128 pages; 60 lb. offset paper; glossy cover; illustrations; photos. "Kerem publishes Jewish religious, creative, literary material—short stories, poetry, personal reflections, text study, prayers, rituals, etc." Estab. 1992.

Needs Jewish: feminist, humor/satire, literary, religious/inspirational. Receives 10-12 unsolicited mss/month. Accepts 1-2 mss/issue. Publishes ms 2-10 months after acceptance. **Publishes 2 new writers/year.** Also publishes literary essays, poetry.

How to Contact Prefers submissions by e-mail. Send SASE for reply, return of ms or send disposable copy of ms. Responds in 2 months to queries; 5 months to mss. Accepts simultaneous, multiple submissions. Sample copy for $8.50. Writer's guidelines online.

Payment/Terms Pays free subscription and 2-10 contributor's copies. Acquires one-time rights.

Tips "Should have a strong Jewish content. We want to be moved by reading the manuscript!"

$ THE KIT-CAT REVIEW

244 Halstead Ave., Harrison NY 10528. (914)835-4833. E-mail: kitcatreview@gmail.com. **Contact:** Claudia Fletcher, editor. Magazine: 8½ × 5½; 75 pages; laser paper; colored card cover stock; illustrations. "The Kit-Cat Review is named after the 18th Century Kit-Cat Club, whose members included Addison, Steele, Congreve, Vanbrugh and Garth. Its purpose is to promote/discover excellence and originality." The Kit-Cat Review is part of the collections of the University of Wisconsin (Madison) and State University of New York (Buffalo). Quarterly.

Needs Ethnic/multicultural, experimental, literary, novel excerpts, slice-of-life vignettes. No stories with "O. Henry-type formula endings. Shorter pieces stand a better chance of publication." No science fiction, fantasy, romance, horror or new age. Receives 40 unsolicited mss/month. Accepts 6 mss/issue; 24 mss/year. Time between acceptance and publication is 6 months. **Publishes 14 new writers/year.** Recently published work by Chayym Zeldis, Michael Fedo, Louis Phillips, Elisha Porat. Length: 5,000 words maximum; average length: 2,000 words. Publishes short shorts. Also publishes literary essays, literary criticism, poetry.

How to Contact Send complete ms. Accepts submissions by disk. Send SASE (or IRC) for return of ms, or send disposable copy of ms and #10 SASE for reply only. Responds in 1 week to queries; 2 months to mss. Accepts simultaneous, multiple submissions. Sample copy for $7 (payable to Claudia Fletcher). Writer's guidelines not available.

Payment/Terms Pays $25-200 and 2 contributor's copies; additional copies $5. Pays on publication for first rights.

LA KANCERKLINIKO

c/o Laurent Septier, 162 rue Paradis, P.O. Box 174, 13444 Marseille Cantini Cedex 6 France. (33) 2-48-61-81-98. Fax: (33) 2-48-61-81-98. E-mail: lseptier@hotmail.com. **Contact:** Laurent Septier. "An Esperanto magazine which appears 4 times annually. Each issue contains 32 pages. La Kancerkliniko is a political and cultural magazine." Quarterly. Circ. 300.

Needs Science fiction, short stories or very short novels. "The short story (or the very short novel) must be written only in Esperanto, either original or translation from any other language." Wants more science fiction. **Publishes 2-3 new writers/year.** Recently published work by Mao Zifu, Manuel de Seabra, Peter Brown and Aldo de'Giorgi.

How to Contact Accepts submissions by e-mail, fax. Accepts disk submissions. Accepts multiple submissions. Sample copy for 3 IRCs from Universal Postal Union.

Payment/Terms Pays in contributor's copies.

LAKE EFFECT

4951 College Dr., Erie PA 16563-1501. (814)898-6281. Fax: (814)898-6032. E-mail: goL1@psu.edu. Website: www.pserie.psu.edu/lakeeffect. **Contact:** George Looney, editor-in-chief. Magazine: 5½ × 8½; 180-200 pages; 55 lb. natural paper; 12 pt. C1S cover. "In addition to seeking strong, traditional stories, Lake Effect is open to more experimental, language-centered fiction as well." Annual. Estab. as Lake Effect, 2001; as Tempest, 1978. Member CLMP.

Needs Experimental, literary, mainstream. "No children's/juvenile, fantasy, science fiction, romance or young adult/teen." Receives 120 unsolicited mss/month. Accepts 5-9 mss/issue. Publishes ms 1 year after acceptance. **Publishes 6 new writers/year.** Recently published work by Edith Pearlman, Francois Camoin, Cris Mazza, Joan Connor, Aimee Parkison, Joanna Howard. Length: 4,500-5,000 words; average length: 2,600-3,900 words. Publishes short shorts. Also publishes literary essays, poetry.

How to Contact Send SASE for return of ms or send a disposable copy of ms and #10 SASE for reply only. Responds in 3 weeks to queries; 4-6 months to mss. Accepts simultaneous submissions. Sample copy for $6. Writer's guidelines for SASE.

Payment/Terms Pays 2 contributor's copies; additional copies $2. Acquires first, one-time rights. Not copyrighted.

Tips "We're looking for strong, well-crafted stories that emerge from character and language more than plot. The language is what makes a story stand out (and a strong sense of voice). Be sure to let us know immediately should a submitted story be accepted elsewhere."

LANDFALL/OTAGO UNIVERSITY PRESS

Otago University Press, P.O. Box 56, Dunedin New Zealand. Fax: (643)479-8385. E-mail: landfall@otago.ac.nz. **Contact:** Landfall Editor.

Needs Publishes fiction, poetry, commentary and reviews of New Zealand books.

How to Contact Send copy of ms with SASE. Sample copy not available.

Tips "We concentrate on publishing work by New Zealand writers, but occasionally accept work from elsewhere."

LAND-GRANT COLLEGE REVIEW

P.O. Box 1164, New York NY 10159-1164. E-mail: editors@lgcr.org. Website: www.lgcr.org. **Contact:** Fiction Submission. Magazine: 6 × 9; 196 pages; 70 lb. Natural Stock paper; 12 point cover stock. "The Land-Grant College Review is a nationally distributed literary journal. Recent contributors include Aimee Bender, Josip Novakovich, Robert Olmstead, Ron Carlson and Stephen Dixon." Annual. Estab. 2002. Circ. 4,000.

- Recent Stories in the magazine have been included in *O. Henry Prize Stories* and *Best American Non-Required Reading.*

Needs Literary. No genre fiction, humor for its own sake, or anything "cutesy-pooh." Accepts 16 mss/issue. Publishes ms 3-4 months after acceptance. Agented fiction 10%. **Publishes 2 new writers/year.** Recently published work by Aimee Bender, Josip Novakovich, Robert Olmstead, Ron Carlson, Arthur Bradford, Alan Chuese. Average length: 2,750 words. Publishes short shorts.

How to Contact Send complete ms. Responds in 6-8 months to mss. Accepts simultaneous submissions. Sample copy for $12. Writer's guidelines online.

Payment/Terms Pays in copies. Acquires first North American serial rights.

Tips "Read the magazine first and familiarize yourself with stories we've selected in the past. Send only your absolute best work."

THE LAUREL REVIEW

Northwest Missouri State University, Dept. of English, Maryville MO 64468. (660)562-1739. E-mail: tlr@nwmissouri.edu. Website: http://catpages.nwmissouri.edu/m/tlr. **Contact:** John Gallaher, Richard Black, or Brenda Lewis. Magazine: 6 × 9; 124-128 pages; good quality paper. "We publish poetry and fiction of high quality, from the traditional to the avant-garde. We are eclectic, open and flexible. Good writing is all we seek." Biannual. Estab. 1960. Circ. 900.

Needs Literary, contemporary. "No genre or politically polemical fiction." Receives 120 unsolicited mss/month. Accepts 3-5 mss/issue; 6-10 mss/year. Reading period: September 1-May 1. Publishes ms 1-12 months after acceptance. **Publishes 1-2 new writers/year.** Recently published work by Albert Goldbarth, Zachary Schomburg, Craig Morgan Teicher, and Ethan Paquin. Also publishes literary essays, poetry.

How to Contact Responds in 4 months to mss. No simultaneous submissions. Sample copy for $5.
Payment/Terms Pays 2 contributor's copies and 1 year subscription. Acquires first rights. Copyright reverts to author upon request.
Tips "Nothing really matters to us except our perception that the story presents something powerfully felt by the writer and communicated intensely to a serious reader. (We believe, incidentally, that comedy is just as serious a matter as tragedy, and we don't mind a bit if something makes us laugh out loud; we get too little that makes us laugh, in fact.) We try to reply promptly, though we don't always manage that. In short, we want good poems and good stories. We hope to be able to recognize them, and we print what we believe to the best work submitted."

THE LEDGE MAGAZINE

40 Maple Ave., Bellport NY 11713-2011. (631)219-5969. E-mail: tkmonaghan@aol.com. Website: www.theledgemagazine.com. **Contact:** Tim Monaghan, publisher. Literary magazine/journal: 6 x 9, 192 pages, offset paper, glossy stock cover. "The Ledge Magazine publishes cutting-edge contemporary fiction by emerging and established wirters." Annual. Estab. 1988. Circ. 1,000.
Needs Erotica, ethnic/multicultural (general), literary. Receives 90 mss/month. Accepts 6-8 mss/issue. Manuscript published 6 months after acceptance. Published Pia Chatterjee, Xujun Eberlein, Franny French, Clifford Garstang, Richard Jespers, Al Sims. Length: 2,500 words (min)-7,500 words (max). Average length: 6,000 words. Also publishes poetry. Rarely comments on/critiques rejected mss.
How to Contact Send complete ms with cover letter. Include estimated word count, brief bio. Responds to queries in 6 weeks. Responds to mss in 8 months. Send SASE (or IRC) for return of ms. Considers simultaneous submissions. Sample copy available for $10. Subscription: $20 (2 issues), $36 (4 issues). Guidelines available for SASE.
Payment/Terms Writers receive 1 contributor's copy. Additional copies $6. Pays on publication. Acquires first North American serial rights. Sends galleys to author. Publication is copyrighted.
Tips "We seek compelling stories that employ innovative language and complex characterization. We especially enjoy poignant stories with a sense of purpose. We dislike careless or hackneyed writing."

LE FORUM

University of Maine, Franco American Center, Orono ME 04469-5719. (207)581-3764. Fax: (207)581-1455. E-mail: lisa_michaud@umit.maine.edu. Website: www.francomaine.org. **Contact:** Lisa Michaud, managing editor. Magazine: 56 pages; illustrations; photos. Publication was founded to stimulate and recognize creative expression among Franco-Americans, all types of readers, including literary and working class. This publication is used in classrooms. Circulated internationally. Quarterly. Estab. 19 72. Circ. 5,000.
Needs "We will consider any type of short fiction, poetry and critical essays having to do with Franco-American experience. They must be of good quality in French or English. We are also looking for Canadian writers with French-North American experiences." Receives 10 unsolicited mss/month. Accepts 2-4 mss/issue. **Publishes some new writers/year.** Length: 750-2,500 words; average length: 1,000 words. Occasionally comments on rejected mss.
How to Contact Include SASE. Responds in 3 weeks to queries; 1 month to mss. Accepts simultaneous submissions and reprints. Sample copy not available.
Payment/Terms Pays 3 copies. Acquires one-time rights.
Tips "Write honestly. Start with a strongly felt personal Franco-American experience. If you make us feel what you have felt, we will publish it. We stress that this publication deals specifically with the Franco-American experience."

THE LISTENING EYE

Kent State University Geauga Campus, 14111 Claridon-Troy Rd., Burton OH 44021. (440)286-3840. E-mail: grace_butcher@msn.com. **Contact:** Grace Butcher, editor. Magazine: 5½ × 8½; 60 pages; photographs. "We publish the occasional very short stories (750 words/3 pages double spaced) in any subject and any style, but the language must be strong, unusual, free from cliché and vagueness. We are a shoestring operation from a small campus but we publish high-quality work." Annual. Estab. 1970. Circ. 250.

Needs Literary. "Pretty much anything will be considered except porn." Reads mss January 1-April 15 only. Publishes ms 3-4 months after acceptance. Recently published work by Elizabeth Scott, Sam Ruddick, H.E. Wright. Publishes short shorts. Also publishes poetry. Sometimes comments on rejected mss.

How to Contact Send SASE for return of ms or disposable copy of ms with SASE for reply only. Responds in 4 weeks to queries; 4 months to mss. Accepts reprint submissions. Sample copy for $3 and $1 postage. Writer's guidelines for SASE.

Payment/Terms Pays 2 contributor's copies; additional copies $3 with $1 postage. Pays on publication for one-time rights.

Tips "We look for powerful, unusual imagery, content and plot. Short, short."

☐ LITERAL LATTE

Word Sci, Inc., 200 East 10th Street Suite 240, New York NY 10003. (212)260-5532. E-mail: litlatte@aol.com. Website: www.literal-latte.com. **Contact:** Jeff Bockman, editor. "Publishes great writing in many flavors and styles. Literal Latte expanded the readership for literary magazines by offering free copies in New York coffeehouses and bookstores. Now online only and free to the world." Bimonthly. Estab. 1994. CLMP.

Needs Experimental, fantasy, literary, science fiction. Receives 4,000 unsolicited mss/month. Accepts 5-8 mss/issue; 40 mss/year. Agented fiction 1%. **Publishes 6 new writers/year.** Length: 500-8,000 words; average length: 4,000 words. Publishes short shorts. Often comments on rejected mss.

How to Contact Send SASE for return of mss or send a disposable copy of ms and e-mail for reply only. Responds in 6 months to mss. Accepts simultaneous, multiple submissions. Sample copy for $3. Writer's guidelines for SASE, e-mail or check website. Reviews fiction.

Payment/Terms Pays annual anthology. First rights. May request additional rights to put piece in annual anthology. Pays on publication for first, one-time rights. Sponsors awards/contests.

Tips "Keeping free thought free and challenging entertainment are not mutually exclusive. Words make a manuscript stand out, words beautifully woven together in striking and memorable patterns."

☐ ☒ THE LITERARY REVIEW

An International Journal of Contemporary Writing, 285 Madison Ave., Madison NJ 07940. (973)443-8564. Fax: (973)443-8364. E-mail: tlr@fdu.edu. Website: www.theliteraryreview.org. **Contact:** Minna Proctor, Editor-In-Chief. Magazine: 6 × 9; 200 pages; professionally printed on textpaper; semigloss card cover; perfect-bound. "Literary magazine specializing in fiction, poetry and essays with an international focus. Our audience is general with a leaning toward scholars, libraries and schools." Quarterly. Estab. 1957. Circ. 2,000.

- Work published in *The Literary Review* has been included in *Editor's Choice, Best American Short Stories* and *Pushcart Prize* anthologies.

Needs Works of high literary quality only. Does not want to see "overused subject matter or pat resolutions to conflicts." Receives 90-100 unsolicited mss/month. Accepts 20-25 mss/year. Does not read submissions June 1-September 1. Publishes ms 1-2 years after acceptance. Agented fiction 1-2%. **Publishes 80% new writers/year.** Recently published work by Irvin Faust, Todd James Pierce, Joshua Shapiro, Susan Schwartz Senstadt. Also publishes literary essays, literary criticism, poetry. Occasionally comments on rejected mss.

How to Contact Responds in 6-12 months to mss. Submit online at www.theliteraryreview.org/submit.html only. Accepts multiple submissions. Sample copy for $8. Writer's guidelines for SASE. Reviews fiction.

Payment/Terms Pays 2 contributor's copies; $4 discount for extras. Acquires first rights.

Tips "We want original dramatic situations with complex moral and intellectual resonance and vivid prose. We don't want versions of familiar plots and relationships. Too much of what we are seeing today is openly derivative in subject, plot and prose style. We pride ourselves on spotting new writers with fresh insight and approach."

☐ THE LONG STORY

18 Eaton St., Lawrence MA 01843. (978)686-7638. E-mail: rpburnham@mac.com. Website: web.me.com/rpburnham/Site/LongStory.html. **Contact:** R.P. Burnham. Magazine: 5½ × 8½; 160 pages; 60 lb. cover stock; illustrations (b&w graphics). For serious, educated, literary people. Annual. Circ. 600.

Needs Ethnic/multicultural, feminist, literary, contemporary. "No science fiction, adventure, romance, etc. We publish high literary quality of any kind but especially look for stories that have difficulty getting published elsewhere—committed fiction, working class settings, left-wing themes, etc." Receives 30-50 unsolicited mss/month. Accepts 6-7 mss/issue. Publishes ms 3 months to 1 year after acceptance. **Publishes 90% new writers/year.** Length: 8,000-20,000 words; average length: 8,000-12,000 words.

How to Contact Include SASE. Responds in 2 months to mss. Accepts simultaneous submissions "but not wild about it." Sample copy for $7.

Payment/Terms Pays 2 contributor's copies; $5 charge for extras. Acquires first rights.

Tips "Read us first and make sure submitted material is the kind we're interested in. Send clear, legible manuscripts. We're not interested in commercial success; rather we want to provide a place for long stories, the most difficult literary form to publish in our country."

◪ ◎ LOUISIANA LITERATURE

A Review of Literature and Humanities, SLU 792, Hammond LA 70402. Website: www.louisianaliterature.org. **Contact:** Jack B. Bedell, fiction editor. Magazine: 6 × 9; 150 pages; 70 lb. paper; card cover; illustrations. "Essays should be about Louisiana material; preference is given to fiction and poetry with Louisiana and Southern themes, but creative work can be set anywhere." Semiannual. Circ. 600 paid; 750-1,000 printed.

Needs Literary, mainstream, regional. "No sloppy, ungrammatical manuscripts." Receives 100 unsolicited mss/month. May not read mss June-July. Publishes ms 6-12 after acceptance. **Publishes 4 new writers/year.** Recently published work by Anthony Bukowski, Aaron Gwyn, Robert Phillips, R.T. Smith. Length: 1,000-6,000 words; average length: 3,500 words. Sometimes comments on rejected mss.

How to Contact Include SASE. Responds in 3 months to mss. Sample copy for $8. Reviews fiction.

Payment/Terms Pays usually in contributor's copies. Acquires one-time rights.

Tips "Cut out everything that is not a functioning part of the story. Make sure your manuscript is professionally presented. Use relevant specific detail in every scene. We love detail, local color, voice and craft. Any professional manuscript stands out."

◎ THE LOUISIANA REVIEW

P.O. Box 1129, Eunice LA 70535. (337)550-1315. E-mail: bfonteno@lsue.edu. Website: web.lsue.edu/la-review. **Contact:** Dr. Billy Fontenot, editor. Magazine: 812X512 bound; 100-200 pages; b&w illustrations. "We are looking for excellent work by Louisiana writers as well as those outside the state who tell us their connection to it. Non-Louisiana material is considered, but Louisiana/Gulf Coast themed work gets priority." Annual. Circ. 300-600.

Needs Ethnic/multicultural (Cajun or Louisiana culture), historical (Louisiana-related or setting), regional (Louisiana, Gulf Coast). Receives 25 unsolicited mss/month. Accepts 5-7 mss/issue. Reads year-round. Publishes ms 6-12 months after acceptance. Recently published work by Ronald Frame, Tom Bonner, Laura Cario, Sheryl St. Germaine. Length: up to 9,000 words; average length: 2,000 words. Publishes short shorts. Also publishes poetry and b&w artwork. Sometimes comments on rejected mss.

How to Contact Send SASE for return of ms. Responds in 5 weeks to queries; 10 weeks to mss. Accepts multiple submissions. Sample copy for $5.

Payment/Terms Pays 1 contributor's copy. Pays on publication for one-time rights. Not copyrighted but has an ISSN number.

Tips "We do like to have fiction play out visually as a film would rather than static and undramatized. Louisiana or Gulf Coast settings and themes preferred."

THE MACGUFFIN

18600 Haggerty Rd., Livonia MI 48152-2696. (734)462-4400, ext 5327. E-mail: macguffin@schoolcraft.edu. Website: www.macguffin.org. **Contact:** Steven A. Dolgin, editor; Nicholle Cormier, managing editor; Elizabeth Kircos, fiction editor. Magazine: 6 × 9; 160 pages; 60 lb. paper; 110 lb. cover; b&w illustrations, photos. "*The MacGuffin* is a literary magazine which publishes a range of material including poetry, creative nonfiction, fiction, and art. Material ranges from traditional to experimental. Our periodical attracts a variety of people with many different interests." Triannual. Circ. 500.

Needs Adventure, ethnic/multicultural, experimental, historical (general), humor/satire, literary, mainstream, translations, contemporary, prose poem. "No religious, inspirational, juvenile, romance, horror, pornography." Receives 80-100 unsolicited mss/month. Accepts 14-18 mss/issue; 42-54 mss/year. Publishes ms 6 months to 1.5 years after acceptance. Agented fiction 10-15%. **Publishes 30 new writers/year.** Recently published work by Thomas Lynch, Linda Nemec Foster, Jim Daniels, M. E. Parker, and Daniel Pearlman. Length: 100-5,000 words; average length: 2,000-2,500 words. Publishes short shorts. Also publishes literary essays. Occasionally comments on rejected mss.

How to Contact Send SASE or e-mail. Responds in 4-6 months to mss. Sample copy for $6; current issue for $9. Writer's guidelines free on website or with SASE. Pays 2 contributor's copies. Acquires one-time rights.

Tips "We strive to give promising new writers the opportunity to publish alongside recognized writers. Follow the submission guidelines, proofread your work, and be persistent. When we reject a story, we may accept the next one you send. When we make suggestions for a rewrite, we may accept the revision. Make your characters come to life. Even the most ordinary people become fascinating if they live for your readers."

THE MADISON REVIEW

600 N. Park St., University of Wisconsin, 6193 Helen C. White Hall, Madison WI 53706. E-mail: madisonreview@gmail. Website: www.english.wisc.edu/madisonreview. **Contact:** Fiction Editor. Magazine: 6 × 9; 180 pages. "We are an independent literary journal featuring quality fiction, poetry, artwork and interviews. Both established and emerging writers are encouraged to submit." Semiannual. Circ. 1,000.

Needs "Well-crafted, compelling fiction featuring a wide range of styles and subjects." Receives 300 unsolicited mss/period. Accepts 6 mss/issue. Does not read May-September. Publishes ms 4 months after acceptance. **Publishes 4 new writers/year.** Recently published work by Lori Rader Day and Ian Williams. Average length: 4,000 words. Also publishes poetry.

How to Contact Accepts multiple submissions. Sample copy for $4 via postal service or e-mail.

Payment/Terms Pays 2 contributor's copies; $5 charge for extras. Acquires first North American serial rights.

$ THE MALAHAT REVIEW

P.O. Box 1700, STN CSC, Victoria BC V8W 2Y2 Canada. (250)721-8524. E-mail: malahat@uvic.ca. Website: www.malahatreview.ca. **Contact:** John Barton, editor. "We try to achieve a balance of views and styles in each issue. We strive for a mix of the best writing by both established and new writers." Quarterly. Estab. 1967. Circ. 1,700.

- *The Malahat Review* has received Canada's National Magazine Award for poetry and fiction.

Needs "General fiction, poetry, and creative nonfiction." Accepts 3-4 fiction mss/issue and 1 creative nonfiction ms/issue. Publishes ms within 6 months after acceptance. **Publishes 4-5 new writers/year.** Recently published work by Bill Gaston, Daryl Hine, Jan Zwicky, Stephen Henighan.

How to Contact Send complete ms. "Enclose proper Canadian postage on the SASE (or send IRC)." Responds in 2 weeks to queries; approx. 3 months to mss. No simultaneous submissions. Sample copy for $16.45 (US). Writer's guidelines online.
Payment/Terms Pays $40 CAD/magazine page. Pays on acceptance for second serial (reprint), first world rights.
Tips "We do encourage new writers to submit. Read the magazines you want to be published in, ask for their guidelines and follow them. Check website for information on *Malahat's*novella competition, *Far Horizons for Short Fiction* award, and creative nonfiction award."

$ MANOA

A Pacific Journal of International Writing, English Dept., University of Hawaii, Honolulu HI 96822. (808)956-3070. Fax: (808)956-3083. E-mail: mjournal-l@hawaii.edu. Website: http://manoajournal.hawaii.edu. **Contact:** Frank Stewart, Poetry Editor. Magazine: 7 × 10; 240 pages. Most of each issue devoted to new work from Pacific and Asian nations, including high quality literary fiction, poetry, essays, personal narrative. Please see website for current projects. Authors should query before sending submissions. Semiannual.

- *Manoa*has received numerous awards, and work published in the magazine has been selected for prize anthologies. See website for recently published issues.

How to Contact Please query first before sending in mss. Include SASE. Does not accept submissions by e-mail. Sample copy for $20 (U.S.). Writer's guidelines online.
Payment/Terms Pays $100-500 normally ($25/printed page). Pays on publication for first North American serial, non-exclusive, one-time print rights. Sends galleys to author.

MARGINALIA

Communication Arts, Language and Literature Department of Western State College of Colorado, P.O. Box 258, Pitkin CO 81241. (970) 642-0393. E-mail: marginaliajournal@gmail.com. Website: www.marginaliajournal.com. **Contact:** Alicita Rodriguez, editor. Annual literary magazine/journal. 6 × 9, 150 pages, 100 lb paper. "We like writing that pays close attention to the sentence. Language is not a means to an end. It should not be something that gets used solely to establish plot. We want gorgeous diction, unusual and striking imagery, reversed and playful syntax. We don't want to remember what the story or poem is about; we want to remember how it's told. We welcome any hybrid or unidentifiable genres, though we shun experimentation for experimentation's sake. We don't want work that depends on clever jokes or conceits. We like the odd but well-written traditional story, though we don't see too many of these. No gratuitous violence (especially against women and animals)."
Needs Experimental, literary. Does not want mainstream or genre fiction. List of upcoming themes available on Web site. Receives 40 mss/month. Accepts 20 mss/issue; 20 mss/year. Ms published 6-9 months after acceptance. Publishes 15% new writers/year. Published Brian Evenson, Laird Hunt, Mark Irwin, Steve Katz, Alex Lemon, Harry Matthews, Gina Ochsner, Lance Olsen, George Singleton, Abdelkrim Tabal, Wendy Walker, and Tom Whalen. Average length: 2,000 words. Publishes short shorts. Also publishes literary essays, book reviews, poetry, visual art. Send review copies to P.O. Box 258, Pitkin CO 81241. Sometimes comments on/critiques rejected mss.
How to Contact How to Contact: Submit full ms via email to marginaliajournal@gmail.com or by mail to P.O. Box 258, Pitkin CO 81241. Include estimated word count, brief bio, list of publications. Responds to mss in 6-9 months. Considers simultaneous submissions, multiple submissions. Sample copy available for $9. Sample copy, guidelines available on Web Site: www.marginaliajournal.com. Payment/Terms: Writers receive 3 contributor's copies. Additional copies $5. Pays on acceptance. Acquires first rights. Sends galleys to author. Publication is copyrighted. No contests at this time.

$ THE MASSACHUSETTS REVIEW

University of Massachusetts, South College, Amherst MA 01003-9934. Website: www.massreview.org. **Contact:** Fiction Editor. Magazine: 6 × 9; 172 pages; 52 lb. paper; 65 lb. vellum cover; illustrations; photos. Quarterly. Circ. 1,200.

- Stories from *The Massachusetts Review* have been anthologized in the *100 Best American Short Stories of the Century* and the *Pushcart Prize* anthology.

Needs Short stories. Wants more prose less than 30 pages. Does not read fiction mss May 2-September 30. Publishes ms 18 months after acceptance. Agented fiction Approximately 5%. **Publishes 3-5 new writers/year.** Recently published work by Ahdaf Soueif, Elizabeth Denton, Nicholas Montemarano. Also publishes poetry. Sometimes comments on rejected mss.
How to Contact Send complete ms electronically or by mail. **If submitting online, there is a $3 submission fee**. No returned ms without SASE. Responds in 3 months to mss. Accepts simultaneous, multiple submissions. Sample copy for $8. Writer's guidelines online.
Payment/Terms Pays $50. Pays on publication for first North American serial rights.
Tips "Shorter rather than longer stories preferred (up to 28-30 pages)." Looks for works that "stop us in our tracks." Manuscripts that stand out use "unexpected language, idiosyncrasy of outlook and are the opposite of ordinary."

☐ METAL SCRATCHES

P.O. Box 685, Forest Lake MN 55025. E-mail: metalscratches@aol.com. **Contact:** Kim Mark, editor. Magazine: 5½ × 8½; 35 pages; heavy cover-stock. "Metal Scratches focuses on literary fiction that examines the dark side of humanity. We are not looking for anything that is 'cute' or 'sweet'." Semiannual. Estab. 2000.
Needs Experimental, horror (psychological), literary. "No poetry, science fiction, rape, murder or horror as in gore." Receives 20 unsolicited mss/month. Accepts 5-6 mss/issue; 20 mss/year. Publishes ms 6 months after acceptance. **Publishes 3 new writers/year.** Length: 3,500 words; average length: 3,000 words. Publishes short shorts. Sometimes comments on rejected mss.
How to Contact Send complete ms. Accepts submissions by e-mail. (No attachments.) Send disposable copy of ms and #10 SASE for reply only. Responds in 1 month to mss. Accepts simultaneous, multiple submissions. Sample copy for $5. Writer's guidelines for SASE or by e-mail.
Payment/Terms Pays 2 contributor's copies and one year subscription; additional copies for $3. Pays on publication for one-time rights. Not copyrighted.
Tips "Clean manuscripts prepared according to guidelines are a must. Send us something new and inventive. Don't let rejections from any editor scare you. Keep writing and keep submitting."

$ ☒ MICHIGAN QUARTERLY REVIEW

0576 Rackham Bldg., 915 E. Washington, University, Ann Arbor MI 48109-1070. (734)764-9265. E-mail: mqr@umich.edu. Website: www.umich.edu/~mqr. "An interdisciplinary journal which publishes mainly essays and reviews, with some high-quality fiction and poetry, for an intellectual, widely read audience." Quarterly. Circ. 1,500.

- Stories from *Michigan Quarterly Review* have been selected for inclusion in *The Best American Short Stories, The O. Henry Prize Stories* and *Pushcart Prize* volumes.

Needs Literary. "No genre fiction written for a market. Would like to see more fiction about social, political, cultural matters, not just centered on a love relationship or dysfunctional family." Receives 200 unsolicited mss/month. Accepts 2 mss/issue; 8 mss/year. Publishes ms 1 year after acceptance. **Publishes 1-2 new writers/year.** Recently published work by Robert Boyers, Laura Kasischke, Herbert Gold, Alice Mattison, Joyce Carol Oates, Vu Tran. Length: 1,500-7,000 words; average length: 5,000 words. Also publishes literary essays, poetry.
How to Contact Send complete ms. "I like to know if a writer is at the beginning, or further along, in his or her career. Don't offer plot summaries of the story, though a background comment is welcome." Include SASE. Responds in 2 months to queries; 6 weeks to mss. No simultaneous submissions. Sample copy for $4. Writer's guidelines online.
Payment/Terms Pays $10/published page. Pays on publication. Buys first serial rights. Sponsors awards/contests.
Tips "There's no beating a good plot, interesting characters and a fresh use of the English language. (Most stories fail because they're written in such a bland manner, or in TV-speak.) Be ambitious, try to involve the social world in the personal one, be aware of what the best writing of today

is doing, don't be satisfied with a small slice-of-life narrative but think how to go beyond the ordinary."

MID-AMERICAN REVIEW

Department of English, Bowling Green State University, Bowling Green OH 43403. E-mail: mikeczy@bgnet.bgsu.edu. Website: www.bgsu.edu/midamericanreview. **Contact:** Michael Czyzniejewski, fiction editor. Magazine: 6 × 9; 232 pages; 60 lb. bond paper; coated cover stock. "We try to put the best possible work in front of the biggest possible audience. We publish serious fiction and poetry, as well as critical studies in contemporary literature, translations and book reviews." Semiannual.

Needs Experimental, literary, translations, memoir, prose poem, traditional. "No genre fiction. Would like to see more short shorts." Receives 700 unsolicited mss/month. Accepts 4-8 mss/issue. Publishes ms 6 months after acceptance. Agented fiction 5%. **Publishes 4-8 new writers/year.** Recently published work by Matthew Eck, Becky Hagentson, and Kevin Wilson. Occasionally comments on rejected mss.

How to Contact Send complete ms with SASE. Responds in 4 months to mss. Sample copy for $9 (current issue), $5 (back issue); rare back issues $10. Writer's guidelines online. Reviews fiction.

Payment/Terms Pays $10/page up to $50, pending funding. Pays on publication when funding is available. Acquires first North American serial, one-time rights. Sponsors awards/contests.

Tips "We look for well-written stories that make the reader want to read on past the first line and page. Clicheé themes and sloppy writing turn us off immediately. Read literary journals to see what's being published in today's market. We tend to publish work that is more non-traditional in style and subject, but are open to all literary non-genre submissions."

MINNETONKA REVIEW

Minnetonka Review Press, LLC, P.O. Box 386, Spring Park MN 55384. Website: www.minnetonkareview.com. **Contact:** Troy Ehlers, editor-in-chief. Minnetonka Review Press, LLC, P.O. Box 386, Spring Park MN 55384. E-mail: query@minnetonkareview.com. Website: www.minnetonkareview.com. **Contact:** Troy Ehlers, Editor-in-Chief. Literary magazine/journal. 6x9, 200 pages, recycled natural paper, glossy cover. Contains illustrations. Includes photographs. "We publish work of literary excellence. We are particularly attracted to fiction with careful prose, engaging and tension filled stories, and new perspectives, forms and styles." Semiannual. Estab. 2007. Circ. 1,000.

Needs Literary, mainstream. Receives 100 mss/month. Accepts 7 mss/issue; 15 mss/year. Does not read during the summer between May 15th and October 15th. Ms published 6-8 months after acceptance. **Publishes 6 new writers/year.** Published Bev Jafek, Daniel DiStasio, Nathan Leslie, Robin Lippincott, Megan Cass, Arthur Saltzman, Gary Amdahl, and Arthur Winfield Knight. Length: 1,200 words (min)-6,000 words (best). Will accept up to 10,00 words but must be outstanding. Average length: 4,000 words. Publishes short shorts. Average length of short shorts: 1,200 words. Also publishes literary essays, poetry. Rarely comments on/critiques rejected mss.

How to Contact Send complete ms with cover letter. Accepts submissions by mail or by submission manager online. Include brief bio. Responds to queries in 2 weeks. Responds to mss in 4 months. Send either SASE (or IRC) for return of ms or disposable copy of ms and #10 SASE for reply only. Considers simultaneous submissions. Sample copy available for $9. Guidelines available for SASE, via e-mail, on website.

Payment/Terms Writers receive 3 contributor's copies. Additional copies $7. Pays on publication. Acquires first North American serial rights. Publication is copyrighted. "Two authors from each issue receive a $150 Editor's Prize. Other contests with $1,000 prize are held from time to time. Details are available on our website."

Tips "The trick seems to be holding our attention, whether via novelty, language, style, story, good descriptions or tension. Always be honing your craft, reading and writing. And when you read, it helps to be familiar with what we publish, but in general, you should be reading a number of literary journals and anthologies. Think of your work as a contribution to a greater literary dialogue."

MISSISSIPPI REVIEW

118 College Dr. #5144, Hattiesburg MS 39406-0001. (601)266-4321. Fax: (601)266-5757. E-mail: rief@mississippireview.com. Website: www.mississippireview.com. **Contact:** Rie Fortenberry, managing editor. Semiannual. Circ. 1,500.

Needs Annual fiction and poetry competition. $1,000 awarded in each category plus publication of all winners and finalists. Fiction entries 5,000 words or less. Poetry entry equals 1-3 poems, page limit is 10. $15 entry fee includes copy of prize issue. No limit on number of entries. Deadline October 1. No mss returned. **Publishes 25-30 new writers/year.**

How to Contact Sample copy for $8. Writer's guidelines online.

Payment/Terms Acquires first North American serial rights.

$ THE MISSOURI REVIEW

357 McReynolds Hall, University of Missouri, Columbia MO 65211. E-mail: question@moreview.com. Website: www.missourireview.com. Magazine: 6¾ × 10; 200 pages. "We publish contemporary fiction, poetry, interviews, personal essays, cartoons, special features for the literary and the general reader interested in a wide range of subjects." Circ. 5,500.

- This magazine had stories anthologized in the *Pushcart Prize, Best American Short Stories, The O. Henry Prize Stories, Best American Essays, Best American Mystery Stories, Best American Nature and Science Writing, Best American Erotica,* and *New Stories from The South.*

Needs Literary fiction on all subjects, novel excerpts. Word count is best if between 2,000 and 30,000 words; shorter or longer must be truly exceptional to be published. No genre fiction. Receives 500 unsolicited mss/month. Accepts 5-7 mss/issue; 16-20 mss/year. **Publishes 6-10 new writers/year.** Recently published work by Nat Akin, Jennifer Bryan, Bruce Ducker, William Lychack, Cynthia Morrison Phoel. Also publishes literary essays, poetry. Often comments on rejected mss.

How to Contact Send complete ms. May include brief bio and list of publications. Send SASE for reply, return of ms or send disposable copy of ms. **Online submissions via website with a $3 charge**. Responds in 2 weeks to queries; 12 weeks to mss. Writer's guidelines online.

Payment/Terms Pays $30/printed page up to $750. Offers signed contract. Sponsors awards/contests.

MOBIUS

The Journal of Social Change, 505 Christianson, Madison WI 53714. (608)242-1009. E-mail: fmschep@charter.net. Website: www.mobiusmagazine.com. **Contact:** Fred Schepartz, editor. Magazine: 8½ × 11; 16-24 pages; 60 lb. paper; 60 lb. cover. "Looking for fiction which uses social change as either a primary or secondary theme. This is broader than most people think. Need social relevance in one way or another. For an artistically and politically aware and curious audience." Quarterly.

Needs Ethnic/multicultural, experimental, fantasy, feminist, gay, historical, horror, humor/satire, lesbian, literary, mainstream, science fiction, contemporary, prose poem. "No porn, no racist, sexist or any other kind of -ist. No Christian or spirituality proselytizing fiction." Wants to see more science fiction, erotica "assuming it relates to social change." Receives 15 unsolicited mss/month. Accepts 3-5 mss/issue. Publishes ms 3-9 months after acceptance. **Publishes 10 new writers/year.** Recently published work by Margaret Karmazin, Benjamin Reed, John Tuschen, Ken Byrnes. Length: 500-5,000 words; average length: 3,500 words. Publishes short shorts. Always comments on rejected mss.

How to Contact Include SASE. Responds in 4 weeks to mss. Accepts reprints, but no multiple or simultaneous submissions." Sample copy for $2, 9 × 12 SAE and 3 first class stamps. Writer's guidelines for SASE.

Payment/Terms Acquires one-time electronic rights as well as archival rights. All rights revert back to author after publication.

Tips "Note that fiction and poetry may be simultaneously published in e-version of Mobius. Due to space constraints of print version, some works may be accepted in e-version, but not print version. We like high impact, we like plot and character-driven stories that function like theater of the mind. Looks for first and foremost, good writing. Prose must be crisp and polished; the story must pique my interest and make me care due to a certain intellectual, emotional aspect. Second, *Mobius* is about social change. We want stories that make some statement about the society we live in, either on a macro or micro level. Not that your story neeeds to preach from a soapbox (actually, we prefer that it doesn't), but your story needs to have *something* to say."

NERVE COWBOY

P.O. Box 4973, Austin TX 78765. Website: jwhagins.com/nervecowboy.html. **Contact:** Joseph Shields or Jerry Hagins. Magazine: 7 × 8½; 64 pages; 20 lb. paper; card stock cover; illustrations. "Nerve Cowboy publishes adventurous, comical, disturbing, thought-provoking, accessible poetry and fiction. We like to see work sensitive enough to make the hardest hard-ass cry, funny enough to make the most helpless brooder laugh and disturbing enough to make us all glad we're not the author of the piece." Semiannual. Estab. 1996. Circ. 400.

Needs Literary. No "racist, sexist or overly offensive work. Wants more unusual stories with rich description and enough twists and turns that leave the reader thinking." Receives 40 unsolicited mss/month. Accepts 2-3 mss/issue; 4-6 mss/year. Publishes ms 6-12 months after acceptance. **Publishes 5-10 new writers/year.** Recently published work by Lori Jakiela, Michele Anne Jaquays, Tom Schmidt, David Elsey, Michael A. Flanagan. Length: 1,500 words; average length: 750-1,000 words. Publishes short shorts. Also publishes poetry.

How to Contact Send SASE for reply, return of ms or send a disposable copy of ms. Responds in 6 weeks to queries; 3 months to mss. Accepts reprint submissions. No simultaneous submissions. Sample copy for $6. Writer's guidelines for #10 SASE or online.

Payment/Terms Pays 1 contributor's copy. Acquires one-time rights.

Tips "We look for writing which is very direct and elicits a visceral reaction in the reader. Read magazines you submit to in order to get a feel for what the editors are looking for. Write simply and from the gut."

NEW COLLAGE

New College of Florida, New College of Florida, c/o WRC, 5800 Bayshore Rd., Sarasota FL 34243. E-mail: newcollagemag@gmail.com. Website: newcollagemag.wordpress.com. **Contact:** Alexis Orgera, editor.

Needs "We choose well-written, thought-provoking short fiction. A ms stands out if it interacts with the theme of collage and/or if it has a compelling voice all its own. We like to be surprised by voice and language." Do not send any genre fiction (fantasy, horror, religious, erotic, etc.).

How to Contact E-mail no more than 1500 words in a single Word document. "Do not submit again until you've heard back." Note "submission" in the subject line, as well as the type of work you're submitting." Accepts simultaneous submissions. Reads September-May. Responds in 2-6 months.

Payment/Terms Acquires first serial rights, print and online. All rights revert to author upon publication. Author receives 2 contributor copies.

$ NEW LETTERS

University House, 5101 Rockhill Rd., Kansas City MO 64110-2499. (816)235-1168. Fax: (816)235-2611. E-mail: newletters@umkc.edu. Website: www.newletters.org. **Contact:** Robert STewart, editor-in-chief. Magazine: 6X9, 14 lb. cream paper; illustrations. "New Letters is intended for the general literary reader. We publish literary fiction, nonfiction, essays, poetry. We also publish art." Quarterly. Circ. 2,500.

Needs Ethnic/multicultural, experimental, humor/satire, literary, mainstream, translations, contemporary. No genre fiction. Does not read mss May 1-October 1. Publishes ms 5 months after acceptance. Recently published work by Thomas E. Kennedy, Sheila Kohler, Charlotte Holmes, Rosellen Brown, Janet Burroway. Publishes short shorts. Average length is 3,000-5,000 words.

How to Contact Send complete ms. Do not submit by e-mail. Responds in 1 month to queries; 3 months to mss. "We discourage multiple submissions but appreciate being told if you are simultaneously submitting your work to us and other magazines; we expect to be notified immediately if the work you sent us has been accepted for publication elsewhere." Sample copy for $10 or sample articles on website. Writer's guidelines online.

Payment/Terms Pays $30-75 for fiction and $15 for single poem. Pays on publication for first North American serial rights. Sends galleys to author. $4,500 awarded annually in writing contest for short fiction, essay, and poetry. Visit www.newletters.org for contest guidelines.

Tips "Seek publication of representative chapters in high-quality magazines as a way to the book contract. Try literary magazines first."

NEW MADRID

Murray State University, 7C Faculty Hall, Murray KY 42071. (270)809-4730. E-mail: newmadrid@murraystate.edu. Website: newmadridjournal.org. **Contact:** Ann Neelon, editor. Literary magazine/journal: 160 pages. "New Madrid is the national journal of the low-residency MFA program at Murray State University. It takes its name from the New Madrid seismic zone, which falls within the central Mississippi Valley and extends through western Kentucky." Semiannual. Circ.1,000.

Needs Literary. See website for guidelines and upcoming themes. "We have two reading periods, one from August 15-October 15, and one from January 15-March 15." Also publishes poetry and creative nonfiction. Rarely comments on/critiques rejected mss.

How to Contact Accepts submissions by Online Submissions Manager only. Include brief bio, list of publications. Considers multiple submissions. Guidelines available on website.

Payment/Terms Pays 2 contributor's copies on publication. Acquires first North American serial rights. Publication is copyrighted.

Tips "Quality is the determining factor for breaking into *New Madrid*. We are looking for well-crafted, compelling writing in a range of genres, forms and styles."

$ NEW MILLENNIUM WRITINGS

New Messenger Writing and Publishing, P.O. Box 2463, Knoxville TN 37901. (865)428-0389. E-mail: donwilliams7@charter.net. Website: http://newmillenniumwritings.com. **Contact:** Don Williams, editor. Annual anthology. 6 × 9, 204 pages, 50 lb. white paper, glossy 4-color cover. Contains illustrations. Includes photographs. "Superior writing is the sole criterion." Annual. Circ. 3,000. Received Golden Presscard Award from Sigma Delta Chi (1997)

Needs "While we only accept general submissions January-March, we hold four contests twice each year for all types of fiction, nonfiction, short-short fiction and poetry." Receives average of 200 mss/month. Accepts 60 mss/year. Manuscript published 6 months to one year after acceptance. Agented fiction 0%. Publishes 10 new writers/year. Published Charles Wright, Ted Kooser, Allen Wier, Lucille Clifton, John Updike, and Don Williams. Length: 200 words (min)-6,000 words (max). Average length: 4,000 words for fiction. Publishes short shorts. Also publishes literary essays, poetry. Rarely comments on/critiques rejected manuscripts.

How to Contact Accepts ms through biannual *New Millennium Writing* Awards only. Visit website for more information.

Payment/Terms See listing for *New Millennium Writing* Awards in Contests & Awards section.

Tips "Looks for originality, accessibility, musicality, psychological insight, moral sensibility. E-mail for list of writing tips or send SASE. No charge."

NEW ORLEANS REVIEW

Box 195, Loyola University, New Orleans LA 70118. (504)865-2295. Fax: (504)865-2294. E-mail: noreview@loyno.edu. Website: http://neworleans.org. **Contact:** Christopher Chambers, editor. Journal: 6 × 9; perfect bound; 200 pages; photos. "Publishes poetry, fiction, translations, photographs, nonfiction on literature, art and film. Readership: those interested in contemporary literature and culture." Biannual. Estab. 1968. Circ. 1,500.

- Work from the *New Orleans Review* has been anthologized in *New Stores from The South* and the *Pushcart Prize Anthology. Best American Non required reading, Best American Poetry, O. Henry Prize Anthology*.

Needs "Quality fiction from conventional to experimental." **Publishes 12 new writers/year.** Recently published work by Gordon Lish, Michael Martone, Dylan Landis, Stephen Graham Jones, Carolyn Sanchez and Josh Russell.

How to Contact Responds in 4-6 months to mss. Accepts simultaneous submissions "if we are notified immediately upon acceptance elsewhere." Sample copy for $5. Reviews fiction. Pays 2 copies.
Payment/Terms Pays $25-50 and 2 copies. Pays on publication for first North American serial rights.
Tips "We're looking for dynamic writing that demonstrates attention to the language, and a sense of the medium, writing that engages, surprises, moves us. We're not looking for genre fiction, or academic articles. We subscribe to the belief that in order to truly write well, one must first master the rudiments: grammar and syntax, punctuation, the sentence, the paragraph, the line, the stanza. We receive about 3,000 manuscripts a year, and publish about 3% of them. Check out a recent issue, send us your best, proofread your work, be patient, be persistent."

NEW SOUTH

Georgia State University, Campus P.O. Box 1894, MSC 8R0322 Unit 8, Atlanta GA 30303-3083. (404) 413-5874. Fax: (404) 413-5830. Website: www.review.gsu.edu. **Contact:** Prose Editor. Literary journal. "New South is a biannual literary magazine publishing poetry, fiction, creative nonfiction, and visual art. We're looking for original voices and well-written manuscripts. No subject or form biases." Biannual.
Needs Literary fiction and creative nonfiction. Receives 200 unsolicited mss/month. Publishes and welcomes short shorts.
How to Contact Include SASE for notification. Responds in 3-5 months. Sample copy for $5. Writer's guidelines for SASE or on website.
Payment/Terms Pays in contributor's copy. Acquires one-time rights.

THE NEW WRITER

P.O. Box 60, Cranbrook TN17 2ZR United Kingdom. 01580 212626. E-mail: editor@thenewwriter.com; admin@thenewwriter.com. Website: www.thenewwriter.com. **Contact:** Suzanne Ruthven, editor. Magazine: A4; 56 pages; illustrations; photos. Contemporary writing magazine which publishes "the best in fact, fiction and poetry." Publishes 6 issues per annum. Estab. 1996. Circ. 1,500.
Needs "We will consider most categories apart from stories written for children. No horror, erotic or cosy fiction." Accepts 4 mss/issue; 24 mss/year. Publishes ms 1 year after acceptance. Agented fiction 5%. **Publishes 12 new writers/year.** Recently published work by Sally Zigmond, Lorna Dowell, Wes Lee, Amy Licence, Cathy Whitfield, Katy Darby, Clio Gray. Length: 2,000-5,000 words; average length: 3,500 words. Publishes short shorts. Also publishes literary essays, literary criticism, poetry. Often comments on rejected mss.
How to Contact Query with published clips. Accepts submissions by e-mail, fax. Send SASE (or IRC) for return of ms or send a disposable copy of ms and #10 SASE for reply only. "We consider short stories from subscribers only but we may also commission guest writers." Responds in 2 months to queries; 4 months to mss. Accepts simultaneous submissions. Sample copy for SASE and A4 SAE with IRCs only. Writer's guidelines for SASE. Reviews fiction.
Payment/Terms Pays £10 per story by credit voucher; additional copies for £1.50. Pays on publication for one-time rights. Sponsors awards/contests.
Tips "Hone it—always be prepared to improve the story. It's a competitive market."

NIMROD

International Journal of Prose and Poetry, 800 S. Tucker Dr., Tulsa OK 74104-3189. (918)631-3080. Fax: (918)631-3033. E-mail: nimrod@utulsa.edu. Website: www.utulsa.edu/nimrod/. **Contact:** Gerry McLoud, fiction editor. Magazine: 6 × 9; 192 pages; 60 lb. white paper; illustrations; photos. "We publish one thematic issue and one awards issue each year. A recent theme was 'Crossing Borders,' a compilation of poetry and prose from all over the world. We seek vigorous, imaginative, quality writing. Our mission is to discover new writers and publish experimental writers who have not yet found a 'home' for their work." Semiannual. Circ. 3,000.
Needs "We accept contemporary poetry and/or prose. May submit adventure, ethnic, experimental,

prose poem or translations. No science fiction or romance." Receives 120 unsolicited mss/month. **Publishes 5-10 new writers/year.** Recently published work by Felicia Ward, Ellen Bass, Jeanette Turner Hospital, Kate Small. Also publishes poetry.

How to Contact SASE for return of ms. Accepts queries by e-mail. Does not accept submissions by e-mail unless the writer is living outside the U.S. Responds in 5 months to mss. Accepts simultaneous, multiple submissions.

Payment/Terms Pays 2 contributor's copies.

Tips "We have not changed our fiction needs: quality, vigor, distinctive voice. We have, however, increased the number of stories we print. See current issues. We look for fiction that is fresh, vigorous, distinctive, serious and humorous, unflinchingly serious, ironic—whatever. Just so it is quality. Strongly encourage writers to send #10 SASE for brochure for annual literary contest with prizes of $1,000 and $2,000."

$ THE NORTH AMERICAN REVIEW

University of Northern Iowa, 1222 West 27th St., Cedar Falls IA 50614-0516. Website: www.northamericanreview.org. "The NAR is the oldest literary magazine in America and one of the most respected. Though we have no prejudices about the subject matter of material sent to us, our first concern is quality." Bimonthly. Estab. 1815. Circ. under 5,000.

- Works published in *The North American Review* have won the Pushcart Prize.

Needs Open (literary). "No flat narrative stories where the inferiority of the character is the paramount concern." Wants to see more "well-crafted literary stories that emphasize family concerns. We'd also like to see more stories engaged with environmental concerns." Reads fiction mss all year. Publishes ms an average of 1 year after acceptance. **Publishes 2 new writers/year.** Recently published work by Lee Ann Roripaugh, Dick Allen, Rita Welty Bourke.

How to Contact Accepts submissions by USPS mail only. Send complete ms with SASE. Responds in 3 months to queries; 4 months to mss. No simultaneous submissions. Sample copy for $5. Writer's guidelines online.

Payment/Terms Pays $5/350 words; $20 minimum, $100 maximum. Pays on publication for first North American serial, first rights.

Tips "Stories that do not condescend to the reader or their character are always appealing to us. We also like stories that have characters doing things (acting upon the world instead of being acted upon). We also like a strong narrative arc. Stories tnat are mainly about language need not apply. Your first should be your second best line. Your last sentence should be your best. Everything in the middle should approach the two."

NORTH CAROLINA LITERARY REVIEW

A Magazine of North Carolina Literature, Culture, and History, English Dept., East Carolina University, Greenville NC 27858-4353. E-mail: BauerM@ecu.edu. Website: www.ecu.edu/nclr. **Contact:** Margaret D. Bauer, editor. "Articles should have a North Carolina literature slant. First consideration is always for quality of work. Although we treat academic and scholarly subjects, we do not wish to see jargon-laden prose; our readers, we hope, are found as often in bookstores and libraries as in academia. We seek to combine the best elements of a magazine for serious readers with the best of a scholarly journal." Annual. Circ. 750.

Needs Regional (North Carolina). Must be North Carolina related—either a North Carolina-connected writer or set in North Carolina. Publishes ms 1 year after acceptance. 2011 theme: Environmental Writing in North Carolina.

How to Contact Accepts submissions via online submissions manager. Responds in 1 month to queries; within 6 months to mss. Sample copy for $10-25. Writer's guidelines online.

Payment/Terms Pays on publication for first North American serial rights. Rights returned to writer on request.

NORTH CENTRAL REVIEW, YOUR UNDERGRADUATE LITERARY JOURNAL

North Central College, 30 N. Brainard St., CM #235, Naperville IL 60540. (630)637-5280. Fax: (630) 637-5221. E-mail: nccreview@noctrl.edu. Website: http://orgs.northcentralcollege.edu/

review. **Contact:** Dr. Richard Guzman, advisor. Magazine has revolving editor. Editorial term: Editor changes each year in the Fall. Literary magazine/journal: 5½ × 8½, 120 pages, perfect binding, color card-stock cover. Includes black and white art. "The North Central Review is an undergraduate literary journal soliciting fiction, poetry, nonfiction and drama from around the country and the globe—but only from college students. This offers undergraduates a venue for sharing their work with their peers." Semiannual. Estab. 1936, undergraduate focus as of 2005. Circ. 500-750, depending on funding.

Needs Considers all categories. Deadlines: February 15 and October 15. Does not read February 15-August 15. Accepts 4-8 mss/issue; 8-16 mss/year. Manuscript published 2-3 months after acceptance. Agented fiction 0%. **Publishes "at least half, probably more" new writers/year.** Length: 5,000 words (max). Average length: 2,000 words. Publishes short shorts. Average length of short shorts: 100-700 words. Also publishes literary essays, poetry. Rarely comments on/critiques rejected manuscripts.

How to Contact Send complete ms with cover letter. Accepts submissions by e-mail. Include student (.edu) e-mail address or copy of student ID with ID number marked. Responds to queries in 2 weeks. Responds to mss in 4 months. Send disposable copy of ms and #10 SASE for reply only. Considers multiple submissions. Sample copy free upon request (older issue) or available for $5 (most recent issue). Guidelines available at website, for SASE, via e-mail.

Payment/Terms Writers receive 2 contributors copies. Additional copies $5. Pays on publication. Acquires one-time rights.

Tips "The reading staff changes year to year (and sometimes from one academic term to the next) so tastes change. That said, at least three readers evaluate each submission, and there's usually a widespread agreement on the best ones. While all elements need to work together, readers take notice when one element—maybe setting or character—captivates and even teaches the reader something new. Don't send something you just drafted and printed. Give your work some time, revise it, and polish what you plan to send us. That said, don't hesitate to submit and submit again to the *North Central Review*. Undergraduates are beginners, and we welcome new voices."

NORTH DAKOTA QUARTERLY

University of North Dakota, Merrifield Hall Room 110, 276 Centennial Drive Stop 7209 Grand Forks ND 58202-7209. (701) 777-3322. Fax: (701) 777-2373. E-mail: ndq@und.edu. Website: www.und.nodak.edu/org/ndq. **Contact:** Robert W. Lewis, editor. Magazine: 6 × 9; 200 pages; bond paper; illustrations; photos. "North Dakota Quarterly is a literary journal publishing essays in the humanities; some short stories, some poetry. Occasional special topic issues." General audience. Quarterly. Estab. 1911. Circ. 600.

- Work published in *North Dakota Quarterly* was selected for inclusion in *The O. Henry Prize Stories, The Pushcart Prize Series,* and *Best American Essays*.

Needs Ethnic/multicultural, experimental, feminist, historical, literary, Native American. Receives 125-150 unsolicited mss/month. Accepts 4 mss/issue; 16 mss/year. Publishes ms 2 years after acceptance. **Publishes 4-5 new writers/year.** Recently published work by Louise Erdrich, Robert Day, Maxine Kumin and Fred Arroyo. Average length: 3,000-4,000 words. Also publishes literary essays and criticism. Sometimes comments on rejected mss.

How to Contact SASE. Responds in 3 months to mss. Sample copy for $10. Reviews fiction.

Payment/Terms Pays 2-4 contributor's copies; 30% discount for extras. Acquires one-time rights. Sends galleys to author.

NORTHWEST REVIEW

5243 University of Oregon, Eugene OR 97403. (541)346-3957. Fax: (541)346-0537. E-mail: nweditor@uoregon.edu. Website: nwr.uoregon.edu. **Contact:** Geri Doran, general editor. Contact: Geri Doran, general editor. Magazine: 6 × 9; 140-160 pages; high quality cover stock; illustrations; photos. "A general literary review featuring poems, stories, essays and reviews, circulated nationally and internationally. For a literate audience in avant-garde as well as traditional literary forms; interested in the important writers who have not yet achieved their readership." Triannual. Circ. 1,200.

Needs Experimental, feminist, literary, translations, contemporary. Receives 150 unsolicited mss/

month. Accepts 4-5 mss/issue; 12-15 mss/year. **Publishes some new writers/year.** Recently published work by Diana Abu-Jaber, Madison Smartt Bell, Maria Flook, Charles Marvin. Also publishes literary essays, literary criticism, poetry. Comments on rejected mss "when there is time."

How to Contact Responds in 4 months to mss. No simultaneous submissions. Sample copy for $4. Reviews fiction.

Payment/Terms Pays 3 contributor's copies and 1-year subscription; 40% discount on extras. Acquires first rights.

◪ $ NORTHWOODS JOURNAL

Conservatory of American Letters, P.O. Box 298, Thomaston ME 04861. (207) 226-7528. E-mail: cal@americanletters.org. Website: www.americanletters.org. Magazine: 5½ × 8½; 32-64 pages; white paper; 8 pt. glossy, full color cover; digital printing; some illustrations; photos. "No theme, no philosophy—for writers and for people who read for entertainment." Quarterly. Estab. 1993. Circ. 100.

Needs Adventure, experimental, fantasy (science fantasy, sword and sorcery), literary, mainstream, mystery/suspense (amateur sleuth, police procedural, private eye/hard-boiled, romantic suspense), psychic/supernatural/occult, regional, romance (gothic, historical), science fiction (hard science, soft/sociological), western (frontier, traditional), sports. "Would like to see more first-person adventure. No porn or evangelical." Publishes annual *Northwoods Anthology*. Receives 20 unsolicited mss/month. Accepts 12-15 mss/year. **Publishes 15 new writers/year.** Recently published work by J.F. Pytko, Richard Vaughn, Kelley Jean White. Also publishes literary criticism, poetry.

How to Contact Send SASE for reply, return of ms or send a disposable copy of ms. Responds in 2 days to queries; by next deadline plus 5 days to mss. No simultaneous submissions or electronic submissions. Sample copy for $6.50 next issue, $10 current issue, $14.50 back issue, all postage paid. Or send 7 × 10 SASE with $1.35 postage affixed and $6.50. Writer's guidelines for #10 SASE. Reviews fiction. Reviews editor J. R. Clifford 1537 Oakhurst Dr, Mt Pleasant, SC 29464. Send SASE for rules of submission. Accepts books for review or reviews of small press and self published books.

Payment/Terms Varies "but is generally 1 cent per word or more, based on experience with us. Pays an advance (non refundable) based on sales we can attribute to your influence." Pays on acceptance for first North American serial rights. 50/50 split of additional sales.

Tips "Read guidelines, read the things we've published. Know your market. Anyone submitting to a publication he/she has never seen deserves whatever happens to them."

◪ $ ◘ NOTRE DAME REVIEW

840 Flanner Hall, Notre Dame IN 46556. Website: www.nd.edu/~ndr/review.htm. **Contact:** William O'Rourke. Literary magazine: 6 × 9; 200 pages; 50 lb. smooth paper; illustrations; photos. "The Notre Dame Review is an indepenent, noncommercial magazine of contemporary American and international fiction, poetry, criticism and art. We are especially interested in work that takes on big issues by making the invisible seen, that gives voice to the voiceless. In addition to showcasing celebrated authors like Seamus Heaney and Czelaw Milosz, the Notre Dame Review introduces readers to authors they may have never encountered before, but who are doing innovative and important work. In conjunction with the Notre Dame Review, the online companion to the printed magazine engages readers as a community centered in literary rather than commercial concerns, a community we reach out to through critique and commentary as well as aesthetic experience." Semiannual. Circ. 1,500.

- Pushcart prizes in fiction and poetry. Best American Short stories; Best American Poetry.

Needs No genre fiction. Upcoming theme issues planned. Receives 75 unsolicited mss/month. Accepts 4-5 mss/issue; 10 mss/year. Does not read mss November-January or April-August. Publishes ms 6 months after acceptance. **Publishes 1 new writer/year.** Recently published work by Ed Falco, Jarda Cerverka, David Green. Publishes short shorts. Also publishes literary criticism, poetry.

How to Contact Send complete ms with cover letter. Include 4-sentence bio. Send SASE for response, return of ms, or send a disposable copy of ms. Responds in 6 months to mss. Accepts simultaneous submissions. Sample copy for $6. Writer's guidelines online. Mss sent during summer months will be returned unread.
Payment/Terms Pays $5-25. Pays on publication for first North American serial rights.
Tips "We're looking for high quality work that takes on big issues in a literary way. Please read our back issues before submitting."

OBSIDIAN III

Literature in the African Diaspora, Dept. of English, North Carolina State University, Box 8105, Raleigh NC 27695-8105. (919)515-4153. E-mail: obsidian@gw.ncsu.edu. Website: www.ncsu.edu/chass/obsidian/. **Contact:** Sheila Smith McKoy, editor. Magazine: 130 pages. "Creative works in English by black writers, scholarly critical studies by all writers on black literature in English." Published 2 times/year (spring/summer, fall/winter). Estab. 1975.
Needs Ethnic/multicultural (Pan-African), feminist, literary. Accepts 7-9 mss/year. Publishes ms 4-6 months after acceptance. **Publishes 20 new writers/year.** Recently published work by R. Flowers Rivera, Terrance Hayes, Eugene Kraft, Arlene McKanic, Pearl Bothe Williams, Kwane Dawes, Jay Wright, and Octavia E. Butler.
How to Contact Accepts submissions by e-mail. Responds in 4 months to mss. Sample copy for $10.
Payment/Terms Pays in contributor's copies. Acquires one-time rights. Sponsors awards/contests.
Tips "Following proper format is essential. Your title must be intriguing and text clean. Never give up. Some of the writers we publish were rejected many times before we published them."

OHIO TEACHERS WRITE

644 Overlook Dr., Columbus OH 43214. E-mail: rmcclain@bright.net. **Contact:** Sally Lamping, editor. Editors change every 3 years. Magazine: 8½ × 11; 50 pages; 60 lb. white offset paper; 65 lb. blue cover stock; illustrations; photos. "The purpose of the magazine is three fold: (1) to provide a collection of fine literature for the reading pleasure of teachers and other adult readers; (2) to encourage teachers to compose literary works along with their students; (3) to provide the literate citizens of Ohio a window into the world of educators not often seen by those outside the teaching profession." Annual. Circ. 1,000. Submissions are limited to Ohio Educators.
Needs Adventure, ethnic/multicultural, experimental, fantasy (science fantasy), feminist, gay, historical, humor/satire, lesbian, literary, mainstream, regional, religious/inspirational, romance (contemporary), science fiction (hard science, soft/sociological), western (frontier, traditional), senior citizen/retirement, sports, teaching. Receives 2 unsolicited mss/month. Accepts 7 mss/issue. "We read only in May when editorial board meets." Recently published work by Lois Spencer, Harry R. Noden, Linda J. Rice, June Langford Berkley. Publishes short shorts. Also publishes poetry. Often comments on rejected mss.
How to Contact Send SASE with postage clipped for return of ms or send a disposable copy of ms. Accepts multiple submissions. Sample copy for $6.
Payment/Terms Pays 2 contributor's copies; additional copies $6. Acquires first rights.

N ONE LESS, ART ON THE RANGE

One Less Press, 6 Village Hill Road, Williamsburg MA 01096-9706. E-mail: onelessartontherange@yahoo.com. Website: www.onelessmag.blogspot.com. **Contact:** David Gardner, co-editor. Literary magazine/journal: 6 × 9, 100-200 pages, 60 lb. white paper, 10 pt. cover. Contains illustrations and photographs. "One Less publishes work that challenges artistic conventions and modes of expression. Accepted forms: poetry, prose, short stories, novel excerpts, play excerpts, comics, photography, painting, film stills, drawing and mixed media." Annual. Estab. 2005.

- 2004 Northampton Arts Council/Massachusetts Cultural Council Grant Recipient.

Needs Comics/graphic novels, ethnic/multicultural, experimental, historical, literary. Does not want erotica, romance, religious, young adult/teens, new age, family saga, sports, children's/

juvenile. Receives 1 mss/month. Accepts 5-10 mss/issue; 10-15 mss/year. Manuscript published 3-4 months after acceptance. **Publishes 1-2 new writers/year.** Published Anne Waldman, Lisa Jarnot, Bruce Covey, Elizabeth Robinson, and Ken Rumble. Length: 1 word (min)-1,500 words (max). Average length: 1,200 words. Publishes short shorts. Also publishes literary essays, literary criticism, poetry. Never comments on/critiques rejected manuscripts.
How to Contact Query first. Accepts submissions by e-mail. Include estimated word count, brief bio, list of publications. Responds to queries in 1 week. Responds to mss in 2 months. Send either SASE (or IRC) for return of ms or disposable copy of ms and #10 SASE for reply only. Sample copy available for $10. Guidelines available for SASE, via e-mail, on website.
Payment/Terms Writers receive 1 contributor's copy. Additional copies $10. Pays on publication. Acquires all rights, revert back to writer/artist upon publication. Publication is copyrighted.
Tips "Obtain a copy of our magazine and become familiar with the fiction we publish."

$ ONE-STORY

The Old American Can Factory, 232 Third St., #A111, Brooklyn NY 11215. Website: www.one-story.com. "*One Story* is a literary magazine that contains, simply, one story. It is a subscription-only magazine. Every 3 weeks subscribers are sent *One Story* in the mail. *One Story* is artfully designed, lightweight, easy to carry, and ready to entertain on buses, in bed, in subways, in cars, in the park, in the bath, in the waiting rooms of doctor's, on the couch, or in line at the supermarket. Subscribers also have access to a website, www.one-story.com, where they can learn more about *One Story* authors, and hear about readings and events. There is always time to read *One Story*." Circ. 3,500.
Needs Literary short stories. One Story only accepts short stories. Do not send excerpts. Do not send more than 1 story at a time. Publishes ms 3-6 months after acceptance. Recently published work by John Hodgman, Melanie Rae Thon, Daniel Wallace and Judy Budnitz.
How to Contact Send complete ms. Accepts online submissions only. Responds in 2-6 months to mss. Sample copy for $5. Writer's guidelines online.
Payment/Terms Pays $100. Pays on publication for first North American serial rights. Buys the rights to publish excerpts on website and in promotional materials.

OPEN WIDE MAGAZINE

40 Wingfield Road, Lakenheath, Brandon, Suffolk IP27 9HR United Kingdom. E-mail: contact@openwidemagazine.co.uk. Website: www.openwidemagazine.co.uk. **Contact:** Liz Roberts. Online literary magazine/journal: Quarterly. Estab. 2001.
Needs Christian-based journal enjoys adventure, ethnic/multicultural, experimental, feminist, humor/satire, mainstream, mystery/suspense, principle beat. Receives 100 mss/month. Accepts 25 mss/issue. Manuscript published 3 months after acceptance. **Publishes 30 new writers/year.** Length: 500-4,000. Average length: 2,500. Publishes short shorts. Also publishes poetry, reviews (music, film, art) and interviews. Rarely comments on/critiques rejected mss.
How to Contact Accepts submissions by e-mail. Include estimated word count, brief bio. Send either SASE (or IRC) for return of ms or disposable copy of ms and #10 SASE for reply only.
Payment/Terms Acquires one-time rights. Publication is copyrighted.

OYEZ REVIEW

Roosevelt University, Dept. of Literature and languages, 430 S. Michigan Ave., Chicago IL 60605. (312)341-3770. E-mail: oyezreview@roosevelt.edu. Website: www.roosevelt.edu/oyezreview. **Contact:** Dr. Janet Wondra, editor. Literary magazine/journal. "Oyez Review publishes fiction, creative nonfiction, poetry and art. There are no restrictions on style, theme, or subject matter." Annual. Estab. 1965. Circ. 800.
Needs Publishes short stories and flash fiction from established authors and newcomers. Literary excellence is our goal and our primary criterion. Send us your best work, and you will receive a thoughtful, thorough reading. Recently published J. Weintraub, Lori Rader Day, Joyce Goldenstern, Norman Lock, Peter Obourn, Jotham Burrello.

How to Contact Accepts art and international submissions by e-mail. Sample copy available for $5. Guidelines available on website.
Payment/Terms Writers receive 2 contributors copies. Acquires first North American serial rights.
Tips "Writers should familiarize themselves with a variety of literary magazines in addition to ours in order to understand what contemporary literary magazines do and do not publish. Note that e-mail submissions, simultaneous submissions, work received without an SASE, and mss received before or after our August 1-October 1 reading period will not be read. We read complete manuscripts rather than queries."

OYSTER BOY REVIEW

P.O. Box 1483, Pacifica CA 94044. E-mail: email_2010@oysterboyreview.com. Website: www.oysterboyreview.com. **Contact:** Damon Suave, editor/publisher. Electronic and print magazine. "We publish kick-ass, teeth-cracking stories." Published 2-3 times a year.
Needs No genre fiction. "Fiction that revolves around characters in conflict with themselves or each other; a plot that has a beginning, a middle, and an end; a narrative with a strong moral center (not necessarily 'moralistic'); a story with a satisfying resolution to the conflict; and an ethereal something that contributes to the mystery of a question, but does not necessarily seek or contrive to answer it." Submissions closed for 2009. **Publishes 4 new writers/year.** Recently published work by Todd Goldberg, Ken Wainio, Elisha Porat, Kevin McGowan.
How to Contact *"Submissions are closed through 2010."* Accepts multiple submissions. Sample copy not available.
Tips "Keep writing, keep submitting, keep revising."

☑ PACIFIC COAST JOURNAL

French Bread Publications, P.O. Box 56, Carlsbad CA 92018. E-mail: paccoastj@frenchbreadpublications.com. Website: www.frenchbreadpublications.com/pcj. **Contact:** Stephanie Kylkis, fiction editor. Magazine: 5½ × 8½; 40 pages; 20 lb. paper; 67 lb. cover; illustrations; b&w photos. "Slight focus toward Western North America/Pacific Rim." Quarterly. Estab. 1992. Circ. 200.
Needs Ethnic/multicultural, experimental, feminist, historical, humor/satire, literary, science fiction (soft/sociological, magical realism). "No children's, religious, or hard sci-fi." Receives 150unsolicited mss/month. Accepts 3-4 mss/issue; 10-12 mss/year. Publishes ms 6-18 months after acceptance. Length: 4,000 words; average length: 2,500 words. Publishes short shorts. Also publishes literary essays, poetry. Sometimes comments on rejected mss.
How to Contact Send SASE for reply, return of ms or send a disposable copy of ms. Also accepts e-mail address for response instead of SASE. Responds in 6-9 months to mss. Accepts simultaneous submissions and reprints. Sample copy for $3, 6 × 9 SASE and 3oz. postage. Reviews fiction.
Payment/Terms Pays 1 contributor's copy. Acquires one-time rights.
Tips "*PCJ* is an independent magazine and we have a limited amount of space and funding. We are looking for experiments in what can be done with the short fiction form. The best stories will entertain as well as confuse."

☑ PACIFIC REVIEW

Dept. of English and Comparative Lit., San Diego S, San Diego CA 92182-8140. E-mail: pacificREVIEW_sdsu@yahoo.com. Website: http://pacificREVIEW.sdsu.edu. **Contact:** Lester O'Connor, fiction editor. Magazine: 6 × 9; 200 pages; book stock paper; paper back, extra heavy cover stock; b&w illustrations, b&w photos. "pacific REVIEW publishes the work of emergent literati, pairing their efforts with those of established artists. It is available at West Coast independent booksellers and university and college libraries and is taught as text in numerous university literature and creative writing classes." Circ. 2,000.
Needs "We welcome submissions of previously published poems, short stories, translations, and creative nonfiction, including essays and reviews." For information on theme issues see website. **Publishes 15 new writers/year.** Recently published work by Ai, Alurista, Susan Daitch, Lawrence

Ferlinghetti, William T. Vollmann.

How to Contact Responds in 3 months to mss. Sample copy for $10.

Payment/Terms Pays 2 contributor's copies. Aquires first serial rights. All other rights revert to author.

Tips "We welcome all submissions, especially those created in or in the context of the West Coast/California and the space of our borders."

PACKINGTOWN REVIEW

E-mail: editors@packingtownreview.com. Magazine has revolving editor. Editorial term: 2 years. Next term: 2011. Literary magazine/journal. 812X11, 250 pages. "Packingtown Review publishes imaginative and critical prose by emerging and established writers. We welcome submissions of poetry, scholarly articles, drama, creative nonfiction, fiction, and literary translation, as well as genre-bending pieces." Annual.

Needs Comics/graphic novels, ethnic/multicultural (general), experimental, feminist, gay, glitz, historical (general), literary, mainstream, military/war, translations. Does not want to see uninspired or unrevised work. "We also would like to avoid fantasy, science fiction, overtly religious, or romantic pieces." Ms published max of one year after acceptance. Length: 3,000 words (min)-8,000 words (max). Publishes short shorts. Also publishes literary essays, literary criticism, book reviews, poetry. Send review copies to Jennifer Moore and Matthew Corey Editor. Sometimes comments on/critiques rejected mss.

How to Contact Send complete ms with cover letter. Include estimated word count, brief bio. Responds to queries in 3 weeks. Responds to mss in 3 months. Considers simultaneous submissions. See website for price guidelines. Guidelines available for SASE, via e-mail.

Payment/Terms Writers receive 2 contributor's copies. Pays on publication. Acquires first North American serial rights. Sends galleys to author. Publication is copyrighted.

Tips "We are looking for well-crafted prose. We are open to most styles and forms. We are also looking for prose that takes risks and does so successfully. We will consider articles about prose."

PADDLEFISH

1105 W. 8th Street, Yankton SD 5708. (605) 688-1362. E-mail: james.reese@mtmc.edu. Website: www.mmcpaddlefish.com. **Contact:** Dr. Jim Reese, editor. Literary magazine/journal. 6x9, 150 pages. Includes photographs. "We publish unique and creative pieces." Annual. Estab. 2007.

Needs Adventure, comics/graphic novels, erotica, ethnic/multicultural, experimental, family saga, fantasy, feminist, gay, glitz, historical, horror, humor/satire, lesbian, literary, mainstream, military/war, mystery, new age, psychic/supernatural/occult, religious, romance, science fiction, thriller/espionage, translations, western, young adult/teen. Does not want excessive or gratuitous language, sex or violence. Receives 300 mss/month. Accepts 30 mss/year. Submission period is Nov 1-Feb 28. Ms published 3-9 months after acceptance. **Publishes 5-10 new writers/year.** Published David Lee, William Kloefkorn, David Allen Evans, Jack Anderson and Maria Mazziotti Gillan. Length: 2,500 words (max). Publishes short shorts. Also publishes literary essays, poetry. Rarely comments on/critiques rejected mss.

How to Contact Send complete ms with cover letter. Include estimated word count, brief bio, list of publications. Send disposable copy of ms and #10 SASE for reply only. Guidelines available for SASE.

Payment/Terms Writers receive 1 contributor's copy. Additional copies $8. Pays on publication. Acquires one-time rights. Sends galleys to author. Publication is copyrighted. "Cash prizes are award to Mount Marty students."

PAINTED BRIDE QUARTERLY

Drexel University, Dept. of English, 3141 Chestnut Street, Philadelphia PA 19104. Website: http://webdelsol.com/pbq. "PBQ seeks literary fiction, experimental and traditional." Publishes online each quarter and a print annual each spring. Estab. 1973.

Needs Ethnic/multicultural, experimental, feminist, gay, lesbian, literary, translations. "No genre fiction." "Publishes theme-related work, check website; holds annual fiction contests. **Publishes**

24 new writers/year. Length: 5,000 words; average length: 3,000 words. Publishes short shorts. Also publishes literary essays, literary criticism, poetry. Occasionally comments on rejected mss.
How to Contact Send complete ms. No electronic submissions. Responds in 6 months to mss. Sample copy online. Writer's guidelines online. Reviews fiction.
Payment/Terms Acquires first North American serial rights.
Tips We look for "freshness of idea incorporated with high-quality writing. We receive an awful lot of nicely written work with worn-out plots. We want quality in whatever—we hold experimental work to as strict standards as anything else. Many of our readers write fiction; most of them enjoy a good reading. We hope to be an outlet for quality. A good story gives, first, enjoyment to the reader. We've seen a good many of them lately, and we've published the best of them."

PALO ALTO REVIEW

A Journal of Ideas, 1400 W. Villaret, San Antonio TX 78224. (210)486-3249. Fax: (210)486-3231. E-mail: eshull@alamo.edu. **Contact:** Ellen Shull, editor. Magazine: 8½ × 11; 88 pages; 60 lb. gloss white paper; illustrations; photos. More than half of each issue is devoted to articles and essays. "We select stories that we would want to read again. Not too experimental nor excessively avant-garde, just good fiction." Annual.

- *Palo Alto Review* was awarded the Pushcart Prize for 2001.

Needs Adventure, ethnic/multicultural, experimental, fantasy, feminist, historical, humor/satire, literary, mainstream, mystery/suspense, regional, romance, science fiction, translations, western. Upcoming themes available for SASE. Receives 100-150 unsolicited mss/month. Accepts 2-3 mss/issue; 4-6 mss/year. Publishes ms 2-15 months after acceptance. **Publishes 20 new writers/year.** Recently published work by Char Miller, Naveed Noori, E.M. Schorb, Louis Phillips, Tom Filer, Jo Lecoeur, H. Palmer Hall. Publishes short shorts. Also publishes poetry, essays, articles, memoirs, book reviews. Always comments on rejected mss.
How to Contact Send SASE for reply, return of ms or send a disposable copy of ms. "Request sample copy and guidelines." Accepts submissions by e-mail only if outside the US. Responds in 4 months to mss. Accepts simultaneous submissions. Sample copy for $5. Writer's guidelines for #10 SASE or e-mail to eshull@alamo.edu.
Payment/Terms Pays 2 contributor's copies; additional copies for $5. Acquires first North American serial rights.
Tips "Good short stories have interesting characters confronted by a dilemma working toward a solution. So often what we get is 'a moment in time,' not a story. Generally, characters are interesting because readers can identify with them. Edit judiciously. Cut out extraneous verbiage. Set up a choice that has to be made. Then create tension—who wants what and why they can't have it."

THE PARIS REVIEW

62 White St., New York NY 10013. Website: www.theparisreview.org. **Contact:** Philip Gourevitch, editor; Nathaniel Rich, fiction editor. Magazine: about 192 pages; illustrations; photography portfolios (unsolicited artwork not accepted). Fiction, nonfiction and poetry of superlative quality. "Our contributors include prominent as well as previously unpublished writers. The Writers at Work interview series features important contemporary writers discussing their own work and the craft of writing." Published quarterly.
Needs Fiction, nonfiction, poetry. Receives 2,000 unsolicited mss/month. Recently published work by Karl Taro Greenfeld, J. Robert Lennon, and Belle Boggs.
How to Contact Send complete ms and SASE. Responds in 2 months to fiction mss; 6 months for poetry. Accepts simultaneous, multiple submissions. Sample copy for $12. Writer's guidelines online.
Payment/Terms Payment varies depending on length. Pays on publication for first English-language rights. Sends galleys to author. Sponsors awards/contests.

PASSAGER

Passager Press, c/o The University of Baltimore, Baltimore MD 21201.(410) 837-6047. E-mail: passager@saysomethingloudly.com. Website: www.passagerpress.com. **Contact**: Editors. Literary magazine/journal. 8¼ × 8¼, 84 pages, recycled paper. "Passager has a special focus on older writers. Its mission is to encourage, engage and strengthen the imagination well into old age and to give mature readers oppertunities that are sometimes closed off to them in our youth-oriented culture. We are dedicated to honoring the creativity that takes hold in later years and to making public the talents of those over the age of 50." Semiannual. Estab. 1990. Circ. 1,500. Member CLMP.

Needs Literary. Receives 20 mss/month. Accepts 4 mss/issue; 4 mss/year. Does not read Sept.15 through Feb 15th. Ms published 4 months after acceptance. Publishes 2-3 new writers/year. Published Miriam Karme, Lucille Schulberg Warner, Sally Bellerose and Craig Hartglass. Length: 4,000 words (max). Publishes short shorts. Also publishes poetry and memoir. Never comments on/critiques rejected mss.

How to Contact Send complete ms with cover letter. Check website for guidelines. Include estimated word count, brief bio, list of publications. Responds to mss in 5 months. Send either SASE (or IRC) for return of ms or disposable copy of ms and #10 SASE for reply only. Considers simultaneous submissions. Sample copy available for $10. Guidelines available for SASE, on website. Payment and Terms Writers receive 1 contributor's copy. Additional copies $7. Pays on publication. Acquires first North American serial rights. Publication is copyrighted.

Tips "Stereotyped images of old age will be rejected immediately. Write humorous, tongue-in-cheek essays. Read the publication, or at least visit the website."

PASSAGES NORTH

Northern Michigan University, Department of English, Gries Hall, Rm 229, Marquette MI 49855. (906) 227-1203. Fax: (906) 227-1096. E-mail: passages@nmu.edu. Website: http://myweb.nmu.edu/~passages. **Contact:** Kate Myers Hanson, Editor-in-Chief. Magazine: 7 × 10; 200-300 pgs; 60 lb. paper. "Passages North publishes quality fiction, poetry and creative nonfiction by emerging and established writers." Annual. Estab. 1979. Circ. 1,500.

Needs Ethnic/multicultural, literary, short-short fiction. No genre fiction, science fiction, "typical commercial press work." Receives 200 unsolicited mss/month. Accepts 12-15 mss/year. Reads mss September 1-April 15. **Publishes 10% new writers/year.** Recently published work by John McNally, Steve Almond, Tracy Winn and Midege Raymond. Length: 5,000 words (max). Average length 3,000 words. Publishes short shorts. Average length: 1,000 words. Also publishes literary essays, poetry. Comments on rejected mss when there is time.

How to Contact Send complete ms with cover letter. Responds in 2-4 months to mss. Accepts simultaneous submissions. Sample copy for $3-7. Guidelines for SASE, e-mail, on website.

Payment/Terms Pays 2 contributor's copies. Rights revert to author upon publication. Publication is copyrighted. Occasionally sponsors contests; check website for details.

Tips "We look for voice, energetic prose, writers who take risks. We look for an engaging story in which the author evokes an emotional response from the reader through carefully rendered scenes, complex characters, and a smart, narrative design. Revise, revise. Read what we publish."

THE PATERSON LITERARY REVIEW

Passaic County Community College, One College Blvd., Paterson NJ 07505. (973) 684-6555. Fax: (973) 523-6085. E-mail: mgillan@pccc.edu. Website: www.pccc.edu/poetry. **Contact:** Maria Mazziotti Gillan, editor. Magazine: 6 × 9; 400 pages; 60 lb. paper; 70 lb. cover; illustrations; photos. Annual.

- Work for *PLR* has been included in the *Pushcart Prize* anthology and *Best American Poetry*.

Needs Ethnic/multicultural, literary, contemporary. "We are interested in quality short stories, with no taboos on subject matter." Receives 60 unsolicited mss/month. Publishes ms 6-12 months after acceptance. **Publishes 5% new writers/year.** Recently published work by Robert Mooney and Abigail Stone. Also publishes literary essays, literary criticism, poetry.

How to Contact Send SASE for reply or return of ms. "Indicate whether you want story returned." Accepts simultaneous submissions. Sample copy for $13 plus $1.50 postage. Reviews fiction.
Payment/Terms Pays in contributor's copies. Acquires first North American serial rights.
Tips Looks for "clear, moving and specific work."

PEARL

3030 E. Second St., Long Beach CA 90803. (562)434-4523. E-mail: pearlmag@aol.com. Website: www.pearlmag.com. Magazine: 5½ × 8½; 96 pages; 60 lb. recycled, acid-free paper; perfect bound; coated cover; b &w drawings and graphics. "We are primarily a poetry magazine, but we do publish some very short fiction. We are interested in lively, readable prose that speaks to real people in direct, living language; for a general literary audience." Biannual.
Needs Humor/satire, literary, mainstream, contemporary, prose poem. "We will consider short-short stories up to 1,200 words. Longer stories (up to 4,000 words) may only be submitted to our short story contest. All contest entries are considered for publication. Although we have no taboos stylistically or subject-wise, obscure, predictable, sentimental, or clicheé-ridden stories are a turn-off." Publishes an all-fiction issue each year. Receives 30-40 unsolicited mss/month. Accepts 15-20 mss/issue; 12-15 mss/year. Submissions accepted January-June only. Publishes ms 6-12 months after acceptance. **Publishes 1-5 new writers/year.** Recently published work by Ruth Moon Kempher, Sharon Reitman, Erin Campbell, Michael Lee Phillips, John Stacy, Suzanne Greenberg, Gerald Locklin, Lisa Glatt. Length: 500-1,200 words; average length: 1,000 words. Also publishes poetry.
How to Contact Include SASE. Responds in 2 months to mss. Accepts simultaneous, multiple submissions. Sample copy for $8 (postpaid). Writer's guidelines for #10 SASE.
Payment/Terms Pays 1 contributor's copy. Acquires first North American serial rights. Sends galleys to author. Sponsors awards/contests.
Tips "We look for vivid, *dramatized* situations and characters, stories written in an original 'voice,' that make sense and follow a clear narrative line. What makes a manuscript stand out is more elusive, though—more to do with feeling and imagination than anything else."

$ PEEKS & VALLEYS

E-mail: editor@peeksandvalleys.com. Website: http://peeksandvalleys.com/. **Contact**: Mary Anne DeYoung, editor. "Peeks & Valleys is a fiction journal that seeks traditional, character driven fiction. Our goal is to encourage and offer an outlet for both accomplished and new writers and to cause contemplation on the part of the reader." Quarterly. Estab. 1999, under new ownership as of 2007.
Needs "Please no sci-fi, formulaic, interview/profile or erotica." Receives 50 unsolicited mss/month. Accepts 7-8 mss/issue; 28-32 mss/year. Publishing time after acceptance varies. **Publishes 70% new writers/year.** Length: 5,000 words max; average length: 2,400 words. Also publishes poetry.
How to Contact Send complete ms. or poems electronically only. Check website for guidelines. Responds in 3 months. Accepts simultaneous submissions if advised with submissions. some reprints considered but prefers new, never-before published stories.
Payment/Terms Pays $10.00 plus 2 contributor's copies. Pays on publication for one-time or second serial (reprint) rights.
Tips "Please follow Writer's guidelines carefully. Submissions not following guidelines may not be read. Study the journal to become familiar with the type of material we are seeking."

PENNSYLVANIA ENGLISH

Penn State DuBois, College Place, DuBois PA 15801. (814)375-4814. Fax: (814)375-4784. E-mail: ajv2@psu.edu. **Contact:** Antonio Vallone. Magazine: 5¼ × 8¼; up to 200 pages; perfect bound; full color cover featuring the artwork of a Pennsylvania artist. "Our philosophy is quality. We publish literary fiction (and poetry and nonfiction). Our intended audience is literate, college-educated people." Annual. Circ. 300.
Needs Literary, mainstream, contemporary. "No genre fiction or romance." Reads mss during

the summer. Publishes ms up tp 12 months after acceptance. **Publishes 4-6 new writers/year.** Recently published work by Dave Kress, Dan Leone and Paul West. Publishes short shorts. Also publishes literary essays, literary criticism, poetry. Sometimes comments on rejected mss.

How to Contact SASE. Does not accept electronic submissions. "We are creating Pennsylvania English Online —www.pennsylvaniaenglish.com— for electronic submissions and expanded publishing opportunities." Responds in up to 12 months to mss. Accepts simultaneous submissions. Does not accept previously published work. Sample copy for $10.

Payment/Terms Pays in 2 contributor's copies. Acquires first North American serial rights.

Tips "Quality of the writing is our only measure. We're not impressed by long-winded cover letters detailing awards and publications we've never heard of. Beginners and professionals have the same chance with us. We receive stacks of competently written but boring fiction. For a story to rise out of the rejection pile, it takes more than the basic competence."

◪ PEREGRINE

P.O. Box 1076, Amherst MA 01002. (413)253-3307. E-mail: peregrine@amherstwriters.com. Website: www.amherstwriters.com. **Contact:** Nancy Rose, editor. Magazine: 6x9; 100 pages; 60 lb. white offset paper; glossy cover. "Peregrine has provided a forum for national and international writers since 1983, and is committed to finding excellent work by emerging as well as established writers. We welcome work reflecting diversity of voice. We like to be surprised. We look for writing that is honest, unpretentious, and memorable. We like to be surprised. All decisions are made by the editors." Annual. Member CLMP.

Needs Poetry and prose. "No previously published work. No children's stories." Short pieces have a better chance of publication. No electronic submissions. Accepts 6-12 mss/issue. Reads January-April. Publishes ms 4 months after acceptance. **Publishes 8-10 new writers/year.** Recently published work by Douglas Andrew, Brad Buchanan, Krikor N. Der Hohannesian, Myron Ernst, Laura Hogan, Lucy Honig, Dana Kroos, M.K. Meder, Pat Schneider, John Surowiecki, Edwina Trentham, Sacha Webley, Fred Yannantuono. Publishes short shorts.

How to Contact Enclose sufficiently stamped SASE for return of ms; if disposable copy, enclose #10 SASE (use Forever stamp) for response. Deadline for submission: April 15. Accepts simultaneous submissions. Sample copy for $12. Writer's guidelines for #10 SASE or website.

Payment/Terms Pays contributor's copies. All rights return to writer upon publication.

Tips "Check guidelines before submitting your work. Familiarize yourself with Peregrine. We look for heart and soul as well as technical expertise. Trust your own voice."

◪ PHANTASMAGORIA

Century College English Dept., 3300 Century Ave. N, White Bear Lake MN 55110. (651)779-3410. E-mail: allenabigail@hotmail.com. **Contact**: Abigail Allen, editor. Magazine: 5½ × 8½; 140-200 pages. "We publish literary fiction, poetry and essays (no scholarly essays)." Semiannual. Estab. 2001. Circ. 1,000. Member CLMP.

Needs Experimental, literary, mainstream. "No children's stories or young adult/teen material." Receives 120 unsolicited mss/month. Accepts 20-40 mss/issue; 40-80 mss/year. Publishes ms 6 months after acceptance. Publishes 5-10 new writers/year. Recently published work by Greg Mulcahy, Hiram Goza, Kim Chinquee, Louis E. Bourgeois. Length: 4,000 words; average length: 2,500 words. Publishes short shorts. Also publishes literary essays, poetry.

How to Contact Send SASE (or IRC) for return of ms or send a disposable copy of ms and #10 SASE for reply only. Responds in 2 weeks to queries. Sample copy for $9. Writer's guidelines for SASE. Reviews fiction.

Payment/Terms Pays 2 contributor's copies. Acquires first North American serial rights.

◪ ◎ PHILADELPHIA STORIES

Fiction/Art/Poetry of the Delaware Valley, 2021 S. 11th Street, Philadelphia PA 19148. (215) 551-5889. Fax: (215) 635-0195. E-mail: info@philadelphiastories.org. Website: www.philadelphiastories.org. **Contact:** Carla Spataro, fiction editor/co-publisher. Literary magazine/journal. 8½ × 11; 24 pages; 70# Matte Text, all four-color paper; 70# Matte Text cover. Contains illustrations., photographs.

"Philadelphia Stories Magazine publishes fiction, poetry, essays and art written by authors living in, or originally from, Pennsylvania, Delaware, or New Jersey." Quarterly. Circ. 10,000. Member CLMP.

Needs Experimental, literary, mainstream. "We will consider anything that is well written but are most inclined to publish literary or mainstream fiction. We are NOT particularly interested in most genres (sci fi/fantasy, romance, etc.)." List of upcoming themes available for SASE, on website. Receives 45-80 mss/month. Accepts 3-4 mss/issue for print, additional 1-2 online; 12-16 mss/year for print, 4-8 online. Ms published 1-2 months after acceptance. **Publishes 50% new writers/year.** Published katherine Hill, Jenny Lentz, Tom Larsen, Liz-Abrams-Morley, and Mitchell Sommers. Length: 5,000 words (max). Average length: 4,000 words. Publishes short shorts. Average length of short shorts: 800 words. Also publishes literary essays, book reviews, poetry. Send review queries to: info@philadelphiastories.org. Rarely comments on/critiques rejected mss.

How to Contact Send complete ms with cover letter via online submission form only. Include estimated word count, list of publications, affiliation to the Philadelphia area. Responds to mss in 12 weeks. Considers simultaneous submissions. Sample copy available for $5, on website. Guidelines available on website.

Payment/Terms Writers receive 2+ contributor's copies. Pays on publication. Acquires one-time rights. Publication is copyrighted. "Launched First National Fiction contest in 2009 with $1,000 prize and plans another one for 2010. Visit our website for opportunities."

Tips "All work is screened by three editorial board members, who rank the work. These scores are processed at the end of the quarterly submission period, and then the board meets to decide which pieces will be published in print and online. We look for exceptional, polished prose, a controlled voice, strong characters and place, and interesting subjects. Follow guidelines. We cannot stress this enough. Read every guideline carefully and thoroughly before sending anything out. Send out only polished material. We reject many quality pieces for various reasons; try not to take rejection personally. Just because your piece isn't right for one publication doesn't mean it's bad. Selection is an extremely subjective process."

THE PINCH

Dept. of English, The University of Memphis, Memphis TN 38152. (901)678-4591. E-mail: editor@thepinchjournal.com. Website: www.thepinchjournal.com. **Contact:** Kristen Iverson, editor-in-chief. Magazine: 7 × 10; 168 pages. Semiannual.

Needs Short stories, poetry, creative nonfiction, essays, memoir, travel, nature writing, photography, art. **Publishes some new writers every year.** Recently published work by Chris Fink, George Singleton, Stephen Dunn, Denise Duhamel, Floyd Skloot, and Beth Ann Fennelly.

How to Contact Send complete ms. Responds in 2 months to mss. Sample copy for $12.

Payment/Terms Pays 2 contributor's copies. Acquires first North American serial rights.

Tips "We have a new look and a new edge. We're soliciting work from writers with a national or international reputation as well as strong, interesting work from emerging writers. The Pinch Literary Award (previously River City Writing Award) in Fiction offers a $1,500 prize and publication. Check our website for details."

PINDELDYBOZ

E-mail: editor@pindeldyboz.com. "Pindeldyboz is dedicated to publishing work that challenges what a short story can be. We don't ask for anything specific—we only ask that people take chances. We like heightened language, events, relationships—stories that paint the world a little differently, while still showing us the places we already know." Bimonthly.

Needs Comics/graphic novels, experimental, literary. Reads mss September 1-February 1 only. Publishes ms 3 months after acceptance. Has published work by Tai Dong Huai, Vanessa Wieland, Kyle Minor, Brandi Wells, Alex Burford, Daniel Pinkerton. Length: 250+; average length: 2,000 words. Publishes short shorts. Also publishes literary essays, poetry. Always comments on rejected mss.

How to Contact Send complete copy of ms with cover letter. Accepts mss by e-mail and disk. Include brief bio and phone number with submission. Send SASE (or IRC) for return of the ms and disposable copy of ms and #10 SASE for reply only. Responds in 2 weeks to queries; 3 months to mss. Accepts simultaneous, multiple submissions. Sample copy for $12. Writer's guidelines online.

Payment/Terms Pays 2 contributor's copies; additional copies $10. Pays on publication for one-time rights.

Tips "Good grammar, spelling, and sentence structure help, but what's more important is a willingness to take risks. Surprise us. And we will love it."

PINYON

Mesa State College, Dept. of Languages, Lit and Comm, 1100 North Avenue, Grand Junction CO 81501-3122. E-mail: pinyonpoetry@hotmail.com. **Contact:** fiction editor. Literary magazine/journal: 8½ × 5½, 120 pages, heavy paper. Contains illustrations and photographs. Annual. Estab. 1996. Circ. 200.

Needs Literary. Receives 16-20 mss/month. Accepts 3-4 mss/issue; 3-4 mss/year. Does not read mss January-August. Manuscript published 6 months after acceptance. Length: 1,500 words (min)-5,000 words (max). Average length: 2,500 words. Publishes short shorts. Average length of short shorts: 500 words. Also publishes poetry.

How to Contact Send complete ms with cover letter. Include brief bio. Responds to queries in 1 month. Responds to mss in 6 months. Send either SASE (or IRC) for return of ms or disposable copy of ms and #10 SASE for reply only. Considers simultaneous submissions, multiple submissions. Sample copy available for $4.50. Send SASE for guidelines.

Payment/Terms Writers receive 2 contributor's copies. Acquires one-time rights. Publication is copyrighted.

Tips "Ask yourself if the work is something you would like to read in a publication."

PISGAH REVIEW

Department of Humanities, Brevard College, 400 N. Broad St., Brevard NC 28712. (828)884-8349. E-mail: tinerjj@brevard.edu. **Contact:** Jubal Tiner, editor; Jennifer McGaha, creative nonfiction editor. Literary magazine/journal: 5½ × 8½, 120 pages. Includes cover artwork. "*Pisgah Review* publishes primarily literary short fiction, creative nonfiction and poetry. Our only criteria is quality of work; we look for the best." Semiannual. Circ. 200.

Needs Ethnic/multicultural, experimental, literary, mainstream. Special interests: stories rooted in the theme of place—physical, psychological, or spiritual. Does not want genre fiction or inspirational stories. Receives 85 mss/month. Accepts 6-8 mss/issue; 12-15 mss/year. Manuscript published 6 months after acceptance. **Publishes 5 new writers/year.** Published Ron Rash, Thomas Rain Crowe, Joan Conner, Gary Fincke, and Steve Almond. Length: 2,000 words (min)-7,500 words (max). Average length: 4,000 words. Publishes short shorts. Average length of short shorts: 1,000 words. Also publishes poetry and creative nonfiction. Sometimes comments on/critiques rejected mss.

How to Contact Send complete ms with cover letter. Accepts submissions by e-mail. Responds to mss in 4-6 months. Send either SASE (or IRC) for return of ms or disposable copy of ms and #10 SASE for reply only. Considers simultaneous submissions. Sample copy available for $7. Guidelines available on website.

Payment/Terms Writers receive 2 contributor's copies. Additional copies $7. Pays on publication. Acquires first North American serial rights. Sends galleys to author. Publication is copyrighted.

Tips "We select work only of the highest quality. Grab us from the beginning and follow through. Engage us with your language and characters. A clean manuscript goes a long way toward acceptance. Stay true to the vision of your work, revise tirelessly, and submit persistently."

$ PLANET-THE WELSH INTERNATIONALIST

P.O. Box 44, Aberystwyth Ceredigion Cymru/Wales SY23 3ZZ United Kingdom. E-mail: planet.enquiries@planetmagazine.org.uk. Website: www.planetmagazine.org.uk. **Contact:** Helle Michelsen, Editor. "A literary/cultural/political journal centered on Welsh affairs but also covering international issues, with a strong interest in minority cultures in Europe and elsewhere." Quarterly.

Needs No horror or science fiction. Recently published work by Emyr Humphreys, Anne Stevenson, and Robert Minhinnick.

How to Contact No submissions returned unless accompanied by an SAE. Writers submitting from abroad should send at least 3 IRCs for return of typescript; 1 IRC for reply only. E-mail queries accepted. Sample copy for £5.75. Writer's guidelines online.

Payment/Terms Pays £50/1,000 words.

Tips "We do not look for fiction which necessarily has a 'Welsh' connection, which some writers assume from our title. We try to publish a broad range of fiction and our main criterion is quality. Try to read copies of any magazine you submit to. Don't write out of the blue to a magazine which might be completely inappropriate for your work. Recognize that you are likely to have a high rejection rate, as magazines tend to favor writers from their own countries."

$ PLEIADES

University of Central Missouri, Martin 336, Warrensburg MO 64093. (660)543-4425. Fax: (660)543-8544. E-mail: kdp8106@yahoo.com. Website: www.ucmo.edu/englphil/pleiades. **Contact:** G.B. Crump, Matthew Eck and Phong Nguyen, prose editors. Magazine: 5½ × 8½; 250 pages; 60 lb. paper; perfect-bound; 8 pt. color cover. "We publish contemporary fiction, poetry, interviews, literary essays, special-interest personal essays, reviews for a general and literary audience." Semiannual. Estab. 1991. Circ. 3,000.

- Work from *Pleiades* appears in recent volumes of *The Best American Poetry, Pushcart Prize* and *Best American Fantasy and Horror*.

Needs Ethnic/multicultural, experimental, feminist, gay, humor/satire, literary, mainstream, novel excerpts, regional, translations, magical realism. No science fiction, fantasy, confession, erotica. Receives 100 unsolicited mss/month. Accepts 8 mss/issue; 16 mss/year. "We're slower at reading manuscripts in the summer." Publishes ms 9 months after acceptance. **Publishes 4-5 new writers/year.** Recently published work by Sherman Alexie, Edith Pearlman, Joyce Carol Oates, James Tate. Length: 2,000-6,000 words; average length: 3,000-6,000 words. Also publishes literary essays, literary criticism, poetry. Sometimes comments on rejected mss.

How to Contact Send complete ms. Include 75-100 word bio and list of publications. Send SASE for reply, return of ms or send a disposable copy of ms. Responds in 2 months to queries; 2 months to mss. Accepts simultaneous submissions. Sample copy for $6 (back issue), $8 (current issue). Writer's guidelines for #10 SASE.

Payment/Terms Pays 2 contributor copies. Pays on publication for first North American serial, second serial (reprint) rights. Occasionally requests rights for TV, radio reading, website.

Tips Looks for "a blend of language and subject matter that entices from beginning to end. Send us your best work. Don't send us formula stories. While we appreciate and publish well-crafted traditional pieces, we constantly seek the story that risks, that breaks form and expectations and wins us over anyhow."

$ PLOUGHSHARES

Emerson College, *Ploughshares*, 120 Boylston St., Boston MA 02116. E-mail: pshares@emerson.edu. Website: www.pshares.org. **Contact:** Fiction Editor. "Our mission is to present dynamic, contrasting views on what is valid and important in contemporary literature and to discover and advance significant literary talent. Each issue is guest-edited by a different writer. We no longer structure issues around preconceived themes." Circ. 6,000. Literary, mainstream. "No genre (science fiction, detective, gothic, adventure, etc.), popular formula or commerical fiction whose purpose is to entertain rather than to illuminate." Receives 1,000 unsolicited mss/month. Accepts 30 mss/year. Reads submissions June 1-January 15 (postmark); mss submitted January 16-May 31 will be returned unread. Publishes ms 6 months after acceptance. **Publishes some new writers/year.** Recently published work by ZZ Packer, Antonya Nelson, Stuart Dybek.

PMS, POEMMEMOIRSTORY

University of Alabama at Birmingham, HB 217, 1530 3rd Avenue S, Birmingham AL 35294-4450. Fax: (205)975-5493. E-mail: poemmemoirstory@gmail.com. Website: www.pms-journal.org. **Contact:** Tina Harris, editor-in-chief. Literary magazine/journal: 6X9; 120 pages; recycled white; matte paper; cover photos. "We print one issue a year, our cover price is $7, and our journal publishes fine creative work by women writers from across the nation (and beyond) in the three genres listed in the title. One of our distinctive features is a memoir that we feature in each issue written by a woman who has experienced something of historic, national import but who would not necessarily call herself a writer. Our first issue, for instance, featured a piece by Emily Lyons, the nurse who was critically injured in the 1998 bombing of the Birmingham New Woman All Women clinic. We've published a wide range of these featured pieces including a memoir by a woman who was in the World Trade Center on 9-11, another by a woman who was serving in Iraq, another by a student who lived through Katrina in New Orleans, and another by a woman who married her lesbian partner in a wedding in Boston during that initial window of opportunity. PMS 8 was our first special issue, guest edited by Honorée Fanonne Jeffers and featuring all African-American women writers. We are currently distributed by Ingram Periodicals, Inc." Annual. Estab. 2001. Circ. 1,500. Member Council of Literary Magazines and Presses and the Council of Editors of Learned Journals.

- Work from PMS has been reprinted in a number of award anthologies: *New Stories from the South 2005, The Best Creative Nonfiction 2007* and *2008, Best American Poetry 2003* and *2004,* and *Best American Essays 2005* and*2007.*

Needs Comics/graphic novels, ethnic/multicultural (general), experimental, feminist, literary, translations. "We don't do erotic, mystery work, and most popular forms, per se. We publish short stories and essays including memoirs and other brands of creative nonfiction." Receives 30 mss/month. Accepts 4-6 mss/issue. As of 2009, reading period is January 1 through March 30. Ms published within 6 months after acceptance. **Publishes 5 new writers/year.** Published Vicki Covington, Kim Aubrey, Patricia Brieschke, Gaines Marsh. Length: 4,500 words (max). Average length: 3,500-4,000 words. Publishes short shorts. Average length of short shorts: 300-350 words. Also publishes literary essays, poetry. Rarely comments on/critiques rejected mss.

How to Contact Send complete ms with cover letter. Include list of publications. Responds to queries in 1 month. Responds to mss in 1-4 months. Send disposable copy of ms and #10 SASE for reply only. Considers simultaneous submissions, multiple submissions. Sample copy available for $7. Guidelines available for SASE, on website.

Payment/Terms Writers receive 2 contributor's copies. Additional copies $7. Pays on publication. Acquires one-time rights. Publication is copyrighted.

Tips "Send your best work; excellent work with a strong eye for detail and a sense of a fresh use of the language. Read a lot, write a lot, and get into the habit of sending your work out a lot."

POINTED CIRCLE

Portland Community College-Cascade, 705 N. Killing, Portland OR 97217. E-mail: lutgarda.cowan@pcc.edu. **Contact:** Lutgarda Cowan, English instructor, faculty advisor. Magazine: 80 pages; b&w illustrations; photos. "Anything of interest to educationally/culturally mixed audience." Annual.

Needs Ethnic/multicultural, literary, regional, contemporary, prose poem. "We will read whatever is sent, but encourage writers to remember we are a quality literary/arts magazine intended to promote the arts in the community. No pornography, nothing trite. Be mindful of deadlines and length limits." Accepts submissions only October 1-March 1, for July 1 issue.

How to Contact Accepts submissions by e-mail, mail. Prose up to 3,000 words; poetry up to 6 pages; artwork in high-resolution digital form. Submitted materials will not be returned; SASE for notification only. Accepts multiple submissions.

Payment/Terms Pays 2 copies. Acquires one-time rights.

POLYPHONY H.S., A STUDENT-RUN NATIONAL LITERARY MAGAZINE FOR

HIGH SCHOOL WRITERS

Polyphony H.S., c/o Educational Endeavors, 1535 N. Dayton, Chicago IL 60622. (312) 266-0123. Fax: (312) 643-1036. E-mail: polyphonyhs@gmail.com. Website: www.polyphonyhs.com. **Contact:** Billy Lombardo, managing editor. Literary magazine/journal: 9X6, 70-120 pages, silk finish 80 lb. white paper, silk finish 100 lb. cover. " We are a 501(c)3 organization. Our goal is to seek out the finest high school writers in the country, to work with them to grow as writers, and to exhibit their fiction before a national audience. Every submission is edited, commented upon, by at least three high school editors from around the country. Polyphony H.S. invites high school students to serve as National First readers, and hosts summer workshops National Editors. Just partnered with the Claudia Ann Seaman Awards for Young Writers; 4500 awards for the best poem, best story, best work of creative nonfiction. See website for details." Annual. Estab. 2005. Circ. 2,000.

Needs Poetry, fiction, and creative nonfiction. Receives 500-1,000 mss/year. Accepts 50-75 mss/issue. Publishes new writers/year. Length: 3,000 words (max). Average length: 2,000 words.

How to Contact See website. Online submission process. Deadline: day after Valentine's Day (February 15). Responds in 4-6 weeks. Considers simultaneous submissions. Sample copy available for $7.50 + $2.50 shipping/handling.

Payment/Terms Writers receive 2 contributor's copies. Additional copies $3.50. Pays on publication. Acquires first rights. **d Advice:** "We think this is the most important literary magazine in the world. Inherent in it is the collective value of every other magazine in circulation. If you're a high school teacher, you should have us in your classroom. If you teach in a university you should be paying attention to our writers."

☑ PORTLAND REVIEW

Portland State University, Box 347, Portland OR 97207-0347. E-mail: theportlandreview@gmail.com. Website: www.portlandreview.org. **Contact:** Chris Cottrell, editor. Circ. 500

Needs Unpublished poetry and prose. Fiction/Nonfiction prose of up to 5,000 words or 5 poems per submission. Receives 200 unsolicited mss/week. Accepts up to 24 mss/issue.

How to Contact Ms and SASE for submissions. Review queries via e-mail. Submission guidelines online. All ms submissions not following guidelines are immediately rejected.

Payment/Terms Pays contributor's copies. Acquires first North American serial rights.

☑ POST ROAD

E-mail: ricco@postroadmag.com. Literary magazine/journal. 812x1112, 240 pages, 60 lb. opaque paper, gloss cover. "*Post Road* is a nationally distributed literayy magazine based out of New York and Boston that publishes work in the following genres: art, criticism, fiction, nonfiction, and poetry. Post Road also features two innovations: the Recommendations section, where established writers write 500-1,000 words on a favorite book(s) or author(s); and the Etcetera section, where we publish interviews, profiles, translations, letters, classic reprints, documents, topical essays, travelogues, etc." Estab. 2000. Circ. 2,000.

- Work from *Post Road* has received the following honors: honorable mention in the 2001 O. Henry Prize Issue guest-edited by Michael Chabon, Mary Gordon, and Mona Simpson; the Pushcart Prize; honorable mention in *The Best American Nonfiction* series; and inclusion in the *Best American Short Stories* 2005.

Needs Literary. Receives 100 mss/month. Accepts 4-6 mss/issue; 8-12 mss/year. See website for reading periods. Manuscript published 6 months after acceptance. Published Brian Booker, Louis E. Bourgeois, Becky Bradway, Adam Braver, Ashley Capps, Susan Choi, Lisa Selin Davis, Rebecca Dickson, Rick Moody. Average length: 5,000 words. Average length of short shorts: 1,500 words. Also publishes literary essays, literary criticism, poetry. Sometimes comments on/critiques rejected manuscripts.

How to Contact Accepts submissions by online submissions manager only. Include brief bio. Responds to mss in 1 months. Send SASE (or IRC) for return of ms. Considers simultaneous submissions. Guidelines available on website.

Payment/Terms Writers receive 2 contributor's copies. Pays on publication. Acquires first North American serial rights. Sends galleys to author. Publication is not copyrighted.

Tips "Looking for interesting narrative, sharp dialogue, deft use of imagery and metaphor. Be persistent and be open to criticism."

$ POSTSCRIPTS: THE A TO Z OF FANTASTIC FICTION

PS Publishing LTD., Grosvenor House, 1 New Road, Hornsea HU18-1P9 United Kingdom. 0-11-44-1964 537575. Fax: 0-11-44-1964 537535. E-mail: editor@pspublishing.co.uk. Website: www.pspublishing.co.uk. **Contact:** Peter Crowther, editor/publisher. Literary magazine/journal: digest, 144 pages. Contains illustrations & photographs. "Science fiction, fantasy, horror and crime/suspense. We focus on the cerebral rather than the visceral, with an emphasis on quality literary fiction within the specified areas." Quarterly. Circ. around 1,000.

- PS Publishing has received five British Fantasy Awards, one World Fantasy Award, one International Horror Guild Award, and one Horror Writers Association Award.

Needs Fantasy (space fantasy, sword and sorcery), horror (dark fantasy, futuristic, psychological, supernatural), mystery (amateur sleuth, cozy, police procedural, private eye/hard-boiled), science fiction (hard science/technological, soft/sociological), List of upcoming themes available on website. Receives 20-50 mss/month. Accepts 10 mss/issue; 50 mss/year. Manuscript published up to 2 years after acceptance. Agented fiction less than 10%. **Publishes 4-8 new writers/year.** Length: 3,000 words (min)–8,000 words (max). Average length: 5,000 words. Publishes short shorts. Average length of short shorts: 1,000 words. Rarely comments on/critiques rejected mss.

How to Contact Send complete ms with cover letter. Accepts submissions by mail, e-mail. Include estimated word count, brief bio, list of publications. Responds to queries in 2 weeks; mss in 4 weeks. Send either SASE (or IRC) for return of ms or disposable copy of ms and #10 SASE for reply only. Sample copy available for $10 (and $5 IRCs). Guidelines available on website.

Payment/Terms Writers receive 4–7¢/word, 2 contributor's copies. Additional copies $10 (inc. postage). **Pays on acceptance.** Acquires first worldwide English rights. Publication is copyrighted.

Tips "Read the magazine."

POTOMAC REVIEW

The Journal for Arts & Humanities, Montgomery College, Paul Peck Humanities Institute, Rockville MD 20850. (301)251-7417. Fax: (301)738-1745. E-mail: potomacrevieweditor@montgomerycollege.edu. Website: www.montgomerycollege.edu/potomacreview. **Contact:** Julie Wakeman-Linn, editor. Magazine: 5½ × 8½; 175 pages; 50 lb. paper; 65 lb. color cover. Potomac Review "reflects a view of our region looking out to the world, and in turn, seeks how the world views the region." Bi-annual.

Needs "Stories and poems with a vivid, individual quality that get at 'the concealed side' of life." Flash Fiction accepted. Essays and creative non-fiction pieces welcome. No themes. Receives 300+ unsolicited mss/month. Accepts 40-50 mss/issue. Publishes ms within 1 year after acceptance. Recently published work by Jennine Capo Crucet, T.J. Forrester, Irene Keliher, Myfanwy Collins, Tiger D. Quinn, and Julee Newberger. Length: 5,000 words; average length: 2,000 words.

How to Contact Send SASE with adequate postage for reply and/or return of ms. Responds in 3-6 months to mss. Accepts simultaneous submissions. Sample copy for $10. Writer's guidelines on website.

Payment/Terms Pays 2 or more contributor's copies; additional copies for a 40% discount.

Tips " Send us interesting, well crafted stories. Have something to say in an original, provocative voice. Read recent issue to get a sense of the journal's new direction."

$ THE PRAIRIE JOURNAL

Journal of Canadian Literature, 28 Crowfoot Terrace NW, PO Box 68073, Calgary AB T3G 3N8 Canada. E-mail: prairiejournal@yahoo.com. Website: prairiejournal.org. **Contact:** A.E. Burke, literary editor. Journal: 7 × 8½; 50-60 pages; white bond paper; Cadillac cover stock; cover illustrations. "The audience is literary, university, library, scholarly and creative readers/writers." Semiannual. Estab. 1983.

Needs Literary, regional. No genre (romance, horror, western—sagebrush or cowboys—erotic, science fiction, or mystery). Receives 100 unsolicited mss/month. Accepts 10-15 mss/issue; 20-30 mss/year. Suggested deadlines: April 1 for spring/summer issue; October 1 for fall/winter. Publishes ms 4-6 months after acceptance. **Publishes 60 new writers/year.** Recently published work by Robert Clark, Sandy Campbell, Darcie Hasack, Christopher Blais. Length: 100-3,000 words; average length: 2,500 words. Also publishes literary essays, literary criticism, poetry. Sometimes comments on rejected mss.

How to Contact Send complete ms with SASE (IRC). Include cover letter of past credits, if any. Reply to queries for SAE with 55¢ for postage or IRC. No American stamps. Responds in 2 weeks to queries; 6 months to mss. No simultaneous submissions. No e-mail submissions. Sample copy for $6. Writer's guidelines online. Reviews fiction.

Payment/Terms Pays $10-75. Pays on publication for first North American serial rights. In Canada, author retains copyright with acknowledgement appreciated.

Tips "We like character-driven rather than plot-centered fiction." Interested in "innovational work of quality. Beginning writers welcome! There is no point in simply republishing known authors or conventional, predictable plots. Of the genres we receive, fiction is most often of the highest calibre. It is a very competitive field. Be proud of what you send. You're worth it."

PRAIRIE SCHOONER

201 Andrews Hall, P.O. Box 880334, Lincoln NE 68588-0334. (402)472-0911. Fax: (402)472-9771. E-mail: jengelhardt2@unl.edu. Website: www.unl.edu/schooner/psmain.htm. **Contact:** James Engelhardt, managing editor. Magazine: 6 × 9; 200 pages; good stock paper; heavy cover stock. "A fine literary quarterly of stories, poems, essays and reviews for a general audience that reads for pleasure." Estab. 1926. Circ. 3,000.

- *Prairie Schooner*, one of the oldest publications in this book, has garnered several awards and honors over the years. Work appearing in the magazine has been selected for anthologies including the *Pushcart Prize* anthology and *Best American Short Stories*.

Needs Good fiction (literary). Receives 500 unsolicited mss/month. Accepts 4-5 mss/issue. Mss are read September through May only. **Publishes 5-10 new writers/year.**Recently published work by Robert Olen Butler, Janet Burroway, Aimee Phan, Valerie Sayers, Daniel Stern. Also publishes poetry.

How to Contact Send complete ms with SASE and cover letter listing previous publications—where, when. Responds in 4 months to mss. Sample copy for $6. Writer's guidelines and excerpts online. Reviews fiction.

Payment/Terms Pays in contributor's copies and prize money awarded. Will reassign rights upon request after publication. Sponsors awards/contests.

Tips "*Prairie Schooner* is eager to see fiction from beginning and established writers. Be tenacious. Accept rejection as a temporary setback and send out rejected stories to other magazines. *Prairie Schooner* is not a magazine with a program. We look for good fiction in traditional narrative modes as well as experimental, meta-fiction or any other form or fashion a writer might try. Create striking detail, well-developed characters, fresh dialogue; let the images and the situations evoke the stories' themes. Too much explication kills a lot of otherwise good stories. Be persistent. Keep writing and sending out new work. Be familiar with the tastes of the magazines where you're sending. We are receiving record numbers of submissions. Prospective contributors must sometimes wait longer to receive our reply."

$ PRISM INTERNATIONAL

Dept. of Creative Writing, Buch E462-1866 Main Mall, Univ. of British Columbia, Vancouver BC V6T 1Z1 Canada. (604)822-2514. Fax: (604)822-3616. E-mail: prism@interchange.ubc.ca. Website: prism.arts.ubc.ca. **Contact:** The Editor. Magazine: 6 × 9; 80 pages; Zephyr book paper; Cornwall, coated one-side cover; artwork on cover. "An international journal of contemporary writing—fiction, poetry, drama, creative nonfiction and translation." Readership: "public and university libraries, individual subscriptions, bookstores—a worldwide audience concerned with the contemporary in literature." Quarterly.

- *Prism International* has won numerous magazine awards, and stories first published in Prism International have been included in the *Journey Prize Anthology* every year since 1991.

Needs Experimental, traditional. New writing that is contemporary and literary. Short stories and self-contained novel excerpts (up to 25 double-spaced pages). Works of translation are eagerly sought and should be accompanied by a copy of the original. Would like to see more translations. "No gothic, confession, religious, romance, pornography, or sci-fi." Also looking for creative nonfiction that is literary, not journalistic, in scope and tone. Receives over 100 unsolicited mss/month. Accepts 70 mss/year. "PRISM publishes both new and established writers; our contributors have included Franz Kafka, Gabriel García Maárquez, Michael Ondaatje, Margaret Laurence, Mark Anthony Jarman, Gail Anderson-Dargatz and Eden Robinson." Publishes ms 4 months after acceptance. **Publishes 7 new writers/year.** Recently published work by Ibi Kaslik, Melanie Little, Mark Anthony Jarman. Publishes short shorts. Also publishes poetry.

How to Contact Send complete ms by mail. "Keep it simple. U.S. contributors take note: Do not send SASEs with U.S. stamps, they are not valid in Canada. Send International Reply Coupons instead." Responds in 4 months to queries; 3-6 months to mss. Sample copy for $11 or on website. Writer's guidelines online.

Payment/Terms Pays $20/printed page of prose, $40/printed page of poetry, and 1-year subscription. Pays on publication for first North American serial rights. Selected authors are paid an additional $10/page for digital rights. Cover art pays $300 and 4 copies of issue. Sponsors awards/contests, including annual short fiction and nonfiction contests.

Tips "Read several issues of our magazine before submitting. We are committed to publishing outstanding literary work. We look for strong, believable characters; real voices; attention to language; interesting ideas and plots. Send us fresh, innovative work which also shows a mastery of the basics of good prose writing."

☐ PUERTO DEL SOL

Department of English, P.O. Box 30001, MSC 3E, Las Cruces NM 88003. E-mail: contact@puertodelsol.org. Website: www.puertodelsol.org. **Contact:** Carmen Giménez Smith, editor-in-chief. Magazine: 7 × 9; 200 pages; 60 lb. paper; 70 lb. cover stock. "We publish innovative work from emerging and established writers and artists. Poetry, fiction, nonfiction, drama, theory, artwork, interviews, reviews, and interesting combinations thereof." Semiannual. Circ. 1,500.

Needs Literary, experimental, theory, drama, work in translation. Accepts 8-12 mss/issue; 16-24 mss/year. Does not accept mss April 1-September 14. **Publishes 8-10 new writers/year.** Recently accepted and published work by Kim Chinquee, Joanna Scott, Peter Markus, Shya Scanlon.

How to Contact Submit 2-4 short stories at a time through online submission manager. Responds in 3-6 months to mss. Accepts simultaneous submissions. Sample copy for $8.

Payment/Terms Pays 2 contributor's copies. Acquires one-time print and electronic rights and anthology rights. Rights revert to author after publication.

Tips "We are especially pleased to publish emerging writers who work to push their art form or field of study in new directions."

QUALITY FICTION

(formerly Quarterly Women's Fiction), c/o AllWriters' Workplace & Workshop, 234 Brook St., Unit 2, Waukesha WI 53188. E-mail: qwfsubmissionsusa@yahoo.com. Website: www.allwriters.org (click on QWF) **Contact:** Kathie Giorgio, Editor. Magazine: A5; 100 pages; glossy paper. "Whether a story is about a woman's highest point in her life, or her lowest, the stories must resonate with an emotional chord. All QWF stories must have impact." Published twice a year. Estab. 1994. Circ. 1,000.

Needs Accepts all genres, as long as the main characters are women and the stories are written by women. Receives 300 unsolicited mss/reading period. Accepts 20 mss/issue; 40 mss/year. Only reads during reading periods. Publishes ms in next issue after acceptance. Publishes new writers. Length: up to 5,000 words; average length: 2,500 words. Publishes short shorts. Always comments on rejected mss.

How to Contact Send complete ms. Accepts submissions by e-mail only. Send complete ms as Word document. Responds in 2 months to queries; 2 months to mss. Simultaneous submissions okay, but not preferred. Back issues available for sale on Web site.Payment/Terms Pays in copies. Acquires first rights.
Tips "Evoking emotion is the most important characteristic of a QWF story. There is no room for a dry reporting of the facts here. Rather, the stories should present the expanse that is every woman's emotional lifetime and experience."d

QUARTER AFTER EIGHT

QAE, Ellis Hall, Ohio University, Athens OH 45701. (740)593-2827. E-mail: editor@quarteraftereight.org. Website: www.quarteraftereight.org. **Contact:** Wendy Walker, co-editor-in-chief. Magazine: 6 × 9; 200 pages; 20 lb. glossy cover stock; photos. "We look to publish work which challenges boundaries of genre, style, idea, and voice." Annual.
Needs Condensed novels, ethnic/multicultural, experimental, gay, humor/satire, lesbian, literary, mainstream, translations. "No traditional, conventional fiction." Receives 150-200 unsolicited mss/month. Accepts 40-50 mss/issue. Does not read mss mid-March-mid-September. Publishes ms 6-12 months after acceptance. **Publishes 20-30 new writers/year**. Recently published work by Virgil Suaárez, Maureen Sexton, John Gallagher and Amy England. Length: 10,000 words; average length: 3,000 words. Publishes short shorts. Also publishes literary essays, literary criticism, prose poetry. Occasionally comments on rejected mss.
How to Contact Send SASE for return of ms or send a disposable copy of ms. Responds in 3-5 months to mss. Accepts simultaneous, multiple submissions. Sample copy for $10, 8 × 11 SAE and $1.60 postage. Writer's guidelines for #10 SASE. Reviews fiction.
Payment/Terms Pays 2 contributor's copies; additional back copies $7. Acquires first North American serial rights. Rights revert to author upon publication. Sponsors awards/contests.
Tips "We look for fiction that is experimental, exploratory, devoted to and driven by language—that which succeeds in achieving the QAE aesthetic. Please subscribe to our journal and read what is published. We do not publish traditional lined poetry or straightforward conventional stories. We encourage writers to submit after they have gotten acquainted with the QAE aesthetic."

$ QUARTERLY WEST

255 S. Central Campus Dr., Rm. 3500, University of Utah, Salt Lake City UT 84112. (801)581-3938. E-mail: quarterlywest@yahoo.com. Website: www.utah.edu/quarterlywest. **Contact:** Matt Kirkpatrick & Cami Nelson, editors. Magazine: 7 × 10; 50 lb. paper; 4-color cover stock. "We publish fiction, poetry, and nonfiction in long and short formats, and will consider experimental as well as traditional works." Semiannual. Circ. 1,900.

- *Quarterly West* was awarded First Place for Editorial Content from the American Literary Magazine Awards. Work published in the magazine has been selected for inclusion in the *Pushcart Prize* anthology and *The Best American Short Stories* anthology.

Needs Ethnic/multicultural, experimental, humor/satire, literary, mainstream, novel excerpts, slice-of-life vignettes, translations, short shorts, translations. No detective, science fiction or romance. Receives 300 unsolicited mss/month. Accepts 6-10 mss/issue; 12-20 mss/year. Reads mss between September 1 and May 1 only. "Submissions received between May 2 and August 31 will be returned unread." Publishes ms 6 months after acceptance. **Publishes 3 new writers/year.** Recently published work by Steve Almond, Linh Dinh.
How to Contact Send complete ms. Brief cover letters welcome. Send SASE for reply or return of ms. Responds in 6 months to mss. Accepts simultaneous submissions if notified. Sample copy for $7.50. Writer's guidelines online.
Payment/Terms Pays $15-50, and 2 contributor's copies. Pays on publication for first North American serial rights.
Tips "We publish a special section of short shorts every issue, and we also sponsor a biennial novella contest. We are open to experimental work—potential contributors should read the magazine! We solicit occasionally, but tend more toward the surprises—unsolicited. Don't send more than one story per submission, and wait until you've heard about the first before submitting another."

RAINBOW CURVE

P.O. Box 93206, Las Vegas NV 89193-3206. E-mail: rainbowcurve@sbcglobal.net. Website: www.rainbowcurve.com. **Contact:** Daphne Young and Julianne Bonnet, editors. Magazine: 5½ × 8½; 100 pages; 60 lb. paper; coated cover. "Rainbow Curve publishes fiction and poetry that dabble at the edge; contemporary work that evokes emotion. Our audience is interested in exploring new worlds of experience and emotion; raw, visceral work is what we look for." Semiannual. Estab. 2002. Circ. 500.

Needs Ethnic/multicultural, experimental, feminist, gay, lesbian, literary. "No genre fiction (romance, western, fantasy, sci-fi)." Receives 60 unsolicited mss/month. Accepts 10-15 mss/issue; 20-30 mss/year. Publishes ms 6 months after acceptance. Agented fiction 1%. **Publishes 80% new writers/year.** Recently published work by Jonathan Barrett, Trent Busch, Rob Carney, Peter Fontaine, Bridget Hoida, and Karen Toloui. Length: 500-10,000 words; average length: 7,500 words. Publishes short shorts. Sometimes comments on rejected mss.

How to Contact Send SASE for return of ms or send a disposable copy of ms and #10 SASE for reply only. Responds in 3 months to mss. Accepts simultaneous submissions. Sample copy for $6. Writer's guidelines for SASE or on website.

Payment/Terms Pays 1 contributor's copy; additional copies $5. Acquires one-time rights. Sends galleys to author.

Tips "Unusual rendering of usual subjects and strong narrative voice make a story stand out. Unique glimpses into the lives of others—make it new."

RATTAPALLAX

217 Thompson St., Suite 353, New York NJ 10012. E-mail: info@rattapallax.com. Website: www.rattapallax.com. **Contact:** Alan Cheuse, fiction editor. Literary magazine: 9 × 12; 128 pages; bound; some illustrations; photos. "General readership. Our stories must be character driven with strong conflict. All accepted stories are edited by our staff and the writer before publication to ensure a well-crafted and written work." Semiannual. Circ. 2,000.

Needs Literary. Receives 15 unsolicited mss/month. Accepts 3 mss/issue; 6 mss/year. Publishes ms 3-6 months after acceptance. Agented fiction 15%. **Publishes 3 new writers/year.** Recently published work by Stuart Dybek, Howard Norman, Molly Giles, Rick Moody. Length: 1,000-10,000 words; average length: 5,000 words. Publishes short shorts. Also publishes poetry. Often comments on rejected mss.

How to Contact Send SASE for return of ms. Responds in 3 months to queries; 3 months to mss. Sample copy for $7.95. Writer's guidelines for SASE or on website.

Payment/Terms Pays 2 contributor's copies; additional copies for $7.95. Pays on publication for first North American serial rights. Sends galleys to author.

Tips "Character driven, well crafted, strong conflict."

$ THE RAVEN CHRONICLES

A Magazine of Transcultural Art, Literature and the Spoken Word, 12346 Sand Point Way N.E., Seattle WA 98125. (206)364-2045. E-mail: editors@ravenchronicles.org. Website: www.ravenchronicles.org. Magazine: 8½ × 11; 88-100 pages; 50 lb. book; glossy cover; b&w illustrations; photos. "The Raven Chronicles is designed to promote transcultural art, literature and the spoken word." Biannual. Circ. 2,500-5,000.

Needs Ethnic/multicultural, literary, regional, political, cultural essays. "No romance, fantasy, mystery or detective." Receives 300-400 unsolicited mss/month. Accepts 35-60 mss/issue; 105-150 mss/year. Publishes ms 12 months after acceptance. **Publishes 50-100 new writers/year.** Recently published work by David Romtvedt, Sherman Alexie, D.L. Birchfield, Nancy Redwine, Diane Glancy, Greg Hischak, Sharon Hashimoto. Length: 2,500 words (but negotiable); average length: 2,000 words. Publishes short shorts. Also publishes literary essays, literary criticism, poetry. Sometimes comments on rejected mss.

How to Contact Send complete ms with SASE. Does not accept unsolicited submissions by e-mail (except foreign submissions). Responds in 3 months to mss. Does not accept simultaneous submissions. Sample copy for $5.19-10.19. Writer's guidelines for #10 SASE.

Payment/Terms Pays $10-40 and 2 contributor's copies; additional copies at half cover cost. Pays on publication for first North American serial rights. Sends galleys to author. See website for submission deadlines.

Tips Looks for "clean, direct language, written from the heart, and experimental writing. Read sample copy, or look at *Before Columbus* anthologies and *Greywolf Annual* anthologies."

THE READER

19 Abercromby Square, Liverpool, Merseyside LG9 7ZG United Kingdom. E-mail: info@thereader.org.uk; readers@liv.ac.uk. Website: www.thereader.org.uk. **Contact:** Philip Davis, editor. Literary magazine/journal: 216 X 138 mm, 130 pages, 80 gsm (Silver Offset) paper. Includes photographs. "The Reader is a quarterly literary magazine aimed at the intelligent 'common reader'—from those just beginning to explore serious literary reading to professional teachers, academics and writers. As well as publishing short fiction and poetry by new writers and established names, the magazine features articles on all aspects of literature, language, and reading; regular features, including a literary quiz and 'Our Spy in NY', a bird's-eye view of literary goings-on in New York; reviews; and readers'recommendations of books that have made a difference to them. The Reader is unique among literary magazines in its focus on reading as a creative, important and pleasurable activity, and in its combination of high-quality material and presentation with a genuine commitment to ordinary but dedicated readers." Quarterly. Estab. 1997.

Needs Literary. Receives 10 mss/month. Accepts 1-2 mss/issue; 8 mss/year. Manuscript published 16 months after acceptance. Publishes 4 new writers/year. Published Karen King Arbisala, Ray Tallis, Sasha Dugdale, Vicki Seal, David Constantine, Jonathan Meades, Ramesh Avadhani. Length: 1,000 words (min)-3,000 words (max). Average length: 2,300 words. Publishes short shorts. Average length of short shorts: 1,500 words. Also publishes literary essays, literary criticism, poetry. Sometimes comments on/critiques rejected mss.

How to Contact No email submissions. Send complete ms with cover letter. Include estimated word count, brief bio, list of publications. Responds to queries in 2 months; mss in 2 months. Send SASE (or IRC) for return of ms. Considers simultaneous submissions, multiple submissions. Guidelines available for SASE.

Payment/Terms Additional copies $14. Pays on publication. Sends galleys to author.

Tips "The style or polish of the writing is less important than the deep structure of the story (though of course, it matters that it's well written). The main persuasive element is whether the story moves us—and that's quite hard to quantify—it's something to do with the force of the idea and the genuine nature of enquiry within the story. When fiction is the writer's natural means of thinking things through, that'll get us."

THE RED CLAY REVIEW

M. A. in Professional Writing Program, Dept of English, Bldg. #27, Kennesaw State University, Kennesaw GA 30144-5591. E-mail: redclayreview@gmail.com. Website: http://rcr.kaitopia.com. **Contact:** Dr. Jim Elledge, Director M.A. in Professional Writing Program or student Editor-in-Chief. Magazine has revolving editor. Editorial term: 1 year. Literary magazine/journal. 8½ × 5½, 80-120 pages, 60# white paper, 10 pt matte lam. cover. "The Red Clay Review is dedicated to publishing only the most outstanding graduate literary pieces. It has been established by members of the Graduate Writers Association at Kennesaw State University. It is unique because it only includes the work of graduate writing students. We publish poems (must be limited to 300 words, double spaced, 12 pt. font, 3-5 poems per submission), fiction/non-fiction pieces (must not exceed 10 pages, double spaced, 12 pt. font), and 10 minute plays/scenes (should be limited to 11 total pages since the first page will usually be mostly taken up by character listing/setting description.)" Annual. Estab. 2008.

Needs "We do not have any specific themes or topics, but keep in mind that we are a literary publication. We will read whatever is sent in. We will publish whatever we deem to be great literary writing. So in essence, every topic is open to submission, and we are all interested in a wide variety of subjects. We do not prohibit any topic or subject matter from being submitted. As long as submissions adhere to our guidelines, we are open to reading them. However, subject matter in any area that is too extreme may be less likely to be published because we want to include a broad collection of literary graduate work, but on the other hand, we cannot morally reject great writing." Receives 12 mss/month. Does not read November 1- June 1. Ms published 6 months after acceptance. Length: 2,500 words (min)-8,000 words (max). Publishes short shorts. Also publishes literary essays, poetry. Never comments on/critiques rejected mss.

How to Contact Send complete ms with cover letter. Include brief bio, list of publications, and an e-mail address must be supplied for the student, as well as the student's advisor's contact information (to verify student status). Responds to mss in 12-16 weeks. Considers simultaneous submissions, multiple submissions. Guidelines available on website.

Payment/Terms Writers receive 2 contributor's copies. Pays on publication. Acquires first rights. Publication is copyrighted.

Tips "Because the editors of *RCR* are graduate student writers, we are mindful of grammatical proficiency, vocabulary, and the organizational flow of the submissions we receive. We appreciate a heightened level of writing from fellow graduate writing students; but we also hold it to a standard to which we have learned in our graduate writing experience. Have your submission(s) proofread by a fellow student or professor."

◪ REDIVIDER

120 Boylston St., Emerson College, Boston MA 02116. E-mail: fiction@redividerjournal.com. Website: www.redividerjournal.org. Editors change each year. Magazine: 5½ × 8½; 160 pages; 60 lb. paper. Redivider, a journal of literature and art, is published twice a year by students in the graduate writing, literature and publishing department of Emerson College. Biannual. Estab. 1986. Circ. 1000.

Needs Literary. Receives 100 unsolicited mss/month. Accepts 6-8 mss/issue; 10-12 mss/year. Publishes ms 3-6 months after acceptance. Publishes short shorts. Also publishes poetry. Sometimes comments on rejected mss.

How to Contact We are taking electronic submissions solely through our online submissions manager. Hard copy submissions and inquiries may be sent to the appropriate genre editor through postal mail. Send disposable copy of ms. Accepts simultaneous submissions with notification. Sample copy for $6 with a #10 SASE. Writer's guidelines for SASE or online.

Payment/Terms Pays 2 contributor's copies; additional copies $6. Pays on publication for one-time rights. Sponsors awards/contests.

Tips Our deadlines are July 1 for the Fall issue, and December 1 for the Spring issue.

◪ RED ROCK REVIEW

CSN Dept. of English, J2A, 3200 E. Cheyenne Ave., Las Vegas NV 89030. (702)651-4094. E-mail: RedRockReview@csn.edu; richard.logsdon@csn.edu. Website: sites.csn.edu/english/redrockreview/issue.htm. **Contact:** Dr. Richard Logsdon, senior editor. Magazine: 5 × 8; 125 pages. "We're looking for the very best literature. Stories need to be tightly crafted, strong in character development, built around conflict. Poems need to be tightly crafted, characterised by expert use of language." Semiannual. Circ. 250.

Needs Experimental, literary, mainstream. Receives 350 unsolicited mss/month. Accepts 40-60 mss/issue; 80-120 mss/year. Does not read mss during summer. Publishes ms 3-5 after acceptance. **Publishes 5-10 new writers/year.** Recently published work by Charles Harper Webb, Mary Sojourner, Mark Irwin. Length: less than 7,500 words. Publishes short shorts. Also publishes literary essays, literary criticism, poetry. Sometimes comments on rejected mss.

How to Contact Send SASE (or IRC) for return of ms. Responds in 2 weeks to queries; 3 months to mss. Does not accept general submissions June-August, or in December. Accepts simultaneous, multiple submissions. Sample copy for $5.50. Writer's guidelines for SASE, by e-mail or on website.

Payment/Terms Pays 2 contributor's copies. Pays on acceptance for first rights.

REED MAGAZINE

San Jose State University, Dept. of English, One Washington Square, San Jose CA 95192-0090. (408) 927-4458. E-mail: reed@email.sjsu.edu. Website: http://www.reedmag.org/drupal/. **Contact:** Nick Taylor, editor. Literary magazine/journal. 9 × 5.75, 200 pages, semi-gloss paper, card cover. Contains illustrations. Includes photographs. "Reed Magazine is one of the oldest student-run literary journals west of the Mississippi. We publish outstanding fiction, poetry, nonfiction and art as a service to the South Bay literary community." Annual. Circ. 3500. Member CLMP.

Needs Ethnic/multicultural (general), experimental, feminist, gay, historical (general), humor/satire, lesbian, literary, mainstream, regional (northern California). Does not want children's, young adult, fantasy, or erotic. Receives 30 mss/month. Accepts 5-7 mss/issue. Does not read Nov 2-May 31. Ms published 6 months after acceptance. Publishes 3-4 new writers/year. Published Tommy Mouton, Alan Soldofsky, Gwen Goodkin and Al Young. Length: 2,000 words (min)-6,000 words (max). Average length: 3,500 words. Also publishes literary essays, book reviews, poetry. Send review copies to Nick Taylor, Editor. Never comments on/critiques rejected mss.

How to Contact Submit online. Include estimated word count, brief bio. Responds to mss in 6 months. Considers simultaneous submissions, multiple submissions. Sample copy available for $8. Guidelines available on website.

Payment/Terms Writers receive free subscription to the magazine. Additional copies $5. Pays on publication. Acquires first North American serial rights. Sends galleys to author. Publication is copyrighted. "Sponsors the Steinbeck Award, given annually for the best short story. The prize is $1,000 and there's a $15 entry fee."

Tips "Well-writen, original, clean grammatical prose is essential. Keep submitting! The readers are students and change every year."

$ THE REJECTED QUARTERLY

A Journal of Quality Literature Rejected at Least Five Times, P.O. Box 1351, Cobb CA 95426. E-mail: bplankton@yahoo.com. **Contact:** Daniel Weiss, fiction editor. Magazine: 8½ × 11; 36-44 pages; 60 lb. paper; 10 pt. coated cover stock; illustrations. "We want the best literature possible, regardless of genre. We do, however, have a bias toward the unusual and toward speculative fiction. We aim for a literate, educated audience. The Rejected Quarterly believes in publishing the highest quality rejected fiction and other writing that doesn't fit anywhere else. We strive to be different, but will go for quality every time, whether conventional or not." Semiannual.

Needs Experimental, fantasy, historical, humor/satire, literary, mainstream, mystery/suspense, romance (futuristic/time travel only), science fiction (soft/sociological), sports. Accepts poetry about being rejected. Receives 30 unsolicited mss/month. Accepts 3-6 mss/issue; 8-12 mss/year. Publishes ms 1-12 months after acceptance. **Publishes 2-4 new writers/year.** Recently published work by Sharon Ellis, C. Marcus Parr, Adam Fuller, Tim Kissell, Hannah Gersen and John C. Carter. Length: 8,000 words. Publishes short shorts (literature related), literary criticism, rejection-related poetry. Often comments on rejected mss.

How to Contact Send SASE for reply, return of ms or send a disposable copy of ms. No longer accepting email submissions. Responds in 2-4 weeks to queries; 1-9 months to mss. Accepts reprint submissions. Sample copy for $7.50 (IRCs for foreign requests). Reviews fiction.

Payment/Terms Pays $20 and 1 contributor's copy; additional copies $5. Pays on acceptance for first rights.

Tips "Beginning in June 2010, we will be reading manuscripts from June through August only. We are looking for high-quality writing that tells a story or expresses a coherent idea. We want unique stories, original viewpoints and unusual slants. We are getting far too many inappropriate submissions. Please be familiar with the magazine. Be sure to include your rejection slips! Send out quality rather than quantity."

RIVER OAK REVIEW

Elmhurst College, 190 Prospect Ave, Elmhurst IL 60126-3296. (630) 617-3137. Fax: (630) 617-3609. E-mail: riveroak@elmhurst.edu. Website: www.riveroakreview.org. **Contact:** Ron Wiginton, editor. Literary magazine/journal: 6 × 9, 195 pages; perfect bound paper; glossy, 4 color cover. "We try with each issue to showcase many voices of America, loud and soft, radical and sublime. Each piece we publish, prose or poetry, is an attempt to capture a part of 'us', with the notion that it is through our art that we are defined as a culture." Estab. 1993. Circ. 500.

Needs Ethnic/multicultural (general), experimental, literary, mainstream, translations. Does not want genre fiction or "lessons of morality; 'idea' driven stories usually do not work." Receives 50-75 mss/month. Accepts 7-8 mss/issue; 14-16 mss/year. Ms published 3 months after acceptance. Agented fiction 1%. **Publishes 2-3 new writers/year.** Published Adam Lichtenstein, Robert Moulthrop, J. Malcom Garcia and Laura Hope-Gill. Length: 250 words (min)-7,000 words (max). Average length: 3,000 words. Publishes short shorts. Average length of short shorts: 750 words. Also publishes literary essays, book reviews, poetry. Send review copies to Ron Wiginton, Editor. Sometimes comments on/critiques rejected mss.

How to Contact Send complete ms with cover letter. Accepts submissions by e-mail. Include list of publications. Responds to mss in 6 months. Send disposable copy of ms and #10 SASE for reply only. Considers simultaneous submissions. Sample copy available for $5. Guidelines available for SASE, via e-mail, on website, via fax.

Payment/Terms Writers receive 2 contributor's copies. Additional copies $10. Pays on publication. Acquires first North American serial rights. Publication is copyrighted.

Tips "The voice is what we notice first. Is the writer in command of the language? Secondly, does the story have anything to say? It's not that 'fluff' cannot be good, but we note our favorites stories tend to have meaning beyond the surface of the plot. Thirdly, the story must by populated by 'real' peoples who are also interesting, characters, in other words, who have lives underneath the storyline. Finally, look before you leap."

RIVER STYX

3547 Olive Street Suite 107, St. Louis MO 63103. (314)533-4541. Fax: (314)289-4019. Website: www.riverstyx.org. **Contact:** Richard Newman, editor. Magazine: 6 × 9; 100 pages; color card cover; perfect-bound; b&w visual art. "River Styx publishes the highest quality fiction, poetry, interviews, essays, and visual art. We are an internationally distributed multicultural literary magazine." Mss read May-November. Estab. 1975.

- *River Styx* has had stories appear in *New Stories from the South* and has been included in *Pushcart* anthologies.

Needs Ethnic/multicultural, experimental, feminist, gay, lesbian, literary, mainstream, novel excerpts, translations, short stories, literary. "No genre fiction, less thinly veiled autobiography." Receives 350 unsolicited mss/month. Accepts 2-6 mss/issue; 6-12 mss/year. Reads only May through November. Publishes ms 1 year after acceptance. **Publishes 20 new writers/year.** Recently published work by George Singleton, Philip Graham, Katherine Min, Richard Burgin, Nancy Zafris, Jacob Appel, and Eric Shade. Publishes short shorts. Also publishes poetry. Sometimes comments on rejected mss.

How to Contact Send complete ms. SASE required. Responds in 4 months to mss. Accepts simultaneous submissions "if a note is enclosed with your work and if we are notified immediately upon acceptance elsewhere." Sample copy for $8. Writer's guidelines online.

Payment/Terms Pays 2 contributor copies, plus 1-year subscription; $8/page if funds are available. Pays on publication for first North American serial, one-time rights.

Tips "We want high-powered stories with well-developed characters. We like strong plots, usually with at least three memorable scenes, and a subplot often helps. No thin, flimsy fiction with merely serviceable language. Short stories shouldn't be any different than poetry—every single word should count. One could argue every word counts more since we're being asked to read 10 to 30 pages."

RIVERWIND

3301 Hocking Park Way, Nelsonville OH 45764. (740)753-3591. E-mail: williams_k@hocking.edu. Magazine: 7 × 7; 125-150 pages; 60 lb. offset paper; illustrations; photos. Riverwind is an established magazine that prints fiction, poetry, black and white photos and prints, drawings, creative nonfiction, book reviews and plays. Special consideration is given to writers from the Appalachian region. Annual. Estab. 1976. Circ. 200-400.

Needs Adventure, ethnic/multicultural (Appalachian), humor/satire, literary, mainstream, regional. DOES NOT WANT erotica, fantasy, horror, experimental, religious, children's/juvenile. Receives 25 unsolicited mss/month. Does not read mss June-September. Publishes ms 6-9 months after acceptance. **Publishes many new writers/year.** Recently published work by Gerald Wheeler, Wendy McVicker, Roy Bentley, Perry A. White, Tom Montag, Beau Beadreaux. Length: 500-2,500 words; average length: 1,750 words. Publishes short shorts. Also publishes literary essays, literary criticism, poetry. Rarely comments on rejected mss.

How to Contact Send complete ms. Accepts submissions by e-mail, disk. Send disposable copy of ms and #10 SASE for reply only. Responds in 4 weeks to queries; 8-16 weeks to mss. Accepts simultaneous, multiple submissions. Sample copy for $5. Writer's guidelines for #10 SASE or by e-mail.

Payment/Terms Pays 2 contributor's copies. Pays on publication for first North American serial rights.

Tips "Avoid stereotypical plots and characters. We tend to favor realism but not sentimentality."

◪ $ ROANOKE REVIEW

Roanoke College, 221 College Lane, Salem VA 24153-3794. (540)375-2380. E-mail: review@roanoke.edu. **Contact:** Paul Hanstedt, editor. Magazine: 6 × 9; 200 pages; 60 lb. paper; 70 lb. cover. "We're looking for fresh, thoughtful material that will appeal to a broader as well as literary audience. Humor encouraged." Annual. Estab. 1967. Circ. 500.

Needs Feminist, gay, humor/satire, lesbian, literary, mainstream, regional. Receives 150 unsolicited mss/month. Accepts 5-10 mss/year. Does not read mss February 1-September 1. Publishes ms 6 months after acceptance. **Publishes 1-5 new writers/year.** Recently published work by Siobhan Fallon, Jacob M. Appel, and JoeAnn Hart. Length: 1,000-5,000 words; average length: 3,000 words. Publishes short shorts. Also publishes poetry. Sometimes comments on rejected mss.

How to Contact Send SASE for return of ms or send a disposable copy of ms and #10 SASE for reply only. Responds in 1 month to queries; 6 months to mss. Sample copy for 8 × 11 SAE with $2 postage. Writer's guidelines for SASE.

Payment/Terms Pays $10-50/story (when budget allows) and 2 contributor's copies; additional copies $5. Pays on publication for one-time rights.

Tips "Pay attention to sentence-level writing—verbs, metaphors, concrete images. Don't forget, though, that plot and character keep us reading. We're looking for stuff that breaks the MFA story style."

◪ THE ROCKFORD REVIEW

The Rockford Writers Guild, P.O. Box 858, Rockford IL 61105. E-mail: rosangela.taylor@rockfordwritersguild.com. Website: http://www.rockfordwritersguild.com/review. **Contact:** Rosangela C. Taylor, editor. Magazine: 100 pages; perfect bound; color illustrations; b&w photos. Rockford Writers' Guild is a nonprofit corporation established in 1947 with the mission to promote the literary arts in Rockford, IL and beyond. Monthly meetings, interaction with other writers, writers groups, editorial support, current information and useful resources through the website, discounts on book production, and other benefits are just part of what RWG offers to its members. Semiannual.

Needs Ethnic/multicultural, experimental, fantasy, humor/satire, literary, regional, science fiction (hard science, soft/sociological). "No graphic sex, translations or overly academic work." Recently published work by James Bellarosa, Sean Michael Rice, John P. Kristofco, L.S. Sedishiro. Also publishes literary essays.

How to Contact Please go online and follow the rules for submission: www.rockfordwritersguild.com/submit.html. Please note that submissions rules may change from time to time and for each edition there is a different theme to write about. So, check the website regularly. Be sure your manuscripts conform to the rules, or they may not be considered. Pays 1 contributor's copy and pays two editor's choice awards of $25 each: one for prose and one for poetry

Tips "We're wide open to new and established writers alike—particularly short satire."

$ ROOM

A Canadian Quarterly of Women's Literature and Criticism, P.O. Box 46160, Station D, Vancouver BC V6J 5G5 Canada. E-mail: contactus@roommagazine.com. Website: www.roommagazine.com. **Contact:** Growing Room Collective. Magazine: 112 pages; illustrations; photos. "Room of One's Own is Canada's oldest feminist literary journal. Since 1975, Room has been a forum in which women can share their unique perspectives on the world, each other and themselves." Quarterly. Estab. 1975.

Needs Feminist literature—short stories, creative nonfiction, essays—by, for and about women. "No humor, science fiction, romance." Receives 60-100 unsolicited mss/month. Accepts 18-20 mss/issue; 75-80 mss/year. Publishes ms 1 year after acceptance. **Publishes 15-20 new writers/year.** Publishes poetry by Canadian authors only.

How to Contact We are accepting email submissions on a trial basis. See our guidelines online. Or, send complete ms with a cover letter. Include estimated word count and brief bio. Do not send a SASE. Responds in 6 months to mss. Sample copy for $13 or online. Writer's guidelines online. Reviews fiction.

Payment/Terms Pays $50 (Canadian), 2 contributor's copies, and a 1-year subscription. Pays on publication for first North American serial rights.

SALMAGUNDI

Skidmore College, 815 North Broadway, Saratoga Springs NY 12866. (518)580-5000 ext. 4495. Fax: (518)580-5188. E-mail: salmagun@skidmore.edu. Website: cms.skidmore.edu/salmagundi/index.cfm. Magazine: 8 × 5; 200-300 pages; illustrations; photos. "*Salmagundi* publishes an eclectic variety of materials, ranging from short-short fiction to novellas from the surreal to the realistic. Authors include Nadine Gordimer, Russell Banks, Steven Millhauser, Gordon Lish, Clark Blaise, Mary Gordon, Joyce Carol Oates and Cynthia Ozick. Our audience is a generally literate population of people who read for pleasure." Quarterly. Circ. 4,800. Member CLMP.

- *Salmagundi* authors are regularly represented in *Pushcart* collections and *Best American Short Story* collections.

Needs Ethnic/multicultural (multicultural), experimental, family saga, gay, historical (general), literary, poetry. Receives 300-500 unsolicited mss/month. Accepts 2 mss/year. Read unsolicited mss October 1-May 1 "but from time to time close the doors even during this period because the backlog tends to grow out of control." Publishes ms up to 2 years after acceptance. Agented fiction 10%. Also publishes literary essays, literary criticism, poetry.

How to Contact *Currently not accepting unsolicited mss.* Send complete ms by e-mail (pboyes@skidmore.edu). Responds in 6 months to mss. Sample copy for $5. Writer's guidelines for #10 SASE.

Payment/Terms Pays 6-10 contributor's copies and subscription to magazine. Acquires first, electronic rights.

Tips "I look for excellence and a very unpredictable ability to appeal to the interests and tastes of the editors. Be brave. Don't be discouraged by rejection. Keep stories in circulation. Of course, it goes without saying: Work hard on the writing. Revise tirelessly. Study magazines and send only to those whose sensibility matches yours."

SANTA MONICA REVIEW

1900 Pico Blvd., Santa Monica CA 90405. Website: www.smc.edu/sm_review/. Magazine: 250 pages. "The editors are committed to fostering new talent as well as presenting new work by established writers. There is also a special emphasis on presenting and promoting writers who make their home in Southern California." Circ. 4,000.

Needs Experimental, literary, memoirs. "No crime and detective, mysogyny, footnotes, TV, dog stories. We want more self-conscious, smart, political, humorous, digressive, meta-fiction." Receives 250 unsolicited mss/month. Accepts 10 mss/issue; 20 mss/year. Agented fiction 10%. **Publishes 5 new writers/year.** Recently published work by Charles Baxter, Greg Bills, John Cage,

Bernard Cooper, Mary Jeselnik-Koral, Amy Gerstler, Judith Grossman, Peter Handke, Jim Krusoe, Michelle Latiolais, and Deena Metzger . Also publishes literary essays.
How to Contact Send complete ms. Send disposable copy of ms. Responds in 3 months to mss. Accepts simultaneous, multiple submissions. Sample copy for $7.
Payment/Terms Pays 5 contributor's copies. Acquires first North American serial rights. Sends galleys to author.

THE SARANAC REVIEW

Dept. of English, Champlain Valley Hall, Plattsburgh NY 12901. (518)564-2414. Fax: (518)564-2140. E-mail: saranacreview@plattsburgh.edu. Website: research.plattsburgh.edu/saranacreview. **Contact:** Fiction Editor. Magazine: 5½ × 8½; 180 pages; 80 lb. cover/70 lb. paper; glossy cover stock; illustrations; photos. "*The Saranac Review* is committed to dissolving boundaries of all kinds, seeking to publish a diverse array of emerging and established writers from Canada and the U.S. *The Saranac Review* aims to be a textual clearing in which a space is opened for cross-pollination between American and Canadian writers. In this way the magazine reflects the expansive bright spirit of the etymology of it's name, Saranac, meaning 'cluster of stars."' Annual.
Needs Ethnic/multicultural, historical, literary, flash fiction. Publishes ms 8 months after acceptance. Also publishes poetry and literary/creative nonfiction. Sometimes comments on rejected mss.
How to Contact Send complete ms. Send SASE (or IRC) for return of ms or send disposable copy of the ms and #10 SASE for reply only. Responds in 4 months to mss. Accepts simultaneous submissions. Sample copy for $6. Writer's guidelines online, or by e-mail. "Please send one story at a time." Maximum length: 7,000 words.
Payment/Terms Pays 2 contributor's copies; discount on extras. Pays on publication for first North American serial, first rights.
Tips "We publish serious, generous fiction."

THE SEATTLE REVIEW

Box 354330, University of Washington, Seattle WA 98195. (206)543-2302. E-mail: seaview@u.washington.edu. Website: www.seattlereview.org. **Contact:** Andrew Feld, editor-in-chief. Magazine: 6 × 9; 150 pages; illustrations; photos. "Includes fiction, nonfiction, poetry and one interview per issue with an established writer." Semiannual. Estab. 1978. Circ. 1,000.Needs Literary. Nothing in "bad taste (porn, racist, etc.)." Receives 200 unsolicited mss/month. Accepts 2-4 mss/issue; 4-8 mss/year. Does not read mss May 31-October 1. Publishes ms 1-212 years after acceptance. **Publishes 3-4 new writers/year.** Recently published work by Rick Bass, Lauren Whitehurst, Martha Hurwitz. Length: 4,000 words; average length: 3,000 words.
How to Contact Send complete ms. Send SASE (or IRC) for return of ms or send disposable copy of ms and #10 SASE for reply only. Responds in 4-6 months to mss. No simultaneous submissions, accepts multiple submissions. Sample copy for $8. Writer's guidelines for #10 SASE, online or by e-mail.
Payment/Terms Pays 2 contributor's copies. Acquires first North American serial rights.
Tips "Know what we publish: no genre fiction; look at our magazine and decide if your work might be appreciated."

$ THE SEWANEE REVIEW

735 University Ave., Sewanee TN 37383-1000. (931)598-1246. Website: www.sewanee.edu/sreview/home.html. **Contact:** George Core. "A literary quarterly, publishing original fiction, poetry, essays on literary and related subjects, and book reviews for well-educated readers who appreciate good American and English literature." Quarterly. Estab. 1892.
Needs Literary, contemporary. No erotica, science fiction, fantasy or excessively violent or profane material.
How to Contact Responds in 8-10 weeks to mss. Sample copy for $8.50. Writer's guidelines online, or e-mail Leigh Anne Couch at lcouch@sewanee.edu. Unsolicited works should not be submitted between June 1st and August 31st.
Payment/Terms Pays $10-12/printed pages of prose; $2.50/line of poetry. 2 contributor copies.

Pays on publication for first North American serial, second serial (reprint) rights.

$ SHENANDOAH

Washington and Lee University, Mattingly House, 2 Lee Avenue, Washington and Lee University, Lexington VA 24450-2116. (540) 458-8765. E-mail: shenandoah@wlu.edu. Website: http://shenandoah.wlu.edu. Triannual. Estab. 1950. Circ. 2,000.

Needs Mainstream, novel excerpts. No sloppy, hasty, slight fiction. Publishes ms 10 months after acceptance.

How to Contact Send complete ms. Responds in 2 months to mss. Sample copy for $10. Writer's guidelines online.

Payment/Terms Pays $25/page (cap $250). Pays on publication for first North American serial, one-time rights.

◪ SLEEPINGFISH

E-mail: white@sleepingfish.net. Literary magazine/journal: 6 × 8, 160 pages, 60 lb. vellum paper, card stock cover. More recently publishing a Web version. Contains illustrations. Includes photographs. "Sleepingfish publishes an eclectic mix of flash fiction, prose and visual poetry, experimental texts, text/image and art." Published every 9 months. Circ. 500.

Needs Adventure, comics/graphic novels, ethnic/multicultural, experimental, literary. Does not want to see any fiction or writing that fits into a genre or that is written for any other reason except for the sake of art. Receives 250 mss/month. Accepts 25 mss/issue; 25 mss/year. Manuscript published less than 3 months after acceptance. **Publishes 2-3 new writers/year.**Published Rick Moody, Dawn Raffel, Terese Svoboda, Laird Hunt, Normon Lock, Peter Markus, Kevin Sampsell, Brian Evenson, Thurston Moore, and Kim Chinquee. Length: 1 word (min)-8,000 words (max). Average length: 2,000 words. Publishes short shorts. Average length of short shorts: 1,000 words. Rarely comments on/critiques rejected mss.

How to Contact Send complete ms with cover letter during reading period only. Only accepts submissions by e-mail. See website for next submission period. Include brief bio. Responds to queries in 4 weeks. Responds to mss in 3 months. Send SASE (or IRC) for return of ms. Considers simultaneous submissions, multiple submissions. Guidelines available on website.

Payment/Terms Writers receive 1 contributor copy. Additional copies half price. Pays on publication. Acquires first rights. Sends galleys to author. Publication is copyrighted.

Tips "Write or create what's true to yourself and find a publication where you think your work honestly fits in."

◪ $ SNOWY EGRET

The Fair Press, P.O. Box 9265, Terre Haute IN 47808. **Contact:** Editors. Magazine: 8½ × 11; 60 pages; text paper; heavier cover; illustrations. "We publish works which celebrate the abundance and beauty of nature and examine the variety of ways in which human beings interact with landscapes and living things. Nature writing from literary, artistic, psychological, philosophical and historical perspectives." Semiannual. Estab. 1922. Circ. 400.

Needs "No genre fiction, e.g., horror, western, romance, etc." Receives 25 unsolicited mss/month. Accepts up to 6 mss/issue; up to 12 mss/year. Publishes ms 6 months after acceptance. **Publishes 20 new writers/year.** Recently published work by James Hinton, Ron Gielgun, Tom Noyes, Alice Cross, Maeve Mullin Ellis. Length: 500-10,000 words; average length: 1,000-3,000 words. Publishes short shorts. Sometimes comments on rejected mss.

How to Contact Send complete ms with SASE. Cover letter optional: do not query. Responds in 2 months to mss. Accepts simultaneous submissions if noted. Sample copy for 9 × 12 SASE and $8. Writer's guidelines for #10 SASE.

Payment/Terms Pays $2/page plus 2 contributor's copies. Pays on publication for first North American serial, one-time anthology rights, or reprint rights. Sends galleys to author.

Tips Looks for "honest, freshly detailed pieces with plenty of description and/or dialogue which will allow the reader to identify with the characters and step into the setting; fiction in which nature affects character development and the outcome of the story."

SONORA REVIEW

University of Arizona's Creative Writing MFA Program, University of Arizona, Dept. of English, Tucson AZ 85721. E-mail: sonora@email.arizona.edu. Website: www.coh.arizona.edu/sonora. **Contact:** Jake Levine, Jon Walter, editors. Magazine: 6 × 9; approx. 150 pages; photos. "We look for the highest quality poetry, fiction, and nonfiction, with an emphasis on emerging writers. Our magazine has a long-standing tradition of publishing the best new literature and writers. Check out our website for a sample of what we publish and our submission guidelines, or write us for a sample back issue." Semiannual. Estab. 1980. Circ. 500.

Needs Ethnic/multicultural, experimental, literary, mainstream, novel excerpts. Receives 200 unsolicited mss/month. Accepts 2-3 mss/issue; 6-8 mss/year. Does not read in the summer (June-August). Publishes ms 3-4 months after acceptance. **Publishes 1-3 new writers/year.** Recently published work by Michael Martone, Sawako Nakayasu. Also publishes literary essays, literary criticism, poetry. Sometimes comments on rejected mss.

How to Contact Send complete ms. Send disposable copy of the ms and #10 SASE for reply only. Responds in 2-5 weeks to queries; 3 months to mss. Accepts simultaneous, multiple submissions. Sample copy for $6. Writer's guidelines online. Reviews fiction.

Payment/Terms Pays 2 contributor's copies; additional copies for $4. Pays on publication for first North American serial, one-time, electronic rights.

Tips "Send us your best stuff."

SO TO SPEAK

A Feminist Journal of Language and Art, 4400 University Dr., MSN 2C5, Fairfax VA 22030. E-mail: sts@gmu.edu. Website: www.gmu.edu/org/sts. **Contact:** Angela Panayotopulos, editor-in-chief. Magazine: 5½ × 8½; approximately 100 pages. "We are a feminist journal of language and art." Semiannual. Circ. 1,000.

Needs Ethnic/multicultural, experimental, feminist, lesbian, literary, mainstream, regional, translations. "No science fiction, mystery, genre romance." Receives 100 unsolicited mss/month. Accepts 3-5 mss/issue; 6-10 mss/year. Publishes ms 6 months after acceptance. **Publishes 7 new writers/year.** Length: For fiction, up to 5,000 words; for poetry, 3-5 pages per submission; average length: for fiction, up to 5,000 words; for poetry, 3-5 pages per submission. Publishes flash and short fiction, creative nonfiction, poetry, and visual art.

How to Contact Send complete ms attention Fiction Editor. Include bio (50 words maximum) and SASE for return of ms or send a disposable copy of ms. Include your name, address, phone number, and e-mail address, how you heard about *So to Speak*, and a bio of 75 words or less. Does not accept e-mail. "Fiction submitted during the August 1–October 15 reading period will be considered for our Spring Issue and requires no reading fee. Fiction submitted during the January 1–March 15 reading period will be considered for our Fall annual fiction contest & must be accompanied by a $15 reading fee. See contest guidelines. Contest entries will not be returned." Responds in 6 months to mss. Accepts simultaneous submissions. Sample copy for $7. Reviews fiction.

Payment/Terms Pays contributor copies. Acquires first North American serial rights. Sponsors awards/contests.

Tips "We do not read between March 15 and August 15. Every writer has something they do exceptionally well; do that and it will shine through in the work. We look for quality prose with a definite appeal to a feminist audience. We are trying to move away from strict genre lines. We want high quality fiction, nonfiction, poetry, art, innovative and risk-taking work."

SOUTH CAROLINA REVIEW

611 Strode Tower Box 340522, Clemson University, Clemson SC 29634-0522. (864) 656-5399. Fax: (864) 656-1345. E-mail: cwayne@clemson.edu. Website: www.clemson.edu/caah/cedp. **Contact:** Wayne Chapman, editor. Magazine: 6 × 9; 200 pages; 60 lb. cream white vellum paper; 65 lb. color cover stock. Semiannual. Estab. 1967. Circ. 500.

Needs Literary, mainstream, poetry, essays, reviews. Does not read mss June-August or December. Receives 50-60 unsolicited mss/month. Recently published work by Ronald Frame, Dennis McFadden, Dulane Upshaw Ponder, and Stephen Jones. Rarely comments on rejected mss.

How to Contact Send complete ms. Requires text on disk upon acceptance in WordPerfect or Microsoft Word in PC format. Responds in 2 months to mss. Sample copy for $16 includes postage inside the U.S. Reviews fiction.
Payment/Terms Pays in contributor's copies.

SOUTHERN CALIFORNIA REVIEW

3501 Trousdale Parkway, Mark Taper Hall, THH 355J, Los Angeles CA 90089-4034. E-mail: scr@college.usc.edu. Website: usc.edu/scr. **Contact:** Fiction Editor. Magazine: 150 pages; semiglosss cover stock. "Formerly known as the Southern California Anthology, *Southern California Review* (SCR) is the literary journal of the Master of Professional Writing program at the University of Southern California. It has been publishing fiction and poetry since 1982 and now also accepts submissions of creative nonfiction, plays, and screenplays. Printed every fall and spring with original cover artwork, every issue contains new, emerging, and established authors." Semiannual. Circ. 1,000.
Needs "We accept short shorts but rarely use stories more than 8,000 words. Novel excerpts are acceptable if they can stand alone. We do consider genre work (horror, mystery, romance, sci-fi) if it transcends the boundaries of the genre." Receives 120 unsolicited mss/month. Accepts 10-15 mss/issue. Publishes ms 4 months after acceptance. **Publishes 20-30 new writers/year**. Recently published work by Judith Freeman, Gary Fincke David Francis, Gerald Locklin, Seth Greenland, and interviews with Nathan Englander, Steve Almond, Danzy Senna. Publishes short shorts.
How to Contact Send complete, typed, double-spaced ms. Cover letter should include list of previous publications. Address to the proper editor (Fiction, Poetry, etc.). Please include a cover letter. Be sure your full name and contact information (address, phone, and email) appear on the first page of the manuscript. Response time for submissions is 3 to 6 months. No electronic or email submissions are accepted. Every submission must include a self-addressed stamped envelope (SASE). Sample copy for $10. Writer's guidelines for SASE and on website.
Payment/Terms Pays in 2 contributor copies. Acquires first rights.

SOUTHERN HUMANITIES REVIEW

9088 Haley Center, Auburn University AL 36849. (334)844-4620. Fax: (334) 844-9027. E-mail: english@auburn.edu. Website: www.auburn.edu/english/shr/home.htm. **Contact:** Dan Latimer and Chantel Acevedo, co-editors. Magazine: 6 × 9; 100 pages; 60 lb neutral pH, natural paper; 65 lb. neutral pH medium coated cover stock; occasional illustration; photos. "We publish essays, poetry, fiction and reviews. Our fiction has ranged from very traditional in form and content to very experimental. Literate, college-educated audience. We hope they read our journal for both enlightenment and pleasure." Quarterly. Circ. 800.
Needs Feminist, humor/satire, regional. Slower reading time in summer. Receives 25 unsolicited mss/month. Accepts 1-2 mss/issue; 4-6 mss/year. Recently published work by Chris Arthur, Andrea Deagon, Sheryl St. Germain, Patricia Foster, Janette Turner Hospital, Paula Köhlmeier, David Wagner, Yves Bonnefoy, Neil Grimmett, and Wayne Flynt. Also publishes literary essays, literary criticism, poetry. Sometimes comments on rejected mss.
How to Contact Send complete ms, cover letter with an explanation of the topic chosen—"special, certain book, etc., a little about the author if he/she has never submitted." No e-mail submissions. No simultaneous submissions. Responds in 3 months to mss.
Payment/Terms Pays in contributor copies. Rights revert to author on publication.
Tips "Send us the ms with SASE. If we like it, we'll take it or we'll recommend changes. If we don't like it, we'll send it back as promptly as possible. Read the journal. Send typewritten, clean copy, carefully proofread. We also award the annual Hoepfner Prize of $100 for the best published essay or short story of the year. Let someone whose opinion you respect read your story and give you an honest appraisal. Rewrite, if necessary, to get the most from your story."

$ THE SOUTHERN REVIEW

Old President's House, Louisiana State University, Baton Rouge LA 70803-5001. (225)578-5108. Fax: (225)578-5098. E-mail: southernreview@lsu.edu. Website: www.lsu.edu/thesouthernreview/.

Contact: Jeanne Leiby, editor. Magazine: 6¼ × 10; 240 pages; 50 lb. Glatfelter paper; 65 lb. #1 grade cover stock. Quarterly. Circ. 3,000.

- Several stories published in *The Southern Review* were *Pushcart Prize* selections.

Needs Literary. "We select fiction that conveys a unique and compelling voice and vision." Receives approximately 300 unsolicited mss/month. Accepts 4-6 mss/issue. Reading period: September-May. Publishes ms 6 months after acceptance. Agented fiction 1%. **Publishes 10-12 new writers/year.** Recently published work by Jack Driscoll, Don Lee, Peter Levine, and Debbie Urbanski. Also publishes literary essays, literary criticism, poetry and book reviews.

How to Contact Mail hard copy of ms with cover letter and SASE. No queries. "Prefer brief letters giving author's professional information, including recent or notable publications. Biographical info not necessary." Responds within 10 weeks to mss. Sample copy for $8. Writer's guidelines online. Reviews fiction, poetry.

Payment/Terms Pays $30/page. Pays on publication for first North American serial rights. Sends page proof to author via e-mail. Sponsors awards/contests.

Tips "Careful attention to craftsmanship and technique combined with a developed sense of the creation of story will always make us pay attention."

SOUTHWESTERN AMERICAN LITERATURE

Texas State University-San Marcos, 601 University Dr., San Marcos TX 78666. (512)245-2224. Fax: (512)245-7462. E-mail: swpublications@txstate.edu. Website: swrhc.txstate.edu/cssw/. **Contact:** Twister Marquiss, assistant editor; Mark Busby, co-editor; Dick Maurice Heaberlin, co-editor. Magazine: 6x9; 125 pages; 80 lb. cover stock. "We publish fiction, nonfiction, poetry, literary criticism and book reviews. Generally speaking, we want material covering the Greater Southwest or material written by Southwest writers." Biannual.

Needs Ethnic/multicultural, literary, mainstream, regional. "No science fiction or romance." Receives 10-15 unsolicited mss/month. Accepts 1-2 mss/issue; 4-5 mss/year. Publishes ms 6 months after acceptance. **Publishes 1-2 new writers/year.** Recently published work by Sherwin Bitsui, Alison Hawthorne Deming, Keith Ekiss, Sara Marie Ortiz, Karla K. Morton, Lowell Mick White, John Blanchard, Jeffrey C. Alfier, Carol Hamilton, and Larry D. Thomas. Length: 6,250 words; average length: 4,000 words. Also publishes literary essays, literary criticism, poetry. Sometimes comments on rejected mss.

How to Contact Send complete ms. Include cover letter, estimated word count, 2-5 line bio and list of publications. Accepts e-mail submissions: swpublications@txstate.edu. Include bio and list of publications in e-mail. Responds in 3-6 months to mss. Sample copy for $10. Writer's guidelines free.

Payment/Terms Pays 2 contributor copies. Acquires first rights.

Tips "We look for crisp language, an interesting approach to material; a regional approach is desired but not required. Read widely, write often, revise carefully. We are looking for stories that probe the relationship between the tradition of Southwestern American literature and the writer's own imagination in creative ways. We seek stories that move beyond stereotype and approach the larger defining elements and also ones that, as William Faulkner noted in his Nobel Prize acceptance speech, treat subjects central to good literature—the old verities of the human heart, such as honor and courage and pity and suffering, fear and humor, love and sorrow."

SOUTHWEST REVIEW

P.O. Box 750374, Dallas TX 75275-0374. (214)768-1037. Fax: (214)768-1408. E-mail: swr@smu.edu. Website: www.smu.edu/southwestreview. **Contact:** Jennifer Cranfill, Senior Editor. Magazine: 6 × 9; 150 pages. "The majority of our readers are well read adults who wish to stay abreast of the latest and best in contemporary fiction, poetry, and essays in all but the most specialized disciplines." Quarterly. Estab. 1915. Circ. 1,600.

Needs "High literary quality; no specific requirements as to subject matter, but cannot use sentimental, religious, western, poor science fiction, pornographic, true confession, mystery, juvenile or serialized or condensed novels." Receives 200 unsolicited mss/month. Publishes ms 6-12 months after acceptance. Recently published work by Alice Hoffman, Sabina Murray, Alix

Ohlin. Also publishes literary essays, poetry. Occasionally comments on rejected mss.
How to Contact Mail complete ms to P.O. Box or submit online. Please note that online submissions require a $2.00 administrative fee. Responds in 1-4 months to mss. Accepts multiple submissions. Sample copy for $6. Writer's guidelines for #10 SASE or on website.
Payment/Terms Pays negotiable rate and 3 contributor copies. Acquires first North American serial rights. Sends galleys to author.
Tips "Despite the title, we are not a regional magazine. Before you submit your work, it's a good idea to take a look at recent issues to familiarize yourself with the magazine. We strongly advise all writers to include a cover letter. Keep your cover letter professional and concise and don't include extraneous personal information, a story synopsis, or a resume. When authors ask what we look for in a strong story submission the answer is simple regardless of graduate degrees in creative writing, workshops, or whom you know. We look for good writing, period."

SPOUT

Spout Press, P.O. Box 581067, Minneapolis MN 55458-1067.E-mail: editors@spoutpress.org. Website: www.spoutpress.org. **Contact:** Carrie Eidem, fiction editor. Literary magazine/journal: 5¾ × 8½, 60 pages. Contains illustrations. Includes photographs. "With Spout we strive to publish experimental writing. We don't focus on any certain style, tone or approach for the stories we publish. Spout also has an annual fiction story of the year contest. Please see website for details." Semiannual. Estab. 1989. Member CLMP.
Needs Adventure, comics/graphic novels, ethnic/multicultural (general), experimental, feminist, gay, science fiction. Does not want children's fiction. Receives 15-20 mss/month. Accepts 3-5 mss/issue; 6-10 mss/year. Ms published 1-2 months after acceptance. **Publishes 6-10 new writers/year**. Published Jeri Blazek, Ryan Van Cleave and Mike Tuohy. Length: 500 words (min)-7,000 words (max). Average length: 5,000 words. Publishes short shorts. Average length of short shorts: 500 words. Also publishes poetry. Rarely comments on/critiques rejected mss.
How to Contact Send complete ms with cover letter. Include estimated word count, brief bio. Responds to queries within one month. Responds to mss in 6-8 weeks. Send either SASE (or IRC) for return of ms or disposable copy of ms and #10 SASE for reply only. Considers simultaneous submissions, multiple submissions. Sample copy available for $5. Guidelines available for SASE, via e-mail, on website.
Payment/Terms Writers receive 1 contributor copy. Additional copies $5. Pays on publication. Acquires one-time rights. Publication is not copyrighted. "We take submissions from the fall to spring for our Story of the Year contest. See website for details."
Tips "Please look at our *Spout Magazine* to see if your submissions will fit our journal."

STAND MAGAZINE

North American Office: Department of English, VCU, Richmond VA 23284-2005. (804) 828-1331. E-mail: dlatane@vcu.edu. Website: www.standmagazine.org. "Stand Magazine is concerned with what happens when cultures and literatures meet, with translation in its many guises, with the mechanics of language, with the processes by which the policy receives or disables its cultural makers. Stand promotes debate of issues that are of radical concern to the intellectual community worldwide." Quarterly. Estab. 1952 in Leeds UK. Circ. 3,000 worldwide.
Needs "No genre fiction." Publishes ms 12 months after acceptance.
How to Contact Send complete ms. Responds in 6 weeks to queries; 3 months to mss. Sample copy for $12. Writer's guidelines for #10 SASE with sufficient number of IRCs or online.
Payment/Terms Payment varies. Pays on publication. Aquires first world rights.

$ STONE SOUP

The Magazine by Young Writers and Artists, P.O. Box 83, Santa Cruz CA 95063-0083. (831)426-5557. Fax: (831)426-1161. Website: www.stonesoup.com. **Contact:** Ms. Gerry Mandel, editor. Magazine: 7 × 10; 48 pages; high quality paper; photos. Audience is children, teachers, parents, writers, artists. "We have a preference for writing and art based on real-life experiences; no formula stories or poems. We only publish writing by children ages 8 to 13. We do not publish writing by adults." Bimonthly. Circ. 15,000.

Needs Adventure, ethnic/multicultural, experimental, fantasy, historical, humor/satire, mystery/suspense, science fiction, slice-of-life vignettes, suspense. "We do not like assignments or formula stories of any kind." Receives 1,000 unsolicited mss/month. Accepts 10 mss/issue. Publishes ms 4 months after acceptance. **Publishes some new writers/year.** Also publishes literary essays, poetry.

How to Contact Send complete ms. "We like to learn a little about our young writers, why they like to write, and how they came to write the story they are submitting." Please do not include SASE. Do not send originals. Responds only to those submissions being considered for possible publication. "If you do not hear from us in 4 to 6 weeks it means we were not able to use your work. Don't be discouraged! Try again!" No simultaneous submissions. Sample copy for $5 or online. Writer's guidelines online.

Payment/Terms Pays $40 for stories. Authors also receive 2 copies, a certificate, and discounts on additional copies and on subscriptions. Pays on publication.

Tips Mss are rejected because they are "derivatives of movies, TV, comic books, or classroom assignments or other formulas. Go to our website, where you can see many examples of the kind of work we publish."

$ STORIE

Leconte Press, Via Suor Celestina Donati 13/E, Rome 00167 Italy. (+39) 06 614 8777. Fax: (+39) 06 614 8777. E-mail: storie@tiscali.it. Website: www.storie.it. **Contact**: Gianluca Bassi, editor; Barbara Pezzopane, assistant editor; George Lerner, foreign editor. Magazine: 186 pages; illustrations; photographs. "Storie is one of Italy's leading literary magazines. Committed to a truly crossover vision of writing, the bilingual (Italian/English) review publishes high quality fiction and poetry, interspersed with the work of alternative wordsmiths such as filmmakers and musicians. Through writings bordering on narratives and interviews with important contemporary writers, it explores the culture and craft of writing." Bimonthly. Estab. 1989. Circ. 20,000.

Needs Literary. Receives 150 unsolicited mss/month. Accepts 6-10 mss/issue; 30-50 mss/year. Does not read mss in August. Publishes ms 2 months after acceptance. Publishes 20 new writers/year. Recently published work by Joyce Carol Oates, Haruki Murakami, Paul Auster, Robert Coover, Raymond Carver, T.C. Boyle, Ariel Dorfman, Tess Gallagher. Length: 2,000-6,000 words; average length: 1,500 words. Publishes short shorts. Also publishes literary essays, literary criticism, poetry. Sometimes comments on rejected mss.

How to Contact Accepts submissions by e-mail or on disk. Include brief bio. Send complete ms with cover letter. "Manuscripts may be submitted directly by regular post without querying first; however, we do not accept unsolicited m anus cripts via e-mail. Please query via e-mail first. We only contact writers if their work has been accepted. We also arrange for and oversee a high-quality, professional translation of the piece." Responds in 1 month to queries; 6 months to mss. Accepts multiple submissions. Sample copy for $ 10. Writer's guidelines online.

Payment/Terms Pays $30-600 and 2 contributor's copies. Pays on publication for first (in English and Italian) rights.

Tips "More than erudite references or a virtuoso performance, we're interested in the recording of human experience in a genuine, original voice. *Storie* reserves the right to include a brief review of interesting submissions not selected for publication in a special column of the magazine."

STRAYLIGHT

UW-Parkside, English Dept., 900 Wood Rd., P.O. Box 2000, Kenosha WI 53141. (262)595-2139. Fax: (262)595-2271. E-mail: straylight@litspot.net. Website: www.straylightmag.com. **Contact:** fiction editor. Magazine has revolving editor. Editorial term: 1 years. Literary magazine/journal: 6x9 115 pages, quality paper, uncoated index stock cover. Contains illustrations. Includes photographs. "Straylight publishes high quality, character-based fiction of any style. We tend not to publish strict genre pieces, though we may query them for future special issues. We do not publish erotica." Biannual with special issues. Estab. 2005.

Needs Ethnic/multicultural (general), experimental, gay, lesbian, literary, mainstream, regional. Special interests: genre fiction in special theme issues. Accepts 3-5 mss/issue; 6-10 mss/year. Does not read May-August. Manuscript published 6 months after acceptance. Agented fiction 10%. Length: 2,500 words (min)-6,000 words (max). Average length: 2,500 words. Publishes short shorts. Also publishes poetry. Rarely comments on/critiques rejected mss.
How to Contact Send complete ms with cover letter. Accepts submissions by e-mail. Include brief bio, list of publications. Responds to queries in 2 weeks. Responds to mss in 2 months. Send either SASE (or IRC) for return of ms or disposable copy of ms and #10 SASE for reply only. Sample copy available for $10. Guidelines available for SASE, on website.
Payment/Terms Writers receive 2 contributor's copies. Additional copies $3. Pays on publication. Acquires first North American serial rights. Publication is copyrighted.
Tips "We tend to publish character-based and inventive fiction with cutting-edge prose. We are unimpressed with works based on strict plot twists or novelties. Read a sample copy to get a feel for what we publish."

◪ STRUGGLE

A Magazine of Proletarian Revolutionary Literature, PO Box 28536, Detroit MI 48228. (213)273-9039. E-mail: timhall11@yahoo.com. Website: www.strugglemagazine.net. **Contact:** Tim Hall, editor. Magazine: 5½ × 8½; 36-72 pages; 20 lb. white bond paper; colored cover; illustrations; occasional photos. Publishes material related to "the struggle of the working class and all progressive people against the rule of the rich—including their war policies, repression, racism, exploitation of the workers, oppression of women and general culture, etc." Quarterly.
Needs Ethnic/multicultural, experimental, feminist, historical, humor/satire, literary, regional, science fiction, translations, young adult/teen (10-18), prose poem, senior citizen/retirement. "The theme can be approached in many ways, including plenty of categories not listed here. Readers would like fiction about anti-globalization, the fight against racism, prison conditions, neo-conservatism and the Iraq and Afghanistan wars and the disillusionment with the Obama Administration as it reveals it craven service to the rich billionaires. Would also like to see more fiction that depicts life, work and struggle of the working class of every background; also the struggles of the 1930s and '60s illustrated and brought to life. No romance, psychic, mystery, western, erotica, religious." Receives 10-12 unsolicited mss/month. Recently published work by Billie Louise Jones, Tyler Plosia, Margaret Dimacou. Length: 4,000 words; average length: 1,000-3,000 words. Publishes short shorts. Normally comments on rejected mss.
How to Contact Send complete ms. Accepts submissions by e-mail. "Tries to" report in 3-4 months to queries. Accepts simultaneous, multiple submissions and reprints. Sample copies for $3; $5 for double-size issues; subscriptions $10 for 4 issues; make checks payable to Tim Hall, Special Account, not to *Struggle*.
Payment/Terms Pays 1 contributor's copy. No rights acquired. Not copyrighted.
Tips "Write about the oppression of the working people, the poor, the minorities, women and, if possible, their rebellion against it—we are not interested in anything which accepts the status quo. We are not too worried about plot and advanced technique (fine if we get them!)—we would probably accept things others would call sketches, provided they have life and struggle. For new writers: just describe for us a situation in which some real people confront some problem of oppression, however seemingly minor. Observe and put down the real facts. Experienced writers: try your 'committed'/experimental fiction on us. We get poetry all the time. We have increased our fiction portion of our content in the last few years. The quality of fiction that we have published has continued to improve. If your work raises an interesting issue of literature and politics, it may get discussed in letters and in my editorial. I suggest ordering a sample or going to the website, www.strugglemagazine.net. "

⊞ ◪ $ SUBTERRAIN

P.O. Box 3008, MPO, Vancouver BC V6B 3X5 Canada. (604) 876-8710. Fax: (604) 879-2667. E-mail: subter@portal.ca. Website: www.subterrain.ca. **Contact:** Fiction editor. Magazine: 8¼ × 10-7/8; 56

pages; gloss stock paper; color gloss cover stock; illustrations; photos. "Looking for unique work and perspectives from Canada and beyond." Triannual. Estab. 1988. Circ. 3,000.

Needs Literary. Does not want genre fiction or children's fiction. Receives 100 unsolicited mss/month. Accepts 4 mss/issue; 10-15 mss/year. Publishes ms 4 months after acceptance. Recently published work by John Moore. Also publishes literary essays, literary criticism. Rarely comments on rejected mss.

How to Contact Send complete ms. Include disposable copy of the ms and #10 SASE for reply only. Responds in 2-4 months to mss. Accepts multiple submissions. Sample copy for $5. Writer's guidelines online.

Payment/Terms Pays $25 per page for prose. Pays on publication for first North American serial rights.

Tips "Read the magazine first. Get to know what kind of work we publish."

◪ ◎ $ SUBTROPICS

P. O. Box 112075, Turlington Hall, Univ. of FL, Gainesville FL 32611-2075. (352)392-6650 x 234. Fax: (352)392-0860. E-mail: subtropics@english.ufl.edu. Website: english.ufl.edu/subtropics. **Contact:** David Leavitt, fiction editor. Literary magazine/journal: 9x6, 160 pages. Includes photographs. "Subtropics —headed by fiction editor David Leavitt, poetry editor Sidney Wade, and managing editor Mark Mitchell—is committed to publishing the best new fiction, poetry, literary nonfiction, and translation by emerging and established writers. In addition to new work, Subtropics also, from time to time, republishes important and compelling stories, essays, and poems that have lapsed out of print." Triannual. Circ. 3,500. Member CLMP.

- Stories included in *Best American Short Stories 2007* and *The O. Henry Prize Stories 2007* and 2009. Poems included in *Best American Poetry 2007 and 2008.*

Needs Literary. Does not want genre fiction. Receives 1,000 mss/month. Accepts 5-6 mss/issue; 15-18 mss/year. Does not read between May 1 and August 31. Ms published 3-6 months after acceptance. Agented fiction 33%. **Publishes 1-2 new writers/year.** Published John Barth, Ariel Dorfman, Tony D'Souza, Allan Gurganus, Frances Hwang, Kuzhali Manickavel, Eileen Pollack, Padgett Powell, Nancy Reisman, Jarret Rosenblatt, Joanna Scott, and Olga Slavnikova. Average length: 5,000 words. Publishes short shorts. Average length of short shorts: 400 words. Also publishes literary essays, poetry. Rarely comments on/critiques rejected mss.

How to Contact Send complete ms with cover letter. Responds to mss in 2-6 weeks. Send disposable copy of ms. Replies via e-mail only. Do not include SASE. Considers simultaneous submissions. Sample copy available for $12.95. Guidelines available on website.

Payment/Terms Writers receive $500-1,000, 2 contributor's copies. Additional copies $12.95. Pays on acceptance. Acquires first North American serial rights. Publication is copyrighted.

Tips "Please read the guidelines and at least one issue of the magazine before submitting."

◪ $ THE SUN

107 N. Roberson St., Chapel Hill NC 27516. (919)942-5282. Fax: (919)932-3101. Website: www.thesunmagazine.org. **Contact:** Sy Safransky. Magazine: 8½ × 11; 48 pages; offset paper; glossy cover stock; photos. "We are open to all kinds of writing, though we favor work of a personal nature." Monthly. Circ. 72,000.

Needs Literary. Open to all fiction. Receives 800 unsolicited mss/month. Accepts 20 short stories/year. Publishes ms 12-24 months after acceptance. Recently published work by Alex Mindt, John Tait, Mark Wisniewski, April Wilder, Theresa Williams. Also publishes poetry and nonfiction. No science fiction, horror, fantasy, or other genre fiction.

How to Contact Send complete ms. Accepts reprint submissions. Sample copy for $5. Writer's guidelines online.

Payment/Terms Pays $300-2,000. Pays on publication for first, one-time rights.

Tips "We favor honest, personal writing with an intimate point of view. No science fiction, fantasy, or historical fiction."

SYCAMORE REVIEW

Purdue University, Department of English, 500 Oval Drive, West Lafayette IN 47907. (765) 494-3783. Fax: (765) 494-3780. E-mail: sycamore@purdue.edu. Website: www.sycamorereview.com. **Contact:** Anthony Cook. Magazine: 8 × 8; 130-180 pages; heavy, textured, uncoated paper; heavy laminated cover. "Journal devoted to contemporary literature. We publish both traditional and experimental fiction, personal essay, poetry, interviews, drama and graphic art. Novel excerpts welcome if they stand alone as a story." Semiannual. Estab. 1989. Circ. 1,000.

Needs Experimental, humor/satire, literary, mainstream, regional, translations. "We generally avoid genre literature but maintain no formal restrictions on style or subject matter. No romance, children's." Would like to see more experimental fiction. Publishes ms 11 months after acceptance. Recently published work by Lucia Perillo, Sherman Alexie, G.C. Waldrep, June Armstrong, W.P. Osborn, William Giraldi. Also publishes poetry. Sometimes comments on rejected mss.

How to Contact Send complete ms with SASE, cover letter with previous publications and address. Responds in 3-4 months to mss. Accepts simultaneous submissions. Sample copy for $5. Writer's guidelines for #10 SASE or online.

Payment/Terms Copies of journal/acquires one-time rights.

Tips "We publish both new and experienced authors but we're always looking for stories with strong emotional appeal, vivid characterization and a distinctive narrative voice; fiction that breaks new ground while still telling an interesting and significant story. Avoid gimmicks and trite, predictable outcomes. Write stories that have a ring of truth, the impact of felt emotion. Don't be afraid to submit, send your best."

$ TAKAHE

P.O. Box 13-335, Christchurch 8001 New Zealand. (03)359-8133. Website: http://takahe.org.nz. "Takahe is a hardcopy literary magazine which appears three times a year and publishes short stories, poetry, and artwork by both established and emerging writers. The publisher is Takahe Collective Trust, a non-profit organization formed by established writers to help new writers get into print."

Needs "We are particularly losing interest in stories offer a new perspective; something a little different." **Publishes 20 new writers/year.** Recently published work by Raewyn Alexander, Simon Minto, Claire Baylis, Hayden Williams, Sarah Penwarden, Michael Botur, Doc Drumheller, Andrew McIntyre.

How to Contact Send complete ms. by e-mail (poetry in hardcopy). Include e-mail address, mailing address, 40 word bio and SASE (IRC for overseas submissions). See website for formatting. No simultaneous submissions. Copyright reverts to author on publication.

Payment/Terms NZ residents receive $30 (amount subject to change) and all contributors receive two hard copies of the issue in which their work appears. Overseas contributors receive a one year subscription to *Takahe* in lieu of payment.

Tips "We pay a flat rate to each writer/poet appearing in a particular issue regardless of the number/length of items. Editorials and literary commentaries are by invitation only."

TALKING RIVER

Division of Literature and Languages, 500 8th Ave., Lewiston ID 83501. (208)792-2189. Fax: (208)792-2324. Website: www.lcsc.edu/talkingriverreview. **Contact:** Kevin Goodan, editorial advisor. Magazine: 6 × 9; 150-200 pages; 60 lb. paper; coated, color cover; illustrations; photos. "We look for new voices with something to say to a discerning general audience." Semiannual. Circ. 250.

Needs Ethnic/multicultural, feminist, humor/satire, literary, regional. "Wants more well-written, character-driven stories that surprise and delight the reader with fresh, arresting yet unselfconscious language, imagery, metaphor, revelation." No stories that are sexist, racist, homophobic, erotic for shock value; no genre fiction. Receives 400 unsolicited mss/month. Accepts 5-8 mss/issue; 10-15 mss/year. Reads mss September 1-May 1 only. Publishes ms 1-2 year s after acceptance. **Publishes 10-15 new writers/year.** Recently published work by X.J. Kennedy and Gary Fincke. Length: 4,000 words; average length: 3,000 words. Also publishes literary essays, poetry. Sometimes comments on rejected mss.

How to Contact Send complete manuscript with cover letter. Include estimated word count, 2-sentence bio and list of publications. Send SASE for reply, return of ms or send disposable copy of ms. Responds in 3 months to mss. Does not accept simultaneous submissions. Sample copy for $6. Writer's guidelines for #10 SASE.

Payment/Terms Pays contributor's copies; additional copies $4. Acquires one-time rights.

Tips "We look for the strong, the unique; we reject clichéd images and predictable climaxes."

$ TAMPA REVIEW

401 W. Kennedy Blvd., Box 19F, Tampa FL 33606. (813)253-6266. Website: tampareview.ut.edu. Magazine: 7½ × 10½; hardback; approximately 100 pages; acid-free paper; visual art; photos. An international literary journal publishing art and literature from Florida and Tampa Bay as well as new work and translations from throughout the world. Semiannual. Circ. 800.

Needs Ethnic/multicultural, experimental, fantasy, historical, literary, mainstream, translations. "We are far more interested in quality than in genre. Nothing sentimental as opposed to genuinely moving, nor self-conscious style at the expense of human truth." Accepts 4-5 mss/issue. Reads September-December; reports January-May. Publishes ms 10 months after acceptance. Agented fiction 20%. Recently published work by Elizabeth Spencer, Lee K. Abbott, Lorrie Moore, Gordon Weaver, Tim O'Brien. Publishes short shorts. Also publishes literary essays, poetry.

How to Contact Send complete ms by mail or through online submissions manager. Include brief bio. Responds in 5 months to mss. Accepts multiple submissions. No simultaneous submissions. Sample copy for $7. Writer's guidelines online.

Payment/Terms Pays $10/printed page. Pays on publication for first North American serial rights. Sends digital proofs to author.

Tips "There are more good writers publishing in magazines today than there have been in many decades. Unfortunately, there are even more bad ones. In T. Gertler's Elbowing the Seducer, an editor advises a young writer that he wants to hear her voice completely, to tell (he means 'show') him in a story the truest thing she knows. We concur. Rather than a trendy workshop story or a minimalism that actually stems from not having much to say, we would like to see stories that make us believe they mattered to the writer and, more importantly, will matter to a reader. Trim until only the essential is left, and don't give up belief in yourself. And it might help to attend a good writers' conference."

TAPROOT LITERARY REVIEW

Box 204, Ambridge PA 15003. (724)266-8476. E-mail: taproot10@aol.com. **Contact:** Tikvah Feinstein, editor. Magazine: 5½ × 8½; 93 pages; 20 lb. paper; hardcover; attractively printed; saddle-stitched. "We select on quality, not topic. Variety and quality are our appealing features." Annual. Circ. 500.

Needs Literary. "No pornography, religious, popular, romance fiction. Wants more stories with multicultural themes, showing intensity, reality and human emotions that readers can relate to, learn from, and most importantly—be interesting." The majority of ms published are received through annual contest. Receives 20 unsolicited mss/month. Accepts 6 mss/issue. **Publishes 2-4 new writers/year.** Recently published work by Bruce Mikkiff, Derrick Harrison Hurd, Faith Romeo Cataffa, B.Z. Niditch, Alicia Stakay, Alena Horowitz, Shirley Barasch, and Tikvah Feinstein. Publishes short shorts. Also publishes poetry. Sometimes comments on rejected mss.

How to Contact Accepts submissions by e-mail. Send for guidelines first. Send complete ms with a cover letter. Include estimated word count and bio. Responds in 6 months to mss. No simultaneous submissions. "The best way for fiction writers to break into Taproot is through the annual contest. Send a SASE for guidelines. Sample copy for $5, 6 × 12 SAE with 5 first-class stamps. Writer's guidelines for #10 SASE.

Payment/Terms Awards $25 in prize money for first place fiction and poetry winners each issue; certificate for 2nd and 3rd place; 1 contributor's copy.

Tips "*Taproot* is getting more fiction submissions, and every one is read entirely. This takes time, so response can be delayed at busy times of year. Our contest is a good way to start publishing. Send for a sample copy and read it through. Ask for a critique and follow suggestions. Don't be offended by any suggestions—just take them or leave them and keep writing. Looks for a story that speaks in its unique voice, told in a well-crafted and complete, memorable style, a style of signature to the author. Follow writer's guidelines. Research markets. Send cover letter. Don't give up."

THE TEXAS REVIEW

P.O. Box 2146, Huntsville TX 77341-2146. (936)294-1992. Fax: (936)294-3070 (inquiries only). E-mail: eng_pdr@shsu.edu. Website: www.shsu.edu/~www_trp/. **Contact:** Paul Ruffin, editor. Magazine: 6×9; 148-190 pages; best quality paper; 70 lb. cover stock; illustrations; photos. "We publish top quality poetry, fiction, articles, interviews and reviews for a general audience." Semiannual. Circ. 1,200. A member of the Texas A&M University Press consortium.

Needs Humor/satire, literary, mainstream, contemporary fiction. "We are eager enough to consider fiction of quality, no matter what its theme or subject matter. No juvenile fiction." Receives 40-60 unsolicited mss/month. Accepts 4 mss/issue; 6 mss/year. Does not read mss May-September. Publishes ms 6-12 months after acceptance. **Publishes some new writers/year.** Recently published work by George Garrett, Ellen Gilchrist, Fred Chappell. Also publishes literary essays, literary criticism, poetry. Sometimes comments on rejected mss.

How to Contact Send complete ms. No mss accepted via fax. Send disposable copy of ms and #10 SASE for reply only. Responds in 2 weeks to queries; 3-6 months to mss. Accepts multiple submissions. Sample copy for $5. Writer's guidelines for SASE and on website.

Payment/Terms Pays contributor's copies and one year subscription. Pays on publication for first North American serial, one-time rights. Sends galleys to author.

Tips "Submit often; be aware that we reject 90% of submissions due to overwhelming number of mss sent."

$ THEMA

Box 8747, Metairie LA 70011-8747. (504)940-7156. E-mail: thema@cox.net. Website: members.cox.net/thema. **Contact:** Virginia Howard, editor. Magazine: 5½×8½; 150 pages; Grandee Strathmore cover stock; b&w illustrations. "Thema is designed to stimulate creative thinking by challenging writers with unusual themes, such as ' rage over a lost penny.' Appeals to writers, teachers of creative writing, and general reading audience." Circ. 350.

Needs Adventure, ethnic/multicultural, experimental, fantasy, historical, humor/satire, literary, mainstream, mystery/suspense, novel excerpts, psychic/supernatural/occult, regional, religious/inspirational, science fiction, slice-of-life vignettes, western, contemporary, sports, prose poem. "No erotica." Themes with deadlines for submission in 2011 (publication in 2012): "Your Reality or Mine?" (March 1); "Wisecracks & Poems" (July 1); "Who Keeps Them Tidy?" (November 1). For more information, visit *THEMA*'s website. Publishes ms within 6 months after acceptance. **Publishes 9 new writers/year.** Recently published work by Michael Fontana, Sky Andrews Gerspacher, Malaika Favorite, and Mark Krieger. Publishes short shorts. Also publishes poetry. Sometimes comments on rejected mss.

How to Contact Send complete ms with SASE, cover letter, include "name and address, brief introduction, specifying the intended target issue for the mss." SASE. Responds in 1 week to queries; 5 months to mss. Accepts simultaneous, multiple submissions and reprints. Does not accept e-mailed submissions. Sample copy for $10. Writer's guidelines for #10 SASE.

Payment/Terms Pays $10-25. Pays on acceptance for one-time rights.

Tips "Do not submit a manuscript unless you have written it for a specified theme. If you don't know the upcoming themes, send for guidelines first before sending a story. We need more stories told in the Mark Twain/O. Henry tradition in magazine fiction."

THIRD COAST

Dept. of English, Western Michigan University, Kalamazoo MI 49008-5331. (269)387-2675. Fax: (269)387-2562. E-mail: editors@thirdcoastmagazine.com. Website: www.thirdcoastmagazine.com. **Contact:** Fiction Editors. Magazine: 6×9; 176 pages. "We will consider many different types of fiction and favor those exhibiting a freshness of vision and approach." Twice-yearly. Circ. 2,875.

- *Third Coast* has received *Pushcart Prize* nominations. The section editors of this publication change with the university year.

Needs Literary. "While we don't want to see formulaic genre fiction, we will consider material that plays with or challenges generic forms." Receives 200 unsolicited mss/month. Accepts 6-8 mss/issue; 15 mss/year. Recently published work by Bonnie Jo Campbell, Peter Ho Davies, Moira Crone, Lee Martin, John McNally, and Peter Orner. Also publishes literary essays, poetry, one-act plays. Sometimes comments on rejected mss.

How to Contact Visit our website for guidelines. *Third Coast* only accepts submissions submitted to its online submission manager. All hard copy submissions will be returned unread. Reads mss from August through May of each year.

Payment/Terms Pays 2 contributor's copies as well as a 1 year subscription to the publication; additional copies for $4. Acquires first North American serial rights.

Tips "We seek superior fiction from short-shorts to 30-page stories."

$ THIRD WEDNESDAY: A LITERARY ARTS MAGAZINE

174 Greenside Up, Ypsilanti MI 48197. (734)434-2409. E-mail: submissions@thirdwednesday.org; LaurenceWT@aol.com. Website: http://thirdwednesday.org. **Contact:** Laurence Thomas, editor. Literary magazine/journal. 60-65 pages. Contains illustrations. Includes photographs. "Third Wednesday publishes quality (a subjective term at best) poetry, short fiction and artwork by experienced writers and artists. We welcome work by established writers/artists, as well as those who are not yet well known, but headed for prominence." Quarterly. Estab. 2007.

Needs Experimental, fantasy, humor/satire, literary, mainstream, romance, translations. Does not want "purely anecdotal accounts of incidents, sentimentality, pointless conclusions, or stories without some characterization or plot development." Receives 5-10 mss/month. Accepts 3-5 mss/issue. Ms published 3 months after acceptance. Length: 1,500 words (max). Average length: 1,000 words. Publishes short shorts. Also publishes poetry. Sometimes comments on/critiques rejected mss.

How to Contact Send complete ms with cover letter. Accepts submissions by e-mail. Include estimated word count, brief bio. Responds to mss in 6-8 weeks. Considers simultaneous submissions. Sample copy available for $8. Guidelines available for SASE, via e-mail.

Payment/Terms Writers receive $3, 1 contributor's copy. Additional copies $8. Pays on acceptance. Acquires first rights.

Tips "Of course, originality is important along with skill in writing, deft handling of language and meaning which goes hand in hand with beauty, whatever that is. Short fiction is specialized and difficult, so the writer should read extensively in the field."

TICKLED BY THUNDER

Helping Writers Get Published Since 1990, 14076 86A Ave., Surrey BC V3W 0V9 Canada. (604)591-6095. E-mail: info@tickledbythunder.com. Website: www.tickledbythunder.com. **Contact:** Larry Lindner, publisher. Magazine: digest-sized; 24 pages; bond paper; bond cover stock; illustrations; photos. "Tickled By Thunder is designed to encourage beginning writers of fiction, poetry and nonfiction." Quarterly. Estab. 1990.

Needs Fantasy, humor/satire, literary, mainstream, mystery/suspense, science fiction, western. "No overly indulgent horror, sex, profanity or religious material." Receives 25 unsolicited mss/month. Accepts 3 mss/issue; 12 mss/year. Publishes ms 3-9 months after acceptance. **Publishes 5 new writers/year.** Recently published work by John Connors and J-Ann Godfrey. Length: 2,000 words; average length: 1,500 words. Also publishes literary essays, literary criticism, poetry.

How to Contact Send complete ms. Include estimated word count and brief bio. Send SASE or IRC for return of ms; or send disposable copy of ms and #10 SASE for reply only. Only subscribers may send e-mail submissions online. Responds in 3 months to queries; 6 months to mss. Accepts simultaneous, multiple submissions and reprints. Writer's guidelines online.

Payment/Terms Pays on publication for first, second serial (reprint) rights.

Tips "Allow your characters to breathe on their own. Use description with action."

TRANSITION

An International Review, 104 Mount Auburn St., 3R, Cambridge MA 02138. (617)496-2845. Fax: (617)496-2877. E-mail: transition@fas.harvard.edu. Website: www.transitionmagazine.com. **Contact:** Vincent Brown, Glenda Carpio, and Tommie Shelby, editors. Magazine: 9½ × 6½; 150-175 pages; 70 lb. Finch Opaque paper; 100 lb. White Warren Lustro dull cover; illustrations; photos. "Transition magazine is a trimestrial international review known for compelling and controversial writing from and about Africa and the diaspora. This prestigious magazine is edited at Harvard University, and editorial board members include such heavy-hitters as Toni Morrison, Jamaica Kincaid and bell hooks. The magazine also attracts famous contributors such as Spike Lee, Philip Gourevitch and Carolos Fuentes." Quarterly. Circ. 3,000.

- Essays first published in a recent issue of *Transition* were selected for inclusion in *Best American Essays 2008, Best American Nonrequired Reading 2008,* and *Best African American Writing 2009.* Four-time winner of the Alternative Press Award for international reporting (2001, 2000, 1999, 1995); finalist in the 2001 National Magazine Award in General Excellence category.

Needs Ethnic/multicultural, historical, humor/satire, literary, regional (African diaspora, Third World, etc.). Receives 40 unsolicited mss/month. Accepts 2-4 mss/year. Publishes ms 6-8 months after acceptance. Agented fiction 30-40%. **Publishes 5 new writers/year.** Recently published work by Wole Soyinka, Nuruddin Farah, Chimamanda Adichie, John Wideman, and Emily Raboteau. Length: 4,000-8,000 words; average length: 7,000 words. Also publishes literary essays, literary criticism. Sometimes comments on rejected mss.

How to Contact Query with published clips or send complete ms. Include brief bio and list of publications. Send disposable copy of ms and #10 SASE for reply only. Responds in 2 months to queries; 6 months to mss. Accepts simultaneous submissions. Sample copy not available. Writer's guidelines for #10 SASE.

Payment/Terms 2 contributor's copies. Sends galleys to author.

Tips "We look for a non-white, alternative perspective, dealing with issues of race, ethnicity and identity in an upredictable, provocative way."

UNDER HWY 99

Showcasing the Untold Story Seattle WA. E-mail: info@underhwy99.com. Website: http://underhwy99.com. **Contact:** Erica Goodkind, editor. Literary magazine/journal: 8.5X11; 25-35 pages; 60# paper; 80# glossy cover. Contains illustrations, photographs. "The 'untold story' is the story that is most important to you—the one you feel most compelled to tell. This is a publication for people who like a good read, and for those who have an undying devotion to and special knack for writing." Biannual. Estab. 2008. Circ. 300.

Needs Adventure, ethnic/multicultural (general), historical (general), humor/satire, literary, mainstream. Special interests: slice-of-life, music inspired prose. Does not want horror, romance, science fiction, evangelic. Receives 20-30 mss/month. Accepts 5-15 mss/issue; 15-30 mss/year. Manuscript published 2-4 months after acceptance. **Publishes 75% new writers/year.** Length: 3,500 words (max). Average length: 2,500 words. Publishes short shorts. Average length of short shorts: 500 words. Sometimes comments on/critiques rejected mss.

How to Contact Send complete ms with cover letter. Accepts submissions by e-mail only. Include estimated word count, brief bio. Responds to queries in 4 weeks; mss in 2 months. Considers simultaneous submissions, multiple submissions. Sample copy available for $4.95. Guidelines available on website.

Payment/Terms Writers receive 1 contributor's copy. Additional copies $4.95. Pays on publication. Acquires first rights, electronic rights. Publication is not copyrighted.

Tips "We have weakness for smart, imaginative pieces that bring out the uniqueness in any given situation. We tend to find stories that cast ordinary things in an unusual light and unusual things in an ordinary light particularly irresistible. Pieces should balance all other usual elements of any good piece of literature: character, setting, theme, voice, pacing, etc."

UNDERSTANDING

Dionysia Press, 127 Milton Rd. West, 7 Duddingston House Courtyard, Edinburgh Scotland EH15 1JG United Kingdom. Magazine: A5; 200 pages. Annual. Estab. 1989. Circ. 500. Member: Scottish Publishing Association.

Needs Translations. Publishes ms 10 months after acceptance. **Publishes 100 new writers/year.** Publishes short shorts. Also publishes literary essays, poetry. Sometimes comments on rejected mss.

How to Contact Responds in 1 year to queries. Sample copy for $4.50 + postage. Writer's guidelines for SASE.

Payment/Terms Pays in contributor's copies.

UNMUZZLED OX

105 Hudson St., New York NY 10013. (212)226-7170. Unmuzzled Ox Foundation Ltd., 105 Hudson St., New York NY 10013. (212)226-7170. E-mail: mandreox@aol.com. **Contact:** Michael Andre, editor. Magazine: 5½ × 8½. "Magazine about life for an intelligent audience." Irregular frequency. Estab. 1971. Circ. 7,000.

- Recent issues of this magazine have included art, poetry and essays only. Check before sending submissions.

Needs Literary, mainstream, translations, prose poetry. "No commercial fiction." Receives 20-25 unsolicited mss/month. Also publishes poetry. Sometimes comments on rejected mss.

How to Contact "Please no phone calls and no e-mail submissions. Correspondence by *mail* only. Cover letter is significant." Responds in 1 month to queries; 1 month to mss. Sample copy not available.

Payment/Terms Pays in contributor's copies.

Tips "You may want to check out a copy of the magazine before you submit."

UPSTREET

Ledgetop Publishing, P.O. Box 105, Richmond MA 01254-0105. (413) 441-9702. E-mail: editor@upstreet-mag.org. Website: www.upstreet-mag.org. Literary magazine/journal. 7x8.5, 224 pages, 60# white offset paper. "A literary annual containing the best new fiction, poetry, and creative nonfiction available. First four issues feature interviews with Jim Shepard, Lydia Davis, Wally Lamb, and Michael Martone. Independently owned and published, nationally distributed. Founded by Vivian Dorsel, former managing editor of The Berkshire Review for eight years, who selected the members of the editorial staff for their love of the written word, their high standards of literary judgment, and their desire to offer a voice to prose writers and poets who might not find publication opportunities in more mainstream journals." Annual. Estab. 2005. Circ. 4,000. Member CLMP.

Needs Ethnic/multicultural (general), experimental, humor/satire, literary, mainstream. Does not want juvenile/YA, religious, or "any genre fiction that is not 'literary' (i.e., imaginative, sophisticated, innovative)." Does not read March-September. Ms published 2-4 months after acceptance. Length: 5,000 words (max). Publishes short shorts. Also publishes literary essays, poetry. Rarely comments on/critiques rejected mss.

How to Contact Submit complete ms via online submissions manager. Include estimated word count, brief bio, contact information. Considers simultaneous submissions, multiple submissions. Sample copy available for $10 plus postage. Guidelines available via e-mail.

Payment/Terms Writers receive 1 contributor's copy. Additional copies $10. Pays on publication. Acquires first North American serial rights. Publication is copyrighted.

VERSAL

wordsinhere, Amsterdam NT Canada. E-mail: versaljournal@wordsinhere.com. Website: www.wordsinhere.com. **Contact:** Megan M. Garr, editor. Literary magazine/journal: 20 cm x 20 cm, 100 pages, offset, perfect-bound, acid-free color cover. Includes artwork. "Versal is the only English-language literary magazine in the Netherlands and publishes new poetry, prose and art from around the world. We publish writers with an instinct for language and line break, content and form that is urgent, involved and unexpected." Annual. Circ. 750.

Needs Experimental, literary. Receives 125 mss/month. Accepts 10 mss/year. Does not read mss January 16-September 14. Manuscript published 4-7 months after acceptance. **Publishes 4 new writers/year.** Published Derek White, Alissa Nutting, Russell Edson, Sawako Nakayasu. Length: 1,000 words (max). Publishes short shorts. Average length of short shorts: 1,500 words. Also publishes poetry. Sometimes comments on/critiques rejected mss.
How to Contact Send complete ms with cover letter. Accepts submissions electronically only. Include brief bio. Responds to queries in 1 week. Responds to mss in 2 months. Considers simultaneous submissions. Guidelines available on website.
Payment/Terms Writers receive 1 contributor copy. Additional copies $15. Pays on publication. Acquires one-time rights. Sends galleys to author. Publication is copyrighted.
Tips "We like to see that a story is really a story, or, regardless of your definition of story, that the text has a shape. Often, we receive excellent ideas or anecdotes that have no real sense of development, evolution, or involution. Because we have a story limit of 3,000 words, the best stories have carefully considered their shape. A good shape for an 8,000 word story will rarely be successful in a two- or three thousand word story. We prefer work that has really thought through and utilized detail/imagery which is both vivid and can carry some symbolic/metaphoric weight. While we like stories that test or challenge language and syntax, we do publish plenty of amazing stories that emply traditional syntax. Even in these stories, however, it is clear that the writers pay close attention to sound and language, which allows the stories to best display their power."

◪ $ VIRGINIA QUARTERLY REVIEW

One West Range, P.O. Box 400223, Charlottesville VA 22904-4223. (434)924-3124. Fax: (434)924-1397. E-mail: vqr@vqronline.org; k.morrissey@virginia.edu. Website: www.vqronline.org. **Contact:** Kevin Morrissey, managing editor. "A national journal of literature and discussion, featuring nonfiction, fiction, and poetry for educated general readers." Quarterly. Circ. 6,000.
Needs Ethnic/multicultural, feminist, historical, humor/satire, literary, mainstream, mystery/suspense, novel excerpts, translations. Accepts 3 mss/issue; 20 mss/year. Publishes ms 3-6 months after acceptance.
How to Contact Submit complete ms. online. No queries. Word count: 2,000-8,000 words. Submissions are limited to one prose piece and three poems every six months. Responds in 3-4 months to mss. Sample copy for $14. Writer's guidelines online. Occasionally closes submissions to catch up on backlog; check website to find when submissions are open.
Payment/Terms Pays $.20/word. $5 per line for poetry. Pays on publication for first North American rights and nonexclusive online rights. Submissions only accepted online.

◪ WESTERN HUMANITIES REVIEW

English Dept, 255 S. Central Campus Dr., LNCO 3500, Salt Lake City UT 84112-0494. (801)581-6070. Fax: (801)585-5167. E-mail: whr@mail.hum.utah.edu. Website: www.hum.utah.edu/whr. **Contact:** Dawn Lonsinger, managing editor. Circ. 1,300.
Needs "Looking for work that continues to resonate after reading is over. Especially interested in experimental and innovative fiction." Does not want genre (romance, sci-fi, etc.). Receives 100 mss/month. Accepts 5-6 mss/issue; 6-8 mss/year. Does not read April-September. Publishes ms up to 1 year after acceptance. **Publishes 3-5 new writers/year.** Recently published work by Michael Martone, Steve Almond, Craig Dworkin, Benjamin Percy, Francois Camoin, Kate Bernheimer, Lidia Yuknavitch. Publishes short shorts. Also innovative literary criticism and poetry. Rarely comments on rejected mss.
How to Contact Send one story per reading period. No email submissions or queries. Sample copy for $10. Writer's guidelines online.
Payment/Terms Pays in contributor's copies on publication.Additional Information Runs Utah Writers' Contest every fall.

◪ WHISKEY ISLAND MAGAZINE

Cleveland State University, Dept. of English, Rhodes Tower 1636, Cleveland OH 44115-2214. Website: www.csuohio.edu/whiskey_island. Editors change each year. Magazine of fiction, creative nonfiction, theater writing, poetry and art. "We provide a forum for new writers, for themes and points of view that are both traditional and experimental." Semiannual. Press run: 1,000.

Needs "From flash fiction to 5,000 words." Receives 100 unsolicited mss/month. Accepts 46 mss/issue. Recently published work by Carolyn Furnish, Carl Peterson, and Shannon Robinson. "Most recent issue features three writers' first publications. We nominate for *Pushcart Prize.*"

How to Contact Send complete ms. Accepts submissions by mail and e-mail. Accepts simultaneous submissions. Responds in 6 months. Sample copy for $6. Subscription $12.

Payment/Terms Pays 2 contributor copies and 1-year subscription. Acquires one-time rights. Sponsors annual fiction contest with $500 prize and publication. $10 per entry.

Tips "We read manuscripts year round. We seek engaging writing of any style."

WHITE FUNGUS: AN EXPERIMENTAL ARTS MAGAZINE

P.O. Box 6173, Wellington, Aotearoa, New Zealand. (64) 4 382 9113. E-mail: whitefungusmail@yahoo.com. Website: www.whitefungus.com. **Contact:** Ron Hanson, Editor. Literary magazine/journal. Oversize A5, 104 pages, matte paper, matte card cover. Contains illustrations, photographs. "White Fungus covers a range of experimental arts including literature, poetry, visual arts, comics and music. We are interested in material that is bold, innovative and well-researched. Independence of thought and meaningful surprises are a high priority." Semiannual. Estab. 2004. Circ. 2,000.

Needs Comics/graphic novels, ethnic/multicultural, experimental, feminist, gay, historical (general), humor/satire, lesbian, literary, science fiction. "*White Fungus* considers submissions on the basis of quality rather than genre." Receives 20 mss/month. Accepts 3 mss/issue; 6 mss/year. Ms published 1-12 months after acceptance. **Publishes 2 new writers/year.** Published Hamish Low, Cyril Wong, Aaron Coyes, Hamish Wyn, Tim Bollinger, Kate Montgomery, Tessa Laird and Tobias Fischer. Average length: 1,200 words. Publishes short shorts. Average length of short shorts: 1,000 words. Also publishes literary criticism, poetry. Sometimes comments on/critiques rejected mss.

How to Contact Query with clips of published work. Accepts submissions by e-mail, on disk. Include brief bio, list of publications. Responds to queries in 1 week. Responds to mss in 1 week. Send either SASE (or IRC) for return of ms or disposable copy of ms and #10 SASE for reply only. Considers simultaneous submissions, multiple submissions. Sample copy available for $10. Guidelines available via e-mail.

Payment/Terms Writers receive 10 contributor's copies, free subscription to the magazine. Additional copies $6. Pays on publication. Acquires first rights. Publication is copyrighted.

Tips "We like writing that explores the world around it rather than being self-obsessed. We're not interested in personal fantasies or self-projections, just an active critical response to one's environment. Be direct, flexible and consider how your work might be considered in an international context. What can you contribute or shed light on?"

WILLARD & MAPLE

163 South Willard Street, Freeman 302, Box 34, Burlington VT 05401. (802)860-2700 ext. 2462. E-mail: willardandmaple@champlain.edu. **Contact:** fiction editor. Magazine: perfect bound; 125 pages; illustrations; photos. "Willard & Maple is a student-run literary magazine from Champlain College that publishes a wide array of poems, short stories, creative essays, short plays, pen and ink drawings, black and white photos, and computer graphics. We now accept color." Annual. Estab. 1996.

Needs We accept all types of mss. Receives 20 unsolicited mss/month. Accepts 1 mss/year. Does not read mss March 31-September 1. Publishes ms within 1 year after acceptance. **Publishes 10 new writers/year.** Recently published work by Ian Frisch, Mark Belair, Rachel Chalmers, Robin Gaines, W.J. Everts, and Shirley O. Length: 5,000 words; average length: 2,500 words. Publishes short shorts. Also publishes literary essays, poetry. Sometimes comments on rejected mss.

How to Contact Send complete mss. Send SASE for return of ms or send disposable copy of mss and #10 SASE for reply only. Responds in 6 months to queries; 6 months to mss. Accepts simultaneous, multiple submissions. Sample copy for $10. Writer's guidelines for SASE or send e-mail. Reviews fiction.

Payment/Terms Pays 2 contributor's copies; additional copies $12. Pays on publication for one-time rights.
Tips "The power of imagination makes us infinite."

THE WILLIAM AND MARY REVIEW

The College of William and Mary, Campus Center, P.O. Box 8795, Williamsburg VA 23187-8795. (757)221-3290. E-mail: review@wm.edu. Website: www.wm.edu/so/wmreview. **Contact:** Address all prose submissions ATTN: Prose Editor. Magazine: 6 × 9; 96 pages; coated paper; 4-color card cover; photos. "Our journal is read by a sophisticated audience of subscribers, professors, and university students." Annual. Estab. 1962. Circ. 1,600.
Needs Experimental, family saga, historical, horror (psychological), humor/satire, literary, mainstream, science fiction, thriller/espionage, short stories. "We do not want to see typical genre pieces. Do not bother sending fantasy or erotica." Receives 35 unsolicited mss/month. Accepts 4-5 mss/year. Does not read mss from February to August. Publishes ms 1-2 months after acceptance. **Publishes 1-2 new writers/year.** Length: 250-7,000 words; average length: 3,500 words. Publishes short shorts. Also publishes poetry. Rarely comments on rejected mss.
How to Contact Send complete ms. Send SASE (or IRC) for return of the mss or send disposable copy of the ms and #10 SASE for reply only. Include a cover letter. Responds in 5-6 months to queries. Accepts simultaneous, multiple submissions but requires identification of those that are simultaneous and notification if they are accepted elsewhere. Sample copy for $5.50.
Payment/Terms Pays 5 contributor's copies; additional copies $5. Pays on publication for first North American serial rights.
Tips "We do not give much weight to prior publications; each piece is judged on its own merit. New writers should be bold and unafraid to submit unorthodox works that depart from textbook literary tradition. We would like to see more quality short shorts and nonfiction works. We receive far too many mediocre genre stories."

WILLOW SPRINGS

501 N Riverpoint Blvd, Ste. 425, Spokane WA 99202. (509) 359-7435. E-mail: willowspringsweb@gmail.com. Website: willowsprings.ewu.edu. **Contact:** Samuel Ligon, editor. Magazine: 9 × 6; 120 pages; 80 lb. matte cover. "We publish quality contemporary fiction, poetry, nonfiction, interviews with notable authors, and works in translation." Semiannual. Circ. 1,500. Member CLMP, AWP.

- *Willow Springs* has received grants from the NEA and a CLMP excellence award.

Needs Literary short shorts, nonfiction, translations, short stories, prose poems, poems. "No genre fiction, please." Receives 200 unsolicited mss/month. Accepts 2-4 mss/issue; 4-8 mss/year. Reads mss year round, but expect slower response between July and October. Publishes ms 4 months after acceptance. **Publishes some new writers/year.** Recently published work by Imad Rahman, Deb Olin Unferth, Jim Daniels, Kirsten Sundberg Lunstrum, Robert Lopez, Stacey Richter. Also publishes literary essays, literary criticism, poetry. Rarely comments on rejected mss.
How to Contact Send complete ms. Prose submissions now accepted online. Responds in 2 months to queries; 2 months to mss. Simultaneous submissions encouraged. Sample copy for $10. Writer's guidelines for #10 SASE.
Payment/Terms Pays 2 contributor's copies. Acquires first North American serial, first rights.
Tips "We hope to attract good fiction writers to our magazine, and we've made a commitment to publish 3-4 stories per issue. We like fiction that exhibits a fresh approach to language. Our most recent issues, we feel, indicate the quality and level of our commitment."

WINDHOVER

University of Mary Hardin-Baylor, P.O. Box 8008, 900 College St., Belton TX 76513. (254)295-4561. E-mail: windhover@umhb.edu. **Contact:** D. Audell Shelburne, editor. Magazine: 6 × 9; white bond paper. "We accept poetry, short fiction, nonfiction, creative nonfiction. Windhover is devoted to promoting writers and literature with a Christian perspective and with a broad definition of that perspective." Annual. Estab. 1997. Circ. 500.
Needs Ethnic/multicultural, experimental, fantasy, historical, humor/satire, literary. No erotica.

Receives 30 unsolicited mss/month. Accepts 5 mss/issue; 5 mss/year. Publishes ms 1 year after acceptance. **Publishes 5 new writers/year.** Recently published work by Walt McDonald, Cleatus Rattan, Greg Garrett, Barbara Crooker. Length: 1,500-4,000 words; average length: 3,000 words. Publishes short shorts. Also publishes literary essays, poetry. Sometimes comments on rejected mss.

How to Contact Send complete ms. Estimated word count, brief bio and list of publications. Include SASE postcard for acknowledgement. No submissions by e-mail. "Deadlines for submissions in June 1st for next issue. Editors read during summer months and notify writers in early September." Accepts simultaneous submissions. Sample copy for $10. Writer's guidelines by e-mail.

Payment/Terms Pays 2 contributor copies. Pays on publication for first rights.

Tips "Be patient. We have an editorial board and it sometimes take s longer than I like. We particularly look for convincing plot and character development."

$ WITHERSIN MAGAZINE, DARK, DIFFERENT; PLEASANTLY SINISTER

(951) 795-5498. E-mail: withersin@hotmail.com. Literary magazine/journal. 6 × 9, 100 pages. Contains illustrations. Includes photographs. "A literary chimera, Withersin explores the bittersweet stain of the human condition. Comprised of an impressive array of original razor wire fiction, oddments and incongruities, obscure historical footnotes, unconventional research articles, delectable interviews, highlights, reviews and releases in film, music and print; all sewn together with threads of deviant art." Triannual. Circ. 600.

Needs Comics/graphic novels, experimental, historical (general), horror, literary, psychic/supernatural/occult, regional (specific and unique places; legends and lore). Does not want romance, erotica (read: pornography), or politically charged pieces. List of upcoming themes available for SASE, on website. Receives 100-300 mss/month. Accepts 3-5 mss/issue; 9-15 mss/year. Does not read July-March. Ms published 9-18 months after acceptance. **Publishes 5 new writers/year.** Published David Bain, Robert Heinze, Edward Morris, Michael Pignatella, M.W. Anderson, Sunil Sadanand, David Sackmyster, Mark Allan Gunnells and Chet Gottfried. Length: 500 words (min)-3,000 words (max). Average length: 2,000 words. Publishes short shorts. Average length of short shorts: 500 words. Also publishes literary essays, literary criticism, book reviews, poetry. Often comments on/critiques rejected mss.

How to Contact Send complete ms with cover letter. Accepts submissions by e-mail, on disk. Include estimated word count, brief bio. Responds to queries in 2-3 weeks. Responds to mss in 4-6 weeks. Send either SASE (or IRC) for return of ms or disposable copy of ms and #10 SASE for reply only. Considers previously published submissions (reprints have different pay scale), multiple submissions. Sample copy available for $7.25, on website. Guidelines available for SASE, via e-mail, on website.

Payment/Terms Writers receive 1-5¢ per word, 3000 word payment cap, 1 contributor's copy. Additional copies $7.25. Pays on publication. Acquires first North American serial rights, one-time rights. Publication is copyrighted. Occasionally sponsors contests, check website for details. "We also sponsor videography contests on www.youtube.com/withersin."

Tips "Beyond an interesting plot structure and ideology, we definitely look for 'complete' pieces i.e. short works that have a distinct beginning, middle and end—Emphasis on END. It is actually difficult to complete a work of short fiction with all of these elements present, and it is important to continue to work and rework your piece until this comes to fruition. Your work should be free of errors, and each sentence should flow well into the next. Stand out works feature looking at the world from an odd, oblique angle. Make us think. Look outside the box, and tell us what you see—Elements of horror can always be presented in a non-traditional, yet still somehow gut-wrenching and unsettling way. Stay away from clicheé. Before turning in your manuscript, read it aloud. Then have someone else unfamiliar with the piece read it aloud to you. This will highlight any unintentional snafus in grammar, spelling, sentence structure and flow. It will also allow you some great feedback. Look for open endings and correct them. Remember, you must articulate your writing so the reader can understand your message."

THE WORCESTER REVIEW

1 Ekman St., Worcester MA 01607. (508)797-4770. Website: wreview.homestead.com. **Contact:** Rodger Martin, managing editor. Magazine: 6 × 9; 100 pages; 60 lb. white offset paper; 10 pt. CS1 cover stock; illustrations; photos. "We like high quality, creative poetry, artwork and fiction. Critical articles should be connected to New England." Annual. Circ. 1,000.

Needs Literary, prose poem. "We encourage New England writers in the hopes we will publish at least 30% New England but want the other 70% to show the best of writing from across the U.S." Receives 20-30 unsolicited mss/month. Accepts 2-4 mss/issue. Publishes ms 11 months after acceptance. Agented fiction less than 10%. Recently published work by Robert Pinsky, Marge Piercy, Wes McNair, Ed Hirsch. Length: 1,000-4,000 words; average length: 2,000 words. Publishes short shorts. Also publishes literary essays, literary criticism, poetry. Sometimes comments on rejected mss.

How to Contact Send complete ms. Responds in 1 year to mss. Accepts simultaneous submissions only if other markets are clearly identified. Sample copy for $8. Writer's guidelines free.

Payment/Terms Pays 2 contributor copies and honorarium if possible. Acquires one-time rights.

Tips "Send only one short story—reading editors do not like to read two by the same author at the same time. We will use only one. We generally look for creative work with a blend of craftsmanship, insight and empathy. This does not exclude humor. We won't print work that is shoddy in any of these areas."

$ WORKERS WRITE!

Blue Cubicle Press, LLC, P.O. Box 250382, Plano TX 75005-0382. (972)824-0646. E-mail: info@workerswritejournal.com. Website: www.workerswritejournal.com. **Contact:** David LaBounty, editor. Literary magazine/journal: 100-164 pages, 20 lb. bond paper paper, 80 lb. cover stock cover. "We publish stories that center on a particular workplace." Annual.

Needs Ethnic/multicultural (general), humor/satire, literary, mainstream, regional. Receives 100 mss/month. Accepts 12-15 mss/year. Manuscript published 3-4 months after acceptance. **Publishes 1 new writer/year**. Length: 500 words (min)-5,000 words (max). Average length: 3,000 words. Publishes short shorts. Also publishes poetry. Often comments on rejected mss.

How to Contact Send complete ms with cover letter. Accepts submissions by e-mail. Responds to queries in 1 weeks. Responds to mss in 2-3 months. Send either SASE (or IRC) for return of ms or disposable copy of ms and #10 SASE for reply only. Considers simultaneous submissions, previously published submissions, multiple submissions. Sample copy available for $8. Guidelines available for SASE, via e-mail, on website.

Payment/Terms Pays $50 maximum and contributor's copies. Additional copies $4. Pays on publication.

Tips "We publish stories from the worker's point of view."

N $ THE YALE REVIEW

Yale University, P.O. Box 208243, New Haven CT 06520-8243. (203)432-0499. Fax: (203) 432-0510. Website: www.yale.edu/yalereview. **Contact:** J.D. McClatchy, editor. "*The Yale Review* is the nation's oldest literary quarterly." Quarterly. Circ. 7,000.

Needs Publishes ms 6 months after acceptance.

How to Contact Submit complete ms with SASE. Responds in 3 months to queries; 2 months to mss. Sample copy for $9, plus postage. All submissions should be sent to the editorial office.

Payment/Terms Pays $400-500. Pays prior to publication. Acquires one-time rights.

THE YALOBUSHA REVIEW

The Literary Journal of the University of Mississippi, Dept of English, University of Miss, P.O. Box 1848, University MS 38677-1848. E-mail: yreditor@yahoo.com. Website: www.olemiss.edu/yalobusha. **Contact:** Editor. Magazine: 5 × 10; 125 pages; illustrations; photos. Annual. "Literary journal seeking quality submissions from around the world." Circ. 500.

Needs Experimental, historical, humorous, literary, novel excerpts, short shorts. Does not want sappy confessional or insights into parenthood. Receives 100 unsolicited mss/month. Accepts

3-6 mss/issue. Reading period: July 15-November 15. Publishes ms 4 months after acceptance. **Publishes 2-4 new writers/year.** Recently published work by John Brandon, Steve Almond, Shay Youngblood, Dan Chaon. Length: 10,000 words; average length: 4,000 words. Publishes short shorts. Also publishes nonfiction, poetry.

How to Contact Send complete ms. Include a brief bio. and #10 SASE for reply only. Does not accept electronic submissions unless from outside the U.S. Accepts simultaneous submissions; no previously published work. Send disposable copy of ms and #10 SASE for reply only. Responds in 2-4 months to mss. Reading period is July 15-November 15. Sample copy for $10. Writer's guidelines for #10 SASE.

Payment/Terms Pays 2 contributor's copies. Pays honorarium when funding available. Acquires first North American serial rights.

Tips "We look for writers with a strong, distinct voice and good stories to tell. Thrill us from the first page."

N ☐ $ ZEEK, A JEWISH JOURNAL OF THOUGHT AND CULTURE

Metatronics Inc., 104 West 14th St., 4th Floor, New York NY 10011. E-mail: zeek@zeek.net. Website: www.zeek.net. **Contact** Dan Friedman, fiction editor. Literary magazine/journal, online magazine: 96 pages, card cover. Contains illustrations. Includes photographs. "Zeek is a new Jewish journal of thought and culture. Our mission is to present alternative Jewish voices of criticism, literature and religious thought, in an intelligent, but non-academic, context. Zeek exists both online and in print, in semi-annual journal form. Zeek believes in expansive definitions of what constitutes Jewish writing and culture, and is dedicated toward enriching those definitions within its pages. While it would be reductive to label any writing produced by Jews as 'Jewish writing,' Zeek believes that vibrant Jewish writing embraces a wide variety of media, opinions and perspectives that often express their Jewishness in subtle and unexpected ways, and often presents Jewish readings of non-Jewish culture. This may mean, for example, expressing an ethical/humanist sensibility in art criticism, or engaging the alterity of Jewishness with that of queer sexuality, or immersing oneself in the many diasporic cultures of Jewish character, from New York's Broadway to Marxism. Sometimes it may mean content that grapples with explicitly Jewish cultural themes, and sometimes it may mean Jews interacting with other cultures in a way in which Jewishness is relevant and informative." Semiannual. Estab. 2003. Circ. 2000. Member IPA.

Needs Comics/graphic novels, ethnic/multicultural (general, Jewish), feminist, gay, historical (general, Jewish), humor/satire, lesbian, literary, religious (Jewish), translations. Does not want "cynical, inspirational. No ethnocentric writing or simplistic ranting. If someone else can say it, let them; define new boundaries." Receives 20 mss/month. Accepts 2-4 (with more online) mss/issue; 4-8 (with more online) mss/year. Manuscript published 4 months after acceptance. Agented fiction 0%. **Publishes 5-7 new writers/year.** Published David Ehrlich, Dalia Rosenfeld, Rebecca Mostov (debut), Joshua Henkin, Hayyim Obadiah. Length: 750 words-2,500 words. Average length: 1,500 words. Publishes short shorts. Average length of short shorts: 500 words. Also publishes literary essays, literary criticism, book reviews, poetry. Send review copies to Review Editor. Often comments on/critiques rejected mss.

How to Contact Accepts submissions by e-mail. Send ms attachment and cover letter to zeek@zeek.net. Include estimated word count, brief bio, list of publications. Responds to queries in 4 weeks. Responds to mss in 8 weeks. Send disposable copy of ms and #10 SASE for reply only, but strongly prefers e-mail submissions. Considers simultaneous submissions, multiple submissions. Guidelines available on website.

Payment/Terms Writers receive $25-$50 flat-rate payment, contributor's copies, free subscription to the magazine. Additional copies $7/each. Pays on publication. Acquires first rights. Publication is copyrighted.

Tips "Seeks quality, freshness of perspective. Something intangibly Jewish and questioning of Jewish mores. Read the online archives. Ask yourself what questions your fiction poses."

$ ZYZZYVA

The Last Word: West Coast Writers & Artists, P.O. Box 590069, San Francisco CA 94159-0069. (415)752-4393. Fax: (415)752-4391. E-mail: editor@zyzzyva.org. Website: www.zyzzyva.org. **Contact:** Howard Junker, editor. "We feature work by writers currently living on the West Coast or in Alaska and Hawaii only. We are essentially a literary magazine, but of wide-ranging interests and a strong commitment to nonfiction." Circ. 2,500.

Needs Ethnic/multicultural, experimental, humor/satire, mainstream. Receives 300 unsolicited mss/month. Accepts 15 mss/issue; 45 mss/year. Publishes ms 3 months after acceptance. Agented fiction 1%. **Publishes 15 new writers/year.** Recently published work by Rick Barot, Jackson Bliss, Dust Wells. Publishes short shorts. Also publishes literary essays, poetry.

How to Contact Send complete ms. Responds in 1 week to queries; 1 month to mss. Sample copy for $7 or online. Writer's guidelines online.

Payment/Terms Pays $50. Pays on acceptance for first North American serial and one-time anthology rights.

Small Circulation Magazines

This section of *Novel & Short Story Writer's Market* contains general interest, special interest, regional and genre magazines with circulations under 10,000. Although these magazines vary greatly in size, theme, format and management, the editors are all looking for short stories. Their specific fiction needs present writers of all degrees of expertise and interests with an abundance of publishing opportunities. Among the diverse publications in this section are magazines devoted to almost every topic, every level of writing, and every type of writer. Some of the markets listed here publish fiction about a particular geographic area or by authors who live in that locale.

Although not as high-paying as the large-circulation consumer magazines, you'll find some of the publications listed here do pay writers 1-5¢/word or more. Also, unlike the big consumer magazines, these markets are very open to new writers and relatively easy to break into. Their only criterion is that your story be well written, well presented and suitable for their particular readership.

In this section you will also find listings for zines. Zines vary greatly in appearance as well as content. Some paper zines are photocopies published whenever the editor has material and money, while others feature offset printing and regular distribution schedules. A few have evolved into very slick four-color, commercial-looking publications.

SELECTING THE RIGHT MARKET

First, zero in on those markets most likely to be interested in your work. Begin by looking at the Category Index starting on page 591. If your work is more general—or conversely, very specialized—you may wish to browse through the listings, perhaps looking up those magazines published in your state or region. Also check the Online Markets section for other specialized and genre publications.

In addition to browsing through the listings and using the Category Index, check the openness icons at the beginning of listings to find those most likely to be receptive to your work. This is especially true for beginning writers, who should look for magazines that say they are especially open to new writers (☐) and for those giving equal weight to both new and established writers (◪). For more explanation about these icons, see the inside covers of this book.

Once you have a list of magazines you might like to try, read their listings carefully. Much of the material within each listing carries clues that tell you more about the magazine. You've Got a Story, starting on page 1, describes in detail the listing information common to all the markets in our book.

The physical description appearing near the beginning of the listings can give you clues about the size and financial commitment to the publication. This is not always an indication of quality, but chances are a publication with expensive paper and four-color artwork on the cover has more prestige than a photocopied publication featuring a clip-art cover. For more information on some of the paper, binding and printing terms used in these descriptions, see Printing and Production Terms Defined on page 540.

FURTHERING YOUR SEARCH

It cannot be stressed enough that reading the listing is only the first part of developing your marketing plan. The second part, equally important, is to obtain fiction guidelines and read the actual magazine. Reading copies of a magazine helps you determine the fine points of the magazine's publishing style and philosophy. There is no substitute for this type of hands-on research.

Unlike commercial magazines available at most newsstands and bookstores, it requires a little more effort to obtain some of the magazines listed here. You may need to send for a sample copy. We include sample copy prices in the listings whenever possible. See The Business of Fiction Writing on page **49** for the specific mechanics of manuscript submission. Above all, editors appreciate a professional presentation. Include a brief cover letter and send a self-addressed, stamped envelope for a reply. Be sure the envelope is large enough to accommodate your manuscript, if you would like it returned, and include enough stamps or International Reply Coupons (for replies from countries other than your own) to cover your manuscript's return. Many publishers today appreciate receiving a disposable manuscript, eliminating the cost to writers of return postage and saving editors the effort of repackaging manuscripts for return.

Most of the magazines listed here are published in the U.S. You will also find some English-speaking markets from around the world. These foreign publications are denoted with a 🌐 symbol at the beginning of listings. To make it easier to find Canadian markets, we include a 🍁 symbol at the start of those listings.

🌐 ◪ ◎ THE ABIKO ANNUAL WITH JAMES JOYCE

c/o T. Hamada, Hananoi 1787-28, Kashiwa-shi 277-0812, Japan. (011) 81-471-69-8036. E-mail: hamada-tatsuo@jcom.home.ne.jp. Website: http://members.jcom.home.ne.jp/hamada-tatsuo/. **Contact**: Tatsuo Hamada. Magazine: A5; 350 pages; illustrations; photos. "We primarily publish James Joyce Finnegans Wake essays from writers here in Japan and abroad." Annual. Estab. 1989. Circ. 300.

Needs Experimental (in the vein of James Joyce), literary, inspirational. Also essays on James Joyce's *Finnegans Wake* from around the world. Receives very few unsolicited mss/month. Also publishes literary essays, literary criticism, poetry. Always comments on rejected mss.

How to Contact Send a disposable copy of ms or e-mail attachment. Responds in 1 week to queries; 3 months to mss. Accepts multiple submissions. Sample copy for $20. Guidelines for SASE. Reviews fiction.

Payment/Terms Pays 1 contributor's copy; additional copies $25. Copyright reverts to author upon publication.

Tips "We require camera-ready copy. The writer is welcome to accompany it with appropriate artwork."

$ ALBEDO ONE

(353)1 8730 177. E-mail: bobn@yellowbrickroad.ie. Website: www.albedo1.com. Magazine: A4; 64 pages. "We hope to publish interesting and unusual fiction by new and established writers. We will consider anything, as long as it is well written and entertaining, though our definitions of both may not be exactly mainstream. We like stories with plot and characters that live on the page. Most of our audience are probably committed genre fans, but we try to appeal to a broad spectrum of readers." Triannual. Circ. 900.

Needs Experimental, fantasy, horror, literary, science fiction. Receives more than 80 unsolicited mss/month. Accepts 15-18 mss/year. Publishes ms 1 year after acceptance. **Publishes 6-8 new writers/year.** Length: 2,000-9,000 words; average length: 4,000 words. Also publishes literary criticism. Sometimes comments on rejected mss.

How to Contact Responds in 3 months to mss. PDF—electronic—sample copies are available for download at a reduced price. Guidelines available by e-mail or on website. Reviews fiction.

Payment/Terms Pays €3 per 1,000 words, and 1 contributor's copy; additional copies $5 plus p&p. Pays on publication for first rights.

Tips "We look for good writing, good plot, good characters. Read the magazine, and don't give up."

THE ALEMBIC

Providence College, English Dept., Providence College, Providence RI 01918. (401) 865-2751. E-mail: cdeniord@providence.edu. **Contact:** Magazine has revolving editor. Editorial term: one year. Magazine: 6 × 9, 80 pages. Contains illustrations, photographs. "We publish strong work from both emerging and established writers." Annual. Estab. 1940. Circ. 600.

Needs "We are open to all styles of fiction." Receives 200 mss/month. Accepts 5 mss/issue; 5 mss/year. Does not read January-September. Ms published 6 months after acceptance. **Publishes 15 new writers/year.** Published Bruce Smith, Robin Behn, Rane Arroyo, Sharon Dolin, Jeff Friedman, Khalid Mattawa. Length: 20 pages or words (min)-6000 words (max). Average length: 5000 words. Publishes short shorts. Average length of short shorts: 200 words. Also publishes literary essays, literary criticism, book reviews, poetry. Send review copies to Chard deNiord. Never comments on/critiques rejected mss.

How to Contact Send complete ms with cover letter. Include brief bio. Responds to queries in 1 month; mss in 8 months. Send SASE (or IRC) for return of ms. Considers simultaneous submissions. Sample copy available for $12. Guidelines available for SASE, via e-mail.

Payment/Terms Writers receive 2 contributor's copies. Additional copies $12. Pays on publication. Acquires first rights. Publication is not copyrighted.

Tips "We're looking for stories that are wise, memorable, grammatical, economical, poetic in the right places, and end strongly. Take Heraclitus' claim that 'character is fate' to heart and study the strategies, styles and craft of such masters as Anton Chekov, J. Cheever, Flannery O'Connor, John Updike, Rick Bass, Phillip Roth, Joyce Carol Oates, William Treavor, Lorrie Moore and Ethan Canin."

ANY DREAM WILL DO REVIEW

Short Stories and Humor from the Secret Recesses of our Minds, 250 Jeanell Dr., Carson City NV 89703. (775)786-0345. E-mail: cassjmb@intercomm.com. Website: www.willigocrazy.org/Ch08.htm. **Contact:** Dr. Jean M. Bradt, editor and publisher. Magazine: 5½ × 8½; 52 pages; 20 lb. bond paper; 12pt. Carolina cover stock. "The Any Dream Will Do Review showcases a new literary genre, Fiction In The Raw, which attempts to fight the prejudice against consumers of mental-health services by touching hearts, that is, by exposing the consumers' deepest thoughts and emotions. In the Review's stories, accomplished authors honestly reveal their most intimate secrets. See www.willigocrazy.org/Ch09a.htm for detailed instructions on how to write Fiction In The Raw." Published every 4 or 5 years.

Needs Adapted ethnic/multicultural, mainstream, psychic/supernatural/occult, romance (contemporary), science fiction (soft/sociological), all of which must follow the guidelines at website. No pornography, true-life stories, black humor, political material, testimonials, experimental fiction, or depressing accounts of hopeless or perverted people. Accepts 10 mss/issue; 5 mss/year. Publishes ms 12 months after acceptance. **Publishes 2 new writers/year.** Publishes short shorts. Often comments on rejected mss.

How to Contact Send complete ms. Accepts submissions by e-mail (cassjmb@intercomm.com). Please submit by e-mail. If you must submit by hardcopy, please send disposable copies. No queries, please. Responds in 8 weeks to mss. Sample copy for $4 plus postage. Writer's guidelines online.

Payment/Terms Pays in contributor's copies; additional copies $4 plus postage. Acquires first North American serial rights.

Tips "Read several stories on www.willigocrazy.org before starting to write. Proof your story many times before submitting. Make the readers think. Above all, present people (preferably diagnosed with mental illness) realistically rather than with prejudice."

$ APEX SCIENCE FICTION AND HORROR DIGEST

Apex Publications, P.O. Box 24323, Lexington KY 40524. (859) 312-3974. E-mail: jason@apexdigest.com. Website: www.apexdigest.com. **Contact:** Jason Sizemore, editor-in-chief. Magazine: 5½ × 8½, 128 pages, 70 lb. white offset paper, glossy #120 cover. Contains illustrations. "We publish dark sci-fi with horror elements. Our readers are those that enjoy speculative fiction with dark themes." Monthly. Estab. 2005. Circ. 3,000.

Needs Dark science fiction. "We're not fans of 'monster' fiction." Receives 200-250 mss/month. Accepts 2 mss/issue; 24 mss/year. Manuscript published 3 months after acceptance. **Publishes 10 new writers/year**. Published Brian Keene, Cherie Priest, Ben Bova, William F. Nolan, Tom Piccirilli, M.M. Buckner, JA Rourath, and James P. Hogan. Length: 200 words (min)-7,500 words (max). Average length: 4,000 words. Publishes short shorts. Average length of short shorts: 500 words. Often comments on/critiques rejected manuscripts.

How to Contact Send complete ms with cover letter. Include estimated word count, brief bio. Responds to queries in 3-4 weeks. Responds to mss in 3-4 weeks. E-mail submissions only. Guidelines available via e-mail, on website.

Payment/Terms Writers receive 5¢/word. Pays on publication. Acquires first North American web rights. Non-exclusive print anthology rights. Publication is copyrighted.

Tips "Be professional. Be confident. Remember that any criticisms offered are given for your benefit."

$ THE APUTAMKON REVIEW: VOICES FROM DOWNEAST MAINE AND THE CANADIAN MARITIMES (OR THEREABOUTS)

the WordShed, LLC, P.O. Box 190, Jonesboro MA 04648. (207) 434-5661. Fax: (207) 434-5661. E-mail: thewordshed@tds.net. **Contact:** Les Simon, Publisher. Magazine. Approx. 160 pages. Contains b&w illustrations. Includes photographs. "All age groups living in downeast Maine and the Canadian Maritimes, or thereabouts, are invited to participate. The Aputamkon Review will present a mismash of truths, half truths and outright lies, including but not limited to short fiction, tall tales, creative non-fiction, essays, (some) poetry, haiku, b&w visual arts, interviews, lyrics and music, quips, quirks, quotes that should be famous, witticisms, follies, comic strips, cartoons, jokes, riddles, recipes, puzzles, games. Stretch your imagination. Practically anything goes." Annual. Estab. 2006. Circ. 500. Member Maine Writers and Publishers Alliance.

Needs Adventure, children's/juvenile, comics/graphic novels, ethnic/multicultural, experimental, family saga, fantasy, glitz, historical, horror, humor/satire, literary, mainstream, military/war, mystery, psychic/supernatural/occult, religious, romance, science fiction, thriller/espionage, translations, western, young adult/teen. Does not want mss which are heavy with sex or religion. Receives 1-20 mss/month. Accepts 10-20 mss/year. Ms published max of 12 months after acceptance. Length: 50 words (min)-4,000 words (max). Average length: 500 words. Publishes short shorts. Also publishes literary essays, literary criticism, poetry. Rarely comments on/critiques rejected mss.

How to Contact Send complete ms with cover letter. Accepts submissions by e-mail, on disk. Submission period is twelve months a year; reading January 1 through April 1. Responds by June 30th. Include age if under 18, and a bio will be requested upon acceptance of work. Responds to queries in 2-4 weeks. Responds to mss in 1-6 months. Send SASE (or IRC) for return of ms or a disposable copy of ms and #10 SASE for reply only. Considers simultaneous submissions, multiple submissions. Sample copy available for $12 plus s/h. Guidelines available for SASE, via e-mail, via fax.

Payment/Terms Submissions accepted $10-35 depending on medium. Pays on acceptance. Acquires first North American serial rights. Publication is copyrighted. All rights revert back to the contributors upon publication.

Tips "Be colorful, heartfelt not mainstream. Write what you want and then submit."

THE BINNACLE

University of Maine at Machias, 9 O'Brien Ave., Machias ME 04654. E-mail: ummbinnacle@maine.edu. Website: www.umm.maine.edu/binnacle. "We are looking for the fresh voices of people who know what dirt under their fingernails, a belly laugh, and hard luck feel like, and of writers who are not afraid to take a chance." Semiannual, plus annual Ultra-Short Competition editon. Estab. 1957. Circ. 300.

Needs Ethnic/multicultural, experimental, humor/satire, mainstream, slice-of-life vignettes. No extreme erotica, fantasy, horror, or religious, but any genre attuned to a general audience can work. Publishes ms 3 months after acceptance.

How to Contact Submissions by e-mail preferred. Responds in 1 month to queries; 3 months to mss. Accepts simultaneous submissions. Sample copy for $7. Writer's guidelines online at website or by e-mail.

Payment/Terms $300 in prizes for Ultra-Short. $50 per issue for one work of editor's choice. Acquires one-time rights.

☐ ◎ $ BLACK LACE

P.O. Box 83912, Los Angeles CA 90083-0912. (310)410-0808. Fax: (310)410-9250. E-mail: newsroom@blk.com. Website: www.blacklace.org. **Contact:** Editor. Magazine: 8-1/8 × 10-5/8; 48 pages; book stock; color glossy cover; illustrations; photos. "*Black Lace* is a lifestyle magazine for African-American lesbians. Its content ranges from erotic imagery to political commentary." Quarterly.

Needs Ethnic/multicultural, lesbian. Wants "full-length erotic fiction of 2,000-4,000 words detailing the exploits of black women in the life. Avoid interracial stories of idealized pornography." Accepts 4 mss/year. Recently published work by Nicole King, Wanda Thompson, Lynn K. Pannell, Sheree Ann Slaughter, Lyn Lifshin, JoJo and Drew Alise Timmens. Publishes short shorts. Also publishes literary essays, literary criticism, poetry.

How to Contact Query with published clips or send complete ms. Send a disposable copy of ms. No simultaneous submissions. Accepts electronic submissions. Sample copy for $7. Writer's guidelines free.

Payment/Terms Pays $50 and 2 contributor's copies. Acquires first North American serial rights. Right to anthologize.

Tips "*Black Lace* seeks erotic material of the highest quality. The most important thing is that the work be erotic and that it feature black lesbians or themes. Study the magazine to see what we do and how we do it. Some fiction is very romantic, other is highly sexual. Most articles in *Black Lace* cater to black lesbians between two extremes."

N ☐ BROKEN PENCIL

P.O. Box 203 STN P, Toronto ON M5S 2S7 Canada. (416)204-1700. E-mail: editor@brokenpencil.com. Website: www.brokenpencil.com. **Contact:** Hal Niedzviecki, fiction editor. Magazine. "Founded in

1995 and based in Toronto, Canada, Broken Pencil is a website and print magazine published four times a year. It is one of the few magazines in the world devoted to underground culture and the independent arts. We are a great resource and a lively read. A cross between the Utne Reader, an underground Reader's Digest, and the now defunct Factsheet15, Broken Pencil reviews the best zines, books, Web sites, videos, and artworks from the underground and reprints the best articles from the alternative press. Also, ground-breaking interviews, original fiction, and commentary on all aspects of the independent arts. From the hilarious to the perverse, Broken Pencil challenges conformity and demands attention." Quarterly. Estab. 1995. Circ. 5,000.

Needs Adventure, erotica, ethnic/multicultural, experimental, fantasy, historical, horror, humor/satire, amateur sleuth, romance, science fiction. Accepts 8 mss/year. Manuscript published 2-3 months after acceptance. Length: 500-3,000 words.

How to Contact Accepts submissions by e-mail.

Payment/Terms Acquires first rights.

Tips "Write to receive a list of upcoming themes and then pitch us stories based around these themes. If you keep your ear to the ground in alternative and underground arts communities, you will be able to find content appropriate for *Broken Pencil.*"

$ CONCEIT MAGAZINE

P.O. Box 884223, San Francisco CA 94188-4333 or P.O. Box 8544, Emeryville CA 94662. (415) 401-8370. Fax: (415) 401-8370. E-mail: conceitmagazine2007@yahoo.com. Website: www.myspace.com/conceitmagazine. **Contact:** Perry Terrell, Editor. Magazine. 8½ × 5½, 44 pages, copy paper paper. Contains illustrations, photographs. "If it's on your mind, write it down and send it to Perry Terrell at Conceit Magazine. Writing is good therapy." Monthly. Estab. 2007. Circ. 300+.

Needs Adventure, children's/juvenile, ethnic/multicultural, experimental, family saga, fantasy, feminist, gay, historical, horror (futuristic, psychological, supernatural), humor/satire, lesbian, literary, mainstream, military/war, mystery, new age, psychic/supernatural/occult, religious, romance (contemporary, futuristic/time travel, historical, regency, suspense), science fiction (soft/sociological), thriller/espionage, translations, western, young adult/teen (adventure, easy-to-read, fantasy/science fiction, historical, mystery/suspense, problem novels, romance, series, sports, western). Does not want profanity, porn, gruesomeness. List of upcoming themes available for SASE and on website. Receives 40-50 mss/month. Accepts 20-22 mss/issue; up to 264 mss/year. Ms published 3-10 months after acceptance. **Publishes 150 new writers/year.** Published Dr. C. David Hay, D. Neil Simmers, Tamara Fey Turner, Zachary Nahrstadt, Eve J. Blohm, Barbara Hantman, Wayne Sheer. Length: 100 words (min)-3,000 words (max). Average length: 1,500-2,000 words. Publishes short shorts. Average length of short shorts: 50-500 words. Also publishes literary essays, literary criticism, book reviews, poetry. Send review copies to Perry Terrell. Sometimes comments on/critiques rejected mss.

How to Contact Query first or send complete ms with cover letter. Accepts submissions by e-mail, by fax, mail and on disk. Include estimated word count, brief bio, list of publications. Responds to queries in 1-2 weeks. Responds to mss in 1-4 weeks. Send either SASE (or IRC) for return of ms or disposable copy of ms and #10 SASE for reply only. Considers simultaneous submissions, previously published submissions, multiple submissions. Sample copy free with SASE. Guidelines available for SASE, via e-mail, on website, via fax.

Payment/Terms Writers receive 1 contributor copy and subscribers vote on who receives a $100 monthly stipend. Additional copies $4.50. Pays on publication. Acquires one-time rights. Publication is copyrighted. "Occassionly sponsors contests. Send SASE or check blog on website for details."

Tips "Uniqueness and creativity make a manuscript stand out. Be brave and confident. Let me see what you created."

$ THE COUNTRY CONNECTION

Pinecone Publishing, P.O. Box 100, Boulter ON K0L 1G0 Canada. (613) 332-3651. E-mail: editor@pinecone.on.ca. Website: www.pinecone.on.ca. "The Country Connection is a magazine for true nature lovers and the rural adventurer. Building on our commitment to heritage, cultural, artistic, and environmental themes, we continually add new topics to illuminate the country experience of people living within nature. Our goal is to chronicle rural life in its many aspects, giving 'voice' to the countryside." Estab. 1989. Circ. 5,000.

Needs Ontario history and heritage, humor/satire, nature, environment, the arts, country living. "Canadian material by Canadian authors only." Publishes ms 4 months after acceptance.

How to Contact Send complete ms. Accepts submissions by e-mail, disk. Sample copy for $ 6.68. Writer's guidelines online.

Payment/Terms Pays 10¢/word. Pays on publication for first rights.

☐ CREATIVE WITH WORDS PUBLICATIONS

P.O. Box 223226, Carmel CA 93922. Fax: (831)655-8627. E-mail: geltrich@mbay.net. Website: creativewithwords.tripod.com. **Contact:** Brigitta Geltrich, publisher/editor.

Needs Ethnic/multicultural, humor/satire, mystery/suspense (amateur sleuth, private eye), regional (folklore), young adult/teen (adventure, historical). "Do not submit essays." No violence or erotica, overly religious fiction or sensationalism. "Twice a year we publish *the*Eclectics written by adults only (20 and older); throughout the year we publish thematic anthologies written by all ages." List of upcoming themes available for SASE. Limit poetry to 20 lines or less, 46 characters per line or less. Receives 50-200 unsolicited mss/month. Accepts 50-80 mss/anthology. Publishes ms 1-2 months after acceptance. Recently published work by Najwa Salam Brax, Sirock Brighton, Roger D. Coleman, Antoinette Garrick and Maria Dickerhof. Sometimes comments on rejected mss.

How to Contact Send complete ms with a cover letter with SASE. Include estimated word count. Responds in 2 weeks to queries; 1-2 months after a specific theme's due date to mss. Please request a list of themes with SASE before sending manuscript. Sample copy for $7. Writer's guidelines for #10 SASE.

Payment/Terms 20% reduction cost on 1-9 copies ordered, 30% reduction on 10 to 19 copies, 40% reduction on each copy on order of 20 or more. Acquires one-time rights.

Tips "We offer a great variety of themes. We look for clean family-type fiction/poetry. Also, we ask the writer to look at the world from a different perspective, research topic thoroughly, be creative, apply brevity, tell the story from a character's viewpoint, tighten dialogue, be less descriptive, proofread before submitting and be patient. We will not publish every manuscript we receive. It has to be in standard English, well written, proofread. We do not appreciate receiving manuscripts where we have to do the proofreading and the correcting of grammar."

☐ DAN RIVER ANTHOLOGY

Conservatory of American Letters, P.O. Box 298, Thomaston ME 04861. (207)226-7528. Website: www.americanletters.org. **Contact**: R.S. Danbury III, editor. Book: 6 × 9; 192 pages; 60 lb. paper; gloss 10 pt. full-color cover. Deadline every year is March 31, with acceptance/rejection by May 15, proofs out by June 15, and book released December 7. Annual. Estab. 1984. Circ. 750.

Needs Adventure, ethnic/multicultural, experimental, fantasy, historical, horror, humor/satire, literary, mainstream, psychic/supernatural/occult, regional, romance (contemporary and historical), science fiction, suspense, western, contemporary, prose poem, senior citizen/retirement. "Virtually anything but porn, evangelical, juvenile. Would like to see more first-person adventure." Reads "mostly in April." Length: 800-3,500 words; average length: 2,000-2,400 words. Also publishes poetry.

How to Contact Send complete ms. No simultaneous submissions. Submit disk in rich text format (.RTF), disk must be single spaced, do not justify, do not indent paragraphs. Be sure sase is large enought if you want your disk back. Send cd or floppy. We can not accept anything not on disk. Nothing previously published. Sample copy for $16.95 paperback, $39.95 cloth, plus $3.50 shipping. Writer's guidelines available for #10 SASE or online.

Payment/Terms Payment "depends on your experience with us, as it is a nonrefundable advance against royalties on all sales that we can attribute to your influence. For first-timers, the advance is about 1¢/word." Pays on acceptance for first rights.

Tips "Read an issue or two, know the market. Don't submit without reading guidelines on the Web or send #10 SASE."

$ DARK DISCOVERIES

Dark Discoveries Publications, 142 Woodside Drive, Longview WA 98632. (360) 425-5796. E-mail: ddsubmissions@gmail.com; info@darkdiscoveries.com; darkdiscoveries@msn.com. Website: www.darkdiscoveries.com. **Contact:** James R. Beach, Editor-in-Chief/Publisher. Magazine. 8 12 × 11, 64 pages. Published on recycled paper with vegetable-based inks. Contains illustrations. Includes photographs. "We publish dark fiction in the horror/fantasy realm with a lean towards the psychological side. We do publish mystery and supernatural as well. We also feature interviews and articles. Themed issues such as Twilight Zone, Lovecraft, etc." Quarterly.

- Seven stories published in Dark Discoveries have been Honorable Mentions in the Year's Best Fantasy & Horror and 5 stories have been nominated for the Bram Stoker Awards. Magazine was runner-up for Best Horror Magazine in the first Black Quill Awards.

Needs Horror (dark fantasy). Does not want straight science fiction or mystery, "but will look at hybrid horror stories with elements of each. No straight sword and sorcery or fantasy either." Receives 150-200 mss/month. Accepts 25 mss/year. Ms published within 12 months after acceptance. **Publishes 2-4 new writers/year.** Published fiction by Richard Matheson, William F. Nolan, Brian Lumley, Elizabeth Engstrom, Kealan Patrick Burke, Jay Lake, Tony Richards, Tim Lebbon, Gary A. Braunbeck, John Everson, Tim Waggoner, Cindy Foster, Stephen Mark Rainey, Kurt Newton, and Brian Knight. Length: 500-5,000 words. Average length: 4,000 words. Publishes short shorts. Average length of short shorts: 500 - 1,000 words. Also publishes literary essays, literary criticism, book reviews. Please send queries on review copies to James R. Beach. Often comments on/critiques rejected mss.

How to Contact Send complete ms with cover letter. Encourages submissions by e-mail to help the environment. Include estimated word count, brief bio, list of publications. Submission period is October 1st to July 1st yearly. Responds to queries in 1-2 weeks. Responds to mss in 3-4 months. Send either SASE (or IRC) for return of ms or disposable copy of ms and #10 SASE for reply only. Only publishing select "Classic" reprints at this point (besides new stories). No simultaneous submissions. Sample copy available for $8.99 in the US (add $2 for Canada and $6 for overseas). Please note Writer's market discount. Guidelines available for SASE, via e-mail, on website. Payment/Terms Writers receive ¢.05 per word up to 5000 words, 2 contributor's copies. Additional copies at 40% of cover price. Pays within 60 days of publication.

Tips "I look for well-written and thought provoking tales. I don't like to see the same well-tread themes. Be it a new or established writer, I like to see the writer's voice show through. Take our suggestions to heart, and if you don't succeed at catching our eye at first keep trying."

$ DARK TALES

Dark Tales, 7 Offley Street, Worcester WR3 8BH United Kingdom. E-mail: sean@darktales.co.uk. Website: www.darktales.co.uk. **Contact:** Sean Jeffery, editor. Magazine: Contains illustrations. "We publish horror and speculative short fiction from anybody, anywhere, and the publication is professionally illustrated throughout." Circ. 350+.

Needs Horror (dark fantasy, futuristic, psychological, supernatural), science fiction (soft/sociological). Receives 25+ mss/month. Accepts 10-15 mss/issue; 25-40 mss/year. Ms published 6 months after acceptance. **Publishes 20 new writers/year.** Published Davin Ireland, Niall McMahon, David Robertson, Valerie Robson, K.S. Dearsley and Mark Cowley. Length: 500-3,500 words. Average length: 2,500 words. Publishes short shorts. Average length of short shorts: 500 words. Sometimes comments on/critiques rejected mss. Has occasional contests; see website for details.

How to Contact Send complete ms with cover letter. Include estimated word count, list of publications. Responds to queries in 1 week. Responds to mss in 12 weeks. Send disposable copy of ms and #10 SASE for reply only. Sample copy available for $3. Guidelines available on website.
Payment/Terms Writers receive $5 per thousand words. Additional copies $7.10. Pays on publication. Acquires first British serial rights. Sends galleys to author. Publication is copyrighted.
Tips "Have a believable but inspiring plot, sympathetic characters, an original premise, and a human heart no matter how technical or disturbing a story. Read a copy of the magazine! Make sure you get your writing basics spot-on. Don't rehash old ideas—if you must go down the werewolf/vampire route, put a spin on it."

☐ DOWN IN THE DIRT

The Publication Revealing all your Dirty Little Secrets, 829 Brian Court, Gurnee IL 60031-3155. (847)281-9070. E-mail: alexrand@scars.tv. Website: scars.tv.. **Contact:** Alexandria Rand, editor. Magazine: 5½ × 8½; perfect-bound 84-page book. Monthly.
Needs Adventure, ethnic/multicultural, experimental, fantasy, feminist, gay, historical, horror, lesbian, literary, mystery/suspense, New Age, psychic/supernatural/occult, science fiction. No religious or rhyming or family-oriented material. Publishes ms within 1 year after acceptance. Recently published work by Pat Dixon, Mel Waldman, Ken Dean Aeon Logan, Helena Wolfe. Average length: 1,000 words. Publishes short shorts. Also publishes poetry. "Contact us if you are interested in submitting very long stories, or parts of a novel (if accepted, it would appear in parts in multiple issues)." Always, if asked, comments on rejected mss.
How to Contact Query with e-mail submission. "99.5% of all submissions are via e-mail only, so if you do not have electronic access, there is a strong chance you will not be considered. Responds in 1 month to queries; 1 month to mss. Accepts simultaneous, multiple submissions and reprints. Sample copy for $6. Writer's guidelines for SASE, e-mail or on the website.

$ DREAMS & VISIONS

Skysong Press, 35 Peter St. S., Orillia ON L3V 5A8 Canada. (705) 329-1770. E-mail: skysong@bconnex.net. Website: www.bconnex.net/~skysong. **Contact:** Steve Stanton, editor. Magazine: 5½ × 8½; 60 pages; 20 lb. bond paper; glossy cover. "Innovative literary fiction for adult Christian readers." Semiannual. Estab. 1988. Circ. 300.
Needs Experimental, fantasy, humor/satire, literary, mainstream, mystery/suspense, novel excerpts, religious/inspirational, science fiction, slice-of-life vignettes. "We do not publish stories that glorify violence or perversity. All stories should portray a Christian worldview or expand upon Biblical themes or ethics in an entertaining or enlightening manner." Receives 20 unsolicited mss/month. Accepts 5 mss/issue; 10 mss/year. Publishes ms 4-8 months after acceptance. **Publishes 3 new writers/year.** Recently published work by Fred McGavran, Steven Mills, Donna Farley, and Michael Vance. Length: 2,000-6,000 words; average length: 2,500 words.
How to Contact Send complete ms. Responds in 3 weeks to queries; 3 months to mss. Accepts simultaneous submissions and reprints. Sample copy for $ 5.95. Writer's guidelines online.
Payment/Terms Pays 1¢/word (Canadian). Pays on publication for one-time rights.
Tips "In general we look for work that has some literary value, that is in some way unique and relevant to Christian readers today. Our first priority is technical adequacy, though we will occasionally work with a beginning writer to polish a manuscript. Ultimately, we look for stories that glorify the Lord Jesus Christ, stories that build up rather than tear down, that exalt the sanctity of life, the holiness of God, and the value of the family."

$ THE FIRST LINE

P.O. Box 250382, Plano TX 75025-0382. (972)824-0646. E-mail: submission@thefirstline.com. Website: www.thefirstline.com. **Contact:** Robin LaBounty, manuscript coordinator. Magazine: 8 × 5; 64-72 pages; 20 lb. bond paper; 80 lb. cover stock. "We only publish stories that start with the first line provided. We are a collection of tales—of different directions writers can take when they start from the same place. Quarterly. Circ. 1,200.

Needs Adventure, ethnic/multicultural, fantasy, gay, humor/satire, lesbian, literary, mainstream, mystery/suspense, regional, romance, science fiction, western. Receives 200 unsolicited mss/month. Accepts 12 mss/issue; 48 mss/year. Publishes ms 1 month after acceptance. **Publishes 6 new writers/year.** Length: 300-3,000 words; average length: 1,500 words. Publishes short shorts. Also publishes literary essays, literary criticism. Often comments on rejected mss.

How to Contact Send complete ms. Accepts submissions by e-mail. Send SASE for return of ms or disposable copy of the ms and #10 SASE for reply only. Responds in 1 week to queries; 3 months to mss. Accepts multiple submissions. No simultaneous submissions. Sample copy for $3.50. Writer's guidelines for SASE, e-mail or on website. Reviews fiction.

Payment/Terms Pays $20 maximum and contributor's copy; additional copy $2. Pays on publication.

Tips "Don't just write the first story that comes to mind after you read the sentence. If it is obvious, chances are other people are writing about the same thing. Don't try so hard. Be willing to accept criticism."

◪ ◎ $ HARDBOILED

Gryphon Publications, P.O. Box 209, Brooklyn NY 11228. Website: www.gryphonbooks.com. **Contact:** Gary Lovisi, editor. Magazine: Digest-sized; 100 pages; offset paper; color cover; illustrations. "Hard-hitting crime fiction and private-eye stories—the newest and most cutting-edge work and classic reprints." Semiannual. Estab. 1988. Circ. 1,000.

Needs Mystery/suspense (private eye, police procedural, noir), hard-boiled crime, and private-eye stories, all on the cutting edge. No "pastiches, violence for the sake of violence." Wants to see more non-private-eye hard-boiled. Receives 40-60 unsolicited mss/month. Accepts 10-20 mss/issue. Publishes ms 18 months after acceptance. **Publishes 5-10 new writers/year.** Recently published work by Andrew Vachss, Stephen Solomita, Joe Hensley, Mike Black. Sometimes comments on rejected mss.

How to Contact Query with or without published clips or send complete ms. Accepts submissions by fax. Query with SASE only on anything over 3,000 words. All stories must be submitted in hard copy. If accepted, e-mail as an attachment in a Word document. Responds in 2 weeks to queries; 1 month to mss. Accepts simultaneous submissions and reprints. Sample copy for $10 or double issue for $20 (add $1.50 book postage). Writer's guidelines for #10 SASE.

Payment/Terms Pays $5-50. Pays on publication for first North American serial, one-time rights.

Tips By "hardboiled" the editor does not mean rehashing of pulp detective fiction from the 1940s and 1950s but rather realistic, gritty material. We look for good writing, memorable characters, intense situations. Lovisi could be called a pulp fiction "afficionado," however he also publishes *Paperback Parade* and holds an annual vintage paperback fiction convention each year. "It is advisable new writers try a subscription to the magazine to better see the type of stories and writing I am looking for. $35 gets you the next 4 hard-hitting issues."

◪ ◎ IRREANTUM

Exploring Mormon Literature, P.O. Box 970874, Orem UT 84097-0874. (801)582-2090. Website: irreantum.mormonletters.org. **Contact:** Managing Editor. Magazine or Zine: 8½ × 7½; 100-120 pages; 20 lb. paper; 20 lb. color cover; illustrations; photos. "While focused on Mormonism, *Irreantum* is a cultural, humanities-oriented magazine, not a religious magazine. Our guiding principle is that Mormonism is grounded in a sufficiently unusual, cohesive, and extended historical and cultural experience that it has become like a nation, an ethnic culture. We can speak of Mormon literature at least as surely as we can of a Jewish or Southern literature. Irreantum publishes stories, one-act dramas, stand-alone novel and drama excerpts, and poetry by, for, or about Mormons (as well as author interviews, essays, and reviews). The magazine's audience includes readers of any or no religious faith who are interested in literary exploration of the Mormon culture, mindset, and worldview through Mormon themes and characters. Irreantum is currently the only magazine devoted to Mormon literature." Bi-annual. Circ. 300.

Needs "High quality work that explores the Mormon experience, directly or by implication, through literature. We acknowledge a broad range of experience with Mormonism, both as a faith and as a culture—on the part of devoted multi-generation Mormons, ethnic Mormons, new converts, and people outside the faith and culture who interact with Mormons and Mormon culture. We are committed to respectful exploration of Mormonism through literature. Receives 5 unsolicited mss/month. Accepts 3 mss/issue; 6 mss/year. Publishes ms 3-12 months after acceptance. **Publishes 3 or more new writers/year.** Recently published work by Orson Scott Card, Terryl Givens, Jack Harrell, Eric Samuelsen, Michael Collins, Phyllis Barber, Paul Swenson. Length: 1,000-5,000 words; average length: 5,000 words. Publishes short shorts. Also publishes literary essays, literary criticism, poetry. Sometimes comments on rejected mss. Annual fiction contest and annual personal essay contest with cash prizes.

How to Contact Accepts submissions by email only in Microsoft Word or rich text files only. Accepts critical essays to criticalessaysubmissions@mormonletter.org. "The fiction and personal essay/creative nonfiction we publish is selected from the contest entries for the annual fiction contest and annual personal essay contest with offer cash prizes. There is a submission window—January 1-May 31st—for fiction and creative nonfiction submissions. All unsolicited fiction and creative nonfiction must be submitted according to contest rules which can be found on the website." Winner will receive a copy of the Irreantum issue in which their work appears. Send complete ms. with cover letter. Include a brief bio and list of publications. Responds in 2 weeks to queries, 2 months to mss. Accepts simultaneous and reprints, multiple submissions. Sample copy $15. Writer's guidelines on website. Reviews fiction.

Payment/Terms Pays $0-100. Pays on publication for one-time rights.

Tips "*Irreantum* is not interested in didactic or polemical fiction that primarily attempts to prove or disprove Mormon doctrine, history or corporate policy. We encourage beginning writers to focus on human elements first, with Mormon elements introduced only as natural and organic to the story. Readers can tell if you are honestly trying to explore the human experience or if you are writing with a propagandistic agenda either for or against Mormonism. For conservative, orthodox Mormon writers, beware of sentimentalism, simplistic resolutions, and foregone conclusions."d

◪ ◎ ITALIAN AMERICANA

80 Washington Street, Providence RI 02903-1803. E-mail: bonomoal@etal.uri.edu. Website: www.italianamericana.com. **Contact:** C.B. Albright, editor. Magazine: 6 × 9; 240 pages; varnished cover; perfect bound; photos. "Italian Americana contains historical articles, fiction, poetry and memoirs, all concerning the Italian experience in the Americas." Semiannual. Circ. 1,200.

Needs Literary, Italian American. No nostalgia. Wants to see more fiction featuring "individualized characters." Receives 10 unsolicited mss/month. Accepts 3 mss/issue; 6-7 mss/year. Publishes ms up to 1 year after acceptance. Agented fiction 5%. **Publishes 2-4 new writers/year.** Publishing 2 issues a year of historical articles, fiction, memoir, poetry and reviews. Seeking historical articles. Award winning authors in all categories, such as Mary Caponegro, Sal La Puma, Dana Gioia (past poetry editor).

How to Contact Send complete ms (in duplicate) with a cover letter. Include 3-5 line bio, list of publications. Responds in 1 month to queries; 2 months to mss. No simultaneous submissions. Subscription: $20/year; $35/2 years. Sample copy for $7. Writer's guidelines for #10 SASE. Reviews fiction.

Payment/Terms 1 contributor's copy; additional copies $7. Acquires first North American serial rights.

Tips "Check out our new website supplement to the journal at www.italianamericana.com. Read *Wild Dreams: The Best of Italian Americana* (Fordham University Press), the best stories, poems and memoirs in the journal's 35- year history."

KELSEY REVIEW

Mercer County College, P.O. Box B, Trenton NJ 08690. (609) 586-4800. Fax: (609) 586-2318. E-mail: kelsey.review@mccc.edu. Website: www.mccc.edu. **Contact**: Ed Carmien, Holly-Katherine Mathews, editors. Magazine: 7 × 14; 98 pages; glossy paper; soft cover. "Must live or work in Mercer County, NJ." Annual. Estab. 1988. Circ. 2,000.

Needs Regional (Mercer County, NJ only), open. Receives 10 unsolicited mss/month. Accepts 24 mss/issue. Reads mss only in May. **Publishes 10 new writers/year.** Recently published work by Thom Beachamps, Janet Kirk, Bruce Petronio. Publishes short shorts. Also publishes literary essays, poetry.

How to Contact SASE for return of ms. Responds no later than September 1 to mss. Accepts multiple submissions. Sample copy free.

Payment/Terms 3 contributor's copies. Rights revert to author on publication.

Tips Look for "quality, intellect, grace and guts. Avoid sentimentality, overwriting and self-indulgence. Work on clarity, depth and originality."

KRAX MAGAZINE

63 Dixon Lane, Leeds Yorkshire LS12 4RR United Kingdom. **Contact:**A. Robson, co-editor. "Krax publishes lighthearted, humorous and whimsical writing. It is for anyone seeking light relief at a gentle pace. Our audience has grown middle-aged along with us, especially now that we're annual and not able to provide the instant fix demanded by teens and twenties."

Needs "No war stories, horror, space bandits, boy-girl soap opera. We publish mostly poetry of a lighthearted nature but use comic or spoof fiction, witty and humorous essays. Would like to see more whimsical items, trivia ramblings or anything daft." Accepts 1 mss/issue. **Publishes 1 new writer/year.** Recently published work by Aaron Dabrowski, Rovert L. Voss.

How to Contact No specific guidelines but cover letter appreciated. Sample copy for $2.

Tips "Look at what you enjoy in all forms of fiction—from strip cartoons to novels, movies to music lyrics—then try to put some of this into your own writing. Go for the idea first, then find the scenery to set it in. There are plenty of unreal worlds out there."

$ LADY CHURCHILL'S ROSEBUD WRISTLET

150 Pleasant St., #306, Easthampton MA 01027. E-mail: smallbeerpress@gmail.com. Website: www.smallbeerpress.com/lcrw. **Contact:** Gavin Grant, editor. Zine: half legal size; 60 pages; 60 lb. paper; glossy cover; illustrations; photos. Semiannual. Circ. 1,000.

Needs Comics/graphic novels, experimental, fantasy, feminist, literary, science fiction, translations, short story collections. Receives 100 unsolicited mss/month. Accepts 4-6 mss/issue; 8-12 mss/year. Publishes ms 6-12 months after acceptance. **Publishes 2-4 new writers/year.** Recently published work by Ted Chiang, Gwenda Bond, Alissa Nutting, Charlie Anders. Length: 200-7,000 words; average length: 3,500 words. Also publishes literary essays, poetry. Sometimes comments on rejected mss.

How to Contact Send complete ms with a cover letter. Include estimated word count. Send SASE (or IRC) for return of ms, or send a disposable copy of ms and #10 SASE for reply only. Responds in 4 weeks to queries; 3-6 months to mss. Sample copy for $5. Writer's guidelines online. Reviews fiction.

Payment/Terms Pays 1¢/word, $20 minimum and 2 contributor's copies; additional copies contributor's discount 40%. Pays on publication for first, one-time and electronic rights.

Tips "I like fiction that tends toward the speculative."

LEADING EDGE

Magazine of Science Fiction and Fantasy, 4087 JKB, Provo UT 84602. (801)378-4455. E-mail: fiction@leadingedgemagazine.com. Website: www.leadingedgemagazine.com. **Contact:** Fiction Director. Magazine specializing in science fiction and fantasy. Leading Edge is dedicated to helping new writers make their way into publishing. "We send back critiques with every story. We don't print anything with explicit language, graphic violence or sex." Semiannual.

Needs Fantasy and science fiction short stories, poetry, and artwork. Receives 50 unsolicited mss/month. Accepts 6 mss/issue; 12 mss/year. Publishes ms 1-6 months after acceptance. **Publishes 9-10 new writers/year.** Have published work by Orson Scott Card, Brandon Sanderson, and Dave Wolverton. Max length: 15,000; average length: 10,000 words.

How to Contact Send complete ms with cover letter and SASE. Include estimated word count. Send #10 SASE for reply only if disposable ms. Responds in 4-6 months to mss. Sample copy for $5.95. Writer's guidelines on website or send a SASE.

Payment/Terms 1¢/word for fiction; $10 for first 4 pages of poetry, $1.50 for each subsequent page; 2 contributor's copies; additional copies $4.95. Pays for publication for first North American serial rights. Sends galleys to author.

Tips "Buy a sample issue to know what is currently selling in our magazine. Also, make sure to follow the writer's guidelines when submitting."

LEFT CURVE

P.O. Box 472, Oakland CA 94604-0472. (510)763-7193. E-mail: editor@leftcurve.org. Website: www.leftcurve.org. **Contact:** Csaba Polony, editor. Magazine: 8½ × 11; 144 pages; 60 lb. paper; 100 pt. C1S gloss layflat lamination cover; illustrations; photos. "Left Curve is an artist-produced journal addressing the problem(s) of cultural forms emerging from the crises of modernity that strive to be independent from the control of dominant institutions, based on the recognition of the destructiveness of commodity (capitalist) systems to all life." Published irregularly. Circ. 2,000.

Needs Ethnic/multicultural, experimental, historical, literary, regional, science fiction, translations, contemporary, prose poem, political. "No topical satire, religion-based pieces, melodrama. We publish critical, open, social/political-conscious writing." Receives 50 unsolicited mss/month. Accepts 3-4 mss/issue. Publishes ms 6-12 months after acceptance. Recently published work by Mike Standaert, Ilan Pappe, Terrence Cannon, John Gist. Length: 500-5,000 words; average length: 1,200 words. Publishes short shorts. Sometimes comments on rejected mss.

How to Contact Send complete ms. Accepts submissions by e-mail (editor@leftcurve.org). Send complete ms with cover letter. Include "statement of writer's intent, brief bio and reason for submitting to *Left Curve*." Accepts electronic submissions and hard copy, though for accepted work we request e-mail copy, either in body of text or as attachments." Responds in 6 months to mss. Sample copy for $12. Writer's guidelines available with SASE.

Payment/Terms Contributor's copies. Rights revert to author.

Tips "We look for continuity, adequate descriptive passages, endings that are not simply abandoned (in both meanings). Dig deep; no superficial personalisms, no corny satire. Be honest, realistic and gouge out the truth you wish to say. Understand yourself and the world. Have writing be a means to achieve or realize what is real."

$ THE LONDON MAGAZINE

Review of Literature and the Arts, 11 Queen's Gate, London En SW7 5ELU UK. +44 (0)20 7584 5977. E-mail: admin@thelondonmagazine.net. Website: www.thelondonmagazine.net. **Contact:** Editor.

$ MAMAZINA

Mom Writer's Productions, LLC., Mamazina Magazine, 6224 Deer Run Rd., Libery Township OH, 45044 (877) 382-6771. E-mail: managingeditor@mamazina.com. Website: www.momwriterslitmag.com. **Contact:** Kris Underwood, Managing Editor. Mom Writer's Productions, LLC., P.O. Box 447, St. Johnsbury, VT 05719. (877)382-6771. Online and print literary magazine. Print: 8x10, 84 pages. Contains illustrations. Includes photographs. "*Mamazina*—formerly Mom Writer's Literary Magazine—is a publication written by moms for moms across the globe who come together to share their stories. We publish creative nonfiction essays, fiction, columns, book reviews, profiles about mom writers and visual art. *Mamazina* seeks writing that is vivid, complex and practical. We are not looking for 'sugar-coated' material. We believe the art of Motherhood is deserving of literary attention. We are a literary magazine for mothers with something to say. We're proud to have published essays that are emotionally moving, smart, raw and, sometimes, humorous. *Mamazina* honors the fulfilling and tedious work that women do by making their stories visible through print." Semiannual. Estab. 2005-Online, 2007- Print. Circ. 6,000. Member Mom Writers Publishing Cooperative.

- *Mom Writer's Literary Magazine* was picked by *Writer's Digest* magazine as one of the Best Web Sites for Writers in 2006, 2007, and 2008.

Needs Adventure, ethnic/multicultural, family saga, feminist, literary, mainstream, romance (contemporary, suspense). Special interests: motherhood. Does not want children/juvenile, religious, horror, or western. Receives 20-30 mss/month. Accepts 2 mss/issue; 4 mss/year. Ms published 1-4 months after acceptance. **Publishes 2 new writers/year.** Length: 800-1,500 words. Average length: 1,400 words. Publishes short shorts. Average length of short shorts: 1,200 words. Also publishes literary essays, book reviews, poetry. Send review copies to Kathy Schlaeger, Reviews Editor, Mom Writer's Literary Magazine, 6224 Deer Run Road Liberty Township, OH 45044. Rarely comments on/critiques rejected mss.

How to Contact MAMAZINA does not accept any submissions by snail mail. Please send all submissions via e-mail. Please do not send attachments. Send complete ms with cover letter. Include estimated word count, brief bio. For all essay and poetry submissions—we read submissions in January and July. All submissions carry a $10 reading fee, payable by using the PayPal on our website. Please read our letter explaining the new submission procedure. Responds to mss in 1-3 months. Considers simultaneous submissions. Guidelines available on website.

Payment/Terms Writers receive $100 max., 1 contributor's copy. Additional copies $10. Pays on publication. Acquires one-time rights. Publication is copyrighted.

Tips "May be any genre. Story must flow smoothly and really get our attention (all editors). Must be within the word limits and submitted correctly. Also, please have a title for your story."

THE NOCTURNAL LYRIC

Journal of the Bizarre, P.O. Box 542, Astoria OR 97103. E-mail: nocturnallyric@melodymail.com. Website: www.angelfire.com/ca/nocturnallyric. **Contact:** Susan Moon, editor. "Annual magazine. Magazine: 8½ × 11; 40 pages; illustrations. Fiction and poetry submitted should have a bizarre horror theme. Our audience encompasses people who stand proudly outside of the mainstream society."

Needs Horror (dark fantasy, futuristic, psychological, supernatural, satirical). "No sexually graphic material—it's too overdone in the horror genre lately." Receives 25-30 unsolicited mss/month. Accepts 10-11 mss/issue; 10-11 mss/year. Publishes ms 1 year after acceptance. Publishes 20 new writers/year. Recently published work by Murphy Edwards, Tim Scott, Richard Grebe, Melissa S. Mutlu, and Jessica Brown. Length: 2,000 words maximum; average length: 1,500 words. Publishes short shorts. Also publishes literary essays, poetry. Rarely comments on rejected mss.

How to Contact Send complete ms with cover letter. Include estimated word count. Responds in 3 month to queries; 8 months to mss. Accepts simultaneous, multiple submissions and reprints. Sample copy for $2 (back issue); $3 (current issue). Writer's guidelines online. Pays with discounts on subscriptions and discounts on copies of issue. Pays on acceptance. Not copyrighted.

$ NOVA SCIENCE FICTION MAGAZINE

Nova Publishing Company, 17983 Paseo Del Sol, Chino Hills CA 91709-3947. (909)393-0806. **Contact:** Wesley Kawato, editor. Zine specializing in evangelical Christian science fiction: 8½ × 5½; 64 pages; cardstock cover. "We publish religious science fiction short stories, no fantasy or horror. One story slot per issue will be reserved for a story written from an evangelical Christian viewpoint." Biannual. Estab. 1999. Circ. 25.

Needs Science fiction (hard science/technological, soft/sociological, religious). "No stories where the villain is a religious fanatic and stories that assume the truth of evolution." Accepts 6 mss/issue; 12 mss/year. Publishes ms 3 months after acceptance. **Publishes 7 new writers/year.** Recently published work by Jonathan Cooper, Lawrence Dagstine, Don Kerr, Gary Carter, Wesley Lambert, Susan Taylor, Erik Leinhart, David Baumann, Francis Alexander, Mark Galbert, Howard Bowman. Length: 250-7,000 words; average length: 4,000 words. Publishes short shorts. Sometimes comments on rejected mss.

How to Contact Query first. Include estimated word count and list of publications. Responds in 3 months to queries and mss. Send SASE (or IRC) for return of ms. Accepts reprints, multiple submissions. Sample copy for $6. Guidelines free for SASE.

Payment/Terms Pays $1.25-35. Pays on publication for first North American serial rights. Not copyrighted.

Tips "Make sure your plot is believable and describe your characters well enough so I can visualize them. If I like it, I buy it. I like happy endings and heroes with a strong sense of faith."

NTH DEGREE

The Fiction and Fandom 'Zine, 3502 Fernmoss Ct., Charlotte NC 28269. E-mail: submissions@nthzine.com. Website: www.nthzine.com. **Contact:** Michael Pederson. Magazine: 8½ × 11; 48 pages; 50 lb. white off-set paper; 80 lb. glossy cover stock; illustrations; photos. "We print the best SF/Fantasy from the genre's newest writers and run artwork by the hottest new artists. Our goal is to help make it easier for new artists and writers to break into the field." Quarterly. Circ. 3,500.

Needs Fantasy (space fantasy, sword and sorcery), historical (alternate history), horror (dark fantasy, futuristic, psychological, supernatural), humor/satire, science fiction (hard science/technological), young adult/teen (fantasy/science fiction), comic strips. Receives 3 unsolicited mss/month. Accepts 4 mss/issue; 6 mss/year. Publishes ms 6 months after acceptance. **Publishes 6 new writers/year.** Recently published work by Robert E. Waters, Scott D. Coon, and Helen Lloyd Montgomery. Length: 2,000-7,000 words; average length: 3,500 words. Publishes short shorts. Also publishes poetry. Always comments on rejected mss.

How to Contact Send complete ms. Accepts submissions by e-mail, disk. Send SASE (or IRC) for return of ms, or send disposable copy of the ms and #10 SASE for reply only. Responds in 2 weeks to queries; 2 months to mss. Accepts simultaneous, multiple submissions. Sample copy for $3. Writer's guidelines online, or by e-mail.

Payment/Terms Pays 5 contributor's copies and free subscription to the magazine. Pays on publication for one-time rights.

Tips "Don't submit anything that you may be ashamed of ten years later."

NUTHOUSE

Twin Rivers Press, P.O. Box 119, Ellenton FL 34222. **Contact:** Dr. Ludwig "Needles" Von Quirk, chief of staff. Zine: digest-sized; 12-16 pages; bond paper; illustrations; photos. "Humor of all genres for an adult readership that is not easily offended." Published every 2-3 months. Estab. 1993. Circ. 100.

Needs Humor/satire (erotica, experimental, fantasy, feminist, historical [[general]], horror, literary, main-stream/contemporary, mystery/suspense, psychic/supernatural/occult, romance, science fiction and westerns). Receives 30-50 unsolicited mss/month. Accepts 5-10 mss/issue; 50-60 mss/year. Publishes ms 6-12 months after acceptance. **Publishes 10-15 new writers/year.** Recently published work by Michael Fowler, Dale Andrew White, and Jim Sullivan. Length: 100-1,000 words; average length: 500 words. Publishes short shorts. Also publishes literary essays, literary criticism, poetry. Often comments on rejected mss.

How to Contact Send complete ms with a cover letter. Include estimated word count, bio (paragraph) and list of publications. SASE for return of ms or send disposable copy of ms. Sample copy for $1. 50 (payable to Twin Rivers Press). Writer's guidelines for #10 SASE.

Payment/Terms Pays 1 contributor's copy. Acquires one-time rights. Not copyrighted.

Tips Looks for "laugh-out-loud prose. Strive for original ideas; read the great humorists—Saki, Woody Allen, Robert Benchley, Garrison Keillor, John Irving—and learn from them. We are turned off by sophomoric attempts at humor built on a single, tired, overworked gag or pun; give us a story with a beginning, middle and end."

THE OAK

1530 Seventh Street, Rock Island IL 61201. (309)788-3980. **Contact:** Betty Mowery, editor. Magazine: 8½ × 11; 8-10 pages. "To provide a showcase for new authors while showing the work of established authors as well; to publish wholesome work, something with a message." Bimonthly. Estab. 1991. Circ. 300.

Needs Mainstream, contemporary, poems. Fiction up to 500 words. No erotica or love poetry. "No killing of humans or animals." "Gray Squirrel" appears as a section in Oak, accepts poetry and fiction from seniors age 50 and up. Length: 500 words. Receives 25 unsolicited mss/month. Accepts 12 mss/issue. Publishes ms 3 months after acceptance. **Publishes 25 new writers/year.**

How to Contact Send complete ms. Responds in 1 week to mss. Accepts simultaneous, multiple submissions. Sample copy for $4; subscription $12. Writer's guidelines for #10 SASE.

Payment/Terms None, but not necessary to buy a copy in order to be published. Acquires first rights.

Tips "I do not want erotica, extreme violence or killing of humans or animals for the sake of killing. Just be yourself when you write. Also, write tight. Please include SASE or manuscripts will be destroyed. Be sure name and address are on the manuscript. Study the markets for length of manuscript and what type of material is wanted. *The Shepherd* needs inspirational fiction up to 500 words, poetry, and Biblical character profiles. Same address as *The Oak*. Sample $3; subscription $12."

$ ON SPEC

P.O. Box 4727, Station South, Edmonton AB T6E 5G6 Canada. (780)413-0215. Fax: (780)413-1538. E-mail: onspec@onspec.ca. Website: www.onspec.ca/. **Contact:** Diane L. Walton, editor. Magazine: 5¼ × 8; 112-120 pages; illustrations. "We publish speculative fiction by new and established writers, with a strong preference for Canadian authored works. We are moving towards offering a digital version of our issues in addition to our print circulation." Quarterly. Estab. 1989. Circ. 2,000.

Needs Fantasy, horror, science fiction, magic realism. No media tie-in or shaggy-alien stories. No condensed or excerpted novels, Religious/inspirational stories, fairy tales. "We would like to see more horror, fantasy, science fiction—well-developed stories with complex characters and strong plots." Receives 100 unsolicited mss/month. Accepts 10 mss/issue; 40 mss/year. "We read manuscripts during the month after each deadline: February 28/May 31/August 31/November 30." Publishes ms 6-18 months after acceptance. **Publishes 10-15 new writers/year.** Recently published work by Mark Shainblum, Hugh Spencer, Kate Riedel, and Leah Bobet. Length: 1,000-6,000 words; average length: 4,000 words. Also publishes poetry. Often comments on rejected mss.

How to Contact Send complete ms. Accepts submissions by disk. SASE with Canadian postage for return of ms or send a disposable copy of ms plus #10 SASE for response. Include Canadian postage or IRCs. No e-mail or fax submissions. Responds in 2 weeks to queries; 4 months after deadline to mss. Accepts simultaneous submissions. Sample copy for $8. Writer's guidelines for #10 SASE or on website.

Payment/Terms Pays $50-200 for fiction. Short stories (under 1,000 words): $50 plus 1 contributor's copy. Pays on acceptance for first North American serial rights.

Tips "We're looking for original ideas with a strong SF element, excellent dialogue, and characters who are so believable, our readers will really care about them."

OPIUM MAGAZINE

Literary Humor for the Deliriously Captivated, 166 Albion St., San Francisco, CA 94110. (347)229-2443. E-mail: todd@opiummagazine.com. Website: www.opiumden.org. **Contact:** Todd Zuniga, editor-in-chief. Biannual magazine. Contains black and white cartoons, illustrations, and photographs. "Opium Magazine displays an eclectic mix of stories, poetry, reviews, cartoons, interviews and much more. It features 'estimated reading times' that precede each piece. While the focus is often humorous literature, we love to publish heartbreaking, serious work. Our rule is that all work must be well written and engaging from the very first sentence. While we publish traditional pieces, we're primarily engaged by writers who take risks." Updated daily. Estab. 2001. Circ. 25,000 hits/month. Member CLMP.

Needs Comics/graphic novels, experimental, humor/satire, literary, mainstream. "Vignettes and first-person 'look at what a whacky time I had going to Spain' stories aren't going to get past first base with us." Receives 200 mss/month. Accepts 60 mss/year. Manuscript published 4 months after acceptance. Agented fiction 10%. **Publishes 10-12 new writers/year**. Published Etgar Keret, Art Spiegelman, Jack Handey, Terese Svoboda. Length: 50-1,200 words. Average length: 700 words. Publishes short shorts. Average length of short shorts: 400 words. Also publishes literary essays, literary criticism, poetry. Sometimes comments on/critiques rejected mss.

How to Contact Send complete ms with cover letter by e-mail only. Ms received via snail mail will not be read. Include estimated word count, brief bio, list of publications, and your favorite book. Responds to queries in 2 weeks. Responds to mss in 15 weeks. Considers simultaneous submissions. Guidelines available via e-mail or on website.

Payment/Terms Acquires first North American serial rights. Publication is copyrighted.

Tips "If you don't strike out in that first paragraph to expose something definitive or new, then you better by the second. We get scores of stories, and like the readers we want to attract, we demand to be engaged immediately. Tell us it's your first time, we'll be gentle, and our editors usually give thoughts and encouragement if a piece has promise, even if we reject it."

ORACLE STORY & LETTERS

7510 Lake Glen Drive, Glen Dale MD 20769. (301)352-2533. Fax: (301)352-2529. E-mail: hekwonna@aol.com. **Contact:** Obi H. Ekwonna, publisher. Magazine: 5½ × 8½; 60 lb. white bound paper. Quarterly. Estab. 1989. Circ. 1,000.

Needs Adventure, children's/juvenile (adventure, fantasy, historical, mystery, series), comics/graphic novels, ethnic/multicultural, family saga, fantasy (sword and sorcery), historical, literary, mainstream, military/war, romance (contemporary, historical, suspense), thriller/espionage, western (frontier saga), young adult/teen (adventure, historical). Does not want gay/lesbian or erotica works. Receives 10 unsolicited mss/month. Accepts 7 mss/issue. Publishes ms 4 months after acceptance. **Publishes 5 new writers/year.** Recently published work by Joseph Manco, I.B.S. Sesay. Publishes short shorts. Also publishes literary essays, literary criticism, poetry. Rarely comments on rejected mss.

How to Contact Send complete ms. Accepts submissions by disk. Send SASE (or IRC) for return of the ms, or send a disposable copy of the ms and #10 SASE for reply only. Responds in 1 month to mss. Accepts multiple submissions. Sample copy for $10. Writer's guidelines for #10 SASE, or by e-mail.

Payment/Terms Pays 1 contributor's copy. Pays on publication for first North American serial rights.

Tips "Read anything you can lay your hands on."

OUTER DARKNESS

Outer Darkness Press, 1312 N. Delaware Place, Tulsa OK 74110. Website: http://members.cox.net/outerdarkness. **Contact**: Dennis Kirk, editor. Zine: 8½ × 5½; 50-60 pages; 20 lb. paper; perfect-bound, 90 lb. glossy cover; illustrations. Specializes in imaginative literature. "Variety is something I strive for in Outer Darkness. In each issue we present readers with great tales of science fiction and horror along with poetry, cartoons and interviews/essays. I seek to provide readers with a magazine which, overall, is fun to read. My readers range in age from 16 to 70." Quarterly. Estab. 1994. Circ. 500.

- Fiction published in *Outer Darkness* has received honorable mention in *The Year's Best Fantasy and Horror.*

Needs Fantasy (science), horror, mystery/suspense (with horror slant), psychic/supernatural/occult, romance (gothic), science fiction (hard science, soft/sociological). No straight mystery, pure fantasy—works which do not incorporate elements of science fiction and/or horror. Also, no slasher horror with violence, gore, sex instead of plot. Wants more "character driven tales—especially in the genre of science fiction and well-developed psychological horror. I do not publish works with children in sexual situations, and graphic language should be kept to a minimum." Receives 75-100 unsolicited mss/month. Accepts 5-7 mss/issue; 2 0-25 mss/year. **Publishes 2-5 new writers/year.** Recently published work by John Sunseri, Christopher Fulbright, Melinda Arnett, and James M. Steimle. Length: 1,500-5,000 words; average length: 3,000 words. Also publishes poetry. Comments on rejected mss when possible.

How to Contact Send complete ms with a cover letter. Include estimated word count, 50- to 75-word bio, list of publications and "any awards, honors you have received." Send SASE for reply, return of ms, or send a disposable copy of ms. Responds in 2 weeks to queries; 4 months to mss. Accepts simultaneous, multiple submissions. Sample copy for $4.95. Writer's guidelines for #10 SASE.

Payment/Terms Pays 2 contributor's copies for fiction; 1 for poetry and 2 for art. Pays on publication for one-time rights.

Tips "I look for strong characters and well -developed plot. And I definitely look for suspense. I want stories which move—and carry the reader along with them. Be patient and persistent. Often it's simply a matter of linking the right story with the right editor. I've received many stories which were good, but not what I wanted at the time. However, these stories worked well in another horror-sci-fi zine."

◙ PARADOXISM

200 College Rd., Gallup NM 87301. Fax: (503)863-7532. E-mail: smarand@unm.edu. Website: www.gallup.unm.edu/~smarandache/a/paradoxism.htm. **Contact:** Dr. Florentin Smarandache. Magazine: 8½ × 11; 100 pages; illustrations. "Paradoxism is an avant-garde movement based on excessive use of antinomies, antitheses, contraditions, paradoxes in the literary creations set up by the editor in the 1980s as an anti-totalitarian protest." Annual. Circ. 500.

Needs Experimental, literary. "Contradictory, uncommon, experimental, avant garde." Plans specific themes in the next year. Publishes annual special fiction issue or anthology. Receives 5 unsolicited mss/month. Accepts 10 mss/issue. Recently published work by Mircea Monu, Doru Motoc and Patrick Pinard. Publishes short shorts. Also publishes literary essays, literary criticism, poetry. Sometimes comments on rejected mss.

How to Contact Send a disposable copy of ms. Responds in 2 months to mss. Accepts simultaneous submissions. Sample copy for $19.95 and 8½ × 11 SASE. Writer's guidelines online.

Payment/Terms Pays subscription. Pays on publication. Not copyrighted.

Tips "We look for work that refers to the paradoxism or is written in the paradoxist style. The Basic Thesis of the paradoxism: everything has a meaning and a non-meaning in a harmony with each other. The Essence of the paradoxism: a) the sense has a non-sense, and reciprocally B) the non-sense has a sense. The Motto of the paradoxism: 'All is possible, the impossible too!' The Symbol of the paradoxism: a spiral—optic illusion, or vicious circle."

☐ ◙ PRAYERWORKS

Encouraging God's people to do real work of ministry—intercessory prayer, P.O. Box 301363, Portland OR 97294-9363. (503)761-2072. E-mail: vannm1@aol.com. Website: www.prayerworksnw.org. **Contact:** V. Ann Mandeville, editor. Newsletter: 5½ × 8; 4 pages; bond paper. "Our intended audience is 70% retired Christians and 30% families. We publish 350-500 word devotional material—fiction, nonfiction, biographical, poetry, clean quips and quotes. Our philosophy is evangelical Christian serving the body of Chirst in the area of prayer."

Needs Religious/inspirational. "No nonevangelical Christian. Subject matter may include anything which will build relationship with the Lord—prayer, ways to pray, stories of answered prayer, teaching on a Scripture portion, articles that will build faith, or poems will all work." We even use a series occasionally. Publishes ms 2-6 months after acceptance. **Publishes 30 new writers/year.** Recently published work by Allen Audrey and Petey Prater. Length: 350-500 words; average length: 350-500 words. Publishes short shorts. Also publishes poetry. Often comments on rejected mss.
How to Contact Send complete ms with cover letter. Include estimated word count and a very short bio. Responds in 1 month to mss. Accepts simultaneous, multiple submissions and reprints. Writer's guidelines for #10 SASE.
Payment/Terms Pays free subscription to the magazine and contributor's copies. Pays on publication. Not copyrighted.
Tips Stories "must have a great take-away—no preaching; teach through action. Be thrifty with words—make them count."

☐ $ PURPOSE

616 Walnut Ave., Scottdale PA 15683-1999. (724) 887-8500. Fax: (724) 887-3111. E-mail: horsch@mph.org. Website: www.mph.net. **Contact:** James E. Horsch, editor. Magazine: 5-3/8 × 8-3/8; 8 pages; illustrations; photos. Monthly. Estab. 1968. Circ. 8,500.
Needs Historical (related to discipleship theme), humor/satire, religious/inspirational. No militaristic, narrow patriotism, or racist themes. Receives 150 unsolicited mss/month. Accepts 12 mss/issue; 140 mss/year. Publishes ms 1 year after acceptance. **Publishes 15-25 new writers/year.** Length: 600 words; average length: 400 words. Occasionally comments on rejected mss.
How to Contact Send complete ms. Send all submissions by Word attachment via e-mail. Responds in 3 months to queries. Accepts simultaneous submissions, reprints, multiple submissions. Sample copy and writer's guidelines for $2, 6 × 9 SAE and 2 first-class stamps. Writer's guidelines online.
Payment/Terms Pays up to 7¢/word for stories, and 2 contributor's copies. Pays on acceptance for one-time rights.
Tips "Many stories are situational, how to respond to dilemmas. Looking for first-person storylines. Write crisp, action moving, personal style, focused upon an individual, a group of people, or an organization. The story form is an excellent literary device to help readers explore discipleship issues. The first two paragraphs are crucial in establishing the mood/issue to be resolved in the story. Work hard on the development of these."

☐ ☐ ☐ $ QUEEN'S QUARTERLY

Queen's Quarterly, 144 Barrie St. Kingston ON K7L 3N6 Canada. (613)533-2667. Fax: (613)533-6822. E-mail: queens.quarterly@queensu.ca. Website: www.queensu.ca/quarterly. **Contact**: Boris Castel, editor. Magazine: 6 × 9; 800 pages/year; illustrations. "A general interest intellectual review, featuring articles on science, politics, humanities, arts and letters. Book reviews, poetry and fiction." Quarterly. Estab. 1893. Circ. 3,000.
Needs Historical, literary, mainstream, novel excerpts, short stories, women's. "Special emphasis on work by Canadian writers." Accepts 2 mss/issue; 8 mss/year. Publishes ms 6-12 months after acceptance. **Publishes 5 new writers/year.** Recently published work by Gail Anderson-Dargatz, Tim Bowling, Emma Donohue, Viktor Carr, Mark Jarman, Rick Bowers and Dennis Bock. Also publishes literary essays, literary criticism, poetry.
How to Contact "Send complete ms with SASE and/or IRC. No reply with insufficient postage." Responds in 2-3 months to queries. Sample copy online. Writer's guidelines online. Reviews fiction.
Payment/Terms Pays $100-300 for fiction, 2 contributor's copies and 1-year subscription; additional copies $5. Pays on publication for first North American serial rights. Sends galleys to author.

SILENT VOICES

Ex Machina Press, LLC, P.O. Box 11180, Glendale CA 91226. (818)244-7209. E-mail: exmachinapag@aol.com. Website: www.exmachinapress.com. **Contact:** Peter Balaskas, editor. Literary magazine/journal. "*Silent Voices* is an annual literary anthology whose purpose is to publish fiction of a variety of styles and genres. By taking stories of a diverse nature and placing them in a specific order, we produce a creative mosaic that tells a larger story." Annual. Estab. 2004. Circ. 1,000.

Needs Adventure, erotica, ethnic/multicultural, experimental, fantasy, historical, horror, humor/satire, mainstream, mystery, religious, romance, science fiction, western. Manuscript published 4-5 months after acceptance. Length: 10,000 words. "*We are not accepting new fiction submissions at this time.* Please check website for updates."

How to Contact Send complete ms with cover letter via e-mail only. Considers simultaneous submissions. Guidelines available on website. Please read website guidelines before submitting.

Payment/Terms Pays 2 contributor's copies. Acquires first North American serial rights.

SLATE & STYLE

Magazine of the National Federation of the Blind Writers Division, 2704 Beach Drive, Merrick NY 11566. E-mail: qobells@roadrunner.com; loristay@aol.com. Website: www.nfb-writers-division.org. **Contact:** Shelley Alongi, editor. Quarterly magazine: 28-32 print/40 Braille pages; available by e-mail, cassette and in large print. "Accepts articles of interest to writers, and resources for blind writers." Needs Adventure, fantasy, humor/satire, contemporary, blindness. No erotica. "Avoid theme of death." Does not read mss in June or July. Publishes 2 new writers/year. Recently published work by Bruce Adkins, Patricia Hubschman, Kristen Diaz, and Amy Krout-horn. Accepts short stories up to 2,000 words. Publishes short shorts. Also publishes literary criticism, poetry. Sometimes comments on rejected mss. Accepts submissions by e-mail. Responds in 3-6 weeks to queries; 3-6 weeks to mss. Sample copy for $3. Pays in contributor's copies. Acquires one-time rights. Sponsors awards/contests.

Tips "The best advice I can give is to send your work out; manuscripts left in a drawer have no chance at all."

SOLEADO

IPFW, CM 267 2101 E. Coliseum Blvd., Fort Wayne IN 46805. (260)481-6630. Fax: (260)481-6985. E-mail: summersj@ipfw.edu. Website: www.soleado.org. **Contact:** Jason Summers, editor. Magazine. "We are looking for good literary writing in Spanish, from Magical Realism á la García Márquez, to McOndo-esque writing similiar to that of Edmundo Paz-Soldá and Alberto Fuguet, to Spanish pulp realism like that of Arturo Pérez-Reverte. Testimonials, experimental works like those of Diamela Eltit, and women's voices like Marcela Serrano and Zoé Valdés are also encouraged. We are not against any particular genre writing, but such stories do have to maintain their hold on the literary, as well as the genre, which is often a difficult task. Please do not send anything in English. We publish a very limited selection of work in Spanglish—Do not send us anything without having read what we have already published." Annual. Estab. 2004.

Needs Children's/juvenile, ethnic/multicultural, experimental, fantasy, historical, humor/satire, mainstream, mystery, science fiction. Accepts 2-6 mss/year. Length: 8,000 words (max).

How to Contact Send complete ms with cover letter. Accepts submissions by e-mail. Responds to queries in 2 weeks. Responds to mss in 3 months. Guidelines available on website.

Payment/Terms Acquires first rights, first North American serial rights, one-time rights, electronic rights.

$ SPACE AND TIME MAGAZINE: THE MAGAZINE OF FANTASY, HORROR, AND SCIENCE

HDi Consulting, Inc., 1308 Centennial Ave, Ste 101, Piscataway NJ 08854. (732)512-8789. E-mail: hildy@spaceandtimemagazine.com. Website: spaceandtimemagazine.com. **Contact:** Gerard Houarner, fiction editor. Magazine. 812x11, 48 pages, matte paper, glossy cover. Contains illustrations.

"We love stories that blend elements—horror and science fiction, fantasy with SF elements, etc. We challenge writers to try something new and send us their unclassifiable works—what other publications reject because the work doesn't fit in their 'pigeonholes.'" Quarterly. Circ. 2,000.

Needs Fantasy (high, sword and sorcery, modern), horror (dark fantasy, futuristic, psychological, supernatural), romance (futuristic/time travel), science fiction (hard science/technological, soft/sociological). Does not want anything without some sort of speculative element. Receives 250 mss/reading period. Accepts 8 mss/issue; 32 mss/year. Only open during announced reading periods. Check website to see if submissions are open. Ms published 3-6 months after acceptance. **Publishes 2-4 new writers/year.** Published PD Cacek, AR Morlan, Jeffrey Ford, Charles De Lint and Jack Ketchum. Length: 1,000-10,000 words. Average length: 6,500 words. Publishes short shorts. Average length of short shorts: 1,000 words. Also publishes poetry, occasional book reviews. Send review copies to Publisher Hildy Silverman, hildy@spaceandtimemagazine.com. Sometimes comments on/critiques rejected mss.

How to Contact Send complete ms with cover letter. Accepts submissions by e-mail only. Include estimated word count, brief bio, list of publications. Responds to queries in 4-6 weeks. Responds to mss in 4-6 weeks. Send disposable query letter and #10 SASE for reply only if unable to email submission. Sample copy available for $5. Guidelines available via e-mail, on website.

Payment/Terms Writers receive 1¢ per word, 2 contributor's copies. Additional copies $ 5. Pays on publication. Acquires first North American serial rights, one-time rights. Publication is copyrighted.

Tips "Be well written—that means proper grammar, punctuation and spelling. Proofread! The greatness of your story will not supersede sloppy construct. Strong internal logic no matter how 'far out' the story. New twists on familiar plots or truly unique offerings will make your manuscript stand out. Blend genre elements in a new and interesting way, and you'll get our attention."

☐ $ THE STORYTELLER

A Writer's Magazine, 2441 Washington Road, Maynard AR 72444. (870)647-2137. E-mail: storyteller1@hightowercom.com. Website: http://freewebz.com/fossilcreek. **Contact:** Regina Williams, editor. Tabloid: 8½ × 11; 72 pages; typing paper; glossy cover; illustrations. "This magazine is open to all new writers regardless of age. I will accept short stories in most genres and poetry in any type. Please keep in mind, this is a family publication." Quarterly.

- Offers *People's Choice Awards* and nominates for a *Pushcart Prize.*

Needs Adventure, historical, humor/satire, literary, mainstream, mystery/suspense, religious/inspirational, romance, western, senior citizen/retirement, sports. "I will not accept pornography, erotica, science fiction, new age, foul language, graphic horror or graphic violence." No children's stories or young adult. Wants more well-plotted mysteries. Publishes ms 3-9 months after acceptance. **Publishes 30-50 new writers/year.** Recently published work by Jodi Thomas, Jory Sherman, David Marion Wilkinson, Dusty Richards and Tony Hillerman. Publishes short shorts. Also publishes literary essays, poetry. Sometimes comments on rejected mss. Word length 2,500.

How to Contact Send complete ms with cover letter. Include estimated word count and 5-line bio. Submission by mail only. Responds in 1-2 weeks to mss. No queries. Accepts simultaneous submissions and reprints. Sample copy for $6. Writer's guidelines for #10 SASE.

Payment/Terms Pays ¼ ¢ per word. Sponsors awards/contests.

Tips "Follow the guidelines. No matter how many times this has been said, writers still ignore this basic and most important rule." Looks for "professionalism, good plots and unique characters. Purchase a sample copy so you know the kind of material we look for." Would like more "well-plotted mysteries and suspense and a few traditional westerns. Avoid sending anything that children or young adults would not (or could not) read, such as really bad language. Polish, polish, polish before sending anything out."

STUDIO

A Journal of Christians Writing, 727 Peel Street, Albury 2640 Australia. E-mail: studio00@bigpond.net.au. **Contact:** Paul Grover, managing editor.

Needs "*Studio* publishes prose and poetry of literary merit, offers a venue for new and aspiring writers, and seeks to create a sense of community among Christians writing." Accepts 30-40 mss/year. **Publishes 40 new writers/year.** Recently published work by Andrew Lansdown and Benjamin Gilmour.

How to Contact Accepts submissions by e-mail. Send SASE. "Overseas contributors must use International postal coupons in place of stamped envelope." Responds in 1 month to mss. Sample copy for $10 (Aus).

Payment/Terms Pays in copies; additional copies are discounted. Subscription $60 (Australian) for 4 issues (1 year). International draft in Australian dollars and IRC required, or Visa and Mastercard facilities available. "Copyright of individual published pieces remains with the author, while each collection is copyright to *Studio*."

$ TALES OF THE TALISMAN

P.O. Box 2194, Mesilla Park NM 88047-2194. E-mail: hadrosaur@zianet.com. Website: www.talesofthetalisman.com. **Contact:** David L. Summers, editor. Zine specializing in science fiction: 8½ × 10½; 90 pages; 60 lb. white stock; 80 lb. cover. "*Tales of the Talisman* is a literary science fiction and fantasy magazine published 4 times a year. We publish short stories, poetry, and articles with themes related to science fiction and fantasy. Above all, we are looking for thought-provoking ideas and good writing. Speculative fiction set in the past, present, and future is welcome. Likewise, contemporary or historical fiction is welcome as long as it has a mythic or science fictional element. Our target audience includes adult fans of the science fiction and fantasy genres along with anyone else who enjoys thought-provoking and entertaining writing." Quarterly. Circ. 200.

- Received an honorable mention in *The Year's Best Science Fiction 2004* edited by Gardner Dozois.

Needs Fantasy (space fantasy, sword and sorcery), horror, science fiction (hard science/technological, soft/sociological). "We do not want to see stories with graphic violence. Do not send 'mainstream' fiction with no science fictional or fantastic elements. Do not send stories with copyrighted characters, unless you're the copyright holder." Receives 60 unsolicited mss/month. Accepts 7-10 mss/issue; 21-30 mss/year. Publishes ms 9 months after acceptance. **Publishes 8 new writers/year.** Recently published work by Tyree Campbell, Carol Hightshoe Ed Cox, Richard Harland, Janni Lee Simner and Jill Knowles. Length: 1,000-6,000 words; average length: 4,000 words. Also publishes poetry. Often comments on rejected mss.

How to Contact Send complete ms. Accepts submissions by e-mail (hadrosaur@zianet.com). Accepts submissions from January 1-February 15 and July 1-August 15. Include estimated word count, brief bio and list of publications. Send SASE (or IRC) for return of ms or send a disposable copy of ms and #10 SASE for reply only. Responds in 1 week to queries; 1 month to mss. Sometimes comments on rejected works. Accepts reprint submissions. No simultaneous submissions. Sample copy for $8. Writer's guidelines online.

Payment/Terms Pays $6-10. Pays on acceptance for one-time rights.

Tips "First and foremost, I look for engaging drama and believable characters. With those characters and situations, I want you to take me someplace I've never been before. The story I'll buy is the one set in a new world or where the unexpected happens, but yet I cannot help but believe in the situation because it feels real. Read absolutely everything you can get your hands on, especially stories and articles outside your genre of choice. This is a great source for original ideas."

TEA, A MAGAZINE

Olde English Tea Company, Inc., 3 Devotion Road P.O. Box 348, Scotland CT 06264. (860)456-1145. Fax: (860)456-1023. E-mail: teamag@teamag.com. Website: www.teamag.com. **Contact:** Jobina

Miller, assistant. Magazine. "An exciting quarterly magazine all about tea, both as a drink and for its cultural significance in art, music, literature, history and society." Quarterly. Circ. 9,500.

Needs Needs fiction that is tea related.

How to Contact Send complete ms with cover letter. Responds to mss in 6 months. Guidelines available for SASE.

Payment/Terms Pays on publication. Acquires all rights.

☑ $ TIMBER CREEK REVIEW

8969 UNCG Sta, Greensboro NC 27413. E-mail: timber_creek_review@hoopsmail.com. **Contact:** John M. Freiermuth, editor and Willa Schmidt, associate editor. Newsletter: 5½ × 8½; 76-80 pages; computer generated on copy paper; saddle-stapled with colored paper cover; some illustrations. "Fiction, humor/satire, poetry and travel for a general audience." Quarterly. Circ. 140-150.

Needs Adventure, ethnic/multicultural, feminist, historical, humor/satire, literary, mainstream, mystery/suspense, regional, western, literary nonfiction, and one-act plays. "No religious, children's, gay, modern romance, and no reprints please!" Receives 50-60 unsolicited mss/month. Accepts 30-40 stories and 80-90 poems a year. Publishes ms 2-6 months after acceptance. Length: 3,500-6,000 words. **Publishes 0-3 new writers/year.** Recently published work by Linda L. Dunlap, Robert McGee, W.S. Bell, Reilly Maginn, Dennis Vannatta, Margaret A. Young, Darcy Cummings, Deborah H. Doolittle, Maria Bennett, and Robert Cooperman.

How to Contact Cover letter expected. Accepts simultaneous submissions. Sample copy for $5.00, subscription $18. Overseas mail add $8 for postage.

Payment/Terms Pays $10-35, plus subscription for first story. Acquires first North American serial rights. Not copyrighted.

Tips "Stop watching TV and read that literary magazine where your last manuscript appeared. There are no automatons here, so don't treat us like machines. We may not recognize your name at the top of the manuscript. Include a statement that the mss have previously not been published on paper nor on the internet, nor have they been accepted by others. A few lines about yourself breaks the ice, the names of three or four magazines that have published you in the last year or so would show your reality, and a bio blurb of 27 + /- words including the names of 2 or 3 of the magazines you send the occasional subscription check (where you aspire to be?) could help. If you are not sending a check to some little magazine that is supported by subscriptions and the blood, sweat and tears of the editors, why would you send your manuscript to any of them and expect to receive a warm welcome? No requirement to subscribe or buy a sample, but they're available and are encouraged. There are no phony contests and never a reading fee. We read all year long, but may take 3-8 months to respond."

☐ ◎ TRAIL OF INDISCRETION

Fortress Publishing, Inc., 3704 Hartzdale Dr., Camp Hill PA 17011. (717) 350-8760. E-mail: fortresspublishinginc@yahoo.com. Website: www.fortresspublishinginc.com. **Contact:** Brian Koscienski, editor in chief. Zine specializing in genre fiction: digest (5½ × 8½), 48 pages, 24 lb. paper, glossy cover. "We publish genre fiction—sci-fi, fantasy, horror, etc. We'd rather have a solid story containing great characters than a weak story with a surprise 'trick' ending." Quarterly. Estab. 2006. Circ. 100.

Needs Adventure, fantasy (space fantasy, sword and sorcery), horror (dark fantasy, futuristic, psychological, supernatural), humor/satire, psychic/supernatural/occult, science fiction (hard science/technological, soft/sociological). Does not want "touchy-feely 'coming of age' stories or stories where the protagonist mopes about contemplating his/her own mortality." Accepts 5-7 mss/issue. Manuscript published 3-9 months after acceptance. **Publishes 2-10 new writers/year.** Published Cliff Ackman (debut), Roger Arnold, Susan Kerr (debut), Kristine Ong Muslim, Tala Bar, CJ Henderson, Danielle Ackley-McPhail. Length: 5,000 words (max). Average length: 3,000 words. Publishes short shorts. Sometimes comments on/critiques rejected mss.

How to Contact Send complete ms with cover letter. Accepts submissions by e-mail. Include estimated word count, brief bio, list of publications. Responds to queries in 1-2 weeks. Responds to mss in 1-10 weeks. Send either SASE (or IRC) for return of ms or disposable copy of ms and #10 SASE for reply only. Considers simultaneous submissions, previously published submissions. Sample copy available for $4 or on website. Guidelines available for SASE, via e-mail, on website.
Payment/Terms Writers receive 1 contributor copy. Additional copies $2.50. Pays on publication. Acquires one-time rights. Publication is copyrighted.
Tips "If your story is about a 13-year-old girl coping with the change to womanhood while poignantly reflecting the recent passing of her favorite aunt, then we *don't* want it. However, if your story is about the 13-year-old daughter of a vampire cowboy who stumbles upon a government conspiracy involving unicorns and aliens while investigating the grizzly murder of her favorite aunt, then we'll look at it. Please read the magazine to see what we want." "Love your story, but listen to advice."

TRANSCENDENT VISIONS

Toxic Evolution Press, 251 S. Olds Blvd., 84-E, Fairless Hills PA 19030-3426. (215)547-7159. **Contact:** David Kime, editor. Zine: letter size; 50-60 pages; xerox paper; illustrations. "Transcendent Visions is a literary zine by and for people who have been labeled mentally ill. Our purpose is to illustrate that we are creative and articulate people." Annual. Estab. 1992. Circ. 250.

- *Transcendent Visions* has received excellent reviews in many underground publications.

Needs Experimental, feminist, gay, humor/satire, lesbian. Especially interested in material dealing with mental illness. "I do not like stuff one would find in a mainstream publication. No porn." Would like to see more "quirky, non-mainstream fiction." Receives 5 unsolicited mss/month. Accepts 7 mss/year. Publishes ms 3-8 months after acceptance. Recently published work by White Elephant, Gabe Kaufman, Jamey Damert, Marc Pernaino, Teacup Mary, K.J. Kabza, and Arthur Longworth. Publishes short shorts. Also publishes poetry.
How to Contact Send complete ms with cover letter. Include half-page bio. Send disposable copy of ms. Responds in 3-4 months to mss. Accepts simultaneous submissions and reprints. Sample copy for $3.
Payment/Terms Pays 1 contributor's copy. Pays on publication for one-time rights.
Tips "We like unusual stories that are quirky. We like shorter pieces. Please do not go on and on about what zines you have been published in or awards you have won, etc. We just want to read your material, not know your life story. Please don't swamp me with tons of submissions. Send up to five stories. Please print or type your name and address."

$ WATERMEN

Fine & Finer Graphic, 2428 Gramercy Ave, Torrance CA 90501. (310) 850-6431. E-mail: tomlockie@sbcglobal.net. Website: http://freedivingfilms.com/watermen.htm. **Contact:** Tom Lockie, Editor. Magazine. 8.5 × 11, 32 pages. Contains illustrations. Includes photographs. "Watermen is a term referring to the lifequarding, bodysurfing, surfing, spearfishing, SCUBA diving lifestyle. The magazine is dedicated to the ocean lifestyle, arts, fashion and sports: diving, surfing, kayaking, paddleboating, underwater photography. We publish stories and articles dealing with adventure travel and above all ecological issues—protecting oceans and water health. Also publishes medical articles, travel articles, poems and short stories." Semiannual. Estab. 2006. Circ. 5,000.
Needs Adventure, humor/satire, literary, mainstream. Special interests: watersport stories. Receives 10-12 mss/month. Accepts 2-3 mss/issue; 4-6 mss/year. Ms published 1-5 months after acceptance. Agented fiction 10%. **Publishes 1-2 new writers/year.** Published Brian Donahue and Matteo Verna. Length: 500-1,500 words. Average length: 1,200 words. Publishes short shorts. Average length of short shorts: 400-500 words. Also publishes book reviews, poetry. Send review copies to Tom Lockie; has to be watersport based. Sometimes comments on/critiques rejected mss.

How to Contact Accepts submissions by e-mail only. Please query first. Include brief bio. Responds to queries in 3 weeks. Responds to mss in 1 months. Sample copy free with 812X11 SASE and $2.60 postage. Guidelines available via e-mail.
Payment/Terms Writers receive $20 per page. Additional copies $5 & $1.90 postage. Pays on publication. Acquires electronic rights, archive rights. Publication is not copyrighted.
Tips "Writer must be seriously involved in watersports to stand out. Pay some heavy dues in the water."

$ WEBER, THE CONTEMPORARY WEST

1214 University Circle, Ogden UT 84408-1214. (801)626-6473. E-mail: weberjournal@weber.edu. Website: weber journal.weber.edu. **Contact**: Michael Wutz, editor. Magazine: 7½ × 10; 120-140 pages; coated paper; 4-color cover; illustrations; photos. "We seek the following themes: preservation of and access to wilderness, environmental cooperation, insight derived from living in the West, cultural diversity, changing federal involvement in the region, women and the West, implications of population growth, a sense of place, etc. We love good writing that reveals human nature as well as natural environment." Triannual. Estab. 1984. Circ. 1,000.
Needs Adventure, comics/graphic novels, ethnic/multicultural, experimental, feminist, historical, humor/satire, literary, mainstream, military/war, mystery/suspense, New Age, psychic/supernatural/occult, regional (contemporary western US), translations, western (frontier sage, tradtional, contemporary), short story collections. No children's/juvenile, erotica, religious or young adult/teen. Receives 50 unsolicited mss/month. Accepts 3-6 mss/issue; 9-18 mss/year. Publishes ms up to 18 months after acceptance. **Publishes "few" new writers/year.** Recently published work by Gary Gildner, Stephen Dunn, Ron McFarland and Carolyn Forché. Publishes short shorts. Also publishes literary essays, poetry, art. Sometimes comments on rejected mss.
How to Contact Send complete ms with a cover letter. Include estimated word count, bio (if necessary), and list of publications (not necessary). Responds in 3 months to mss. Accepts multiple submissions. Sample copy for $10.
Payment/Terms Pays $150-$300. Pays on publication for first, electronic rights. Requests electronic archive permission. Sends galleys to author.
Tips "Is it true? Is it new? Is it interesting? Will the story appeal to educated readers who are concerned with the contemporary western United States? Declining public interest in reading generally is of concern. We publish both print media and electronic media because we believe the future will expect both options. The Dr. Neila C. Seshachari Fiction Award, a $500 prize, is awarded annually to the best fiction appearing in *Weber* each year."

$ WEIRD TALES

P.O. Box 38190, Tallahassee FL 32315. E-mail: weirdtales@gmail.com. Website: www.weirdtales.net. Magazine: 8½ × 11; 80-96 pages; white, newsprint paper; glossy 4-color cover; illustrations and comics. "We publish fantastic fiction, supernatural horror for an adult audience." Published 6 times a year. Circ. 5,000.
Needs Fantasy (sword and sorcery), horror, psychic/supernatural/occult, translations. No hard science fiction or non-fantasy. "Looking for darkly fantastical fiction, work that is unique and unusual. Stories that are recognized as weird tales for the 21st Century." Receives 1,200 unsolicited mss/month. Accepts 8 mss/issue; 48 mss/year. Publishes ms 6-18 months after acceptance. Agented fiction 10%. **Publishes 8 new writers/year.** Recently published work by Michael Moorcock, Tanith Lee, Thomas Ligotti, Darrell Schweitzer, Sarah Monette and Michael Boatman. Length: up to 10,000 words, but very few longer than 8,000; average length: 4,000 words. Publishes short shorts.
How to Contact Send complete ms via email. Responds in 6-8 weeks to mss. Accepts simultaneous submissions. No multiple submissions. Also accepts email submissions to weirdtales@gmail.com. For hardcopy submissions through the mail: provide an SASE with proper postage to ensure a response. If the postage is not enough to return the manuscript, it will be considered disposable.

Weird Tales is not responsible for loss or damage to any unsolicited work Sample copy for $6. Writer's guidelines for #10 SASE or by e-mail. Reviews books of fantasy fiction.

Payment/Terms Pays 3-4¢/word and 2 contributor's copies on acceptance. Acquires First North American publication rights, covering all print and electronic versions of the magazine, plus nonexclusive rights to reprint stories for an additional fee in translated and collected editions drawn from the magazine.

Tips "Traditional fantasy tropes are fine as long as it's a new and different take on the genre. Do not send any familiar story lines and do not send any pastiches of Lovecraft."

$ THE WILLOWS

E-mail: editor@thewillowsmagazine.com. Website: www.thewillowsmagazine.com. **Contact:** Ben Thomas, lead editor. Literary magazine/journal. 812X11, 70-90 pages, matte paper, glossy cover. Contains illustrations. "Founded to give voice to a unique but neglected corner of horror literature, The Willows strives to publish only the best in true classic-style weird fiction. We pride ourselves on our gentlemanly aesthetic, as well as our love of mad science, strange monstrosities, and ethereal wonder. Our readers share our passion for this bygone age, and the scientific romances of its greatest literary minds." Bimonthly. Estab. 2007. Circ. 50.

Needs Horror (dark fantasy, supernatural). Special interests: classic-style weird fiction. Does not want gory horror, slashers, splatterpunk, or "anything not fitting to be told over brandy in a gentleman's lounge in 1920s London." Receives 50-60 mss/month. Accepts 10 mss/issue; 60 mss/year. Manuscript published 2-4 months after acceptance. **Publishes 5 new writers/year.**Published Paul Melniczek, Charles Muir, Paul Marlowe, Nike Bourke, Nickolas Cook, G.W. Thomas, Lawrence Dagstine, Kristine Ong Muslim, Sarah Monette, and Steven Shrewsbury. Length: 1,000-5,500 words. Average length: 3,500 words. Publishes short shorts. Average length of short shorts: 500 words. Also publishes literary essays, literary criticism, poetry. Often comments on/critiques rejected mss.

How to Contact Send complete ms with cover letter. Accepts submissions by e-mail. Include estimated word count, brief bio, list of publications, expression of interest in the classic weird tale genre. Responds to queries in 2 weeks. Responds to mss in 1 month. Considers previously published submissions. Guidelines available on website.

Payment/Terms Writers receive $25. Additional copies $5 each. Pays on publication. Acquires first North American serial rights. Sends galleys to author. Publication is copyrighted.

Tips "We love work set in Victorian times, in the European countryside, in a twisted fairyland, in the underbelly of an enchanted city, or in the ruins of an undiscovered civilization. We want tales of cosmic fright; eerie fireside memories of nature's deadly mystery; adventures among the aether, the hemera, the spirit realm; tragedies of mad academics who take science too far; warnings of monstrosities that lurk in the sea, in the air, beneath the ground; stories of strange mechanical devices with unholy purposes; or anything else fitting the classic weird motifs. We do not accept stories set in postmodern times. This means nothing after the 1940s. In fact, we prefer stories that are timeless, or at least set in Victorian or Edwardian times. Weird fiction does not merely mean 'stories that are weird.' Weird Fiction refers to a specific genre, and if this genre is one with which you are unfamiliar, we ask that you not submit here until you have become sufficiently familiar."

$ ZAHIR

A Journal of Speculative Fiction, 315 South Coast Hwy. 101, Suite U8, Encinitas CA 92024. E-mail: zahirtales@gmail.com. Website: www.zahirtales.com. **Contact:** Sheryl Tempchin, editor. Online magazine. "We publish literary speculative fiction." Quarterly.

Needs Fantasy, literary, psychic/supernatural/occult, science fiction, surrealism, magical realism. No children's stories, excessive violence or pornography. Accepts 5-8 mss/issue; 20-25 mss/year. Publishes ms 2-12 months after acceptance. **Publishes 6 new writers/year.** Sometimes comments on rejected mss.

How to Contact Send complete ms. Send SASE (or IRC) for return of ms, or send disposable copy of the ms and #10 SASE or email address for reply only. E-mail queries okay. Email submissions okay

Small Circulation

through online submission form on our website. Responds in 1-2 weeks to queries; 1-3 months to mss. Accepts reprints submissions. Accepts simultaneous submissions. No multiple submissions. Writer's guidelines for #10 SASE, by e-mail, or online.
Payment/Terms Pays $10 and one copy of annual print anthology. Pays on publication for electronic rights and first, second serial (reprint) rights.
Tips "The stories we are most likely to buy are well written, have interesting, well-developed characters and/or ideas that fascinate, chill, thrill, or amuse us. They must have some element of the fantastic or surreal."

MARKETS

Online Markets

As production and distribution costs go up and the number of subscribers falls, more and more magazines are giving up print publication and moving online. Relatively inexpensive to maintain and quicker to accept and post submissions, online fiction sites are growing fast in numbers and legitimacy. The benefit for writers is that your stories can get more attention in online journals than in small literary journals. Small journals have small print runs—500-1,000 copies—so there's a limit on how many people will read your work. There is no limit when your work appears online.

There is also no limit to the types on online journals being published, offering outlets for a rich and diverse community of voices. These include genre sites, particular those for science fiction/fantasy and horror, and mainstream short fiction markets. Online literary journals range from the traditional to those with a decidedly more quirky bent. Writers will also find online outlets for more highly experimental and multimedia work.

While the medium of online publication is different, the traditional rules of publishing apply to submissions. Writers should research the site and archives carefully, looking for a match in sensibility for their work. Follow submission guidelines exactly and submit courteously. True, these sites aren't bound by traditional print schedules, so your work theoretically may be published more quickly. But that doesn't mean online journals have larger staffs, so exercise patience with editors considering your manuscript.

Also, while reviewing the listings in this market section, notice they are grouped differently from other market listings. In our Literary Magazines section, for example, you'll find primarily publications searching for only literary short fiction. But Online Markets are grouped by medium, so you'll find publishers of mystery short stories listed next to those looking for horror next to those specializing in flash fiction, so review with care. In addition, online markets with print counterparts can be found listed in the print markets sections.

A final note about online publication: Like literary journals, the majority of these markets are either nonpaying or very low paying. In addition, writers will not receive print copies of the publications because of the medium. So in most cases, do not expect to be paid for your exposure.

5-TROPE

E-mail: editor.5trope@gmail.com. Website: www.5trope.com. **Contact:** Gunnar Benediktsson, editor. Online literary journal. "We aim to publish the new and original in fiction, poetry and new media. We are seeking writers with a playful seriousness about language and form." Quarterly. Estab. 1999. Circ. 5,000.

Needs Avant-garde prose, experimental, literary. "No religious, horror, fantasy, espionage." Receives 75 unsolicited mss/month. Accepts 6 mss/issue; 18 mss/year. Publishes ms 6-12 months after acceptance. **Publishes 5 new writers/year.** Recently published work by Cole Swensen, Carol Novack, Christopher Kennedy, Mike Topp, Norman Lock, Jeff Johnson, Peter Markus, Mandee Wright, and Jane Unrue. Length: 25-5,000 words; average length: 1,000 words. Publishes short shorts. Also publishes poetry. Sometimes comments on rejected mss.

How to Contact Accepts submissions by e-mail. Send complete mss electronically. Sample copy online.

Payment/Terms Acquires first rights. Sends galleys to author.

Tips "Before submitting, please visit our site, read an issue, and consult our guidelines for submission. Include your story within the body of an e-mail, not as an attachment. Include a descriptive subject line to get around spam filters. Experimental work should have a clarity about it, and should never be sentimental. Our stories are about the moment of rupture, not the moment of closure."

◪ THE 13TH WARRIOR REVIEW

P.O. Box 5122, Seabrook NJ 08302-3511. E-mail: theeditor@asteriusonline.com. Website: www.asteriuspress.com. **Contact:** John C. Erianne, Editor. Published 2-3 times/year.

Needs Literary/mainstream, erotica, experimental, magical realism, meta-fiction. Receives 500 unsolicited mss/month. Accepts 4-8 mss/issue; 10-15 mss/year. Publishes ms 6 months after acceptance. **Publishes 1-2 new writers/year.** Recently published work by Cindy Rosmus, Jeff Blechle, Elizabeth Farren, and Andrew Hellem. Length: 500-6,000 words; average length: 1,800 words. Publishes short shorts. Also publishes literary essays, literary criticism, poetry, and book reviews. Sometimes comments on rejected mss.

How to Contact Send complete ms. Include estimated word count, brief bio and address/e-mail. Send SASE or IRC for return of ms or send a disposable copy of ms and #10 SASE for reply only. Accepts submissions by e-mail (will accept file attachments, but prefers text in message body). Responds in 1 week to queries; 1-2 months to mss. Accepts simultaneous submissions. Sample copy online at www.13thwr.org. Reviews fiction.

Payment/Terms Acquires first rights, Internet archival rights.

◪ $ ALIENSKIN MAGAZINE

An Online Science Fiction, Fantasy & Horror Magazine, 465 Market St., Beaver PA 15009. E-mail: alienskin@alienskinmag.com. Website: www.alienskinmag.com. **Contact:** Kay Patterson (flash fiction); Phil Adams (micro fiction). Online magazine. "Our magazine was created to promote genre fiction." Bimonthly. Circ. 5,500 + internet.

Needs Fantasy (dark fantasy, sword and sorcery), horror (dark fantasy, futuristic, psychological, psychic/supernatural/occult), science fiction (hard science/technological, soft/sociological). "No excessive blood, gore, erotica, vulgarity or child abuse. No experimental or speculative fiction that does not use basic story elements of character, conflict, action and resolution. No esoteric ruminations." Receives 250-400 unsolicited mss/month. Accepts 25-28 mss/issue; 150-168 mss/year. Publishes ms 30-60 days after acceptance. **Publishes 18-42 new writers/year.** Recently published work by Michael A. Kechula, Francis W. Alexander, Ev Bishop, and Abby Rustad. Length: 500-1,000 words; average length: 995 words. Publishes micro fiction of exactly 150 words and Fibonacci sequence poetry (6 lines, 20 syllables). Always comments on rejected mss.

How to Contact Send complete ms. Accepts submissions by e-mail only. Include estimated word count, brief bio, legal name, mailing address. Responds in 1-2 weeks to queries; 2 months to mss.

Accepts multiple submissions; no simultaneous submissions or previously published material. Sample copy and writer's guidelines online.

Payment/Terms $10 flat fee for 500-1,000 words. Exposure only for 150 word micro fiction and Fibonacci poetry. Pays on publication for first, electronic rights. Sponsors a pro-payment contest each year.

Tips "We look for interesting stories, offering something unique; stories that use basic story elements of character, conflict, action and resolution. We like the dark, twisted side of SFFH genres. Read our guidelines and follow the rules. Treat the submission process as a serious business transaction. Only send stories that have been spell-checked, and proofread at least twice. Try to remember: editors who offer a critique on manuscripts do so to help you as a writer, not to hamper or dissuade you as a writer."

☐ ◎ $ ☐ ALLEGORY

Tri-Annual Online Magazine of SF, Fantasy & Horror, 1225 Liberty Bell Dr., Cherry Hill NJ 08003. E-mail: submissions@allegoryezine.com. Website: www.allegoryezine.com. **Contact:** Ty Drago, editor. Online magazine specializing in science fiction, fantasy and horror. "We are an e-zine by writers for writers. Our articles focus on the art, craft and business of writing. Our links and editorial policy all focus on the needs of fiction authors." Triannual.

- Peridot Books won the Page One Award for Literary Contribution.

Needs Fantasy (space fantasy, sword and sorcery, sociological), horror (dark fantasy, futuristic, supernatural), science fiction (hard science/technological, soft/sociological). "No media tie-ins (Star Trek, Star Wars, etc., or space opera, vampires)." Receives 150 unsolicited mss/month. Accepts 8 mss/issue; 24 mss/year. Publishes ms 1-2 months after acceptance. Agented fiction 5%. **Publishes 10 new writers/year.** Length: 1,500-7,500 words; average length: 4,500 words. Also publishes literary essays, literary criticism. Often comments on rejected mss.

How to Contact All submissions should be sent by e-mail (no letters or telephone calls please) in either text or RTF format. Please place "Submission (Title)-(first and last name) in the subject line. Include the following in both the body of the email and the attachment: Your name, name to use on the story (byline), if different, your preferred e-mail address, your mailing address, the story's title and the story's word count. Responds in 8 weeks to mss. Accepts simultaneous submissions and reprints. Writer's guidelines online.

Payment/Terms $15/story-article. Pays on publication for one-time, electronic rights.

Tips "Give us something original, preferably with a twist. Avoid gratuitous sex or violence. Funny always scores points. Be clever, imaginative, but be able to tell a story with proper mood and characterization. Put your name and e-mail address in the body of the story. Read the site and get a feel for it before submitting."

☐ ☐ ANDERBO.COM

Anderbo Publishing, 270 Lafayette St., Suite 1412, New York NY 10012-3364. E-mail: editors@anderbo.com. Website: www.anderbo.com. **Contact:** Rick Rofihe, editor-in-chief. Online literary magazine/journal. "Quality fiction, poetry, 'fact' and photography on a website with 'print-feel' design." Member CLMP.

- Received the Best New Online Magazine or Journal, *storySouth* Million Writers Award in 2005.

Needs Literary. Does not want any genre literature. "We're interested only in literary fiction, poetry, and literary 'fact.'" Receives 200 mss/month. Accepts 20 mss/year. Ms published one month after acceptance. **Publishes 6 new writers/year.** Published Lisa Margonelli, Margot Berwin, Jeffrey Lent and Susan Breen. Length: 3,500. Average length: 1,750 words. Publishes short shorts. Average length of short shorts: 1,400 words. Also publishes literary essays, poetry. Rarely comments on/critiques rejected mss.

How to Contact Send complete ms with cover letter. Accepts submissions by e-mail. Include brief bio, list of publications. Responds to queries in 2 weeks. Responds to mss in 2 weeks. Considers simultaneous submissions. Guidelines available on website.
Payment/Terms Acquires first rights, first North American serial rights, one-time rights, electronic rights. Publication is copyrighted.
Tips "We are looking for fiction that is unique, urgent, accessible and involving. Look at our site and read what we've already published."

APPLE VALLEY REVIEW, A JOURNAL OF CONTEMPORARY LITERATURE

Queen's Postal Outlet, Box 12, Kingston ON K7L 3R9 Canada. E-mail: editor@leahbrowning.net. Website: www.applevalleyreview.com. **Contact:** Leah Browning, editor. Online literary magazine. Includes photographs/artwork on cover. "Each issue features a selection of beautifully crafted poetry, short fiction and essays. We prefer work that has both mainstream and literary appeal. As such, we avoid erotica and very explicit work. Our audience includes teens and adults of all ages." Semiannual. Member CLMP.
Needs Ethnic/multicultural (general), experimental, humor/satire, literary, mainstream, regional (American South, Southwest), translations, literary women's fiction (e.g. Barbara Kingsolver, Anne Tyler, Lee Smith, Elinor Lipman, Perri Klass). Does not want strict genre fiction, erotica, work containing explicit language, or anything extremely violent or depressing. Receives 100+ mss/month. Accepts 1-3 mss/issue; 2-12 mss/year. Manuscript published 3-6 months after acceptance. Published Barry Jay Kaplan, Jenny Steele, Tai Dong Huai, Matthew Grice, Arrie Brown. Length: 100-3,000 words. Average length: 2,000 words. Publishes short shorts. Average length of short shorts: 1,200 words. Also publishes literary essays, poetry. Sometimes comments on/critiques rejected mss.
How to Contact Send complete ms with cover letter. Accepts submissions only via e-mail. Include estimated word count, brief bio. Responds to mss in 1 week-2 months. No simultaneous submissions. Guidelines available on website. Sample copy on website.
Payment/Terms Acquires first rights, right to archive online. Publication is copyrighted.
Tips "Excellent writing always makes a manuscript stand out. Beyond that, I look for stories and poems that I want to read again, and that I want to give to someone else to read—work so interesting for one reason or another that I feel compelled to share it. Please read at least some of the previously published work to get a feel for our style, and follow the submission guidelines as closely as possible. We accept submissions only via e-mail."

ASCENT ASPIRATIONS

Aspirations for Artists, 1560 Arbutus Dr., Nanoose Bay BC C9P 9C8 Canada. E-mail: ascentaspirations@shaw.com. Website: www.ascentaspirations.ca. **Contact:** David Fraser, Editor. Ascent Aspirations Magazine. E-zine specializing in short fiction (all genres) and poetry, essays, visual art: 40 electronic pages; illustrations; photos. Ascent publishes one additional issues in print each year. "Ascent Aspirations Magazine publishes monthly online and once in print. The print issues are operated as contests. Please refer to current guidelines before submitting. Ascent Aspirations is a quality electronic publication dedicated to the promotion and encouragement of aspiring writers of any genre. The focus however is toward interesting experimental writing in dark mainstream, literary, science fiction, fantasy and horror. Poetry can be on any theme. Essays need to be unique, current and have social, philosophical commentary." Monthly online.
Needs Erotica, experimental, fantasy (space fantasy), feminist, horror (dark fantasy, futuristic, psychological, supernatural), literary, mainstream, mystery/suspense, New Age, psychic/supernatural/occult, science fiction (hard science/technological, soft/sociological). Receives 100-200 unsolicited mss/month. Accepts 40 mss/issue; 240 mss/year. Publishes ms 3 months after acceptance. **Publishes 10-50 new writers/year.** Recently published work by Taylor Graham, Janet Buck, Jim Manton, Steve Cartwright, Don Stockard, Penn Kemp, Sam Vargo, Vernon Waring, Margaret Karmazin, Bill Hughes. Length: 1,000 words or less. Publishes short shorts. Also publishes

literary essays, literary criticism, poetry. Sometimes comments on rejected mss.

How to Contact "Query by e-mail with Word attachment." Include estimated word count, brief bio and list of publications. If you have to submit by mail because it is your only avenue, provide a SASE with either International Coupons or Canadian stamps only. Responds in 1 week to queries; 3 months to mss. Accepts simultaneous, multiple submissions, and reprints. Guidelines by e-mail or on website. Reviews fiction and poetry collections.

Payment/Terms "No payment at this time. Rights remain with author."

Tips "Short fiction should, first of all tell, a good story, take the reader to new and interesting imaginary or real places. Short fiction should use language lyrically and effectively, be experimental in either form or content and take the reader into realms where they can analyze and think about the human condition. Write with passion for your material, be concise and economical and let the reader work to unravel your story. In terms of editing, always proofread to the point where what you submit is the best it possibly can be. Never be discouraged if your work is not accepted; it may just not be the right fit for a current publication."

$ ATOMJACK

Susurrus Press, 409 Alabama Street, Huntington WV 25704. (304) 634-9867. E-mail: atomjackmagazine@yahoo.com. Website: http://atomjackmagazine.com. **Contact:** Adicus Ryan Garton, editor. Online magazine. Contains illustrations. Includes photographs. "There are many online science fiction magazines, but they rarely combine a visual aesthetic with powerful stories. Atomjack, being a Susurrus publication, strives to achieve the prominence and quality of big print magazines in a free online publication. Atomjack is aimed at adults, as some stories have excessive violence or language unsuited for most children." Quarterly. Estab. 2006. Circ. 300-600 viewers per month.

Needs Comics/graphic novels, fantasy (space fantasy, science fantasy), horror (futuristic), science fiction (hard science/technological, soft/sociological). Does not want any stories that do NOT contain an element of science fiction."*Atomjack* very rarely considers romance or erotic stories, though we do not entirely discount them." List of upcoming themes available for SASE, on website. Receives 200 mss/month. Accepts 8-12 mss/issue; 40 mss/year. Ms published 2 months after acceptance. **Publishes 10 new writers/year.** Published Lawrence Dagstine, Kristine Ong Muslim, Anthony Bernstein, Amanda Underwood, and Cameron Pierce. Length: 100 words-5,000 words. Average length: 3,500 words. Publishes short shorts. Average length of short shorts: 500 words. Also publishes literary criticism. Always comments on/critiques rejected mss.

How to Contact Send complete ms with cover letter. Accepts submissions by e-mail only. Include estimated word count, brief bio. Responds to queries in 2 weeks. Responds to mss in 3 months. Considers simultaneous submissions, previously published submissions, multiple submissions. Sample copy, guidelines available on website.

Payment/Terms Writers receive $20. Pays on publication. Acquires electronic rights. Sends galleys to author. Publication is not copyrighted.

Tips "Character development and plot are the most important aspect of an *Atomjack*story. We routinely publish stories that have great characters in unique situations in what may not be an original SF environment. We also reject many stories with an amazing concept but no story to reinforce it. Atomjack occasionally gives a curt response for some stories. Queries about rejections welcome. Re-submit. Atomjack has published stories that were rewritten with the critique in mind and re-submitted."

BABEL

E-mail: submissions@towerofbabel.com. Website: www.towerofbabel.com. Multicultural Online Journal and Community of Arts and Electronic zine. "Recognized by the United Nations as one of the most important social and human sciences online periodicals." Publishes "regional reports from international stringers all over the planet, as well as features, round table discussions, fiction, columns, poetry, erotica, travelogues, and reviews of all of the arts and editorials. We are an online community involving an extensive group of artists, writers, programmers and translators representing 250 of the world's languages."

Needs "There are no specifc categories of fiction we are not interested in. Possible exceptions: lawyers/vampires, different genders hailing from different planets, cold war military scenarios and things that go bump in the suburban night." Recently published work by Nicholas P. Snoek, Yves Jaques, Doug Williamson, A.L. Fern, Laura Feister, Denzel J. Hankinson, and Pete Hanson.

How to Contact Send queries/mss by email. "Please send submissions with a resumé/cover letter or biography attached to the email." Reviews novels and short story collections.

Tips "We would like to see more fiction with first-person male characters written by female authors, as well as more fiction first-person female characters written by male authors. We would also like to see that dynamic in action when it comes to other languages, cultures, races, classes, sexual orientations and ages. The best advice we could give to writers wanting to be published in our publication is simply to know what you are writing about and write passionately about it."

THE BARCELONA REVIEW

Correu Vell 12-2, Barcelona 08002 Spain. E-mail: editor@barcelonareview.com. Website: www.barcelonareview.com. **Contact:** Jill Adams, editor. "TBR is an international review of contemporary, cutting-edge fiction published in English, Spanish and Catalan. Our aim is to bring both new and established writers to the attention of a larger audience. Well-known writers such as Alicia Erian in the U.S., Michel Faber in the U.K., Carlos Gardini in Argentina, and Nuria Amat in Spain, for example, were not known outside their countries until appearing in TBR. Our multilingual format increases the audience all the more. Internationally known writers, such as Irvine Welsh and Douglas Coupland, have contributed stories that ran in small press anthologies available only in one country. We try to keep abreast of what's happening internationally and to present the best finds every two months. Our intended audience is anyone interested in high-quality contemporary fiction that often (but not always) veers from the mainstream; we assume that our readers are well read and familiar with contemporary fiction in general."

Needs Short fiction. "Our bias is towards potent and powerful cutting-edge material; given that general criteria, we are open to all styles and techniques and all genres. No slice-of-life stories, vignettes or reworked fables, and nothing that does not measure up, in your opinion, to the quality of work in our review, which we expect submitters to be familiar with." **Publishes 20 new writers/year.** Recently published work by Niall Griffiths, Adam Haslett, G.K. Wuori, Adam Johnson, Mary Wornov, Emily Carter, Jesse Shepard and Julie Orringer.

How to Contact Send submissions by e-mail as an attached file. Hard copies accepted but cannot be returned. No simultaneous submissions. Reply takes 8 weeks.

Payment/Terms "In lieu of pay we sometimes offer a highly professional Spanish translation to English language writers and vice versa to Spanish writers. Work is showcased along with two or more known authors in a high quality literary review with an international readership. Author retains all rights although for the Internet only we ask for exclusive rights for the time period agreed upon."

Tips "Send top drawer material that has been drafted two, three, four times—whatever it takes. Then sit on it for a while and look at it afresh. Keep the text tight. Grab the reader in the first paragraph and don't let go. Keep in mind that a perfectly crafted story that lacks a punch of some sort won't cut it. Make it new, make it different. Surprise the reader in some way. Read the best of the short fiction available in your area of writing to see how yours measures up. Don't send anything off until you feel it's ready and then familiarize yourself with the content of the review/magazine to which you are submitting."

BLACKBIRD

An online journal of literature and the arts, Virginia Commonwealth University Department of Fic, Richmond VA 23284. (804)225-4729. E-mail: blackbird@vcu.edu. Website: www.blackbird.vcu.edu. **Contact:** Mary Flinn, Gregory Donovan, editors. Online journal: 80+ pages if printed;

illustrations; photos. "We strive to maintain the highest quality of writing and design, bringing the best things about a print magazine to the outside world. We publish fiction that is carefully crafted, thoughtful and suprising." Semiannual. Estab. 2001. Circ. 30,000 readers per month.
Needs Literary, novel excerpts. Does not want science fiction, religious/inspirational, condensed novels, horror, romance, children's. Receives 400-600 unsolicited mss/month. Accepts 4-5 mss/issue; 8-10 mss/year. Does not read from April 15-November 1. Publishes ms 3-6 months after acceptance. **Publishes 1-2 new writers/year.** Length: 5,000-10,000 words; average length: 5,000-6,500 words. Also publishes literary essays, literary criticism, poetry. Sometimes comments on rejected mss.
How to Contact Send complete ms. In clude cover letter, name, address, telephone number, brief biographical comment. Responds in 6 months to mss. Accepts simultaneous submissions. Sample copy online. Writer's guidelines online.
Payment/Terms Pays $200 for fiction, $40 for poetry. Pays on publication for first North American serial rights.
Tips "We like a story that invites us into its world, that engages our senses, soul and mind."

$ THE CAFE IRREAL

E-mail: editors@cafeirreal.com. E-zine: illustrations. "The Cafe Irreal is a webzine focusing on short stories and short shorts of an irreal nature." Quarterly.
Needs Experimental, fantasy (literary), science fiction (literary), translations. "No horror or 'slice-of-life' stories; no genre or mainstream science fiction or fantasy." Accepts 8-10 mss/issue; 30-40 mss/year. Recently published work by Ignacio Padilla, Charles Simic, Michal Ajvaz, Marianne Villanueva, and Bruce Holland Rogers. Length: 2,000 words (max). Publishes short shorts. Also publishes literary essays, literary criticism. Sometimes comments on rejected mss.
How to Contact Accepts submissions by e-mail. "No attachments, include submission in body of e-mail. Include estimated word count." Responds in 2-4 months to mss. No simultaneous submissions. Sample copy online. Writer's guidelines online.
Payment/Terms Pays 1¢/word, $2 minimum. Pays on publication for first-time electronic rights. Sends galleys to author.
Tips "Forget formulas. Write about what you don't know, take me places I couldn't possibly go, don't try to make me care about the characters. Read short fiction by writers such as Franz Kafka, Kobo Abe, Donald Barthelme, Magnus Mills, Ana Maria Shua and Stanislaw Lem. Also read our website and guidelines."

$ ORSON SCOTT CARD'S INTERGALACTIC MEDICINE SHOW

Hatrack River Publications, P.O. Box 18184, Greensboro NC 27419. Website: InterGalacticMedicineShow.com. **Contact:** Edmund R. Schubert, editor. E-zine specializing in science fiction and fantasy. Contains illustrations. "We like to see well-developed milieus and believeable, engaging characters. We also look for clear, unaffected writing. Asimov, Niven, Tolkien, Yolen and Hobb are more likely to be our literary exemplars than James Joyce." Bi-monthly.
Needs fantasy (space fantasy, sword and sorcery), horror (dark fantasy, futuristic), science fiction (hard science/technological, soft/sociological), young adult/teen (fantasy/science fiction). Receives 300-400 mss/month. Accepts 7 mss/issue; 30+ mss/year. Ms published 4-9 months after acceptance. Agented fiction 5%. **Publishes 4-6 new writers/year.** Published Peter S. Beagle, Tim Pratt, Eugie Foster, James Maxey, Eric James Stone, Alethea Kontis, Steven Savile and Cat Rambo. Length: 1000 words (min)-10000 words (max). Average length: 4000-7000 words. Publishes short shorts. Average length of short shorts: 750 words. Also publishes book reviews. Sometimes comments on/critiques rejected mss.
How to Contact Submit ms via submission form on website. Include estimated word count, email address. Responds to queries in 2 weeks. Responds to mss in 3-6 months. Considers simultaneous submissions, previously published submissions (if obscure publication). Guidelines available on website.

Payment/Terms Writers receive ¢6 per word for first 7500 words, ¢5 per word beyond 7500, contributor's copy. Pays on publication. Acquires first North American serial rights, electronic rights. Publication is copyrighted.
Tips "Plain and simple, we want to see plots that go somewhere, filled with people we care about. Stories that show the author has a real undersanding of the subtleties of human nature. Proper manuscript formatting and up-to-date contact information are overlooked by more writers than you could imagine. Also, please bear in mind that all stories must be PG-13 suitable. Gratuitous sex, violence or language will get you rejected right away."

CEZANNE'S CARROT, A LITERARY JOURNAL OF FRESH OBSERVATIONS

Spiritual, Transformational & Visionary Art, Inc., P.O. Box 6037, Santa Fe NM 87502-6037. E-mail: query@cezannescarrot.org. Website: www.cezannescarrot.org. **Contact:** Barbara Jacksha and Joan Kremer, editors. Online magazine. "*Cezanne's Carrot* publishes "high quality literary fiction and creative nonfiction that explores spiritual, metaphysical, transformational, visionary, or mind-expanding themes. We are most interested in stories that push us into a transcendent realm, that give us a higher understanding of our expanding, multi-dimensional selves."
Needs Experimental, fantasy (speculative), literary, new age, psychic/supernatural/occult, science fiction (soft/sociological), magical realism, irrealism, visionary, surrealism, metaphysical, spiritual, "and other genres, as long as the work is literary and embraces the journal's metaphysical mission and theme. Does not want horror, gore, murder, serial-killers, abuse stories, drug stories, vampires or other monsters, political stories, war stories, stories written for children, stories that primarily promote an agenda or a particular religion. We're not interested in dogma in any form." Receives 100-200 mss/month. Accepts 24-36 mss/issue; 40-60 mss/year. Manuscript published 4-12 weeks after acceptance. **Publishes 1-5 new writers/year.** Published Bruce Holland Rogers, Tamara Kaye Sellman, Utahna Faith, Margaret Frey, Corey Mesler, Christine Boyka kluge, and Charles P. Ries. Length: 100 words (min)-3,000 words (max). Average length: 1,800 words. Publishes short shorts.
How to Contact Send complete ms with cover letter. Accepts submissions by e-mail only. Include estimated word count, brief bio, list of publications. Responds to mss in 1-4 months. Considers simultaneous submissions, previously published submissions. Guidelines available on website.
Payment/Terms Pays $10 per story upon publication. Acquires one-time rights, reprint rights.
Tips "We only accept work with a strong tie to our journal's mission and theme. Read our guidelines and mission statement carefully. Read previous issues to understand the kind of work we're looking for. Only submissions sent to the correct e-mail address will be considered. Submissions sent as attachments or that exceed our maximum word count will not be read or responded to."

$ CHIZINE: TREATMENT OF LIGHT AND SHADE IN WORDS

E-mail: savory@rogers.com. Website: www.chizine.com. **Contact:** Brett Alexander Savory, editor-in-chief. E-zine. "Subtle, sophisticated dark fiction with a literary bent." Quarterly. Estab. 1997.

- Received Bram Stoker Award for Other Media in 2000

Needs Experimental, fantasy, horror (dark fantasy, futuristic, psychological, supernatural), literary, mystery, science fiction (soft/sociological), Does not want "tropes of vampires, werewolves, mummies, monsters, or anything that's been done to death." Receives 100 mss/month. Accepts 3-4 mss/issue; 12-16 mss/year. Does not read June, July and August due to Chizine/Leisure Short Story Contest. Length: 4,000 words (max). Publishes short shorts. Average length of short shorts: 500 words. Also publishes poetry. Send to savory@rogers.com to query. Always comments on/critiques rejected mss.
How to Contact Send complete ms with cover letter. Accepts only submissions by e-mail. Include estimated word count, brief bio. Responds to queries in 1 week. Responds to mss within 3 months. Considers simultaneous submissions so long as we're told it is simultaneous. Guidelines available on website.
Payment/Terms Writers receive 7¢/word, with a $280 max. Pays on publication. Acquires all rights

for 90 days, then archival rights for one year. Sends any edits to author. Publication is copyrighted. Sponsors the Chizine/Leisure Short Story contest. Guidelines posted on website around May. See entry in Contests & Awards section.

CONTE ONLINE, A JOURNAL OF NARRATIVE WRITING

E-mail: robert.lieberman@gmail.com; prose@conteonline.net. Biannual online magazine. "We aim to publish narrative writing of all kinds. Relating a sequence of events is a primary method of human communication; we are interested in the narrative form as a means of relating ideas, experiences, and emotions, and we love how the act of telling a story unites the perspectives of listeners and speakers. We are dedicated to the concept of disseminating fresh, stellar writing to as many people as possible, as quickly and as often as possible, hence our online basis. We are enthusiastic about publishing the latest works of writers from all backgrounds and of varying experience. We hope Conte will be a mechanism not only for publication, but communication among writers as well as between readers and authors, and above all that we continue the ancient and perhaps sacred tradition of telling a good yarn."

Needs "We'll consider fiction on essentially any topic; our primary focus is the effective use of narrative. We discourage fiction which does not present a clear (sequential or non-sequential) narrative progression; work without a distinctive and engaging plot of some form isn't what we are looking for. We tend to be frustrated by stories that merely raise questions but don't attempt to address them, or that end early without seeming complete." Receives 20-30 mss/month. Accepts 5-7 mss/issue; 10-14 mss/year. Manuscript published 2-3 months or less after acceptance. Agented fiction <5%. **Publishes 4 new writers/year.** Published poetry by William Hathaway, Jim Daniels, Roger Weingarten, Erika Meitner, and E. Ethelbert Miller, among others. Length: 8,000 words (max). Average length: 5,000 words. Publishes short shorts. Average length of short shorts: 1,000 words. Also publishes poetry. Sometimes comments on/critiques rejected mss.

How to Contact Send complete ms with cover letter. Accepts submissions by e-mail only. Include estimated word count, brief bio. Responds to queries in 3-4 weeks. Responds to mss in 8-10 weeks. Considers simultaneous submissions. Guidelines available via e-mail, on website.

Payment/Terms Acquires electronic rights. Sends galleys to author. Publication is not copyrighted.

Tips "We love to see stories that let us take something away—a fact, a perspective, a great bit of dialogue, some piece of the world you create we can keep with us after it's over. Writing that leads us somewhere unexpected is always a delight; immersive worlds and characters are the hallmarks of our favorite fiction. Stories that investigate the overlooked and show us the significance of something often missed are likely to grab our attention. In all, the clarity of the senses you lend us, the adroitness of your storytelling, and the joy we take in reading your tale are the primary barometers of our selection process. Tell your story completely; if you start us on a journey, we want to be taken all the way to the end. Details and imagery are what make a narrative come alive, but try not to lose momentum in them. Have the confidence to tell your story the way it needs to be told; we love reading, so we're already on your side to begin with."

$ CONTRARY

3133 S. Emerald Ave., Chicago IL 60616-3299. E-mail: chicago@contrarymagazine.com (no submissions). Website: www.contrarymagazine.com. **Contact:** Jeff McMahon, editor. Online literary magazine/journal. Contains illustrations. "Contrary publishes fiction, poetry, literary commentary, and prefers work that combines the virtues of all those categories. Founded at the University of Chicago, it now operates independently and not-for-profit on the South Side of Chicago. We like work that is not only contrary in content, but contrary in its evasion of the expectations established by its genre. Our fiction defies traditional story form. For example, a story may bring us to closure without ever delivering an ending. We don't insist on the ending, but we do insiste on the closure. And we value fiction as poetic as any poem." Quarterly. Circ. 38,000 unique readers. Member CLMP.

Needs Literary. Receives 650 mss/month. Accepts 6 mss/issue; 24 mss/year. Ms published no more than 21 days after acceptance. **Publishes 1 new writer/year.** Published Sherman Alexie, Andrew Coburn, Amy Reed, Clare Kirwan, Stephanie Johnson, Laurence Davies, and Edward McWhinney. Length: 2,000 words (max). Average length: 750 words. Publishes short shorts. Average length of short shorts: 750 words. Also publishes literary essays, poetry. Rarely comments on/critiques rejected mss.
How to Contact Accepts submissions through website only. www.contrarymagazine.com/Contrary/Submissions.html. Include estimated word count, brief bio, list of publications. Responds to queries in 2 weeks. Responds to mss in 3 months. Considers simultaneous submissions. Guidelines available on website.
Payment/Terms Pays $20-60. Pays on publication. Acquires first rights and perpetual archive and anthology rights. Publication is copyrighted.
Tips "Beautiful writing catches our eye first. If we realize we're in the presence of unanticipated meaning, that's what clinches the deal. Also, we're not fond of expository fiction. We prefer to be seduced by beauty, profundity and mystery than to be presented with the obvious. We look for fiction that entrances, that stays the reader's finger above the mouse button. That is, in part, why we favor microfiction, flash fiction and short-shorts. Also, we hope writers will remember that most editors are looking for very particular species of work. We try to describe our particular species in our mission statement and our submission guidelines, but those descriptions don't always convey nuance. That's why many editors urge writers to read the publication itself; in the hope that they will intuit an understanding of its particularities. If you happen to write that particular species of work we favor, your submission may find a happy home with us. If you don't, it does not necessarily reflect on your quality or your ability. It usually just means that your work has a happier home somewhere else."

◪ ◙ THE COPPERFIELD REVIEW

E-mail: info@copperfieldreview.com. "We are an online literary journal that publishes historical fiction and articles, reviews and interviews related to historical fiction. We believe that by understanding the lessons of the past through historical fiction we can gain better insight into the nature of our society today, as well as a better understanding of ourselves." Quarterly.
Needs Historical (general), romance (historical), western (frontier saga, traditional). "We will consider submissions in most fiction categories, but the setting must be historical in nature. We don't want to see anything not related to historical fiction." Receives 30 unsolicited mss/month. Accepts 7-10 mss/issue; 28-40 mss/year. Responds to mss during the months of January, April, July and October. **Publishes "between 30 and 40 percent" new writers/year.** Publishes short shorts. Also publishes literary essays, literary criticism, poetry. Seldom comments on rejected mss.
How to Contact Send complete ms. Accepts submissions by e-mail. Responds in 6 weeks to queries. Accepts simultaneous, multiple submissions and reprints. Sample copy online. Writer's guidelines online. Reviews fiction.
Payment/Terms Acquires one-time rights.
Tips "We wish to showcase the very best in literary historical fiction. Stories that use historical periods and details to illuminate universal truths will immediately stand out. We are thrilled to receive thoughtful work that is polished, poised and written from the heart. Be professional, and only submit your very best work. Be certain to adhere to a publication's submission guidelines, and always treat your e-mail submissions with the same care you would use with a traditional publisher. Above all, be strong and true to your calling as a writer. It is a difficult, frustrating but wonderful journey. It is important for writers to review our online submission guidelines prior to submitting."

◙ DARGONZINE

E-mail: dargon@dargonzine.org. E-zine specializing in fantasy fiction. "DargonZine is an E-zine that prints original fantasy fiction by aspiring fantasy writers. The Dargon Project is a shared world anthology whose goal is to provide a way for aspiring fantasy writers to meet and improve their writing skills through mutual contact and collaboration as well as contact with a live readership via the Internet."

Needs Fantasy. "Our goal is to write fantasy fiction that is mature, emotionally compelling, and professional. Membership in the Dargon Project is a requirement for publication." **Publishes 1-3 new writers/year.** Guidlines available on website. Sample copy online. "As a strictly noncommercial magazine, our writers' only compensation is their growth and membership in a lively writing community. Authors retain all rights to their stories."

Tips "The Readers and Writers FAQs on our website provide much more detailed information about our mission, writing philosophy and the value of writing for *DargonZine*."

◎ THE DEAD MULE SCHOOL OF SOUTHERN LITERATURE

117 North Brown St., Washington NC 27889. E-mail: submit.mule@gmail.com. Website: www.deadmule.com. **Contact:** Valerie MacEwan, editor (MacEwan@assemblagist.com); Rebekah Cowell, fiction editor (use submit.mule@gmail.com but with "Attn: Rebekah" in subject line).. "The Dead Mule School of Southern Literature Institutional Alumni Association recruits year 'round. Want to join the freshman class of 2015? Submit today. The Mule proudly claims the longest running online magazine devoted to Southern literary excellence."

Needs Fiction, creative nonfiction, interviews with Southerners, essays, poetry. "Always, always, stories about mules."

How to Contact Send complete ms. You can send it as a .doc attachment but also include your submission in the body of your e-mail. "Read and follow the guidelines online—you need a Southern Legitimacy Statement. What's an SLS? It's mostly about you entertaining us and capturing our interest. Everyone is South of Somewhere, go ahead, check us out."

Tips "You are a writer - obviously, or you would not be reading this book and trying to find a place to send your work. So: remember to follow submission guidelines; match your work to the publication; spellcheck and edit your work before submitting; and don't track mud all over your mother's clean floor. Don't send a personally published blog entry to an online journal—you're wasting good bandwidth when you do that. If sending a.doc is beyond your level of expertise, spend some quality time playing technological catch-up. And remember to be patient, we're southern, so haste is not a word in our vocabulary. No good Southern fiction is complete without a dead mule."

◪ DIAGRAM

A Magazine of Art, Text, and Schematic, University of Arizona, ML 445, P.O. Box 210067, Tucson AZ 85721. E-mail: editor@thediagram.com. Website: http://thediagram.com. "We specialize in work that pushes the boundaries of traditional genre or work that is in some way schematic. We do publish traditional fiction and poetry, too, but hybrid forms (short stories, prose poems, indexes, tables of contents, etc.) are particularly welcome! We also publish diagrams and schematics (original and found). Bimonthly. Circ. 300,000 + hits/month. Member CLMP.

Needs Experimental, literary. "We don't publish genre fiction, unless it's exceptional and transcends the genre boundaries." Receives 100 unsolicited mss/month. Accepts 2-3 mss/issue; 15 mss/year. **Publishes 6 new writers/year.** Average length: 250-2,000 words. Publishes short shorts. Also publishes literary essays, poetry. Often comments on rejected mss.

How to Contact Send complete ms. Accepts submissions by Web submissions manager; no e-mail please. If sending by post, send SASE for return of the ms, or send disposable copy of the ms and #10 SASE for reply only. Responds in 2 weeks to queries; 1-2 months to mss. Accepts simultaneous submissions. Sample copy for $12 for print version. Writer's guidelines online.

Payment/Terms Acquires first, serial, electronic rights.

Tips "We value invention, energy, experimentation and voice. When done very well, we like traditional fiction, too. Nearly all the work we select is propulsive and exciting, but first the sentences have to be beautiful."

DUCTS

P.O. Box 3203, Grand Central Station, New York NY 10163. E-mail: department: fiction@ducts.org, essays@ducts.org. Website: http://ducts.org.. **Contact:** Jonathan Kravetz. DUCTS is a Webzine of personal stories, fiction, essays, memoirs, poetry, humor, profiles, reviews and art. "DUCTS was founded in 1999 with the intent of giving emerging writers a venue to regularly publish their compelling, personal stories. The site has been expanded to include art and creative works of all genres. We believe that these genres must and do overlap. DUCTS publishes the best, most compelling stories and we hope to attract readers who are drawn to work that rises above." Semiannual. Estab. 1999. Circ. 12,000. CLMP.

Needs Ethnic/multicultural, humor/satire, literary, mainstream. "Please do not send us genre work, unless it is extraordinarily unique." Receives 50 unsolicited mss/month. Accepts 40 mss/issue; 80 mss/year. Publishes ms 1-6 months after acceptance. **Publishes 10-12 new writers/year.** Recently published work by Charles Salzberg, Mark Goldblatt, Richard Kostelanz, and Helen Zelon. Publishes short shorts. Also publishes literary essays, literary criticism, poetry. Sometimes comments on rejected mss.

How to Contact Reading period is January 1 through August 31. Send complete ms. Accepts submissions by e-mail to appropriate departments. Responds in 1-4 weeks to queries; 1-6 months to mss. Accepts simultaneous and reprints submissions. Writer's guidelines on ducts.org.

Payment/Terms $15. Acquires one-time rights.

Tips "We prefer writing that tells a compelling story with a strong narrative drive."

THE EXTERNALIST: A JOURNAL OF PERSPECTIVES

c/o Larina Warnock, P.O. Box 2052, Corvallis OR 97339. E-mail: editor@theexternalist.com; fiction@theexternalist.com. Website: www.theexternalist.com. **Contact:** Larina Warnock. Online magazine, PDF format, 45-60 pgs. "The Externalist embraces the balance between craft, entertainment and substance with a focus on subjects that are meaningful in human context. The externalist writer is the writer who is driven by a desire to write well while also writing in such a way that others can understand their perspective (even if they disagree or can't relate), and in this way, keeps an eye on the world outside of self. Externalism values craft and content equally. It recognizes there are still important lessons to be learned, there is still a need to understand and relate to the world around us, and differences are as important as similiarites, and vice versa. The externalist believes there are significant human concerns across the globe and here in the United States, and that good litereature has the power to create discussion around these concerns. The externalist also believes the multiplicity of perspectives found in today's quickly changing world can (and should) be valued as a means to comprehension—a way to change the things that do not work and give force to the things that do." Bimonthly. Estab. 2007. Circ. approx.1,000 unique visitors a month.

- *The Externalist* has been nominated for "Best of the Web" and "Best of the Net." Nominates for the *Pushcart Prize*.

Needs Adventure, ethnic/multicultural, family saga, fantasy, feminist, gay, historical, horror, humor/satire, lesbian, literary, mainstream, military/war, mystery, new age, psychic/supernatural/occult, religious, science fiction, thriller/espionage, and western, but "all fiction must have an externalist focus regardless of genre." Does not want children's or young adult literature, erotica or pornography, or standard romance. "We do not publish any work that is designed to inspire hate or violance against any population. Highly experimental work is strongly discouraged. Slice-of-life fiction that does not deal with a significant social issue will not be accepted." List of upcoming themes available on website. Receives 20-25 mss/month. Accepts 2-3 mss/issue; 12-18 mss/year. Ms published 4 months after acceptance. **Publishes 10-15 new writers/year.** Published Bill Tietelbaum, Lois Shapley Bassen, and Shaul Hendel. Length: 500-5,000 words. Average length: 3,500 words. Publishes short shorts. Average length of short shorts: 750 words. Also publishes literary essays, literary criticism, poetry. Often comments on/critiques rejected mss.

How to Contact E-mail submissions only. Include estimated word count, brief bio. Responds to queries in 2-3 weeks. Responds to mss in 6-8 weeks. Considers simultaneous submissions, previously published submissions. Guidelines available on website.
Payment/Terms Contributor's link on Web page (see website for details). Acquires first North American serial rights. Sends galleys to author. Publication is copyrighted. "All work published in *The Externalist* is eligible for Editor's Choice (each issue) and our annual Best of *The Externalist* anthology."
Tips "The fiction that appears in *The Externalist* is well-crafted and speaks subtly about significant social issues in our world today. The more thought-provoking the story, the more likely we will accept it for publication. The editor has a soft spot for well written satire. However, read the work we publish before submitting. Familiarize yourslef with externalism. This information is on our website free of charge, and even a brief look at the material we publish will improve your chances. Follow the guidelines! We do not open unsolicated attachments, and manuscripts that do not follow our e-mail formatting guidelines stand a good chance of hitting our junk mail folder and not being seen."

FAILBETTER.COM

2022 Grove Avenue, Richmond VA 23221. E-mail: tdidato@failbetter.com; submissions@failbetter.com. Website: www.failbtetter.com. **Contact:** Thom Didato, publisher.

THE FAIRFIELD REVIEW

19 Norman Ave., E. Norwalk CT 06855. E-mail: fairfieldreview@hpmd.com. Website: www.fairfieldreview.org. **Contact:** Edward G. Happ, editor. Electronic magazine. "Our mission is to provide an outlet for poetry, short stories and essays, from both new and established writers and students. We are accessible to the general public."
Needs Literary. Would like to see more stories "rich in lyrical imagery and those that are more humorous." **Publishes 20 new writers/year.** Recently published work by Nan Leslie (Pushcart nominee) and Richard Boughton.
How to Contact Requires submissions by e-mail. "No snail mail please." Replies by e-mail only. Right to retain publication in online archive issues, and the right to use in "Best of The Fairfield Review" anthologies. Sample copy online.
Payment/Terms Acquires first rights.
Tips "We encourage students and first-time writers to submit their work. In addition to the submission guidelines found in each issue on our website, we recommend reading the essay 'Writing Qualities to Keep in Mind' from our Editors and Authors page on the website. Keep to small, directly experienced themes; write crisply using creative, poetic images, avoid the trite expression."

FICKLE MUSES

E-mail: fiction2@ficklemuses.com. Online magazine. Contains illustrations. Includes photographs. "We feature poetry and short stories that re-imagine old myths or reexamine mythic themes contemporarily." Weekly.
Needs Literary. "Stories may cross over into any genre as long as the story is based in a myth or legend. Does not want stories that treat myth as a false belief or stereotype (e.g. the myth of beauty). No pure genre (romance, horror, mystery, etc.)." Receives 13-15 mss/month. Accepts 12-24 mss/year. Ms published up to 3 months after acceptance. **Publishes approx 10% new writers/year.** Published Neil de la Flor, Maureen Seaton, Virginia Mohlere and M.M. De Voe. Length: 1,000-5,000 words. Average length: 2,000 words. Publishes short shorts. Average length of short shorts: 500 words. Also publishes literary essays, literary criticism, book reviews, poetry. Send review query to fiction@ficklemuses.com. Rarely comments on/critiques rejected mss.
How to Contact Send complete ms with cover letter. Accepts submissions by e-mail only. Include estimated word count and "a brief description of the myth or legend your story is based on if it is

not standard knowledge." Responds to queries in 3 weeks. Responds to mss in 3 weeks. Considers simultaneous submissions, previously published submissions. Guidelines available on website.
Payment/Terms Acquires one-time rights. Publication is not copyrighted.
Tips "Originality. An innovative look at an old story. I'm looking to be swept away. Get a feel for our website."

☐ $ FLASH ME MAGAZINE: THE ONLINE MAGAZINE EXCLUSIVELY FOR FLASH FICTION STORIES

Winged Halo Productions, P.O. Box 803, O'Fallon, IL 62269-0803. E-mail: info@wingedhalo.com. Website: www.wingedhalo.com. **Contact:** Jennifer Dawson, Editor-in-Chief. Online magazine. "Flash Me Magazine is a quartly magazine, accepting all genres of fiction, as long as the story is under 1000 words. There are no restrictions on content, though we will not publish stories with excess gore, violence, profanity or sex." Quarterly. Estab. 2003. Circ. 1,000 visitors per month. Member Small Press Co-op.
Needs Fantasy (space fantasy, sword and sorcery), historical, horror (dark fantasy, futuristic, psychological, supernatural), humor/satire, literary, mainstream, military/war, mystery, romance (contemporary, futuristic/time travel, gothic, historical, regency, suspense), science fiction (soft/sociological). Receives 100 mss/month. Accepts 6-12 mss/issue; 24-48 mss/year. Ms published 3 months or less after acceptance. **Publishes 20 new writers/year.** Published Debbie Mumford, Bruce Holland Rogers, Angie Smibert and Amy Herlihy. Publishes short shorts only. Average length of short shorts: 750, max 1,000 words. Also publishes book reviews. Send review queries to reviews@wingedhalo.com. Always comments on/critiques rejected mss.
How to Contact Send complete ms with cover letter. Accepts submissions by e-mail. Include brief bio. Responds to queries in 1 week. Responds to mss in 3 months. Considers previously published submissions, multiple submissions. Guidelines available on website.
Payment/Terms Writers receive $5-20. Pays on publication. Acquires electronic rights. Sends galleys to author. Publication is copyrighted.
Tips "Anything well-written stands a chance, and anything with a good plot, as well. To really catch our eye though, a story has be unique and memorable. Read our guidelines carefully before submitting work."

◪ $ FLASHQUAKE

An Online Journal of Flash Literature, P.O. Box 2154, Albany NY 12220-0154. E-mail: dorton@flashquake.org. Website: www.flashquake.org. **Contact:** Debi Orton, publisher. E-zine specializing in flash literature. "flashquake is a quarterly online literary journal featuring flash literature—flash fiction, flash nonfiction, and short poetry. Send us works that will leave readers thinking. We define flash as works less than 1,000 words, shorter pieces will impress us. Poetry can be up to 35 lines; prose poetry up to 300 lines. We want the best story you can tell us in the fewest words you need to do it! Move us, engage us, give us a complete story with characters, plot, and a beginning, middle and end."
Needs Ethnic/multicultural (general), experimental, literary, flash literature of all types: fiction, memoir, creative nonfiction, poetry and artwork. "Not interested in romance, graphic sex, graphic violence, gore, jokey humor, vampires, or work of a religious nature." Receives 200-250 unsolicited mss/month. Accepts 30 mss/issue. Publishes ms 1-3 months after acceptance. Publishes only short shorts. Comments on most rejected mss.
How to Contact Accepts submissions by e-mail (submit@flashquake.org) only. No land mail. Include brief bio, mailing address and e-mail address. Guidelines and submission instructions on website.
Payment/Terms Pays $5-25 plus CD copy of site. Pays within two weeks of publication for electronic rights. Sponsors occasional awards/contests.
Tips "Read our submission guidelines before submitting. Proofread your work thoroughly! We will instantly reject your work for spelling and grammar errors. Save your document as plain text and

paste it into an e-mail message. We do not open attachments. We like experimental work, but that is not a license to forget narrative clarity, plot, character development or reader satisfaction."

FLUENT ASCENSION

Fierce Concepts, P.O. Box 14581, Phoenix AZ 85063. E-mail: submissions@fluentascension.com. Website: www.fluentascension.com. **Contact:** Warren Norgaard, editor. Online magazine. Quarterly. Estab. 2003.

Needs Comics/graphic novels, erotica, ethnic/multicultural, experimental, gay, humor/satire, lesbian, literary, translations. Receives 6-10 unsolicited mss/month. Accepts 1-3 mss/issue. Publishes short shorts. Also publishes literary essays, literary criticism, poetry. Sometimes comments on rejected mss.

How to Contact Send complete ms. Accepts submissions by e-mail. Include estimated word count, brief bio and list of publications. Send SASE (or IRC) for return of ms or send disposable copy of ms and #10 SASE for reply only. Responds in 8-12 weeks to queries; 8-12 weeks to mss. Accepts simultaneous, multiple submissions. Sample copy online. Writer's guidelines online.

Payment/Terms Acquires electronic rights. Sponsors awards/contests.

FULLOSIA PRESS

P.O. Box 280, Ronkonkoma NY 11779. E-mail: deanofrpps@aol.com. Website: rpps_fullosia_press.tripod.com. **Contact:** J.D. Collins, editor; Geoff Jackson, associate editor. E-zine. "Part-time publisher of fiction and non-fiction. Our publication is right wing and conservative, leaning to views of Patrick Buchanan but amenable to the opposition's point of view. We promote an independent America. We are anti-global, anti-UN. Collects unusual news from former British or American provinces. Fiction interests include military, police, private detective, courthouse stories." Monthly. Circ. 175.

Needs Historical (American), military/war, mystery/suspense, thriller/espionage. Christmas, St. Patrick's Day, Fourth of July. Publishes ms 1 week after acceptance. **Publishes 10 new writers/year.** Recently published work by Geoff Jasckson, 'Awesome' Dave Lawrence, John Grey, James Davies, Andy Martin and Michael Levy. Length: 500-2,000 words; average length: 750 words. Publishes short shorts. Also publishes literary essays. Always comments on rejected mss.

How to Contact Query with or without published clips. Accepts submissions by e-mail. Include brief bio and list of publications. Mail submissions must be on 314 floppy disk. Responds in 1 month to mss. Please avoid mass mailings. Sample copy online. Reviews fiction.

Payment/Terms Acquires electronic rights.

Tips "Make your point quickly. If you haven't done so, after five pages, everybody hates you and your characters."

THE FURNACE REVIEW

16909 N. Bay Rd. #305, Sunny Isles FL 33160. E-mail: editor@thefurnacereview.com. Website: www.furnacereview.com. **Contact:** Ciara LaVelle, editor. "We reach out to a young, well-educated audience, bringing them new, unique, fresh work they won't find elsewhere." Quarterly. Estab. 2004.

Needs Experimental, literary, mainstream. Does not want children's, science fiction, or religious submissions. Receives 50-60 unsolicited mss/month. Accepts 1-5 mss/issue; 5-8 mss/year. **Publishes 10-20 new writers/year.** Recently published work by Amy Greene, Dominic Preziosi, and Sandra Soson. Length: 7,000 words; average length: 4,000 words. Publishes short shorts. Also publishes poetry.

How to Contact Send complete ms. Accepts submissions by e-mail only. Responds in 4 month to queries. Accepts simultaneous submissions.

Payment/Terms Acquires first North American serial rights.

THE GREEN HILLS LITERARY LANTERN

Published by Truman State University, Division of Language & Literature, Kirksville MO 63501. (660) 785-4487. E-mail: adavis@truman.edu. Website: http://ll.truman.edu/ghllweb. **Contact:** Fiction editor. "The mission of GHLL is to provide a literary market for quality fiction writers, both established and beginners, and to provide quality literature for readers from diverse backgrounds. We also see ourselves as a cultural resource for North Missouri. Our publication works to publish the highest quality fiction—dense, layered, subtle—and, at the same time, fiction which grabs the ordinary reader. We tend to publish traditional short stories, but we are open to experimental forms." Annual. Estab. 1990. The GHLL is now an online, open-access journal.

Needs Ethnic/multicultural, experimental, feminist, humor/satire, literary, mainstream, regional. "Our main requirement is literary merit. Wants more quality fiction about rural culture. No adventure, crime, erotica, horror, inspirational, mystery/suspense, romance." Receives 40 unsolicited mss/month. Accepts 15-17 mss/issue. Publishes ms 6-12 months after acceptance. **Publishes 0-3 new writers/year.** Recently published work by Karl Harshbarger, Mark Jacobs, J. Morris, Gary Fincke, Dennis Vannatta. Length: 7,000 words; average length: 3,000 words. Publishes short shorts. Also publishes poetry. Sometimes comments on rejected mss.

How to Contact SASE for return of ms. Responds in 4 months to mss. Accepts simultaneous, multiple submissions. Electronic submissions in.doc or.txt format also acceptable from writers livingoutside North America, but our manuscript readers still prefer hardcopy. E-mail attachment to adavis@truman.edu.

Payment/Terms No payment. Acquires one-time rights.

Tips "We look for strong character development, substantive plot and theme, visual and forceful language within a multilayered story. Make sure your work has the flavor of life, a sense of reality. A good story, well crafted, will eventually get published. Find the right market for it, and above all, don't give up."

HYCO REVIEW ARTS AND LITERARY JOURNAL

Piedmont Community College, P.O. Box 1197, Roxboro NC 27573. (336)599-1181. E-mail: reflect@piedmont.cc.nc.us. Website: www.piedmontcc.edu. **Contact:** Dawn Langley, editor. Online magazine. 100-150 pages.

Needs Literary. "Accepts mss from Person and Caswell county, NC authors only (residents or natives). If time and space permit, we'll consider submissions from other North Carolina authors." Publishes mss 6-10 months after acceptance. **Publishes 3-5 new writers/year.** Recently published work by Maureen Sherbondy, Dainiel Green, Betty Moffett, Lian Gouw, Sejal Badani Ravani, Donna Conrad. Max Length: 4,000 words; average length: 2,500 words. Publishes short shorts. Also publishes poetry and essays, photographs, videos, digital animation, and artwork.

How to Contact Send SASE for return of ms or #10 SASE for reply only. Sample copy for $5. Writer's guidelines for SASE or by e-mail.

Payment/Terms Publication is online. Acquires first North American serial rights. Sponsors awards/contests.

Tips "We look for good writing with a flair, which captivates an educated lay audience. Don't take rejection letters personally. We turn away many submissions simply because we don't have room for everything we like or because the author is not from our region. For that reason, we're more likely to accept shorter well-written stories than longer stories of the same quality. Also, stories containing profanity that doesn't contribute to the plot, structure or intended tone are rejected immediately."

$ IDEOMANCER

E-mail: publisher@ideomancer.com. Website: www.ideomancer.com. Online magazine. Contains illustrations. "Ideomancer publishes speculative fiction and poetry that explores the edges of ideas; stories that subvert, refute and push the limits. We want unique pieces from authors willing to explore non-traditional narratives and take chances with tone, structure and execution, balance ideas and character, emotion and ruthlessness. We also have an eye for more traditional tales told with excellence." Quarterly.

Needs fantasy (mythic, urban, historical, low, literary), horror (dark fantasy, futuristic, psychological, supernatural), science fiction (hard science/technological, soft/sociological). Special interests: slipstream, hyperfiction and poetry. Does not want fiction without a speculative element. Receives 160 mss/month. Accepts 3 mss/issue; 9-12 mss/year. Does not read February, May, August and November. Ms published within 12 months of acceptance. **Publishes 1-2 new writers/year.** Published Sarah Monette, Ruth Nestvold, Christopher Barzak, Nicole Kornher-Stace, Tobias Buckell, Yoon Ha Lee, and David Kopaska-Merkel. Length: 7,000 words (max). Average length: 4,000 words. Publishes short shorts. Average length of short shorts: 1,000 words. Also publishes book reviews, poetry. *Requests only* to have a novel or collection reviewed should be sent to the publisher. Often comments on/critiques rejected mss.

How to Contact Send complete ms with cover letter. Accepts submissions by e-mail only. Include estimated word count. Responds to queries in 1 week. Responds to mss in 4 weeks. Guidelines available on website.

Payment/Terms Writers receive 3¢ per word, max of $40. Pays on acceptance. Acquires electronic rights. Publication is copyrighted.

Tips "Beyond the basics of formatting the fiction as per our guidelines, good writing and intriguing characters and plot, where the writer brings depth to the tale, make a manuscript stand out. We receive a number of submissions which showcase good writing, but lack the details that make them spring to life for us. Visit our website and read some of our fiction to see if we're a good fit. Read our submission guidelines carefully and use rtf formatting as requested. We're far more interested in your story than your cover letter, so spend your time polishing that."

MAD HATTERS' REVIEW: EDGY AND ENLIGHTENED ART, LITERATURE AND MUSIC IN THE AGE OF DEMENTIA

E-mail: madhattersreview@gmail.com. Website: www.madhattersreview.com. Online magazine. "*Mad Hatters' Review* is a socially aware/progressive, multi-media/literary journal, featuring original works of fiction, flash fiction, poetry, creative/literary nonfiction, whatnots, drama, collages, audios, book reviews, columns, contests and more. We also feature cartoons and comic strips, including the 'The Perils of Patriotic Polly' and 'Coconuts.' All of our contributing authors' writings are accompanied by original art created specifically for the material, as well as original, custom made music or recitations by authors. We are proud of our spectacular featured artists' galleries, as well as our mini-movies, parodies, and featured foreign sections. Our staff musicians and visual artists are wonderful. Webdelsol took us on board (the first and only multimedia) in 2006 and hosts our site." Semiannual. Member CLMP.

- *Mad Hatters' Review* has received an Artistry Award from Sixty Plus Design, 2006-7 Web Design Award from Invision Graphics, and a Gold Medal Award of Excellence for 2006-7 from ArtSpace2000.com.

Needs Inventive works, mixed media, translations, humor, literary prose and poetry that demonstrate a unique, unconventional, intellectual, sophisticated and emotional perspective on the world and a delight in craft. Does not want mainstream prose/story that doesn't exhibit a love of language and a sophisticated mentality. No religious or inspirational writings, confessionals, boys sowing oats, sentimental and coming of age stories. Accepts 3-6 mss/issue. Submissions are open briefly for each issue: check guidelines periodically for dates or subscribe free to newsletter. Ms published 5-6 months after acceptance. **Publishes 1 new writer/year.** Published Alastair Gray, Kass Fleisher, Vanessa Place, Harold Jaffe, Andrei Codrescu, Sheila Murphy, Simon Perchik, Terese Svoboda, Niels Hav, Martin, Nakell, and Juan Jose Millas (translated from the Spanish). Length: 3,000 words (max). Average length of fictions: 1,500-2,500 words. Publishes short shorts. Average length of short shorts: 500-800 words. Also publishes literary essays, literary criticism, book reviews, and interviews. Send review queries to madhattersreview@gmail.com. Sometimes comments on/critiques rejected mss.

How to Contact Accepts submissions by e-mail only. Include estimated word count, brief bio. Now has a submission form for most issues. Responds to queries in 1 week. Responds to mss in 1-6 weeks. Considers simultaneous submissions. Guidelines available on website. **Payment/Terms** Acquires first rights. Sends galleys to author. "We offer contests in most issues."
Tips "Imagination, skill with and appreciation of language, inventivesness, rhythm, sense of humor/irony/satire and compelling style make a manuscript stand out. Read the magazine. Don't necessarily follow the rules you've been taught in the usual MFA program or workshop."

MCSWEENEY'S

849 Valencia Street, San Francisco CA 94110. E-mail: printsubmissions@mcsweeneys.net; websubmissions@mcsweeneys.net. Website: www.mcsweeneys.net. Online literary journal. "Timothy McSweeney's Internet Tendency is an offshoot of Timothy McSweeney's Quarterly Concern, a journal created by nervous people in relative obscurity, and published four times a year." Daily.
Needs Literate humor. Sometimes comments on rejected mss.
How to Contact Accepts submissions by e-mail. "For submissions to the website, paste the entire piece into the body of an e-mail. Absolute length limit of 1,500 words, with a preference for pieces significantly shorter (700-1,000 words)." Sample copy online. Writer's guidelines online.
Tips "Do not submit your work to both the print submissions address and the Web submissions address, as seemingly hundreds of writers have been doing lately. If you submit a piece of writing intended for the magazine to the Web submissions address, you will confuse us, and if you confuse us, we will accidentally delete your work without reading it, and then we will laugh and never give it another moment's thought, and sleep the carefree sleep of young children. This is very, very serious."

◘ ◙ MICROHORROR: SHORT STORIES. ENDLESS NIGHTMARES

P.O. Box 32259, Pikesville MD 21282-2259. (443) 670-6133. E-mail: microhorror@gmail.com. Website: www.microhorror.com. **Contact:** Nathan Rosen, editor. Online magazine. "MicroHorror is not a magazine in the traditional sense. Instead, it is a free online archive for short-short horror fiction. With a strict limit of 666 words, MicroHorror showcases the power of the short-short horror to convey great emotional impact in only a few brief paragraphs." Estab. 2006.

- Golden Horror Award from Horrorfind.com in 2007.

Needs Horror (dark fantasy, futuristic, psychological, supernatural), young adult/teen (horror). Receives 25 mss/month. Accepts 300 mss/year. Ms published 1-3 days after acceptance. **Publishes 50 new writers/year.** Published Chris Allinotte, Kevin G. Bufton, Santiago Eximeno, Oonah V Joslin, Brian Laing, Caroline Robinson, and Chris Yodice. Length: 666 words (max). Publishes short shorts. Average length of short shorts: 500 words. Often comments on/critiques rejected mss.
How to Contact Send complete ms with cover letter. Accepts submissions by e-mail. Include estimated word count, brief bio. Responds to queries in 1 week. Responds to mss in 1 week. Send either SASE (or IRC) for return of ms or disposable copy of ms and #10 SASE for reply only. Considers simultaneous submissions, previously published submissions, multiple submissions. Guidelines available on website.
Payment/Terms Acquires one-time rights. Publication is copyrighted.
Tips "This is horror. Scare me. Make shivers run down my spine. Make me afraid to look behind the shower curtain. Pack the biggest punch you can into a few well chosen sentences. Read all the horror you can, and figure out what makes it scary. Trim away all the excess trappngs until you get right to the core, and use what you find."

◘ MIDNIGHT TIMES

E-mail: editor@midnighttimes.com. Website: www.midnighttimes.com. Midnight Times is an online literary magazine dedicated to publishing quality poetry and fiction by both previously

unpublished as well as published writers. The primary theme is darkness, but this doesn't necessarily mean evil. There can be a light at the end of the tunnel. Quarterly. Estab. 2003.
Needs Fantasy (sword and sorcery), horror (dark fantasy, futuristic, psychological, supernatural), literary, mainstream, psychic/supernatural/occult, science fiction, vampires. No pornography. Accepts 5-9 mss/issue; 20-36 mss/year. Publishes ms 3-9 months after acceptance. **Publishes many new writers/year. Length:** Short fiction from 1,000-10,000 words maximum. Vignettes from 500-1,000 words. Poetry from 1 to 5 pages max. Average length: 4,000 words. Publishes short shorts. Sometimes comments on rejected mss.
How to Contact Send complete ms. Submissions accepted by e-mail only. Responds in 2 months to mss. Accepts simultaneous, multiple submissions and reprints. Writer's guidelines on website.
Payment/Terms No payment. Acquires one-time, electronic rights.
Tips "Please read the submission guidelines on MidnightTimes.com before submitting your work! Thanks."

◪ MIDWAY JOURNAL

P.O. Box 14499, St. Paul MN 55114. (612) 825-4811. E-mail: editors@midwayjournal.com. Website: www.midwayjournal.com. **Contact:** Ralph Pennel, fiction editor. Online magazine. "Midway Journal accepts submissions of aesthetically ambitious work that occupies the realms between the experimental and trasitional. Midway, or its position is midway, is a place of boundary crossing, where work complicates and even questions the boundaries between forms, binaries and genres." Bimonthly. Member CLMP.
Needs Comics/graphic novels, ethnic/multicultural (general), experimental, feminist, gay, historical (general), humor/satire, lesbian, literary, science fiction (soft/sociological), translations. Does not want new age, young adult/teen, children/juvenile or erotica. "Writers should visit current and back issues to see what we have or have not published in the past." Receives 30 mss/month. Accepts 3-4 mss/issue; 18-24 mss/year. Does not read June 1-Nov 30. Ms published 4-12 months after acceptance. Agented fiction 1%. **Publishes 2-5 new writers/year.** Published Steve Almond, Alden Jones, Scott T. Hutchinson, and Marjorie Maddox. Length: 250-25,000 words. Average length: 3,000 words. Publishes short shorts. Average length of short shorts: 600 words. Also publishes literary essays, poetry, and drama. Sometimes comments on/critiques rejected mss.
How to Contact Send complete ms with cover letter. Accepts international submissions by e-mail. Include estimated word count, brief bio, list of publications. Responds to queries in 1-2 weeks. Please see website for submission guidelines. Send either SASE (or IRC) for return of ms or disposable copy of ms and #10 SASE for reply only. Considers simultaneous submissions, previously published submissions. Guidelines available on website.
Payment/Terms Acquires one-time rights. Publication is copyrighted.
Tips "An interesting story with engaging writing, both in terms of style and voice, make a manuscript stand out. Round characters are a must. Writers who take chances either with content or with form grab an editor's immediate attention. Spend time with the words on the page. Spend time with the language. The language and voice are not vehicles, they, too, are tools."

☐ ◙ $ MINDFLIGHTS

Double-Edged Publishing, 9618 Misty Brook Cove, Cordova TX 38016. (901) 213-3768. E-mail: editor@mindflights.com. Website: http://www.Mindflights.com. **Contact:** Selena Thomason, Managing Editor. Magazine/E-zine. "Publishes science fiction, fantasy, and all genres of speculative fiction and poetry. We want work that is grounded in a Christian or Christian-friendly worldview, without being preachy. Please see our vision and guidelines page for details. MindFlights is the merging of two established magazines: The Sword Review and Dragons, Knights, & Angels." Monthly e-zine, annual print edition.
Needs Fantasy (space fantasy, sword and sorcery), science fiction (hard science/technological, soft/sociological), special interests: speculative fiction and poetry with Christian themes. Does not want to see work "that would be offensive to a Christian audience. Also, we are a family-friendly

market and thus do not want to see explicit sex, illicit drug use, gratuitous violence or excessive gore." Receives 30 mss/month. Accepts 4 mss/issue; 48 mss/year. Ms published 2 months after acceptance. **Publishes 6-12 new writers/year.** Length: 500-5,000 words. Average length: 3,000 words. Publishes short shorts. Average length of short shorts: 700 words. Also publishes poetry. Always comments on/critiques rejected mss.

How to Contact Send complete ms via online form. Include estimated word count. Responds to queries in 2 weeks. Responds to mss in 4 weeks. Considers previously published submissions, multiple submissions. Guidelines available on website.

Payment/Terms Writers receive 1/2¢ per word, $5 min and $25 max, 1 contributor's copy if selected for print edition. Additional copies $7.50. Pays on acceptance. Acquires first rights, first North American serial rights, one-time rights, electronic rights. Sends galleys to author. Publication is copyrighted. Occasional contests. "Details and entry process would be on our website when contest is announced."

Tips "We look for speculative fiction that entertains, enlightens, and uplifts. We also prefer work that is family-friendly and grounded in a Christian world-view. We especially seek work that successfully melds the speculative with Christian themes. Please read our guidelines and proof your work carefully. (It is helpful to also have someone else proof your work as writers often miss typos in their own work.) Please do not submit work that is clearly inappropriate for our magazine and/or is full of typos, misspellings, and grammar errors."

N ◪ ◎ $ MOUTH FULL OF BULLETS

P.O. Box 138, Mathews LA 70375. (985) 532-3186. E-mail: bjbourg@bjbourg.com. Website: www.mouthfullofbullets.com. **Contact:** BJ Bourg, Owner & Acquisitions Editor. Online magazine. "I'm dedicated to offering writers a place where they can showcase their writing talent to as wide an audience as possible. To that end, I provide both a print and an online edition of the magazine. All original works appear exclusively in the print publication for a three-month period. After the exclusivity period has lapsed, the original works are then archived in the online edition, offering exposure to a much larger reading audience. In order to reach as many readers as possible, I don't require that readers subscribe or sign up in order to read the online content, and I make it available for free. Mouth of Bullets was started by a mystery writer to help other mystery writers, and I'm dedicated to doing everything I can to promote their work—at no cost to them. I strive to publish the best short stories, flash fiction and poems from some of the best new and vetren voices in the business." Quarterly. Estab. 2006. Circ. 1,000+ hits per month. d

- A story published in MFOB was a finalist in the 2007 Deffinger Awards

Needs Children's/juvenile (mystery), mystery (amateur sleuth, cozy, police procedural, private eye/hard-boiled), religious (mystery/suspense), romance (suspense), young adult/teen (mystery/suspense). Does not want erotica or anything that does not contain a crime. Receives 20-50 mss/month. Accepts 20-25 mss/issue; 85-90 mss/year. Does not read January, April, July and October. Ms published 6 months after acceptance. **Publishes 12 new writers/year.** Published Jillian Berg, John M. Floyd, Herschel Cozine, SF Johnston, Stephen D. Rogers, Anita Page and Kimberly Brown. Length: 1,000-3,000 words. Average length: 2,000 words. Publishes short shorts. Average length of short shorts: 700 words. Also publishes book reviews, poetry. Send review copies to Kevin R. Tipple (kevin_tipple@att.net). Rarely comments on/critiques rejected mss.

How to Contact Send complete ms with cover letter. Accepts submissions by e-mail. Include estimated word count, brief bio, list of publications, mailing address, email address. Responds to mss in 1-3 months. Considers previously published submissions. Guidelines available on website. Sample copy for $6 (US funds only, check or money order).

Payment/Terms Writers receive $3-20. Pays on publication. Acquires first North American serial rights and anthology rights. Publication is copyrighted.

Tips "I want stories that feature believable characters who speak naturally, realistic situations that bleed conflict and surprise endings that stay with me long after I reach the final period. I love to be surprised. I hate it when I can figure out the ending halfway through a story. Now, while I love to be surprised, the twist at the end has to be plausible. Read and adhere to submission guidelines. I'm surprised by the number of writers who fail to follow this elementary rule of writing. Check your work for errors or omissions. Everyone's entitled to a few mistakes, but too many detract from the story. Be courteous. Above all else, surprise me!"

NECROLOGY SHORTS: TALES OF MACABRE AND HORROR

Isis International, P.O. Box 510232, Saint Louis MO 63151. E-mail: editor@necrologyshorts.com; submit@necrologyshorts.com. Website: www.necrologyshorts.com. **Contact:** John Ferguson, Editor. Circulation: 10,000. Consumer publication published online daily and through Amazon Kindle. "We will also be publishing an annual collection for each year in print, e-book reader, and Adobe PDF format. Our main genre is suspense horror similar to H.P. Lovecraft and/or Robert E. Howard. We also publish science fiction and fantasy. We would love to see work continuing the Cthulhu Mythos, but we accept all horror."

Needs "*Necrology Shorts* is an online publication which publishes fiction, articles, cartoons, artwork, and poetry daily. Embracing the internet, e-book readers, and new technology, we aim to go beyond the long time standard of a regular publication to bringing our readers a daily flow of entertainment."

How to Contact Submit complete ms. by e-mail to submit@necrologyshorts.com. Buys 1,000 mss/year. Responds in 1 month. Guidelines on website. We review submissions in the order we receive them. Please allow 1-2 weeks for us to review your work. If your submission passes review it will be added to Necrology Shorts within 72 hours. You will be notified when your submission is posted. If your submission does not pass review we will notify you of any problems and reasons. Submission can be resubmitted once it is corrected.

Tips "*Necrology Shorts* is looking to break out of the traditional publication types to use the internet, e-book readers, and other technology. We not only publish works of authors and artists, we let them use their published works to brand themselves and further their profits of their hard work. We love to see traditional short fiction and artwork, but we also look forward to those that go beyond that to create multimedia works. The best way to get to us is to let your creative side run wild and not send us the typical fare. Don't forget that we publish horror, sci-fi, and fantasy. We expect deranged, warped, twisted, strange, sadistic, and things that question sanity and reality."

NUVEIN ONLINE

(626)401-3466. E-mail: editor@nuvein.com. Website: www.nuvein.com. Online magazine published by the Nuvein Foundation for Literature and the Arts. "We are open to short fiction, poetry and essays that explore topics divergent from the mainstream. Our vision is to provide a forum for new and experienced voices rarely heard in our global community."

- *Nuvein Online* has received the Visionary Media Award.

Needs Fiction, poetry, plays, movie/theatre reviews/articles and art. Wants more "experimental fiction, ethnic works, and pieces dealing with the exploration of gender and sexuality, as well as works dealing with the clash of cultures." **Publishes 20 new writers/year.** Recently published work by J. Knight, Paul A. Toth, Rick Austin, Robert Levin and Scott Essman, as well as interviews with film directors Guillermo Del Toro, Alejandro Gonzalez Iñarritu and Frank Darabont.

How to Contact Query. Accepts submissions by e-mail. Send work as attachment. Sample copy online.

Tips "Read over each submission before sending it, and if you, as the writer, find the piece irresistable, e-mail it to us immediately!"

$ ON THE PREMISES: A GOOD PLACE TO START

On The Premises, LLC, 4323 Gingham Court, Alexandria, VA 22310. (202)262-2168. E-mail: questions@onthepremises.com. Website: www.OnThePremises.com. **Contact:** Tarl Roger Kudrick or Bethany Granger, Co-Publishers. E-zine. "Stories published in On the Premises are winning entries in contests that are held every four months. Each contest challenges writers to produce a great story based on a broad premise that our editors supply as part of the contest. On the Premises aims to promote newer and/or relatively unknown writers who can write what we feel are creative, compelling stories told in effective, uncluttered and evocative prose. Entrants pay no fees, and winners recieve cash prizes in addition to publication." Triannual. Estab. 2007. Member Small Press Promotions.

Needs Adventure, ethnic/multicultural (general), experimental, family saga, fantasy, feminist, historical (general), horror, humor/satire, literary, mainstream, military/war, mystery, new age, psychic/supernatural/occult, romance, science fiction, thriller/espionage, western. Does not want young adult fiction, children's fiction, x-rated fiction. "In general, we don't like stories that were written solely to make a social or political point, especialy if the story seems to assume that no intelligent person could possibly disagree with the author. Save the idealogy for editorial and opinion pieces, please. But above all, we NEVER EVER want to see stories that do not use the contest premise! Use the premise, and make it 'clear' and 'obvious' that you are using the premise." Themes are announced the day each contest is launched. List of past and current premises available on website. Receives 10-40 mss/month. Accepts 3-6 mss/issue; 9-18 mss/year. Does not read February, June and October. Ms published a month or less after acceptance. **Publishes 3-6 new writers/year.** Published A'llyn Ettien, Cory Cramer, Mark Tullius, Michael Van Ornum, Ken Liu and K. Stodard Hayes. Length: 1000 words (min)-5000 words (max). Average length: 3500 words. Sometimes comments on/critiques rejected mss.

How to Contact Send complete ms with cover letter."We are a contest-based magazine and we strive to judge all entries 'blindly.' We request that an author's name and contact information be in the body of the email." Accepts submissions by e-mail only. Responds to mss in 2 weeks after contest deadline. Guidelines available on website.

Payment/Terms Writers receive $25-140. Pays on acceptance. Acquires electronic rights. Sends galleys to author. Publication is copyrighted.

Tips "Make sure you use the premise, not just interpret it. If the premise is 'must contain a real live dog,' then think of a creative, compelling way to use a real dog. Revise you draft, then revise again and again. Remember, we judge blindly, so craftmanship and creativety matter, not how well known you are."

THE ORACULAR TREE

The Oracular Tree, 29 Hillyard St., Chatham ON N7L 3E1 Canada. E-mail: editor@oraculartree.com. Website: www.oraculartree.com. **Contact:** Jeff Beardwood, editor. E-zine specializing in practical ideas for transforming our lives. "The stories we tell ourselves and each other predict the outcome of our lives. We can affect gradual social change by transforming our deeply rooted cultural stories. The genre is not as important as the message and the high quality of the writing. We accept stories, poems, articles and essays which will reach well-educated, open-minded readers around the world. We offer a forum for those who see a need for change, who want to add their voices to a growing search for positive alternatives." Monthly. Estab. 1997. Circ. 250,000 hits/month.

Needs Serial fiction, poetry, essays, novels and novel excerpts, visual art, short fiction, news. "We'll look at any genre that is well written and can examine a new cultural paradigm. No tired dogma, no greeting card poetry, please." Receives 20-30 unsolicited mss/month. Accepts 80-100 mss/year. Publishes ms 3 months after acceptance. **Publishes 20-30 new writers/year.** Recently published work by Elisha Porat, Lyn Lyfshin, Rattan Mann, and Dr. Elaine Hatfield. Publishes short shorts. Also publishes literary essays, poetry. Often comments on rejected mss.

How to Contact Send complete ms. Accepts submissions by e-mail. Responds in 2 weeks to queries; 2 months to mss. Accepts simultaneous, multiple submissions and reprints. Sample copy online. Writer's guidelines online.

Payment/Terms Author retains copyright; one-time archive posting.

Tips "The underlying idea must be clearly expressed. The language should be appropriate to the tale, using creative license and an awareness of rhythm. We look for a juxtaposition of ideas that creates resonance in the mind and heart of the reader. Write from your honest voice. Trust your writing to unfold."

OUTER ART

The University of New Mexico, 200 College Road, Gallup NM 87301. (505) 863-7647. Fax: (505) 863-7532. E-mail: smarand@unm.edu. Website: www.gallup.unm.edu/~smarandache/a/outer-art.htm. **Contact:** Florentin Smarandache, editor. E-zine. Annual. Estab. 2000.

Needs Experimental, literary, outer-art. Publishes ms 1 month after acceptance. Publishes short shorts. Also publishes literary essays, literary criticism.

How to Contact Accepts submissions by e-mail. Send SASE (or IRC) for return of the ms. Responds in 1 month to mss. Accepts simultaneous submissions and reprints. Writer's guidelines online.

OXFORD MAGAZINE

Bachelor Hall, Miami University, Oxford OH 45056. (513) 529-1279. E-mail: oxmagfictioneditor@muohio.edu. Website: www.oxfordmagazine.org. **Contact:** Fiction editor. Annual. Estab. 1985. Circ. 1,000.

- *Oxford* has been awarded two Pushcart Prizes.

Needs Wants quality fiction and prose, genre is not an issue but nothing sentimental. Receives 150 unsolicited mss/month. **Publishes some new writers/year.** Recently published work by Stephen Dixon, Andre Dubus and Stuart Dybek. Publishes short shorts. Also publishes poetry.

How to Contact Responds in 2 months, depending upon time of submissions; mss received after December 31 will be returned. Accepts simultaneous submissions if notified. Sample copy for $5.

Payment/Terms Acquires one-time rights.

Tips "*Oxford Magazine* accepts fiction, poetry, and essays (this last genre is a catch-all, much like the space under your couch cushions, and includes creative nonfiction, critical work exploring writing, and the like). Appearing once a year, *OxMag* is a Web-based journal that acquires first North American serial rights, one-time anthology rights and online serial rights. Simultaneous submissions are okay if you would kindly let us know if and when someone beats us to the punch."

PAPERPLATES

A magazine for fifty readers, 19 Kenwood Ave., Toronto ON M6C 2R8 Canada. (416)651-2551. E-mail: magazine@paperplates.org. Website: www.paperplates.org. **Contact:** Bethany Gibson, fiction editor. Electronic magazine. Quarterly. Estab. 1990.

Needs Condensed novels, ethnic/multicultural, feminist, gay, lesbian, literary, mainstream, translations. "No science fiction, fantasy or horror." Receives 12 unsolicited mss/month. Accepts 2-3 mss/issue; 6-9 mss/year. Publishes ms 6-8 months after acceptance. Recently published work by Lyn Fox, David Bezmozgis, Fraser Sutherland and Tim Conley. Length: 1,500-3,500 words; average length: 3,000 words. Publishes short shorts. Also publishes literary essays, literary criticism, poetry.

How to Contact Accepts submissions by e-mail and land mail. Responds in 6 weeks to queries; 6 months to mss. Accepts simultaneous submissions. Sample copy online. Writer's guidelines online.

Payment/Terms No payment. Acquires first North American serial rights.

THE PAUMANOK REVIEW

E-mail: submissions@paumanokreview.com. Website: www.paumanokreview.com. **Contact:** Katherine Arline, editor. Online literary magazine. "TPR is dedicated to publishing and promoting the best in world art and literature." Quarterly. Estab. 2000.

- J.P. Maney's *Western Exposures* was selected for inclusion in the *E2INK Best of the Web Anthology*.

Needs Mainstream, narrative, experimental, historical, mystery, horror, western, science fiction, slice-of-life vignette, serial, novel excerpt. Receives 100 unsolicited mss/month. Accepts 6-8 mss/issue; 24-32 mss/year. Publishes ms 6 weeks after acceptance. **Publishes 4 new writers/year.** Recently published work by Patty Friedman, Elisha Porat, Barry Spacks and Walt McDonald. Length: 1,000-6,000 words; average length: 3,000 words. Publishes short shorts. Also publishes literary essays, poetry. Usually comments on rejected mss.

How to Contact Send complete ms as attachment (Word, RTF, HTML, TXT) or pasted in body of e-mail. Include estimated word count, brief bio, two ways to contact you, list of publications, and how you discovered *TPR*. Responds in 1 week to queries; 1 month to mss. Accepts simultaneous submissions and reprints. No multiple submissions. Sample copy online. Writer's guidelines online.

Payment/Terms Acquires one-time, anthology rights. Galleys offered in HTML or PDF format.

Tips "Though this is an English-language publication, it is not US-or UK-centric. Please submit accordingly. *TPR* is a publication of Wind River Press, which also publishes *Critique* magazine and select print and electronic books."d

$ THE PEDESTAL MAGAZINE

Pedestal Enterprises, Inc., 6815 Honors Court, Charlotte NC 28210. (704)643-0244. E-mail: pedmagazine@carolina.rr.com. Website: www.thepedestalmagazine.com. **Contact:** Nathan Leslie, editor; John Amen, editor-in-chief. Online literary magazine/journal. "We publish poetry, fiction, reviews and interviews. We are committed to the individual voice and publish an eclectic mix of high-quality work." Bimonthly. Member CLMP.

Needs Adventure, ethnic/multicultural, experimental, family saga, fantasy, feminist, gay, glitz, historical, horror, humor/satire, lesbian, literary, mainstream, military/war, mystery, new age, psychic/supernatural/occult, romance, science fiction, thriller/espionage. Receives 100-150 mss/month. Accepts 3-5 mss/issue; 18-24 mss/year. Closed to submissions at the following times: January, March, May, July, September, November: from the 12th-19th; February, April, June, August, October, December: from the 14th-28th. Ms published 1-3 weeks after acceptance. **Publishes 1-2 new writers/year.** Published Grant Tracy, Mary Grabar, Karen Heuler, James Scott Iredell, Don Shea, Mary Carroll-Hackett, R.T. Smith and Richard Peabody. Publishes short shorts. Also publishes book reviews, poetry. Send review query to pedmagazine@carolina.rr.com. Rarely comments on/critiques rejected mss.

How to Contact Submit via the online form provided on the website. Include brief bio, list of publications. Responds to queries in 2-3 days. Responds to mss in 4-6 weeks. Considers simultaneous submissions, multiple submissions. Guidelines available on website.

Payment/Terms Writers receive 8¢/word. Pays on publication. Acquires first rights. Sends galleys to author. Publication is copyrighted.

Tips "Strong characterization, imagery and a distinct voice are always important. Also, we always look for startling or unusual themes and content. Writers we publish should be willing to push their readers and themselves into unfamiliar terrain. We read too many generic stories that read like bad television. Read the magazine to get a sense of what we publish. Polish your work as much as possible before submitting. Be professional."

PERSIMMON TREE: MAGAZINE OF THE ARTS BY WOMEN OVER SIXTY

1534 Campus Drive, Berkeley CA 94708. E-mail: editor@persimmontree.org. Website: www.persimmontree.org. **Contact:** Nan Gefen, editor. Online magazine. "Persimmon Tree is a showcase for the talent and creativity of women over sixty, but the magazine appeals to readers of all ages." Quarterly. Estab. 2007. Member Council of Literary Magazines.

Needs ethnic/multicultural (general), experimental, family saga, feminist, gay, historical (general), humor/satire, lesbian, literary, mainstream. Receives 80-100 mss/month. Accepts 2-3 mss/issue; 8-12 mss/year. Ms published 3-6 months after acceptance. **Publishes 2-3 new writers/year.** Published Grace Paley, Paula Gunn Allen, Daphne Muse, Carole Rosenthal and Sandy Boucher.

Length: 1200 words (min)-3000 words (max). Average length: 2000 words. Publishes short shorts. Also publishes literary essays, literary criticism, book reviews, poetry.

How to Contact Send complete ms with cover letter. Accepts submissions by e-mail only. Include estimated word count, brief bio, list of publications. Responds to mss in 3-6 months. Considers simultaneous submissions, multiple submissions. Guidelines available on website.

Payment/Terms Acquires one-time rights. Sends galleys to author. Publication is copyrighted.

Tips "High quality of writing, an interesting or unique point of view, make a manuscript stand out. Make it clear that you're familiar with the magazine. Tell us why the piece would work for our audience."

$ PSEUDOPOD, THE SOUND OF HORROR

Escape Artists, Inc., PO Box 965609, Marietta GA 30066. Fax: (866)373-8739. E-mail: editor@pseudopod.org. Website: http://pseudopod.org. Online audio magazine. 25-40 min weekly episode, 5-10 min for sporadic specials like flash fiction or movie/book reviews. "Pseudopod is a genre magazine in audio form. We're looking for horror: dark, weird fiction. We run the spectrum from grim realism or magic-realism to blatantly supernatural dark fantasy. We publish highly literary stories reminiscent of Poe or Lovecraft, as well as vulgar, innovative, and/or shock-value-focused pulp fiction. We don't split hairs about genre definitions, and we don't have any hard and fast taboos about what kind of content can appear in our stories. Originality demands that you're better off avoiding vampires, zombies, and other recognizable horror tropes unless you have put a very original spin on them. (Ghosts are currently somewhat more smiled upon, mainly because they haven't settled into such predictably canonical treatment; you don't know what a ghost can do until the author establishes it, so fear of the unknown is intact - which is the real lesson here.) What matters most is just that the stories are dark and entertaining." Weekly. Circ. 5,500.

- Episode 27 was a finalist nominee for the 2007 Parsec (podcasting) award for Best SF Story (short form)

Needs Horror (dark fantasy, futuristic, psychological, supernatural, sentimental, literary, erotic, splatterpunk, romantic, humorours). Does not want archetypical vampire, zombie, or werewolf fiction. Receives 100 mss/month. Accepts 1 mss/issue; 70 mss/year. Manuscript published 1 month after acceptance. **Publishes 20 new writers/year.** Published Joel Arnold, Kevin J. Anderson, Richard Dansky, Scott Sigler, Paul Jessup, Nicholas Ozment, and Stephen Gaskell. Length: 2,000-6,000 words. Average length: 3,000 words. Publishes short shorts. Average length of short shorts: 800 words. Often comments on/critiques rejected manuscripts.

How to Contact Send complete ms with cover letter. Accepts submissions by e-mail. Include estimated word count, brief bio, brief list of publications. Responds to queries in 2 weeks. Responds to mss in 2 months. Considers simultaneous submissions, previously published submissions. Sample copy, guidelines available on website.

Payment/Terms Writers receive $20 over 2,000 words, $100 over 2,000 words. Pays on acceptance.

Tips "Since we're an audio magazine, our audience can't skim past the boring parts, so stories with beautiful language at the expense of plot don't translate well. We're looking for fiction with strong pacing, well-defined characters, engaging dialogue, and clear action. It can be beautiful too, if you've got all those other bases covered."

$ RAVING DOVE

E-mail: editor@ravingdove.org. Website: www.ravingdove.org. Online literary magazine. "Raving Dove publishes writing, poetry, and art with universal, anti-violence, anti-hate, human rights, and social justice themes. We share sentiments that oppose physical and psychological violence in all its forms, including war, discrimination against sexual orientation, and every shade of bigotry." Quarterly.

Needs Literary, mainstream. "*Raving Dove* is not a political publication. Material for or against one specific person or entity will not be considered, fictitious or otherwise." Ms published up to 3

months after acceptance. Length: 2,000 words (max). Also publishes poetry.
How to Contact Accepts submissions by e-mail only. Include brief bio, submission genre, i.e., fiction, nonfiction, poetry, etc., in the e-mail subject line. Responds to mss in 3 months. Considers simultaneous submissions. Guidelines available on website.
Payment/Terms Not currently a paying market. (Check website for current information.) Acquires one-time North American and Internet serial rights, exclusive for the duration of the edition in which the work appears (3 months).

REALPOETIK

E-mail: salasin@scn.org. Website: RealPoetik.blogspot.com. **Contact:** Fiction Editor. "We publish the new, lively, exciting and unexpected in vernacular English. Any vernacular will do." Weekly. Estab. 1993.
Needs "We do not want to see anything that fits neatly into categories. We subvert categories." Publishes ms 2-4 months after acceptance. **Publishes 20-30 new writers/year.** Average length: 250-500 words. Publishes short shorts. Also publishes literary essays, literary criticism, poetry. Sometimes comments on rejected mss.
How to Contact Query with or without published clips or send complete ms. Accepts submissions by e-mail. Responds in 1 month to queries. Sample copy online.
Payment/Terms Acquires one-time rights. Sponsors awards/contests.
Tips "Be different but interesting. Humor and consciousness are always helpful. Write short. We're a post-modern e-zine."

RESIDENTIAL ALIENS

ResAliens Press, 7412 E Brookview Cir., Wichita KS 67226. E-mail: resaliens@gmail.com. Website: www.resaliens.com. **Contact:** Lyn Perry, founding editor. Online magazine/E-zine. "Because reading and writing speculative fiction is a strong interest of mine, I thought I'd contribute to the genre of faith-informed spec fic by offering other writers and readers of science fiction, fantasy, spiritual and supernatural thrillers a quality venue in which to share their passion. You could say ResAliens is speculative fiction with a spiritual thread." Monthly.
Needs Fantasy (space fantasy, sword and sorcery), horror (supernatural), science fiction (soft/sociological), thriller. Does not want horror, gore, erotica. Will publish another Sci-Fi/Fantasy anthology. List of upcoming themes available for SASE, on website. Receives 20 mss/month. Accepts 5-6 mss/issue; 65-75 mss/year. Ms published 1-2 months after acceptance. **Publishes 25 new writers/year.**Published George L. Duncan (author of novel *A Cold and Distant Memory*), Patrick G. Cox (author of novel *Out of Time*), Merrie Destefano (editor of *Victorian Homes Magazine*), Brandon Barr (co-author of upcoming novel *When the Sky Fell*), Ilaria Dal Brun (short story "Foul Breath"), Alex Moisi (short story "Up or Down"), Curtis Schweitzer (short story "Colossus"), and Glyn Shull (short story "Demonic Intent"). Length: 500-5,000 words. Average length: 3,500 words. Publishes short shorts. Average length of short shorts: 900 words. Will take serial novellas of 2-5 installments (up to 20,000 words). Also publishes book reviews. Send review copies to resaliens@gmail.com. Often comments on/critiques rejected mss.
How to Contact Send complete ms with cover letter via e-mail. Include estimated word count, brief bio. Responds to queries in 2-5 days; to mss in 1-2 weeks. Considers simultaneous submissions, previously published submissions, multiple submissions. Sample copy and guidelines available on website.
Payment/Terms Writers receive PDF file as their contributor's copy. Acquires one-time rights, electronic rights, 6 month archive rights. Sends galleys to author. Publication is copyrighted. "Occasionally sponsors contests."
Tips "We want stories that read well and move quickly. We enjoy all sorts of speculative fiction, and 'tried and true' forms and themes are fine as long as the author has a slightly different take or a fresh perspective on a topic. For example, time machine stories are great—how is yours unique or interesting?"

R-KV-R-Y, A QUARTERLY LITERARY JOURNAL

90 Meetings in 90 Days Press, 499 North Canon Dr., Suite 400, Beverly Hills CA 90210. (323)217-5162. Fax: (323)852-1535. E-mail: victoriapynchon@gmail.com. Website: rkvry.com. **Contact:** Victoria Pynchon, editor-in-chief. Online magazine. 100 Web pages. Contains illustrations. Includes photographs. "R-KV-R-Y publishes half a dozen short stories of high literary quality every quarter. We publish fiction that varies widely in style. We prefer stories of character development, psychological penetration, and lyricism, without sentimentality or purple prose. We ask that all submissions address issues related to recovery from any type of physical, psychological, or cultural loss, dislocation or oppression. We include but do not limit ourselves to issues of substance abuse. We do not publish the standard 'what it was like, what happened and what it is like now' recovery narrative. Works published by R-KV-R-Y embrace almost every area of adult interest related to recovery: literary affairs, history, folklore, fiction, poetry, literary criticism, art, music, and the theatre. Material should be presented in a fashion suited to a quarterly that is neither journalistic nor academic. We welcome academic articles from varying fields. We encourage our academic contributors to free themselves from the constraints imposed by academic journals, letting their knowledge, wisdom, and experience rock and roll on these pages. Our intended audience is people of discriminating taste, original ideas, heart, and love of narrative and language." Quarterly. Estab. 2004. Circ. 15,000 quarterly readers.

Needs Literary. List of upcoming themes available on website. Receives 10 mss/month. Accepts 5 mss/issue; 20 mss/year. Manuscript published 2-3 months after acceptance. Agented fiction 10%. **Publishes 5-6 new writers/year.** Published Rita Coleman (debut fiction), Anne LaBorde (debut literary nonfiction), Richard Wirick, Joseph Mockus, Birute Serota, Zoe Kiethley, Lee Patton, Nathan Leslie, Kathleen Wakefield, Sherry Lynne Maze (debut). Length: 5,000 words (max). Average length: 2,000 words. Publishes short shorts. Average length of short shorts: 1,000 words. Also publishes literary essays, book reviews, poetry. Sometimes comments on/critiques rejected manuscripts.

How to Contact Send complete ms with cover letter. Accepts submissions by e-mail. Include brief bio, list of publications. Responds to queries in 2 weeks. Responds to mss in 1-3 months. Considers simultaneous submissions, previously published submissions. Guidelines available on website.

Payment/Terms Acquires electronic rights. Posts proof pages on site. Publication is copyrighted.

Tips "Wants strong focus on character development and lively writing style with strong voice. Read our present and former issues (archived online) as well as fiction found in such journals and magazines as *Granta, The New Yorker, Tri-Quarterly, The Atlantic, Harper's, Story*and similar sources of the highest quality fiction."

$ THE ROSE & THORN LITERARY E-ZINE

E-mail: BAQuinn@aol.com. Website: www.theroseandthornezine.com. **Contact:** Barbara Quinn, fiction editor, publisher, managing editor. E-zine specializing in literary works of fiction, nonfiction, poetry and essays. "We created this publication for readers and writers alike. We provide a forum for emerging and established voices. We blend contemporary writing with traditional prose and poetry in an effort to promote the literary arts." Quarterly. Circ. 120,000.

Needs Adventure, ethnic/multicultural, experimental, fantasy, historical, horror (dark fantasy, futuristic, psychological, supernatural), humor/satire, literary, mainstream, mystery/suspense, New Age, regional, religious/inspirational, romance (contemporary, futuristic/time travel, gothic, historical, regency, romantic suspense), science fiction, thriller/espionage, western. Receives "several hundred" unsolicited mss/month. Accepts 8-10 mss/issue; 40-50 mss/year. **Publishes many new writers/year.** Publishes short shorts. Also publishes literary essays, poetry. Sometimes comments on rejected mss.

How to Contact Query with or without published clips or send complete ms. Accepts submissions by e-mail. Include estimated word count, 150-word bio, list of publications and author's byline. Responds in 1 week to queries; 1 month to mss. Accepts simultaneous submissions and reprints. Sample copy free. Writer's guidelines online. Length: 2,000 word limit.

Payment/Terms Writer retains all rights. Sends galleys to author. Pays $5 for each piece published.
Tips "Clarity, control of the language, evocative stories that tug at the heart and make their mark on the reader long after it's been read. We look for uniqueness in voice, style and characterization. New twists on old themes are always welcome. Use all aspects of good writing in your stories, including dynamic characters, strong narrative voice and a riveting original plot. We have eclectic tastes, so go ahead and give us a shot. Read the publication and other quality literary journals so you'll see what we look for. Always check your spelling and grammar before submitting. Reread your submission with a critical eye and ask yourself, 'Does it evoke an emotional response? Have I completely captured my reader?' Check your submission for 'it' and 'was' and see if you can come up with a better way to express yourself. Be unique."

SLOW TRAINS LITERARY JOURNAL

E-mail: editor@slowtrains.com. Website: www.slowtrains.com.
Needs Literary. No romance, sci-fi, or other specific genre-writing. Receives 100+ unsolicited mss/month. Accepts 10-15 mss/issue; 40-50 mss/year. Publishes ms 3 months after acceptance. **Publishes 20- 40 new writers/year.** Length: 1,000-5,000 words; average length: 3,500 words. Publishes short shorts. Also publishes literary essays, poetry. Rarely comments on rejected mss.
How to Contact Accepts submissions by e-mail pasted into the body of the text. Responds in 2 months. Accepts simultaneous and reprints submissions. Sample copy online. Writer's guidelines online.
Payment/Terms Pays 2 contributor's copies. Acquires one-time, electronic rights with optional archiving.
Tips "The first page must be able to pull the reader in immediately. Use your own fresh, poetic, compelling voice. Center your story around some emotional truth, and be sure of what you're trying to say."

SNREVIEW

Starry Night Review—A Literary E-Zine, 197 Fairchild Ave., Fairfield CT 06825-4856. (203)366-5991. E-mail: editor@snreview.org. Website: www.snreview.org. **Contact:** Joseph Conlin, editor. E-zine and print edition specializing in literary short stories, essays and poetry. "We search for material that not only has strong characters and plot but also a devotion to imagery." Now available in a print edition. Quarterly.
Needs Literary, mainstream. Receives 200 unsolicited mss/month. Accepts 40+ mss/issue; 150 mss/year. Publishes ms 6 months after acceptance. **Publishes 50 new writers/year.** Recently published work by Frank X. Walker, Adrian Louis, Barbara Burkhardt, E. Lindsey Balkan, Marie Griffin and Jonathan Lerner. Length: 1,000-7,000 words; average length: 4,000 words. Also publishes literary essays, literary criticism, poetry.
How to Contact Accepts submissions by e-mail only. Copy and paste work into the body of the email. Don't send attachments. Include 100 word bio and list of publications. Responds in 7 months to mss. Accepts simultaneous submissions. Sample copy online. Writer's guidelines online. A printed edition of SNReview is now available from an on-demand printer.
Payment/Terms Acquires first electronic and print rights.

$ SPACEWESTERNS: THE E-ZINE OF THE SPACE WESTERN SUB-GENRE

P.O. Box 93, Parker Ford, PA 19457. (610) 410-7400. E-mail: submissions2018@spacewesterns.com. Website: www.spacewesterns.com. **Contact:** N.E. Lilly, Editor-in-chief. E-zine. "Aside from strictly short stories we also like to see stage plays, screen plays, comics, audio files of stories, short form videos and animation." Weekly. Estab. 2007.
Needs Adventure, comics/graphic novels, ethnic/multicultural, fantasy (space fantasy), horror (dark fantasy, futuristic, psychological, supernatural), humor/satire, mystery, science fiction (hard

science/technological, soft/sociological), western (frontier saga, traditional), but it *must be space western*, science fiction western. List of upcoming themes available on website. Receives 12 mss/month. Accepts 52 mss/year. Ms published within 6 months after acceptance. **Publishes 12 new writers/year.** Published Camille Alexa, Vonnie Winslow Crist, Jens Rushing, Amanda Spikol, Donald Jacob Uitvlugt, John M. Whalen, A.R. Yngve, Filamena Young. Length: 2,500-7,500 words. Average length: 4,000-5,000 words. Also publishes literary essays, literary criticism, book reviews, poetry. Send review copies to N. E. Lilly. Often comments on/critiques rejected mss.

How to Contact Send complete ms with cover letter. Accepts submissions by e-mail only. Include estimated word count. Responds to queries immediately. Responds to mss in 6 weeks. Considers previously published submissions, multiple submissions. Guidelines available on website.

Payment/Terms Writers receive 1¢ per word, $50 max. Pays on publication. Publication is copyrighted.

Tips "First of all, have a well-crafted manuscript (no spelling or grammar errors). Secondly, a good idea—many errors will be forgiven for a solid concept and fresh idea. Be yourself. Write what you love. Familiarize yourself with the scope of the Universe and astronomical concepts."

STILL CRAZY: AN ONLINE LITERARY MAGAZINE

(614)746-0859. E-mail: editor@crazylitmag.com. Website: www.crazylitmag.com. "*Still Crazy* publishes writing by people over age 50 and writing by people of any age if the topic is about people over 50. The editor is particularly interested in material that challenges the stereotypes of older people and that portrays older people's inner lives as rich and rewarding." Semiannual.

Needs Feminist. Special interests: seniors (over 50). "Does not want material that is too sentimental or inspirational, 'Geezer' humor, or anything too grim." Accepts 3-4 mss/issue; 6-8 mss/year. Manuscript published 6-12 months after acceptance. Length: 4,000 words (max) under 3,000 words more likely to be published. Publishes short shorts. Also publishes poetry and short nonfiction 1,500 words or less. Sometimes comments on/critiques rejected mss. Paper copies $9; downloads $3.

How to Contact Submit via e-mail form on website. Attach MS Word doc or cut and paste into text of email. Include estimated word count, brief bio, age of writer or "Over 50." Responds to mss in 3-5 months. Considers simultaneous submissions, previously published submissions (please indicate when and where), multiple submissions. Guidelines available on website.

Payment/Terms Acquires one-time rights. Publication is not copyrighted. Pays one contributor copy.

Tips Looking for "interesting characters and interesting situations that might interest readers of all ages. Humor and Lightness welcome."

STIRRING: A LITERARY COLLECTION

323 Oglewood Ave, Knoxville TN 37917. (607)765-6751. E-mail: eesmith81@gmail.com. Website: www.sundress.net/stirring/. **Contact:** Erin Elizabeth Smith, managing editor.

How to Contact For fiction and creative nonfiction, please send your submission as a Word or RTF document to Josh Webster at stirring.fiction@gmail.com. For all submissions, please include a brief biography in the body of the email.

STORY BYTES

E-mail: editor@storybytes.com. Website: www.storybytes.com. **Contact:** M. Stanley Bubien, editor. Electronic zine. "We are strictly an electronic publication, appearing on the Internet in three forms. First, the stories are sent to an electronic mailing list of readers. They also get placed on our website, both in PDF and HTML format."

Needs "Stories must be very short—having a length that is the power of 2, specifically: 2, 4, 8, 16, 32, etc." No sexually explicit material. "Would like to see more material dealing with religion—not necessarily 'inspirational' stories, but those that show the struggles of living a life of faith in a realistic manner." **Publishes 33% new writers/year.** Recently published work by Richard K.

Weems, Joseph Lerner, Lisa Cote and Thomas Sennet.

How to Contact Please query first. Query with or without published clips or send complete ms. Accepts submissions by e-mail. "I prefer plain text with story title, authorship and word count. Only accepts electronic submissions. See website for complete guidelines." Sample copy online. Writer's guidelines online.

Tips "In Story Bytes the very short stories themselves range in topic. Many explore a brief event—a vignette of something unusual, unique and at times something even commonplace. Some stories can be bizarre, while others quite lucid. Some are based on actual events, while others are entirely fictional. Try to develop conflict early on (in the first sentence if possible!), and illustrate or resolve this conflict through action rather than description. I believe we'll find an audience for electronic published works primarily in the short story realm."

STORYSOUTH

The Best From New South Writers, 5603B W. Friendly Ave., Suite 282, Greensboro NC 27410. E-mail: terry@storysouth.com. Website: www.storysouth.com. **Contact:** Terry Kennedy, editor. "*storySouth* is interested in fiction, creative nonfiction, and poetry by writers from the New South. The exact definition New South varies from person to person and we leave it up to the writer to define their own connection to the southern United States." Quarterly.

Needs Experimental, literary, regional (south), translations. Receives 70 unsolicited mss/month. Accepts 5 mss/issue; 20 mss/year. Publishes ms 1 month after acceptance. **Publishes 5-10 new writers/year.** Average length: 4,000 words. Publishes short shorts. Also publishes literary essays, literary criticism, poetry. Often comments on rejected mss.

How to Contact Send complete ms. Accepts online submissions only. Responds in 4 months to mss. No simultaneous submissions. Writer's guidelines online.

Payment/Terms Acquires one-time rights.

Tips "What really makes a story stand out is a strong voice and a sense of urgency—a need for the reader to keep reading the story and not put it down until it is finished."

$ STRANGE HORIZONS

Strange Horizons, Inc., P.O. Box 1693, Dubuque IA 52004-1693. E-mail: fiction@strangehorizons.com. Website: http://strangehorizons.com. **Contact:** Susan Groppi, Editor-in-Chief. Online magazine. "We're a science fiction magazine dedicated to showcasing new voices in the genre." Weekly. Estab. 2000.

Needs Fantasy (space fantasy, sword and sorcery), feminist, science fiction (hard science/technological, soft/sociological). Does not want horror; see website. Receives 300 mss/month. Accepts 48 or 50 mss/year. Does not read December. Ms published 2-4 months after acceptance. **Publishes 5-10 new writers/year.** Published Liz Williams, Charlie Anders, Elizabeth Bear, Carrie Vaughn, Benjamin Rosenbaum and Ruth Nestvold. Length: 2,000-8,000 words. Average length: 3,600 words. Publishes short shorts rarely. Also publishes literary essays, literary criticism, book reviews, poetry. Send review queries to reviews@strangehorizons.com. Rarely comments on/critiques rejected mss.

How to Contact Accepts submissions by e-mail. Responds to queries in 1 week. Responds to mss in 3 months. Guidelines available on website.

Payment/Terms Writers receive 5¢ per word. Pays on acceptance. Acquires first rights,.

$ THE SUMMERSET REVIEW

25 Summerset Dr., Smithtown NY 11787. E-mail: editor@summersetreview.org. Website: www.summersetreview.org. **Contact:** Joseph Levens, editor. Magazine: illustrations and photographs. "Our goal is simply to publish the highest quality literary fiction and essays intended for a general audience. This is a simple online literary journal of high quality material, so simple you can call it unique." Periodically releases print issues. Quarterly.

Needs Literary. No sci-fi, horror, or graphic erotica. Receives 150 unsolicited mss/month. Accepts

4 mss/issue; 18 mss/year. Publishes ms 2-3 months after acceptance. **Publishes 5-10 new writers/ year.** Length: 8,000 words; average length: 3,000 words. Publishes short shorts. Also publishes literary essays. Usually critiques on mss that were almost accepted.

How to Contact Send complete ms. Accepts submissions by e-mail. Responds in 1-2 weeks to queries; 4-12 weeks to mss. Accepts simultaneous and reprints submissions. Writer's guidelines online.

Payment/Terms Complimentary copy of back issue in print. Acquires no rights other than one-time publishing, although we request credit if first published in *The Summerset Review*. Sends galleys to author.

Tips "Style counts. We prefer innovative or at least very smooth, convincing voices. Even the dullest of premises or the complete lack of conflict make for an interesting story if it is told in the right voice and style. We like to find little, interesting facts and/or connections subtly sprinkled throughout the piece. Harsh language should be used only if/when necessary. If we are choosing between light and dark subjects, the light will usually win."

TERRAIN.ORG: A JOURNAL OF THE BUILT & NATURAL ENVIROMENTS

Terrain.org, P.O. Box 19161, Tucson AZ 19161. (520)241-7390. Website: www.terrain.org. **Contact:** Simmons Buntin, editor/publisher. "Terrain.org is searching for that interface-the integration-among the built and natural enviroments, that might be called the soul of place. The works contained within Terrain.org ultimately examine the physical realm around us, and how those enviroments influence us and each other physically, mentally, emotionally and spiritually." Semiannual.

- PLANetizen Top 50 Website 2002 & 2003.

Needs Adventure, ethnic/multicultural, experimental, family saga, fantasy, feminist, historical, horror, humor/satire, literary, mainstream, military/war, mystery, psychic/supernatural/occult, science fiction, thriller/espionage, translations, western. Special interests: enviromental. Does not want erotica. All issues are theme-based. List of upcoming themes available on website. Receives 25 mss/month. Accepts 3-5 mss/issue; 6-10 mss/year. Does not read August 1-September 30 and February 1-March 30. Manuscript published five weeks to 18 months after acceptance. Agented fiction 5%. **Publishes 1-3 new writers/year.** Published Al Sim, Jacob MacAurthur Mooney, T.R. Healy, Deborah Fries, Andrew Wingfield, Martin Ott, Scott Spires and Tiel Aisha Ansari. Length: 1,000-8,000 words. Average length: 5,000 words. Publishes short shorts. Average length of short shorts: 750 words. Also publishes literary essays, literary criticism, book reviews, poetry, articles, and artwork. Send review copies to Simmon Buntin. Sometimes comments on/critiques rejected mss.

How to Contact Send complete ms with cover letter. Accepts submissions online@ http://sub.terrain.org. Include brief bio. Responds to queries in 2 weeks. Responds to mss in 4-8 weeks. Considers simultaneous submissions, previously published submissions. Guidelines available on website.

Payment/Terms Acquires one-time rights. Sends galleys to author. Publication is copyrighted.

Tips "We have three primary criteria in reviewing fiction: 1) The story is compelling and well-crafted. 2) The story provides some element of surprise; i.e., whether in content, form or delivery we are unexpectedly delighted in what we've read. 3) The story meets an upcoming theme, even if only peripherally. Read fiction in the current issue and perhaps some archived work, and if you like what you read—and our overall enviromental slant—then send us your best work. Make sure you follow our submission guidelines (including cover note with bio), and that your manuscript is as error-free as possible."

TOASTED CHEESE

E-mail: editors@toasted-cheese.com. Website: www.toasted-cheese.com. E-zine specializing in fiction, creative nonfiction, poetry and flash fiction. "Toasted Cheese accepts submissions of previously unpublished fiction, flash fiction, creative nonfiction and poetry. Our focus is on quality of work, not quantity. Some issues will therefore contain fewer/more pieces than previous issues.

We don't restrict publication based on subject matter. We encourage submissions from innovative writers in all genres." Quarterly.

Needs Adventure, children's/juvenile, ethnic/multicultural, fantasy, feminist, gay, historical, horror, humor/satire, lesbian, literary, mainstream, mystery/suspense, New Age, psychic/supernatural/occult, romance, science fiction, thriller/espionage, western. "No fan fiction. No chapters or excerpts unless they read as a stand-alone story. No first drafts." Receives 150 unsolicited mss/month. Accepts 1-10 mss/issue; 5-30 mss/year. **Publishes 15 new writers/year.** Publishes short shorts. Also publishes poetry.

How to Contact Send complete ms in body of e-mail; no attachments. Accepts submissions by e-mail. Responds in 4 months to mss. No simultaneous submissions. Sample copy online. Writer's guidelines online.

Payment/Terms Acquires electronic rights. Sponsors awards/contests.

Tips "We are looking for clean, professional writing from writers of any level. Accepted stories will be concise and compelling. We are looking for writers who are serious about the craft: tomorrow's literary stars before they're famous. Take your submission seriously, yet remember that levity is appreciated. You are submitting not to traditional 'editors' but to fellow writers who appreciate the efforts of those in the trenches."

$ TOWER OF LIGHT FANTASY FREE ONLINE

9701 Harford Road, Carney MD 21234. (410) 661-3362. E-mail: tol@tolfantasy.com. Website: www.tolfantasy.com **Contact:** Michael Southard, editor. Online magazine. "To publish great fantasy stories, especially the genre-blending kind such as dark fantasy, urban, science, and superhero fantasy. Romantic fantasy (not erotic, however) is also acceptable. And Tower of Light would very much like to showcase new work by beginning writers." Biannual. Estab. 2007.

Needs Fantasy (space fantasy, sword and sorcery), horror (dark fantasy, futuristic, supernatural), psychic/supernatural/occult, religious (fantasy), romance (fantasy). Does not want erotic fantasy, or anything that does not have a mystical or supernatural element. List of upcoming themes available on website. Receives 15-30 mss/month. Accepts 6 mss/issue; 12 mss/year. Reading period: Jan 1-Mar 31; July 1-Aug 31. Ms published 6-12 months after acceptance. Published Ian Whates, Christopher Heath, Tom Williams, Daniel Henderson, Alice M. Roelke, Matthew Baron, Eric S. Brown, Ryder Patzuk-Russell and Mischell Lyne. Length: 500-4,000 words. Average length: 3,500 words. Publishes short shorts. Also publishes book reviews. Send review copies to Michael Southard. Sometimes comments on/critiques rejected mss.

How to Contact Send ms in the body of e-mail. Unfortunately, artwork must be sent as an attachment. Responds to mss in 6-12 weeks. Considers previously published submissions, multiple submissions. Guidelines, sample copy available on website.

Payment/Terms Writers and artists receive $5. Pays on publication. Acquires one-time rights, electronic rights. Occasionally sends galleys to author. Publication is not copyrighted.

Tips "Strong, well-developed characters that really elicit an emotional response, good writing, original plots and world-building catch my attention. Send me a good story, and make sure to check your spelling and grammar. I don't mind a couple of errors, but when there's more than half a dozen, it gets really irritating. Make sure to study the guidelines thoroughly; I'm looking for character-driven stories, preferably in third person limited point-of-view."

UGLY ACCENT

A Literary Adversaria Brought to You by the Midwest, 2310 40th Pl NW, #302, Washington DC 20007. E-mail: editor@uglyaccent.com. Website: www.uglyaccent.com. **Contact:** Juli Obudzinski, Fiction Editor. Online and print literary magazine: 8.5 × 11; 40 pages; newsprint paper; contains illustrations, photographs. "Ugly Accent is an emerging literary journal out of Madison, Wisconsin. The focus of our journal is not only to publish exceptional writing, but also to glorify the cesspool of talent this region breeds. We put forth a challenge to our submitters to find that inherent degree of separation from the good ole heartland." Semiannual. Estab. 2006. Circ. 2,000. **Needs**

Experimental, feminist, gay, humor/satire, lesbian, literary, regional (midwest). Does not want pieces containing unnessesary violence or those that are sexist, racist or homophobic in nature. Receives 10 mss/month. Accepts 2-7 mss/issue; 15-20 mss/year. Ms published 6 months after acceptance. **Publishes 5-10 new writers/year**. Published Susan Yount, Brian Nealon, C.J. Krueger, Joseph Fronczak, Ryan Chapman, Shanley Erin Kane, Bayard Godsave, Erica Goodkind, Louis Bourgeois, Erin Pringle,and Nicolette Kittinger. Length: 1,000-6,000 words. Average length: 3,000 words. Publishes short shorts. Average length of short shorts: 1,000 words. Also publishes literary essays, literary criticism, book reviews, poetry. Send review copies to Juli Obudzinski. Often comments on/critiques rejected mss.

How to Contact Send complete ms with cover letter. Include estimated word count, brief bio, list of publications. Responds to queries in 2-4 weeks; mss in 4-6 months. Send disposable copy of ms and #10 SASE for reply only. Considers simultaneous submissions, previously published submissions. Sample copy available on website. Guidelines available on website. **Payment/Terms** Writers receive contributor's copies. Pays on publication. Acquires one-time rights, electronic rights. Publication is not copyrighted.

Tips "We are looking for writers with subtlety and a predilection for experimentation with language and form. We believe that prose should test the elasticity of language and utilize the form for all its worth. We seek literary pieces that challenge everything else that ends up filling the shelves of chain stores littered across the country. Those looking for fame need not apply. Instead, those whose writing challenges the mold, works against the metaphorical grain. We like good writing, who doesn't, but it also has to catch our attention somehow. Satires, absurdity, form stretching free style prose are all goodies for us. We like when you bend the rules a little and things become messy and a little strange."

VERBSAP.COM, CONCISE PROSE. ENOUGH SAID.

E-mail: editor@verbsap.com. Website: www.verbsap.com. **Contact:** Laurie Seider, editor. Online magazine. "Verbsap showcases an eclectic selection of the finest in concise prose by established and emerging writers." Published quarterly. Estab. 2005. Needs Literary, mainstream. Does not want violent, racist or pornographic content. Accepts 200 mss/year. Ms published 2-4 weeks after acceptance. Length: 3,000 words (max). Average length: 2,000 words. Publishes short shorts. Average length of short shorts: 900 words. Also publishes literary essays, author and artist interviews, and book reviews. Always comments on/critiques rejected mss.

How to Contact Follow online guidelines. Accepts submissions by e-mail. Responds to mss in 1-3 weeks. Considers simultaneous submissions. Guidelines available on website.

Payment/Terms Sends galleys to author. Publication is copyrighted.

Tips "We're looking for stark, elegant prose. Make us weep or make us laugh, but move us. You might find our 'Editor's Notebook' essays helpful."

Online Markets

WEB DEL SOL

Wed del Sol Association, 2020 Pennsylvania Ave. NW, Suite 443, Washington, D.C. 20006 E-mail: dspress@webdelsol.com. Website: www.webdelsol.com. **Contact:** Michael Neff, editor-in-chief. Electronic magazine. "The goal of Web Del Sol is to use the medium of the Internet to bring the finest in contemporary literary arts to a larger audience. To that end, WDS not only web-publishes collections of work by accomplished writers and poets, but hosts over 25 literary arts publications on the WWW such as Del Sol Review, North American Review, Global City Review, The Literary Review and The Prose Poem." Estab. 1994.

Needs Literary. "*WDS* publishes work considered to be literary in nature, i.e. non-genre fiction. *WDS* also publishes poetry, prose poetry, essays and experimental types of writing." **Publishes 100-200 new writers/year.**

How to Contact "Submissions by e-mail from September through November and from January through March only. Submissions must contain some brief bio, list of prior publications (if any), and a short work or portion of that work, neither to exceed 1,000 words. Editors will contact if the balance of work is required." Sample copy online.

Tips "*WDS* wants fiction that is absolutely cutting edge, unique and/or at a minimum, accomplished with a crisp style and concerning subjects not usually considered the objects of literary scrutiny. Read works in such publications as *Conjunctions* (www.conjunctions.com) and *North American Review* (webdelsol.com/NorthAmReview/NAR) to get an idea of what we are looking for."

WILD VIOLET

P.O. Box 39706, Philadelphia PA 19106-9706. E-mail: wildvioletmagazine@yahoo.com. Website: www.wildviolet.net. **Contact:** Alyce Wilson, editor. Online magazine: illustrations, photos. "Our goal is to make a place for the arts: to make the arts more accessible and to serve as a creative forum for writers and artists. Our audience includes English-speaking readers from all over the world, who are interested in both 'high art' and pop culture." Quarterly.

Needs Comics/graphic novels, ethnic/multicultural, experimental, fantasy (space fantasy, sword and sorcery), feminist, gay, horror (dark fantasy, futuristic, psychological, supernatural), humor/satire, lesbian, literary, New Age, psychic/supernatural/occult, science fiction. "No stories where sexual or violent content is just used to shock the reader. No racist writings." Receives 30 unsolicited mss/month. Accepts 5 mss/issue; 20 mss/year. **Publishes 30 new writers/year.** Recently published work by Rik Hunik, Wayne Scheer, Jane McDonald, Mark Joseph Kiewlak, T. Richard Williams, and Susan Snowden. Length: 500-6,000 words; average length: 3,000 words. Also publishes literary essays, literary criticism, poetry. Sometimes comments on rejected mss.

How to Contact Send complete ms. Accepts submissions by e-mail. Include estimated word count and brief bio. Send SASE for return of ms or send a disposable copy of ms and #10 SASE for reply only. Responds in 1 week to queries; 3-6 months to mss. Accepts simultaneous, multiple submissions. Sample copy online. Writer's guidelines by e-mail.

Payment/Terms Writers receive bio and links on contributor's page. Request limited electronic rights, for online publication and archival only. Sponsors awards/contests.

Tips "We look for stories that are well-paced and show character and plot development. Even short shorts should do more than simply paint a picture. Manuscripts stand out when the author's voice is fresh and engaging. Avoid muddying your story with too many characters and don't attempt to shock the reader with an ending you have not earned. Experiment with styles and structures, but don't resort to experimentation for its own sake."

WORD RIOT

A Communication-Breakdown Production, P.O. Box 414, Middletown NJ 07748-3143. (732)706-1272. Fax: (732)706-5856. E-mail: wr.submissions@gmail.com. Website: www.wordriot.org. **Contact:** Jackie Corley, publisher. Online magazine. Monthly. Member, CLMP.

Needs Humor/satire, literary, mainstream. "No fantasy, science fiction, romance." Accepts 20-25 mss/issue; 240-300 mss/year. Publishes ms 1-2 months after acceptance. Agented fiction 5%. Publishes 8-10 new writers/year. Length: 300-6,000 words; average length: 2,700 words. Publishes flash fiction, short stories, creative non-fiction and poetry. Also publishes literary essays, poetry. Often comments on rejected mss.

How to Contact Accepts submissions by e-mail only. Do not send submissions by mail. Include estimated word count and brief bio. Responds in 4-6 weeks to mss. Accepts multiple submissions. Sample copy online. Writer's guidelines online.

Payment/Terms Acquires electronic rights. Not copyrighted. Sponsors awards/contests.

Tips "We're always looking for something edgy or quirky. We like writers who take risks."

WORDS ON WALLS

3408 Whitfield Ave. Apt 4, Cincinnati OH 45220. (513) 961-1475. E-mail: editor@wordsonwalls.net. Website: http://wordsonwalls.net. **Contact:** Kathrine Wright; Ariana-Sophia Kartsonis. Quarterly. Estab. 2003.

Needs Experimental, feminist, gay, literary. Receives 25-35 unsolicited mss/month. Accepts 2-3 mss/issue; 6-12 mss/year. Responds to mss in 12 weeks. Publishes ms 3-4 months after acceptance. Publishes short shorts. Also publishes literary essays, poetry. Often comments on rejected mss.
How to Contact Accepts submissions by e-mail. Accepts simultaneous, multiple submissions and reprints. Writer's guidelines online.
Payment/Terms Writer retains all rights.
Tips "We like work that is edgy, beautifully written with a strong sense of voice and music."

MARKETS

Consumer Magazines

In this section of *Novel & Short Story Writer's Market* are consumer magazines with circulations of more than 10,000. Many have circulations in the hundreds of thousands or millions. And among the oldest magazines listed here are ones not only familiar to us, but also to our parents, grandparents and even great-grandparents: *The Atlantic Monthly* (1857); *Esquire* (1933); and *Ellery Queen's Mystery Magazine* (1941).

Consumer periodicals make excellent markets for fiction in terms of exposure, prestige and payment. Because these magazines are well known, however, competition is great. Even the largest consumer publications buy only one or two stories an issue, yet thousands of writers submit to these popular magazines.

Despite the odds, it is possible for talented new writers to break into print in the magazines listed here. Your keys to breaking into these markets are careful research, professional presentation and, of course, top-quality fiction.

TYPES OF CONSUMER MAGAZINES

In this section you will find a number of popular publications, some for a broad-based, general-interest readership and others for large but select groups of readers—children, teenagers, women, men and seniors. There are also religious and church-affiliated magazines, publications devoted to the interests of particular cultures and outlooks, and top markets for genre fiction.

SELECTING THE RIGHT MARKET

Unlike smaller journals and publications, most of the magazines listed here are available at newsstands and bookstores. Many can also be found in the library, and guidelines and sample copies are almost always available by mail or online. Start your search by reviewing the listings, then familiarize yourself with the fiction included in the magazines that interest you.

Don't make the mistake of thinking that just because you are familiar with a magazine, their fiction is the same today as when you first saw it. Nothing could be further from the truth. Consumer magazines, no matter how well established, are constantly revising their fiction needs as they strive to expand their audience base.

In a magazine that uses only one or two stories an issue, take a look at the nonfiction articles and features as well. These can give you a better idea of the audience for the publication and clues to the type of fiction that might appeal to them.

If you write genre fiction, look in the Category Index beginning on page 591. There you will find a list of markets that say they are looking for a particular subject.

FURTHERING YOUR SEARCH

See You've Got a Story (page 1) for information about the material common to all listings in this book. In this section in particular, pay close attention to the number of submissions a magazine receives in a given period and how many they publish in the same period. This will give you a clear picture of how stiff your competition can be.

While many of the magazines listed here publish one or two pieces of fiction in each issue, some also publish special fiction issues once or twice a year. When possible, we have indicated this in the listing information. We also note if the magazine is open to novel excerpts as well as short fiction, and we advise novelists to query first before submitting long work.

The Business of Fiction Writing, beginning on page 49, covers the basics of submitting your work. Professional presentation is a must for all markets listed. Editors at consumer magazines are especially busy, and anything you can do to make your manuscript easy to read and accessible will help your chances of being published. Most magazines want to see complete manuscripts, but watch for publications in this section that require a query first.

As in the previous section, we've included our own comments in many of the listings, set off by a bullet (•). Whenever possible, we list the publication's recent awards and honors. We've also included any special information we feel will help you in determining whether a particular publication interests you.

The maple leaf symbol (🍁) identifies our Canadian listings. You will also find some English-speaking markets from around the world. These foreign magazines are denoted with (🌐) at the beginning of the listings. Remember to use International Reply Coupons rather than stamps when you want a reply from a country other than your own.

ADVOCATE, PKA'S PUBLICATION

1881 Little Westkill Rd. CO2, Prattsville NY 12468. (518)299-3103. Tabloid: 9-3/8 × 12¼; 20-24 pages; newsprint paper; line drawings; color and b&w photographs. "Eclectic for a general audience." Bimonthly. Estab. 1987. Circ. 10,000.

Needs Adventure, children's/juvenile (5-9 years), ethnic/multicultural, experimental, fantasy, feminist, historical, humor/satire, literary, mainstream, mystery/suspense, regional, romance, science fiction, western, young adult/teen (10-18 years), contemporary, prose poem, senior citizen/retirement, sports. "Nothing religious, pornographic, violent, erotic, pro-drug or anti-environment. Currently looking for equine (horses) stories, poetry, art, photos and cartoons. *The Gaited Horse Newsletter* is currently published within the pages of PKA's *Advocate*." Receives 60 unsolicited mss/month. Accepts 6-8 mss/issue; 34-48 mss/year. Publishes ms 4 months to 1 year after acceptance. Also publishes poetry. Sometimes comments on rejected mss.

How to Contact Send a complete ms with cover letter. Responds in 2 months to mss. No simultaneous submissions. "No work that has appeared on the Internet." Sample copy for $5 (US currency for inside US; $6.50 US currency for Canada). Writer's Guidelines with purchase of sample copy.

Payment/Terms Pays contributor copies. Acquires first rights.

Tips "The highest criterion in selecting a work is its entertainment value. It must first be enjoyable reading. It must, of course, be orginal. To stand out, it must be thought provoking or strongly emotive, or very cleverly plotted. Will consider only previously unpublished works by writers who do not earn their living principally through writing. We are currently very backed up on short stories. We are mostly looking for art, photos and poetry."

AFRICAN VOICES

270 W. 96th St., New York NY 10025. Fax: (212)316-3335. E-mail: general@africanvoices.com. Website: www.africanvoices.com. Magazine: 52 pages; illustrations; photos. "*African Voices* is dedicated to highlighting the art, literature, and history of people of color." Quarterly. Circ. 20,000.

Needs Adventure, children's/juvenile, condensed novels, erotica, ethnic/multicultural, experimental, fantasy, gay, historical (general), horror, humor/satire, literary, mainstream, mystery/suspense, novel excerpts, psychic/supernatural/occult, religious/inspirational, romance, science fiction, serialized novels, slice-of-life vignettes, suspense, young adult/teen (adventure, romance), African-American. List of upcoming themes available for SASE. Publishes special fiction issue. Receives 20-50 unsolicited mss/month. Accepts 20 mss/issue. Publishes ms 3-6 months after acceptance. Agented fiction 5%. **Publishes 30 new writers/year.** Recently published work by Anton Nimblett, Latoya Wolfe, and novelist Ngugiwa Thiong'o. Length: 500-2,500 words; average length: 2,000 words. Publishes short shorts. Also publishes literary essays, poetry.

How to Contact Send complete ms. Include short bio. Send SASE for return of ms. Responds in 3 months to queries. Accepts simultaneous and reprints submissions. Sample copy for $5 or online. Writer's guidelines online. Reviews fiction.

Payment/Terms Pays $25-50. Pays on publication for first North American serial rights.

Tips "A manuscript stands out if it is neatly typed with a well-written and interesting story line or plot. Originality encouraged. We are interested in more horror, erotic and drama pieces. *AV* wants to highlight the diversity in our culture. Stories must touch the humanity in us all."

$ ANALOG SCIENCE FICTION & FACT

Dell Magazine Fiction Group, 475 Park Ave. S., 11th Floor, New York NY 10016. (212) 686-7188. Fax: (212) 686-7414. E-mail: analog@dellmagazines.com. Website: www.analogsf.com. **Contact:** Stanley Schmidt, editor. Magazine: 144 pages; illustrations; photos. Monthly. Estab. 1930. Circ. 50,000.

- Fiction published in *Analog* has won numerous Nebula and Hugo Awards.

Needs Science fiction (hard science/technological, soft/sociological). "No fantasy or stories in which the scientific background is implausible or plays no essential role." Receives 500 unsolicited mss/month. Accepts 6 mss/issue; 70 mss/year. Publishes ms 10 months after acceptance. Agented fiction 5%. **Publishes 3-4 new writers/year.** Recently published work by Ben Bova, Stephen Baxter, Larry Niven, Michael F. Flynn, Timothy Zahn, Robert J. Sawyer, and Joe Haldeman. Length: 2,000-80,000 words; average length: 10,000 words. Publishes short shorts. Sometimes comments on rejected mss.

How to Contact Send complete ms with a cover letter. Accepts queries for serials and fact articles only; query by mail. Include estimated word count. Send SASE for return of ms or send a disposable copy of ms and #10 SASE for reply only. Responds in 1 month to queries. Accepts multiple submissions. No simultaneous submissions. Sample copy for $5. Writer's guidelines online. Reviews fiction.

Payment/Terms Pays 4¢/word for novels; 5-6¢/word for novelettes; 6-8¢/word for shorts under 7,500 words; $450-600 for intermediate lengths. Pays on acceptance for first North American serial, nonexclusive foreign serial rights. Sends galleys to author. Not copyrighted.

Tips "I'm looking for irresistibly entertaining stories that make me think about things in ways I've never done before. Read several issues to get a broad feel for our tastes, but don't try to imitate what you read."

$ THE ANNALS OF SAINT ANNE DE BEAUPRE

9795 St. Anne Blvd., St. Anne de Beaupre QC G0A 3C0 Canada. (418)827-4538. Fax: (418)827-4530. E-mail: mag@revuesaintanne.ca (for subscriptions only). **Contact:** Fr. Guy Desrochers, C.Ss.R, editor. Magazine: 32 pages; glossy paper; photos. "Promotes Catholic family values and devotion to St. Anne." Bimonthly. Estab. 1885. Circ. 25,000.

Needs Religious/inspirational. "No senseless mockery." Receives 50-60 unsolicited mss/month. Recently published work by Beverly Sheresh. Always comments on rejected mss.

How to Contact Send complete ms. Include estimated word count. Send SASE for reply or return of ms. Responds in 4-6 weeks to queries; send SASE for reply or return of ms. No disc or e-mail submission. Rights must be clearly stated. Typed manuscripts only. Included estimated word count.

Payment/Terms Pays $40 for Adult/Religious fiction (one page only, 700 words). Pays on acceptance for first North American serial rights. Please state "rights" for sale.

Tips "Writing must be uplifting and inspirational, clearly written, not filled with long quotations. We tend to stay away from extreme controversy and focus on the family, good family values, devotion, and Christianity. Most open to Christian education, Christian living, Christian growth, Church life and testimonies. Write a well-researched, current story with "across the board" appeal.

$ ART TIMES

P.O. Box 730, Mount Marion NY 12456-0730. (914)246-6944. Fax: (914)246-6944. Website: www.arttimesjournal.com. **Contact:** Raymond J. Steiner, fiction editor. Magazine: 12 × 15; 24 pages; Jet paper and cover; illustrations; photos. "Art Times covers the art fields and is distributed in locations most frequented by those enjoying the arts. Our copies are distributed throughout the Northeast region as well as in most of the galleries of Soho, 57th Street and Madison Avenue in the metropolitan area; locations include theaters, galleries, museums, cultural centers and the like. Our readers are mostly over 40, affluent, art-conscious and sophisticated. Subscribers are located across U.S. and abroad (Italy, France, Germany, Greece, Russia, etc.)." Monthly. Estab. 1984. Circ. 28,000.

Needs Adventure, ethnic/multicultural, fantasy, feminist, gay, historical, humor/satire, lesbian, literary, mainstream, science fiction, contemporary. "We seek quality literary pieces. Nothing violent, sexist, erotic, juvenile, racist, romantic, political, etc." Receives 30-50 unsolicited mss/month. Accepts 1 mss/issue; 10 mss/year. Publishes ms 3 years after acceptance. **Publishes 6 new writers/year.** Publishes short shorts.

How to Contact Send complete ms with SASE. Responds in 6 months to mss. Accepts simultaneous, multiple submissions. Sample copy for 9 × 12 SAE and 6 first-class stamps. Writer's guidelines for #10 SASE or on website.
Payment/Terms Pays $25 maximum (honorarium) and 1 year's free subscription. Pays on publication for first North American serial, first rights.
Tips "Competition is greater (more submissions received), but keep trying. We print new as well as published writers."

$ ASIMOV'S SCIENCE FICTION

267 Broadway, Fourth Floor, New York NY 10007. (212)686-7188. Fax: (212)686-7414. E-mail: asimovssf@dellmagazines.com. Website: www.asimovs.com. **Contact:** Sheila Williams, editor. Magazine: 5-7/8 x 8-5/8 (trim size); 112 pages; 30 lb. newspaper; 70 lb. to 8 pt. C1S cover stock; illustrations; rarely photos. Magazine consists of science fiction and fantasy stories for adults and young adults. Publishes "the best short science fiction available." Estab. 1977. Circ. 50,000.

- Named for a science fiction "legend," *Asimov's* regularly receives Hugo and Nebula Awards. Editor Gardner Dozois has received several awards for editing including Hugos and those from *Locus*magazine.

Needs Fantasy, science fiction (hard science, soft sociological). No horror or psychic/supernatural. Would like to see more hard science fiction. Receives approximately 800 unsolicited mss/month. Accepts 10 mss/issue. Publishes ms 6-12 months after acceptance. Agented fiction 10%. **Publishes 10 new writers/year.** Recently published work by Robert Silverberg and Larry Niven. Publishes short shorts. Sometimes comments on rejected mss.
How to Contact Send complete ms with SASE. Responds in 2 months to queries; 3 months to mss. No simultaneous or reprint submissions. Sample copy for $5. Writer's guidelines for #10 SASE or online. Reviews fiction.
Payment/Terms Pays 5-8¢/word. Pays on acceptance. Buys first North American serial, nonexclusive foreign serial rights; reprint rights occasionally. Sends galleys to author.
Tips "We are looking for character stories rather than those emphasizing technology or science. New writers will do best with a story under 10,000 words. Every new science fiction or fantasy film seems to 'inspire' writers—and this is not a desirable trend. Be sure to be familiar with our magazine and the type of story we like; workshops and lots of practice help. Try to stay away from trite, clicheéd themes. Start in the middle of the action, starting as close to the end of the story as you possibly can. We like stories that extrapolate from up-to-date scientific research, but don't forget that we've been publishing clone stories for decades. Ideas must be fresh."

$ BABYBUG

Carus Publishing Co., 70 E. Lake, Suite 300, Chicago IL 60601. (312)701-1720. Website: www.cricketmag.com. "Babybug is 'the listening and looking magazine for infants and toddlers,' intended to be read aloud by a loving adult to foster a love of books and reading in young children ages 6 months-2 years." Estab. 1994. Circ. 45,000.
Needs Very simple stories for infants and toddlers.
How to Contact Send complete ms. Accepts simultaneous submissions. Sample copy for $5. Writer's guidelines online.
Payment/Terms Pays $25 and up. Pays on publication for variable rights.
Tips "*Babybug* is a board-book magazine. Study back issues before submitting."

$ BACKROADS

Motorcycles, Travel & AdventureBackroads, Inc., P.O. Box 317, Branchville NJ 07826. (973)948-4176. Fax: (973)948-0823. E-mail: editor@backroadsusa.com. Website: www.backroadsusa.com. "Backroads is a motorcycle tour magazine geared toward getting motorcyclists on the road and traveling. We provide interesting destinations, unique roadside attractions and eateries, plus Rip &

Ride Route Sheets. We cater to all brands. If you really ride, you need Backroads." Monthly. Estab. 1995. Circ. 50,000.

Needs Travel, motorcycle-related stories. Publishes ms 3 months after acceptance. Articles must be motorcycle-related and include images of motorcycles to accompany story. It helps if you actually ride a motorcycle.

How to Contact Query. Accepts submissions by e-mail. Sample copy for $5. Writer's guidelines on website.

Payment/Terms Pays 5¢/word. Pays on publication for one-time rights.

$ THE BEAR DELUXE MAGAZINE

E-mail: bear@orlo.org. Website: www.orlo.org. Magazine: 9 × 12; 48 pages; newsprint paper; Kraft paper cover illustrations; photos. "The Bear Deluxe Magazine provides a fresh voice amid often strident and polarized environmental discourse. Street level, solution-oriented, and nondogmatic, The Bear Deluxe presents lively creative discussion to a diverse readership." Semiannual. Estab. 1993.

- *The Bear Deluxe* has received publishing grants from the Oregon Cultural Trust, Regional Arts and Culture Council, Oregon Council for the Humanities, Literary Arts, Regional Arts and Culture Council, Tides Foundation.

Needs Adventure, condensed novels, historical, horror, humor/satire, mystery/suspense, novel excerpts, western. "No detective, children's or horror." Enviromentally focused: humor/satire, literary, science fiction. "We would like to see more nontraditional forms." List of upcoming themes available for SASE. Receives 20-30 unsolicited mss/month. Accepts 2-3 mss/issue; 8-12 mss/year. Publishes ms 3 months after acceptance. **Publishes 5-6 new writers/year.** Recently published work by Peter Houlahan, John Reed and Karen Hueler. Length: 750-4,500 words; average length: 2,500 words. Publishes short shorts. Also publishes literary essays, literary criticism, poetry. Sometimes comments on rejected mss.

How to Contact Query with or without published clips or send complete ms. Send disposable copy of mss. Responds in 3 months to queries; 6 months to mss. Accepts simultaneous submissions and reprints. Sample copy for $5. Writer's guidelines for #10 SASE or on website. Reviews fiction. Also send SASE for guides to new Doug Fir Fiction Award ($1,000 top prize).

Payment/Terms Pays free subscription to the magazine, contributor's copies and 5¢/word; additional copies for postage. Pays on publication for first, one-time rights.

Tips "Keep sending work. Write actively and focus on the connections of man, nature, etc., not just flowery descriptions. Urban and suburban environments are grist for the mill as well. Have not seen enough quality humorous and ironic writing. Interview and artist profile ideas needed. Juxtaposition of place welcome. Action and hands-on great. Not all that interested in environmental ranting and simple 'walks through the park.' Make it powerful, yet accessible to a wide audience."

$ BOMB MAGAZINE

80 Hanson Place, Suite 703, Brooklyn NY 11217. (718)636-9100. E-mail: firstproof@bombsite.com; generalinquiries@bombsite.com. Website: www.bombsite.com. **Contact:** Monica de la Torre. Magazine: 9 X 11.5; 104 pages; 70 lb. glossy cover; illustrations; photos. Written, edited and produced by industry professionals and funded by those interested in the arts. Publishes writing which is unconventional and contains an edge, whether it be in style or subject matter. Quarterly. Experimental, novel excerpts, contemporary. No genre: romance, science fiction, horror, western. Receives 200 unsolicited mss/month. Accepts 6 mss/issue; 24 mss/year. Publishes ms 3-6 months after acceptance. Agented fiction 70%. **Publishes 2-3 new writers/year.** Recently published work by Lynne Tillman, Dennis Cooper, Susan Wheeler, and Laurie Sheck.

Tips "We are committed to publishing new work that commercial publishers often deem too dangerous or difficult. The problem is, a lot of young writers confuse difficult with dreadful. Read the magazine before you even think of submitting something."

$ BOSTON REVIEW

35 Medford Street, Suite 302, Somerville MA 02143. 617-591-0505. Fax: 617-591-0440. E-mail: review@bostonreview.net. Website: www.bostonreview.net. **Contact:** Junot Diaz. Magazine: 10¾ × 14¾; 60 pages; newsprint. "The editors are committed to a society and culture that foster human diversity and a democracy in which we seek common grounds of principle amidst our many differences. In the hope of advancing these ideals, the Review acts as a forum that seeks to enrich the language of public debate." Bimonthly. Estab. 1975. Circ. 20,000.

- *Boston Review* is the recipient of a Pushcart Prize in poetry.

Needs Ethnic/multicultural, experimental, literary, regional, translations, contemporary, prose poem. Receives 150 unsolicited mss/month. Accepts 4-6 mss/year. Publishes ms 4 months after acceptance. Recently published work by Dagberto Gilb, Charles Johnson, Deb Olin Unferth, T.E. Holt, and Yvonne Woon. Length: 1,200-5,000 words; average length: 2,000 words. Occasionally comments on rejected mss.

How to Contact Send complete ms with SASE or submit through online submissions manager. Responds in 4 months to queries. Accepts simultaneous submissions if noted. Sample copy for $5 or online. Writer's guidelines online. Reviews fiction. "The editors are looking for fiction in which a heart struggles against itself, in which the messy unmanageable complexity of the world is revealed. Sentences that are so sharp they cut the eye." *Boston Review* reads fiction submissions between September 15 and May 15 each year.

Payment/Terms Pays $300, and 3 contributor's copies. Acquires first North American serial, first rights.

BRAIN, CHILD

The Magazine for Thinking Mothers, March Press, P.O. Box 714, Lexington VA 24450. (540)463-4817. E-mail: editor@brainchildmag.com. Website: www.brainchildmag.com. **Contact:** Jennifer Niesslein and Stephanie Wilkinson, co-editors. Magazine: 7¼ × 10; 60-100 pages; 80lb. matte cover; illustrations; photos. "Brain, Child reflects modern motherhood—the way it really is. We like to think of Brain, Child as a community, for and by mothers who like to think about what raising kids does for (and to) the mind and soul. Brain, Child isn't your typical parenting magazine. We couldn't cupcake-decorate our way out of a paper bag. We are more 'literary' than 'how-to,' more New Yorker than Parents. We shy away from expert advice on childrearing in favor of first-hand reflections by great writers (Jane Smiley, Barbara Ehrenreich, Anne Tyler) on life as a mother. Each quarterly issue is full of essays, features, humor, reviews, fiction, art, cartoons, and our readers' own stories. Our philosophy is pretty simple: Motherhood is worthy of literature. And there are a lot of ways to mother, all of them interesting. We're proud to be publishing articles and essays that are smart, down to earth, sometimes funny, and sometimes poignant." Quarterly. Estab. 2000. Circ. 30,000. Member, IPA, ASME.

Needs Literary, mainstream, literary. No genre fiction. Receives 200 unsolicited mss/month. Accepts 1 mss/issue; 4 mss/year. Publishes ms 6 months after acceptance. Recently published work by Anne Tyler, Barbara Kingsolver and Jane Smiley. Length: 800-5,000 words; average length: 2,500 words. Also publishes literary essays. Sometimes comments on rejected mss.

How to Contact Send complete ms. Accepts submissions by e-mail only (be sure to copy and paste the ms into the body of the e-mail). Include estimated word count, brief bio and list of publications. Responds in 1 month to queries; 1-3 months to mss. Accepts simultaneous and reprints, multiple submissions. Sample copy online. Writer's guidelines online. Reviews fiction.

Payment/Terms Payment varies. Pays on publication for first North American serial, electronic rights. *Brain, Child* anthology rights. Sends galleys to author.

Tips "We only publish fiction with a strong motherhood theme. But, like every other publisher of literary fiction, we look for well-developed characters, a compelling story, and an ending that is as strong as the rest of the piece."

$ BUGLE

(406)523-4570. Fax: (406)523-4550. E-mail: bugle@rmef.org. Website: www.elkfoundation.org. Magazine: 114-172 pages; 55 lb. Escanaba paper; 80 lb. Steriling cover, b&w, 4-color illustrations; photos. Bugle is the membership publication of the Rocky Mountain Elk Foundation, a nonprofit wildlife conservation group. "Our readers are predominantly hunters, many of them conservationists who care deeply about protecting wildlife habitat." Bimonthly. Circ. 155,000.

Needs Adventure, children's/juvenile, historical, humor/satire, novel excerpts, slice-of-life vignettes, western, human interest, natural history, conservation, as long as they related to elk. "We accept fiction and nonfiction stories pertaining in some way to elk, other wildlife, hunting, habitat conservation, and related issues. We would like to see more humor." Receives 20-30 unsolicited mss/month. Accepts 3-4 mss/issue; 18-24 mss/year. Publishes ms 1-36 months after acceptance. **Publishes 12 new writers/year.** Length: 1,500-4,500 words; average length: 2,500 words. Publishes short shorts. Also publishes literary essays and poetry about elk.

How to Contact Query with or without published clips or send complete ms. Prefers submissions by e-mail. Send SASE for reply, return of ms or send a disposable copy of ms. Responds in 1 month to queries; 3 months to mss. Accepts reprints, multiple submissions. Sample copy for $5. Writer's guidelines online.

Payment/Terms Pays 20¢/word. Pays on acceptance for one-time rights.

Tips "Hunting stories and essays should celebrate the hunting experience, demonstrating respect for wildlife, the land, and the hunt. Articles on elk behavior or elk habitat should include personal observations and entertain as well as educate. No freelance product reviews or formulaic how-to articles accepted. Straight action-adventure hunting stories are in short supply, as are "Situation Ethics" manuscripts."

$ CALLIOPE

Exploring World History, 30 Grove St., Peterborough NH 03458-1454. (603)924-7209. Fax: (603)924-7380. E-mail: cfbakeriii@meganet.net. Website: www.cobblestonepub.com. **Contact:** Lou Waryncia, Editorial Director. Magazine published 9 times/year. "Calliope covers world history (East/West), and lively, original approaches to the subject are the primary concerns of the editors in choosing material."

- 2010 themes include: Isabella of Spain-Queen of a New World; Michelangelo; Dutch East India Company; Exploring Africa with Stanley & Livingstone; Meaning of Numbers; Shades of Indigo; The Nile river, and the Zodiac.

Needs Middle readers and young adults: adventure, folktales, plays, history, biographical fiction. Material must relate to forthcoming themes. Word length: up to 800.

How to Contact "A query must consist of the following to be considered (please use nonerasable paper): a brief cover letter stating subject and word length of the proposed article; a detailed one-page outline explaining the information to be presented in the article; an bibliography of materials the author intends to use in preparing the article; a self-addressed stamped envelope. Writers new to Calliope should send a writing sample with query. In all correspondence, please include your complete address as well as a telephone number where you can be reached. A writer may send as many queries for one issue as he or she wishes, but each query must have a separate cover letter, outline and bibliography as well as a SASE. Telephone and e-mail queries are not accepted. Handwritten queries will not be considered. Queries may be submitted at any time, but queries sent well in advance of deadline may not be answered for several months. Go-aheads requesting material proposed in queries are usually sent five months prior to publication date. Unused queries will be returned approximately three to four months prior to publication date."

Payment/Terms Buys all rights for mss and artwork. Pays 20-25¢/word for stories/articles. Pays on an individual basis for poetry, activities, games/puzzles. Sample copy for $5.95 and SAE with $2 postage. Writer's guidelines for SASE.

CANADIAN WRITER'S JOURNAL

P.O. Box 1178, New Liskeard ON P0J 1P0 Canada. (705)647-5424. E-mail: editor@cwj.ca; cwj@cwj.ca. Website: www.cwj.ca. Accepts well-written articles by all writers. Annual. Estab. 1984.

Needs Requirements being met by annual contest. Send SASE for rules, or see guidelines on website. "Does not want gratuitous violence, sex subject matter." Publishes ms 9 months after acceptance. **Publishes 40 new writers/year.** Also publishes poetry. Rarely comments on rejected mss.

How to Contact Accepts submissions by e-mail. Responds in 2 months to queries. Writer's guidelines online.

Payment/Terms Pays on publication for one-time rights.

$ CLUBHOUSE JR.

Focus on the Family, 8605 Explorer Drive, Colorado Springs CO 80920. (719)531-3400. Website: www.clubhousejr.com. **Contact**: Jamie Dangers, editorial assistant. Magazine: 8½ × 11; 24 pages; illustrations; photos. Clubhouse Jr. is designed to inspire, entertain, and teach Christian values to children 4-8. Estab. 1988. Circ. 57,000.

Needs Children's/juvenile (adventure, animal, preschool, sports), ethnic/multicultural, religious/inspirational. Receives 160 unsolicited mss/month. Accepts 1 mss/issue; 12 mss/year. Publishes ms 1 year after acceptance. **Publishes 2-3 new writers/year.** Recently published work by Laura Sassi, Nancy Sanders, Manfred Koehler, and Mary Manz Simon. Length: 250-1,000 words; average length: 250-700 words. Publishes short shorts. Also publishes poetry. Sometimes comments on rejected mss.

How to Contact Send complete ms. Send SASE (or IRC) for return of the ms or send disposable copy of the ms and #10 SASE for reply only. Responds in 6-8 weeks to mss. Does not accept simultaneous submissions. Sample copy for $1.25. Writer's guidelines for #10 SASE.

Payment/Terms Pays $125-200. Pays on acceptance for all rights.

Tips "Fresh, inviting, creative; stories that explore a worthy theme without an obvious *moral*. Characters are well-developed, story line fast-moving and interesting; built on Christian beliefs and values."

$ CRICKET

Carus Publishing Co., 70 E. Lake, Suite 300, Chicago IL 60601. (312)701-1720. Website: www.cricketmag.com. Marianne Carus, editor-in-chief. **Contact:** Submissions Editor. Magazine: 8 × 10; 64 pages; illustrations; photos. Magazine for children, ages 9-14. Monthly. Estab. 1973. Circ. 73,000.

- *Cricket* has received a Parents' Choice Award, and awards from EdPress. Carus Corporation also publishes *Spider, the Magazine for Children*; *Ladybug, the Magazine for Young Children;Babybug*; and *Cicada*.

Needs Adventure, children's/juvenile, ethnic/multicultural, fantasy, historical, humor/satire, mystery/suspense, novel excerpts, science fiction, suspense, thriller/espionage, western, folk and fairy tales. No didactic, sex, religious, or horror stories. All issues have different "mini-themes." Receives 1,100 unsolicited mss/month. Accepts 150 mss/year. Publishes ms 6-24 months after acceptance. Agented fiction 1-2%. **Publishes some new writers/year.** Recently published work by Aaron Shepard, Arnold Adoff, and Nancy Springer.

How to Contact Send complete ms. Responds in 3 months to mss. Accepts reprints submissions. Sample copy for $5 and 9 × 12 SAE. Writer's guidelines for SASE and on website.

Payment/Terms Pays 25¢/word maximum, and 6 contributor's copies; $2.50 charge for extras. Pays on publication. Rights vary. Sponsors awards/contests.

Tips "Do not write *down* to children. Write about well-researched subjects you are familiar with and interested in, or about something that concerns you deeply. Children *need* fiction and fantasy. Carefully study several issues of *Cricket* before you submit your manuscript."

$ DISCIPLESWORLD

DisciplesWorld, Inc., 6325 N. Guilford Ave., Dyr. 213, Indianapolis IN 46202. E-mail: editor@disciplesworld.com. Website: www.disciplesworld.com. "We are the journal of the Christian Church (Disciples of Christ) in North America. Our denomination numbers roughly 800,000. Disciples are a mainline Protestant group. Our readers are mostly laity, active in their churches, and interested in issues of faithful living, political and church news, ethics, and contemporary social issues." Monthly. Estab. 2002. Circ. 14,000.

Needs Ethnic/multicultural, mainstream, religious/inspirational, slice-of-life vignettes. "We're a religious publication, so use common sense! Stories do not have to be overtly 'religious,' but they should be uplifting and positive." Publishes ms 6 months after acceptance.

How to Contact Send complete ms. Accepts submissions by e-mail (editor@disciplesworld.com). Responds in 2 weeks to queries; 2 months to mss. Accepts simultaneous submissions. Sample copy for #10 SASE. Writer's guidelines online.

Payment/Terms Pays 16¢/word. Pays on publication for first North American serial rights.

$ ESQUIRE

Hearst, 300 West 57th Street, 21st Floor, New York NY 10019. (212)649-4050. Website: www.esquire.com. **Contact:** Adrienne Miller, literary editor. Magazine. Monthly magazine for smart, well-off men. General readership is college educated and sophisticated, between ages 30 and 45. Written mostly by contributing editors on contract. Rarely accepts unsolicited manuscripts. Monthly. Estab. 1933. Circ. 750,000.

- *Esquire*is well respected for its fiction and has received several National Magazine Awards. Work published in *Esquire* has been selected for inclusion in the *Best American Short Stories* and *O. Henry* anthologies.

Needs Novel excerpts, short stories, some poetry, memoirs, and plays. No "pornography, science fiction or 'true romance' stories." Publishes special fiction issue in July. Receives 800 unsolicited mss/month. Rarely accepts unsolicited fiction. Publishes ms 2-6 months after acceptance. Recently published work by Russell Banks, Tim O'Brien, Richard Russo and David Means.

How to Contact Send complete ms. Accepts simultaneous submissions. Writer's guidelines for SASE.

Payment/Terms Pays in cash on acceptance, amount undisclosed. Retains first worldwide periodical publication rights for 90 days from cover date.

Tips "Submit one story at a time. We receive over 10,000 stories a year, so worry a little less about publication, a little more about the work itself."

$ EVANGEL

Free Methodist Publishing House, P.O. Box 535002, Indianapolis IN 46253-5002. (317)244-3660. Magazine: 5½ × 8½; 8 pages; 2 and 4-color illustrations; color and b&w photos. Sunday school take-home paper for distribution to adults who attend church. Fiction involves people coping with everday crises, making decisions that show spiritual growth. Weekly distribution. Printed quarterly. Estab. 1897. Circ. 10,000.

Needs Religious/inspirational. "No fiction without any semblance of Christian message or where the message clobbers the reader. Looking for devotional style short pieces 500 words or less." Receives 300 unsolicited mss/month. Accepts 3-4 mss/issue; 156-200 mss/year. Publishes ms 18-36 months after acceptance. **Publishes 7 new writers/year.** Recently published work by Kelli Wise and Hope Byler.

How to Contact Send complete ms. Responds in 4-6 weeks to queries. Accepts multiple submissions. Sample copy and writer's guidelines for #10 SASE.

Payment/Terms Pays 4¢/word and 2 contributor's copies. Pays on publication. Buys second serial (reprint) or one-time rights.

Tips "Desire, concise, tight writing that supports a solid thesis and fits the mission expressed in the quidelines."

$ FIFTY SOMETHING MAGAZINE

Linde Graphics Co., 1168 S. Beachview Rd., Willoughby OH 44094. (440)951-2468. Fax: (440)951-1015. "We are focusing on the 50-and-better reader." Quarterly. Estab. 1990. Circ. 10,000.

Needs Adventure, confessions, ethnic/multicultural, experimental, fantasy, historical, humor/satire, mainstream, mystery/suspense, novel excerpts, romance, slice-of-life vignettes, suspense, western. No erotica or horror. Receives 150 unsolicited mss/month. Accepts 5 mss/issue. Publishes ms 6 months after acceptance. **Publishes 20 new writers/year.** Recently published work by Gail Morrisey, Sally Morrisey, Jenny Miller, J. Alan Witt, and Sharon McGreagor. Length: 500-1,000 words; average length: 1,000 words. Publishes short shorts.

How to Contact Send complete ms. Responds in 3 months to queries; 3 months to mss. Accepts simultaneous submissions and reprints. Sample copy for 9 × 12 SAE and 4 first-class stamps. Writer's guidelines for #10 SASE.

Payment/Terms Pays $10-100. Pays on publication for one-time, second serial (reprint), simultaneous rights.

N $ FLAUNT MAGAZINE

1422 North Highland Avenue, Los Angeles CA 90028. (323)836-1000. E-mail: info@flauntmagazine.com. Website: www.flaunt.com. **Contact:** Andrew Pogany, senior editor. Magazine. "10 times a year Flaunt features the bold work of emerging photographers, writers, artists, and musicians. The quality of the content is mirrored in the sophisticated, interactive format of the magazine, using advanced printing techniques, fold-out articles, beautiful papers, and inserts to create a visually stimulating, surprisingly readable, and intelligent book that pushes the magazine into the realm of art-object. Flaunt magazine has for the last eight years made it a point to break new ground, earning itself a reputation as an engine and outlet for the culture of the cutting edge. Flaunt takes pride in reinventing itself each month, while consistently representing a hybrid of all that is interesting in entertainment, fashion, music, design, film, art, and literature." Estab. 1998. Circ. 110,000.

Needs Experimental, urban, academic. We publish 3 fiction peices a year. Length: 500-5,000 words.

How to Contact Guidelines available via e-mail.

Payment/Terms Acquires one-time rights and first option to reprint. Pays one-time flat-rate to be determined upon correspondence.

$ FUNNY TIMES

A Monthly Humor Review, P.O. Box 18530, Cleveland Heights OH 44118. (216)371-8600. Fax: (216)371-8696. Website: www.funnytimes.com. **Contact:** Ray Lesser and Susan Wolpert, editors. Zine specializing in humor: tabloid; 24 pages; newsprint; illustrations. "Funny Times is a monthly review of America's funniest cartoonists and writers. We are the Reader's Digest of modern American humor with a progressive/peace-oriented/environmental/politically activist slant." Monthly. Circ. 70,000.

Needs Humor/satire. "Anything funny." Receives hundreds unsolicited mss/month. Accepts 5 mss/issue; 60 mss/year. Publishes ms 3 months after acceptance. Agented fiction 10%. **Publishes 10 new writers/year.** Publishes short shorts.

How to Contact Query with published clips. Include list of publications. Send SASE for return of ms or disposable copy of ms. Responds in 3 months to mss. Accepts simultaneous and reprints submissions. Sample copy for $3 or 9 × 12 SAE with 4 first-class stamps ($1.22 postage). Writer's guidelines online.

Payment/Terms Pays $50-150. Pays on publication for one-time, second serial (reprint) rights.

Tips "It must be funny."

HARPER'S MAGAZINE

666 Broadway, 11th Floor, New York NY 10012. (212)420-5720. Fax: (212)228-5889. Website: www.harpers.org. **Contact:** Ben Metcalf. Magazine: 8 × 10¾; 80 pages; illustrations. "*Harper's Magazine*

encourages national discussion on current and significant issues in a format that offers arresting facts and intelligent opinions. By means of its several shorter journalistic forms—Harper's Index, Readings, Forum, and Annotation—as well as with its acclaimed essays, fiction, and reporting, *Harper's* continues the tradition begun with its first issue in 1850: to inform readers across the whole spectrum of political, literary, cultural, and scientific affairs." Monthly. Estab. 1850. Circ. 230,000.

Needs Humor/satire. Stories on contemporary life and its problems. Receives 50 unsolicited mss/month. Accepts 12 mss/year. Publishes ms 3 months after acceptance. **Publishes some new writers/year.** Recently published work by Rebecca Curtis, George Saunders, Haruki Murakami, Margaret Atwood, Allan Gurganus, Evan Connell and Dave Bezmosgis.

How to Contact Query by mail, except for submissions to the Readings section, which can be submitted via readings@harpers.org. Responds in 3 months to queries. Accepts reprints submissions. SASE required for all unsolicited material. Sample copy for $6.95.

Payment/Terms Generally pays 50¢-$1/word. Pays on acceptance. Vary with author and material. Sends galleys to author.

$ HIGHLIGHTS FOR CHILDREN

Manuscript Submissions, 803 Church St., Honesdale PA 18431-1824. Website: www.highlights.com. **Contact:** Christine French Clark. Magazine: 42 pages; uncoated paper; coated cover stock; illustrations; photos. "This magazine of wholesome fun is dedicated to helping children grow in basic skills and knowledge, in creativeness, in ability to think and reason, in sensitivity to others, in high ideals and worthy ways of living—for children are the world's most important people. Publishes stories for children up to age 12; up to 500 words for beginners (ages 3-7), up to 800 words for advanced (ages 8-12)." Monthly.

- *Highlights* has won the Parent's Guide to Children's Media Award, Parent's Choice Award, and Editorial Excellence Awards from the Association of Educational Publishers.

Needs Adventure, fantasy, mystery, historical, humor, mystery, animal, contemporary, retellings of folktales, multicultural, sports. Prefers stories appealing to both girls and boys and stories with good characterization, strong emotional appeal, action, strong plot, believable setting. Receives 600-800 unsolicited mss/month. **Publishes 30 new writers/year**.

How to Contact Send complete ms. Responds in 4 to 6 weeks. Accepts multiple submissions. Sample copy free. Writer's guidelines in "About Us" section of website.

Payment/Terms Pays $150 minimum, plus 2 contributor's copies. **Pays on acceptance.** Sends galleys to author.

Tips "We accept a story on its merit whether written by an unpublished or an experienced writer. Mss are rejected because of poor writing, lack of plot, trite or worn-out plot, or poor characterization. Children *like* stories and learn about life from stories. Children learn to become lifelong fiction readers by enjoying stories. Feel passion for your subject. Create vivid images. Write a child-centered story; leave adults in the background."

ALFRED HITCHCOCK'S MYSTERY MAGAZINE

Dell Magazines, 475 Park Ave. S., 11th Floor, New York NY 10016. Website: www.themysteryplace.com. **Contact:** Linda Landrigan, editor. Mystery fiction magazine: 5½ × 8; 112 pages; 28 lb. newsprint paper; 70 lb. machine-coated cover stock; illustrations; photos. 10 issues/year (2 double). Estab. 1956. Readership: 100,000.

- Stories published in *Alfred Hitchcock's Mystery Magazine* have won Edgar Awards for "Best Mystery Story of the Year," Shamus Awards for "Best Private Eye Story of the Year" and Robert L. Fish Awards for "Best First Mystery Short Story of the Year."

Needs Mystery/suspense (amateur sleuth, private eye, police procedural, suspense, etc.). No sensationalism. Number of mss/issue varies with length of mss. Recently published work by Rhys Bowen, Doug Allyn, I.J. Parker, and Martin Limón.

How to Contact Send complete ms. Responds in 4 months to mss. Sample copy for $5. Writer's guidelines for SASE or on website.
Payment/Terms Payment varies. Pays on publication for first serial, foreign rights.

JEWISH CURRENTS MAGAZINE

45 E. 33rd Street, New York NY 10016-1919. (845) 626-2427. E-mail: lawrencebush@earthlink.net. **Contact:** Lawrence Bush. Magazine: 8½ × 11; 48 pages. A secular, progressive, independent Jewish bimonthly, printing fiction, poetry articles and reviews on Jewish politics and history. Holocaust/Resistance; Mideast peace process, Black-Jewish relations; labor struggles, women's issues. Audience is secular, left/progressive, Jewish, mostly urban. Bimonthly. Estab.1946. Circ.16,000.
Needs Ethnic/multicultural, feminist, historical, humor/satire, translations, contemporary. "No no porn or hard sex, no escapist stuff. Go easy on experimentation, but we're interested." Must be well written! We are interested in *authentic* experience and readable prose; humanistic orientation. Jewish themes." Receives 6-10 unsolicited mss/month. Accepts 1-2 mss/issue; 6-12 mss/year. Publishes ms 2-24 months after acceptance. Recently published work by Elizabeth Swados, Esther Cohen, Lawrence Bush, David Rothenberg, Paul Buhle, Mikhail Horowitz. Length: 1,000-3,000 words; average length: 2,000 words. Publishes short shorts. Also publishes literary essays, literary criticism, poetry.
How to Contact Send complete ms with cover letter. "Writers should include brief biographical information, especially their publishing histories." SASE. Responds in 2 months to mss. Sample copy for $3 with SAE and 3 first class stamps. Reviews fiction.
Payment/Terms Pays complimentary one-year subscription and 6 contributor's copies. "We readily give reprint permission at no charge." Sends galleys to author.

KALEIDOSCOPE

Exploring the Experience of Disability Through Literature and the Fine Arts, 701 S. Main St., Akron OH 44311-1019. (330)762-9755. Fax: (330)762-0912. E-mail: kaleidoscope@udsakron.org. Website: www.udsakron.org. **Contact:** Gail Willmott, editor-in-chief. Magazine: 8½ × 11; 64 pages; non-coated paper; coated cover stock; illustrations (all media); photos. Subscribers include individuals, agencies, and organizations that assist people with disabilities and many university and public libraries. Open to new writers but appreciates work by established writers as well. Especially interested in work by writers with a disability, but features writers both with and without disabilities. "Writers without a disability must limit themselves to our focus, while those with a disability may explore any topic (although we prefer original perspectives about experiences with disability)." Semiannual. Estab. 1979. Circ. 1,000.

- *Kaleidoscope* has received awards from the American Heart Association, the Great Lakes Awards Competition and Ohio Public Images.

Needs "We look for well-developed plots, engaging characters and realistic dialogue. We lean toward fiction that emphasizes character and emotions rather than action-oriented narratives. No fiction that is stereotypical, patronizing, sentimental, erotic, or maudlin. No romance, religious or dogmatic fiction; no children's literature." Receives 35-40 unsolicited mss/month. Accepts 20 mss/year. Agented fiction 1%. **Publishes 2 new writer/year.** Recently published work by Carole hall, Deshae E. Lott, and Natalie E. Illum. Also publishes poetry.
How to Contact Accepts submissions by fax and e-mail, double-spaced with full address. Query first or send complete ms and cover letter. Include author's education and writing background and, if author has a disability, how it influenced the writing. SASE. Responds in 3 weeks to queries; 6 months to mss. Accepts simultaneous, multiple submissions and reprints. Sample copy for $6 prepaid. Writer's guidelines online.
Payment/Terms Pays $10-125, and 2 contributor's copies; additional copies $6. Pays on publication for first rights, reprints permitted with credit given to original publication. Rights revert to author upon publication.

Tips "Read the magazine and get submission guidelines. We prefer that writers with a disability offer original perspectives about their experiences; writers without disabilities should limit themselves to our focus in order to solidify a connection to our magazine's purpose. Do not use stereotypical, patronizing and sentimental attitudes about disability."

$ KENTUCKY MONTHLY

106-C St. James Ct., Frankfort KY 40601. (502)227-0053. E-mail: steve@kentuckymonthly.com. Website: www.kentuckymonthly.com. **Contact:** Stephen Vest, editor. Vested Interest Publications, 213 St. Clair St., Frankfort KY 40601. (502)227-0053. Fax: (502)227-5009. E-mail: amanda@kentuckymonthly.com. Website: www.kentuckymonthly.com. **Contact:** Amanda Hervy, associate editor. "We publish stories about Kentucky and by Kentuckians, including stories written by those who live elsewhere." Monthly. Estab. 1998. Circ. 40,000.

Needs Adventure, historical, mainstream, novel excerpts. Publishes ms 3 months after acceptance.

How to Contact Query with published clips. Accepts submissions by e-mail, fax. Responds in 3 weeks to queries; 1 month to mss. Accepts simultaneous submissions. Sample copy online. Writer's guidelines online.

Payment/Terms Pays $50-100. Pays within 3 months of publication. Acquires first North American serial rights.

$ LADYBUG

The Magazine for Young Children, 70 E. Lake St., Suite 300, Chicago IL 60601. (312)701-1720. Website: www.ladybugmagkids.com. **Contact:** Alice Letvin, editor; Jenny Gillespie, associate editor. Magazine: 8 × 10; 36 pages plus 4-page pullout section; illustrations. "We look for quality writing—quality literature, no matter the subject. For young children, ages 3-6." Monthly. Circ. 134,000.

- *Ladybug* has received the Parents Choice Award; the Golden Lamp Honor Award and the Golden Lamp Award from Ed Press, and Magazine Merit awards from the Society of Children's Book Writers and Illustrators.

Needs "Looking for age-appropriate read-aloud stories for preschoolers."

How to Contact Send complete ms. SASE. Responds in 6-8 months to mss. Accepts reprints submissions. Sample copy for $5 and 9 × 12 SAE. Writer's guidelines online.

Payment/Terms Pays 25¢/word (less for reprints). Pays on publication. Rights purchased vary. For recurring features, pays flat fee and copyright becomes property of Cricket Magazine Group.

Tips Looks for "well-written stories for preschoolers: age-appropriate, not condescending. We look for rich, evocative language and sense of joy or wonder."

$ LIGUORIAN

One Liguori Dr., Liguori MO 63057-9999. (636)464-2500. Fax: (636)464-8449. E-mail: liguorianeditor@liguori.org. Website: www.liguorian.org. **Contact:** Cheryl Plass, managing editor. Magazine: 40 pages; 4-color illustrations; photos. "Our purpose is to lead our readers to a fuller Christian life by helping them better understand the teachings of the gospel and the church and by illustrating how these teachings apply to life and the problems confronting them as members of families, the church, and society." Estab. 1913. Circ. 145,000.

- *Liguorian* received Catholic Press Association awards each year in numerous categories.

Needs Religious/inspirational, young adult/teen, senior citizen/retirement. "Stories submitted to *Liguorian* must have as their goal the lifting up of the reader to a higher Christian view of values and goals. We are not interested in contemporary works that lack purpose or are of questionable moral value." Receives 25 unsolicited mss/month. Accepts 10 mss/year. **Publishes 8-10 new writers/year.**

How to Contact Send complete mss of 400-2,000 words. Accepts submissions by e-mail, fax, disk. Responds in 3 months to mss. Sample copy for 9 × 12 SASE with 3 first-class stamps or online. Writer's guidelines for #10 SASE and on website.

Payment/Terms Pays 10-15¢/word and 5 contributor's copies. Pays on acceptance. Buys first rights.

Tips "First read several issues containing short stories. We look for originality and creative input in each story we read. Since most editors must wade through mounds of manuscripts each month, consideration for the editor requires that the market be studied, the manuscript be carefully presented and polished before submitting. Our publication uses only one story a month. Compare this with the 25 or more we receive over the transom each month. Also, many fiction mss are written without a specific goal or thrust, i.e., an interesting incident that goes nowhere is *not a story*. We believe fiction is a highly effective mode for transmitting the Christian message and also provides a good balance in an unusually heavy issue."

LIMP WRIST MAGAZINE

E-mail: dustin@limpwristmag.com.

How to Contact Submit 1 story up to 5,000 words by e-mail only in the body of the message to Heather Hughes (heather@limpwristmag.com). No attachments. "Don't forget: Include the following statement (and mean it!) with your submissions: 'The work submitted is my own original work and has notbeen previously published.'"

$ LISTEN MAGAZINE

Celebrating Positive Choices, 55 W. Oak Ridge Dr., Hagerstown MD 21740. (301)393-4082. Fax: (301)393-4055. E-mail: editor@listenmagazine.org. Website: www.listenmagazine.org. **Contact:** Celeste Perrino-Walker, editor. Magazine: 16 pages; glossy paper; illustrations; photos. "Listen is used in many high school classes and by professionals: medical personnel, counselors, law enforcement officers, educators, youth workers, etc. Listen publishes true lifestories about giving teens choices about real-life situations and moral issues in a secular way." Monthly. Circ. 12,000.

Needs Young adult/teen (hobbies, sports), anti-drug, alcohol, tobacco, positive role models, life skills. Publishes ms 6 months after acceptance. Length: 350-700; average length: 500 words.

How to Contact Query with published clips or send complete ms. Accepts submissions by e-mail. Prefers submissions by e-mail. Considers manuscripts once a year-around October. Accepts simultaneous and multiple submissions, and reprints. Sample copy for $2 and 9 × 12 SASE. Writer's guidelines for SASE, by e-mail, fax or on website.

Payment/Terms Pays $50-200, and 3 contributor's copies; additional copies $2. Pays on acceptance for first rights.

$ LIVE

A Weekly Journal of Practical Christian Living, 1445 N. Boonville Ave., Springfield MO 65802-1894. (417)862-2781. Fax: (417)862-6059. E-mail: rl-live@gph.org. Website: www.radiantlife.org. **Contact:** Richard Bennett, editor. "LIVE is a take-home paper distributed weekly in young adult and adult Sunday school classes. We seek to encourage Christians to live for God through fiction and true stories which apply Biblical principles to everyday problems." Weekly. Circ. 38,000.

Needs Religious/inspirational, inspirational, prose poem. No preachy fiction, fiction about Bible characters, or stories that refer to religious myths (e.g., Santa Claus, Easter Bunny, etc.). No science fiction or Biblical fiction. No controversial stories about such subjects as feminism, war or capital punishment, 'city, ethnic, racial settings.' Accepts 2 mss/issue. Publishes ms 18 months after acceptance. **Publishes 50-70 new writers/year.** Recently published work by Tim Woodruff, Barbara Bryden, Katherine Crawford, Roy Borges.

How to Contact Send complete ms. Accepts submissions by e-mail or regular mail. Responds in 6 weeks to mss. Accepts simultaneous submissions. Sample copy for #10 SASE. Writer's guidelines for #10 SASE or by e-mail request.

Payment/Terms Pays 7-10¢/word. Pays on acceptance for first, second serial (reprint) rights.
Tips "Write good, inspirational stories that will encourage people to become all they can be as Christians. Stories should go somewhere! Action, not just thought life; interaction, not just insights. Heroes and heroines, suspense and conflict. Avoid simplistic, pietistic, preachy, or critical conclusions or moralizing. We don't accept science fiction or Biblical fiction. Stories should be encouraging, challenging, humorous. Even problem-centered stories should be upbeat. Reserves the right to change the titles, abbreviate length and clarify flashbacks for publication."

$ THE LUTHERAN JOURNAL

7010 6th St. N., Oakdale MN 55128. (651)702-0176. Fax: (651)702-0074. E-mail: christianad2@msn.com. "A family magazine providing wholesome and inspirational reading material for the enjoyment and enrichment of Lutherans." Annual. Circ. 200,000.
Needs Literary, religious/inspirational, romance (historical), young adult/teen, senior citizen/retirement. Must be appropriate for distribution in the churches. Accepts 3-6 mss/issue.
How to Contact Send complete ms. Responds in 4 months to queries. Accepts simultaneous submissions. Sample copy for 9 × 12 SASE with 60¢ postage.
Payment/Terms Pays $50-300 and one contributor's copy. Pays on publication for first rights.

$ THE MAGAZINE OF FANTASY & SCIENCE FICTION

P.O. Box 3447, Hoboken NJ 07030. (201) 876-2551. E-mail: fandsf@aol.com. Website: www.fandsf.com. **Contact:** Gordon Van Gelder, editor. Magazine: 5 × 8; 240 pages; groundwood paper; card stock cover; illustrations on cover only. "For almost sixty years, we have been one of the leading publishers of fantastic fiction (which includes fantasy stories, science fiction, and some horror fiction). Our vision has changed little over six decades—we remain committed to publishing great stories without regard for whether they're classified as sf or fantasy. The Magazine of Fantasy and Science Fiction publishes various types of science fiction and fantasy short stories and novellas, making up about 80% of each issue. The balance of each issue is devoted to articles about science fiction, a science column, book and film reviews, cartoons, and competitions." Monthly. Circ. 30,000.

- The *Magazine of Fantasy and Science Fiction* won a Nebula Award for Best Novelet for "The Merchant and the Alchemist's Gate" by Ted Chiang in in 2008. Also won the 2007 World Fantasy Award for Best Short Story for "Journey into the Kingdom" by M. Rickert. Editor Van Gelder won the Hugo Award for Best Editor (short form), 2007 and 2008.

Needs Adventure, fantasy (space fantasy, sword and sorcery), horror (dark fantasy, futuristic, psychological, supernatural), psychic/supernatural/occult, science fiction (hard science/technological, soft/sociological), young adult/teen (fantasy/science fiction, horror). "We're always looking for more science fiction." Receives 600-900 unsolicited mss/month. Accepts 5-10 mss/issue; 60-100 mss/year. Publishes ms 6-9 months after acceptance. **Publishes 3-6 new writers/year.** Agented fiction 5%. Recently published work by Peter S. Beagle, Ursula K. Le Guin, Alex Irvine, Pat Murphy, Joyce Carol Oates, Gene Wolfe, Ted Chiang, S.L. Gilbow and Robert Silverberg. Length: Up to 25,000 words; average length: 7,500 words. Publishes short shorts. Send book review copies to Gordon Van Gelder. Sometimes comments on rejected mss.
How to Contact Send complete ms with SASE (or IRC). Include list of publications, estimated word count. No electronic submissions. Responds in 2 months to queries, 6-8 weeks to mss. Accepts reprint submissions. Sample copy for $6. Writer's guidelines for SASE or on website.
Payment/Terms Pays 6-9¢/word, 2 contributor's copies; additional copies $4.20. Pays on acceptance for first North American serial rights. Sends galleys to author. Publication is copyrighted.
Tips "Good storytelling makes a submission stand out. Regarding manuscripts, a well-prepared manuscript (i.e., one that follows the traditional format, like that describted here: http://www.sfwa.org/writing/vonda/vonda.htm) stands out more than any gimmicks. Read an issue of the magazine before submitting. New writers should keep their submissions under 15,000 words—we rarely publish novellas by new writers."

MATURE LIVING

A Magazine for Christian Senior Adults, Lifeway Christian Resources, One Lifeway Plaza, Nashville TN 37234-0175. (615)251-2000. E-mail: matureliving@lifeway.com. Website: www.lifeway.com. **Contact:** Rene Holt, content editor. Magazine: 8½ × 11; 52 pages; slick cover stock; full-color illustrations; photos. "Our magazine is Christian in content, and the material required is what would appeal to 55 and over age group: inspirational, informational, nostalgic, humorous. Our magazine is distributed mainly through churches (especially Southern Baptist churches) that buy the magazine in bulk and distribute it. Circ. 315,000.

Needs Humor/satire, religious/inspirational, senior citizen/retirement. No reference to liquor, dancing, drugs, gambling; no pornography, profanity or occult. Accepts 8-10 mss/issue. Publishes ms 7-8 months after acceptance. Length: 600-1,200 words preferred; average length: 1,000 words.

How to Contact Send complete ms. by email or postal mail. "No queries please." Responds in 2 months to mss. Sample copy for 9 × 12 SAE with 4 first-class stamps. Writer's guidelines for #10 SASE.

Payment/Terms Pays $85-115 for feature articles; 3 contributor's copies. Pays on publication.

Tips Mss are rejected because they are too long or subject matter unsuitable. "Our readers seem to enjoy an occasional short piece of fiction. It must be believable, however, and present senior adults in a favorable light."

$ MATURE YEARS

201 Eighth Ave. S., Nashville TN 37202-0801. (615)749-6292. Fax: (615)749-6512. E-mail: matureyears@umpublishing.org. **Contact:** Marvin Cropsey, editor. Magazine: 8½ × 11; 112 pages; illustrations; photos. Magazine "helps persons in and nearing retirement to appropriate the resources of the Christian faith as they seek to face the problems and opportunities related to aging." Quarterly. Circ. 55,000.

Needs Humor/satire, religious/inspirational, slice-of-life vignettes, retirement years issues, intergenerational relationships. "We don't want anything poking fun at old age, saccharine stories or anything not for older adults. Must show older adults (age 55 plus) in a positive manner." Accepts 1 mss/issue; 4 mss/year. Publishes ms 1 year after acceptance. **Publishes some new writers/year.** Recently published work by Harriet May Savitz, Donita K. Paul and Ann Gray.

How to Contact Send complete ms. Responds in 2 weeks to queries; 2 months to mss. No simultaneous submissions. Sample copy for $6 and 9 × 12 SAE. Writer's guidelines for #10 SASE or by e-mail.

Payment/Terms Pays $60-125. Pays on acceptance for first North American serial rights.

Tips "Practice writing dialogue! Listen to people talk; take notes; master dialogue writing! Not easy, but well worth it! Most inquiry letters are far too long. If you can't sell me an idea in a brief paragraph, you're not going to sell the reader on reading your finished article or story."

$ MSLEXIA

For Women Who Write, P.O. Box 656, Newcastle Upon Tyne NE99 1PZ United Kingdom. +44 (0)191 233 3860. Fax: +44 (0)191 233 3882. E-mail: postbag@mslexia.co.uk. Website: www.mslexia.co.uk.. **Contact:** Daneet Steffens, editor. Magazine: A4; 6 8 pages; some illustrations; photos. "Mslexia is for women who write, who want to write, who have a specialist interest in women's writing or who teach creative writing. Mslexia is a blend of features, articles, advice, listings, and original prose and poetry. Many parts of the magazine are open to submission from any women. Please request contributors' guidelines prior to sending in work." Quarterly. Circ. 20,000.

Needs No work from men accepted, except on letters' page. Prose and poetry in each issue is to a specific theme (e.g. sins, travel, rain). Send SASE for themes. Publishes ms 1-2 months after acceptance. **Publishes 40-50 new writers/year**. Length: 2,200 words; average length: 2,000 words. Publishes short shorts to a specific theme and autobiography (900 words). Recent themes have been: The Four Elements, Idols, Skin. Also publishes poetry.

How to Contact Accepts submissions by post, and by e-mail from overseas only (postbag@mslexia.co.uk). See www.mslexia.co.uk to read contributors' guidelines before submitting. Responds in 3 months to mss. Guidelines for SAE, e-mail, fax or on website.
Payment/Terms Pays £25 per poem; £15 per 1,000 words prose; features by negotiation. Plus contributors' copies.
Tips "Well structured, short pieces preferred. We look for intelligence and a strong sense of voice and place. Consider the obvious interpretations of the theme—then try to think of a new slant. Dare to be different. Make sure the piece is strong on craft as well as content. Extracts from novels are unlikely to be suitable."

$ THE NEW YORKER

4 Times Square, New York NY 10036. (212) 286-2860. Website: www.newyorker.com. A quality magazine of interesting, well-written stories, articles, essays and poems for a literate audience. Weekly. Circ. 750,000.
Needs Accepts 1 mss/issue.
How to Contact Send complete ms as .pdf attachments via online e-mail manager. No more than 1 story or 6 poems should be submitted. No attachments. Responds in 3 months to mss. No simultaneous submissions. Writer's guidelines online.
Payment/Terms Payment varies. Pays on acceptance.
Tips "Be lively, original, not overly literary. Write what you want to write, not what you think the editor would like. Send poetry to Poetry Department."

N $ OCEAN MAGAZINE

P.O. Box 84, Rodanthe, NC 27968. (252)256-2296. E-mail: diane@oceanmag.com. Website: www.oceanmag.org. **Contact:** Diane Buccheri, editor. Magazine. "Ocean Magazine serves to celebrate and protect the greatest, most comprehensive resource for life on earth, our world's ocean. Ocean publishes articles, stories, poems, essays, and photography about the ocean—observations, experiences, scientific and environmental discussions—written with fact and feeling, illustrated with images from nature." Quarterly. Estab. 2003. Circ. 10,000.
Needs Adventure, fantasy, historical, romance. Accepts 1-2 mss/year. Length: 100-2,000 words.
How to Contact Query first. Accepts submissions by e-mail. Responds to queries in 2 weeks. Responds to mss in 1 month. Considers simultaneous submissions, previously published submissions.
Payment/Terms Pays on publication. Acquires one-time rights. Pays $75-200.

$ OUTLOOKS

#1B, 1230A 17th Avenue SW, Calgary AB T2T 0B8 Canada. (403) 228-1157. Fax: (403) 228-7735. E-mail: main@outlooks.ca. Website: www.outlooks.ca. **Contact:** Roy Heale, editor. Magazine. "National lifestyle publisher for Canada's Gay and Lesbian community." Monthly. Estab. 1997. Circ. 37,500.
Needs Adventure, erotica, humor/satire. Accepts 10 mss/year. Manuscript published 2 months after acceptance. Length: 1,200-1,600 words.
How to Contact Query with clips of published work. Responds to queries in 2 weeks. Guidelines available on website.
Payment/Terms Acquires first rights. Pays between $120-$160 for fiction. Publication is copyrighted.

$ PAKN TREGER

National Yiddish Book Center, 1021 West Street, Amherst MA 01002. (413)256-4900. Fax: (413)256-4700. E-mail: aatherley@bikher.org. Website: www.yiddishbookcenter.org. **Contact:** Anne Atherley, editor's assistant. Literary magazine/journal. "Pakn Treger is looking for high-quality writing for a secular audience interested in Yiddish and Jewish history, literature, and culture." Biannual. Circ. 30,000.

Needs Historical, humor/satire, mystery. Accepts 2 mss/year. Manuscript published 4 months after acceptance. Length: 1,200-5,000 words.

How to Contact Query first. Accepts submissions by e-mail. Responds to queries in 2 weeks; mss in 2 months. Sample copy available via e-mail request or viewed on website. Guidelines available via e-mail.

Payment/Terms Acquires one-time rights.

Tips "Read the magazine and visit website."

$ POCKETS

The Upper Room, 1908 Grand Ave., P.O. Box 340004, Nashville TN 37203-0004. (615) 340-7333. Fax: (615) 340-7267. E-mail: pockets@upperroom.org. Website: www.pockets.org. **Contact**: Lynn W. Gilliam, editor. Magazine: 7 × 11; 48 pages; some photos. "Pockets is a Christian, inter-denominational publication for children 6-11 years of age. Each issue reflects a specific theme." Estab. 1981. Circ. 96,000.

- *Pockets*has received honors from the Educational Press Association of America.

Needs Adventure, ethnic/multicultural, historical (general), religious/inspirational, slice-of-life vignettes. No fantasy, science fiction, talking animals. "All submissions should address the broad theme of the magazine. Each issue is built around one theme with material which can be used by children in a variety of ways. Scripture stories, fiction, poetry, prayers, art, graphics, puzzles and activities are included. Submissions do not need to be overtly religious. They should help children experience a Christian lifestyle that is not always a neatly-wrapped moral package, but is open to the continuing revelation of God's will. Seasonal material, both secular and liturgical, is desired. No violence, horror, sexual, racial stereotyping or fiction containing heavy moralizing." Receives 200 unsolicited mss/month. Accepts 3-4 mss/issue; 33-44 mss/year. Publishes ms 1 year to 18 months after acceptance. **Publishes 15 new writers/year.** Length: 600-1,400 words; average length: 1,200 words.

How to Contact Send complete ms. Cover letter not required. Responds in 6 weeks to mss. Accepts one-time reprints, multiple submissions. For a sample copy, themes and/or guidelines send 9 × 12 SASE with 4 first-class stamps. Writer's guidelines, themes, and due dates available online.

Payment/Terms Pays 14¢/word, plus 2-5 contributor's copies. Pays on acceptance for first North American serial rights. Sponsors an annual fiction-writing contest.

Tips "We receive many inappropriate maunscripts. Study guidelines and themes before submitting. Many manuscripts we receive are simply inappropriate. New themes published in December of each year. We strongly advise sending for themes or reading them on the website before submitting." Include SASE with all submissions.

$ PORTLAND MONTHLY

722 Congress St., Portland ME 04102. (207)775-4339. Fax: (207)775-2334. E-mail: editor@portlandmonthly.com. Website: www.portlandmagazine.com. **Contact:** Colin Sargent, editor. Magazine: 200 pages; 60 lb. paper; 100 lb. cover stock; illustrations; photos. "City lifestyle magazine—fiction, style, business, real estate, controversy, fashion, cuisine, interviews and art relating to the Maine area." Monthly. Estab. 1986. Circ. 100,000.

Needs Contemporary, literary (Maine connection). Query first. Receives 20 unsolicited mss/month. Accepts 1 ms/issue; 10 mss/year. **Publishes 50 new writers/year.** Recently published work by Rick Mood y, Ann Hood, C.D.B Bryan, Joan Connor, Mameve Medwed, Jason Brown, Sarah Graves, Tess Gerritsor and Sebastian Junger.

How to Contact Send complete ms. SASE.

Payment/Terms Pays on publication for first North American serial rights.

Tips "We publish ambitious short fiction featuring everyone from Rick Moody to newly discovered fiction by Edna St. Vincent Millay."

$ ELLERY QUEEN'S MYSTERY MAGAZINE

267 Broadway, 4th Floor, New York NY 10007. (212)686-7188. Fax: (212)686-7414. E-mail: elleryqueenmm@dellmagazines.com. Website: www.themysteryplace.com/eqmm. **Contact:** Janet Hutchings, editor. Magazine: 5⅞ × 8⅝, 112 pages with special 192-page combined March/April and September/October issues. "Ellery Queen's Mystery Magazine welcomes submissions from both new and established writers. We publish every kind of mystery short story: the psychological suspense tale, the deductive puzzle, the private eye case, the gamut of crime and detection from the realistic (including the policeman's lot and stories of police procedure) to the more imaginative (including "locked rooms" and "impossible crimes"). EQMM has been in continuous publication since 1941. From the beginning, three general criteria have been employed in evaluating submissions: We look for strong writing, an original and exciting plot, and professional craftsmanship. We encourage writers whose work meets these general criteria to read an issue of EQMM before making a submission." Magazine for lovers of mystery fiction. Estab. 1941. Circ. 100,000 readers.

- *EQMM* has won numerous awards and sponsors its own award yearly for the best EQMM stories nominated by its readership.

Needs Mystery/suspense. No explicit sex or violence, no gore or horror. Seldom publishes parodies or pastiches. "We accept only mystery, crime, suspense and detective fiction." 2,500-8,000 words is the preferred range. Also publishes minute mysteries of 250 words; novellas up to 20,000 words from established authors. Publishes ms 6-12 months after acceptance. Agented fiction 50%. **Publishes 10 new writers/year.** Recently published work by Jeffery Deaver, Joyce Carol Oates and Margaret Maron. Sometimes comments on rejected mss.

How to Contact Send complete ms with SASE for reply. No e-mail submissions. No query necessary. Responds in 3 months to mss. Accepts simultaneous, multiple submissions. Sample copy for $5.50. Writer's guidelines for SASE or online.

Payment/Terms Pays 5-8¢/ a word, occasionally higher for established authors. Pays on acceptance for first North American serial rights.

Tips "We have a Department of First Stories and usually publish at least one first story an issue, i.e., the author's first published fiction. We select stories that are fresh and of the kind our readers have expressed a liking for. In writing a detective story, you must play fair with the reader, providing clues and necessary information. Otherwise you have a better chance of publishing if you avoid writing to formula."

$ SEEK

8805 Governor's Hill Drive, Suite 400, Cincinnati OH 45239. (513)931-4050, ext. 351. Website: www.standardpub.com. Magazine: 5½ × 8½; 8 pages; newsprint paper; art and photo in each issue. "Inspirational stories of faith-in-action for Christian adults; a Sunday School take-home paper." Quarterly. Circ. 27,000.

Needs Religious/inspirational, Religious fiction and religiously slanted historical and humorous fiction. No poetry. List of upcoming themes available online. Accepts 150 mss/year. Publishes ms 1 year after acceptance.

How to Contact Send complete ms. Accepts submissions by e-mail. Prefers submissions by e-mail. Writer's guidelines online.

Payment/Terms Pays 7¢/word. Pays on acceptance for first North American serial, pays 5¢ for second serial (reprint) rights.

Tips "Write a credible story with a Christian slant—no preachments; avoid overworked themes such as joy in suffering, generation gaps, etc. Most manuscripts are rejected by us because of irrelevant topic or message, unrealistic story, or poor charater and/or plot development. We use fiction stories that are believable."

$ SHINE BRIGHTLY

P.O. Box 7259, Grand Rapids MI 49510. (616)241-5616. Fax: (616)241-5558. E-mail: shinebrightly@gemsgc.org. Website: www.gemsgc.org. **Contact:** Sara Hilton, senior editor. Monthly with combined

summer issue. Circ. 17,000. "SHINE brightly is designed to help girls ages 9-14 see how God is at work in their lives and in the world around them."
Needs adventure, animal, contemporary, health, history, humorous, multicultural, nature/environment, problem-solving, religious, sports. Does not want "unrealistic stories and those with trite, easy endings. We are interested in manuscripts that show how girls can change the world." Buys 30 mss/year. Length: 400-1,000 words; average length: 800 words.
How to Contact Send complete ms within body of e-mail. No attachments. Responds to mss in 1 month. Will consider simultaneous submissions. Guidelines are on website.
Payment/Terms Pays $35/story. Pays on publication for first North American serial, second serial (reprint), simultaneous rights. Original artwork not returned at job's completion.
Tips "Please check our website before submitting. We have a specific style and theme that deals with how girls can impact the world. The stories should be current, deal with pre-adolescent problems and joys, and help girls see God at work in their lives through humor as well as problem-solving."

$ STANDARD

Nazarene Publishing House, 2923 Troost, Kansas City MO 64109. (816) 931-1900. Fax: (816)412-8306. E-mail: clyourdon@wordaction.com. Website: www.wordaction.com. **Contact:** Charlie L. Yourdon, editor; Everett Leadingham, senior editor. Magazine: 8½ × 11; 8 pages; illustrations; photos. Inspirational reading for adults. "In Standard we want to show Christianity in action, and we prefer to do that through stories that hold the reader's attention." Weekly. Estab. 1936. Circ. 100,000.
Needs "Looking for stories that show Christianity in action." Accepts 200 mss/year. Publishes ms 14-18 months after acceptance. **Publishes some new writers/year.**
How to Contact Accepts submissions by e-mail. Postal submissions: send complete ms. SASE. Accepts simultaneous submissions but pays at reprint rates. Writer's guidelines and sample copy for SAE with 2 first-class stamps or available by e-mail request.
Payment/Terms Pays 312¢/word for first rights; 2¢/word for reprint rights, and contributor's copies. Pays on acceptance for one-time rights, whether first or reprint rights.
Tips "Be conscientious in your use of Scripture; don't overload your story with quotations. When you quote the Bible, quote it exactly and cite chapter, verse, and version used. (We prefer NIV.) *Standard* will handle copyright matters for Scripture. Except for quotations from the Bible, written permission for the use of any other copyrighted material (especially song lyrics) is the responsibility of the writer. Keep in mind the international audience of *Standard* with regard to geographic ref erences and holidays. We cannot use stories about cultural, national, or secular holidays. Do not mention specific church affiliations. *Standard* is read in a variety of denominations. Do not submit any man uscrip ts which has been submitted to or published in any of the following: *Vista, Wesleyan Advocate, Holiness Today, Preacher's Magazine, World Mission, Women Alive,* or various teen and children's publications produced by WordAction Publishing Company. These are overlapping markets."

$ ST. ANTHONY MESSENGER

28 W. Liberty St., Cincinnati OH 45202-6498. (513) 241-5615. Fax: (513) 241-0399. E-mail: patm@americancatholic.org. Website: www.americancatholic.org. **Contact:** Father Pat McCloskey, O.F.M., editor. Magazine: 8 × 10¾; 60 pages; illustrations; photos. "St. Anthony Messenger is a Catholic family magazine which aims to help its readers lead more fully human and Christian lives. We publish articles which report on a changing church and world, opinion pieces written from the perspective of Christian faith and values, personality profiles, and fiction which entertains and informs." Estab. 1893. Circ. 308,884.

- This is a leading Catholic magazine, but has won awards for both religious and secular journalism and writing from the Catholic Press Association, the International Association of Business Communicators, and the Society of Professional Journalists.

Needs Mainstream, religious/inspirational, senior citizen/retirement. "We do not want mawkishly sentimental or preachy fiction. Stories are most often rejected for poor plotting and characterization; bad dialogue—listen to how people talk; inadequate motivation. Many stories say nothing, are 'happenings' rather than stories." No fetal journals, no rewritten Bible stories. Receives 60-70 unsolicited mss/month. Accepts 1 mss/issue; 12 mss/year. Publishes ms 1 year after acceptance. **Publishes 3 new writers/year.** Recently published work by Geraldine Marshall Gutfreund, John Salustri, Beth Dotson, Miriam Pollikatsikis and Joseph Pici. Sometimes requests revisions before acceptance.
How to Contact Send complete ms. Accepts submissions by e-mail, fax. "For quickest response send self-addressed stamped postcard with choices: "Yes, we're interested in publishing; Maybe, we'd like to hold for future consideration; No, we've decided to pass on the publication." Responds in 3 weeks to queries; 2 months to mss. No simultaneous submissions. Sample copy for 9 × 12 SASE with 4 first-class stamps. Writer's guidelines online. Reviews fiction.
Payment/Terms Pays 16¢/word maximum and 2 contributor's copies; $1 charge for extras. Pays on acceptance for first North American serial, electronic rights.
Tips "We publish one story a month and we get up to 1,000 a year. Too many offer simplistic 'solutions' or answers. Pay attention to endings. Easy, simplistic, deus ex machina endings don't work. People have to feel characters in the stories are real and have a reason to care about them and what happens to them. Fiction entertains but can also convey a point and sound values."

$ THE STRAND MAGAZINE

P.O. Box 1418, Birmingham MI 48012-1418. (248)788-5948. Fax: (248)874-1046. E-mail: strandmag@strandmag.com. Website: www.strandmag.com. **Contact:** A.F. Gulli, editor. "After an absence of nearly half a century, the magazine known to millions for bringing Sir Arthur Conan Doyle's ingenious detective, Sherlock Holmes, to the world has once again appeared on the literary scene. First launched in 1891, The Strand included in its pages the works of some of the greatest writers of the 20th century: Agatha Christie, Dorothy Sayers, Margery Allingham, W. Somerset Maugham, Graham Greene, P.G. Wodehouse, H.G. Wells, Aldous Huxley and many others. In 1950, economic difficulties in England caused a drop in circulation which forced the magazine to cease publication." Quarterly. Estab. 1998. Circ. 50,000.
Needs Horror, humor/satire, mystery/suspense (detective stories), suspense, tales of the unexpected, tales of terror and the supernatural "written in the classic tradition of this century's great author's. "We are NOT interested in submissions with any sexual content." Stories can be set in any time or place, provided they are well written and the plots interesting and well thought out." Publishes ms 4 months after acceptance.
How to Contact SASE (IRCs if outside the US). Query first. Responds in 1 month to queries. Sample copy not available. Writer's guidelines for #10 SASE.
Payment/Terms Pays $50-175. Pays on acceptance for first North American serial rights.

$ WASHINGTON RUNNING REPORT

13710 Ashby Rd, Rockville MD 20853. (301) 871-0006. Fax: (301) 871-0005. E-mail: kathy@runwashington.com. Website: www.runwashington.com. **Contact:** Kathy Freedman, editor. Magazine. "Written by runners for runners, Washington Running Report covers the running and racing scene in metropolitan Washington DC. Features include runner rankings, training tips and advice, feature articles on races, race results, race calendar, humor, product reviews and other articles of interest to runners." Bimonthly. Estab. 1984. Circ. 35,000.
Needs Adventure, fantasy, historical, humor/satire, mainstream, mystery. Accepts 1-2 mss/year. Manuscript published 2-4 months after acceptance. Length: 750-1,500 words. Stories must be about running.
How to Contact Send complete ms with cover letter. Accepts submissions by e-mail. Responds to queries in 2-3 weeks. Responds to mss in 1-2 months. Considers simultaneous submissions, previously published submissions. Sample copy free upon request.

Payment/Terms Acquires first rights, one-time rights, electronic rights.

$ WITCHES AND PAGANS

BBI, Inc., P.O. Box 687, Forest Grove OR 97116. (503)430-8817. E-mail: annel@bbimedia.com; meditor@newwitch.com. Website: www.newwitch.com. **Contact:** Anne Niven, editor. Magazine. "Witches and Pagans is dedicated to Witches, Wiccans, Neo-Pagans, and various other earth-based, ethnic, pre/post-christian, shamanic and magical practitioners. We hope to reach not only those already involved in what we cover, but also the curious and completely new as well." Quarterly.

Needs Needs contemporary Pagan-themed fiction only. Does not accept fictionalized retellings of real events. Avoid gratuitous sex and violence: in movie rating terms think PG-13. Also avoid gratuitous sentimentality and Pagan moralizing: don't beat our readers with the Rede or the Threefold Law. Accepts 3-4 mss/year. Length: 1,000 words (min)-5,000 words (max).

How to Contact Send complete ms with cover letter. Accepts submissions by e-mail. Responds to queries in 1-2 weeks. Responds to mss in 1 month. Sample copy available for. Guidelines available on website.

Tips "Read the magazine, do your research, write the piece, send it in. That's really the only way to get started as a writer: Everything else is window dressing."

▦ $ WOMAN'S WEEKLY

IPC Magazines, The Blue Fin Building, 110 Southward Street, London SE1 OSU United Kingdom. **Contact:** Gaynor Davies. Publishes 1 serial and at least 2 short stories/week.

Needs "Short stories can be on any theme, but must have depth. No explicit sex or violence. Serials need not be written in installments. They are submitted as complete manuscripts and we split them up, or send first installment of serial (4,000 words) and synopsis of the rest."

How to Contact Send an sae for Writers' Guidelines.

Payment/Terms Short story payment starts at £100 and rises as writer becomes a more regular contributor. Serial payments start at around £600/installment. Writers also receive contributor's copies.

Tips "Read the magazine and try to understand who the publication is aimed at."

▦ ☐ $ WRITERS' FORUM

Select Publisher Services, P.O. Box 6337, Bournemouth BH1 9EH United Kingdom. (44)1202 586848. E-mail: carl@selectps.com. Website: www.writers-forum.com. **Contact**: Carl Styants, editor. Monthly: A4; 68 pages; illustrations; photos. "In each issue Writers' Forum covers the who, why, what, where, when and how of writing. You will find the latest on markets, how-to articles, courses/holidays for writers and much more. There is also a short story competition in every issue a poetry competition, and a young writer's competition in every issue with cash prizes and all winning entries and runners-up printed in the magazine. Prizes range from £300 to £100. Monthly. Estab. 1995.

Needs Historical, horror (psychological), literary, mainstream, mystery/suspense (cozy, private eye/hardboiled), romance (contemporary, futuristic/time travel, historical, romantic suspense), science fiction (soft/sociological), thriller/espionage, western (frontier saga, traditional), young adult/teen (adventure, easy-to-read, historical, problem novels, romance). Receives hundreds unsolicited mss/month. Accepts 3-4 mss/issue; 33 mss/year. Publishes ms 2-3 months after acceptance. Length: 1,000-3,000 words; average length: 1,800 words. Also publishes literary essays, literary criticism, and poetry. Full critique on all rejected competition mss.

How to Contact Query. Accepts submissions by e-mail, post; $15 fee per competition entry. Send SASE (or IRC) for return of ms or send disposable copy of the ms and #10 SASE for reply only. Responds in 2-3 weeks to queries; 3-4 weeks to mss. Accepts simultaneous submissions. Sample copy online. Writer's guidelines online. Reviews fiction.

Payment/Terms Pays £300 maximum and 1 contributor's copy; additional copies $6. Pays 1 month following publication. Acquires first rights. Sponsors awards/contests.

Tips "A good introduction and a original slant on a common theme. Always read the competition rules and our guidelines."

$ WRITERS' JOURNAL

The Complete Writer's Magazine, P.O. Box 394, Perham MN 56573-0394. (218)346-7921. Fax: (218)346-7924. E-mail: editor@writersjournal.com. Website: www.writersjournal.com. "WRITERS' Journal is read by thousands of aspiring writers whose love of writing has taken them to the next step: Writing for money. We are an instructional manual giving writers the tools and information necessary to get their work published. We also print works by authors who have won our writing contests." Bimonthly.

Needs "We publish fiction stories from winners of our contests—16 contests/year." Receives 200 contest entries mss/month. Publishes article submissions 5-7 mss/issue; 30-40 mss/year. **Publishes 100 new writers/year.** Also publishes poetry.

How to Contact Postal mail only. Responds in 6 weeks to queries; 6 months to article mss. Accepts unpublished simultaneous submissions. Sample copy for $6.

Payment/Terms Pays prize money on publication for one-time rights.

MARKETS

Book Publishers

In this section, you will find many of the "big name"' book publishers. Many of these publishers remain tough markets for new writers or for those whose work might be considered literary or experimental. Indeed, some only accept work from established authors, and then often only through an author's agent. Although having your novel published by one of the big commercial publishers listed in this section is difficult, it is not impossible. The trade magazine *Publishers Weekly* regularly features interviews with writers whose first novels are being released by top publishers. Many editors at large publishing houses find great satisfaction in publishing a writer's first novel.

On page 534, you'll find the publishing industry's "family tree," which maps out each of the large book publishing conglomerates' divisions, subsidiaries and imprints. Remember, most manuscripts are acquired by imprints, not their parent company, so avoid submitting to the conglomerates themselves.

Also listed here are "small presses" publishing four or more titles annually. Included among them are independent presses, university presses and other nonprofit publishers. Introducing new writers to the reading public has become an increasingly important role of these smaller presses at a time when the large conglomerates are taking fewer chances on unknown writers. Many of the successful small presses listed in this section have built their reputations and their businesses in this way and have become known for publishing prize-winning fiction.

These smaller presses also tend to keep books in print longer than larger houses. And, since small presses publish a smaller number of books, each title is equally important to the publisher, and each is promoted in much the same way and with the same commitment. Editors also stay at small presses longer because they have more of a stake in the business—often they own the business. Many smaller book publishers are writers themselves and know firsthand the importance of a close editor-author or publisher-author relationship.

TYPES OF BOOK PUBLISHERS

Large or small, the publishers in this section publish books "for the trade." That is, unlike textbook, technical or scholarly publishers, trade publishers publish books to be sold to the general consumer through bookstores, chain stores or other retail outlets. Within the trade book field, however, there are a number of different types of books.

The easiest way to categorize books is by their physical appearance and the way they are marketed. Hardcover books are the more expensive editions of a book, sold through bookstores and carrying a price tag of around $20 and up. Trade paperbacks are soft-bound books, also sold mostly in bookstores, but they carry a more modest price tag of usually around $10 to $20. Today a lot of fiction is published in this form because it means a lower financial risk than hardcover.

Mass market paperbacks are another animal altogether. These are the smaller "pocket-size" books available at bookstores, grocery stores, drug stores, chain retail outlets, etc. Much genre or category fiction is published in this format. This area of the publishing industry is very open to the work of talented new writers who write in specific genres such as science fiction, romance and mystery.

At one time publishers could be easily identified and grouped by the type of books they produce. Today, however, the lines between hardcover and paperback books are blurred. Many publishers known for publishing hardcover books also publish trade paperbacks and have paperback imprints. This enables them to offer established authors (and a very few lucky newcomers) hard-soft deals in which their book comes out in both versions. Thanks to the mergers of the past decade, too, the same company may own several hardcover and paperback subsidiaries and imprints, even though their editorial focuses may remain separate.

CHOOSING A BOOK PUBLISHER

In addition to checking the bookstores and libraries for books by publishers that interest you, you may want to refer to the Category Index at the back of this book to find publishers divided by specific subject categories. The subjects listed in the Index are general. Read individual listings to find which subcategories interest a publisher. For example, you will find several romance publishers listed, but read the listings to find which type of romance is considered—gothic, contemporary, regency or futuristic. See You've Got a Story on page 1 for more on how to refine your list of potential markets.

The icons appearing before the names of the publishers will also help you in selecting a publisher. These codes are especially important in this section, because many of the publishing houses listed here require writers to submit through an agent. The symbol indicates that a publisher accepts agented submissions only. A icon identifies those that mostly publish established and agented authors, while a points to publishers most open to new writers. See the inside front cover of this book for a complete list and explanations of symbols used in this book.

IN THE LISTINGS

As with other sections in this book, we identify new listings with a symbol. In this section, most with this symbol are not new publishers, but instead are established publishers who were unable or decided not to list last year and are therefore new to this edition.

In addition to the symbol indicating new listings, we include other symbols to help you in narrowing your search. English-speaking foreign markets are denoted by a . The maple leaf symbol identifies Canadian presses. If you are not a Canadian writer but are interested in a Canadian press, check the listing carefully. Many small presses in Canada receive grants and other funds from their provincial or national government and are, therefore, restricted to publishing Canadian authors.

We also include editorial comments set off by a bullet (•) within listings. This is where we include information about any special requirements or circumstances that will help you know even more about the publisher's needs and policies. The star signals that this market is an imprint or division of a larger publisher. The symbol identifies publishers who have recently received honors or awards for their books. The denotes publishers who produce comics and graphic novels.

Each listing includes a summary of the editorial mission of the house, an overarching principle that ties together what they publish. Under the heading **Contact** we list one or more editors, often with their specific area of expertise.

Book editors asked us again this year to emphasize the importance of paying close attention to the **Needs** and **How to Contact** subheads of listings for book publishers. Unlike magazine editors who want to see complete manuscripts of short stories, most of the book publishers listed here ask that writers send a query letter with an outline and/or synopsis and several chapters of their novel. The Business of Fiction Writing, beginning on page 49 of this book, outlines how to prepare work to submit directly to a publisher.

There are no subsidy book publishers listed in *Novel & Short Story Writer's Market*. By subsidy, we mean any arrangement in which the writer is expected to pay all or part of the cost of producing, distributing and marketing his book. We feel a writer should not be asked to share in any cost of turning his manuscript into a book. All the book publishers listed here told us that they *do not charge writers* for publishing their work. **If any of the publishers listed here ask you to pay any part of publishing or marketing your manuscript, please let us know.** See our Complaint Procedure on the copyright page of this book.

A NOTE ABOUT AGENTS

Some publishers are willing to look at unsolicited submissions, but most feel having an agent is in the writer's best interest. In this section more than any other, you'll find a number of publishers who prefer submissions from agents. That's why we've included a section of agents open to submissions from fiction writers (page 106). For even more agents along with a great deal of helpful articles about approaching and working with them, refer to *Guide to Literary Agents* (Writer's Digest Books).

If you use the Internet or another resource to find an agent not listed in this book, be wary of any agents who charge large sums of money for reading a manuscript. Reading fees do not guarantee representation. Think of an agent as a potential business partner and feel free to ask tough questions about his or her credentials, experience and business practices.

☐ ABERDEEN BAY

5676 Ridge View Dr., Alexandria VA 22310. E-mail: zhangqandy@gmail.com. Website: www.aberdeenbay.com. **Contact:** Joan Roberts, Acquisition Director. "We're a growing independent publisher who publishes trade paperback originals with outstanding quality." Publishes paperback originals, paperback reprints, e-books. Format: POD printing. Published 14 new titles last year. Plans 10 debut novels this year. Averages 18 total titles/year; 12 fiction titles/year. Distributes/promotes titles through various retailers.

Needs Needs ethnic/multicultural (Asian), family saga, feminist, gay, glitz, historical, lesbian, literary, mainstream, young adult/teen (adventure, easy-to-read, historical, mystery/suspense, problem novels, romance, series, sports, western).

◪ ABSEY & CO.

23011 Northcrest Drive, Spring TX 77389. (281)257-2340. E-mail: abseyandco@aol.com; info@absey.biz. Website: www.absey.biz. **Contact:** Edward Wilson, editor-in-chief. "We are interested in book-length fiction of literary merit with a firm intended audience." Publishes hardcover, trade paperback and mass market paperback originals. **Published 3-5 debut authors within the last year.** Averages 6-10 total titles, 6-10 fiction titles/year.

Needs Juvenile, mainstream/contemporary, short story collections. Published *Where I'm From*, by George Ella Lyon; *Blast Man Standing*, by Robert V. Spelleri.

How to Contact Accepts unsolicited mss. Query with SASE. Responds in 3 months to queries; 6-9 months to mss. No simultaneous submissions, electronic submissions.
Terms Royalty and advance vary. Publishes ms 1 year after acceptance. Ms guidelines online.

ACADEMY CHICAGO PUBLISHERS

363 W. Erie St., 4W, Chicago IL 60654. (312)751-7300. E-mail: info@academychicago.com. Website: www.academychicago.com. **Contact:** Anita Miller, senior editor. Estab. 1975. Midsize independent publisher. Publishes hardcover originals and trade paperback reprints. Averages 15 total titles/year.
Needs Historical, mainstream/contemporary, military/war, mystery. "We look for quality work, but we do not publish experimental, avant-garde novels." Biography, history, academic and anthologies. Only the most unusual mysteries, no private-eyes or thrillers. No explicit sex or violence. Serious fiction, no romance/adventure. "We will consider historical fiction that is well researched. No science fiction/fantasy, no religious/inspirational, no how-to, no cookbooks. In general, we are very conscious of women's roles. We publish very few children's books." Published *Clean Start*, by Patricia Margaret Page (first fiction); *Cutter's Island: Caesar in Captivity*, by Vincent Panella (first fiction, historical); *Murder at the Paniomic Games*, by Michael B. Edward.
How to Contact Accepts unsolicited mss. Do not submit by e-mail or fax. Submit 3 sample chapter(s), synopsis. Accepts queries by mail. Include cover letter briefly describing the content of your work. Send SASE or IRC. "Manuscripts without envelopes will be discarded. *Mailers* are a *must* even from agents." Responds in 3 months to queries. No electronic submissions.
Terms Pays 7-10% royalty on wholesale price. Average advance: modest. Publishes ms 18 months after acceptance. Ms guidelines online.

AGELESS PRESS

3759 Collinst St., Sarasota FL 34232. E-mail: irishope@comcast.net. Website: http://irisforrest.com. **Contact:** Iris Forrest, editor. Independent publisher. Publishes paperback originals. Books: acid-free paper; notched perfect binding; no illustrations. Averages 1 total title/year.
Needs Experimental, fantasy, humor, literary, mainstream/contemporary, mystery, new age/mystic, science fiction, short story collections, thriller/espionage. Looking for material "based on personal computer experiences." Stories selected by editor. Published *Computer Legends, Lies & Lore*, by various (anthology); and *Computer Tales of Fact and Fantasy*, by various (anthology).
How to Contact Does not accept unsolicited mss. Query with SASE. Accepts queries by e-mail, fax, mail. Responds in 1 week to queries; 1 week to mss. Accepts simultaneous submissions, electronic submissions, submissions on disk. Sometimes comments on rejected mss.
Terms Average advance: negotiable. Publishes ms 6-12 months after acceptance.

ALGONQUIN BOOKS OF CHAPEL HILL

P.O. Box 2225, Chapel Hill NC 27515-2225. E-mail: inquiry@algonquin.com. Website: www.algonquin.com. **Contact:** Editorial Department. Publishes hardcover originals. Averages 24 total titles/year.
Needs Literary fiction and nonfiction, cookbooks and lifestyle books (about family, animals, food, flowers, adventure, and other topics of interest). No poetry, genre fiction (romance, science fiction, etc.) or children's books. Recently published *Saving the World*, by Julia Alvarez; *Which Brings Me to You*, by Steve Almond and Julianna Baggott; *Hope and Other Dangerous Pursuits*, by Laila Lalami.
How to Contact Send a 20-page sample of your work, along with a cover letter, SASE, and a check for return postage (if you wish to have your mss returned). No email queries or submissions.
Terms Ms guidelines online.

AMERICAN ATHEIST PRESS

P.O. Box 5733, Parsippany NJ 07054-6733. (908)276-7300. Fax: (908)276-7402. E-mail: editor@atheists.org; info@atheists.org. Website: www.atheists.org. **Contact:** Framl Zindler, editor. Publishes trade paperback originals and reprints. Publishes monthly journal, American Atheist, for which are needed articles of interest to atheists. **Published 40-50% debut authors within the last year.** Averages 12 total titles/year.

Imprints Gustav Broukal Press

Needs Humor (satire of religion or of current religious leaders), anything of particular interest to atheists. "We rarely publish any fiction. But we have occasionally released a humorous book. No mainstream. For our press to consider fiction, it would have to tie in with the general focus of our press, which is the promotion of atheism and free thought."

How to Contact Submit outline, sample chapter(s). Responds in 4 months to queries. Accepts simultaneous submissions.

Terms Pays 5-10% royalty on retail price. Publishes ms within 2 years after acceptance. Ms to be submitted as MS Word attachments with e-mail. Hard copy may be requested.

ANNICK PRESS, LTD.

15 Patricia Ave., Toronto ON M2M 1H9 Canada. (416)221-4802. Fax: (416)221-8400. E-mail: annickpress@annickpress.com. Website: www.annickpress.com. Publisher of children's books. Publishes hardcover and trade paperback originals. Average print order; 9,000. First novel print order: 7,000. Plans 18 first novels this year. Averages 25 total titles/year. Distributes titles through Firefly Books Ltd.

- *Does not accept unsolicited mss.*

Needs Juvenile, young adult. fiction, and non-fiction.

How to Contact Query with SASE. Responds in 1 month queries; 3 months to mss. No simultaneous submissions, electronic submissions. Sometimes comments on rejected mss.

Terms Publishes ms 2 years after acceptance. Ms guidelines online.

ANTARCTIC PRESS

7272 Wurzbach, Suite 204, San Antonio TX 78240. (210)614-0396. Website: www.antarctic-press.com. "Antarctic Press is a Texas-based company that was started in 1984. Since then, we have grown to become one of the largest publishers of comics in the United States. Over the years we have produced over 850 titles with a total circulation of over 5 million. Among our titles are some of the most respected and longest-running independent series in comics today. Since our inception, our main goal has been to establish a series of titles that are unique, entertaining, and high in both quality and profitability. The titles we currently publish exhibit all these traits, and appeal to a wide audience." Publishes comic books, graphic novels.

Terms Pays royalty on net receipts. Ms guidelines online.

ANVIL PRESS

278 East First Avenue, Vancouver BC V5T 1A6 Canada. E-mail: info@anvilpress.com. Website: www.anvilpress.com. **Contact:** Brian Kaufman, publisher. Estab. 1988. "Three-person operation with volunteer editorial board." Publishes trade paperback originals. Canadian authors only. Books: offset or web printing; perfect bound.**Published some debut authors within the last year.** Averages 8-10 total titles/year.

Needs Experimental, literary, short story collections. Contemporary, modern literature—no formulaic or genre. Published *Stolen*, by Annette Lapointe (novel); *Suburban Pornography*, by Matthew Firth (stories); *Elysium and Other Stories*, by Pamela Stewart; *Dirtbags*, by Teresa McWhirter (novel); *Black Rabbit and Other Stories* by Salvatore DiFalco.

How to Contact Accepts unsolicited mss, or query with SASE. Include estimated word count, brief bio. Send SASE for return of ms or send a disposable ms and SASE for reply only. No email submissions. Responds in 2 months to queries; 6 months to mss. Accepts simultaneous submissions.

Terms Pays 15% royalty on net receipts. Average advance: $500. Publishes ms 8 months after acceptance. Book catalog for 9 × 12 SAE with 2 first-class stamps. Ms guidelines online.

ARCHAIA

586 Devon St., 3rd Floor, Kearny NJ 07032-2804. E-mail: editorial@aspcomics.com. Website: www.archaiasp.com. **Contact:** Comics Submissions Department. "Archaia was founded as a home originally for Mark S. Smylie's comic Artesia. Now Mark and publishing partner Aki Liao have expanded ASP to include a line of idiosyncratic and creator-driven comic books and graphic novels in the fantasy, science fiction, and horror genres, as well as translations of several of Europe's best titles."

Needs "Archaia Studios Press (ASP) is interested in publishing creator-owned comic books in the adventure, fantasy, horror, pulp noir, and science fiction genres that contain idiosyncratic and atypical writing and art. ASP does not hire freelancers or arrange for freelance work, so submissions should only be for book and series proposals. ASP is primarily interested in full-color projects, but proposals for black & white projects will also be considered."

How to Contact Query with outline/synopsis and photocopies of completed pages. Prefers email lsubmissions. Accepts queries by snail mail. Include estimated page count and other technical details."

Terms Writer's guidelines on website.

ARIEL STARR PRODUCTIONS, LTD.

P.O. Box 17, Demarest NJ 07627. E-mail: darkbird@aol.com. **Contact:** Acquisitions department. Publishes paperback originals. **Published 2 debut authors within the last year.**

How to Contact Submit outline, 1 sample chapter. Accepts queries by e-mail. Include brief bio. Send SASE or IRC. Responds in 6 weeks to queries; 4 months to mss. Sometimes comments on rejected mss.

Terms Publishes ms one year after acceptance.

ARSENAL PULP PRESS

341 Water Street, Suite 200, Vancouver BC V6B 1B8 Canada. Website: www.arsenalpulp.com. **Contact:** Editorial Board. Estab. 1980. Literary press. Publishes hardcover and trade paperback originals, and trade paperback reprints. **Published some debut authors within the last year.** Plans 1,500 first novels this year. Plans 2 first novels this year. Averages 20 total titles/year. Distributes titles through Whitecap Books (Canada) and Consortium (U.S.). Promotes titles through reviews, excerpts and print advertising.

Needs Gay/lesbian, literary fiction and nonfiction, multicultural, regional (British Columbia), cultural studies, pop culture, political/sociological issues, cookbooks. No poetry at this time. We do not publish children's books.

How to Contact Accepts unsolicited mss. Submit outline, 2-3 sample chapter(s), synopsis. Include list of publishing credits. Send copy of ms and SASE (or with International Reply Coupons if sent from outside Canada) OR include e-mail address if manuscript does not need to be returned. Agented fiction 10%. Responds in 2 months to queries; 4 months to mss. Accepts simultaneous submissions. Sometimes comments on rejected mss.

Terms Publishes ms 1 year after acceptance. Book catalog and submission guidelines on website.

ARTEMIS PRESS

236 W. Portal Avenue #525, San Francisco CA 94127. (866)216-7333. E-mail: submissions@artemispress.com. Website: www.artemispress.com. **Contact:** Susan R. Skolnick, publisher and editor-in-chief. "Publisher of short fiction of interest to the worldwide women's community. We specialize in lesbian-related titles but are interested in all women-centered titles. We are open

to working with new authors." Publishes electronic editions of original, previously published material. **Published no debut authors within the last year.** Titles distributed and promoted online to target market.

Needs Mystery, suspense, romance, erotica, psychic/supernatural, and science fiction. Published *The Ladies Next Door*, by Jacqui Singleton (humor/satire); *Selects Her Own*, by Claire Garden (humor/satire); *Clicking Stones*, by Nancy Tyler Glenn (New Age/mystic); *Moon Madness and Other Stories*, by Liann Snow (short story collection); *Faith in Love*, by Liann Snow (humor/satire); *Luna Ascending: Stories of Love and Magic*, by Renee Brown (short story collection); *Windrow Garden*, by Janet McClellan (romance); *Never Letting Go*, by Suzanne Hollo (humor/satire); *Minding Therapy*, by Ros Johnson (humor/satire).

How to Contact Does not accept unsolicited mss. Agented fiction 5%. Responds in 3 months to queries. Does not accept simultaneous submissions.

Terms Buys all rights. Publishes ms 6 months after acceptance. Ms guidelines online.

ARTE PUBLICO PRESS

University of Houston, 452 Cullen Performance Hall, Houston TX 77204-2004. Fax: (713)743-3080. Website: www.artepublicopress.com. "Small press devoted to the publication of contemporary U.S.-Hispanic literature." Publishes hardcover originals, trade paperback originals and reprints. Averages 36 total titles/year.

- Arte Publico Press is the oldest and largest publisher of Hispanic literature for children and adults in the United States.

Imprints Pinata Books featuring children's and young adult literature by U.S.-Hispanic writers.

Needs Ethnic, literary, mainstream/contemporary, written by U.S.-Hispanic authors. Published *Project Death*, by Richard Bertematti (novel, mystery); *A Perfect Silence*, by Alba Ambert; *Song of the Hummingbird*, by Graciela Limoón; *Little Havana Blues: A Cuban-American Literature Anthology*.

How to Contact Accepts unsolicited mss. Query with SASE or submit 2 sample chapter(s), synopsis or submit complete ms. Agented fiction 1%. Responds in 2-4 months to queries; 3-6 months to mss. Accepts simultaneous submissions. Sometimes comments on rejected mss.

Terms Pays 10% royalty on wholesale price. Provides 20 author's copies; 40% discount on subsequent copies. Average advance: $1,000-3,000. Publishes ms 2 years after acceptance. Ms guidelines online.

ASPEN MOUNTAIN PRESS

18121-C East Hampden Ave., Aurora CO 80013. E-mail: submissions@aspenmountainpress.com. Website: www.AspenMountainPress.com. **Contact:** Sandra Hicks, Editor-in-Chief. "We are a small electronic press that specializes in e-books. A few outstanding stories are considered for print. We currently encourage newer, outstanding writers to take their craft to the next level. The bulk of our stories are romantic with varying degrees of sensuality/sexuality. We encourage romances between consenting adults. We encourage discussion among our authors; we frequently discuss marketing, we take author input into covers seriously, we pay every month royalties are earned." Publishes e-books. Format: POD printing; perfect bound. Average print order: 250-500. Debut novel print order: 250. **Published 30 debut writers last year in e-book**. Plans 25-30 debut novels this year. Averages 65 fiction titles/year. Member RWA, CIPA. Distributes/promotes titles through Fictionwise, AllRomance eBooks, Mobipocket, Amazon, 1Romance eBooks, Bookstrand.

Needs erotica, fantasy (space fantasy, sword and sorcery), gay, historical (erotic regency), horror (dark fantasy, futuristic, psychological, supernatural), lesbian, mystery/suspense (amateur sleuth, cozy, police procedural, private eye/hardboiled), psychic/supernatural, romance (contemporary, futuristic/time travel, gothic, regency, romantic suspense), science fiction (hard science/technological, soft/sociological), western (frontier saga, traditional, gay). Special interests: "We want heroes the reader can identify with and science fiction romance—No first person!" Published *Cold Warriors*, by Clare Dargin (science fiction romance); *Del Fantasma: Texas Tea*, by Maura Anderson (erotic paranormal romance); and Cover Me, by L.B. Gregg (erotic gay thriller). "We are also opening a regency line late summer 2010. See our website for details regarding Aurora Regency.

How to Contact Query with outline/synopsis and 4 sample chapters. Accepts queries by e-mail only; does not accept mail. Include estimated word count, brief bio, list of publishing credits, and indicate whether the ms is finished. Responds to queries in 3 months. Accepts unsolicited mss. Often critiques/comments on rejected mss. Responds to mss in 3-4 months.

Terms Sends pre-production galleys to author. Ms published 3-12 months after acceptance. Writer's guidelines on website. Pays royalties of 8% min for print, 35-40% max for e-books, 50% of net from resellers.

ATHENEUM BOOKS FOR YOUNG READERS

1230 Avenue of the Americas, New York NY 10020. (212)698-2715. Fax: (212)698-2796. E-mail: Emma.Dryden@simonandschuster.com. Website: http://imprints.simonandschuster.biz/atheneum. **Contact:** Caitlyn Dlouhy, editorial director. Estab. 1960. Atheneum Books for Young Readers is a hardcover imprint with a focus on literary fiction and fine picture books for preschoolers through young adults. Publishes special interest, first novels and new talent. Publishes 20+ picture books/year; 20+ middle readers/year; 20+ young adult titles/year.

- In recent years, Atheneum has received the Newberry Medal for *Kira-Kira* by Cynthia Kadohata and *The Higher Power of Lucky* by Susan Patron; the Caldecott Honor for international bestseller *Olivia* written and illustrated by Ian Falconer; the Siebert Honor for *Lightship* written and illustrated by Brian Floca; and National Book Award finalists *Skin Hunger* by Kathleen Duey and *The Underneath* by Kathi Appelt.

Needs Middle grade and YA adventure, fantasy, humor, mainstream/contemporary, mystery, suspense, and picture books. "We do not need how-to pamphlets, ABC books, coloring books, or board books." **How to Contact** "*We do not accept unsolicited queries, partial, or full manuscript submissions, unless from an agent.*"

Terms Average print order is 10,000 -15,000 for a first middle grade or young adult book; 7,500-20,000 for a first picture book. Pays royalty on hardcover retail price: 10% fiction; 5% author, 5% illustrator (picture book). Offers $5,000-$8,000 advance for new authors. Publishes ms up to 3 years after acceptance.

AUNT LUTE BOOKS

P.O. Box 410687, San Francisco CA 94141. (415)826-1300. Fax: (415)826-8300. E-mail: books@auntlute.com. Website: www.auntlute.com. **Contact:** Acquisitions editor. Small feminist and women-of-color press. Publishes hardcover and paperback originals. Does not publish single-author collections of poetry. Averages 4 total titles/year.

Needs Ethnic, feminist, lesbian. We encourage you to consult our catalog to get a sense of the areas in which we publish and the audiences we currently serve.

How to Contact Accepts unsolicited ms queries. Please include SASE. Please do not send manuscripts by certified mail or return receipt requested. We do not accept emailed submissions. Alternately, submit cover letter, two sample chapters (approx 50 pages), brief synopsis, and SASE. Responds in 3 months.

Terms Pays royalty.

AURORA PUBLISHING

3655 Torrance Blvd., Suite 430, Torrance CA 90503. (310)540-2800. Fax: (310)540-2877. E-mail: info@aurora-publishing.com. Website: www.aurora-publishing.com. It is Aurora's mission to introduce the highest quality manga titles to the wider population of North America and to the rest of the world, and to develop the manga market for a more mature audience.

AVALON BOOKS

160 Madison Ave., 5th Floor, New York NY 10016. (212)598-0222. Fax: (212)979-1862. E-mail: editorial@avalonbooks.com. Website: www.avalonbooks.com. **Contact:** Faith Black, editorial assistant. Estab. 1950. Publishes hardcover originals. **Published some debut authors within the last year.** Under its **AVALON BOOKS** imprint, Thomas Bouregy & Co., Inc. is a publisher of hardcover Romances, Mysteries, and Westerns focusing primarily on the library market. There is no explicit sexual content or profanity in any of our novels. It is the author's responsibility to heighten the romantic atmosphere by developing love scenes with tenderness, emotion, and perception. We publish 60 books a year in bimonthly cycles of ten. A cycle consists of four Contemporary Romances, two Historical Romances, two Mysteries, and two Westerns. Books range in length from a minimum of 50,000 words to a maximum of 70,000 words. However, if the manuscript is exceptional, we will accept somewhat longer books. Please address any inquiries regarding manuscript submissions to: **editorial@avalonbooks.com.** Distributes titles through Baker & Taylor, libraries, Barnes&Noble.com and Amazon.com. Promotes titles through Library Journal, Booklist, Publishers Weekly and local papers.

Needs "We publish wholesome contemporary romances, mysteries, historical romances and westerns. Our books are read by adults as well as teenagers, and the main characters are all adults. All mysteries are contemporary. We publish contemporary romances, historical romances, mysteries and westerns. Submit first 3 sample chapters, a 2-3 page synopsis and SASE. The manuscripts should be between 50,000 to 70,000 words. Manuscripts that are too long will not be considered. Time period and setting are the author's preference. The historical romances will maintain the high level of reading expected by our readers. The books shall be wholesome fiction, without graphic sex, violence or strong language." Published *Death in the French Quarter*, by Kent Conwell (mystery); *Judgment at Gold Butte,*, by Terrell L. Bowers (western); *Adieu, My Love*, by Lynn Turner (historical romance); *Everything But a Groom*, by Holly Jacobs (romantic comedy).

How to Contact *We do not accept unagented material. Unsolicited ms will be returned.* We accept queries by email but not partials. Query with SASE or IRC. Responds in 1 month to queries; 6-8 months to mss.

Terms Average advance: $1,000. Publishes ms 8-12 months after acceptance. Ms guidelines online.

AVATAR PRESS

515 N. Century Blvd, Rantoul IL 61866. Fax: (217)893-9671. E-mail: submissions@avatarpress.net. Website: www.avatarpress.com.

Needs Comic books both freelance artists working within company-owned storylines, or creator-owned comics. Published Warren Ellis' *Anna Mercury*, George A. Romero's *Night of the Living Dead*, Frank Miller's *Robocop*, Alan Moore's *The Courtyard* and more.

How to Contact *Not currently seeking script-only submissions at this time.* "Send us an 8-12 page story with panel to panel descriptions and in full script format. The story should feature an adventure by any Avatar Press company-owned character. Do not send us stories featuring characters owned by other comic companies or any creator-owned characters (even if the creator who owns the character is you - if you want to submit a creator-owned project see our listed guidelines for that). E-mail submissions are OK. If you have been previously published you may send copies of those comics. Don't forget to include your name, address, e-mail address and/or a phone number at which you can be contacted."

Terms Writer's guidelines on website.

AVON BOOKS

Harper Collins Publishers, 10 E. 53 Street, New York NY 10022. Website: www.harpercollins.com. **Contact:** Michael Morrison, publisher. Estab. 1941. "Avon has been publishing award-winning books since 1941. It is recognized for having pioneered the historical romance category and

continues to bring the best of commercial literature to the broadest possible audience." Publishes hardcover and paperback originals and reprints. Averages 400 total titles/year.
Imprints Avon, EOS.
Needs Historical, literary, mystery, romance, science fiction, young adult, health, pop culture.
How to Contact *Does not accept unsolicited mss.* Query with SASE. Send SASE or IRC.
Terms Varies.

B & H PUBLISHING

127 Ninth Ave. N., Nashville TN 37234. Website: www.bhpublishinggroup.com. Estab. 1934. Publishes hardcover and paperback originals. B & H is the book division of LifeWay, the world's largest publisher of Christian materials. Averages 90 total titles, 20 fiction titles/year. Member: ECPA.
Needs Religious/inspirational (contemporary women's fiction, suspense, romance, thriller, historical romance). Engaging stories told from a Christian worldview. Published*Elvis Takes a Back Seat,* by Leanna Ellis (contemporary); *Snow Angel,* by Jamie Carie (romance); *The Moon in the Mango Tree,* by Pamela Binnings Ewin (historical); *Shade,* by John B. Olson (thriller); and *Forsaken,* by James David Jordan (suspense).
How to Contact *At this time B&H only accepts manuscripts from literary agents**. For additional information, the agent may call us at 615-251-2438. Writer's Guidelines are available by sending a self-addressed stamped envelope to: Pat Carter: Writer's Guidelines, B&H Publishing Group, 127 9th Avenue North, MSN 115. Accepts simultaneous submissions.
Terms Pays negotiable royalty. Publishes ms 10-12 months after acceptance. Ms guidelines for #10 SASE.

BAKER BOOKS

Baker Book House Company, P.O. Box 6287, Grand Rapids MI 49516-6287. (616)676-9185. Fax: (616)676-2315. Website: www.bakerbooks.com. **Contact:** Jeanette Thomason, special projects editor (mystery, literary, women's fiction); Lonnie Hull DuPont, editoral director (all genres); Vicki Crumpton, aquisitions editor (all genres). Estab. 1939. "Midsize publisher of work that interests Christians." Publishes hardcover and trade paperback originals and trade paperback reprints. Books: web offset print. Plans 5 first novels this year. Averages 200 total titles/year. Distributes titles through Ingram and Spring Arbor into both CBA and ABA markets worldwide.
Needs Literary, mainstream/contemporary, mystery, picture books, religious. "We are mainly seeking fiction of two genres: contemporary women's fiction and mystery." Published *Praise Jerusalem!* and *Resting in the Bosom of the Lamb,* by Augusta Trobaugh (contemporary women's fiction); *Touches the Sky,* by James Schaap (western, literary); and *Face to Face,* by Linda Dorrell (mystery); *Flabbergasted,* by Ray Blackston; *The Fisherman,* by Larry Huntsberger.
How to Contact Does not accept unsolicited mss.
Terms Pays 14% royalty on net receipts. Offers advance. Publishes ms within 1 year after acceptance. Ms guidelines for #10 SASE.

BALLANTINE BOOKS

1745 Broadway, New York NY 10019. (212)782-9000. Website: www.randomhouse.com/BB. "Ballantine's list encompasses a large, diverse offering in a variety of formats." Publishes hardcover, trade paperback, mass market paperback originals
Imprints Ballantine Books; Del Ray; Fawcett (mystery line); Ivy (romance); The Modern Library; One World; Strivers Row; Presidio Press; Random House Trade Paperbacks; Villard Books.
Needs Confession, ethnic, fantasy, feminist, gay/lesbian, historical, humor, literary, mainstream/contemporary (women's), military/war, multicultural, mystery, romance, short story collections, spiritual, suspense, general fiction.
How to Contact *Agented submissions only.*
Terms Pays 8-15% royalty. Average advance: variable. Ms guidelines online.

BANCROFT PRESS

P.O. Box 65360, Baltimore MD 21209-9945. (410)358-0658. Fax: (410)764-1967. E-mail: bruceb@bancroftpress.com. Website: www.bancroftpress.com. **Contact:** Bruce Bortz, publisher (health, investments, politics, history, humor); FictionEditor (literary novels, mystery/thrillers, young adult). "Small independent press publishing literary and commercial fiction." Publishes hardcover and trade paperback originals. Also packages books for other publishers (no fee to authors). **Published 5 debut authors within the last two years.** Averages 4-6 fiction titles/year.

- *The Re-Appearance of Sam Webber*, by Jonathon Scott Fugua is an ALEX Award winner; *Uncovering Sadie's Secrets*, by Libby Sternberg, is an Edgar Award finalist.

Needs Ethnic (general), family saga, feminist, gay/lesbian, glitz, historical, humor, lesbian, literary, mainstream/contemporary, military/war, mystery (amateur sleuth, cozy, police procedural, private eye/hard-boiled), new age/mystic, regional, science fiction (hard science/technological, soft/sociological), thriller/espionage, young adult (historical, problem novels, series. "Our current focuses are young adult fiction, women's fiction, and literary fiction." Published *The Re-Appearance of Sam Webber*, by Scott Fugua (literary); *Hume's Fork*, by Ron Cooper (literary); *The Case Against My Brother*, by Libby Sternberg (historical/young adult), *Finn* by Matthew Olshan (young adult); and *The Sinful Life of Lucy Burns,* by Elizabeth Leikness (fantasy/women's).

How to Contact Accepts unsolicited mss. Query with SASE or submit outline, 2 sample chapter(s), synopsis, by mail or e-mail or submit complete ms. Accepts queries by e-mail, fax. Include brief bio, list of publishing credits. Send SASE for return of ms or send a disposable ms and SASE for reply only. Agented fiction 100%. Responds in 6-12 months to mss. Accepts simultaneous submissions. Sometimes comments on rejected mss.

Terms Pays various royalties on retail price. Average advance: $1500. Publishes ms up to 3 years after acceptance. Ms guidelines online.

BANTAM DELL PUBLISHING GROUP

1745 Broadway, New York NY 10019. E-mail: bdpublicity@randomhouse.com. Website: www.bantamdell.com. "In addition to being the nation's largest mass market paperback publisher, Bantam publishes a select yet diverse hardcover list." Publishes hardcover, trade paperback and mass market paperback originals; mass market paperback reprints. Averages 350 total titles/year.

Imprints Bantam Hardcover; Bantam Trade Paperback; Bantam Mass Market; Crimeline; Dell; Delta; Domain; DTP; Delacorte Press; The Dial Press; Fanfare; Island; Spectra.

Needs Adventure, fantasy, horror.

How to Contact *Agented submissions only.*

Terms Offers advance. Publishes ms 1 year after acceptance.

BARBOUR PUBLISHING, INC.

P.O. Box 719, Uhrichsville OH 44683. (740)922-6045. E-mail: fictionsubmit@barbourbooks.com. Website: www.barbourbooks.com. **Contact:** Rebecca Germany, senior editor (fiction). Estab. 1981. Publishes hardcover, trade paperback and mass market paperback originals and reprints. **Published 40% debut authors within the last year.** Averages 250 total titles/year.

Imprints Heartsong Presents; Barbour Books.

Needs Historical, contemporary, religious, romance, western, mystery. All submissions must be Christian mss. "Heartsong romance is 'sweet'—no sex, no bad language. All stories must have Christian faith as an underlying basis. Common writer's mistakes are a sketchy proposal, an unbelieveable story, and a story that doesn't fit our guidelines for inspirational romances." Published *A Sister's Secret*, by Wanda E. Brunstetter (fiction).

How to Contact Submit 3 sample chapter(s), synopsis by e-mail only. For submission of your manuscripts, please follow the link online to download the appropriate guidelines. From time to time, we do look for specific types of manuscripts. These are usually announced through various writers' organizations including the American Christian Writers'. For submission of your manuscripts and the types of manuscripts that we are currently seeking, please follow the online link to download the appropriate guidelines. You can follow a link for a submission form and email address that you can send your questions to. Responds in 6 months to mss. Accepts simultaneous submissions.

Terms Pays 8-16% royalty on net price. Average advance: $1,000-8,000. Publishes ms 1-2 years after acceptance. Book catalog online or for 9 × 12 SAE with 2 first-class stamps; ms guidelines for #10 SASE or online.

FREDERIC C. BEIL, PUBLISHER, INC.

609 Whitaker St., Savannah GA 31401. (912)233-2446. E-mail: beilbook@beil.com; editor@beil.com. Website: www.beil.com. **Contact:** Frederic C. Beil III, president; Mary Ann Bowman, editor. **Contact:** Estab. 1982. "Our objectives are (1) to offer to the reading public carefully selected texts of lasting value; (2) to adhere to high standards in the choice of materials and bookmaking craftsmanship; (3) to produce books that exemplify good taste in format and design; and (4) to maintain the lowest cost consistent with quality." Publishes hardcover originals and reprints. Books: acid-free paper; offset printing; Smyth-sewn, hardcover binding; illustrations. Plans 3 first novels this year. Averages 10 total titles, 4 fiction titles/year.

Imprints The Sandstone Press, Hypermedia.

Needs History, biography, fiction. Published *Dancing by The River*, by Marlin Barton; *Joseph Jefferson*, by Arthur Bloom (biography); *The Invisible Country*, by H.E. Francis (fiction).

How to Contact *Does not accept unsolicited mss.* We prefer postal mail queries. Query with SASE. Responds in 3 days to queries. Accepts simultaneous submissions.

Terms Pays 712% royalty on retail price. Publishes ms 20 months after acceptance.

BELLEVUE LITERARY PRESS

Dept. of Medicine, NYU School of Medicine, 550 First Avenue, OBV A-640, New York NY 10016. (212) 263-7802. Fax: (212) 263-7803. E-mail: egoldman@blreview.org. Website: http://blpress.org. **Contact:** Erika Goldman, editorial director (literary fiction); Leslie Hodgkins, editor (literary fiction). Estab. 2005. "We're a small literary press that publishes nonfiction and fiction that ranges the intersection of the sciences (or medicine) and the arts." Publishes hardcover originals, paperback originals. Debut novel print order: 3000. Plans 2 debut novels this year. Averages 8 total titles/year; 2 fiction titles/year. Member CLMP. Distributes/promotes titles through Consortium.

Needs Literary. Published *The Cure*, by Varley O'Connor; *The Leper Compound*, by Paula Nangle (literary); *A Proper Knowledge*, by Michelle Latiolais; and *Tinkers*, by Paul Harding.

How to Contact Send query letter or query with outline/synopsis and 3 sample chapters. Accepts queries by snail mail, e-mail. Include estimated word count, brief bio, list of publishing credits. Send disposable copy of ms and SASE for reply only. Agented fiction: 75%. Responds to queries in 2 weeks. Accepts unsolicited mss. Considers simultaneous submissions. Rarely critiques/comments on rejected mss. Responds to mss in 6 weeks.

Terms Sends pre-production galleys to author. Manuscript published 8-12 months after acceptance. Writer's guidelines not available. Pays royalties 6-15%, advance $1,000. Book catalogs on website.

BILINGUAL REVIEW PRESS

Hispanic Research Center, Arizona State University, P.O. Box 875303, Tempe AZ 85287-5303. (480)965-3867. Fax: (480)965-0315. E-mail: brp@asu.edu. Website: www.asu.edu/brp. **Contact:** Gary Keller, publisher. Estab. 1973. "University affiliated." Publishes hardcover and paperback originals and reprints. Books: 60 lb. acid-free paper; single sheet or web press printing; perfect-bound.

Needs Ethnic, literary, short story collections. Always seeking Chicano, Puerto Rican, Cuban-American or other U.S. Hispanic themes with strong and serious literary qualities and distinctive and intellectually important themes. Does *not* publish children's literature or trade genres such as travelogues and adventure fiction. Novels set in a pre-Columbian past are not likely to be published.

Published *Moving Target: A Memoir of Pursuit*, by Ron Arias; *Contemporary Chicano and Chicana Art: Artists, Works, Culture, and Education*, Gary Keller, et al; *Triumph of Our Communities: Four Decades of Mexican American Art*, Gary Keller et al; *Assumption and Other Stories*, by Daniel A. Olivas; *Renaming Ecstasy: Latino Writings on the Sacred*, edited by Orlando Ricardo Menes.
How to Contact Accepts unsolicited mss. Query with SASE or submit 2-3 sample chapter(s). Accepts queries by email, mail. Include brief bio, list of publishing credits. Send SASE or IRC. Responds in 6 weeks to queries; 2-6 months to mss.
Terms Pays 10% royalty. Average advance: $500. Publishes ms 2 years after acceptance. Ms guidelines by email.

BIRCH BROOK PRESS

P.O. Box 81, Delhi NY 13753. Fax: (607)746-7453. E-mail: birchbrook@copper.net. Website: www.birchbrookpress.info. **Contact:** Tom Tolnay. Small publisher of popular culture and literary titles in mostly handcrafted letterpress editions. Specializes in fiction anthologies with specific theme, and an occasional novella. "Not a good market for full-length novels." Occasionally publishes hardcover and trade paperback originals. Books: 80 lb. vellum paper; letterpress printing; wood engraving illustrations. Averages 5 total titles, 2 fiction titles/year. Member, Small Press Center, Publishers Marketing Association, Academy of American Poets. Distributes titles through Barnes&Noble.com, Amazon.com, Gazelle Book Services in Europe, Multicultural Books in Canada. Promotes titles through website, catalogs, direct mail and group ads.
Imprints Birch Brook Press, Persephone Press and Birch Brook Impressions.
Needs Literary, regional (Adirondacks), popular culture, special interest (flyfishing, baseball, books about books, outdoors). "Mostly we do anthologies around a particular theme generated inhouse. We make specific calls for fiction when we are doing an anthology." Published *The Bells of Moses Henry*, by Peter Skinner; *Magic and Madness in the Library* (fiction collection); *Life & Death of a Book*, by William MacAdams; *Kilimanjaro Burning*, by John B. Robinson; *The Suspense of Loneliness* (anthology); *Tales for the Trail* (anthology); *Sexy Sixties*, by Harry Smith; *The Alchemy of Words*, by Edward Francisco; *Where Things Are When You Lose Them*, by Martin Golan; *The Sea-Crossing of St. Brendan*, by Matthew Brennan; *Baseball & the Game of Life* (anthology).
How to Contact Query with SASE or submit sample chapter(s), synopsis. Responds in 2 months to queries. Accepts simultaneous submissions. Sometimes comments on rejected mss.
Terms Modest flat fee on anthologies. Usually publishes ms 10-18 months after acceptance. Ms guidelines for #10 SASE.

BKMK PRESS

5101 Rockhill Rd., Kansas City MO 64110-2499. (816)235-2558. Fax: (816)235-2611. E-mail: bkmk@umkc.edu. Website: www.umkc.edu/bkmk. **Contact:** Ben Furnish, managing editor. Estab. 1971. Publishes trade paperback originals. Averages 4 total titles/year.
Needs Literary, short story collections. Not currently acquiring novels.
How to Contact Query with SASE or submit 2-3 sample stories between January 1 and June 30. Responds in 8 months to mss. Accepts simultaneous submissions.
Terms Pays 10% royalty on wholesale price. Publishes ms 1 year after acceptance. Ms guidelines online.

BLACK HERON PRESS

P.O. Box13396, Mill Creek WA 98082. E-mail: Jgoldheron@aol.com; heron@blackheron.mav.net. Website: www.blackheronpress.com. Two-person operation; no immediate plans to expand. "We're known for literary fiction. We've done several Vietnam titles and several surrealistic fictions." Publishes hardcover and trade paperback originals. **Published 1-2 debut authors within the last year.** Averages 4 total titles, 4 fiction titles/year.

- Ten books published by Black Heron Press have won regional or national awards.

Needs Experimental, humor, literary, mainstream/contemporary, science fiction (surrealism), war novels (literary). Published *Infinite Kindness*, by Laurie Blauner (historical fiction); and *Moses in Sinai*, by Simone Zelitch (historical fiction).

How to Contact Query letter with first 30 pages of completed manuscript, and SASE with SASE. Responds in 3 months to queries; 6 months to mss. Accepts simultaneous submissions.

Terms Pays 8% royalty on retail price.

BLACK LYON PUBLISHING, LLC

P.O. Box 567, Baker City OR 97814. E-mail: info@blacklyonpublishing.com. Website: www.blacklyonpublishing.com. **Contact:** The Editors (romance & general fiction love stories). Estab. 2007. "Black Lyon Publishing is a small, independent publisher. We produce 1-2 romance or general fiction novels each month in both 5x8 trade paperback and PDF e-books formats. We are very focused on giving new novelists a launching pad into the industry." Publishes paperback originals, e-books. **Published 4 new writers last year.** Plans 12 debut novels this year. Averages 15-20 fiction titles/year. Distributes/promotes titles through website, Ingram and Baker & Taylor, bookstores, and major online retailers.

- "We are now seeking novella submissions for our upcoming Lyonettes imprint. Please see information online."

Needs romance (contemporary, futuristic/time travel, gothic, historical, regency period, romantic suspense). Special interests: ancient times. Published *Cast in Stone*, by Kerry A. Jones (paranorma romance); *The Medallion of Solaus*, by Kimberly Adkins (paranormal romance); *Maya's Gold*, by Mary Vine (contemporary romance).

How to Contact Send query letter. Query with outline/synopsis and sample chapters. Accepts queries by e-mail. Include estimated word count, brief bio, list of publishing credits. Send SASE or IRC for return of ms or disposable copy of ms and SASE/IRC for reply only. Responds to queries in 2 weeks. No unsolicited mss. Considers simultaneous submissions, submissions on CD or disk, e-mail submissions. Often critiques/comments on rejected mss. Responds to mss in 1 week.

Terms Sends pre-production galleys to author. Ms published within 6 months after acceptance. Writer's guidelines on website. Pays royalties and author's copies. Book catalogs on website.

JOHN F. BLAIR, PUBLISHER

1406 Plaza Dr., Winston-Salem NC 27103-1470. (336)768-1374. Fax: (336)768-9194. Website: www.blairpub.com. **Contact:** Carolyn Sakowski, president. Small, independent publisher. Publishes hardcover originals and trade paperbacks. Books: Acid-free paper; offset printing; illustrations. Averages 20 total titles/year.

Needs Prefers regional material dealing with southeastern U.S. "We publish one work of fiction per season relating to the Southeastern U.S. Our editorial focus concentrates mostly on nonfiction." Published *The Minotaur Takes a Cigarette Break*, by Steven Sherrill; *Rocks That Float*, by Kathy Steele.

How to Contact Accepts unsolicited mss. Any fiction submitted should have some connection with the Southeast, either through setting or author's background. Send a cover letter, giving a synopsis of the book. Include the first two chapters (at least 50 pages) of the manuscript. You may send the entire manuscript if you wish. If you choose to send only samples, please include the projected word length of your book and estimated completion date in your cover letter. Send a biography of the author, including publishing credits and credentials. Responds in 3 months to queries. Accepts simultaneous submissions.

Terms Royalty negotiable. Offers advance. Publishes ms 18 months after acceptance. Book catalog online.

BLIND EYE BOOKS

1141 Grant Street, Bellingham WA 98225. E-mail: editor@blindeyebooks.com. Website: www.blindeyebooks.com. **Contact:** Nicole Kimberling, editor. "Blind Eye Books publishes science fiction, fantasy and paranormal romance novels featuring gay or lesbian protagonists. We do not publish short story collections, poetry, erotica, horror or non-fiction. We would hesitate to publish any manuscript that is less than 70,000 or over 150,000 words."

Needs Science fiction, fantasy, and paranormal romance novels featuring gay or lesbian protagonists. Published *The Archer's Heart* by Astrid Amara, *Tangle* (anthology), and *Wicked Gentlemen* by Ginn Hale.

How to Contact Submit complete ms with cover letter. Accepts queries by snail mail. Send disposable copy of ms and SASE for reply only. Does not return rejected mss.

Terms Writer's guidelines on website.

BLOODFIRE STUDIOS

P.O Box 710451, San Diego CA 92171. E-mail: likewecare@bloodfire.com. Website: www.bloodfire.com. **Contact:** Dennis Greenhil, VP of Publishing. Estab. 1997. "Midsize Independent Publisher working mostly in Sci/Fi, Horror, and Manga. We pride ourselves on maintaining a high level of quality comparable to the big publishers. Art, Story, paper, etc meet or exceed Marvel and DC standards." Publishes paperback originals, paperpack reprints. Format: 60-80 lb gloss paper; saddle stitch, perfect bound binding; illustrations. **Publishes 4 debut writers/year.** Publishes 6-10 titles/year. Various distributors including Diamond Comics, direct sales, conventions, etc. Advertising and self-promotion through various channels;

- *"No longer able to accept unsolicited submissions."*

How to Contact Prefers submissions from writers, artists, writer-artists, creative teams. BloodFire Studios is not actively looking for new stories or character ideas. Writing submissions should be submitted in a script format like a play or movie (novel and short story formats are usually passed over). Presentation is important so make sure its easy to read. A 12 point font and double spaced lines are recommended. It also helps to make sure it's clean. Submission can be sent via email but ONLY AS HYPERLINKS. Use the "Click here to email us" button online and enter "Writing submission" in the subject line. It will be forwarded to the appropriate editor. Follow guidelines posted on website closely or submissions will be trashed. "We attend major industry shows such as San Diego Comic Con, Wizard World LA and Wizard World Chicago." Responds to mss/art packets in a few weeks. Considers simultaneous submissions. Often comments on rejected mss.

Terms Payment and rights varies on contract terms for each book. Ms published about a year after acceptance. Writer's and artist's guidelines, book catalog on website.

BL PUBLISHING

Willow Road, Lenton, Nottingham NG7 2WS Wales. (44) (115) 900-4100. Fax: (44) (115) 900-4111. E-mail: contact@blacklibrary.com; publishing@games-workshop.co.uk. Website: www.blacklibrary.com. **Contact:** Christian Dunn. Estab. 1997. Publishes paperback originals. Published 3 new writers last year. Averages 65 total titles/year; 65 fiction titles/year.

Imprints Black Library, Solaris.

Needs Fantasy (space fantasy, sword and sorcery), horror (dark fantasy, futuristic), science fiction (hard science/technological, soft/sociological), short story collection, young adult/teen (fantasy/science fiction, horror). Published *The Summoner*, by Gail Z. Martin (fantasy); *Horus Rising*, by Dan Abnett (science fiction); *The Vampire Genevieve*, by Jack Yeovil (fantasy).

How to Contact Our 2010 submissions window opens on 4 May 2010 and closes on 31 July 2010. Writers whose work we consider fit for publication will be contacted within 8 weeks of the window closing. Rejected submissions will not receive a response. Accepts queries by snail mail, e-mail. Include brief bio, list of publishing credits. Send SASE or IRC for return of ms or disposable copy of ms and SASE/IRC for reply only. Agented fiction: 5%. Responds to mss in 3 months. No unsolicited mss. Considers simultaneous submissions, e-mail submissions. Rarely critiques/comments on rejected mss.

Terms Sends pre-production galleys to author. Writer's guidelines on website.

BOOKS FOR ALL TIMES, INC.

Box 202, Warrenton VA 20188. (540)428-3175. E-mail: staff@bfat.com. Website: www.bfat.com. **Contact:** Joe David, publisher & editor. Estab. 1981. One-man operation. Publishes paperback originals.

Needs Literary, mainstream/contemporary, short story collections. "No novels at the moment; hopeful, though, of publishing a collection of quality short stories. No popular fiction or material easily published by the major or minor houses specializing in mindless entertainment. Only interested in stories of the Victor Hugo or Sinclair Lewis quality."

How to Contact Query with SASE. Responds in 1 month to queries. Sometimes comments on rejected mss.

Terms Pays negotiable advance. "Publishing/payment arrangement will depend on plans for the book."

BRANDEN PUBLISHING CO., INC.

P.O. Box 812094, Wellesley MA 02482. (781)235-3634. Fax: (781)235-3634. E-mail: branden@brandenbooks.com. Website: www.brandenbooks.com. **Contact:** Adolph Caso, editor. Publishes hardcover and trade paperback originals, reprints and software. Books: 55-60 lb. acid-free paper; case—or perfect-bound; illustrations. Averages 15 total titles, 5 fiction titles/year.

Imprints I.P.L; Dante University Press; Four Seas; Branden Publishing Co., Branden Books.

Needs Ethnic (histories, integration), historical, literary, military/war, religious (historical-reconstructive), short story collections. Looking for "contemporary, fast pace, modern society." Published *I, Morgain*, by Harry Robin; *The Bell Keeper*, by Marilyn Seguin; and *The Straw Obelisk*, by Adolph Caso; *Priest to Mafia Don* by Father Bascio; Erebus—Nightmare of a Social Worker, by Sam Saladino.

How to Contact Does not accept unsolicited mss. Query with SASE. Responds in 1 month to queries.

Terms Pays 5-10% royalty on net receipts. 10 author's copies. Average advance: $1,000 maximum. Publishes ms 10 months after acceptance.

BRIDGE WORKS PUBLISHING CO.

Box 1798, 221 Bridge Lane, Bridgehampton NY 11932. (631)537-3418. Fax: (631)537-5092. **Contact:** Barbara Phillips, editorial director. Box 1798, 221 Bridge Lane, Bridgehampton NY 11932. (631)537-3418. Fax: (631)537-5092. **Contact:** Barbara Phillips, editorial director. Estab. 1992. "Bridge Works is very small, publishing only 1-6 titles a year." **Publishing some debut authors.** Distributes titles through National Book Network. "Our books are routinely reviewed in major publications, and we work closely with authors in both the editorial and marketing processes."

Needs Publishes mainstream quality fiction and nonfiction, also thrillers. "Query with SASE before submitting ms. Recent publications include *Mineral Spirits*, by Heather Sharfeddin and *Chest Pains*, by Janet Nichols Lynch.

How to Contact Write to address above, including synopsis and estimated word count. Responds in one month to query and 50 pages, two months to entire ms. Sometimes comments on rejected mss. Query with SASE before submitting ms. Distributes titles through National Book Network. "Our books are routinely reviewed in major publications, and we work closely with authors in both the editorial and marketing processes." Does not read simultaneous submissions.

Terms Pays 8% of net received from wholesalers and bookstores. Average advance: $1,000. Publishes ms 1 year after acceptance. Book catalog and ms guidelines for #10 SASE.

BROADWAY BOOKS

1745 Broadway, New York NY 10019. (212)782-9000. Fax: (212)782-9411. Website: www.broadwaybooks.com. **Contact:** William Thomas, editor-in-chief. Estab. 1995. Broadway publishes general interest nonfiction and fiction for adults. Publishes hardcover and trade paperback originals and reprints.

Needs Broadway Books publishes a variety of nonfiction books across several categories including memoir, health & fitness, inspiration & spirituality, history, current affairs & politics, marriage & relationships, animals, travel & adventure narrative, pop culture, humor, and personal finance. Publishes a limited list of commercial literary fiction. Published *Freedomland*, by Richard Price.
How to Contact *Agented submissions only.*

CALAMARI PRESS

E-mail: derek@calamaripress.com. "Calamari Press publishes book objects of literary text and art and experimental fiction." Publishes paperback originals. Format: 60 lb. natural finch opaque paper; digital printing; perfect or saddle-stitched bound. Average print order: 500-1,000. Debut novel print order: 300. Averages 2-3 total titles/year; 2 fiction titles/year.
Needs Adventure, comics/graphic novels, ethnic/multicultural, experimental, literary, short story collections. Published *Land of the Snow Men*, by George Belden (Norman Lock) (fictional literary canard with illustrations); *The Singing Fish*, by Peter Markus (prose poem/short fiction collection); *The Night I Dropped Shakespeare On The Cat*, by John Olson; *The Revisionist*, by Miranda Mellis; *Part of the World*, by Robert Lopez; *Ever*, by Blake Butler; reissued *Motorman*, by David Ohle, and *Stories in the Worst Way*, by Gary Lutz.
How to Contact Query with outline/synopsis and 3 sample chapters. Accepts queries by e-mail only. Include brief bio. Send SASE or IRC for return of ms. Responds to queries in 2 weeks. Accepts unsolicited mss. Considers e-mail submissions only. Sometimes critiques/comments on rejected mss. Responds to mss in 2 weeks.
Terms Sends pre-production galleys to author. Manuscript published 2-6 months after acceptance. Writer's guidelines on website. Pays in author's copies.

CALYX BOOKS

P.O. Box B, Corvallis OR 97339-0539. (541)753-9384. Fax: (541)753-0515. E-mail: info@calyxpress.org. Website: http://www.proaxis.com/~calyx/. **Contact:** The Editor. Estab. 1986 for Calyx Books; 1976 for Calyx, Inc. "Calyx exists to publish women's literary and artistic work and is committed to publishing the works of all women, including women of color, older women, lesbians, working-class women, and other voices that need to be heard." Publishes fine literature by women, fiction, nonfiction and poetry. Publishes hardcover and paperback originals. Books: offset printing; paper and cloth binding. **Published 1 debut author within the last year.** Averages 1-2 total titles/year. Distributes titles through Consortium Book Sale and Distribution. Promotes titles through author reading tours, print advertising (trade and individuals), galley and review copy mailings, presence at trade shows, etc.

- "Due to the high volume of book manuscripts received, CALYX Books is currently closed for manuscript submissions until further notice except for the Sarah Lantz Poetry Book Prize."

Needs Ethnic, experimental, feminist, gay/lesbian, lesbian, literary, mainstream/contemporary, short story collections. Published *Forbidden Stitch: An Asian American Women's Anthology; Women and Aging: Present Tense; Writing and Art by Young Women*; and *A Line of Cutting Women*.
How to Contact Closed to submissions until further notice.
Terms Pays 10-15% royalty on net receipts. Average advance: depends on grant support. Publishes ms 2 years after acceptance. Ms guidelines for #10 SASE.

CAROLINA WREN PRESS

120 Morris St., Durham NC 27701. E-mail: carolinawrenpress@earthlink.net. Website: www.carolinawrenpress.org. **Contact:** Andrea Selch, president. Estab. 1976. "We publish poetry, fiction, nonfiction, biography, autobiography, literary nonfiction work by and/or about people of color, women, gay/lesbian issues, health and mental health topics in children's literature." Books: 6 × 9 paper; typeset; various bindings; illustrations. **Published 2 debut authors within the last year.** Distributes titles through Amazon.com, Barnes & Noble, Borders, Ingram and Baker & Taylor and on their website.

Needs "Though we accept unsolicited manuscripts of fiction and nonfiction September-December, we very rarely accept any. We suggest you submit to our Doris Bakwin Award for Writing by a Woman; contest is held in fall of odd-numbered years" Does not publish genre fiction or religious texts or self-help books. Published *Downriver* by Jeanne Leiby in 2007.
How to Contact Reads unsolicited mss in September only. Accepts queries by e-mail, mail. Include brief bio. Send SASE or IRC. Responds in 3 months to queries; 6 months to mss. "Please query before you send or else plan to enter one of our contests; entry fee is required. Guidelines on our website in summer."
Terms Publishes ms 2 year after acceptance. Ms guidelines online.

CHAMPAGNE ROSE PRESS

P.O. Box 708, Adam's Basin NY 14410. E-mail: queryus@thewildrosepress.com. Website: www.thewildrosepress.com. **Contact:** Roseann Armstrong, editor. "The Champagne Rose line is the contemporary romance line of the Wild Rose Press. Our contemporary stories are filled with sexual tension and passionate chemistry. The setting can take place anywhere in the world today. Champagne Rose couples explore their relationship both emotionally and physically. In each full-length novel, there must be one fully consummated love scene. In the case of short stories, if this isn't realistic for the plot of the story, then the physical encounters must be ripe with tension. The characters should leave us remembering them long after we turn the last page. We should feel their feelings, share their joys and their heartaches. And, as with all romances, we should close the book completely satisfied by the happy-ever-after ending." Publishes paperback originals, reprints, and e-books in a POD format. **Published 25 debut authors last year**. Publishes approximately 60 fiction titles/year. Member: EPIC, Romance Writers of America. Distributes/promotes titles through major distribution chains, including Ingrams, Baker & Taylor, Sony, Amazon.com, Kindle, as well as smaller and online distributors.
Needs contemporary, futuristic/time travel, gothic, historical, regency, romantic suspense, erotic, and paranormal romances. Plans several anthologies "in several lines of the company in the next year, including Cactus Rose, Yellow Rose, American Rose, Black Rose, and Scarlet Rose." Has published *Calendar of Love*, by Susan Lyons; *Seduction's Stakes*, by Claire Ashgrove; and *A Perfect Fit*, by Sheridon Smythe.
How to Contact *Does not accept unsolicited mss*. Send query letter with outline and synopsis of up to 5 pages. Prefers queries by e-mail; accepts by mail. Include estimated word count, brief bio, and list of publishing credits. Send SASE or IRC for return of ms. Agented fiction less than 1%. Responds to queries in 4 weeks; to mss in 12 weeks. Does not consider simultaneous submissions. Always comments on rejected mss.
Terms Pays royalty of 7% minimum; 35% maximum. Sends prepublication galleys to author. Time between acceptance and publication is approximately 1 year. Writer's guidelines available on website.

CHANGELING PRESS LLC

P.O. Box 1046, Martinsburg WV 25402. E-mail: Submissions@changelingpress.com. Website: www.changelingpress.com. **Contact:** Sheri Ross Fogarty, editor-in-chief. Publishes print and e-books.
Needs Special interests: "We publish Sci-Fi, Futuristic, Paranormal, Fantasy, Suspense, Horror, and Humor, BDSM, and Fetish Love Stories. We publish Interludes and Novellas only, from 8,000 to 25,000 words total length — NO 100,000 word sagas, please! (Series and Serials welcome)."
How to Contact Submit complete ms with cover letter via e-mail only. Responds to queries in 2 months. Accepts unsolicited mss. Considers e-mail submissions.
Terms Pays royalties of 35% gross paid monthly.

CHARLESBRIDGE PUBLISHING

85 Main St., Watertown MA 02472. (800)225-3214. Fax: (800)926-5775. E-mail: schoolmarketing@charlesbridge.com. Website: www.charlesbridge.com/school. Publishes hardcover and paperback

nonfiction and fiction children's picture books, early readers, and middle-grade chapter books. Averages 36 total titles/year.

Needs Multicultural, nature, science, social studies, bedtime, math, etc. Recently published *The Searcher and Old Tree*, by David McPhail; *Wiggle and Waggle*, by Caroline Arnold.

How to Contact Submit complete ms as exclusive submission for three months. Responds only to ms of interest. Please do not include SASE.

Terms Royalty and advance vary. Publishes ms 2 years after acceptance. Ms guidelines online.

CHRONICLE BOOKS FOR CHILDREN

Chronicle Books; Submissions Editor, 680 Second St., 6th Floor, San Francisco CA 94105. E-mail: kided@chroniclebooks.com. Website: www.chroniclekids.com. **Contact:** Victoria Rock, publisher and editor-at-large. Publishes hardcover and trade paperback originals. **Published 5% debut authors within the last year.** Averages 90 total titles/year.

Needs Mainstream/contemporary, multicultural, young adult, picture books, middle grade fiction, young adult projects. Published *Wave*, by Suzy Lee (all ages, picture book); Ivy and Bean series, by Annie Barrows, illustrated by Sophie Blackwell (ages 6-11, chapter book); *Delicious: The Art and Life of Wayne Theibaud*, by Susan Goldman Rubin (ages 9-14, chapter book).

How to Contact Submit complete ms (picture books); submit outline synopsis and 3 sample chapters (for older readers). Prefers email ssubmissions. Responds to queries in 1 month; will not respond to submissions unless interested. Do not send SASE; send SASP to confirm receipt.

Terms Royalty varies. Average advance: variable. Publishes ms 18-24 months after acceptance. Ms guidelines online.

CLARION BOOKS

215 Park Ave. S., New York NY 10003. Website: www.houghtonmifflinbooks.com. **Contact:** Dinah Stevenson, vice-president and publisher (YA, middle-grade, chapter book); Jennifer B. Greene, senior editor (YA, middle-grade, chapter book); Jennifer Wingertzahn, editor (YA, middle-grade, chapter book); Marcia Leonard, editor (middle-grade, chapter book), Lynne Polvino, editor (YA, middle-grade, chapter book). Estab. 1965. "Clarion is a strong presence in the fiction market for young readers. We are highly selective in the areas of historical and contemporary fiction. We publish chapter books for children ages 7-10 and middle-grade novels for ages 9-12, as well as picture books and nonfiction." Publishes hardcover originals for children. Averages 50 total titles/year.

- *"We are no longer responding to your unsolicited submission unless we are interested in publishing it. Please do not include a self-addressed stamped envelope. Submissions will be recycled, and you will not hear from us regarding the status of your submission unless we are interested. We regret that we cannot respond personally to each submission, but we do consider each and every submission we receive."*

Needs Adventure, historical, humor, mystery, suspense, strong character studies. Clarion is highly selective in the areas of historical fiction, fantasy and science fiction. A novel must be superlatively written in order to find a place on the list. Mss are not responded to unless there is an interest in publishing. Accepts fiction translations. Published *A Taste for Red*, by Lewis Harris (contemporary, middle-grade); *The Wednesday Wars*, by Gary D. Schmidt (historical fiction); *Keeping Score*, by Linda Sue Park (middle-grade historical fiction).

How to Contact Submit complete ms. Responds in 2 months to queries. Prefers no multiple submissions of mss.

Terms Pays 5-10% royalty on retail price. Average advance: start at $6,000. Publishes ms 2 years after acceptance. Ms guidelines available at website.

CLEIS PRESS

Viva Editions, 2246 Sixth St., Berkeley CA 94710. E-mail: cleis@cleispress.com. Website: www.cleispress.com. **Contact:** Brenda Knight. Estab. 1980. "Cleis Press publishes provocative works by women and men in the areas of gay and lesbian studies sexual politics, fiction, feminism, self-help, erotica, gender studies, and human rights." Publishes trade paperback originals and reprints. **Published some debut authors within the last year.** Averages 20 total titles, 5 fiction titles/year.

Needs Feminist, gay/lesbian, literary. "We are looking for high quality fiction by women and men." *Black Like Us* (fiction); *Arts and Letters*, by Edmund White (essays); and *A Fragile Union*, by Joan Nestle (essays), which won a Lambda Literary Award.

How to Contact Accepts unsolicited mss. Submit complete ms. Accepts queries by email. Include brief bio, list of publishing credits. Send SASE for return of ms or send a disposable ms and SASE for reply only. Agented fiction 10%. Responds in 1 month to queries.

Terms Pays variable royalty on retail price. Publishes ms 2 years after acceptance.

COFFEE HOUSE PRESS

79 Thirteenth Ave. NE, Ste. 110, Minneapolis MN 55413. Fax: (612)338-4004. Website: www.coffeehousepress.org. **Contact:** Chris Fischbach, senior editor. "Nonprofit publisher with a small staff. We publish literary titles: fiction and poetry." Publishes trade paperback originals. Books: acid-free paper; cover illustrations. **Published some debut authors within the last year.** Averages 12 total titles, 6 fiction titles/year.

- This successful nonprofit small press has received numerous grants from various organizations including the NEA, the McKnight Foundation and Target.

Needs Ethnic, experimental, literary, mainstream/contemporary, short story collections, novels. Publishes anthologies, but they are closed to unsolicited submissions. Published *German for Travelers*, by Norah Labiner (novel); *Firmin*, by Sam Savage (novel); *Fugue State*, by Brian Evenson (stories).

How to Contact Accepts unsolicited mss except for when otherwise posted on website to catch up on backlog. Query with SASE. Agented fiction 10%. Responds in 1 month to queries; up to 4 months to mss. No electronic submissions.

Terms Pays 8% royalty on retail price. Provides 15 author's copies. Publishes ms 18 months after acceptance. Book catalog and ms guidelines for #10 SASE with 2 first-class stamps. Ms guidelines for #10 SAE with 1 first-class stamps.

CONSTABLE & ROBINSON, LTD.

3 The Lanchesters, 162 Fulham Palace Rd., London En WG 9ER United Kingdom. 0208-741-3663. Fax: 0208-748-7562. E-mail: enquiries@constablerobinson.com. Website: http://constablerobinson.co.uk/. **Contact:** Krystyna Green, editorial director (crime fiction). Publishes hardcover and trade paperback originals. Averages 160 total titles/year.

Needs Publishes "crime fiction (mysteries) and historical crime fiction." Length 80,000 words minimum; 130,000 words maximum. Recently published *Roma* and *The Judgement of Caesar*, by Steven Saylor; *The Yeane's Midnight*, by Ed O'Connor; *The More Deceived*, by David Roberts.

How to Contact *Agented submissions only.* No e-mail submissions. Submit by post 3 sample chapter(s), synopsis and cover letter. Responds in 1 month to queries; 3 months to mss. Accepts simultaneous submissions.

Terms Pays royalty. Offers advance. Publishes ms 1 year after acceptance.

COTEAU BOOKS

2517 Victoria Ave., Regina SK S4P 0T2 Canada. (306)777-0170. Fax: (306)522-5152. E-mail: coteau@coteaubooks.com. Website: www.coteaubooks.com. **Contact:** Nik. L. Burton, managing editor. AKA Thunder Creek Publishing Co-operative Ltd. "Coteau Books publishes the finest Canadian fiction, poetry, drama and children's literature, with an emphasis on western writers." Publishes trade paperback originals and reprints. Books: offset printing; perfect bound; 4-color illustrations. Averages 16 total titles, 4-6 fiction titles/year. Distributes titles through Fitzhenry & Whiteside.

Needs Ethnic, fantasy, feminist, gay/lesbian, historical, humor, juvenile, literary, mainstream/contemporary, multicultural, multimedia, mystery, regional, short story collections, spiritual, sports, young adult. Canadian authors *only*. Published *The Knife Sharpener's Bell*, by Rhea Tregebov (novel); *Passchendaele: Canada's Triumph and Tragedy on the Fields of Flanders*, by Norman Leach (adult nonfiction); *We Want You to Know*, by Deborah Ellis (juvenile nonfiction); *Summer of Fire*, by Karen Bass (teen novel).

How to Contact Accepts unsolicited mss. Fiction accepted from January 1-April 30; Children's/Teen novels from May 1-August 31; poetry from September 1-December 31; nonfiction accepted year round. Submit complete manuscript, or 3-4 sample chapter(s), author bio. Responds in 2-3 months to queries; 6 months to mss. No simultaneous submissions. Sometimes comments on rejected mss.

Terms Pays 10% royalty on retail price. "We're a co-operative and receive subsidies from the Canadian, provincial and local governments. We do not accept payments from authors to publish their works." Publishes ms 1-2 years after acceptance. Ms guidelines online.

COVENANT COMMUNICATIONS, INC.

920 E. State Rd., American Fork UT 84003-0416. (801)756-9966. E-mail: info@covenant-lds.com. Website: www.covenant-lds.com. Averages 80+ total titles/year.

Needs Historical fiction, suspense, mystery, romance, children's; all submissions must have strong LDS (Church of Jesus Christ of Latter-day Saints, or "Mormons") content.

How to Contact Email your manuscript, along with a one-page cover letter, a one- to two-page plot summary, and the Author Questionnaire. We request that all submissions be submitted via email as Microsoft Word attachments. If you cannot email your submission, please burn the Word document onto a CD and mail it. Follow submission guidelines on website. Requires electronic submission. Responds in 4 months to mss.

Terms Pays 612-15% royalty on retail price. Generally publishes ms 6-12 months after acceptance. Ms guidelines online.

CROWN BOOKS FOR YOUNG READERS

1540 Broadway, New York NY 10171. (212)572-2600 or (800)200-3552. Website: www.randomhouse.com/kids. See listing for Bantam, Doubleday, Dell/Delacorte, Knopf and Crown Books for Young Readers.

- Random House Children's Publishing only accepts submissions through agents.

CROWN PUBLISHING GROUP

1745 Broadway, New York NY 10019. (212)572-2600. Fax: (212)940-7408. E-mail: crownbiz@randomhouse.com. Website: www.randomhouse.com/crown. Estab. 1933. "The group publishes a selection of popular fiction and nonfiction by both established and rising authors."

Imprints Crown, Harmony Books; Shaye Areheart Books; Three Rivers Press; The Princeton Review; Watson-Guptill.

How to Contact *Agented submissions only.*

JOHN DANIEL AND CO.

P.O. Box 2790, McKinleyville CA 95519. (707)839-3495. Fax: (707)839-3242. E-mail: dandd@danielpublishing.com. Website: www.danielpublishing.com. **Contact:** John Daniel, publisher. "We publish small books, usually in small editions, but we do so with pride." Publishes hardcover originals and trade paperback originals. Publishes poetry, fiction and nonfiction. Averages 4 total titles/year. Distributes through SCB Distributors. Promotes through direct mail, reviews.

Needs Literary, short story collections. Publishes poetry, fiction and nonfiction; specializes in belles lettres, literary memoir. Published *Murder in Los Lobos*, by Sue McGinty (mystery novel); *Wolf Tones*, by Irving Weinman (novel).

How to Contact Currently closed to fiction submissions.

Terms Pays 10% royalty on wholesale price. Average advance: $0-500. Publishes ms 1 year after acceptance. Ms guidelines online.

DARK HORSE COMICS, INC.

10956 SE Main St., Milwaukie OR 97222. (503)652-8815. Fax: (503) 654-9440. E-mail: dhcomics@darkhorse.com. Website: www.darkhorse.com. **Contact:** Submissions Editor. "In addition to publishing comics from top talent like Frank Miller, Mike Mignola, Stan Sakai and internationally-renowned humorist Sergio Aragonés, Dark Horse is recognized as the world's leading publisher of licensed comics."

Needs Comic books, graphic novels. Published *Astro Boy Volume 10 TPB*, by Osamu Tezuka and Reid Fleming; *Flaming Carrot Crossover #1* by Bob Burden and David Boswell.

How to Contact Submit synopsis. See website for detailed submission guidelines and submission agreement, which must be signed. Include a full script for any short story or single-issue submission, or the first eight pages of the first issue of any series. Submissions can no longer be mailed back to the sender.

MAY DAVENPORT, PUBLISHERS

26313 Purissima Rd., Los Altos Hills CA 94022. E-mail: mdbooks@earthlink.net. Website: www.maydavenportpublishers.com. **Contact:** May Davenport, editor/publisher. Estab. 1976. "We prefer books which can be used in high schools as supplementary readings in English or creative writing courses. Reading skills have to be taught, and novels by humourous authors can be more pleasant to read than Hawthorne's or Melville's novels, war novels, or novels about past generations. Humor has a place in literature." Publishes hardcover and paperback originals. Averages 4 total titles/year. Distributes titles through direct mail order.

- Books with contemporary themes, are specifically written for TV- and computer-oriented teens and young adults. The emphasis is on enjoying the printed page so as to acquire literary skills to write beyond the Internet "chat room" style.

Imprints md Books (nonfiction and fiction).

Needs Humor, literary. "We want to focus on novels junior and senior high school teachers can share with the reluctant readers in their classrooms." Published *Charlie and Champ*, by Allyson Wagoner; *Senioritis*, by Tate Thompson; *A Life on The Line*, by Michael Horton; *Matthew Livingston & The Prison of Souls*, by Marco Conelli; *Summer of Suspense*, by Frances Drummond Waines.

How to Contact Query with SASE. Responds in 1 month to queries.

Terms Pays 15% royalty on retail price. Publishes ms 1 year after acceptance. Ms guidelines for #10 SASE.

DAW BOOKS, INC.

375 Hudson St., 3rd Floor, New York NY 10014-3658. E-mail: daw@penguinputnam.com. Website: www.dawbooks.com. **Contact:** Peter Stampfel, submissions editor. Estab. 1971. Publishes hardcover and paperback originals and reprints. Averages 60 total titles/year.

Needs Fantasy, science fiction. "We are interested in science fiction and fantasy novels. We are also interested in paranormal romantic fantasy. We like character-driven books. We accept both agented and unagented manuscripts. Long books are not a problem. We are not seeking short stories, poetry, or ideas for anthologies. We do not want any nonfiction manuscripts."

How to Contact Submit complete ms with SASE. Do not submit your only copy of anything. Responds within 3 months to mss. The average length of the novels we publish varies but is almost never less than 80,000 words. Send us the entire manuscript with a cover letter. We do not accept electronic submissions of any kind

Terms Pays in royalties with an advance negotiable on a book-by-book basis. Ms guidelines online.

DELACORTE BOOKS FOR YOUNG READERS

1745 Broadway, New York NY 10019. Website: www.randomhouse.com/kids;www.randomhouse.com/teens. Random House Children's Books, 1540 Broadway, New York NY 10036. (212)782-900.

Website: . Distinguished literary fiction and commercial fiction for the middle grade and young adult categories.

Needs Random House, Inc. does not accept unsolicited submissions, proposals, manuscripts, or submission queries via e-mail at this time.

Terms Ms guidelines online.

DEL REY BOOKS

1745 Broadway, 18th Floor, New York NY 10019. (212)782-9000. Website: www.delreybooks.com. **Contact:** Betsy Mitchell, editor-in-chief. "We are a long-established imprint with an eclectic frontlist. We're seeking interesting new voices to add to our best-selling backlist. Publishes hardcover, trade paperback, and mass market originals and mass market paperback reprints. Averages 120 total titles, 80 fiction titles/year.

Imprints Del Rey Manga, managed by Dallas Middaugh, publishes translations of Japanese comics as well as original graphic novels.

Needs Fantasy (should have the practice of magic as an essential element of the plot), science fiction (well-plotted novels with good characterizations and interesting extrapolations), alternate history. Published *Gentlemen of the Road*, by Michael Chabon; Kraken, by China Mieville; *His Majesty's Dragon*, by Naomi Novik; *The Man With the Iron Heart*, by Harry Turtledove; and *Star Wars: Order 66*, by Karen Traviss.

How to Contact Does not accept unsolicited mss. *Agented submissions only.*

Terms Pays royalty on retail price. Average advance: competitive. Publishes ms 1 year after acceptance. Ms guidelines online.

DIAL BOOKS FOR YOUNG READERS

345 Hudson St., 14th Floor, New York NY 10014. (212)366-2000. E-mail: lauri.hornik@us.penguingroup.com. Website: www.penguin.com. **Contact:** Submissions Editor. Estab. 1961. Trade children's book publisher. Publishes hardcover originals. Averages 50 total titles/year.

Needs Adventure, fantasy, juvenile, picture books, young adult. Especially looking for "lively and well-written novels for middle grade and young adult children involving a convincing plot and believable characters. The subject matter or theme should not already be overworked in previously published books. The approach must not be demeaning to any minority group, nor should the roles of female characters (or others) be stereotyped, though we don't think books should be didactic, or in any way message-y. No topics inappropriate for the juvenile, young adult and middle grade audiences. No plays." Published *A Year Down Yonder*, by Richard Peck; *The Missing Mitten Mystery*, by Steven Kellog.

How to Contact Accepts unsolicited mss. "Submit entire picture book manuscript or the first three chapters of longer works. Please include a cover letter with brief bio and publication credits. Please note that, unless interested in publishing your book, Dial will not respond to unsolicited submissions. Please do NOT include a SASE. If Dial is interested, expect a reply from us within four months."

Terms Pays royalty. Average advance: varies.

DOUBLEDAY

1745 Broadway, New York NY 10019. E-mail: ddaypub@randomhouse.com. Website: www.randomhouse.biz. Knopf Doubleday Broadway Publishing Group, Random House, Inc. Estab. 1897. Publishes hardcover originals. Averages 70 total titles/year.

Imprints Nan A. Talese, Doubleday Religion, Currency, Black Ink/Harlem Moon, Doubleday Graphic Novels.

Needs Adventure, confession, ethnic, experimental, feminist, gay/lesbian, historical, humor, literary, mainstream/contemporary, religious, short story collections.

How to Contact *Agented submissions only.* Does not accept unsolicited mss by email. No simultaneous submissions.

Terms Pays royalty on retail price. Offers advance. Publishes ms 1 year after acceptance.

DOUBLEDAY BOOKS FOR YOUNG READERS

1540 Broadway, New York NY 10036. (212)782-9000. Website: www.randomhouse.com/kids.

- Only accepts manuscripts submitted by an agent.

DOWN EAST BOOKS

Down East, Attn: Books, PO Box 679, Camden ME 04843-0679. Fax: (207)594-7215. E-mail: editors@downeast.com; msteere@downeast.com. Website: www.downeast.com. **Contact:** Michael Steere, managing editor. "We are primarily a regional publisher concentrating on Maine or New England." Publishes hardcover and trade paperback originals, trade paperback reprints. First print order: 3,000. Averages 20-24 total titles/year.

- *Down East Books does not accept unsolicited manuscripts.*

Needs Juvenile, mainstream/contemporary, regional. "We publish 1-2 juvenile titles/year (fiction and nonfiction), and 1-2 adult fiction titles/year." See bookshelf on our website.

How to Contact If you feel like your book is a good fit for Down East, then send us a letter, either through the mail or by email, no more than one page long, with a short description of your project and a little bit about you. In the case of a non-fiction book maybe tell us why you are qualified to write your book. You may also include the first two pages (no more than 1,000 words) of your book if you'd like. We prefer email queries. Or query with SASE. Responds in 3 months to queries. Accepts simultaneous submissions.

Terms Pays 10-15% royalty on net receipts. Average advance: $500 average. Publishes ms 18 months- 2 years after acceptance. Ms guidelines for 9 × 12 SAE with 2 first-class stamps.

DRAGON MOON PRESS

3521 43A Ave., Red Deer AB T4N 3E9 Canada. E-mail: publisher@dragonmoonpress.com. Website: www.dragonmoonpress.com. **Contact:** Gwen Gaddes, publisher. Estab. 1994. "Dragon Moon Press is dedicated to new and exciting voices in science fiction and fantasy." Publishes trade paperback and electronic originals. Books: 60 lb. offset paper; short run printing and offset printing. Average print order: 250-3,000. **Published several debut authors within the last year.** Plans 5 first novels this year. Averages 4-6 total titles, 4-5 fiction titles/year. Distributed through Baker & Taylor. Promoted locally through authors and online at leading retail bookstores like Amazon, Barnes & Noble, Chapters, etc.

Imprints Dragon Moon Press, Gwen Gades publisher (fantasy and science fiction).

Needs At present, we are only accepting solicited manuscripts via referral from our authors and partners. All manuscripts already under review will still be considered by our readers, and we will notify you of our decision. For solicited submissions: Market: We prefer manuscripts targeted to the adult market or the upper border of YA. No middle grade or children's literature, please. Fantasy, science fiction (soft/sociological). No horror or children's fiction, short stories or poetry. "We seek out quality manuscripts and authors who are eager to participate in the marketing of their book.

How to Contact Please visit our website at www.dragonmoonpress.com for submission guidelines. Accepts simultaneous submissions. No submissions on disk. "All submissions are requested electronically—do not mail submissions, as we will not respond. All mailed submissions are shredded and recycled. All queries should be emailed to eic@dragonmoonpress.com with the words BOOK SUBMISSION: and your book title in the subject line."

Terms Pays 8-15% royalty on retail price. Publishes ms 2 years after acceptance.

DREAMCATCHER BOOKS & PUBLISHING

55 Canterbury St. #8 & 9, Saint John NB E2L 2C6 Canada. (506)632-4008. Fax: (506)632-4009. E-mail: dreamcatcherpub@nb.aibn.com. Website: www.dreamcatcherpublishing.ca. **Contact:** Elizabeth Margaris, publisher. Publishes mainstream fiction, with first consideration to Atalantic Canadian

writers. "Especially interested in green themes, hope & inspiration (including autobiographies) with a humourous twist." **Imprints:** Magi Press (vanity press).;

DUTTON (ADULT TRADE)

375 Hudson St., New York NY 10014. (212)366-2000. Website: us.penguingroup.com. **Contact:** Brian Tart, Publisher. Estab. 1852. Publishers hardcover originals. Averages 40 total titles/year.

Needs Adventure, historical, literary, mainstream/contemporary, mystery, short story collections, suspense. Published *The Darwin Awards II,* by Wendy Northcutt (humor); *Falling Angels*, by Tracy Chevalier (fiction); *The Oath*, by John Lescroart (fiction).

How to Contact *Agented submissions only.* Responds in 6 months to queries. Accepts simultaneous submissions.

Terms Pays royalty. Average advance: negotiable. Publishes ms 12-18 months after acceptance.

DUTTON CHILDREN'S BOOKS

345 Hudson St., New York NY 10014. (212)414-3700. Fax: (212)414-3397. Website: www.penguin.com/youngreaders. **Contact:** Lauri Hornik, president and publisher. Dutton Children's Books publishes fiction and nonfiction for readers ranging from preschoolers to young adults on a variety of subjects. Publishes hardcover originals as well as novelty formats Averages 50 titles/year. 10% of books form first-time authors.

Needs Dutton Children's Books has a diverse, general-interest list that includes picture books and fiction for all ages, from middle grade to young adult novels. Published *Big Chickens Fly the Coop*, by Leslie Helakoski, illustrated by Henry Cole (picture book); *Antsy Does Time*, by Neal Shusterman (middle-grade novel); *Paper Towns*, by John Green (young adult novel).

How to Contact Query letter only; include SASE

Terms Pays royalty on retail price. Offers advance

EDGE SCIENCE FICTION AND FANTASY PUBLISHING/TESSERACT BOOKS

Box 1714, Calgary AB T2P 2L7 Canada. (403)254-0160. Fax: (403)254-0456. E-mail: publisher@hadespublications.com. Website: www.edgewebsite.com. **Contact:** Editorial Manager. Estab. 1996. "We are an independent publisher of science fiction and fantasy novels in hard cover or trade paperback format. We produce high-quality books with lots of attention to detail and lots of marketing effort. We want to encourage, produce and promote thought-provoking and fun-to-read science fiction and fantasy literature by 'bringing the magic alive: one world at a time' (as our motto says) with each new book released." Publishes hardcover and trade paperback originals. Books: natural offset paper; offset/web printing; HC/perfect binding; b&w illustration only. Average print order: 2,000-3,000. Plans 20 first novels this year. Averages 16-20 total titles/year. Member of Book Publishers Association of Alberta (BPAA), Independent Publishers Association of Canada (IPAC), Publisher's Marketing Association (PMA), Small Press Center.

Imprints Dragon Moon Press, Alien Vistas, Riverbend.

Needs Fantasy (space fantasy, sword and sorcery), science fiction (hard science/technological, soft/sociological). "We are looking for all types of fantasy and science fiction, horror except juvenile/young adlut, erotica, religious fiction, short stories, dark/gruesome fantasy, or poetry." Length: 75,000-100,000/words. Published *Stealing Magic*, by Tanya Huff; *Forbidden Cargo*, by Rebecca K. Rowe, *The Hounds of Ash and other tales of Fool Wolf* by Greg Keyes.

How to Contact Accepts unsolicited mss. Submit first 3 chapters and synopsis, Check website for guidelines or send SAE & IRCs for same. Include estimated word count. Responds in 4-5 months to mss. No simultaneous submissions, electronic submissions. Rarely comments on rejected mss.

Terms Pays 10% royalty on wholesale price. Average advance: negotiable. Publishes ms 18-20 months after acceptance. Ms guidelines online.

ENGLISH TEA ROSE PRESS

P.O. Box 708, Adams Basin NY 14410-0708. (585)752-8770. E-mail: queryus@thewildrosepress.com. Website: www.thewildrosepress.com. **Contact:** Nicole D'Arienzo, editor. "In the English Tea Rose line we have conquering heroes, high seas adventure, and scandalous gossip. The love stories that will take you back in time. From the windswept moors of Scotland, to the Emerald Isle, to the elegant ballrooms of Regency England, the men and women of this time are larger than life and willing to risk it all for the love of a lifetime. English Tea Rose stories encompass historical romances set before 1900 which are not set on American soil. Send us your medieval knights, Vikings, Scottish highlanders, marauding pirates, and ladies and gentlemen of the Ton. English Tea Rose romances should have strong conflict and be emotionally driven; and, whether the story is medieval, Regency, set during the renaissance, or any other pre-1900 time, they must stay true to their period in historical accuracy and flavor. English Tea Roses can range from sweet to spicy, but should not contain overly explicit language."Publishes paperback originals, reprints, and e-books in a POD format. Published 5 debut authors last year. Publishes approximately 10 fiction titles/year. Member: EPIC, Romance Writers of America. Distributes/promotes titles through major distribution chains, including Ingrams, Baker & Taylor, Sony, Amazon.com, Kindle, as well as smaller and online distributors.

Imprints American Rose (American historical romance), Nicole D'Arienzo, editor

Needs contemporary, futuristic/time travel, gothic, historical, regency, romantic suspense, erotic, and paranormal romances. Plans several anthologies "in several lines of the company in the next year, including Cactus Rose, Yellow Rose, American Rose, Black Rose, and Scarlet Rose." Has published *Nothing to Commend Her*, by Jo Barrett; *The Dragon & The Rose*, by Gini Rifkin; and *Wish for the Moon*, by Sandra Jones.

How to Contact *Does not accept unsolicited mss.* Send query letter with outline and a list of publishing credits. Include estimated word count, brief bio, and list of publishing credits. Agented fiction less than 1%. Responds to queries in 4 weeks; to mss in 12 weeks. Does not consider simultaneous submissions. Always comments on rejected mss.

Terms Pays royalty of 7% minimum; 35% maximum. Sends prepublication galleys to author. Time between acceptance and publication is approximately 1 year. Writer's guidelines available on website. **Advice** "Polish your manuscript, make it as error free as possible, and follow our submission guidelines."

FAERY ROSE

P.O. Box 708, Adams Basin NY 14410-0708. (585)752-8770. E-mail: queryus@thewildrosepress.com. Website: www.thewildrosepress.com. **Contact:** Amanda Barnett, editor. "Fairy Tales are not just for children. The Faery Rose line is a place where you can allow your imagination a free rein to create romance with mystical and mythical characters. Picture if you will, a faery hero who is a strong sensual male who knows what he wants and goes after his leading lady. Dragons don't just frolic in the mist but turn into mortal men and women with love and lust on their minds. Elves have minds and hearts, looking for love with a bit of mischief thrown in. Ghosts who come back to life for the love of their life and wizards, warlocks, and witches who crank up the romance like they spit out a spell. Futuristic worlds, filled with science fiction warriors who can wield a sword as well as a laser and not afraid, be they woman or man, to go after what their heart desires. Time travels moving through centuries with the hero and heroine seeking not the secrets of the ages but love." Publishes paperback originals, reprints, and e-books in a POD format. Published 25 debut authors last year. Publishes approximately 60 fiction titles/year. Member: EPIC, Romance Writers of America. Distributes/promotes titles through major distribution chains, including Ingrams, Baker & Taylor, Sony, Amazon.com, Kindle, as well as smaller and online distributors.

Needs contemporary, futuristic/time travel, gothic, historical, regency, romantic suspense, erotic, and paranormal romances. Plans several anthologies "in several lines of the company in the next year, including Cactus Rose, Yellow Rose, American Rose, Black Rose, and Scarlet Rose." Has published *It Takes Two*, by Sheridon Smythe; *Ties That Bind*, by Keena Kincaid; and *Human Touch*, by J.L. Wilson. *Does not accept unsolicited mss.*

FARRAR, STRAUS & GIROUX

18 West 18th St., New York NY 10011. (212)741-6900. E-mail: fsg.editorial@fsgbooks.com. Website: http://us.macmillan.com/FSG.aspx. **Contact:** Eric Chinski, editor-in-chief. Publishes hardcover and trade paperback books. Averages 180 total titles/year.

Needs Literary.

How to Contact "Unsolicited submissions are accepted at Farrar, Straus and Giroux. All submissions must be submitted through the mail—we do not accept electronic submissions, or submissions delivered in person. Please include a cover letter describing your submission, along with the first 50 pages of the manuscript. If you are submitting poems, please include 3-4 poems. If you wish to hear back from us, please include a SASE with your submission. We will reply in 6-8 weeks of the receipt of the submission."

FARRAR, STRAUS & GIROUX BOOKS FOR YOUNG READERS

Children's Editorial Dept., 175 Fifth Ave., New York NY 10010. (212)741-6900. E-mail: childrens-editorial@fsgbooks.com. Website: http://www.fsgbooks.com/. **Contact:** Margaret Ferguson, editorial director (children's); Wesley Adams, executive editor (children's); Jill Davis, executive editor (children's); Janine O'Malley, senior editor (children's). "We publish original and well-written materials for all ages." Publishes hardcover originals and trade paperback reprints. **Published some debut authors within the last year.** Averages 75 total titles/year.

Imprints Frances Foster Books, edited by Frances Foster (children's); Melanie Kroupa Books, edited by Melanie Kroupa (children's).

Needs Children's/juvenile, picture books, middle grade, young adult, narrative nonfiction. "Do not query picture books; just send manuscript. Do not fax queries or manuscripts." Published *Adele and Simon*, by Barbara McClintock; *The Cabinet of Wonders*, by Marie Rutkoski.

How to Contact For novels and other longer mss, query with SASE and three sample chapters. Do not query picture books, just send ms with cover letter. Include brief bio, list of publishing credits. Agented fiction 50%. Responds in 2 months to queries; 4 months to mss. Accepts simultaneous submissions. No electronic submissions or submissions on disk.

Terms Pays 2-6% royalty on retail price for paperbacks, 3-10% for hardcovers. Average advance: $3,000-25,000. Publishes ms 18 months after acceptance. Book catalog for 9 × 12 SAE with $2.00 postage. Ms guidelines for #10 SASE.

FARRAR, STRAUS & GIROUX PAPERBACKS

18 West 18th St., New York NY 10011. (212)741-6900. Website: http://www.fsgbooks.com/. FSG Paperbacks emphasizes literary nonfiction and fiction, as well as poetry. Publishes hardcover and trade paperback originals and reprints. Averages 180 total titles/year.

Needs Literary. Published *The Corrections*, by Jonathan Franzen; *The Haunting of L.*, by Howard Norman.

How to Contact Unsolicited submissions are accepted at Farrar, Straus and Giroux. All submissions must be submitted through the mail—we do not accept electronic submissions, or submissions delivered in person. Please include a cover letter describing your submission, along with the first 50 pages of the manuscript. If you are submitting poems, please include 3-4 poems.

FLORIDA ACADEMIC PRESS

P.O. Box 540, Gainesville FL 32602. (352)332-5104. Fax: (352)331-6003. E-mail: fapress@worldnet.att.net. **Contact:** Florence Dusek, assistant editor (fiction). Publishes hardcover and trade paperback originals. **Published 90% debut authors within the last year.** Averages 10 total titles/year.

Needs Serious fiction and scholarly social science manuscripts. Does not want "children's books, poetry, science fiction, religious tracts, anthologies, or booklets."

How to Contact Submit complete ms. Responds in 4-12 weeks to mss.

Terms Pays 5-8% royalty on retail price, depending if paperback or hardcover. Publishes ms 3-5 months after acceptance.

FORGE AND TOR BOOKS

175 Fifth Ave. 14th Floor, New York NY 10010. Website: www.tor.com. "Tor Books are science fiction, fantasy and horror, and occasionally, related nonfiction. Forge books are everything else—general fiction, historical fiction, mysteries and suspense, women's fiction and nonfiction. Orb titles are trade paperback reprint editions of science fiction, fantasy and horror books." Publishes hardcover, trade paperback and mass market paperback originals, trade and mass market paperback reprints. **Published some debut authors within the last year.**

- Tor was named Best Publisher at the Locus Awards for the sixteenth consecutive year.

Imprints Forge, Tor, Orb.
Needs Historical, horror, mainstream/contemporary, mystery (amateur sleuth, police procedural, private eye/hard-boiled), science fiction, suspense, thriller/espionage, western (frontier saga, traditional), thriller; general fiction and fantasy.
How to Contact Accepts unsolicited mss. Do not query; "submit only the first three chapters of your book and a synopsis of the entire book. Your cover letter should state the genre of the submission and previous sales or publications if relevant." Include estimated word count, brief bio, list of publishing credits. Agented fiction 95%. Sometimes comments on rejected mss. Responds in 4-6 months. No simultaneous submissions. Additional guidelines on website.
Terms Paperback: Pays 6-8% royalty for first-time authors, 8-10% royalty for established authors. Hardcover: Pays 10% first 5,000; 1212% second 5,000; 15% thereafter. Offers advance. Publishes ms 12-18 months after acceptance.

FREYA'S BOWER

P.O. Box 4897, Culver City CA 90231. E-mail: mbaun@freyasbower.com. Website: http://www.freyasbower.com. **Contact:** Marci Baun, publisher. "Freya's Bower is a small, independent press that started out in March 2006. We are known for working with newer/unpublished authors and editing to the standards of NYC publishers. We respond promptly to submissions." Publishes paperback originals, e-books. Average print order: 50-200. Debut novel print order: 50. **Published over 30 new writers last year.** Plans 10-15 debut novels this year. Averages 75 total titles/year; 75 fiction titles/year. Member EPIC. Distributes/promotes titles through Ingram, All Romance eBooks, Fictionwise, Mobipocket, Amazon, Omnilit, and website.
Needs Erotica and romance of all genres. Has published *Love Bites Back*, by Christopher C. Newman (vampire/paranormal novella); *Dark Succession*, by Teresa D'Amario (a shapeshifter/paranormal novel); *The Art of Losing*, by Lisa Troy (a contemporary erotica novel); *Two Hearts and a Crow*, by Jane Toombs (a contemporary romance novella).
How to Contact Query with outline/synopsis and one sample chapter. Accepts queries by e-mail only. Include estimated word count, brief bio. Writers submit material per submissions guidelines. See website for details. Responds to queries in 2-4 weeks. Accepts unsolicited mss. Often critiques/comments on rejected mss. Responds to mss in 6-8 weeks. Does not accept simultaneous submissions.
Terms Sends pre-production galleys to author. Ms published 2-5 months after acceptance. Writer's guidelines on website. Pays royalties 10-40%. Book catalogs on website.

FRONT STREET

815 Church St., Honesdale PA 18431. (570)253-1164. E-mail: contact@boydsmillspress.com. Website: www.frontstreetbooks.com.
Needs Adventure, ethnic, historical, humor, juvenile, literary, picture books, young adult (adventure, fantasy/science fiction, historical, mystery/suspense, problem novels, sports). "We look for fresh voices for children and young adults. Titles on our list entertain, challenge, or enlighten, always employing novel characters whose considered voices resonate." Published *The Bear Makers* by

Andrea Cheng; *Drive* by Nathan Clement; *The Adventurous Deeds of Deadwood Jones* by Helen Hemphill.

How to Contact Accepts unsolicited and international mss. Query with outline/synopsis, first 3 chapters, and SASE and label the package "Manuscript Submission." Agented fiction 30%. Responds in 3 months to mss. Accepts simultaneous submissions.

Terms Pays royalty on retail price. Offers advance.

GENESIS PRESS, INC.

(662)329-9927. Fax: (662)329-9399. E-mail: customerservice@genesis-press.com. Website: www.genesis-press.com. Publishes hardcover and trade paperback originals and reprints. **Published 50% debut authors within the last year**. Averages 30 total titles/year.

- *Tomorrow's Promise*, by Leslie Esdale won a Gold Pen Award.

Needs Erotica, ethnic, literary, multicultural, romance, women's. Published *Cherish the Flame*, by Beverly Clark; *No Apologies*, by Seressia Glass.

How to Contact Query with SASE or submit 3 sample chapter(s), synopsis. Responds in 2 months to queries; 4 months to mss.Terms Pays 6-12% royalty on invoice price. Average advance: $750-5,000. Publishes ms 1 year after acceptance. Ms guidelines online.

◪ GERTRUDE PRESS

P.O. Box 83948, Portland OR 97283. (503)515-8252. E-mail: edelehoy@fc.edu. Website: www.gertrudepress.org. **Contact:** Justus Ballard (all fiction). "Gertrude Press is a nonprofit organization developing and showcasing the creative talents of lesbian, gay, bisexual, trans, queer-identified and allied individuals. We publish limited-edition fiction and poetry chapbooks plus the biannual literary journal, Gertrude." Format: 60 lb. paper; high-quality digital printing; perfect (lit mag) or saddle-stitch (chapbook) bound. Average print order: 350. Published 5-10 new writers last year. Averages 4 total titles/year; 1 fiction title/year.

Needs Ethnic/multicultural, experimental, feminist, gay, humor/satire, lesbian, literary, mainstream, short story collections.

How to Contact Submit complete ms with cover letter. Submissions accepted year-round. Accepts queries by snail mail, e-mail. Include estimated word count, brief bio, list of publishing credits. Send disposable copy of ms and SASE for reply only. Responds to queries in 3-4 weeks; mss in 3-6 months. Accepts unsolicited mss. Considers simultaneous submissions, e-mail submissions. Sometimes critiques/comments on rejected mss.

Terms Manuscript published 3 months after acceptance. Writer's guidelines on website. Pays in author's copies (1 for lit mag, 50 for chapbook). Book catalogs not available.

N GHOST ROAD PRESS

(303)758-7623. E-mail: matt@ghostroadpress.com; evan@ghostroadpress.com. Website: www.ghostroadpress.com.

Needs "Genre-based mss in literary, science fiction, young adult, fantasy, mystery, and crime fiction."

How to Contact *Not currently accepting submissions.* "Send an attachment (word or.rtf only) that includes a complete synopsis, a description of your marketing plan and platform, and the first three chapters. To view a complete list of our titles and changing submission guidelines, please visit website." Responds in 2-3 months. Accepts simultaneous submissions.

▢ GIVAL PRESS

P.O. Box 3812, Arlington VA 22203. (703)351-0079. E-mail: givalpress@yahoo.com. Website: www.givalpress.com. **Contact:** Robert L. Giron, Publisher. A small, award-winning independent publisher that publishes quality works by a variety of authors from an array of walks of life. Works are in English, Spanish and French and have a philosophical or social message. Publishes paperback originals and reprints and e-books. Books: perfect-bound. Average print order: 500. **Publishes**

established and debut authors. Publishes 2 novels/year. Member AAP, PMA, Literary Council of Small Presses and Magazines. Distributes books through Ingram and BookMasters, Inc.
Needs Literary, multicultural, GLBT. "Looking for French books with English translation." The Annual Gival Press Novel Award contest deadline is May 30th. The Annual Gival Press Short Story Award contest deadline is August 8th. Guidelines on website. Recently published *That Demon Life*, by Lowell Mick White. *Twelve Rivers of the Body*, by Elizabeth Oness, and *A Tomb of the Periphery*, by John Domini.
How to Contact Does not accept unsolicited mss. Query by e-mail first. Include description of project, estimated word count, brief bio, list of publishing credits. Agented fiction 5%. Responds by e-mail within 2-3 weeks. Rarely comments on rejected mss.
Terms Pays 20 contributor's copies. Offers advance. Publishes ms 1 year after acceptance. For book catalog send SASE and on website. Ms guidelines by SASE or on website.

THE GLENCANNON PRESS

P.O. Box 1428, El Cerrito CA 94530. (510)528-4216. Fax: (510)528-3194. E-mail: merships@yahoo.com. Website: www.glencannon.com. **Contact:** Bill Harris (maritime, maritime children's). "We publish quality books about ships and the sea." Publishes hardcover and paperback originals and hardcover reprints. Books: Smyth: perfect binding; illustrations. Average print order: 1,000. First novel print order: 750. Averages 4-5 total titles, 1 fiction titles/year. Member PMA, BAIPA. Distributes titles through Quality Books, Baker & Taylor. Promotes titles through direct mail, magazine advertising and word of mouth.
Imprints Palo Alto Books (any except maritime); Glencannon Press (merchant marine and Navy).
Needs Adventure, children's/juvenile (adventure, fantasy, historical, mystery, preschool/picture book), ethnic (general), historical (maritime), humor, mainstream/contemporary, military/war, mystery, thriller/espionage, western (frontier saga, traditional maritime), young adult (adventure, historical, mystery/suspense, western). Currently emphasizing children's maritime, any age. Recently published *Good Shipmates*, by Ernest F. Imhoff (anthology, merchant marine); *Fort Ross*, by Mark West (Palo Alto Books, western).
How to Contact Accepts unsolicited mss. Submit complete ms. Include brief bio, list of publishing credits. Send SASE for return of ms or send a disposable ms and SASE for reply only. Responds in 1 month to queries; 2 months to mss. Accepts simultaneous submissions. Often comments on rejected mss.
Terms Pays 10-20% royalty. Publishes ms 6-24 months after acceptance.

GOOSE LANE EDITIONS

500 Beaverbrook Court, Suite 300, Fredericton NB E3B 5X4 Canada. (506)450-4251. Fax: (506)459-4991. E-mail: info@gooselane.com. Website: www.gooselane.com. **Contact:** Managing editor. Estab. 1954. Publishes hardcover and paperback originals and occasional reprints. Books: some illustrations. Average print order: 3,000. First novel print order: 1,500. Averages 16-18 total titles, 6-8 fiction titles/year. Distributes titles through University of Toronto Press (UTP).
Needs Literary (novels), mainstream/contemporary, short story collections. "Our needs in fiction never change: substantial, character-centered literary fiction." Published *Reading by Lightning*, by Joan Thomas.
How to Contact Accepts unsolicited mss. Query with SASE. Responds in 6-8 months to mss. No simultaneous submissions.
Terms Pays 8-10% royalty on retail price. Average advance: $200-1,000, negotiable. Ms guidelines online.

GOTHIC CHAPBOOK SERIES

2272 Quail Oak, Baton Rouge LA 70808. E-mail: gothicpt12@aol.com. Website: www.gothicpress.com. "One person operation on a part-time basis." Publishes paperback originals. Books: printing or photocopying. Average print order: 150-200. Distributes titles through direct mail and book dealers.

Needs Horror (dark fantasy, psychological, supernatural). Need novellas and short stories.

How to Contact *Submissions are sought by invitation only.* Include estimated word count, brief bio, list of publishing credits. Send SASE for return of ms or send a disposable ms and SASE for reply only. Responds in 2 weeks to queries; 2 months to mss. Sometimes comments on rejected mss.

Terms Pays 10% royalty. Ms guidelines for #10 SASE.

GRAYWOLF PRESS

250 Third Avenue North, Suite 600, Minneapolis MN 55401. E-mail: wolves@graywolfpress.org. Website: www.graywolfpress.org. **Contact:** Steve Woodward, editorial assistant. Growing independent literary press, nonprofit corporation. Publishes trade cloth and paperback originals. Books: acid-free quality paper; offset printing; hardcover and soft binding. Average print order: 3,000-10,000. First novel print order: 3,000-7,500. Averages 27 total titles, 8-10 fiction titles/year. Distributes titles nationally through Farrar, Straus and Giroux.

Needs Literary novels, short story collections. "Familiarize yourself with our list before submitting your work." Published *The Adderall Diaries*, by Stephen Elliot; *Castle*, by J. Robert Lennon; *The Heyday of the Insensitive Bastards*, by Robert Boswell; *I Am Not Sidney Poitier*, by Percival Everett.

How to Contact Send full ms during open submission period including SASE/IRC, estimated word count, brief bio, list of publishing credits. Agented fiction 90%. Does not accept unsolicited queries, book proposals, or sample chapters. Responds in 3-6 months to submissions. Accepts simultaneous submissions.

Terms Pays royalty on retail price, author's copies. Average advance: $2,500-15,000. Publishes ms 18-24 months after acceptance. Ms guidelines online.

GUERNICA EDITIONS

Att'n: Editor, Series, 489 Strathmore Blvd., Toronto ON M4C 1N8 Canada. (416)658-9888. E-mail: guernicaeditions@cs.com; antoniodalfonso@cs.com. Website: www.guernicaeditions.com. **Contact:** Antonio D'Alfonso, fiction editor (novel and short story). Estab. 1978. "Guernica Editions is a small press that produces works of fiction and nonfiction on the viability of pluriculturalism." Publishes trade paperback originals, reprints and software. Books: various paper; offset printing; perfect binding. Average print order: 1,000. **Published 4 debut authors within the last year.** Averages 25 total titles, 18-20 fiction titles/year. Distributes titles through professional distributors.

- Three titles by Guernica Editions have won American Book Awards.

Imprints Prose Series (original); Picas Series (reprints).

Needs literary, multicultural. "We wish to open up into the fiction world and focus less on poetry. We specialize in European, especially Italian, translations." Publishes anthology of Arab women/Italian women writers. Published *At the Copa*, by Marisa Labozzetta; *In the Claws of the Cat*, by Claude Forand; *Unholy Stories*, by Carole David; *girls Closed In*, by France Theoret.

How to Contact Accepts unsolicited mss. Query with SASE. Must have Canadian postage. Include estimated word count, brief bio, list of publishing credits. Responds in 1 month to queries; 1 year to mss. No simultaneous submissions.

Terms Pays 8-10% royalty on retail price. Or makes outright purchase of $200-5,000. Average advance: $200-2,000. Publishes ms 15 months after acceptance.

HADLEY RILLE BOOKS

P.O. Box 25466, Overland Park KS 66225. E-mail: contact@hadleyrillebooks.com. Website: http://www.hadleyrillebooks.com. **Contact:** Eric T. Reynolds, Editor (science fiction, fantasy). Estab. 2005. "Small publisher, one to two person operation. The first 9 titles are anthologies, mostly science fiction, with a little fantasy (in two titles). We've published new works by well-know authors (for example, new works by Sir Arthur C. Clarke, Mike Resnick, Stephen Baxter, Jay Lake, G. David Nordley, Robert Sheckley, Terry Bisson) as well as up-and-coming and new authors. At present time, about half of our anthologies are by invitation only, the other half are open to unsolicited submissions. We publish the kind of innovative anthologies that are generally not considered by larger publishers (somewhat common in the SF genre). Some of our anthologies are experimental, for example, the first title (Golden Age SF) had well-known authors write 'Golden Age' SF stories as if they were living during that time. The second title, Visual Journeys, asked each contributing author to choose a work of space art and write a story based on it. We included color plates of the art with each story. We're currently in the middle of a Ruins anthology series with stories that are set in or are about ruins. An anthology in 2009 will feature stories that deal with the consequences of global warming. Well-known futurists and SF writers are writing for this." Publishes hardcover originals, paperback originals. Format: Offset and POD printing. Published 50 new writers last year. Averages 6 fiction titles/year. Distributes/promotes titles via distributors, promotes at conventions, online advertising and by reviews.

- One story from *Golden Age SF: Tales of a Bygone Future* (2006) selected for David Hartwell and Kathryn Cramer's *Year's Best SF* #12, another selected for Rich Horton's *Space Opera 2007*. Two stories reprinted in Gardner Dozois' *The Year's Best Science Fiction #2* and ten stories received honorable mentions.

Needs Science fiction, fantasy, short story collections. Check website for current needs. Some anthologies are and will be open to unsolicited submissions, and will be announced on website. Published *Golden Age SF: Tales of a Bygone Future* (science fiction), *Visual Journeys: A Tribute to Space* (science fiction), *Ruins Terra* (SF/fantasy/horror).

How to Contact Send query letter. Accepts queries by e-mail. Include estimated word count, brief bio. Agented fiction: less than 5%. Accepts unsolicited mss. Often critiques/comments on rejected mss.

Terms Sends pre-production galleys to author. Ms published generally 6 months after acceptance. Writer's guidelines on website. Pays royalties of 12 of the ratio of 1 to the number of stories in the book, advance of $30 for unsolicited work. Book catalogs on website.

HARCOURT CHILDREN'S BOOKS

215 Park Ave. South, New York NY 10003. E-mail: adah.nuchi@hmhpub.com. Website: www.harcourtbooks.com/htm/childrens_index.asp. **Contact:** Adah Nuchi. 20% of books by first-time authors; 75% of books from agented writers. "Harcourt Children's Books publishes hardcover picture books and fiction only."

- Harcourt Children's Books no longer accepts unsolicited manuscripts, queries, or illustrations. Recent Harcourt titles: *Jessica's Guide to Dating on the Dark Side*, by Beth Fantaskey; *Graceling*, by Kristin Cashore; *Life as We Knew It*, by Susan Beth Pfeffer; *A Crooked Kind of Perfect*, by Linda Urban; *Evil Genius*, by Catherine Jinks; and *Each Little Bird That Sings*, by Deborah Wiles, a 2005 finalist for the National Book Award

How to Contact Only interested in agented material. Illustration Only interested in agented material.

Terms Pays authors royalty based on retail price. Sends preproduction galleys to authors.

HARLEQUIN BLAZE

225 Duncan Mill Road, Don Mills ON M3B 3K9 Canada. (416)445-5860. Website: www.eharlequin.com. **Contact:** Brenda Chin, associate editor. "Harlequin Blaze is a red-hot series. It is a vehicle to build and promote new authors who have a strong sexual edge to their stories. It is also the place to be for seasoned authors who want to create a sexy, sizzling, longer contemporary story." Publishes paperback originals. Books: newspaper print; web printing; perfect bound. **Published some debut authors within the last year.**

Needs Romance (contemporary). "Sensuous, highly romantic, innovative plots that are sexy in premise and execution. The tone of the books can run from fun and flirtatious to dark and sensual.

Submissions should have a very contemporary feel—what it's like to be young and single today. We are looking for heroes and heroines in their early 20s and up. There should be a strong emphasis on the physical relationship between the couples. Fully described love scenes along with a high level of fantasy and playfulness."

How to Contact No simultaneous submissions, electronic submissions, submissions on disk.

Terms Pays royalty. Offers advance. Ms guidelines online.

HARLEQUIN HISTORICALS

Eton House, 18-24 Paradise Road, Richmond Surrey TW9 1SR United Kingdom. Website: www.eharlequin.com. **Contact:** Linda Fildew, senior editor. "The primary element of a Harlequin Historical novel is romance. The story should focus on the heroine and how her love for one man changes her life forever. For this reason, it is very important that you have an appealing hero and heroine, and that their relationship is a compelling one. The conflicts they must overcome—and the situations they face—can be as varied as the setting you have chosen, but there must be romantic tension, some spark between your hero and heroine that keeps your reader interested." Publishes paperback originals and reprints. Books: newsprint paper; perfect bound. **Published some debut authors within the last year.**

Needs Romance (historical). "We will not accept books set after 1900. We're looking primarily for books set in North America, England or France between 1100 and 1900 A.D. We do not buy many novels set during the American Civil War. We are, however, flexible and will consider most periods and settings. We are not looking for gothics or family sagas, nor are we interested in the kind of comedy of manners typified by straight Regencies. Historical romances set during the Regency period, however, will definitely be considered." Length: 70,000-75,000/words.

How to Contact Submit the first three chapters along with a 1-2 page synopsis of your novel.

Terms Pays royalty. Offers advance. Ms guidelines online.

HARLEQUIN MILLS & BOON, LTD.

Eton House, 18-24 Paradise Rd., Richmond Surrey TW9 1SR United Kingdom. Website: www.millsandboon.co.uk. **Contact:** Editorial Department. Estab. 1908-1909. Publishes mass market paperback originals. **Published some debut authors within the last year.** Plans 3-4 first novels this year.

- Send "first three chapters and a short synopsis of the story. The synopsis of your story should give a clear idea of both your plot and characters and be no more than two pages. Your cover letter should outline pertinent facts about yourself as a writer including your familiarity with the romance genre and previous publishing experience. Please indicate what series you think your project is appropriate for, and if it is completed."

Imprints Mills & Boon Modern Romance (Harlequin Presents); Mills & Boon Tender Romance (Harlequin Romance); Mills & Boon Historicals; Mills & Boon Medicals.

Needs Romance (contemporary, historical, regency period, medical).

How to Contact Send query letter. Accepts queries or submissions by email. Please send any email submissions as a Word document attachment. No simultaneous submissions.

Terms Pays advance against royalty. Publishes ms 2 years after acceptance. Ms guidelines online.

HARLEQUIN SUPERROMANCE

225 Duncan Mill Road, Don Mills ON M3B 3K9 Canada. Website: www.eharlequin.com. **Contact:** Laura Shin, senior editor. "The aim of Superromance novels is to produce a contemporary, involving read with a mainstream tone in its situations and characters, using romance as the major theme. To achieve this, emphasis should be placed on individual writing styles and unique and topical ideas." Publishes paperback originals. Books: newspaper print; perfect bound. **Published 5 debut authors in 2006.**

Needs Romance (contemporary). "The criteria for Superromance books are flexible. Aside from length, the determining factor for publication will always be quality. Authors should strive to break free of stereotypes, clicheés and worn-out plot devices to create strong, believable stories with depth and emotional intensity. Superromance novels are intended to appeal to a wide range of romance readers."

How to Contact Accepts unsolicited submissions. Submit 3 sample chapter(s) and synopsis. Send SASE for return of ms or send a disposable ms and SASE for reply only. No simultaneous submissions, electronic submissions, submissions on disk.

Terms Pays royalty. Offers advance. Ms guidelines online.

HARPERCOLLINS GENERAL BOOKS GROUP

10 East 53 Street, New York NY 10022. (212)207-7000. Fax: (212)207-7633. Website: www.harpercollins.com. "HarperCollins, one of the largest English language publishers in the world, is a broad-based publisher with strengths in academic, business and professional, children's, educational, general interest, and religious and spiritual books, as well as multimedia titles." Publishes hardcover and paperback originals and paperback reprints.

Imprints Amistad Press, Avon, Caedmon, Ecco, Eos, Haper Perennial, HarperAudio, HarperCollins, HarperEntertainment, HarperLargePrint, HarperSanFranciso, HarperTorch PerfectBound, Rayo, ReganBooks, William Morrow.

How to Contact *Does not accept unsolicited manuscripts.* See imprint for specific guidelines.

HENDRICK-LONG PUBLISHING CO., INC.

10635 Tower Oaks, Ste. D, Houston TX 77070. (832)912-7323; (800)544-3770. Fax: (832)912-7353. E-mail: hendrick-long@worldnet.att.net. Website: hendricklongpublishing.com. **Contact:** Michael Long. Estab. 1969. Only considers manuscripts with Texas theme. Publishes hardcover and trade paperback originals and hardcover reprints. Averages 4 total titles/year.

Needs Juvenile, young adult.

How to Contact Submit outline, 2 sample chapter(s), synopsis. Responds in 3 months to queries. No simultaneous submissions. Please, no e-mail submissions.

Terms Pays royalty on selling price. Offers advance. Publishes ms 18 months after acceptance. Book catalog for 8½ × 11 or 9 × 12 SASE with 4 first-class stamps. Ms guidelines online.

HESPERUS PRESS

4 Rickett Street, London En SW6 1RU United Kingdom. 44 20 7610 3331. E-mail: info@hesperuspress.com. Website: www.hesperuspress.com. Hesperus is a small independent publisher mainly of classic literary fiction translated fiction, and biographies of literary figures. Publishes paperback originals. Books: munken paper; traditional printing; sewn binding. Average print order: 5,000. Distributes titles through Trafalgar Square in the US, Grantham Book Services in the UK.

Needs Literary. Published *Carlyle's House*, by Virginia Woolf (rediscovered modern classic); *No Man's Land*, by Graham Greene (rediscovered modern classic); *The Princess of Mantua*, by Marie Ferranti (award-winning fiction in translation); *The Maytrees*, by Annie Dillard (new fiction).

How to Contact Does not accept unsolicited mss. *Agented submissions only.* Query with SASE. Accepts queries by mail. Include estimated word count, brief bio, list of publishing credits. Agented fiction 100%. Responds in 8-10 weeks to queries; 8-10 weeks to mss. Accepts simultaneous submissions. No submissions on disk.

HIGHLAND PRESS PUBLISHING

P.O. Box 2292, High Springs FL 32655. (386) 454-3927. Fax: (386) 454-3927. E-mail: The.Highland.Press@gmail.com. Website: http://www.highlandpress.org. **Contact:** Leanne Burroughs, CEO (fiction); she will forward all mss to appropriate editor. "With our focus on historical romances, Highland Press Publishing is known as your 'Passport to Romance.' We focus on historical romances and our award-winning anthologies. Many people have told us they can once again delight in reading with the anthologies, since they do not have to feel guilty about reading and then putting a book down before it is finished. With the short stories/novellas, they can read a heart warming story, yet still get back to the demands of today's busy lives. As for our historicals, we publish historical novels like many of us grew up with and loved. History is a big part of the story and is tactfully woven throughout the romance." Publishes paperback originals, paperback reprints. Format: off set printing; perfect bound. Average print order: 1000. Debut novel print order: 1,000. **Published 15 new writers last year.** Plans 25 debut authors this year. Averages 30 total titles/year; 30 fiction titles/year. Distributes/promotes titles through Ingrams, Baker & Taylor, Nielsen, Powells.

- *Highland Wishes* was a Finalist, 2005 Readers and Booksellers Best and 2006 Winner, Reviewers International Award of Excellence. *Faery Special Romances* was a nominee for 2007 Night Owl Romances. *Blue Moon Enchantment* won the 2007 P.E.A.R.L. Award (two separate stories). *Christmas Wishes* had several stories nominated for the 2007 P.E.A.R.L. Award and received the 2007 Linda Howard Award of Excellence. *Her Highland Rogue* recieved the 2006 Reviewer's International Award, the 2006 National Readers Choice Award, and was a 2007 finalist for Readers and Booksellers Best. *Cat O'Nine Tales* had several stories as finalists or win the 2007 P.E.A.R.L. Award, 2007 Linda Howard Award of Excellence, and the 2007 Reviewers International Organization Award of Excellence.

Imprints Grace (inspirationals), A Wee Dram (short stories/novellas), The Wee Ones (children's illustrated), Regency Royale (Regency/romance), Thistle (Scottish historicals), Eire (Irish historicals), Pandora (young adult), Western (western/romance), Paranormal, Tea Time (Victorian to gaslight Britain), Americana (American historical), Circles of Gold (contemporary romance), Stirling (historical Britain), Mystery/Suspense, Reference (nonfiction writers' reference).

Needs Children's/juvenile (adventure, animal, easy-to-read, fantasy, historical, mystery, preschool/picture book, series), Comedy (romance/suspense), Contemporary (romance/mystery/suspense); Family saga, Fantasy (space fantasy), historical, horror (dark fantasy, futuristic, supernatural), mainstream, military/war, mystery/suspense (amateur/sleuth, cozy, police, private eye/hardboiled), religious (children's, general, family, inspirational, fantasy, mystery/suspense, thriller, romance), romance (contemporary, futuristic/time travel, gothic, historical, regency period, suspense), short story collections, thriller/espionage, western (frontier saga, traditional), young adult/teen (adventure, paranormal, fantasy/science fiction, historical, horror, mystery/suspense, romance, series, western, chapter books). Special interests: Children's ms must come with illustrator. "We will always be looking for good historical manuscripts. In addition, we are actively seeking inspirational romances and Regency period romances." Numerous romance anthologies are planned. Topics and word count are posted on the Website. Writers should query with their proposal. After the submission deadline has passed, editors select the stories.

How to Contact Send query letter. Query with outline/synopsis and sample chapters. Accepts queries by snail mail, e-mail. Include estimated word count, target market. Send disposable copy of ms and SASE for reply only. Agented fiction: 10%. Responds to queries in 8 weeks. Accepts unsolicited mss. Considers simultaneous submissions, e-mail submissions. Sometimes critiques/comments on rejected mss. Responds to mss in 3-12 months.

Terms Sends pre-production galleys to author. Ms published within 12 months after acceptance. Writer's guidelines on Website. Pays royalties 7.5-8%. Book catalogs on Website.

◙ HENRY HOLT & CO. BOOKS FOR YOUNG READERS

175 Fifth Avenue, New York NY 10010. (646)307-5282. Website: www.henryholtchildrensbooks.com. Henry Holt Books for Young Readers publishes excellent books of all kinds (fiction, nonfiction, illustrated) for all ages, from the very young to the young adult. Publishes hardcover originals of picture books, chapter books, middle grade and young adult novels. Averages 70-80 total titles/year.

Needs Adventure, fantasy, historical, mainstream/contemporary, multicultural, picture books, young adult. Juvenile: adventure, animal, contemporary, fantasy, history, multicultural. Picture books: animal, concept, history, mulitcultural, sports. Young adult: contemporary, fantasy, history, multicultural, nature/environment, problem novels, sports. Published *When Zachary Beaver Came* *to Town*, by Kimberly Willis Holt (middle grade fiction); *The Gospel According to Larry*, by Janet Tashjian (YA fiction); *Visiting Langston*, by Willie Perdomo, illustrated by Bryan Collier (picture book); *Keeper of the Night*, by Kimberly Willis Holt; *Alphabet Under Construction*, by Denise Fleming (picture book).

How to Contact *Does not accept unsolicited submissions.*

Terms See website for complete guidelines, www.henryholtchildrensbooks.com/submissions.htm.

HOUGHTON MIFFLIN BOOKS FOR CHILDREN

222 Berkeley St., Boston MA 02116. E-mail: children's_books@hmco.com. Website: www.houghtonmifflinbooks.com. **Contact:** Submissions coordinator. "Houghton Mifflin gives shape to ideas that educate, inform and, above all, delight." Publishes hardcover originals and trade paperback originals and reprints. **Published 12 debut authors within the last year.** Averages 100 total titles/year. Promotes titles through author visits, advertising, reviews.

Imprints Clarion Books, New York City, Graphia Boston; Sand Pipers, Boston.

Needs Adventure, ethnic, historical, humor, juvenile (early readers), literary, mystery, picture books, suspense, young adult, board books. Published *Trainstop*, by Barbara Lehman; *The Willowbys*, by Lois Lowry; *Just Grace Walker the Dog*, by Cherise Mericle Harper.

How to Contact Accepts unsolicited mss. Responds only if interested. Do not send SASE. Accepts simultaneous submissions. No electronic submissions.

Terms Pays 5-10% royalty on retail price. Average advance: variable. Publishes ms 18-24 months after acceptance. Book catalog for 9 × 12 SASE with 3 first-class stamps. Ms guidelines online.

HOUGHTON MIFFLIN HARCOURT CO.

222 Berkeley St., Boston MA 02116. (617)351-5000. Website: www.hmco.com. Estab. 1832. Publishes hardcover originals and trade paperback originals and reprints. **Published 5 debut authors within the last year.** Averages 250 total titles/year.

Needs Literary. "We are not a mass market publisher. Study the current list." Published *Extremely Loud and Incredibly Close*, by Jonathan Safran Foer; *The Plot Against America*, by Philip Roth; *Heir to the Glimmering World*, by Cynthia Ozick.

How to Contact Does not accept unsolicited mss. *Agented submissions only.* Accepts simultaneous submissions.

Terms Hardcover: pays 10-15% royalty on retail price, sliding scale or flat rate based on sales; paperback: 712% flat rate, but negotiable. Average advance: variable. Publishes ms 3 years after acceptance.

IMAGE COMICS

Submissions, 2134 Allston Way, 2nd Floor, Berkeley CA 94704. E-mail: submissions@imagecomics.com; ericstephenson@imagecomics.com. Website: http://www.imagecomics.com/. **Contact:** Eric Stephenson, publisher. "Image is a comics and graphic novels publisher formed by seven of Marvel Comics' best-selling artists: Erik Larsen, Jim Lee, Rob Liefeld, Todd McFarlane, Whilce Portacio, Marc Silvestri, and Jim Valentino. Since that time, Image has gone on to become the third largest comics publisher in the United States."

Needs "We are not looking for any specific genre or type of comic book. We are looking for comics that are well written and well drawn, by people who are dedicated and can meet deadlines."

How to Contact Query with 1 page synopsis and 5 pages or more of samples. "We do not accept writing (that is plots, scripts, whatever) samples! If you're an established pro, we might be able to find somebody willing to work with you but it would be nearly impossible for us to read through every script that might find its way our direction. Do not send your script or your plot unaccompanied by art — it will be discarded, unread." Accepts queries by snail mail, e-mail. Sometimes critiques/comments on rejected mss.

Terms Writer's guidelines on website.

INSOMNIAC PRESS

520 Princess Ave., London ON N6B 2B8 Canada. (416)504-6270. Fax: (416)504-9313. E-mail: mike@insomniacpress.com. Website: www.insomniacpress.com. **Contact:** Mike O'Connor, publisher. Estab. 1992. "Midsize independent publisher with a mandate to produce edgy experimental fiction." Publishes trade paperback originals and reprints, mass market paperback originals, and electronic originals and reprints. First novel print order: 3,000. **Published 15 debut authors within the last year.** Plans 4 first novels this year. Averages 20 total titles, 5 fiction titles/year.

Needs Comic books, ethnic, experimental, gay/lesbian, humor, literary, mainstream/contemporary, multicultural, mystery, suspense. We publish a mix of commercial (mysteries) and literary fiction. Published *Pray For Us Sinners,* by Patrick Taylor (novel).

How to Contact Accepts unsolicited mss. Accepts queries by email. Include estimated word count, brief bio, list of publishing credits. Send SASE for return of ms or send a disposable ms and SASE for reply only. Agented fiction 5%. Responds in 1 week to queries; 2 months to mss. Accepts simultaneous submissions. Sometimes comments on rejected mss.

Terms Pays 10-15% royalty on retail price. Average advance: $500-1,000. Publishes ms 6 months after acceptance. Ms guidelines online.

INTERLINK PUBLISHING GROUP, INC.

46 Crosby St., Northampton MA 01060. (413)582-7054. Fax: (413)582-7057. E-mail: editor@interlinkbooks.com. Website: www.interlinkbooks.com. **Contact:** Pam Thompson, editor. Estab. 1987. "Midsize independent publisher specializing in world travel, world literature, world history and politics." Publishes hardcover and trade paperback originals. Books: 55 lb. Warren Sebago Cream white paper; web offset printing; perfect binding. Average print order: 5,000. **Published new writers within the last year.**Averages 50 total titles, 2-4 fiction titles/year. Distributes titles through Baker & Taylor. Promotes titles through book mailings to extensive, specialized lists of editors and reviews; authors read at bookstores and special events across the country.

Imprints Interlink Books and Olive Branch Press.

Needs Ethnic, international. "Adult—We are looking for translated works relating to the Middle East, Africa or Latin America." Recently published *Everything Good Will Come,* by Sefi Atta (first novel); *The Gardens of Light,* by Amin Maalouf (novel translated from French); *War in the Land of Egypt,* by Yusef Al-Qaid (novel translated from Arabic).

How to Contact Become familiar with the kinds of books we publish. Request a catalog or read them at your local library, If you believe your ms might fit our list, please send a query letter to the attention of Pam Thompson. The query letter may (but doesn't have to) include any of the following: a writing sample (preferably the opening of the book) of no more than 10 pages, a brief synopsis and bio. Send an SASE as well. The only fiction we publish falls into our "Interlink WorldFiction" series. Most of these books, as you can see in our catalog, are translated fiction from around the world. The idea behind the series is to bring fiction from other countries to a North American audience. So unless you were born outside the United States, your novel will not fit into the series. All of our children's books are picture books designed for ages 3-8. We publish very few of them, and most are co-published with overseas publishing houses. We do not consider unsolicited manuscripts of children's books. Query with SASE and a brief sample. Responds in 3 months to queries. Accepts simultaneous submissions. No electronic submissions.

Terms Pays 6-8% royalty on retail price. Average advance: small. Publishes ms 18 months after acceptance. Ms guidelines online.

INVERTED-A

P.O. Box 267, Licking MO 65542. E-mail: amnfn@well.com. **Contact:** Aya Katz, chief editor (poetry, novels, political); Nets Katz, science editor (scientific, academic). Publishes paperback originals. Books: offset printing. Average print order: 1,000. Average first novel print order: 500. Distributes through Baker & Taylor, Amazon, Bowker.

Needs Utopian, political. Needs poetry submission for our newsletter, *Inverted-A Horn.*

How to Contact Does not accept unsolicited mss. Query with SASE. Reading period open from January 2 to March 15. Accepts queries by e-mail. Include estimated word count. Responds in 1 month to queries; 3 months to mss. Accepts simultaneous submissions. Sometimes comments on rejected mss.

Terms Pays in 10 author's copies. Publishes ms 1 year after acceptance. Ms guidelines for SASE.

◎ ION IMAGINATION PUBLISHING

P.O. Box 210943, Nashville TN 37221-0943. Fax: (615)646-6276. E-mail: ionimagin@aol.com. Website: www.flumpa.com. **Contact:** Keith Frickey, editor. Small independent publisher of science-related children's fiction, multimedia and audio products. Publishes hardcover and paperback originals. Average first novel print order: 10,000. Member SPAN and PMA.

- Received the Parents' Choice, National Parenting Centers Seal of Approval, Dr. Toy, Parent Council.

Needs Children's/juvenile (adventure, animal, preschool/picture book, science).

How to Contact Does not accept unsolicited mss. Query with SASE. Include brief bio, list of publishing credits. Responds in 1 month to queries. Accepts simultaneous submissions. Sometimes comments on rejected queries.

Terms Pays royalty.

◪ ◎ ITALICA PRESS

595 Main St., Suite 605, New York NY 10044-0047. (212)935-4230. E-mail: inquiries@italicapress.com. Website: www.italicapress.com. **Contact:** Ronald G. Musto and Eileen Gardiner, Ph.D., publishers. Estab. 1985. Small independent publisher of Italian fiction in translation. "First-time translators published. We would like to see translations of Italian writers who are well-known in Italy who are not yet translated for an American audience." Publishes trade paperback originals. Books: 50-60 lb. natural paper; offset printing; illustrations. Average print order: 1,500. Averages 6 total titles, 2 fiction titles/year. Distributes titles through website. Promotes titles through website.

Needs Translations of 20th century Italian fiction. Published *Game Plan for a Novel*, by Gianna Manzini; *The Great Bear*, by Ginevra Bompianai; *Sparrow*, by Giovanni Verga.

How to Contact Accepts unsolicited mss. Query with SASE. Accepts queries by e-mail, fax. Responds in 1 month to queries; 2 months to mss. Accepts simultaneous submissions, electronic submissions, submissions on disk.

Terms Pays 7-15% royalty on wholesale price. Pays author's copies. Publishes ms 1 year after acceptance. Ms guidelines online.

◪ ◎ JUNO BOOKS

E-mail: editor@juno-books.com; submissions@juno-books.com. Website: www.juno-books.com. An imprint of Pocket Books, Juno publishes hardcover originals, paperback originals, paperback reprints, e-books. Format: offset printing; mass market paperback or trade paperback bound. Average print order: mmp first printing 10,000-25,000, trade 2,000-5,000. Debut novel print order: mmp 10,000, trade 2,000.

Needs "We welcome a cross-genre mix of contemporary and traditional FANTASY with mystery, thriller, paranormal romance, sf, adventure, historical fiction, detective, sensual, etc. We're looking for contemporary and urban fantasy featuring strong female protagonists with 'kickassitude.'" Published *Dancing With Werewolves*, by Carole Nelson Douglas; *Personal Demons*, by Stacia Kane; *Matters of the Blood* by Maria Lima.

How to Contact *Currently closed to submissions.* See website for when submissions will open again. Query with outline/synopsis and 3 sample chapters. Accepts queries by e-mail only. Include estimated word count, brief bio, list of best publishing credits. Agented fiction: 30%. Responds to queries in 3 months. Accepts unsolicited mss. Considers simultaneous submissions. Sometimes critiques/comments on rejected mss.

Terms Sends pre-production galleys to author. Ms published 6-24 months after acceptance. Writer's guidelines on website. Pays 6-10% royalties, average $1000 advance, author's copies. Advance is negotiable. Book catalog on website.

JUST US BOOKS, INC.

(973)672-7701. Fax: (973)677-7570. E-mail: katura_hudson@justusbooks.com; cheryl_hudson@justusbooks.com. Website: www.justusbooks.com. Estab. 1988. Small independent publisher of children's books that focus on Black history, culture, and experiences (fiction and nonfiction). Publishes hardcover originals, paperback originals, hardcover reprints and paperback reprints (under its Sankofa Books imprint for previously published titles). Averages 4-8 total titles, 2-4 fiction titles/year. Member, Small Press Association; Children Book Council.

Needs Ethnic (African American), young adult (adventure, easy-to-read, historical, mystery/suspense, problem novels, series, sports). Published *Path to my African Eyes*, by Ermila Moodley; *12 Brown Boys*, by Omar Tyree.

How to Contact Currently accepting queries for young adult titles only. We are not considering picture books, poetry, activity books or any other manuscripts at this time. Query with SASE, ms synopsis and pitch letter by mail only. Include brief bio, list of publishing credits. Send SASE for reply. Responds to queries in 10-12 weeks. Accepts simultaneous submissions.

Terms Pays royalty. Ms guidelines for SASE or on website.

KAEDEN BOOKS

P.O. Box 16190, Rocky River, OH 44116-6190. E-mail: lstenger@kaeden.com. Website: www.kaeden.com. **Contact:** Lisa Stenger, Editor. Kaeden Books produces high-quality children's books for the educational market.

Needs Stories with humor, surprise endings and interesting characters suitable for the education market. "Must have well-developed plots with clear beginnings, middles and endings. No adult or religious themes." Word count range: 25-2,000.

How to Contact Submit complete ms; include SASE. Do not send originals. Respond within 1 year. For complete guidelines see www.kaeden.com. No phone calls please.

Terms Work purchased outright from authors. Pays royalties to previous authors.

KEARNEY STREET BOOKS

P.O. Box 2021, Bellingham WA 98227. (360)738-1355. E-mail: garyrmc@mac.com. Website: http://kearneystreetbooks.com.

Needs Only publishes books about music or musicians. Published *Such a Killing Crime*, Robert Lopresti (mystery); *Tribute to Orpheus* (short story collection).

How to Contact Send query letter. Accepts queries by e-mail. Send disposable copy of ms and SASE for reply only. Responds to queries in 1 week. Accepts unsolicited mss. Responds to mss in 6-10 months. Considers simultaneous submissions, submissions on CD or disk. Never critiques/comments on rejected mss. Does not return rejected mss.

Terms Sends pre-production galleys to author. Manuscript published 18 months after acceptance. Pays "after expenses, profits split 50/50."

KENSINGTON PUBLISHING CORP.

119 West 40th St., New York NY 10018. (800)221-2647; (212)407-1500. E-mail: kensingtonmarketing@kensingtonbooks.com. Website: www.kensingtonbooks.com. **Contact:** John Scognamiglio, editor in chief. Estab. 1975. Full service trade commercial publisher, all formats. Publishes hardcover and trade paperback originals, mass market paperback originals and reprints. Averages over 500 total titles/year.

Needs Book-length fiction and nonfiction for popular audiences. Adult and YA.

How to Contact Accepts unsolicited and unagented mss. You may **QUERY ONLY** by email. Do not attach manuscripts or proposals to email queries. An editor will respond if he or she is interested in seeing your material based on your query. Submit to one editor only. Responds in 1 month to queries; 4 months to mss. Accepts simultaneous submissions.

Terms Advance against royalties based on net sales. Publishes ms 12-24 months after acceptance.

ALLEN A. KNOLL, PUBLISHERS

200 W. Victoria Street, Santa Barbara CA 93101. (805)564-3377. E-mail: bookinfo@knollpublishers.com. Website: www.knollpublishers.com. **Contact:** Submissions. Small independent publisher, a few titles a year. Specializes in 'books for intelligent people who read for fun.' Publishes hardcover originals. Books: offset printing; sewn binding. Titles distributed through Ingram, Baker & Taylor.

Needs Published *They Fall Hard*, by Alistair Boyle (mystery); *To Die For*, by David Champion (mystery); *The Duchess to the Rescue*, by Alexandra Eden (children's fiction).

How to Contact Does not accept unsolicited mss.

Terms Varies.

ALFRED A. KNOPF

1745 Broadway, 21st Floor, New York NY 10019. Website: http://knopf.knopfdoubleday.com. **Contact:** Senior Editor. Estab. 1915. Publishes hardcover and paperback originals. **Published some debut authors within the last year.** Averages 200 total titles/year.

Needs Publishes book-length fiction of literary merit by known or unknown writers. Length: 40,000-150,000 words. Published *Gertrude and Claudius*, by John Updike; *The Emperor of Ocean Park*, by Stephen Carter; *Balzac and the Little Chinese Seamstress*, by Dai Sijie.

How to Contact *Agented submissions only.* Query with SASE or submit sample chapter(s). Responds in 2-6 months to queries. Accepts simultaneous submissions.

Terms Pays 10-15% royalty. Royalty and advance vary. Offers advance. Must return advance if book is not completed or is unacceptable. Publishes ms 1 year after acceptance. Book catalog for 7½ × 10½ SAE with 5 first-class stamps.

KNOPF PUBLISHING GROUP

1745 Broadway, New York NY 10019. (212)751-2600. Website: www.randomhouse.com/knopf. Division of Random House, Inc. "Throughout history, Knopf has been dedicated to publishing distinguished fiction and nonfiction." Publishes hardcover and paperback originals.

Imprints Everyman's Library; Alfred A. Knopf; Pantheon Books; Shocken Books; Vintage Anchor Publishing, Doubleday, and Nan A. Talese.

LACHESIS PUBLISHING

2221 Millar Rd. West, RR 4, Spencerville Ontario K0E 1X0 Canada. Fax: (902) 590-9667. E-mail: write2dar@gmail.com. Website: www.lachesispublishing.com. **Contact:** Carole Spencer, publisher. "Midsize independent publisher. Will assess all fiction but no poetry, collections of short stories or children's stories." Publishes paperback originals, paperback reprints, e-books. Format: POD printing;some illustrations. Debut novel print order: 150. **Published 12 new writers last year.** Plans 8 debut novels this year. Averages 12 fiction titles/year. **Imprint(s)** LBF Books; Sinful Moments Press.

Needs Adventure, juvenile (fantasy, mystery, series), erotica, family saga, fantasy, gay, historical, horror, mainstream, military/war, mystery/suspense, regional, romance, science fiction, thriller/espionage, western, young adult/teen. Need erotica, gay and lesbian, and all types of romance

How to Contact Query with outline/synopsis and 3 sample chapters. Accepts queries by e-mail; no snail mail. Include estimated word count, brief bio, list of publishing credits, any connection with a writer's association. Responds to queries in 2 weeks. Accepts unsolicited mss. Considers simultaneous submissions. Always critiques/comments on rejected mss. Responds to mss in 3-5 months.

Terms Ms published 18 months after acceptance. Writer's guidelines on website. Pays royalties 10% min for print, 20% max for e-book.

LEAPFROG PRESS

Box 2110, Teaticket MA 02536. (508)349-1925. Fax: (508)349-1180. E-mail: leapfrog@leapfrogpress.com. Website: www.leapfrogpress.com. **Contact:** Tasha Enseki, acquisitions editor. "We search for beautifully written literary titles and market them aggressively to national trade and library accounts. We also sell film, translation, foreign, and book club rights." Publishes paperback originals. Books: acid-free paper; sewn binding. Average print order: 3,000. First novel print order: 2,000 (average). Member, Publishers Marketing Association, PEN. Distributes titles through Consortium Book Sales and Distribution, St. Paul, MN. Promotes titles through all national review media, bookstore readings, author tours, website, radio shows, chain store promotions, advertisements, book fairs.

- *The Devil and Daniel Silverman* by Theodore Rosak was nominated for the American Library Association Stonewall Award and was a San Francisco Chronicle best seller. *The German Money* by Lev Raphael was a Booksense 76 pick.

Needs "Genres often blur; look for good writing. We are most interested in works that are quirky, that fall outside of any known genre,and of course well written and finely crafted. We are most interested in literary fiction." Published *The War at Home*, by Nora Eisenberg; *Junebug*, by Maureen McCoy; *Paradise Dance*, by Michael Lee; *Waiting for Elvis*, by Toni Graham; and *Losing Kei*, by Suzanne Kamata. See web site for more recent titles.

How to Contact Query by e-mail only. Send letter and first 5 to 10 ms pages within e-mail message. No attachments. Responds in 2-3 weeks to queries by e-mail; 6 months to mss. may consider simultaneous submissions.

Terms Pays 4-8% royalty on net receipts. Average advance: negotiable. Publishes ms 1-2 years after acceptance.

LEAPING DOG PRESS AND ASYLUM ARTS PUBLISHING

Literature with bark and bite, P.O. Box 90473, Raleigh NC 27675-0473. (877)570-6873. Fax: (877)570-6873. E-mail: editor@leapingdogpress.com. Website: www.leapingdogpress.com. **Contact:** Jordan Jones, editor & publisher. Member: CLMP, SPAN, and PMA. "Leaping Dog Press and Asylum Arts Press publish accessible, edgy, witty, and challenging contemporary poetry, fiction, and works in translation, with Asylum Arts Press having an additional focus on surrealism and the avant garde."

Needs "Please bear in mind that we are a small press that publishes only 4-6 titles a year. Additionally, we are currently under contract for titles through calendar year 2008, so the soonest newly accepted titles could appear is 2011." Does not want "genre fiction, self help, dog books, etc."

How to Contact Query by mail with a cover letter "containing your reasons for considering LPD or AA and your ideas for marketing your title; a proposed table of contents; a bio or CV and a list of publications; two chapters or 20 pages of fiction." Does not accept e-mail or electronic submissions or queries. Include SASE.

LEE & LOW BOOKS INC.

95 Madison Ave., Suite 1205, New York NY 10016. (212)779-4400. Fax: (212) 683-1894. Website: www.leeandlow.com. **Contact:** Submissions Editor. Publishes 12-14 children's books/year. 25% of books by first-time authors. Lee & Low Books publishes books with diverse themes. "One of our goals is to discover new talent and produce books that reflect the diverse society in which we live.

- "Lee & Low Books is dedicated to publishing culturally authentic literature. The company makes a special effort to work with writers and artists of color and encourages new voices."

Needs Picture books, young readers: anthology, contemporary, history, multicultural, poetry. "We are not considering folktales or animal stories." Picture book, middle reader: contemporary, history, multicultural, nature/environment, poetry, sports. Average word length: picture books—1,000-1,500 words. Recently published *Amazing Faces*, by Lee Bennett Hopkins, illustrated by Chris Soentpiet; *The Can Man*, by Laura E. Williams, illustrated by Craig Orback.

How to Contact Fiction/nonfiction: Submit complete ms. No e-mail submissions. Publishes a book 1-2 years after acceptance. Will consider simultaneous submissions. Guidelines on website. No SASE. Writer will be notified within 6 monthsif we have interest in the work. Manuscripts will not be returned.

Terms Pays authors advances against royalty. Pays illustrators advance against royalty. Photographers paid advance against royalty. Book catalog available for 9 × 12 SAE and $1.65 postage; ms and art guidelines available via website or with SASE.

LEISURE BOOKS

Dorchester Publishing Co., 200 Madison Ave., Suite 2000, New York NY 10016. (212)725-8811. Fax: (212)532-1054. Website: www.dorchesterpub.com. **Contact:** Editorial Department. Estab. 1970. Publishes mass market paperback originals and reprints. Publishes romances, westerns, horrors, and thrillers. Books: newsprint paper; offset printing; perfect bound. Average print order: variable. First novel print order: variable. Plans 25 first novels this year. Averages 255 total titles/year. Promotes titles through national reviews, ads, author readings, promotional items and on the website.

Imprints Leisure Books, Love Spell.

Needs Horror, romance, western, and thrillers. "We strongly back first time writers. All historical romance should be set pre-1900. Horrors and westerns are growing as well. No sweet romance, science fiction, cozy mysteries." Published *When Love Comes*, by Leigh Greenwood (historical romance); *A Tale of Two Demon Slayers*, by Angie Fox (paranormal romance); *Darkness on the Edge of Town*, by Brian Keene (horror); *The Outlaw Josey Wales*, by Forrest Carter (western).

How to Contact Accepts unsolicited mss. Query with SASE or submit outline, first 3 sample chapters, synopsis in hard copy or e-mail as an attachment to submissions@dorchesterpub.com. Agented fiction 70%. Responds in 6-8 months to queries. No simultaneous submissions, electronic submissions.

Terms Pays royalty on retail price. Average advance: negotiable. Publishes ms 12 months after acceptance. Book catalog for free (800)481-9191. Ms guidelines online.

LERNER PUBLISHING GROUP

241 First Ave. N., Minneapolis MN 55401. (612)332-3344. Fax: (612)332-7615. E-mail: info@lernerbooks.com. Website: www.lernerbooks.com. Primarily publishes books for children ages PreK-18. List includes titles in geography, natural and physical science, current events, ancient and modern history, high interest, sports, world cultures, and numerous biography series.

- Starting in 2007, Lerner Publishing Group no longer accepts submission in any of their imprints except for Kar-Ben Publishing.

How to Contact "We will continue to seek targeted solicitations at specific reading levels and in specific subject areas. The company will list these targeted solicitations on our website and in national newsletters, such as the SCBWI *Bulletin*."

LETHE PRESS

E-mail: editor@lethepressbooks.com. Website: www.lethepressbooks.com. "Named after the Greek river of memory and forgetfulness (and pronounced Lee-Thee), Lethe Press is a small press devoted to ideas that are often neglected or forgotten by mainstream, profit-oriented publishers." Distributes/promotes titles Lethe Books are distributed by Ingram Publications and Bookazine, and are available at all major bookstores, as well as the major online retailers.

Needs *Rarely accepts unsolicited mss.* Primarily interested in gay fiction, poetry and non-fiction titles. Has imprint for gay spirituality titles. Also releases work of occult and supernatural, sci-fi, and east asian interests.

How to Contact Send query letter. Accepts queries by e-mail.

ARTHUR A. LEVINE BOOKS

557 Broadway, New York NY 10012. (212)343-4436. Website: www.scholastic.com. **Contact:** Arthur Levine, VP, publisher. "Arthur A. Levine is looking for distinctive literature, for children and young adults, for whatever's extraordinary." Averages 18-20 total titles/year.

Needs Juvenile, picture books, young adult, middle grade novels. Published *Peaceful Heroes*, by Jonah Winter, illustrated by Sean Addy; *Blue Mountain Trouble*, by Martin Mordecai; *Marcelo In The Real World*, by Francisco X Stork; *Lips Touch*, by Laini Taylor, illustrations by Jim Di Bartolo.

How to Contact Query with SASE.

Terms Pays variable royalty on retail price. Average advance: variable. Book catalog for 9 × 12 SASE.

LIQUID SILVER BOOKS

E-mail: raven@liquidsilverbooks.com; support@liquidsilverbooks.com. Website: www.liquidsilverbooks.com. "Romance is the key to our stories. The stories must hold on their own if the sex scenes are omitted. Stories must have well developed characters, with depth and explosive chemistry that entice the reader to like and/or identify with them. Mix in an imaginative and fully realized plot, vivid settings, and clear dialog and you've got the ingredients for a story we'd be interested in publishing." Publishes paperback originals and e-books.

Needs Contemporary, gay and lesbian, paranormal, supernatural, sci-fi, fantasy, historical, suspense, and western romances.

How to Contact Query with outline/synopsis and three sample chapters in.rtf form, ariel 12 pt font only. Accepts queries by e-mail. Include estimated word count, author bio, thoughts on e-Publishing, and a snapshot synopsis of book including title and series title, if applicable, in body of e-mail. Mss must include pen name, real name, snail mail, and e-mail contact information on first page top left corner. No headers, footers, or page numbers. Responds to queries in 4-6 weeks.

Terms Manuscript published 4 months after acceptance. Writer's guidelines on website. We pay 35% royalties on eBook retail sales from those sales originating from the Liquid Silver Books website. For other retail distributors, we pay 35% royalties on minus the distribution costs. Our contract is for electronic rights for one year. If your book is chosen for print, the contract will be amended to reflect the print terms.

LITTLE, BROWN AND CO. ADULT TRADE BOOKS

237 Park Ave., New York NY 10017. E-mail: publicity@littlebrown.com. Website: www.hachettebookgroup.com. **Contact:** Michael Pietsch, publisher. "The general editorial philosophy for all divisions continues to be broad and flexible, with high quality and the promise of commercial success as always the first considerations." Publishes hardcover originals and paperback originals and reprints. Averages 100 total titles/year.

Imprints Little, Brown; Arcade Books; Back Bay Books; Bulfinch Press.

Needs Literary, mainstream/contemporary. Published *Cross Country*, by James Patterson; *Outliers*, by Malcolm Gladwell; *The Historian*, by Elizabeth Kostova; *When You Are Engulfed in Flames*, by David Sedaris.

How to Contact *Agented submissions only.*

Terms Pays royalty. Offers advance. Ms guidelines online.

LITTLE, BROWN AND CO. BOOKS FOR YOUNG READERS

237 Park Ave., New York NY 10017. (212)364-1100. E-mail: pamela.gruber@hbgusa.com. Website: www.twbookmark.com/children. **Contact:** Submissions Editor. "We are looking for strong writing and presentation but no predetermined topics." Publishes hardcover originals, trade paperback reprints. Averages 100-150 total titles/year.

Imprints Poppy; LB Kids; Megan Tingley Books (Megan Tingley, VP publisher).

Needs Adventure, ethnic, fantasy, historical, humor, juvenile, mystery, novelty, picture books, science fiction, suspense, young adult. "We are looking for strong fiction for children of all ages in any area, including multicultural. We always prefer full manuscripts for fiction."

How to Contact *Agented submissions only.*

Terms Pays royalty on retail price. Average advance: negotiable. Publishes ms 2 years after acceptance. Ms guidelines online.

LIVINGSTON PRESS

Univ. of West Alabama, Station 22, Livingston AL 35470. E-mail: jwt@uwa.edu. Website: www.livingstonpress.uwa.edu. **Contact:** Joe Taylor, literary editor. "Small university press specializing in offbeat and/or Southern literature." Publishes hardcover and trade paperback originals. Books: acid free; offset; some illustrations. Average print order: 2,500. First novel print order: 2,500. Plans 5 first novels this year. Averages 10 fiction titles/year.

- Our standing policy is to read over-the-transom, open submission, ONLY in June of every year. We have we have committed to books until Fall 2011, and we will be reading only Tartts entries until June 2010. Our next Tartts Story Collection Contest closes on December 31, 2010. See Tartts Fiction Award on our website. When we are reading over the transom, we accept only fiction—either story collections or novels.

Imprints Swallow's Tale Press.

Needs Experimental, literary, short story collections, off-beat or southern. "We are interested in form and, of course style." Published *The Gin Girl*, by River Jordan (novel); *Pulpwood*, by Scott Ely (stories); *Live Cargo*, by Paul Toutonghi (stories).

How to Contact Query with SASE. Include estimated word count, brief bio, list of publishing credits. Send SASE for return of ms or send a disposable ms and SASE for reply only. Responds in 1 month to queries; 1 year to mss. Accepts simultaneous submissions. Send only in June and July.

Terms Pays 10% of 1,500 print run, 150 copies; thereafter pays a mix of royalties and books. Publishes ms 18 months after acceptance. Book catalog for SASE. Ms guidelines online.

◎ LOOSE ID

P.O. Box 425690, San Francisco CA 94142-5960. E-mail: submissions@loose-id.com. Website: www.loose-id.com. **Contact:** Treva Harte, editor-in-chief. "*Loose Id* is love unleashed. We're taking romance to the edge." Publishes e-books. Distributes/promotes titles "The company promotes itself through web and print advertising wherever readers of erotic romance may be found, creating a recognizable brand identity as the place to let your id run free and the people who unleash your fantasies. It is currently pursuing licensing agreements for foreign translations, and has a print program of 2 to 5 titles per month."

Needs Wants non-traditional erotic romance stories, including gay, lesbian, heroes and heroines, multi-culturalism, cross-genre, fantasy, and science fiction, straight contemporary or historical romances.

How to Contact Query with outline/synopsis and three sample chapters. Accepts queries by e-mail. Include estimated word count, list of publishing credits, and why your submission is "Love Unleashed[PItm]". Responds to queries in 1 months. Considers e-mail submissions.

Terms Manuscript published within 1 year after acceptance. Writer's guidelines on website. Pays e-book royalties 35%.

◪ ◎ LOST HORSE PRESS

105 Lost Horse Lane, Sandpoint ID 83864. (208)255-4410. Fax: (208)255-1560. E-mail: losthorsepress@mindspring.com. Website: http://losthorsepress.org. **Contact:** Christine Holbert, publisher. Estab. 1998. Publishes hardcover and paperback originals. Books: 60-70 lb. natural paper; offset printing; b&w illustration. Average print order: 500-2,500. First novel print order: 500. **Published 2 debut authors within the last year.** Averages 4 total titles/year. Distributed by Eastern Washington University Press.

- *Woman on the Cross*, by Pierre Delattre, won the *ForeWord Magazine's* 2001 Book of the Year Award for literary fiction.

Needs Literary, regional (Pacific NW), short story collections, poetry. Published *Tales of a Dalai Lama*, by Pierre Delattre (literary fiction); *Love*, by Valerie Martin (short stories); *The Baseball Field At Night Poems*, by Patricia Goedicke; *Thistle*, by Melissa Kwasny; *Willing To Choose* and *Composing Voices*, by Robert Pack.

How to Contact "Regrettably, Lost Horse Press is *no longer accepting unsolicited manuscripts for review*. However, we welcome submissions for The Idaho Prize for Poetry, a national competition offering $1,000 prize money plus publication for a book-length manuscript. Please check The Idaho Prize for Poetry submission guidelines for more information."

Terms Publishes ms 6 months-1 year after acceptance. Please check submission guidelines on website before submitting ms.

LOVE SPELL

200 Madison Ave., Suite 2000, New York NY 10016. (212)725-8811. Fax: (212)532-1054. E-mail: adavis@dorchesterpub.com. Website: www.dorchesterpub.com. **Contact:** Alissa Davis, editorial assistant. Love Spell publishes the quirky sub-genres of romance: time-travel, paranormal, futuristic. "Despite the exotic settings, we are still interested in character-driven plots." Publishes mass market paperback originals. Books: newsprint paper; offset printing; perfect bound. Average print order: varies. First novel print order: varies. Averages 48 total titles/year.

Needs Romance (futuristic, time travel, paranormal, historical), whimsical contemporaries. "Books industry-wide are getting shorter; we're interested in 90,000 words." Published *Deep Magic*, by Joy Nash (historical romance); *Immortals: The Calling*, by Jennifer Ashley (paranormal romance).

How to Contact Accepts unsolicited mss. Query with SASE or submit 3 sample chapter(s), synopsis. Send SASE or IRC. Agented fiction 70%. Responds in 6-8 months to mss. No simultaneous submissions.

Terms Pays royalty on retail price. Average advance: varies. Publishes ms 1 year after acceptance. Book catalog for free (800)481-9191. Ms guidelines online.

MARINE TECHNIQUES PUBLISHING, INC.

126 Western Ave., Suite 266, Augusta ME 04330-7252. (207)622-7984. Fax: (207)621-0821. E-mail: info@marinetechpublishing.com. Website: www.marinetechpublishing.com. **Contact:** James L. Pelletier, president/owner. **Published 15% debut authors within the last year.** Averages 3-5 total titles/year.

Needs Must be commercial maritime/marine related.

How to Contact Submit complete ms. Responds in 2 months to queries; 6 months to mss. Accepts simultaneous submissions.

Terms Pays 25-43% royalty on wholesale or retail price. Publishes ms 6-12 months after acceptance.

MARVEL COMICS

417 5th Ave., New York NY 10016. (212)576-4000. Fax: (212)576-8547. Website: www.marvel.com. Publishes hardcover originals and reprints, trade paperback reprints, mass market comic book originals, electronic reprints. Averages 650 total titles/year.

Needs Adventure, comic books, fantasy, horror, humor, science fiction, young adult. "Our shared universe needs new heroes and villains; books for younger readers and teens needed."

How to Contact "Please send us an inquiry letter, detailing your writing experience and why you would like to write for Marvel. Based on your inquiry letter, we may request to read a sample of your work. Please note: Unsolicited writing samples will not be read. *Any unsolicited or solicited writing sample received without a signed Marvel Idea Submission Form will be destroyed unread.*" (Download Marvel Idea Submission Form from website). Responds only if interested in 3-5 weeks.

Terms Pays on a per page work-for-hire basis which is contracted. Ms guidelines online.

MCBOOKS PRESS

10 Booth Building, 520 N. Meadow St., Ithaca NY 14850. (607)272-2114. Fax: (607)273-6068. E-mail: jackie@mcbooks.com. Website: www.mcbooks.com. **Contact:** Jackie Swift, editorial director. Small independent publisher. Publishes Julian Stockwin, John Biggins, Colin Sargent, and Douglas W. Jacobson. Publishes trade paperback and hardcover originals and reprints. Averages 8 fiction titles/year. Distributes titles through Independent Publishers Group.

Needs "We are looking for a few good novels and are open to almost any genre or style, except romance, inspirational, science fiction, fantasy, and children's. Our main criteria is an exceptionally strong story combined with an author who can show he/she has a good grasp on self-promotion through networking, personal appearances, and tireless internet presence."

How to Contact Does not accept unsolicited mss. Submission guidelines available on website. Query with SASE or via e-mail. Include list of publishing credits and a well thought-out marketing plan. Responds in 3 months to queries. Accepts simultaneous submissions.

Terms Pays 5-10% royalty on retail price. Average advance: $1,000-5,000.

MEDALLION PRESS, INC.

8988 South Sheridan Road, Suite L, Box 216, Tulsa OK 74133. Website: www.medallionpress.com., Suite L, Box 216, Tulsa OK 74133. 630-513-8316. E-mail: info@medallionpress.com. Website: www.medallionpress.com. **Contact:** Emily Steele, editorial director, emily@medallionpress.com. Estab. 2003. "We are an independent publisher looking for books that are outside of the box. Please do not submit to us if you are looking for a large advance. We reserve our funds for marketing the books." Publishes paperback originals. Average print order: 5,000. **Published 20+ debut authors within the last year.**

Imprints Platinum/Hardcover; Gold/Mass Market; Silver/Trade Paper; Bronze/Young Adult; Jewel/Romance; Amethyst/Fantasy, Sci-Fi, Paranormal; Emerald/Suspense; Ruby/Contemporary; Sapphire/Historical.

Needs Adventure, ethnic, fantasy (space fantasy, sword and sorcery), glitz, historical, horror (dark fantasy, futuristic, psychological, supernatural), humor, literary, mainstream/contemporary, military/war, mystery (amateur slueth, police procedural, private eye/hard-boiled), romance, science fiction (hard science/technological, soft/sociological), thriller/espionage, western (frontier saga), young adult. Published *Siren's Call*, by Mary Ann Mitchell (horror); *Grand Traverse*, by Michael Beres (mainstream fiction); *Memories of Empire*, by Django Wexler (epic fantasy).

How to Contact "Minimum word count 80K for adult fiction, 55K for YA, no exceptions." No poetry, anthologies, erotica or inspirational. Submit first 3 consecutive chapters and a chapter-by-chapter synopsis. "Without the synopsis, the submission will be rejected." Accepts queries only by email. Include estimated word count, brief bio, list of publishing credits. Send SASE or IRC. Responds in 4-8 months to mss. Accepts simultaneous submissions. Sometimes comments on rejected mss.

Terms Offers advance. Publishes ms 1-2 years after acceptance. Ms guidelines online.

MERIWETHER PUBLISHING, LTD.

885 Elkton Dr., Colorado Springs CO 80907-3557. (719)594-4422. Fax: (719)594-9916. E-mail: editor@meriwether.com. Website: www.meriwetherpublishing.com; www.contemporarydrama.com. **Contact:** Rhonda Wray, associate editor (church plays); Ted Zapel, editor (school plays, comedies, books).

Needs Mainstream/contemporary, comedy, religious (children's plays and religious Christmas and Easter plays), suspense—all in playscript format. Published *Pirates and Petticoats*, by Pat Cook (a two-act pirate comedy); *Let Him Sleep Until it's Time for His Funeral*, by Peg Kehret (two-act play).

How to Contact Accepts unsolicited mss. Query with SASE. Accepts queries by e-mail. Include list of publishing credits. Send SASE for return of ms or send a disposable ms and SASE for reply only.

Responds in 3 weeks to queries; 2 months to mss. Accepts simultaneous submissions. Sometimes comments on rejected mss.

Terms Pays 10% royalty on retail price or makes outright purchase. Publishes ms 6-12 months after acceptance. Book catalog and ms guidelines for $2 postage.

MID-LIST PRESS

4324 12th Ave S., Minneapolis MN 55407-3218. (612)432-8062. Fax: (612)823-8387. E-mail: guide@midlist.org. Website: www.midlist.org. **Contact:** Acquisitions director. Estab. 1989. "We are a nonprofit literary press dedicated to the survival of the mid-list, those quality titles that are being neglected by the larger commercial houses. Our focus is on new and emerging writers." Publishes hardcover and trade paperback originals. Mid-List publishes only book-length works. Fiction and nonfiction manuscripts must be at least 50,000 words in length. Poetry collections must be at least 60 pages in length (single-spaced, each poem beginning a new page). Mid-List Press does not publish children's books. Books: acid-free paper; offset printing; perfect or Smyth-sewn binding. Average print order: 2,000. Averages 4 total titles, 1 fiction titles/year. Distributes titles through Baker & Taylor, Midwest Library Service, Brodart, Follett and Emery Pratt. Promotes titles through publicity, direct mail, catalogs, author's events and review and awards.

Needs General fiction. Published *The Woman Who Never Cooked*, by Mary L. Tabor; *The Echo of Sand*, by Gail Chehab (first novel).

How to Contact Accepts unsolicited mss. Agented fiction less than10%. Do not include SASE. No email or fax queries. Responds only if interested by telephone or e-mail. Accepts simultaneous submissions. Ms guidelines online.

Terms Pays 40-50% royalty on net receipts. Average advance: $1,000. Publishes ms 12-18 months after acceptance.

MILKWEED EDITIONS

1011 Washington Ave. S., Suite 300, Minneapolis MN 55415. (612)332-3192. Fax: (612)215-2550. Website: www.milkweed.org. **Contact:** The Editors. Nonprofit publisher. Publishes hardcover originals, paperback originals and reprints. Books: book text quality—acid-free paper; offset printing; perfect or hardcover binding. Average print order: 4,000. First novel print order depends on book. **Published some debut authors within the last year.** Averages 15 total titles/year. Distributes through Publisher's Group West. Each book has its own marketing plan involving print ads, tours, conferences, etc.

Needs Literary. Novels for adults and for readers 8-13. High literary quality. For adult readers: literary fiction, nonfiction, poetry, essays; for children (ages 8-13): literary novels. Translations welcome for both audiences. Published *The Blue Sky*, by Galsan Tschinag (translation); *Driftless*, by David Rhodes; *The Farther Shore*, by Matthew Eck.

How to Contact Submit complete ms via submission manager. Responds in 2 months to queries; 6 months to mss. Accepts simultaneous submissions.

Terms Variable royalty on retail price. Average advance: varied. Publishes ms 1-2 years after acceptance. Book catalog for $1.50 postage. Ms guidelines online.

MILKWEED FOR YOUNG READERS

1011 Washington Ave. South, Open Book, Suite 300, Minneapolis MN 55415. Website: www.milkweed.org. **Contact:** Daniel Slager, Publisher; Children's reader. Estab. 1984. "Milkweed for Young Readers are works that embody humane values and contribute to cultural understanding." Publishes hardcover and trade paperback originals. Averages 1-2 total titles/year. Distributes titles through Publishers Group West. Promotes titles individually through print advertising, website and author tours.

- *Perfect*, by Natasha Friend, was chosen as a Book Sense 76 Children's Book selection. **Needs** Adventure, historical, humor, mainstream/contemporary, animal, environmental. For ages 8-13. Published *The Cat*, By Jutta Richter, and *The Linden Tree* by Ellie Mathews. **How to**

Contact Query with SASE. Agented fiction 30%. Responds in 2 months to queries. Accepts simultaneous submissions. **Terms** Pays 6% royalty on retail price. Average advance: variable. Publishes ms 1 year after acceptance. Book catalog for $1.50. Ms guidelines for #10 SASE or on the website. **Advice** "Familiarize yourself with our books before submitting. You need not have a long list of credentials—excellent work speaks for itself."

How to Contact Authors can now submit and manage their submissions through Milkweed's Submission Manager. If you have any problems, contact us through email. If you send by postal mail, please address submissions to: Fiction Reader (or Nonfiction, Poetry, Children's, as appropriate). See guidelines online.

$ MONDIAL

203 W. 107th St., Suite 6C, New York NY 10025. (212)851-3252. E-mail: contact@mondialbooks.com. Website: www.mondialbooks.com.

Needs adventure, erotica, ethnic, gay, historical, literary, mainstream, multicultural, mystery, poetry, romance, short, translation. Published *Two People*, by David Windham; *Bitterness*, by Malama Katulwende; *Winter Ridge: A Love Story*, by Bruce Kellner.

How to Contact Query through online submission form. Responds to queries in 3 months. Terms Pays 10% royalty of the selling price of each book copy sold.

MONSOON BOOKS

52 Telok Blangah Road, 098829, 139527 Singapore. Website: www.monsoonbooks.com.sg. **Contact:** Philip Tathum, publisher (fiction). "Monsoon Books is an independent publisher of fiction and nonfiction with Asian themes, based in Singapore with worldwide distribution." Unsolicited manuscripts are welcomed from published and unpublished authors alike. Publishes paperback originals, paperback reprints. Books: Mungken 80 gram paper; offset printing; threadsewn binding. Average print order: 3,000. First novel print order: 3,000. **Published 7 new writers last year**. Plans 10 first novels this year. Averages 20 total titles/year; 12 fiction titles/year. Distributes titles through Worldwide Distribution and promotes through Freelance Publicists for USA and Asia.

Needs erotica, ethnic/multicultural, family saga, gay, historical, horror (supernatural), humor satire, literary, mainstream, military/war, mystery/suspense (police procedural, private eye/hard-boiled), regional (Asia), thriller/espionage, translations, young adult (romance). Special interests: Southeast Asia. Published *Rouge Raider*, by Nigel Barley (historical fiction); *Straights and Narrow*, by Grace McClurg (thriller); *Private Dancer*, by Stephen Leather (general fiction/international relationships).

How to Contact Query with outline/synopsis and submit complete ms with cover letter. Accepts queries by snail mail, fax and e-mail. Please include estimated word count, brief bio, list of publishing credits, and list of three comparative titles. Send SASE or IRC for return of ms. Agented fiction 20%. Responds in 1 week to queries; 12 weeks to manuscripts. Accepts simultaneous submissions, submissions on CD or disk. Rarely comments on rejected manuscripts.

Terms Pays 7-10% royalty. Advance is negotiable. Publishes ms 6-12 months after acceptance. Guidelines online.

MOODY PUBLISHERS

820 N. LaSalle Blvd., Chicago IL 60610. E-mail: pressinfo@moody.edu. Website: www.moodypublishers.org. **Contact:** Acquisitions Coordinator. Estab. 1894. Small, evangelical Christian publisher. "We publish fiction that reflects and supports our evangelical worldview and mission." Publishes hardcover, trade and mass market paperback originals. Averages 70 total titles, 10-12 fiction titles/year. Member, CBA. Distributes and promotes titles through sales reps, print advertising, promotional events, Internet, etc.

- Moody Publishers does not accept unsolicited manuscripts in any category unless submitted via:— a professional literary agent— an author who has published with us— an associate from a Moody Bible Institute ministry— personal contact at a writers conference.

Needs Contemporary, historical, literary, mystery, suspense, science fiction. Recently published *My Hands Came Away Red*, by Lisa McKay (suspense novel); *Feeling for Bones*, by Bethany Pierce (contemporary/literary).

How to Contact Accepts unsolicited fiction mss. proposal with SASE and two chapters. Accepts queries by mail only (no electronic submissions). Include estimated word count, brief bio, list of publishing credits. Send SASE for return of ms or send a disposable ms and SASE for reply only. Agented fiction 75%. Responds in 4-5 months to queries. Accepts electronic submissions.

Terms Royalty varies. Average advance: $1,000-10,000. Publishes ms 9-12 months after acceptance. Ms guidelines for SASE and on website.

MOUNTAINLAND PUBLISHING, INC

P.O. Box 150891, Ogden UT 84415. E-mail: editor@mountainlandpublishing.com. Website: www.mountainlandpublishing.com. **Contact:** Michael Combs, managing editor. Estab. 2001. Publishes paperback originals, e-books. Published 50% new writers last year. Averages 6-10 total titles/year.

Needs adventure, fantasy, historical, horror, humor, juvenile, literary, mainstream, military/war, multicultural, mystery, regional, religious, romance, science fiction, short story collections, suspense, western, young adult.

How to Contact Online submissions only. Considers simultaneous submissions.

Terms Manuscript published 3 months after acceptance. Pays royalties.

NBM PUBLISHING

40 Exchange Pl., Ste. 1308, New York NY 10005. E-mail: nbmgn@nbmpub.com. Website: nbmpub.com. **Contact:** Terry Nantier, editor/art director. "One of the best regarded quality graphic novel publishers. Our catalog is determined by what will appeal to a wide audience of readers." Publishes hardcover originals, paperback originals. Format: offset printing; perfect binding. Average print order: 3,000-4,000; average debut writer's print order: 2,000. Publishes 1-2 debut writers/year. Publishes 30 titles/year. Member: PMA, CBC. Distributed/promoted "ourselves." Imprints: ComicsLit (literary comics), Eurotica (erotic comics).

Needs Literary fiction mostly, children's/juvenile (especially fairy tales, classics), creative nonfiction (especially true crime), erotica, ethnic/multicultural, humor (satire), manga, mystery/suspense, translations, young adult/teen. Does not want superhero or overly violent comics.

How to Contact Prefers submissions from writer-artists, creative teams. Send a one-page synopsis of story along with a few pages of comics (copies NOT originals) and a SASE. Attends San Diego Comicon. Agented submissions: 2%. Responds to queries in 1 week; to ms/art packages in 3-4 weeks. Sometimes comments on rejected manuscripts.

Terms Royalties and advance negotiable. Publishes ms 6 months to 1 year after acceptance. Writer's guidelines on website. Artist's guidelines on website. Book catalog free upon request.

NEW ISSUES POETRY & PROSE

1903 W. Michigan Ave., Kalamazoo MI 49008-5463. (269)387-8185. Fax: (269)387-2562. E-mail: new-issues@wmich.edu. Website: wmich.edu/newissues. **Contact:** Managing Editor. Publishes hardcover originals and trade paperback originals. Averages 8 titles/year. Has recently published *We Agreed to Meet Just Here*, by Scott Blackwood; *Missing Her*, by Claudia Keelan; *Tall If*, by Mark Irwin; *Please*, by Jericho Brown.

Needs Literary, poetry, translations.

How to Contact Query first. All unsolicited mss returned unopened. 50% of books published are by first time authors. Agented submissions: less than 5%. Responds to mss in 6 months.

Terms Pays 10-12% royalty on wholesale price. Manuscript published 18 months after acceptance. Accepts simultaneous submissions. Writer's guidelines by SASE, e-mail, or online.

NEW VICTORIA PUBLISHERS

P.O. Box 13173, Chicago IL 60613-0173. (773)793-2244. E-mail: newvictoriapub@att.net. Website: www.newvictoria.com. **Contact:** Patricia Feuerhaken, president. Estab. 1976. "Publishes mostly lesbian fiction—strong female protagonists. Most well known for Stoner McTavish mystery series." Publishes trade paperback originals. Averages 2-3 total titles/year. Distributes titles through Amazon Books, Bella books, Bulldog Books (Sydney, Australia), and Women and Children First Books (Chicago). Promotes titles "mostly through lesbian feminist media."

- *Mommy Deadest*, by Jean Marcy, won the Lambda Literary Award for Mystery.

Needs Lesbian, feminist fiction including adventure, erotica, fantasy, historical, humor, mystery (amateur sleuth), or science fiction. "Looking for strong feminist, well drawn characters, with a strong plot and action. We will consider any original, well written piece that appeals to the lesbian/feminist audience." Publishes anthologies or special editions. Published *Sparkling rain*, by Barbara Summerhawk and Kimberly Hughes (2008); *Killing at the Cat*, by Carlene Miller (mystery); *Queer Japan*, by Barbara Summerhawk (anthology); *Skin to Skin*, by Martha Miller (erotic short fiction); *Talk Show*, by Melissa Hartman (novel); *Flight from Chador*, by Sigrid Brunel (adventure); *Owl of the Desert*, by Ida Swearingen (novel).

How to Contact Accepts unsolicited mss, but prefers query first. Submit outline, synopsis, and sample chapters (50 pages). No queries by e-mail or fax; please send SASE or IRC. No simultaneous submissions.

Terms Pays 10% royalty. Publishes ms 1 year after acceptance. Ms guidelines for SASE.

W.W. NORTON CO., INC.

500 Fifth Ave., New York NY 10110. Fax: (212)869-0856. E-mail: manuscripts@wwnorton.com. Website: www.wwnorton.com. **Contact:** Acquisitions editor. Midsize independent publisher of trade books and college textbooks. Publishes literary fiction. Estab. 1923. Publishes hardcover and paperback originals and reprints. Averages 300 total titles/year.

Needs Literary, poetry, poetry in translation, religious. High-quilty literary fiction. Published *Ship Fever*, by Andrea Barrett; *Oyster*, by Jannette Turner Hospital; *Power*, by Linda Hogan.

How to Contact *Does not accept unagented submissions or unsolicited mss.* If you would like to submit your proposal (6 pages or less) by e-mail, paste the text of your query letter and/or sample chapter into the body of the e-mail message. Do not send attachments. Responds in 2 months to queries. No simultaneous submissions.

Terms Pays royalty. Offers advance. Ms guidelines online.

OAK TREE PRESS

140 E. Palmer St., Taylorville IL 62568. E-mail: oaktreepub@aol.com. Website: www.oaktreebooks.com. **Contact:** Acquisitions Editor. Estab. 1998. "Small independent publisher with a philosophy of author advocacy. Welcomes first-time authors, and sponsors annual contests in which the winning entries are published." Publishes hardcover, trade paperback and mass market paperback originals and reprints. Books: acid-free paper; perfect binding. First novel print order: 1,000. **Published 5 debut authors within the last year.** Plans 8 first novels this year. Averages 12 total titles, 8 fiction titles/year. Member: SPAN, SPAWN. Distributes through Ingram, Baker & Taylor and Amazon.com. Promotes through website, conferences, PR, author tours.

- *Affinity for Murder*, by Anne White, was an Agatha Award finalist. *Timeless Love*, by Mary Montague Sikes, received a Prism Award.

Imprints Oak Tree Press, Dark Oak Mysteries (also has an annual contest), Timeless Love (also has an annual contest), CopTales (also has an annual contest), Acorn Books for Children (children's, YA).

Needs Adventure, confession, ethnic, fantasy (romance), feminist, humor, mainstream/contemporary, mystery (amateur sleuth, cozy, police procedural, private eye/hard-boiled), new age/mystic, picture books, romance (contemporary, futuristic/time travel, romantic suspense), suspense, thriller/espionage, young adult (adventure, mystery/suspense, romance). Emphasis

on mystery and romance novels. Recently published *The Poetry of Murder*, by Bernadette Steele (mystery); *Media Blitz*, by Joe Nowlan(mystery); *Lake Meade*, by Heather Mosko (romance); *Secrets by the Sea*, by Mary Montague Sikes (paranormal romance); *Easy Money*, by Norm Maher (memoir-police officer), and *The Last Stop: Lincoln and the Mud Circuit*, by Alan Bower (history).
How to Contact Does not accept or return unsolicited mss. Query with SASE. Accepts queries by e-mail. Include estimated word count, brief bio, list of publishing credits, brief description of ms. Send SASE for return of ms or send a disposable ms and SASE for reply only. Agented fiction 5%. Responds in 4-6 weeks to queries; 2 months to proposals; 3-6 months to mss. Accepts simultaneous submissions, electronic submissions. No submissions on disk. Rarely comments on rejected mss.
Terms Pays 10-20% royalty on wholesale price. Average advance: negotiable. Publishes ms 9-18 months after acceptance. Book catalog for SASE or on website www.oaktreebooks.com. Ms guidelines for SASE or on website.

ORCA BOOK PUBLISHERS

P.O. Box 5626, Victoria BC V8R 6S4 Canada. (250)380-1229. Fax: (250)380-1892. E-mail: orca@orcabook.com. Website: www.orcabook.com. **Contact:** Christi Howes, editor (picture books); Sarah Harvey, editor (young readers); Andrew Wooldridge, editor (juvenile fiction, teen fiction); Bob Tyrrell, publisher (YA, teen). Only publishes Canadian authors. Publishes hardcover and trade paperback originals, and mass market paperback originals and reprints. Books: quality 60 lb. book stock paper; illustrations. Average print order: 3,000-5,000. First novel print order: 3,000-5,000. Averages 30 total titles/year.
Needs Hi-lo, juvenile (5-9 years), literary, mainstream/contemporary, young adult (10-18 years). "Ask for guidelines, find out what we publish." Looking for "children's fiction."
How to Contact Query with SASE or submit proposal package including outline, 2-5 sample chapter(s), synopsis, SASE. Agented fiction 20%. Responds in 1 month to queries; 1-2 months to mss. No simultaneous submissions. Sometimes comments on rejected mss.
Terms Pays 10% royalty. Publishes ms 12-18 months after acceptance. Book catalog for 8½ × 11 SASE. Ms guidelines online.

OUTRIDER PRESS, INC.

2036 North Winds Drive, Dyer IN 46311. (219)322-7270. Fax: (219)322-7085. E-mail: outriderpress@sbcglobal.net. Website: www.outriderpress.com. **Contact:** Whitney Scott, editor. Small literary press and hand bindery; publishes many first-time authors. Publishes paperback originals. Books: 70 lb. paper; offset printing; perfect bound. Average print order: 2,000. **Published 25-30 debut authors within the last year.** Distributes titles through Baker & Taylor.

- Was a *Small Press Review* "Pick" for 2000.

Needs Ethnic, experimental, family saga, fantasy (space fantasy, sword and sorcery), feminist, gay/lesbian, historical, horror (psychological, supernatural), humor, lesbian, literary, mainstream/contemporary, mystery (amateur slueth, cozy, police procedural, private eye/hard-boiled), new age/mystic, psychic/supernatural, romance (contemporary, futuristic/time travel, gothic, historical, regency period, romantic suspense), science *fiction (soft/sociological), short story collections, thriller/espionage, western (frontier saga, traditional). Published Telling Time*, by Cherie Caswell Dost; *If Ever I Cease to Love*, by Robert Klein Engler; *62000 Reasons*, by Paul Miller; *Aquarium Octopus*, by Claudia Van Gerven; and *Heat*, by Deborah Thompson.
How to Contact Accepts unsolicited mss. Query with SASE. Accepts queries by mail. Include estimated word count, brief bio, list of publishing credits. Agented fiction 10%. Responds in 6 weeks to queries; 4 months to mss. Accepts simultaneous submissions, electronic submissions, submissions on disk. Sometimes comments on rejected mss. In affiliation with Tallgrass Writers Guild, publishes an annual anthonlogy with cash prizes. 2010 anthology theme is: "'Flight and Risk.' As always, broadly interpreted with a variety of historic/geographic settings welcomed." Deadline is February 27, 2011. For details and complete guidelines, e-mail outriderpress@sbcglobal.net.
Terms Pays honorarium. Publishes ms 6 months after acceptance. Ms guidelines for SASE.

PANTHEON BOOKS

Random House, Inc., 1745 Broadway, 3rd Floor, New York NY 10019. E-mail: pantheonpublicity@randomhouse.com. Website: www.pantheonbooks.com. "Small but well-established imprint of well-known larger house." Publishes hardcover and trade paperback originals and trade paperback reprints.

Needs Quality fiction and nonfiction. Published *Crooked Little Heart,* Anne Lamott.

How to Contact *Does not accept unsolicited mss.* Send SASE or IRC. No simultaneous submissions.

Terms Pays royalty. Offers advance.

PAYCOCK PRESS

3819 No. 13th St., Arlington VA 22201. (703)525-9296. E-mail: hedgehog2@erols.com. Website: www.gargoylemagazine.com. **Contact:** Lucinda Ebersole and Richard Peabody. "Too academic for underground, too outlaw for the academic world. We tend to be edgy and look for ultra-literary work." Publishes paperback originals. Books: POD printing. Average print order: 500. Averages 1 total title/year. Member CLMP. Distributes through Amazon and website.

Needs Experimental, literary, short story collections.

How to Contact Accepts unsolicited mss. Accepts queries by e-mail. Include brief bio. Send SASE for return of ms or send a disposable ms and SASE for reply only. Agented fiction 5%. Responds in 1 month to queries; 4 months to mss. Accepts simultaneous submissions, electronic submissions. Rarely comments on rejected mss.

Terms Publishes ms 12 months after acceptance.

PEACHTREE PUBLISHERS, LTD.

1700 Chattahoochee Ave., Atlanta GA 30318-2112. E-mail: jackson@peachtree-online.com. Website: www.peachtree-online.com. **Contact:** Helen Harriss, acquisitions. Publishes 30-35 titles/year. Peachtree currently publishes the following categories: Children's fiction and nonfiction picture books, chapter books, middle readers, young adult books; Education, parenting, self-help, and health books of interest to the general trade.

Needs Picture books, young readers: adventure, animal, concept, history, nature/environment. Middle readers: adventure, animal, history, nature/environment, sports. Young adults: fiction, mystery, adventure. Peachtree does **not** publish historical novels (except children's/young adult), science fiction, fantasy, romance, westerns, horror, poetry, short stories, plays, business, scientific or technical reference, or books intended specifically as textbooks.

How to Contact Submit complete ms (picture books) or 3 sample chapters (chapter books), bio by postal mail only. Responds to queries/mss in 6-7 months. Publishes a book 1-2 years after acceptance. Will consider simultaneous submissions.

Terms "Manuscript guidelines for SASE, visit website or call for a recorded message. No fax or e-mail submittals or queries please."

PEDLAR PRESS

P.O. Box 26, Station P, Toronto ON M5S 2S6 Canada. (416)534-2011. E-mail: feralgrl@interlog.com. **Contact:** Beth Follett, owner/editor. Publishes hardcover and trade paperback originals. **Published 50% debut authors within the last year.** Averages 7 total titles/year. Distributes in Canada through LitDistCo.; in the US distributes directly through publisher.

Needs Experimental, feminist, gay/lesbian, literary, picture books, short story collections. Canadian writers only. Published Black Stars in a White Night Sky, by Jonarno Lawson, illustrated by Sherwin Tjia.

How to Contact Query with SASE, sample chapter(s), synopsis.

Terms Pays 10% royalty on retail price. Average advance: $200-400. Publishes ms 1 year after acceptance. Ms guidelines for #10 SASE.

PELICAN PUBLISHING CO.

1000 Burmaster St., Gretna LA 70055. (504)368-1175. Fax: (504) 368-1195. E-mail: editorial@pelicanpub.com. Website: www.pelicanpub.com. **Contact:** Nina Kooij, editor-in-chief. "We seek writers on the cutting edge of ideas. We believe ideas have consequences. One of the consequences is that they lead to a best-selling book." Publishes hardcover, trade paperback and mass market paperback originals and reprints. Books: hardcover and paperback binding; illustrations sometimes. Buys juvenile mss with illustrations. Averages 65 total titles/year. Distributes titles internationally through distributors, bookstores, libraries. Promotes titles at reading and book conventions, in trade magazines, in radio interviews, print reviews and TV interviews.

- *The Warlord's Puzzle*, by Virginia Walton Pilegard, was #2 on *Independent Bookseller's Book Sense 76* list.

Needs Considers picture books for young readers or Louisiana historical middle-grade novels. All writers should send us a query letter and SASE, describing the project briefly and concisely. Multiple (or "simultaneous") or e-mail queries are not considered.

How to Contact Does not accept unsolicited mss except for picture books (1,100 words). For Louisiana historical middle-grade novels, submit outline, 2 sample chapters. Responds in 1 month to queries; 3 months to mss. No simultaneous or multiple submissions. Rarely comments on rejected mss.

Terms Pays royalty on actual receipts. Average advance: considered. Publishes ms 9-18 months after acceptance. Book catalog for SASE or on website. Writer's guidelines for SASE or on website.

PEMMICAN PUBLICATIONS

150 Henry Ave., Main Floor RM 12, Winnipeg MB R3B 0J7 Canada. (204)589-6346. Fax: (204)589-2063. E-mail: mcilroy@pemmican.mb.ca. Website: www.pemmican.mb.ca. **Contact:** Randal McIlroy, managing editor. Metis adult and children's books. Publishes paperback originals. Books: stapled-bound smaller books and perfect-bound larger ones; 4-color illustrations, where applicable. Average print order: 1,500. First novel print order: 1,000. **Published some debut authors within the last year.** Averages 6 total titles/year. Distributes titles through press releases, website, fax, catalogues, and book displays.

Needs Stories by and about the Canadian Metis experience, especially from a modern adult or young-adult perspective. Recently published *Flight of the Wild Geese* (YA fiction), by T.D. Thompson; *River of Tears* (adult fiction), by Linda Ducharme; and *Kawlija's Blueberry Promise* (children's fiction), by Audrey Guiboche.

How to Contact Accepts unsolicited mss by conventional mail only. Submit samples and synopsis. Send SASE for return of ms or send a disposable ms and SASE for reply only. Return postage for outside of Canada must be provided in IRC's. Accepts simultaneous submissions.

Terms Pays 10% royalty. Provides 10 author's copies. Average advance: $350.

PENGUIN GROUP USA

375 Hudson St., New York NY 10014. (212)366-2000. Website: www.penguin.com. "The company possesses perhaps the world's most prestigious list of best-selling authors and a backlist of unparalleled breadth, depth and quality." General interest publisher of both fiction and nonfiction.

Imprints Viking (hardcover); Dutton (hardcover); The Penguin Press (hardcover); Daw (hardcover and paperback); G P Putnam's Sons (hardcover and children's); Riverhead Books (hardcover and paperback); Tarcher (hardcover and paperback); Grosset/Putnam (hardcover); Putnam (hardcover); Avery; Viking Compass (hardcover); Penguin (paperback); Penguin Classics (paperback); Plume (paperback); Signet (paperback); Signet classics (paperback); Onyx (paperback); Roc (paperback); Topaz (paperback); Mentor (paperback); Meridian (paperback); Berkley Books (paperback); Jove (paperback); Ace (paperback); Prime Crime (paperback); HPBooks (paperback); Penguin Compass (paperback); Dial Books for Young Readers (children's); Dutton Children's Books (children's); Viking Children's Books (children's); Puffin (children's); Frederick Warne (children's); Philomel

Books (children's); Grosset and Dunlap (children's); Wee Sing (children's); PaperStar (children's); Planet Dexter (children's); Berkely (hardcover); Gothom (hardcover and paperback); Portfolio (hard and paperback); NAL (hardcover).

How to Contact "Due to the high volume of manuscripts we receive, Penguin Group (USA) Inc. imprints do not normally accept unsolicited manuscripts. On rare occasion, however, a particular imprint may be open to reading such. The Penguin Group (USA) web site features a listing of which imprints (if any) are currently accepting unsolicited manuscripts." Continue to check website for updates to the list.

Terms Pays advance and royalties, depending on imprint.

THE PERMANENT PRESS

Attn: Judith Shepard, 4170 Noyac Rd., Sag Harbor NY 11963. (631)725-1101. E-mail: info@thepermanentpress.com; shepard@thepermanentpress.com. Website: www.thepermanentpress.com. **Contact:** Judith and Martin Shepard, publishers. Mid-size, independent publisher of literary fiction. "We keep titles in print and are active in selling subsidiary rights." Publishes hardcover originals. Average print order: 1,500. Averages 12 total titles, 11 fiction titles/year. Distributes titles through Baker & Taylor and Brodart. Promotes titles through reviews.

Needs Literary, mainstream/contemporary, mystery. Especially looking for high-line literary fiction, "artful, original and arresting." Accepts any fiction category as long as it is a "well-written, original full-length novel." Published *The Last Refuge, Two Time and Head Wounds* by Chris Knopf; *The Contractor,* by Charles Holdefer; *The Night Battles* by M.F. Bloxam; *A Richer Dust* by Amy Boaz.

How to Contact Accepts unsolicited mss. Send SASE for return of ms or send a disposable ms and SASE for reply only. Responds in 12 weeks to queries; 8 months to mss. Accepts simultaneous submissions.

Terms Pays 10-15% royalty on wholesale price. Offers $1,000 advance for Permanent Press books; royalty only on Second Chance Press titles. Publishes ms 18 months after acceptance. Ms guidelines for #10 SASE.

DAVID PHILIP PUBLISHERS

P.O. Box 46962, Claremont 7702 South Africa. Fax: (21)6743358. E-mail: info@newafricabooks.co.za. Website: www.newafricabooks.co.za.

Needs "Fiction with southern African concern or focus. Progressive, often suitable for school or university prescription, literary, serious but with commercial potential."

How to Contact Submit 1 sample chapter(s), detailed synopsis and letter of motivation.

Terms Pays royalty. Write for guidelines.

PICADOR USA

175 Fifth Ave., New York NY 10010. (212)674-5151. E-mail: david.saint@picadorusa.com; pressinquiries@macmillanusa.com. Website: www.picadorusa.com. **Contact:** Frances Coady, publisher (literary fiction). Estab. 1994. Picador publishes high-quality literary fiction and nonfiction. "We are open to a broad range of subjects, well written by authoritative authors." Publishes hardcover and trade paperback originals and reprints. Averages 70-80 total titles/year. Titles distributed through Von Holtzbrinck Publishers. Titles promoted through national print advertising and bookstore co-op.

- *The Amazing Adventures of Kavalier & Clay,* by Michael Chabon, won the Pulitzer Prize for fiction; *In America,* by Susan Sontag, won National Book Award; Jame Crace's *Being Dead* won the National Book Critics Circle Award.

Needs Literary. Published *No One Thinks of Greenland,* by John Griesmer (first novel, literary); *Summerland,* by Malcolm Knox (first novel, literary fiction); *Half a Heart,* by Rosellen Brown (literary fiction).

How to Contact Does not accept unsolicited mss. *Agented submissions only.* Accepts queries by e-mail, fax, mail. Responds in 2 months to queries. Accepts simultaneous submissions.

Terms Pays 712-15% royalty on retail price. Average advance: varies. Publishes ms 18 months after acceptance. Book catalog for 9 × 12 SASE and $2.60 postage; ms guidelines for #10 SASE or online.

PINATA BOOKS

University of Houston, 452 Cullen Performance Hall, Houston TX 77204-2004. (713)743-2841. Fax: (713)743-3080. E-mail: submapp@uh.edu. Website: www.latinoteca.com. **Contact:** Nicolas Kanellos. Piñata Books is dedicated to the publication of children's and young adult literature focusing on U.S. Hispanic culture by U.S. Hispanic authors. Books published under this imprint include bilingual picture books for children and entertaining novels and short-story collections for young adults by authors such as Pat Mora, Diane Gonzales Bertrand, Victor Villaseñor, Ofelia Dumas Lachtman, and many others. Publishes hardcover and trade paperback originals. **Published some debut authors within the last year.** Averages 10-15 total titles/year.

Needs Adventure, juvenile, picture books, young adult. Published *Trino's Choice*, by Diane Gonzales Bertrand (ages 11-up); *Delicious Hullabaloo/Pachanga Deliciosa*, by Pat Mora (picture book); and *The Year of Our Revolution*, by Judith Ortiz Cofer (young adult).

How to Contact Does not accept unsolicited mss. Query with SASE or submit 2 sample chapter(s), synopsis, SASE. Responds in 1 month to queries; 6 months to mss. Accepts simultaneous submissions.

Terms Pays 10% royalty on wholesale price. Average advance: $1,000-3,000. Publishes ms 2 years after acceptance. Book catalog and ms guidelines available via website or with #10 SASE.

PINEAPPLE PRESS, INC.

P.O. Box 3889, Sarasota FL 34230. (941)359-0886. Fax: (941)351-9988. E-mail: info@pineapplepress.com. Website: www.pineapplepress.com. **Contact:** June Cussen, editor. Small independent trade publisher. Publishes hardcover and trade paperback originals. Books: quality paper; offset printing; Smyth-sewn or perfect bound; illustrations occasionally. Averages 25 total titles/year. Distributes titles through Pineapple, Ingram, and Baker & Taylor. Promotes titles through reviews, advertising in print media, direct mail, author signings, and the World Wide Web.

Needs Will only consider fiction set in Florida.

How to Contact Does not accept unsolicited mss. Query with sample, SASE. Responds in 2 months to queries. Accepts simultaneous submissions.

Terms Pays 612-15% royalty on net receipts. Average advance: rare. Publishes ms 18 months after acceptance. Book catalog for 9 × 12 SAE with $1.34 postage.

PIPERS' ASH, LTD.

Pipers' Ash, Church Rd., Christian Malford, Chippe, Wiltshire SN15 4BW United Kingdom. Fax: +44 0870 0568917. E-mail: pipersash@supamasu.com. Website: www.supamasu.com. **Contact:** Manuscript Evaluation Desk. "Small press publisher. Considers all submitted manuscripts fairly—without bias or favor. This company is run by book lovers, not by accountants." Publishes hardcover and electronic originals. **Published 18 debut authors within the last year.** Averages 18 total titles, 18 fiction titles/year. Distributes and promotes titles through press releases, catalogues, website shopping basket, direct mail and the Internet.

Needs Adventure, children's/juvenile (adventure), confession, feminist, historical, literary, mainstream/contemporary, military/war, regional, religious, romance (contemporary, romantic suspense), science fiction (hard science/technological, soft/sociological), short story collections, sports, suspense, young adult (adventure, science fiction). "We publish 30,000-word novellas and short story collections. Visit our website for submission guidelines and tips. Authors are invited to submit collections of short stories and poetry for consideration for our ongoing programs." Published *Belly-Button Tales and Other Things*, by Sandra McTavish; *Cosmic Women*, by Margaret Karamazin; *A Sailor's Song*, by Leslie Wilkie.

How to Contact Accepts unsolicited mss. Query with SASE or IRC or submit sample chapter(s), 25-word synopsis (that sorts out the writers from the wafflers). Accepts queries by e-mail, fax, phone. Include estimated word count. Send SASE or IRC for return of ms or send a disposable ms and SASE or IRC for reply only. Responds in 1 month to queries; 3 months to mss. Accepts electronic submissions, submissions on disk. No simultaneous submissions. Always comments on rejected mss.

Terms Pays 10% royalty on wholesale price. Also gives 5 author's copies. Publishes ms 6 months after acceptance. Ms guidelines online, www.supumasu.com.

☐ POCOL PRESS

6023 Pocol Dr., Clifton VA 20124. (703)830-5862. E-mail: chrisandtom@erols.com. Website: www.pocolpress.com. **Contact:** J. Thomas Hetrick, editor (baseball history and fiction). Pocol Press publishes first-time, unagented authors. Our fiction deals mainly with single author short story collections from outstanding niche writers. Publishes paperback originals. Books: 50 lb. paper; offset printing; perfect binding. Average print order: 500. **Published 2 debut authors within the last year**. Averages 4-6 total titles, 3 fiction titles/year. Member: Small Press Publishers Association. Distributes titles through website, authors, e-mail, word-of-mouth and readings.

Needs Horror (psychological, supernatural), literary, mainstream/contemporary, short story collections, baseball. Published *Gulf*, by Brock Adams (short fiction); *The Last of One*, by Stephan Solberg (novel); *A Good Death*, by David E. Lawrence.

How to Contact Does not accept or return unsolicited mss. Query with SASE or submit 1 sample chapter(s). Accepts queries by mail only. Include estimated word count, brief bio, list of publishing credits. Responds in 2 weeks to queries; 2 months to mss. No simultaneous submissions, submissions on disk. Sometimes comments on rejected mss.

Terms Pays 10-12% royalty. Publishes ms 1 year or less after acceptance. Book catalog for SASE or on website. Ms guidelines for SASE or on website.

☐ ◙ ◘ POISONED PEN PRESS

6962 E. 1st Ave. #103, Scottsdale AZ 85251. (480)945-3375. Fax: (480)949-1707. E-mail: info@poisonedpenpress.com. Website: www.poisonedpenpress.com. **Contact:** Jessica Tribble. 6962 E. 1st Ave. #103, Scottsdale AZ 85251. (480) 945-3375. Fax: (480) 949-1707. E-mail: info@poisonedpenpress.com. Website: www.poisonedpenpress.com. **Contact:** editor@poisonedpenpress.com (mystery, fiction). Estab. 1997. Publishes hardcover originals and paperback reprints. Books: 60 lb. paper; offset printing; hardcover binding. Average print order: 3,500. First novel print order: 3,000. **Published 4 debut authors within the last year.** Plans 5 first novels this year. Member Publishers Marketing Associations, Arizona Book Publishers Associations, Publishers Association of West. Distributes through Ingram, Baker & Taylor, Brodart.

- Was nominated in 2002 for the LA Times Book Prize. Also the recipient of several Edgar and Agatha Awards.

Needs Mystery (amateur sleuth, cozy, police procedural, private eye/hard-boiled, historical). Published *Sweeping Up Glass*, by Carolyn D. Wall (mystery/fiction); *Impulse*, by Frederick Ramsay (mystery/fiction); *Murder in the Dark*, by Kerry Greenwood(mystery/fiction); *Drive*, by James Sallis (mystery/fiction).

How to Contact Accepts unsolicited mss. Electronic queries only. Accepts queries by e-mail to editor@poisonedpenpress.com. Responds in 1-3 weeks to queries; 6-9 months to mss. Only accepts electronic submissions. No simultaneous submissions. Often comments on rejected mss.

Terms Pays 9-15% royalty. Average advance: $1,000. Publishes ms 12-15 months after acceptance. Ms guidelines online.

◘ ◪ ◙ PRAIRIE JOURNAL PRESS

P.O. Box 68073, Calgary AB T3G 3N8 Canada. E-mail: prairiejournal@yahoo.com. Website: www.geocities.com/prairiejournal/. **Contact:** Anne Burke, literary editor. Estab. 1983. Small-press, noncommercial literary publisher. Publishes paperback originals. Books: bond paper; offset printing; stapled binding; b&w line drawings. **Published some debut authors within the last year.** Distributes titles by mail and in bookstores and libraries (public and university). Promotes titles through direct mail, reviews and in journals.

- Prairie Journal Press authors have been nominees for The Journey Prize in fiction and finalists and honorable mention for the National Magazine awards.

Needs Literary, short story collections. Published *Prairie Journal Fiction, Prairie Journal Fiction II* (anthologies of short stories); *Solstice* (short fiction on the theme of aging); and *Prairie Journal Prose.*

How to Contact Accepts unsolicited mss. Sometimes comments on rejected mss.

Terms Pays 1 author's copy; honorarium depends on grant/award provided by the government or private/corporate donations. SAE with IRC for individuals. No U.S. stamps please.

$ PS BOOKS

2021 S. 11th St., Philadelphia PA 19148. (215)551-5889. Fax: (215)635-0195. E-mail: info@psbookspublishing.org. Website: www.psbookspublishing.org. **Contact:** Marc Schuster, acquisitions editor. "In 2008, the publishers of Philadelphia Stories magazine launched a books division called PS Books. The needs of PS Books closely mirror those of the magazine; we are looking for novel-length fiction and narrative nonfiction manuscripts featuring polished prose, a controlled voice, strong characters, and interesting subjects. Please read our current titles to get a sense of what we publish. For information on submitting a query package, please visit our website." Publishes paperback originals. Format: cougar smooth paper;off-set commercial printing;perfect-bound. Average print order: 500-1,000. Debut novel print order: 500-1,000. Plans 1 debut novel this year. Averages 2 total titles/year; 1-2 fiction titles/year. Member CLMP. Distributes/promotes titles Baker & Taylor, direct marketing.

Needs Humor, Literary, Mainstream, Regional (Delaware valley, greater Philadelphia). Anthologies planned include *The Best of Philadelphia Stories, vol. 2*; *By Any Other Name*. Published *Broad Street*, by Christine Weiser (upmarket commercial fiction); *The Singular Exploits of Wonder Mom and Party Girl*, by Marc Schuster (literary fiction).

How to Contact Query with outline/synopsis and first 20 pages. Accepts queries by e-mail only. Include estimated word count, brief bio, list of publishing credits. Send disposable copy of ms and SASE for reply only. Responds to queries in 2 months. Considers simultaneous submissions, e-mail submissions. Rarely critiques/comments on rejected mss. Responds to mss in 3 months.

Terms Manuscript published within 1 year after acceptance.

PUFFIN BOOKS

345 Hudson St., New York NY 10014. (212)366-2000. E-mail: Sharyn.November@us.penguingroup.com. Website: www.penguinputnam.com. **Contact:** Kristin Gilson, editorial director. Puffin Books publishes high-end trade paperbacks and paperback reprints for preschool children, beginning and middle readers, and young adults. Publishes trade paperback originals and reprints. Averages 175-225 total titles/year.

Needs Young adult, middle grade; easy-to-read grades 1-3. "We publish paperback reprints and original titles. We do not publish original picture books." Noted Puffin picture book authors and illustrators include Jan Brett, Eric Carle, Graeme Base, Tomie de Paola, Ezra Jack Keats, Rosemary Wells, Paul Zelinsky, E. B. Lewis, Jon Scieszka, Lane Smith, David Catrow, Patricia Polacco. Published *Three Cups of Tea, Young Readers Edition,* by Greg Mortenson and David Oliver Relin, adapted for young readers by Sarah Thomson.

How to Contact Does not accept unsolicited mss. Send SASE or IRC. Responds in 3 months to mss. No simultaneous submissions.

Terms Royalty varies. Average advance: varies. Publishes ms 1 year after acceptance. Book catalog for 9 × 12 SAE with 7 first-class stamps; send request to Marketing Department.

PUREPLAY PRESS

350 Judah St., Suite 302, San Francisco CA 94122. E-mail: info@pureplaypress.com; editor@pureplaypress.com. Website: www.pureplaypress.com. **Contact:** David Landau. "We are a small, niche publisher devoted to Cuba's history and culture. We publish high-quality books that people will want to read for years to come." Books are in English, Spanish and bilingual formats. Publishes hardcover and paperback originals. Ms guidelines online.

Needs "Founded in 2001 by writers and editors who felt the need to publish works about Cuba's history and culture. At present we have 12 books in print, all with Cuban themes, and we are beginning to publish on other subjects. Our byword is freedom from the status quo. The qualities we prize in the written word are sincerity, simplicity, elegance and clarity of expression. We are convinced that culture is infinite, and creativity general. We strive to be considerate to readers and encouraging to writers. Our books are closely edited, carefully designed, printed with high-quality materials and then marketed by all plausible means, including the World Wide Web. We are interested in fiction, history, poetry, politics and culture."

How to Contact "While we cannot receive unsolicited manuscripts, we will consider proposals of up to 250 words in length. The most effective proposal is a statement about the work that might serve as copy for a book-jacket or a back cover."

G.P. PUTNAM'S SONS

Penguin Putnam, Inc., 375 Hudson, New York NY 10014. (212)366-2000. Fax: (212)366-2664. E-mail: susan.kochan@us.penguingroup.com. Website: www.penguinputnam.com. **Contact:** Susan Kochan, associate editorial director. Penguin Putnam Books For Young Readers, 345 Hudson St., New York NY 10014. (212)414-3610. Website: www.us.penguingroup.com. **Manuscript Acquisitions:** Publishes 25 picture books/year; 15 middle readers/year; 5 young adult titles/year. 5% of books by first-time authors; 50% of books from agented authors.

- G. Putnam's Sons 2007 titles *Slam*, by Nick Hornby and *The Three Snow Bears*, by Jan Brett were #1 on the New York Times Bestseller List.

Needs Juvenile picture books: animal, concept, contemporary, humor, multicultural. Young readers: adventure, contemporary, history, humor, multicultural, special needs, suspense/mystery. Middle readers: adventure, contemporary, history, humor, fantasy, multicultural, problem novels, sports, suspense/mystery. Young adults: contemporary, history, fantasy, problem novels, special needs. Does not want to see series. Average word length: picture books—200-1,000; middle readers—10,000-30,000; young adults—40,000-50,000. Recently published *Good Night, Goon: A Parody* by Michael Rex (ages 4-8); *Geek Magnet*, by Kieran Scott (ages 12 and up).

How to Contact Accepts unsolicited mss. No SASE required, as will only respond if interested. Picture books: send full mss. Fiction: Query with outline/synopsis and 10 manuscript pages. When submitting a portion of a longer work, please provide an accompanying cove letter that briefly describes your manuscript's plot, genre, the intended age group, and your publishing credits, if any. Do not send art unless requested. Responds to mss within 4 months if interested. Will consider simultaneous submissions.

Terms Pays authors royalty based on retail price. Sends prepublication galleys to authors.

QUIXOTE PRESS

3544 Blakslee St., Wever IA 52658. (800)571-2665. Fax: (319)372-7485. **Contact:** Bruce Carlson. Quixote Press specializes in humorous and/or regional folklore and special-interest cookbooks. Publishes trade paperback originals and reprints. **Published many debut authors within the last year.**

Needs Humor, short story collections. Published *Eating Ohio*, by Rus Pishnery (short stories about Ohio); *Lil' Red Book of Fishing Tips*, by Tom Whitecloud (fishing tales); *How to Talk Hoosier*, by Netha Bell (humor); *Cow Whisperer*, by Skip Holmes (humor); *Flour Sack Bloomers*, by Lucy Fetterhoff (history).

How to Contact Query with SASE. Accepts simultaneous submissions.

Terms Pays 10% royalty on wholesale price. Publishes ms 1 year after acceptance.

RANDOM HOUSE, INC.

1745 Broadway, New York NY 10013. Website: www.randomhouse.com. "Random House has long been committed to publishing the best literature by writers both in the United States and abroad."

Imprints Alfred A. Knopf; Anchor Books; Shaye Areheart Books; Ballantine Books; Bantam Hardcover; Bantam Mass Market; Bantam Trade Paperbacks; Bell Tower; Black Ink/Harlem Moon; Broadway; Clarkson Potter; Crown Books for Young Readers; Crown Publishers, Inc; Currency; Del Ray; Del Ray/Lucas; Delacorte; Dell; Dell Dragonfly; Dell Laurel-Leaf; Dell Yearling; Delta; The Dial Press; Domain; Doubleday; Doubleday Religion; Doubleday Graphic Novels; DTP; Everyman's Library; Fanfare; Fawcett; David Fickling Books; First Choice Chapter Books; Fodor's; Grammercy Book; Harmony Books; Island; Ivy; Knopf Books for Young Readers; Knopf Paperbacks; Library of Contemporary Thought; Main Street Books; The Modern Library; Nan A. Talese; One World; Pantheon Books; Picture Yearling; Presidio Press; Random House Children's Publishing; Random House Large Print Publishing; Shocken Books; Spectra; Strivers Row; Three Rivers Press; Times Books; Villard Books; Vintage Books; Wings Books.

How to Contact *Agented submissions only.*

Terms Pays royalty. Offers advance. Ms guidelines online.

RANDOM HOUSE CHILDREN'S BOOKS

1745 Broadway, New York NY 10019. (212)782-9000. Fax: (212)782-9452. Website: www.randomhouse.com/kids. **Contact:** Kate Klimo, editorial director of Random House Golden Books Young Readers Group. Estab. 1925. "Producing books for preschool children through young adult readers, in all formats from board to activity books to picture books and novels, Random House Children's Books brings together world-famous franchise characters, multimillion-copy series and top-flight, award-winning authors and illustrators."

Imprints *For Knopf Delacorte Dell Young Readers Group*—Doubleday, Alfred A. Knopf, Crown, Delacorte Press, Wendy Lamb Books, David Fickling Books, Dragonfly Books, Yearling Books, Laurel-Leaf Books, Bantam, Swartz & Wade Books. *For Random House/Golden Books Young Readers Group*—Picturebacks, Beginner Books, Step Into Reading, Stepping Stone Books, Landmark Books, Disney Books for Young Readers, First Time Books, Sesame Workshop.

Needs "Random House publishes a select list of first chapter books and novels, with an emphasis on fantasy and historical fiction." Chapter books, middle-grade readers, young adult.

How to Contact Does not accept unsolicited mss. *Agented submissions only.* Accepts simultaneous submissions.

RANSOM PUBLISHING

Radley House, 8 St. Cross Road, Winchester Hampshire SO23 9HXUK United Kingdom. +44 (0) 01962 862307. Fax: +44 (0) 05601 148881. E-mail: ransom@ransom.co.uk. Website: www.ransom.co.uk. **Contact:** Jenny Ertle, editor. Estab. 1995. Independent UK publisher with distribution in English speaking markets throughout the world. Specializes in books for reluctant and struggling readers. Our high quality, visually stimulating, age appropriate material has achieved wide acclaim for its ability to engage and motivate those who either can't or won't read. One of the few English language publishers to publish books with very high interest age and very low reading age. Has a developing list of children's books for home and school use. Specializes in phonics and general reading programs. Publishes paperback originals. **Published 5 debut authors within the last year.** Member BESA (UK), IPG (UK).

Needs Easy reading for young adults. Books for reluctant and struggling readers.

How to Contact Accepts unsolicited mss. Query with SASE or submit outline/proposal. Prefers queries by e-mail. Include estimated word count, brief bio, list of publishing credits. Responds in

3-4 weeks to queries. Accepts simultaneous submissions, electronic submissions, submissions on disk. Never comments on rejected mss.

Terms Pays 10% royalty on net receipts. Ms guidelines by e-mail.

RED DEER PRESS

195 Allstate Pkwy, Markham ON L3R 4TB Canada. (905)477-9700. Fax: (905)477-9179. E-mail: rdp@reddeerpress.com; dionne@reddeerpress.com; val@reddeerpress.com. Website: www.reddeerpress.com. **Contact:** Richard Dionne, publisher. Estab. 1975. Publishes young adult, adult non-fiction, science fiction, fantasy, and paperback originals "focusing on books by, about, or of interest to Canadians." Books: offset paper; offset printing; hardcover/perfect-bound. Average print order: 5,000. First novel print order: 2,500. Distributes titles in Canada and the US, the UK, Australia and New Zealand.

- Red Deer Press has received numerous honors and awards from the Book Publishers Association of Alberta, Canadian Children's Book Centre, the Governor General of Canada and the Writers Guild of Alberta.

Imprints Robert J Sawyer Books (Sci-fi), Flea Circus Books (fantasy).

Needs Young adult (juvenile and early reader), contemporary. No romance or horror. Published *A Fine Daughter*, by Catherine Simmons Niven (novel); *The Kappa Child*, by Hiromi Goto (novel); *The Dollinage*, by Martine Leavitt; and *The Game*, by Teresa Toten (nominated for the Governor General's Award); *The Drum Calls Softly*, by David Bouchard (Aboriginal Picture Book); *Greener Grass*, by Caroline Pignat (Winner of the Governor General's Award); *Big Big Sky*, by Kristyn Dunnion (novel).

How to Contact Accepts unsolicited mss. Query with SASE. Responds in 6 months to mss. Accepts simultaneous submissions. No submissions on disk.

Terms Pays 8-10% royalty. Advance is negotiable. Publishes ms 1 year after acceptance. Book catalog for 9 × 12 SASE.

RED TUQUE BOOKS, INC.

477 Martin St.,, Unit #6, Penticton BC V2A 5L2 Canada. (778)476-5750. Fax: (778)476-5651. Website: www.redtuquebooks.ca. **Contact:** David Korinetz, executive editor. "Red Tuque Books is a new small publisher/distributor specializing in new and established Canadian authors." Publishes paperback originals, reprints, and ebooks. Average first novel print order 1,200-2,000. Publishes up to 4 debut authors each year. Publishes 4 fiction titles each year.

Needs Adventure, short story collections, young adult and teen (specifically adventure and science fiction), graphic novels, and fantasy (space fantasy, sword and sorcery).

How to Contact Submit a query letter and first five pages. Include total word count. A one-page synopsis is optional. Accepts queries by e-mail and mail. SASE for reply only. Responds in 3 weeks. Does not consider simultaneous submissions. Sometimes comments on rejected mss. $250 advance, royalties are 5-7% on net sales. Time between acceptance and publication is one year. Writer's guidelines and book catalogs on website.

RIVER CITY PUBLISHING

1719 Mulberry St., Montgomery AL 36106. E-mail: publicity@rivercitypublishing.com; jgilbert@rivercitypublishing.com. Website: www.rivercitypublishing.com. **Contact:** Jim Gilbert, editor. Estab. 1989. Midsize independent publisher (8-10 books per year). "We publish books of national appeal, with an emphasis on Southern writers and Southern stories." Publishes hardcover and trade paperback originals. Averages 6 total titles, 2 fiction titles/year.

- Had three nominees to *Foreword* fiction book of the year awards (2002); won Ippy for Short Fiction (2005).

Needs Literary fiction, narrative nonfiction, regional (southern), short story collections. No poetry, memoir, or children's books. Published *Murder Creek*, by Joe Formichella (true crime); *Breathing Out the Ghost*, by Kirk Curnutt (novel); *The Bear Bryant Funeral Train*, by Brad Vice (short story collection).

How to Contact Accepts unsolicited submissions and submissions from unagented authors, as well as those from established and agented writers. Submit 5 consecutive sample chapters or entire manuscript for review. "Please include a short biography that highlights any previous writing and publishing experience, sales opportunities the author could provide, ideas for marketing the book, and why you think the work would be appropriate for River City." Send appropriate-sized SASE or IRC, "otherwise, the material will be recycled." Also accepts queries by e-mail. "Please include your electronic query letter as inline text and not an as attachment; we do not open unsolicited attachments of any kind. Please do not include sample chapters or your entire manuscript as inline text. We do not field or accept queries by telephone." Agented fiction 25%. Responds in three to nine months; "please wait at least 3 months before contacting us about your submission." Accepts simultaneous submissions. No multiple submissions. Rarely comments on rejected mss.
Terms Pays 10-15% royalty on retail price. Average advance: $500-5,000. Publishes ms 1 year after acceptance.

RIVERHEAD BOOKS

375 Hudson Street, Office #4079, New York NY 10014. E-mail: ecommerce@us.penguingroup.com. Website: www.riverheadbooks.com. **Contact:** Megan Lynch, senior editor.
Needs Literary, mainstream, contemporary. Among the award-winning writers whose careers Riverhead has launched so far are Pearl Abraham (*The Romance Reader*; *Giving Up America*), Jennifer Belle (*Going Down*; *High Maintenance*), Adam Davies (*The Frog King*), Junot Diíaz (*Drown*), Alex Garland (*The Beach*; *The Tesseract*), Nick Hornby (*High Fidelity*; *About a Boy*; *How to Be Good*), Khaled Hosseini (*The Kite Runner*), ZZ Packer (*Drinking Coffee Elsewhere*), Iain Pears (*The Dream of Scipio*; *Instance of the Fingerpost*), Danzy Senna (*Caucasia*), Gary Shteyngart (*The Russian Debutante's Handbook*), Aryeh Lev Stollman (*The Far Euphrates*; *The Illuminated Soul*; *The Dialogues of Time and Entropy*), Sarah Waters (*Tipping the Velvet*; *Affinity*; *Fingersmith*).
How to Contact Submit through agent only. No unsolicited mss.

RONSDALE PRESS

3350 W. 21st Ave., Vancouver BC V6S 1G7 Canada. (604)738-4688. Fax: (604)731-4548. E-mail: ronsdale@shaw.ca. Website: www.ronsdalepress.com. **Contact:** Ronald B. Hatch, president/editor. Ronsdale Press is "dedicated to publishing books that give Canadians new insights into themselves and their country." Publishes trade paperback originals. Books: 60 lb. paper; photo offset printing; perfect binding. Average print order: 1,500. **Published some debut authors within the last year.** Averages 11 total titles, 3 fiction titles/year. Sales representation: Literary Press Group. Distribution: LitDistco. Promotes titles through ads in BC Bookworld and Globe & Mail and interviews on radio.
Needs Literary, short story collections, novels. Canadian authors *only*. Published *The City in the Egg*, by Michel Tremblay (novel); *River of Gold*, by Susan Dobbie (novel); and *What Belongs*, by F.B. Andreé (short story collection).
How to Contact Accepts unsolicited mss. Accepts short queries by e-mail. Send SASE or IRC. Responds in 2 weeks to queries; 2 months to mss. Accepts simultaneous submissions. Sometimes comments on rejected mss.
Terms Pays 10% royalty on retail price. Publishes ms 1 year after acceptance. Ms guidelines online.

SAMHAIN PUBLISHING, LTD

577 Mulberry Street, Ste. 1520, Macon GA 31201. (478)314-5144. Fax: (478)314-5148. E-mail: editor@samhainpublishing.com. Website: samhainpublishing.com. **Contact:** Laurie M. Rauch, executive editor. "A small, independent publisher, Samhain's motto is 'It's all about the story.' We look for fresh, unique voices who have a story to share with the world. We encourage our authors to let their muse have its way and to create tales that don't always adhere to current trends. One

never knows what the next hot genre will be or when it will start, so write what's in your soul. These are the books that, whether the story is based on formula or is an original, when written from the heart will earn you a life-time readership." Publishes e-books and paperback originals. Format: POD/offset printing; line illustrations. **Published 20-30 new writers last year.** Plans 20 or more debut novels this year. Averages 300 fiction titles/year. Distributes/promotes titles through Ingrams Publisher Services and through a variety of media outlets both online and offline.

- Preditor and Editors Best Publisher 2006

Needs Needs erotica and all genres and all heat levels of romance (contemporary, futuristic/time travel, gothic, historical, paranormal, regency period, romantic suspense, fantasy, action/adventure, etc.), as well as fantasy, urban fantasy or science fiction with strong romantic elements, with word counts between 12,000 and 120,000 words. Anthologies planned include red hot fairy tales, steampunk romance and red hot winter. Open calls for submissions are available on the website. Full manuscript is required for special anthologies and the editor in charge of anthology selects final stories. Published *Here Kitty, Kitty,* by Shelly Laurenston (paranormal); *Unbroken*, by Maya Banks (contemporary erotic romance); *Silent Blade,* by Ilona Andrews (scifi/futuristic).

How to Contact Query with outline/synopsis and either 3 sample chapters or the full manuscript. Accepts queries by e-mail only. Include estimated word count, brief bio, list of publishing credits, and "how the author is working to improve craft: association, critique groups, etc." Responds to queries and mss within 10-16 weeks. Accepts unsolicited mss. Sometimes critiques/comments on rejected mss. Guidelines on website.

Terms Sends pre-production galleys to author. Ms published 6-18 months after acceptance. Writers' guidelines on website. Pays royalties 30-40% for e-books, average of 8% for trade paper, and author's copies (quantity varies). Book catalogs on website.

SARABANDE BOOKS, INC.

2234 Dundee Rd., Suite 200, Louisville KY 40205. E-mail: info@sarabandebooks.org. Website: www.sarabandebooks.org. **Contact:** Sarah Gorham, editor-in-chief. Estab. 1994. "Small literary press publishing poetry, short fiction and literary nonfiction." Publishes trade paperback originals. **Published some debut authors within the last year.** Averages 12 total titles, 3-4 prose titles/year. Distributes titles through Consortium Book Sales & Distribution. Promotes titles through advertising in national magazines, sales reps, brochures, newsletters, postcards, catalogs, press release mailings, sales conferences, book fairs, author tours and reviews.

- Marjorie Sander's story collection *Portrait of My Mother Who Posed Nude in Wartime* won the 2004 National Jewish Book Award. *When It Burned to the Ground,* by Yolanda Barnes won the 2006 Independent Publisher Award for Best Multicultural Fiction.

Needs Literary, novellas, short novels, 250 pages maximum, 150 pages minimum. We consider novels and non-fiction in a wide variety of genres and subject matters with a special emphasis on mysteries and crime fiction. We do not consider science fiction, fantasy, or horror. Our target length is 70-90,000 words. Queries can be sent via email, fax or regular post. Submissions to Mary McCarthy Prize in Short Fiction accepted January through February. Published *Other Electricities*, by Ander Monson; *More Like Not Running Away*, by Paul Shepherd, and *Water: Nine Stories*, by Alyce Miller.

How to Contact See website for McCarthy Contest entry form. Accepts simultaneous submissions. **Charges $10 handling fee** with alternative option of purchase of book from website (email confirmation of sale must be included with submission).

Terms Pays royalty of 10% on actual income received. Publishes ms 18 months after acceptance. Ms guidelines for #10 SASE.

SCHOLASTIC CANADA, LTD.

604 King St. West, Toronto ON M5V 1E1 Canada. (416)915-3500. Fax: (416)849-7912. E-mail: NWoodrow@scholastic.ca. Website: www.scholastic.ca. **Contact:** Editor, children's books. Publishes hardcover and trade paperback originals. Imprints: Scholastic Canada; North Winds

Press; Les Editions Scholastic. Publishes 70 titles/year; imprint publishes 4 titles/year. 3% of books from first-time authors; 50% from unagented writers. Canadian authors, theme or setting required.

- At press time Scholastic Canada was not accepting unsolicited manuscripts. For up-to-date information on their current submission policy, call their publishing status line at (905)887-7323, ext. 4308 or view their submission guidelines on their website.

Needs Juvenile picture books, young readers, young adult. Average word length: picture books—under 1,000; young readers—7,000-10,000; middle readers—15,000-30,000; young adult—25,000-40,000.

How to Contact Query with synopsis, 3 sample chapters and SASE. Nonfiction: Query with outline, 1-2 sample chapters and SASE (IRC or Canadian stamps only). Responds in 3 months. Publishes book 1 year after acceptance.

Terms Pays authors royalty of 5-10% based on retail price. Offers advances. Book catalog for 8½ × 11 SAE with $2.55 postage stamps (IRC or Canadian stamps only).

☐ ◙ SEAL PRESS

1700 4th Street, Berkeley CA 94710. (510)595-3664. E-mail: Seal.Press@perseusbooks.com. Website: www.sealpress.com. **Contact:** Ingrid Emerick, editor/publisher. Estab. 1976. "Midsize independent feminist book publisher interested in original, lively, radical, empowering and culturally diverse books by women." Publishes mainly trade paperback originals. Books: 55 lb. natural paper; Cameron Belt, Web or offset printing; perfect binding; illustrations occasionally. Averages 22 total titles/year. Titles distributed by Publishers Group West.

Imprints Adventura (women 's travel/outdoors), Live Girls (Third-Wave, pop culture, young feminist).

Needs Ethnic, feminist, gay/lesbian, literary, multicultural. "We are interested in alternative voices." Published *Valencia*, by Michelle Tea (fiction); *Navigating the Darwin Straits*, by Edith Forbes (fiction); and *Bruised Hibiscus*, by Elizabeth Nunez (fiction).

How to Contact Does not accept fiction at present. Query with SASE or submit outline, 2 sample chapter(s), synopsis. See guidelines online. Responds in 2 months to queries. Accepts simultaneous submissions.

Terms Pays 7-10% royalty on retail price. Pays variable advance. Publishes ms 18 months after acceptance. Book catalog and ms guidelines for SASE or online. Ms guidelines online.

☐ ◙ SILHOUETTE DESIRE

233 Broadway, Suite 1001, New York NY 10279. (212)553-4200. Website: www.eharlequin.com. **Contact:** Krista Stroever. "Desire novels are sensual reads and a love scene or scenes are still needed. But there is no set number of pages that needs to be fulfilled. Rather, the level of sensuality must be appropriate to the storyline. Above all, every Silhouette Desire novel must fulfill the promise of a powerful, passionate and provocative read." Publishes paperback originals and reprints. Books: newspaper print; web printing; perfect bound. **Published some debut authors within the last year.**

Needs Romance. Looking for novels in which "the conflict is an emotional one, springing naturally from the unique characters you've chosen. The focus is on the developing relationship, set in a believable plot. Sensuality is key, but lovemaking is never taken lightly. Secondary characters and subplots need to blend with the core story. Innovative new directions in storytelling and fresh approaches to classic romantic plots are welcome." Manuscripts must be 50,000-55,000 words.

How to Contact Does not accept unsolicited mss. Query with word count, brief bio, publishing history, synopsis (no more than 2 single-spaced pages), SASE/IRC. No simultaneous submissions.

Terms Pays royalty. Offers advance. Detailed ms guidelines for SASE or on website.

SILVER LEAF BOOKS, LLC

P.O. Box 6460, Holliston MA 01746. (508)429-6270. E-mail: editor@silverleafbooks.com. Website: www.silverleafbooks.com. **Contact:** Brett Fried, editor. "Silver Leaf Books is a small press featuring primarily new and upcoming talent in the fantasy, science fiction, mystery, thrillers, suspense, and horror genres. Our editors work closely with our authors to establish a lasting and mutually beneficial relationship, helping both the authors and company continue to grow and thrive." Publishes hardcover originals, trade paperback originals, paperback originals, paperback reprints. Average print order: 3,000. Debut novel print order: 3,000. **Published 1 new writer last year**. Plans 4 debut novels this year. Averages 6 total titles/year; 6 fiction titles/year. Distributes/promotes titles through Baker & Taylor Books and Ingram.

Needs Fantasy (space fantasy, sword and sorcery), horror (dark fantasy, futuristic, psychological, supernatural), mystery/suspense (amateur sleuth, cozy, police procedural, private eye/hard-boiled), science fiction (hard science/technological, soft/sociological), young adult (adventure, fantasy/science fiction, horror, mystery/suspense). Published *The Apprentice of Zoldex* and *The Darkness Within*, by Clifford B. Bowyer, and *When the Sky Fell* by Mike Lynch and Brandon Barr.

How to Contact Query with outline/synopsis and 3 sample chapters. Accepts queries by snail mail. Include estimated word count, brief bio and marketing plan. Send SASE or IRC for return of ms or disposable copy of ms and SASE/IRC for reply only. Agented fiction: 25%. Responds to queries in 6 months. Responds to mss in 4 months. Accepts unsolicited mss. Sometimes critiques/comments on rejected mss.

Terms Manuscript published 12-24 months after acceptance. Writer's guidelines on website. Pays royalties, and provides author's copies.

SIMON & SCHUSTER

1230 Avenue of the Americas, New York NY 10020. (212)698-7000. Website: www.simonsays.com.

Imprints Simon & Schuster Adult Publishing Group: Simon & Schuster; Scribner (Scribner, Lisa Drew, Simple Abundance Press); The Free Press; Atria Books; Kaplan; Touchstone; Scribner Paperback Fiction; S&S Libros en Espanol; Simon & Schuster Source; Wall Street Journal Books; Pocket Books (Pocket Star; Washington Square Press; MTV Books; Sonnet Books; Star Trek; The New Fogler Shakespeare; VH-1 Books; WWF Books). Simon & Schuster Children's Publishing: Aladdin Paperbacks; Atheneum Books for Young Readers (Richard Jackson Books); Beach Lane Books; Little Simon (Simon Spotlight; Rabbit Ears Books & Audio); Margaret K. McElderry Books, (Archway Paperbacks; Minstreal Books); Simon & Schuster Books for Young Readers (Paula Wiseman Books).

How to Contact Agented submissions only.

Terms Pays royalty. Offers advance. Ms guidelines online.

SIMON & SCHUSTER ADULT PUBLISHING GROUP

1230 Avenue of the Americas, New York NY 10020. E-mail: ssonline@simonsays.com; Lydia.Frost@simonandschuster.com. Website: www.simonsays.com. (formerly Simon & Schuster Trade Division, Division of Simon & Schuster) , The Simon & Schuster Adult Publishing Group includes a number of publishing units that offer books in several formats. Each unit has its own publisher, editorial group and publicity department. Common sales and business departments support all the units. The managing editorial, art, production, marketing, and subsidiary rights departments have staff members dedicated to the individual imprints. Estab. 1924.

Imprints H&R Block; Lisa Drew Books; Fireside; The Free Press; Pocket Book Press; Rawson Associates; Scribner; Scribner Classics; Scribner Paperback Fiction; Scribner Poetry; S&S—Libros en Espanol; Simon & Schuster; Simon & Schuster Source; Simple Abundance Press; Touchstone; Wall Street Journal Books.

How to Contact *Agented submissions only.*

SMALL BEER PRESS

150 Pleasant St., #306, Easthampton MA 01027. (413) 203-1636. Fax: (413) 203-1636. E-mail: info@smallbeerpress.com. Website: www.smallbeerpress.com. **Contact:** Gavin J. Grant. Averages 3-6 fiction titles/year.

- Small Beer Press also publishes the zine *Lady Churchill's Rosebud Wristlet*. SBP's books have been Hugo and Locus Award winners, as well as BookSense Picks and finalists for The Story Prize.

Needs Literary, experimental, speculative, story collections. Recently published *Hound, A Debut Novel,* by Vincent McCaffrey; *A Life on Paper: Stories* by Georges-Olivier Chateaureynaud and translated by Edward Gauvin; and*Redemption in Indigo*, a debut novel by Karen Lord.

How to Contact "We do not accept unsolicited novel or short story collection manuscripts. Queries are welcome. Please send queries with an SASE by mail."

SOFT SKULL PRESS INC.

19 West 21st, Suite 1101, New York NY 10010. 718-643-1599. Fax: 510-704-0268. E-mail: editorial@softskull.com. Website: www.softskull.com. **Contact:** Fiction or Graphic Novel editor (whichever is appropriate). Publishes hardcover and trade paperback originals Averages 10 total titles/year.

Needs Confession, experimental, historical, gay/lesbian, erotica, graphic novels and comics, literary, mainstream/contemporary, multicultural, short story collections. Agented submissions encouraged.

How to Contact Soft Skull Press accepts unsolicited submissions. Email with a subject heading of "SUBMISSION OF Fiction/Nonfiction/Graphic Novel" (whichever is appropriate). Include contact information on your attachment/s, be that a sample chapter or the whole manuscript. Attachments should be no bigger than 2 megabytes. For graphic novels, send a minimum of five fully inked pages of art, along with a synopsis of your storyline. Responds in 2 months to proposals; 3 months to mss. No simultaneous submissions.

Terms Pays 7-10% royalty. Average advance: $100-15,000. Publishes ms 6 months after acceptance. Book catalog free or on website. Ms guidelines online.

SOHO PRESS, INC.

853 Broadway, New York NY 10003. (212)260-1900. Fax: (212)260-1902. E-mail: soho@sohopress.com. Website: www.sohopress.com. **Contact:** Katy Herman, editor; Mark Doten, managing editor; Bronwen Hruska, Publisher. "Independent publisher known for sophisticated fiction, mysteries set abroad, women's interest (no genre) novels and multicultural novels." Publishes hardcover and trade paperback originals and reprint editions. Books: perfect binding; halftone illustrations. First novel print order varies. **Published 7 debut authors within the last year.** Averages 70 total titles, 65 fiction titles/year. Distributes titles through Consortium Book Sales & Distribution in the US and Canada, Turnaround in England.

Imprints Soho Crime: procedural series set abroad.

Needs Adventure, ethnic, feminist, historical, literary, mainstream/contemporary, mystery (police procedural), suspense, multicultural. Published *Thirty-Three Teeth,* by Colin Cotterill; *When Red is Black,* by Qiu Xiaolong; *Murder on the Ile Saint-Louis,* by Cara Black; *The Farming of Bones,* by Edwidge Danticat; *The Darkest Child,* by Delores Phillips; *The First Wave,* by James R. Benn.

How to Contact Send first three chapters. Include estimated word count, brief bio, list of publishing credits. Send SASE for return of ms or send a disposable ms and SASE for reply only. Agented fiction 85%. Responds in 3 months to queries; 3 months to mss. Accepts simultaneous submissions. No electronic submissions. Sometimes comments on rejected mss.

Terms Pays 10-15% royalty on retail price for harcovers, 7.5% on trade paperbacks. Offers advance. Publishes ms 18-24 months after acceptance. Ms guidelines online.

SOURCEBOOKS LANDMARK

P.O. Box 4410, Naperville IL 60567-4410. E-mail: info@sourcebooks.com. Website: www.sourcebooks.com. "Our fiction imprint, Sourcebooks Landmark, publishes a variety of commercial fiction, including specialties in historical fiction and Austenalia. We are interested first and foremost in books that have a story to tell."

- We publish a variety of titles. We are currently only reviewing agented fiction manuscripts with the exception of Romance fiction. Find out more information about our Romance fiction submission guidelines online at our website.

How to Contact Responds to queries in 6-8 weeks.

SOUTHERN METHODIST UNIVERSITY PRESS

P.O. Box 750415, Dallas TX 75275-0415. (214)768-1433. Fax: (214)768-1428. E-mail: klang@smu.edu. Website: www.tamu.edu/upress. **Contact:** Kathryn Lang, Senior Editor. "Small university press publishing in areas of Southwest life and letters, medical humanities, sports (with emphasis on baseball), creative nonfiction and contemporary fiction." Publishes hardcover and trade paperback originals and reprints. Books: acid-free paper; perfect bound; some illustrations. Average print order: 1,500. **Published 2 debut authors within the last year.** Averages 8 total titles, 3-4 fiction titles/year. Distributes titles through Texas A&M University Press Consortium. Promotes titles through writers' publications.

Needs Literary, short story collections, novels. "We are willing to look at 'serious' or 'literary' fiction." No "mass market, science fiction, formula, thriller, romance." Published *Mrs. Somebody Somebody: A Linked Story Collection*, by Tracy Winn; and *God's Dogs: A Novel In Stories*, by Mitch Wieland.

How to Contact Accepts unsolicited mss. Query with SASE. Responds in 2 weeks to queries; up to 1 year to mss. No simultaneous submissions. Sometimes comments on rejected mss.

Terms Pays 10% royalty on wholesale price, 10 author's copies. Average advance: $500. Publishes ms 1 year after acceptance. Ms guidelines online.

SPEAK UP PRESS

P.O. Box 100506, Denver CO 80250. (303)715-0837. Fax: (303)715-0793. E-mail: info@speakuppress.org. Website: www.speakuppress.org. "Speak Up Press is a small, nonprofit publisher of young adult fiction and nonfiction." Publishes paperback originals. Plans 2 debut novels this year. Averages 2 fiction titles/year.

Needs Young adult fiction, contemporary, problem novels novels only and nonfiction contemporary social issues only.

How to Contact Query only. Accepts queries by snail mail, e-mail. Send disposable copy of ms and SASE for reply only. Responds to queries in 6 weeks. Considers simultaneous submissions, e-mail submissions. Never critiques/comments on rejected mss.

Terms Writer's guidelines on website. Payment is determined "per individual author depending on book."

SPIRE PRESS

217 Thompson St., Suite 298, New York NY 10012. E-mail: editor@spirepress.org. Website: www.spirepress.org. **Contact:** Shelly Reed. Publishes 5-6 books/year. **Publishes 1-2 new writers/year.**

Needs Literary story collections. Also publishes memoir, poetry. No novels. No horror, romance, or religious work. Length: 30,000+ words. Recently published work by Damiam Dressick.

How to Contact Send first 15 pages and synopsis in August only. Send disposable copy and #10 SASE for reply only. Responds in 3 months. Accepts simultaneous submissions. Rarely comments on rejected queries. Writer's guidelines online.

Terms Pays in advance copies and 15% royalty.

SPOUT PRESS

P.O. Box 581067, Minneapolis MN 55458. (612) 782-9629. E-mail: editors@spoutpress.org. Website: www.spoutpress.org. **Contact:** Carrie Eidem, fiction editor. Estab. 1989. "Small independent publisher with a permanent staff of five—interested in experimental fiction for our magazine and books." Publishes paperback originals. Books: perfect bound; illustrations. Average print order: 1,000. **Published 1 debut author within the last year.** Distibutes and promotes books through the website, events and large Web-based stores such as Amazon.com.

Needs Ethnic, experimental, literary, short story collections. Published *I'm Right Here*, by Tony Rauch. Runs annual. Accepts submissions all year around fall through spring. See website for specific dates and details.

How to Contact Does not accept unsolicited mss. Query with SASE. Accepts queries by mail. Include estimated word count, brief bio, list of publishing credits. Send SASE for return of ms or send a disposable ms and SASE for reply only. Responds in 1 month to queries; 3-5 months to mss. Accepts simultaneous submissions. Rarely comments on rejected mss.

Terms Individual arrangement with author depending on the book. Publishes ms 12-15 months after acceptance. Ms guidelines for SASE or on website.

STARCHERONE BOOKS

P.O. Box 303, Buffalo NY 14201-0303. (716)885-2726. E-mail: starcherone@gmail.com; publisher@starcherone.com. Website: www.starcherone.com. **Contact:** Ted Pelton, publisher. Estab. 2000. Non-profit publisher of literary and experimental fiction. Publishes paperback originals and reprints. Books: acid-free paper; perfect bound; occasional illustrations. Average print order: 1,000. Average first novel print order: 1,000. **Published 2 debut authors within the last year.** Member CLMP. Titles distributed through website, Small Press Distribution, Amazon, independent bookstores.

Needs Experimental, literary. Published *Quinnehtukqut*, by Joshua Harmon (debut author, novel); *Hangings*, by Nina Shope (debut author, short stories); *My Body in Nine Parts*, by Raymond Federman (experimental).

How to Contact Accepts queries by mail or e-mail during August and September of each year. WE WILL NOT BE ACCEPTING ANY MANUSCRIPTS OR QUERIES OUTSIDE OF OUR CONTEST UNTIL THE 2010 CONTEST IS CONCLUDED. Submissions of unsolicited manuscripts will risk being returned or discarded, unread. Include brief bio, list of publishing credits. Always query before sending ms. Responds in 2 months to queries; 6-10 months to mss. Accepts simultaneous submissions if noted in cover letter.

Terms Pays 10-12.5% royalty. Publishes ms 9-18 months after acceptance. Guidelines and catalog available on website.

STEEPLE HILL

233 Broadway, Suite 1001, New York NY 10279. (212) 553-4200. Website: www.eharlequin.com. **Contact:** Joan Marlow Golan, Krista Stroever, senior editors. Publishes mass market paperback originals.

Imprints Love Inspired; Steeple Hill Love Inspired Suspense; Steeple Hill Love Inspired Historical; Steeple Hill Woman's Fiction; Steeple Hill Café.

Needs Romance (Christian, 70,000-75,000 words). Wants all genres of inspirational woman's fiction including contemporary and historical romance, chick/mom-lit, relationship novels, romantic suspense, mysteries, family sagas, and thrillers. Published *A Mother at Heart*, by Carolyne Aarsen.

How to Contact No unsolicited mss. Query with SASE, synopsis. No simultaneous submissions.

Terms Pays royalty. Offers advance. Detailed ms guidelines online.

ST. MARTIN'S PRESS

175 Fifth Ave., New York NY 10010. (212)674-5151. Website: www.stmartins.com. General interest publisher of both fiction and nonfiction. Publishes hardcover, trade paperback and mass market originals. Averages 1,500 total titles/year.

Imprints Bedford Books; Buzz Books; Thomas Dunne Books; Forge; Minotaur; Picador USA; Stonewall Inn Editions; TOR Books; Griffin.

Needs Fantasy, historical, horror, literary, mainstream/contemporary, mystery, science fiction, suspense, western (contemporary), general fiction; thriller.

How to Contact *Agented submissions only.*

Terms Pays royalty. Offers advance. Ms guidelines online.

SYNERGEBOOKS

E-mail: synergebooks@aol.com. E-mail: synergebooks@aol.com. Website: www.synergebooks.com. **Contact:** Debra Staples, editor. Estab. 1999. Small press publisher, specializing in quality e-books from talented new writers in a myriad of genres, including print-on-demand. SynergEbooks "works together" with the author to edit and market each book. Publishes paperback originals and e-books. Books: 60 lb. paper; print-on-demand; perfect bound. Average first novel print order: 30. **Published 10-20 debut authors within the last year.** Averages 50 total titles, 30 fiction titles/year.

- Authors have received EPPIES and other awards.

Needs Adventure, business, family saga, fantasy (space fantasy, sword and sorcery), historical, horror, humor, mainstream/contemporary, mystery, new age/mystic, religious (children's religious, inspirational, religious fantasy, religious mystery/suspense, religious thriller, religious romance), romance (contemporary, futuristic/time travel, historical, regency period, romantic suspense), science fiction, short story collections, western (frontier saga, traditional), young adult (adventure, fantasy/science fiction, historical, horror, mystery/suspense, romance), native american, new age, and spirituality. Welcomes series books (1-9 in a series, with at least 1 title completed at time of submission.) Published *A Talent to Deceive: Who REALLY Killed the Lindberg Baby?*, by William Norris (nonfiction); *The Witchlock Series*, by Cyrese Covelli (fantasy/young adult); *A Banana Patch*, by Michael David (new age).

How to Contact Accepts unsolicited mss. Query via e-mail or snail mail, email preferred, 1-3 sample chapter(s), synopsis via attached mail in.doc format. Include estimated word count, brief bio, list of publishing credits, and e-mail address. Agented fiction 1%. Responds in 3 weeks to queries; 3 months to mss. Accepts simultaneous submissions, submissions on disk. Sometimes comments on rejected mss.

Terms Pays 15-40% royalty. Publishes ms 3-6 months after acceptance. Ms guidelines online.

THIRD WORLD PRESS

P.O. Box 19730, 7822 S. Dobson Ave., Chicago IL 60619. (773)651-0700. Fax: (773)651-7286. E-mail: TWPress3@aol.com. Website: www.thirdworldpressinc.com. **Contact:** Gwendolyn Mitchell, editor. "Black-owned and operated independent publisher of fiction and nonfiction books about the black experience throughout the Diaspora." Publishes hardcover and trade paperback originals and reprints. Averages 20 total titles/year. Distibutes titles through Independent Publisher Group. Needs Materials for literary, ethnic, contemporary, juvenile and children's books. "We publish nonfiction, primarily, but will consider fiction." Published *The Covenant with Black America*, with an introduction by Tavis Smiley; 1996, by Gloria Naylor.

How to Contact Accepts unsolicited mss. Submit outline, 5 sample chapter(s), synopsis. Responds in 8 weeks to queries; 5 months to mss. Accepts simultaneous submissions.

Terms Pays royalty on net revenues. Individual arrangement with author depending on the book, etc. Publishes ms 18 months after acceptance. Ms guidelines for #10 SASE.

TIGHTROPE BOOKS

602 Markham St., Toronto ON M6G 2L8 Canada. (647) 348-4460. Website: tightropebooks.com. **Contact:** Shirarose Wilensky, editor (fiction, poetry, nonfiction).

TIN HOUSE BOOKS

(503)473-8663. Fax: (503)473-8957. E-mail: meg@tinhouse.com. Website: www.tinhouse.com. "We are a small independent publisher dedicated to nurturing new, promising talent as well as showcasing the work of established writers. Our Tin House New Voice series features work by authors who have not previously published a book." Publishes hardcover originals, paperback originals, paperback reprints. **Plans 3 debut novels/year.** Averages 8-10 total titles/year; 4-6 fiction titles/year. Distributes/promotes titles through Publishers Group West.

Needs Literary, novels, short story collections, poetry, translations. Publishes A New Voice series.

How to Contact Agented mss only. Accepts queries by snail mail, e-mail, phone. Include brief bio, list of publishing credits. Send SASE or IRC for return of ms or disposable copy of ms and SASE/IRC for reply only. Agented fiction 80%. Responds to queries in 2-3 weeks. Responds to mss in 2-3 months. Considers simultaneous submissions. Sometimes critiques/comments on rejected mss.

Terms Sends pre-production galleys to author. Manuscript published approximately one year after acceptance. Writer's guidelines on website. Advance is negotiable. Book catalogs not available.

TITAN PRESS

PMB 17897, Encino CA 91416. E-mail: titan91416@yahoo.com. Website: www.calwriterssfv.com. **Contact:** Stefanya Wilson, editor. Publishes hardcover originals and paperback originals. Books: recycled paper; offset printing; perfect bound. Average print order: 2,000. Average first novel print order: 1,000. **Published 3 debut authors within the last year.** Averages 12 total titles, 6 fiction titles/year. Distributed at book fairs and through the Internet and at Barnes & Noble.

Needs Literary, mainstream/contemporary, short story collections. Published *Orange Messiahs*, by Scott Alixander Sonders (fiction).

How to Contact Does not accept unsolicited mss. Query with SASE. Include brief bio, social security number, list of publishing credits. Agented fiction 50%. Responds in 3 months to mss. Accepts simultaneous submissions. Sometimes comments on rejected mss.

Terms Pays 20-40% royalty. Publishes ms 1 year after acceptance. Ms guidelines for #10 SASE.

TOKYOPOP

5900 Wilshire Blvd., 20th Floor, Los Angeles CA 90036-5020. (323)692-6700; (323)692-6730. E-mail: info@tokyopop.com. Website: www.tokyopop.com. **Contact:** Marco Pavia, Associate Publisher.

Needs *TOKYOPOP* is not accepting submissions at this time.

TORQUERE PRESS

P.O. Box 2545, Round Rock TX 78680. (512)586-6921. Fax: (866)287-4860. E-mail: torquere@torquerepress.com. Website: www.torquerepress.com. **Contact:** Shawn Clements, submission editor (homoerotica, suspense) and Lorna Hinson, senior editor (gay and lesbian romance, historical). Estab. 2003. "We are a gay and lesbian press focusing on romance. We particularly like paranormal and western romance." Publishes paperback originals. Averages 140 total titles/year.

- Please read our writers' guidelines. Look for new contests coming soon.

Imprints Top Shelf—Shawn Clements, editor; Screwdrivers—M. Rode, editor; Single Shot—Jane Davitt, editor.

Needs All categories gay and lesbian themed. Adventure, erotica, historical, horror, mainstream, multicultural, mystery, occult, romance, science fiction, short story collections, suspense, western. Published *Broken Road*, by Sean Michael (romance); *Soul Mates: Bound by Blood*, by Jourdan Lane (paranormal romance). Imprints accepting submissions.

How to Contact Query with outline/synopsis and 3 sample chapters. Responds to queries in 2 months; mss in 3-4 months. Electronic submissions preferred. Send query to submissions@torquerepress.com. No simultaneous submissions.

Terms Manuscript published 6 months after acceptance. Pays royalties. Book catalogs on website.

TRADEWIND BOOKS

202-1807 Maritime Mews, Vancouver BC V6H 3W7 Canada. (604)662-4405. Fax: (604)730-0454. E-mail: tradewindbooks@yahoo.com. Website: www.tradewindbooks.com. **Contact:** Michael Katz, publisher, Manuscript Acquisitions; R. David Stephens, Senior Editor. Publishes 2 picture books; 2 chapter books, 3 young adult titles/year; 1 book of poetry. 15% of books by first-time authors.

Needs Juvenile Picture books: adventure, multicultural, folktales. Average word length: 900 words. Recently published *City Kids*, by X.J. Kennedy; *Roxy*, by P.J. Reece; *Viva Zapata*, by Emelie Smith.

How to Contact Picture books: submit complete ms. YA novels by Canadian authors only. Chapter books by US authors considered. Will consider simultaneous submissions. Do not send query letter. Responds to mss in 12 weeks. Unsolicited submissions accepted only if authors have read a selection of books published by Tradewind Books. Submissions must include a reference to these books.

Terms Royalties negotiable. Offers advances against royalties. Catalog available on website.

TURNSTONE PRESS

206-100 Arthur St., Winnipeg MB R3B 1H3 Canada. (204)947-1555. Fax: (204)942-1555. E-mail: info@turnstonepress.com. Website: www.ravenstonebooks.com. **Contact:** Jamis Paulson, Associate Publisher. "Turnstone Press is a literary press that publishes Canadian writers with an emphasis on writers from, and writing on, the Canadian west." Focuses on eclectic new writing, prairie writers, travel writing and regional mysteries. Publishes trade paperback originals. Books: offset paper; perfect-bound. First novel print order: 1,500. **Published 5 debut authors within the last year.** Averages 8-12 total titles/year. Distributes titles through Lit DistCo (Canada and US). Promotes titles through Canadian national and local print media and select US print advertising.

- Turnstone Press is a past nominee for Small Press Publisher of the Year. In addition to winning a Governor General's award, Turnstone Press has been shortlisted for numerous national and regional writing awards including The Giller Prize, The Leacock Award, the Arthur Ellis awards and the ReLit Awards.

Imprints Ravenstone.

Needs Contemporary literary novels, short story collections, cultural non-fiction and poetry. Canadian authors only. Published *An Unexpected Break in the Weather* (novels), *mama dada* (poetry) and *The Finger's Twist* (Ravenstone, action/thriller).

How to Contact Accepts unsolicited mss. Include list of publishing credits. Send SASE or IRC. Responds in 4 months to queries. No simultaneous submissions.

Terms Pays 10% royalty on retail price. and 10 author's copies. Offers advance. Publishes ms 1 year after acceptance. Ms guidelines online.

UNBRIDLED BOOKS

200 North 9th Street, Suite A, Columbia MO 65201. Website: http://unbridledbooks.com. 200 North 9th Street, Suite A, Columbia MO 65201. 573-256-4106. Fax: 573-256-5207. Website: www.unbridledbooks.com. **Contact**: Greg Michalson and Fred Ramey, editors. Estab. 2004. "Unbridled Books is a premier publisher of works of rich literary quality that appeal to a broad audience." Publishes both fiction and creative nonfiction. Hardcover and trade paperback originals. **Published 6 debut authors within the last year.** Averages 10-12 total titles, 8-10 fiction titles/year.

Needs Literary, nonfiction, memoir. *The Green Age of Asher Witherow*, by M. Allen Cunningham; *The Distance Between Us*, by Masha Hamilton; *Fear Itself*, by Candida Lawrence; *Lucky Strike*, by Nancy Zafris.

How to Contact Query with SASE. Accepts queries by mail. No electronic submissions.

UNIVERSITY OF IOWA PRESS

100 Kuhl House, Iowa City IA 52242-1000. (319)335-2000. Fax: (319)335-2055. Website: www.uiowapress.org. **Contact:** Holly Carver, director; Joe Parsons, acquisitions editor. Publishes paperback originals. Average print run for a first book is 1,000-1,500. Averages 40 total titles/year.

Needs Currently publishes the Iowa Short Fiction Award selections.

How to Contact See website for details.

Terms Pays 7-10% royalty on net receipts. Publishes ms 1 year after acceptance. Ms guidelines online.

UNIVERSITY OF NEVADA PRESS

MS 0166, Reno NV 89557. (775)682-7393. Fax: (775)784-6200. E-mail: MDalrymple@unpress.nevada.edu. Website: www.unpress.nevada.edu. **Contact:** Margaret Fisher Dalrymple, Acquisitions Editor: Basque Studies, Fiction, Natural History. Estab. 1961. "Small university press. Publishes fiction that primarily focuses on the American West." Publishes hardcover and paperback originals. Averages 25 total titles, 2 fiction titles/year. Member: AAUP

- *Strange White Male,* by Gerald Haslam won the WESTAF Award for Fiction in 2000 and *Foreword Magazine's* second place winner for Book of the Year.

Needs "We publish in Basque Studies, Gambling Studies, Western literature, Western history, Natural science, Environmental Studies, Travel and Outdoor books, Archeology, Anthropology, and Political Studies, all focusing on the West". The Press also publishes creative nonfiction and books on regional topics for a general audience. Has published *The Mechanics of Falling and Other Stories*, by Catherine Brady; *Little Lost River*, by Pamela Johnston; *Moon Lily*, by Susan Lang.

How to Contact Submit outline, 2-4 sample chapter(s), synopsis. Include estimated word count, brief bio, list of publishing credits. Send SASE or IRC. Responds in 2 months to queries. No simultaneous submissions. No email submissions.

Terms Publishes ms 18 months after acceptance. Book catalog and ms guidelines free Ms guidelines online.

UNIVERSITY OF WISCONSIN PRESS

1930 Monroe Street, 3rd Floor, Madison WI 53711. E-mail: uwiscpress@uwpress.wisc.edu. Website: www.wisc.edu/wisconsinpress. **Contact:** Raphael Kadushin, senior acquisitions editor. Publishes hardcover originals, paperback originals and paperback reprints. **Published 5-8 debut authors within the last year.** Averages 98 total titles, 15 fiction titles/year. Member, AAUP Distributes titles through ads, reviews, catalog, sales reps, etc.

Imprints Terrace Books, Library of American Fiction, Library of World Fiction.

Needs Gay/lesbian, historical, lesbian, mystery, regional (Wisconsin), short story collections. Recently published *A Friend of Kissinger*, by David Milofsky; *Beijing*, by Philip Gambone; *Latin Moon in Manhattan*, by Jaime Manrique.

How to Contact Does not accept unsolicited mss. Query with SASE or submit outline, 1-2 sample chapter(s), synopsis. Accepts queries by e-mail, mail, fax. Include estimated word count, brief bio. Send copy of ms and SASE. Direct your inquiries in the areas of autobiography/memoir, biography, classical studies, dance and performance studies, film, food, gender studies, GLBT studies, Jewish studies, Latino/a memoirs, and travel to Raphael Kadushin, kadushin@wisc.edu. Agented fiction 40%. Direct non-fiction inquiries in the areas of African studies, anthropology, environmental studies, human rights, Irish studies, Latin American studies, Slavic studies, Southeast Asian studies, and U.S. History to: Gwen Walker, gcwalker@uwpress.wisc.edu. See website for more contact info. Responds in 2 weeks to queries; 8 weeks to mss. Rarely comments on rejected mss.

Terms Pays royalty. Publishes ms 9-18 months after acceptance. Ms guidelines online.

VANHOOK HOUSE

925 Orchard St., Charleston WV 25302. E-mail: editor@vanhookhouse.com. Website: www.vanhookhouse.com. **Contact:** Jim Whyte, acquisitions, all fiction/true crime/military/war.

VÈHICULE PRESS

Box 125, Place du Parc Station, Montreal QC H2X 4A3 Canada. (514)844-6073. Fax: (514)844-7543. E-mail: vp@vehiculepress.com. Website: www.vehiculepress.com. **Contact:** Andrew Steinmetz, fiction editor. Estab. 1973. Small publisher of scholarly, literary and cultural books. Publishes trade paperback originals by Canadian authors only. Books: good quality paper; offset printing; perfect and cloth binding; illustrations. Average print order: 1,000-3,000. Averages 15 total titles/year.

Imprints Signal Editions (poetry), Esplande Books (fiction).

Needs Literary, regional, short story collections. Published *Optique*, by Clayton Bailey; *Seventeen Tomatoes: Tales from Kashmir*, by Jaspreet Singh; *A Short Journey by Car*, by Liam Durcan.

How to Contact Query first with SASE. We mostly publish Canadian atuhors. Responds in 4 months to queries.

Terms Pays 10-15% royalty on retail price. Average advance: $200-500. "Depends on press run and sales. Translators of fiction can receive Canada Council funding, which publisher applies for." Publishes ms 1 year after acceptance. Book catalog for 9 × 12 SAE with IRCs.

VERTIGO

Vertigo-DC Comics, 1700 Broadway, New York NY 10019. Website: www.dccomics.com.

Needs "We're seeking artists for all our imprints, including the DC Universe, Vertigo, WildStorm, Mad magazine, Minx, kids comics and more!"

How to Contact "The DC TALENT SEARCH program is designed to offer aspiring artists the chance to present artwork samples directly to the DC Editors and Art Directors. The process is simple: during your convention visit, drop off photocopied samples of your work and enjoy the show! No lines, no waiting. If the DC folks like what they see, a time is scheduled for you the following day to meet a DC representative personally and discuss your artistic interests and portfolio.: At this time, DC Comics does not accept unsolicited writing submissions by mail. See submission guidelines online.

VIKING CHILDREN'S BOOKS

345 Hudson St., New York NY 10014. E-mail: averystudiopublicity@us.penguingroup.com. Website: www.penguin.com. **Contact:** Catherine Frank. A division of Penguin Young Readers Group, "Viking Children's books publishes high quality trade hardcover books for children through young adults. These include fiction and nonfiction." Publishes hardcover originals. **Published some debut authors within the last year.** Averages 70 total titles/year. Promotes titles through press kits, institutional ads.

Needs Juvenile, picture books, young adult. Published *Just Listen*, by Sarah Dessen (novel); *Llama, Llama Red Pajama*, by Anna Dewdney (picture book).

How to Contact Only accepts solicited mss. Submit complete ms. Send SASE. Responds in 12 months to queries.

Terms Pays 5-10% royalty on retail price. Average advance: negotiable. Publishes ms 1 year after acceptance.

VINTAGE ANCHOR PUBLISHING

1745 Broadway, New York NY 10019. E-mail: vintageanchorpublicity@randomhouse.com. Website: www.randomhouse.com. **Contact:** Furaha Norton, editor. The Knopf Publishing Group, A Division of Random House, Inc. Publishes trade paperback originals and reprints.

Needs Literary, mainstream/contemporary, short story collections. Published *Snow Falling on Cedars*, by Guterson (contemporary); *Martin Dressler*, by Millhauser (literary).

How to Contact *Agented submissions only.* Accepts simultaneous submissions. No electronic submissions.
Terms Pays 4-8% royalty on retail price. Average advance: $2,500 and up. Publishes ms 1 year after acceptance.

VIZ MEDIA LLC

P.O. Box 77010, 295 Bay Street, San Francisco CA 94133. (415)546-7073. E-mail: evelyn.dubocq@viz.com. Website: www.viz.com. "VIZ Media, LLC is one of the most comprehensive and innovative companies in the field of manga (graphic novel) publishing, animation and entertainment licensing of Japanese content. Owned by three of Japan's largest creators and licensors of manga and animation, Shueisha Inc., Shogakukan Inc., and Shogakukan-Shueisha Productions, Co., Ltd., VIZ Media is a leader in the publishing and distribution of Japanese manga for English speaking audiences in North America, the United Kingdom, Ireland, and South Africa and is a global ex-Asia licensor of Japanese manga and animation. The company offers an integrated product line including magazines such as SHONEN JUMP and SHOJO BEAT, graphic novels, and DVDs, and develops, markets, licenses, and distributes animated entertainment for audiences and consumers of all ages."
Needs VIZ Media is currently accepting submissions and pitches for original comics. Keep in mind that all submissions must be accompanied by a signed release form.
How to Contact Accepts queries by snail mail.

THE WATERBROOK MULTNOMAH PUBLISHERS GROUP.

12265 Oracle Blvd. Suite 200, Colorado Springs CO 80921. 719-590-4999. Fax: 719-590-8977. Website: www.waterbrookmultnomah.com. **Contact:** Steve Cobb, president. Midsize independent publisher of evangelical fiction and nonfiction. Publishes hardcover and trade paperback originals. Books: perfect binding. Average print order: 15,000. Averages 75 total titles/year.

- Multnomah Books has received several Gold Medallion Book Awards from the Evangelical Christian Publishers Association.

Imprints Multnomah Books ("Christian living and popular theology books"); Multnomah Fiction ("Changing lives through the power of story"); Multnomah Gift ("Substantive topics with beautiful, lyrical writing").
Needs Adventure, historical, literary, mainstream/contemporary, mystery, religious (inspirational, religious mystery/suspense, religious thriller, religious romance), romance (contemporary, historical), science fiction, spiritual, suspense. Published *A Name of Her Own*, by Jane Kirkpatrick (historical); *Women's Intuition*, by Lisa Samson (contemporary); *Thorn in My Heart*, by Liz Curtis Higgs (historical).
How to Contact Does not accept unsolicited mss. *Agented submissions only.* Accepts simultaneous submissions.
Terms Pays royalty. Publishes ms 11 months after acceptance. Ms guidelines online.

WHITE MANE KIDS

P.O. Box 708, Shippensburg PA 17257. (717)532-2237. Fax: (717)532-6110. E-mail: marketing@whitemane.com. Website: www.whitemane.com. **Contact:** Editor. Publishes hardcover originals and paperback originals.
Needs Children's/juvenile (historical), young adult (historical). Published *Anybody's Hero: Battle of Old Men & Young Boys*, by Phyllis Haslip; *Crossroads at Gettysburg*, by Alan Kay.
How to Contact Accepts unsolicited mss. Query with SASE. Accepts queries by fax, mail. Include estimated word count, brief bio, summary of work and marketing ideas. Send SASE for return of ms or send a disposable ms and SASE for reply only. Responds in 1 month to queries; 3-4 months to mss. Accepts simultaneous submissions. Rarely comments on rejected mss.
Terms Pays royalty. Publishes ms 12-18 months after acceptance. Ms guidelines for #10 SASE.

WILD CHILD PUBLISHING

PO Box 4897, Culver City CA 90231. (310) 721-4461. Website: www.wildchildpublishing.com. **Contact:** Marci Baun, editor-in-chief (genres not covered by other editors); Faith Bicknell-Brown, managing editor (horror and romance); S.R. Howen, editor (science fiction and non-fiction). Wild Child Publishing is a small, independent press that started out as a magazine in September 1999. We are known for working with newer/unpublished authors and editing to the standards of NYC publishers. Publishes paperback originals, e-books. Format: POD printing; perfect bound. Average print order: 50-200. Debut novel print order: 50. **Published 12 new writers last year.** Plans 10 debut novels this year. Averages 12 fiction titles/year. Member EPIC. Distributes/promotes titles through Ingrams and own website, Mobipocket Kindle, Amazon, and soon with Fictionwise. Freya's Bower already distributed with through Fictionwise.

- Was named a Top 101 Writers' Web sites in 2005.

Imprints Freya's Bower.

Needs Adventure, children's/juvenile, erotica for Freya's Bower only, ethnic/multicultural, experimental, fantasy, feminist, gay, historical, horror, humor/satire, lesbian, literary, mainstream, military/war, mystery/suspense, New Age/mystic, psychic/supernatural, romance, science fiction, short story collections, thriller/espionage, western, young adult/teen (fantasy/science fiction). Multiple anthologies planned. Writers should submit material per our submissions guidelines. Published *Weirdly: A Collection of Strange Tales*, by Variety(horror/psychological thriller); *Quits: Book 2: Devils*, by M.E. Ellis (horror, psychological thriller, paranormal).

How to Contact Query with outline/synopsis and 1 sample chapter. Accepts queries by e-mail only. Include estimated word count, brief bio. Responds to queries in 2-4 weeks. Often critiques/comments on rejected mss. Responds to mss in 2-4 weeks.

Terms Sends pre-production galleys to author. Ms published 2-4 months after acceptance. Pays royalties 10-40%. Book catalogs on website.

WILDE PUBLISHING

P.O. Box 4581, Alburquerque NM 87196. Fax: (419)715-1430. E-mail: wilde@unm.edu. Website: www.unm.edu/~wilde. **Contact:** Josiah Simon, Dusty, McGowan, and David Wilde. Publishes hardcover and paperback originals. **Published 6 debut authors within the last year.**

Needs Children's/juvenile, fantasy (sword and sorcery), historical, literary, military/war, mystery, psychic/supernatural, romance, short story collections, thriller/espionage, western, young adult. Published *Scuttlebut*, by David Wilde (military) and *Harry The Magician*, by Dusty McGowan (children).

How to Contact Does not accept unsolicited mss. Query with SASE. Accepts queries by e-mail, fax, mail. Include brief bio, list of publishing credits. Send SASE for return of ms or send a disposable ms and SASE for reply only. Accepts submissions on disk. No simultaneous submissions.

Terms Pay depends on grants/awards. Publishes ms 12 after acceptance. Ms guidelines for #10 SASE.

THE WILD ROSE PRESS

P.O. Box 708, Adams Basin NY 14410. (585) 752-8770. E-mail: queryus@thewildrosepress.com; rpenders@thewildrosepress.com. Website: http://www.thewildrosepress.com. **Contact:** Nicole D'Arienzo, editor. "The American Rose line publishes stories about the French and Indian wars; Colonial America; the Revolutionary War; the war of 1812; the War Between the States; the Reconstruction era; the dawn of the new century. These are the struggles at the heart of the American Rose story. The central romantic relationship is the key driving force, set against historically accurate backdrop. These stories are for those who long for the courageous heroes and heroines who fought for their freedom and settled the new world; for gentle southern belles with spines of steel and the gallant gentlemen who sweep them away. This line is wide open for writers with a love of American history." Publishes paperback originals, reprints, and e-books in a POD format. Published 5 debut authors last year. Publishes approximately 10 fiction titles/year. Member:

EPIC, Romance Writers of America. Distributes/promotes titles through major distribution chains, including Ingrams, Baker & Taylor, Sony, Kindle, Amazon.com, as well as smaller and online distributors.

Imprints American Rose (American historical romance), Nicole D'Arienzo, editor; Climbing Roses (YA), Jill Williamson, editor; and more.

Needs contemporary, futuristic/time travel, gothic, historical, regency, romantic suspense, erotic and paranormal. Plans several anthologies "in several lines of the company in the next year, including Cactus Rose, Yellow Rose, American Rose, Black Rose, and Scarlet Rose." Has published *Enemy of the King*, by Beth Trissel; *An April to Remember*, by Lauri Robinson; and *Hero For Hire*, by Sheridon Smythe.

How to Contact *Does not accept unsolicited mss*. Send query letter with outline and synopsis of up to 5 pages. Accepts all queries by e-mail. Include estimated word count, brief bio, and list of publishing credits. Agented fiction less than 1%. Responds to queries in 4 weeks; to mss in 12 weeks. Does not consider simultaneous submissions. Always comments on rejected mss.

Terms Pays royalty of 7% minimum; 35% maximum. Sends prepublication galleys to author. Time between acceptance and publication is approximately 1 year. Writer's guidelines available on website.

WILSHIRE BOOK CO.

9731 Variel Ave., Chatsworth CA 91311-4315. (818)700-1522. Fax: (818)700-1527. E-mail: mpowers@mpowers.com. Website: www.mpowers.com. **Contact:** Melvin Powers, publisher, editorial department. "You are not only what you are today, but also what you choose to become tomorrow." Looking for adult fables that teach principles of psychological growth. Publishes trade paperback originals and reprints. **Published 7 debut authors within the last year.** Averages 25 total titles/year. Distributes titles through wholesalers, bookstores and mail order. Promotes titles through author interviews on radio and television.

Needs Adult allegories that teach principles of psychological growth or offer guidance in living. Minimum 25,000 words. Published *The Princess Who Believed in Fairy Tales*, by Marcia Grad; *The Knight in Rusty Armor*, by Robert Fisher; *The Dragon Slayer With a Heavy Heart*, by Marcia Powers.

How to Contact Accepts unsolicited mss. Query with SASE or submit 3 sample chapter(s), synopsis or submit complete ms. Accepts queries by e-mail. Responds in 2 months to queries. Accepts simultaneous submissions.

Terms Pays standard royalty. Offers advance. Publishes ms 6 months after acceptance. Ms guidelines online.

WINDRIVER PUBLISHING, INC.

72 N. Windriver Lane, Silverton ID 83867-0446. E-mail: info@windriverpublishing.com. Website: www.windriverpublishing.com. Estab. 2003. Publishes hardcover originals and reprints, trade paperback originals, mass market originals. Averages 8 total titles/year.

Needs Adventure, fantasy, historical, humor, juvenile, literary, military/war, mystery, religious, science fiction, spiritual, suspense, young adult.

How to Contact WindRiver Publishing does not accept manuscript submissions via e-mail. Authors interested in publishing with us should review our Publishing Guidelines page. Responds in 2 months to queries; 4-6 months to mss. Accepts simultaneous submissions. Website is used to accept manuscripts for all four imprints of WindRiver Publishing, Inc.: Silverton House Publishing, Mapletree Publishing Company, WindRiver Publishing, Trumpet Media. These four imprints each deal with non-overlapping genres. Whether you submit online or as hard copy, the imprint will be determined based on the genre you assign for your project.

Terms Pays 8-15% royalty on wholesale price. Publishes ms 12-18 months after acceptance. Ms guidelines online.

WOODLEY MEMORIAL PRESS

English Dept., Washburn University, Topeka KS 66621. E-mail: karen.barron@washburn.edu. Website: www.washburn.edu/reference/woodley-press. **Contact:** Kevin Rabas, Acquisitions Editor. English Dept., Washburn University, Topeka KS 66621. Website: www.washburn.edu/reference/woodley-press. **Contact:** Kevin Rabas, acquisitions editor at Dept. of English, Box 4019, Emporia State University, 1200 Commercial St., Emporia KS 66801. Estab. 1980. "Woodley Memorial Press is a small, nonprofit press which publishes novels and fiction collections by Kansas writers only; by 'Kansas writers' we mean writers who reside in Kansas or have a Kansas connection." Publishes paperback originals.

Needs Literary, mainstream/contemporary, short story collections. Published KS Notable Book winner *Great Blues*, by Steve Semken; *The Trouble With Campus Security*, by G.W. Clift; and *Loading The Stone*, by Harley Elliot.

How to Contact Accepts unsolicited mss. Accepts queries by e-mail. Responds in 2 weeks to queries; 6 months to mss. Often comments on rejected mss.

Terms Publishes ms 1 year after acceptance. Ms guidelines online.

WRITERS DIRECT

4330 Kauai Beach Dr., Suite G21, Lihue HI 96766. (808)822-7449. Fax: (808)822-2312. E-mail: sales@hshawaii.com. Website: www.bestplacesonearth.com. **Contact:** Rob Sanford, editor. "Small independent publishing house founded and run by published authors." Publishes hardcover and paperback orginals and reprints. Books: recycled paper; digital printing; perfect binding; illustrations.

Needs Adventure, humor, literary, mainstream/contemporary, new age/mystic, regional (Hawaii), inspirational, religious mystery/suspense, religious thriller, thriller/espionage.

How to Contact Send 1st chapter and synopsis. Include estimated word count, why author wrote book and marketing plan. Send SASE for return of ms or send a disposable ms and SASE for reply only. Responds in 1 month to queries; 3 months to mss. Accepts simultaneous submissions. Sometimes comments on rejected mss.

Terms Pays 15-35% royalty.

YELLOW SHOE FICTION SERIES

P.O. Box 25053, Baton Rouge LA 70894-5053. Website: www.lsu.edu/lsupress. **Contact:** Michael Griffith, Editor. Literary fiction series. Averages 2 titles/year.

Needs Literary. "Looking first and foremost for literary excellence, especially good manuscripts that have fallen through the cracks at the big commercial presses. I'll cast a wide net." Published *If the Heart is Lean*, by Margaret Luongo; new and upcoming titles from Allison Amend, Josh Russell, Chris Bachelder.

How to Contact Does not accept unsolicited mss. Accepts queries by mail, Attn: John Easterly. No electronic submissions.

Terms Pays royalty. Offers advance. Ms guidelines online.

Contests & Awards

In addition to honors and, quite often, cash prizes, contests and awards programs offer writers the opportunity to be judged on the basis of quality alone without the outside factors that sometimes influence publishing decisions. New writers who win contests may be published for the first time, while more experienced writers may gain public recognition of an entire body of work.

Listed here are contests for almost every type of fiction writing. Some focus on form, such as short stories, novels or novellas, while others feature writing on particular themes or topics. Still others are prestigious prizes or awards for work that must be nominated, such as the Pulitzer Prize in Fiction. Chances are, no matter what type of fiction you write, there is a contest or award program that may interest you.

SELECTING & SUBMITTING TO A CONTEST

Use the same care in submitting to contests as you would sending your manuscript to a publication or book publisher. Deadlines are very important, and where possible, we've included this information. At times contest deadlines were only approximate at our press deadline, so be sure to write, call or look online for complete information.

Follow the rules to the letter. If, for instance, contest rules require your name on a cover sheet only, you will be disqualified if you ignore this and put your name on every page. Find out how many copies to send. If you don't send the correct amount, by the time you are contacted to send more, it may be past the submission deadline. An increasing number of contests invite writers to query by e-mail, and many post contest information on their Web sites. Check listings for e-mail and website addresses.

One note of caution: Beware of contests that charge entry fees that are disproportionate to the amount of the prize. Contests offering a $10 prize, but charging $7 in entry fees, are a waste of your time and money.

If you are interested in a contest or award that requires your publisher to nominate your work, it's acceptable to make your interest known. Be sure to leave the publisher plenty of time, however, to make the nomination deadline.

AEON AWARD

c/o 8 Bachelor's Walk, Dublin 1 Ireland. +353 1 8730177. E-mail: fraslaw@yahoo.co.uk. Website: www.albedo1.com. **Contact:** Frank Ludlow, event coordinator. "We aim to encourage new writers into the genre and to encourage existing writers to push at their boundaries" Annual. Competition/award for short stories. Prize: First prize €1,000, second €200, and third €100. The top three stories are guaranteed publication in Albedo One. Categories: any speculative genre, "i.e. fantasy, SF horror or anything in between or unlcassifiable (like slipstream)." A short list is drawn up by the Albedo One editorial team and the final decision is made by renowned author Ian Watson. Entry Fee: € 7. Pay via website. Guidelines available in December. Accepts inquiries by fax, e-mail. The best stories of each submission period are shortlisted for the grand prize. **The competition is run in four quarterly periods with probable deadlines of the end of March, June, September and November.** Check the website for definite dates. Entries should be unpublished. Award open to "anyone with € 7 and a burning desire to be the best." Length: under 8,000 words. Cover letter should include name, address, e-mail, word count, novel/story title. It is essential the story is marked so it can be identified with its author. Writers may submit own work. "As the contest is initially judged by the editorial staff of Albedo One, I think it is fair to say that choices will be influenced by the individual tastes of these people. You can see what they like in Albedo One on a regular basis. I wish I could say there is a certain formula, but we pick the best stories submitted to us and although there can often be little evidence of genre influence visible on the page, we always feel that the stories are informed by the author's genre sensibilities. In other words, we like stories by authors who used to like/write science fiction. Confused? Pick up an issue of the magazine and check it out." Results announced within two months of the final deadline. Winners notified by e-mail, and at event/banquet. Winners in 2007 were announced at Eurocon in Copenhagen. Results made available to entrants on website.

AHWA FLASH & SHORT STORY COMPETITION

c/o Post Office, Elphinstone, Victoria 3448 Australia. E-mail: competitions@australianhorror.com. Website: australianhorror.com. **Contact:** David Carroll, competitions officer. "To showcase the diversity and talent of writers of horror fiction." Annual. Competition/award for short stories and flash fiction. The writers of the winning story in each category will receive an engraved plaque, plus the stories will be published om Midnight Echo, the magazine of the Australian Horror Writers Association at paying rates. "We're after horror stories, tales that frighten, yarns that unsettle us in our comfortable homes. All themes in this genre will be accepted, from the well-used (zombies, vampires, ghosts etc) to the highly original, so long as the story is professional and well written. No previously published entries will be accepted—all tales must be an original work by the author. Stories can be as violent or as bloody as the storyline dictates, but those containing gratuitous sex or violence will not be considered. Please check your entries for spelling and grammar mistakes and follow standard submission guidelines (eg, 12 point font, Ariel, Times New Roman, or Courier New, one and a half spacing between lines, with title and page number on each page)." There are 2 categories: short stories (1,001 to 8,000 words) and flash fiction (less than 1,000 words). Writers may submit to one or both categories, but entry is limited to 1 story per author per category. Please send your submission as an attached rtf or doc to competitions@australianhorror.com. Alternatively, contact us to arrange postal submissions. Entry free for AHWA members; for non-members, $5 for flash, $10 for short story. Payment can be made via our secure Paypal option using ahwa@australianhorror.com. Alternatively, contact us and we can arrange other payment methods (eg, direct debit). Cheques will not be accepted due to the cost associated with banking them. Full guidelines available from on website. Accepts inquiries by e-mail. Entry deadline each year is May 31. Results announced July/August.

ALABAMA STATE COUNCIL ON THE ARTS INDIVIDUAL ARTIST FELLOWSHIP

201 Monroe St., Montgomery AL 36130-1800. (334) 242-4076, ext. 224. Fax: (334) 240-3269. E-mail: randy.shoults@arts.alabama.gov. Website: www.arts.state.al.us. **Contact:** Randy Shoults,

literature program manager. "To recognize the achievements and potential of Alabama writers." Judged by independent peer panel. Guidelines available in January. For guidelines, fax, e-mail, visit website. Accepts inquiries by fax, e-mail and phone. "Two copies of the following should be submitted: a résumé and a list of published works with reviews, if available. A minimum of 10 pages of poetry or prose, but no more than 20 pages. Please label each page with title, artist's name and date. If published, indicate where and the date of publication." Winners announced in June and notified by mail. List of winners available for SASE, fax, e-mail or visit website. No entry fee. Deadline: March 1 and applications can be submitted by egrant. Competition receives 25 submissions annually. Two-year residency required.

ALLIGATOR JUNIPER'S NATIONAL WRITING CONTEST

Alligator Juniper, 220 Grove Ave, Prescott AZ 86301. (928) 350-2012. Fax: (928) 776-5137. E-mail: aj@prescott.edu. Website: http://www.prescott.edu/highlights/alligator_juniper/index.html. **Contact:** Jeff Fearnside, managing editor. Annual. Competition/award for short stories. Prize: Winner receives $500 and publication. Finalists are published and receive copies. Categories: fiction, creative nonfiction, poetry. "All entries are read and discussed by advanced writing students at Prescott College enrolled in the Alligator Juniper practicum class. This class is overseen by two faculty members, each of whom is a working writer in the genres of poetry, fiction and creative nonfiction. All entrants receive a personal letter from one of our staff regarding the status of their submission. We usually inform in late January. The individual attention we devote to each manuscript takes time. We appreciate your patience." Entry fee: $15 (includes copy of issue). Make checks payable to Alligator Juniper. Accepts inquiries by fax, e-mail, phone. **Submission period is May 1-October 1.** Entries should be unpublished. Deadline: **October 15 through December 15 (postmark).** Anyone may enter contest. Length: Prose should be under 30 pages; poetry 5 poems or less. Cover letter should include name, address, phone, e-mail, word count, novel excerpt/story title. Writers may submit own work. "Send us your best work; we often don't know what we're looking for until we read it. Historically, winning work has grappled poetically and honestly with issues of race, sexuality, patriotism, politics, the environment, and language itself. We publish work that is both long and short, traditional and experimental in its approaches. Our editorial staff is composed of savvy, college-aged readers; do your best to wow us." Results announced January. Winners notified by phone, by e-mail. Winners announced December. Results made available to entrants with SASE, by fax, by e-mail, on website.

AMERICAN LITERARY REVIEW SHORT FICTION AWARD

P.O. Box 311307, University of North Texas, Denton TX 76203-1307. (940)565-2755. E-mail: americanliteraryreview@gmail.com. Website: www.engl.unt.edu/alr. American Literary Review, P.O. Box 311307, University of North Texas, Denton TX 76203-1307. (940)565-2755. Website: www.engl.unt.edu/alr. "To award excellence in short fiction." Prize: $1,000 and publication. Judged by rotating outside writer. Past judges have included Marly Swick, Antonya Nelson and Jonis Agee. Entry fee: $15. For guidelines, send SASE or visit website. Accepts inquiries by email and phone. Deadline: September 1. Entries must be unpublished. Contest open to anyone not affiliated with the University of North Texas. "Only solidly crafted, character-driven stories will have the best chance for success." Winners announced and notified by mail and phone in February. List of winners available for SASE.

AMERICAN MARKETS NEWSLETTER SHORT STORY COMPETITION

1974 46th Ave., San Francisco CA 94116. E-mail: sheila.oconnor@juno.com. Award is "to give short story writers more exposure." Accepts fiction and nonfiction up to 2,000 words. Entries are eligible for cash prizes and all entries are eligible for worldwide syndication whether they win or not. Send double-spaced manuscripts with your story/article title, byline, word count and address on the first page above your article/story's first paragraph (no need for separate cover page). There is no limit to the number of entries you may send. Prize: 1st Place: $300; 2nd Place: $100; 3rd

Place: $50. Judged by a panel of independent judges. Entry fee: $12 per entry; $20 for 2; $25 for 3; $30 for 4; $5 each entry thereafter. For guidelines, send SASE, fax or e-mail. **Deadline: June 30 and December 31.** Contest offered biannually. Published and unpublished stories are actively encouraged. Add a note of where and when previously published. Open to any writer. "All kinds of fiction are considered. We especially want women's pieces—romance, with a twist in the tale—but all will be considered." Results announced within 3 months of deadlines. Winners notified by mail if they include SASE.

ART AFFAIR SHORT STORY AND WESTERN SHORT STORY CONTESTS

P.O. Box 54302, Oklahoma City OK 73154. E-mail: artaffair@aol.com. Website: www.shadetreecreations.com. **Contact:** Barbara Shepherd. The annual Art Affair Writing Contests include (General) Short Story, Mystery Short Story, and Western Short Story categories and offer 1st Prize: $50 and certificate; 2nd Prize: $25 and certificate; and 3rd Prize: $15 and certificate in all three categories. Honorable Mention certificates will be awarded at the discretion of the judges. Open to any writer. All short stories must be unpublished. Multiple entries accepted in both categories with separate entry fees for each. Submit original stories on any subject and timeframe for general Short Story category, submit original mystery (or suspense) short stories for Mystery Short Story, and submit original western stories for Western Short Story - word limit for all entries is 5,000 words. (Put word count in the upper right-hand corner of first page; mark "Mystery" or"Western" if applicable). All ms. must be double-spaced on 8½x11 white paper. Type title of short story on first page and headers on following pages. Include cover page with writer's name, address, phone number, and ms title. Do not include SASE; mss will not be returned. Guidelines available on website. **Deadline: October 1, 2009 (postmark). Entry Fee:** $5 per story. Make check payable to Art Affair. Winners' list will be published on the Art Affair website in December.

ARTIST TRUST FELLOWSHIP AWARD

1835 12th Ave, Seattle WA 98122. (209) 467-8734 ext 9. Fax: (206) 467-9633. Website: artisttrust.org. **Contact:** Monica Miller, director of programs. "Artist Trust Fellowship awards practicing professional Washington State artists of exceptional talent and demonstrated ability." Annual. Prize: $7,500. "The Fellowship awards are multidisciplinary awards. The categories for 2011 are Literary, Music, Media and Craft. Accepted genres for Literary are: poetry, fiction, graphic novels, experimental works, creative non-fiction, screen plays, film scripts and teleplays." Receives about 175 entries per category. Entries are judged by work samples as specified in the guidelines. Winners are selected by a multidisciplinary panel of artists and arts professionals. No entry fee. Guidelines available around December, please check website. Accepts inquiries by e-mail, phone. Submission period is January-February. **Deadline is approximately the 4th Friday of January.** website should be consulted for the exact date. Entries can be unpublished or previously published. Washington State residents only. Length: up to 15 pages for poetry, fiction, graphic novels, experimental works and creative non-fiction, and up to 20 pages for screen plays, film scripts and teleplays. All mss must be typed with a 12-pnt font size or larger and cannot be single spaced (except for poetry). Include artist statement and resume with name, address, phone, e-mail, and novel/story title. "The Fellowship awards are highly competitive. Please follow guidelines with care." Results announced in the spring. Winners notified by mail. Results made available to entrants on website.

THE ART OF MUSIC ANNUAL WRITING CONTEST

The Art of Music, Inc., P.O. Box 85, Del Mar CA 92014-0085. (619) 884-1401. Fax: (858) 755-1104. E-mail: info@theartofmusicinc.org. Website: www.theartofmusicinc.org. **Contact:** Elizabeth C. Axford. Offered annually. Categories are: essay, short story, poetry, song lyrics, and illustrations for cover art. All writings must be on music-related topics. The purpose of the contest is to promote the art of music through writing. Acquires one-time rights. All entries must be accompanied by an entry form indicating category and age; parent signature is required of all writers under age 18. Poems may be of any length and in any style; essays and short stories should not exceed five double-spaced, typewritten pages. All entries shall be previously unpublished (except poems and song lyrics) and the original work of the author. Guidelines and entry form for SASE, on website or by e-mail. Prize: Cash, medal, certificate, publication in the anthology titled The Art of Music: A Collection of Writings, and copies of the book. Judged by a panel of published poets, authors and songwriters. Entry fee: $20 fee. Inquiries accepted by e-mail, phone. **Deadline: June 30.** Short stories should be no longer than five pages typed and double spaced. Open to any writer. "Make sure all work is fresh and original. Music-related topics only." Results announced October 31. Winners notified by mail. For contest results, send SASE or visit website.

AWP INTRO JOURNALS PROJECT

One University Drive, Bluffton OH 45817-2104. E-mail: awp@gmu.edu. Website: www.awpwriter.org. **Contact:** Susan Streeter Carpenter. "This is a prize for students in AWP member university creative writing programs only. Authors are nominated by the head of the creative writing department. Each school may nominate no more than one work of nonfiction, one work of short fiction and three poems. Nominations must be accompanied by a cover letter from the program director, which verifies that the enclosed nominations are by students currently enrolled in the university's creative writing program. In the letter, the program must provide a permanent address for each nominated student." Winners will be contacted in the spring of 2010. Each will receive an award letter, publication in a participating journal, and a $100 cash honorarium. Winning works will appear in the fall or winter issues of Hayden's Ferry Review, Mid-American Review, Colorado Review, Puerto del Sol, Controlled Burn, Quarterly West, Tampa Review, and Artful Dodge. Categories: Short stories, nonfiction and poetry. Judged by AWP. No entry fee. **Deadline: first week of December** (postmark). Entries must be unpublished. Open to students in AWP Member University Creative Writing Programs only. Accepts inquiries by e-mail, fax and phone. Guidelines available for SASE or on website. Results announced in Spring. Winners notified by mail in Spring. For contest results, send SASE or visit website.

BARD FICTION PRIZE

P.O. Box 5000, Annandale-on-Hudson NY 12504-5000. (845)758-7087. Fax: (845)758-7043. E-mail: bfp@bard.edu. Website: www.bard.edu/bfp. **Contact:** Irene Zedlacher. The Bard Fiction Prize is intended to encourage and support young writers of fiction to pursue their creative goals and to provide an opportunity to work in a fertile and intellectual environment. Prize: $30,000 cash award and appointment as writer-in-residence at Bard College for 1 semester. Judged by committee of 5 judges (authors associated with Bard College). No entry fee. Cover letter should include name, address, phone, e-mail and name of publisher where book was previously published. Guidelines available by SASE, fax, phone, e-mail or on website. Deadline: July 15. Entries must be previously published. Open to US citizens aged 39 and below. Accepts inquiries by fax, e-mail and phone. Results announced by October 15. Winners notified by phone. For contest results, e-mail or visit website.

BEST LESBIAN EROTICA

BLE 2010, 31-64 21st St., #319, Long Island City NY 11106. E-mail: kwarnockble@gmail.com. **Contact:** Kathleen Warnock, series editor. Categories: Novel excerpts, short stories, other prose; poetry will be considered but is not encouraged. No entry fee. Include cover page with author's name, title of submission(s), address, phone, fax, e-mail. All submissions must be typed and double-spaced. You may submit double-sided copies. Length: 5,000 words. You may submit 2 different pieces of work. Submit 2 hard copies of each submission. Will only accept e-mail copies if the following conditions apply: You live outside of North America or Europe, the cost of postage would be prohibitive from your home country, the post office system in your country is dreadful (U.S. does not count); the content of your submission may be illegal to send via postal mail in your home country. Accepts both previously published and unpublished material, but does not accept simultaneous submissions to another annual erotica anthology. Open to any writer. All submissions must include SASE or an e-mail address for response. If no e-mail address, then please include SASP. No mss will be returned.

BINGHAMTON UNIVERSITY JOHN GARDNER FICTION BOOK AWARD

P.O. Box 6000, Binghamton NY 13902. (607)777-2713. Fax: (607)777-2408. E-mail: cwpro@binghamton.edu. Website: english.binghamton.edu/cwpro. **Contact:** Maria Mazziotti Gillan, director. Award's purpose is "to serve the literary community by calling attention to outstanding books of fiction." Prize: $1,000. Categories: novels and short story collections. Judged by "rotating outside judges." No entry fee. Entry must have been published in book form with a minimum press run of 500. Each book submitted must be accompanied by an application form, available online or send SASE to above address. Submit three copies of the book; copies will not be returned. Publishers may submit more than one book for prize consideration. **Deadline: March 1**. Entries must have appeared in print between January 1 and December 31 of the year preceding the award. Open to any writer. Results announced in Summer. Winners notified by e-mail or phone. For contest results, send SASE or visit website.

IRMA S. AND JAMES H. BLACK AWARD

610 W. 112th St., New York NY 10025. (212)875-4450. Fax: (212)875-4558. E-mail: kfreda@bankstreet.edu. Website: bankstreet.edu/childrenslibrary/irmasimontonblackhome.html. **Contact:** Kristin Freda, award director.

JAMES TAIT BLACK MEMORIAL PRIZES

Department of English Literature, University of Edinburgh, David Hume Tower, George Square, Edinburgh Scotland EH8 9JX United Kingdom. (44-13) 1650-3619. Fax: (44-13) 1650-6898. E-mail: s.strathdee@ed.ac.uk. Website: www.englit.ed.ac.uk/jtbinf.htm. **Contact:** Sheila Strathdee, Department of English Literature. "Two prizes each of £10,000 are awarded: one for the best work of fiction, one for the best biography or work of that nature, published during the calendar year January 1 to December 31." Judged by professors of English Literature with the assistance of teams of postgraduate readers. No entry fee. Accepts inquiries by fax, e-mail, phone. **Deadline: December 1.** Entries must be previously published. "Eligible works are those written in English and first published or co-published in Britain in the year of the award. Works should be submitted by publishers." Open to any writer. Winners notified by phone, via publisher. Contact department of English Literature for list of winners or check website.

THE BRIDPORT PRIZE

P.O. Box 6910, Dorset DT6 9QB United Kingdom. +44 (0)1308 428 333. E-mail: frances@bridportprize.org.uk. Website: www.bridportprize.org.uk. **Contact:** Frances Everitt, administrator. Award to "promote literary excellence, discover new talent." Prize: £5,000 sterling; £1,000 sterling; £500 sterling, plus various runners-up prizes and publication of approximately 13 best stories and 13 best poems in anthology. Categories: short stories and poetry and flash fiction. Judged by 1 judge for fiction (in 2010, Zoë Heller) and 1 judge for poetry (in 2010, Michael Laskey). 2010 introduced a new category for flash fiction. £1,000 sterling first prize for the best short, short story of under 250 words. Entry fee: £6 sterling for poems, £7 for fiction, and £5 for flash fiction. **Deadline: June 30.** Entries must be unpublished. Length: 5,000 maximum for short stories; 42 lines for poetry, and 250 words for flash fiction.

BURNABY WRITERS' SOCIETY CONTEST

6584 Deer Lake Ave., Burnaby BC V5G 3T7 Canada. E-mail: info@bws.bc.ca. Website: www.bws.bc.ca. Blogsite: http:burnabywritersnews.blogspot.com. Offered annually for unpublished work. Open to all residents of British Columbia. Categories vary from year to year. Send SASE for current rules. Purpose is to encourage talented writers in all genres. Prize: 1st Place: $200; 2nd Place: $100; 3rd Place: $50; and public reading. Entry fee: $5. Guidelines available by e-mail, for SASE or on website. Accepts inquiries by e-mail. Deadline: May 31. Results announced in September. Winners notified by mail, phone, e-mail. Results available for SASE or on website and blog.

THE CAINE PRIZE FOR AFRICAN WRITING

51a Southwark St., London SE1 1RU United Kingdom. E-mail: info@caineprize.com. Website: www.caineprize.com. **Contact:** Nick Elam, administrator. Annual award for a short story (3,000-10,000 words) by an African writer. "An 'African writer' is normally taken to mean someone who was born in Africa, who is a national of an African country, or whose parents are African, and whose work has reflected African sensibilities." Entries must have appeared for the first time in the 5 years prior to the closing date for submissions, which is January 31 each year. Publishers should submit 6 copies of the published original with a brief cover note (no pro forma application). "Please indicate nationality or passport held." Prize: £10,000. Judged by a panel of judges appointed each year. No entry fee. Cover letter should include name, address, phone, e-mail, title and publication where story was previously published. Deadline: January 31. Entries must be previously published. Word length: 3,000-10,000 words. Manuscripts not accepted. Entries must be submitted by publishers not authors. Results announced in mid-July. Winners notified at event/banquet. For contest results, send fax, e-mail or visit our website.

JOHN W. CAMPBELL MEMORIAL AWARD FOR BEST SCIENCE FICTION NOVEL OF THE YEAR

English Department, University of Kansas, Lawrence KS 66045. (785)864-3380. Fax: (785)864-1159. E-mail: jgunn@ku.edu. Website: www.ku.edu/~sfcenter. **Contact:** James Gunn, professor and director. Award to "honor the best science fiction novel of the year." Prize: Trophy. Winners receive an expense-paid trip to the university to receive their award. Their names are also engraved on a permanent trophy. Categories: novels. Judged by a jury. No entry fee. Deadline: see website. Entries must be previously published. Open to any writer. Accepts inquiries by e-mail and fax. "Ordinarily publishers should submit work, but authors have done so when publishers would not. Send for list of jurors." Results announced in July. For contest results, send SASE.

CRAZYHORSE FICTION PRIZE

College of Charleston, Dept. of English, 66 George St., Charleston SC 29424. (843)953-7740. E-mail: crazyhorse@cofc.edu. Website: crazyhorse.cofc.edu. **Contact:** Editors.

THE CRUCIBLE POETRY AND FICTION COMPETITION

Barton College, College Station, Wilson NC 27893. (252)399-6343. E-mail: crucible@barton.edu. Website: www.barton.edu/academics/english.crucible.htm. **Contact:** Terrence L. Grimes, editor. Offered annually for unpublished short stories. Prize: $150 (1st Prize); $100 (2nd Prize) and publication in Crucible. Competition receives 300 entries. Categories: Fiction should be 8,000 words or less. Judged by in-house editorial board. No entry fee. Entries should be submitted electronically. Guidelines available online. **Deadline: April**. Open to any writer. "The best time to submit is December through April." Results announced in late summer. Winners notified by e-mail. For contest rules, see website.

DEAD OF WINTER

E-mail: editors@toasted-cheese.com. Website: www.toasted-cheese.com. The contest is a winter-themed horror fiction contest with a new topic each year. Topic and word limit announced Nov. 1. The topic is usually geared toward a supernatural theme. Prize: Amazon gift certificates in the amount of $20, $15 and $10; publication in Toasted Cheese. Also offers honorable mention. Categories: short stories. Judged by two Toasted Cheese editors who blind judge each contest. Each judge uses her own criteria to rate entries. No entry fee. Cover letter should include name, address, e-mail, word count and title. **Deadline: December 21.** Entries must be unpublished. Word limit varies each year. Open to any writer. Guidelines available in November on website. Accepts inquiries by e-mail. "Follow guidelines. Write a smart, original story. We have further guidelines on the website." Results announced January 31. Winners notified by e-mail. List of winners on website.

DELAWARE DIVISION OF THE ARTS

820 N. French St., Wilmington DE 19801. (302)577-8278. Fax: (302)577-6561. Website: www.artsdel.org. **Contact:** Kristin Pleasanton, art and artist services coordinator. Award "to help further careers of emerging and established professional artists." For Delaware residents only. Prize: $10,000 for masters; $6,000 for established professionals; $3,000 for emerging professionals. Judged by out-of-state, nationally recognized professionals in each artistic discipline. No entry fee. Guidelines available after May 1 on website. Accepts inquiries by e-mail, phone. Expects to receive 25 fiction entries. Deadline: August 1. Open to any Delaware writer. Results announced in December. Winners notified by mail. Results available on website. "Follow all instructions and choose your best work sample."

EATON LITERARY AGENCY'S ANNUAL AWARDS PROGRAM

P.O. Box 49795, Sarasota FL 34230. (941)366-6589. Fax: (941)365-4679. E-mail: eatonlit@aol.com. Website: www.eatonliterary.com. **Contact:** Richard Lawrence, Vice President. Offered biannually for unpublished mss. Prize: $2,500 (over 10,000 words); $500 (under 10,000 words). Judged by an independent agency in conjunction with some members of Eaton's staff. No entry fee. Guidelines available for SASE, by fax, e-mail, or on website. Accepts inquiries by fax, phone and e-mail. Deadline: **March 31** (mss under 10,000 words); **August 31** (mss over 10,000 words). Entries must be unpublished. Open to any writer. Results announced in April and September. Winners notified by mail. For contest results, send SASE, fax, e-mail or visit website.

THE VIRGINIA FAULKNER AWARD FOR EXCELLENCE IN WRITING

201 Andrews Hall, P.O. Box 880334, Lincoln NE 68588-0334. (402)472-0911. Fax: (402)472-9771. E-mail: jengelhardt2@unl.edu. Website: prairieschooner.unl.edu. **Contact:** Hilda Raz, editor. Offered annually for work published in Prairie Schooner in the previous year. Prize: $1,000. Categories: short stories, essays, novel excerpts and translations. Judged by Editorial Board. No entry fee. Guidelines for SASE or on website. Accepts inquiries by fax and e-mail. "We only read mss from September 1 through May 1." Winning entry must have been published in Prairie Schooner in the year preceeding the award. Results announced in the Spring issue. Winners notified by mail in February or March.

GEORGETOWN REVIEW PRIZE

400 East College St., Box 227, Georgetown KY 40324. (502) 863-8308. Fax: (502) 863-8888. E-mail: gtownreview@georgetowncollege.edu. Website: http://georgetownreview.georgetowncollege.edu. **Contact:** Steve Carter, editor. "Contest for short stories, poetry and creative nonfiction." Annual. Competition/award for short stories. Prize: $1,000 and publication; runners-up receive publication. Receives about 400 entries for each category. Entries are judged by the editors. Entry fee: $10 for first entry, $5 for each one thereafter. Make checks payable to Georgetown Review. Guidelines available in July. Accepts inquiries by e-mail. **Entry deadline is Nov. 15th, 2009.** Entries should be unpublished. Contest open to anyone except family, friends of the editors. Cover letter, ms should include name, address, phone, e-mail, novel/story title. Writers may submit own work. "We're just looking to publish quality work. Sometimes our contests are themed, so check the website for details." Results announced Feb or March. Winners notified by e-mail. Results made available to entrants with SASE.

GIVAL PRESS NOVEL AWARD

P.O. Box 3812, Arlington VA 22203. (703)351-0079. E-mail: givalpress@yahoo.com. Website: www.givalpress.com. **Contact:** Robert L. Giron, Publisher. "To award the best literary novel." Annual. Prize: $3,000 (USD), publication and author's copies. Categories: literary novel. Receives about 100-120 entries per category. Final judge is announced after winner is chosen. Entries read anonymously. Entry fee: $50 (USD). Make checks payable to Gival Press, LLC. Guidelines with SASE, by phone, by e-mail, on website, in journals. Accepts inquiries by e-mail. **Deadline: May 30 of each year.** Entries should be unpublished. Open to any author who writes original work in English. Length: 30,000-100,000 words. Cover letter should include name, address, phone, e-mail, word count, novel title. Only the title and word count should appear on the actual ms. Writers may submit own work. "Review the types of mss Gival Press has published. We stress literary works." Results announced late fall of same year. Winners notified by phone. Results made available to entrants with SASE, by e-mail, on website.

☐ GIVAL PRESS SHORT STORY AWARD

P.O. Box 3812, Arlington VA 22203. (703)351-0079. E-mail: givalpress@yahoo.com. Website: www.givalpress.com. **Contact:** Robert L. Giron, Publisher. "To award the best literary short story." Annual. Prize: $1,000 and publication on website. Category: literary short story. Receives about 100-150 entries per category. Entries are judged anonymously. Entry fee: $25. Make checks payable to Gival Press, LLC. Guidelines available online, via e-mail, or by mail. Deadline: Aug. 8th of every year. Entries must be unpublished. Open to anyone who writes original short stories in English. Length: 5,000-15,000 words. Include name, address, phone, e-mail, word count, title on cover letter. Only the title and word count should be found on ms. Writers may submit their own ficiton. "We publish literary works." Results announced in the fall of the same year. Winners notified by phone. Results available with SASE, by e-mail, on website.

GLIMMER TRAIN'S FAMILY MATTERS

1211 NW Glisan St. Suite 207, Portland OR 97209. (503)221-0836. Fax: (503)221-0837. Website: www.glimmertrain.org. **Contact:** Susan Burmeister-Brown, co-editor. Offered twice a year for unpublished stories about family. Word count should not exceed 12,000. Prize: 1st place: $1,200, publication in Glimmer Train Stories, and 20 copies of that issue; 1st/2nd runners up receive $500/$300, respectively, and possible publication in Glimmer Train Stories. Entry fee: $15. **Contest open the months of April and October.** Open to all writers. Make your submissions online at www.glimmertrain.org. Winners will be notified and results will be posted two months after the close of each competition.

☐ GLIMMER TRAIN'S FICTION OPEN

1211 NW Glisan St., Suite 207, Portland OR 97209. (503)221-0836. Fax: (503)221-0837. Website: www.glimmertrain.com. **Contact:** Susan Burmeister-Brown, co-editor. Offered quarterly for unpublished stories on any theme. Word count should not exceed 20,000. Prize: 1st place: $2,000, publication in Glimmer Train Stories, and 20 copies of that issue; 1st/2nd runners-up: $1,000/$600 respectively, and possible publication in Glimmer Train Stories. Entry fee: $20/story. **Contest open during the months of March, June, September and December.** Make your submissions online (www.glimmertrain.org). Winners will be called and results announced two months after the close of each contest.

☐ GLIMMER TRAIN'S SHORT STORY AWARD FOR NEW WRITERS

1211 NW Glisan St., Suite 207, Portland OR 97209. (503)221-0836. Fax: (503)221-0837. Website: www.glimmertrain.com. **Contact:** Susan Burmeister-Brown, co-editor. Offered quarterly for any writer whose fiction hasn't appeared in a nationally-distributed publication with a circulation over 5,000. Word count should not exceed 12,000 words. Stories must be previously unpublished. **Entry fee**: $15/story. **Contest open in the months of February, May, August, and November**. Make your submissions online at www.glimmertrain.org. Prize: First place: receives $1,200, publication in Glimmer Train Stories, and 20 copies of that issue. First/second runners-up receive $500/$300, respectively, and possible publication in Glimmer Train Stories. Winners will be called and results announced two months after the close of each contest. "We are very open to the work of new writers. Of the 100 distinguished short stories listed in a recent edition of the Best American Short

Stories, 10 first appeared in Glimmer Train Stories, more than in any other publication, including the New Yorker. 3 of those 10 were the author's first publication."

GLIMMER TRAIN'S VERY SHORT FICTION AWARD

1211 NW Glisan St., Suite 207, Portland OR 97209. (503)221-0836. Fax: (503)221-0837. Website: www.glimmertrain.com. **Contact:** Susan Burmeister-Brown, co-editor. Award to encourage the art of the very short story. "We want to read your original, unpublished, very short story—word count not to exceed 3,000 words." Prize: $1,200 and publication in Glimmer Train Stories and 20 author's copies (1st place); First/Second runners-up: $500/$300 respectively and possible publication. Entry fee: $15/story. **Contest open in the months of January and July**. Open to all writers. Make your submissions online at www.glimmertrain.org. Winners will be called and results announced two months after the close of each contest.

GRANTS FOR ARTIST'S PROJECTS

1835 12th Ave, Seattle WA 98122. (206) 467-8734. Fax: (206) 467-9633. E-mail: info@artisttrust.org. Website: www.artisttrust.org. **Contact:** Monica Miller, Director of Programs. "The GAP Program provides support for artist-generated projects, which can include (but are not limited to) the development, completion or presentation of new work." Annual. Prize: maximum of $1,500 for projects. Accepted are poetry, fiction, graphic novels, experimental works, creative non-fiction, screen plays, film scripts and teleplays. Entries are judged by work sample as specified in the guidelines. Winners are selected by a discipline-specific panel of artists and artist professionals. No entry fee. Guidelines available in May. Accepts inquiries by mail, phone. Submission period is May-June. **Deadline is approximately the 4th Friday of June.** Website should be consulted for exact date. Entries can be unpublished or previously published. Washington state residents only. Length: 8 pages max for poetry, fiction, graphic novels, experimental work and creative nonfiction; up to 12 pages for screen plays, film scripts and teleplays. All mss must be typed with a 12-point font size or larger and cannot be single-spaced (except for poetry). Include application with project proposal and budget, as well as resume with name, address, phone, e-mail, and novel/story title. "GAP awards are highly competitive. Please follow guidelines with care." Results announced in the fall. Winners notified by mail. Results made available to entrants by mail and on website.

GREAT LAKES COLLEGES ASSOCIATION NEW WRITERS AWARD

535 W. William, Suite 301, Ann Arbor MI 48103. (734)661-2350. Fax: (734)661-2349. E-mail: shackelford@glca.org. **Contact:** Greg Wegner. Award for first publication, one in each category of fiction, creative non-fiction and poetry. Writer must be nominated by publisher or can submit work if self-published. Prize: Winners are invited to tour the GLCA colleges. An honorarium of $500 will be guaranteed the author by each GLCA member college they visit. Judged by professors from member colleges. No entry fee. **Deadline: July 25, 2010 for 2011 competition**. Open to any writer. Submit 4 copies of the book to Greg Wegner. Guidelines available early 2010. Accepts inquiries by e-mail. Results announced in winter.

THE GRUB STREET BOOK PRIZE IN FICTION

160 Boylston Street, Boston MA 02116. (617) 695-0075. Fax: (617) 695-0075. E-mail: info@grubstreet.org. Website: grubstreet.org. **Contact:** Christopher Castellani, artistic director. "Supports writers who are publishing beyond their first or second, third, fourth (or beyond...) book, and who live outside of New England." Annual. Competition/award for short story collections, novels. Prize: Each winner receives a $1,000 honorarium and a Friday night reading/book party at Grub Street's event space in downtown Boston. The reading and party are co-sponsored by a local independent bookstore, which will sell books at the event. Winners will lead a two-hour informal craft class on a topic of their choice for a small group of aspiring Grub Street writers. Winners also invited as guest authors to *Muse and the Marketplace* literary conference. Grub Street provides accommodations for all time in Boston and covers all travel and meal expenses. Categories: Fiction, Poetry, and

Non-fiction. Different deadlines apply for each category. Entries are judged by a guest judge and committee of readers drawn from the Grub Street staff. Committee members negotiate their top picks at a meeting facilitated by the guest judge. **Entry fee: $10**. Send credit card information or make checks payable to Grub Street. Guidelines available in June. Accepts inquiries by fax, e-mail, phone. **Entry deadline is October 15th**. Entries should be previously published or under contract. Publication date must be in 2010 or 2011, and the hardcover or paperback original must be available to booksellers by the time of the winner's visit to Boston. Galleys may be submitted for the contest as long as the first edition is published by May 1, 2011. All applicants must have at least one previously published novel or short story collection (self-publication not eligible), and must not primarily reside in the following states: Massachusetts, Vermont, Maine, Connecticut, New Hampshire or Rhode Island. Cover letter should include name, address, phone, e-mail, novel/story title. Also include a curriculum vitae and a 500-word synopsis of the proposed craft class. Writers may submit own work. "Grub Street's top criterion is the overall literary merit of the work submitted, the award committee especially encourages writers publishing with small presses, writers of short story collections, and writers of color to apply. Grub Street also wants the award to benefit writers for whom a trip to Boston will likely expand their readership in a meaningful way. Please give careful thought to your proposal for the craft class, and please plan it as a 2-hour gathering for a group of 15 adult writers of mixed experience." Results announced 2-3 months after submission deadline. Previous winners: Alan Cheuse's *To Catch the Lightning*, Dinty W. Moore's *Between Panic and Desire*, and Rick Barot's *The Darker Fall*.

☐ LORIAN HEMINGWAY SHORT STORY COMPETITION

P.O. Box 993, Key West FL 33041-0993. (305)294-0320. E-mail: shortstorykw@gmail.com. Website: www.shortstorycompetition.com. **Contact:** Jeff Baker, co-director; Joanne Denning, contest development director. Award to "encourage literary excellence and the efforts of writers whose voices have yet to be heard." Competition for short stories. Prize: $1,000 (first prize), $500 (second prize), $500 (third prize), honorable mentions. *The Saturday Evening Post* will be in addition ot the first-place prize of $1,000. Judged by a panel of writers, editors and literary scholars selected by author Lorian Hemingway. Guidelines available in January for SASE, by e-mail or on website.

☐ ◙ HIGHLIGHTS FOR CHILDREN FICTION CONTEST

803 Church St., Honesdale PA 18431-1824. (570)253-1080. Fax: (570)251-7847. E-mail: eds@highlights-corp.com. Website: www.Highlights.com. **Contact:** Joëlle Dujardin, Associate Editor.

☐ TOM HOWARD/JOHN H. REID SHORT STORY CONTEST

(866)946-9748. Fax: (413)280-0539. E-mail: johnreid@mail.qango.com. Website: www.winningwriters.com. This award honors the best short stories, essays and other works of prose being written today." Annual. Prize: $3,000 (first prize), $1,000 (second prize), $400 (third prize), $250 (fourth prize). There will also be five High Distinction Awards of $200 each and six Most Highly Commended Awards of $150 each. The top ten entries will be published on the Winning Writers website and announced in Tom Howard Contest News and the Winning Writers Newsletter. Categories: All entries are judged in one category. "We received 1,641 entries for the 2009 contest." Judged by a former journalist and magazine editor, John H. Reid. Mr. Reid has judged literary contests for over 15 years. He has published several novels, a collection of poetry, a guide to winning literary contests, and 15 books of film criticism and movie history. He is assisted by Dee C. Konrad, a leading educator and published author, who served as Associate Professor of English at Barat College of DePaul University and dean of Liberal Arts and Sciences for the year 2000-2001. Entry fee: $15 per entry. Make checks payable to Winning Writers (U.S. funds only, please). Guidelines available in July on website. Prefers inquiries by e-mail. **Deadline: March 31, 2010.** "Both published and unpublished works are accepted. In the case of published work, the contestant must own the online publication rights." Open to all writers. Length: 5,000 words max per entry. Cover letter should include name, address, phone, e-mail, story title, place(s) where story was previously published (if any). Only the title should be on the actual ms. Writers may submit own work. "Read past winning entries at www.winningwriters.com/contests/tomstory/ts_pastwinners.php." Results announced September 15. Winners notified by e-mail. Results made available to entrants on website.

THE JULIA WARD HOWE/BOSTON AUTHORS AWARD

79 Moore Rd, Wayland MA 01778. (617) 783-1357. E-mail: bostonauthors@aol.com. Website: www.bostonauthorsclub.org. **Contact:** Alan Lawson. This annual award honors Julia Ward Howe and her literary friends who founded the Boston Authors Club in 1900. It also honors the membership over 111 years, consisting of novelists, biographers, historians, governors, senators, philosophers, poets, playwrights, and other luminaries. There are 2 categories: trade books and books for young readers (beginning with chapter books through young adult books). Works of fiction, nonfiction, memoir, poetry, and biography published in current year (2010 for 2011 prize) are eligible. Authors must live or have lived (college counts) within a 100-mile radius of Boston. Subsidized books, cook books and picture books are not eligible. No fee. **Deadline: January 15**. Prize: $1,000 in each category.

◙ INDIANA REVIEW ½ K (SHORT-SHORT/PROSE-POEM) CONTEST

BH 465/Indiana University, 1020 E. Kirkwood Ave., Bloomington IN 47405-7103. (812)855-3439. Fax: (812)855-4253. E-mail: inreview@indiana.edu. Website: www.indianareview.edu. **Contact:** Alessandra Simmons, editor. ICompetition for fiction and prose poems no longer than 500 words. Prize: $1,000 plus publication, contributor's copies and a year's subscription. All entries considered for publication. Judged by Indiana Review staff and outside judges. Entry fee: $15 fee for no more than 3 pieces (includes a year's subscription, two issues). Make checks payable to Indiana Review. **Deadline: June.** Entries must be unpublished. Guidelines available in March for SASE, by phone, e-mail, on website, or in publication. Length: 500 words, 3 mss per entry. Open to any writer. Cover letter should include name, address, phone, e-mail, word count and title. No identifying information on ms. "We look for command of language and form." Results announced in August. Winners notified by mail. For contest results, send SASE or visit website. See website for detailed guidelines.

❑ INDIANA REVIEW FICTION CONTEST

BH 465/Indiana University, 1020 E. Kirkwood Ave., Bloomington IN 47405-7103. (812)855-3439. Fax: (812)855-4253. E-mail: inreview@indiana.edu. Website: www.indianareview.org. **Contact:** Alessandra Simmons, editor. Contest for fiction in any style and on any subject. Prize: $1,000, publication in the Indiana Review and contributor's copies. Judged by Indiana Review staff and outside judges. Entry fee: $15 fee (includes a year's subscription). Deadline: Mid-October. Entries must be unpublished. Mss will not be returned. No previously published work, or works forthcoming elsewhere, are eligible. Simultaneous submissions accepted, but in the event of entrant withdrawal, contest fee will not be refunded. Length: 35 pages maximum, double spaced. Open to any writer. Cover letter must include name, address, phone number and title of story. Entrant's name should appear only in the cover letter, as all entries will be considered anonymously. Results announced January. Winners notified by mail. For contest results, send SASE. "We look for a command of language and structure, as well as a facility with compelling and unusual subject matter. It's a good idea to obtain copies of issues featuring past winners to get a more concrete idea of what we are looking for." See website for updates to guidelines.

INTERNATIONAL READING ASSOCIATION CHILDREN'S BOOK AWARDS

P.O. Box 8139, 800 Barksdale Rd., Newark DE 19714-8139. (302)731-1600, ext. 221. E-mail: exec@reading.org. "This award is for newly published authors of children's books who show unusual promise in the children's book field." Offered annually for an author's first or second published book in fiction and nonfiction in 3 categories: primary (preschool-age 8), intermediate (ages 9-13), and young adult (ages 14-17). Guidelines and deadlines for SASE. Prize: 6 awards of $1,000 each, and a medal for each category. Categories: fiction and nonfiction. No entry fee. The book will be considered one time during the year of first copyright in English. **Deadline: November 1**. For guidelines with specific information write to Executive Office, International Reading Association.

☐ E.M. KOEPPEL SHORT FICTION AWARD

P.O. Box 140310, Gainesville FL 32614-0310. Website: www.writecorner.com. **Contact:** Mary Sue Koeppel, editor. Award for short stories. Prize: $1,100 first prize, and $100 for Editors' Choices. Judged by award-winning writers. Entry fee: $15 first story, $10 each additional story. Make checks payable to Writecorner Press. Send 2 title pages: One with title only and one with title, name, address, phone, e-mail, short bio. Place no other identification of the author on the ms that will be used in the judging. Guidelines available for SASE or on website. Accepts inquiries by e-mail and phone. Expects 300+ entries. **Deadline: October 1-April 30.** Entries must be unpublished. Open to any writer. Winning stories published on website. Winners notified by mail, phone in July (or earlier). For results, send SASE or see website.

◙ LAWRENCE FOUNDATION PRIZE

0576 Rackham Building, Ann Arbor MI 48109-1070. (734)764-9265. E-mail: mqr@umich.edu. Website: www.umich.edu/~mqr. **Contact:** Vicki Lawrence, Managing Editor. Competition for short stories. Prize: $1,000. Judged by editorial board. No entry fee. No deadline. "An annual cash prize awarded to the author of the best short story published in Michigan Quarterly Review each year. Stories must be already published in Michigan Quarterly Review. This is not a competition in which manuscripts are read outside of the normal submission process." Guidelines available for SASE or on website. Accepts inquires by e-mail and phone. Results announced in December. Winners notified by phone or mail.

◙ LEAGUE OF UTAH WRITERS CONTEST

P.O. Box 1359, St. George UT 84771. (435)619-0331. E-mail: marybawriter@msn.com. Website: www.luwrite.com. **Contact:** Mary Barnes, membership chair. "The LUW Contest has been held since 1935 to give Utah writers an opportunity to get their works read and critiqued. It also encourages writers to keep writing in an effort to get published." Competition for short stories and novels. Offers cash prizes, see rules and guidelines for details. "Separate categories include speculative fiction, children's and teens' books, plus full-length book categories and more." Judged by professional authors, editors, and publishers. Entry fee: see guidelines. Guidelines available after February 15 for SASE or on website. Accepts inquiries by fax, e-mail and phone. Deadline: June 16. Entries must be unpublished. Open to any writer. "Read the contest rules and guidelines. Don't skim over them. Rules change and are revised from year to year. Don't forget to enclose your entry fee when mailing your entries." Winners announced at the Annual Writers Round-Up in September. List of winners available after September 30th for SASE.

N ◙ LESBIAN WRITERS FUND

116 E. 16th St., 7th flr, New York NY 10003. (212) 529-8021. E-mail: grants@astraeafoundation.org. Website: www.astraeafoundation.org. "This award is to support the work of emerging lesbian writers, and to acknowledge the contributions of established writers to our movement and culture." Annual. Competition/award for short stories, novels, story collections and poetry. Prize: First place awardees and two runners-up in the poetry and fiction categories will receive cash awards ($10,000 for awardee; $1,500 for runners-up). Each year a new set of judges reviews applications. An independent team of 2 judges in each genre selects the winners unanimously. The names of applicants will not be known to the judges until the decisions are made and all applicants have been notified by mail. All applications will be reviewed by a panel of lesbian writers who will remain anonymous until after the process has been completed. **Entry fee: $5**. Make checks payable to Astraea Lesbian Foundation for Justice. Accepts inquiries by e-mail, phone. **Entry deadline is July**

15, 2010. Entries may be published or unpublished. "To be eligible for an award from the Lesbian Writers Fund, you must satisfy all of the following: You are a lesbian-identified writer of poetry and/or fiction. Your submission is a poetry or fiction sample in English (non-fiction, screenplays, or plays are ineligible). You reside in the United States. Your submitted work includes some lesbian content (e.g. lesbian desire, identity, and/or perspective). You have published at least one piece of your writing (in any genre) in a newspaper, magazine, journal, anthology, or professional web publication (excluding personal or self-produced homepages). You have not published more than one book, including a chapbook, in any subject or genre with a publisher. If a second book has been accepted by a publisher, but has not been published yet, you are not eligible to apply. Published books or anthologies you have edited do not count towards the maximum. If awarded, you agree to be acknowledged publicly as a lesbian writer and agree to have your work publicized as Astraea sees fit. This may include an announcement or profile in our website and newsletter. All previous finalists, except for first place winners are eligible to apply. Past judges are excluded. Current staff and Board members of the Astraea Foundation are ineligible to apply." Write to grants@astraeafoundation.org for complete guidelines and application instructions. Submit up to 20 pages from a novel or a collection of short stories. Mss must be double spaced. "While there is no minimum page limit for fiction submissions, we recommend that you submit at least 10 pages, so that the judges gain a deeper understanding of your work." Name should not appear on ms; all pages must have identification number provided with application. Writers must submit own work. Results announced December 2010. Winners notified by mail.

LITERAL LATTÉ FICTION AWARD

200 East 10th Street Suite 240, New York NY 10003. (212)260-5532. E-mail: litlatte@aol.com. Website: www.literal-latte.com. **Contact:** Edward Estlin, contributing editor. Award "to provide talented writers with three essential tools for continued success: money, publication and recognition." Offered annually for unpublished fiction. Guidelines for SASE or on website. Open to any writer. Prize: $1,000 and publication in Literal Latté (first prize), $300 (second prize), $200 (third prize), up to 7 honorable mentions. Judged by the editors. Entry fee: $10/story. Guidelines available for SASE, by e-mail or on website. Accepts inquiries by e-mail. Deadline: January 15. Entries must be unpublished. Length: 8,000 words maximum. Guidelines available by e-mail or on website. Accepts inquiries by e-mail or on website. "Celebrating fifteen years of supporting great, new writers." Winners notified by phone. List of winners available in late April for SASE or by e-mail.

LONG STORY CONTEST, INTERNATIONAL

P.O. Box 383, Fox River Grove IL 60021. (847)639-9200. E-mail: wecspress@aol.com. Website: http://members.aol.com/wecspress. **Contact:** Frank E. Smith, publisher.

THE HUGH J. LUKE AWARD

201 Andrews Hall, P.O. Box 880334, Lincoln NE 68588-0334. (402)472-0911. Fax: (402)472-9771. E-mail: jengelhardt2@unl.edu. Website: prairieschooner.unl.edu/. **Contact:** Hilda Raz, editor-in-chief. Offered annually for work published in Prairie Schooner in the previous year. Prize: $250. Judged by editorial staff of Prairie Schooner. No entry fee. Work is nominated by the editorial staff. Guidelines for SASE or on website. Results announced in the Spring issue. Winners notified by mail in February or March.

WALTER RUMSEY MARVIN GRANT

274 E. First Ave., Suite 300, Columbus OH 43201. (614)466-3831. Fax: (614)728-6974. E-mail: ohioana@ohioana.org. Website: www.ohioana.org. **Contact:** Linda Hengst. Award "to encourage young, unpublished writers 30 years of age or younger." Competition for short stories. Prize: $1,000. **No entry fee.** Up to 6 pieces of prose may be submitted; maximum 60 pages, minimum 10 pages double-spaced, 12-point type. Deadline: January 31. Entries must be unpublished. Open to unpublished authors born in Ohio or who have lived in Ohio for a minimum of five years. Must

be 30 years of age or younger. Guidelines for SASE or on website. Winner notified in May or June. Award given in October.

DAVID NATHAN MEYERSON PRIZE FOR FICTION

Southwest Review, P.O. Box 750374, Dallas TX 75275-0374. (214) 768-1037. Fax: (214) 768-1408. E-mail: swr@smu.edu; tlewers@smu.edu. Website: www.smu.edu/southwestreview. **Contact:** Jennifer Cranfill, senior editor. Prize will consist of $1,000 and publication in the Southwest Review. Open to writers who have not yet published a first book of fiction. Submissions must be no longer than 8,000 words. $25 entry reading fee must accompany each submission. Work should be printed without the author's name. Name and address should appear only on the cover letter. Submissions will not be returned. For notification of the winning submission, include a S.A.S.E. Postmarked deadline for entry is May 1, 2010. Winner announced in August.

◎ A MIDSUMMER TALE

E-mail: editors@toasted-cheese.com; amtsummer10@toasted-cheese.com. Website: www.toasted-cheese.com. A Midsummer Tale is a summer-themed creative nonfiction contest. Topic changes each year. Send entries to: amtcontest10@toasted-cheese.com with the subject line: A Midsummer Tale Contest Entry. Stories must be about something that took place during the warm months of the year. The word range is 3,000—5,000 words. Check website for current focus and word limit. "We usually receive around 20 entries." Prize: First prize: $20 Amazon gift certificate, publication; Second prize: $15 Amazon gift certificate, publication; Third prize: $10 Amazon gift certificate, publication. Some feedback is often given to entrants. Categories: creative nonfiction. Judged by two Toasted Cheese editors who blind-judge each contest. Each judge has her own criteria for selecting winners. No entry fee. Guidelines, including the e-mail address to which you should send your entry and instructions for what to include and how to format, are available May 1 on website. Accepts inquiries by e-mail. **Deadline: June 21.** Entries must be unpublished. Open to any writer. Results announced July 31 on website. Winners notified by e-mail.

MILKWEED EDITIONS NATIONAL FICTION PRIZE

1011 Washington Ave. S., Suite 300, Minneapolis MN 55415. (612)332-3192. Fax: (612)215-2550. E-mail: editor@milkweed.org. Website: www.milkweed.org. **Contact:** The Editors. Annual award for unpublished works. "Looking for a novel, novella, or a collection of short stories. Manuscripts should be of high literary quality and must be double-spaced and between 150-400 pages in length. Milkweed Editions prefers submissions through its online submissions manager." Winner will be chosen from the mss Milkweed accepts for publication each year. All mss submitted to Milkweed will automatically be considered for the prize. Submission directly to the contest is no longer necessary. Must be written in English." Catalog available on request for $1.50. Guidelines for SASE or online. Prize: Publication by Milkweed Editions, and a cash advance of $5,000 against royalties agreed upon in the contractual arrangement negotiated at the time of acceptance. Judged by Milkweed Editions. No entry fee. Deadline: rolling. Entries must be unpublished. Previous winners: The Father Shore, by Matthew Eck; Visigoth, by Gary Amdahl; Crossing Bully Creek, by Margaret Erhart; Ordinary Wolves, by Seth Kantner; Roofwalker, by Susan Power—this is the caliber of fiction we are searching for." Winners are notified by phone.

◎ MILLION WRITERS AWARD

5603B W. Friendly Ave., Suite 282, Greensboro NC 27410. E-mail: editors@storysouth.com. Website: www.storysouth.com. **Contact:** Jason Sanford, editor emeritus. Contest "to honor and promote the best fiction published annually in online journals and magazines. The reason for the Million Writers Award is that most of the major literary prizes for short fiction (such as the O. Henry Awards) ignore Web-published fiction. This award aims to show that world-class fiction is being published online and to promote this fiction to the larger reading and literary community." Prize: Cash prize and publicity for the author and story. Categories: short stories. Judged by StorySouth judges. No entry fee. Cover letter should include e-mail address, word count, title and publication where story was previously published. Guidelines available in winter on website. Deadline: varies. Entries must be previously published. All stories must be 1,000 words or longer. Open to any writer. Results announced in spring on website. Winners notified by e-mail.

☐ NATIONAL WRITERS ASSOCIATION NOVEL WRITING CONTEST

10940 S. Parker Rd #508, Parker CO 80134. (303)841-0246. Fax: (303)841-2607. E-mail: anitaedits@aol.com; natlwritersassn@hotmail.com. Website: www.nationalwriters.com. **Contact:** Sandy Whelchel, director. Annual contest "to help develop creative skills, to recognize and reward outstanding ability, and to increase the opportunity for the marketing and subsequent publication of novel manuscripts." Prize: 1st place: $500; 2nd place: $300; 3rd place: $200. Judges' evaluation sheets sent to each entry with SASE. Categories: Open to any genre or category. Judged by editors and agents. Entry fee: $35. Opens December 1. **Deadline: April 1.** Entries must be unpublished. Length: 20,000-100,000 words. Open to any writer. Entry form and information available on Benefits section of website.

NELLIGAN PRIZE FOR SHORT FICTION

9105 Campus Delivery, Dept of English,, Colorado State University, Fort Collins CO 80523-9105. (970) 491-5449. E-mail: creview@colostate.edu. Website: http://coloradoreview.colostate.edu. **Contact:** Stephanie G'Schwind, editor/director. "The Nelligan Prize for Short Fiction was established in memory of Liza Nelligan, a writer, editor, and friend of many in Colorado State University's English Department, where she received her master's degree in literature in 1992. By giving an award to the author of an outstanding short story each year, we hope to honor Liza Nelligan's life, her passion for writing, and her love of fiction." Annual. Competition/award for short stories. Prize: $1,500 plus publication in Colorado Review. Receives approximately 900 stories. All entries are read blind by Colorado Review's editorial staff. Fifteen entries are selected to be sent on to a final judge. Entry fee: $15. Send credit card information or make checks payable to Colorado Review. Payment also accepted via PayPal link from website. Guidelines available in August 2009. Accepts inquiries by e-mail, phone. **Entry deadline March 12, 2011.** Entries must be unpublished and under 50 pages. Anyone may enter contest. Cover letter should include name, address, phone, e-mail, and novel/story title. "Authors should provide two cover sheets: one with name, address, phone, e-mail, and title of story, and a second with only the title of the story. Manuscripts are read 'blind,' so authors'names should not appear anywhere else in the manuscript." Writers may submit own work. "Successful short story writers are those who are reading contemporary short fiction (short story collections, literary magazines, annual prize anthologies), reading about the craft, and actively engaging in the practice of writing." Results announced in July of each year. Winners notified by phone. Results made available to entrants with SASE.

☐ NEW LETTERS LITERARY AWARDS

5101 Rockhill Rd., Kansas City MO 64110-2499. (816)235-1168. Fax: (816)235-2611. E-mail: newletters@umkc.edu. Award to "find and reward good writing from writers who need the recognition and support." Award has 3 categories (fiction, poetry and creative nonfiction) with 1 winner in each. Offered annually for previously unpublished work. Prize: 1st place: $1,500, plus publication; all entries are considered for publication. Judged by 2 rounds of regional writers (preliminary judging). Winners picked by an anonymous judge of national repute. Entry fee: $15/entry (includes year's subscription). Make checks payable to New Letters or send credit card information. **Deadline**: May 18. Entries must be unpublished. Open to any writer. Guidelines available in January for SASE, e-mail, on website and in publication. Cover letter should include name, address, phone, e-mail and title. Results announced in September. Winners notified by phone. For contest results, send SASE, e-mail or visit website.

☐ NEW MILLENNIUM WRITING AWARDS

Room M2, P.O. Box 2463, Knoxville TN 37901. (423)428-0389. Fax: (865)428-2302. E-mail: DonWilliams7@charter.net. Website: www.newmillenniumwritings.com/awards.html. **Contact:** Don Williams, editor. Award "to promote literary excellence in contemporary fiction." Offered twice annually for unpublished fiction, poetry, essays or nonfiction prose to encourage new fiction writers, poets and essayists and bring them to attention of publishing industry. Entrants receive an issue of NMW in which winners appear. Prize: $1,000 (fiction, poetry, nonfiction and short-short fiction, 1,000 words or less); winners published in NMW and on website. Judged by novelists and short story writers. Entry fee: $17 for each submission. **Deadline**: November 17 and June 17. Entries must be unpublished. Biannual competition. Length: 1,000-6,000 words. Guidelines available year round for SASE and on website at www.writingawards.com. "Provide a bold, yet organic opening line, sustain the voice and mood throughout, tell an entertaining and vital story with a strong ending. New Millennium Writings is a forward-looking periodical for writers and lovers of good reading. It is filled with outstanding poetry, fiction, essays and other speculations on subjects both topical and timeless about life in our astonishing times. Our pages brim with prize-winning essays, humor, illustration, writing advice and poetry from writers at all stages of their careers. First-timers find their work displayed alongside such well-known writers as Shel Silverstein, Khaled Hosseini, Ted Kooser, Lucille Clifton, John Updike, Sharyn McCrumb, Lee Smith, Norman Mailer, Madison Smartt Bell and Cormac McCarthy." Results announced October and April. Winners notified by mail and phone. All entrants will receive a list of winners, plus a copy of the annual anthology. Send letter-sized SASE with entry for list.

SEAN O'FAOLAIN SHORT STORY PRIZE

Frank O'Connor House, 84 Douglas Street, Cork Ireland. +353-214319255. E-mail: munsterlit@eircom.net. Website: www.munsterlit.ie. **Contact:** Patrick Cotter, artistic director. The Munster Literature Centre, "To reward writers of outstanding short stories" Annual. Prize: 1st prize €1500 (approx US $2,200); 2nd prize €500 (approx $730). Four runners-up prizes of €100 (approx $146). All six stories to be published in Southword Literary Journal. Receives about 700 entries. Guest judge reads each and every story anonymously. Judge in 20098 was Philip O Ceallaigh. Entry fee: $20. Make checks payable to Munster Literature Centre. Guidelines available in November. Accepts inquiries by e-mail, phone. **Entry deadline is July 31.** Entries should be unpublished. Anyone may enter contest. Length: 3,000 words max. Cover letter should include name, address, phone, e-mail, word count, novel/story title. No identifying information on ms. "Read previous winners in Southword Journal. " Results announced last day of Frank O'Connor International Short Story Festival in third weekend of September. Winners notified by mail or by e-mail. Results made available to entrants on website. 2010 Judge: Tania Hershman.

(ALICE WOOD MEMORIAL) OHIOANA AWARD FOR CHILDREN'S LITERATURE

274 E. First Ave., Suite 300, Columbus OH 43201. (614)466-3831. Fax: (614)728-6974. E-mail: ohioana@ohioana.org. Website: www.ohioana.org. **Contact:** Linda Hengst, executive director. Offered to an author whose body of work has made, and continues to make, a significant contribution to literature for children or young adults and through their work as a writer, teacher, or administrator and through their community service, interest in children's literature has been encouraged and children have become involved with reading. Nomination forms for SASE. Recipient must have been born in Ohio or lived in Ohio at least 5 years. Prize: $1,000. No entry fee. Deadline: December 31. Guidelines for SASE. Accepts inquiries by phone and e-mail. Results announced in August or September. Winners notified by letter in May. For contest results, call or e-mail.

$ ON THE PREMISES CONTEST

4323 Gingham Court, Alexandria VA 22310. (202) 262-2168. E-mail: questions@onthepremises.com. Website: www.onthepremises.com. **Contact:** Tarl Roger Kudrick or Bethany Granger, co-publishers. "On the Premises aims to promote newer and/or relatively unknown writers who can write what we feel are creative, compelling stories told in effective, uncluttered and evocative prose. Each contest challenges writers to produce a great story based on a broad premise that our editors supply as part of the contest." Competition/award for short stories. Prize: First prize is $140, Second prize $100, Third prize $70, and Honorable Mentions recieve $25. All prize winners are published in On the Premises magazine in HTML and PDF format. Entries are judged blindly by a panel of judges with professional editing and writing experience. No entry fee. Submissions are accepted by e-mail only. Contests held every four months. Check website for exact dates. Entries should be unpublished. Open to everyone. Length: min 1,000 words, max 5,000. Email should include name, address, e-mail, novel/story title, with ms attached. No name or contact info should be in ms. Writers may submit own work. "Write something compelling, creative and well-crafted. Above all, clearly use the contest premise. Results announced within 2 weeks of contest deadline. Winners notified via newsletter and with publication of On the Premises. Results made available to entrants on website, in publication.

☐ PEARL SHORT STORY PRIZE

3030 E. Second St., Long Beach CA 90803-5163. (562)434-4523. E-mail: Pearlmag@aol.com. Website: www.pearlmag.com. **Contact:** Marilyn Johnson, fiction editor. Award to "provide a larger forum and help widen publishing opportunities for fiction writers in the small press and to help support the continuing publication of Pearl." Prize: $250, publication in Pearl and 10 copies of the journal. Judged by the editors of Pearl: Marilyn Johnson, Joan Jobe Smith, Barbara Hauk. Entry fee: $10/story. Include a brief bio and SASE for reply or return of mss. Accepts simultaneous submissions, but asks to be notified if story is accepted elsewhere. **Submission period: April 1-May 31 (postmark).** Entries must be unpublished. "Although we are open to all types of fiction, we look most favorably on coherent, well-crafted narratives containing interesting, believable characters in meaningful situations." Length: 4,000 words maximum. Open to any writer. Guidelines for SASE or on website. Accepts queries by e-mail or fax. Results announced in September. Winners notified by mail. For contest results, send SASE, e-mail or visit website.

☐ KATHERINE ANNE PORTER PRIZE IN SHORT FICTION

1155 Union Cir., #311336, Denton TX 76203-5017. (940)565-2142. Fax: (940)565-4590. E-mail: karen.devinney@unt.edu. Website: web3.unt.edu/untpress. **Contact:** Laura Kopchick, Univ. of Texas at Arlington. Contest is offered annually. Prize is awarded to a collection of short fiction." No limitations to entrants. In years when the judge is announced, we ask that students of the judge not enter to avoid a perceived conflict. All entries should contain identifying material ONLY on the one cover sheet. Entries are read anonymously. Entries may include both unpublished and previously published stories, but collection as a whole has to be previously unpublished." Entry must be postmarked between May 1 and June 30. Entry fee: $25. Prize: $1000 and publication by University of North Texas Press (standard author contract). Judged by a different eminent writer each year. Some prefer to remain anonymous until conclusion of contest.

PRAIRIE SCHOONER BOOK PRIZE SERIES

201 Andrews Hall, P.O. Box 880334, Lincoln NE 68588-0334. Website: prairieschooner.unl.edu. **Contact:** Attn: Fiction. Annual. Competition/award for story collections. Prize: $3,000 and publication through the University of Nebraska Press for one book of short fiction and one book of poetry. Entry fee: $25. Make checks payable to Prairie Schooner. Deadline: Submissions are accepted between January 15 and March 15; check website for updates. Entries should be unpublished. Send full manuscript (the author's name should not appear anywhere on the ms). Send two cover pages: one listing only the title of the ms, and the other listing the title, author's name, address, telephone number, and e-mail address. Send SASE for notification of results. All mss will be recycled. You may also send an optional SAS postcard for confirmation of receipt of ms. Winners notified by phone, by e-mail. Results made available to entrants on website, in publication.

PRAIRIE SCHOONER GLENNA LUSCHEI AWARDS

201 Andrews Hall, P.O. Box 880334, Lincoln NE 68588-0334. (402)472-0911. Fax: (402)472-9771. E-mail: jengelhardt2@unl.edu. **Contact:** Hilda Raz, editor-in-chief. Awards to honor work published the previous year in Prairie Schooner, including poetry, essays and fiction. Prize: $250 in each category. Judged by editorial staff of Prairie Schooner. No entry fee. For guidelines, send SASE or visit website. "Only work published in Prairie Schooner in the previous year is considered." Work nominated by the editorial staff. Results announced in the Spring issue. Winners notified by mail in February or March.

PUSHCART PRIZE

P.O. Box 380, Wainscott NY 11975. (516)324-9300. Website: www.pushcartprize.com. **Contact:** Bill Henderson, president. Award to "publish and recognize the best of small press literary work." Prize: Publication in Pushcart Prize: Best of the Small Presses anthology. Categories: short stories, poetry, essays on any subject. No entry fee. Deadline: December 1. Entries must be previously published. Must have been published during the current calendar year. Open to any writer. Nomination by small press publishers/editors only.

THE RED HOUSE CHILDREN'S BOOK AWARD

2 Bridge Wood View, Horsforth,, Leeds, West Yorkshire LS18 5PE United Kingdom. E-mail: info@rhcba.co.uk. Website: www.redhousechildrensbookaward.co.uk. **Contact:** Sinead Kromer, national co-ordinator. (formerly The Children's Book Award), Owned and co-ordinated by the Federation of Children's Book Groups (Reg. Charity No. 268289). Purpose of the award is to enable children choose the best works of fiction published in the UK. Prize: trophy and silver bookmarks, portfolio of children's letters and pictures. Categories: Books for Younger Children, Books for Younger Readers, Books for Older Readers. No entry fee. **Closing Date is December 31.** Either author or publisher may nominate title. Guidelines available on website. Accepts enquiries by email and phone. Shortlist announced in February and winners announced in May. Winners notified at award ceremony and dinner at the Birmingham Botanical Gardens and via the publisher. For contest results, visit the website.

THE SCARS EDITOR'S CHOICE AWARDS

829 Brian Court, Gurnee IL 60031-3155. E-mail: editor@scars.tv. Website: http://scars.tv. **Contact:** Janet Kuypers, editor/publisher. Award "to showcase good writing in an annual book." Prize: publication of story/essay and 1 copy of the book. Categories: short stories. Entry fee: $18/short story. Deadline: revolves for appearing in different upcoming books as winners. Entries may be unpublished or previously published. Open to any writer. For guidelines, visit website. Accepts inquiries by e-mail. Length: "We appreciate shorter works. Shorter stories, more vivid and more real storylines in writing have a good chance." Results announced at book publication, online. Winners notified by mail when book is printed. For contest results, send SASE or e-mail or look at the contest page at website. "

THE SCENT OF AN ENDING™

P.O. Box 383, Fox River Grove IL 60021-0383. (847)639-9200. E-mail: scentofanending@aol.com. Website: http://thescentofanending.com. **Contact:** Frank Edmund Smith, publisher.

A. DAVID SCHWARTZ FICTION PRIZE

Dept. of English; University of Wisconsin-Milwaukee, Milwaukee WI 53201. (414) 229-4708. E-mail: info@creamcityreview.org. Website: www.creamcityreview.org. **Contact:** Jay P. Johnson, editor-in-chief. Purpose: "to recognize what the judge determines to be the most original, well-crafted work of previously unpublished short fiction. We are devoted to publishing memorable and energetic fiction, poetry, and creative non-fiction by new and established writers. Cream city review is particularly interested in publishing new voices; our reputation and long publishing history attracts well-known writers, often leading to unpublished writers appearing next to poet laureates. Our contest is open to all writers in all places, so long as the work is in English, original and previously unpublished." Annual. Competition/award for short stories. Prize: $1,000 plus publication in cream city review. Receives about 50-250 entries. Entries are judged by guest-judges; 2009 was Kelly Link; 2010: David Treuer. Entry fee: $15. Fee includes the award-winners issue. Make checks payable to cream city review. **Deadline: early December.** Guidelines available on website. Anyone may enter contest. Length: A work of more than 30 pages would have to be particularly impressive. Cover letter should include name, address, phone, e-mail, novel/story title. Also include on first page of ms. Writers may submit own work. "See aesthetic statement; read previous issues of cream city review to gain an understanding of the work we are interested in publishing; familiarize yourself with the work of the judge." Results announced at time of publication (April/May). Winners notified by e-mail. Winners announced February/March. Results made available to entrants with SASE, on website.

SCRIPTAPALOOZA TELEVISION WRITING COMPETITION

7775 Sunset Blvd., PMB #200, Hollywood CA 90046. (323)654-5809. E-mail: info@scriptapalooza.com. Website: www.scriptapaloozatv.com. "Seeking talented writers who have an interest in American television writing." Prize: $500, $200, and $100 in each category (total $3,200), production company consideration. Categories: sitcoms, pilots, one-hour dramas and reality shows. Entry fee: $40; accepts Paypal credit card or make checks payable to Scriptapalooza. **Deadline: April 30 and October 1 of each year.** Length: standard television format whether one hour, one-half hour or pilot. Open to any writer 18 or older. Guidelines available now for SASE or on website. Accepts inquiries by e-mail, phone. "Pilots should be fresh and new and easy to visualize. Spec scripts should stay current with the shows, up-to-date story lines, characters, etc." Winners announced February 15 and August 15. For contest results, visit website.

SHORT GRAIN WRITING CONTEST

Box 67, Saskatoon SK S7K 3K1 Canada. (306)244-2828. Fax: (306)244-0255. E-mail: grainmag@sasktel.net. Website: www.grainmagazine.ca. **Contact:** Mike Thompson, business administrator (inquiries only). The annual Short Grain Contest includes a category for poetry of any style up to 100 lines, offering 4 prizes with a first prize of $1,250 plus publication in Grain Magazine (see separate listing in Magazines/Journals). Each entry must be original, unpublished, not submitted elsewhere for publication or broadcast, nor accepted elsewhere for publication or broadcast, nor entered simultaneously in any other contest or competition for which it is also eligible to win a prize. Entries must be typed on 8½ x 11 paper. It must be legible. Faxed and/or electronic entries not accepted. No simultaneous submissions. A separate covering page must be attached to the text of your entry, and must provide the following information: writer's name, complete mailing address, telephone number, e-mail address, entry title, category name, and line count. An absolutely accurate word or line count is required. No identifying information on the text pages. Entries will not be returned. Include SASE for results only. Entry fee: $30 CAD; $36 US and international entrants; includes 1 year subscription to Grain Magazine. **Deadline: April 1.** Winning entries will be posted on the Grain Magazine website the following August.

SKIPPING STONES HONOR BOOK AWARDS

P.O. Box 3939, Eugene OR 97403-0939. Phone/fax: (541)342-4956. E-mail: editor@skippingstones.org. Website: www.skippingstones.org. **Contact:** Arun N. Toké. Annual awards since 1994 to "promote multicultural and/or nature awareness through creative writings for children and teens and their educators." Prize: honor certificates; seals; reviews; press release/publicity. Categories: short stories, novels, story collections, poetry and nonfiction. Judged by "a multicultural committee of teachers, librarians, parents, students and editors." Entry fee: $50. **Deadline: February 1.** Entries must be previously published. Open to published books and teaching resources that appeared in print during a two year period prior to the deadline date. Guidelines for SASE or e-mail and on website. Accepts inquiries by e-mail, fax, phone. "We seek authentic, exceptional, child/youth friendly books that promote intercultural, international, intergenerational harmony and understanding through creative ways. Writings that come out of your own experiences and cultural understanding seem to have an edge." Results announced in May each year. Winners notified through personal notifications, press release and by publishing reviews of winning titles in the summer issue. Attractive gold honor seals available for winners. For contest results, send SASE, e-mail or visit website.

SKIPPING STONES YOUTH AWARDS

P.O. Box 3939, Eugene OR 97403-0939. Phone/fax: (541)342-4956. E-mail: editor@skippingstones.org. Website: www.skippingstones.org. **Contact:** Arun N. Toké. Annual awards to "promote creativity as well as multicultural and nature awareness in youth." Prize: publication in the Autumn issue, honor certificate, subscription to magazine, plus 5 multicultural or nature books. Categories: short stories. Entry fee: $3/entry, make checks payable to Skipping Stones. Cover letter should include name, address, phone and e-mail. Deadline: June 20. Entries must be unpublished. Length: 1,000 words maximum. Open to any writer between 7 and 17. Guidelines available by SASE, e-mail or on website. Accepts inquiries by e-mail or phone. "Be creative. Do not use stereotypes or excessive violent language or plots. Be sensitive to cultural diversity." Results announced in the September-October issue. Winners notified by mail. For contest results, visit website. Everyone who enters receives the issue which features the award winners.

THE BERNICE SLOTE AWARD

201 Andrews Hall, P.O. Box 880334, Lincoln NE 68588-0334. (402)472-0911. Fax: (402)472-9771. E-mail: jengelhardt2@unlnotes.unl.edu. Website: prairieschooner.unl.edu. **Contact:** Hilda Raz, editor-in-chief. Offered annually for the best work by a beginning writer published in Prairie Schooner in the previous year. Prize: $500. Categories: short stories, essays and poetry. Judged by editorial staff of Prairie Schooner. No entry fee. For guidelines, send SASE or visit website. "Only work published in the journal during the previous year will be considered." Work is nominated by the editorial staff. Results announced in the Spring issue. Winners notified by mail in February or March.

KAY SNOW WRITING AWARDS

9045 SW Barbur Blvd., Suite 5A, Portland OR 97219. (503)452-1592. E-mail: wilwrite@teleport.com. Website: www.willamettewriters.com. **Contact:** Pat MacAodha. Contest offered annually to "offer encouragement and recognition to writers with unpublished submissions." Acquires right to publish excerpts from winning pieces 1 time in their newsletter. Prize: 1st place: $300; 2nd place: $150; 3rd place: $50; excerpts published in Willamette Writers newsletter, and winners acknowledged at banquet during writing conference. Student writers win $50 in categories for grades 1-5, 6-8, and 9-12. $500 Liam Callen Memorial Award goes to best overall entry. Entry fee: $15 fee; no fee for student writers. **Deadline: April 23.** Guidelines for #10 SASE, fax, by e-mail or on website. Accepts inquires by fax, phone and e-mail. Winners notified by mail and phone. For contest results, send SASE. Prize winners will be honored at the two-day August Willamette Writers' Conference. Press releases will be sent to local and national media announcing the winners, and excerpts from winning entries may appear in our newsletter.

SOUTH DAKOTA ARTS COUNCIL

711 E. Wells Avenue, Pierre SD 57501-3369. (605)773-3301. E-mail: sdac@state.sd.us. Website: www.artscouncil.sd.gov. **Contact:** Michael Pangburn, executive director. " Artist Fellowships ($5,000), Artist Project Grants (1,000- 2,000) and Artist Collaboration Grants (up to $6,000) are planned for fiscal 2011." No entry fee. Deadline: March 1. Open to South Dakota residents only. Students pursuing an undergraduate or graduate degree are ineligible. Guidelines and application available on website only. Applicants must submit signature page through the mail. All other

materials are submitted on line through an e-grant system. Application materials include current résumé no longer than 5 pages; appropriate samples of artistic work (see guidelines); up to 5 pages additional documentation; SASE with adequate postage for return of ms (if desired).

SOUTHWEST WRITERS (SWW) CONTESTS

3721 Morris St. NE, Suite A, Albuquerque NM 87111-3611. (505)265-9485. E-mail: Swwriters@juno.com. Website: www.southwestwriters.org. **Contact:** Contest Chair. The SouthWest Writers (SWW) Contest encourages and honors excellence in writing. There are 14 categories, including Christian Novel. (Please see rules on website for more details.) Prizes: Finalists in all categories are notified by mail and are listed on the SWW website with the title of their entry. First, second and third place winners in each category also receive cash prizes of $150, $100, and $50 (respectively), as well as a certificate of achievement. First place winners also compete for the $1,000 Storyteller Award. Winners will be honored at a contest awards banquet (date and time TBA). Categories: Mainstream/Literary Novel, Mystery/Suspense/Thriller/Adventure Novel, Science Fiction/Fantast/Horror Novel, Historical Novel, Middle Grade or YA Novel, Memoir Book, Memoir Article, Mainstream/Literary Article, Nonfiction Essay/Article, Personal Essay/Column, Nonfiction Book, Children's Fiction or Nonfiction Picture Book, Screenplay, Poetry. Judged by editors and agents (most from New York publishing houses) who are chosen by the contest chairs. Screening panel sends top 15 entries in each category to judges. Judges rank and critique the top three entries in each category. All entries may receive an optional written critique by a qualified consultant. Entry fee: Early deadline with no critique, $20 for members; $30 for nonmembers; Poetry $10 for first poem, $5 for each additional poem; late deadline, an additional $5. Early deadline with critique, $45 for members; $55 for nonmembers; late deadline, an additional $5. Cash, check (made out to SouthWest Writers), money order or credit card. No cover letter is required; send copy of the SWW Contest Entry Form. Personal information should not appear anywhere on ms. Please follow detailed instructions for submission in Category Specific Guidelines on website. Deadline: May 1; late deadline: May 15. Entries must be unpublished. Open to all writers from around the world. All entries should be submitted in English and follow standard ms format. "Entrants should read the SWW Contest Rules for complete information on the SWW website." Guidelines available in January by SASE, e-mail, on website or in SouthWest Sage SWW newsletter. Accepts inquiries by e-mail, phone. Mail SASE to receive rules, entry form in hard copy. Do not use certified mail to send submissions as they will be returned unopened; enclose an SASP to verify receipt.

SPUR AWARDS

1080 Mesa Vista Hall MSC06 3770, 1 University of New Mexico, Albuquerque NM 87131. (615)791-1444. E-mail: wwa@unm.edu. Website: www.westernwriters.org. **Contact:** Awards Coordinator. Purpose of award is "to reward quality in the fields of western fiction and nonfiction." Prize: Trophy. Categories: short stories, novels, poetry, songs, scripts and nonfiction. No entry fee. **Deadline: January 10.** Entries must be published during the contest year. Open to any writer. Guidelines available in Sept./Oct. for SASE, on website or by phone. Inquiries accepted by e-mail or phone. Results announced annually in Summer. Winners notified by mail. For contest results, send SASE.

THEODORE STURGEON MEMORIAL AWARD FOR BEST SHORT SF OF THE YEAR

English Department, University of Kansas, Lawrence KS 66045. (785)864-3380. Fax: (785)864-1159. E-mail: jgunn@ku.edu. Website: www.ku.edu/~sfcenter. **Contact:** James Gunn, professor and director. Award to "honor the best science fiction short story of the year." Prize: Trophy. Winners receive expense-paid trip to the University and have their names engraved on permanent trophy. Categories: short stories. Judged by jury. No entry fee. Entries must be previously published. Guidelines available in December by phone, e-mail or on website. Accepts inquiries by e-mail and fax. Entrants for the Sturgeon Award are by nomination only. Results announced in July. For contest results, send SASE.

SYDNEY TAYLOR MANUSCRIPT COMPETITION

204 Park St., Montclair NJ 07042. (201)862-0312. Fax: (201)862-0362. E-mail: aidonna@aol.com; stmacajl@aol.com. Website: www.jewishlibraries.org. **Contact:** Aileen Grossberg, coordinator.

TORONTO BOOK AWARDS

100 Queen St. West, City Hall, 10th Floor, West Tower, Toronto ON M5H 2N2 Canada. (416)392-8191. Fax: (416)392-1247. E-mail: bkurmey@toronto.ca. Website: www.toronto.ca/book_awards. **Contact:** Bev Kurmey, protocol officer. The Toronto Book Awards honor authors of books of literary or artistic merit that are evocative of Toronto. Annual award for short stories, novels, poetry or short story collections. Prize: $15,000. Each short-listed author (usually 4-6) receives $1,000 and the winner receives the remainder. Categories: No separate categories—novels, short story collections, books of poetry, biographies, history, books about sports, children's books—all are judged together. Judged by jury of five who have demonstrated interest and/or experience in literature, literacy, books and book publishing. No entry fee. Cover letter should include name, address, phone, e-mail and title of entry. Six copies of the entry book are also required. **Deadline: last week of March.** Entries must be previously published. Guidelines available in September on website. Accepts inquires by fax, e-mail, phone. Finalists announced in June; winners notified in September at a gala reception. Guidelines and results available on website.

WABASH PRIZE FOR FICTION

Department of English, 500 Oval Dr., Purdue University, West Lafayette IN 47907. E-mail: sycamore@purdue.edu. Website: www.sycamorereview.com. **Contact:** Mehdi Okasi, editor-in-chief. Submit one short story (not to exceed 10,000 words). No identifying information should appear on the manuscript. Include cover letter with all identifying information along with a word count. Include SASE to receive notification of the winner and check made payable to Sycamore Review for entry.

THE ROBERT WATSON LITERARY PRIZE IN FICTION AND POETRY

3302 Hall for Humanities, UNCG, P.O. Box 26170, Greensboro NC 27402-6170. (336)334-5459. E-mail: jlclark@uncg.edu. Website: www.greensbororeview.org. **Contact:** Jim Clark, editor. Offered annually for fiction (7,500 word limit) and poetry(3-5 poems). Sample issue for $8. Prize: $1,000 each for best short story and poem. Judged by editors of *The Greensboro Review*. Guidelines for SASE or on website. **Deadline: September 15. Fee:** $14. Entries must be unpublished. No submissions by e-mail. Open to any writer. Winners notified by mail, phone or e-mail. List of winners published in Spring issue. "All manuscripts meeting literary award guidelines will be considered for cash award as well as for publication in the Spring issue of The Greensboro Review."

WORLD FANTASY AWARDS

P.O. Box 43, Mukilteo WA 98275-0043. E-mail: sfexecsec@gmail.com. Website: www.worldfantasy.org. **Contact:** Peter Dennis Pautz, president. Awards "to recognize excellence in fantasy literature worldwide." Offered annually for previously published work in several categories, including life achievement, novel, novella, short story, anthology, collection, artist, special award-pro and special award-nonpro. Works are recommended by attendees of current and previous 2 years' conventions and a panel of judges. Prize: Bust of HP Lovecraft. Judged by panel. No entry fee. Guidelines available in December for SASE or on website. **Deadline: June 1.** Entries must be previously published. Published submissions from previous calendar year. Word length: 10,000-40,000 for novella, 10,000 for short story. "All fantasy is eligible, from supernatural horror to Tolkien-esque to sword and sorcery to the occult, and beyond." Cover letter should include name, address, phone, e-mail, word count, title and publications where submission was previously published, submitted to the address above and the panel of judges when they appear on the website. Results announced November 1 at annual convention. For contest results, visit website.

☐ WRITERS-EDITORS NETWORK 28TH ANNUAL INTERNATIONAL WRITING COMPETITION

P.O. Box A, Stratford NH 03590-0167. E-mail: contest@writers-editors.com. Website: www.writers-editors.com. **Contact:** Dana K. Cassell, executive director. Annual award "to recognize publishable talent." Divisions & Categories: Nonfiction (previously published article/essay/column/nonfiction book chapter; unpublished or self-published article/essay/column/nonfiction book chapter); Fiction (unpublished or self-published short story or novel chapter); Children's Literature (unpublished or self-published short story/nonfiction article/book chapter/poem); Poetry (unpublished or self-published free verse/traditional). Prize: 1st Place: $100, plus certificate; 2nd Place: $75, plus certificate; 3rd Place: $50, plus certificate. Honorable Mention certificates will be awarded in each category as warranted. Judged by editors, librarians and writers. Entry fee: $5 (active or new CNW/FFWA members) or $10 (nonmembers) for each fiction/nonfiction entry under 3,000 words; $10 (members) or $20 (nonmembers) for each entry of 3,000 words or longer; and $3 (members) or $5 (nonmembers) for each poem. Guidelines for SASE or on website. Accepts inquiries by e-mail, phone and mail. Deadline: March 15. Open to any writer. Results announced May 31. Winners notified by mail and posted on website. Results available for SASE or visit website.

☐ WRITERS' JOURNAL ANNUAL FICTION CONTEST

P.O. Box 394, Perham MN 56573. (218)346-7921. Fax: (218)346-7924. E-mail: writersjournal@writersjournal.com. Website: www.writersjournal.com. **Contact:** Leon Ogroske, editor (editor@writersjournal.com). Offered annually for previously unpublished fiction up to 5,000 words. Open to any writer. Prize: 1st Place: $500; 2nd Place: $200; 3rd Place: $100, plus honorable mentions. Prize-winning stories and selected honorable mentions published in WRITERS' Journal July/August issue. Entry fee: $15 reading fee. Guidelines and entry forms available for SASE and on website. Accepts inquiries by fax, e-mail and phone. **Deadline: January 30.** "Writer's name must not appear on submission. A separate cover sheet must include name of contest, title, word count and writer's name, address, phone and e-mail (if available)." Results announced in July/August. Winners notified by mail. A list of winners is published in July/August issue and posted on website or available for SASE. Receives fewer than 350 entries.

☐ ◙ WRITERS' JOURNAL ANNUAL ROMANCE CONTEST

P.O. Box 394, Perham MN 56573. (218)346-7921. Fax: (218)346-7924. E-mail: writersjournal@writersjournal.com. Website: www.writersjournal.com. **Contact:** Leon Ogroske, editor. Offered annually for previously unpublished works. Open to any writer. Prize: 1st place: $250; 2nd place: $100; 3rd place: $50, plus honorable mentions. Prize-winning stories and selected honorable mentions published in WRITERS' Journal. Entry fee: $7 fee. No limit on entries per person. Guidelines for SASE, by fax, phone, e-mail, on website and in publication. Accepts inquiries by fax, e-mail, phone. **Deadline: July 30.** Length: 2,000 words maximum. Open to any writer. Cover letter should include name, address, phone, e-mail, word count and title; just title on ms. Results announced in January/February issue. Winners notified by mail. Winners list published in WRITERS' Journal and on website. Enclose SASE for winner's list. Receives fewer than 150 entries.

◙ WRITERS' JOURNAL ANNUAL SCIENCE FICTION/FANTASY CONTEST

P.O. Box 394, Perham MN 56573. (218)346-7921. Fax: (218)346-7924. E-mail: writersjournal@writersjournal.com. Website: www.writersjournal.com. **Contact:** Leon Ogroske, editor. Annual contest for previously unpublished fiction up to 2,000 words. Open to any writer. Prize: 1st Place: $250; 2nd Place: $100; 3rd Place: $50, plus honorable mentions. Prize-winning stories and selected honorable mentions published in WRITERS' Journal. Entry fee: $7 reading fee. Guidelines available for SASE and on website. Accepts inquiries by fax, e-mail and phone. **Deadline: November 30.** Writer's name must not appear on submission. A separate cover sheet must include name of contest, title, word count and writer's name, address, phone and e-mail (if available)." Results announced in May/June. Receives fewer than 200 entries. Winners notified by mail. A list of winners is published in May/June issue and posted on website or available for SASE. Receives more than 250 entries.

◪ ZOETROPE SHORT STORY CONTEST

916 Kearny St., San Francisco CA 94133. (415)788-7500. E-mail: contests@all-story.com. Website: www.all-story.com. Zoetrope: All-Story, 916 Kearny St., San Francisco CA 94133. (415) 788-7500. Fax: (415) 989-7910. E-mail: contests@all-story.com. Website: www.all-story.com. **Contact:** Krista Halverson, managing editor. Annual contest for unpublished short stories. Prize: 1st place: $1,000; 2nd place: $500, 3rd place: $250; plus 7 honorable mentions. Judged by Elizabeth McCracken in 2008. Entry fee: $15. Guidelines for SASE, by e-mail, in publication, or on website. **The 2010 Short Fiction Contest opens July 1, 2010. Deadline: October 1.** Entries must be unpublished. Word length: 5,000 words maximum. Open to any writer. "Please mark envelope clearly 'short fiction contest'." For details, please visit the website this summer, or email us. Winners notified by phone or e-mail December 1. Results announced December 1. A list of winners will be posted on website and published in spring issue. The winning story will be published at the website as a special supplement to the spring issue.

Conferences & Workshops

Why are conferences so popular? Writers and conference directors alike tell us it's because writing can be such a lonely business—at conferences writers have the opportunity to meet (and commiserate) with fellow writers, as well as meet and network with publishers, editors and agents. Conferences and workshops provide some of the best opportunities for writers to make publishing contacts and pick up valuable information on the business, as well as the craft, of writing.

The bulk of the listings in this section are for conferences. Most conferences last from one day to one week and offer a combination of workshop-type writing sessions, panel discussions and a variety of guest speakers. Topics may include all aspects of writing from fiction to poetry to scriptwriting, or they may focus on a specific type of writing, such as those conferences sponsored by the Romance Writers of America (RWA) for writers of romance or by the Society of Children's Book Writers and Illustrators (SCBWI) for writers of children's books.

Workshops, however, tend to run longer—usually one to two weeks. Designed to operate like writing classes, most require writers to be prepared to work on and discuss their fiction while attending. An important benefit of workshops is the opportunity they provide writers for an intensive critique of their work, often by professional writing teachers and established writers.

Each of the listings here includes information on the specific focus of an event as well as planned panels, guest speakers and workshop topics. It is important to note, however, some conference directors were still in the planning stages for 2011 when we contacted them. If it was not possible to include 2011 dates, fees or topics, we have provided information from 2010 so you can get an idea of what to expect. For the most current information, it's best to check the conference website or send a self-addressed, stamped envelope to the director in question about three months before the date(s) listed.

FINDING A CONFERENCE

Many writers try to make it to at least one conference a year, but cost and location count as much as subject matter or other considerations when determining which conference to attend. There are conferences in almost every state and province and even some in Europe open to North Americans.

To find a conference based on the month in which it occurs, check out our Conference Index by Date at the back of this book.

LEARNING & NETWORKING

Besides learning from workshop leaders and panelists in formal sessions, writers at conferences also benefit from conversations with other attendees. Writers on all levels enjoy sharing insights. Often, a conversation over lunch can reveal a new market for your work or let you know which editors are most receptive to the work of new writers. You can find out about recent editor changes and about specific agents. A casual chat could lead to a new contact or resource in your area.

Many editors and agents make visiting conferences a part of their regular search for new writers. A cover letter or query that starts with "I met you at the Green Mountain Writers Conference," or "I found your talk on your company's new romance line at the Moonlight and Magnolias Writer's Conference most interesting . . ." may give you a small leg up on the competition.

While a few writers have been successful in selling their manuscripts at a conference, the availability of editors and agents does not usually mean these folks will have the time there to read your novel or six best short stories (unless, of course, you've scheduled an individual meeting with them ahead of time). While editors and agents are glad to meet writers and discuss work in general terms, usually they don't have the time (or energy) to give an extensive critique during a conference. In other words, use the conference as a way to make a first, brief contact.

SELECTING A CONFERENCE

Besides the obvious considerations of time, place and cost, choose your conference based on your writing goals. If, for example, your goal is to improve the quality of your writing, it will be more helpful to you to choose a hands-on craft workshop rather than a conference offering a series of panels on marketing and promotion. If, on the other hand, you are a science fiction novelist who would like to meet your fans, try one of the many science fiction conferences or "cons" held throughout the country and the world.

Look for panelists and workshop instructors whose work you admire and who seem to be writing in your general area. Check for specific panels or discussions of topics relevant to what you are writing now. Think about the size—would you feel more comfortable with a small workshop of eight people or a large group of 100 or more attendees?

If your funds are limited, start by looking for conferences close to home, but you may want to explore those that offer contests with cash prizes—and a chance to recoup your expenses. A few conferences and workshops also offer scholarships, but the competition is stiff and writers interested in these should find out the requirements early. Finally, students may want to look for conferences and workshops that offer college credit. You will find these options included in the listings here. Again, send a self-addressed, stamped envelope for the most current details.

ABROAD WRITERS CONFERENCES

17363 Sutter Creek Rd., Sutter Creek CA 95685. (209)296-4050. E-mail: abroadwriters@yahoo.com. Website: http://www.abroad-crwf.com/index.html. Conferences are held throughout the year in various places worldwide. See website for scheduling details. Conference duration: 7-10 days. "Instead of being lost in a crowd at a large conference, Abroad Writers' Conference prides itself on holding small group meetings where participants have personal contact with everyone. Stimulating talks, interviews, readings, Q&A's, writing workshops, film screenings, private consultations and social gatherings all take place within a week to ten days. Abroad Writers' Conference promises you true networking opportunities and full detailed feedback on your writing."

Costs Prices start at $2,750. Discounts and upgrades may apply. See website for pricing details.

Additional Information Agents participate in conference.

ALABAMA WRITERS' CONCLAVE

137 Sterline Dr., Hueytown AL 35023. E-mail: irenelatham@charter.net. Website: www.alabamawritersconclave.org. Contact: Irene Latham, program chair; Don Johnson, treasurer. Estab. 1923. Last event held July 16-18, 2010. Average attendance: 80-100. Conference to promote all phases of writing. Also offers ms critiques and eight writing contests. Site: Four Points Sherataon at the University of Alabama campus in Tuscaloosa, Alabama.

Costs Fees for conference are $150 (member)/$175 (nonmember), includes 2 meals. Critique fee $25 (member)/$30 (nonmember). Membership $25.

Accommodations Special conference rates.

Additional Information "We have major speakers and faculty members who conduct intensive, energetic workshops. Our annual writing contest guidelines and all other information is available at www.alabamawritersconclave.org."

ALTERNATIVE PRESS EXPO (APE)

Comic-Con International, P.O. Box 128458, San Diego CA 92112-8458. (619)491-2475. Fax: (619)414-1022. E-mail: cci-info@comic-con.org. Website: www.comic-con.org/ape/. **Contact:** Eddie Ibrahim, director of programming. Annual. Last conference held October 16-17, 2010, in San Francisco. Conference duration: 2 days. "Hundreds of artists and publishers converge for the largest gathering of alternative and self-published comics in the country." Includes panels on graphic novels, Web comics, how to pitch your comic to publishers, and the traditional APE 'queer cartoonists' panel. Site: Large conference or expo center in host city. Check website for 2010 location. 2010 special guests are Lynda Barry, Daniel Clowes, Rich Koslowski, and Tony Millionaire.

Costs $7 single day; $10 both days.

Accommodations Does not offer overnight accommodations. Provides list of area hotels or lodging options on website.

Additional Information For brochure, visit website. Editors participate in conference.

AMERICAN CHRISTIAN WRITERS CONFERENCES

P.O. Box 110390, Nashville TN 37222. (800)21-WRITE. Fax: (615)834-7736. E-mail: ACWriters@aol.com. Website: www.ACWriters.com. Annual. Conferences held throughout the year in over 2 dozen cities. Conference duration: 2 days. Average attendance: 30-80. Conference's purpose is to promote all forms of Christian writing. Site: Usually located at a major hotel chain like Holiday Inn.

Costs $150 for 1 day; $250 for 2 days. Plus meals and accommodations.

Accommodations Special rates available at host hotel.

Additional Information Conference information available for SASE, e-mail, phone or fax. Accepts inquiries by fax, e-mail, phone, SASE.

AMERICAN INDEPENDENT WRITERS (AIW) AMERICAN WRITERS

CONFERENCE

1001 Connecticut Ave. NW, Ste. 701, Washington DC 20036. (202) 775-5150. Fax: (202) 775-5810. E-mail: info@amerindywriters.org. Website: www.amerindywriters.org. **Contact:** Donald Graul Jr, Executive Director. Annual conference held in June. Conference duration: Saturday. Average attendance: 350. "Gives participants a chance to hear from and talk with dozens of experts on book and magazine publishing as well as meet one-on-one with literary agents." Site: George Washington University Conference Center. Past keynote speakers included Erica Jong, Diana Rehm, Kitty Kelley, Lawrence Block, John Barth, Stephen Hunter, Francine Prose.

ANNUAL NEW YORK ROUND TABLE WRITERS' CONFERENCE

20 West 44th Street, New York NY 10036. (212) 764-7021. E-mail: smallpress@aol.com. Website: www.writersconferencenyc.com. **Contact:** Karin Taylor, director. Estab. 2004. Annual. Next conference held in April, 2010. Conference duration: 2 days. Average attendance: 200. "The purpose is to educate writers about the business of getting published." Site: The conference takes place at the New York Center for Independent Publishing, based in Midtown Manhattan. Panels in 2008 included Birth of a Book, Memoir Writing, Writing Process and Fiction Writing. Speakers for 2008 included Brigid Hughes (A Public Space), Marjorie Braman (HarperCollins) and authors Sharon Mesmer, Alice Hoffman, John Berendt, and Lincoln Child.

Costs In 2009, $250 (1 day) to $350 (2 days).

Accommodations Does not offer overnight accommodations. Provides list of area hotels or lodging options.

Additional Information Information available in January. For brochure, fax request, call, e-mail or visit website. Agents and editors participate in conference. "We try to provide writers with useful tools to help increase their chances of finding a literary agent or publisher."

ANTIOCH WRITERS' WORKSHOP

P.O. Box 494, Yellow Springs OH 45387. (937)475-7357. E-mail: info@antiochwritersworkshop.com. Website: www.antiochwritersworkshop.com. **Contact:** Sharon Short, director. Annual conference held July 10-16, 2010. Conference duration: 1 week for full week experience; "A La Carte" options include morning only classes; Focus on Form afternoon seminar, and one-day Saturday seminar. Average attendance: 80. Workshop concentration: fiction, creative nonfiction, poetry, personal essay, memoir. Workshop located at Antioch University McGregor and at various sites in the Village of Yellow Springs. 2010 faculty include Sigrid Nunez, Ralph Keyes, Ann Hagedorn, Donald Ray Pollock, Cathy Smith Bowers, John Drury, and many others. 2010 visiting agents: April Eberhardt and Janet Reid. Tuition is $735 (regular) or $675 (alumni and local participants), or $575.00 for Ohio college/university students and faculty, which includes a nonrefundable $125 registration fee.) Accommodations are available in local homes through the village host program ($150 for the week) or at area hotels and B&Bs. Presented in partnership with Antioch University McGregor. Continuing education and college level credit options available. Full week experience also includes small group lunches with faculty, agent pitch sessions, optional ms critiques.

ARKANSAS WRITERS' CONFERENCE

AR Penwomen Pioneer Branch of the National League of American Penwomen, 13005 Misty Creek, Little Rock AR 72211. (501)224-5823. E-mail: pvining@aristotle.net. Website: http://groups.yahoo.com/group/arpenwomen. **Contact:** Send SASE to: Peggy Vining, at the address listed above. Estab. 1944. Annual. Conference held first weekend in June. Average attendance: 175. "We have a variety of subjects related to writing. We have some general sessions, some more specific, but we try to vary each year's subjects."

Costs Registration: $15; luncheon: $19; banquet: $20; contest entry $10 (2006 rates).

Accommodations "We meet at a Holiday Inn Presidential in Little Rock. Rooms available at reduced rate." Holiday Inn has a bus to bring our attendees from the airport. Rooms average $79.

Additional Information "We have 36 contest categories. Some are open only to Arkansans, most are open to all writers. Our judges are not announced before the conference. All are qualified, many from out of state." Conference information available February 15. For brochures or inquiries send SASE with full mailing address, call or fax. "We have had 226 people attending from 12 states—over 2,000 contest entries from 40 states and New Zealand, Mexico and Canada."

ART WORKSHOPS IN GUATEMALA

4758 Lyndale Ave. S, Minneapolis MN 55419-5304. (612)825-0747. E-mail: info@artguat.org. Website: www.artguat.org. **Contact:** Liza Fourre, director. Annual. Workshops held year-round. Maximim class size: 10 students per class. Workshop titles include: Fiction Writing: New Directions in Travel Writing with Richard Harris; Poetry: Snapshots in Words with Rosanne Lloyd; and Creative Writing: Journey of the Soul with Sharon Doubiago. Costs $1,745 (includes tuition, lodging in a lovely colonial style B&B, and ground transportation, and some pretty interesting field trips).

Accommodations All transportation and accommodations included in price of conference.

Additional Information Conference information available now. For brochure/guidelines visit website, e-mail, fax or call. Accepts inquiries by e-mail, phone.

ASPEN SUMMER WORDS WRITING RETREAT & LITERARY FESTIVAL

110 E. Hallam St., #116, Aspen CO 81611. (970)925-3122. Fax: (970)925-5700. E-mail: info@aspenwriters.org. Website: www.aspenwriters.org. **Contact:** Natalie Lacy, programs manager. Estab. 1976. Annual. 2009 conference held June 21-26. Conference duration: 5 days. Average attendance: writing retreat, 150; literary festival, 300+, 1,800 visitors. Retreat includes intensive workshops in fiction (beginning through advanced), creative nonfiction, poetry, wirting for young readers, young wirters' workshop, magazine writing and food writing, plus a "Readers' Retreat" which in 2008 focused on Indian Literature. Literary festival features approximately 18 events (craft talks, author readings, and interviews; publishing panel discussions; agent/editor meeting; and social gatherings) for readers and writers. Festival theme for 2008 was "Passage to India". Retreat faculty for 2009: Ron Carlson (Advanced Fiction); Hallie Ephron (Mystery); Gary Ferguson (Magazine Writing and Nature Writing); William Loizeaux (Narrative Nonfiction); Christopher Merrill (Poetry); Pamela Painter (Fiction); and Nic Pizzolatto (Beginning Fiction). Festival presenters for 2009 were Salman Rushdie, Anita Rau Badami, Chitra Banerjee Divakaruni, David Davidar, Indu Sundaresan, Manil Suri, and Shashi Tharoor.

Costs As of 2008, $475/retreat; $250/2 day symposia; $175/2-day reader's retreat. Tuition includes daily continental breakfast and lunch, plus one evening reception. $200 festival pass; retreat students receive a $50 discount when they sign up for the literary festival. Festival registration includes two wine and hors d'oeuvres receptions. $35/private meetings with agents and editors.

Accommodations Discount lodging at the conference site will be available. 2011 rates to be announced. Free shuttle around town.

Additional Information Application deadline: April 6. Mss must be submitted by late May for review by faculty, for most workshops. 10 page limit for workshop application mss. A limited number of partial-tuition scholarships are available. Deadline for agent/editor meeting registration is May 25th. Brochures available for SASE, by e-mail and phone request, and on website.

N ATLANTIC CENTER FOR THE ARTS

1414 Art Center Ave, New Smyrna Beach FL 32618. (386)427-6975. Website: atlanticcenterforthearts.org. **Contact:** program department. Three week long residency offered several times a year. "Associates selected will get one-on-one experience with a Master Artist. The Master Artist selects Associate Residents from the applications."

Costs $850; $25 non-refundable application fee. Financial aid is available.

Accommodations "Van transportation is provided from ACA two days per week at regularly scheduled times to the shopping center and art supply stores. Many artists do bring their own vehicles and car-pooling may be an option. ACA does provide van transportation to outreaches, when possible. Master Artists are supplied with a car. Bikes are available at ACA." Offers overnight accommodations.

AWP ANNUAL CONFERENCE AND BOOKFAIR

MS 1E3, George Mason University, Fairfax VA 22030. (703)993-4540. E-mail: conference@awpwriter.org; bookfair@awpwriter.org. Website: www.awpwriter.org. **Contact:** Matt Burriesci, associate director. MS 1E3, George Mason University, Fairfax VA 22030. (703)993-4301 Fax: (703)993-4302. E-mail: conference@awpwriter.org. Website: www.awpwriter.org. Annual. Conference duration: 4 days. AWP holds its Annual Conference in a different region of North America in order to celebrate the outstanding authors, teachers, writing programs, literary centers, and small press publishers of that region. The Annual Conference typically features 350 presentations: readings, lectures, panel discussions, and Forums plus hundreds of book signings, receptions, dances, and informal gatherings. The conference attracts more than 8,000 attendees and more than 500 publishers. All genres are represented. Site: Washington, DC at the Marriott Wardman Park & Omni Shoreham Hotels. "We will offer 175 panels on everything from writing to teaching to critical analysis." In 2009, Art Spiegelman was the keynote speaker. Others readers were Charles Baxter, Isaiah Sheffer, Z.Z. Packer, Nareem Murr, Marilynne Robinson; 2008: John Irving, Joyce Carol Oates, among others.

Costs Early registration fees: $40 student; $140 AWP member; $160 non-member.

Accommodations Provide airline discounts and rental-car discounts. Special rate at Hilton.

Additional Information Please note: The date is now February 2-5, 2011. Check website for more information. (For editorial guidelines, submissions, information about the AWP Award Series and other AWP contests, information about *The Writer's Chronicle*, or information about the AWP Official Guide to Writing Programs, e-mail chronicle@awpwriter.org.)

N BACKSPACE WRITERS CONFERENCE & AGENT AUTHOR SEMINAR

P.O. Box 454, Washington MI 48094. (732)267-6449. E-mail: karendionne@bksp.org. Website: http://www.backspacewritersconference.com. **Contact:** Christopher Graham or Karen Dionne, co-founders. Annual. Estab. 2004. 2010 dates: May 27th, 28th, and 29th. Dates for the November 2010 Agent-Author Seminar: Nov. 5th and 6th. Conference duration: 3 days. Average attendance: 150-200. Conference. "We focus on all genres, from nonfiction to literary fiction and everything in between, covering all popular genres from mysteries, and thrillers to young adult and romance. Formal pitch sessions are a staple at most writers'conferences. However, in planning our Backspace events, we discovered that agents hate conducting pitch sessions almost as much as authors dread doing them. In fact, many of the agents we've talked to are happy to sit on a panel or conduct a workshop, but decline to participate in formal pitch sessions. The goal of the Backspace Agent-Author Seminars is to help authors connect with agents - lots of agents - thereby giving authors the opportunity to ask questions specific to their interests and concerns. We facilitate this through small group workshops of usually no more than 10 writers and 2 agents. Workshops concentrate on query letters and opening pages. That's why we've built so much free time into the program. The full fifteen minutes between panels also allows plenty of opportunity for seminar registrants to talk to agents. Many of the agents will also be available during the noon hour. Remember, agents attend conferences because they want to help authors. They're looking for new talent, and welcome the chance to hear about your work. Instead of a tense, angst-filled pitch session where it's difficult for all but the most confident authors to put their best foot forward, an interesting, relaxed, enjoyable conversation leaves a much more positive impression. And even if authors don't get the chance to mention their project, the pleasant conversation gives the author a point of reference when sending a formal query letter to the agent's office after the seminar is over." Site: The Radisson Martinique in Manhattan NY located in Mid-town Manhattan just a few blocks from Madison Square Garden/NY Penn Station. 2008 agents in attendance: Jeff Kleinman, Noah Lukeman, Paul Cirone, Kristin Nelson, Colleen Lindsay, Jason Allen Ashlock, Scott Hoffman, 2010 speakers: Lorenzo Carcaterra, #1 New York Times bestselling author, screenwriter; Neil S. Nyren, Sr. Vice President, Publisher and Editor-in-Chief of G.P. Putnam's Sons. Also featured editors and over 35 authors.

Costs $200-700; offers member, group, and student discounts along with additional workshops that are priced separately.
Accommodations "We offer a special conference rate at the Radisson Martinique for conference attendees. Average price of $199-279/night, must be booked 30 days in advance."
Additional Information See website for more information. Brochures available in January. Accepts inquiries by e-mail and phone. Agents and editors attend conference. "

BALTIMORE COMIC-CON

Baltimore Convention Center, One West Pratt St., Baltimore MD 21201. (410)526-7410. E-mail: cardscomicscollectibles@yahoo.com. Website: http://www.comicon.com/baltimore. **Contact:** Marc Nathan. Estab. 1999. Annual. August 28-29. Conference, "promoting the wonderful world of comics to as many people as possible." Comic-Con 20109: Special Guest Todd McFarlane. The Baltimore Comic-Con welcomes the return of The Harvey Awards: Hosted by Scott Kurtz. Nomination ballots are online now. Other guests are Mike Allred, Geoff Johns, Sergio Aragones, Frank Cho, JG Jones, James Robinson, Walter Simonson, Terry Moore and many more.
Costs Two day pass: $25; Saturday or Sunday only: $15.
Accommodations Does not offer overnight accommodations. Provides list of area hotels or lodging options.
Additional Information For brochure, visit website.

BAY TO OCEAN WRITERS' CONFERENCE

Presented by the Eastern Shore Writers Association, P.O. Box 544, St. Michaels MD 21663. (443)786-4536. E-mail: info@baytoocean.com. Website: www.baytoocean.com. **Contact:** Wilson Wyatt, Jr., Coordinator. Annual. Conference held last Saturday in February. Average attendance: 150. Approximately 25 speakers conduct workshops on publishing, agents, editing, marketing, craft, the internet, writing for television and movies, poetry, fiction, nonfiction and freelance writing. Site: Chesapeake College, Rt. 213 and Rt. 50, Wye Mills, on Maryland's historic Eastern Shore. Accessible to individuals with disabilities.
Costs $80-100, students $55. Includes choice of 5 of 19 sessions, continental breakfast and networking lunch.
Additional Information Mail-in registration form available on website in December prior to the conference. Pre-registration is required, no registration at door. Conference usually sells out one month in advance. Conference is for all levels of writers.

BIG APPLE CON

401 Seventh Ave., 33rd St., New York, NY 10001-2062. (347)581-6166. E-mail: mikecarbo@gmail.com. Website: http://bigapplecon.com. **Contact:** Michael Carbonaro, director; Brian Schutzer, director. Annual conference held in October 1-3, 2010. Conference duration: 3 days. "The Big Apple Con is the oldest and longest-running comic, art and toy, Sci-Fi show in New York City." Site: Located directly across from Madison Square Garden and Penn Station.

BIG APPLE WRITING WORKSHOPS, MEET THE AUTHORS/MEET THE AGENTS

IWWG, P.O. Box 810, Gracie Station NY 10028. (212) 737-7536. Fax: (212) 737-9469. E-mail: dirhahn@aol.com. Website: www.iwwg.org. **Contact:** Hannalore Hahn, founder & executive director. Estab. 1980. Semi-annual. October 2010, April 2011, October 2011. Conference duration: 2 days. Average attendance: 150. Workshop. "The three-fold purpose entails: 1) A full day writing workshop; 2) A panel discussion with 12 recently published IWWG members about how they became authors, found agents and publishers; 3) An open house with 8 agents for authors to meet." Site: Scandinavia House is the official building for Sweden, Norway, Finland, Iceland and Denmark. It is a modern building on Park Avenue in midtown Manhattan. It offers two comfortable lecture halls and a cafeteria (with Scandinavian food). Previous panels include "Fiction and

Nonfiction: Writing and Selling on Both Sides of the Aisle" and "The Writer at Work: Writing Adrift/Writing a Draft."

Costs $130 for members of IWWG/$160 for non-members for both days. Individual sections may be selected and paid for if not attending full conference.

Accommodations Does not offer overnight accommodations. Provides list of area hotels or lodging options.

Additional Information For brochure, send SASE, fax request, call, e-mail, visit website. Agents and editors participate in conference. "We've had over 50 Meet the Author/Meet the Agent events. Close to 4,000 books have been published by IWWG members since our inception in 1976."

BLOCKBUSTER PLOT INTENSIVE WRITING WORKSHOPS (SANTA CRUZ)

E-mail: contact@blockbusterplots.com. Website: www.blockbusterplots.com. Held four times per year. Conference duration: 2 days. Average attendance: 20. Workshop is intended to help writers create an action, character and thematic plotline for a screenplay, memoir, short story, novel or creative nonfiction. Site: Conference hall.

Costs $95 per day.

Accommodations Provides list of area hotels and lodging options.

Additional Information Brochures available by e-mail or on website. Accepts inquiries by e-mail.

⌗ BLOODY WORDS MYSTERY CONFERENCE

Phone/fax: (416) 497-5293. E-mail: soles@sff.net. Website: www.bloodywords.com. **Contact:** Caro Soles, chair. Estab. 1999. Annual. Last conference held June May 28-30, 2010. Average attendance: 300. Focus: Mystery/true crime/forensics, with Canadian slant. Purpose: To bring readers and writers of the mystery genre together in a Canadian setting. Site: Ottawa: Ottawa Marriott Hotel. Conference includes two workshops and two tracks of panels, one on factual information such as forensics, agents, scene of the crime procedures, etc. and one on fiction, such as "Death in a Cold Climate," "Murder on the Menu," "Elementary, My Dear Watson," and a First Novelists Panel. Canadian Guest of Honer in 2009: Louise Penny; International Guest of Honor: Denise Mina.

Costs $175 (Canadian include the banquet and all panels, readings, dealers' room and workshop.

Accommodations Offers block of rooms in hotel; list of optional lodging available. Check website for details.

Additional Information Sponsors short mystery story contest—5,000 word limit; judges are experienced editors of anthologies; fee is $5 (entrants must be registered). Conference information is available now. For brochure visit website. Accepts inquiries by e-mail and phone. Agents and editors participate in conference. "This is a conference for both readers and writers of mysteries, the only one of its kind in Canada. We also run 'The Mystery Cafe,' a chance to get to know a dozen or so authors, hear them read and ask questions (half hour each)."

BLUE RIDGE MOUNTAINS CHRISTIAN WRITERS CONFERENCE

(800) 588-7222. E-mail: ylehman@bellsouth.net. Website: www.lifeway.com/christianwriters. **Contact:** Yvonne Lehman, director. Estab. 1999. Annual. Last conference held May 16-20, 2010. Average attendance: 380. All areas of Christian writing including fiction, nonfiction, devotionals, women's fiction, romance, suspense, romance, craft of writing, etc. For beginning and advanced writers. Site: LifeWay/Ridgecrest Conference Center, 20 miles east of Asheville, NC. Companies represented May 18-22, 2008 include AMG Publications, B&H, Focus on the Family, Howard Books, The Upper Room, LifeWay Christian Resources, Christian Writers Guild, Living Ink Books, Hensley Publishing, Today's Christian Woman, Benrey Literary Agency, Les Stobbe Agency, Bethan House, Big Idea (Veggie Tales), MacGregor Literary Agency, The Nashville Group, WinePress, William K. Jensen Literary Agency, et al. Faculty includes professional authors, agents and editors.

Costs 2010: $315, which includes all sessions, breaks, and a special Wednesday evening Awards Ceremony. Additional on-campus meal package available for $98/person.

Accommodations LifeWay Ridgecrest Conference Center. See website for on-campus room rates.

Additional Information The Blue Ridge "Autumn in the Mountains" Novel retreat will be held annually in October at Ridgecrest/Life Way Conference Center (www.lifeway.com/novelretreat). Sponsors contests for unpublished writers. Awards include trophy and $200 scholarship toward next year's conference. See website for critique service and daily schedule-offering keynote sessions, continuing classes and workshops.

JAMES BONNET'S STORYMAKING: THE MASTER CLASS

6, Rue de Chateau, 25330 Nans Sous Ste. Anne, France. +33 3 81 86 56 83. USA: (818)567-0521. E-mail: bonnet@storymaking.com. Website: www.storymaking.com. **Contact:** James Bonnet. Estab. 1990. Seminars held February and October. Conference duration: 2 days. Average attendance: 25. Conferences focus on fiction, mystery and screenwriting. Site: Los Angeles, California. Workshops/ Retreats held May and September. Workshop duration: 7 days. Average attendance: "limited to 4." Site: Nans Sous Ste. Anne, France. "Seminars focus on mastery of the novel and screenwriting arts through an understanding of story and guiding writers from inspiration to the final draft. Topics include The High Concept Great Idea, The Creative Unconscious, Metaphor, The Character Archetypes, The Fundamentals of Plot, Structure, Genre, Conflict, Suspense, and more. Workshops/ Retreats include weekend seminar plus 5 days working one-on-one with James Bonnet. James Bonnet will be the speaker.

Costs $350 for weekend seminar. $1,500 for 7 day workshop/retreat.

Accommodations Provides a list of area hotels or lodging options.

Additional Information For brochure send SASE, e-mail, visit website, or call. Accepts inquiries by SASE, e-mail, phone and fax. "James Bonnet is the author of *Stealing Fire From the Gods* and *The Complete Guide to Story for Writers and Filmmakers*."

BOOMING GROUND

Buch E-462, 1866 Main Mall, Creative Writing Program, UBC, Vancouver BC V6T 121 Canada. (604) 822-2469. Fax: (604) 822-3616. E-mail: apply@boominground.com. Website: www.boomingground.com. **Contact:** Brianna Brash-Nyberg. Estab. 1998. Average attendance: 30 per session. Writing mentorships geared toward beginner, intermediate, and advanced levels in novel, short fiction, poetry, nonfiction, and children's writing. Open to students. Online mentorship program-students work for 4-8 months with a mentor by e-mail, allowing up to 120-240 pages of material to be created. Site: Online and by e-mail.

Costs $780 (Canadian) for online mentorships; individual manuscript evaluation also available.

Additional Information Workshops are based on works-in-progress. Writers must submit ms with application. For guidelines visit website, or e-mail brianna@boomingground.com. Accepts inquiries by e-mail and via website. "Classes are offered for writers at all levels—from early career to mid-career. Our mentorships are ideal for long-form work such as novels, collections of poetry, and short fiction."

Conferences

BOUCHERCON

Website: www.bouchercon.com. Conference held October 14-17, 2010, in Indianapolis. The Bouchercon is "the world mystery and detective fiction event." Site: Hyatt Regency Indianapolis. See website for details. Special guests include Michael Connelly.

Costs $150 (prior to July 1, 2007), $250 (after July 1) registration fee covers writing workshops, panels, reception, etc.

Additional Information Sponsors Anthony Award for published mystery novel; ballots due prior to conference. Information available on website.

BREAD LOAF WRITERS' CONFERENCE

Middlebury VT 05753. (802)443-5286. Fax: (802)443-2087. E-mail: ncargill@middlebury.edu. Website: www.middlebury.edu/~blwc. **Contact:** Noreen Cargill, administrative manager. Estab. 1926. Annual. Last conference held August 11-21, 2010. Conference duration: 11 days. Average

attendance: 230. For fiction, nonfiction, poetry. Site: Held at the summer campus in Ripton, Vermont (belongs to Middlebury College). 2007 faculty and staff included William Kittredge, Percival Everett, Sigrid Nunez, Joanna Scott, Susan Orlean.
Costs In 2007, $2,260 (included room and board). Fellowships available.
Accommodations Accommodations are at Ripton. Onsite accommodations included in fee.
Additional Information 2010 conference information available December 2009 on website. Accepts inquiries by fax, e-mail and phone.

N BROOKLYN BOOK FESTIVAL

209 Joralemon St., Brooklyn NY 11201. (718)802-3852. E-mail: ekoch@brooklynbp.nyc.gov. Website: www.brooklynbookfestival.org. **Contact:** Liz Koch. Estab. 2005. Annual 1 day festival. "The Brooklyn Book Festival is a huge, free public event presenting an array of local, national, and international literary stars and emerging authors who represent the exciting world of literature today."
Additional Information For brochure visit website.

BYU WRITING FOR YOUNG READERS WORKSHOP

348 HCEB, Brigham Young University, Provo UT 84602. (801)422-2568. E-mail: cw348@byu.edu. Website: http://wfyr.byu.edu. **Contact:** Bill Kelly. Estab. 2000. Annual. Workshop held June or July each year. Average attendance: 150. Conference focuses on "all genres for children and teens." Site: Brigham Young University's Conference Center. Mornings feature small group workshop sessions with a published author. Afternoon breakout sessions on a variety of topics of interest to writers. Sessions for picture book, novel, illustration, fantasy, beginners, general writing. Two editors and an agent are in attendance. Faculty for 2010 include Laurie Halse Anderson, Patricia MacLachlan, Brandon Mull, Kadir Nelson, Elizabeth Partridge, David Shannon.
Costs $399 conference fee and closing banquet.
Accommodations Provides list of area hotels.
Additional Information Brochures available in March by phone and on website. Accepts inquiries by SASE, e-mail, phone. Agents and editors participate in conference. "Bring the manuscript you are currently working on."

N CAPE COD WRITERS' CONFERENCE

P.O. Box 408, Osterville MA 02655. (508)420-0200. E-mail: writers@capecodwriterscenter.org. Website: www.capecodwriterscenter.org. **Contact:** Anne Elizabeth Tom, executive director. Annual Conference. Duration: Two-part (back to back), each part three-days, 7.5 hours; two different Master Classes; six one-day workshops; offers workshops in poetry, fiction, and creative nonfiction, and getting published, as well as manuscript evaluation/mentoring sessions with faculty." Site: Held at the Craigville Conference center in a Cape Cod village overlooking Nantucket Sound. **Costs** $30 per course hour; manuscript evaluation/mentoring sessions (1.5 hours) $225; $50 registration fee for non-members.

CENTRAL OHIO FICTION WRITERS ANNUAL CONFERENCE

P.O. Box 912, Worthington OH 43085. E-mail: cae@carolannerhardt.com. Website: www.cofw.org. **Contact:** Carol Ann Erhardt, president. Central Ohio Fiction Writers (COFW), P.O. Box 912, Worthington OH 43085.Estab. 1990. Annual. Conference held in Worthington, OH. 2010 Conference dates October 1-2, 2010. Average attendance: 120. COFW is a chapter of Romance Writers of America. The conference focuses on all romance subgenres and welcomes published writers, pre-published writers and readers. Conference theme: celebrates and fosters writers at every stage of their careers. Best-selling authors provide motivation and instruction; workshops, speakers, and materials cover a broad spectrum of topics. Two agents and two editors will speak and take short appointments. Appointments to early registrants who have completed at least one manuscript.

Keynote speaker is Suzanne Brockmann. Suzanne will teach workshops Friday evening & two on Saturday. See others online.

Costs COFW members - $118, Others - $128. Price includes Friday evening buffet and Saturday lunch. Registration is completely electronic though you can pay by check. There is a $15 late fee for registrations received after Sept. 27th.

Accommodations See www.cofw.org for exact location. 2010: Holiday Inn Worthington-Columbus, 7007 N. High Street, Worthington, OH 43085, 614-436-0700. There will be a special conference rate for hotel rooms of $99. www.HolidayInn.com/WorthingtonOh. (For $99 roomrate use Group code COF).

Additional Information Registration form and information available on website or by e-mail.

CENTRUM'S PORT TOWNSEND WRITERS' CONFERENCE

P.O. Box 1158, Port Townsend WA 98368-0958. (360)385-3102. E-mail: info@centrum.org; jordan@centrum.org. Website: www.centrum.org. **Contact:** Jordan Hartt, director of programs. Estab. 1974. Annual. Conference held mid-July. 2010: July 18-25. Average attendance: 180. Conference to promote poetry, fiction, creative nonfiction "featuring many of the nation's leading writers." Two different workshop options: "New Works" and "Works-in-Progress." Site: The conference is held at Fort Worden State Park on the Strait of Juan de Fuca. "The site is a Victorian-era military fort with miles of beaches, wooded trails and recreation facilities. The park is within the limits of Port Townsend, a historic seaport and arts community, approximately 80 miles northwest of Seattle, on the Olympic Peninsula." Guest speakers participate in addition to full-time faculty.

Costs Tuition for the Conference is $595. Room and board options range from $205 to $515. Admission to afternoon workshops only is $50 per workshop or $275 for unlimited access to all afternoon workshops. Admission to freewrites or morning writing exercises only is $25 per session. All freewrites, morning writing exercises, and afternoon workshops are free for those who are registered for the core morning workshops. Register online at website.

Accommodations "Modest room and board facilities on site." Also list of hotels/motels/inns/bed & breakfasts/private rentals available.

Additional Information Brochures/guidelines available for SASE or on website. "The conference focus is on the craft of writing and the writing life, not on marketing."

CHILDREN'S LITERATURE CONFERENCE

239 Montauk Hwy, Southampton NY 11968-6700. (631)632-5030. Fax: (631)632-2578. Website: www.stonybrook.edu/writers. **Contact:** Adrienne Unger, administrative coordinator. *Application deadline extended to June 15, 2010!*. Annual conference held in July: 2010: July 28-Aug. 1, 2010. "The seaside campus of Stony Brook Southampton is located in the heart of the Hamptons, a renowned resort area only 70 miles from New York City. During free time, participants can draw on inspiration from the Atlantic beaches or explore the charming seaside towns." Faculty have included Richard Peck, Tor Seidler, Cindy Kane, Gahan Wilson James McMullan, and Mitchell Kriegman.

Costs Application fee: $15; tuition, room and board: $1270; tuition only $1125 (includes breakfast and lunch).

Accommodations On-campus housing, doubles and small singles with shared baths, is modest but comfortable. Housing assignment is by lottery. Supplies list of lodging alternatives.

Additional Information "Applicants must complete an application and submit a writing sample of original, unpublished work. See Web for details. Brochure available in January by phone, e-mail, and on website. Accepts inquiries by e-mail, phone, and fax."

CLARION SCIENCE FICTION AND FANTASY WRITERS' WORKSHOP

UCSD 9500 Gilman Drive # 0410, La Jolla CA 92097-0410. (858) 534-2115. E-mail: clarion@ucsd.edu. Website: http://clarion.ucsd.edu. **Contact:** Hadas Blinder, Program Coordinator. Estab. 1968. Annual. Conference duration: Six-week residency in summer (late June-early Aug.). Average attendance: 18. Workshop. "Clarion is a short-story writing workshop focused on fundamentals particular to the writing of science fiction, fantasy and horror." Site: The workshop is held at the UC San Diego campus in the beautiful beach town of La Jolla. Participants reside in campus apartments and attend workshop sessions in a seminar room. Beaches and shopping are within easy reach by public transportation. Summer temperatures in San Diego are normally 70-80°F, dry and comfortable. Our 2010 writers in residence are Delia Sherman, George R.R. Martin, Dale Bailey, Samuel R. Delany, Jeff VanderMeer, and Ann VanderMeer. June 27-Aug. 7, 2010.

Costs The fees for 2009 (application, tuition, room and board) were approximately $4,500. Scholarships were available.

Accommodations Participants make their own travel arrangements to and from the campus. Campus residency is required. Participants are housed in semi-private accommodations (private bedroom, shared bathroom) in student apartments. The room and board fee includes three meals a day at a campus dining facility. In 2009 the room and board fee for the six-week residency were approximately $2,500 (included in the $4,500 workshop fee).

Additional Information "Workshop participants are selected on the basis of their potential for highly successful writing careers. Applications are judged by a review panel composed of the workshop instructors. Applicants submit an application ($50) and two complete short stories, each between 2,500 words and 6,000 words in length. The application deadline (typically, March 1) is posted on the Clarion website." Information available in September. For brochure, visit website. Agents and editors frequently participate in Clarion as instructors or guest speakers.

CLARION WEST WRITERS' WORKSHOP

P.O. Box 31264, Seattle WA 98103-1264. (206)322-9083. E-mail: info@clarionwest.org. Website: www.clarionwest.org. **Contact:** Leslie Howle, executive director. Annual. Workshop usually held in late June through July. Average attendance: 18. "Conference to prepare students for professional careers in science fiction and fantasy writing." Deadline for applications: March 1. Site: Conference held in Seattle's University district, an urban site close to restaurants and cafes, but not too far from downtown. Faculty: 6 teachers (professional writers and editors established in the field). "Every week a new instructor—each a well-known writer chosen for the quality of his or her work and for professional stature—teaches the class, bringing a unique perspective on speculative fiction. During the fifth week, the workshop is taught by a professional editor."

Costs Workshop tuition, dormitory housing and most meals: $3,200. ($100 discount if application received by February 1).

Accommodations Students stay on site in workshop housing at one of the University of Washington's sorority houses.

Additional Information "Students write their own stories every week while preparing critiques of all the other students' work for classroom sessions. This gives participants a more focused, professional approach to their writing. The core of the workshop remains science fiction, and short stories (not novels) are the focus." Conference information available in Fall. For brochure/guidelines send SASE, visit website, e-mail or call. Accepts inquiries by e-mail, phone, SASE. Limited scholarships are available, based on financial need. Students must submit 20-30 pages of ms with 4-page biography and $30 fee for applications sent by mail or e-mail to qualify for admission.

N CONFLUENCE

P.O. Box 3681, Pittsburgh PA 15230-3681.(412)344-0456. E-mail: confluence@spellcaster.org. Website: http://www.parsec-sff.org/confluence/whatis.html. Estab. 1996. Annual. July 23-25, 2010. Conference. Site: Doubletree Hotel Pittsburgh Airport. Science Fiction Guest of Honor: John Scalzi.

DESERT DREAMS CONFERENCE: REALIZING THE DREAM

P.O. Box 27407, Tempe AZ 85285. (623)910-0524. E-mail: info@rwawnational.org. Website: www.desertroserwa.org. **Contact:** Conference coordinator. Estab. 1986. Biennial. Last conference held April 4-6, 2008. Next conference Spring 2010. Average attendance: 250. Conference focuses on romance fiction. Site: 30th Annual RWA Conference will be held at The Walt Disney World Swan and Dolphin Resort in Orlando, Florida, July 28–31, 2010. The RWA Conference registration rate remains $425 for members/$500 for nonmembers through July 1. After July 1, the registration rate goes up to $475 for members/$550 for nonmembers. Hotel rooms for RWA Conference attendees are available at the fantastic rate of $149 per night, single or double if booked by July 10, 2010. If more than two guests share a room, the cost will increase by $25 per person per night. Children under 18 may stay for free in their parents' room using existing bedding. .Past panels included: Plotting, Dialogue, Manuscript Preparation, website Design, Synopsis, Help for the Sagging Middle. Keynote speakers in 2006 included Debbie Macomber, Lisa Gardner, Jennifer Cruise and Debra Dixon. Guest editors/agents from St. Martin's Press, Harlequin, Irene Goodman Literary Agency, Borders Group, Ellora's Cave, Spectrum Literary Agency and more.

Costs Vary each year; approximately $175-228 for full conference.

Accommodations Hotels may vary for each conference; it is always a resort location in the Phoenix area.

Additional Information Sponsors contest as part of conference, open to conference attendees only. For brochure, inquiries, contact by e-mail, phone, fax, mail or visit website. Agents and editors participate in conference.

EAST TEXAS CHRISTIAN WRITER'S CONFERENCE

East Texas Baptist University, School of Humanities, 1209 N. Grove, Marshall TX 75670. (903)923-2083. E-mail: jhopkins@etbu.edu; jcornish@etbu.edu. Website: www.etbu.edu. **Contact:** Joy Cornish. Annual. Conference held the second weekend in April, Friday and Saturday, April 9-10, 2010. Conference duration: 2 days (Friday & Saturday). Average attendance: 190. "Primarily we are interested in promoting quality Christian writing that would be accepted in mainstream publishing." Site: We use the classrooms, cafeterias, etc. of East Texas Baptist University. Past conference themes were Back to Basics, Getting Started in Fiction, Writers & Agents, Writing Short Stories, Writing for Newspapers, The Significance of Style, Writing Fillers and Articles, Writing Devotionals, Blogging for Writers, Christian Non-Fiction, Inspirational Writing, E-Publishing, Publishing on Demand, and Editor and Author Relations. Past conference speakers/workshop leaders were David Jenkins, Bill Keith, Pete Litterski, Joe Early, Jr., Mary Lou Redding, Marie Chapian, Denny Boultinghouse, Vickie Phelps, Michael Farris, Susan Farris, Pamela Dowd, Donn Taylor, Terry Burns, Donna Walker-Nixon, Lexie Smith, Marv Knox, D.D. Turner, Jim Pence, Andrea Chevalier, Marie Bagnull, and Leonard Goss.

Costs $75 for individuals before March 19, 2010; after will be $80; $60 students before March 19, after $70. Price includes meal prior to early registration deadline. Conference workshops $30 before March 19; after $40.

Additional Information "We have expanded to include publishers, small presses, publish-on-demand opportunities, e-publishing and agents. A bookstore is provided with a variety of materials for writers."

WRITERS IN PARADISE

(727) 864-7994. Fax: (727) 864-7575. E-mail: cayacr@eckerd.edu. Annual. January. Conference duration: 8 days. Average attendance: 84 max. Workshop. Offers college credit. "Writers in Paradise Conference offers workshop classes in fiction (novel and short story), poetry and nonfiction. Working closely with our award-winning faculty, students will have stimulating opportunities to ask questions and learn valuable skills from fellow students and authors at the top of their form. Most importantly, the intimate size and secluded location of the Writers in Paradise experience allows you the time and opportunity to share your manuscripts, critique one another's work and

discuss the craft of writing with experts and peers who can help guide you to the next level." Site: Located on 188 acres of waterfont property in St. Petersburg, Florida, Eckerd College is a private, coeducational college of liberal arts and sciences. In 2010, lectures were given on the craft of writing fiction by Anita Shreve, Sheri Reynolds, Dennis Lehane, and Denise Duhamel. Fiction faculty also led discussions during two mornings of informal roundtables. 2010 Faculty and Guest Faculty included: Sheri Reynolds (*The Rapture of Canaan*), Ann Rittenberg (Ann Rittenberg Literary Agency), David Hale Smith (DHS Literary), Ben Sevier (Dutton), Johnny Temple (Akashic Books), Amy Schiffman (IPGM), Richard Mathews (University of Tampa Press), Sterling Watson (*Sweet Dream Baby*), Beth Ann Fennelly (*Unmentionables*), Ann Hood (*Comfort*), and more.

Costs 2010 tuition fee: $675.

Accommodations Does not offer overnight accommodations. Provides list of area hotels or lodging options.

Additional Information Application materials are required of all attendees. Acceptance is based on a writing sample and a letter detailing your writing background. Submit one short story (25 pg max) or the opening 25 pages of a novel-in-progress, plus a two-page synopsis of the book. Deadline for application materials is December 1st. "Writers in Paradise is a conference for writers of various styles and approaches. While admission is selective, the admissions committee accepts writers with early potential as well as those with strong backgrounds in writing." Sponsors contest. "At the final Evening Reading Series Event, Co-directors Dennis Lehane and Sterling Watson will announce 'The Best of' nominees of the Writers in Paradise Conference. Winners will be published in *Sabal—A Review Featuring the Best Writing of the Writers in Paradise Conference at Eckerd College*. One winner and one honorable mention will be selected from each workshop based on the material brought into the workshop for discussion. Selection will be made by the faculty member leading the workshop. There are no additional fees or entry forms needed." Information available in October 2010. For brochure, send SASE, call, e-mail. Agents participate in conference. Editors participate in conference. "The tranquil seaside landscape sets the tone for this informal gathering of writers, teachers, editors and literary agents. After 8 days of workshopping and engagemnt with peers and professionals in your field, you will leave this unique opportunity with solid ideas about how to find an agent and get published, along with a new and better understanding of your craft."

N ⊟ EMERALD CITY COMICON

800 Convention Place, Seattle WA 98037. (425)744-2767. Fax: (425)675-0737. E-mail: info@emeraldcitycomicon.com; george@emeraldcitycomicon.com. Website: www.emeraldcitycomicon.com. **Contact:** George Demonakos, operations director. Estab. 2002. Annual. 9th Annual ECCC: March 4th - 6th, 2011.| Conference duration: 2 days. "The premiere comic book convention of the Pacific Northwest. Includes comic creators and media guests, various creative and publishing panels, exhibitors, dealers and much more." Site: Washington State Convention & Trade Center. Guests include Jim Cheung, Cully Hamner, Steve McNiven, Yanick Paquette, Pete Woods and many more.

Costs $15/day or $25/weekend pre-sale, $20/Sat, $15/Sun or $30/weekend on-site. Subject to change.

Accommodations Offers overnight accommodations. Discounted rate at Roosevelt Hotel, Crowne Plaza and Red Lion in Seattle.

Additional Information For information, visit website. Editors participate in conference.

FESTIVAL OF FAITH AND WRITING

1795 Knollcrest Circle SE, Grand Rapids MI 49546. (616)526-6770. E-mail: ffw@calvin.edu. Website: www.calvin.edu/academic/engl/festival.htm. **Contact:** English Dept.. Biennial. Conference usually held in April of even years. Conference duration: 3 days. Average attendance: 1,800. The Festival of Faith and Writing encourages serious, imaginative writing by all writers interested in the intersections of literature and belief. Site: The festival is held at Calvin College in Grand Rapids,

MI, 180 miles north of Chicago. Focus is on fiction, nonfiction, memoir, poetry, drama, children's, young adult, literary criticism, film and song lyrics. Past speakers have included Annie Dillard, John Updike, Katherine Paterson, Elie Wiesel, Joyce Carol Oates, Leif Enger, Salman Rushdie, and Marilynne Robinson.

Costs Registration: consult festival website. Registration includes all sessions during the 3-day event but does not include meals, lodging or evening concerts.

Accommodations Shuttles are available to and from select local hotels. Consult festival website for a list of hotels with special conference rates.

Additional Information Some agents and editors attend the festival and consult with prospective writers.

FISHERMAN'S WHARF WRITERS CONFERENCE

Fort Mason, San Francisco CA (800)250-8290. E-mail: algonkian@webdelsol.com. Website: fwwc.algonkianconferences.com. 2010 dates: May 12-16. Annual. Conference duration: 5 days. "Using our unique model-and-context method, Algonkian students will study and apply techniques of craft, structure, and style culled from over 20 successful authors (and dramatists) including Ann Patchett, Ken Kesey, Annie Proulx, F. Scott Fitzgerald, Tennessee Williams, Michael Chabon, Gail Godwin, Ernest Hemingway, V. Nabokov, Flannery O'Connor, Barbara Kingsolver, and Robert Graves."

Costs $495

FLATHEAD RIVER WRITERS CONFERENCE

P.O. Box 7711, Kalispell MT 59904. E-mail: conference@authorsoftheflathead.org. Website: http://authorsoftheflathead.org/conference.asp. **Contact:** Betty Kuffel. Annual. Next general conference October 2-3, 2010. Attendance limited to 100. Deals with all aspects of writing, including short and long fiction and nonfiction. Site: Flathead Valley Community College, Kalilspell, Montana. Recent speakers: Cricket Pechstein (agent) and Sandy Novack-Gottshall (fiction.)

Costs Cost: $180 for two-day conference, $150 for early bird. Includes breakfast and lunch, not lodging. Many local lodging accommodations, at all price levels.

Additional Information "We limit attendance to 100 to assure friendly, easy access to presentations."

THE GLEN WORKSHOP

3307 Third Avenue W, Seattle WA 98119. (206)281-2988. E-mail: glenworkshop@imagejournal.org. Website: www.imagejournal.org. Registration for the 2010 Glen Workshop is open until the deadline of June 1. Some workshops are already full, so consider registering soon to ensure a place in your workshop of choice. Writing classes. Art classes. A seminar on arts and aesthetics. A retreat option. The Glen Workshop combines an intensive learning experience with a lively festival of the arts. It takes place in the stark, dramatic beauty of the Sangre de Cristo mountains and within easy reach of the rich cultural, artistic, and spiritual traditions of northern New Mexico. Estab. 1991. Annual. Held first full week in August. 2010: August 1-8, Santa Fe, NM. Theme: Creativity from the Margins: Art as Witness. Conference duration: 1 week. Average attendance: 150-200. Workshop focuses on "fiction, poetry, spiritual writing, songwriting, playwriting, painting, drawing, and mixed media. Run by Image, a literary journal with a religious focus. The Glen welcomes writers who practice or grapple with religious faith." Site: features "presentations and readings by the faculty." Faculty has included Lauren F. Winner (spiritual writing), B.H. Fairchild and Marilyn Nelson (poetry), Mark St. Germain (playwriting), and Over the Rhine (songwriting).

Costs $440-1,050, including room and board; $440-520 for commuters (tuition & lunch only).

Accommodations Arrange transportation by shuttle. Accommodations included in conference cost.

Additional Information Prior to arrival, participants may need to submit workshop material depending on the teacher. "Usually 10-25 pages." Conference information is available in January/

February. For brochure e-mail, visit website, or call. "Like *Image*, the Glen is grounded in a Christian perspective, but its tone is informal and hospitable to all spiritual wayfarers."

GOTHAM WRITERS' WORKSHOP

555 8th Ave, Suite 1402, New York NY 10018. (212)974-8377. Fax: (212)307-6325. E-mail: dana@write.org. Website: www.writingclasses.com. **Contact:** Dana Miller, director of student affairs. "Classes held throughout the year. There are four terms, beginning in January, April, June/July, September/October." Conference duration: 10-week, 6-week, 1-day, and online courses offered. Average attendance: approximately 1,300 students per term, 6,000 students per year. Offers craft-oriented creative writing courses in fiction writing, screenwriting, nonfiction writing, memoir writing, novel writing, children's book writing, playwriting, poetry, songwriting, mystery writing, science fiction writing, romance writing, television writing, documentary film writing, feature article writing, travel writing, creative writing, and business writing. Also, Gotham Writers' Workshop offers a teen program, private instruction and classes on selling your work. Site: Classes are held at various schools in New York City as well as online at www.writingclasses.com. View a sample online class on the website.

Costs 10-week and online courses—$420 (includes $25 registration fee); 6-week courses-$320 (includes $25 registration fee); 1-day courses—$150 (includes $25 registration fee). Meals and lodging not included.

Additional Information "Participants do not need to submit workshop material prior to their first class." Sponsors a contest for a free 10-week online creative writing course (value = $420) offered each term. Students should fill out a form online at www.writingclasses.com to participate in the contest. The winner is randomly selected. For brochure send e-mail, visit website, call or fax. Accepts inquiries by e-mail, phone, fax. Agents and editors participate in some workshops.

GREATER LEHIGH VALLEY WRITERS GROUP 'THE WRITE STUFF' WRITERS CONFERENCE

350 Nazareth Pile, PMB #136, Bethlehem PA 18020-1115. (610)844-2949. E-mail: write@glvwg.org. Website: www.glvwg.org. **Contact:** Tammy Burke, chair. Estab. 1993. Annual. Last conference was March 25-27, 2010. Conference duration: 3 days. Average attendance: 140. This conference features workshops in all genres. Site: "The Four Points Sheraton is located in the beautiful Lehigh Valley. The spacious hotel has an indoor swimming pool and newly renovated conference rooms. Our keynote speaker James N. Frey addressed the conference over a delicious hot meal."

Costs Members, $100 (includes all workshops, 2 meals, and a chance to pitch to an editor or agent); non-members, $120. Late registration, $135.

Additional Information "The Writer's Flash contest is judged by conference participants. Write 100 words or less in fiction, creative nonfiction, or poetry. Brochures available in January by SASE, or by phone, e-mail, or on website. Accepts inquiries by SASE, e-mail or phone. Agents and editors attend conference. For updated info refer to the website, and our conference blog Http://glvwritersconferences.blogspot.com/. Greater Lehigh Valley Writer's Group hosts a friendly conference has remained one of the most friendly conferences and we give the most for your money. Breakout rooms offer craft topics, business of publishing, editor and agent panels. Book fair with book signing by published authors and presenters."

GREAT RIVER ARTS

33 Bridge Street, P.O. Box 48, Bellows Falls VT 05101. (802)463-3330. E-mail: info@greatriverarts.org. Website: www.greatriverarts.org. **Contact:** Tonia Fleming, administrator. Estab. 1999. Year-round workshops. Conference duration: 2-5 days. Average attendance: 6-8 per class. Master class and workshops in the visual and literary arts. Site: Classes are held in the Bellows Falls, Vermont/Walpole, New Hampshire region located on the shores of the Connecticut River. Classes are given in poetry, memoir, fiction and children's book arts.

Costs 2008 rates were $500-750. Does not include lodging or meals.

Accommodations Provides list of area hotels.
Additional Information Participants may need to submit material prior to arrival depending on course. Workshops for 2009 were available on website. Accepts inquiries by e-mail, phone, fax.

GREEN LAKE CHRISTIAN WRITERS CONFERENCE

W2511 State Hwy 23, Green Lake WI 54941. (920)294-7364. Fax: (920)294-3848. E-mail: janwhite@glcc.org. Website: www.glcc.org. **Contact:** Jan White. "Come learn, write and celebrate with us!" Sunday afternoon-Friday morning, August 22-27, 2010, our 62nd annual conference. "Affordable, inspirational conference for new or well-published writers. May write for the secular or Christian market or both. Workshop leaders are well-published and are experienced teachers. Spend 12 hours of classroom time in any of these areas: fiction, nonfiction, poetry, inspiratiional, curriculum, publishing for pastors. Special features: writers' contest, manuscript review, one-on-one with leaders, vespers, devotions, music, bookstore, writers' own area for display and sales, Writers' Showcase celebration. A dozen or more optional afternoon seminars and evening panels which cover marketing, internet use, specialized writing, and more." Site: South Central WI on the state's deepest lake, with 212 miles of shoreline and 1,000 acres of land, including outstanding golf course.
Accommodations Hotels, lodges and all meeting rooms are a/c. Affordable rates, excellent meals.
Additional Information Party & writers' showcase. Brochure and scholarship info from website or contact Jan White (920)294-3323.

GREEN MOUNTAIN WRITERS CONFERENCE

47 Hazel St., Rutland VT 05701. (802)775-5326. E-mail: ydaley@sbcglobal.net. Website: www.vermontwriters.com. **Contact:** Yvonne Daley. Estab. 1999. Annual. 2010 date: August 2-6. Conference duration: 5 days. Average attendance: 40. "The conference is an opportunity for writers at all stages of their development to hone their skills in a beautiful, lakeside environment where published writers across genres share tips and give feedback." Site: Conference held at Tinmouth Pavilion, an old dance pavillion on a 5-acre site on a remote pond in Tinmouth, VT. Past features include Place in story: The Importance of Environment; Creating Character through Description, Dialogue, Action, Reaction, and Thought; The Collision of Real Events and Imagination. Costs $500 before June 15, $525 after. Fee includes lunch, snacks, beverages, readings. 2010 staff: Yvonne Daley, Stephen Sandy, Joni B. Cole, Chuck Clarino, Tom Smith, Brad Kessler and Verandah Porche. This year, along with these professional authors, several writers who have self-published their books or worked with small publishers will share their experiences and offer advice to those who want to explore this option: Stephen Sandy and Brad Kessler. Both have publishing careers and experience in leading writing workshops.
Accommodations Offers list of area hotels and lodging.
Additional Information Participants' mss can be read and commented on at a cost. Sponsors contests. Conference publishes a literary magazine featuring work of participants. Brochures available in January on website or for SASE, e-mail. Accepts inquiries by SASE, e-mail, phone. "We offer the opportunity to learn from some of the nation's best writers at a small, supportive conference in a lakeside setting that allows one-to-one feedback. Participants often continue to correspond and share work after conferences." Further information available on website, by e-mail or by phone.

HEART TALK

5511 SE Hawthorne Blvd., Portland OR 97215-3367. (503)517-1931 or (877)517-1800. Fax: (503)517-1889. E-mail: wcm@westernseminary.edu. Website: www.westernseminary.edu/women/. **Contact:** Kenine Stein, administrative associate. Conference duration: 1 day. Average attendance: 100+. Every other year (alternates with speaker's conferences). March 12, 2011 will be next writer's conference. Information will be available on website as it develops. Previous keynote speakers have included Robin Jones Gunn, Patricia Rushford, Deborah Hedstrom-Page, and more. Workshop sessions and 1:1 consultation with professional writers/editors. Topics for new and advanced

writers may include: publishing, editing, fiction, market trends, dialogue, screenwriting, websites, book proposals, critique groups, nonfiction, and more. "Heart Talk provides inspirational training for men and women desiring to write for publication and/or speak publicly." Site:
Costs 2008: $65. See website for more information.
Accommodations Western Seminary has a chapel and classrooms to accommodate various size groups. The campus has a peaceful, park-like setting with beautiful lawns, trees, and flowers, plus an inviting fountain and pond. Please check website for further details as they become available.
Additional Information Contact by mail, e-mail, or phone. "Conference is open to Christians who desire to write for publication. To be added to our Heart Talk mailing list, please e-mail contact information."

HIGHLAND SUMMER CONFERENCE

Box 7014, Radford University, Radford VA 24142-7014. (540)831-5366. Fax: (540)831-5951. E-mail: rbderrick@radford.edu. Website: www.radford.edu/~arsc.. Annual conference held in June. 2010 date: June 7-18. Conference duration: 2 weeks. Average attendance: 25. Covers fiction, nonfiction, poetry, and screenwriting. This year's Highland Summer Conference will be conducted the first week by Pamela Duncan. The second week of the Conference will be conducted by author George Ella Lyon. Special evening readings by Dot Jackson and Charles Swanson. Go to website for more information.
Costs The cost is based on current Radford tuition for 3 credit hours, plus an additional conference fee. On-campus meals and housing are available at additional cost. In 2009, conference tuition was $815/in-state undergraduates, $1,944/forout-of-state undergraduates, $900/in-state graduates, and $1,728/out-of-state graduates.
Accommodations "We do not have special rate arrangements with local hotels. We do offer accommodations on the Radford University campus in a recently refurbished residence hall. The 2009 cost was $29-36/night."
Additional Information "Conference leaders typically critique work done during the 2-week conference, but do not ask to have any writing submitted prior to the conference. Conference brochures/guidelines are available in March for a SASE."

HIGHLIGHTS FOUNDATION FOUNDERS WORKSHOPS

814 Court St., Honesdale PA 18431. (570)253-1192. Fax: (570)253-0179. E-mail: contact@highlightsfoundation.org. Website: www.highlightsfoundation.org. **Contact:** Kent L. Brown, Jr.. Estab. 2000. "Workshops geared toward those interested in writing and illustrating for children, intermediate and advanced levels." Classes offered include: Writing Novels for Young Adults, Biography, Nonfiction Writing, Writing Historical Fiction, Wordplay: Writing Poetry for Children, Heart of the Novel, Nature Writing for Kids, Visual Art of the Picture Book, The Whole Novel Workshop, and more (see website for updated list).
Costs Range from $695 and up, including tuition, meals, conference supplies, and private housing.
Additional Information "Call for application and more information."

HIGHLIGHTS FOUNDATION WRITERS WORKSHOP AT CHATAUQUA

814 Court St., Honesdale PA 18431. (570)253-1192. Fax: (570)253-0179. E-mail: contact@highlightsfoundation.org. Website: www.highlightsfoundation.org. **Contact:** Kent L. Brown, Jr.. Workshops geared toward those interested in writing for children; beginner, intermediate and advanced levels. Dozens of Classes include: Writing Poetry, Book Promotion, Characterization, Developing a Plot, Exploring Genres, The Publishing Business, What Makes a Good Book, and many more. Annual workshop. Held at the Chautauqua Institution, Chautauqua, NY. Registration limited to 100. 26th Annual Writers Workshop at Chautauqua is July 17-24, 2010.
Costs Cost includes tuition, meals, conference supplies. Call for availability and pricing. Scholarships are available for first-time attendees. Call for more information or visit the website.

TONY HILLERMAN WRITER'S WEEKEND

304 Calle Oso, Santa FE NM 87501. (505)471-1565. E-mail: wordharvest@wordharvest.com. Website: www.wordharvest.com. **Contact:** Jean Schaumberg, co-director. Estab. 2004. Annual. November. 11-13, 2010. Conference duration: 4 days. Average attendance: 160. Site: The Inn and Spa at Loretto. First day: Author/teacher Margaret Coel, focuses on the art of creating fascinating characters and irresistable dialog. The second, led by motivational speaker and much-published author Bill O'Hanlon, concentrates on the business of writing and selling your book. We'll honor the winner of the 2010 Tony Hillerman Prize for best first mystery at a dinner with keynote speaker Valerie Plame Wilson, a former CIA covert operations officer. As a bonus, author/editor/publisher Judith Van Gieson will offer optional first chapter critiques and a class on how to write a great opening to your novel or non-fiction book. The first winner of the Tony Hillerman Prize, Christine Barber, will join us at the conference. There was no conference in 2009.

Costs Previous year's costs: $395 per-registration.

Accommodations The Inn and Spa at Loretto offers $109 single or double occupancy, (plus tax and a nightly $6 resort fee) for stays Nov. 11-14. Book on line with the hotel, or call 1-800-727-5531.

Additional Information Sponsors a $10,000 first mystery novel contest with Thomas Dunne Books. Brochures available in July for SASE, by phone, e-mail, fax and on website. Accepts inquiries by SASE, phone, e-mail. Deadline for the Hillerman Mystery Competition is June 1, 2010.

HOW TO BE PUBLISHED WORKSHOPS

P.O. Box 100031, Birmingham AL 35210-3006. E-mail: mike@writing2sell.com. Website: www.writing2sell.com. **Contact:** Michael Garrett. Workshops are offered continuously year-round at various locations. Conference duration: 1 session. Average attendance: 10-15. Workshops to "move writers of category fiction closer to publication." Focus is not on how to write, but how to get published. Site: Workshops held at college campuses and universities. Themes include marketing, idea development and manuscript critique.

Costs $55-89.

Additional Information "Special critique is offered, but advance submission is not required." Workshop information available on website. Accepts inquiries by e-mail.

✪ HUMBER SCHOOL FOR WRITERS SUMMER WORKSHOP

3199 Lake Shore Blvd. West, Toronto ON M8V 1K8 Canada. (416)675-6622 ext. 3448. E-mail: antanas.sileika@humber.ca. Website: www.humber.ca/creativeandperformingarts. **Contact:** Antanas Sileika, Artistic Director. Annual. Workshop held second week in July. Conference duration: 1 week. Average attendance: 100. Focuses on fiction, poetry, creative nonfiction. Site: Humber College's Lakeshore campus in Toronto. Panels cover success stories, small presses, large presses, agents. Faculty: Changes annually. 2009 included Martin Amis, Rachel Kushner, Joe Kertes, Alistair Macleod, David Mitchell, Nino Ricci, Wayson Choy, Bruce Jay Friedman, Kim Moritsugu, Olive Senior.

Costs Workshop fee is $950 Canadian.

Accommodations Provides lodging. Residence fee is $450 Canadian.

Additional Information Participants "must submit sample writing no longer than 15 pages approximately 4 weeks before workshop begins." Brochures available mid-February for e-mail, phone, fax. Accepts inquiries by e-mail, phone, fax. Agents and editors participate in conference.

INDIANA UNIVERSITY WRITERS' CONFERENCE

464 Ballantine Hall, Bloomington IN 47405-7103. (812)855-1877. Fax: (812)855-9535. E-mail: writecon@indiana.edu. Website: www.indiana.edu/~writecon. **Contact:** Bob Bledsoe, director. Estab. 1940. Annual. Conference/workshops held in June. 2010: June 6-11. Average attendance: 115. "The Indiana University Writers' Conference believes in a craft-based teaching of fiction writing. We emphasize an exploration of creativity through a variety of approaches, offering workshop-

based craft discussions, classes focusing on technique, and talks about the careers and concerns of a writing life." 2009: fiction faculty: Julia Glass, Manuel Munoz, Alyce Miller, Danit Brown.

Costs 2009 cost: 4500 for workshop (included all classes); $250 for classes only. $50 application fee. Information on accommodations available on website.

Additional Information Fiction workshop applicants must submit up to 25 pages of prose. Registration information available for SASE, by e-mail, or on website. Spaces still available in all workshops and classes for 2010.

INTERNATIONAL COMIC-CON

Comic-Con International, P.O. Box 128458, San Diego CA 92112-8458. (619)491-2475. Fax: (619)414-1022. E-mail: cci-info@comic-con.org. Website: www.comic-con.org/cci/. **Contact:** Gary Sassaman, director of print/publications. Annual. July 22-25, 2010. Conference duration: 4 days. Average attendance: 104,000. "The comics industry's largest expo, hosting writers, artists, editors, agents, publishers, buyers and sellers of comics and graphic novels." Site: San Diego Convention Center. "Nearly 300 programming events, including panels, seminars and previews, on the world of comics, movies, television, animation, art, and much more." Legendary comics creator Neal Adams is a special guest for 2010, plus a diverse line up of special guests. We're also, of course, featuring Golden and Silver Age creators, sf/fantasy writers and artists, and longtime Comic-Con friends. 2006 special guests included Ray Bradbury, Forrest J. Ackerman, Sergio Aragones, John Romita Sr., J. Michael Straczynski, Daniel Clowes, George Perez.

Costs $50 by April 19, $55 by June 7, $65 at the door. Special discounts for children and seniors.

Accommodations Does not offer overnight accommodations. Provides list of area hotels or lodging options. Special conference hotel and airfare discounts available. See website for details.

Additional Information For brochure, visit website. Agents and editors participate in conference.

INTERNATIONAL MUSIC CAMP CREATIVE WRITING WORKSHOP

111-11th Ave SW, Minot ND 58701. (701)838-8472. E-mail: info@internationalmusiccamp.com. Website: www.internationalmusiccamp.com. **Contact:** Dr. Timothy Wollenzien, camp director. Annual. Last conference held June 27-July 3, 2010. Average attendance: 35. "The workshop offers students the opportunity to refine their skills in thinking, composing and writing in an environment that is conducive to positive reinforcement. In addition to writing poems, essays and stories, individuals are encourgaged to work on their own area of interest with conferencing and feedback from the course instructor." Site: International Peace Garden on the border between the US and Canada. "Similar to a university campus, several dormitories, classrooms, lecture halls and cafeteria provide the perfect site for such a workshop. The beautiful and picturesque International Peace Garden provides additional inspiration to creative thinking." Instructor still to be determined.

Costs $360, includes tuition, room and board. Early bird registration (postmarked by May 1) $345.

Accommodations Airline and depot shuttles are available upon request. Housing is included in the $345 fee.

Additional Information Conference information is available in September. For brochure visit website, e-mail, call or fax. Accepts inquiries by e-mail, phone and fax.

INTERNATIONAL READERS THEATRE WORKSHOPS

P.O. Box 421262, San Diego CA 92142. (858)277-4274. Fax: (858)277-4222. E-mail: marlene1@san.rr.com. Website: www.readerstheatreinstitute.com. **Contact:** Arlene McCoy, general manager. 2010 workshop July 11-24. Average attendance: 25-35. Workshop on "all aspects of Readers Theatre with emphasis on scriptmaking." Site: Chicago, IL

Costs "$1,975 includes housing for two weeks (twin accommodations), continental breakfast, complimentary mid-morning coffee break on class days, textbook for first time participants and Institute fees."

Additional Information "One-on-one critiques available between writer and faculty (if members)." For reservation form and guidelines visit website, e-mail, fax, or call. Conference offers "up to 12 graduate credits. For more information on credit, contact Larisa Kruze, University of Southern Maine at (207)780-5942.

IOWA SUMMER WRITING FESTIVAL

C215 Seashore Hall, University of Iowa, Iowa City IA 52242-1802. (319)335-4160. E-mail: iswfestival@uiowa.edu. Website: www.uiowa.edu/~iswfest.. **Contact:** Amy Margolis, director. Annual. Festival held in June and July. Workshops are one week or a weekend. Average attendance: limited to 12/class—over 1,500 participants throughout the summer. "We offer workshops across the genres, including novel, short story, poetry, essay, memoir, humor, travel, playwriting, screenwriting, writing for children and more. All writers 21 and over are welcome. You need only have the desire to write." Site: University of Iowa campus. 2011 speakers are undetermined at this time. Readers and instructors have included Lee K. Abbott, John Dalton, Amber Dermont, Ann Harleman, Bret Anthony Johnston, Diana Ossana, Mark Jude Poirier, Michelle Wildgen, and Bart Yates.
Costs $560 for full week; $280 for weekend workshop. Housing and meals are separate.
Accommodations Sheraton, $104/night, Heartland Inn, $70/night (rates subject to change).
Additional Information Conference information available in February. Accepts inquiries by fax, e-mail, phone. "Register early. Classes fill quickly."

IWWG EARLY SUMMER CONFERENCE

P.O. Box 810, Gracie Station NY 10028-0082. (212)737-7536. Fax: (212)737-7536. E-mail: iwwg@iwwg.com. Website: www.iwwg.com. **Contact:** Hannelore Hahn, exec. director. 2011 dates: March 11-13. Location: California. More information to come. Average attendance: 500 maximum. Open to all women. Around 65 workshops offered each day. 2009 poetry staff includes Barbara Garro, Marj Hahne, D.H. Melhem, Myra Shapiro, and Susan Baugh.
Accommodations 2009 cost: $1,085 (single), $945 (double) for IWWG members; $1,330 (single), $990 (double), $1,034 (single). Includes program and room and board for 7 nights, 21 meals at Skidmore College. Shorter conference stays available, such as 5 days or weekend. Commuters welcome.
Additional Information Post-conference retreat weekend also available. information available for SASE, by e-mail, or on web site.

IWWG MEET THE AGENTS AND EDITORS: THE BIG APPLE WORKSHOPS

P.O. Box 810, Gracie Station, New York NY 10028-0082. (212)737-7536. Fax: (212)737-9469. E-mail: iwwg@iwwg.com. Website: www.iwwg.com. **Contact:** Hannelore Hahn, executive director. Estab. 1976. Biannual. Workshops held in April and October. Average attendance: 150. Workshops to promote creative writing and professional success. October 16-17, 2010 (Weekend) "Myth and Memoir: What's Mythical About an 'Ordinary' Life?" Workshop with Maureen Murdock (Saturday) Open House: Meet the Authors/Meet the Agents (Sunday). The National Arts Club, 15 Gramercy Park South (just east of East 20th St.) New York City. Register online via PayPal. Saturday: 1-day writing workshop. Sunday afternoon: open house/meet the agents, independent presses and editors.
Costs $130 for members; $155 for non-members for the weekend.
Accommodations Information on transportation arrangements and overnight accommodations available.
Additional Information Accepts inquiries by fax, e-mail, phone.

JACKSON HOLE WRITERS CONFERENCE

Jackson WY. (307)766-2938. Fax: (307)766-3914. E-mail: tim@jacksonholewritersconference.com. Website: http://jacksonholewritersconference.com/. **Contact:** Tim Sandlin, director. Annual. June 24-27, 2010. Conference duration: 4 days. Average attendance: 100. The Jackson Hole Writers

Conference draws a wide range of participants, from beginners to published writers. Site: Center for the Arts. The conference is directed toward fiction, poetry, travel/adventure magazine, young adult playwriting and creative nonfiction, offering programs relevant to all 6 disciplines: story structure, character development, narrative thrust, work habits and business techniques. In addition, separate sessions deal with skills particular to each specialty. "We offer three one-on-one manuscript critiques to each participant." Featuring Janet Fitch, Winifred Gallagher, Jeff Chu, and Tim Cahill.

Costs $325 conference pre-registration; $300 conference pre-registration for past participants; $75 spouse/guest registration; $50 ms evaluation; $75 extended ms evaluation. "You must register for conference to be eligible for manuscript evaluation."

Accommodations $135/night for single or double; $145/night triple; $155/night quadruple.

Additional Information The conference faculty's goal is to help our writers get published. Agent and editor roundtable discussions are geared specifically to teach you how your writing can be crafted, shaped and packaged for sale. Ms evaluations are also available. See website for details.

JAMES RIVER WRITERS CONFERENCE

ArtWorks Studios 136, 320 Hull St., #136, Richmond VA 23224. (804)433-3790. Fax: (804)291-1466. E-mail: info@jamesriverwriters.com; fallconference@jamesriverwriters.com; anne@jamesriverwriters.com. Website: www.jamesriverwriters.com. **Contact:** Anne Westrick, admin. director. Estab. 2003. Annual. Thursday-Friday, October 8-9, 2010. Average attendance: 250. Conference. "The James River Writers Conference offers two days of cross-genre sessions to bring aspiring writers together with professionals to share the ups and downs of the writing life. By seeking to build and inspire the community of writers, the sessions address a myriad of topics related to the craft and business of writing fiction, nonfiction, poetry, fantasy/sci-fi, children's, magazine articles, short stories, memoir, biography, and romance. The purpose is to energize the creative literary community." Site: Artworks Studios. Past years'conference guests have included Sheri Reynolds, Sharyn McCrumb, Claudia Emerson, Eric VanLustbader, Mark Bowden, Rosalind Miles, Dennis McFarland, David L. Robbins, Dean King, James Campbell and Hampton Sides.

Costs In 2008 the cost was $140 early registration and $155 after September 1, 2008. A continental breakfast and box lunch were included in the fee.

Accommodations Richmond is easily accessibly by air and train. Does not offer overnight accommodations. Provides list of area hotels or lodging options. "Each year we arrange for special conference rates at an area hotel."

Additional Information Workshop material is not required, however we have offered an option for submissions: the first pages critique session in which submissions are read before a panel of agents and editors who are seeing them for the first time and are asked to react on the spot. No additional fee. No guarantee that a particular submission will be read. Details posted on the website, www.jamesriverwriters.com. Information available in June. For brochure, visit website. Agents participate in conference. Editors participate in conference.

N JOURNEY INTO THE IMAGINATION: A WEEKEND WRITING WORKSHOP

995 Chapman Rd, Yorktown NY 10598. (914)962-4432. E-mail: emily@emilyhanlon.com. Website: www.thefictionwritersjourney.com. **Contact:** Emily Hanlon. Estab. 2004. Annual. April 30-May 2, 2010. Held the first weekend in May. Average attendance: 15-20. "Purpose of workshop: fiction, memoir, short story, creativity and the creative process." Site: Wisdom House Retreat Center in Litchfield, CT. "We stay in an old farmhouse on the retreat center grounds. Excellent food and lovely surroundings and accommodations. The core of this weekend's work is welcoming the unknown into your writing. We will go on a magical mystery tour to find and embrace new characters and to deepen our relationship to characters who already may people our stories. Bring something on which you are already working or simply bring along your Inner Writer, pen and a journal, and let the magic unfold!"

Costs 2009: $450-650, dependent on choice of room.

Additional Information For brochure, visit website.

KENYON REVIEW WRITERS WORKSHOP

The Kenyon Review, Kenyon College, Gambier OH 43022. (740) 427-5207. Fax: (740) 427-5417. E-mail: writers@kenyonreview.org. Website: www.kenyonreview.org. **Contact:** Anna Duke Reach, director. Estab.1990. Annual. Workshop held mid to late June. Conference duration: 8 days. Average attendance: 60-70. Participants apply in poetry, fiction or literary nonfiction, and then participate in intensive daily workshops which focus on the generation and revision of significant new work. Site: The conference takes place on the campus of Kenyon College in the rural village of Gambier, Ohio. Students have access to college computing and recreational facilities and are housed in campus housing. Workshop leaders have included David Baker, Ron Carlson, Rebecca McClanahan, Meghan O'Rourke, Linda Gregorson, Dinty Moore, Tara Ison and Nancy Zafris.

Costs $1,995 including room and board.

Accommodations The workshop operates a shuttle to and from Gambier and the airport in Columbus, Ohio. Offers overnight accommodations. Participants are housed in Kenyon College student housing. The cost is covered in the tuition.

Additional Information Application includes a writing sample. Admission decisions are made on a rolling basis. Workshop information is available November 1. For brochure send e-mail, visit website, call, fax. Accepts inquiries by SASE, e-mail, phone, fax.

KILLER NASHVILLE

P.O. Box 680686, Franklin TN 37068-0686. (615)599-4032. E-mail: contact@killernashville.com. Website: www.KillerNashville.com. **Contact:** Clay Stafford, founder. Estab. 2006. Annual. Next event: August 20-22, 2010. Conference duration: 4 days. Average attendance: 180+. "Conference designed for writers and fans of mysteries and thrillers, including authors (fiction and nonfiction), playwrights, and screenwriters. Sponsors include Middle Tennessee State University, Barnes & Noble Booksellers, Mystery Writers of America, Sisters in Crime, First Tennessee Bank, Landmark Booksellers, and The Nashville Scene. Law enforcement workshop parters include the Federal Bureau of Investigation (FBI), The Tennessee Bureau of Investigations (TBI), Alcohol, Tobacco, & Firearms (ATF), Franklin Police Department, Brentwood Police Department, and Wilson County Sheriff's Department. Agents, editors and industry professionals include Carey Nelson Burch (William Morris Agency), Lucienne Diver (The Knight Literary Agency), Miriam Kress (Irene Goodman Literary Agency), and Maryglenn McCombs (Oceanview Publishing). Event includes book signings and panels." Past panelists included authors Michael Connelly, Carol Higgins Clark, Bill Bass, Gregg Hurwitz, Hallie Ephron, Chris Grabenstein, Rhonda Pollero, P.J. Parrish, Reed Farrel Coleman, Kathryn Wall, Mary Saums, Don Bruns, Bill Moody, Richard Helms, Alexandra Sokoloff, and Steven Womack.

Costs Signings events are free; current prices for events available on website.

Additional Information "Additional information about registration is provided at www.KillerNashville.com."

LA JOLLA WRITERS CONFERENCE

P.O. Box 178122, San Diego CA 92177. (858)467-1978. Fax: (858)467-1971. E-mail: jkuritz@strategiespr.com. Website: www.lajollawritersconference.com. **Contact:** Jared Kuritz, director.

Additional Information Private Read & Critiques for an additional fee of $50 each.

LAMB'S SPRINGFED WRITING RETREAT

P.O. Box 304, Royal Oak MI 48068-0304. (248)589-3913. Fax: (248)589-9981. E-mail: johndlamb@ameritech.net. Website: www.springfed.org. **Contact:** John D. Lamb, director. (formally Walloon Writer's Retreat)Estab. 1999. Annual. Last conference held October 8-11, 2009. Average attendance: 75. Focus includes fiction, poetry, screenwriting and nonfiction. Site: The Birchwood Inn, Harbor Spring, MI. Attendees stay in comfortable rooms, and seminars are held in conference rooms with fieldstone fireplaces and dining area. Past faculty included Billy Collins, Michael Moore, Jonathan Rand, Jacquelyn Mitchard, Jane Hamilton, Thomas Lux, Joyce Maynard, Jack Driscoll, Dorianne Laux, and Cornelius Eady.

Costs Single occupancy is $625, $560 (3 days, 2 nights, all meals included). $360 non-lodging.

Accommodations Shuttle rides from Traverse City Airport or Pellston Airport. Offers overnight accommodations. Provides list of area lodging options.

Additional Information Optional: Attendees may submit 3 poems or 5 pages of prose for conference with a staff member. Brochures available mid-June by e-mail, on website or by phone. Accepts inquiries by SASE, e-mail, phone.

N LAS VEGAS WRITERS CONFERENCE

Henderson Writers' Group, 614 Mosswood Dr., Henderson NV 89015. (702)564-2488. E-mail: president@hendersonwritersgroup.com. Website: www.lasvegaswritersconference.com. **Contact:** Jo Wilkens, president. Annual. April. Conference duration: 4 days. Average attendance: 150 maximum. "Join writing professionals, agents, industry experts and your colleagues for four days in Las Vegas, NV, as they share their knowledge on all aspects of the writer's craft. While there are formal pitch sessions, panels, workshops, and seminars, the faculty is also available throughout the conference for informal discussions and advice. Plus, you're bound to meet a few new friends, too. Workshops, seminars and expert panels will take you through writing in many genres including fiction, creative nonfiction, screenwriting, poetry, journalism and business and technical writing. There will be many Q&A panels for you to ask the experts all your questions." Site: Sam's Town Hotel and Gambling Hall in Las Vegas.

Costs $400 Early Bird or $436 after February 1; $450 at the door. One day registration $250.

Additional Information Sponsors contest. Agents and editors participate in conference.

LEDIG HOUSE INTERNATIONAL WRITERS RESIDENCY

55 Fifth Ave., 15th Floor, New York NY 10003. (212)206-6114. Website: www.artomi.org/ledig. Residency duration: 2 weeks to 2 months. Average attendance: Up to 20 writers per session. Residency. Site: "Up to 20 writers per session—10 at a given time—live and write on the stunning 300 acre grounds and sculpture park that overlooks the Catskill Mountains."

Accommodations Residents provide their own transportation. Offers overnight accommodations.

Additional Information "Agents and editors from the New York publishing community are invited for dinner and discussion. Bicycles, a swimming pool, and nearby tennis court are available for use."

LESLEY UNIVERSITY WRITER'S CONFERENCE

29 Everett Street, Cambridge MA 02138. (617) 349-8298. Fax: (617) 349-8335. E-mail: jwadling@lesley.edu; lrice@lesley.edu. Website: www.lesley.edu/info/luwc. **Contact:** Joyce Wadlington, dir. continuing ed. Estab. 2007. Annual. 2010 to be announced on website. 2009 Conference July 26-July 31. Conference duration: one week. Average attendance: 40-60 people. Workshop/residency. "We focus on fiction, nonfiction, children's book writing, and poetry." Workshop limit: 10. Site: Lesley University Campus, Cambridge, MA. 2009 faculty included Marcie Hershman (Safe in America), Michael Lowenthal (Charity Girl), Afas M. Weaver (Timber and Prayer, 1996 Pulitzer Prize finalist), and David Elliot (And Here's to You !). Guest faculty included Julia Glass (Three Junes, 2002 National Book Award), M.T. Anderson (Octavian Nothing, 2006 National Book Award for Young People), and Gail Mazur (Nightfire).

Costs 2009: tuition $770 plus $30 registration fee.

Accommodations Participants commute or stay in the residence halls; commuter and resident meal plans are available. Parking available for a fee.

Additional Information Admission is selective and based on evaluation of applicant's work. For brochure, call or e-mail.

THE MACDOWELL COLONY

100 High St., Peterborough NH 03458. (603)924-3886. Fax: (603)924-9142. E-mail: admissions@macdowellcolony.org. Website: www.macdowellcolony.org. **Contact:** Admissions Director. Open to writers and playwrights, composers, visual artists, film/video artists, interdisciplinary artists and architects. Site: includes main building, library, 3 residence halls and 32 individual studios on over 450 mostly wooded acres, 1 mile from center of small town in southern New Hampshire. Available up to 8 weeks year-round. Provisions for the writer include meals, private sleeping room, individual secluded studio. Accommodates variable number of writers, 10 to 20 at a time.

Costs "There are no residency fees. Grants for travel to and from the Colony are available based on need. The MacDowell Colony is pleased to offer grants up to $1,000 for artists in need of financial assistance during a residency at MacDowell. At the present time, only artists reviewed and accepted by the admissions panel are eligible for this grant." Application forms available. Application deadline: January 15 for summer (June 1-Sept. 30), April 15 for fall (Oct. 1-Jan. 31), September 15 for winter/spring (Feb. 1-May 31). Submit application form online. Mail 6 copies of a writing sample, no more than 25 pages, along with copies of the completed application form. Please refer to work sample guidelines. Work in progress strongly recommended. Brochure/guidelines available; SASE required for return of work sample.

MARYMOUNT MANHATTAN COLLEGE WRITERS' CONFERENCE

221 E. 71st St., New York NY 10021. (212)774-4810. Fax: 212-774-0792. E-mail: lfrumkes@mmm.edu. **Contact:** Lewis Burke Frumkes or Karen Arfi. Annual. June. Conference duration: "Actual conference is one day, and there is a three-day intensive preceeding." Average attendance: 200. "We present workshops on several different writing genres and panels on publicity, editing and literary agents." Site: College/auditorium setting. 2008 conference featured 2 fiction panels, a children's book writing panel, a mystery/thriller panel and a literary agent panel. Keynote speaker for 2008 was Stuart Woods. The conference itself included more than 50 authors.

Costs $175, includes lunch and reception.

Accommodations Provides list of area lodging.

Additional Information 2009 conference information will be available in March by fax or phone. Also accepts inquiries by e-mail. Editors and agents sometimes attend conference.

MEGACON

5757 74th Trace, Live Oak FL 32060. (386)364-1826. E-mail: info@megaconvention.com. Website: www.megaconvention.com. 5757 74th Trace, Live Oak FL 32060.(386)364-1826. Fax: (386)364-1828. E-mail: info@megaconvention.com. Website: www.megaconvention.com. Annual. March 25th - 27th, 2011. Orange County Convention Center Hall D, 9899 International Drive, Orlando, FL 32819. Conference duration: 3 days. "MegaCon is the southeast's largest comic book, science fiction/fantasy, anime, gaming, toys multi-media event!"

Costs Advance Online (online, over phone or by mail) $23.96 for one day advance ticket, $56.45 for three days. At the Door $25.00 for one day, $60.00 for three days. 10 & under(with paid adult) Free! All prices include 6.5% sales tax.

MONTEVALLO LITERARY FESTIVAL

Sta. 6420, University of Montevallo, Montevallo AL 35115. (205)665-6420. Fax: (205)665-6422. E-mail: murphyj@montevallo.edu. Website: www.montevallo.edu/english. **Contact:** Dr. Jim Murphy, director. Annual. Last festival held: April 23, 2010. Average attendance: 60-100. "Readings, panels, and workshops on all literary genres and on literary editing/publishing. Master class workshops in fiction and poetry." Site: Several sites on a bucolic liberal arts university campus. 2010 fiction workshop leader was Lorraine López. Past fiction workshop faculty included Anthony Grooms, Inman Majors, Patricia Foster, Tom Franklin, Sheri Joseph, Sena Jeter Naslund, Brad Vice, Brad Watson, and John Dufresne. See website for 2011 dates and speakers.

Costs In 2010: $45 for festival, including meals; $95 for festival, including meals and workshop.

Accommodations Free on-campus parking. Offers overnight accommodations at Ramsay Conference Center on campus. Rooms $40/night. Call (205)665-6280 for reservations. Visit www.montevallo.edu/cont_ed/ramsay.shtm for information.

Additional Information To enroll in a fiction workshop, contact Bryn Chancellor (bchancellor@montevallo.edu). Information for upcoming festival available in February For brochure, visit website. Accepts inquiries by mail (with SASE), e-mail, phone, and fax. Editors participate in conference. "This is a friendly, relaxed festival dedicated to bringing literary writers and readers together on a personal scale."

MONTROSE CHRISTIAN WRITER'S CONFERENCE

5 Locust Street, Montrose Bible Conference, Montrose PA 18801-1112. (570)278-1001 or (800)598-5030. Fax: (570)278-3061. E-mail: mbc@montrosebible.org. Website: www.montrosebible.org. **Contact:** Donna Kosik, MBC secretary/registrar. Annual. Conference held in July. Average attendance: 85. "We try to meet a cross-section of writing needs, for beginners and advanced, covering fiction, poetry and writing for children. It is small enough to allow personal interaction between conferees and faculty. We meet in the beautiful village of Montrose, Pennsylvania, situated in the mountains. The Bible Conference provides hotel/motel-like accommodation and good food. The main sessions are held in the chapel with rooms available for other classes. Fiction writing has been taught each year."

Costs In 2009 registration (tuition) was $155.

Accommodations Will meet planes in Binghamton, NY and Scranton, PA. On-site accomodations: room and board $285-330/conference; $60-70/day including food (2009 rates). RV court available.

Additional Information "Writers can send work ahead of time and have it critiqued for a small fee." The attendees are usually church related. The writing has a Christian emphasis. Conference information available in April. For brochure send SASE, visit website, e-mail, call or fax. Accepts inquiries by SASE, e-mail, fax, phone.

MOUNT HERMON CHRISTIAN WRITERS CONFERENCE

P.O. Box 413, Mount Hermon CA 95041-0413. (831)335-4466. Fax: (831)335-9413. E-mail: info@mhcamps.org. Website: www.mounthermon.org/writers. **Contact:** Rachel Williams, director. Annual. Held Palm Sunday weekend, Friday through Tuesday. "A working, how-to conference with over 10 major morning tracks and 70 options afternoon workshops about the craft of writing fiction, children's books, poetry, nonfiction, articles, and educational curriculum, with varying levels of writing proficiency addressed. Site: "The conference is sponsored by and held at the 440-acre Mount Hermon Christian Conference Center near San Jose, California, in the heart of the coastal redwoods. The faculty/student ratio is about 1:6 or 7. Faculty is made up of editors and publisher representatives from major Christian publishing houses nationwide."

Costs Registration fees include tuition, all major morning sessions, keynote sessions, and refreshment breaks. Room and board varies depending on choice of housing options. See website for current costs.

Accommodations Registrants stay in hotel-style accommodations, and full board is provided as part of conference fees. Housing is not required of registrants, but about 96% of our registrants use Mount Hermon's housing facilities. Meals are buffet style, with faculty joining registrants and are required and included in fees. For those flying, shuttle service is available from the San Jose International airport. Check website for current cost of this service.

Additional Information Registrants may submit 2 mss for critique in advance of the conference. No advance work is required, however. Conference brochures/guidelines are available online annually in December. Accepts inquiries by e-mail, fax. "The residential nature of our conference makes this a unique setting for one-on-one interaction with faculty/staff. There is an intentional spiritual flavor to the conference, with genreal sessions by well-known speakers a highlight. Come rested, with plenty of business cards and samples of works in progress."

NATCHEZ LITERARY AND CINEMA CELEBRATION

P.O. Box 1307, Natchez MS 39121-1307. (601)446-1208. Fax: (601)446-1214. E-mail: carolyn.smith@colin.edu. Website: www.colin.edu/NLCC.. **Contact:** Carolyn Vance Smith, co-chairman. Annual. Conference held February 25-28, 2010. Average attendance: 3,000. Conference focuses on "all literature, including film scripts." Site: 500-seat auditorium, various sizes of break-out rooms. Theme: "Southern Humor." Scholars will speak on humor in history, literature, film, and real life. Costs about $100, includes a meal, receptions, book signings, workshops. Lectures/panel discussions are free.

Costs About $100, includes a meal, receptions, book signings, workshops. Lectures/panel discussions are free.

Accommodations Groups can ask for special assistance. Usually they can be accommodated. Call 866-296-6522.

Additional Information Conference information is available in Fall. For brochure send SASE, e-mail, visit website, call or fax. Accepts inquiries by SASE, e-mail, phone and fax. Agents and editors participate in conference.

NY STATE SUMMER WRITERS INSTITUTE

815 N. Broadway, Saratoga Springs NY 12866. (518)580-5592. Fax: (518)580-5549. E-mail: summerwriters@skidmore.edu. Website: www.skidmore.edu/summer. **Contact:** Darcy Bourassa, student services assistant. Estab. 1987. Annual. Conference duration: Two-week or four-week session. Average attendance: 100 per two-week session. This event features fiction, nonfiction, and poetry workshops. College credit is available for four-week attendees. Site: held on Skidmore campus—dorm residency and dining hall meals. "Summer in Saratoga is beautiful." Past faculty has included Amy Hempel, Nick Delbanco, Margot Livesey, Jay McInerney, Rick Moody and Lee K. Abbott. Visiting writers have included Joyce Carol Oates, Russell Banks, Ann Beattie, Michael Cunningham and Michael Ondaatje.

Additional Information For pricing information and how to apply, visit the website.

ODYSSEY FANTASY WRITING WORKSHOP

P.O. Box 75, Mont Vernon NH 03057-1420. Phone/fax: (603)673-6234. E-mail: jcavelos@sff.net. Website: www.odysseyworkshop.org. **Contact:** Jeanne Cavelos, director. Annual. Last workshop held June 7 to July 16, 2010. Conference duration: 6 weeks. Average attendance: limited to 16. "A workshop for fantasy, science fiction and horror writers that combines an intensive learning and writing experience with in-depth feedback on students' manuscripts. The only six-week workshop to combine the overall guidance of a single instructor with the varied perspectives of guest lecturers. Also, the only such workshop run by a former New York City book editor." Site: conference held at Saint Anselm College in Manchester, New Hampshire. Previous guest lecturers included: George R.R. Martin, Harlan Ellison, Ben Bova, Dan Simmons, Jane Yolen, Elizabeth Hand, Terry Brooks, Nancy Kress, Patricia McKillip and John Crowley.

Costs In 2010: $1,900 tuition, $775 housing (double room), $1,550 (single room); $35 application fee, $400-600 food (approximate), $450 processing fee to receive college credit.

Accommodations "Workshop students stay at Saint Anselm College Apartments and eat at college."

Additional Information Students must apply and include a writing sample. Application deadline April 10. Students' works are critiqued throughout the 6 weeks. Workshop information available in October. For brochure/guidelines send SASE, e-mail, visit website, call or fax. Accepts inquiries by SASE, e-mail, fax, phone.

OXFORD CONFERENCE FOR THE BOOK

Center for the Study of Southern Culture, Univ. of Mississippi, University MS 38677-1848. (662)915-5993. Fax: (662)915-5814. E-mail: aabadie@olemiss.edu. Website: www.oxfordconferenceforthebook.com or www.olemiss.edu/depts/south. **Contact:** Ann J. Abadie. Estab. 1993. Annual. Conference held in March or April. Average attendance: 300. "The conference celebrates books, writing and reading and deals with practical concerns on which the literary arts depend, including literacy, freedom of expression and the book trade itself. Each year's program consists of readings, lectures and discussions. Areas of focus are fiction, poetry, nonfiction and—occasionally—drama. We have, on occasion, looked at science fiction and mysteries. We always pay attention to children's literature." Site: University of Mississippi campus. Annual topics include Submitting Manuscripts/ Working One's Way into Print; Finding a Voice/Reaching an Audience; The Endangered Species: Readers Today and Tomorrow. The 2010 was dedicated to Barry Hannah, one of Mississippi's most distinguished contemporary writers. Among the more than 50 speakers were William Dunlap, Noel Polk, Tom Franklin and Amy Hempel; Daniel E. Williams, who taught the first course on Hannah's work; and his former students Anne Rapp and Cynthia Shearer, Nicholas A. Basbane, known as "the leading authority of books about books." There was a celebration of National Poetry Month, with poets E. Ethelbert Miller, of Washington, D.C., and Mark Jarman, a professor at Vanderbilt University, reading their work. Donna Hemans, John Brandon, and others read from their fiction, and journalist Curtis Wilkie and New Yorker columnist Hendrick Hertzberg discussed books about politics.

Costs "The conference is open to participants without charge."

Accommodations Provides list of area hotels.

Additional Information Brochures available in February by e-mail, on Website, by phone, by fax. Accepts inquiries by e-mail, phone, fax. Agents and editors participate in conference.

PACIFIC NORTHWEST WRITERS CONFERENCE

P.O. Box 2016, Edmonds WA 98020-9516. (425)673-2665. Fax: (425)771-9588. E-mail: pnwa@pnwa.org. Website: www.pnwa.org. **Contact:** Kelly Liddane. PMB 2717-1420 NW Gilman Blvd., Ste 2, Issaquah, WA 98027. (425)673-2665. Fax: (206)824-4559. E-mail: pnwa@pnwa.org. Website: www.pnwa.org. Annual. 2010 conference held July 22-August 25, 2010 at Seattle Airport Hilton, Seattle, WA 98188. Average attendance: 450. "Meet agents and editors, learn craft from renowned authors, uncover new marketing secrets, and more."

Additional Information Literary Contest featuring 12 categories: Mainstream, Inspirational, Romance, Mystery/Thriller, Science Fiction/Fantasy, Young Adult Novel, Nonfiction Book/Memoir, Screen Writing, Poetry, Short Story, Children's Picture Book or Chapter Book, Adult Short Topics (article, essay, short memoir). Contest deadline: February 19, 2010. For Conference and Contest information please visit website.

PHILADELPHIA WRITERS' CONFERENCE

(215)619-7422. E-mail: dresente@mc3.edu. Annual. Conference held June 11-13 for 2010. Average attendance: 160-200. Conference covers many forms of writing, "novel, short story, genre fiction, nonfiction book, magazine writing, juvenile, poetry." Site: Entire wing of Independence Mall Holiday Inn.

Costs 2010: Six workshops + features was $205 if registered byt April 15; $225 after April 15 and for walk-in. Buffet and banquet $40 each for Friday and Saturday.

Accommodations "Hotel offers discount for early registration."

Additional Information Sponsors contest. "Length generally 2,500 words for fiction or nonfiction. First prize in addition to cash and certificate gets free tuition for following year." Also offers ms critique. Brochures available usually in January for SASE, by e-mail and on website. Accepts inquiries by e-mail and SASE. Agents and editors attend conference. 2002 guest editors and agents included Juris Jurjevics, Soho Press; Dan Simon, Seven Stories Press; Lynn Rosen, Running Press; Samantha Mandok, Berkley Publishing Group; Toni Lopopolo, Toni Lopopolo Literary Agency; Meredith Bernstein, Meredith Bernstein Literary Agency; Jim Fitzgerald, Carl Wahn Agency; Lucienne Diver, Spectrum Literary Agency.

PIKES PEAK

427 E. Colorado Ave. #116, Colorado Springs CO 80903. (719)531-5723. E-mail: info@pikespeakwriters.com. Website: pikespeakwriters.com. Annual. Conference duration: 3 days. Conference. "The Pikes Peak Writers Conference is a project of the Pikes Peak Writers, a nonprofit organization. This conference is underwritten by the Marriott Hotel in Colorado Springs."

Accommodations Offers overnight accommodations.

Additional Information For brochure, visit website. Agents and editors participate in conference.

THE POWER OF WORDS

Goddard College, 123 Pitkin Rd., Plainfield VT 05667. (802)454-8311. E-mail: tlaconference@goddard.edu. Website: www.goddard.edu; www.tlanetwork.org/conference. **Contact:** Heather A. Mandell, TLA network coordinator. Estab. 2003. Annual. This year's conference is September 23-26, 2010 at Goddard College in Plainfield, VT, featuring Gregory Orr, Kim Rosen, Greg Greenway, Katherine Towler, Nancy Mellon, S. Pearl Sharp and many others. Conference duration: 4 days. Average attendance: 150. "Purpose is to explore social and personal transformation through the spoken, written and sung word and to share resources for making a living using writing, storytelling, drama, narrative medicine, etc. in local communities." Site: A small college campus nestled in the Green Mountains of Vermont; campus was once historic farm, and historic buildings still in use—features woodlands (with trails), dorms, meeting halls and offices. This year the conference will feature a number of TLA practitioners as keynote speakers and special guests, including the following: Gregory Orr, Nancy Mellon, Greg Greenway, S. Pearl Sharp, Kim Rosen, Katherine Towler, Yvette Hyater-Adams, Vanita Leatherwood. See themes on the website.

Costs $220 early bird special by March 15; $250 until July 15; /$280 thereafter.

Accommodations Offers overnight accommodations. Average is $40-60/night plus $12/meal.

Additional Information Submit workshop proposals prior to conference; deadline for proposals is January 15. Visit website for more information.

ROMANCE WRITERS OF AMERICA NATIONAL CONFERENCE

14615 Benfer Rd., Houston TX 77069. (832)717-5200, ext. 121. Fax: (832)717-5201. E-mail: info@rwanational.org. Website: www.rwanational.org. **Contact:** Judy Scott, PR manager. Annual. Average attendance: 2,000. Over 100 workshops on the craft of writing, researching and the business side of being a working writer. Publishing professionals attend and accept appointments. Site: Conference held in Washington DC in 2009 and Nashville in 2010. Keynote speaker for 2009 was New York Times bestselling author Linda Howard.

Costs In 2009, early registration was $425 for RWA members and $500 for nonmembers.

Additional Information Annual RITA awards are presented for romance authors. Annual Golden Heart awards are presented for unpublished writers. Conference brochures/guidelines and registration forms are available on website in January. Accepts inquiries by SASE, e-mail, fax, phone.

SAGE HILL WRITING EXPERIENCE

Box 1731, Saskatoon SK S7K 3S1 Canada. Phone/fax: (306)652-7395. E-mail: sage.hill@sasktel.net. Website: www.sagehillwriting.ca. **Contact:** Paula Jane Remlinger. Annual. Workshops held in July and May. Conference duration: 10-14 days. Average attendance: Summer, 30-40; Spring, 6-8. "Sage Hill Writing Experience offers a special working and learning opportunity to writers at different stages of development. Top quality instruction, low instructor-student ratio and the beautiful Sage Hill setting offer conditions ideal for the pursuit of excellence in the arts of fiction, and poetry." Site: The Sage Hill location features "individual accommodation, in-room writing area, lounges, meeting rooms, healthy meals, walking woods and vistas in several directions." Various classes are held: Introduction to Writing Fiction & Poetry; Fiction Workshop; Fiction Colloquium, Poetry Workshop; Poetry Colloquium; Writing for Young Adults Lab.

Costs Summer program, $1,095 (Canadian) includes instruction, accommodation, meals and all facilities. Spring Colloquium: $1,395 (Canadian).

Accommodations On-site individual accommodations for Summer and Fall programs located at Lumsden, 45 kilometers outside Regina.

Additional Information Application requirements for Introduction to Creative Writing: A 5-page sample of your writing or a statement of your interest in creative writing; list of courses taken required. For workshop and colloquium programs: A résumé of your writing career and a 12-page sample of your work-in-progress, plus 5 pages of published work required. Application deadline for the Summer Program is in April. Spring program deadline in March. Guidelines are available for SASE, e-mail, fax, phone or on website. Scholarships and bursaries are available.

SCBWI SOUTHERN BREEZE FALL CONFERENCE

Writing and Illustrating for Kids '10, P.O. Box 26282, Birmingham AL 35260. E-mail: jskittinger@gmail.com. Website: www.southern-breeze.org. **Contact:** Jo Kittinger, co-regional advisor. Estab. 1992. Annual. Conference held the third Saturday in October. Average Attendance: 160. This conference is designed to educate and inspire creators of quality children's literature. **Costs:** About $125 for SCBWI members, $145 for non-members.

Accommodations Nearby hotel offers a group rate to Southern Breeze conference attendees. The conference is held in a fabulous school.

Additional Information This Southern Breeze conference offers an amazing lineup of 28 workshops on craft and the business of writing and illustrating. Tracks are included for the novice or professional. Speakers generally include editors, agents, authors, art directors, writers, and illustrators - all professionals in children's books. Come prepared to be WOWED! Manuscript and portfolio critiques available for an additional fee; manuscripts must be sent by deadline. Conference information is included in the Southern Breeze News, mailed in available online by Mid-August. Visit website for details. Accepts inquiries by SASE or e-mail.

SCBWI WINTER CONFERENCE ON WRITING AND ILLUSTRATING FOR CHILDREN

8271 Beverly Blvd., Los Angeles CA 90048. (323)782-1010. Fax: (323)782-1892. E-mail: scbwi@scbwi.org. Website: www.scbwi.org. **Contact:** Stephen Mooser. (formerly SCBWI Midyear Conference), Society of Children's book Writers and Illustrators. Annual. Conference held in February. Average attendance: 800. Conference is to promote writing and illustrating for children: picture books; fiction; nonfiction; middle grade and young adult; network with professionals; financial planning for writers; marketing your book; art exhibition; etc. Site: Manhattan.

Costs See website for current cost and conference information.

Additional Information SCBWI also holds an annual summer conference in August in Los Angeles. See the listing in the West section or visit website for details.

SCWG CONFERENCE

Holiday Inn, 1300 North Atlantic Ave., Cocoa Beach FL 32931. (321)956-7193. Website: scwg.org/conference.asp. **Contact:** Joyce Henderson. Annual. Conference duration: 2 days. Conference held the fourth weekend in January.

Costs $210 for guild members; $220 non-members. One day rates are available; see website for rates.

Additional Information Agents and editors participate in conference.

SEACOAST WRITERS ASSOCIATION SPRING AND FALL CONFERENCES

59 River Road, Stratham NH 03885-2358. E-mail: patparnell@comcast.net. **Contact:** Pat Parnell, conference coordinator. Annual. Conferences held in May and October. Conference duration: 1 day. Average attendance: 60. "Our conferences offer workshops covering various aspects of fiction, nonfiction and poetry." Site: McConnell Center, 61 Locust St., Dover NH. (603)742-1030.

Costs Approximately $50.

Additional Information "We sometimes include critiques. It is up to the workshop presenter." Spring meeting includes a contest. Categories are fiction, nonfiction (essays) and poetry. Judges vary from year to year. Conference and contest information available for SASE November 1, April 1, and September 1. Accepts inquiries by SASE, e-mail and phone. For further information, check the website www.seacoastwritersassociation.org.

SOAPSTONE: A WRITING RETREAT FOR WOMEN

5252 NE 57th Ave., Portland OR 97218. (503) 327-1042. E-mail: director@soapstone.org. Website: www.soapstone.org. Duration: 1-4 weeks. Average attendance: 30 writers/year. Retreat/residency. "Soapstone provides women writers with a stretch of uninterrupted time for their work and the opportunity to live in semi-solitude close to the natural world. In addition to that rare but essential commodity for a writer-a quiet space away from jobs, children, and other responsibilities-Soapstone provides something less tangible but also invaluable: the validation and encouragement necessary to embark upon or sustain a long or difficult writing project." Site: Located in Oregon's Coast Range, nine miles from the ocean, the retreat stands on twenty-two acres of densely forested land along the banks of Soapstone Creek and is home to much wildlife. The writers in residence enjoy a unique opportunity to learn about the natural world and join us in conscious stewardship of the land.

Costs $4 per day. $20 non-refundable application fee.

Accommodations Residents must provide all of their own transportation. See website for more information. Offers overnight accommodations.

Additional Information Application materials required include 3 copies of the completed application, a writing sample (no more than 3 pages of poetry or 5 pages, double-spaced, of prose), and application fee. Applications must be postmarked between July 1-August 1 each year.

SOUTH COAST WRITERS CONFERENCE

P.O. Box 590, 29392 Ellensburg Avenue, Gold Beach OR 97444. (541)247-2741. Fax: (541)247-6247. E-mail: scwc@socc.edu. Website: www.socc.edu/scwriters. **Contact:** Karim Shumaker, coordinator. Annual. Conference held President's Day weekend. Workshops held Friday and Saturday. Average attendance: 100. "We try to cover a broad spectrum: fiction, historical, poetry, children's, nature." Site: "Friday workshops are held at The Event Center on the Beach. Saturday workshops are held at the high school." 2010 keynote speaker will be John Daniel. Other presenters include Linda Barnes, Heidi Connolly, Jayel Gibson, Kim Griswell, Diane Hammond, Marianne Monson, Rebecca Olson, Dennis Powers, Keith Scales, and Erica Wheeler. **Costs** $60 before January 31; $70 after. Friday workshops are an additional $55. No meals or lodging included.

Accommodations Provides list of area hotels.

Additional Information Sponsors contest. Bob Simons Scholarship open to anyone. Contact SCWC for details.

SOUTHWEST WRITERS CONFERENCE

3271 Morris NE, Albuquerque NM 87111. (505)265-9485. Fax: (505)265-9483. E-mail: swwriters@juno.com. Website: www.southwestwriters.org. **Contact:** Conference Chair. Annual. Conferences held throughout the year. Average attendance: 50. "Conferences concentrate on all areas of writing and include appointments and networking." Workshops and speakers include writers, editors and agents of all genres for all levels from beginners to advanced.

Costs $99 and up (members); $159 and up (nonmembers); includes conference sessions and lunch.

Accommodations Usually have official airline and discount rates. Special conference rates are available at hotel. A list of other area hotels and motels is available.

Additional Information Sponsors an annual contest judged by authors, editors and agents from New York, Los Angeles, etc., and from other major publishing houses. Many categories. Deadline, fee structure on website. For brochures/guidelines send SASE, visit website, e-mail, call. "An appointment (10 minutes, one-on-one) may be set up at the conference with the editor/agent of your choice on a first-registered/first-served basis."

SQUAW VALLEY COMMUNITY OF WRITERS

P.O. Box 1416, Nevada City CA 95959-1416. (530)470-8440. Website: www.squawvalleywriters.org. **Contact:** Brett Hall Jones, executive director. Annual conference held in August. Conference duration: 7 days. Average attendance: 124. "These writers workshops in fiction, nonfiction and memoir assist talented writers by exploring the art and craft as well as the business of writing." Offerings include daily morning workshops led by writer-teachers, editors, or agents of the staff, limited to 12-13 participants; seminars; panel discussions of editing and publishing; craft colloquies; lectures; and staff readings. Past themes and panels included Personal History in Fiction, Narrative Structure, Promise and Premise: Recognizing Subject; The Nation of Narrative Prose: Telling the Truth in Memoir and Personal Essay, and Anatomy of a Short Story. The workshops are held in a ski lodge at the foot of this spectacular ski area. Literary agent speakers have recently included Julie Barer, Michael Carlisle, Henry Dunow, Theresa Park, B.J. Robbins, Janet Silver and Peter Steinberg.

Costs Tuition is $775, which includes 6 dinners.

Accommodations The Community of Writers rents houses and condominiums in the Valley for participants to live in during the week of the conference. Single room (one participant): $600/week. Double room (twin beds, room shared by conference participant of the same sex): $350/week. Multiple room (bunk beds, room shared with 2 or more participants of the same sex): $210/week. All rooms subject to availability; early requests are recommended. Can arrange airport shuttle pick-ups for a fee.

Additional Information Admissions are based on submitted ms (unpublished fiction, one or two stories or novel chapters); requires $35 reading fee. Submit ms to Brett Hall Jones, Squaw Valley Community of Writers, P.O. Box 1416, Nevada City, CA 95959. Brochure/guidelines available March by phone, e-mail or visit website. Accepts inquiries by SASE, e-mail, phone. Agents and editors attend/participate in conferences.

STEAMBOAT SPRINGS WRITERS GROUP

P.O. Box 774284, Steamboat Springs CO 80477. (970)879-8079. E-mail: susan@steamboatwriters.com. Website: www.steamboatwriters.com. **Contact:** Susan de Wardt, director. Group meets year-round on Thursdays, 12:00 to 2:00 at Arts Depot; guests welcome. Annual conference held in July. Conference duration: 1 day. Average attendance: 35. "Our conference emphasizes instruction within the seminar format. Novices and polished professionals benefit from the individual attention and camaraderie which can be established within small groups. A pleasurable and memorable learning experience is guaranteed by the relaxed and friendly atmosphere of the old train depot. Registration is limited." Site: Restored train depot.

Costs $50 before May 25, $60 after. Fee covers all seminars and luncheon.

Accommodations Lodging available at Steamboat Resorts.

Additional Information Optional dinner and activities during evening preceding conference. Accepts inquiries by e-mail, phone, mail.

SUMMER WRITING PROGRAM

Naropa University, 2130 Arapahoe Ave., Boulder CO 80302. (303)245-4600. Fax: (303)546-5287. E-mail: swpr@naropa.edu; clesser@naropa.edu. Website: www.naropa.edu/swp. **Contact:** Julie Kazimer, registration manager. Annual. Workshops held: June 14-July 11. Workshop duration: 4 weeks. Average attendance: 250. Offers college credit. "With 13 workshops to choose from each of the four weeks of the program, students may study poetry, prose, hybrid/cross-genre writing, small press printing, or book arts." Site: All workshops, panels, lectures and readings are hosted on the Naropa University main campus. Located in downtown Boulder, the campus is within easy walking distance of restaurants, shopping and the scenic Pearl Street Mall. Prose-related panels include

Ecology, Poetics of Prose, Telling Stories, The Informant "Other." 2010 faculty included Samual R. Delany, Linh Dinh, Dolores Dorantes, Penny Arcade, Bhanu Kapil, Akilah Oliver, Selah Saterstrom, Steven Taylor, Bob Holman, Anne Waldman, Xi Chuan, and many others.

Costs In 2010: $475/week, $1,800 for all four weeks (non-credit students); $1140/week (BA students); $1,550/week (MFA students).

Accommodations Offers overnight accommodations. Housing is available at Snow Lion Apartments. Single room is $45/night or $315/week, single bedroom apartment is $64/night or $448/week.

Additional Information If students would like to take the Summer Writing Program for academic credit, they must submit a non-degree seeking academic credit student application, transcripts, a letter of intent, and 5-10 pages of their creative work. Information available in January. For catalog of upcoming program, fill out catalog request form on website. Accepts inquiries by e-mail, phone.

THRILLERFEST

P.O. Box 311, Eureka CA 95502. E-mail: infocentral@thrillerwriters.org. Website: thrillerwriters.org/thrillerfest. **Contact:** Dennis Kennett. Annual. July 7-10 in Manhattan. Conference duration: 4 days. Average attendance: 700. Workshop/conference/festival. "A great place to learn the craft of writing the thriller. Classes taught by NYT best-selling authors. A fabulous event for fans/readers to meet and spend a few days with their favorite authors and packed with terrific programming." Speakers have included David Morrell, James Patterson, Sandra Brown, Ken Follett, Eric Van Lustbader, David Baldacci, Brad Meltzer, Steve Martini, R.L. Stine, Steve Berry, Kathleen Antrim, Douglas Preston, Gayle Lynds, Harlan Coben, Lee Child, Lisa Scottolini, Katherine Neville, Robin Cook, Andrew Gross, Kathy Reichs, Brad Thor, Clive Cussler, Donald Maass, MJ Rose, and Al Zuckerman. Two days of the conference are CraftFest, where the focus is on the craft of writing, and two days are ThrillerFest, which showcase the author-fan relationship. Also featured: AgentFest—a unique event where authors can pitch their work face-to-face to over forty top literary agents, and the International Thriller Awards and Banquet.

Costs $200-1000 depending on which events are selected. Various package deals are available offering savings, and Early Bird pricing is offered beginning in August each year.

Accommodations Grand Hyatt in New York City.

Additional Information Information available in September. For brochure, call or e-mail. Agents and editors participate in conference. "AgentFest is a three-hour event in which authors have the oppertunity to 'speed pitch' their story to dozens of agents in a single setting. ThrillerFest boasts a very congenial, relaxed and friendly atmosphere in which the best and the brightest in our field can mix and interact comfortably with those dreaming of becoming just that."

TMCC WRITERS' CONFERENCE

5270 Neil Road Rm 216, Reno NV 89502. (775)829-9010. Fax: (775)829-9032. E-mail: wdce@mcc.edu. Website: wdce.tmcc.edu. Annual. 2010 conference held in April. Average attendance: 125. Conference focuses on strengthening mainstream/literary fiction and nonfiction works and how to market them to agents and publisher. Site: Truckee Meadows Community College in Reno, Nevada.

Costs $99 for lectures; $29 for one-on-one appointment with an agent.

Accommodations A wide range of affordable accommodations are available nearby.

Additional Information Brochures are available the end of November through the website, e-mail or mail. Accepts inquires by phone or e-mail. Multiple agents, along with successful authors, participate in this event. "This conference features a supportive, informal atmosphere where questions are encouraged."

MARK TWAIN CREATIVE WRITERS WORKSHOPS

5101 Rockhill Rd., Kansas City MO 64110-2499. (816)235-1168. Fax: (816)235-2611. E-mail: BeasleyM@umkc.edu. Website: www.newletters.org. **Contact:** Betsy Beasley, administrative

associate. Annual. Held 3 weeks of June, from 9:30 to 12:30 each weekday morning. Conference duration: 3 weeks. Average attendance: 40. "Focus is on fiction, poetry and literary nonfiction." Site: University of Missouri-Kansas City Campus. Panels planned for next conference include the full range of craft essentials. Staff includes Robert Stewart, editor-in-chief of New Letters magazine and BkMk Press, and Michael Pritchett, director of creative writing and English professor.
Costs Fees for regular and noncredit courses.
Accommodations Offers list of area hotels or lodging options.
Additional Information Submit for workshop 6 poems/one short story prior to arrival. Conference information is available in March by SASE, e-mail or on website. Editors participate in conference.

TY NEWYDD WRITERS' CENTRE

Llanystumdwy, Cricieth Gwynedd LL52 0LW United Kingdom. E-mail: post@tynewydd.org. Website: www.tynewydd.org. **Contact:** Sally Baker. Year-round. Regular courses held throughout the year.Most courses run Monday-Saturday. Average attendance: 14. "To give people the opportunity to work side-by-side with professional writers, in an informal atmosphere." Site: Ty Newydd, large manor house, last home of the prime minister, David Lloyd George. Situated in North Wales -between mountains and sea.
Costs Single room, £525, shared room, £450 for Monday - Saturday (includes full board, tuition).
Accommodations Transportation from railway stations arranged. Accommodation in Ty Newydd (onsite).
Additional Information Course information available by mail, phone, e-mail, fax or visit website. Accepts inquiries by SASE, e-mail, fax, phone."More and more people come to us from the U.S. often combining a writing course with a tour of Wales."

VIRGINIA FESTIVAL OF THE BOOK

145 Ednam Dr., Charlottesville VA 22903. (434)924-7548. Fax: (434)296-4714. E-mail: vabook@virginia.edu. Website: www.vabook.org. **Contact:** Nancy Damon, program director. Annual. Festival held in March. 2010 Dates are March 17-21. Average attendance: 22,000. Festival held to celebrate books and promote reading and literacy. Site: Held throughout the Charlottesville/Albemarle area.
Costs See website for 2011 rates. Most events are free and open to the public. Two luncheons, a breakfast, and a reception require tickets.
Accommodations Overnight accommodations available.
Additional Information "The festival is a five-day event featuring authors, illustrators, and publishing professionals. Authors must apply to the festival to be included on a panel. Preferred method of application is by use of online form. Information is available on the website and inquiries can be made via e-mail, fax, or phone."

WESLEYAN WRITERS CONFERENCE

(860)685-3604. Fax: (860)685-2441. E-mail: agreene@wesleyan.edu. Annual. Conference held the third week of June. Average attendance: 100. For novel, short story, fiction techniques, poetry, short- and long-form nonfiction, journalism, memoir, multi-media work, digital media. Site: The conference is held on the campus of Wesleyan University, in the hills overlooking the Connecticut River. Meals and lodging are provided on campus. Features daily seminars, readings, lectures, panels, workshops, mss consultations, publishing advice; faculty of award-winning writers and guest speakers.
Costs In 2010, day student $850 (tuition, no meals), day student with meals $1,125 (includes tuition, meals), boarding student $1,298 (includes tuition, meals, and room for 5 nights).
Accommodations "Participants may stay on campus in new air-conditioned dorms or in local hotels. Conference meals and meetings are held in the university's new Usdan University Center. Participants usually drive to campus, fly to Hartford or take Amtrak to Meriden, CT. We are happy

to help participants make travel arrangements."

Additional Information "Both experienced writers and new writers are welcome." Scholarships and teaching fellowships are available, including the Joan Jakobson Scholarships for writers of fiction, poetry and nonfiction and the Jon Davidoff Scholarships for journalists." Accepts inquiries by e-mail, phone, fax.

WINCHESTER WRITERS' CONFERENCE, FESTIVAL AND BOOKFAIR, AND WEEKLONG WRITING WORKSHOPS

University of Winchester, Winchester Hampshire WA S022 4NR United Kingdom. 44 (0) 1962 827238. E-mail: Barbara.Large@winchester.ac.uk. Website: www.writersconference.co.uk. **Contact:** Barbara Large. The 31st Winchester Writers' Conference, Festival; and Bookfair will be held on the weekend of 1-3 July, 2011 and followed by the In-depth Weeklong Writing Workshops at the University of Winchester, Winchester, Hampshire S022 4NR. Sir Terry Pratchett OBE, internationally famed for his Discworld series, will give the Keynote Address and will lead an outstanding team of 65 professional writers who will offer during 13 mini courses, 43 workshops, 60 lectures and 500 one to one appointments to help writers harness their creative ideas into marketable work. Participate by entering some of the 18 writing competitions, even if you can't attend. Over 100 writers have now reported major publishing successes as a direct result of their attendance at past conferences. This leading literary event offers a magnificent source of information and network of support from tutors who are published writers and industry specialists, a support that continues throughout the year with additional short courses. Enjoy a creative writing holiday in the oldest city in England, yet within an hour of London. Tours planned to Jane Austen's home and Study Centre, the haunts of Keats and the 12th century Winchester Bible.To receive the 66-page conference programme including all the competition details please contact us.

WINTER POETRY & PROSE GETAWAY IN CAPE MAY

18 North Richards Ave., Ventnor NJ 08406. (888)887-2105. E-mail: info@wintergetaway.com. Website: www.wintergetaway.com. **Contact:** Peter E. Murphy. January 14-17, 2011. Conference duration: 3 days. Average attendance: 200 (10 or fewer participants in each workshop). "Now in its 18th year, the Winter Poetry and Prose Getaway is not your typical writers' conference. Energize your writing with challenging and supportive workshops that focus on starting new material. Advance your craft with feedback from our award-winning faculty, including Pulitzer Prize and National Book Award winners. But the focus isn't on our faculty, it's on helping you improve and advance your skills." Offers a variety of poetry and prose workshops, each with 10 or fewer participants. Featured workshops include Finishing Your Novel, Focusing Your Fiction, Revising a Short Story Toward Publication, Writing and Publishing New Fiction, Writing for the Children's Market, The Art and Craft of Creative Nonfiction, Turning Memory into Memoir, and Reimagining Memoir. Previous faculty has included Renee Ashley, Julianna Baggott, Christian Bauman, Anndee Hochman, Laura McCullough, Sondra Perl, Carol Plum-Ucci, Robbie Clipper Sethi, David Schwartz, Mimi Schwartz, Terese Svoboda, Richard K. Weems, and many more.

Costs $385 for 2009; includes all workshops, 2 lunches, 2 receptions, and a tutorial for poets. Room packages from $225. A $25 Early Bard discount is available if paid in full by November 15.

WOMEN WRITERS WINTER RETREAT

Homestead House B&B, 38111 West Spaulding, Willoughby OH 44094. (440)946-1902. E-mail: deencr@aol.com. Website: www.deannaadams.com. **Contact:** Deanna Adams, director. Estab. 2007. Annual. Last retreat held February 27, 2009-March 1, 2009.Conference duration: 1-3 days. Average attendance: 35-40. Retreat. "The Women Writers' Winter Retreat was designed for aspiring and professional women writers who cannot seem to find enough time to devote to honing their craft. Each retreat offers class time and workshops facilitated by successful women writers, as well as allows time to do some actual writing, alone or in a group. A Friday night dinner and Keynote kick-starts the weekend, followed by Saturday workshops, free time, meals, and an open mic to read your works. Sunday wraps up with one more workshop and fellowship. All genres welcome. Choice of overnight stay or commuting." Site: Located in the heart of downtown Willoughby, this warm and attractive bed and breakfast is easy to find, around the corner from the main street, Erie Street, and behind a popular Arabica coffee house. Door prizes and book sale/author signings throughout the weekend.

Costs Single room: $269. Shared Room: $199 (includes complete weekend package, with B&B stay and all meals and workshops); weekend commute: $135; Saturday only: $100 (prices include lunch and dinner).

Additional Information "Brochures for the writers retreat are available by December. Accepts inquiries and reservations by e-mail or phone. See website for additional information."

WRITE FROM THE HEART

9827 Irvine Avenue, Upper Lake CA 95485. (707) 275-9011. E-mail: Halbooks@HalZinaBennet.com. Website: www.HalZinaBennet.com. **Contact:** Hal. Offered 4 to 6 times a year. Conference duration: 3-5 days. Average attendance: 15-30. "Open to all genres, focusing on accessing the author's most individualized sources of imagery, characterization, tensions, content, style and voice." Site: Varies; California's Mt. Shasta, Mendocino California coast, Chicago, Colorado. Instructor: Hal Zina Bennett.

Costs $350 and up.

Accommodations No Arrangements for transportation. Provides list of area hotels.

Additional Information Brochures available. Request by SASE, e-mail, phone, fax or on website. Editors participate in conference. "Hal is the author of 30-plus successful books and is a writing coach with over 200 published clients, including several national bestsellers."

WRITE IT OUT

P.O. Box 704, Sarasota FL 34230-0704. (941)359-3824. E-mail: rmillerwio@aol.com. Website: www.writeitout.com. **Contact:** Ronni Miller, director. Workshops held 2-3 times/year in March, June, July and August. Conference duration: 5-10 days. Average attendance: 4-10. Workshops retreats on "expressive writing and painting, fiction, poetry, memoirs. We also offer intimate, motivational, in-depth free private conferences with instructors." Site: Workshops in Italy in a Tuscan villa, in Sarasota at a hotel, Cape Cod and the North Carolina mountains at inns. Past speakers included Arturo Vivante, novelist.

Costs 2010 fees: Italy, $800; Cape Cod, $400. Price includes tuition, private conferences and salons. Room, board, and airfare not included.

Additional Information "Critiques on work are given at the workshops." Conference information available year round. For brochures/guidelines e-mail, call or visit website. Accepts inquiries by phone, e-mail. Workshops have "small groups, option to spend time writing and not attend classes, with personal appointments with instructors."

WRITE ON THE SOUND WRITERS' CONFERENCE

700 Main Street, Edmonds WA 98020. (425)771-0228. Fax: (425)771-0253. E-mail: wots@ci.edmonds.wa.us. **Contact:** Kris Gillespie, conference organizer. Annual. Last conference held October 1-3, 2010. Conference duration: 2.5 days. Average attendance: 180. "Conference is limited to 200 participants, good for networking, and focuses on the craft of writing." Site: "Edmonds is a beautiful community on the shores of Puget Sound, just north of Seattle. View brochure at www.ci.edmonds.wa.us/artscommission/wots.stm."

Costs $119 by Sept. 3, $139 after Sept. 3 for 2 days, $74 for 1 day (2010); includes registration, morning refreshments and 1 ticket to keynote lecture.

Additional Information Brochures available August 1. Accepts inquiries by phone, e-mail, fax.

WRITERS ONLINE WORKSHOPS

4700 E. Galbraith Rd., Cincinnati OH 45236. (800)759-0963. E-mail: wdwowadmin@fwmedia.com. Website: www.writersonlineworkshops.com. Online workshop; ongoing. Course duration: From 4-28 weeks. Average attendance: 10-15 per class. "We have workshops in fiction, nonfiction, memoir, poetry, proposal writing and more." Site: Internet-based, operated entirely on the website. Current fiction-related courses include Fundamentals of Fiction, Focus on the Novel, Focus on the Short Story, Advanced Novel Writing, Creating Dynamic Characters, Writing Effective Dialogue, Writing the Novel Proposal, Essentials of Mystery Writing, Essentials of Science Fiction & Fantasy Writing, Essentials of Romance Writing, Essentials of Writing to Inspire, Voice and Viewpoint, Marketing Short Stories, and workshops based on books from Writer's Digest. New in 2010-11: 12 Weeks to Your First Draft, Art of Self- and Group Critique, and others."

Costs $150-775.

Additional Information Additional information always available on website. Accepts inquiries by e-mail and phone.

THE WRITERS' RETREAT

E-mail: info@writersretreat.com. "This is the only organization featuring a network of worldwide residential retreats opened year-round with on-site mentoring. The retreats cater to writers of all genres and offer support such as mentoring, workshops, editing, and lodging; some retreats offer scholarships."

Costs Residency varies between $475-$1,200 per week depending on location of the retreat. To join The Writers' Retreat as a retreat operator, please submit application by e-mail.

Additional Information Accepts inquiries by e-mail.

THE WRITERS WORKSHOP

PO Box 329, Langley WA 98260. E-mail: bob@bobmayer.org. Website: www.bobmayer.org. **Contact:** Bob Mayer. Held every 3 months. Last conference: January 2010. Conference duration: 2 days. Site: various locations around the country.

Costs varies depending on venue

Additional Information Limited to eight participants and focused on their novel and marketability.

WRITERS WORKSHOP IN SCIENCE FICTION

Lawrence KS 66045-2115. (785)864-3380. Fax: (785)864-1159. E-mail: jgunn@ku.edu. Website: www.ku.edu/~sfcenter. **Contact:** James Gunn, professor. Annual. Workshop held in late June to early July. Conference duration: 2 weeks. Average attendance: 10-14. The workshop is "small, informal and aimed at writers on the edge of publication or regular publication." For writing and marketing science fiction and fantasy. Site: "Housing is provided and classes meet in university housing on the University of Kansas campus. Workshop sessions operate informally in a lounge." Past guests included Frederik Pohl, SF writer and former editor and agent; John Ordover, writer and editor; George Zebrowski, Pamela Sargent, Kij Johnson and Christopher McKittrick, writers; Lou Anders, editor. A novel workshop in science fiction and fantasy is also available.

Costs $400 tuition. Housing and meals are additional.

Accommodations Several airport shuttle services offer reasonable transportation from the Kansas City International Airport to Lawrence. During past conferences, students were housed in a student dormitory at $14/day double, $28/day single.

Additional Information "Admission to the workshop is by submission of an acceptable story. Two additional stories should be submitted by the end of May. These three stories are distributed to other participants for critiquing and are the basis for the first week of the workshop; one story is rewritten for the second week. The workshop offers a 3-hour session manuscript critiquing each afternoon. The rest of the day is free for writing, study, consultation and recreation." Information available in December. For brochures/guidelines send SASE, visit website, e-mail, fax, call. The workshop concludes with The Campbell Conference, a round-table discussion of a single topic, and the presentation of the Campbell and Sturgeon Awards for the Best SF Novel and Short Story of the Year. "The Writers Workshop in Science Fiction is intended for writers who have just started to sell their work or need that extra bit of understanding or skill to become a published writer."

WRITE-TO-PUBLISH CONFERENCE

9118 W. Elmwood Dr., Suite 1G, Niles IL 60714-5820. (847)296-3964. Fax: (847)296-0754. E-mail: lin@writetopublish.com. Website: www.writetopublish.com. **Contact:** Lin Johnson, director.

Costs approximately $475.

Accommodations In campus residence halls or discounted hotel rates. Cost approximately $225-310.

Additional Information Optional ms evaluation available. College credit available. Conference information available in January. For details, visit website, or e-mail brochure@writetopublish.com. Accepts inquiries by e-mail, fax, phone.

YADDO

Box 395, Saratoga Springs NY 12866-0395. (518)584-0746. Fax: (518)584-1312. E-mail: yaddo@yaddo.org. Website: www.yaddo.org. **Contact:** Candace Wait, program director (chwait@yahoo.org). Two seasons: large season is in mid-May-August; small season is late September-May (stays from 2 weeks to 2 months; average stay is 5 weeks). Average attendance: 220/year. Accommodates approximately 34 artists in large season, 16 in the small season. "Those qualified for invitations to Yaddo are highly qualified writers, visual artists, composers, choreographers, performance artists and film and video artists who are working at the professional level in their fields. Artists who wish to work collaboratively are encouraged to apply. An abiding principle at Yaddo is that applications for residencies are judged on the quality of the artists' work and professional promise." Site: includes four small lakes, a rose garden, woodland.

Costs No fee is charged; residency includes room, board and studio space. Limited travel expenses are available to artists accepted for residencies at Yaddo.

Accommodations Provisions include room, board and studio space. No stipends are offered.

Additional Information To apply: Filing fee is $30, or $40 for visual artists submitting work samples digitally via the SlideRoom website (checks payable to Corporation of Yaddo). Two letters of recommendation are requested. Applications are considered by the Admissions Committee and invitations are issued by March 15 (deadline: January 1) and October 1 (deadline: August 1). Information available for SASE (63¢ postage), by e-mail, fax or phone and on website. Accepts inquiries by e-mail, fax, SASE, phone.

RESOURCES

Publishers and Their Imprints

The publishing world is in constant transition. With all the buying, selling, reorganizing, consolidating, and dissolving, it's hard to keep publishers and their imprints straight. To help make sense of these changes, here's a breakdown of major publishers (and their divisions)—who owns whom and which imprints are under each company umbrella. Keep in mind that this information changes frequently. The Web site of each publisher is provided to help you keep an eye on this ever-evolving business.

HACHETTE BOOK GROUP USA

www.hachettebookgroupusa.com

Center Street

FaithWords

Grand Central Publishing
Business Plus
5-Spot
Forever
Springboard Press
Twelve
Vision
Wellness Central

Hachette Book Group Digital Media
Hachette Audio

Little, Brown and Company
Back Bay Books
Bulfinch
Reagan Arthur Books

Little, Brown Books for Young Readers
LB Kids
Poppy

Orbit

Yen Press

HARLEQUIN ENTERPRISES

www.eharlequin.com

Harlequin
Harlequin American Romance
Harlequin Bianca
Harlequin Blaze
Harlequin Deseo
Harlequin Historical
Harlequin Intrigue
Harlequin Jazmin
Harlequin Julia
Harlequin Medical Romance
Harlequin NASCAR
Harlequin NEXT
Harlequin Presents
Harlequin Romance
Harlequin Superromance
Harlequin eBooks

Harlequin Special Releases
Harlequin Nonfiction
Harlequin Historical Undone
HQN Books
HQN eBooks
LUNA
Luna eBooks
MIRA
Mira eBooks
Kimani Press
Kimani Press Arabesque
Kimani Press Kimani Romance
Kimani Press Kimani TRU
Kimani Press New Spirit
Kimani Press Sepia
Kimani Press Special Releases
Kimani Press eBooks
Red Dress Ink
Red Dress eBooks
Silhouette
Silhouette Desire
Silhouette Nocturne
Silhouette Romantic Suspense
Silhouette Special Edition
SPICE
SPICE Books
SPICE Briefs
Steeple Hill
Steeple Hill Café©
Steeple Hill Love Inspired
Steeple Hill Love Inspired Historical
Steeple Hill Love Inspired Suspense
Steeple Hill Women's Fiction
Worldwide Library
Rogue Angel
Worldwide Mystery

HARPERCOLLINS

www.harpercollins.com

HarperMorrow
Amistad
Avon
Avon A
Avon Inspire
Avon Red
Collins
Collins Business
Collins Design
Collins Living
Ecco
Eos
Harper
Harper Mass Market
Harper Perennial
Harper Perennial
Modern Classics
Harper Audio
HarperCollins
HarperCollins e-Books
HarperEntertainment
HarperLuxe
HarperOne
HarperStudio
William Morrow
Morrow Cookbooks
Rayo
HarperCollins Children's Books
Amistad
Eos
Greenwillow Books
HarperCollins
Children's Audio
Harper Festival
HarperTeen
HarperTrophy
HarperCollins U.K.
Harper Press
Blue Door
Fourth Estate
The Friday Project
HarperPress
HarperFiction
Voyager
Avon
HarperCollins Childrens Books
Collins
Times
Jane's
HarperCollins Canada
HarperCollinsPublishers
Collins Canada

HarperPerennial Canada
HarperTrophyCanada
Phyllis Bruce Books
HarperCollins Australia
HarperCollins India
HarperCollins New
Zealand Zondervan
Zonderkids
Vida

MACMILLAN US (HOLTZBRINCK)

http://us.macmillan.com

MacMillan
Farrar, Straus & Giroux
Faber and Faber, Inc
Farrar, Straus
Hill & Wang
North Point Press
First Second
Henry Holt
Henry Holt Books for Young Readers
Holt Paperbacks
Metropolitan
Times
MacMillan Children's
Feiwel & Friends
Farrar, Straus and Giroux Books for Young Readers
Kingfisher
Holt Books for Young Readers
Priddy Books
Roaring Brook Press
Square Fish
Picador
Palgrave MacMillan
Tor/Forge Books
Tor
Forge
Orb
Tor/Seven Seas
St. Martin's Press
Minotaur Press
Thomas Dunne Books
Griffin
St. Martin's Press Paperbacks
Let's Go
Truman Talley Books
Bedford, Freeman & Worth Publishing Group
Bedford/St. Martin's
Hayden-McNeil
W.H. Freeman
Worth Publishers
MacMillan Audio

PENGUIN GROUP (USA), INC.

www.penguingroup.com

Penguin Adult Division
Ace
Alpha
Amy Einhorn Books/Putnam
Avery
Berkley
Dutton
Gotham
HPBooks
Hudson Street Press
Jeremy P. Tarcher
Jove NAL
Penguin
Penguin Press
Perigree
Plume
Portfolio
Riverhead
Sentinel
Viking
Price Stern Sloan
Young Readers Division
Dial
Dutton
Firebird
Frederick Warne
Grosset & Dunlap
Philomel

Puffin Books
Putnam
Razorbill
Speak
Viking

RANDOM HOUSE, INC. (BERTELSMANN)

www.randomhouse.com

Crown Publishing Group
Broadway Business
Crown
Crown Business
Crown Forum
Clarkson Potter
Doubleday Business
Doubleday Religion
Harmony
Potter Craft
Potter Style
Three Rivers Press
Shaye Areheart Books
Waterbrook
Multnomah
Knopf Doubleday Publishing Group
Alfred A. Knopf
Anchor Books
Doubleday
Doubleday Religion
Flying Dolphin Press
Broadway
Everyman's Library
Nan A. Talese
Pantheon Books
Schocken Books
Vintage
Monacelli Press
Random House Publishing Group
Ballantine Books
Bantam Dell
Del Rey
Del Rey/Lucas Books
The Dial Press
The Modern Library
One World
Random House Trade Group
Random House Trade Paperbacks
Reader's Circle
Spectra
Spiegel and Grau
Strivers Row Books
Villard Books
Random House Audio Publishing Group
Listening Library
Random House Audio Random House Children's Books
Kids@Random
Golden Books
Alfred A. Knopf Children's Books
Bantam Beginner Books
Crown Children's Books
David Fickling Books
Delacorte Press
Disney Books for Young Readers
Doubleday Children's Books
Dragonfly
First Time Books
Landmark Books
Laurel-Leaf
Picturebacks
Random House Books for Young Readers
Robin Corey Books
Schwartz and Wade Books
Sesame Workshop
Step into Reading
Stepping Stone Books
Wendy Lamb Books
Yearling Random House Information Group
Fodor's Travel
Living Language
Prima Games
Princeton Review
RH Puzzles & Games
RH Reference Publishing
Sylvan Learning
Random House International
Arete
McClelland & Stewart Ltd.
Plaza & Janes
RH Australia
RH of Canada Limited
RH Mondadori

RH South America
RH United Kingdom
Transworld UK
Verlagsgruppe RH

SIMON & SCHUSTER

www.simonsays.com

Simon & Schuster Adult Publishing
Atria Books
Washington Square Press
Beyond Words
Free Press
Howard Books
Pocket Books
Scribner
Simon & Schuster
Strebor
The Touchstone & Fireside Group
Simon & Schuster Audio
Pimsleur
Simon & Schuster Audioworks
Encore
Sound Ideas
Nightingale Conant
Simon & Schuster Children's Publishing
Aladdin Paperbacks
Atheneum Books for Young Readers
Libros
Para Nin´os
Little Simon®
Little Simon
Inspirations
Margaret K. McElderry Books
Simon & Schuster Books for Young Readers
Simon Pulse
Simon Scribbles
Simon Spotlight®
Simon Spotlight Entertainment
Simon & Schuster International
Simon & Schuster Australia
Simon & Schuster Canada
Simon & Schuster UK

Canadian Writers Take Note

While much of the information contained in this section applies to all writers, here are some specifics of interest to Canadian writers:

Postage: When sending an SASE from Canada, you will need an International Reply Coupon ($3.50). Also be aware, a GST tax is required on postage in Canada and for mail with postage under $5 going to destinations outside the country. Since Canadian postage rates are voted on in January of each year (after we go to press), contact a Canada Post Corporation Customer Service Division (located in most cities in Canada) or visit www.canadapost.ca for the most current rates.

Copyright: For information on copyrighting your work and to obtain forms, write Canadian Intellectual Property Office, Industry Canada, Place du Portage I, 50 Victoria St., Room C-114, Gatineau, Quebec K1A 0C9 or call (866)997-1936. Web site: www.cipo.gc.ca.

The public lending right: The Public Lending Right Commission has established that eligible Canadian authors are entitled to payments when a book is available through a library. Payments are determined by a sampling of the holdings of a representative number of libraries. To find out more about the program and to learn if you are eligible, write to the Public Lending Right Commission at 350 Albert St., P.O. Box 1047, Ottawa, Ontario K1P 5V8 or call (613)566-4378 or (800)521-5721 for information. Web site: www.plr-dpp.ca. The Commission, which is part of The Canada Council, produces a helpful pamphlet, *How the PLR System Works* > , on the program.

Grants available to Canadian writers: Most province art councils or departments of culture provide grants to resident writers. Some of these, as well as contests for Canadian writers, are listed in our Contests and Awards section. For national programs, contact The Canada Council, Writing and Publishing Section, 350 Alberta St., P.O. Box 1047, Ottawa, Ontario K1P 5V8 or call (613)566-4414 or (800)263-5588 for information. Fax: (613)566-4410. Web site: www.canadacouncil.ca.

For more information: Contact The Writer's Union of Canada, 90 Richmond St. E, Suite 200, Toronto, Ontario M5C 1P1; call them at (416)703-8982 or fax them at (416)504-9090. E-mail: info@writersunion.ca. Web site: www.writersunion.ca. This organization provides a wealth of information (as well as strong support) for Canadian writers, including specialized publications on publishing contracts; contract negotiations; the author/editor relationship; author awards, competitions and grants; agents; taxes for writers, libel issues and access to archives in Canada.

Printing & Production Terms Defined

In most of the magazine listings in this book, you will find a brief physical description of each publication. This material usually includes the number of pages, type of paper, type of binding and whether or not the magazine uses photographs and/or illustrations.

Although it is important to look at a copy of the magazine to which you are submitting, these descriptions can give you a general idea of what the publication looks like. This material can provide you with a feel for the magazine's financial resources and prestige. Do not, however, rule out small, simply produced publications, as these may be the most receptive to new writers. Watch for publications that have increased their page count or improved their production from year to year. This is a sign the publication is doing well and may be accepting more fiction.

You will notice a wide variety of printing terms used within these descriptions. We explain here some of the more common terms used in our listing descriptions. We do not include explanations of terms such as Mohawk and Karma which are brand names and refer to the paper manufacturer.

PAPER

A5: An international paper standard; 148 × 210 mm or 5.8 × 8.3 in.

acid-free: Paper that has low or no acid content. This type of paper resists deterioration from exposure to the elements. More expensive than many other types of paper, publications done on acid-free paper can last a long time.

bond: Bond paper is often used for stationery and is more transparent than text paper. It can be made of either sulphite (wood) or cotton fiber. Some bonds have a mixture of both wood and cotton (such as "25 percent cotton" paper). This is the type of paper most often used in photocopying or as standard typing paper.

coated/uncoated stock: Coated and uncoated are terms usually used when referring to book or text paper. More opaque than bond, it is the paper most used for offset printing. As the name implies, uncoated paper has no coating. Coated paper is coated with a layer of clay, varnish or other chemicals. It comes in various sheens and surfaces depending on the type of coating, but the most common are dull, matte and gloss.

cover stock: Cover stock is heavier book or text paper used to cover a publication. It comes in a variety of colors and textures and can be coated on one or both sides.

CS1/CS2: Most often used when referring to cover stock, CS1 means paper that is coated only on one side; CS2 is paper coated on both sides.

newsprint: Inexpensive absorbent pulp wood paper often used in newspapers and tabloids.

text: Text paper is similar to book paper (a smooth paper used in offset printing), but it has been given some texture by using rollers or other methods to apply a pattern to the paper.

vellum: Vellum is a text paper that is fairly porous and soft.

Some notes about paper weight and thickness: Often you will see paper thickness described in terms of pounds such as 80 lb. or 60 lb. paper. The weight is determined by figuring how many pounds in a ream of a particular paper (a ream is 500 sheets). This can be confusing, however, because this figure is based on a standard sheet size and standard sheet sizes vary depending on the type of paper used. This information is most helpful when comparing papers of the same type. For example, 80 lb. book paper versus 60 lb. book paper. Since the size of the paper is the same it would follow that 80 lb. paper is the thicker, heavier paper.

Some paper, especially cover stock, is described by the actual thickness of the paper. This is expressed in a system of points. Typical paper thicknesses range from 8 points to 14 points thick.

PRINTING

There are many other printing methods but these are the ones most commonly referred to in our listings.

letterpress: Letterpress printing is printing that uses a raised surface such as type. The type is inked and then pressed against the paper. Unlike offset printing, only a limited number of impressions can be made, as the surface of the type can wear down.

offset: Offset is a printing method in which ink is transferred from an image-bearing plate to a "blanket" and from the blanket to the paper.

sheet-fed offset: Offset printing in which the paper is fed one piece at a time.

web offset: Offset printing in which a roll of paper is printed and then cut apart to make individual sheets.

BINDING

case binding: In case binding, signatures (groups of pages) are stitched together with thread rather than glued together. The stitched pages are then trimmed on three sides and glued into a hardcover or board "case'' or cover. Most hardcover books and thicker magazines are done this way.

comb binding: A comb is a plastic spine used to hold pages together with bent tabs that are fed through punched holes in the edge of the paper.

perfect binding: Used for paperback books and heavier magazines, perfect binding involves gathering signatures (groups of pages) into a stack, trimming off the folds so the edge is flat and gluing a cover to that edge.

saddle stitched: Publications in which the pages are stitched together using metal staples. This fairly inexpensive type of binding is usually used with books or magazines that are under 80 pages.

Smythe-sewn: Binding in which the pages are sewn together with thread. Smythe is the name of the most common machine used for this purpose.

spiral binding: A wire spiral that is wound through holes punched in pages is a spiral bind. This is the binding used in spiral notebooks.

Glossary

Advance. Payment by a publisher to an author prior to the publication of a book, to be deducted from the author's future royalties.

Adventure story. A genre of fiction in which action is the key element, overshadowing characters, theme and setting. The conflict in an adventure story is often man against nature. A secondary plot that reinforces this kind of conflict is sometimes included. In Allistair MacLean's *Night Without End*, for example, the hero, while investigating a mysterious Arctic air crash, also finds himself dealing with espionage, sabotage and murder.

All rights. The rights contracted to a publisher permitting a manuscript's use anywhere and in any form, including movie and book club sales, without additional payment to the writer.

Amateur sleuth. The character in a mystery, usually the protagonist, who does the detection but is not a professional private investigator or police detective.

Anthology. A collection of selected writings by various authors.

Association of Authors' Representatives (AAR). An organization for literary agents committed to maintaining excellence in literary representation.

Auction. Publishers sometimes bid against each other for the acquisition of a manuscript that has excellent sales prospects.

Backlist. A publisher's books not published during the current season but still in print.

Biographical novel. A life story documented in history and transformed into fiction through the insight and imagination of the writer. This type of novel melds the elements of biographical research and historical truth into the framework of a novel, complete with dialogue, drama and mood. A biographical novel resembles historical fiction, save for one aspect: Characters in a historical novel may be fabricated and then placed into an authentic setting; characters in a biographical novel have actually lived.

Book producer/packager. An organization that may develop a book for a publisher based upon the publisher's idea or may plan all elements of a book, from its initial concept to writing and marketing strategies, and then sell the package to a book publisher and/or movie producer.

Cliffhanger. Fictional event in which the reader is left in suspense at the end of a chapter or episode, so that interest in the story's outcome will be sustained.

Clip. Sample, usually from a newspaper or magazine, of a writer's published work.

Cloak-and-dagger. A melodramatic, romantic type of fiction dealing with espionage and intrigue.

Commercial. Publishers whose concern is salability, profit and success with a large readership.

Contemporary. Material dealing with popular current trends, themes or topics.

Contributor's copy. Copy of an issue of a magazine or published book sent to an author whose work is included.

Copublishing. An arrangement in which the author and publisher share costs and profits.

Copyediting. Editing a manuscript for writing style, grammar, punctuation and factual accuracy.

Copyright. The legal right to exclusive publication, sale or distribution of a literary work.

Cover letter. A brief letter sent with a complete manuscript submitted to an editor.

"Cozy" (or "teacup") mystery. Mystery usually set in a small British town, in a bygone era, featuring a somewhat genteel, intellectual protagonist.

Cyberpunk. Type of science fiction, usually concerned with computer networks and human-computer combinations, involving young, sophisticated protagonists.

Electronic rights. The right to publish material electronically, either in book or short story form.

E-zine. A magazine that is published electronically.

Electronic submission. A submission of material by e-mail or on computer disk.

Ethnic fiction. Stories and novels whose central characters are black, Native American, Italian-American, Jewish, Appalachian or members of some other specific cultural group. Ethnic fiction usually deals with a protagonist caught between two conflicting ways of life: mainstream American culture and his ethnic heritage.

Experimental fiction. Fiction that is innovative in subject matter and style; avant-garde, non-formulaic, usually literary material.

Exposition. The portion of the storyline, usually the beginning, where background information about character and setting is related.

Fair use. A provision in the copyright law that says short passages from copyrighted material may be used without infringing on the owner's rights.

Fanzine. A noncommercial, small-circulation magazine usually dealing with fantasy, horror or science-fiction literature and art.

Fictional biography. The biography of a real person that goes beyond the events of a person's life by being fleshed out with imagined scenes and dialogue. The writer of fictional biographies strives to make it clear that the story is, indeed, fiction and not history.

First North American serial rights. The right to publish material in a periodical before it appears in book form, for the first time, in the United States or Canada.

Flash fiction. See short short stories.

Galleys. The first typeset version of a manuscript that has not yet been divided into pages.

Genre. A formulaic type of fiction such as romance, western or horror.

Gothic. This type of category fiction dates back to the late 18th and early 19th centuries. Contemporary gothic novels are characterized by atmospheric, historical settings and feature young, beautiful women who win the favor of handsome, brooding heroes-simultaneously dealing successfully with some life-threatening menace, either natural or supernatural. Gothics rely on mystery, peril, romantic relationships and a sense of foreboding for their strong, emotional effect on the reader. A classic early gothic novel is

Emily Bronte's *Wuthering Heights*. The gothic writer builds a series of credible, emotional crises for his ultimately triumphant heroine. Sex between the woman and her lover is implied rather than graphically detailed; the writer's descriptive talents are used instead to paint rich, desolate, gloomy settings in stark mansions and awesome castles. He composes slow-paced, intricate sketches that create a sense of impending evil on every page.

Graphic novel. A book (original or adapted) that takes the form of a long comic strip or heavily illustrated story of 40 pages or more, produced in paperback. Though called a novel, these can also be works of nonfiction.

Hard science fiction. Science fiction with an emphasis on science and technology.

Hard-boiled detective novel. Mystery novel featuring a private eye or police detective as the protagonist; usually involves a murder. The emphasis is on the details of the crime and the tough, unsentimental protagonist usually takes a matter-of-fact attitude towards violence.

High fantasy. Fantasy with a medieval setting and a heavy emphasis on chivalry and the quest.

Historical fiction. A fictional story set in a recognizable period of history. As well as telling the stories of ordinary people's lives, historical fiction may involve political or social events of the time.

Horror. Howard Phillips (H.P.) Lovecraft, generally acknowledged to be the master of the horror tale in the 20th century and the most important American writer of this genre since Edgar Allan Poe, maintained that "The oldest and strongest emotion of mankind is fear, and the oldest and strongest kind of fear is fear of the unknown. These facts few psychologists will dispute, and their admitted truth must establish for all time the genuineness and dignity of the weirdly horrible tale as a literary form." Lovecraft distinguishes horror literature from fiction based entirely on physical fear and the merely gruesome. "The true weird tale has something more than secret murder, bloody bones or a sheeted form clanking chains according to rule. A certain atmosphere of breathless and unexplainable dread of outer, unknown forces must be present; there must be a hint, expressed with a seriousness and portentousness becoming its subject, of that most terrible concept of the human brain-a malign and particular suspension or defeat of the fixed laws of Nature which are our only safeguards against the assaults of chaos and the daemons of unplumbed space." It is that atmosphere-the creation of a particular sensation or emotional level-that, according to Lovecraft, is the most important element in the creation of horror literature. Contemporary writers enjoying considerable success in horror fiction include Stephen King, Robert Bloch, Peter Straub and Dean Koontz.

Hypertext fiction. A fictional form, read electronically, which incorporates traditional elements of storytelling with a nonlinear plot line, in which the reader determines the direction of the story by opting for one of many author-supplied links.

Imprint. Name applied to a publisher's specific line (e.g. Owl, an imprint of Henry Holt).

Interactive fiction. Fiction in book or computer-software format where the reader determines the path the story will take by choosing from several alternatives at the end of each chapter or episode.

International Reply Coupon (IRC). A form purchased at a post office and enclosed with a letter or manuscript to a international publisher, to cover return postage costs.

Juveniles, Writing for. This includes works intended for an audience usually between the ages of 2 and 18. Categories of children's books are usually divided in this way: (1) picture books and storybooks (ages 2 to 8); (2) young readers or easy-to-read books (ages 5 to 8); (3) middle readers or middle grade (ages 9 to 11); (4) young adult books (ages 12 and up).

Libel. Written or printed words that defame, malign or damagingly misrepresent a living person.

Literary fiction. The general category of fiction which employs more sophisticated technique, driven as much or more by character evolution than action in the plot.

Literary fiction vs. commercial fiction. To the writer of literary, or serious, fiction, style and technique are often as important as subject matter. Commercial fiction, however, is written with the intent of reaching as wide an audience as possible. Commercial fiction is sometimes called genre fiction because books of this type often fall into categories, such as western, gothic, romance, historical, mystery and horror.

Literary agent. A person who acts for an author in finding a publisher or arranging contract terms on a literary project.

Mainstream fiction. Fiction which appeals to a more general reading audience, versus literary or genre fiction. Mainstream is more plot-driven than literary fiction and less formulaic than genre fiction.

Malice domestic novel. A mystery featuring a murder among family members, such as the murder of a spouse or a parent.

Manuscript. The author's unpublished copy of a work, usually typewritten, used as the basis for typesetting.

Mass market paperback. Softcover book on a popular subject, usually around 4 × 7, directed to a general audience and sold in drugstores and groceries as well as in bookstores.

Middle reader. Also called middle grade. Juvenile fiction for readers aged 9 to 11.

Ms(s). Abbreviation for manuscript(s).

Multiple submission. Submission of more than one short story at a time to the same editor. Do not make a multiple submission unless requested.

Mystery. A form of narration in which one or more elements remain unknown or unexplained until the end of the story. The modern mystery story contains elements of the serious novel: a convincing account of a character's struggle with various physical and psychological obstacles in an effort to achieve his goal, good characterization and sound motivation.

Narration. The account of events in a story's plot as related by the speaker or the voice of the author.

Narrator. The person who tells the story, either someone involved in the action or the voice of the writer.

New Age. A term including categories such as astrology, psychic phenomena, spiritual healing, UFOs, mysticism and other aspects of the occult.

Noir. A style of mystery involving hard-boiled detectives and bleak settings.

Nom de plume. French for "pen name"; a pseudonym.

Nonfiction novel. A work in which real events and people are written [about] in novel form, but are not camouflaged, as they are in the roman a clef. In the nonfiction novel, reality is presented imaginatively; the writer imposes a novelistic structure on the actual events, keying sections of narrative around moments that are seen (in retrospect) as symbolic. In this way, he creates a coherence that the actual story might not have had. *The Executioner's Song*, by Norman Mailer, and *In Cold Blood*, by Truman Capote, are notable examples of the nonfiction novel.

Novella (also novelette). A short novel or long story, approximately 20,000-50,000 words.

#10 envelope. 4 × 9½ envelope, used for queries and other business letters.

Offprint. Copy of a story taken from a magazine before it is bound.

One-time rights. Permission to publish a story in periodical or book form one time only.

Outline. A summary of a book's contents, often in the form of chapter headings with a few sentences outlining the action of the story under each one; sometimes part of a book proposal.

Over the transom. A phrase referring to unsolicited manuscripts, or those that come in "over the transom."

Payment on acceptance. Payment from the magazine or publishing house as soon as the decision to print a manuscript is made.

Payment on publication. Payment from the publisher after a manuscript is printed.

Pen name. A pseudonym used to conceal a writer's real name.

Periodical. A magazine or journal published at regular intervals.

Plot. The carefully devised series of events through which the characters progress in a work of fiction.

Police procedural. A mystery featuring a police detective or officer who uses standard professional police practices to solve a crime.

Popular fiction. Generally, a synonym for category or genre fiction; i.e., fiction intended to appeal to audiences for certain kinds of novels. Popular, or category, fiction is defined as such primarily for the convenience of publishers, editors, reviewers and booksellers who must identify novels of different areas of interest for potential readers.

Print on demand (POD). Novels produced digitally one at a time, as ordered. Self-publishing through print on demand technology typically involves some fees for the author. Some authors use POD to create a manuscript in book form to send to prospective traditional publishers.

Proofreading. Close reading and correction of a manuscript's typographical errors.

Proofs. A typeset version of a manuscript used for correcting errors and making changes, often a photocopy of the galleys.

Proposal. An offer to write a specific work, usually consisting of an outline of the work and one or two completed chapters.

Protagonist. The principal or leading character in a literary work.

Psychological novel. A narrative that emphasizes the mental and emotional aspects of its characters, focusing on motivations and mental activities rather than on exterior events. The psychological novelist is less concerned about relating what happened than about exploring why it happened. The term is most often used to describe 20th-century works that employ techniques such as interior monologue and stream of consciousness. Two examples of contemporary psychological novels are Judith Guest's *Ordinary People* and Mary Gordon's *The Company of Women*.

Public domain. Material that either was never copyrighted or whose copyright term has expired.

Pulp magazine. A periodical printed on inexpensive paper, usually containing lurid, sensational stories or articles.

Query. A letter written to an editor to elicit interest in a story the writer wants to submit.

Reader. A person hired by a publisher to read unsolicited manuscripts.

Reading fee. An arbitrary amount of money charged by some agents and publishers to read a submitted manuscript.

Regency romance. A subgenre of romance, usually set in England between 1811-1820.

Remainders. Leftover copies of an out-of-print book, sold by the publisher at a reduced price.

Reporting time. The number of weeks or months it takes an editor to report back on an author's query or manuscript.

Reprint rights. Permission to print an already published work whose rights have been sold to another magazine or book publisher.

Roman á clef. French "novel with a key." A novel that represents actual living or historical characters and events in fictionalized form.

Romance novel. A type of category fiction in which the love relationship between a man and a woman pervades the plot. The story is often told from the viewpoint of the heroine, who meets a man (the hero), falls in love with him, encounters a conflict that hinders their relationship, then resolves the conflict. Romance is the overriding element in this kind of story: The couple's relationship determines the plot and tone of the book. The theme of the novel is the woman's sexual awakening. Although she may not be a virgin, she has never before been so emotionally aroused. Despite all this emotion, however, characters and plot both must be well developed and realistic. Throughout a romance novel, the reader senses the sexual and emotional attraction between the heroine and hero. Lovemaking scenes, though sometimes detailed, are not generally too graphic, because more emphasis is placed on the sensual element than on physical action.

Royalties. A percentage of the retail price paid to an author for each copy of the book that is sold.

SAE. Self-addressed envelope.

SASE. Self-addressed stamped envelope.

Science fiction [vs. fantasy]. It is generally accepted that, to be science fiction, a story must have elements of science in either the conflict or setting (usually both). Fantasy, on the other hand, rarely utilizes science, relying instead on magic, mythological and neomythological beings and devices and outright invention for conflict and setting.

Second serial (reprint) rights. Permission for the reprinting of a work in another periodical after its first publication in book or magazine form.

Self-publishing. In this arrangement, the author keeps all income derived from the book, but he pays for its manufacturing, production and marketing.

Sequel. A literary work that continues the narrative of a previous, related story or novel.

Serial rights. The rights given by an author to a publisher to print a piece in one or more periodicals.

Serialized novel. A book-length work of fiction published in sequential issues of a periodical.

Setting. The environment and time period during which the action of a story takes place.

Short short story. A condensed piece of fiction, usually under 1,000 words.

Simultaneous submission. The practice of sending copies of the same manuscript to several editors or publishers at the same time. Some editors refuse to consider such submissions.

Slant. A story's particular approach or style, designed to appeal to the readers of a specific magazine.

Slice of life. A presentation of characters in a seemingly mundane situation which offers the reader a flash of illumination about the characters or their situation.

Slush pile. A stack of unsolicited manuscripts in the editorial offices of a publisher.

Social fiction. Fiction written with the purpose of bringing about positive changes in society.

Soft/sociological science fiction. Science fiction with an emphasis on society and culture versus scientific accuracy.

Space opera. Epic science fiction with an emphasis on good guys versus bad guys.

Speculation (or Spec). An editor's agreement to look at an author's manuscript with no promise to purchase.

Speculative fiction (SpecFic). The all-inclusive term for science fiction, fantasy and horror.

Splatterpunk. Type of horror fiction known for its very violent and graphic content.

Subsidiary. An incorporated branch of a company or conglomerate (e.g. Alfred Knopf, Inc., a subsidiary of Random House, Inc.).

Subsidiary rights. All rights other than book publishing rights included in a book contract, such as paperback, book club and movie rights.

Subsidy publisher. A book publisher who charges the author for the cost of typesetting, printing and promoting a book. Also called a vanity publisher.

Subterficial fiction. Innovative, challenging, nonconventional fiction in which what seems to be happening is the result of things not so easily perceived.

Suspense. A genre of fiction where the plot's primary function is to build a feeling of anticipation and fear in the reader over its possible outcome.

Synopsis. A brief summary of a story, novel or play. As part of a book proposal, it is a comprehensive summary condensed in a page or page and a half.

Tabloid. Publication printed on paper about half the size of a regular newspaper page (e.g. *The National Enquirer*).

Tearsheet. Page from a magazine containing a published story.

Techno-Thriller. This genre utilizes many of the same elements as the thriller, with one major difference. In techno-thrillers, technology becomes a major character. In Tom Clancy's *The Hunt for Red October* for example, specific functions of the submarine become crucial to plot development.

Theme. The dominant or central idea in a literary work; its message, moral or main thread.

Thriller. A novel intended to arouse feelings of excitement or suspense. Works in this genre are highly sensational, usually focusing on illegal activities, international espionage, sex and violence. A thriller is often a detective story in which the forces of good are pitted against the forces of evil in a kill-or-be-killed situation.

Trade paperback. A softbound volume, usually around 5X8, published and designed for the general public, available mainly in bookstores.

Traditional fantasy. Fantasy with an emphasis on magic, using characters with the ability to practice magic, such as wizards, witches, dragons, elves and unicorns.

Unsolicited manuscript. A story or novel manuscript that an editor did not specifically ask to see.

Urban fantasy. Fantasy that takes magical characters such as elves, fairies, vampires or wizards and places them in modern-day settings, often in the inner city.

Vanity publisher. See subsidy publisher.

Viewpoint. The position or attitude of the first- or third-person narrator or multiple narrators, which determines how a story's action is seen and evaluated.

Western. Genre with a setting in the West, usually between 1860-1890, with a formula plot about cowboys or other aspects of frontier life.

Whodunit. Genre dealing with murder, suspense and the detection of criminals.

Work-for-hire. Work that another party commissions you to do, generally for a flat fee. The creator does not own the copyright and therefore cannot sell any rights.

Young adult. The general classification of books written for readers 12 and up.

Zine. Often one- or two-person operations run from the home of the publisher/editor. Themes tend to be specialized, personal, experimental and often controversial.

Genre Glossary

Definitions of Fiction Subcategories

The following were provided courtesy of The Extended Novel Writing Workshop, created by the staff of Writers Online Workshops (www.writersonlineworkshops.com).

MYSTERY SUBCATEGORIES

The major mystery subcategories are listed below, each followed by a brief description and the names of representative authors, so you can sample each type of work. Note that we have loosely classified "suspense/thriller" as a mystery category. While these stories do not necessarily follow a traditional "whodunit" plot pattern, they share many elements with other mystery categories. In addition, many traditional mysteries are marketed as suspense/thriller because of this category's current appeal in the marketplace. Since the lines between categories are frequently blurred, it seems practical to include them all here.

Classic Mystery (Whodunit). A crime (almost always a murder or series of murders) is solved. The detective is the viewpoint character; the reader never knows any more or less about the crime than the detective, and all the clues to solving the crime are available to the reader.

Amateur detective. As the name implies, the detective is not a professional detective (private or otherwise), but is almost always a professional something. This professional association routinely involves the protagonist in criminal cases (in a support capacity), gives him or her a special advantage in a specific case, or provides the contacts and skills necessary to solve a particular crime. (Jonathan Kellerman, Patricia Cornwell, Jan Burke)

Courtroom Drama. The action takes place primarily in the courtroom; the protagonist is generally a defense attorney out to prove the innocence of his or her client by finding the real culprit. (Scott Turow, Steve Martini, Richard North Patterson, John Grisham)

Cozy. A special class of the amateur detective category that frequently features a female protagonist. (Agatha Christie's Miss Marple stories are the classic example.) There is less on-stage violence than in other categories and the plot is often wrapped up in a final scene where the detective identifies the murderer and explains how the crime was solved. In contemporary stories, the protagonist can be anyone from a chronically curious housewife to a mystery-buff clergyman to a college professor, but he or she is usually quirky, even eccentric. (Susan Isaacs, Andrew Greeley, Lillian Jackson Braun)

Espionage. The international spy novel is less popular since the end of the cold war, but stories can still revolve around political intrigue in unstable regions. (John le Carré, Ken Follett)

Heists and Capers. The crime itself is the focus. Its planning and execution are seen in detail and the participants are fully-drawn characters that may even be portrayed sympathetically. One character is the obvious leader of the group (the "brains"); the other members are often brought together by the leader specifically for this job and may or may not have a previous association. In a heist, no matter how clever or daring the characters are, they are still portrayed as criminals and the expectation is that they will be caught and punished (but not always). A caper is more light hearted, even comedic. The participants may have a noble goal (something other than personal gain) and often get away with the crime. (Eric Ambler, Tony Kenrick, Leslie Hollander)

Historical. May be any category or subcategory of mystery, but with an emphasis on setting, the details of which must be diligently researched. But beyond the historical details (which must never overshadow the story), the plot develops along the lines of its contemporary counterpart. (Candace Robb, Caleb Carr, Anne Perry)

Juvenile/Young adult. Written for the 8-12 age group (Middle Grade) or the 12 and up age group (Young Adult), the crime in these stories may or may not be murder, but it is serious. The protagonist is a kid (or group of kids) in the same age range as the targeted reader. There is no graphic violence depicted, but the stories are scary and the villains are realistic. (Mary Downing Hahn, Wendy Corsi Staub, Cameron Dokey, Norma Fox Mazer)

Medical thriller. The plot can involve a legitimate medical threat (such as the outbreak of a virulent plague) or the illegal or immoral use of medical technology. In the former scenario, the protagonist is likely to be the doctor (or team) who identifies the virus and procures the antidote; in the latter he or she could be a patient (or the relative of a victim) who uncovers the plot and brings down the villain. (Robin Cook, Michael Palmer, Michael Crichton, Stanley Pottinger)

Police procedurals. The most realistic category, these stories require the most meticulous research. A police procedural may have more than one protagonist since cops rarely work alone. Conflict between partners, or between the detective and his or her superiors is a common theme. But cops are portrayed positively as a group, even though there may be a couple of bad or ineffective law enforcement characters for contrast and conflict. Jurisdictional disputes are still popular sources of conflict as well. (Lawrence Treat, Joseph Wambaugh, Ridley Pearson, Julie Smith)

Private detective. When described as "hard-boiled," this category takes a tough stance. Violence is more prominent, characters are darker, the detective—while almost always licensed by the state operates on the fringes of the law, and there is often open resentment between the detective and law enforcement. More "enlightened" male detectives and a crop of contemporary females have brought about new trends in this category. (For female P.I.s—Sue Grafton, Sara Paretsky; for male P.I.s—John D. MacDonald, Lawrence Sanders, Robert Parker)

Suspense/Thriller. Where a classic mystery is always a whodunit, a suspense/thriller novel may deal more with the intricacies of the crime, what motivated it, and how the villain (whose identity may be revealed to the reader early on) is caught and brought to justice. Novels in this category frequently employ multiple points of view and have a broader scope than a more traditional murder mystery. The crime may not even involve murder—it may be a threat to global economy or regional ecology; it may be technology run amok or abused at the hands of an unscrupulous scientist; it may involve innocent citizens victimized for personal or corporate gain. Its perpetrators are kidnappers, stalkers, serial killers, rapists, pedophiles, computer hackers, or just about anyone with an evil intention and the means to carry it out. The protagonist may be a private detective or law enforcement official, but is just as likely to be a doctor, lawyer, military officer or other individual in a unique position to identify the villain and bring him or her to justice. (James Patterson, John J. Nance, Michael Connelly)

Technothriller. These are replacing the traditional espionage novel, and feature technology as an integral part of not just the setting, but the plot as well. (Tom Clancy, Stephen Coonts)

Woman in Jeopardy. A murder or other crime may be committed, but the focus is on the woman (and/or her children) currently at risk, her struggle to understand the nature of the danger, and her eventual victory over her tormentor. The protagonist makes up for her lack of physical prowess with intellect or special skills, and solves the problem on her own or with the help of her family (but she runs the show). Closely related to this category is the Romantic Suspense. But, while the heroine in a romantic suspense is certainly a "woman in jeopardy," the mystery or suspense element is subordinate to the romance. (Mary Higgins Clark, Mary Stewart, Jessica Mann)

ROMANCE SUBCATEGORIES

These categories and subcategories of romance fiction have been culled from the *Romance Writer's Sourcebook* (Writer's Digest Books) and Phyllis Taylor Pianka's *How to Write Romances* (Writer's Digest Books). We've arranged the "major'' categories below with the subcategories beneath them, each followed by a brief description and the names of authors who write in each category, so you can sample representative works.

Category or Series. These are published in "lines'' by individual publishing houses (such as Harlequin and Silhouette); each line has its own requirements as to word length, story content and amount of sex. (Debbie Macomber, Nora Roberts, Glenda Sanders)

Christian. With an inspirational, Christian message centering on the spiritual dynamic of the romantic relationship and faith in God as the foundation for that relationship; sensuality is played down. (Janelle Burnham, Ann Bell, Linda Chaikin, Catherine Palmer, Dee Henderson, Lisa Tawn Bergen)

Glitz. So called because they feature (generally wealthy) characters with high-powered positions in careers that are considered to be glamorous—high finance, modeling/acting, publishing, fashion—and are set in exciting or exotic (often metropolitan) locales such as Monte Carlo, Hollywood, London or New York. (Jackie Collins, Judith Krantz)

Historical. Can cover just about any historical (or even prehistorical) period. Setting in the historical is especially significant, and details must be thoroughly researched and accurately presented. For a sampling of a variety of historical styles try Laura Kinsell (*Flowers from the Storm*), Mary Jo Putney (*The Rake and the Reformer*) and Judy Cuevas (*Bliss*). Some currently popular periods/themes in historicals are:

- *Gothic:* historical with a strong element of suspense and a feeling of supernatural events, although these events frequently have a natural explanation. Setting plays an important role in establishing a dark, moody, suspenseful atmosphere. (Phyllis Whitney, Victoria Holt)
- *Historical fantasy:* with traditional fantasy elements of magic and magical beings, frequently set in a medieval society. (Amanda Glass, Jayne Ann Krentz, Kathleen Morgan, Jessica Bryan, Taylor Quinn Evans, Carla Simpson, Karyn Monk)

- *Early American:* usually Revolution to Civil War, set in New England or the South, but "frontier" stories set in the American West are quite popular as well. (Robin Lee Hatcher, Elizabeth Lowell, Heather Graham)
- *Native American:* where one or both of the characters are Native Americans; the conflict between cultures is a popular theme. (Carol Finch, Elizabeth Grayson, Karen Kay, Kathleen Harrington, Genell Dellim, Candace McCarthy)
- *Regency:* set in England during the Regency period from 1811-1820. (Carol Finch, Elizabeth Elliott, Georgette Heyer, Joan Johnston, Lynn Collum)

Multicultural. Most currently feature African-American or Hispanic couples, but editors are looking for other ethnic stories as well. Multiculturals can be contemporary or historical, and fall into any sub-category. (Rochelle Alers, Monica Jackson, Bette Ford, Sandra Kitt, Brenda Jackson)

Paranormal. Containing elements of the supernatural or science fiction/fantasy. There are numerous subcategories (many stories combine elements of more than one) including:

- *Time travel:* One or more of the characters travels to another time—usually the past—to find love. (Jude Devereaux, Linda Lael Miller, Diana Gabaldon, Constance O'Day Flannery)
- *Science fiction/Futuristic:* S/F elements are used for the story's setting: imaginary worlds, parallel universes, Earth in the near or distant future. (Marilyn Campbell, Jayne Ann Krentz, J.D. Robb [Nora Roberts], Anne Avery)
- *Contemporary fantasy:* From modern ghost and vampire stories to "New Age" themes such as extraterrestrials and reincarnation. (Linda Lael Miller, Anne Stuart, Antoinette Stockenberg, Christine Feehan)

Romantic Comedy. Has a fairly strong comic premise and/or a comic perspective in the author's voice or the voices of the characters (especially the heroine). (Jennifer Crusie, Susan Elizabeth Phillips)

Romantic Suspense. With a mystery or psychological thriller subplot in addition to the romance plot. (Mary Stewart, Barbara Michaels, Tami Hoag, Nora Roberts, Linda Howard, Catherine Coulter)

Single title. Longer contemporaries that do not necessarily conform to the requirements of a specific romance line and therefore feature more complex plots and nontraditional characters. (Mary Ruth Myers, Nora Roberts, Kathleen Gilles Seidel, Kathleen Korbel)

Young Adult. Focus is on first love with very little, if any, sex. These can have bittersweet endings, as opposed to the traditional romance happy ending, since first loves are often lost loves. (YA historical—Nancy Covert Smith, Louise Vernon; YA contemporary—Mary Downing Hahn, Kathryn Makris)

SCIENCE FICTION SUBCATEGORIES

Peter Heck, in his article "Doors to Other Worlds: Trends in Science Fiction and Fantasy," which appears in the 1996 edition of *Science Fiction and Fantasy Writer's Sourcebook* (Writer's Digest Books), identifies some science fiction trends that have distinct enough characteristics to be defined as categories. These distinctions are frequently the result of marketing decisions as much as literary ones, so understanding them is important in deciding where your novel idea belongs. We've supplied a brief description and the names of authors who write in each category. In those instances where the author writes in more than one category, we've included titles of appropriate representative works.

Hard science fiction. Based on the logical extrapolation of real science to the future. In these stories the scientific background (setting) may be as, or more, important than the characters. (Larry Niven)

Social science fiction. The focus is on how the characters react to their environments. This category includes social satire. (George Orwell's *1984* is a classic example.) (Margaret Atwood, *The Handmaid's Tale*; Ursula K. Le Guin, *The Left Hand of Darkness*; Marge Piercy, *Woman on the Edge of Time*)

Military science fiction. Stories about war that feature traditional military organization and tactics extrapolated into the future. (Jerry Pournelle, David Drake, Elizabeth Moon)

Cyberpunk. Characters in these stories are tough outsiders in a high-tech, generally near-future society where computers have produced major changes in the way that society functions. (William Gibson, Bruce Sterling, Pat Cadigan, Wilhelmina Baird)

Space opera. From the term "horse opera," describing a traditional good-guys-vs-bad-guys western, these stories put the emphasis on sweeping action and larger-than-life characters. The focus on action makes these stories especially appealing for film treatment. (The Star Wars series is one of the best examples, also Samuel R. Delany.)

Alternate history. Fantasy, sometimes with science fiction elements, that changes the accepted account of actual historical events or people to suggest an alternate view of history. (Ted Mooney, *Traffic and Laughter*; Ward Moore, *Bring the Jubilee*; Philip K. Dick, *The Man in the High Castle*)

Steampunk. A specific type of alternate history science fiction set in Victorian England in which characters have access to 20th-century technology. (William Gibson; Bruce Sterling, *The Difference Engine*)

New Age. A category of speculative fiction that deals with subjects such as astrology, psychic phenomena, spiritual healing, UFOs, mysticism and other aspects of the occult. (Walter Mosley, *Blue Light*; Neil Gaiman)

Science fantasy. Blend of traditional fantasy elements with scientific or pseudo-scientific support (genetic engineering, for example, to "explain" a traditional fantasy creature like the dragon). These stories are traditionally more character driven than hard science fiction. (Anne McCaffrey, Mercedes Lackey, Marion Zimmer Bradley)

Science fiction mystery. A cross-genre blending that can either be a more-or-less traditional science fiction story with a mystery as a key plot element, or a more-or-less traditional whodunit with science fiction elements. (Philip K. Dick, Lynn S. Hightower)

Science fiction romance. Another genre blend that may be a romance with science fiction elements (in which case it is more accurately placed as a subcategory within the romance genre) or a science fiction story with a strong romantic subplot. (Anne McCaffrey, Melanie Rawn, Kate Elliot)

Young Adult. Any subcategory of science fiction geared to a YA audience (12-18), but these are usually shorter novels with characters in the central roles who are the same age as (or slightly older than) the targeted reader. (Jane Yolen, Andre Norton)

FANTASY SUBCATEGORIES

Before we take a look at the individual fantasy categories, it should be noted that, for purposes of these supplements, we've treated fantasy as a genre distinct from science fiction. While these two are closely related, there are significant enough differences to warrant their separation for study purposes. We have included here those science fiction categories that have strong fantasy elements, or that have a significant amount of crossover (these categories appear in both the science fiction and the fantasy supplements), but "pure" science fiction categories are not included below. If you're not sure whether your novel is fantasy or science fiction, consider this definition by Orson Scott Card in *How to Write Science Fiction and Fantasy* (Writer's Digest Books):

> "Here's a good, simple, semi-accurate rule of thumb: If the story is set in a universe that follows the same rules as ours, it's science fiction. If it's set in a universe that doesn't follow our rules, it's fantasy.
>
> Or in other words, science fiction is about what could be but isn't; fantasy is about what couldn't be."

But even Card admits this rule is only "semi-accurate." He goes on to say that the real boundary between science fiction and fantasy is defined by how the impossible is achieved: "If you have people do some magic, impossible thing [like time travel] by stroking a talisman or praying to a tree, it's fantasy; if they do the same thing by pressing a button or climbing inside a machine, it's science fiction."

Peter Heck, in his article "Doors to Other Worlds: Trends in Science Fiction and Fantasy," which appears in the 1996 edition of the *Science Fiction and Fantasy Writer's Sourcebook* (Writer's Digest Books), does note some trends that have distinct enough characteristics to be defined as separate categories. These categories are frequently the result of marketing decisions as much as literary ones, so understanding them is important in deciding where your novel idea belongs. We've supplied a brief description and the names of authors who write in each category, so you can sample representative works.

Arthurian. Re-working of the legend of King Arthur and the Knights of the Round Table. (T.H. White, *The Once and Future King*; Marion Zimmer Bradley, *The Mists of Avalon*)

Contemporary (also called "urban") fantasy. Traditional fantasy elements (such as elves and magic) are incorporated into an otherwise recognizable modern setting. (Emma Bull, *War for the Oaks*; Mercedes Lackey, *The SERRAted Edge*; Terry Brooks, the Knight of the Word series)

Dark fantasy. Closely related to horror, but generally not as graphic. Characters in these stories are the "darker" fantasy types: vampires, witches, werewolves, demons, etc. (Anne Rice; Clive Barker, *Weaveworld*, *Imajica*; Fred Chappell)

Fantastic alternate history. Set in an alternate historical period (in which magic would not have been a common belief) where magic works, these stories frequently feature actual historical figures. (Orson Scott Card, *Alvin Maker*)

Game-related fantasy. Plots and characters are similar to high fantasy, but are based on a particular role-playing game. (Dungeons and Dragons; Magic: The Gathering; Dragonlance Chronicles; Forgotten Realms; Dark Sun)

Heroic fantasy. The fantasy equivalent to military science fiction, these are stories of war and its heroes and heroines. (Robert E. Howard, the Conan the Barbarian series; Elizabeth Moon, *Deed of Paksenarion*; Michael Moorcock, the Elric series)

High fantasy. Emphasis is on the fate of an entire race or nation, threatened by an ultimate evil. J.R.R. Tolkien's Lord of the Rings trilogy is a classic example. (Terry Brooks, David Eddings, Margaret Weis, Tracy Hickman)

Historical fantasy. The setting can be almost any era in which the belief in magic was strong; these are essentially historical novels where magic is a key element of the plot and/or setting. (Susan Schwartz, *Silk Road and Shadow*; Margaret Ball, *No Earthly Sunne*; Tim Powers, *The Anubis Gates*)

Juvenile/Young adult. Can be any type of fantasy, but geared to a juvenile (8-12) or YA audience (12-18); these are shorter novels with younger characters in central roles. (J.K. Rowling, Christopher Paolini, C.S. Lewis)

Science fantasy. A blend of traditional fantasy elements with scientific or pseudo-scientific support (genetic engineering, for example, to "explain" a traditional fantasy creature like the dragon). These stories are traditionally more character driven than hard science fiction. (Anne McCaffrey, Mercedes Lackey, Marion Zimmer Bradley)

HORROR SUBCATEGORIES

Subcategories in horror are less well defined than in other genres and are frequently the result of marketing decisions as much as literary ones. But being familiar with the terms used to describe different horror styles can be important in understanding how your own novel might be best presented to an agent or editor. What follows is a brief description of the most commonly used terms, along with names of authors and, where necessary, representative works.

Dark Fantasy. Sometimes used as a euphemistic term for horror in general, but also refers to a specific type of fantasy, usually less graphic than other horror subcategories, that features more "traditional" supernatural or mythical beings (vampires, werewolves, zombies, etc.) in either contemporary or historical settings. (Contemporary: Stephen King, *Salem's Lot*; Thomas Tessier, *The Nightwalker*. Historical: Brian Stableford, *The Empire of Fear*; Chelsea Quinn Yarbro, *Werewolves of London*.)

Hauntings. "Classic" stories of ghosts, poltergeists and spiritual possessions. The level of violence portrayed varies, but many writers in this category exploit the reader's natural fear of the unknown by hinting at the horror and letting the reader's imagination supply the details. (Peter Straub, *Ghost Story*; Richard Matheson, *Hell House*)

Juvenile/Young Adult. Can be any horror style, but with a protagonist who is the same age as, or slightly older than, the targeted reader. Stories for middle grades (eight to 12 years old) are scary, with monsters and violent acts that might best be described as "gross," but stories for young adults (12-18) may be more graphic. (R.L. Stine, Christopher Pike, Carol Gorman)

Psychological horror. Features a human monster with horrific, but not necessarily supernatural, aspects. (Thomas Harris, *The Silence of the Lambs*, *Hannibal*; Dean Koontz, *Whispers*)

Splatterpunk. Very graphic depiction of violence—often gratuitous—popularized in the 1980s, especially in film. (*Friday the 13th*, *Halloween*, *Nightmare on Elm Street*, etc.)

Supernatural/Occult. Similar to the dark fantasy, but may be more graphic in its depiction of violence. Stories feature satanic worship, demonic possession, or ultimate evil incarnate in an entity or supernatural being that may or may not have its roots in traditional mythology or folklore. (Ramsey Campbell; Robert McCammon; Ira Levin, *Rosemary's Baby*; William Peter Blatty, *The Exorcist*; Stephen King, *Pet Sematary*)

Technological horror. "Monsters" in these stories are the result of science run amok or technology turned to purposes of evil. (Dean Koontz, *Watchers*; Michael Crichton, *Jurassic Park*)

Professional Organizations

AGENTS' ORGANIZATIONS

Association of Authors' Agents (AAA), 20 John St., London WC1N 2DR, United Kingdom. (44)(20)7405-6774. E-mail: aaa@apwatt. Web site: www.agentsassoc.co.uk.

Association of Authors' Representatives (AAR), 676A 9th Ave., #312, New York NY 10036. (212)840-5777. E-mail: aarinc@mindspring.com. Web site: www.aar-online.org.

Association of Talent Agents (ATA), 9255 Sunset Blvd., Suite 930, Los Angeles CA 90069. (310)274-0628. Fax: (310)274-5063. E-mail: shellie@agentassociation.com. Web site: www.agentassociation.com.

WRITERS' ORGANIZATIONS

Academy of American Poets, 584 Broadway, Suite 604, New York NY 10012-5243. (212)274-0343. Fax: (212)274-9427. E-mail: academy@poets.org. Web site: www.poets.org.

American Crime Writers League (ACWL), 17367 Hilltop Ridge Dr., Eureka MO 63205. Web site: www.acwl.org.

American Medical Writers Association (AMWA), 40 W. Gude Dr., Suite 101, Rockville MD 20850-1192. (301)294-5303. Fax: (301)294-9006. E-mail: amwa@amwa.org. Web site: www.amwa.org.

American Screenwriters Association (ASA), 269 S. Beverly Dr., Suite 2600, Beverly Hills CA 90212-3807. (866)265-9091. E-mail: asa@goasa.com. Website: www.asascreenwriters.com.

American Translators Association (ATA), 225 Reinekers Lane, Suite 590, Alexandria VA 22314. (703)683-6100. Fax: (703)683-6122. E-mail: ata@atanet.org. Web site: www.atanet.org.

Education Writers Association (EWA), 2122 P St. NW, Suite 201, Washington DC 20037. (202)452-9830. Fax: (202)452-9837. E-mail: ewa@ewa.org. Web site: www.ewa.org.

Garden Writers Association (GWA), 10210 Leatherleaf Ct., Manassas VA 20111. (703)257-1032. Fax: (703)257-0213. Web site: www.gardenwriters.org.

Horror Writers Association (HWA), 244 5th Ave., Suite 2767, New York NY 10001. E-mail: hwa@horror.org. Web site: www.horror.org.

The International Women's Writing Guild (IWWG), P.O. Box 810, Gracie Station, New York NY 10028-0082. (212)737-7536. Fax: (212)737-9469. E-mail: dirhahn@iwwg.org. Web site: www.iwwg.com.

Mystery Writers of America (MWA), 17 E. 47th St., 6th Floor, New York NY 10017. (212)888-8171. Fax: (212)888-8107. E-mail: mwa@mysterywriters.org. Web site: www.mysterywriters.org.

National Association of Science Writers (NASW), P.O. Box 890, Hedgesville WV 25427. (304)754-5077. Fax: (304)754-5076. E-mail: diane@nasw.org. Web site: www.nasw.org.

National Association of Women Writers (NAWW), 24165 IH-10 W., Suite 217-637, San Antonio TX 78257. Web site: www.naww.org.

Organization of Black Screenwriters (OBS). Web site: www.obswriter.com.

Outdoor Writers Association of America (OWAA), 121 Hickory St., Suite 1, Missoula MT 59801. (406)728-7434. Fax: (406)728-7445. E-mail: krhoades@owaa.org. Web site: www.owaa.org.

Poetry Society of America (PSA), 15 Gramercy Park, New York NY 10003. (212)254-9628. Web site: www.poetrysociety.org.

Poets & Writers, 72 Spring St., Suite 301, New York NY 10012. (212)226-3586. Fax: (212)226-3963. Web site: www.pw.org.

Romance Writers of America (RWA), 16000 Stuebner Airline Rd., Suite 140, Spring TX 77379. (832)717-5200. E-mail: info@rwanational.org. Web site: www.rwanational.org.

Science Fiction and Fantasy Writers of America (SFWA), P.O. Box 877, Chestertown MD 21620. E-mail: execdir@sfwa.org. Web site: www.sfwa.org.

Society of American Business Editors & Writers (SABEW), University of Missouri, School of Journalism, 385 McReynolds, Columbia MO 65211. (573)882-7862. Fax: (573)884-1372. E-mail: sabew@missouri.edu. Web site: www.sabew.org.

Society of American Travel Writers (SATW), 1500 Sunday Dr., Suite 102, Raleigh NC 27607. (919)861-5586. Fax: (919)787-4916. E-mail: satw@satw.org. Web site: www.satw.org.

Society of Children's Book Writers & Illustrators (SCBWI), 8271 Beverly Blvd., Los Angeles CA 90048. (323)782-1010. Fax: (323)782-1892. E-mail: scbwi@scbwi.org. Web site: www.scbwi.org.

Washington Independent Writers (WIW), 1001 Connecticut Ave. NW, Suite 701, Washington DC 20036. (202)775-5150. Fax: (202)775-5810. E-mail: info@washwriter.org. Web site: www.washwriter.org.

Western Writers of America (WWA). E-mail: wwa@unm.edu. Web site: www.westernwriters.org.

INDUSTRY ORGANIZATIONS

American Booksellers Association (ABA), 200 White Plains Rd., Tarrytown NY 10591. (914)591-2665. Fax: (914)591-2720. E-mail: info@bookweb.org. Web site: www.bookweb.org.

American Society of Journalists & Authors (ASJA), 1501 Broadway, Suite 302, New York NY 10036. (212)997-0947. Fax: (212)937-2315. E-mail: execdir@asja.org. Web site: www.asja.org.

Association for Women in Communications (AWC), 3337 Duke St., Alexandria VA 22314. (703)370-7436. Fax: (703)370-7437. E-mail: info@womcom.org. Web site: www.womcom.org.

Association of American Publishers (AAP), 71 5th Ave., 2nd Floor, New York NY 10003. (212)255-0200. Fax: (212)255-7007. Or, 50 F St. NW, Suite 400, Washington DC 20001. (202)347-3375. Fax: (202)347-3690. Web site: www.publishers.org.

The Association of Writers & Writing Programs (AWP), The Carty House, Mail stop 1E3, George Mason University, Fairfax VA 22030. (703)993-4301. Fax: (703)993-4302. E-mail: services@awpwriter.org. Web site: www.awpwriter.org.

The Authors Guild, Inc., 31 E. 32nd St., 7th Floor, New York NY 10016. (212)563-5904. Fax: (212)564-5363. E-mail: staff@authorsguild.org. Web site: www.authorsguild.org.

Canadian Authors Association (CAA), Box 419, Campbellford ON K0L 1L0 Canada. (705)653-0323. Fax: (705)653-0593. E-mail: admin@canauthors.org. Web site: www.canauthors.org.

Christian Booksellers Association (CBA), P.O. Box 62000, Colorado Springs CO 80962-2000. (800)252-1950. Fax: (719)272-3510. E-mail: info@cbaonline.org. Web site: www.cbaonline.org.

The Dramatists Guild of America, 1501 Broadway, Suite 701, New York NY 10036. (212)398-9366. Fax: (212)944-0420. Web site: www.dramaguild.com.

National League of American Pen Women (NLAPW), 1300 17th St. NW, Washington DC 20036-1973. (202)785-1997. Fax: (202)452-8868. Website: www.americanpenwomen.org.

National Writers Association (NWA), 10940 S. Parker Rd., #508, Parker CO 80134. (303)841-0246. Fax: (303)841-2607. E-mail: anitaedits@aol.com. Web site: www.nationalwriters.com.

National Writers Union (NWU), 113 University Place, 6th Floor, New York NY 10003. (212)254-0279. Fax: (212)254-0673. E-mail: nwu@nwu.org. Web site: www.nwu.org.

PEN American Center, 588 Broadway, Suite 303, New York NY 10012-3225. (212)334-1660. Fax: (212)334-2181. E-mail: pen@pen.org. Web site: www.pen.org.

The Playwrights Guild of Canada (PGC), 54 Wolseley St., 2nd Floor, Toronto ON M5T 1A5 Canada. (416)703-0201. Fax: (416)703-0059. E-mail: info@playwrightsguild.ca. Web site: www.playwrightsguild.com.

Volunteer Lawyers for the Arts (VLA), One E. 53rd St., 6th Floor, New York NY 10022. (212)319-2787. Fax: (212)752-6575. Web site: www.vlany.org.

Women in Film (WIF), 8857 W. Olympic Blvd., Suite 201, Beverly Hills CA 90211. (310)657-5144. E-mail: info@wif.org. Web site: www.wif.org.

Women in the Arts Foundation (WIA), 32-35 30th St., D24, Long Island City NY 11106. (212)941-0130. E-mail: reginas@anny.org. Web site: www.anny.org/2/orgs/womeninarts/.

Women's National Book Association (WNBA), 2166 Broadway, #9-E, New York NY 10024. (212)208-4629. Web site: www.wnba-books.org.

Writers Guild of Alberta (WGA), 11759 Groat Rd., Edmonton AB T5M 3K6 Canada. (780)422-8174. Fax: (780)422-2663. E-mail: mail@writersguild.ab.ca. Web site: writersguild.ab.ca.

Writers Guild of America-East (WGA), 555 W. 57th St., Suite 1230, New York NY 10019. (212)767-7800. Fax: (212)582-1909. Web site: www.wgaeast.org.

Writers Guild of America-West (WGA), 7000 W. Third St., Los Angeles CA 90048. (323)951-4000. Fax: (323)782-4800. Web site: www.wga.org.

Writers Union of Canada (TWUC), 90 Richmond St. E., Suite 200, Toronto ON M5C 1P1 Canada. (416)703-8982. Fax: (416)504-9090. E-mail: info@writersunion.ca. Web site: www.writersunion.ca.

Literary Agents Category Index

Action

Adventure

Cartoon

Comic Books

Commercial

Confession

Contemporary

Contemporary Issues

Crime

Detective

Erotica

Ethnic

Experimental

Family

Family Saga

Fantasy

Feminist

Frontier

Gay

Glitz

Gothic

Historical

Horror

Humor

Inspirational

Juvenile

Lesbian

Literary

Mainstream

Military

Multicultural

Multimedia

Mystery

New Age

Occult

Picture Books

Police

Psychic

Regency

Regional

Religious

Romance

Satire

Science

Science Fiction

Short Story Collections

Spiritual

Sports

Supernatural

Suspense

Thriller

Westerns

Women's

Conference Index by Date

Our conference index organizes all conferences listed in this edition by the month in which they are held. If a conference bridges two months, you will find its name and page number under both monthly headings. If a conference occurs multiple times during the year (seasonally, for example), it will appear under each appropriate monthly heading. Turn to the listing's page number for exact dates and more detailed information.

January

February

March

April

May

June

July

August

September

October

November

December

Category Index

Our category index makes it easy for you to identify publishers who are looking for a specific type of fiction. Publishers who are not listed under a fiction category either accept all types of fiction or have not indicated specific subject preferences. Also not appearing here are listings that need very specific types of fiction, e.g., "fiction about fly fishing only."

To use this index to find markets for your work, go to category title that best describes the type of fiction you write and look under either Magazines or Book Publishers (depending on whom you're targeting). Finally, read individual listings *carefully* to determine the publishers best suited to your work.

For a listing of agents and the types of fiction they represent, see the Literary Agents Category Index beginning on page 560.

BOOK PUBLISHERS

Adventure

Children's Juvenile

Comics/Graphic Novels

Erotica

Ethnic/Multicultural

Experimental

Family Saga

Fantasy

Feminist

Gay

Glitz

Historical

Horror

Humor Satire

Lesbian

Literary

Mainstream

Military/War

Mystery/Suspense

Psychic/Supernatural

Regional

Religious

Romance

Science Fiction

Short Story Collections

Thriller/Espionage

Category Index

Translations

Western

Young Adult/Teen

MAGAZINES

Adventure

Children's/Juvenile

Comics/Graphic Novels

Erotica

Ethnic/Multicultural

Experimental

Family Saga

Fantasy

Feminist

Gay

Glitz

Historical

Category Index

Horror

Humor/Satire

Lesbian

Literary

Mainstream

Category Index

Military/War

Mystery/Suspense

Category Index

New Age

Psychic/Supernatural/Occult

Regional

Religious

Romance

Science Fiction

Thriller/Espionage

Translations

Westerns

Young Adult/Teen

General Index

B

I

J

K

M

W

Y

Z